TEXT, CASES AND MATERIALS ON MEDICAL LAW

Routledge
Taylor & Francis

D0609995

TEXT, CASES AND MATERIALS ON MEDICAL LAW

Third Edition

Marc Stauch MA (Oxon)
Solicitor, Lecturer and Researcher,
The Centre for British Studies, Humboldt-Universität zu Berlin

and

Kay Wheat BA
Solicitor, Senior Lecturer in Law,
Nottingham Trent University

with

John Tingle BA, MEd
Barrister, Reader in Health Care Law,
Nottingham Trent University

Routledge·Cavendish
Taylor & Francis Group

Fifth edition published 2006
by Routledge·Cavendish
2 Park Square, Milton Park, Abingdon, Oxon, OX14 4RN

Simultaneously published in the USA and Canada
by Routledge·Cavendish
270 Madison Ave, New York, NY 10016

Routledge·Cavendish is an imprint of the Taylor & Francis Group, an informa business

First published as *Sourcebook on Medical Law* in 1998
by Cavendish Publishing Ltd
Reprinted 1999 and 2000
Second edition published in 2002
by Cavendish Publishing Ltd
Reprinted 2004 (twice)

© 1998, 2002, 2006 M Stauch, K Wheat and J Tingle

Typeset by Newgen Imaging Systems (P) Ltd, Chennai, India
Printed and bound in Great Britain

British Library Cataloguing in Publication Data
A catalogue record for this book is available from the British Library

Library of Congress Cataloging in Publication Data
A catalog record for this book has been requested

PREFACE

Medical law is an exciting and challenging subject, whose dilemmas are the focus of intense and ongoing public debate. The fact that it is a relatively young discipline, which must attempt to keep pace with the constant advance of medical science, makes it of considerable jurisprudential interest. Moreover, the questions which it addresses are ones of fundamental human concern, bearing ineluctably upon the lives of each one of us and the shape of the society we inhabit. In fact, few other legal subjects display so clearly the interaction between law and morality.

Sourcebook on Medical Law aims to draw together a wide range of material (much of it very recent), including extracts from statutes, judgments and academic commentaries. It is primarily designed for use as a core text by law students taking medical (or health care) law at undergraduate level. However, it is hoped that it may also be of some interest to postgraduate students, including those in the burgeoning field of bioethics, as well as to health care professionals.

While the authors take collective responsibility for the book, primary responsibility for the individual chapters was as follows: Marc Stauch, Chapters 6, 7, 8, 11 and 12; Kay Wheat, Chapters 1, 4, 5 and 9; Marc Stauch and Kay Wheat, Chapter 3. Finally, Chapter 2 was contributed to by all three authors, although overall responsibility was taken by all three authors.

We should like to express our thanks to Terry Hanstock and Angela Donaldson of The Nottingham Trent University Library and Information Services for their assistance in tracking down material and references for inclusion in the work.

Crown copyright is reproduced with the permission of the Controller of Her Majesty's Stationery Office. Every effort has been made to trace copyright holders, but if any have been inadvertently overlooked the publishers will be pleased to make the necessary arrangements.

In this new edition, the law is current upto 1 Augest 2005 but we have been able to incorporate later material in a few instances.

Marc Stauch, Kay Wheat and John Tingle

August 2005

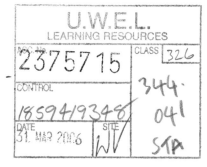

CONTENTS

TABLE OF CASES

TABLE OF STATUTES

STATUTORY INSTRUMENTS

TABLE OF TREATIES AND EU LEGISLATION

ABBREVIATIONS

Atlantic Reporter	A
Appeal Cases	AC
Australian Law Journal Reports	ALJR
All England Law Reports	All ER
American Journal of Law and Medicine	Am J Law & Med
British Columbia Law Reports	BCLR
British Medical Journal	BMJ
Butterworths Medico-Legal Reports	BMLR
Californian Appellate Cases	Cal App
Californian Reporter	Cal Rptr
Chancery Division	Ch
Chancery Division	Ch D
Cambridge Law Journal	CLJ
Current Legal Problems	CLP
Cox's Criminal Cases	Cox
Criminal Appeal Reports	Cr App R
Criminal Law Review	Crim LR
Dominion Law Reports	DLR
European Human Rights Reports	EHRR
Federal Reporter	F
Family Division	Fam
Family Law	Fam Law
Family Law Reports	FLR
Industrial Relations Law Reports	IRLR
Journal of Social Welfare Law	J Soc Wel L
Journal of Law and Society	JLS
Journal of Medical Ethics	JME
King's Bench Law Reports	KB
Knight's Industrial Reports	KIR
Lloyd's Law Reports: Medical	Lloyd's Rep Med
Law Quarterly Review	LQR
Massachusetts Supreme Judicial Court Reports	Mass
Medical Law Reports	Med LR
Medical Law Review	Med L Rev
Modern Law Review	MLR
North Eastern Reporter	NE
New Jersey Supreme Court Reports	NJ
New Law Journal	NLJ
New Law Journal Reports	NLJR
Nottingham Law Journal	Nott LJ

New South Wales Law Reports	NSWLR
North Western Reporter	NW
New York Court of Appeal Reports	NY
New York Supplement	NYS
New Zealand Law Reports	NZLR
Oxford Journal of Legal Studies	OJLS
Ontario Reports	OR
Pacific Reporter	P
Pennsylvania District and County Reports	Pa D & C
Public Law	PL
Queen's Bench Law Reports	QB
Road Traffic Reports	RTR
Supreme Court Reporter	S Ct
South Australian State Reports	SASR
Session Cases	SC
Canada Law Reports: Supreme Court	SCR
Solicitor's Journal	SJ
Scots Law Times	SLT
Southern Reporter	SO
South Western Reporter	SW
United States Supreme Court Reports	US
United States Law Week	USLW
Victorian Reports	VR
Weekly Law Reports	WLR
Western Weekly Reports	WWR

PART I

GENERAL PRINCIPLES

CHAPTER 1

ETHICS AND MEDICINE

INTRODUCTION TO ETHICS

This chapter will examine the ways in which ethical issues are part of the practice of medicine. In this first section we will look, briefly, at a number of ethical theories and concepts and the ways in which they might relate to medicine. Next, we consider the doctor–patient relationship and the way in which medicine has given rise to particular ways of describing this relationship and its ethical implications. Although it is by no means a clear-cut dichotomy, generally it can be said that many of the problems in medical ethics, and certainly many of the conflicting opinions, are based upon the debate between paternalism and the patient's right to autonomy. First, the view that paternalism is central to the doctor–patient relationship means that because of the doctor's superior knowledge and his ethical obligation to do good, the medical view of what is best for the patient should prevail. The opposing view is that the patient has a right to autonomous decision-making and that this should not be overridden by 'doctor knows best'. Later in the chapter we will study these two different ways of looking at the doctor–patient relationship, question whether it is helpful to use either of these models as frameworks for medical decision-making, and look at alternatives. Finally, we will look at justice and fairness in the allocation of treatment between competing patients when resources dictate that not all can be treated, and at the distribution of health care resources on a national level.

However, although the current chapter looks at general principles, when appropriate, ethical problems in particular areas of medical practice will be examined in other chapters.

Why study ethics?

Why should ethics be so important in medicine? In other fields of activity, such as commerce, ethics plays a small role. As long as business is operated on the right side of the law, little consideration is given to whether it is practised ethically. Although many may protest, for example, that 'it isn't fair' for large supermarkets to put small shops out of business, the 'ethics' of this plays a minor role in the general discourse about such matters, which is much more likely to be concerned with convenience and consumer choice. That is not to say that it is not relevant. It is simply that the language of ethics has not permeated the world of business in the way in which it has the practice of medicine. The reason may be that much of medicine is about issues of life and death: for example, abortion, infertility treatment, the threat to life through negligent treatment, or insufficiency of health resources, the treatment of the terminally ill and so on. Perhaps the heart of the doctor–patient relationship is this: the doctor does things to the body of the patient, thereby invading his physical integrity. This is neither good nor bad in itself, but is instrumentally good if the likely effect is the cure or amelioration of the patient's condition, and if it is done with the real consent and co-operation of the patient. However, in so far as it can be ascertained, it must be done in the patient's best medical interests. If there is no real consent, or if the treatment is unsuitable or negligently carried out, then it could be regarded as a violation of the patient's physical integrity.

Although, as we shall see, there is some argument that the doctor–patient relationship has been wrongly accorded this special status, there is no doubt that since the time of ancient Greece, it has given rise to ethical codes prescribing the extent of the doctor's duties:

Mason, JK and McCall Smith, RA, *Law and Medical Ethics*, 4th edn, 1994, London: Butterworths, p 4:

Medicine in the Middle East

The first effective example of organised medicine is to be found in Egypt where the father figure of medicine practised – Imhotep, who was the archetypal combination of physician, priest and court official. The Papyri discovered in the 19th century indicate that Egyptian medicine was comparatively advanced as early as the second millennium BC. Several features of that organisation are outstanding in their relation to modern practice. In the first place, the concept of a national health service seems to have been well developed – patients were not charged for visits to the healers who, themselves, were supported by the community. Secondly, rather rigid rules were laid down as to experimental treatment – there was no culpability in failure to cure so long as the standard textbooks were followed. Severe penalties were, however, threatened for those who ignored the instructions, the reason being that very few men would be expected to know better than the best specialists who had gone before – an interesting attitude towards negligence which was still being adopted by the courts at the turn of this century ... More importantly, the notion of specialisation was deeply instilled. Medical treatment, however, remained very much the practice of the priest caste – indeed, the aura of mystique surrounding the physician in comparison with the overt technical expertise of his surgical colleagues has persisted until recent times.

The extension of surgical practice into lay hands was steady and was demonstrated in the parallel practice of Babylonian medicine.

It is from here that the first known legal code originated – the Code of Hammurabi (c 1900 BC). This contained an element of medical ethics and laid down, *inter alia*, a system of payment based on results and, to some extent, on the ability to pay and on the status of the patient; it also tabled penalties for negligent failure, some of which were draconian to an extent which must have deterred many from entering the profession.

Greek medicine

For the origin of our modern ethics, however, one must look to Greece where early medical practice must have been derived from both Egypt and Babylon. By 500 BC, the originally strong influence of the priest had waned and had been taken over by the philosophers who, through the processes of logical thought, observation and deduction, transformed the practice of medicine. Inevitably, this led to the formation of schools involving close association, paternalism and the elements of the 'closed shop'; a code of intraprofessional conduct evolved – the dawn of what has become known as medical etiquette. In addition, the new concepts of practice dictated that the physician went to the patient rather than the patient to the temple. A standard of practice relevant to the new ideals was required and has survived as the Hippocratic Oath ...

Hippocrates remains as the most famous figure in Greek philosophical medicine but he was not alone and, indeed, it is probable that the Oath predates his own school. It therefore indicates a prevailing ethos rather than a professorial edict and it is still regarded as the fundamental governance of the medical profession. We are not, here, concerned with medical etiquette. As to medical ethics, the Oath lays down certain guidelines. First, it implies the need for co-ordinated instruction and registration of doctors – the public is to be protected, so far as is possible, from the dabbler or the charlatan. Secondly, it is clearly stated that a doctor is there for the benefit of his patients – to the best of his ability he must do them good and he must do nothing which he knows will cause harm. Thirdly, euthanasia and abortion are proscribed; the reference to lithotomy probably prohibits mutilating operations (castration) but has been taken by many to indicate a proper limitation of practice to that in which one has expertise. Fourthly, the nature of the doctor–patient relationship is outlined and an undertaking is given not to take advantage of that relationship. Finally, the Oath expresses the doctrine of medical confidentiality.

In fact, the Hippocratic Oath did not become an integral part of ethical teaching until well into the Christian era; it lapsed with the decline of Greek civilisation and was restored with the evolution of university medical schools. It is doubtful if any British medical school now requires a reiteration of the Oath at graduation – although Edinburgh, for one, requires assent by students to a modified version – but, avowed or not, all doctors would admit to its persuasive influence. The language of the Oath is, however, archaic and a modernised version was introduced by the World Medical Association as the Declaration of Geneva. This was amended at Sydney in 1968 and provides the basis of an International Code of Medical Ethics.

What is the study of ethics about? The purpose of ethics is to try and find principles for living good lives. It will be seen that there is much overlap between ethical theories, and within each, there are contradictions and tensions. Words such as 'equality', 'rights' and 'liberty' all sound good, and we all like to think that we approve of these things. However, in deciding what we mean by them we may find that we are making all sorts of value judgments and interpretations which suit the end we would like to achieve.

A fundamental starting point in discussions about ethics is universalisation. This means that one must move away from what is right or beneficial for the individual and seek principles that can apply to everyone. Peter Singer describes the way this has permeated ethical thinking:

Singer, P, *Practical Ethics*, 1979, Cambridge: CUP, p 10:

From ancient times, philosophers and moralists have expressed the idea that ethical conduct is acceptable from a point of view that is somehow universal. The 'Golden Rule' attributed to Moses tells us to go beyond our own personal interests and 'do unto others as we would have them do unto us'. The same idea of putting oneself in the position of another is involved in the Christian commandment that we love our neighbour as ourselves. The Stoics held that ethics derives from a universal natural law. Kant developed this idea into his famous formula: 'Act only on that maxim through which you can at the same time will that it should become a universal law.' Kant's theory has itself been modified and developed by RM Hare, who sees 'universalisability' as a logical feature of moral judgments. The 18th century British philosophers Hutcheson, Hume and Adam Smith appealed to an imaginary 'impartial spectator' as the test of a moral judgment, and this theory has its modern version in the Ideal Observer Theory. Utilitarians from Jeremy Bentham to JJC Smart take it as axiomatic that in deciding moral issues 'each counts for one and none for more than one'; while John Rawls, a leading contemporary critic of utilitarianism, incorporates essentially the same axiom into his own theory by deriving basic ethical principles from an imaginary choice in which those choosing do not know whether they will be the ones who gain or lose by the principles they select. Even Continental philosophers like the existentialist Jean-Paul Sartre and the Marxist Jürgen Habermas, who differ in many ways from their English-speaking colleagues – and from each other – agree that ethics is in some sense universal.

One could argue endlessly about the merits of each of these characterisations of the ethical; but what they have in common is more important than their differences. They agree that the justification of an ethical principle cannot be in terms of any partial or sectional group. Ethics takes a universal point of view. This does not mean that a particular ethical judgment must be universally applicable. Circumstances alter causes, as we have seen. What it does mean is that in making ethical judgments we go beyond our own likes and dislikes. From an ethical point of view the fact that it is I who benefit from, say, a more equal distribution of income and you, say, who lose by it, is irrelevant. Ethics requires us to go beyond 'I' and 'you' to the universal law, the universalisable judgment, the standpoint of the impartial spectator or ideal observer, or whatever we choose to call it.

Can we use this universal aspect of ethics to derive an ethical theory which will give us guidance about right and wrong? Philosophers from the Stoics to Hare and Rawls have attempted this. No attempt has met with general acceptance. The problem is that if we describe the universal aspect of ethics in bare, formal terms, a wide range of ethical theories, including quite irreconcilable ones, are compatible with this notion of universality; if, on the other hand, we build up our description of the universal aspect of ethics so that it leads us ineluctably to one particular ethical theory, we shall be accused of smuggling our own ethical beliefs into our definition of the ethical – and this definition was supposed to be broad enough, and neutral enough, to encompass all serious candidates for the status of 'ethical theory'.

As Singer says, the principle of universalisation has appealed to many and it cannot be said to belong to any particular theory.

Consequences v deontological absolutes

One way of deciding whether an action is ethically right or wrong is to look at the consequences of *this* act; or we might consider it important to look at the consequences of translating this act into an ethical proposition about what should be done generally, ie, by framing an ethical principle which will produce the best consequences. So, for example, we might make a rule about keeping promises which is generally a good thing to do, even though in some circumstances the consequences of breaking a promise may be better than keeping it. Another way is to ask whether the act or principle would be right or wrong *regardless of its consequences*. This leads to a somewhat crude distinction between theories which judge the moral correctness of an action by its consequences alone, and those which state there are certain principles, rights or whatever, which are inviolable, whatever the consequences. However, it is by no means a neat division. Most consequentialists try to incorporate certain things such as respect for individual rights into their theories with varying degrees of success. Those who believe in the paramountcy of absolute values cannot disregard consequences entirely. Advocates of certain principles such as the sanctity of life (one of those so called inviolable principles) may oppose, say, the withdrawal of nutrition from a permanently unconscious patient (see Chapter 12). However, they may argue that one of the reasons for their view is the 'slippery slope' argument, which says that once a certain course of action is carried out (as here), then the next step will be to withdraw food from a patient who is gravely disabled, but not unconscious. This argument is an appeal to consequentialism.

Consequentialism

The theory that the rightness of a course of action is to be judged by its consequences is an attractive one and it is tempting to embrace this view as being self-evidently right. Human actions have outcomes. We believe that we need to know what these are in order to decide what is the right thing to do. However, a moment's reflection will make us realise that whilst it may be correct, as it stands, it is full of holes. First, consequences for whom? If we are looking at types of medical treatment or the allocation of health resources we must ask whether we are looking at these sorts of patients or society as a whole? What sorts of consequences are going to be relevant? If the consequences of treating these patients may be that they will live, but live in pain or be dependent upon others for their most basic needs, is this right?

The most well known consequentialist view is that of utilitarianism. This theory, of whom Jeremy Bentham was one of the earliest exponents, states that ethical principles should produce the greatest happiness for the greatest number of people, and 'happiness' is defined by means of pleasure. The rightness of a decision is judged by deciding whether it produces, on balance, more pleasure than pain. When we consider the treatment of say, very seriously disabled new-born children, we might discount treating them because they will live (we believe) painful lives. But we also tend to think that there is more to life than the pursuit of pleasure and the avoidance of pain. JC Smart has put forward the example of the 'pleasure machine' (see his contribution to *Utilitarianism: For and Against*, 1993, Cambridge: CUP). This is a machine that can be connected to the brain to give pleasure, without the 'inconvenience' of the means of obtaining pleasure, for example, from books, sex, sport and so on. Once we acknowledge the absurdity of this and realise that we do not pursue pleasure as such, but an infinite number of pursuits, the pain–pleasure dichotomy is not so attractive. We tend to think that to be human is to be more than the repository of the sensations of pleasure and pain. Although the most well known utilitarian philosopher, John Stuart Mill, referred to the maximising of pleasure, and described utilitarianism as the 'happiness' theory, he was aware that this might be interpreted as pandering to selfish and, perhaps, base, tastes. Mill tried to deal with this by distinguishing between different kinds of pleasure:

Mill, JS, *Utilitarianism*, 1863, London: Routledge, p 15:

It must be admitted ... that utilitarian writers in general have placed the superiority of mental over bodily pleasures chiefly in the greater permanency, safety, uncostliness, etc, of the former – that is, in their circumstantial advantages rather than in their intrinsic nature. And, on all these points, utilitarians have fully proved their case, but they might have taken the other, and, as it may be called, higher ground, with entire consistency. It is quite compatible with the principle of utility to recognise the fact that some *kinds* of pleasure are more desirable and more valuable than others. It would be absurd that while, in estimating all other things, quality is considered as well as quantity, the estimation of pleasures should be supposed to depend on quantity alone.

Singer describes his own version of utilitarianism:

Singer, P, *Practical Ethics*, 1979, Cambridge: CUP, p 12:

Suppose I then begin to think ethically, to the extent of recognising that my own interests cannot count for more, simply because they are my own, than the interests of others. In place of my own interests, I now have to take account of the interests of all those affected by my decision. This requires me to weigh up all these interests and adopt the course of action most likely to maximise the interests of those affected. Thus I must choose the course of action which has the best consequences, on balance, for all affected. This is a form of utilitarianism. It differs from classical utilitarianism in that 'best consequences' is understood as meaning what, on balance, furthers the interests of those affected, rather than merely what increases pleasure and reduces pain. (It has, however, been suggested that classical utilitarians like Bentham and John Stuart Mill used 'pleasure' and 'pain' in a broad sense which allowed them to include achieving what one desired as a 'pleasure' and the reverse as a 'pain'. If this interpretation is correct, the difference between classical utilitarianism and utilitarianism based on interests disappears.)

What does this show? It does not show that utilitarianism can be deduced from the universal aspect of ethics. There are other ethical ideals – like individual rights, the sanctity of life, justice, purity and so on – which are universal in the required sense, and are, at least in some versions, incompatible with utilitarianism. It does show that we very swiftly arrive at an initially utilitarian position once we apply the universal aspect of ethics to simple, pre-ethical decision-making. This, I believe, places the onus of proof on those who seek to go beyond utilitarianism. The utilitarian position is a minimal one, a first base which we reach by universalising self-interested decision-making. We cannot, if we are to think ethically, refuse to take this step. If we are to be persuaded that we should go beyond utilitarianism and accept non-utilitarian moral rules or ideals, we need to be provided with good reasons for taking this further step. Until such reasons are produced, we have some grounds for remaining utilitarians.

It has been suggested that utilitarianism fails to deal with the problem of people's unacceptable preferences:

Beauchamp, TL and Childress, JF, *Principles of Biomedical Ethics*, 2001, Oxford: OUP, pp 345–46:

Problems arise for utilitarians who are concerned about the maximization of individual preferences when some of these individuals have what our considered judgments tell us are morally unacceptable preferences. For example, if a researcher derived supreme satisfaction from inflicting pain on animals or on human subjects in experiments, we would condemn this preference and would seek to prevent it from being actualized. Utilitarianism based on subjective preferences is a defensible theory only if we can formulate a range of *acceptable* preferences and determine 'acceptability' independently of agents' preferences. This task seems inconsistent with a pure preference approach.

Critics of utilitarianism have pointed out that the theory can be upheld and still permit an awful lot of wrongdoing. In other words, the great majority of society can be wealthy and healthy, but a small minority may live in appalling circumstances, with no access whatsoever to basic facilities, such as health care. This is a powerful argument. Although Mill does incorporate concepts such as justice into his theory, is this not coming perilously close to maintaining that there are ideals or principles which are worthy and must be supported regardless of the consequences? Consequentialist theories do not have to be utilitarian, ie, the maximisation of happiness or welfare can be replaced by some other concept of what is good. For example, one may try to incorporate some role for distributive justice. This may be possible, but it is not necessarily part of a consequentialist theory, which may lead us to conclude that judging actions by consequences alone is an insufficient guide to ethical behaviour.

Utilitarianism, however, is an attractive theory when one considers certain specific issues such as the doctor's obligation of confidentiality, where the obligation can be justified on the basis that patients would be less than candid when consulting a doctor if they had doubts that the information would be kept confidential (see Chapter 5). The fact that the obligation can be broken if it is in the public interest to do so is also an appeal to consequentialism.

Absolutism/deontology

Having recognised the inadequacies of consequentialism, John Mackie considers alternatives:

Mackie, JL, *Ethics: Inventing Right and Wrong*, 1977, Harmondsworth: Penguin, p 149:

... we could reject the consequentialist structure, and develop a moral system built not round the notion of some goal that is to be attained, but rather round the notions of rules or principles of action or duties or rights or virtues, or some combination of these – in a very broad sense, some kind of deontological system. Of course a consequentialist theory will usually give some place to items of all these sorts, but a subordinate place: a utilitarian takes virtues, for example, to be good just because and in so far as they tend to issue in behaviour that increases the general happiness. But in a deontological theory actions of the kinds held to be virtuous are seen as being intrinsically obligatory or admirable, and goodness of character too may be seen as having intrinsic value; actions and characters may have a merit of their own not wholly derived from what they bring about.

The term 'deontology' comes from *deon* – the Greek word for 'duty'. Probably the most well known exponent of this is Immanuel Kant:

Paton, HJ, *The Moral Law*, 1948, London: Hutchinson University Library, p 19:

A human action is morally good, not because it is done from immediate inclination – still less because it is done from self-interest – but because it is done for the sake of duty.

This is Kant's first proposition about duty, though he does not state it in this general form.

An action – even if it accords with duty and is in that sense right – is not commonly regarded as morally good if it is done solely out of self-interest. We may, however, be inclined to attribute moral goodness to right actions done solely from some immediate inclination – for example, from a direct impulse of sympathy or generosity. In order to test this we must *isolate* our motives: we must consider first an action done solely out of inclination and *not* out of duty, and then an action done solely out of duty and *not* out of inclination. If we do this, then, we shall find – to take the case most favourable to immediate inclination – that an action done solely out of natural sympathy may be right and praiseworthy, but that nevertheless it has no distinctively moral worth. The same kind of action done solely out of duty does have distinctively moral worth. The goodness shown in helping others is all the more conspicuous if a man does this for the sake of duty at a time when he is fully occupied with his own troubles and when he is not impelled to do so by his natural inclinations.

Kant's doctrine would be absurd if it meant that the presence of a natural inclination to good actions (or even of a feeling of satisfaction in doing them) detracted from their moral worth. The ambiguity of his language lends some colour to this interpretation, which is almost universally accepted. Thus he says that a man shows moral worth if he does good, not from inclination, but from duty. But we must remember that he is here contrasting two motives taken in *isolation* in order to find out which of them is the source of moral worth. He would have avoided the ambiguity if he had said that a man shows moral worth, not in doing good from inclination, but in doing it for the sake of duty. It is the motive of duty, not the motive of inclination, that gives moral worth to an action.

Just as happiness was central to Mill's view, it plays a significant role in Kant's philosophy: '... the natural end which all men seek is their own happiness.' However, this happiness will only be produced, says Kant, if human beings, as rational beings, make rules to govern their own lives and the lives of others, and have reverence for the moral law. Crucial to Kant's philosophy is the maxim that no one should be treated merely as a means to an end, but always, as well, as an end in themselves. As we shall see, this Kantian rule is particularly pertinent to issues such as medical research and organ donation (see Chapters 10 and 11).

Beauchamp and Walters comment on deontological theories as follows:

Beauchamp, TL and Walters, L, *Contemporary Issues in Bioethics,* **1982, Belmont, Calif: Wadsworth Publishing, p 19:**

Deontological theories

We have seen that utilitarianism conceives the moral life in terms of intrinsic value and the means to produce this value. Deontologists, by contrast, argue that moral standards exist independently of utilitarian ends and that the moral life should not be conceived in terms of means and ends ... An act or rule is right, in the view of a deontologist, in so far as it satisfies the demands of some overriding principle(s) of obligation.

Deontologists urge us to consider that actions are morally wrong not because of their consequences but because the action type – the class of which the actions are instances – involves a moral violation. Because of the wide diversity in these theories it is hard to find the unity, but the following two conditions are close to the heart of deontological theories. First, the justification of principles and actions is not entirely by appeal to the consequences of adopting the principles or performing the actions. Second, some principles must be followed or actions performed irrespective of the consequences. Thus, there are not only justificatory grounds of obligation that are independent of the production of good consequences, but these grounds are at least sometimes sufficient to defeat the consequences no matter what the consequences are.

A radical deontologist will argue that consequences are irrelevant to moral evaluations: an act is right if and only if it conforms to an overriding moral obligation and wrong if and only if it violates the overriding moral duty or principle. Many deontological theories are not so radical, however, holding that moral rightness is only in part independent of utilitarian conceptions of goodness. The fairness of distribution, keeping a personal promise, repaying a debt, and abiding by a contract would be right, according to these theories, whether or not utility was maximised.

Deontologists believe that our duties to others are manifold and diverse, some springing from special relationships that utilitarians unjustifiably ignore. These relationships include, for example, those of parent and child, physician and patient, and employer and employee. Physicians have obligations to their patients that they do not have to other individuals, no matter the utilitarian outcome of treating their patients and not treating others. Children incur special obligations to their parents, and vice versa; parents have a moral obligation to oversee and support the health and welfare needs of their children that they do not have in regard to other children in their neighbourhood. This is not to suggest that utilitarians denigrate or downgrade these relationships. They do not. The point is that deontologists do not believe that these relationships can be justified on consequentialist grounds.

Deontologists also believe that utilitarians give too little consideration to the performance of acts in the past that create obligations in the present. If a person has promised something or has entered into a contract, he or she is bound to the terms of the agreement, no matter what the consequences of keeping it are. If one person harms another, the person who inflicted the injury is bound to compensate the injured one, whether the compensation serves utilitarian goals or not.

As an example of differences in utilitarian and deontological thinking, consider a survey conducted by researchers K Ann Coleman Stolurow and Dale W Moeller. Stolurow and Moeller were interested in the frequency with which x-rays are routinely used as part of dental checkups. They conducted a telephone survey of dental offices in the Boston area and found that in 95% of the offices surveyed x-ray procedures are customarily ordered in connection with the initial investigation of new patients, and that in nearly half of those offices the procedures employed involve full-mouth x-rays to obtain accurate information. These researchers misrepresented themselves over the telephone as new residents in the Boston area inquiring about available dental services and they asked a series of specific questions that followed a prepared written survey instrument wholly undisclosed to the dentists or their offices. This misrepresentation apparently contributed significantly to the accuracy of the results, because the data obtained showed a frequency of dental x-ray use far greater than that reported by an earlier study in which the researchers did not conceal their purposes.

This use of deception raises ethical issues of whether the researchers violated the moral rights of the participants or unjustifiably invaded privacy. Many act utilitarians would likely consider this study justifiable: there are public benefits of obtaining accurate information about dental x-rays. The information, for instance, might form the basis on which the American Dental Association would refocus its ongoing efforts to reduce unnecessary x-ray exposure, from lessening dosage levels to cutting down on the frequency of exposure. One also might draw an analogy with consumer surveys, noting that the survey seeks to evaluate a contractual service between providers and customers. The utilitarian could then argue that the terms of the contract give potential customers grounds to know accurate information about the service, and that this customer interest overrides conflicting rights of dental office owners and employees. A deontologist, by contrast, may find indefensible the deception and invasion of privacy essential to the conduct of the study. In any event, the deontologist will not frame the moral problem exclusively in terms of a weighing of consequences.

Since deontologists believe that moral standards are independent of utilitarian ends, what is the source of these standards and how is moral obligation based on these standards? Throughout the history of philosophy deontologists have identified starkly different ultimate principles of obligation as the final moral standards. Although these many different views cannot be surveyed here, it is possible to briefly distinguish several different grounds to which they have appealed. Perhaps the best known deontological account is the divine command theory. The will of God is the ultimate standard in this account and an action or action type is right or wrong if and only if commanded or forbidden by God. Other deontologists hold that some actions or action types are naturally right or wrong, good or evil, requiring no reason having to do with religion, politics, or social organisation.

Finally, some deontologists appeal to a social contract reached under conditions of absolute fairness as the source of moral obligation. The ultimate principle of obligation is action in accordance with moral rules fairly derived from a situation of mutual agreement. Many writers in this volume appeal to the recent work of John Rawls on the topic of justice, and Rawls is one representative of the social contract point of view.

We also talk about absolutism, ie the belief in absolute values which can be regarded as inviolable, regardless of what they may bring about in any given set of circumstances. For example, it could be said that torture is *always* wrong. This is illustrated by the prohibition on torture in the Declaration of Tokyo, issued by the World Medical Association:

Declaration of Tokyo 1975:

1 -The doctor shall not countenance, condone or participate in the practice of torture or other forms of cruel, inhuman or degrading procedures, whatever the offence of which the victim of such procedures is suspected, accused or guilty, and whatever the victim's beliefs or motives, and in all situations, including armed conflict and civil strife ...

This implies that under no circumstances could torture ever be justified, but it is by no means clear that we can be sure about this. Simmonds gives the following example:

Simmonds, NE, *Central Issues in Jurisprudence*, 1986, London: Sweet & Maxwell, p 34:

... if a madman had hidden a nuclear device which was set to destroy the whole of South East England at a pre-set time, we might feel justified in torturing him if this really was the only way of discovering the location of the bomb so as to defuse it.

The sanctity of life principle might also be said to be an absolute, but, again, this is questionable. Most people accept the fact that innocent people's lives will be lost in the cause of a just war. In medicine, the right of people to refuse life-saving treatment is respected, even though it conflicts with the sanctity of life principle, and, as we shall see in Chapter 12, many doctors believe that it is right not to treat a person if the treatment will not 'benefit' him, even if his death will result because of this.

Gillon describes the view of the intuitionist philosopher WD Ross, and his account of what happens when principles conflict:

Gillon, R, *Philosophical Medical Ethics*, 1985, Chichester: John Wiley, p 18:

Ross described various moral principles that he believed any reflective person would intuitively accept: duties of fidelity (the obligations to keep promises and not to deceive); duties of beneficence (obligations to try and help others); the duty of non-maleficence (the obligations, more stringent than the obligation to help others, not to harm others); duties of justice (obligations to promote the distribution of happiness or pleasure in accord with merits – probably meaning deserts – of the persons concerned); duties of reparation (obligation to compensate others for harms we have caused them); duties of gratitude (obligations to repay in some way those who have helped us); and a duty of self-improvement.

According to Ross, it is self-evident to any mature person on reflection that all these principles of conduct are *prima facie* moral obligations or moral rules of conduct that should undoubtedly prevail unless to obey them would result in a clash with some other rule of conduct. Although he did not claim that the list was exhaustive, he had no doubts that it was 'correct as far as it goes', and that the 'moral order expressed in these propositions is just as much part of the fundamental nature of the universe ... as is the spatial or numerical structure expressed in the axioms of geometry or arithmetic'.

What should be done when these *prima facie* principles conflict in any given circumstances? Ross did not believe that they could be immutably ranked or weighted so that we could know in advance which principles should take precedence over which. He also did not believe in any decisive overarching principle such as the Kantian supreme moral principle or the utilitarian greatest happiness principle by reference to which moral conflicts could be settled. Our moral life was far more complicated than the systematisers and simplifiers of ethics accepted, and when it came to specific cases of moral conflict we could only have opinions, not knowledge about which principle took precedence.

This idea that principles can be weighed up against each other depending upon the circumstances is attractive and is reflected in the writings of Ronald Dworkin, who describes the role principles have in legal decision-making (see *Taking Rights Seriously*, 1977, London: Duckworth). As we shall see, this 'weighing up' of different principles is frequently a feature of medical law cases.

Rights, duties and liberties

When considering absolutist theories we questioned whether there was, for example, a right not to be tortured which could never be overridden. It leads us to try to get to grips with what we mean by rights. Rights are often described in terms of the corresponding duties which go with them. The jurist WN Hohfeld was a well known exponent of this, incorporating into his scheme the role of liberties and powers:

Simmonds, NE, *Central Issues in Jurisprudence*, 1986, London: Sweet & Maxwell, p 133:

Correlativity of rights and duties

In Hohfeld's analytical scheme, claim-rights are correlative to duties in a very strict way. When we say that X has a claim-right of a certain kind, a part of what we mean (according to Hohfeld) is that Y owes a duty of some kind to X. Liberties are not correlative to duties: they are correlative to the absence of a claim-right, or what Hohfeld calls a 'no-right' (thus if X has a liberty to wear a hat, Y has 'no-right' that X should not wear a hat). Powers are correlative to liabilities (being liable to have one's legal position changed by the act of another) and immunities are correlative to disabilities (ie, the inability to change another person's legal position).

The idea of strict correlativity between rights (ie, claim-rights) and duties is a controversial one, and the controversy is important for two quite different sets of reasons, which we may summarise as follows:

1 If rights are strictly correlative to duties, then a person has established legal rights only in so far as there are established duties corresponding to those rights. The law on this account has a static appearance: it could be represented as a long list of duties. If, on the other hand, it makes sense to talk of established rights without established correlative – we may think of the law as imposing duties, and perhaps creating new duties, in order to protect established rights. On this account, there may at any one time be established legal rights which are inadequately protected by legal duties: such rights provide a legal reason for creating new legal duties.

Seen from this perspective, the law is not static but has an inner dynamic of its own. It is not a long list of duties that is added to whenever moral and policy considerations make this desirable: new duties may be recognised as a response to specifically legal considerations, in the attempt to give better legal protection to established legal rights.

2   Politicians and others make frequent use of the concept of rights. People are said to have rights of this and that kind, and rights are generally regarded as a 'good thing'. But if rights (in this case moral, rather than legal, rights) are correlative to duties, such claims are always open to the question 'on whom do the correlative duties rest?' People are much more willing to assert the existence of rights to various amenities than they are to ascribe specific duties. Moreover, if rights are correlative to duties, we may feel that they are not necessarily an unqualified good: for if rights entail duties, they entail greater restrictions on freedom. If therefore we believe that freedom is a 'good thing' we will not wish to see an unlimited expansion in people's rights (meaning, I repeat, 'claim-rights').

Kant distinguished between perfect and imperfect duties. Paton gives examples of these:

Paton, HJ, _The Moral Law_, 1948, London: Hutchinson University Library, p 31:

A perfect duty is one which admits of no exception in the interests of inclination. Under this heading the examples given are the ban on suicide and on making a false promise in order to receive a loan. We are not entitled to commit suicide because we have a strong inclination to do so, nor are we entitled to pay our debt to one man and not to another because we happen to like him better. In the case of imperfect duties the position is different: we are bound only to adopt the maxim of developing our talents and of helping others, and we are to some extent entitled to decide arbitrarily which persons we will help. There is here a certain 'latitude' or 'playroom' for mere inclination.

In terms of medicine, this could be translated as follows. Doctors are under a perfect duty to be just in the way in which they decide who to treat. They have only an imperfect duty to provide medical treatment to everyone who requests it. Under the Hohfeldian scheme there is no right to medical treatment, only the right to be considered in accordance with just criteria. In the next chapter we refer to the European Social Charter of 1961, which enshrines the 'right to protection of health, and the right to social and medical assistance'. However, as we shall see, in the context of the provision of medical treatment, the clinical discretion of the doctor as to the provision of treatment is paramount.

We might look for perfect duties in medical law, or we might consider the question the other way round and ask whether there are any absolute rights. Ronald Dworkin argues that there is a right to be treated with equal respect (see _Taking Rights Seriously_, 1977, London: Duckworth). Are mentally impaired people to be treated with the same respect as the non-impaired? There are a number of controversial cases where mentally impaired young women have been sterilised for contraceptive purposes even though there was little likelihood of them becoming pregnant (see Chapter 4). Were they being treated with the same respect as non-impaired women?

The principle of self-determination is frequently asserted in medical law and ethics. It could be said that there is an absolute right to self-determination as long as the person has the capacity to make decisions. We often talk of people being competent to make decisions. Problems may arise in deciding whether the person is competent, but once it is established then the right to physical integrity seems to be inviolable. But could the right still be overridden – for example, in an emergency? As we shall see, this 'right' is overridden when the doctor has no time to consult with, for example, an unconscious patient: he will successfully raise the defence of necessity to an action in battery. However, is it arguable that the right to self-determination has not been overridden at all because the patient was incapable of exercising it? In English law the foetus has no legal 'rights'. We will examine this in Chapter 8, below, in relation, in particular, to abortion and women who refuse Caesarean section operations, even though the refusal may gravely risk their own lives and the survival of the foetuses. Does the foetus have no rights because it cannot enforce them? If this were the case, then children and the seriously mentally disordered would not have rights, but we often speak about the rights of children and the mentally ill. In one of the sterilisation cases referred to above it was said that a woman's 'right' to reproduce meant nothing to her *(Re B (A Minor) (Wardship: Sterilisation)* [1988] AC 199). Because of the dangers of dismissing rights in this way, it might be preferable to consider the rights of the incompetent in terms of the duties others have towards them. With regard to children, Carl Wellman states:

Wellman, C, *An Approach to Rights,* **1997, Dordrecht: Kluwer Academic, p 132:**

The moral right to freedom of movement contains several other associated elements, but let me mention only one – the State's moral duty to enforce the parental duty of non-interference with the child's freedom of movement. Although this duty is very limited in scope, it can be of crucial importance in extreme cases. Imagine that a parent keeps a young child restrained in a crib so much of the time that the child has no opportunity to learn to walk … Under such circumstances, the State would have a moral obligation to intervene in the family and force the parent to cease and desist from such grossly unjustified interference with the freedom of movement of the child. Although this moral duty of the State begins as merely a duty regarding the child, in due course it grows into a moral duty to the child when the child becomes capable of claiming State intervention vis à vis the parent.

Wellman goes on to examine the right of the child to protection. In medical law the tension between granting the child the freedom it needs to develop and the protection it may need will be apparent when we look at the ability of the child to consent to treatment (see Chapter 4).

Liberty and equality are two other general ethical concepts that are open to a number of different interpretations. In Mill's philosophy they are interdependent. Mill stresses that the liberty of the individual is paramount, and his liberty to pursue his own choices has to be no more than the equal liberty of everyone else. He can only be restrained from any activity which interferes with the liberty of others:

Mill, JS, *On Liberty,* **1982, Harmondsworth: Penguin, p 68:**

The object of this essay is to assert one very simple principle, as entitled to govern absolutely the dealings of society with the individual in the way of compulsion and control, whether the means used be physical force in the form of legal penalties or the moral coercion of public opinion. That principle is that the sole end for which mankind are warranted, individually or collectively, in interfering with the liberty of action of any of their number is self-protection. That the only purpose for which power can be rightfully exercised over any member of a civilised community, against his will, is to prevent harm to others. His own good, either physical or moral, is not a sufficient warrant.

Mill's principle is reflected in the right to self-determination.

Respect for persons

We have referred to Dworkin's equal respect for persons, but do we know what we mean by a person? This may sound like a silly question, but if we pose the question in a different way and ask what we mean by respect for human life it is not an easy one to answer. (There are those who argue that respect for life generally is what matters, so that animals should be treated with respect, and this has relevance to medical research and the development of xenotransplantation (animal to human): see Chapter 11.)

Harris asks when human life begins to matter morally and examines the potentiality argument which says that human life begins when the human egg is fertilised, ie when there is the potential for human life:

Harris, J, *The Value of Life*, 1985, London: Routledge & Kegan Paul, p 11:

There are two sorts of difficulty with the potentiality argument which are jointly and severally fatal to it. The first is that the bare fact that something will become X (even if it will inevitably become X, which is far from being the case with the fertilised egg and the adult human being) is not a good reason for treating it now as if it were in fact X. We will all inevitably die, but that is, I suppose, an inadequate reason for treating us now as if we were dead.

The second difficulty is that it is not only the fertilised egg that is potentially a human being. The unfertilised egg and the sperm are equally potentially a human being. The unfertilised egg and the sperm are equally potentially new human beings. To say that a fertilised egg is potentially a human being is just to say that if certain things happen to it (like implantation), and certain other things do not (like spontaneous abortion), it will eventually become a human being. But the same is also true of the unfertilised egg and the sperm. If certain things happen to the egg (like meeting a sperm) and certain things happen to the sperm (like meeting an egg) and thereafter certain other things do not (like meeting a contraceptive), then they will eventually become a new human being.

It is sometimes objected that it is only the fertilised egg that has all the necessary potential present in one place, so to speak, and it is this that is crucial. It is only when the egg has been fertilised, so the argument goes, that a new unique entity exists that itself has all the potential necessary to become a new human being. This seems plausible enough until we remember that something had the potential to become that fertilised egg; and whatever had that potential, had also the potential to become whatever it is that the fertilised egg has the potential to become!

If then we ignore the first difficulty with the potentiality argument, and concede that we are somehow morally required to actualise all human potential, we are all in for a highly exhausting time. And it is clear that if we put the maximal effort into procreation that this imperative demands, our endeavours will ultimately be self-defeating.

Harris goes on to say that what we really value is *a person*:

Harris, J, *The Value of Life*, 1985, London: Routledge & Kegan Paul, p 18:

... a person will be any being capable of valuing its own existence. Apart from the advantage of its simplicity, this account has two other major advantages. The first is that it is value- and species-neutral. It does not imply that any particular kind of being or any particular mode of existence is more valuable than any other so long as the individual in question can value its mode of existence. Once this threshold is crossed, no individual is more of a person or more valuable than any other. This concept of the person sets out to identity which individuals and which forms of life have the sort of value and importance that makes appropriate and justifies our according to them the same concern, respect and protections as we grant to one another. And it tries to do so without begging any questions as to the sort of creatures that will be found to qualify.

The second advantage is that it is capable of performing the two tasks we require of a concept of a person. These are that it should give us some grasp of why persons are valuable and make intelligible the moral difference between persons and other beings. The second task is that it should enable us, in principle, to tell persons from non-persons.

On this concept of the person, the moral difference between persons and non-persons lies in the value that people give to their own lives. The reasons it is wrong to kill is that to do so robs that individual of something they value, and of the very thing that makes possible valuing anything at all. To kill a person not only frustrates their wishes for their own futures, but frustrates every wish a person has. Creatures that cannot value their own existence cannot be wronged in this way, for their death deprives them of nothing that they can value.

Of course non-persons can be harmed in other ways, by being subjected to pain for example, and there are good reasons for avoiding subjecting any sentient creatures to pain if this can be avoided.

It is important to note that Harris is talking about the *capacity* to value one's own existence, so a new-born child would have that capacity. However, would a foetus also have the capacity?

Justice

By now it will be apparent that the language of morals can slip easily between rights, duties and liberties. The concept of 'justice' is no less an elusive concept. Although its importance usually lies in the realm of politics, it can be relevant both to the wider issues of allocating health resources on a national basis, and when deciding which patients to treat when local resources are limited. This will be examined further at the end of this chapter and in Chapter 2.

Relativism and feminist ethics

It is arguable that we approach ethical problems from the standpoint of a white Western man (see Hart's criticism of Mill, p 30, below). Increasingly, therefore, there are thinkers who want to move away from this and explore the issues from the perspective of women or of people from different cultures.

We commenced this section with the suggestion that ethical principles are universal. Some would argue that this does not address the way in which cultural differences might give rise to different ethical norms:

Beauchamp, TL and Walters, L, *Contemporary Issues in Bioethics*, 1982, Belmont, Calif: Wadsworth Publishing, p 8:

[Cultural] relativists defend their position by appeal to anthropological data indicating that moral rightness and wrongness vary from place to place and that there are no absolute or universal moral standards that could apply to all persons at all times. They add that rightness is contingent on cultural beliefs and that the concepts of rightness and wrongness are therefore meaningless apart from the specific contexts in which they arise. The claim is that patterns of culture can only be understood as unique wholes and that moral beliefs about normal behaviour are thus closely connected in a culture to other cultural characteristics, such as language and fundamental political institutions. Studies show, they maintain, that what is deemed worthy of moral approval or disapproval in one society varies, both in detail and as a whole pattern, from moral standards in other societies.

Similarly, some feminists have taken the view that the language of moral philosophy is male-centred, and dominated by an undue reverence for 'reason'. This is particularly pertinent to medical ethics, as the medical profession has traditionally been dominated by men, particularly in its upper reaches. It has been said that the traditional approach to medical ethics reinforces the practice of patriarchal medicine and the patriarchal institutions within society (for example, by Susan Sherwin – see 'Feminist and medical ethics: two different approaches to contextual ethics', in Bequaert Holmes, H and Purdy, LM, *Feminist Perspectives in Medical Ethics*, 1992, Bloomington: Indiana UP). Some feminist writers have spoken of the need for an 'ethics of care', whereby the emotions have an important role to play in ethical theories (see Gilligan, C, *In a Different Voice*, 1982, Cambridge, Mass: Harvard UP). Beauchamp and Childress describe the care ethic as follows:

Beauchamp, TL and Childress, JF, *Principles of Biomedical Ethics*, 2001, Oxford: OUP, pp 373–74:

Having a certain emotional attitude and expressing the appropriate emotion in action are morally relevant factors, just as having the appropriate motive for an action is morally relevant. The person seems morally deficient who acts from rule-governed obligations without appropriately aligned feelings such as worry when a friend suffers. In addition to expressing their feelings in their responses, agents also need to attend to the feelings of persons toward whom they act. Insight into the needs of others and considerate attentiveness to their circumstances often come from the emotions more than reason.

In the history of human experimentation, for example, those who first recognised that some subjects of research were being brutalised, subjected to misery, or placed at unjustifiable risk were persons who were able to feel compassion, disgust, and outrage through insight into the situation of these research subjects. They exhibited emotional discernment of and sensitivity to the feelings of subjects, where others lacked comparable responses. This emphasis on the emotional dimension of the moral life does not reduce moral response to emotional response. Caring also has a cogntive dimension, because it involves insight into and understanding of another's circumstances, needs, and feelings. As Hume pointed out, emotions motivate us and tell us much about a person's character, but human understanding directs us in choosing a path of action.

The care ethic, however, has its weaknesses, in that it is arguable that it is not sufficient as a moral theory. Beauchamp and Childress comment as follows:

Beauchamp, TL and Childress, JF, *Principles of Biomedical Ethics*, 2001, Oxford: OUP, p 374:

On at least some occasions we need an impartial judgment to arbitrate between conflicting moral judgments or feelings. Many who endorse the ethics of care do not want to exclude all impartial judgments and considerations of justice and the public good. But the problem remains about the extent to which this approach can successfully incorporate these moral notions without losing much of its critical thrust and uniqueness. The ethic of care, as Gilligan and others have defended it, recognises that two perspectives exist, but can they be made *coherent*? ...

Some feminists [eg Susan Sherwin] have sharply criticised the ethics of care, despite its feminist origins, on the grounds that it attends to women's experiences as givers of care in traditional roles of self-sacrifice, but often neglects their oppression. ...

... without a broader framework, the ethics of care is too confined to the *private* sphere of intimate relationships and may serve to reinforce an uncritical adherence to traditional social patterns of assigning caretaker roles to women.

The medical humanities movement

A similar move away from the scientific emphasis that is so much a part of western medicine is the medical humanities movement. It has been around in the USA for some time, but only for the past four or five years has it found a voice in the UK. A relatively new journal 'Medical Humanities' published by the Journal of Medical Ethics aims to promote this:

Greaves, D, and Evans, M, 'Editorial' (2000) J Med Ethics: Medical Humanities 26(1):

... [medical humanities] is a second generational response to the shortcomings of a medical culture dominated by scientific, technical and managerial approaches ... [there are] two main formulations of medical humanities ... [t]he first is concerned with complementing medical science and technology through the contrasting perspective of the arts and humanities, but without either side impinging on the other. The second aims to refocus the whole of medicine in relation to an understanding of what it is to be fully human; the reuniting of technical and humanistic knowledge and practice is central to this enterprise.

It is not clear how far the first of these aims is particularly related to medicine unless it is to point up the statement often made: 'medicine is not an exact science'. This relates particularly to the role played by patient psychology in the development of illness and recovery. The second formulation might be a way of moving to what is often described as patient centred medicine, which seeks to emphasise all the non-medical components of medical decision-making, and in particular emphasises communication skills in the doctor–patient relationship. See, for example, Evans, RG, 'Patient centred medicine: reason, emotion, and human spirit? Some philosophical reflections on being with patients' (2003) J Med Ethics: Medical Humanities 29:8.

It is useful to consider these sorts of approaches when making decisions about a patient's capacity to make medical decisions (see Chapter 3) and what might be in the best interests of a patient who lacks capacity (see Chapter 4).

THE DOCTOR–PATIENT RELATIONSHIP

Beneficence

Doctors are generally regarded as having a positive duty to do good. Raanan Gillon comments as follows:

Gillon, R, *Philosophical Medical Ethics*, 1985, Chichester: John Wiley, p 73:

Whatever the case in general ethics, it is undoubtedly true that members of the medical profession undertake to place the interests of their patients before their own in many circumstances. This undertaking differentiates them from, for instance, merchants, who, while they may also on occasion put their clients' interests first, will do so (*qua* merchants) only to further their own longer term interests – for example, when it is good for business to put themselves out for their clients. Although an element of such self-interest undoubtedly exists in the practice of medicine and although the grandiose claim that interests of patients always come first is false as a description and undesirable as a prescription, the medical profession nonetheless conceives itself, and is conceived by society, as having a duty of beneficence to the sick in general and to its patients in particular. One does not hear the Tannoy ringing out during a ball with the request, 'Would any architect present please report to the manager's office', and if one did, no architect there would feel the slightest moral obligation to respond.

Is this a sentimental view of the role of doctors and can it be justified? Gillon uses the example of an architect, but what about a plumber – might not he be called upon to act in an emergency? Referring to the duty of the doctor as going beyond what can reasonably be expected of everyone else, Downie comments:

Downie, RS, 'Traditional medical ethics and economics in health care: a critique', in Mooney, G and McGuire, A (eds), *Medical Ethics and Economics in Health Care,* **1988, Oxford: OUP, p 45:**

[A main ingredient in a code of medical or other professional ethics] consists of some generalised exhortations to care for patients, which can be summed up by saying that the medical and perhaps all the professions are governed to a much greater extent than other jobs by the principle of benevolence. Indeed, Gillon (1986) goes so far as to describe the doctor's duty as one of supererogatory benevolence, in that it goes beyond what can reasonably be expected of the rest of us.

A short way to dispose of this claim might be to argue that it confuses conceptual points about the definition of the aims of a profession with moral duties; definitional 'oughts' have been confused with moral 'oughts'. Thus, it sounds like a high ideal to say that the doctor ought to care for the health or the welfare of his patient, but in fact this is simply a definition of the job of a doctor. The shepherd *qua* shepherd ought to care for his sheep, the gardener *qua* gardener ought to care for his flower beds and grass, and the pilot *qua* pilot ought to aim at transporting his passengers with safety. These are just definitions of occupations in terms of their aims. Of course, one might say that the person who happens to be a doctor ought to do the best he can as a doctor. Yes, and the person who happens to be a gardener ought to do the best he can for his flower beds. We all ought to work hard in our respective spheres. In other words, if medical ethics is made to seem grander than ordinary morality it is because a conceptual claim has become confused with a perfectly ordinary moral claim.

An argument of this kind is usually thought by doctors to be too superficial. They reply that patients are vulnerable and that health care must be delivered through the uniquely special doctor–patient relationship. But that uniquely special relationship requires a special morality to protect it, and so we need medical ethics as traditionally understood.

Yet what is uniquely special about the doctor–patient relationship? What emerges after any attempt to answer this question is that it is difficult to find a set of necessary and sufficient conditions, which justify the description 'uniquely special' of the doctor–patient relationship. Note to begin with that there is no one relationship which is *the* doctor–patient relationship. For example, an anaesthetist might see a patient once before an operation, but adding this to the anaesthetist's function during an operation hardly creates a 'relationship', and in any case it is certainly different from the 'relationship' which a community health doctor might have with the population who live in a given geographical area. But even waiving this objection and concentrating on certain typical sorts of doctor–patient relationships we cannot easily say what is *uniquely* special about them. Certainly, patients are lacking in information and power when, say, a coronary artery bypass operation is prescribed, but so are most of us when the garage mechanic prescribes an engine transplant! In each case most of us must trust in the knowledge, skills, and good faith of our helpers. Perhaps car engines are not so important as our bodies, but then we also commit the latter to the care of airline pilots and taxi drivers. Again, doctors may have access to our bodies; but teachers, clergymen, and advertisers have access to our minds and can influence to varying degrees our very perceptions of our own identities. The conclusion seems to be that if there are uniquely defining conditions of the doctor–patient relationship they are likely to be trivial and not special in the sense of important, and if there are special or important features they are likely to be shared with a variety of occupations such as the lifeboat service, the police, the clergy, teachers, and many others, some of which are 'professions' and some not. It seems more profitable, then, to drop the whole idea of uniquely special features of the doctor–patient relationship and to draw attention to 'family resemblances' between that relationship and a whole variety of others.

To argue, as I have done, that there is nothing uniquely special about the doctor–patient relationship certainly weakens the claim that there is a need for a special sort of morality. But it does not dispose of it entirely. I wish now to argue that medical ethics as traditionally understood is actually harmful to health care, and that the need is really to drop the traditional approach and to reassert the claims of ordinary morality (Downie and Calman, 1987).

The first respect in which traditional medical ethics has been harmful to health care concerns the distortions it has created in the doctor–patient relationship. For example, traditional codes are expressed in terms of the duties of the doctor, and while this has certainly inspired an idealistic practice it has also created a professional ethos of elitism and paternalism. Thus, generations of medical students have been given the impression that there is an esoteric set of rules – 'medical ethics' – which govern their professional activities. It is easy to extrapolate from this to the conclusion that such a code is different from and superior to ordinary morality. Doctors are not as other men; other men are guided by right and wrong, but doctors have medical ethics. For example, in ordinary life the assumption, if not the reality, is that people speak the truth to each other, but this is not an assumption of those governed by medical ethics; for medical ethics says that the first responsibility of the doctor is to the well being of his patient, and it is generally thought to follow that it is up to the doctor to decide how far, in his opinion, a patient's well being will be furthered by telling the truth. Medical ethics in this respect distorts the doctor–patient relationship, for any true human relationship must have sincerity as its necessary condition, and that condition is discouraged by the attitude built into traditional medical ethics: benevolence (if that is what it is) has swamped sincerity. This criticism might be summed up by saying that the duties of doctors should not be regarded, as they are in the tradition, as duties of benevolence, but rather as duties correlative to the *rights of patients*. To give this emphasis to the doctor–patient relationship is to cut out the distortion caused by the tradition. Indeed, an emphasis on rights – consumer rights, social and political rights, human rights of all kinds – is one moral characteristic of our time.

A second criticism which can be made of the tradition is that its fraternal, inward-looking nature discourages frank and open co-operation with other caring professions. For example, nurses and social workers are not part of the fraternity, so it has been a matter for debate how far they should be admitted into the inner counsels. One consequence of this is inefficiency in the delivery of health care due to uncertainty or lack of co-operation among all the members of a health care team. Where objectives are not shared and discussed among the caring professions there is a diminution of job satisfaction, friction, and a consequent damage to patient care. For example, one member of a team, a nurse, say, may not know how much a patient has been told or what the overall prognosis is. It is then difficult for the nurse to be fully supportive of the patient. This is not good morality.

A third respect in which the traditional approach to medical ethics is deficient is that it suggests that morality is about selected issues, rather than that it is all-pervasive. The discussion of medical ethics has tended to highlight the dramatic issues which happen to be topical at any one time. Although euthanasia, abortion, resuscitation, surrogate motherhood, and human experimentation are undoubtedly important matters, their prominence has obscured the fact that, not just once but many times in the course of a working day, moral stances, value judgments and decisions will result in actions considered to be right or wrong by the doctor. This is partly, but only partly, due to the uncertain nature of medical diagnosis and prognosis. The doctor, lacking certainty, must estimate what in his opinion is for the total good of the patient. This concept of 'total good' is not just a matter of technical expertise but involves values. For example, let us imagine a 70 year old man who wants to be allowed home soon after an operation. The doctor's judgment here will involve technical expertise, but will also involve economic and value judgments of a total good, including knowledge of the home circumstances and many other factors. Again, whether we do a job only moderately well when we are capable of doing it better is a question of morality, of deciding which direction we want to take. Allowing ourselves to become professionally socialised into routinised working patterns which keep things going but diminish patients' dignity and freedom requires as much a moral justification as a sociological explanation. These moral demands are all-pervasive and inescapable in health care.

Fourth, the traditional distinction between 'medical ethics' and 'private morality' suggests that one can deal with moral questions in a professional context without examining personal values and convictions. But I am arguing that it follows from the inescapable and all-pervasive nature of morality that we encounter moral problems in our personal lives which are not fundamentally different from those we may have to explore in our working environment. Whatever values we may feel to be important to us as individuals are almost certainly influencing and directing the decisions that we make as professional health care workers. If we have or lack the skills which allow us to approach moral dilemmas in a rational and methodical way in ordinary life, this will affect how we attempt to solve moral problems in a professional context. In other words, morality is 'indivisible'.

On the other hand, this fundamental assumption about the 'indivisibility' of morality does not lead to a rejection of the very special place that the maintenance of acceptable professional standards of behaviour must have in the work of people whose primary responsibility is to care for vulnerable fellow men and women. The potential harm that can come to people who are in some ways and by definition dependent on the knowledge and skills of others will undoubtedly heighten the moral concern in situations which, outside the professional context, might not be perceived as quite so threatening or acute. For example, a critical or sarcastic remark, which might be acceptable in ordinary circumstances, could be devastating to a sick person.

Another aspect of the 'indivisibility' of morality is that hospitals and other health care organisations ought not to be immune to general attitudinal changes in society. Moral dilemmas arise frequently from the attempts which the professions make or do not make to accommodate social change. Likewise, what professional people do, or often more pertinently what they would refuse to do, reflects the moral standards of their society in the same way in which actions of the individual doctor or nurse, psychologist or speech therapist, social worker or dietician reflect his or her standards of personal morality. The dilemmas created by social change can be obscured by an emphasis on medical ethics traditionally understood as a product.

A fifth criticism of traditional medical ethics is that it tends to underestimate the fact that medical decisions ought to be made in the real world of technological and economic facts. This point is much stressed in the papers of Mooney and McGuire, and Jennett ... Traditionally medical ethics tends to be seen in terms of pure moral absolutes – the doctor must do all that is medically possible for his (or her) patient regardless of the cost. I am asserting that in the real world compromises must be made. As an example of compromise we can point to renal dialysis. It is not helpful to say that there is an absolute value on human life if there are two patients who would benefit from dialysis but facilities for treating only one. The moral requirement here is to reflect on the scientific and economic facts of the cases as well as the quality of life of the potential recipients. This point can be expressed in the form of a distinction between compromising our consciences, which is wrong, and conscientious compromises, which consist in making the moral best of a bad job in the light of scientific and economic constraints. This distinction is compatible with the view that in some circumstances no compromises should be made.

These five criticisms of traditional medical ethics ... suggest that an enlightened medical ethics will be in terms of a 'process' – the process of applying the principles of everyday morality to the scientific and economic complexities of patient care. Moral decisions in medicine are what can be called 'consequential' or 'resultant' in that they arise out of the professional, economic, and legal facts of given cases. Ethics is no substitute for a good diagnosis of the problem, skillfully carried out treatment or clearly communicated information, but equally in doing these things the doctor is at the same time engaging in moral and economic activity. [© Gavin Mooney and Alistair McGuire 1988. Reprinted from *Medical Ethics and Economics in Health Care* edited by Gavin Mooney and Alistair McGuire (Oxford Medical Publications, 1988) by Oxford University Press.]

However, it may be arguable that there is a difference between a doctor and others who provide vital services. It might be said that if a doctor were to refuse to treat in an emergency, he would be the subject of moral condemnation in a way that, say, an off-duty fireman who refused to help in a rescue, would not. It is important to remember that here we are talking about moral, not legal obligations. In the UK, a doctor has no legal obligation to stop at the scene of an accident and treat the injured. If he does, then he is obliged to treat with reasonable skill and care and he may be liable in negligence (see Chapter 6). The position of a non-medically qualified volunteer who assists at the scene of an accident is exactly the same – it is simply that the standard of care is different. The legal duty not to harm is the same for doctor and lay person alike. Is the doctor's moral obligation different? Harris suggests it is not:

Harris, J, *The Value of Life*, 1985, London: Routledge & Kegan Paul, p 54:

We believe ... that we should rescue trapped miners and other victims of accidents, or those shipwrecked, or the victims of hijackers of other hostage-takers; and, not least, those who can be rescued only by medical care. Some of these rescues can be performed by anyone who is on hand; others require all sorts of expertise from that of potholers, sailors, miners, engineers, firemen and so on, to specialised military personnel and those with medical skills. Very often, those of us who lack these skills can best help, and thus discharge our obligation to those at risk, by keeping well out of the way. All of this is perhaps obvious enough, but it helps us to see two important features of the obligation of health care professionals. The first is that *there is nothing special about their obligation in particular*. Just as there is no special category of person whose unique and first obligation it is to refrain from inflicting death, injury or suffering on the rest of us, so there is no one who is specially required, morally speaking, to undertake rescues.

It is also illuminating to consider the duty of beneficence in terms of Kant's perfect/imperfect duties. Kant considers generosity or beneficence as imperfect duties, which an individual has no right to demand, as he has a right, for example, to demand justice.

Of course, the doing of 'good' may, in the short term, necessitate the infliction of pain. Beauchamp and McCullough describe the 'balancing exercise' that may arise as follows:

Beauchamp, TL and McCullough, LB, *Medical Ethics,* **1984, Englewood Cliffs: Prentice Hall, p 30:**

The basic roles and concepts that give substance to the principle of beneficence in medicine are as follows: the positive benefit the physician is under obligation to seek is the cure of disease and injury if there is a reasonable hope of cure; the harms to be avoided, prevented, or removed are the pain and suffering of injury and disease. In addition, the physician is enjoined from doing harm. This consideration, too must be included in the beneficence model because physician interventions themselves can inflict unnecessary pain and suffering on patients. The Hippocratic texts hold that inflicting pain and suffering is permissible in those cases in which the physician is attempting to reverse a threat to health, eg, administering an emetic after the accidental ingestion of a poison. Inflicting such pain and suffering on a patient in order to eliminate a deadly substance from the body is justified because the patient is on balance benefited. When the patient cannot be benefited by further intervention, the inflicted pain and suffering is unnecessary and to be avoided. Thus, in its first formulation in Western medical ethics, the beneficence model of moral responsibility adapts the principle of beneficence to patient care by providing a medically oriented account of how to balance goods over harms.

The rosy spectacled view of the special role of beneficence is questioned by Pellegrino and Thomasma:

Pellegrino, ED and Thomasma, DC, *For the Patient's Good: The Restoration of Beneficence in Health Care,* **1988, Oxford: OUP, p 4:**

According to the Hippocratic Oath, the physician promises to 'follow that system of regimen which according to my ability and judgment I consider for the benefit of my patients'. Nowhere in the Hippocratic corpus is there any provision for the patient's view of things. In fact, in one place the relationship is described as being between 'one who orders and one who obeys'.

We shall see that this traditional principle, however, may be tempered to take into account the wishes of the patient (see p 38, below).

The work of a doctor in the late 20th century is often highly technical in nature, depending upon pharmacy, engineering, computer technology and so on. It might be argued that this diminishes the particular duty of beneficence in some way. Beauchamp and McCullough suggest that it does not:

Beauchamp, TL and McCullough, LB, *Medical Ethics,* **1984, Englewood Cliffs: Prentice Hall, p 35:**

In the history of medicine, the physician has primarily functioned in care-giving and comforting roles, with beneficence serving as the moral foundation of these roles. As medical science exploded in the 20th century, medicine was transformed into a more scientific and technical enterprise. It might be argued that this change has transformed the physician's role, stripping it of its moral core and making it a sheerly technical enterprise. However, this hypothesis is misleading. Beneficent intervention remains, as ever, the moral foundation of the physician's role, a role powerfully augmented by medical science and technology. These remarkable new capacities created some moral problems in medicine, especially problems concerning the physician's authority, but they did not destroy medicine's tradition of beneficence.

But is this confidence that the traditional role of the physician has not been undermined misplaced? Much of the research which leads to treatment at the disposal of the physician has not been developed by physicians at all. Developments in genetics are a case in point. Once opportunities for genetic manipulation, for example, have been unleashed, how much power does the physician have to resist them?

The principle of beneficence is at work when we consider the doctrine of 'double effect'. Imagine a gravely ill patient in the last stages of terminal cancer. The patient is in pain and only a substantial dose of morphine will relieve the pain. However, such a large dose will also hasten the patient's death. As far as the law is concerned this is not homicide (see Chapter 12), and as far as medical ethics is concerned, the principle of beneficence means that the doctor's only intention is to do good, ie relieve pain. The fact that death would also be hastened does not undermine the beneficent motive of the doctor. However, as we shall see, there are aspects of medical law where the principle of beneficence is undermined. First, in medical research patients may be subjected to randomised clinical trials (RCTs) (see Chapter 10). This means that some patients will not be receiving any treatment at all but, unknown to them, will be given placebos, so that the researchers can compare their progress with that of the patients who are given drug treatment. It is arguable that this can never be consistent with the principle of beneficence unless the principle is interpreted as meaning beneficence towards patients in the sense of a *general* benefit to the sick. Similarly, it is accepted that doctors may breach their duty of confidentiality in respect of an individual patient in the wider public interest. In these circumstances, it can be argued, the principle of beneficence is only upheld if it is equated with some form of consequentialism.

Non-maleficence

The traditional duty to do good has been accompanied by the obligation to do no harm – *primum non nocere* (first, do no harm). Gillon describes this in terms of Kant's perfect/imperfect duties distinction, and sees this as a wider obligation than that of beneficence:

Gillon, R, *Philosophical Medical Ethics*, 1985, Chichester: John Wiley, p 81:

The claim that avoiding harm has priority over doing good is vigorously contested in moral philosophy. An interesting sample of the detailed arguments appears in a paper by Phillippa Foot in which she argues for the claim that 'other things being equal, the obligation not to harm people is more stringent that the obligation to benefit people' [Foot, P, 'The problem of abortion and the doctrine of double effect', reprinted in Steinbock, *Killing and Letting Die*, 1980, Englewood Cliffs: Prentice Hall] and in a detailed criticism of her paper Nancy Davis, who argues, primarily by counterexamples, that no such general priority can be defended [Davis, N, 'The priority of avoiding harm', reprinted in Steinbock] ... At first sight Foot's thesis is undoubtedly plausible. We seem to have what Kant called a perfect (though, many would add, only *prima facie*) duty to all other people not to harm them. On the other hand, we do not have a duty to benefit all other people; apart from everything else it is incoherent to talk of a duty which is impossible to fulfil. Thus at most we can have a duty only to benefit some other people (an imperfect duty), while we have a perfect duty to everybody not to harm them.

> While it seems entirely plausible to claim that we owe non-maleficence, but not beneficence, to everybody, it does not follow from this that avoidance of doing harm (non-maleficence) takes priority over beneficence. All that follows is that the scope of non-maleficence is general, encompassing all other people, whereas the scope of beneficence is more specific, applying only to some people not to harm them. Thus we can accept that each of us has a (*prima facie*) moral duty not to harm anybody else without being committed to believing that this *prima facie* duty must always take priority if it conflicts with any duty, including any duty of beneficence, we may have to particular people or groups of people.

This principle might, for example, be used to justify the 'acts and omissions' distinction in the law relating to euthanasia. As we shall see (Chapter 12), in the case of a very seriously ill patient, a doctor may not be obliged to continue to treat that patient. In other words, he can withdraw or omit to treat, and remain within the confines of the law. This is because the doctor may decide that the treatment is not benefiting the patient. That is consistent with the principle of beneficence because the doctor will say that the treatment is not, or would not, benefit the patient. The omission to treat is acceptable. However, the doctor is not legally permitted to give the patient a lethal injection to bring about death, even when 'natural' death is very close, as, it is argued, it would infringe the principle of non-maleficence. But it is arguable that the lethal injection would not be harmful as it might be the kindest way of treating a patient who is terminally ill and in great pain.

The nature of illness

Why is it necessary to consider this? It could be said that the presence of 'illness' or 'disease' is a straightforward factual matter. However, it is interesting to try and formulate a definition. Culver and Gert review the medical literature and select a number of definitions:

Culver, CM and Gert, B, *Philosophy in Medicine*, 1982, New York: OUP, p 66:

Some past definitions of 'disease'

There have been many attempts to set out a formal definition of 'disease,' but among physicians only rarely has a distinction among 'disease', 'illness', 'injury' and related terms been recognised. Consequently, 'illness' is often used interchangeably with 'disease', and injuries are regarded merely as a subclass of diseases. What most of the following authors have intended to define is what we call a malady, so that in addition to diseases they have included injuries, illnesses, headaches and the like in their definitions. By not realising what they have done, however, they have often been misled by some particular feature of the term 'disease'.

Some definitions are general, vague, and too inclusive. Thus, a pathology textbook (Peery and Miller, 1971) states:

> Disease is any disturbance of the structure or function of the body or any of its parts; an imbalance between the individual and his environment; a lack of perfect health.

This seems to offer three separate but equivalent definitions. According to the first definition, clipping nails and puberty are diseases, as well as asymptomatic *situs inversus* (right-left reversal of position of bodily organs) and being tied to a chair. The second definition is too vague to be of any use, and the third is circular. A textbook on internal medicine (Talso and Remenchik, 1968) says:

> ... disease may be defined as deprivation or lack of ease, a discomfort or an annoyance, or a morbid condition of the body or of some organ or part thereof.

There are similar problems here. Two separate definitions are offered. The first is too sweeping and would include inflation, quarrelsome in-laws, poor television reception, and ill-fitting shoes, while the second is circular and depends on the phrase 'morbid condition', which is merely a synonym for 'disease'.

Most texts on medicine and pathology make no attempt to define disease, which is appropriate enough since the exercise is irrelevant to their purposes. Thus, it might be said in defence of the above attempts that they were probably not meant to be taken very seriously.

One cluster of definitions which is meant to be taken seriously utilises a dynamic metaphor in which a person is pictured as constantly interacting and adapting to changes in his environment; disease then corresponds to a failure in that adaptation. An early expression of this definition is found in White's 1926 book, *The Meaning of Disease*:

> Disease can only be that state of the organism that for the time being, at least, is fighting a losing game whether the battle be with temperature, water, micro-organisms, disappointment or what not. In any instance, it may be visualised as the reaction of the organism to some sort of energy impact, addition or deprivation.

Thus, one wrestler held down by another is suffering a disease. A more modern version is found in Engel's 1962 book, *Psychological Development in Health and Disease*:

> When adaptation or adjustment fail and the pre-existing dynamic steady state is disrupted, then a state of disease may be said to exist until a new balance is restored which may again permit the effective interaction with the environment.

Aside from the ambiguities and the question begging inherent in 'adaptation' and 'balance', the emphasis in this definition (and the preceding one) on the deterioration of a previously more normal state seems to rule out all congenital and hereditary diseases ...

JG Scadding (1959, 1963, 1967) has written a series of papers on the definition of disease. In the most recent of these, he offers the following 'formal definition':

> A disease is the sum of the abnormal phenomena displayed by a group of living organisms in association with a specified common characteristic or set of characteristics by which they differ from the norm for their species in such a way as to place them at a biological disadvantage.

Scadding's definition is an improvement over those previously cited. He explicitly introduces the notion of deviation from a norm for a species which, though it does not deserve the prominence he gives it, is necessary for understanding the essential elements of the concept of malady. His 'biological disadvantage' criterion also points in the right direction but is too vague. Kendell, in a recent paper (1975), interprets 'biological disadvantage' as meaning decreased fertility or longevity. But this does not work. Even Kendell recognises that his revision of Scadding's definition leaves one with the 'rather disconcerting' result that a condition such as psoriasis would not qualify as a disease.

Several recent authors have also correctly identified aspects of disease. Spitzer and Endicott (1978) include in their definition of 'a medical disorder' that it is intrinsically associated with distress, disability, or certain types of disadvantage. We think this definition is on the right track. Goodwin and Guze (1979) consider as a disease 'any condition associated with discomfort, pain, disability, death, or an increased liability to these states, regarded by physicians and the public as properly the responsibility of the medical profession ...'

Note the concluding phrase 'regarded by physicians and the public as properly the responsibility of the medical profession'. Is 'illness' that which a doctor thinks should be treated? A doctor faced with a hypochondriac may well form the conclusion that the symptoms complained of are imagined and that the person is not ill, and therefore no treatment is given regardless of the fact that the patient may have some organic disorder, which would be treated by another doctor who did not know about the hypochondria. This may sound simplistic, but consider treatment for infertile people. Are they ill? Or diseased? The answer is no, but they receive 'treatment' because doctors think that they should. It may be argued that it is society which decides what conditions merit treatment and what do not, but does that underestimate the power of information and medical technology, concentrated as it is, if not in the hands of doctors exclusively, in the hands of medical science? Society did not demand heart transplants until the first operation had been performed. The developments in genetic research have implications here. There is evidence that genes which 'cause' things such as baldness may be isolated and eradicated. This would be a 'medical' procedure. Would it mean that baldness would become an illness?

THE CASE FOR PATERNALISM

Introduction

In this and the following sections, we will look at the arguments which may be advanced, respectively, in favour of a paternalistic approach to medicine, and in favour of the primacy of patient autonomy. These two theories are described by Pellegrino and Thomasma:

Pellegrino, ED and Thomasma, DC, *For the Patient's Good: The Restoration of Beneficence in Health Care*, 1988, Oxford: OUP, p 3:

Two major ethical theories are today vying for dominance in medical ethics. The first, inherited from the Enlightenment, stresses the liberty and autonomy of the individual. It gathered strength in the 19th century in response to the depreciation of personal worth that accompanied the Industrial Revolution. This theory grounds ethics in rights, duties and obligations. The second theory stresses social utility rather than individual autonomy. Ironically, it too gained ascendancy during the Industrial Revolution to counter the social atomism of a purely individualistic ethic. This theory stresses social good, rules of conduct, and social accountability. Mill laid the foundation for such theories when he proposed the principle of autonomy, on the one hand, and the principle of utility, on the other.

Applied to physician–patient relationship, the first theory imposes on the physician the obligation of respect for the patient's self-determination. The second theory requires that the physician act to maximise benefits and goods even if this might demand acting without the patient's consent. It sanctions overriding the patient's autonomous decision if that decision is not judged by the physician to be in the patient's or society's good.

When considering the respective positions of the paternalist and the anti-paternalist, it is important to consider two things. First, as we shall see, the consent of the patient is necessary before any medical treatment can take place. This might be said to reflect the anti-paternalist view. The patient can refuse simple life-saving treatment and there is no mechanism for imposing it upon him. However, at least in English law, the arbiter of what the patient needs to know before he consents or refuses is the doctor. It might be said that this reflects a paternalist viewpoint. Secondly, the patient must be competent, ie have sufficient mental capacity to make a treatment decision. The doctor will decide whether the patient is competent. If he lacks competence, he may be treated in his 'best interests'. When reading the following, keep these points in mind.

What is paternalism?

When we considered the principle of beneficence, we noted that it is a one-sided principle: the doctor is *doing good to/for the patient*. Beneficence does not mean the same as paternalism (the recognition of the patient's right to self-determination may be part of beneficence), but a narrower view of beneficence is compatible with paternalism. The paternalistic doctor 'knows best' and regards himself as being the best judge as to what is for the patient's own good. It is interesting to consider the duty of beneficence in relation to the parent–child relationship (the term paternalistic meaning to act like a father): although the parent may be said to have a duty of non-maleficence towards his child, does he have a positive duty to do good?

John Harris distinguishes paternalism from moralism:

Harris, J, *The Value of Life*, 1985, London: Routledge & Kegan Paul, p 194:

When health care professionals accept that their first duty is to act always in the best interests of their patients they are in effect saying that they are concerned for the welfare of their patients and that this is in no way inconsistent with manifesting 'respect for persons'. Welfare is not here used as a technical term – it means what it usually means, 'the state or condition of doing or being well', which will include things like happiness, health and living standards.

An initial problem is that concern for the welfare of others is compatible both with paternalism and with moralism. Briefly, paternalism is the belief that it can be right to order the lives of others for their own good, irrespective of their own wishes or judgments. The characteristic cry of the paternalist is: 'Don't do that, it isn't good for you.' *Moralism*, on the other hand, is the belief that it can be right to order the lives of others so that 'morality' may be preserved. The characteristic cry of the moralist is: 'Don't do that, it's wicked.'

Both the paternalist and the moralist are genuinely concerned for the welfare of others. They argue that it cannot be in your interest, nor can it be conducive to your being in a state of doing or being well, if you either do what isn't good for you or act immorally. Despite the genuineness of this moral concern, both paternalism and moralism involve treating the agent as an incompetent. They deny the individual control over her own life and moral destiny and treat her as incompetent to run her own life as she chooses. While both involve genuine concern for the welfare of others, neither can lay claim to demonstrating respect for their wishes.

But although Harris is right in saying that we are not respecting the wishes of the person whom we exhort to do good, or refrain from doing bad, we would nevertheless argue that we are entitled to do it. If you intervene to prevent another from picking someone's pocket, you are certainly not respecting the pickpocket's wishes, but you are not wrong to do this. Cannot we say the same thing about paternalism? The paternalist's argument would be that, although you are not respecting the patient's wishes when he says he does not want a life-saving operation and you go ahead and perform it anyway, nevertheless you are not wrong to save his life.

Hart describes paternalism as the protection of people against themselves, and maintains that, although respect for individual autonomy is very much a part of 20th century life, there has been a general decline in the belief that we are the best judges of our own best interests. Referring to the libertarian views of JS Mill, Hart says:

Hart, HLA, *Law, Liberty and Morality*, 1963, Oxford: OUP, p 33:

[There is] an increased awareness of a great range of factors which diminish the significance to be attached to an apparently free choice or to consent. Choices may be made or consent given without adequate reflection or appreciation of the consequences; or in pursuit of merely transitory desires; or in various predicaments when the judgment is likely to be clouded; or under inner psychological compulsion; or under pressure by others of a kind too subtle to be susceptible of proof in a law court. Underlying Mill's extreme fear of paternalism there perhaps is a conception of what a normal human being is like which now seems not to correspond to the facts. Mill, in fact, endows him with much of the psychology of a middle-aged man whose desires are relatively fixed, not liable to be artificially stimulated by external influences; who knows what he wants and what gives him satisfaction or happiness; and who pursues these things when he can.

As far as medicine is concerned, this argument states that paternalism is justified when, in the judgment of the doctor, the patient does not exhibit sufficient of the features of Hart's middle-aged man. The patient may be too young; the patient may have limited intelligence or limited education or may have a volatile personality given to acts of impetuosity. The doctor, on the other hand, is educated, impartial, knowledgeable and has only the best interests of the patient at heart. This grading of patients – and in consequence the way in which a doctor is entitled to regard them – is reflected in some of the case law (see, for example, the case of *Sidaway v Board of Governors of the Bethlem Royal Hospital and the Maudsley Hospital* [1985] AC 871, where Lord Diplock (p 895) states that an educated judge would 'naturally' want to ask questions about the risks of medical treatment before he consented to it – see further Chapter 3).

Strong and weak paternalism

It is arguable that the above view, ie that some patients do not have sufficient education, etc, to make valid decisions, does not support paternalism in any form, but only where the patient's views are disregarded because of the circumstances, or something in the patient's own character. Writers sometimes refer to the difference as that between 'strong' and 'weak' (or 'limited') paternalism.

Childress describes the justification for limited paternalism as follows:

Childress, JF, *Who Should Decide? Paternalism in Health Care*, 1982, Oxford: OUP, p 102:

Conditions for justified paternalism

The principle of limited paternalism

Parents sometimes override their children's wishes in order to protect them. Such parental actions are often justified because of children's incompetence and risk of harm or loss of some good. This example from familial relations yields two conditions that are frequently invoked to justify medical paternalism: (1) the defects, encumbrances, and limitations of a person's decision-making and acting; and (2) the probability of harm to that person unless there is intervention.

If the second condition – probable harm – is held to be sufficient to justify paternalism, apart from the person's incapacity for decision-making, we have extended or strong paternalism. According to this position, paternalistic interventions can be justified when a patient's risk-benefit analysis is unreasonable even though he is competent and his wishes, choices, or actions are informed and voluntary. If, however, the first set of conditions is held to be necessary, we have limited or weak paternalism, which allows paternalistic interventions only when a person's wishes, choices, or actions are defective because of incompetence, ignorance, or some internal or external constraint.

Both conditions, yet to be explained and amplified, are jointly necessary to justify active paternalism … To intervene merely because a person suffers some defect, encumbrance, or limitation in decision-making or in acting is unwarranted. It would be intervention for the sake of intervention. As 'paternalism' implies, intervention requires justification in terms of the patient's interests as well as in terms of the patient's defects in deciding or acting. If the patient is not at risk, intervention is not warranted, however much his or her capacity to make decisions is reduced. Even a person with diminished capacity for decision-making should be free except when he or she is at risk. This is an implication of holding that both conditions are jointly necessary.

If these two conditions are jointly necessary for justified active paternalism, and if only limited paternalism is justified, we are able to express both the principle of beneficence and the principle of respect for persons. In limited paternalism, agents meet the needs of other persons without insulting them. For example, if another person is incompetent to make decisions and is also at risk, interventions even against that person's express wishes do not signify disrespect or constitute an indignity. Not to intervene might even violate the principle of respect for persons; certainly, it would violate the principle of beneficence in some circumstances.

Since both of these conditions are necessary to justify paternalistic acts, it is possible to start with either one. An apparent reason to start with prevention or removal of harm, or provision of benefit, is that this consideration frequently triggers paternalistic actions. In the order of experience, perception of risk to the patient, apart from intervention, usually precedes and provokes an assessment of the patient's competence to decide. Indeed … Carlton's studies indicate that a patient's competence to consent to treatment is rarely examined unless there is a conflict between the physician's recommendation and the patient's wishes. Thus, an apparent conflict of values provides the occasion for an examination of the patient's competence. In view of customary medical practice, there are two good reasons for beginning with the patient's incompetence as a necessary condition for justified paternalism. First, to begin with the prevention or removal of harm may appear to give this condition priority and may play into the hands of strong paternalists. Second, even though in practice there may be little interest in the patient's competence unless there are risks, from a moral point of view the assessment of the patient's competence should be somewhat independent of the risks. Otherwise, strong paternalism could masquerade as weak paternalism, since – the argument might go – no competent person would knowingly and voluntarily accept some risks.

Culver and Gert put forward two examples of paternalism, one of which they maintain is justified, the other not:

Culver, CM and Gert, B, *Philosophy in Medicine*, 1982, New York: OUP, p 146:

Case 8–1

Mr K was brought to the emergency room by his wife and a police officer. Mrs K had confessed to her husband earlier that evening that she was having an affair with one of his colleagues. He had become acutely agitated and depressed and, after several hours of mounting tension, told her he was going to kill himself so 'you'll have the freedom to have all the lovers you want'. She became frightened and called the police because there were loaded guns in the house and she knew her husband was an impulsive man.

In the emergency room Mr K would do little more than glower at Dr T, his wife, and the officer. He seemed extremely tense and agitated. Dr T decided that for Mr K's own protection he should be hospitalised but Mr K refused. Dr T therefore committed Mr K to the hospital for a 72 hour emergency detention.

How could Dr T attempt to justify his paternalistic commitment of Mr K? He could claim that by depriving Mr K of his freedom, there was a great likelihood that he was preventing the occurrence of a much greater evil: Mr K's death, or serious injury. Dr T could further claim that in his professional experience the overwhelming majority of persons in Mr K's condition who were hospitalised did subsequently recover from their state of agitated depression and acknowledge the irrational character of their former suicidal desires.

Note that Dr T need not claim that self-inflicted death is an evil of such magnitude that paternalistic intervention to prevent it is always justified. Rather, he could claim that it is justified in Mr K's case on several counts. First, Mr K's desire to kill himself seems irrational; while one may explain his desire, using psychodynamic concepts, he appears to have no adequate reason for killing himself. An adequate reason would be a belief on his part that his death would result in the avoiding of great evil(s) or the attaining of great goods for himself or others. (His statement to his wife ['You'll have ... all the lovers you want'] sarcastically expresses an altruistic reason which, even if taken literally, would not be an adequate reason for his suicide.) Second, there is evidence that he suffers from a condition that is well known to be transient. Third, the violation of a moral rule (deprivation of freedom) which Dr T has carried out results in Mr K's suffering a much lesser evil than the evil (death) which Mr K may perpetrate on himself.

But it is not sufficient justification for Dr T merely to show that the evils prevented for Mr K by his paternalistic action outweigh the evils caused to Mr K; he must also be willing to publicly advocate the deprivation of Mr K's freedom in these circumstances. That is, he must be willing to advocate to all rational persons that in these circumstances everyone may be deprived of his freedom for a limited period of time. We believe that, accepting the case as described, not only could Dr T advocate to all rational persons that Mr K may be deprived of his freedom but also that, if they accepted the facts of the case and the conditions of public advocacy, all rational persons would agree with Dr T's judgment completely. Thus, Dr T's paternalistic behaviour is strongly justified.

By contrast, Culver and Gert consider the following:

Case 8–2

Mrs R, a 29 year old mother, is hospitalised with symptoms of abdominal pain, weight loss, weakness, and swelling of the ankles. An extensive medical workup is inconclusive, and exploratory abdominal surgery is carried out which reveals a primary ovarian cancer with extensive spread to other abdominal organs. Her condition is judged to be too far advanced for surgical relief, and her life expectancy is estimated to be at most a few months. Despite her oft-repeated requests to be told 'where I stand and what I face', Dr E tells both the patient and her husband that the diagnosis is still unclear but that he will see her weekly as an out-patient. At the time of discharge she is feeling somewhat better than at admission, and Dr E hopes that the family will have a few happy weeks together before her condition worsens and they must be told the truth.

Dr E's behaviour is clearly paternalistic: he has deceived Mrs R for what he believes is her benefit; he knows that he is violating the moral rule against deception without her consent; and he views her as someone who is competent to give or refuse valid consent to being told the truth.

Dr E could attempt to justify his paternalistic act by claiming that the evil – psychological suffering – he hoped to prevent by his deception is significantly greater than the evil, if any, he caused by lying. While this might be true in this particular case, it is by no means certain. By his deception, Dr E is depriving Mrs R and her family of the opportunity to make those plans that would enable her family to deal more adequately with her death. In the circumstances of this case as described, Mrs R's desire to know the truth is a rational one; in fact, there is no evidence of any irrational behaviour or desires on her part. This contrasts sharply to Mr K's desire to kill himself, which is clearly irrational. Furthermore, although we regard Mr K's desire not to be deprived of freedom, considered in isolation, as a rational one, we would not consider it rational for one to choose a high probability of death over the loss of a few days of freedom.

Arguably, we can see a weak form of paternalism operating when we consider our attitude to organ donation and non-therapeutic medical research. It is unlawful in the UK to sell a non-regenerative organ for transplant (see Chapter 11). Similarly, we prevent anything other than modest payments for those who undergo non-therapeutic research (ie healthy volunteers). Many people who would not regard themselves as paternalists in the context of medical treatment might support these prohibitions on the basis that it is offensive for there to be a 'trade' in human organs or for people to sell their bodies for the purposes of research. However, is this not a form of paternalism, albeit one based upon the principle of non-maleficence (as opposed to paternalism in relation to medical treatment which is based upon the principle of beneficence)?

Paternalism and the sanctity of life principle

Both Mill and Kant would accept the sanctity of life principle as this stems from the inherent value of the individual. The duty of beneficence has this principle at its heart. A paternalist might argue that the doctor's duty to do good and to uphold the sanctity of life principle will, on occasion, justifiably, override patient autonomy. For example, in Chapter 8 we look at several cases where the courts have had to consider the refusal by women of consent to Caesarean section operations to deliver their children. It has been held that the women's refusals must be respected, even if there is a strong likelihood that both mother and foetus will not survive. However, there is an argument that the principle of the sanctity of life might, in certain circumstances, override the woman's refusal.

Paternalism and the doctor's duty of beneficence

It might be said that it is bad for those involved in health care to be forced to stand helpless in the face of a refusal of life-saving treatment and witness an unnecessary death. This view might be illustrated by the role of doctors and other health care workers in the treatment of suicide attempts. Someone who attempts to take their own life can be treated without their consent. From what arises the right to override the patient's wish to die? Is it because the true wishes of the patient may not be known (it could be a 'cry for help' or an accident), or is it because of the dominance of the sanctity of life principle? It should be noted that health authorities have been held liable when a patient has committed suicide whilst under their care, if there has been inadequate supervision (see Chapter 3). Again, arguably, this is about sanctity of life and beneficence: it is inappropriate that hospitals should be places of avoidable and self-inflicted deaths; they are places for healing and the saving of lives.

Paternalism and a duty to oneself?

In Culver and Gert's example of the patient at risk of suicide, it was assumed that paternalism would eventually give way to autonomy. Is there a sustainable ethical argument that one has a duty to oneself to live and to live a healthy life, and, therefore, treatment against one's wishes may be justifiable? It will be recalled that the intuitionist philosopher, WD Ross, said that one of the intuitively good principles was the duty of self-improvement.

Similarly, Kant, whose moral philosophy stated that human life is intrinsically valuable, puts duty before 'natural inclinations'. for example, he thought suicide permissible only if it was to avoid moral degradation. this was based upon the principle that only human beings can uphold the moral law and, therefore, for as long as they are not morally degraded, they have a duty to do that. would this justify medical paternalism on the basis that the patient has a duty to live a healthy life and if, in the opinion of his doctors, he is not doing so, he must be treated against his will?

THE CASE FOR PATIENT AUTONOMY

Paternalism has an old-fashioned ring to it. Two American academics, Pellegrino and Thomasma, comment as follows:

Pellegrino, ED and Thomasma, DC, *For the Patient's Good: The Restoration of Beneficence in Health Care*, 1988, Oxford: OUP, p 5:

The sources of ... resistance to medical paternalism are many: the political and ethical philosophy of individual rights; the higher educational level of today's public; the latter's awareness of the powers and dangers of medical technology; a distrust of experts; the rise of consumerism; and the moral challenges of the Vietnam War, the civil rights movement, and the campus revolts of the '60s and early '70s. The convergence of these forces has been powerful enough to erode the 2,500 year old tradition of medical status contained in beneficent authoritarianism.

Autonomy

It is in the assertion that the right to autonomous medical decision-making is paramount that Mill's libertarian philosophy is most evident: the only justification for imposing medical treatment on a patient against his will is to prevent harm to others. (In the section on utilitarianism and autonomy we will consider whether non-consensual medical treatment may ever by justified on the basis that it will prevent harm to others, but let us assume for the present that it will not.) Beauchamp and McCullough describe the development of the autonomy principle:

Beauchamp, TL and McCullough, LB, *Medical Ethics*, 1984, Englewood Cliffs: Prentice Hall, p 42:

A key feature of the principle of respect for autonomy has been developed in legal contexts, where 'self-determination' has a venerable history and is taken to be synonymous with what we are calling autonomy – that is, the ability to understand one's situation and pursue personal goals free of governing constraints. The principle of self-determination means that one has sovereignty over one's life – a sovereignty that protects privacy as well as rights to control what happens to one's person and property. In its original development in the law, the intrinsic worth of the individual, including the right to personal sovereignty, was advanced primarily as a check or limit on the authority of the State or another person. For example, the Bill of Rights and the 'due process' amendments to the United States Constitution were so fashioned. The central theme is that a person's sovereignty limits the sphere into which others may legitimately intrude.

Individual sovereignty needs protection for two reasons. First, there is a danger of imbalance in power between the individual and the State (or other parties) in favour of the latter. Individual rights provide a corrective to this imbalance by ensuring that individuals as individuals will be given due consideration and respect. Second, conflicts arise between an individual's perception of his or her best interests and another's perception of those interests. Rights of individual sovereignty protect an individual's freedom to choose his or her best interests. The legal principle of respect for self-determination is applied to questions concerning the physician's responsibility because patients and physicians are unequal in their possession of information and their power to control the circumstances under which they meet. Typically, one party is fit and medically knowledgeable, the other sick and medically ignorant. Legal rights are a way of limiting the physician's power and of protecting the patient from unwarranted intrusions – such as surgery without consent, involuntary commitment to a mental institution, and public disclosure of information contained in hospital records.

Conflicts also arise between medicine's understanding of a patient's best interests and the patient's understanding of those interests. This conflict occurs in the case [of a young woman who wishes to be sterilised as a contraceptive measure as she had decided that her life would be better without children] A physician ... may view this patient's best interests in quite another way by following the beneficence model. Thus, the law dictates that the physician who performs an invasive procedure without the patient's permission may be found guilty of a *battery*, though usually only *negligence* is charged. The underlying rationale behind the battery theory of liability for failure to obtain the patient's agreement has been closely linked in law to autonomy. This rationale burst on the scene in a crucial 1914 case and has since been widely offered as the basic right underlying the legal doctrine of informed consent: 'Every human being of adult years and sound mind has a right to determine what shall be done with his own body; and a surgeon who performs an operation without his patient's consent commits an assault.'

This right is an autonomy right. The language in which the law has expressed it is quite striking. Among the most important formulations is the following from a 1960 landmark case, *Natanson v Kline*: 'A doctor might well believe that an operation or form of treatment is desirable or necessary, but the law does not permit him to substitute his own judgment for that of the patient by any form of artifice or deception.' In a later case, Warren Burger, who later became Chief Justice of the United States Supreme Court, amplified the legal concept of self-determination, with a reflection on the character of the reasons or values of a patient that are meant to be protected. He argued that nothing in the right to be left alone means that an individual possesses these rights only regarding sensible beliefs, reasonable emotions, and the like. Hence many eccentric and even absurd ideas may validly form the basis of a patient's autonomous choices.

Much of the debate surrounding the principle of autonomy concerns the right of a patient to refuse life-saving treatment. Earlier we considered how far there may be an obligation to prevent suicide. It is interesting to note that it has been said that the liberty to commit suicide may be seen as 'an index of high civilisation', because the act goes against the most basic of our instincts, that of self-preservation (see Alvarez, A, *The Savage God: A Study of Suicide*, 1971, London: Weidenfeld & Nicolson).

The right to self-determination

Is the principle of autonomy equivalent to the right to self-determination? Is this 'right' really a liberty in the sense that there is no claim against anyone in the Hohfeldian sense? Certainly the right to self-determination could not be relied upon to impose duties on others to provide medical treatment.

There is some debate as to whether autonomy is part of the right to privacy. Wellman considers the issue:

Wellman, C, *An Approach to Rights*, 1997, Dordrecht: Kluwer Academic, p 185:

... how is this right [to privacy] related to personal autonomy? A tempting hypothesis is that autonomy is located within one portion of this right because one of the constitutionally protected areas of privacy is that of private decisions. Thus, even though the right to privacy is not the liberty-right to make and act on private decisions, it includes the claim-right that others not interfere with these private decisions, for any such interference would be an invasion of a protected area of privacy. I very much doubt, however, that this direct and essential connection between privacy and autonomy has ever been recognised by the courts. For one thing, the expression 'a private decision' is conspicuous by its absence from the opinions in the privacy cases, even in *Roe [v Wade]* and *Quinlan* that centre on the abortion decision and the decision to refuse medical treatment, respectively. Moreover, this interpretation misrepresents the reasoning of the courts. The argument in *Roe* is not that the abortion decision is constitutionally protected because it is a private decision, but that it is encompassed by the right to privacy because it involves the exercise of one of the fundamental liberties recognised in the US Constitution. Hence, the emphasis is upon how fundamental, not how personal and private, the decision is.

The political approach and the rejection of 'social control'

Those who support the overriding importance of the autonomy principle are lent support by the way in which psychiatry was used in the former Soviet Union, where some political dissidents were diagnosed as being 'psychiatrically ill' and compulsorily detained in hospital. The writer Thomas Szasz, whose work is considered further in Chapter 9, cites this abuse of medicine in a number of his publications (see, for example, Szasz, TS, *Law, Liberty and Psychiatry: An Inquiry into the Social Uses of Mental Health Practices*, 1974, London: Routledge & Kegan Paul). The argument is that illness is a value-laden concept and any form of paternalism runs the risk of doctors branding patients with 'illness' and subsequent treatment. It is easy to see how this abuse can take place with something as nebulous as mental illness, but could this sort of abuse take place in respect of other forms of illness? Perhaps alcoholism, for example, could be so regarded – and see p 28 above, where it is suggested that 'imperfections' such as baldness might be categorised as illnesses.

Utilitarianism and autonomy

It is interesting to consider the interaction of these two concepts, because both were embraced in the philosophy of JS Mill. His libertarian views imply that one must be free to pursue a conception of life that is conducive to human flourishing. However, is there one conception of the good life, and if not, how do we maximise welfare? Similarly, if one is looking at the consequences of actions, if the exercise of one's autonomy adversely affects other people, then are not the two principles incompatible? In the context of refusal of life-saving treatment, it may be said that the right to self-determination is in conflict with utility because the consequences of the refusal may be bad for the family left behind: the loss of a breadwinner (the family is now dependent upon society for support) and the infliction of grief. It is arguable that this reflects one of the deficiencies in the utilitarian approach: it allows only a limited role for basic rights. Alternatively, it could be said that subjecting people to violation of their physical integrity has worse consequences for society than does respecting their bodily integrity. If this argument were accepted then respect for autonomy would be an essential element of any utilitarian account of medical ethics.

Rationality

Giving effect to autonomy in relation to medical treatment presupposes that the patient is competent to make decisions about such treatment. Do these decisions have to be rational? GEM Anscombe (see *Intention*, 1963, Oxford: Blackwells) gives an interesting example of having a reason for doing something. She cites the example of a man who wants a saucer of mud. He is asked whether he wants it to study its chemistry, whether he finds mud aesthetically pleasing, whether he has a practical use for it and so on; he answers all questions in the negative: he just wants a saucer of mud for no reason. Surely we would want to conclude that he doesn't want a saucer of mud at all. By analogy, there would have to be reasons for making decisions about medical treatment. However, these can be, and as we shall see, often are, bizarre. Do we conclude that, because of this, the patient lacks decision-making capacity? As we shall see from examining the case law in Chapter 3, the answer is 'no'. Decision-making capacity may be present despite the fact that a patient holds a number of strange and, apparently unsupportable, beliefs. Perhaps the correct view is that if these beliefs are genuinely held, and form part of the patient's 'world view', then they should be respected. In other words, unlike the man who wants the saucer of mud for no reason whatsoever, the patient has reasons that *make sense to him* and, as such, should be respected.

Autonomy and beneficence

Even the most ardent proponent of the principle of autonomy would accept that it would be wrong to deny someone medical treatment because they were incapable of consenting. If it were otherwise, no mentally incompetent patient would ever receive treatment. However, the argument would be that in the cases of children and adults lacking capacity, such treatment is not contrary to the principle of autonomy because they are not autonomous human beings. Similarly, people suffering from certain forms of mental disorder may be compulsorily detained and treated for that disorder without consent, and it is argued that this is carried out to *restore* their autonomy, and therefore entirely consistent with the principle (see Chapter 9).

PATERNALISM V AUTONOMY – A FALSE DICHOTOMY?

Using the principle of beneficence, the paternalist will justify treating patients against their will, or withholding information from them which is 'bad for them'. We have seen that, even within the philosophy of autonomy, there may be justified intervention, although the advocate of autonomy would argue that the patient in those cases is not truly autonomous. However, when we look at decision-making capacity in Chapter 3, we will find that it is by no means easy to decide whether someone has sufficient capacity to make truly autonomous decisions. It might be thought that this adds fuel to the argument of the paternalists. However, it is arguable that precisely because it can be difficult to assess capacity, it is all the more important to guard against the paternalist declaring someone incapable in order to do what he thinks is best for them. These difficulties might make us wonder whether the traditional opposition of paternalism and autonomy might not give way to something which recognises the best in each of them. Some writers have endeavoured to find a more conciliatory approach, which accommodates both models.

Collaborative decision-making

Pellegrino and Thomasma say that there can never be a single model to describe the doctor–patient relationship adequately. They set down a beneficence model as follows:

Pellegrino, ED and Thomasma, DC, *For the Patient's Good: The Restoration of Beneficence in Health Care*, 1988, Oxford: OUP, p 32:

... one of the seductions of the autonomy and paternalism models is their comparative ease of decision-making: Either the physician makes all the decisions or the patient does so. Both models abandon the trials and rewards of a mutual dialogue and exchange between doctor and patient. Both also can assault the moral agency of the patient or the physician ...

... The values of patient autonomy – which translate into the corresponding moral duties of beneficence and respect for persons – may come into conflict with each other. In our view, however, these duties cannot remain in conflict if medicine is to achieve its goal of healing.

But healing, as we define it, is a form of assistance in making the patient whole again by working through his or her body. If the values of patient welfare and patient autonomy remain in conflict, then authentic healing cannot take place. A physician, therefore, must become both a moderate autonomist and a moderate welfarist ...

Another way of arriving at this position is to consider the principle of respect for persons. This principle leads to at least two moral duties. The first is to respect the self-determination or autonomy of others. The second, often neglected duty is to help restore that autonomy or help establish it when it is absent. Looked at in this way, beneficence is seen to be a direct consequence of a fundamental moral principle and the guiding duty of medicine. If this is true, then the autonomy model is necessarily incomplete. So, too, is the paternalistic model.

In this regard, other writers have suggested that it would be preferable for medical decision-making to be conceived of as a kind of collaborative effort:

Teff, H, 'Consent to medical procedures: paternalism, self-determination or therapeutic alliance' (1985) 101 LQR 450:

It has been argued that the pursuit of a therapeutic alliance, in the sense of a genuine collaborative effort, is desirable in so far as it can facilitate a beneficial outcome. Quite apart from the fact that for many medical conditions there is either no specific remedy or the effectiveness of treatment is unknown, the doctor cannot intuitively know precisely what constitutes health or well being for a particular patient. The optimum 'outcome' is not necessarily to be equated with the technically successful result of a given operation, but may embrace a prognosis of the patient's subsequent medical and psychological condition and ability to function, as well as other social and financial considerations where relevant.

When medical procedures, especially invasive ones, are contemplated, doctor–patient relationships are often fraught with uncertainty and ambiguity. There is no *a priori* reason to assume that a doctor or surgeon possesses the kind of psychological or moral insight that would enable him to decide unaided what is most appropriate. The relative importance which patients attach, for example, to quality as against length of life, and to physical integrity or appearance as against diminution of pain, may reflect personal values, circumstances and priorities of which the surgeon, in particular, is initially unaware and may never become sufficiently apprised. It is apparently common practice in English hospitals for the information deemed relevant to patient consent to be provided by 'the most junior and inexperienced doctor, who will not perform the operation and who knows nothing of the likely complications' ...

A fiduciary relationship

That the doctor–patient relationship might be a fiduciary relationship has yet to be accepted by the English courts (see, for example, the judgment of Lord Scarman in *Sidaway v Board of Governors of the Bethlem Royal Hospital and the Maudsley Hospital* [1985] AC 871). However, some commentators have suggested that this may be a plausible analysis of the relationship. What is a fiduciary relationship? Peter Bartlett describes it as follows:

Bartlett, P, 'Doctors as fiduciaries: equitable regulation of the doctor–patient relationship' (1997) Med L Rev 193:

A fiduciary relationship attracts the attention of equity. The term apparently arose in the 19th century, when a variety of relationships held by equity to be 'on trust' were no longer necessarily flowing from 'trusts' themselves in any meaningful sense. With this motley origin, it is not surprising that fiduciary relationships themselves differ widely in the duties equity imposes on them. Consider the examples of lawyers and trustees. Certainly, one would expect a duty of undivided loyalty to the beneficiary or client in each case, and one would not expect the fiduciary to make a profit from the relationship outside that expressly authorised. There are equally firm differences, however. Unless inconsistent with his or her duty to the court, the lawyer acts on the instructions of the client, even when the instructions do not reflect the lawyer's view of the client's best interest. Trustees, by comparison, act in the beneficiary's best financial interest in any event. Where the beneficiary is in a relatively weak position in the control of the trust, the client is in control of the legal matter.

This has led a number of scholars to argue that it is inappropriate to think of the application of fiduciary relationships as a class at all, but rather specific relationships attracting specific collections of fiduciary duties ...

Further flexibility is introduced through the distinction between fact-based and status-based fiduciary obligations, the latter being based in relationships traditionally recognised by equity and attracting a broader array of fiduciary obligations, and the former based in specific fact situations and attracting only some fiduciary obligations. The advantage of this approach is that the courts may perceive an increased flexibility to extend obligations beyond the traditional fiduciary situations to offer specific equitable remedies in specific situations, without setting broad precedent.

Is it arguable that the fiduciary model could remove the paternalism-autonomy divide? For example, could the relationship of trust justify paternalistic treatment as long as the doctor was totally candid with the patient? But there may be an inherent problem here: if the doctor is candid and the patient refuses the treatment, then the 'fiduciary' nature of the relationship does not assist in resolving the problem. However, it is clear that aspects of the doctor–patient relationship can be fiduciary in nature, such as the duty of confidentiality and, whilst the English courts have been reluctant to accept the model in the context of access to medical records, a fiduciary duty may be applicable (see Chapter 5).

JUSTICE IN THE ALLOCATION OF HEALTH RESOURCES

The foregoing sections have considered the treatment of patients when they have not wanted treatment, or where the patients' medical conditions have not been fully revealed to them, or where treatment information has been withheld or restricted. A scenario we have not yet considered consists of a patient requiring treatment, and being refused, or a doctor ready and willing to treat a patient, but unable to do so because of lack of resources.

Most of us would agree that resources should be distributed fairly, or in accordance with justice. However, this bland statement gets us nowhere unless we decide the basis of a fair distribution. Concepts of justice often present three different models for distribution. First, resources may be distributed in accordance with merit. This would mean that the most deserving persons, for example, in terms of moral worth or contribution to society, would receive health care as a matter of priority. Secondly, resources may be distributed 'equally'. However, this presupposes that we have a test for deciding whether the persons concerned are equal. Certainly they are entitled to equal respect and consideration, but that in itself may not be enough. This tempts us to adopt the third model, which is that resources be distributed in accordance with need.

What effect does a shortage of resources have on the doctor–patient relationship? Christopher Newdick argues as follows:

Newdick, C, *Who Should We Treat?*, 1995, Oxford: Clarendon, p 277:

A Rationing and the Hippocratic Oath

One of the most pressing problems in medical law concerns the current status of the Hippocratic Oath and the many international codes which have followed it. Under the Oath doctors promise: 'I will follow that system of regimen which, according to my ability and judgment, I consider for the benefit of my patients ... Into whatever house I enter, I will go into them [*sic*] for the benefit of the sick.'

The modern statement of the principle is contained in the Declaration of Geneva, published by the World Health Organisation. It says, *inter alia*, that the 'health of my patient will be my first consideration'. Similarly, the International Code of Medical Ethics provides that 'a physician shall act only in the patient's best interests when providing medical care which might have the effect of weakening the physical and mental condition of the patient'.

Exactly what counts as a patient's 'best interests' is not, and probably never could be, specified in detail. Patients present doctors with an infinite variety and combination of illnesses and reasonable doctors will naturally differ as to the best way of responding to them. Also, although the Hippocratic Oath presumes that doctors will always promote the best interests of the individual, finite resources have long meant that difficult decisions between patients may sometimes be unavoidable. In all this, however, there is nothing new. Resources have never been infinite and unenviable decisions between patients have always been made, though in a manner less visible in the past. Doctors care for groups of patients and know very well that the use of a bed or operating theatre for one patient may mean that the treatment of another will be delayed or denied altogether. For this reason elderly people have found it more difficult to be referred for surgery, infertility treatment has not always been made available, those suffering mental illness have not always obtained care in hospital, and kidney dialysis has been available to relatively few. In reality, therefore, the idea of absolute clinical freedom may long have been an unaffordable myth. It is debatable whether true clinical freedom in fact ever existed and, if it did, whether it should have been allowed. [Reprinted from *Who Should We Treat?: Law, Patients and Resources in the NHS* by Christopher Newdick (1995) by permission of Oxford University Press.]

Our ethical dilemmas have previously been about the nature of the doctor–patient relationship in a one to one sense. Now we are looking at the relationship between the doctor and many of his patients. Does this undermine the cosy beneficence model, where the doctor's only concern is to do his best for the patient?

Newdick comments further on the issue of clinical freedom:

Newdick, C, *Who Should We Treat?*, 1995, Oxford: Clarendon, p 278:

... pressure is now being exerted on doctors to comply with clinical practice guidelines, to undertake medical audit of their procedures, and to be prepared to justify substantial differences between them. To what extent will the differing instincts of doctors continue to be supportable? Some have individual patients uppermost in their minds and have always prescribed the best available treatment. Others with an eye on reducing expenditure may try a 'second best' treatment first, and use the best only if that fails. Modern medical ethics demands that doctors understand the economic impact of their decisions, of what economists call 'opportunity costs', ie, the range of treatments, the opportunities, that will be forgone if the money to pay for them is diverted elsewhere. Thus, the British Medical Association has said: 'Wastage of resources is unethical because it diminishes society's capacity to relieve suffering through the other uses that could be made of the wasted resources. Doctors working within the NHS need to be aware of cost-effectiveness as well as clinical effectiveness in the care provided for the patient.'

But 'waste' is not a neutral word. Governments, health service managers, doctors and patients all have differing ideas about how resources should be spent. Used as a way of insisting that individual patients receive only the most effective treatment, it may not threaten the idea of clinical freedom. Doctors will be eager to uphold this usage of the word. Many believe the relationship of trust between doctor and patient is precious and that doctors should never compromise their clinical commitment to the individual. The General Medical Council endorses this view and encourages doctors to adhere to their traditional Hippocratic priorities. Recognising the importance of limited resources, it says: 'The Council endorses the principle that a doctor should always seek to give priority to the investigation and treatment of patients solely on the basis of clinical need.'

By contrast, health economists will stress the need to distribute national resources efficiently and give 'waste' a different meaning. They will stress the 'macro' goals and priorities of health spending. This approach tends to emphasise the clinical benefits to whole communities, rather than to individuals, and could have considerable potential in modifying the relationship between doctors and patients. One set of guidelines, for example, has recommended that the distribution of resources by hospitals and doctors should always be consistent with the policies established by governments at national level so that: 'Health care professionals at the clinical level ought not to make any treatment decision that undermines legitimate attempts at a higher level to establish just and efficient use of resources.'

This view is likely to gain ground although it is currently still in its infancy because firm evidence of the cost and effectiveness of medical treatment is unavailable. Its implications, however, are important. Were such an approach to be adopted, doctors would become more openly involved in shaping and implementing social and economic policies and their clinical freedom with respect to individuals would have to be modified as a result. This poses the most clear and coherent threat to the traditional notion of the Hippocratic Oath. On the other hand, in this most delicate and fundamental area of practice, doctors have little training in the principles (whatever they may be) which might assist them. 'Unfortunately, physicians have little experience with the task of bringing moral and social norms to bear on particular disputes and situations. [And] ethicists and jurists are not familiar with the medical and emotional nuances associated with the care of acutely ill and dying patients.'

There is an urgent need for both doctors and the community to address the questions raised by these pressures. [Reprinted from *Who Should We Treat?: Law, Patients and Resources in the NHS* by Christopher Newdick (1995) by permission of Oxford University Press.]

The administration and efficient running of the National Health Service is considered further in Chapter 2.

It is highly likely in practice that many doctors will frequently have to choose who to treat, or who to treat as a matter of priority, and that this will mean that he is not doing his best for those who are not treated, or not treated in a timely fashion. Some doctors have been frank about these issues and have suggested to their patients that a ballot takes place to decide on priority:

'Editorial' (1980) 6 JME 171:

Who shall die?

A British gynaecologist recently chose by ballot the patients who were to be admitted to the inadequate number of beds at his disposal. He had already selected those patients with gynaecologically urgent problems, and finding not much to choose medically between the rest, he obtained their consent to select by lot. He was subsequently criticised on radio by a medically qualified administrator for not using a better method of selection.

Well, what is a better method? The question – an extremely complex one – is raised in a more obviously serious context by two articles in this issue of the *Journal*. In the first Drs Parsons and Lock discuss the results of a survey they carried out among British nephrologists on their criteria for triage among patients with chronic renal failure. In the second Gavin H Mooney, the health economist, argues for the central importance of cost-benefit analysis in the allocation of limited medical resources.

Parsons and Lock, disturbed by increasingly inadequate funds for dialysis and transplantation, asked 25 British nephrologists to reject 10 out of 40 realistically described patients, ticking their reasons for rejection from a checklist under the categories of age, marital status, home facilities, underlying disease, and additional disease. All the nephrologists completed the questionnaire except for one who felt unable to accept any of the reasons suggested as valid grounds for rejection. Their responses make important reading. Interestingly, of the 10 patients most generally rejected, 'we found that at least six of them had been successfully treated by our own unit'; and not one of the patients was rejected by all the respondents.

Accepting for the time being that such choices must in practice be made, whereby some individuals are to be allocated life-saving resources while others with the same problem are to be refused them (microallocation or triage) it may be worthwhile distinguishing different criteria upon which such choices might conceivably be made. Perhaps the one most commonly used in practice is that favoured by many of the respondents, notably the medical or technical criterion, whereby triage is based on the probability of successful medical outcome. In clear cases this criterion seems unproblematic; for example, other things being equal, a doctor faced with two patients needing blood transfusion and only enough blood for one would surely be not merely absurd but downright wicked to transfuse the patient with an incompatible blood group when the other's blood group matched that of the available blood. The criterion for proper choice here is quite clearly likelihood of medical success.

The first of the criteria, the probability of successful medical outcome, seems, as the editorial states, unproblematic. However, the example given of the blood transfusion is perhaps too simplistic. It is beyond doubt that in this example there is one, and only one, ethical choice. Indeed there is no ethical dilemma here at all. Many predictions of 'successful medical outcome', however, might be covert value judgments. From time to time the newspapers report cases of smokers being refused heart surgery. Hospitals are at pains to point out that the refusal is not because they are smokers, but because the cardiac specialists state that the surgery will not be a lasting success if the patient, who has no plans to give up smoking, continues to smoke. However, might, at least in part, these decisions be based on other factors?:

'Editorial' (1980) 6 JME 171:

A second criterion for selection might be the candidates' value or disvalue to society; thus those respondents who rejected patients positive for Australia antigen on grounds of the risk to other patients and staff of potentially lethal hepatitis were explicitly or implicitly using this social criterion, as were any respondents who wished to stop treatment on the grounds that resources are being drained by the heavily handicapped and homeless from other less demanding patients.

There may be concern about the restriction on treatment in the cases of elderly people. Doctors may well find it easier to justify this on the basis of successful medical outcome. Is age a good reason for refusing treatment? The following are some of the arguments explored by Harris for and against:

Harris, J, *The Value of Life*, 1985, London: Routledge & Kegan Paul, p 89:

The anti-ageist argument

All of us who wish to go on living have something that each of us values equally, although for each it is different in character, for some a much richer prize than for others, and we none of us know its true extent. This thing is of course 'the rest of our lives'. So long as we do not know the date of our deaths, then for each of us the 'rest of our lives' is of indefinite duration. Whether we are 17 or 70, in perfect health or suffering from a terminal disease, we each have the rest of our lives to lead. So long as we each fervently wish to live out the rest of our lives, however long that turns out to be, then if we do not deserve to die, we each suffer the same injustice if our wishes are deliberately frustrated and we are cut off prematurely. Indeed there may well be a double injustice in deciding that those whose life expectation is short should not benefit from rescue or resuscitation. Suppose I am told today that I have terminal cancer with only approximately six months or so to live, but I want to live until I die, or at least until I decide that life is no longer worth living. Suppose I then am involved in an accident and because my condition is known to my potential rescuers and there are not enough resources to treat all who could immediately be saved I am marked among those who will not be helped. I am then the victim of a double tragedy and a double injustice. I am stricken first by cancer and the knowledge that I have only a short time to live and I'm then stricken again when I'm told that because of my first tragedy a second and more immediate one is to be visited upon me. Because I have once been unlucky I'm now no longer worth saving.

The point is a simple but powerful one. However short or long my life will be, so long as I want to go on living it then I suffer a terrible injustice when that life is prematurely cut short. Imagine a group of people all of an age, say a class of students all in their mid twenties. If fire trapped all in the lecture theatre and only 20 could be rescued in time should the rescuers shout 'youngest first!'? Suppose they had time to debate the question or had been debating it 'academically' before the fire? It would surely seem invidious to deny some what all value so dearly merely because of an accident of birth. It might be argued that age here provides no criterion precisely because although the lifespans of such a group might be expected to vary widely, there would be no way of knowing who was most likely to live longest. But suppose a reliable astrologer could make very realistic estimates or, what amounts to the same thing, suppose the age range of the students to be much greater, say 17 to 55. Does not the invidiousness of selecting by birth-date remain? Should a 17 year old be saved before a 29 year old or she before the 45 year old and should the 55 year old clearly be the last to be saved or the first to be sacrificed?

Our normal intuitions would share this sense of the invidiousness of choosing between our imaginary students by reason of their respective ages, but would start to want to make age relevant at some extremes, say if there were a 2 day old baby and a 90 year old grandmother. We will be returning to discuss a possible basis for this intuition in a moment. However, it is important to be clear that the anti-ageist argument denies the relevance of age or life expectancy as a criterion absolutely. It argues that even if I know for certain that I have only a little space to live, that space, however short, may be very precious to me. Precious, precisely because it is all the time I have left, and just as precious to me on that account as all the time you have left is precious to you, however much those two timespans differ in length. So that where we both want, equally strongly, to go on living, then we each suffer the same injustice when our lives are cut short or are cut further short.

It might seem that someone who would insist on living out the last few months of his life when by 'going quietly' someone else might have the chance to live for a much longer time would be a very selfish person. But this would be true only if the anti-ageist argument is false. It will be true only if it is not plausible to claim that living out the rest of one's life could be equally valuable to the individual whose life it is irrespective of the amount of unelapsed time that is left. And this is of course precisely the usual situation when individuals do not normally have anything but the haziest of ideas as to how long it is that they might have left.

I think the anti-ageist argument has much plausibility. It locates the wrongness of ending an individual's life in the evil of thwarting that person's desire to go on living and argues that it is profoundly unjust to frustrate that desire merely because some of those who have exactly the same desire, held no more strongly, also have a longer life expectancy than the others. However, there are a number of arguments that pull in the opposite direction and these we must now consider.

The fair innings argument

One problem with the anti-ageist argument is our feeling that there is something unfair about a person who has lived a long and happy life hanging on grimly at the end, while someone who has not been so fortunate suffers a related double misfortune, of losing out in a lottery in which his life happened to be in the balance with that of the grim octogenarian. It might be argued that we could accept the part of the anti-ageist argument which focuses on the equal value of unelapsed time, if this could be tempered in some way. How can it be just that someone who has already had more than her fair share of life and its delights should be preferred or even given an equal chance of continued survival with the young person who has not been so favoured? One strategy that seems to take account of our feeling that there is something wrong with taking steps to prolong the lives of the very old at the expense of those much younger is the fair innings argument.

The fair innings argument takes the view that there is some span of years that we consider a reasonable life, a fair innings. Let's say that a fair share of life is the traditional three score and 10, 70 years. Anyone who does not reach 70 suffers, on this view, the injustice of being cut off in their prime. They have missed out on a reasonable share of life; they have been short-changed. Those, however, who do make 70 suffer no such injustice, they have not lost out but rather must consider any additional years a sort of bonus beyond that which could reasonably be hoped for. The fair innings argument requires that everyone be given an equal chance to have a fair innings, to reach the appropriate threshold but, having reached it, they have received their entitlement. The rest of their life is the sort of bonus which may be cancelled when this is necessary to help others reach the threshold.

The attraction of the fair innings argument is that it preserves and incorporates many of the features that made the anti-ageist argument plausible, but allows us to preserve our feeling that the old who have had a good run for their money should not be endlessly propped up at the expense of those who have not had the same chance. We can preserve the conclusion of the anti-ageist argument, that so long as life is equally valued by the person whose life it is, it should be given an equal chance of preservation, and we can go on taking this view until the people in question have reached a fair innings.

There is, however, an important difficulty with the fair innings argument. It is that the very arguments which support the seeing of the threshold at an age which might plausibly be considered to be a reasonable lifespan, equally support the setting of the threshold at any age at all, so long as an argument from fairness can be used to support so doing. Suppose that there is only one place available on the dialysis programme and two patients are in competition for it. One is 30, and the other 40 years of age. The fair innings argument requires that neither be preferred on the grounds of age since both are below the threshold and are entitled to an equal chance of reaching it. If there is no other reason to choose between them we should do something like toss a coin. However, the 30 year old can argue that the considerations which support the fair innings argument require that she be given the place. After all, what's fair about the fair innings argument is precisely that each individual should have an equal chance of enjoying the benefits of a reasonable lifespan. The younger patient can argue that from where she's standing, the age of 40 looks much more reasonable a span than that of 30, and that she should be given the chance to benefit from those 10 extra years.

This argument generalised becomes a reason for always preferring to save younger rather than older people, whatever the age difference, and makes the original anti-ageist argument begin to look again the more attractive line to take. For the younger person can always argue that the older has had a fairer innings, and should now give way. It is difficult to stop whatever span is taken to be a fair innings collapsing towards zero under pressure from those younger candidates who see their innings as less fair than that of those with a larger share.

But perhaps this objection to the fair innings argument is mistaken? If 70 years is a fair innings it does not follow that the nearer a span of life approaches 70 years, the fairer an innings it is. This may be revealed by considering a different sort of threshold. Suppose that most people can run a mile in seven minutes, and that two people are given the opportunity to show that they can run a mile in that time. They both expect to be given seven minutes. However, if one is in fact given only three minutes and the other only four, it's not true that the latter is given a fairer running time: for people with average abilities four minutes is no more realistic a time in which to run a mile than is three. Four minutes is neither a fair threshold in itself, nor a fairer one than three minutes would be.

Nor does the argument that establishes seven minutes as an appropriate threshold lend itself to variation downwards. For that argument just is that seven is the number of minutes that an average adult takes to run a mile. Why then is it different for lifespans? If three score and ten is the number of years available to most people for getting what life has to offer, and is also the number of years people can reasonably expect to have, then it is a misfortune to be allowed anything less, however much less one is allowed, if nothing less than the full span normally suffices for getting what can be got out of life. It's true that the 40 year old gets more time than the 30 year old, but the frame of reference is not time only, but time normally required for a full life.

This objection has some force, but its failure to be a good analogy reveals that two sorts of considerations go to make an innings fair. For while living a full or complete life, just in the sense of experiencing all the ages of man, is one mark of a fair innings, there is also value in living through as many ages as possible. Just as completing the mile is one value, it is not the only one. Runners in the race of life also value ground covered, and generally judge success in terms of distance run.

What the fair innings argument needs to do is to capture and express in a workable form the truth that while it is always a *misfortune* to die when one wants to go on living, it is not a tragedy to die in old age; but it is on the other hand, both a tragedy and a misfortune to be cut off prematurely. Of course, ideas like 'old age' and 'premature death' are inescapably vague, and may vary from society to society, and over time as techniques for postponing death improve. We must also remember that while it may be invidious to choose between a 30 and a 40 year old on the grounds that one has had a fairer innings than the other, it may not be invidious to choose between the 30 and the 65 year old on those grounds.

If we remember, too, that it will remain wrong to end the life of someone who wants to live or to fail to save them, and that the fair innings argument will only operate as a principle of selection where we are forced to choose between lives, then something workable might well be salvaged.

While 'old age' is irredeemably vague, we can tell the old from the young, and even the old from the middle-aged. So that without attempting precise formulation, a reasonable form of the fair innings argument might hold; and might hold that people who had achieved old age or who were closely approaching it would not have their lives further prolonged when this could only be achieved at the cost of the lives of those who were not nearing old age. These categories could be left vague, the idea being that it would be morally defensible to prefer to save the lives of those who 'still had their lives before them' rather than those who had 'already lived full lives'. The criterion to be employed in each case would simply be what reasonable people would say about whether someone had had a fair innings. Where reasonable people would be in no doubt that a particular individual was nearing old age *and* that that person's life could only be further prolonged at the expense of the life of someone that no reasonable person would classify as nearing old age, then the fair innings argument would apply, and it would be justifiable to save the younger candidate.

In cases where reasonable people differed or it seemed likely that they would differ as to whether people fell into one category or the other, then the anti-ageist argument would apply and the inescapable choice would have to be made arbitrarily.

But again it must be emphasised that the fair innings argument would only operate as a counsel of despair, when it was clearly impossible to postpone the deaths of all those who wanted to go on living. In all other circumstances the anti-ageist argument would apply.

One influential proposal for allocating health care resources fairly has been by means of calculating QALYs (quality distinguished life year) (see, for example, *The Measurement of Health*, published by the Office of Health Economics in 1985; and Williams, A, 'The value of QALYs' (1985) Health and Social Services Journal). John Harris describes this approach as follows:

Harris, J, 'QALYfying the value of life' (1987) 13 JME 117:

1 What are QALYs?

It is important to be as clear as possible as to just what a QALY is and what it might be used for. I cannot do better than let Alan Williams, the architect of QALYs, tell you in his own words:

The essence of a QALY is that it takes a year of healthy life expectancy to be worth one, but regards a year of unhealthy life expectancy as worth less than one. Its precise value is lower the worse the quality of life of the unhealthy person (which is what the 'quality adjusted' bit is all about). If being dead is worth zero, it is, in principle, possible for a QALY to be negative, ie, for the quality of someone's life to be judged worse than being dead.

The general idea is that a beneficial health care activity is one that generates a positive amount of QALYs, and that an efficient health care activity is one where the cost-per-QALY is as low as it can be. A high priority health care activity is one where the cost-per-QALY is low, and a low priority activity is one where cost-per-QALY is high.

The plausibility of the QALY derives from the idea that given the choice, a person would prefer a shorter healthier life to a longer period of survival in a state of severe discomfort and disability. The idea that any rational person would endorse this preference provides the moral and political force behind the QALY. Its acceptability as a measurement of health then depends upon its doing all the theoretical tasks assigned to it, and on its being what people want, or would want, for themselves.

Harris subsequently became involved in a debate with John McKie *et al* about the application of QALYs (a series of articles was published in (1996) 22 JME 204–21). Part of the debate centred on John Rawls's famous 'veil of ignorance' argument in *A Theory of Justice*, 1972, Oxford: OUP. Rawls was attempting to find a system of distributive justice whilst accepting the proposition that people tend to be self-interested rather than altruistic. The scenario he envisages is as follows. Imagine that you are one of a number of people who are aware of the way in which the so called laws of economics work, but do not know their place in society. So, for example, you may be rich and powerful, or you may be unemployed with no resources whatsoever. Behind this 'veil of ignorance' you are asked to agree a set of principles which will govern the way in which the benefits and burdens in society are distributed. Assume, too, that you are motivated by self-interest. Rawls argues that because you do not know your position in society you will take care to ensure that conditions for those at the bottom of the pile are as good as possible. Rawls's theory is open to the objection that it assumes that the self-interested person will choose to play safe in this way. It can be argued that those behind the veil might choose to take a gamble. McKie *et al* state that QALYs would be chosen by those behind the veil of ignorance because QALYs maximise utility. In other words, they take a wider view of self-interest. Harris states that they would not, because the persons behind the veil, ie typical human beings, are cautious risk-averse persons, who would weigh the downside more than the upside. This is a difficult dispute to resolve. Does it depend upon the view one takes of human psychology, and won't there always be at least two views?

Harris also maintains that the problem with the QALY approach is that a person's life is valued more even if the difference in life expectation is very small. For example, the patient who would survive for just two days more than another would be preferred. McKie *et al* acknowledge this, but point out that Harris's insistence upon treating all needy patients equally means that the patient who would survive for 30 years if treated, and the patient who would survive for two days if treated, would be regarded as equally deserving of that treatment. Is the Harris-McKie debate another example of utility versus absolutism? On the basis of the former, at least the traditional way of looking at utilitarianism, some pretty ruthless decisions could be made about health care rationing. So, for example, the denial of treatment to anyone over 75 years old would provide more resources for younger people who would be in the majority. The utilitarian response would be that such a rule would morally impoverish society, leaving many people to suffer a painful and distressing old age, a spectacle which, far from being good for the majority of younger people, would make them positively unhappy.

Both Harris and McKie agree that any form of resource allocation which creates social divisiveness is wrong. But if the wider issues relating to health are examined, there is a great deal of evidence that poverty and health are inextricably linked. See, for example, Black *et al, Inequalities in Health: The Black Report*, 1982, Harmondsworth: Penguin. The latter produced evidence on the link between health and wealth, and reported that life expectancy at birth was seven years higher in social class one (professional) than in social class five (manual). There is therefore a cogent argument in favour of a redistribution of health resources to redress the imbalance. Furthermore, it points up the fact that 'health care' decisions are strongly linked to economic policy and social justice.

CHAPTER 2

HEALTH CARE IN ENGLAND AND WALES

BACKGROUND

The international framework

The UK Government has committed itself under international law to the promotion of its citizens' health and the prevention of disease. The key aspirations to this end are contained in the European Social Charter of 1961 (as revised in 1996), which is an offshoot from the scheme of political and civil rights found in the 1950 European Convention for the Protection of Human Rights and Fundamental Freedoms and is overseen by the same body, the Council of Europe. Articles 11 and 13 of the Social Charter provide as follows:

Article 11 – The right to protection of health

With a view to ensuring the effective exercise of the right to protection of health, the Parties undertake, either directly or in co-operation with public or private organisations, to take appropriate measures designed *inter alia*:

1   to remove as far as possible the causes of ill health;

2   to provide advisory and educational facilities for the promotion of health and the encouragement of individual responsibility in matters of health;

3   to prevent as far as possible epidemic, endemic and other diseases, as well as accidents.

Article 13 – The right to social and medical assistance

With a view to ensuring the effective exercise of the right to social and medical assistance, the Parties undertake:

1   to ensure that any person who is without adequate resources and who is unable to secure such resources either by his own efforts or from other sources, in particular by benefits under a social security scheme, be granted adequate assistance, and, in case of sickness, the care necessitated by his condition;

2   to ensure that persons receiving such assistance shall not, for that reason, suffer from a diminution of their political or social rights …

National provisions

Unlike the position in respect of the Convention, the failure by a state to protect these social 'rights' will not allow one of its citizens to complain to the European Court of Human Rights. However, the broad commitment on this country's part to the goal of access to health care for all is clear, and, in fact, predates the salient international law: it is found in the existence and operation of the National Health Service (NHS), which was established in 1948.

The National Health Service Act 1977

The National Health Service (NHS) Act 1977, which consolidated a number of previous statutes in the area, remains the key piece of legislation governing the obligations of the Government – as devolved to the relevant minister, the Secretary of State for Health, and the Department of Health under him – to make provision for health care. The key provisions of this Act are as follows:

1 Secretary of State's duty as to health service

(1) It is the Secretary of State's duty to continue the promotion in England and Wales of a comprehensive health service designed to secure improvement–

   (a) in the physical and mental health of the people of those countries; and

   (b) in the prevention, diagnosis and treatment of illness, and for that purpose to provide or secure the effective provision of services in accordance with this Act.

(2) The services so provided shall be free of charge except in so far as the making and recovery of charges is expressly provided for by or under any enactment, whenever passed.

2 Secretary of State's general power as to services

Without prejudice to the Secretary of State's powers apart from this section, he has power–

(a) to provide such services as he considers appropriate for the purpose of discharging any duty imposed on him by this Act; and

(b) to do any other thing whatsoever which is calculated to facilitate, or is conducive or incidental to, the discharge of such a duty.

This section is subject to s 3(3), below.

3 Services generally

(1) It is the Secretary of State's duty to provide throughout England and Wales, to such extent as he considers necessary to meet all reasonable requirements–

   (a) hospital accommodation;

   (b) other accommodation for the purpose of any service provided under this Act;

   (c) medical, dental, nursing and ambulance services;

   (d) such other facilities for the care of expectant and nursing mothers and young children as he considers are appropriate as part of the health service;

   (e) such facilities for the prevention of illness, the care of persons suffering from illness and the after-care of persons who have suffered from illness as he considers are appropriate as part of the health service;

   (f) such other services as are required for the diagnosis and treatment of illness.

(2) Where any hospital provided by the Secretary of State in accordance with this Act was a voluntary hospital transferred by virtue of the National Health Service Act 1946, and–

   (a) the character and associations of that hospital before its transfer were such as to link it with a particular religious denomination; then

   (b) regard shall be had in the general administration of the hospital to the preservation of that character and those associations.

(3) Nothing in s 2 above or in this section affects the provisions of Part II of this Act (which relates to arrangements with practitioners for the provision of medical, dental, ophthalmic and pharmaceutical services).

4 Special hospitals

The duty imposed on the Secretary of State by s 1, above to provide services for the purposes of the health service includes a duty to provide and maintain establishments (in this Act referred to as 'special hospitals') for persons subject to detention under the Mental Health Act 1959 who in his opinion require treatment under conditions of special security on account of their dangerous, violent or criminal propensities.

5 Other services

(1) It is the Secretary of State's duty–

(a) to provide for the medical inspection at appropriate intervals of pupils in attendance at schools maintained by local education authorities or at grant-maintained schools and for the medical treatment of such pupils;

(b) to arrange, to such extent as he considers, necessary to meet all reasonable requirements in England and Wales, for the giving of advice on contraception, the medical examination of persons seeking advice on contraception, the treatment of such persons and the supply of contraceptive substances and appliances.

(1A) It is also the Secretary of State's duty to provide, to such extent as he considers necessary to meet all reasonable requirements–

(a) for the dental inspection of pupils in attendance at schools maintained by local education authorities or at grant-maintained schools;

(b) for the dental treatment of such pupils; and

(c) for the education of such pupils in dental health.

(2) The Secretary of State may–

(a) provide invalid carriages for persons appearing to him to be suffering from severe physical defect or disability and, at the request of such a person, may provide for him a vehicle other than an invalid carriage (and the additional provisions set out in Sched 2 to this Act have effect in relation to this paragraph);

(b) arrange to provide accommodation and treatment outside Great Britain for persons suffering from respiratory tuberculosis;

(c) provide a microbiological service, which may include the provision of laboratories, for the control of the spread of infectious diseases and carry on such other activities as in his opinion can conveniently be carried on in conjunction with that service;

(d) conduct, or assist by grants or otherwise (without prejudice to the general powers and duties conferred on him under the Ministry of Health Act 1919) any person to conduct, research into any matters relating to the causation, prevention, diagnosis or treatment of illness, and into any such other matters connected with any service provided under this Act as he considers appropriate.

(2A) Charges may be made for services or materials supplied by virtue of para (c) of sub-s (2) above; and the powers conferred by that paragraph may be exercised both for the purposes of the health service and for other purposes …

Outside the hospital setting, general practitioners (GPs) are required to provide general medical services (known as 'primary care') to patients registered with them pursuant to a statutory contract with the relevant health authority, whose terms are fixed under the NHS (General Medical Services) Regulations 2004 SI 2004/291. (Further statutory provisions for community and primary care – provided, *inter alia*, by community nurses – are found in a number of miscellaneous statutes and statutory instruments, including s 2(1) of the Chronically Sick and Disabled Persons Act 1970, s 47 of the National Health Service and Community Care Act 1990, the National Health Service (General Medical Services) Amendment (No 2) Regulations 1999, the National Health Service (Primary Care) Act 1997 and the National Health Service (Primary Medical Services) Regulations 2005 SI 2005/893.)

The NHS is a vast public health care system (the largest organisation in Europe) as the following statistics illustrate: in 2002/2003 total expenditure was £55.8 billion; in 2003/2004 it was £61.3 billion; in 2004/2005 it was £67.4 billion. Expenditure is set to continue to rise, with a projection for 2007/2008 of £90.2 billion. Expenditure will therefore almost have doubled in the five years from 2002/2003 (see *Departmental Report 2004*, Department of Health, 2004, which can be located on the Department's website: www.doh.gov.uk).

Nevertheless, the NHS has remained the focus of continued and deeply felt public concern and debate, and the service has, from time to time, been the subject of important reforms. The major controversies have centred on achieving accountability within the NHS in relation to two issues: *cost of provision* and *quality of care*. We shall next be looking in more detail at the mechanisms which have been tried in order to ensure that the NHS delivers both efficient and high quality care, before returning later in the chapter to the question of how far, in law, the individual citizen enjoys a right to obtain the particular treatment he desires.

STRUCTURE OF HEALTH CARE IN THE UK

In economic terms, health care as a commodity has the clear potential for generating an anti-competitive market situation, given that the demand for services is in the hands of the same profession (doctors making patient referrals) as is responsible for its supply. The manner in which this may encourage inefficiency in the delivery of care has been commented upon by Christopher Newdick:

Newdick, C, *Who Should We Treat?*, 1995, Oxford: Clarendon, pp 41–43:

Two features of expenditure in the NHS prompted the Government to reconsider its system of funding. The first was a method of distributing financial resources to hospitals largely according to the perceived 'needs' of a resident population, to its mortality and morbidity [propensity for illness], without considering the 'efficiency' of the hospitals responsible for providing treatment. This became known as the 'efficiency trap'. Those hospitals which reduced their unit costs and became more efficient were unable to admit more patients because they were limited by their financial allocation. Arguably, hospitals which are funded simply according to the requirements of their population's needs may feel no incentive to manage their funds as effectively as those whose funding is performance-related. Indeed, when there is no relationship between the amount of money allocated to a district and the number of patients it is able to treat, the more efficient hospital appears to suffer a penalty. By treating more patients it spends its allocation more quickly and exhausts its funds before the end of the financial year. [A Enthoven] who influenced the eventual shape of the health service reforms, wrote of the NHS in 1984:

> The NHS runs on the ability and dedication of the many people who work in it ... But other than the satisfaction of a job well done – which I do not wish to minimise – the system contains no serious incentives to guide the NHS in the direction of better quality care and service at reduced cost ... In the non-competitive NHS, the manager who attempts to implement efficiency-improving changes is more likely to be seen as a cause of problems.

> In fact, the structure of the NHS contains perverse incentives. For example, a District that develops an excellent service in some specialty that attracts more referrals is likely to get more work without getting more resources to do it. A District that does a poor job will 'export' patients and have less work, but not correspondingly less resources, for its reward ... management and consultants in a District risk weakening the case for a new hospital wing they have been campaigning for by solving their waiting list problem by referring patients to other districts with excess capacity ... [and] GPs have weak or no incentives to reduce referrals. They have neither the incentives nor the resources to make extra efforts to keep people out of hospital.

> One solution to this trap is to enable efficient hospitals with spare capacity to offer their services to larger numbers of patients. Obviously, an incentive is required for such a hospital to fund the additional work and logic suggests that the money ought to come from those hospitals which work below full capacity. Those hospitals which achieve most, at least cost and at highest quality, ought to receive more funding than those that do less.

> The second feature of the system which gave cause for concern was that those responsible for spending had no direct interest in controlling costs. The argument was: so long as GPs and consultants are not asked to account for the medicines they prescribe or the procedures they recommend, there may be a tendency to overtreat patients. Why refuse to prescribe antibiotics to a patient who mistakenly expects that they will cure his cold, or antidepressants to the patient who, for entirely non-medical reasons, has good reason to be depressed? Not only might it cause the patient upset and distress, but also doctors are increasingly concerned about the time, expense, and anxiety caused by patients' complaints. On one view, it makes more sense to satisfy patients' misplaced expectations than to spend time trying to explain the medical risks associated with pointless treatment. [Reprinted from *Who Should We Treat?: Law, Patients and Resources in the NHS* by Christopher Newdick (1995) by permission of Oxford University Press.]

In a drive to make the NHS more competitive and better serve the interests of patients, the previous Conservative Government experimented with an 'internal market' within the health service. Under this system (set out in the National Health Service and Community Care Act 1990) NHS management and funding were organised on the principle of separating the 'purchasers' and 'providers' of care. The former were local health authorities and GP fund-holders, responsible for assessing the health needs of their local populations or patients and for purchasing the best possible care for them. Providers, such as hospitals, ambulance and community services, were intended to compete among each other for 'contracts' with purchasers to provide the required care services.

However, on assuming office in 1997, the Labour Government quickly signalled its intent to introduce major changes into the NHS. These were highlighted in the

Government White Paper, *The New NHS: Modern, Dependable* Cm 3807, 1997, London: The Stationery Office and *Executive Summary*, 1997, London: DoH. The Government was committed to abolishing the internal market and replacing it with a system of integrated care based on partnerships between NHS bodies and other local agencies.

Department of Health, *Executive Summary*, December 1997, London: DoH, pp 8–9:

New roles and responsibilities

The new NHS will mean new roles and responsibilities for Health Authorities and NHS trusts and the Department of Health. Primary Care Groups will be developed across the country ...

Health Authorities will be leaner bodies with stronger powers to improve the health of their residents and oversee the effectiveness of the NHS locally. Over time, they will relinquish direct commissioning responsibility. Working with local authorities, NHS trusts and Primary Care Groups, they will take the lead in drawing up three year Health Improvement Programmes which will provide the framework within which all local NHS bodies will operate. These will be backed by a new duty of partnership. Health Authorities will allocate funds to Primary Care Groups on an equitable basis, and hold them to account. Links with social services will be strengthened. Fewer Health Authorities covering larger areas will emerge as a product of these changes.

Primary Care Groups comprising all GPs in an area together with community nurses will take responsibility for commissioning services for the local community. They will work closely with social services. There will be four options for the form that Primary Care Groups can take ... including the opportunity to become free standing Primary Care trusts, with responsibility for running community hospitals and community health services. None of these options affects the independent contractor status of GPs. The new arrangements will replace the thousands of existing commissioning and fund-holding groups. Typical Groups may serve about 100,000 patients, but this will vary according to local circumstances. Primary Care Groups will mean fewer commissioners with more clout. They will have freedom to make decisions about how to use their resources, consistent with the Health Improvement Programme. They will control a single unified budget which will give maximum choice to GPs and community nurses about how best to meet individual patient needs, since no individual elements within it will be artificially capped.

NHS trusts will have devolved operational responsibility, but will also be party to the local Health Improvement Programme. They will agree long term service agreements with Primary Care Groups. These service agreements will generally be organised around a particular care group (such as children) or disease area (such as heart disease) linked to the new National Service Frameworks. In this way, hospital clinicians will be able to make a more significant contribution to service planning. NHS trusts will have new statutory duties of quality and partnerships. NHS trusts will also be more accountable to the public and will publish details of their performance. They will need to demonstrate the development and involvement of their staff.

Following the White Paper, the reforms to the NHS were introduced by the Health Act 1999. As will be seen from the provisions of the Act extracted below, a key organisational building block in the new scheme is the Primary Care Trust:

1 Repeal of law about fund-holding practices

In the National Health Service and Community Care Act 1990, sections 14 to 17 (which make provision in relation to fund-holding practices) are to cease to have effect.

2 Primary Care Trusts

(1) After section 16 of the National Health Service Act 1977 there is inserted–

'16A Primary Care Trusts

(1) The Secretary of State may establish bodies to be known as Primary Care Trusts with a view, in particular, to their–

    (a) providing or arranging for the provision of services under this Part of this Act;

    (b) exercising functions in relation to the provision of general medical services under Part II of this Act; and

    (c) providing services in accordance with section 28C arrangements.

(2) Each Primary Care Trust shall be established by an order made by him (referred to in this Act as a PCT order).

(3) A Primary Care Trust shall be established for the area specified in its PCT order and shall exercise its functions in accordance with any prohibitions or restrictions in the order.

(4) If any consultation requirements apply, they must be complied with before a PCT order is made.

(5) In this section, 'consultation requirements' means requirements about consultation contained in regulations (and the regulations must impose requirements where a PCT order establishes a Primary Care Trust).

(6) Schedule 5A to this Act (which makes further provision about Primary Care Trusts) shall have effect.

16B Exercise of functions by Primary Care Trusts

(1) This section applies to functions which are exercisable by a Primary Care Trust under or by virtue of this Act (including this section), the National Health Service and Community Care Act 1990 or any prescribed provision of any other Act.

(2) Regulations may provide for any functions to which this section applies to be exercised–

    (a) by another Primary Care Trust;

    (b) by a Special Health Authority; or

    (c) jointly with any one or more of the following: Health Authorities, NHS trusts and other Primary Care Trusts.

(3) Regulations may provide–

    (a) for any functions to which this section applies to be exercised, on behalf of the Primary Care Trust by whom they are exercisable, by a committee, sub-committee or officer of the trust;

    (b) for any functions which, under this section, are exercisable by a Special Health Authority to be exercised, on behalf of that authority, by a committee, sub-committee or officer of the authority;

    (c) for any functions which, under this section, are exercisable by a Primary Care Trust jointly with one or more Health Authorities or other Primary Care Trusts (but not with any NHS trusts) to be exercised, on behalf of the health service bodies in question, by a joint committee or joint sub-committee.'

(2) Schedule 1 (which inserts the new Schedule 5A in the 1977 Act) is to have effect.

... 5 Primary Care Trusts: provision of services etc

After section 18 of the 1977 Act there is inserted–

'Primary Care Trusts: further functions

18A Provision of services etc

(1) A Primary Care Trust may provide services under an agreement made under section 28C below, and may do so as a member of a qualifying body (within the meaning of section 28D).

(2) A Primary Care Trust may arrange for the provision by the trust to another health service body of goods or services (including accommodation) which are of the same description as those which, at the time of making the arrangement, the trust has power to provide in carrying out its other functions.

(3) A Primary Care Trust may provide premises for the use of persons–

(a) providing general medical, general dental, general ophthalmic or pharmaceutical services; or

(b) performing personal medical or personal dental services under an agreement made under section 28C below, on any terms it thinks fit.

(4) A Primary Care Trust which manages any hospital may make accommodation or services available there for patients who give undertakings (or for whom undertakings are given) to pay any charges imposed by the trust in respect of the accommodation or services.

(5) A Primary Care Trust has power to do anything specified in section 7(2) of the Health and Medicines Act 1988 (provision of goods, services etc), other than make accommodation or services available for patients at any hospital it manages, for the purpose of making additional income available for improving the health service.

(6) A Primary Care Trust may only exercise a power conferred by subsection (4) or (5) above–

(a) to the extent that its exercise does not to any significant extent interfere with the performance by the trust of its functions or of its obligations under NHS contracts; and

(b) in circumstances specified in directions under section 17 above, with the Secretary of State's consent.

(7) In this section 'hospital' means a health service hospital and includes any establishment or facility managed for the purposes of the health service.'

A useful summary of the manner in which the NHS is presently organised is provided in the following extract, which is taken from the NHS's website:

About the NHS (http://www.nhs.uk/england/aboutthenhs/default.cmsx (28 April 2005))

Department of Health

This is the department that supports the government to improve the health and well being of the population.

The Department of Health has recently started a programme of change, designed to make sure they provide leadership to the NHS and social care. The Department is responsible for:

• Setting overall direction and leading transformation of the NHS and social care

- Setting national standards to improve quality of services
- Securing resources and making investment decisions to ensure that the NHS and social care are able to deliver services

...

Shifting the Balance of Power

Shifting the Balance of Power is the name for the programme of changes that are reforming the way the NHS works. The aim is to design a service centred around patients, which puts them first. It will be faster, more convenient and offer them more choice.

The main feature of the change has been to give locally-based **Primary Care Trusts** (PCTs) the role of running the NHS and improving health in their areas. This has also meant creating new **Strategic Health Authorities** which cover larger areas and have a more strategic role.

Special Health Authorities

These are health authorities which provide a health service to the whole of England, not just to a local community – for example, the National Blood Authority.

Strategic Health Authorities

In April 2002, 28 new, larger Strategic Health Authorities (SHAs) were set up to develop strategies for the NHS, and to make sure their local NHS organisations were performing well.

The new health authorities are responsible for:

- Developing plans for improving health services in their local area
- Making sure local health services are of a high quality and are performing well
- Increasing the capacity of local health services – so they can provide more services
- Making sure national priorities – for example, programmes for improving cancer services – are integrated into local health service plans.

They manage the NHS locally and are a key link between the Department of Health and the NHS.

Primary Care

This is the care provided by people you normally see when you first have a health problem. It might be a visit to a doctor or dentist, an optician for an eye test, or just a trip to a pharmacist to buy cough mixture. NHS Walk-in Centres, and the phone line **NHS Direct**, are also part of primary care. All the people offering primary care are now managed by new local health organisations called **Primary Care Trusts** (PCTs).

Primary Care Trusts

Primary Care Trusts (PCTs) are local health organisations responsible for managing health services in your local area. They work with local authorities and other agencies that provide health and social care locally to make sure the community's needs are being met.

PCTs are now at the centre of the NHS and will get 75% of the NHS budget. As they are local organisations, they are in the best position to understand the needs of their community, so they can make sure that the organisations providing health and social care services are working effectively.

For example, PCTs must make sure there are enough services for people in their area and that they are accessible to patients. They must also make sure that all other health services are provided, including hospitals, dentists, opticians, mental health services, NHS Walk-in Centres, NHS Direct, patient transport (including accident and emergency), population screening, pharmacies and opticians. They are also responsible for getting health and social care systems working together to the benefit of patients.

Doctors/GPs

Doctors look after the health of people in their local community and deal with a whole range of health problems. They also give health education and advice on things like smoking and diet, run clinics, give vaccinations and carry out simple surgical operations.

Doctors usually work with a team including nurses, health visitors and midwives, as well as a range of other health professionals such as physiotherapists and occupational therapists. If a Doctor cannot deal with your problem themselves, they'll usually refer you to a hospital for tests, treatment or to see a consultant with specialised knowledge.

Every UK citizen has a right to be registered with a local Doctor and visits to the surgery are free.

The UK Government's vision for the future of the NHS is further set out in the Department of Health publication, *Shifting the Balance of Power: The Next Steps*, 2002, London: DoH, which makes reference to the 10-year plan for the NHS published by the government in July 2000:

Department of Health, *Shifting the Balance of Power: The Next Steps*, Executive Summary, 2002, London: DoH:

1.2 Why Change is Necessary

1.2.1 The NHS Plan sets out an ambitious vision for a service designed around the patient – a service of high quality and national standards which is fast, convenient and uses modern methods to provide care where and when it is needed. Such a service will not only be designed around patients but also be responsive to them, offer them choices and involve them in decision making and planning.

1.2.2 *Shifting the Balance of Power* recognises that we need to reform the way the NHS works in order to achieve the vision. Central policy can create the framework for reform but we need reform locally to create the environment in every PCT [Primary Care Trust] and Trust where patients truly experience a changed health service. This reform will create new working partnerships between patients and frontline staff who have the skills and knowledge to design, develop and deliver services geared to the needs and concerns of local communities. And it will also ensure they have the authority to do so.

1.2.3 This reform will also make sure that the public can be more involved in shaping the services they use, given more information about decisions affecting their care and have more influence on how that care is delivered.

1.2.4 PCTs will have a leading role in this change. They have a unique perspective across community, hospital and primary care and across both the NHS and local authorities. They also have a very clear relationship both with frontline staff and with patients. These features will allow them to become the cornerstone of the modernised NHS. As such they will take over many of the current functions of health authorities. The smaller number of health authorities will in turn take on an increasingly strategic role including the performance management of both PCTs and NHS Trusts.

1.2.5 Structural change in itself does not necessarily make people work differently – how successful the NHS is in changing its culture and truly shifting the balance will depend on the determination, behaviour, attitudes and actions of healthcare staff at every level.

1.2.6 Achieving our vision for the NHS will involve all these elements of cultural and organisational change with the key elements being:

- empowering front line staff to use their skills and knowledge to develop innovative services with more say in how services are delivered and resources are allocated;
- empowering patients to become informed and active partners in their care involving them in the design, delivery and development of local services;
- changing the NHS culture and structure by devolving power and decision-making to frontline staff and PCTs led by clinicians and local people, and by building clinical networks across organisations.

... 1.4 Changes in Roles and Relationships

1.4.1 The main organisational changes which will underpin these changes in culture are:

- giving PCTs new powers and control over resources to shape and commission services across the whole spectrum of hospital, community and primary services and from the whole range of possible providers in the public, private or voluntary sectors;
- leaving NHS Trusts with their current responsibilities whilst holding them to account through Strategic Health Authorities and requiring them to develop further patient and staff involvement in their own organisations and engage in creating networks for care with their partners externally;
- replacing health authorities by fewer and smaller Strategic Health Authorities with the responsibility for developing strategy and performance managing PCTs, NHS Trusts and Workforce Development Confederations so as to secure delivery and consistency of approach. They will in effect manage the NHS on behalf of the Department;
- reducing the Department's direct role in management, abolishing its eight regional offices and creating four Directors of Health and Social Care to support and develop the NHS, provide local contact and performance manage the Strategic Health Authorities. This will leave the Department better able to do those things which only it can do: in ensuring the development of national standards, securing resources and setting direction.

1.4.2 These organisational changes have also provided the opportunity to review the way significant functions are delivered across the NHS with new more appropriate arrangements being introduced for, amongst others, public health, clinical leadership, information management and technology and communications.

(See also the Department of Health Command Paper, *Delivering the NHS Plan*, Cm 5503, 2002, London: DoH.)

A controversial development, however, is contained Part One of the Health and Social Care (Community Health and Standards) Act 2003. This provides for the setting up of 'foundation hospitals'. These are independent of the Secretary of State for Health, and will be regulated instead by an independent regulator who will monitor their performance. The proposal is that they will be managed locally by a board of governors who will represent the health care professionals delivering the service, the community served by the trust and any local partner organisations. The controversy lies in the independence of the hospitals; some might be concerned that this is a move towards 'privatising' the NHS. However, Davies has argued that because of the regulation of the provision of health care (eg by the Healthcare Commission, see below) and the concern within the NHS about 'accountability', this will effectively prevent foundation hospitals from exercising a meaningful degree of autonomy (see Davies, ACL, 'Foundation hospitals: a new approach to accountability and autonomy in the delivery of public services?' [2004] PL Winter 808).

The private sector

The private sector is subject to statutory regulation pursuant to the Care Standards Act 2000. This provides for the National Care Standards Commission, a statutory authority set up under the Act, to operate a system of registration and inspection in respect of private hospitals and residential care homes, and is designed to ensure that patients are offered a suitable standard of care. Moreover, as Jonathan Montgomery notes, as well as being vulnerable, like their NHS counterparts, to malpractice actions brought in negligence (see Chapter 6), private hospitals can also be sued for breach of contract:

Montgomery, J, *Health Care Law*, 1997, Oxford: OUP, p 166:

Outside the NHS actions may also be brought in contract law. This is not possible under the NHS, because NHS patients do not have a contract with those who treat them. In private medicine, where patients pay their professionals (even if the fees are later reimbursed under some form of insurance), there will be a contract. The patient would be able to sue in both negligence and contract. In theory it is possible for a health professional to contract to provide a standard of care that is higher than that required in negligence. However, the courts have shown themselves very reluctant to accept that they have done so.

REGULATING THE QUALITY OF HEALTH CARE

As previously noted, one perennial concern in relation to the NHS is ensuring that minimum standards are maintained throughout the service in terms of all aspects of provision and care. Clearly, this is also an important way of reducing the expenditure of resources on the fighting and settling of malpractice suits brought by dissatisfied patients (a subject dealt with at length in Chapter 6). In this section, we shall first consider the role of a number of agencies, which oversee and influence the implementation of decision making within the service at the 'macro level', before moving on to address the mechanisms to regulate and provide redress in the context of individual treatment decisions (the 'micro level'). In respect of the latter, there is the possibility for complaints to be brought by aggrieved patients either through the complaints system of the NHS or, where unprofessional conduct on the part of a particular member of the NHS medical staff is alleged, through the latter's professional licensing body – in the case of a doctor, the General Medical Council (GMC).

The 'macro' level: the role of regulatory bodies

In its 1997 White Paper, *The New NHS – Modern, Dependable* (Cm 3807), the government introduced the concept of 'clinical governance', involving the increased use of risk-management techniques and 'evidence-based medicine' 'to assure and improve clinical standards at local level throughout the NHS'. A central role in this initiative was given to two, complementary organisations, the National Institute for Clinical Excellence (NICE), and the Commission for Health Improvement (CHI).

NICE began its work as a Special Health Authority on 1 April 1999, pursuant to the National Institute for Clinical Excellence (Establishment and Constitution) Order 1999 SI 1999/220, and is responsible for disseminating 'best practice' guidance to healthcare professionals working within the NHS. Its role is more fully described in the following extract, which is taken from the Institute's response to Professor Ian Kennedy's report into the Bristol heart surgery scandal (in which it was revealed that inept cardiac surgery on children at a Bristol hospital had led to a significant number of extra deaths and disabilities among them):

National Institute for Clinical Excellence, *Response to the Report of the Bristol Royal Infirmary Inquiry*, 2001, NICE:

Introduction

The Report of the Bristol Royal Infirmary Inquiry is of fundamental importance to the NHS. It describes failures in the arrangements for securing high standards of care and makes recommendations for change and improvement which will effect everyone involved in the health service. The Institute is committed to playing a full part in achieving the goals set out in the Report ...

The Institute is currently constituted as a Special Health Authority with the responsibility to advise health professionals, working in the National Health Service (NHS), on measures to ensure that they are able to provide patients with the highest attainable standards of care. Its guidance takes several forms:

1   It advises health professionals on the appropriate use, within the NHS, of specific health technologies (including pharmaceuticals, devices, procedures, diagnostic and health promotion techniques). In doing so it is required to take account of both the clinical and cost effectiveness of these technologies by the process of 'technology appraisal'.

2   It advises health professionals on the appropriate management of specific conditions (including both diseases such as hypertension, and symptoms such as acute breathlessness). Its guidance may also include advice on appropriate referral for specialist advice. In drawing up clinical guidelines it is required to take into account both clinical and cost effectiveness.

3   The Institute has inherited responsibility for a suite of service delivery guidelines, for cancer, that will be completed within the next 2 years.

These are intended to advise commissioners and purchasers of health care, in the NHS, on the infra-structure necessary to support health professionals provide high standards of care. The Institute has no plans to expand this programme at the present time. Instead, it proposes to incorporate service delivery issues within its clinical guidelines but there may be circumstances, in the future, when separate advice on service reconfiguration would be helpful to the NHS.

4 It advises health professionals with methodological advice on monitoring adherence to its technology appraisal advice, and its clinical guidelines, by means of clinical audit. This includes proposing audit criteria and audit methods.

5 It has responsibility for commissioning and supporting national clinical audits conducted by its National Collaborating Centres (NCCs).

6 It has responsibility for commissioning and supporting the National Confidential Enquiries and for disseminating, to the NHS, specific advice on reducing mortality and other serious adverse events.

However, since 1 April 2005, NICE has joined with the Health Development Agency to become the new National Institute for Health and Clinical Excellence (also to be known as NICE). It is described as 'a single excellence-in-practice organisation' responsible for providing national guidance on the promotion of good health and the prevention and treatment of ill health in three areas: public health; health technologies and clinical practice.

For its part, the CHI, which was established by s 19 of the Health Act 1999, has now been abolished (see Part II of the Health and Social Care (Community Health and Standards) Act 2003) and replaced by the Commission for Healthcare Audit and Inspection (CHAI) and the Commission for Social Care Inspection (CSCI). In addition to these, however, there are a network of other organisations (eg the National Patient Safety Agency, and the National Clinical Assessment Authority) that have been set up to regulate and to improve standards. These are described by the Department of Health as 'arm's length' bodies to indicate their degree of independence from the department. However, the plethora of these organisations causes overlap and confusion and at present there are proposals to 'reconfigure' them (see *Reconfiguring the Department of Health's Arm's Length Bodies*, 2004, London: DoH). In addition to the workings of the above organisations, it should also be noted that a statutory duty to achieve quality in health care is imposed directly upon NHS bodies by s 45 of the Health and Social Care (Community Health and Standards) Act 2003 (replacing s 18 of the Health Act 1999).

The Freedom of Information Act 2000 is also relevant to 'macro' level regulation. This came into force on 1 January 2005 and provides for a public right of acces to information held by public bodies. This includes the NHS, but there is some pre-emption of this as the government has proposed to make available much of the type of information that might be requested, eg information about a trust's performance (see *Better Information, Better Choices and Better Health*, 2004, London: DoH). Information for which disclosure is not provided could be obtained under the Act, but note that (*inter alia*) a request for information can be refused if it would be disproportionately expensive to answer (s 12), the request is vexatious (s 14) and there is a long list of exemptions which include commercial interest, that the information relates to health and safety or is confidential, or if the information is accessible by other means. There is also a public interest exemption (see Part II of the Act, and see Chapter 5 for a discussion of public interest considerations and what 'confidential information' might be.)

The 'micro' level: complaints and discipline

In relation to decisions or other conduct bearing upon the treatment of individual patients, there are a number of mechanisms in place for monitoring the quality of care. We look first at the procedures in place to deal with complaints brought by patients in respect of their treatment (which are an important alternative to formal litigation in the courts), before considering the wider question of disciplinary sanctions available against health professionals who are shown to have behaved in an unbefitting manner.

The complaints system

After widespread and long standing criticism of its excessive complexity and bureaucracy, the NHS complaints system was the subject of radical reform in the light of the recommendations of a government committee of inquiry chaired by Professor Alan Wilson (*Being Heard*, 1994, London: DoH). A new system of NHS complaints procedures was set up and subsequently reviewed and replaced. The history of the complaints system, its shortcomings and recommendations for reform are contained in the Parliamentary and Health Service Ombudsman's Report on the 2004/2005 session:

> **Health Service Ombudsman for England, *Making things Better? A Report on Reform of the NHS Complaints Procedure in England*, 2005, London: The Stationery Office**
>
> **Chapter 1 – A brief history of proposals for reform**
>
> ...
>
> **1996 Single complaints system introduced**
>
> 1. The single complaints system, introduced in April 1996, was a radical improvement on a previously fragmented and partial system. For the first time the same complaints system covered hospital, community and primary care services (family doctors, dentists, opticians and pharmacists), and could handle concerns about both administration and clinical treatment. Complaints were first considered and responded to by the service provider. This first stage was known as local resolution. If complainants remained dissatisfied they could ask a convener (generally a non-executive member of the organisation complained about) to arrange a review by a panel of lay people, with access to any necessary clinical advice. This was known as the second, or independent review stage. But there was no automatic right to such a review. Where complainants remained dissatisfied, or had been refused an independent review, they could complain to the Health Service Ombudsman.
>
> **1999–2001 Evaluation and listening exercise**
>
> 2. It soon became clear that there were major difficulties with the single complaints system. The Department of Health had always intended to evaluate the effectiveness of the system and commissioned a research study, which ran from 1999 to 2000. The results, published in September 2001, revealed that many complainants felt a high level of dissatisfaction with the operation of the system, both at the local resolution and independent review stages. The main causes of dissatisfaction were unhelpful, aggressive or arrogant attitudes of staff, poor communication and a lack of information and support. The most important structural failure was the 'perceived lack of independence in the convening decision and in the review process generally'. The results of the evaluation resonated strongly with the experience of the Ombudsman's office.

3. The Department of Health's evaluation report, *NHS Complaints Procedure: National Evaluation*, made 27 recommendations aimed at improvements throughout the system, including:

- a uniform national procedure, applied equally to primary care and hospital services, with clear and consistent time limits;

- dissemination of good practice, and more use of conciliation to achieve results swiftly and effectively;

- clear guidance on how the complaints procedure should be applied, and standard targets nationally for managing the performance of staff handling complaints;

- clear lines of responsibility for making sure the complaints system is run properly, with Chairs and Chief Executives answerable to the Department of Health for their performance;

- a responsibility on Trust Boards to ensure this work is funded properly, staff are trained appropriately to handle complaints and that their clinical governance framework reflects complaints work as core business;

- a system of quarterly reporting by complaints staff to the Trust Board, summarising the causes and trends underlying complaints, and making recommendations for action. These reports to be copied to relevant patient representative organisations, and the Board to be responsible for implementing recommendations;

- support from Primary Care Groups (PCGs) (predecessors of Primary Care Trusts – PCTs) for practices in managing the system, with a named individual responsible for handling practice complaints;

- regional NHS bodies, or a new independent national complaints authority, to be responsible for holding panels to account and managing their performance;

- wide circulation of the panels' final reports to relevant patient representative bodies and the Commission for Health Improvement (CHI), with the Trust Board being responsible for implementing any recommendations for remedial action;

- new options for how panels should be convened: by the Health Authority, neighbouring Trusts/Health Authorities, or introducing a separate regional or sub-regional panel.

2001 The Department consults on key questions

...

2003 Proposals for the new procedure

6. The Department of Health's response, in January 2002, to the Report of the Public Inquiry into children's heart surgery at the Bristol Royal Infirmary said that they intended to have a new NHS complaints procedure in place by December 2002. However, no new procedure was proposed until April 2003, when the Department published *NHS Complaints Reform, Making things right*. This described the vision of a new complaints procedure:

- open and easy to access – flexible about the ways people could complain and with effective support for people wishing to do so;

- fair and independent – emphasising early resolution so minimising the strain and distress for all those involved;

- responsive – providing appropriate and proportionate response and redress;

- providing an opportunity for learning and developing – ensuring complaints are viewed as a positive opportunity to learn from patients' views to drive continual improvement in services.

...

2004 Partial implementation

9. In December 2003 draft regulations for the new NHS procedure were issued for consultation. The intention had been to implement the regulations on 1 June 2004. However abbreviated regulations, the *National Health Service (Complaints) Regulations 2004*, were eventually laid before Parliament on 9 July 2004 and came into force on 30 July. Ministers had decided on a phased implementation to take account of recommendations of the Shipman Inquiry. The Inquiry's 5th report was likely to address complaints handling in some detail and was due to be published later in 2004. Reports from other inquiries about doctors who had repeatedly failed to observe proper standards of care were also expected later in 2004.

10. The July 2004 Regulations left the local resolution stage of the complaints procedure broadly unchanged. They consolidated and rationalised the statutory requirements for local resolution by NHS bodies and introduced a reformed independent review stage to be carried out by the Healthcare Commission. The Department intends to issue revised regulations in 2005 following consideration of the 5th Shipman report.

11. Whilst the new complaints procedure was in gestation there were a number of inquiries into situations where serious failings in systems or in standards of clinical care continued for lengthy periods and affected significant numbers of patients.

12. The *Bristol Inquiry* reported in 2001, the *Neale* and *Ayling* Inquiries in September 2004, the final part of the *Shipman Inquiry* in January 2005, and the Haslam and Kerr Inquiry reports are expected later in 2005.

13. Each of the inquiries has considered why existing systems, including the complaints system, did not mean that the problems were fully recognised and acted upon far sooner. Each has pressed for a more patient-focused approach. They have also produced specific recommendations on complaint handling.

14. The Neale and Ayling inquiries called for:

- advocacy;

- an independent element to the system;

- early resolution of complaints;

- accessible and easily-used systems;

- better communication;

- training in complaints handling for all staff;

- special training in handling sensitive matters for Patient Advice and Liaison Services (PALS) and Independent Complaints Advocacy Services (ICAS) staff;

- the establishment of systems to ensure that complaints about the same practitioner working in different organisations could be linked.

15. The Shipman Inquiry report recommended key changes to handling complaints about GPs including:

- all complaints about GPs should be reported to the PCT and patients could lodge complaints direct with the PCT; and

- PCTs should develop the ability to investigate complaints properly and refer to the Healthcare Commission where necessary.

In 2004, the new NHS complaints procedure was introduced and is governed by the National Health Service (Complaints) Regulations 2004. The procedure stresses that, wherever possible, complaints should be dealt with and resolved locally. If this cannot be done, the complainant has a right to have his/her case reviewed by the Healthcare Commission. Thereafter, if the issue has not been resolved, there is a right of appeal to the Health Service Ombudsman. However, the Ombudsman's Report of 2005 is critical of these reforms:

Health Service Ombudsman for England, *Making things Better? A Report on Reform of the NHS Complaints Procedure in England*, 2005, London: The Stationery Office

23. There are five key weaknesses in the current system and approach, which the interim changes introduced in 2004 have not resolved:

- complaints systems are fragmented within the NHS, between the NHS and private health care systems, and between health and social care;

- the complaints system is not centred on the patient's needs;

- there is a lack of capacity and competence among staff to deliver a quality service;

- the right leadership, culture and governance are not in place;

- just remedies are not being secured for justified complaints.

- There are, in addition, a number of problems which arise from the way the interim changes were implemented.

- Fragmentation in complaints

Chapter 3 – Key elements of a new system

94. It is only right that, if we are to express such significant concerns about the present system, we should also make clear what we believe needs to be done. The essential elements in the new system should be those that ensure:

- coherent and comprehensive coverage;

- customer focus, accessibility, flexibility and transparency;

- a quality service;

- leadership, culture and governance;

- the provision of just remedies;

- improvements in service as a result of learning from complaints.

To be effective such new arrangements must be introduced in a planned and project managed way.

...

Chapter 4 – Recommendations

108. The outcomes we seek to achieve from the complaints system are clear. The pause in the implementation of a revised complaints process, prompted, in

particular, by the Shipman Inquiry, presents the opportunity for the Department of Health to take a lead and ensure that these outcomes are finally secured for complainants in a new health and social care complaints system.

109. The history of proposals for reform, described in *Chapter 1* of this report, shows that there is remarkable consensus about what an effective complaints system should look like and what it needs to deliver. The Department of Health's publication, *Making things Right*, echoed the recommendations that emerged from the 'listening exercise' and the Bristol Inquiry, and has been reinforced by the recommendations of the *Ayling*, *Neale* and *Shipman* Inquiries. We do not dissent from that vision – indeed we have positively welcomed it.

110. The challenge, therefore, is not in determining the vision of an effective complaints system, but in avoiding the mistakes of the past and turning the aspirations of *Making things Right* into a reality for patients and their families and NHS staff. Our recommendations are framed to that end.

111. A number of bodies need to work together to ensure that we now create the modern, responsive, patient-focused system to which we all aspire. In particular we see clear roles for the Department of Health, the Healthcare Commission and all providers of NHS healthcare.

It should be noted that in addition to the NHS complaints procedure the Healthcare Commissioner has an independent investigative role pursuant to powers grant under the Health Service Commissioners Act 1993.

Discipline

Following the Wilson Committee's report, discipline is the subject of separate procedures to those which govern complaints. Nevertheless, it may become apparent as the result of a complaint (or, indeed, in the course of a malpractice action, see Chapter 6) that the conduct of a particular medical professional is deserving of censure. In this regard, there are two parallel systems for disciplining the professional concerned.

First, disciplinary procedures internal to the NHS may be invoked. However, with regard to these there has been much disquiet because of their time-consuming and costly nature (an estimated £40 million caused just by delay) and, in consequence, a new national disciplinary framework has been devised which came into force on 1 June 2005 (see *Maintaining High Professional Standards in the Modern NHS*, 2005, London: DoH). In the second place, and perhaps of even greater consequence for professionals, their conduct may be investigated by the responsible governing and licensing body for their profession. In respect of doctors this is the GMC, and the equivalent body for nurses is the Nursing and Midwifery Council (NMC). (There are also two general regulatory bodies for health care professionals: the Council for Healthcare Regulatory Excellence and the Health Professions Council – a further extension of the government's apparently insatiable appetite for regulatory bodies in the field of healthcare, this time provoked by the *Harold Shipman* case.) Self-regulatory organisations have a long tradition of enunciating and administering the standards of professional practice to which their members are required to adhere, and their power to discipline and, ultimately, to 'strike off' the register the names of those found guilty of serious misconduct has been codified in statute. In the case of the GMC, the relevant provisions are found in Pt V of the Medical Act 1983 (as amended):

Professional conduct and fitness to practise

35 General Council's power to advise on conduct or ethics

The powers of the General Council shall include the power to provide, in such manner as the Council think fit, advice for members of the medical profession on standards of professional conduct or on medical ethics.

35A General Council's power to require disclosure of information

(1) For the purpose of assisting the General Council or any of their committees in carrying out functions in respect of professional conduct, professional performance or fitness to practise, a person authorised by the Council may require–

    (a) a practitioner (except the practitioner in respect of whose professional conduct, professional performance or fitness to practise the information or document is sought); or

    (b) any other person,

who in his opinion is able to supply information or produce any document which appears relevant to the discharge of any such function, to supply such information or produce such a document.

...

35B Notification and disclosure by the General Council

(1) As soon as is reasonably practicable after the relevant date, the General Council shall notify the following of the making of a decision [to refer a practitioner to the Preliminary Proceedings Committee]–

    (a) the Secretary of State, the Scottish Ministers and the National Assembly for Wales; and

    (b) any person in the United Kingdom of whom the General Council are aware–
        (i) by whom the practitioner concerned is employed to provide services in, or in relation to, any area of medicine; or
        (ii) with whom he has an arrangement to do so.

(2) The General Council may disclose to any person any information relating to a practitioner's professional conduct, professional performance or fitness to practise which they consider it to be in the public interest to disclose.

36 Professional misconduct and criminal offences

(1) Where a fully registered person–

    (a) is found by the Professional Conduct Committee to have been convicted in the British Islands of a criminal offence, whether while so registered or not; or

    (b) is judged by the Professional Conduct Committee to have been guilty of serious professional misconduct, whether while so registered or not,

the Committee may, if they think fit, direct–

        (i) that his name shall be erased from the register;
        (ii) that his registration in the register shall be suspended (that is to say, shall not have effect) during such period not exceeding 12 months as may be specified in the direction; or
        (iii) that his registration shall be conditional on his compliance, during such period not exceeding three years as may be specified in the direction,

with such requirements so specified as the Committee think fit to impose for the protection of members of the public or in his interests.

(2) Where a fully registered person whose registration is subject to conditions imposed under sub-s (1) above by the Professional Conduct Committee or under section 41A by the Interim Orders Committee or the Professional Conduct Committee is judged by the Professional Conduct Committee to have failed to comply with any of the requirements imposed on him as conditions of his registration the Committee may, if they think fit, direct–

(a) that his name shall be erased from the register; or

(b) that his registration in the register shall be suspended (that is to say, shall not have effect) during such period not exceeding 12 months as may be specified in the direction ...

Erasure from the register is clearly a very serious sanction for professionals, in that, henceforth, (unless they succeed at some future date in having their names restored to it) they will be deprived of their professional livelihoods. In so far as a doctor is unhappy with the decision of the GMC in this matter, he or she may appeal (pursuant to s 40 of the 1983 Act) to the Privy Council. A case in point, in which the meaning of 'serious professional misconduct' under s 36 of the Act was considered, is that of *McCandless v GMC* [1996] 1 WLR 167:

McCandless v GMC **[1996] 1 WLR 167**

Lord Hoffmann: Dr David McCandless, a general practitioner in Deeside, appeals against a determination and direction of the Professional Conduct Committee of the General Medical Council. At a hearing on 16 March 1995 the Committee found that he was guilty of serious professional misconduct and directed that his name should be erased from the Register of Medical Practitioners.

The charges alleged errors in his diagnoses of three patients and failure to refer them to hospital. Two subsequently died and the other was found on her eventual admission to hospital to be seriously ill. It is not necessary to go further into the details because Mr Mitting, who appeared for Dr McCandless, accepted that the Committee's findings of fact were not open to any material dispute. He also accepted that in each case Dr McCandless had been negligent. The chairman of the Committee gave the following brief reasons for its finding that he had been guilty of serious professional misconduct:

Dr McCandless, the Committee take a very serious view of the evidence which they have heard about the poor standard of medical care which you provided to all three patients in this case. The care which you provided fell deplorably short of the standard which patients are entitled to expect from their general practitioners.

Mr Mitting submits that these reasons reveal an error of law by the Committee. He says that the Committee applied the wrong test for what amounts to serious professional misconduct. It thought that it was enough that the treatment given to the three patients fell 'deplorably short' of the standard which would reasonably be expected. Mr Mitting says that poor treatment is not enough. The doctor may nevertheless have been doing his best. He may have been overworked or just not particularly good at the job. But 'serious professional misconduct' means, he said, conduct which is morally blameworthy. This cannot be determined simply by deciding whether the treatment measured up to an objective standard. One has to look at why the doctor gave the treatment which he did. If it fell short of a reasonable standard because he was, for example, too lazy or drunk to examine the patient properly, then he would be guilty of misconduct. But not if he made an honest mistake.

Their Lordships think that some support can be found for Mr Mitting's submission in old cases on the meaning of 'infamous conduct in a professional respect' – the words which were used in 19th century Medical Acts and which continued to be used until replaced by the words 'serious professional misconduct' in the Medical Act 1969 ...

[However,] ... the authorities on the old wording do not speak with one voice and ... they are of little assistance in the interpretation of the new. Secondly, although there remains the single disciplinary offence now styled 'serious professional misconduct', the possible penalties available to the Committee, which used to be confined to the ultimate sanction of erasure, have been extended to include suspension and the imposition of conditions upon practice. This suggests that the offence was intended to include serious cases of negligence. Thirdly, the public has higher expectations of doctors and members of other self-governing professions. Their governing bodies are under a corresponding duty to protect the public against the genially incompetent as well as the deliberate wrongdoers. Fourthly, the meaning of the new wording has been authoritatively stated by this Board in *Doughty v General Dental Council* [1988] AC 164, p 173 in objective terms:

> ... judged by proper professional standards in the light of the objective facts about the individual patients ... the dental treatments criticised as unnecessary [were] treatments that no dentist of reasonable skill exercising reasonable care would carry out.

This test appears to their Lordships to be, *mutatis mutandis*, equally applicable to treatment by doctors ...

Once it is accepted that seriously negligent treatment can amount to serious professional misconduct, then it seems to their Lordships that the appeal must fail. The eminent medical practitioners who sat on the Committee came to the conclusion that Dr McCandless' treatment of his three patients fell deplorably short of the standard to which patients are entitled to expect from general practitioners. In the circumstances, it is scarcely surprising that they concluded that Dr McCandless was guilty of serious professional misconduct. Their Lordships can see no basis for interfering with that conclusion. Nor can they see any ground for interfering with the Committee's decision that the offences merited the penalty of erasure from the register.

Subsequently, in *Roylance v GMC (No 2)* [2000] 1 AC 311, it was confirmed that, provided there was 'a link with the profession of medicine', serious professional misconduct could extend beyond clinical conduct to organisational and managerial failures.

In *R (On the Application of Campbell) v GMC* [2005] EWCA Civ 250 the issue was whether mitigating factors were relevant to a decision as to whether conduct amounted to serious misconduct. The Court of Appeal held that such an approach was flawed; personal mitigating factors were only relevant to the second stage of the procedure, ie the appropriate sanction to be imposed.

In 2002 the Government announced a number of reforms to the GMC, including a new role of regularly revalidating a doctor's licence to practise (to ensure that his practice remains up to date and of a high standard): see *Reform of the GMC: A Paper for Consultation*, 2002, London: DoH. The GMC has subsequently set up a new system of dealing with complaints, the key feature of which is the separation of functions. The proposal is that the fitness to practise procedures will be divided into two stages: investigation and adjudication. This is to avoid the traditional criticism of certain professional regulatory bodies who could be accused of acting as police, prosecution and judiciary when dealing with their own members. There is also a proposed new validation procedure whereby doctors will require a licence to practise which will be renewed every five years. The new procedures were due to come into force in April 2005. However, the revalidation procedure is based upon fitness to practise in the sense of being medically competent and does not specifically deal with non-clinical misconduct. In consequence, this issue was highlighted by the publication of the Fifth Report on the Harold Shipman case (*The Fifth Report, Safeguarding Patents: Lessons from the Past – Proposals for the Future*, 2004, London: Shipman Inquiry) and, following publication, it was decided that the government's Chief Medical Officer should review the new procedures and the April 2005 launch was postponed.

It should also be noted that the Naional Health Service Reform and Health Care professions Act 2002 established the Council for the Regulation of Health Care Professionals. The function of this body is to oversee, and, indeed, to scrutinise, the performance of the individual professional regulatory bodies including the GMC and the regulatory bodies of other health care professionals such as nurses, dentists and pharmacists.

Role of (criminal) law

Of course, the disciplinary mechanisms with which we have so far been concerned operate alongside, and independently of, the sanctions provided by the legal system in relation to doctors and other persons who, by their conduct, inflict harm upon others. In Chapters 3 and 6 we shall be focusing upon the civil remedies, in the torts of battery and negligence respectively, available to patients in relation to maltreatment they receive during medical care. However, it is important to note that the criminal law may also be of relevance in some cases. In this regard, where a patient is injured, or simply handled non-consensually, a doctor could in theory be prosecuted for an offence, either in battery at common law, or under the Offences Against the Person Act 1861. Where the patient actually dies, then a charge in murder or manslaughter may be brought, depending on the *mens rea* of the doctor. The former charge, in particular, is a possibility in certain cases of euthanasia (see further Chapter 12).

Although it is generally very rare for criminal charges to be preferred against doctors (it usually not thought to be in the public interest for prosecutions to be brought), the fact that ultimately doctors do not belong to any special category of citizen – and must answer for the serious consequences of deficient conduct – was illustrated by the conviction for manslaughter of an anaesthetist in *R v Adomako* [1994] 5 Med LR 27:

R v Adomako **[1994] 5 Med LR 27 (Lord Mackay of Clashfern LC, Lords Keith, Goff, Browne-Wilkinson and Woolf)**

Lord Mackay of Clashfern LC: The conviction arose out of the conduct of an eye operation carried out at the Mayday Hospital, Croydon on 4 January 1987. The appellant was, during the latter part of that operation, the anaesthetist in charge of the patient.

The operation was carried out by two surgeons supported by a team of five nurses and a theatre sister. Anaesthesia commenced at about 9.45 am ...

At approximately 11.05 am a disconnection occurred at the endotracheal tube connection. The supply of oxygen to the patient ceased and this led to cardiac arrest at 11.14 am. During this period the appellant failed to notice or remedy the disconnection.

The appellant first became aware that something was amiss when an alarm sounded on the Dinamap machine, which monitors the patient's blood pressure. From the evidence it appears that some four and a half minutes would have elapsed between the disconnection and the sounding of this alarm. When this alarm sounded the appellant responded in various ways by checking the equipment and by administering atropine to raise the patient's pulse. But at no stage before the cardiac arrest did he check the integrity of the endotracheal tube connection. The disconnection itself was not discovered until after resuscitation measures had been commenced.

For the prosecution it was alleged that the appellant was guilty of gross negligence in failing to notice or respond appropriately to obvious signs that a disconnection had occurred and that the patient had ceased to breathe. In particular the prosecution alleged that the appellant had failed to notice at various stages during the period after disconnection and before the arrest either occurred or became inevitable that the patient's chest was not moving, the dials on the mechanical ventilating machine were not operating, the disconnection in the endotracheal tube, that the alarm on the ventilator was not switched on and that the patient was becoming progressively blue. Further the prosecution alleged that the appellant had noticed but failed to understand the correct significance of the fact that during this period the patient's pulse had dropped and the patient's blood pressure had dropped.

Two expert witnesses gave evidence for the prosecution. Professor Payne described that standard of care as 'abysmal' while Professor Adams stated in that in his view a competent anaesthetist should have recognised the signs of disconnection within 15 seconds and that the appellant's conduct amounted to 'a gross dereliction of care'.

On behalf of the appellant it was conceded at his trial that he had been negligent. The issue was therefore whether his conduct was criminal ...

... [I]n my opinion the ordinary principles of the law of negligence apply to ascertain whether or not the defendant has been in breach of a duty of care towards the victim who has died. If such breach of duty is established the next question is whether that breach of duty caused the death of the victim. If so, the jury must go on to consider whether that breach of duty should be characterised as gross negligence and therefore as a crime. This will depend on the seriousness of the breach of duty committed by the defendant in all the circumstances in which the defendant was placed when it occurred. The jury will have to consider whether the extent to which the defendant's conduct departed from the proper standard of care incumbent upon him, involving as it must have done a risk of death to the patient, was such that it should be judged criminal.

It is true that to a certain extent this involves an element of circularity, but in this branch of the law I do not believe that is fatal to its being correct as a test of how far conduct must depart from accepted standards to be characterised as criminal. This is necessarily a question of degree and an attempt to specify that degree more closely is I think likely to achieve only a spurious precision. The essence of the matter which is supremely a jury question is whether, having regard to the risk of death involved, the conduct of the defendant was so bad in all the circumstances as to amount in their judgment to a criminal act or omission ...

In my view the summing up of the learned judge in the present case was a model of clarity in analysis of the facts and in setting out the law in a manner which was readily comprehensible by the jury. The summing up was criticised in respect of the inclusion of the following passage ([1991] 2 Med LR 291):

> Of course you will understand it is not for every humble man of the profession to have all that great skill of the great men in Harley Street but, on the other hand, they are not allowed to practise medicine in this country unless they have acquired a certain amount of skill. They are bound to show a reasonable amount of skill according to the circumstances of the case, and you have to judge them on the basis that they are skilled men, but not necessarily so skilled as more skillful men in the profession, and you can only convict them criminally if, in your judgment, they fall below the standard of skill which is the least qualification which any doctor should have. You should only convict a doctor of causing a death by negligence if you think he did something which no reasonably skilled doctor should have done.

The criticism was particularly of the latter part of this quotation in that it was open to the meaning that if the defendant did what no reasonably skilled doctor should have done it was open to the jury to convict him of causing death by negligence. Strictly speaking this passage is concerned with the statement of a necessary condition for a conviction by preventing a conviction unless that condition is satisfied. It is incorrect to treat it as stating a sufficient condition for conviction. In any event I consider that this passage in the context was making the point forcefully that the defendant in this case was not to be judged by the standard of more skilled doctors but by the standard of a reasonably competent doctor. There were many other passages in the summing up which emphasised the need for a high degree of negligence if the jury were to convict and read in that context I consider that the summing up cannot be faulted.

For these reasons I am of the opinion that this appeal should be dismissed ...

(Lords Keith, Goff, Browne-Wilkinson and Woolf agreed.)

In *R v Amit Misra, R v Rajeev Srivastava* [2004] EWCA Crim 2375 two doctors who had been convicted of manslaughter by gross negligence appealed. One of their arguments (the other related to the admission of fresh evidence) was that the offence lacked certainty and therefore was incompatible with Articles 7 and 6 of the European Convention on Human Rights. The Court of Appeal rejected this argument, stating that the requirement for legal certainty of an offence was sufficient rather than absolute certainty and the European Convention had not changed this. The question for the jury to decide was whether the behaviour was grossly negligent and consequently criminal and this was a question of fact.

ACCESS TO HEALTH CARE

Background – scarcity of NHS resources

Demand for NHS resources has always outstripped supply:

Timmins, N, *NHS 50th Anniversary: A History of the NHS*, 1996, London: DoH, p 3:

The new service uncovered a vast well of unmet need. GPs of the time recall women with prolapsed uteruses, who had been unable to afford the hospital treatment, suddenly pouring into the surgery, along with men with huge hernias held in by trusses. Bevan, who had declared the NHS would 'lift the shadow from millions of homes', had been right.

But there was also some abuse as GPs were inundated with people wanting wigs, or free cotton wool for padding, and free surgical spirit and aspirin. 'One would think the people saved up their illness for the first free day', one GP complained and Bevan himself, when the service had been running for 18 months, declared: 'I shudder to think of the ceaseless cascade of medicine which is pouring down British throats at the present time.'

Nonetheless, the NHS transformed health care – and not just for the poor, who were spared the indignity of means tests, but also for the middle classes, who no longer faced the fear of bills. It did so too for doctors. 'I used to charge 1/6d for a consultation,' one Clydeside GP recalled. 'They laid the money on the desk as they came in. It was all rather embarrassing. I used to charge 2/6d to 7/6d for a visit, the highest rate for foremen and undermanagers. We'd send out the bills, but about a quarter would be bad debts and some you simply didn't bill because you knew they couldn't pay. The NHS thankfully got rid of all that.'

In doing so, however, the service instantly faced the first of the great financial crises which were periodically to mark its history. Spending in the first nine months proved two thirds higher than expected. The sea of unmet need, the sheer difficulty of predicting in advance the costs of the new service, the rising expectations it generated and the costs of medical advance had all combined to blow the early budgets.

If this sounds familiar it is because it is the history of health services the world over. Take medical advance. The first antibiotic – penicillin – had become available, for troops, during the war. But the year 1948 saw new types of penicillin developed. Streptomycin, the first drug to successfully tackle tubercular meningitis – TB in the forties was a major scourge – became available. In both Britain and America, other new antibiotics were developed. Tubocurarine, the muscle relaxant still used in surgery today, was introduced.

Clearly, pressures on NHS resources are not simply a consequence of inefficiencies in the way the service is run (the issue that various governmental reforms have sought to address). Rather, in the light of constant advances in medical technology, they are to be regarded as inherent and inescapable in nature. As Christopher Newdick writes:

Newdick, C, *Who Should We Treat?*, 1995, Oxford: Clarendon, pp 5–6:

Medicine no longer focuses on opportunist and acute illness. It routinely deals with chronic conditions such as the diseases of the cardiovascular system, of the respiratory system, the gastrointestinal system, the central nervous system, and joint diseases such as arthritis. Treatments for these conditions are usually long term, and often last many years. Combined together, they accounted for some 63.6% of the total drugs bill in England in 1992. These are the diseases associated with relative affluence and old age which, for the moment, are likely to put increasing pressure on resources. As a result of these pressures, some treatments are not routinely provided by the NHS. For example, tattoo removal is often not offered by hospitals, and many health authorities have restricted the availability of *in vitro* fertilisation, gender reassignment, reversal of sterilisation, cosmetic surgery, and complementary medicine.

Matters will soon become more complicated still. The pharmaceutical industry stands on the edge of a new generation of medicines which will revolutionise our ideas about sickness and health. But they may be so expensive that health service providers will be forced to reassess the question of priorities. Just the past year has seen a paradigm shift in modern biology because it is revealing so much information about the basic mechanisms of disease for which drugs can be developed. In the past, pharmaceutical firms relied on serendipity to find new drugs. In future that is not the way to go if the idea is to produce medicines of value.

Today, as a result of the Human Genome Project, we have sufficient knowledge of the basic structures of DNA in the human body to consider genetic treatments for chronic conditions of illness which were hitherto entirely beyond the reach of doctors and medicines. We may soon be in a position to attack the genetic causes of chronic illness. Cystic fibrosis, for example, is being treated in this way. Similar developments are occurring in the field of medical devices and technology, in both diagnosis and treatment of illness. Such techniques offer the potential for considerable savings on conventional, long term treatment of conditions such as heart and liver disease, diabetes and cancer and may be attractive on health and financial grounds. On the other hand, their cost may be so prohibitive as to threaten the availability of other, less expensive treatments. They also raise fundamental questions about the meaning of the words 'health' and 'illness'. Curative treatment may become available for a range of conditions which are explained in societal or personal terms, rather than as illnesses. Obesity, alcoholism, cigarette smoking and drug addiction provoke arguments of this nature. Should they qualify for care in the same way as other conditions? These issues raise questions about the very purpose of a 'health' service. [Reprinted from *Who Should We Treat?: Law, Patients and Resources in the NHS* by Christopher Newdick (1995) by permission of Oxford University Press.]

Disputes over obtaining treatment

In the 10-year NHS plan, launched by the government in July 2000, ambitious targets (backed by increased funding) have been laid down for the NHS to achieve in terms of faster patient access to the most effective treatments:

Department of Health, *The NHS Plan, A Plan for Investment, A Plan for Reform*, 2000, London: DoH, Annex 3, Department of Health Public Service Agreement:

Aim

A3.1 To transform the health and social care system so that it produces faster, fairer services that deliver better health and tackles health inequalities.

Objectives and performance targets

Objective I: improving health outcomes for everyone

A3.2 Reduce substantially the mortality rates from major killers by 2010: from heart disease by at least 40% in people under 75; from cancer by at least 20% in people under 75; and from suicide and undetermined injury by at least 20%. Key to the delivery of this target will be implementing the National Service Frameworks for coronary heart disease and mental health and the National Cancer Plan.

A3.3 Our objective is to narrow the health gap in childhood and throughout life between socio-economic groups and between the most deprived areas and the rest of the country. Specific national targets will be developed in consultation with external stakeholders and experts early in 2001.

Objective II: improving patient and carer experience of the NHS and social services

A3.4 Patients will receive treatment at a time that suits them in accordance with their clinical need: two thirds of all outpatient appointments and inpatient elective admissions will be pre-booked by 2003/04 on the way to 100% pre-booking by 2005.

A3.5 Reduce the maximum wait for an outpatient appointment to three months and the maximum wait for inpatient treatment to 6 months by the end of 2005.

A3.6 To secure year-on-year improvements in patient satisfaction, including standards of cleanliness and food, as measured by independently audited local surveys.

Objective III: effective delivery of appropriate care …

Objective IV: fair access

A3.10 Guaranteed access to a primary care professional within 24 hours and to a primary care doctor within 48 hours by 2004.

Objective V: value for money

A3.11 The cost of care commissioned from trusts which perform well against indicators of fair access, quality and responsiveness, will become the benchmark for the NHS. Everyone will be expected to reach the level of the best over the next 5 years, with agreed milestones for 2003/04.

Statement of accountability

A3.11 The Secretary of State for Health is accountable for the delivery of the targets set out in this Public Service Agreement.

However, it is apparent that the above 'agreement' functions primarily to define targets for NHS bodies to aim at, rather than conferring a set of enforceable rights upon patients. In terms of such latter rights, the patient remains dependent upon the action in the courts. What, then, are the available legal mechanisms through which a patient may challenge the denial of NHS treatment?

Judicial review

Given the public status of the health service, and the constituent bodies within it (that is, health authorities, NHS trusts, etc), a decision not to provide some given treatment may be susceptible to challenge in public law. This means that such a decision, if viewed as *Wednesbury* unreasonable (see *Associated Provincial Picture Houses v Wednesbury Corp* [1947] 2 All ER 680), can be quashed by the courts. Lord Diplock in *Council of Civil Service Unions v Minister for the Civil Service* [1985] AC 374, p 410, described the power of judicial review in the following terms:

> **Lord Diplock**: It applies to a decision which is so outrageous in its defiance of logic or of accepted moral standards that no sensible person who had applied his mind to the question to be decided could have arrived at it. Whether a decision falls within this category is a question that judges by their training and experience should be well equipped to answer, or else there would be something badly wrong with our judicial system.

In the course of a number of actions brought in judicial review, however, the courts have shown themselves to be unwilling to interfere with decisions of NHS bodies in relation to the treatment of individual patients. In so doing, judges have recognised that the NHS has limited resources and that it is not for them to assume the role of organisers and arbiters of hospital waiting lists.

One of the first cases in which patients invoked judicial review in an attempt to assert a direct right to receive specified health care was that of *R v Secretary of State for Social Services et al ex p Hincks and Others* (1980) 1 BMLR 93:

R v Secretary of State for Social Services, West Midlands RHA and Birmingham AHA (Teaching) ex p Hincks and Others (1980) 1 BMLR 93, CA (Lord Denning MR, Bridge and Oliver LJJ)

This case was principally concerned with the meaning of s 3(1) of the National Health Service Act 1977 (see p 52, above), and in particular whether it imposed an absolute duty on the Secretary of State to provide services regardless of available funding. Four people who had been on the waiting list for orthopaedic surgery sought a declaration that the Secretary of State was in breach of his duty when plans for additional orthopaedic services at a hospital could not be carried out because of lack of funding. In refusing the declaration, the Court of Appeal noted that the Secretary of State has to have regard to the money made available to him:

> **Lord Denning MR**: Mr Blom-Cooper has urged before us all that can be said. He has referred us to the fact that there are no provisions in the statute which limit the expenditure of the Department. Section 3(1) of the National Health Service Act 1977 provides:
>
>> It is the Secretary of State's duty to provide throughout England and Wales, to such extent as he considers necessary to meet all reasonable requirements – (a) hospital accommodation ... (c) medical, dental, nursing and ambulance services ... (f) such other services as are required for the diagnosis and treatment of illness.
>
> So that is his duty. It is a short point, and an important point that Mr Blom-Cooper raises. He says that that duty must be fulfilled. If the Secretary of State needs money to do it, then he must see that Parliament gives it to him. Alternatively, if Parliament does not give it to him, then a provision should be put in the statute to excuse him from his duty. Mr Blom-Cooper says that that duty is plain and imperative, and it ought to be fulfilled by the Secretary of State.
>
> That is an attractive argument, because there is no express limitation on the duty of the Secretary of State in the statute. But, in the course of the argument, many illustrations have been taken showing how necessary it is for a Secretary of State to have regard to forward planning (as it is called), to estimated changes in the population, for instance – or maybe the ageing population. He has to estimate for the future. For instance, when in 1971 the Good Hope Hospital scheme was approved, it was necessarily contemplated that it would be possible within the resources available. Indeed, as the discussion proceeded, it seemed to me inevitable that this provision had to be implied into s 3, 'to such extent as he considers necessary to meet all reasonable requirements such as can be provided within the resources available'. That seems to me to be a very necessary implication to put on that section, in accordance with the general legislative purpose. It cannot be supposed that the Secretary of State has to provide all the latest equipment. As Oliver LJ said in the course of argument, it cannot be supposed that the Secretary of State has to provide all the kidney machines which are asked for, or for all the new developments such as heart transplants in every case where people would benefit from them. It cannot be that the Secretary of State has a duty to provide everything that is asked for in the changed circumstances which have come about. That includes the numerous pills that people take nowadays: it cannot be said that he has to provide all these free for everybody.
>
> I would like to read a few words from the judgment of Wien J, who gave a very comprehensive and good judgment in this matter.
>
> He said:
>
>> The question remains: has there been a breach duty? Counsel for the (Secretary of State) submits that s 3 does not impose an absolute duty. I agree.

He further submits it does, by virtue of the discretion given, include an evaluation of financial resources or the lack of them is at the root of the whole problem in this case.

If funds were unlimited, then of course regions and areas could go ahead and provide all sorts of services. But funds are not unlimited. The funds are voted by parliament, and the health service has to do the best it can with the total allocation of financial resources.

I agree with that approach of the judge in this case. But there is a further aspect which he dealt with.

He said, instead of looking at the health service as a whole, could you pinpoint a particular hospital or a particular area like the Good Hope Hospital in Birmingham, and say, that does require an extension, and it is a breach of duty for the Secretary of State not to provide for that hospital and that area? It seems to me – as, indeed, Mr Roland Moyle said in the course of his letter – that you cannot pinpoint any particular hospital or any particular area. The Secretary of State has to do his best having regard to his wide responsibilities. For instance, there are 12 hospitals in this particular area. The service has to be provided over the whole country. Upon that point, the judge said:

I have come to the conclusion that it is impossible to pinpoint any breach of statutory duty on the part of the Secretary of State. If he is entitled to take into account financial resources, as in my judgment he is, then it follows that every thing that can be done within the limit of the financial resources available has been done in the region and in the area. I doubt very much whether under s 3(1) it is permissible to put the spotlight, as it were, upon one particular department of one particular hospital and say that conditions there are unsatisfactory.

It seems to me that those two paragraphs in the judge's judgment express the position very accurately. It is an interesting point, and it is important from the public point of view because of the grievances which many people feel nowadays about the long waiting list to get into hospital. So be it. The Secretary of State says that he is doing the best he can with the financial resources available to him: and I do not think that he can be faulted in the matter.

I think that the judge was quite right, and I would dismiss the appeal.

The decision shows the very difficult health resource policy issues involved and the extent to which to which there are often no immediate solutions. The lives of patients can be seen to be at stake in some of the cases:

R v Central Birmingham HA ex p Walker, R v Secretary of State for Social Services and Another ex p Walker (1987) 3 BMLR 32 (MacPherson J)

David Barber Walker was a premature baby who needed a heart operation. He had been cared for in hospital since his birth and was not in any immediate danger. His operation had been postponed on a number of occasions because of a shortage of specially trained nurses in the intensive care unit where he would have to go after the operation. His mother applied for leave to apply for judicial review of the decision to postpone the operation, seeking certiorari to quash the decision to postpone on the ground that it had been arrived at unlawfully and unreasonably, and mandamus to require the authority to carry out the operation:

MacPherson J: It seems to me that this case is not truly an attack upon the actual decision made (although that is the matter set out in the application itself) and I detect a general criticism of the decisions as to the staffing and financing of the National Health Service and of those who provide its funds and facilities. It has been said before, and I say it again, that this court can no more investigate that on the facts of this case than it could do so in any other case where the balance of available money and its distribution and use are concerned. Those, of course, are questions which are of enormous public interest and concern – but they are questions to be raised, answered and dealt with outside the court.

I am wholly convinced that this decision of the health authority is not justiciable, that is to say that it is not a matter in which the court should intervene. If it were so, then any question of priority or clinical judgment of which case came first could be subject to review where it may depend on the location of available facilities.

I pause to say that there is no possible basis for suggesting that there could be any 'policy' of the health authority to deprive the hospital of staff other than for financial and general reasons which are well known.

In my judgment the court would do a great disservice to those who have to work in difficult and straitened circumstances if it were to contemplate making an order in this case. No surgeon should be ordered to perform an operation by the court in the circumstances which this case reveals. I deprecate any suggestion that patients should be encouraged to think that the court has a role in a case of this kind.

Mr De Mello has to satisfy me that he has an arguable case, upon the facts set out in this application and in the light of the principles which govern judicial review. He has wholly failed so to persuade me. Of course everybody hopes that this matter will be resolved as soon as is humanly possible. But in my judgment I would simply raise false hopes by giving leave. I am convinced that there are no prospects of success in this court in this application – and it must be dismissed.

The applicant's appeal to the Court of Appeal (Sir John Donaldson MR, Nicholls LJ and Caulfield J) was dismissed:

Sir John Donaldson MR: It is not for this court, or indeed any court, to substitute its own judgment for the judgment of those who are responsible for the allocation of resources. This court could only intervene where it was satisfied that there was a *prima facie* case, not only of failing to allocate resources in the way in which others would think that resources should be allocated, but of a failure to allocate resources to an extent which was *Wednesbury* unreasonable, if one likes to use the lawyers' jargon, or, in simpler words, which involves a breach of a public law duty ... Even then, of course, the court has to exercise a judicial discretion. It has to take account of all the circumstances of the particular case with which it is concerned.

(See also the subsequent decision of the Court of Appeal in *R v Central Birmingham HA ex p Collier* (1988) LEXIS Transcript, 6 January.)

A more recent case which considered the meaning of s 3(1) of the NHS Act 1977, and the scope of a health authority's duty to provide medical services was *R v Sheffield HA ex p Seale* (1994) 25 BMLR 1:

R v Sheffield HA ex p Seale (1994) 25 BMLR 1, QBD (Auld J)

Julie Anne Seale sought *in vitro* fertilisation treatment from the respondent health authority. She was refused it on the grounds that, at 37 years of age, she was outside the age range within which the authority provided such treatment:

Auld J: Mr Straker challenges the decision made in this case, based on the criteria set out in the letter of 22 April 1994, under three heads. The first is illegality. As I understand his submission, it is that as the Secretary of State has given no directions or imposed no limitations on the provision of *in vitro* fertilisation, and it is not for the district health authority, once it has committed itself to providing such a service, to restrict that provision if in the case of any patient there is a chance, a reasonable probability, a possibility – I do not quite know where the line is to be drawn – of the treatment being effective. As I understand Mr Straker's argument, it is that if any such qualification beyond efficacy is to be introduced, that is for the Secretary of State, and she has not done it here.

In my view, it is not possible to erect out of the absence of a direction by the Secretary of State, or of the imposition by her of a limitation on the provision of such a service, a denial to the regional or district health authority of itself determining the circumstances in which such a service can be provided. It is not arguable, in my view, that it is bound, simply because it has undertaken to provide such a service, to provide it on demand to any individual patient for whom it may work, regardless of financial and other constraints upon the authority. Accordingly, I reject as unarguable any submission based on illegality here.

In my view it is clear that if the Secretary of State has not limited or given directions as to the way in which such a service, once undertaken, should be provided; the authority providing it is entitled to form a view as to those circumstances and when they justify provision and when they do not.

The second argument of Mr Straker is that the decision here is irrational, that is, absurd. That is what he has to show as arguable to succeed on this application for leave. He says it is irrational because it is not founded on any sustainable, clinical approach. The basis of that argument appears to be that there is more than one view of the appropriate 'cut-off' age for such treatment. In short, he submits, and refers me to the views of other doctors, that 35 years old is too low an age. It is possible to achieve success certainly up to the age of 42. I cannot, nor could the court when deciding the matter as a substantive issue, if it came to that, form a view as to the rightness or wrongness of competing medical views on the effective cut-off date for the utility of such treatment. The decision letter does not say that the treatment cannot be effective after the age of 35, but merely that it is 'generally less effective in women aged over 35 years'.

If that is so, can Mr Straker challenge the decision as irrational on the basis that it is absurd to apply the age of 35 years as a blanket cut-off point, taking no account of individual circumstances? His submission is that every case should be considered individually. Clinically speaking there is no doubt good sense in such a submission. And a clinical decision on a case by case basis is clearly desirable and, in cases of critical illness, a necessary approach. However, it is reasonable, or it is at least not *Wednesbury* unreasonable (see *Associated Provincial Picture Houses Ltd v Wednesbury Corp* [1947] 2 All ER 680), of an authority to look at the matter in the context of the financial resources available to it to provide this and the many other services for which it is responsible under the National Health Service legislation. I cannot say that it is absurd for this authority, acting on advice that the efficacy of this treatment decreases with age and that it is generally less effective after the age of 35, to take that as an appropriate criterion when balancing the need for such a provision against its ability to provide it and all the other services imposed upon it under the legislation.

The third matter upon which Mr Straker relied as part of his argument based on irrationality was a reference to a particular condition from which this applicant suffers for which pregnancy is said to be a cure. However, that matter does not appear to have loomed large, or at all, in the circumstances giving rise to the decision of 22 April. Nor does it appear to have been particularly prominent as a reason for special treatment in this case in the correspondence that followed that decision.

Under the heading of 'Irrationality' Mr Straker relies upon the fact that privately paying patients can secure such treatment until the age of 42. It seems to me that that argument does not meet the central problem here of an authority coping with a finite budget and a myriad of services which it is bound to provide under it. I am, therefore, of the view that there is no arguable case that this decision was irrational, applying the high test that that word imports under the *Wednesbury* decision.

Lastly, Mr Straker submits that there was a procedural impropriety here. I confess I find it difficult to see any procedural hook on which Mr Straker could base his application. It seems to me, to whatever extent there was a procedural element upon which he relied, it falls to be considered under the heading of 'Irrationality'. I certainly can see no procedural basis upon which he can challenge this decision.

Accordingly, despite the very well organised and highly persuasive arguments of Mr Straker, I feel bound to refuse this application.

(On the provision of fertility treatment generally, see further Chapter 7.)

Seale is a useful decision as it shows a slightly less resolute approach being taken to resource allocation issues compared with cases such as *Walker*. Christopher Newdick has commented on the case as follows:

Newdick, C, 'Resource allocation in the NHS' (1997) 23(2–3) Am J Law & Med 291:

Although the application was refused on its merits the case distinguishes between 'critical', and other, illnesses. If critical illness necessitates an individual clinical decision of the case the *Wednesbury* test of managerial reasonableness is presumably limited to other areas of elective or optional health care. Note how uncomfortably this approach to clinical merits sits with *Collier*. This case is useful on its own facts for identifying that some care may fall into a category in which a clinical assessment is necessary. It says nothing however, about the components of such a decision, who is responsible for making it, or where the line should be drawn.

It does not, of course, follow from the fact that the patient may sometimes be entitled to have his or her own circumstances and condition clinically assessed, that treatment need actually be provided. Indeed, as a corollary of the general ethical obligation on doctors to act in their patients' best interests, it may be that in a particular case no doctor will be found who is willing to carry it out, for example, where it involves serious side effects for the patient and is believed to be of little or no therapeutic benefit. Certainly, the fact that the patient, where competent, wishes to receive the treatment will usually be a strong indicator that such treatment is in his best interests. Nevertheless, there will be exceptions, especially where terminal illness has been diagnosed, and claims for treatment brought on behalf of incompetent patients may also present difficulties.

A well known case, which raised issues of this nature, as well as the question of how far financial considerations should play a part in the deliberations of the treatment provider, was that of *R v Cambridge HA ex p B (A Minor)* (1995) 23 BMLR 1:

R v Cambridge HA ex p B (A Minor) (1995) 23 BMLR 1, CA (Sir Thomas Bingham MR, Sir Stephen Brown P, Simon Brown LJ)

In this case a 10 year old girl was refused the resources for further remedial treatment. She was suffering from acute myeloid leukaemia. The doctors responsible for her care believed that no further treatment could be usefully given to her beyond palliative care. Her father sought further medical treatment by chemotherapy with a view to a second bone marrow transplant. Taking into account clinical judgment, the nature of the treatment requested and its very low chances of success, the health authority declined the father's request. He sought judicial review of the health authority's decision, which was granted by Laws J at first instance. The authority appealed:

Sir Thomas Bingham MR: In the course of his judgment, quashing the decision of the authority, the judge made four criticisms of the manner in which the authority had reached its decision. Before I turn to those, however, it is important that I should state very clearly, as the judge did, that this is a case involving the life of a young patient and that that is a fact which must dominate all consideration of all aspects of the case. Our society is one in which a very high value is put on human life. No decision affecting human life is one that can be regarded with other than the greatest seriousness.

The second general comment which should be made is that the courts are not, contrary to what is sometimes believed, arbiters as to the merits of cases of this kind. Were we to express opinions as to the likelihood of the effectiveness of medical treatment, or as to the merits of medical judgment, then we should be straying far from the sphere which under our constitution is accorded to us. We have one function only, which is to rule upon the lawfulness of decisions. That is a function to which we should strictly confine ourselves.

The four criticisms made by the judge of the authority's decision were these. First, he took the view that Dr Zimmern as the decision maker had wrongly failed to have regard to the wishes of the patient, as expressed on behalf of the patient by her family, and in particular by her father. Our attention was directed to the affidavits that I have mentioned. The point was made that nowhere does one see an express statement that among the factors that led Dr Zimmern to his decision was a consideration of the wishes of the family. In that situation, the judge held that the authority had failed to take a vitally important factor into consideration and that the decision was accordingly flawed.

I feel bound for my part to differ from the judge. It seems to me that the judge's criticism entirely fails to recognise the realities of this situation. When the case was first presented to the authority, it was presented on behalf of the patient, B, as a case calling for the co-operation and funding of the authority. At all times Dr Zimmern was as vividly aware as he could have been of the fact that the family, represented by B's father, were urgently wishing the authority to undertake this treatment; by 'undertake' I mean, of course, provide the funding for it. He was placed under considerable pressure by the family and, in the first instance, perhaps unfortunately, made reference to his policy of not corresponding directly with patients or their relatives about what he called 'extra-contractual referrals', meaning requests for the purchase of medical services outside the health authority.

The inescapable fact is, however, that he was put under perfectly legitimate, but very obvious, pressure by the family to procure this treatment and he was responding to that pressure. It was because he was conscious of that pressure that he obviously found the decision which he had to make such an agonising one and one calling for such careful consideration. To complain that he did not in terms say that he had regard to the wishes of the patient as expressed by the family, is to shut one's eyes to the reality of the situation with which he was confronted. It is also worthy of note, and there is no hint of criticism in this, that the accusation that he did not take the patient's wishes into account was not made in the grounds annexed to Form 86A. It was not, therefore, recognised as an accusation calling for a specific rebuttal.

The second criticism that is made is of the use of the expression 'experimental' to describe this treatment. The judge took the view, and Mr McIntyre on behalf of B urges, that that is not a fair or accurate description given the estimates of success which have been put by reputable practitioners, and given the willingness of Dr Gravett to accept that there was a worthwhile chance of success. The fact, however, is that even the first course of treatment had a chance of success of something between 10 and 20%. It was only if, contrary to the probabilities, that was totally successful, that it would be possible to embark on the second phase of the treatment which itself had a similar chance of success.

The plain fact is that, unlike many courses of medical treatment, this was not one that had a well tried track record of success. It was, on any showing, at the frontier of medical science. That being so, it does not, in my judgment, carry weight to describe this decision as flawed because of the use of this expression.

The third criticism that is made by the judge is of the reference to resources. The learned judge held that Dr Zimmern's evidence about money consisted only of grave and well rounded generalities. The judge acknowledged that the court should not make orders with consequences for the use of health service funds in ignorance of the knock-on effect on other patients. He went on to say that 'where the question is whether the life of a 10 year old child might be saved by however slim a chance, the responsible Authority ... must do more than toll the bell of tight resources'. The judge said that 'They must explain the priorities that have led them to decline to fund the treatment', and he found they had not adequately done so here.

I have no doubt that in a perfect world any treatment which a patient, or a patient's family, sought, would be provided if doctors were willing to give it, no matter how much it cost, particularly when a life was potentially at stake. It would, however, in my view, be shutting one's eyes to the real world if the court were to proceed on the basis that we do live in such a world. It is common knowledge that health authorities of all kinds are constantly pressed to make ends meet. They cannot pay their nurses as much as they would like; they cannot provide all the treatments they would like; they cannot purchase all the extremely expensive medical equipment they would like; they cannot carry out all the research they would like; they cannot build all the hospitals and specialist units they would like. Difficult and agonising judgments have to be made as to how a limited budget is best allocated to the maximum advantage of the maximum number of patients. That is not a judgment which the court can make. In my judgment, it is not something that a health authority such as this authority can be fairly criticised for not advancing before the court.

Mr McIntyre went so far as to say that if the authority has money in the bank which it has not spent, then they would be acting in plain breach of their statutory duty if they did not procure this treatment. I am bound to say that I regard that submission as manifestly incorrect. Unless the health authority had sufficient money to purchase everything which in the interests of patients it would wish to do, then that situation would never ever be reached. I venture to say that no real evidence is needed to satisfy the court that no health authority is in that position.

I furthermore think, differing, I regret, from the judge, that it would be totally unrealistic to require the authority to come to the court with its accounts and seek to demonstrate that if this treatment were provided for B then there would be a patient, C, who would have to go without treatment. No major authority could run its financial affairs in a way which would permit such a demonstration.

The fourth criticism which the judge made was that the authority had wrongly treated the problem which they faced as one of spending £75,000 when, in the first instance, the treatment only involved the expenditure of £15,000. It was therefore a two stage process, so it was held and submitted to us, and not a one stage process, as the authority wrongly thought. Again, I regret that I differ from the judge's view. It is, of course, true that if the first stage were unsuccessful, then £15,000, or even less than £15,000, would be the maximum that the authority would end up spending. It would not, however, be reasonable for the authority to embark on this expenditure on that basis since, quite plainly, they would have to continue if, having expended the £15,000, it proved successful and the call for the second stage of the treatment came. It was, therefore, an inescapable decision whether they should embark on this process at all. Having weighed the matter up and taken advice, particularly bearing in mind the suffering which even embarking on the treatment would inflict, the authority thought that they should not fund the treatment at all. I regret that I find it impossible to fault that process of thinking on their part.

The treatment was subsequently paid for by an anonymous benefactor, although B eventually died in March 1996. She did, however, survive well beyond the six to eight weeks' estimate that the health authority had originally given her to live.

Richard Mullender has commented upon the case as follows:

Mullender, R, 'Judicial review and the rule of law' (1996) 112 LQR 182:

Laws J [at first instance] takes the novel step, in his judgment, of treating the fundamental right to life as providing a constraint upon the health authority's decision making discretion. To justify doing so, he first expresses 'the greatest doubt' as to *Wednesbury's* adequacy as a standard of review (on account of its uncertainty) and, secondly, notes that, where such uncertainty exists, there are *dicta* which support the view that fundamental rights (viz, those occupying a place of central importance in the European Convention for the Protection of Human Rights and Fundamental Freedoms (Cmnd 8969, 1953)) can be invoked in order to resolve uncertainties in the common law ... With this justification for invoking the right to life in place, he determines that the health authority's decision constitutes an interference with it and addresses the question as to whether they have provided a substantial public interest justification for doing so. This question he answers in the negative, rejecting both their argument that further remedial treatment would not be in B's interests (because of the suffering to which it would expose her) and their argument that funding the treatment would not be an effective use of their limited resources. In the light of these findings, he concludes that B's right to life has been violated and quashes the respondent's decision. While the bulk of the judge's analysis concerns the right to life, he, nonetheless, states that the same result can be reached by applying *Wednesbury* and identifies four forms of unreasonableness manifested by the health authority: viz, failure to consider the wishes of B's family, wrongly characterising the treatment sought as 'experimental', failure to explain the priorities that led to the decision not to provide it, and an inaccurate estimate of its cost.

In contrast to the judgment of Laws J, the right to life plays no part in that of Bingham MR, notwithstanding his observing both that 'our society is one in which a very high value is put on human life' and that 'no decision affecting human life ... can be regarded with other than the greatest seriousness'. While, in the light of these comments, the Master of the Rolls' decision not to invoke the right to life might seem surprising, his not doing so can be explained by his commitment to the principle that, in judicial review proceedings, judges must merely scrutinise the lawfulness of a public body's decision and must not adjudicate upon its merits – a commitment to which he gives emphatic expression thus: ' ... we have one function only, which is to rule upon the lawfulness of decisions. That is a function to which we should strictly confine ourselves.' It is, hence, unsurprising to find him basing his decision not on the right to life, but, rather, on the ground of *Wednesbury* unreasonableness, which specifies a modest standard of review and, thus, leaves public bodies with broad scope for making discretionary decisions. The interpretation placed by Bingham MR on *Wednesbury* diverges radically from that of Laws J: he rescinds the judge's quashing order, identifying as unsustainable all four of the grounds on which the latter found the health authority's denial of treatment to be unreasonable.

It might be thought that, following the incorporation of the European Convention on Human Rights (ECHR) into national law by the Human Rights Act 1998, the approach of Laws J would henceforth be the norm in this type of case. However, indications so far are that the courts are proceeding cautiously, generally remaining faithful to the *Wednesbury* test. In *R v North West Lancashire HA ex p A, D and G* [1999] Lloyd's Rep Med 399, a case decided shortly before the 1998 Act entered force, three transsexuals brought an action in judicial review after the respondent health authority refused to fund their gender reassignment surgery. The Court of Appeal was robust in rejecting what it termed 'unfocused recourse' to the ECHR. As Auld LJ commented:

> **Auld LJ**: As to the European Convention of Human Rights, it is not yet part of our domestic law and is relevant only, in an appropriate case, to the Court's consideration of rationality. Mr Blake indicated that the purpose of his fairly detailed submissions and references to Strasbourg jurisprudence was merely to show that transsexualism is a sufficiently serious condition 'to raise human rights problems'. Such an unfocused recourse to that jurisdiction, whether before or after the statutory absorption of part of the Convention into the law of England and Wales, is not helpful to the Court. Indeed, it is positively unhelpful, cluttering up its consideration of adequate and more precise domestic principles and authorities governing the issues in play. Thus, the deployment of generalised propositions from the ECHR that a person's sexual identity is of sufficient importance to attract the protection of the right to respect for private and family life under Article 8, or that a denial of medical treatment may, if sufficiently serious, amount to 'inhuman or degrading treatment' under Article 3, contributes nothing to resolution of the issues here (see, eg, *Rees v United Kingdom* (1988) 9 EHRR 56; *Cossey v United Kingdom* (1991) 13 EHRR 622; and the dissenting opinion of Judge Pettiti in *B v France* (1992) 16 EHRR 1, pp 40–41). It is common ground in this case that transsexualism is an illness; the issues are whether the Authority's policy for the public funding of treatment of it properly reflects that and whether it makes proper provision for consideration of each application for treatment on its individual merits.
>
> In any event, Article 8 imposes no positive obligations to provide treatment ... As Hidden J observed, in rejecting similar submissions below:
>
> > The Convention does not give the applicants rights to free healthcare in general or to gender reassignment surgery in particular. Even if the applicants had such a right it would be qualified by the respondent's right to determine healthcare priorities in the light of its limited resources.

It remains uncertain how far the courts would take the same approach in cases where life-saving treatment is at issue (and the patient's right to life under Art 2 of the ECHR is engaged). However, as Butler-Sloss P noted in *NHS Trust A v M, NHS Trust B v H* [2001] Fam 348, it is clear that the positive obligation upon a state to safeguard life is not an absolute one. In that case, her Ladyship held that, insofar as it accords with respectable medical opinion, a decision to withhold life-sustaining treatment considered not to be in the patient's best interests, would not breach the Article (see further Chapter 12). For a general examination of the role of judicial review in the light of the Human Rights Act 1998, see the judgment of Lord Walker in *R (On the Application of Pro-Life Alliance) v BBC* [2003] UKHL 23, in particular examining the concepts of 'proportionality' and 'margin of appreciation'.

On the other hand, what does seem clear is that in cases where decisions by health authorities not to fund treatment impinge upon the fundamental interests of patients, the court will subject it to a greater degree of scrutiny in order to be satisfied that it passes the *Wednesbury* test. As Phil Fennell, commenting on *Ex p A, D and G*, has argued:

Fennell, P, 'Substantive review of decisions to refuse treatment' (2000) 8 Med L Rev 129:

An array of arguments based on the European Convention of Human Rights and EU law was given short shrift by their Lordships, their preferred approach being through principles of English administrative law. Although the Court of Appeal judges were unanimous in holding that no Convention rights were engaged here, they nevertheless approached the question from the point of view that a fundamental interest was at stake. Therefore the decision-makers had to substantially consider their decision, and the courts would scrutinise carefully that decision to ensure that they have weighed their justification for interfering with that interest against the importance of the interest. 'Careful scrutiny' may differ in intensity from the 'anxious scrutiny' which has been held appropriate in cases where Convention Rights are engaged. Nevertheless, the basic approach remains as described by Lord Woolf MR in *R v Lord Saville of Newdigate ex p A* [1999] 4 All ER 860, where he said:

[W]hen a fundamental right such as the right to life is engaged, the options open to a reasonable decision-maker are curtailed. They are curtailed because it is unreasonable to reach a decision which contravenes or could contravene a human right unless there are sufficiently significant countervailing considerations. In other words it is not open to the decision-maker to risk interfering with fundamental rights in the absence of compelling justification. Even the broadest discretion is constrained by the need for there to be countervailing circumstances to justify interference with human rights. The courts will anxiously scrutinise the strength of the countervailing circumstances and the degree of interference with the human right involved and then apply the test accepted by Lord Bingham MR in *R v Ministry of Defence ex p Smith* [1996] 1 All ER 257, p 263.

In other words where Convention Rights are engaged, the courts will apply a sliding scale in judging whether to intervene on substantive grounds with the exercise of an administrative discretion on grounds of *Wednesbury* unreasonableness. The more substantial the interference with human rights posed by the decision which is subject to challenge, 'the more the court will require by way of justification before it is satisfied that the decision is reasonable'.

In this case, where a 'fundamental interest' rather than a human right was at stake, a similar sliding scale operated (*per* Buxton LJ [1999] Lloyd's Rep Med 399, p 412):

The more important the interest of the citizen that the decision affects, the greater will be the degree of consideration that is required of the decision-maker. A decision that, as is the evidence in this case, seriously affects the citizen's health will require substantial consideration, and be subject to careful scrutiny by the court as to its rationality. That will particularly be the case in respect of decisions which involve the refusing of any, or any significant, treatment in respect of an identified and substantial medical condition.

Applying this approach in *Ex p A, D and G*, the Court of Appeal upheld the judgment of the High Court (Hidden J) that the refusal by the health authority to fund the gender reassignment surgery was *Wednesbury* unreasonable. In particular, although it had recognised gender identity dysmorphia (the condition from which the applicants suffered) as an illness, the authority's policy in relation to it amounted, in effect, to a blanket ban on the generally accepted treatment. As Buxton LJ noted, such a policy could not be regarded as rational:

> **Buxton LJ**: [A]s the evidence in this application demonstrated ... there is a strong and respectable body of medical opinion that considers gender reassignment procedures to be effective in suitable and properly selected cases ... I emphasise that the mere fact that a body of medical opinion supports the procedure does not put the health authority under any legal obligation to provide the procedure: the standard here is far removed from the *Bolam* approach in cases of medical negligence. However, where such a body of opinion exists it is in my view not open to a rational health authority simply to determine that a procedure has no proven clinical benefit while giving no indication of why it considers that that is so ...
>
> I am therefore driven to the conclusion that the health authority has not demonstrated that degree of rational consideration that can reasonably be expected of it before it decides in effect to give no funding at all to a procedure supported by respectable clinicians and psychiatrists, which is said to be necessary in certain cases to relieve extreme mental distress.

Similarly, the maintenance by a health authority of a policy directly opposed to Department of Health circulars and advice will – in the absence of the clearest justifying reasons – fail the *Wednesbury* test. This was established in the case of *R v North Derbyshire HA ex p Fisher* [1997] 8 Med LR 327:

R v North Derbyshire HA ex p Fisher [1997] 8 Med LR 327, QBD (Dyson J)

Kenneth Fisher, who suffered from the relapsing/remitting form of multiple sclerosis, challenged the refusal of his health authority, North Derbyshire, to finance his treatment with a new form of drug therapy, beta-interferon, which he had been assessed as suitable to receive by doctors at the NHS trust in Sheffield where he was being treated. North Derbyshire's refusal reflected the view of its own experts that beta-interferon (which was expensive) was of unproven therapeutic benefit, but contrasted with the terms of an NHS Circular, EL (95) 97, in which the NHS Executive asked health authorities to assist in implementing the use of the drug:

> **Dyson J**: [The] lawfulness [of the authority's policy] must be judged in accordance with *Wednesbury* principles against the background of national policy which was set out fully and firmly in the guidance to be found in the Circular. The respondents had to have regard to that national policy. They were not obliged to follow the policy, but if they decided to depart from it, they had to give clear reasons for so doing, and those reasons would have been susceptible to a *Wednesbury* challenge ... Moreover, if the respondents failed properly to understand the Circular, then their policy would be as defective as if no regard had been paid to the policy at all. It is accepted on behalf of the respondents that they were under a duty to give serious consideration to each aspect of the Circular. Mr Seys Llewllyn submits that the respondents' policy was an honest and conscientious way of managing the introduction into the NHS of the new drug, and was at least consistent with the Circular.

In my judgment the policy was plainly not in accordance with the Circular. The Circular asked for purchasing authorities and providers:

> To develop and implement local arrangements to manage the entry of such drugs into the NHS ... and in particular to initiate a continued prescribing of beta-interferon through hospitals.

One of the key aims was to 'target the drug appropriately at patients who were most likely to benefit from treatment'. In other words, the Circular was giving guidance as to how most effectively beta-interferon could be introduced into the NHS as a drug to be prescribed to treat patients ... I do not consider that the respondents' policy could at any time have fairly been described as a reasonable way of giving effect to the Circular. The respondents, like others, no doubt honestly and conscientiously believed that the efficacy of beta-interferon had not been sufficiently tested. The assumption that underpinned the Circular was that it had been sufficiently tested ... This is not a case in which a health authority departed from the national policy because there were special factors which it considered exceptionally justified departure. The respondents failed to implement any aspect of national policy, principally because they disagreed with it altogether. They now seek to argue that at least they acted consistently with that policy, although for the reasons that I have given that is plainly not the case. Accordingly, they do not seek to justify their policy as a rational exception to the national policy. That is hardly surprising, since I expect that the situation in which the respondents found themselves when the Circular was issued was not materially different from that faced by most other health authorities. The respondents did not take the Circular into account and decide exceptionally not to follow it. They decided to disregard it altogether throughout 1996, because they were opposed to it. That is something which in my judgment they were not entitled to do.

Another basis on which the courts have proven willing to quash decisions by health authorities in judicial review is that of procedural irregularity. Thus, in *R v North and East Devon HA ex p Coughlan* [2001] QB 213 the Court of Appeal held that the respondent authority's planned closure of the severely disabled applicant's care home, contrary to an earlier promise that it would be her home for life, was an unlawful breach of her legitimate expectations. This can be contrasted with the case of *R (On the Application of Haggerty and Others) v St Helen's Borough Council* [2003] EWHC 803, where a similar complaint was made about the closure of a local authority home for the elderly which service was being taken over by a private contractor, but where the application failed on the basis that there had been no promise of 'a home for life'. (See also the case of *R v North and East Devon HA ex p Pow* (1997) 39 BMLR 77, QBD in which a decision to close a hospital was set aside by the High Court (Moses J) due to the health authority's failure to engage in the required consultation process beforehand.)

So far we have been looking at cases in which the judicial review applications have been made against the bodies (usually health authorities) directly responsible for providing or funding treatment. However, this is not the only possibility. In particular, given the increasing tendency for treatment targets and priorities to be set centrally by the Department of Health, the latter too may find its decisions challenged where a link can be shown between such central guidance and the denial of some particular treatment 'on the ground'. This is illustrated by the lengthy attempt by the drug manufacturerr Pfizer to overturn the government's refusal to approve, other than in exceptional circumstances, the prescription of the drug Viagra (otherwise know as silenafil). In *R v Secretary of State for Health ex p Pfizer* [1999] Lloyd's Rep Med 289 the NHS circular in which this advice was contained

(HSC 1998/158) was successfully challenged by Pfizer. Collins J held that this guidance imposed an unreasonable fetter upon the discretion of GPs (the circular stated that the 'exceptional circumstances' in which the drug could be prescribed had to be cleared with the NHS in advance of prescription). Further, it was in breach of the European 'Transparency Directive' 89/105/EEC. Following this judgment the government took steps to remedy the situation by issuing regulations pursuant to the National Health Service Act 1977 by adding Viagra to the schedule of drugs where availability is limited (Schedule 11, National Health Service (General Medical Services) Regulations 1992 (as amended)). Pfizer mounted a second challenge on the ground that this was still in breach of the directive because this states that the criteria to exclude services in such a situation must be available and transparent (Article 7(3)). Pfizer's argument was that the government's statement to the European Commission ostensibly justifying the decision, only referred to cost and did not explain how the treatment of erectile dysfunction should be compared with that for other non-life threatening conditions. The Court of Appeal (*R (On the Application of Pfizer Limited) v Secretary of State for Health* [2002] EWCA Civ 1566) held that the directive did not require such a statement of competing priorities and therefore there was no breach (see Syrett, K, 'Impotence or importance? Judicial review in an era of explicit NHS rationing' (2004) 67(2) MLR 289).

As noted earlier in this chapter, the government has entrusted a key role in appraising the clinical and cost-effectiveness of various medical treatments, and issuing guidance to health authorities in relation to funding the same, to NICE. Accordingly, it is possible that there will be future challenges to NICE (in its newly constituted form) in judicial review. Keith Syrett discusses the position as follows:

Syrett, K, 'Nice work? Rationing, review and the legitimacy problem in the new NHS' (2002) 10 Med L Rev 1

The tasks which the Government intends NICE to perform within the NHS can best be understood by considering its origin in the evidence-based medicine movement which came to the fore in the early 1990s. This 'new scientism' was swiftly appropriated by those seeking to alleviate the problem of limited NHS resources, the argument being that the use of scientific evidence could enable resources to be freed from ineffective treatments and reduce inappropriate variation in clinical practice. In broad terms, therefore, the Institute may be seen as having two functions. First, it is intended to address the problem of so-called 'postcode prescribing' by reducing 'unacceptable variations in performance and practice' across different regions of the NHS. The controversy which this issue may generate is illustrated by the case of *R v North West Lancashire Health Authority ex p A, D and G*, in which three transsexuals successfully challenged a decision to refuse funding for gender reassignment surgery. It was submitted that 34 out of 41 other authorities made some provision for funding such surgery and that a policy which effectively amounted to a 'blanket ban' in one locality would therefore have the effect that entitlement to treatment would depend upon where the patient lived. The Government's hope is that, by acting as 'a single, national focus for appraisal of significant new and existing interventions' whose recommendations are expected to be followed countrywide, variations – and therefore challenges – of this type will become less frequent as the Institute renders decision-making in the NHS more acceptable by bringing 'greater certainty, greater clarity and greater confidence'.

However, such optimism may be premature because it is clear that NICE has a second role in making 'tough choices' on the allocation of resources. Indeed, notwithstanding assertions to the contrary, the establishment of NICE – especially its technology appraisal function – appears to mark 'the beginning of explicit national rationing' in the NHS. This is significant because it has been powerfully argued that explicit resource allocation decisions are inherently more unstable than decisions which can be presented as based upon clinical necessity, even if these are in reality dictated by resource considerations. The greater visibility of the process thus increases the potential for conflict. This may already be seen in the responses to certain Institute decisions. Refusal to authorise the use of an intervention has been opposed by patients and their representatives. On the other hand, approval has been contested by professionals seeking to preserve their clinical and managerial discretion with the consequence that geographical variations in access to treatment have tended to persist. Elsewhere, patients requiring other services have lost out as resources are diverted to fund 'NICE-approved' interventions. The controversy generated has been manifested in media campaigns, Parliamentary debate and threats of legal action.

The range of interests which may be affected by NICE determinations renders some level of opposition a near-certainty.

Another developing area in the provision of healthcare is the extent to which patients are entitled to require the NHS to fund medical treatment in other Member States of the EU. This brings into play Article 49 of the EC Treaty as it relates to prohibition on restrictions on freedom to provide services and Article 22 of Council Regulation 1408/71 which provides that a person, who is a national of a Member State and is insured under the legislation of the Member State and members of his family residing with him, who is 'authorised by the competent institution to go to the territory of another Member State to receive there the treatment appropriate to his condition', may do so at the expense of the competent institution. In *R (On the Application of Yvonne Watts) v (1) Bedford Primary Care Trust (2) Secretary of State for Health* [2004] EWCA Civ 166 it was held by the Court of Appeal that Article 49 applied but that a reference would be made to the European Court of Justice for a ruling on the correct interpretation of Article 22 on such as case as this. The implications for those who wish to seek medical treatment in other EU Member States to avoid waiting lists is huge.

Breach of statutory duty

Rather than bringing a claim in judicial review, could a claimant challenge a decision over health care resource allocation in private law? Jonathan Montgomery addresses the possibility here of an action being maintained for breach of statutory duty, but sees little scope for the successful use of this tort in relation to the National Health Service Act 1977 (and note that the same considerations could apply to s 45 of the Health and Social Care (Community Health and Standards) Act 2003 – see above):

Montgomery, J, *Health Care Law*, 1997, Oxford: OUP, pp 70–71:

Breach of statutory duty

In an action for the tort of breach of statutory duty, it is alleged that damage has been caused to the plaintiff due to the failure to perform a statutory duty which exists for the benefit of the aggrieved individual, and which parliament intended to be enforceable, through the courts, by that individual. Thus, patients denied services could argue that the NHS body responsible had failed to perform its statutory obligations and had harmed them. The prospects for success of this form of action depend in part upon the particular statutory duty in question. However, the courts have shown themselves to be reluctant to permit actions for the breach of duties to provide welfare services, and it is unlikely that such an action could be brought under the NHS Act 1977.

The House of Lords has noted that there has been no case in which statutory social welfare schemes, established for the benefit of the public at large, have been held to give rise to a private law action for damages. In *Re HIV Haemophilic Litigation*, the Court of Appeal accepted (in a preliminary action) that the general duties to provide services under the 1977 Act did not provide a foundation for such a suit. They also noted that Wien J had taken a similar view, *obiter*, in the High Court in *R v Secretary of State for Social Services ex p Hincks*. However, the point was not considered in the Court of Appeal in that case. Against this authority, there was a suggestion in *R v Ealing DHA ex p Fox* that a specific duty to provide services for discharged mental patients could be spelt out from the provisions of s 3(1) of the NHS Act 1977. It was not necessary for the judge in this case to consider this point, as such a duty was explicitly set out in s 117 of the Mental Health Act 1983, and he was not concerned with the issue of compensation. Consequently, it would be dangerous to rely on his comment.

It is possible that the courts will prove themselves less reticent where the statutory duties are more specific, because it is easier to show that the individual was entitled to expect a service to be provided. Thus, a failure to provide after-care services under the Mental Health Act 1983, s 117, might more readily form the basis of an action for breach of statutory duty. There, it will be clear that the individual patient, who has now been discharged, should be receiving help. It is not a general duty owed to the public, but a specific one owed to an identified individual. It may also be possible to use the action for breach of statutory duty where patients are promised specific services after an assessment of their needs, and are then not given them because the relevant authority failed to execute their decision. However, this sort of failure may be more amenable to a claim in negligence.

Negligence and health resources

Patients who are denied treatment might also attempt to argue that a health authority or trust has acted carelessly towards them and they have suffered injury as a result. General principles of the law of tort would be applied and the action framed as a malpractice suit (see further Chapter 6). To the extent that treatment is provided, then it is apparent that lack of resources cannot be used as an excuse for failure to reach the requisite standard of care: see *Wilsher v Essex AHA* [1987] QB 730, CA and *Bull v Devon AHA* [1993] 4 Med LR 117. However, it is unlikely that an action in negligence would lie where, due to lack of resources, a decision is taken not to treat in the first place. Certainly, where the NHS body simply refused to make a given facility available, it is difficult to see how any duty of care would arise between it and the patient.

Compulsory treatment and care

Finally, it should be noted that, exceptionally, treatment may be *imposed* upon citizens in the wider interests of public health, in particular when they are found to be suffering from serious contagious disease. This area, which is governed by the Public Health (Control of Disease) Act 1984 and associated secondary legislation, is considered further in Chapter 3, in relation to consent.

CHAPTER 3

CONSENT TO TREATMENT

ETHICAL CONSIDERATIONS

The requirement that a patient must give a valid consent to medical treatment and its corollary, that it is the patient's prerogative to refuse treatment, even at the cost of his life, are issues at the heart of medical law. It is necessary, therefore, to examine the essential elements which have to be satisfied in order for a patient to give a valid consent.

However, it is also important to consider the ethical underpinnings of the high regard in which society holds the whole concept of consent. In Chapter 1 we looked at the conflict between the patient's right to autonomous decision-making and medical paternalism and nowhere is this more apparent than in the issue of consent to treatment.

Autonomy

The reason for requiring consent to any form of medical treatment stems from the principle of bodily inviolability. To breach this, even in the most well meaning way, is an affront to our notion of our personal bodily integrity. It will be recalled that Mill's libertarian philosophy is particularly relevant to the issue of consent:

Mill, JS, *On Liberty*, 1982, Harmondsworth: Penguin, p 68:

... [T]he only purpose for which power can be rightfully exercised over any member of a civilised community, against his will, is to prevent harm to others. His own good, either physical or moral, is not a sufficient warrant. He cannot rightfully be compelled to do or forbear because it will be better for him to do so, because it will make him happier, because, in the opinions of others, to do so would be wise, or even right.

This approach also echoes the Kantian view (see Chapter 1) that persons are ends in themselves and not simply a means to the ends of other people. Every student of medical law is familiar with the statement made by Cardozo J in *Schloendorff v New York Hospitals* (1914) 105 NE 92:

Cardozo J: Every human being of adult years and sound mind has a right to determine what shall be done with his own body; and a surgeon who performs an operation without his patient's consent, commits an assault ...

The importance of bodily inviolability is entrenched in the law of Western societies. In *McFall v Shimp* (1978) 10 Pa D & C (3d) 90, a patient required a bone marrow donation to avoid almost certain death. The procedure for donation was virtually risk free, and if a donation from a suitable donor went ahead, the prognosis was excellent. The patient's cousin had volunteered for a compatibility test, but when the test showed him to be a suitable donor, he declined to undergo further tests or to donate the bone marrow. The patient sought an injunction to compel his cousin to make the donation:

Flaherty J: The common law has consistently held to a rule which provides that one human being is under no legal compulsion to give aid or to take action to save that human being or to rescue. A great deal has been written regarding this rule which, on the surface, appears to be revolting in a moral sense. Introspection, however, will demonstrate that the rule is founded upon the very essence of our free society. It is noteworthy that counsel for the plaintiff has cited authority which has developed in other societies in support of the plaintiff's request in this instance. Our society, contrary to many others, has as its first principle, the respect for the individual, and that society and government exist to protect the individual from being invaded and hurt by another. Many societies adopt a contrary view which has the individual existing to service the society as a whole. In preserving such a society as we have it is bound to happen that great moral conflicts will arise, and will appear harsh in a given instance. In this case, the Chancellor is being asked to force one member of society to undergo a medical procedure which would provide that part of that individual's body would be removed from him and given to another so that the other could live. Morally, this decision rests with the defendant, and, in the view of the court, the refusal of the defendant is morally indefensible. For our law to *compel* the defendant to submit to an intrusion of his body would change every concept and principle upon which our society is founded. To do so would defeat the sanctity of the individual, and would impose a rule which would know no limits, and one could not imagine where the line would be drawn.

As we shall see below, the English courts have generally also emphasised the primacy of patient autonomy or self-determination and its effect of blocking the doctor's right (and his duty) to invade the patient's bodily integrity so as to treat the patient. This is so, notwithstanding that the treatment might be regarded as in the latter's best interests. In *Airedale NHS Trust v Bland* [1993] AC 789, Lord Goff commented, at 864:

> **Lord Goff of Chieveley**: ... it is established that the principle of self-determination requires that respect must be given to the wishes of the patient, so that if an adult patient of sound mind refuses, however unreasonably, to consent to treatment or care by which his life would or might be prolonged, the doctors responsible for his care must give effect to his wishes, even though they do not consider it to be in his best interests to do so ... To this extent, the principle of the sanctity of human life must yield to the principle of self-determination ... and, for present purposes perhaps more important, the doctor's duty to act in the best interests of his patient must likewise be qualified.

Paternalism

Doctors who believe that a medical procedure is appropriate and necessary for a patient's well being, can, perhaps, be forgiven for believing that the principle of autonomy should be sacrificed in the best interests of the patient. As we saw in Chapter 1, even a strong libertarian such as Mill accepted a limited form of paternalism when it was necessary to intervene temporarily to restore autonomy. However, this is not, perhaps, true paternalism: if autonomy has to be restored then arguably it could not have been exercised in the first place. One situation where the law is prepared to be overtly paternalistic relates to children who purport to refuse treatment with serious implications for their continued life or health; this attitude is captured in the *dictum* of Ward J (as he then was) in *Re E (A Minor) (Wardship: Medical Treatment)* [1993] 1 FLR 386 that 'a court should be slow to let a child martyr himself'.

In the context of consent to treatment, a decision that autonomy is absent is generally expressed by saying that the patient lacks the necessary mental capacity (ie, understanding) to make valid decisions about treatment. It will be seen, however, that it may be tempting here for the paternalistically inclined to 'reason backwards' and infer that a patient who refuses treatment which the doctor recommends lacks such requisite understanding.

THE LEGAL FRAMEWORK

The protection of bodily integrity

Battery

As regards the position in tort, a valid consent to medical treatment is required because, without it, the doctor will be committing a trespass to the person, ie a battery. This is both a crime and a tort. A battery takes place when there is a non-consensual touching. It is sometimes said that an 'assault' has taken place (see the statement of Cardozo J in *Schloendorff v Society of New York Hospitals* (1914) 105 NE 92, p 95, above). Technically, of course, an assault cannot take place in private law unless the victim apprehends some immediate threat, and this would not be the case if the patient were unconscious. Although for the purposes of the criminal law, assault includes battery, in tort they are distinct (but see *AG's Reference (No 6 of 1980)* [1981] QB 715), and the correct term, in the case of non-consensual touching, is battery.

The favoured opinion is that there is no requirement that the touching be hostile. This is reflected in early case law, such as *Mohr v Williams* (1905) 104 NW 12, which concerned a patient who had consented to an operation on her right ear. During the course of the operation, the doctor discovered that the right ear did not, in fact, need surgery, but the left ear was in a more serious condition which required an operation. He performed the operation, which was successful. The patient sued in battery and was also successful.

In the case of *Wilson v Pringle* [1986] 2 All ER 440, the Court of Appeal suggested that the touching must be 'hostile' in order to constitute a battery. Although the court was prepared to adopt a very wide view of hostility so as not to confine it to acts of ill will, this view has since been questioned by the House of Lords (see *Re F (Mental Patient: Sterilisation)* [1990] 2 AC 1). Further, it must be the case that if a wide definition is adhered to then 'hostile' will mean little more than 'non-consensual', in which case its use is otiose. The reason for the hostility requirement imposed in *Wilson v Pringle* is the need to eliminate actions in battery as a result of things such as physical contact in crowded streets. Lord Goff in *Re F* dealt with the matter by stating that there could simply be no liability for physical contact which is generally acceptable in the ordinary conduct of everyday life.

Maim and statutory criminal offences

As already stated, battery is a crime as well as a tort. However, if one considers the nature of non-consensual surgical procedures, it is clear that more serious offences may be committed. In cases of non-consensual surgery, the statutory offences of wounding and causing grievous bodily harm contrary to ss 18 and 20 of the Offences Against the Person Act 1861 may have been committed, at least in theory (although in practice the DPP is likely to regard charges as not being in the public interest). It is also interesting to contemplate the relevance of the old common law offence of maim. Skegg comments as follows:

Skegg, PDG, *Law, Ethics and Medicine,* **1984, Oxford: Clarendon, p 40:**

In practice, the common law offence of maim has long been supplanted by statutory offences. But it has not been expressly abolished, and a judge has made an extra-judicial statement which suggests that there is at least a theoretical possibility of the offence of maim applying to operations in which a kidney is removed from a healthy living donor, for transplantation into a person who is in need of it. It is therefore desirable to consider the extent to which the offence of maim would apply to medical procedures, and the related issue of whether consent would be effective to prevent liability.

The authorities have long distinguished between acts which permanently disable and weaken a man, rendering him less able in fighting; and acts which simply disfigure. The former are maims, which fall within one category rather than the other ...

The fact that a particular injury has in the past been classified as a maim need not be decisive in any future case. Changes in military practice, or increased medical knowledge, could lead to certain injuries ceasing to be regarded as maims, and other injuries coming to be regarded as maims ...

Most medical procedures do not permanently disable a person and render that person less able in fighting. They therefore fall outside even the potential scope of any offence of maim. This is as true of the removal of a healthy kidney for transplantation as it is of the removal of a diseased appendix. But even if a medical procedure did come within the potential scope of an offence of maim, it would not follow that a doctor would commit an offence of maim in going ahead with it. Just as the infliction of a maim was sometimes permitted in self-defence, so a maiming operation would not amount to the offence of maim if there was a good reason for it. Hence, even if castration could still be regarded as coming within the potential scope of maim, it would be justified if performed for a therapeutic purpose.

As Skegg alludes to in this extract, the patient's consent by itself is not always enough to prevent the commission of a crime. This is because the law, for essentially paternalistic reasons, imposes in many situations an upper limit upon the degree of bodily harm to which a person may consent: see *R v Brown et al* [1993] 2 All ER 75. In other words, a person's autonomy to waive his right to bodily integrity is limited.

We shall look further at the situations where consent will fail to provide a defence to crimes such as maim (or one of the more modern statutory offences) at p 112 below. But why, it may be asked in relation to medical treatment, should consent normally be regarded as making a difference? After all, in many cases (such as amputation or radical surgery) it will occasion harm well above the normally permitted limit. In *Airedale NHS Trust v Bland* [1993] AC 789, Lord Mustill addressed this issue, at 891, as follows:

Lord Mustill: 1. *Consent to bodily invasion.* Any invasion of the body of one person by another is potentially both a crime and a tort. At the bottom end of the scale consent is a defence both to a charge of common assault and to a claim in tort. The concentration in most discussions of this topic on this end of the scale has tended to divert attention from the fact that whatever the scope of the civil defence of *volenti non fit injuria* there is a point higher up the scale than common assault at which consent in general ceases to form a defence to a criminal charge. The precise location of this point is at present under consideration by another Committee of your Lordships' House in *Reg v Brown (Anthony)* ... and I need not explore it here, but that the point exists is beyond question. If one person cuts off the hand of another it is no answer to say that the amputee consented to what was done.

2. *Proper medical treatment.* How is it that, consistently with the proposition just stated, a doctor can with immunity perform on a consenting patient an act which would be a very serious crime if done by someone else? The answer must be that bodily invasions in the course of proper medical treatment stand completely outside the criminal law. The reason why the consent of the patient is so important is not that it furnishes a defence in itself, but because it is usually essential to the propriety of medical treatment. Thus, if the consent is absent, and is not dispensed with in special circumstances by operation of law, the acts of the doctor lose their immunity.

The form and scope of consent

Express consent

In both the NHS and in private health care, the patient will be required to sign a consent form. There is a standard form that covers most forms of medical treatment, although modified types of form are used in certain treatments such as sterilisations. (However, in *Taylor v Shropshire Health Authority* [1998] Lloyd's Rep Med 395, the precise nature of the consent form was described as 'pure window dressing' and the failure to have a specialised consent form at the time was not an indication of negligence.)

By signing the form, it may be thought that the patient is confirming that he has received an explanation of the medical procedures and cannot later deny this. However, in *Chatterton v Gerson* [1981] 1 All ER 257, Bristow J (at 265) stated:

> **Bristow J**: I should add that getting the patient to sign a pro forma expressing consent to undergo the operation 'the effect and nature of which have been explained to me', as was done here in each case, should be a valuable reminder to everyone of the need for explanation and consent. But it would be no defence to an action based on trespass to the person if no explanation had in fact been given. The consent would have been expressed in form only, not in reality.

This approach has been endorsed by the appeal courts (for example, by Lord Donaldson MR in *Re T (Adult: Refusal of Treatment)* [1992] 4 All ER 649) and is acknowledged by the NHS Executive in its 2001 publication, *Reference Guide to Consent for Examination or Treatment*, London: NHS Executive, which gives general guidance to doctors and other health care workers:

> The validity of consent does not depend on the form in which it is given. Written consent merely serves as evidence of consent: if the elements of voluntariness, appropriate information and capacity have not been satisfied, a signature on a form will not make consent valid.

The *Reference Guide* goes on to state that the completion of a consent form will, however, be good practice where a significant invasive procedure, such as surgery, is contemplated.

The present model NHS consent form, which was introduced in 2002, appears on the following pages.

[NHS organisation name]
consent form 1

Patient agreement to investigation
or treatment

Patient details (or pre-printed label)

Patient's surname/family name................................

Patient's first names..

Date of birth...

Responsible health professional..................................

Job title..

NHS number (or other identifier)..................................

Male   Female

Special requirements ....
(eg other language/other communication method)

To be retained in patient's notes

Patient identifier/label

Name of proposed procedure or course of treatment (include brief
explanation if medical term not clear) ....
....
....

Statement of health professional (to be filled in by health professional with appropriate knowledge of proposed procedure, as specified in consent policy)

I have explained the procedure to the patient. In particular, I have explained:

The intended benefits ....
....
....

Serious or frequently occurring risks ....
....
....

Any extra procedures which may become necessary during the procedure

    blood transfusion...

    other procedure (please specify) ....

....

I have also discussed what the procedure is likely to involve, the benefits and risks of any available alternative treatments (including no treatment) and any particular concerns of this patient.

    The following leaflet/tape has been provided ....

This procedure will involve:

    general and/or regional anaesthesia   local anaesthesia   sedation

Signed:...   Date: ....
Name (PRINT) ....   Job title ....

Contact details (if patient wishes to discuss options later).....................................

Statement of interpreter (where appropriate)

I have interpreted the information above to the patient to the best of my ability and in a way in which I believe s/he can understand.

Signed:...   Date:...................................
Name (PRINT)..

Top copy accepted by patient: yes/no (please ring)
Statement of patient   **Patient identifier/label**

Please read this form carefully. If your treatment has been planned in advance, you should already have your own copy of page 2 which describes the benefits and risks of the proposed treatment. If not, you will be offered a copy now. If you have any further questions, do ask – we are here to help you. You have the right to change your mind at any time, including after you have signed this form.

I agree to the procedure or course of treatment described on this form.

I understand that you cannot give me a guarantee that a particular person will perform the procedure. The person will, however, have appropriate experience.

I understand that I will have the opportunity to discuss the details of anaesthesia with an anaesthetist before the procedure, unless the urgency of my situation prevents this. (This only applies to patients having general or regional anaesthesia.)

I understand that any procedure in addition to those described on this form will only be carried out if it is necessary to save my life or to prevent serious harm to my health.

I have been told about additional procedures which may become necessary during my treatment. I have listed below any procedures **which I do not wish to be carried out** without further discussion.

....
....
....
....
....

Patient's signature:...Date:..............................
Name (PRINT)..

A witness should sign below if the patient is unable to sign but has indicated his or her consent. Young people/children may also like a parent to sign here (see notes).

Signature:..Date:.......................................
Name (PRINT)..

Confirmation of consent (to be completed by a health professional when the patient is admitted for the procedure, if the patient has signed the form in advance)

On behalf of the team treating the patient, I have confirmed with the patient that s/he has no further questions and wishes the procedure to go ahead.

Signed:...   Date:.......................................
Name (PRINT).......................... ....   Job title........ ....

Important notes: (tick if applicable)

　　See also advance directive/living will (eg Jehovah's Witness form)

　　Patient has withdrawn consent (ask patient to sign/date here) ....

Implied consent

As we saw above, a signed consent form will not necessarily show that the patient really consented. Conversely, consent may be deemed to have occurred despite the absence of any consent form. Indeed, purely oral consent, at least as regards minor procedures, is commonplace in day-to-day medical practice. Sometimes, the consent may simply be implied – in the absence of words – by the patient's conduct, as in *O'Brien v Cunard Steamship Co* (1891) 28 NE 266, in which a ship's passenger who held out her arm to be vaccinated was subsequently unable to succeed in battery against the doctor.

Problems with the scope of the consent

The extent of the treatment

Difficulty may arise in relation to deciding exactly what it was to which the patient consented. In the case of *Mohr v Williams* (1905) 104 NW 12 (see p 97), the defendant tried to argue (*inter alia*) that the fact that the patient had consented to the operation on her right ear was relevant to the lawfulness of the operation on the other ear. In other words, the suggestion was that the patient had consented to 'an ear operation'. Could it be argued that she had given an implied consent to an operation on the other ear? The judge in that case took the view that there was no implied consent because the diseased condition of the patient's left ear was not discovered in the course of an authorised examination of that ear, but in the course of an examination which had not been authorised.

As we have seen, the patient acknowledges on the form that any other (unconsented to) procedure will only be carried out if it is necessary to save his life or to prevent serious harm to his health. In an earlier version the form had stated that any other procedure would only be carried out if it was necessary and in his best interests and was justifiable for medical reasons. Clearly, the former wording was meaningless as any treatment that was not in the patient's best interests and was not justifiable medically would have attracted an action in negligence, or even battery.

Consider whether the patient's acknowledgment that other treatments may also be carried out is a true consent to those other treatments, even if they are in the patient's best interests. It is a standard form, which most patients will feel they are unable to object to: is there not an element of coercion here? How many patients, about to undergo surgery, are likely to delete or alter a standard consent form? The disturbing consequences of such 'blanket' consent forms were illustrated in the case of *Breen v Baker* (1956) *The Times*, 27 January, where a woman consented to surgery which she believed would be dilatation and curettage, but was subsequently given a total hysterectomy. There was found to be no battery because the consent form stated: 'I agree to leave the nature and extent of the operation to be performed to the discretion of the surgeon.' Commenting upon an earlier version of the NHS consent form which referred to 'additional procedures', Jones stated:

Jones, M, *Medical Negligence*, 1996, London: Sweet & Maxwell, p 295:

Even if it were remotely practical for patients to identify all the potential procedures to which they did not wish to be subjected (which, clearly, it is not), there is no obligation in law for a patient to specify what he does not want to have done to him. In the absence of some valid justification, such as the patient's consent to the specific procedure that is contemplated, or necessity, all other procedures which involve physical contact with the person are unlawful, as battery.

The new consent form remedies this by stating that the patient has already been alerted to the additional procedures which may become necessary and has been given the opportunity to state in advance that he or she would not wish for one or more of these to take place.

However, whether the patient has this opportunity in practice will depend on what was said to him (and if he knew in essence what was to happen). In *Williamson v East London and City HA and Others* [1998] Lloyd's Rep Med 6, the claimant underwent surgery following problems with silicone breast implants, and the operation that was eventually performed was a subcutaneous mastectomy. The consent form had originally referred to a 'replacement breast prosthesis and right open capsulotomy', procedures less radical than a mastectomy. It seems that after the signing of the form, in a pre-operative examination the surgeon found that the more radical surgery was required and claimed that this had been explained to the claimant. The hospital altered the consent form but the form was not further signed by the claimant. The claimant successfully recovered against the surgeon in the tort of negligence: it was found that the latter was in breach of duty by not having explained what was proposed to the claimant, and that the consent form was not altered in her presence. Here, it is arguable that battery would have been the more appropriate cause of action.

We shall be looking further at the patient's right to information, and the remedies in battery and/or in negligence where this right is breached, at pp 131ff.

The person carrying out treatment

The standard NHS consent form requires the patient to acknowledge that the procedure need not be carried out by any particular doctor. There are examples of patients in America who have successfully sued following surgery carried out competently and in accordance with the patient's consent, but performed by a different doctor to that expected by the patient (see *Perna v Pirozzi* 457 A 2d 431 (1983)). However, it is implied by the form that if the procedure is not carried out by this doctor, it will be carried out by *a* doctor. Much controversy surrounds the issue of treatment by medical students, and even nurses:

Kennedy, I and Grubb, A, *Medical Law*, 2nd edn, 1994, London: Butterworths, p168:

There are at least two factual situations ... which do give rise to legal difficulties if the patient is unaware that the person is a student.

First, a student may, in fact, examine (ie, touch) a patient solely so as to acquire knowledge or experience for himself. The touching plays no part in the care of the patient. In such a circumstance, the consent given by the patient is probably invalid since the identity of the person touching affects the nature of what is being done to the patient, ie, training rather than caring.

Secondly, a student may touch a patient as part of the patient's care. Does the lack of awareness by the patient of the identity of the person touching (identity being status here) affect the validity of the patient's consent? ... It could be said that the difference between a lay person and a doctor is material whereas the difference between a medical student (presumably supervised) and a doctor is not. In our view, unless the patient suffered harm and could establish that the medical student was negligent, an English court would reject any claim by a patient.

In *R v Richardson* (1998) 43 BMLR 21, the Court of Appeal held that there had been a valid consent to treatment by a dentist when, unbeknown to the patient, the dentist had been suspended from practice by the General Dentist Council, and her conviction for assault was, therefore, quashed. In *Richardson* it was accepted that she was practising unlawfully following her suspension. However, this fraud was said not to vitiate the consent to treatment because it had not induced a mistaken belief as to the identity of the person carrying out the treatment, nor had it induced a mistaken belief about the nature and quality of the treatment. The Court of Appeal rejected the Crown's submission that the concept of 'identity' should be extended to cover qualifications or attributes of the dentist. If this were the case, it would distort the everyday meaning of the word 'identity'. Furthermore, to argue that there was an assault because there was no 'informed' consent was wrong because such consent had no place in the criminal law (we shall see later that it is a concept that is not entirely at the heart of English civil law either: see p 132, below).

This can be contrasted with the case of *R v Naveed Tabussum* [2000] 2 Cr App R 328, where the Court of Appeal held that there had not been a valid consent and the defendant's conviction for indecent assault was upheld where he had asked women to take part in a breast cancer survey to enable him to prepare a computer software package for doctors. The three complainants had agreed to the defendant showing them how to self-examine for breast lumps, which involved the removal of their clothes and the defendant touching their breasts. The central issue was that the women believed him to be a doctor. The defendant had no medical qualifications but he was a scientist with experience in the field of breast cancer, and he denied that he had ever represented himself to be medically qualified. He denied that he had any sexual motive, and the Court of Appeal said that, in any event, this was irrelevant.

Clearly, when the Court of Appeal considered the case of *Tabussum*, it had to try and distinguish it from *Richardson*. The court regarded *Richardson* as being decided solely on the question of identity and not the nature and quality of the acts. In *Tabussum*, the consent was given to touching 'for medical purposes'. This consent was valid as to the nature of the acts but, as the women said they would not have consented if they had known he was not medically qualified, the consent was not valid as to the quality. It is hard to reconcile these two cases when they both turned on 'qualifications and attributes'. Further, the disparity is highlighted by the fact that, in the case of *Richardson*, there was a deliberate unlawful act, whereas, at least on the defendant's evidence, in *Tabussum* the defendant was doing exactly what he had told the women concerned.

Qualifications as to the effect of consent

Generally speaking, the patient's consent is both necessary and sufficient for the propriety and lawfulness of medical treatment. This is at any rate so where the patient is a competent adult (for the position in respect of incompetent patients and children, see further Chapter 4). However, there are exceptions, which may run in both directions. In the first place, (arguably) at common law, and under statute, there are some circumstances in which treatment *can* occur despite the *absence* of consent. Secondly, and conversely, as alluded to briefly at p 98, above, there may be cases in which treatment *cannot* occur despite the *presence* of consent. We shall look at these various situations in turn.

Countervailing interests that justify non-consensual treatment at common law?

The English courts have made it very clear that, as regards refusals to treatment, the paternalistic wishes of doctors will not be allowed to override a patient's autonomy (see, eg, Lord Goff's *dictum* in *Bland*, at p 96, above). However, might it be argued that a patient's refusal of certain forms of treatment can exceptionally be overriden in order to uphold broader interests on the part of the state? The American courts have adverted to such interests. Thus, in the New Jersey case *In the Matter of Claire Conroy* 486 A 2d 1209 (1985), four state interests with potential for limiting patient rights were identified. These were preserving life, preventing suicide, safeguarding the integrity of the medical profession, and protecting innocent third parties:

> **Schrieber J**: The State's interest in preserving life ... may be seen as embracing two separate but related concerns: an interest in preserving the life of the particular patient, and an interest in preserving the sanctity of life ...
>
> While both of these State interests in life are certainly strong, in themselves they will usually not foreclose a competent person from declining life-sustaining medical

treatment for himself. This is because the life that the State is seeking to protect in such a situation is the life of the same person who has competently decided to forgo the medical intervention; it is not some other actual or potential life that cannot adequately protect itself ...

It may be contended that in conjunction with its general interest in preserving life, this State has a particular legislative policy of preventing suicide ... [However] this State interest in protecting people from direct and purposeful self-destruction is motivated by, if not encompassed within, the State's more basic interest in preserving life. Thus, it is questionable whether it is a distinct State interest worthy of independent consideration.

In any event, declining life-sustaining medical treatment may not properly be viewed as an attempt to commit suicide. Refusing medical treatment merely allows the disease to take its natural course; if death were eventually to occur, it would be the result, primarily, of the underlying disease, and not the result of a self-inflicted injury ...

The third State interest that is frequently asserted as a limitation on a competent patient's right to refuse medical treatment is the interest in safeguarding the integrity of the medical profession. This interest is not particularly threatened by permitting competent patients to refuse life-sustaining medical treatment. Medical ethics do not require medical intervention in disease at all costs ...

Moreover, even if doctors were exhorted to attempt to cure or sustain their patients under all circumstances, that moral and professional imperative, at least in cases of patients who were clearly competent, presumably would not require doctors to go beyond advising the patient of the risks of forgoing treatment and urging the patient to accept the medical intervention ...

The fourth asserted State interest in overriding a patient's decision about his medical treatment is the interest in protecting innocent third parties who may be harmed by the patient's treatment decision. When the patient's exercise of his free choice could adversely and directly affect the health, safety, or security of others, the patient's right of self-determination must frequently give way. Thus, for example, the courts have required competent adults to undergo medical procedures against their will if necessary to protect the public health: *Jacobson v Massachusetts* 197 US 11 ... (1905) (recognising enforceability of compulsory smallpox vaccination law); to prevent a serious risk to prison security: *Myers* ... 379 Mass 263 [379 Mass 255 (1979); 399 NE 2d 452 (1979)] ... (compelling prisoner with kidney disease to submit to dialysis over his protest rather than acquiescing in his demand to be transferred to a lower-security prison) ... or to prevent the emotional and financial abandonment of the patient's minor children: *Application of President and Directors of Georgetown College Inc* 331 F 2d 1000, p 1008 (DC Cir), cert denied, 377 US 978 ... (1964) (ordering mother of seven month old infant to submit to blood transfusion over her religious objections because of the mother's 'responsibility to the community to care for her infant'); *Holmes v Silver Cross Hospital* 340 F Supp 125, p 130 (NDIII 1972) (indicating that patient's status as father of a minor child might justify authorising blood transfusions to save his life despite his religious objections).

The categorisation of the four state interests in *Conroy* has been endorsed in a number of subsequent US authorities, and was adopted by Thorpe J (as he then was) in the English High Court in *Secretary of State v Robb* [1995] 1 All ER 677:

Secretary of State v Robb [1995] 1 All ER 677 (Thorpe J)

The respondent, a prison inmate with a personality disorder, went on hunger strike. The application concerned the question of whether it was lawful for his doctors and nurses to abstain from force feeding him in such circumstances:

Thorpe J: The only reference to the duty of the Home Office in modern authority is the briefest passage in the speech of Lord Keith of Kinkel in *Airedale NHS Trust v Bland* [1993] 1 All ER 821, p 861; [1993] AC 789, p 859, in which he said:

> ... the principle of the sanctity of life ... is not an absolute one. It does not compel a medical practitioner on pain of criminal sanctions to treat a patient, who will die if he does not, contrary to the express wishes of the patient. It does not authorise forcible feeding of prisoners on hunger strike. It does not compel the temporary keeping alive of patients who are terminally ill where to do so would merely prolong their suffering.

There have been much fuller developments in other common law jurisdictions, particularly in the United States, and all counsel have drawn attention to and relied upon a number of decisions, all of which consider the right of the individual to refuse nutrition in differing circumstances. I will refer only to recent decision in the United States that is directly concerned with adult prisoners on hunger strike. The most recent, and for me the most helpful, is the decision of the Supreme Court of California, *Thor v Superior Court* 5 Cal 4th 725 (1993). That authority upheld a decision at first instance that the prison authorities failed in their application for an order authorising force feeding of a quadriplegic prison inmate who had determined to refuse food and medical treatment necessary to maintain his life. The conclusion of the court was that the right of self-determination prevailed, but the court recognised that the right of self-determination was not absolute and that there were four specific State interests that might countervail. They were specifically: (i) preserving life; (ii) preventing suicide; (iii) maintaining the integrity of the medical profession; and (iv) protecting innocent third parties. The other United States case which is relevant to these arguments is the case of *Re Caulk* 125 NH 226 (1984). There, the Supreme Court of New Hampshire identified a very similar balancing exercise but found that the balance tipped against the right of self-determination. It seems that that decision was not specifically considered in the judgments given in the later case of *Thor*, and I have to say that I find more persuasive the dissenting judgment of Douglas J than the judgment of the majority given by Bachelder J.

These decisions are obviously relevant and helpful in reaching a decision as to how the law stands in this jurisdiction. I consider specifically the four countervailing State interests that were set against the individual's right of self-determination.

The first, namely the interest that the State holds in preserving life, seems to me to be but part and parcel of the balance that must be struck in determining and declaring the right of self-determination. The principle of the sanctity of human life in this jurisdiction is seen to yield to the principle of self-determination. It is within that balance that the consideration of the preservation of life is reflected.

The second countervailing State interest, preventing suicide, is recognisable, but seems to me to be of no application in cases such as this where the refusal of nutrition and medical treatment in the exercise of the right of self-determination does not constitute an act of suicide.

The third consideration of maintaining the integrity of the medical profession is one that I find hard to recognise as a distinct consideration. Medical ethical decisions can be acutely difficult and it is when they are at their most acute that applications for declaratory relief are made to the High Court. I cannot myself see that this is a distinct consideration that requires to be set against the right of self-determination of the individual.

The fourth consideration of protecting innocent third parties is one that is undoubtedly recognised in this jurisdiction, as is evidenced by the decision of Sir

Stephen Brown P in *Re S (Adult: Refusal of Medical Treatment)* [1992] 4 All ER 671;
[1993] Fam 123. Also recognised within this jurisdiction is a consideration that was
given weight in the decision of *Re Caulk*, namely the need to preserve the internal
order, discipline and security within the confines of the jail. But neither of these
considerations arise in the present case.

Preservation of life

As a general rule, as we have seen, the state's interest in preserving life is regarded
as subordinate to the patient's autonomous decision to refuse life-saving treatment.
This has been reiterated on many occasions by the courts. In *Re T (An Adult: Medical
Treatment)* [1992] 4 All ER 649, Lord Donaldson MR adverted to the conflict between
the sanctity of life, which the state will wish to uphold, and the patient's right to
self-determination, as follows:

> **Lord Donaldson MR:** This situation gives rise to a conflict between two interests, that
> of the patient and that of the society in which he lives. The patient's interest consists
> of his right to self-determination – his right to live his own life how he wishes, even if
> it will damage his health or lead to his premature death. Society's interest is in
> upholding the concept that all human life is sacred and that it should be preserved if
> at all possible. It is well established that in the ultimate the right of the individual is
> paramount.

Nevertheless, it remains arguable that, in some circumstances, a refusal of life-
saving treatment would entail a breach of the sanctity of life principle in so gross a
manner, that such a refusal may rightly be overruled. One instance may be if a
pregnant woman refused a caesarian section, and a mature foetus stands to rupture
her uterus causing both of them to die. In *Re T*, Lord Donaldson MR clearly wished
to place such cases in a special category: having set out the general right of a
competent adult patient to refuse treatment (above), he continued, 'the only possible
qualification is where the choice will lead to the death of a viable foetus'. However,
he offered no further explanation, and his remarks were seen in some quarters as
favouring foetal over maternal rights (an approach with no juridical foundation, and
which has been roundly rejected by the courts in later cases: see generally the
discussion in Chapter 8, at p 447ff). It is suggested here that it is more plausible to
regard the prospect of the woman's death in such macabre circumstances –
involving special insult to the sanctity of life principle – as providing the real
justification for intervention.

A second group of cases that may arguably be understood, at least partly, in
terms of the State's special interest in preserving life relates to refusal's of life-saving
treatment by 'mature minors' (ie older children, of eg 14 and above, who are judged
competent to make decisions about even highly significant medical interventions).
In such cases, the courts have consistently held that, while the child may be able to
consent to treatment, he cannot refuse it at serious cost to his health or life: see eg *Re
W (A Minor) (Medical Treatment)* [1992] 4 All ER 627 and *Re E (A Minor) (Wardship:
Medical Treatment)* [1993] 1 FLR 386. (The relevant principles and cases are discussed
further in Chapter 4, at p 164ff).

Prevention of suicide

The interest of the state in preventing suicide was considered by the California
Court of Appeal in the case of *Bouvia v Superior Court* 179 Cal App 3d 1127 (1986).
Elizabeth Bouvia was a severely disabled quadriplegic, almost totally immobile,

and entirely dependent upon others for all her needs. In addition, she was in continual and severe pain. Mentally, however, she was intelligent and aware. She was spoon fed, but found it difficult to take sufficient food orally because of nausea. It was, therefore, decided to feed her by nasogastric tube. She sought a court order that such 'treatment' could be refused (see Chapters 9 and 12 on feeding as treatment), and her right to self-determination was upheld. Associate Justice Beach reviewed the Californian authorities and the Presidential Commission for the Study of Ethical Problems in Medicine and Biomedical and Behavioural Research, and concluded:

> **Beach J**: It is ... immaterial that the removal of the nasogastric tube will hasten or cause Bouvia's eventual death. Being competent she has the right to live out the remainder of her natural life in dignity and peace. It is precisely the aim and purpose of the many decisions upholding the withdrawal of life support systems to accord and provide as large a measure of dignity, respect and comfort as possible ...

> Overlooking the fact that a desire to terminate one's life is probably the ultimate exercise of one's right to privacy, we find no substantial evidence to support the [trial] court's conclusion [that Bouvia's refusal of tube feeding amounted to a suicide attempt] ... As a consequence of her changed condition, it is clear she has now merely resigned herself to accept an earlier death, if necessary, rather than live by feedings forced upon her by means of nasogastric tube. Her decision to allow nature to take its course is not equivalent to an election to commit suicide with real parties aiding and abetting therein ...

> Moreover, the trial court seriously erred by basing its decision on the 'motives' behind Elizabeth Bouvia's decision to exercise her rights. If a right exists, it matters not what 'motivates' its exercise. We find nothing in the law to suggest the right to refuse medical treatment may be exercised only if the patient's motives meet someone else's approval. It certainly is not illegal or immoral to prefer a natural, albeit sooner, death than a drugged life attached to a mechanical device.

These issues relating to positive acts of killing and omissions to treat, will be examined further in Chapter 12. Consider, however, what difference (if any) it would have made if Elizabeth Bouvia had stated categorically that she was refusing food, not because it was difficult for her to swallow, but because she wished to die? On the analysis of Beach J, the motives are irrelevant. However, if that is the case, why was he at pains to point out that she did not intend to kill herself? In the English case of *Ms B v An NHS Trust Hospital* [2002] EWHC Fam 429, where a competent patient wished to have her artificial ventilation discontinued, Butler-Sloss P accepted Lord Goff's *dictum* in *Airedale NHS Trust v Bland* [1993] AC 789, at 864, that 'in cases of this kind, there is no question of the patient having committed suicide'.

If, on the other hand, the patient requires life-saving treatment as the result of *self-inflicted* injuries, it is arguable that a doctor may treat them, despite their refusal to consent. As Skegg has written:

> **Skegg, PDG, *Law, Ethics and Medicine*, 1984, Oxford: Clarendon, pp 110–12:**

> Where someone has done something in an apparent attempt to kill himself, doctors will often be justified in taking action to avert the consequences of the action. Prior to the abolition of the offence of suicide, there was no difficulty in explaining the legal basis for a doctor acting to prevent a person from attempting to commit suicide, or to avoid death resulting from such an attempt. Suicide was a felony, so the doctor was simply exercising the general liberty to prevent a felony. [*R v Duffy* [1967] 1 QB 63, p 67] ... However, since the enactment of the Suicide Act 1961 it has continued to be

accepted that doctors are sometimes free – sometimes, indeed, under a duty – to prevent patients from committing suicide.

> In some cases, the person who has apparently attempted to commit suicide will be suffering from a mental disorder which prevents the giving or withholding of consent. But in many cases the person will have a sufficient understanding to give, or withhold, consent. This is so, even though the act will often result from a passing impulse or temporary depression, rather than from a rational and fixed decision. If restrained and given assistance, the majority are glad that their action did not result in death. Hence, even if it is accepted that a person should not be prevented from carrying out a calm or a reasoned decision to terminate his own life, there is an overwhelming case for intervention where there is reason to believe that, if given help, the person will be glad he did not kill, or seriously injure, himself. Doctors are constantly intervening in these circumstances and there can be little doubt that, were their conduct to be questioned, the courts would hold it justified.

In fact, there are some cases where it has been held that there is not merely a right (in terms of having immunity from a battery suit), but may even be a duty in negligence on another party to prevent suicide. In *Selfe v Ilford and District Hospital Management Committee* (1970) 114 SJ 935, damages were recovered from the defendant mental hospital after the patient made a further suicide attempt after being admitted following a drug overdose, and in *Kirkham v Chief Constable of Greater Manchester Police* [1990] 2 WLR 987 the Court of Appeal upheld the claim of a widow of a prisoner who killed himself while on remand in custody. The police had failed to pass on to the prison authorities details of the prisoner's suicidal tendencies. By analogy, a patient, known to be a suicide risk, would be owed the same duty by any hospital authority purporting to care for him. (See also *Knight v Home Office* [1990] 3 All ER 237.)

The above decisions concerned persons 'of unsound mind' (which arguably equates to a lack of capacity as discussed below in this chapter). However, in *Reeves v Commissioner of Police of the Metropolis* [1999] 3 All ER 897, the House of Lords held that the police owed a duty of care to take reasonable steps to prevent the suicide of a 'sane' prisoner. The state of mind of the prisoner was irrelevant to the establishment of such a duty. Admittedly *Reeves*, as well as the other cases, related to the failure to prevent/restrain a person's initial self-harming behaviour. But it would arguably be odd if, having imposed a duty at that stage, the law were to deny such a duty (and *a fortiori* the right to treat) on the part of those subsequently rendering medical assistance.

In *R (On the Application of Pretty) v Director of Public Prosecutions* (2001) 151 NLJ 1572, the Divisional Court stated that Article 2 of the European Convention on Human Rights, which protects the right to life, does not require the state to take positive steps to force life on the unwilling, but nor does it mean that the state is *positively obliged* to stand by and allow someone to take his own life. If that were the case, it would be unlawful to attempt to rescue would-be suicides. The clear implication of the court's reasoning is that such intervention would be lawful (the point was not considered further when *Pretty* reached the House of Lords). However, in the subsequent High Court decision of *Re W (Adult: Refusal of Treatment)* [2002] EWHC Fam 901, Butler-Sloss P held that the prison authorities were debarred from treating a competent prisoner whose self-inflicted wounds were in danger of causing fatal scepticaemia.

A further controversial question is whether, in similar circumstances, the state could justify the force-feeding of prisoners on hunger-strike. In the *Robb* case, Thorpe J gave a negative answer, but a different result was reached in *R v Collins and*

Ashworth Hospital Authority ex p Brady [2000] Lloyd's Rep Med 355. The latter case concerned the convicted Moors murderer, Ian Brady, who was on hunger strike and who, by way of judicial review, challenged the decision of the hospital to force-feed him. The case was principally about capacity and about the application of the Mental Health Act (MHA) 1983, and is considered further in Chapter 9, but one of the submissions on behalf of the hospital was that, whatever the statutory position, the patient's right of self-determination is not absolute and can be overidden by the public interest in the preservation of life, the prevention of suicide and the maintenance of the integrity of the medical profession. The judge declined to make a finding in this respect, as he found that the patient lacked capacity and that the provisions of the MHA 1983 justified force feeding, but he said, nevertheless:

> **Maurice Kay J**: It would be a disappointment to me if I were constrained by authority from finding in favour of [the hospital who wanted to force feed] on this issue. My impression is that I would not be. Moreover, it would seem to me to be a matter for deep regret if the law has developed to a point in this area where the rights of a patient count for everything and other ethical values and institutional integrity count for nothing.

However, it is hard not to conclude that the particular facts of this case were the key persuasive factor in the judge coming to that conclusion. It is arguable that allowing such a notorious criminal to achieve what he wanted would have given rise to considerable adverse public opinion.

Protecting the integrity of the medical profession

As regards the third state interest, protecting the integrity of the medical profession, Schrieber J suggested in *Conroy* that this will not justify overriding a refusal of treatment. However, a different rule would seem to apply in the context of *withdrawing* treatment initiated previously. In the case of *Brophy v New England Sinai Hospital* 497 NE 2d 626 (1986), a Massachusetts court held that a hospital need not compromise its own principles by withdrawing feeding from a patient in PVS (who had made it clear he would not wish to survive in such a state), but should permit his transfer to another hospital sympathetic to this course. A similar approach can be found in the recent English case of *Ms B v An NHS Trust Hospital* [2002] EWHC Fam 429 in which, as noted, the patient wished her life-sustaining ventilation to cease. The clinicians treating her had come to like and respect her and could not bring themselves to disconnect the ventilator. The court accepted evidence from a professor of intensive care medicine from another trust that, in his opinion, the patient should be transferred to another hospital which would be willing to accede to her request.

Protection of innocent third parties

It must be said that the purported limtation on treatment refusals 'to protect innocent parties' is of dubious validity. Whilst public health arguments may, in the right circumstances, result in the overriding of a patient's refusal of treatment, in the UK this would have to be by express statutory provision, (see p 112). The cases referred to in *Conroy* relating to the emotional and financial abandonment of children are not in accordance with US or UK law. There is no principle which regards the parents as a means to the ends of their children. Whilst the welfare of the child is paramount in English law, the necessary protection is given, not by compelling parents to care for their children (except financially), but by removing the children from the parents. It is unthinkable that a parent would be ordered to undergo a blood transfusion on the ground that her children would be motherless if she died.

Similarly, the case of *Re S (Adult: Refusal of Medical Treatment)* [1992] 4 All ER 671, referred to by Thorpe J in *Robb* as instancing such a state interest, is also suspect. The case concerned the refusal of a pregnant woman to submit to a Caesarean necessary to save the life of her foetus and her own life. As discussed above, and in Chapter 8, this type of case is not really to be understood as a matter of the court protecting the foetus (despite the terms of the court's declaration in the case, which referred to the 'vital interests of the ... child'). Rather, to the extent that the decision to intervene in *Re S* was supportable, this is on the basis of the first state interest, 'the preservation/upholding the sanctity of life'.

Statutory exceptions to the need for consent

In addition to the common law rules discussed above, there are a number of statutory exceptions to the need normally to obtain a person's consent prior to giving medical treatment and care. The two most important categories of patient, whose consent may be so dispensed with, namely the mentally incapacitated and the mentally ill, will be the subject of Chapters 4 and 9, respectively. However, there are two further statutory regimes that may also apply in certain circumstances. The first relates to the removal to a place of safety of those who, through age or infirmity, are no longer able to care for themselves:

National Assistance Act 1948:

Removal to suitable premises of persons in need of care and attention

47(1) -The following provisions of this section shall have effect for the purposes of securing the necessary care and attention for persons who–

    (a) -are suffering from grave chronic disease or, being aged, infirm or physically incapacitated, are living in insanitary conditions; and

    (b) -are unable to devote to themselves, and are not receiving from other persons, proper care and attention.

(2) -If the medical officer of health certifies in writing to the appropriate authority that he is satisfied after thorough inquiry and consideration that in the interest of any such person as aforesaid residing in the area of the authority, or for preventing injury to the health of, or serious nuisances to, other persons, it is necessary to remove any such person as aforesaid from the premises in which he is residing, the appropriate authority may apply to the court of summary jurisdiction having jurisdiction in the place where the premises are situated for an order under the next following sub-section.

It is, however, questionable how far this provision extends to the administration of medical treatment, as conventionally understood.

Secondly, a patient who suffers from a contagious disease which may pose risks to the health of the community at large may be compulsorily detained and treated pursuant to the Public Health (Control of Disease) Act 1984. Section 37 of the Act provides:

37 (1) -Where a justice of the peace (acting, if he deems it necessary, ex parte) is satisfied, on the application of the local authority, that a person is suffering from a notifiable disease and–

    (a) -that his circumstances are such that proper precautions to prevent the spread of infection cannot be taken, or that such precautions are not being taken; and

(b) -that serious risk of infection to other persons is thereby caused to other persons; and

(c) -that accommodation for him is available in a suitable hospital vested in the Secretary of State or, pursuant to arrangements made by a health authority (whether under an NHS contract or otherwise), in a suitable hospital vested in an NHS trust, NHS Foundation Trust, Primary Care Trust or other person,

the justice may, with the consent mentioned in subsection (1A) below, order his to be removed to it.

(1A) The consent referred to in subsection (1) above is that of a Primary Care Trust or Health Authority—

(a) any part of whose area falls within that of the local authority, and

(b) which appears to the local authority to be an appropriate Primary Care Trust or Health Authority from whom to obtain consent.

(2) An order under this section may be addressed to such officer of the local authority as the justice may think expedient, and that officer and any officer of the hospital may do all acts necessary for giving effect to the order.

A list of 'notifiable diseases' is contained in the Public Health (Infectious Diseases) Regulations 1988 SI 1988/1546 and includes meningitis, dysentery, polio, typhoid, malaria, tuberculosis and AIDS.

Situations where consent may be insufficient

We are here concerned with the converse position where treatment may be unlawful, notwithstanding that the patient has consented.

As noted earlier, it has been established that there are certain procedures in respect of which consent is no defence at criminal law (see *R v Brown et al* [1993] 2 All ER 75). Usually, problems will not arise in relation to medical procedures because these are almost always therapeutic, and thus clearly in the public interest. However, there are a number of interventions which are not therapeutic and whose acceptability may sometimes be more contentious. The issue of consent to non-therapeutic research and to organ donation will be considered later in Chapters 10 and 11, respectively, which focus on those topics; however, three examples of borderline therapeutic/non-therapeutic, procedures are considered here.

Gender reassignment

This is now generally regarded as therapeutic, as such an operation is normally carried out when the patient has exhibited serious and continuing manifestations of the personality of someone of the opposite sex, and is psychologically disturbed by being 'in the wrong body'. Such operations are performed under the NHS as well as privately, and it is highly unlikely that a challenge to their legality would succeed: indeed, in its recent ruling in *Bellinger v Bellinger* [2003] 2 All ER 593, the House of Lords appears to have taken for granted the lawfulness of this type of surgery. Nonetheless, it is important to note that such an operation, carried out on the cosmetic whim of a patient who did not have a history of doubts about his sexual identity, may well constitute a serious criminal offence.

Sterilisation/vasectomy

Despite the judgment of Denning LJ in *Bravery v Bravery* [1954] 1 WLR 1169, when he suggested that sterilisation operations carried out for contraceptive purposes were injurious to the public interest, there can be no doubt nowadays that such operations are lawful, and, it must be said, even in that 1954 case, Denning LJ was not supported by his fellow Court of Appeal judges.

Circumcision

Female circumcision is a much more drastic procedure than male circumcision, and results in pain, discomfort, sexual and childbirthing difficulties which do not follow in the case of men. As a result of a number of well publicised cases, female circumcision was criminalised by the Prohibition of Female Circumcision Act 1985, which has recently been re-enacted with increased penalties (of up to 14 years' imprisonment) by the Female Genital Mutilation Act 2003.

However, there is no doubt that, even in the male, these operations, when undergone for religious or cultural reasons, are non-therapeutic, yet they are carried out almost without question. Further, they are usually carried out on children, at the behest of their parents, and often without anaesthetic. Although failure to be circumcised may inhibit family relationships, it is also said that it is a practice which results in diminished sexual enjoyment. Christopher Price points out that, historically, the practice has been seen as a means of counteracting excessive lust (12th century), and as a preventive for masturbation (19th century England). He also notes that the medical profession justifies carrying out such operations on the basis that they will be performed anyway, and therefore are better done in a clinical setting. He notes that the Bradford Royal Infirmary provide such a service under the NHS. However, he suggests on a number of grounds that the practice should be outlawed:

> **Price, C, 'Male circumcision: an ethical and legal affront' (1997) Bulletin of Medical Ethics (May) 13:**
>
> Rejoicing in our multicultural society does not mean that we should be blind to practices, whatever their source and motive, which are themselves abusive and discriminatory of others, directly and inevitably diminishing the freedoms, human rights, integrity and dignity of others ...
>
> The UN Convention on the Rights of the Child makes the position clearer in respect to circumcision. Article 24(3) provides: 'States Parties shall take all effective and appropriate measures with a view to abolishing traditional practices prejudicial to the health of children.' Some have sought to argue that this provision was only aimed at female circumcision; but this argument cannot hold when the Convention is read with the interpretative provisions of the Vienna Convention on the Law of Treaties 1969.

Referring to the conflict with religious freedom, Price states:

> Customary international law provides that an individual's exercise of his freedoms can legitimately be restrained when so to exercise them is to damage or deny those freedoms to another. Thus, Art 9(2) of the European Convention on Human Rights provides:
>
>> Freedom to manifest one's religion or beliefs shall be subject only to such limitations as are prescribed by law and are necessary in a democratic society in the interests of public safety, for the protection of public order, health or morals, or *for the protection of the rights and freedoms of others*' (emphasis added).

The Convention thus distinguishes between the unfettered right to freedom of thought, and the more restricted right to manifest one's religion.

... Non-therapeutic circumcision is clearly discriminatory, unethical and illegal. Its prehistoric origins, and its kinship with subincision and other forms of penile mutilation, show its essential barbarity ...

These are strong words, but it is hard to disagree that the procedure is non-therapeutic, and constitutes an assault against the person. Is it tolerated simply to avoid the outcry from the religious communities if action were taken against those who carry it out?

THE ELEMENTS TO A VALID CONSENT

The essential elements to a valid consent to treatment can be summed up as follows:

(a) the patient must have sufficient understanding, variously described as mental capacity or mental competence, to make the decision;

(b) the patient must consent to (or refuse) the treatment of his own free will, with no duress or undue influence; and

(c) the patient must have been given sufficient information about the proposed treatment.

We shall address each of these requirements in turn.

Capacity to consent

In its 1995 report, *Mental Incapacity* (Report No 231, 1995), the Law Commission identified three possible alternative approaches to capacity. These are the 'status', 'outcome' and 'functional' approaches. The status approach is most easily explained in relation to children. This would simply state that a person, eg a child under a certain age, lacked capacity and there would be no examination of other issues such as the person's understanding. The Law Commission rejected this in relation to adult patients as being contrary to a policy of encouraging self-determination.

The 'outcome' approach was described by the Law Commission as follows:

Law Commission, *Mental Incapacity*, Report No 231, 1995, London: HMSO, para 3.4:

An assessor of capacity using the 'outcome' method focuses on the final content of an individual's decision. Any decision which is inconsistent with conventional values, or with which the assessor disagrees, may be classified as incompetent. This penalises individuality and demands conformity at the expense of personal autonomy. A number of our respondents argued that an 'outcome' approach is applied by many doctors; if the outcome of the patient's deliberations is to agree with the doctor's recommendations then he or she is taken to have capacity, while if the outcome is to reject a course which the doctor has advised then capacity is found to be absent.

Again, the Law Commission rejected this approach. It must, in fact, be arguable that such an approach would make a nonsense of the whole issue of consent to treatment. To take an outcome approach would mean that the patient's consent would only be required when a doctor did not recommend a type of treatment, but described a number of alternatives to a patient inviting him to decide which to choose. In any situation when there was one recommendation only, a patient who refused it would be deemed to lack capacity, and the treatment could go ahead on the ground that it was in the best interests of the patient to treat him without consent (see Chapter 4). Not only does it undermine the way in which we have traditionally approached capacity, it would destroy the very basis of the need to obtain a valid consent to treatment at all.

Accordingly, the Law Commission recommended the 'functional' approach. Here, the assessor asks whether an individual is able, at the time when a particular decision has to be made, to understand its nature and effects.

The Commission favoured this view not least because it is reflected in the approach the courts have taken. In *Re T (Adult: Refusal of Treatment)* [1992] 4 All ER 649, Lord Donaldson MR (at 661) stated as follows:

> **Lord Donaldson MR**: Doctors faced with a refusal of consent have to give very careful and detailed consideration to the patient's capacity to decide at the time when the decision was made. It may not be the simple case of the patient having no capacity because, for example, at that time he had hallucinations. It may be the more difficult case of a temporarily reduced capacity at the time when his decision was made. What matters is that the doctors should consider whether at that time he had a capacity which was commensurate with the gravity of the decision which he purported to make. The more serious the decision, the greater the capacity ...

> [T]he patient's right of choice exists whether the reasons for making that choice are rational, irrational, unknown or even non-existent. That his choice is contrary to what is to be expected of the vast majority of adults is only relevant if there are other reasons for doubting his capacity to decide. The nature of his choice or the terms in which it is expressed may then tip the balance.

Until the 1990s, there was surprisingly little authority on capacity to consent to medical treatment, but further guidance was given by the High Court in *Re C (Adult: Refusal of Treatment)* [1994] 1 WLR 290, a case startling in a number of ways.

Re C (Adult: Refusal of Treatment) [1994] 1 WLR 290, Fam Div (Thorpe J)

The patient was an elderly man, diagnosed as suffering from paranoid schizophrenia. He had been a patient in Broadmoor special hospital for 30 years. One of his delusional beliefs was that he had been a great doctor who had never failed to cure a patient. He also believed that he had the ability to cure damaged limbs. Following an injury to his foot in 1993, he was diagnosed as suffering from gangrene and the doctors at the local general hospital considered that, unless his foot was amputated, because of the highly toxic nature of gangrene, he was 85% likely to die.

Mr C objected to amputation and made an application to the court for an injunction restraining the health authorities from amputating his foot then *or at any time in the future*. Consent to treatment, other than treatment for the mental disorder, is required even if the patient is mentally ill, as long as he has the necessary capacity (see s 63 of the MHA 1983 and Chapter 9), so in this case the decision would turn on C's capacity, regardless of his long history as a patient suffering from what is generally regarded as serious mental illness. Thorpe J held that there is a rebuttable presumption in favour of capacity. C's evidence was that he did not believe the gangrene would kill him, that he had been born into the world with four complete limbs and he intended to go out with those limbs, and that he did not believe that God wanted him to have his foot amputated:

> **Thorpe J**: [Counsels'] submissions divide over the definition of the capacity which enables an individual to refuse treatment. Mr Gordon argues for what he calls the minimal competence test, which he defines as the capacity to understand in broad terms the nature and effect of the proposed treatment. It is common ground that C has the legal capacity to initiate these proceedings without a next friend, within the terms of RSC Ord 80. Mr Gordon contends that the capacity to refuse treatment is no higher and is equally no higher than the capacity to contract. I reject that submission. I think that the question to be decided is whether it has been established that C's capacity is so reduced by his chronic mental illness that he does not sufficiently understand the nature, purpose and effects of the proffered amputation.
>
> I consider helpful Dr Eastman's analysis of the decision making process into three stages: first, comprehending and retaining treatment information, second, believing it and, third, weighing it in the balance to arrive at choice. The Law Commission has proposed a similar approach in para 2.20 of Law Commission Consultation Paper No 129, *Mentally Incapacitated Adults and Decision Making*. Applying that test to my findings on the evidence, I am completely satisfied that the presumption that C has the right of self-determination has not been displaced. Although his general capacity is impaired by schizophrenia, it has not been established that he does not sufficiently understand the nature, purpose and effects of the treatment he refuses. Indeed, I am satisfied that he has understood and retained the relevant treatment information, that in his own way he believes it, and that in the same fashion he has arrived at a clear choice.

The prevalence of paternalism in English medical law had been dealt a blow: the patient's beliefs can be more important than medical opinion. (It is also interesting to note that Mr C did, in fact, respond to more conservative treatment.)

The approach in *Re C* was subsequently approved by the Court of Appeal in the important case of *Re MB (Medical Treatment)* [1997] 2 FLR 426. There, a 23 year-old woman had been admitted to hospital when 40 weeks pregnant. Her foetus was in the breech position and because a vaginal delivery would pose a serious risk of death or injury to the foetus, she agreed to a Caesarean operation to deliver it. However, because of a phobia that she had about needles, she panicked and, at the last moment, withdrew her consent. The High Court granted a declaration that it would be lawful to carry out the operation because, on the evidence, the patient was suffering from a temporary impairment to her mental functioning and was, therefore, not competent. This decision was upheld by Court of Appeal:

> **Butler-Sloss LJ (delivering the judgment of the court):**
>
> *Conclusions on Capacity to decide*
>
> ... (1) Every person is presumed to have the capacity to consent to or to refuse medical treatment unless and until that presumption is rebutted ...
>
> ... (4) A person lacks capacity if some impairment or disturbance of mental functioning renders the person unable to make a decision whether to consent to or to refuse treatment. That inability to make a decision will occur when:
>
> (a) the patient is unable to comprehend and retain the information which is material to the decision, especially as to the likely consequences of having or not having the treatment in question;
>
> (b) the patient is unable to use the information and weigh it in the balance as part of the process of arriving at the decision. If, as Thorpe J observed in *Re C*

... a compulsive disorder or phobia from which the patient suffers stifles belief in the information presented to her, then the decision may not be a true one. As Lord Cockburn CJ put it in *Banks v Goodfellow* (1870) LR 5 QB 549, p 569:

... one object may be so forced upon the attention of the invalid as to shut out all others that might require consideration.

(5) The 'temporary factors' mentioned by Lord Donaldson MR in *Re T* (confusion, shock, fatigue, pain or drugs) may completely erode capacity but those concerned must be satisfied that such factors are operating to such a degree that the ability to decide is absent.

(6) Another such influence may be panic induced by fear. Again, careful scrutiny of the evidence is necessary because fear of an operation may be a rational reason for refusal to undergo it. Fear may also, however, paralyse the will and thus destroy the capacity to make a decision.

This approach has been applied in a number of subsequent authorities: see, eg, *St George's Healthcare NHS Trust v S* [1999] Fam 26; *Ms B v An NHS Trust Hospital* [2002] EWHC Fam 429; *Re W (Adult: Refusal of Treatment)* [2002] EWHC Fam 901. Indeed, the common law test has now received statutory endorsement in terms of the definition of 'lack of capacity' (the obverse of capacity) contained in the Mental Capacity Act 2005. This provides, in ss 2 and 3, as follows:

Mental Capacity Act 2005:

2 People who lack capacity

(1) For the purposes of this Act, a person lacks capacity in relation to a matter if at the material time he is unable to make a decision for himself in relation to the matter because of an impairment of, or a disturbance in the functioning of, the mind or brain.

(2) It does not matter whether the impairment or disturbance is permanent or temporary.

(3) A lack of capacity cannot be established merely by reference to–

(a) a person's age or appearance, or

(b) a condition of his, or an aspect of his behaviour, which might lead others to make unjustified assumptions about his capacity ...

3 Inability to make decisions

(1) For the purposes of section 2, a person is unable to make a decision for himself if he is unable–

(a) to understand the information relevant to the decision,

(b) to retain that information,

(c) to use or weigh that information as part of the process of making the decision, or

(d) to communicate his decision (whether by talking, using sign language or any other means).

(2) A person is not to be regarded as unable to understand the information relevant to a decision if he is able to understand an explanation of it given to him in a way that is appropriate to his circumstances (using simple language, visual aids or any other means).

(3) The fact that a person is able to retain the information relevant to a decision for a short period only does not prevent him from being regarded as able to make the decision.

(4) The information relevant to a decision includes information about the reasonably foreseeable consequences of–

(a) deciding one way or another, or

(b) failing to make the decision.

As will be apparent, the wording of these provisions owes much to the decision in *Re MB*, in particular. (One gloss is s 3(1)(d), which allows patients who have capacity in principle, but no means of giving expression to it – ie they are 'locked in' as may happen in rare cases of Guillain Barré syndrome, to be treated as though incapacitated.)

Even so, in practice, the assessment of capacity may be far from straightforward. Such an assessment by its nature requires one person (the assessor) to form a judgment about the 'interior', ie cognitively not directly accessible, mental state of another. The importance in this context of cultural awareness on the part of the assessor was highlighted by Michael Gunn, when examining the Consultation Paper which preceded the Law Commission's Report (*Mental Incapacity*, Report No 231, 1995, London: HMSO):

Gunn, M, 'The meaning of incapacity' (1994) 2 Med L Rev 8:

It is clearly the case that capacity is a value-laden concept. Undoubtedly, the approach recommended by the Law Commission is one very much within the tradition of Western cultures. Care must therefore be taken in its application to people from other cultures. More specifically, any person assessing the competence of another individual must be aware of their own values so that assumptions and decisions are not made which are unjustifiable. It is the values of the person being assessed which must be respected. The assessor needs to be able to identify where her values vary from those of the person being assessed. Values cannot be removed from any assessment, but assessors of capacity can be educated to be aware of their own values and thus to take care in assessing capacity not to be prejudiced when meeting someone with a different value base.

In the context of medical treatment, it will fall in the first instance to the doctors, at the point of treatment, to make the assessment. The law, as noted above, attempts to provide assistance by directing them to focus separately on such elements as the patient's 'understanding', 'retention', and 'ability to weigh' treatment information.

Nonetheless, as we shall see below, such concepts remain relatively fluid.

Assessing capacity

The ability to understand and retain information

General principles

As we have seen, those caring for the patient must be satisfied that he comprehends or understands the treatment information. The latter must be able to act in an autonomous manner and, as a first step, this requires the abilty to identify and process information relevant to his situation. If radical mistake or confusion besets this process, he will be prevented from making a considered decision. Arguably, however, the notion of 'understanding' can be manipulated to facilitate a finding of incapacity: see Lee, S, 'Towards a jurisprudence of consent', in *Oxford Essays in Jurisprudence*, 1987, Oxford: Clarendon, in which Lee states that few adults could meet Lord Scarman's criteria in relation to a child's understanding, set out in *Gillick v West Norfolk and*

Wisbech AHA [1986] 1 AC 112. As noted earlier, and discussed further in Chapter 4, special rules apply to children, so that, even if competent, their refusal of treatment is not binding (see Chapter 4, at p 164). Even so, it remains open as to whether Lord Scarman's approach in *Gillick* was intended simply to stress the importance of certainty in the case of children, whether it was imposing a different test of understanding for children, or whether his criteria were also intended to apply to adults.

The question has also been raised – again in the context of 'mature minors' (although there is no reason to suppose that the position will differ for adults) – as to whether the requirement of 'understanding' means that the patient must actually understand the nature of the information about the treatment and its consequences, or merely that he is capable of understanding:

Kennedy, I and Grubb, A, *Medical Law*, 2nd edn, 1994, London: Butterworths, p 120:

If the test of understanding is *actual understanding* ... then whether or not the girl understands *and therefore is competent* to consent may turn on what she is told. Indeed, this seems to have been Lord Donaldson's approach in *Re R* ... If the girl is not given certain information she may not understand enough, but this would not be the product of any lack of competence but merely that she decided in relative ignorance. It would be an unsatisfactory state of law if doctors could be controlling the information given to a patient and thereby grant or deny her competence ... It must, therefore, be the law that competence is determined by reference to the unvarying conceptual standard of capacity or ability to understand.

(The case of *Re R (A Minor) (Wardship: Consent to Medical Treatment)* [1991] 4 All ER 177, referred to here, concerned a 15 year old girl with a fluctuating mental state, who was refusing antipsychotic drugs: see further Chapter 4, at p 164.)

A further question relates to whether the patient must have 'first hand' experience in relation to the matters he is required to understand. The answer to this is clearly 'no', as illustrated in *Ms B v An NHS Trust Hospital* [2002] EWHC Fam 429. Here the patient was paralysed from the neck downwards, with no prospects of recovery. However, she could be admitted to a spinal rehabilitation unit with a view to rehabilitation into the community. She had declined to participate in this and wanted the ventilator which kept her alive to be disconnected. Dame Butler-Sloss, President of the Family Division, found her to have capacity and, therefore, to be able lawfully to refuse treatment. However, expert evidence on behalf of the trust, which wanted her to go ahead with the rehabilitation, was given by a spinal injuries consultant, who stated that as the patient had not gone through the rehabilitation process she did not have the information necessary to make her decision. This was, rightly, roundly rejected by the president when she said: 'Even in issues of the utmost significance and gravity people, including patients, have to make decisions without experience of the consequences and his requirement is unrealistic.'

As regards the retention of information, an important factor will be the stability of the patient's mental profile. Thus, a fluctuating mental state as in the *Re R* case may impede retention, as can temporary factors such as pain and exhaustion. However, it is important that the latter are stringently defined. There are a number of cases, such as *Re MB (Medical Treatment)* [1997] 2 FLR 426, which concern the refusals of Caesarean sections when, in the course of labour, difficulties have arisen which have put the life of both woman and foetus at risk. In such cases, there could be a temptation to use a blanket argument that the labour process itself has produced temporary factors which have inhibited understanding and/or retention: see, in particular, the judgment of Johnson J in *Rochdale Healthcare (NHS) Trust v C* [1997] 1 FCR 274, where he held that the patient was unable 'to make any valid decision about anything of even the most trivial kind', due to the stress and pain of labour. This was in contrast to the obstetrician's view that the woman had capacity.

In *Re MB*, the Court of Appeal took the opportunity to criticise the evidential basis for Johnson J's finding in the *Rochdale* case. This is not to deny that, on the facts of a given case, there may indeed be evidence of special factors temporarily disruptive of capacity. As we have seen, in *Re MB* itself, the patient's needle-phobia was such a factor (and see also the factually similar case of *Re L (Adult: Non-Consensual Treatment)* [1997] 1 FCR 609).

Belief and its effect upon understanding

In *Re C (Adult: Refusal of Treatment)* [1994] 1 WLR 290, Thorpe J treated the patient's ability to believe the treatment information as a distinct element in the test of capacity. Subsequently, however, in *Re MB*, belief was not accorded separate mention, and nor is it adverted to by the new statutory test in s 3 of the Mental Capacity Act 2005. The reason is probably the difficulty, conceptually, of keeping understanding and belief distinct in this context: to mention belief separately is arguably simply a way of emphasising that the patient must appreciate that the information *pertains to him* (as opposed merely to understanding it abstractly in the way, say, one might follow the plot of a novel).

Certainly, where a patient has certain delusional beliefs in relation to treatment information, one may sometimes be justified in concluding that he is unable to 'understand' it. In this regard, the Court of Appeal suggested in *Re MB* that 'a misperception of reality (eg the blood is poisoned because it is red) ... will be more readily accepted to be a disorder of the mind'. It is important to note that what is at issue here are beliefs about the empirical world, where agreed standards exist for demonstrating their falsehood. (By contrast, religiously grounded beliefs, even if of a minority order and regarded by most as wrongheaded, will provide no basis for inferences as to their holder's mental capacity.)

An American case, which illustrates a fundamental misperception of reality on the part of the patient, is the following:

State of Tennessee v Northern 563 SW 2d 197 (1978), Tenn Ct App

> **Todd J**: On 24 January 1978 the Tennessee Department of Human Services filed this suit alleging that Mary C Northern was 72 years old, with no available help from relatives; that Miss Northern resided alone under unsatisfactory conditions as a result of which she had been admitted to and was a patient in Nashville General Hospital; that the patient suffered from gangrene of both feet which required the removal of her feet to save her life; that the patient lacked the capacity to appreciate her condition or to consent to necessary surgery ...

> Capacity means mental ability to make a rational decision, which includes the ability to perceive, appreciate all relevant facts and to reach a rational judgment upon such facts.

> Capacity is not necessarily synonymous with sanity. A blind person may be perfectly capable of observing the shape of small articles by handling them, but not capable of observing the shape of a cloud in the sky.

> A person may have 'capacity' as to some matters and may lack 'capacity' as to others ...

In the present case, this court has found the patient to be lucid and apparently of sound mind generally. However, on the subjects of death and amputation of her feet, her comprehension is blocked, blinded or dimmed to the extent that she is incapable of recognising facts which would be obvious to a person of normal perception. For example, in the presence of this court, the patient looked at her feet and refused to recognise the obvious facts that the flesh was dead, black, shrivelled, rotting and stinking.

The record also discloses that the patient refuses to consider the eventuality of death which is or ought to be obvious in the face of such dire bodily deterioration.

As described by the doctors and observed by this court, the patient wants to live and keep her dead feet, too, and refuses to consider the impossibility of such a desire. In order to avoid the unpleasant experience of facing death and/or loss of feet, her mind or emotions have resorted to the device of denying the unpleasant reality so that, to the patient, the unpleasant reality does not exist. This is the 'delusion' which renders the patient incapable of making a rational decision as to whether to undergo surgery to save her life or to forgo surgery and forfeit her life.

The physicians speak of probabilities of death without amputation as 90% to 95% and the probability of death with surgery as 50:50 (one in two). Such probabilities are not facts, but the existence and expression of such opinions are facts which the patient is unwilling or unable to recognise or discuss.

If, as repeatedly stated, this patient could and would give evidence of a comprehension of the facts of her condition and could and would express her unequivocal desire in the face of such comprehended facts, then her decision, however unreasonable to others, would be accepted and honoured by the courts and by her doctors. The difficulty is that she cannot or will not comprehend the facts.

Accordingly, the court found that the patient was incompetent. (See also the decision of the English High Court in *Norfolk and Norwich Healthcare (NHS) Trust v W* [1997] Fam Law 17, where a patient, who was admitted to hospital in labour, denied that she was pregnant.)

More difficulties arise in cases where a treatment decision by a patient is based upon a mixture of rational and delusional beliefs. The US case of *Re Maida Yetter* 96 D & C 2d 619 (1973) provides a good example. Here the patient, a chronic schizophrenic, refused breast surgery, potentially needed to alleviate a malignant condition. It was generally accepted that when surgery was first suggested to her, her reasons for refusing were largely based on fear of surgery, and that she appreciated the consequences of refusal, including death:

Williams J: Mrs Yetter was committed to Allentown State Hospital in June 1971, by the Courts of Northampton County, after hearings held pursuant to s 406 of the Mental Health and Mental Retardation Act of 20 October 1966 ... Her diagnosis at that time was schizophrenia, chronic undifferentiated. It appears that late in 1972, in connection with a routine physical examination, Mrs Yetter was discovered to have a breast discharge indicating the possible presence of carcinoma. The doctors recommended that a surgical biopsy be performed together with any additional corrective surgery that would be indicated by the pathology of the biopsy. When this recommendation was first discussed with Mrs Yetter in December of 1972 by her caseworker, Mrs Perhac, who had weekly counselling sessions with Mrs Yetter for more than a year, Mrs Yetter indicated that she would not give her consent to the surgery. Her stated reasons were that she was afraid because of the death of her aunt which followed such surgery and that it was her own body and she did not desire the operation. The caseworker indicated that at this time Mrs Yetter was lucid, rational and appeared to understand that the possible consequences of her refusal included death.

Mr Stauffer, who indicated that he visits his sister regularly, and Dr Bischoff, whose direct contacts with Mrs Yetter have been since March 1973, testified that in the last three or four months it has been impossible to discuss the proposed surgery with Mrs Yetter in that, in addition to expressing fear of the operation, she has become delusional in her reasons for not consenting to surgery. Her tendency to become delusional concerning this problem, although no others, was confirmed by Mrs Perhac. The present delusional nature of Mrs Yetter's reasoning concerning the problem was demonstrated at the hearing when Mrs Yetter, in response to questions by the court and counsel, indicated that the operation would interfere with her genital system, affecting her ability to have babies, and would prohibit a movie career. Mrs Yetter is 60 years of age and without children.

Dr Bischoff testified that Mrs Yetter is oriented as to time, place and her personal environment, and that her present delusions are consistent with the diagnosis and evaluation of her mental illness upon admission to the hospital in 1971. The doctor indicated that, in her opinion, at the present time Mrs Yetter is unable, by reasons of her mental illness, to arrive at a considered judgment as to whether to undergo surgery.

Mr Stauffer testified that the aunt referred to by Mrs Yetter, although she underwent a similar operation, died of unrelated causes some 15 years after surgery. He further indicated that he has been apprised by the physicians of the nature of the proposed procedures and their probable consequences as well as the probable consequences if the procedures are not performed. He indicated that if he is appointed guardian of the person for his sister he would consent to the surgical procedures recommended.

At the hearing Mrs Yetter was alert, interested and obviously meticulous about her personal appearance. She stated that she was afraid of surgery, that the best course of action for her would be to leave her body alone, that surgery might hasten the spread of the disease and do further harm, and she reiterated her fears due to the death of her aunt. On several occasions during the hearing she interjected the statements that she would die if surgery were performed. It is clear that mere commitment to a State hospital for treatment of mental illness does not destroy a person's competency or require the appointment of a guardian of the estate or person: *Ryman* (1940) 139 Pa Superior Ct 212. Mental capacity must be examined on a case by case basis.

In our opinion, the constitutional right of privacy included the right of a mature competent adult to refuse to accept medical recommendations that may prolong one's life and which, to a third person at least, appear to be in his best interests; in short, that the right of privacy includes a right to die with which the State should not interfere where there are no minor or unborn children and no clear and present danger to public health, welfare or morals. If the person was competent while being presented with the decision and in making the decision which she did, the court should not interfere even though the decision might be considered unwise, foolish or ridiculous ...

The testimony of the caseworker with respect to her conversations with Mrs Yetter in December 1972, convinces us that at that time her refusal was informed, conscious of the consequences and would not have been superseded by this court. The ordinary person's refusal to accept medical advice based upon fear is commonly known and while the refusal may be irrational and foolish to an outside observer, it cannot be said to be incompetent in order to permit the State to override the decision.

The obvious difficulty in this proceeding is that in recent months Mrs Yetter's steadfast refusal has been accompanied by delusions which create doubt that her decision is the product of competent, reasoned judgment. However, she has been consistent in expressing the fear that she would die if surgery were performed. The delusions do not appear to us to be her primary reason for rejecting surgery. Are we then to force her to submit to medical treatment because some of her present reasons for refusal are delusional and the result of mental illness? Should we now override her original understanding but irrational decision?

There is no indication that Mrs Yetter's condition is critical or that she is in the waning hours of life, although we recognise the advice of medical experts as to the need for early detection and treatment of cancer symptoms. Upon reflection, balancing the risk involved in our refusal to act in favour of compulsory treatment against giving the greatest possible protection to the individual in furtherance of his own desires, we are unwilling now to overrule Mrs Yetter's original irrational but competent decision.

Arguably, as in this case, where the patient's beliefs concern future events, circumspection is called for before concluding that these are delusional. In *Re C (Adult: Refusal of Treatment)* [1994] 1 WLR 290, the English High Court upheld a treatment refusal, based on similarly 'mixed' beliefs, including some that pertained to the future: C was capable of believing he was going to die, but as a matter of fact did not. He believed that the doctors believed that he was going to die; as Thorpe J said, he believed 'in his own way'.

In other words, provided the patient is free of delusion as to the information he has been given about his condition and the proposed treatment, it is not necessary for him to believe in the prognosis, with or without treatment. There is nothing illogical about this, although it might be argued that the prognosis is inescapably bound up with the belief about the medical condition itself. Unless the prognosis is such that the doctor believes that there is a 100% certainty of death (for example, in the case of a refused blood transfusion), it is arguable that the patient may be told that he has, say, only a 5% chance of survival without treatment, but that it is still not unreasonable for him to believe that he will fall into the 5% category.

Weighing treatment information in the balance

Background

As noted, the second main requirement, to have capacity, is that the patient is able to 'weigh' the treatment information. One aspect of this is that the patient must be capable of acting volitionally in the light of the information. There have in fact been a number of cases where, although capable, in intellectual terms, of 'understanding', patients have found incompetent due to an impediment in their will. This may be true, for example, in the case of a person suffering from a compulsive disorder. In *Re W (A Minor) (Medical Treatment)* [1992] 4 All ER 627, the Court of Appeal took the view (without deciding the issue) that a 17 year old girl suffering from anorexia nervosa was probably incompetent. One of the symptoms of the condition is that the patient wants to decide herself when to eat:

Lord Donaldson MR: ... [I]t is a feature of anorexia nervosa that it is capable of destroying the ability to make an informed choice. It creates a compulsion to refuse treatment or only to accept treatment which is likely to be ineffective. This attitude is part and parcel of the disease and the more advanced the illness, the more compelling it may become. Where the wishes of the minor are themselves something which the doctors reasonably consider need to be treated in the minor's own best interests, those wishes clearly have a much reduced significance.

In the case of *B v Croydon Health Authority* [1994] 2 WLR 294, a 24 year old woman with a compulsion to self-harm, had been detained under the MHA 1983. She subsequently suffered serious weight loss after refusing further sustenance. Thorpe J held that she was competent, but authorised her force-feeding under the 1983 Act (see, further, Chapter 9, at p 482ff). On appeal, the Court of Appeal was clearly doubtful as to B's capacity:

> **Hoffmann LJ:** I am bound to say that I have some difficulty with the judge's conclusion [that B had capacity at common law]. Reading the letter which Ms B wrote to the hospital at the end of March 1994 and the transcript of her evidence given before the judge on 23 June 1994, I am as impressed as the judge was by her intelligence and self-awareness. It is however this very self-awareness and acute self-analysis which leads me to doubt whether, at the critical time, she could be said to have made a true choice in refusing to eat. In her letter she said: 'My basic need is to be understood why I feel the need to punish myself and at present this is by not eating.' In evidence she said:
>
> Q. Are you being told that you may die if you are not tube fed? A. ... They told me ... that they were doing that to save my life.
>
> Q. Did you understand what they were telling you? A. I found it difficult to believe because I felt quite well.
>
> Q. Yes. Did you want to die? A. There are times when you feel so despondent that you do not care whether you live or die but I think deep down I don't. I certainly didn't intend to lose weight. I didn't want to allow myself – I've always enjoyed my food so by denying myself something I endured it as a punishment, but it was never meant as a slow suicide attempt or anything like that.
>
> Q. Do you think you are running risks in what you are doing? A. (Pause). I understand now that with severe loss of weight, as the weight just goes less and less, it does put stress on your heart and risk of heart attack. It is not always easy to believe when you are feeling quite fit really.
>
> Q. Looking at the matter today, do you appreciate that you are running some risks in what you are doing? A. Today I understand why they wanted to tube feed me and I understand that my weight – I can accept that my weight was getting out of hand.
>
> Q. Yes. A. I understand that. As much as some days you just wouldn't – you're crying inside for help but you are so stuck in the routine and self-punishment and that, it's almost like a habit you can't break.
>
> Q. Yes. A. and sometimes you just want somebody to come and break it.
>
> Q. Yes; how? A. I don't know how.
>
> I find it hard to accept that someone who acknowledges that in refusing food at the critical time she did not appreciate the extent to which she was hazarding her life, was crying inside for help but unable to break out of the routine of punishing herself, could be said to be capable of making a true choice as to whether or not to eat.

More recently, in *R v Collins and Ashworth Hospital Authority ex p Brady* [2000] Lloyd's Rep Med 355, it was found that Ian Brady's inability to weigh up the treatment information meant that he lacked capacity:

> **Maurice Kay J:** ... [N]otwithstanding the fact that he is a man of well above average intelligence, he has engaged in his battle of wills in such a way that, as a result of his severe personality disorder, he has eschewed the weighing of information and the balancing of the risks and needs to such an extent that ... his decisions on food refusal and force feeding have been incapacitated.

Must there be 'reasons' for the patient's choice?

Generally, as we have seen, even where the consequences of so doing are likely to be very grave, the patient with sufficient understanding may refuse treatment, provided he is capable of balancing the risks of refusal against his other needs. Carrying out this sort of balancing exercise might, on the face of it, require the patient to provide reasons for those needs, and, if necessary, reasons for preferring those needs to taking the recommended medical treatment. However, to recall Lord Donaldson MR's *dictum* in *Re T (Adult: Refusal of Treatment)* [1992] 4 All ER 649, 'the patient's right of choice exists whether the reasons for making that choice are rational, irrational, unknown or even non-existent'. The denial that the patient need have any reasons for his decision in fact stems from remarks by Lord Templeman in *Sidaway v Board of Governors of the Bethlehem Royal Hospital and the Maudsley Hospital* [1985] AC 871, at 904, and it was reiterated by Butler-Sloss LJ in *Re MB (Medical Treatment)* [1997] 2 FLR 426, at 432:

> **Butler-Sloss LJ** (speaking for the Court): A mentally competent patient has an absolute right to refuse to consent to medical treatment for any reason, rational or irrational, or for no reason at all, even where that decision may lead to his or her own death.

The reference to non-existent reasons raises some interesting questions, which we examined in Chapter 1 (see p 37). It will be recalled that when we there discussed 'rational' decision-making, we concluded that if the decision fitted in with the patient's world view, then it should be respected. If this subjective test is adopted, then genuinely held beliefs that fit in with an internally coherent body of thought will not disqualify the patient from decision-making, even if the 'internal coherence' contains a number of bizarre beliefs which can be clearly shown to be unsustainable, for example, Mr C's belief in the *Re C* case that he had once been a successful doctor. Ian Kennedy favours this approach:

> **Kennedy, I, 'Consent to treatment: the capable person', in Dyer, C (ed), *Doctors, Patients and the Law*, 1992, Oxford: Blackwell Science, p 56:**
>
> ... [I]f the beliefs and values of the patient, though incomprehensible to others, are of long standing and have formed the basis for all the patient's decisions about his life, there is a strong argument to suggest that the doctor should respect and give effect to a patient's decision based on them. That is to say that the doctor should regard such a patient as capable of consenting (or refusing). To argue otherwise would effectively be to rob the patient of his right to his own personality which may be far more serious and destructive than anything that could follow from the patient's decision as regards a particular proposed treatment.

In this regard, could it be argued that a purely functional approach to capacity (see p 115, above), as endorsed by the Law Commission and lying behind the aforementioned judicial *dicta*, is deficient in failing properly to address a patient's refusal of treatment in context? The approach may be thought to pay insufficient regard to the patient autonomy understood in a broader sense:

> **Stauch, M, 'Court-authorised Caesareans and the principle of patient autonomy: the *Re MB* case' (1997) 6 Nott LJ 74:**
>
> Whilst autonomy, as it figures in the writings of jurists and philosophers, lacks a single fixed meaning, it broadly amounts to a right of self-determination; the ability to choose one's own life plan and the values that will inform it, and to shape one's destiny, so far as possible, in accordance with those values. Essentially, it appears to be a medium to long term concept and is thus to be contrasted with 'liberty', which is

used here to denote the freedom to act upon impulses of a more transient nature ... [In many cases] ... it can be assumed that long-term survival is part of [a person's] life plan and is what he, in his collected state, would prefer.

Given this understanding of autonomy, it is more apparent why, in the case of refusals of medical treatment with serious consequences for the patient's future, there is often a temptation towards intervention on the part of doctors and courts. This is especially so, given that a person's interests in life and somatic well-being, which treatment aims to preserve, are, in the terminology of Joel Feinberg, 'welfare interests' 'in the sense that, when they are set back, no other interests in a person's interest-network can advance'.

Of course ... there will be situations in which refusals of medical treatment are consonant with autonomy: this is true where treatment, if given, will at best secure the patient a quality of life insufficient for him to continue to pursue the goals and values central to his conception of himself. It may also be so where the nature of the treatment itself would radically infringe those values (an example here is of a Jehovah's Witness who refuses a blood transfusion because receiving blood is inconsistent with a core value governing the lives of members of that faith). On the other hand, the refusal of treatment on a whim cannot be regarded as falling within such a category.

... To say that an irrational choice may be upheld is ambiguous, so far as giving effect to patient autonomy is concerned, for such a choice may or may not be autonomous. What should instead be required is that the choice 'fits' in the general scheme of the patient's life (though there is no need for the scheme itself to be 'rational', whatever that might mean). Clearly, this is a question which cannot be resolved without some inquiry into the patient's reasons for making the choice.

As discussed earlier, the courts are clearly right not to insist that a competent refusal *must* be a rational one (in according with the patient's best interests, objectively considered). For one thing this would rule out refusals based upon religious grounds, which are in practice regarded as among the most respectable reasons for refusing treatment. Indeed, concentration on the rational/irrational raises the image of a neat dichotomy which is misleading (religious reasons, for example, are neither rational nor irrational: they are best described as 'non-rational'). More generally, as we have seen, many of the factors which influence decisions about medical treatment are difficult to categorise as one or the other. Thus, is a patient's fear of the pain involved in a given operation irrational?

In *Re JT (Adult: Refusal of Medical Treatment)* [1998] 1 FLR 48, Wall J found that an adult patient who suffered from mental disability involving learning difficulties and severe behavioural disturbances, such as to have been compulsorily detained under the MHA 1983, had capacity to refuse renal dialysis, without which she would certainly die. He referred to the *Re C* three-stage test, and, upon the evidence, found it to be satisfied. The patient had said that she objected to dialysis and wanted to die. The judge seemed to be particularly impressed with the evidence of the patient's brother who had said that her refusal was 'anything but a flash in the pan' and that, although the family had tried very hard to persuade her to go ahead with the treatment, they now accepted her decision and supported her. However, there is nothing in the case to indicate why she took this view, for example, fear of pain, and arguably, identifying the reason or reasons for refusal of treatment is a good starting point in a decision on capacity. It may well be that in *Re JT* a significant factor was the need for some degree of co-operation on the patient's part in treatment such as dialysis, which is given whilst the patient is conscious, and which takes some time to complete. Clearly, the patient in that case was not going to co-operate, but, of course, that should be irrelevant as far as capacity is concerned.

Notwithstanding the radical rhetoric of decisions such as *Re MB*, it appears that judges will in other cases subject the patient's reasons for refusing treatment to considerable scrutiny. An example is provided by *Ms B v An NHS Trust Hospital* [2002] EWHC Fam 429, where the question related to whether the paralysed patient was competent to refuse life-sustaining ventilation. Dame Elizabeth Butler-Sloss P (interestingly, the same judge as in *Re MB*) carefully chronicled the evidence before her relating it to Ms B's reasons:

Butler-Sloss P: [39] [Ms B] provided two written statements and gave oral evidence for about an hour and a half. She gave a clear account of her wishes and her feelings. She made it clear in her written and oral evidence that she had never changed her view that she wanted the ventilator withdrawn ...

[47] She was asked by Mr Francis QC, for the Hospital, whether it was her wish to die, or not to remain alive in her present condition, she replied:

'The latter. ... Given the range of choices, I would want to recover and have my life back, or significant enough recovery to have a better quality of life. I am not convinced from the evidence that that is going to happen, and I find the idea of living like this intolerable.'

'My view [about rehabilitation] is that it offers me no real opportunity to recover physically, that, in actual fact, it will be more teaching me to live with my disability and to make use of the technologies available and that sort of thing, working with the carers. But, actually, I will not recover in any way. That is not acceptable to me.'

[48] She was asked by Mr Francis whether the independence gained through rehabilitation would be of value to her, and said,

'I think it is an improvement, certainly. Whether it is sufficient for me or not is where we probably disagree. I don't think it is sufficient, but I can see that it offers opportunities for communication. ... I think it does make a difference to quality of life, but I do not think it is sufficient for me to want to pursue it.'

Ms B was found to have capacity to refuse further ventilation.

Consent must be voluntary

The case of *Freeman v Home Office* [1984] 1 All ER 1036 concerned a prisoner who had been injected with certain drugs, apparently for the treatment of a personality disorder. It gave rise to a number of issues: did the prisoner, as a matter of fact, consent to this treatment, and, more interestingly, could it be argued that a prisoner could not give a valid consent to treatment by a prison medical officer where the officer was not acting in his capacity as a doctor but as a disciplinarian. As to the judge's finding of fact in respect of whether consent had been given, the Court of Appeal refused to disturb this. On the wider point of doctor *qua* disciplinarian, Sir John Donaldson MR stated, at 1044:

Sir John Donaldson MR:

Legal inability to consent

Counsel for the plaintiff submitted that such were the pressures of prison life and discipline that a prisoner could not, as a matter of law, give an effective consent to treatment in any circumstances. This is a somewhat surprising proposition since it would mean that, in the absence of statutory authority, no prison medical officer could ever treat a prisoner. The answer of counsel for the plaintiff was in part that outside medical officers could be brought in, but I am not persuaded that this would reduce the pressures, whatever they may be ...

The maxim *volenti non fit injuria* can be roughly translated as 'You cannot claim damages if you have asked for it', and 'it' is something which is and remains a tort. The maxim, where it applies, provides a bar to enforcing a cause of action. It does not negative the cause of action itself. This is a wholly different concept from consent which, in this context, deprives the act of its tortious character. *Volenti* would be a defence in the unlikely scenario of a patient being held not to have in fact consented to treatment, but having by his conduct caused the doctor to believe that he had consented.

The judge expressed his view on this aspect of the argument by saying ([1983] 3 All ER 589, p 597 ...):

> The right approach, in my judgment, is to say that where, in a prison setting, a doctor has the power to influence a prisoner's situation and prospects, a court must be alive to the risk that what may appear, on the face of it, to be a real consent is not in fact so.

I would accept that as a wholly accurate statement of the law. The judge said that he had borne this in mind throughout the case. The sole question is therefore whether, on the evidence, there was a real consent.

Although *Freeman* endorses the need for particular vigilance when a patient may be in a vulnerable situation, on the evidence in this case, the patient was being administered drugs 'because of his obvious hostility and cantankerous behaviour'. The question arises whether this was treatment at all? The patient had been told that the drugs would 'make him feel like a new man', but there is a very clear indication that the drugs would make him a much easier prisoner to deal with. Arguably a rather complacent view of the medical interests of prison inmates was also taken in the case of *Thor v Superior Court* 5 Cal 4th 725 (1993), in which the Supreme Court of California stated:

> There is no reason to believe that the prison environment, with its possible inadequacy of medical and related support services for ill or injured prisoners, inherently jeopardises the voluntariness of a prisoner's decision to forgo life-sustaining treatment. Any individual who suffers a debilitating or life-threatening disease or injury inevitably faces choices in medical decision making affected or even dictated by his life circumstances, and the prison environment (although in some respects unique) is simply one such circumstance in the individual's personal calculus.

Commenting upon the *Thor* case, Ian Kennedy wrote as follows:

Kennedy, I, 'Commentary on *Thor v Superior Court*' (1994) 2 Med L Rev 224:

Medical law as it relates to those in prison is a distinctly murky world. The California Supreme Court could perhaps be excused for not examining in any detail the tensions between the conflicting claims which arise. The impression which is left, however, is one of too great a willingness to defer to the needs of security over the claims of the prisoner, whether to refuse or, just as important, to obtain medical treatment. English law sadly is no less murky. There is, of course, the statement by Lord Keith in the course of his speech in *Bland* [[1993] 1 All ER 821] that concern for the principle of the sanctity of life 'does not authorise forcible feeding of prisoners on hunger strikes'. But the wider questions of the refusal of medical treatment by prisoners, their ability to gain access to treatment and the involuntary treatment of them with, for example, psychotropic drugs are greatly underexamined. One obvious reason is the inability to obtain reliable information. The instant case should serve as a reminder that such an examination is long overdue. [See now, *Health Care of Detainees in Police Stations*, 1994, London: BMA.]

Given these justifiable concerns, should there be additional criteria for a valid consent in such situations? The earlier US case of *Kaimowitz v Michigan Department of Mental Health* 42 USLW 2063 (1973) had suggested a more protective approach to someone in a potentially coercive situation:

Kaimowitz v Michigan Department of Mental Health 42 USLW 2063 (1973)

It is impossible for an involuntarily detained mental patient to be free of ulterior forms of restraint or coercion when his very release from the institution may depend upon his co-operating with the institutional authorities and giving consent to experimental surgery.

... Even Dr Yudashkin, in his testimony, pointed out that involuntarily confined patients tend to tell their doctors what the patient thinks these people want to hear.

... Involuntarily confined mental patients live in an inherently coercive institutional environment. Indirect and subtle psychological coercion has profound effect upon the patient population. Involuntarily confined patients cannot reason as equals with the doctors and administrators over whether they should undergo psychosurgery. They are not able to voluntarily give informed consent because of the inherent inequality in their position.

What of the possibility of coercive behaviour on the part of doctors in the normal setting of patient care (that is, general hospital or GP's surgery)?:

Culver, CM and Gert, B, *Philosophy in Medicine*, 1982, New York: OUP, p 51:

Valid consent requires the absence of any coercion by the doctor or the medical staff. Coercion involves any threat of sufficient force that no rational person would reasonably be expected to resist it ... A threat of this kind means that the person being threatened has been deprived of his freedom and so has an excuse for doing what he has been coerced to do. We do not regard strong recommendations, forcefully given, as coercive. To extend the term 'coercion', so that any pressure by a doctor on a patient to accept the doctor's recommendations would count as coercive, and hence in need of justification, seems to us undesirable. We wish to allow doctors considerable leeway in supporting their views. Patients often have irrational fears that must be overcome, so we do not want to set unrealistic limits. But, given the tremendous authority of doctors and the vulnerable position of patients, no threats of lack of care should be allowed.

Culver and Gert may be right in stating that 'strong recommendations' are not coercive (in the sense of amounting to duress), but given the power imbalance between doctor and patient, and the likelihood of the latter enjoying reduced autonomy due to illness, does the doctor exercise undue influence?

The question of undue influence exercised by a relative, rather than a doctor, was considered in the case of *Re T (Adult: Refusal of Medical Treatment)* [1992] 4 All ER 649:

Re T (Adult: Refusal of Medical Treatment) [1992] 4 All ER 649, CA (Lord Donaldson MR, Butler-Sloss and Staughton LJJ)

The 20-year-old patient, who was pregnant, was admitted to hospital after a road accident. The patient's mother was a devout Jehovah's Witness, although the patient herself was not of the faith. Shortly after being visited by her mother she informed doctors that she did not want a blood transfusion. She asked doctors if there were alternative treatments and was told that there were. Prior to a Caesarean section she signed a form refusing blood transfusions, but was not told that one might be necessary to save her life or prevent serious injury. After the stillbirth of her baby, the patient's condition deteriorated, and the judge at first instance granted a declaration that it would be lawful to administer a blood transfusion:

Lord Donaldson MR:

The vitiating effect of outside influence

A special problem may arise if at the time the decision is made the patient has been subjected to the influence of some third party. This is by no means to say that the patient is not entitled to receive and indeed invite advice and assistance from others in reaching a decision, particularly from members of the family. But the doctors have to consider whether the decision is really that of the patient. It is wholly acceptable that the patient should have been persuaded by others of the merits of such a decision and have decided accordingly. It matters not how strong the persuasion was, so long as it did not overbear the independence of the patient's decision. The real question in each such case is: does the patient really mean what he says or is he merely saying it for a quiet life, to someone else or because the advice and persuasion to which he has been subjected is such that he can no longer think and decide for himself? In other words, is it a decision expressed in form only, not in reality?

When considering the effect of outside influences, two aspects can be of crucial importance. First, the strength of the will of the patient. One who is very tired, in pain or depressed will be much less able to resist having his will overborne than one who is rested, free from pain and cheerful. Second, the relationship of the 'persuader' to the patient may be of crucial importance. The influence of parents on their children or of one spouse on the other can be, but is by no means necessarily, much stronger than would be the case in other relationships. Persuasion based upon religious belief can also be much more compelling and the fact that arguments based upon religious beliefs are being deployed by someone in a very close relationship with the patient will give them added force and should alert the doctors to the possibility – no more – that the patient's capacity or will to decide has been overborne. In other words the patient may not mean what he says.

Lord Donaldson MR acknowledged that awareness of the possibility of undue influence should not preclude genuine consultation by the patient with others, particularly family members. However, given that the doctors will rarely be privy to these consultations, it is hard to see how they could have sufficient evidence of undue influence, unless this was revealed to them by the patient. It is arguable that the decision in this case should have revolved more around the genuineness of the consent in relation to the information given by the doctors to the patient (that is, risk of death, possibility of no alternative treatment and so on) and/or on the possible temporary incapacity of the patient, rather than on the issue of undue influence.

The position in *Re T* can be contrasted with that in *The Centre for Reproductive Medicine v U* [2002] EWCA Civ 565 where the consent of a man who was described as able, intelligent and educated, with a responsible job and in good health could not be said to have been obtained under duress. He and his wife were undergoing treatment for infertility. He had withdrawn his consent to the posthumous use of his sperm and unfortunately died unexpectedly soon afterwards. The allegation was that the clinical practice manager had pressurised him into the withdrawal. On the evidence, she had clearly warned about the implications of posthumous insemination and would have halted the treatment for further consultation and counselling to take place. At first instance, it was found that the husband had succumbed to the pressure placed on him by the manager, but held that something more than pressure had to be shown; the independence of the patient's decision had to be overborne and that had not taken place in this case. The Court of Appeal upheld the decision.

Informing the patient

Earlier we looked at capacity in terms of the patient's ability to process and act upon information relating to his proposed treatment. Clearly, however, this presupposes something to 'bite upon' in terms of the actual data to be processed: in other words, the patient must also have been provided with information about the treatment in question. It is not uncommon to encounter the expression 'informed consent' as a synonym for consent following the provision to the patient of appropriate information. However, this expression has a number of interpretations (depending on differing views as to what is 'appropriate' and in what legal context) and should be approached with caution.

In fact, as regards the validity of consent to medical treatment, the patient need be informed only as to the latter's nature and purpose. As long as he knows this, much of the further detail can be left out: it does not matter, for example, that a treatment risk that the patient was not informed of later materialises. (It is important, however, to keep in mind that we are here considering the validity of the patient's consent so as to negate a subsequent action in battery, and not whether a doctor may have been *negligent* in not giving certain additional information: as to which, see below, at p 136ff).

The distinction between the 'basic' information required for a valid consent – as opposed to the further disclosure of treatment risks (failing which an action may lie in negligence) – was articulated by Bristow J in *Chatterton v Gerson* [1981] QB 432, QBD:

> **Bristow J**: In my judgment, once the patient is informed in broad terms of the nature of the procedure which is intended, and gives her consent, that consent is real, and the cause of the action on which to base a claim for failure to go into risks and implications is negligence, not trespass. Of course, if information is withheld in bad faith, the consent would be vitiated by fraud. Of course, if by some accident, as in a case in the 1940s in the Salford Hundred Court, where a boy was admitted to hospital for tonsillectomy and due to administrative error was circumcised instead, trespass would be the appropriate cause of action against the doctor, though he was as much the victim of the error as the boy. But in my judgment it would be very much against the interests of justice if actions which are really based on a failure by the doctor to perform his duty adequately to inform were pleaded in trespass.

This approach, of limiting 'trespass' or battery to cases where the patient has, in effect, been deliberately misled or told nothing, was initially employed by US courts (see, eg, *Canterbury v Spence* 464 F 2d 772 (1972)) and was endorsed by the House of Lords in *Sidaway v Board of Governors of the Bethlem Royal Hospital and the Maudsley Hospital and Others* [1985] 1 AC 871. In fact, it is now adopted throughout the common law world. In the case of *Reibl v Hughes* (1980) 114 DLR (3d) 1, Laskin CJ in the Supreme Court of Canada commented as follows:

Laskin CJ: I can appreciate the temptation to say that the genuineness of consent to medical treatment depends on proper disclosure of the risks which it entails, but in my view ... a failure to disclose the attendant risks, however serious, should go to negligence rather than to battery. Although such a failure relates to an informed choice of submitting to or refusing recommended and appropriate treatment, it arises as the breach of an anterior duty of due care, comparable in legal obligation to the duty of due care in carrying out the particular treatment to which the patient has consented. It is not a test of the validity of consent.

However, despite its undoubted pedigree, principled reasons for parcelling up the patient's right to information into, on the one hand, that going to the 'nature' of the treatment, and, on the other, that concerning risks, remain elusive. As Laskin CJ acknowledges, a failure to disclose the latter may also seriously impede a patient's autonomous decision-making. Another problem is the vagueness of the criterion of the 'nature' of the treatment, which may be felt to confer too much discretion upon judges. Andrew Grubb discusses this point in the following extract:

Grubb, Andrew (ed), *Principles of Medical Law,* **2nd edn, 2004 Oxford: OUP:**

3.96 What is meant by the 'nature' of the procedure? The *Oxford English Dictionary* defines, *inter alia,* 'nature' as

> [t]he essential qualities or properties of a thing; the inherent and inseparable combination of properties essentially pertaining to anything and giving it its fundamental character.

In relation to what constitutes the 'nature' of a medical procedure, no general answer can be given other than to say it is a relatively narrow notion encompassing by *description* the character of the act(s) to be done by the doctor and, *qualitatively,* the intended effect(s) of the procedure and its purpose. There is no doubt that 'nature' includes an understanding of the purpose or intended effects of the procedure. Indeed, although initially referring only to the 'nature' of the procedure, for clarity it is now commonplace for judges to talk of the 'nature and purpose' of the procedure.

3.97 The information needs to state in 'broad terms' what is to be done to the patient and why. However, this information need not descend into minute, or indeed any, real detail. In practice, judges have considerable leeway in determining what information is relevant to the 'nature and purpose' of a procedure and what is co-lateral to that and, therefore, immaterial to the reality of the patient's consent. For example, it may be enough that the patient knows that a diagnostic procedure of a certain type is to be undertaken, such as a biopsy, and what that involves in terms of contact with the patient and incision. Even if the doctor had been speaking in terms of a particular biopsy such as a muscle biopsy, knowledge of this will be sufficient to amount to a real consent to a bone biopsy carried out at the same time [see *Brushnett v Cowan* [1991] 2 Med LR 271 ...].

In *Davis v Barking, Havering and Brentwood HA* [1993] 4 Med LR 85, the High Court considered the case of a woman who signed a consent form to undergo a general anaesthetic, but, who subsequently received a caudal block (ie an injection of anaesthetising drug into part of the body to interrupt nerve function), and who suffered some damage as a result of this. McCullough J rejected the argument that the failure to obtain consent to this procedure amounted to a battery:

McCullough J: If one is to treat the administration of an injection for analgesic purposes while the patient is generally anaesthetised (eg, the caudal block given to Mrs Davis) as something requiring separate consent, why should separate consent not also be sought for an injection of, for example, morphine to provide analgesia when the patient begins to come round from the general anaesthetic?

... And once this degree of sectionalisation is accepted, how long will it be before the court is invited to say that separate consent should be sought for separate steps in the surgical procedure itself? A sectionalised approach of this kind would encourage – indeed necessitate – what has been called the 'deplorable' prospect of actions being brought in trespass rather than in negligence.

What of, say, carrying out tests on specimens of bodily fluids or tissue which have not been specifically authorised by the patient, although consent to the taking of specimens was given? This is particularly relevant to HIV testing. In April 1994 a number of Harrods' staff had tests carried out on their blood samples without explicit consent (some were also carried out in the face of an express refusal of consent). In the light of this sort of reasoning, would a battery be found to have taken place here? Unfortunately, there has been no judicial consideration of the issue, and expert opinions have differed. The British Medical Association took advice from Michael Sherrard QC and Ian Gatt, who formed the view the explicit consent is necessary, as did Kennedy and Grubb and Gordon Langley QC, whilst Leo Charles QC, advising the Central Committee for Hospital Medical Services, advised that explicit consent was not necessary.

Commenting upon the difference of opinion, with reference to the 'broad nature of the treatment' test in *Chatterton v Gerson*, John Keown states:

Keown, J, 'The ashes of AIDS and the phoenix of informed consent' (1989) 52 MLR 790:

The doctor who tells the patient that a sample of blood is to be taken for 'tests' has surely discharged this duty. The fact that he does not inform the patient that one of the tests is for HIV does not alter the general nature of the procedure as part of a process of therapeutic diagnosis.

The Sherrard opinion's invention of a distinction between 'routine' and 'non-routine' tests, a distinction which apparently turns on the seriousness of the consequences of a positive result suffers not only from vagueness (what is meant by 'seriousness' and does the requirement to inform extend to other tests and treatments?) but is unsupported by authority or argument, as are the opinion's assertions of an implied representation by the doctor that he will only do 'routine' tests without express consent, and that this representation vitiates the uninformed patient's consent. Curiously, the most copious use of authority in the opinion is its lengthy quotation from the *dissenting* opinion of Lord Scarman in *Sidaway*. Whereas it is understandable that a distinction could be made between 'therapeutic' and 'non-therapeutic' testing (an example of the latter being where the sample is taken purely as part of a research programme) such as to render the latter a procedure of a different nature to the former, a distinction between 'routine' and 'non-routine' seems to be insupportable.

No less insupportable, with respect, is Kennedy and Grubb's analogy between the removal of a sample of blood for HIV testing and off-the-ball kicks and punches on the sports field, an analogy which can hardly be described as obvious.

It is one thing to say that a person cannot, as a matter of public policy, consent to the deliberate infliction of bodily harm without good reason (and hence to regard off-the-ball kicks and punches as assaults). It is quite another to extend this reasoning to touchings which involve no infliction, deliberate or otherwise, of bodily harm.

Not only is no relevant authority cited to warrant such an extension, but the supporting argument that consent should be required because of the possible far-reaching implications of the test presumably entails the conclusion that on those, doubtless many, occasions when a doctor takes a sample from a patient to perform a test which may have far-reaching implications (such as for cancer) the doctor is guilty of battery if he does not obtain the patient's specific consent to it.

A second argument advanced by Kennedy and Grubb is that *Chatterton* in fact supports their case. They argue that although the doctor need only inform the patient in broad terms of the nature of the procedure, the 'procedure' is not merely the use of the syringe to obtain a blood sample, but to obtain a blood sample for an HIV test. Merely to have assented to a particular touching will not necessarily amount to consent if there is no comprehension of the quality of the touching. In support of this argument they cite the case of *Flattery* (as explained by Dunn LJ in *Sidaway*) and state that it is clear that a woman who consents to sexual intercourse, knowing it is sexual intercourse but believing it is being done as a surgical operation, has not given a valid consent to the intercourse because she is unaware of the underlying quality of the touching ...

In sum, *Chatterton* merely requires the patient to be informed in broad terms of the nature of the procedure. The doctor who tells his patient that blood is to be removed for testing, even though he does not say that it is to be tested for HIV, has surely satisfied this requirement.

A further difficulty is posed by the situation where a doctor changes his mind about what to do with blood that he has *previously* removed: he could presumably not be liable retrospectively in battery (as there is now no further touching). However, if that is so, then evidentially a battery action would often founder on the doctor's testimony – if accepted – that his decision to do the HIV test postdated the blood's removal.

More generally, an important factor in the courts' eagerness to stress the distinction between battery and negligence is that otherwise a doctor would theoretically be guilty of a criminal offence, as well as a breach of civil law, if he were found to have battered the patient in failing to give sufficient information. Although such a case would be highly unlikely to be prosecuted (as public policy generally militates against imposing criminal liability upon the doctor), a residual stigma carries over to the civil, battery action. An illustration of the judicial unwillingness so to stigmatise a doctor, provided the latter was acting in good faith, may be seen in *Williamson v East London and City HA and Others* [1998] Lloyd's Rep Med 6. Here, the evidence showed that a patient had not been told that her right breast was to be removed (instead she believed that the operation would replace her silicone breast implant, which had ruptured). Nonetheless, any reference in the judgment to the tort of battery is conspicuously absent: instead Butterfield J awarded the claimant £20,000 for the 'negligent failure on the part of the defendants to acquire her consent to the operative procedure'.

However, while rare, there are cases where doctors have been found to have battered their patients. One example is the Canadian case of *Allan v Mount Sinai Hospital* (1980) 109 DLR (3d) 634, in which an anaesthetic injection was given in the patient's left arm, after she had specifically requested that it not be given there. There are also a few English authorities. In *Cull v Royal Surrey County Hospital* (1932) 1 BMJ 1195, there was a battery when a patient had consented to an abortion but received a sterilisation in addition. The same result was reached in *Devi v West Midlands RHA* [1980] CLY 687, where the patient, who consented to a repair to a perforation in her uterus, was sterilised by the surgeon, believing it to be in her best interests. One area where the courts will clearly protect patients is against deliberate deceptions practised upon them by medical professionals acting in bad faith. Thus, in *Appleton v Garrett* [1997] 8 Med LR 75, where a dentist represented falsely to his patients that they needed dental treatment and then carried out unnecessary treatment, the court had no hesitation in finding a battery.

Battery and mistake

What, finally, of the situation where a doctor mistakenly believes the patient has consented? In *Re T (Adult: Refusal of Medical Treatment)* [1992] 4 All ER 649, at 663, Lord Donaldson MR stated that misinformation, whether given innocently or not, may well vitiate a consent or a refusal. It will be recalled also that, in *Chatterton v Gerson*, Bristow J referred to an unreported 1940s case where, due to an administrative error, a boy who was admitted for a tonsilectomy was circumcised, and which he regarded as a clear instance of battery: there, of course, the patient had not been given information so as to be aware of the broad nature of the procedure. On other occasions the mistake may relate to what the patient consented to, or indeed whether he had capacity to consent. On the latter question of mistake as to capacity, Kennedy and Grubb argue that unreasonable mistakes would give rise *prima facie* to a negligence action. On reasonable mistakes they comment as follows:

Kennedy, I and Grubb, A, *Medical Law,* **3rd edn, 2000, London: Butterworths, p 764:**

Deciding which action may be brought is by no means simple: the difficulty lies in whether the mistaken view of the doctor is as to a matter of fact or of opinion ... If it is a mistake of fact, then on first principles an action in battery would lie since mistake is not ordinarily a defence to such an intentional tort (see *John Lewis and Co Ltd v Tims* [1952] AC 676). There are however exceptions where mistake may be a defence. For example, a policeman making an arrest in the mistaken belief, based on reasonable grounds, that a crime has been committed, would at common law, quite apart from statute, be excused.

Since the House of Lords' decision in *Re F (Mental Patient: Sterilisation)* [1990] 2 AC 1, the doctor will have a defence based upon necessity if on the facts the treatment was in the incompetent patient's best interest. Of course, *Re F* would not apply in the converse position where the doctor decides in good faith that a patient is incompetent when this is not so. *Prima facie* the law in these circumstances would consider the doctor to have committed a battery if he treats the patient in the face of a refusal ...

If, by contrast, in law the mistaken view of the doctor as to the patient's understanding is regarded as relating to a matter of *opinion,* assuming the doctor acts in good faith, then the answer may be different ... On grounds of public policy it may be desirable that the law should recognise a legal excuse for the doctor in these circumstances.

It is submitted that there is, in fact, no obvious reason why mistakes (whether they be as to the patient's capacity, the information they have been given, or what they have consented to) should be treated differently in themselves. In each case it is arguable that non-negligent mistakes should not be actionable; negligent mistakes should sound in negligence and grossly negligent mistakes should result in an action in battery. This would also accord with the courts' desire, as exemplified in the use of negligence to address most instances of inadequate information disclosure, to reserve battery for the most egregious cases of faulty conduct by medical staff.

THE DUTY TO DISCLOSE IN NEGLIGENCE

Introduction

As we have just seen, for his consent to be regarded as valid or 'real' (so as to preclude a subsequent action in *battery* against the doctor), the patient need receive only a relatively low amount of information, *viz* as to the 'nature and purpose' of the treatment. However, even where a patient has been told this much, he will in some cases still be entitled to claim in *negligence* against the doctor: in particular, he may allege that the doctor failed, in breach of his duty, to disclose a given risk or side-effect of the treatment. We shall be dealing with medical negligence as a topic in its own right in Chapter 6, but, given the close link between warnings of risks and patient autonomy (does a patient who is ignorant of some serious risk or side-effect of treatment choose autonomously, even if he knows its 'purpose'?), it is useful to deal with the extent of the specific duty on the part of doctors to give such warnings here.

The standard of care in relation to disclosing treatment risks

The doctrine of 'informed consent'

The legal question here is, what standard of care does the law impose upon doctors, at the time of obtaining consent, or at any rate prior to commencing treatment, as regards disclosure of risks, side-effects and alternative treatment options ('risks' will hereafter be used as shorthand for all three)? Such information is, as we have seen, not regarded as essential for consent to be valid; nonetheless, it may clearly be highly significant to a patient when choosing whether or not to have the treatment.

It is in this context that the doctrine of 'informed consent' (in its strict usage: as indicated above, the expression is not always used with sufficient precision) offers one possible answer. The doctrine, which is primarily American, although it has also found widespread acceptance in other parts of the common law world, defines the doctor's duty to disclose risks by reference to the reasonable patient's desire and need to know of them. For this reason the approach is also often termed 'the prudent patient test'. This approach received its classic exposition in the decision of the US Court of Appeals, District of Columbia circuit, in *Canterbury v Spence* 464 F 2d 772 (1972):

Canterbury v Spence **464 F 2d 772 (1972)**

Robinson J: There are, in our view, formidable obstacles to acceptance of the notion that the physician's obligation to disclose is either germinated or limited by medical practice. To begin with, the reality of any discernible custom reflecting a professional consensus on communication of option and risk information to patient is open to serious doubt. We sense the danger that what in fact is no custom at all may be taken as an affirmative custom to maintain silence, and that physician witnesses to the so called custom may state merely their personal opinions as to what they or others would do under given conditions. We cannot gloss over the inconsistency between reliance on a general practice respecting divulgence and, on the other hand, realisation that the myriad of variables among patients makes each case so differing that its omission can rationally justified only by the effect of its individual circumstances. Nor can we ignore the fact that to bind the disclosure obligation to medical usage is to arrogate the decision on revelation to the physician alone. Respect for the patient's right of self-determination on particular therapy demands a standard set by law for physicians rather than one which physicians may or may not impose upon themselves ...

Once the circumstances give rise to a duty on the physician's part to inform his patient, the next inquiry is the scope of the disclosure the physician is legally obliged to make. The courts have frequently confronted this problem but no uniform standard defining the adequacy of the divulgence emerges from the decisions. Some have said 'full' disclosure, a norm we are unwilling to adopt literally. It seems obviously prohibitive and unrealistic to expect physicians to discuss with their patient every risk of proposed treatment – no matter how small or remote – and generally unnecessary from the patient's viewpoint as well. Indeed, the cases speaking in terms of 'full' disclosure appear to envision something less than total disclosure, leaving unanswered the question of just how much.

The larger number of courts, as might be expected, have applied tests framed with reference to prevailing fashion within the medical profession. Some have measured the disclosure by 'good medical practice', others by what a reasonable practitioner would have done under the circumstances, and still others by what medical custom in the community would demand. We have explored this rather considerable body of law but are unprepared to follow it. The duty to disclose, we have reasoned, arises from phenomena apart from medical custom and practice. The latter, we think, should no more establish the scope of the duty than its existence. Any definition of scope in terms purely of a professional standard is at odds with the patient's prerogative to decide on projected therapy himself. That prerogative, we have said, is at the very foundation of the duty to disclose, and both the patient's right to know and the physician's correlative obligation to tell him are diluted to the extent that its compass is dictated by the medical profession.

In our view, the patient's right of self-decision shapes the boundaries of the duty to reveal. That right can be effectively exercised only if the physician's communications to the patient, then, must be measured by the patient's need, and that need is the information material to the decision. Thus the test for determining whether a particular peril must be divulged is its materiality to the patient's decision: all risks potentially affecting the decision must be unmasked. And to safeguard the patient's interest in achieving his own determination on treatment, the law must itself set the standard for adequate disclosure.

However, as the court noted, a difficulty with the prudent patient test is in deciding whether it is objective or subjective:

Robinson J: Of necessity, the content of the disclosure rests in the first instance with the physician. Ordinarily it is only he who is in a position to identify particular dangers; always he must make a judgment, in terms of materiality, as to whether and to what extent revelation to the patient is called for. He cannot know with complete exactitude what the patient would consider important to his decision, but on the basis of his medical training and experience he can sense how the average, reasonable patient expectably would react. Indeed, with knowledge of, or ability to learn his patient's background and current condition, he is in a position superior to that of most others – attorneys, for example – who are called upon to make judgments on pain of liability in damages for unreasonable miscalculation.

From these considerations we derive the breadth of the disclosure of risks legally to be required. The scope of the standard is not subjective as to either the physician or the patient; it remains objective with due regard for the patient's informational needs and with suitable leeway for the physician's situation. In broad outline, we agree that '[a] risk is thus material when a reasonable person in what the physician knows or should know to be the patient's position would be likely to attach significance to the risks or cluster of risks in deciding whether or not to forgo the proposed therapy'.

Does this ultimately imply an objective or a subjective approach in the court's assessment of what the doctor should tell a patient?

Later, in *Rogers v Whitaker* [1993] 4 Med LR 79, the Australian High Court employed an amended definition of 'material risk', whose effect was to create a fully subjective approach. In *Rogers*, the patient was a woman who had been almost completely blind in her right eye after a childhood injury. Nearly 40 years later she was referred to an eye surgeon who said that removal of the scar tissue would considerably improve the appearance of the eye and might also restore some sight. He failed to warn her that, as a result of surgery, there was a risk (one in 14,000) of her developing sympathetic ophthalmia in her left, good eye. Unfortunately, this risk materialised, leaving the patient totally blind in the left eye and with none of the hoped-for improvement in the right eye. In finding the surgeon in breach of his duty to warn, Mason CJ stated:

> **Mason CJ:** A risk is material if, in the circumstances of the particular case, a reasonable person in the patient's position, if warned of the risk, would be likely to attach significance to it *or if the medical practitioner is or should reasonably be aware that the particular patient, if warned of the risk, would be likely to attach significance to it.* [Emphasis added]

The position in England

Until quite recently, one could have asserted confidently that the doctrine of informed consent, just described, formed no part of the English law. Instead, English judges could be seen as espousing a rather different approach to the standard of risk disclosure required by doctors to discharge their duty in negligence. This approach was often termed the 'prudent doctor test' and in some ways could be seen as diametrically opposed to the US 'informed consent'/'prudent patient' test. Its starting point was to link the standard of risk disclosure required of doctors to accepted medical practice: the doctor would not be negligent if his failure to disclose the risk was endorsed by a responsible body of medical opinion: in short, the general *Bolam* test was applied (on which see further Chapter 6).

However, in the light of the newest developments, the position now is far less certain. Indeed, the previous dichotomy between the *Bolam*-based, prudent doctor, and the prudent patient approaches arguably no longer exists. We shall look at these developments shortly.

The Sidaway *case*

In order to place the newer legal developments in context, we need to begin with *Sidaway v Bethlem Royal Hospital* [1985] 1 AC 871, the House of Lords judgment in which, by a 4:1 majority, their Lordships on the face of it rejected 'informed consent' in favour of the *Bolam*-based approach. (It should also be added that, to this day, *Sidaway* has not been expressly doubted by the courts, let alone overruled.)

Sidaway v Board of Governors of the Bethlem Royal Hospital and the Maudsley Hospital and Others [1985] 1 AC 871, HL (Lords Diplock, Bridge, Scarman, Templeman and Keith)

The patient underwent an operation to relieve her recurrent neck pain, which carried an inherent risk (ie even if performed with all reasonable care) of damage to the spinal cord of between 1 and 2%. The patient was not warned of this risk, and when it subsequently materialised and she became severely disabled, she brought an action in negligence. However, the action failed:

> **Lord Diplock**: My Lords, no convincing reason has in my view been advanced before your Lordships that would justify treating the *Bolam* test as doing anything less than laying down a principle of English law that is comprehensive and applicable to every aspect of the duty of care owed by a doctor to his patient in the exercise of his healing functions as respects that patient. What your Lordships have been asked to do – and it is within your power to do so – is to substitute a new and different rule for that part only of the well established *Bolam* test as comprises a doctor's duty to advise and warn the patient of risks of something going wrong in the surgical or other treatment that he is recommending ...
>
> My Lords, I venture to think that in making this separation between that part of the duty of care that he owes to each individual patient, which can be described as a duty to advise upon treatment and warn of its risks, the courts have misconceived their functions as the finders of fact in cases depending upon the negligent exercise of professional skill and judgment. In matters of diagnosis and the carrying out of treatment the court is not tempted to put itself in the surgeon's shoes; it has to rely upon and evaluate expert evidence, remembering that it is no part of its task of evaluation to give effect to any preference it may have for one responsible body of professional opinion over another, provided it is satisfied by the expert evidence that both qualify as responsible bodies of medical opinion ...
>
> [W]e are concerned here with volunteering unsought information about risks of the proposed treatment failing to achieve the result sought or making the patient's physical or mental condition worse rather than better. The only effect that mention of risks can have on the patient's mind, if it has any at all, can be in the direction of deterring the patient from undergoing the treatment which in the expert opinion of the doctor it is in the patient's interest to undergo. To decide what risks the existence of which a patient should be voluntarily warned and the terms in which such warning, if any, should be given, having regard to the effect that the warning may have, is as much an exercise of professional skill and judgment as any other part of the doctor's comprehensive duty of care to the individual patient, and expert medical evidence on this matter should be treated in just the same way. The *Bolam* test should be applied.

In his speech, Lord Bridge also took a stance which tended to defer to clinical judgment:

> **Lord Bridge**: The important question which this appeal raises is whether the law imposes any, and if so what, different criterion as to the measure of the medical man's duty of care to his patient when giving advice with respect to a proposed course of treatment. It is clearly right to recognise that a conscious adult patient of sound mind is entitled to decide for himself whether or not he will submit to a particular course of treatment proposed by the doctor, most significantly surgical treatment under general anaesthesia. This entitlement is the foundation of the doctrine of 'informed consent' which has led in certain American jurisdictions to decisions, and in the Supreme Court of Canada to *dicta*, on which the appellant relies, which would oust the *Bolam* test and substitute an 'objective' test of a doctor's duty to advise the patient of the advantages and disadvantages of undergoing the treatment proposed and more particularly to advise the patient of the risks involved.
>
> There are, it appears to me, at least theoretically, two extreme positions which could be taken. It could be argued that, if the patient's consent is to be fully informed, the

doctor must specifically warn him of *all* risks involved in the treatment offered, unless he has some sound clinical reason not to do so. Logically, this would seem to be the extreme to which a truly objective criterion of the doctor's duty would lead. Yet this position finds no support from any authority, to which we have been referred, in any jurisdiction. It seems to be generally accepted that there is no need to warn of the risks inherent in all surgery under general anaesthesia. This is variously explained on the ground that the patient may be expected to be aware of such risks or that they are relatively remote. If the law is to impose on the medical profession a duty to warn of risk to secure 'informed consent' independently of accepted medical opinion of what is appropriate, neither of these explanations for confining the duty to special as opposed to general surgical risks seems to me wholly convincing.

At the other extreme it could be argued that, once the doctor has decided what treatment is, on balance of advantages and disadvantages, in the patient's best interest, he should not alarm the patient by volunteering a warning of any risk involved, however grave and substantial, unless specifically asked by the patient. I cannot believe that contemporary medical opinion would support this view, which would effectively exclude the patient's right to decide in the very type of case where it is most important that he should be in a position to exercise that right and, perhaps even more significantly, to seek a second opinion as to whether she should submit himself to the significant risk which has been drawn to his attention.

However, importantly, unlike Lord Diplock, Lord Bridge was prepared to acknowledge some situations in which, notwithstanding its compliance with accepted practice, a failure to disclose a particular risk might still be held to be in breach of duty (in other words, although the starting point, the *Bolam* test would not always furnish the doctor with a complete answer to a charge of negligence):

Lord **Bridge**: I am of the opinion that the judge might in certain circumstances come to the conclusion that disclosure of a particular risk was so obviously necessary to an informed choice on the part of the patient that no reasonably prudent medical man would fail to make it. The kind of case I have in mind would be an operation involving a substantial risk of grave adverse consequences, as, for example, the 10% risk of a stroke from the operation which was the subject of the Canadian case of *Reibl v Hughes*, 114 DLR (3d) 1. In such a case, in the absence of some cogent clinical reason why the patient should not be informed, a doctor, recognising and respecting his patient's right of decision, could hardly fail to appreciate the necessity for an appropriate warning.

Lord Keith concurred with Lord Bridge; and Lord Templeman, although his speech makes no express reference to the *Bolam* test at all, appears to have taken a similar view:

Lord **Templeman**: The patient is free to decide whether or not to submit to treatment recommended by the doctor and therefore the doctor impliedly contracts to provide information which is adequate to enable the patient to reach a balanced judgment, subject always to the doctor's own obligation to say and do nothing which the doctor is satisfied will be harmful to the patient. When the doctor himself is considering the possibility of a major operation the doctor is able, with his medical training, with his knowledge of the patient's medical history and with his objective position to make a balanced judgment as to whether the operation should be performed or not ... The duty of the doctor in these circumstances, subject to his overriding duty to have regard to the best interests of the patient, is to provide the patient with information which will enable the patient to make a balanced judgment if the patient chooses to make a balanced judgment.

Elsewhere, Lord Templeman referred rather mysteriously to a distinction between general and special risks:

> **Lord Templeman:** In the case of a general danger the court must decide whether the information afforded to the patient was sufficient to alert the patient to the possibility of serious harm of the kind in fact suffered. If the practice of the medical profession is to make express mention of particular kind of danger, the court will have no difficulty in coming to the conclusion that the doctor ought to have referred expressly to this danger unless the doctor can give reasons to justify the form or absence of warning adopted by him. Where the practice of the medical profession is divided or does not include express mention, it will be for the court to determine whether the harm suffered is an example of a general danger inherent in nature of the operation.

What is the real difference between general and special risks, and is the distinction a useful one? Lord Templeman seems to be saying that they would be treated differently *by the court*, as opposed to the medical profession, and to suggest that *Bolam* only applies to special risks and, even then, will not apply if the medical profession is divided. However, it will be seen in Chapter 6 that if the profession is divided, the usual application of *Bolam* means that the doctor will not have been negligent just because there is a body of medical opinion which differs from the body of opinion to which he belongs.

As we have seen, Lord Diplock denied in *Sidaway* that the giving of information differed from other aspects of the doctor's duty of care to the patient (ie regarding such matters as diagnosis and treatment). However, an arguable distinction is that the decision about what to tell a patient is not really a *medical* one. This was pointed out by Lord Scarman, who (while agreeing that Mrs Sidaway's appeal failed on its facts) delivered a dissenting judgment on this aspect of the law. His speech accorded much more with the US 'prudent patient' approach:

> **Lord Scarman:** My Lords, I think the *Canterbury* propositions reflect a legal truth which too much judicial reliance on medical judgment tends to obscure. In a medical negligence case where the issue is the advice and information given to the patient as to the treatment proposed, the available options, and the risk, the court is concerned primarily with a patient's right. The doctor's duty arises from his patient's rights. If one considers the scope of the doctor's duty by beginning with the right of the patient to make his own decision whether he will or will not undergo the treatment proposed, the right to be informed of significant risk and the doctor's corresponding duty are easy to understand: for the proper implementation of the right requires that the doctor be under a duty to inform his patient of the material risks inherent in the treatment ...
>
> Ideally, the court should ask itself whether in the particular circumstances the risk was such that this particular patient would think it significant if he was told it existed. I would think that, as a matter of ethics, this is the test of the doctor's duty. The law, however, operates not in Utopia but in the world as it is: and such an inquiry would prove in practice to be frustrated by the subjectivity of its aim and purpose. The law can, however, do the next best thing, and require the court to answer the question, what would a reasonably prudent patient think significant if in the situation of this patient? ...

As we have seen, the *Canterbury v Spence* approach, favoured by Lord Scarman, very much equates the need for information and the right to decide upon its materiality, with the patient's right of self-determination. Subsequently, similar arguments to those of Lord Scarman were endorsed by the High Court of Australia in *Rogers v Whitaker* [1993] 4 Med LR 79:

> **Mason CJ**: One consequence of the application of the *Bolam* principle to cases involving the provision of advice or information is that, even if a patient asks a direct question about the possible risks or complications, the making of that inquiry would logically be of little or no significance; medical opinion determines whether the risk should or should not be disclosed and the express desire of a particular patient for information or advice does not alter that opinion or the legal significance of that opinion ...
>
> There is a fundamental difference between, on the one hand, diagnosis and treatment and, on the other hand, the provision of advice or information to the patient. In diagnosis and treatment, the patient's contribution is limited to the narration of symptoms and relevant history; the medical practitioner provides diagnosis and treatment according to his or her level of skill. However, except in cases of emergency or necessity, all medical treatment is preceded by the patients choice to undergo it. In legal terms, the patient's consent to the treatment may be valid once he or she is informed in broad terms of the nature of the procedure which is intended. But the choice is, in reality, meaningless unless it is made on the basis of relevant information and advice. Because the choice to be made calls for a decision by the patient on information known to the medical practitioner but not to the patient, it would be illogical to hold that the amount of information to be provided by the medical practitioner can be determined from the perspective of the practitioner alone or, for that matter, of the medical profession.

Developments post-Sidaway

The Court of Appeal, in *Gold v Haringey HA* [1988] 1 QB 481, followed the *Bolam* approach to disclosure of risks, relying upon the unequivocal judgment of Lord Diplock in *Sidaway*. In the case the court had to consider whether there was any difference between information given in the context of non-therapeutic treatment. The 'non-therapeutic' treatment here was a sterilisation carried out for contraceptive purposes, and the allegation was a negligent failure to warn the claimant of the risk of failure of the operation, and of the respective failure rate of vasectomy operations. Lloyd LJ endorsed the application of the *Bolam* test:

> **Lloyd LJ**: In the first place the line between therapeutic and non-therapeutic medicine is elusive. A plastic surgeon carrying out a skin graft is presumably engaged in therapeutic surgery; but what if he is carrying out a face-lift, or some other cosmetic operation?
>
> In the second place, a distinction between advice given in a therapeutic context and advice given in a non-therapeutic context would be a departure from the principle on which the *Bolam* test is itself grounded. The principle does not depend on the context in which any act is performed, or any advice given. It depends on a man professing skill or competence in a field beyond that possessed by the man on the Clapham omnibus. If the giving of contraceptive advice required no special skill, then I could see an argument that the *Bolam* test should not apply. But that was not, and could not have been, suggested. The fact (if it be the fact) that giving contraceptive advice involves a different sort of skill and competence from carrying out a surgical operation does not mean that the *Bolam* test ceases to be applicable. It is clear from Lord Diplock's speech in *Sidaway* that a doctor's duty of care in relation to diagnosis, treatment and advice, whether the doctor be a specialist or general practitioner, is not to be dissected into its component parts. To dissect a doctor's advice into that given in a therapeutic context and that given in a contraceptive context would be to go against the whole thrust of the decision of the majority of the House of Lords in that case. So I

would reject Mr Lewis's argument under this head, and hold that judge was not free, as he thought, to form his own view of what warning and information ought to have been given, irrespective of any body of responsible medical opinion to the contrary.

In another decision, *Blyth v Bloomsbury HA* [1993] 4 Med LR 151, the Court of Appeal also applied the *Bolam* test to the issue of the doctor's duty to answer questions put by the patient. The case concerned a patient (a qualified nurse) who was given an injection of the contraceptive Depo-Provera following her pregnancy. She alleged it had caused numerous side effects and maintained that she would not have had the drug if she had known of these. The trial judge had accepted that some of the side effects had been caused by the drug, and that the health authority were negligent in failing to answer inquiries made by her. However, this was reversed upon appeal:

> **Kerr LJ**: In the particulars of negligence the plaintiff included an allegation that the defendants were negligent by '(iv) failing to answer the plaintiff's inquiries concerning Depo-Provera accurately and of failing to obtain answers to her questions before attempting to give her the said assurances about the said drug' ...
>
> The question of what a plaintiff should be told in answer to a general inquiry cannot be divorced from the *Bolam* test, any more than when no such inquiry is made. In both cases the answer must depend upon the circumstances, the nature of the inquiry, the nature of the information which is available, its reliability, relevance, the condition of the patient, and so forth. Any medical evidence directed to what would be the proper answer in the light of responsible medical opinion and practice – that is to say, the *Bolam* test – must in my view equally be placed in the balance in cases where the patient makes some inquiry, in order to decide whether the response was negligent or not.

Neill LJ gave a short judgment supporting this view and Balcombe LJ agreed with both of them. This is a surprising decision given that, in *Sidaway*, Lord Bridge unequivocally posited a duty to answer questions, quite independent of the *Bolam* test. His Lordship had commented, at 898:

> **Lord Bridge**: I should perhaps add at this point, although the issue does not strictly arise in this appeal, that, when questioned specifically by a patient of apparently sound mind about risks involved in a particular treatment proposed, the doctor's duty must, in my opinion, be to answer both truthfully and as fully as the questioner requires.

In fact even Lord Diplock, the hard-liner in *Sidaway* when it came to *Bolam*, had made the confident assertion that a doctor would tell an inquiring patient 'whatever it was the patient wanted to know'.

However, as alluded to earlier, there have since been developments in the law, which has moved away from a strict *Bolam* approach. In particular, the courts have shown themselves more willing to impugn failures by doctors to disclose risk even where there is an accepted practice not to do so (see, for example, the judgment of Morland J in *Smith v Tunbridge Wells HA* [1994] 5 Med LR 334). This more pro-patient approach was endorsed by the Court of Appeal in *Pearce v United Bristol Healthcare NHS Trust* [1999] PIQR P53:

Pearce v United Bristol Healthcare NHS Trust [1999] PIQR P53, CA (Lord Woolf MR, Roch and Mummery LJJ)

The claimant claimed damages as a result of the stillbirth of her child. The birth was overdue, but the consultant obstetrician advised against inducement or a Caesarean.

In giving this advice, he did not warn the claimant of the increased risk of stillbirth as a result of non-intervention (of 0.1 to 0.2%). The Court of Appeal upheld the decision of the trial judge to dismiss her claim. The Court held that *Bolam* was the correct starting point, but Lord Woolf MR, giving the judgment of the court went on to say:

> **Lord Woolf MR**: [21] In a case where it is being alleged that a plaintiff has been deprived of the opportunity to make a proper decision as to what course he or she should take in relation to treatment, it seems to me to be the law ... that if there is a significant risk which would affect the judgment of a reasonable patient, then in the normal course it is the responsibility of a doctor to inform the patient of that significant risk, if the information is needed so that the patient can determine for him or herself as to what course he or she should adopt.
>
> [22] In the *Sidaway* case Lord Bridge recognises that position. He refers to a 'significant risk' as being a risk of something in the region of 10%. When one refers to a 'significant risk' it is not possible to talk in precise percentages, but I note, and it may be purely coincidental, that one of the expert doctors who gave evidence before the judge gave the following answer in evidence. I refer to the evidence of Mr Pearson:
>
> > A. If she hadn't asked I wouldn't have mentioned the subject as she was already distressed and the risk is excessively small. I generally practise according to the belief that it is not the doctor's duty to warn of very small risks. If the risk, however, was of the order, of 10 per cent, for instance, then of course it would be my duty to warn against such a level of risk.
>
> ... [24] Turning to the facts of this case, the next question is, therefore, 'Was there a significant risk? To what extent was the risk of Jacqueline being a stillborn child increased by delay?' Miss Edwards, on behalf of the respondent, has referred us to the relevant passages in the transcript. They show that, on any basis, the increased risk of the still birth of Jacqueline, as a result of additional delay, was very small indeed. The statistical material which was available can be broken down into different classes. Even looked at comprehensively it comes to something like 0.1 to 0.2 per cent. The doctors called on behalf of the defendants did not regard that risk as significant, nor do I.

These remarks are somewhat ambiguous. Thus, on one view, *Pearce* could be seen as simply reiterating the approach of Lord Bridge in *Sidaway* (which, despite a good claim to being the majority approach, had subsequently been lost sight of by the Court of Appeal in the *Gold* and *Blyth* cases). This is so if Lord Woolf MR's 'a significant risk' is read as equivalent to Lord Bridge's category of 'a substantial risk of grave adverse consequences', which should always be disclosed to the patient. On the other hand, what is new is the Master of the Rolls' reference to the patient's perspective as well ('a significant risk *which would affect the judgment of a reasonable patient*'), which has echoes of the 'informed consent' doctrine. The ambiguity in the judgment stems from the uncertainty as to how far the risk's effect upon the judgment of a reasonable patient is *part* of what makes it significant.

Lord Woolf's judgment in the *Pearce* case was cited with approval by the Lord Steyn in House of Lords in its important recent decision in *Chester v Afshar* [2004] UKHL 41. The latter case did not directly concern the standard of risk disclosure required of doctors (as the defendant's breach of duty in this regard had already been conceded). Rather, as we shall see at p 152ff below, it dealt with problems of causation that may arise in this context. Nonetheless, the *obiter* remarks of the Law

Lords in relation to the disclosure of treatment risks are naturally of high persuasive value:

Stauch, M, 'Causation and confusion in respect of medical non-disclosure: *Chester v Afshar'* **(2005) 14 Nott LJ 66:**

In *Chester*, the House of Lords –without expressly doubting *Sidaway-* acknowledged that in the intervening years the law in England ... has moved towards recognising the patient's right to know of significant risks to the treatment the doctor is proposing. In his speech, Lord Steyn [at para 14] specifically embraced the language of 'informed consent', noting that, '[t]he court is the final arbiter of what constitutes informed consent. Usually, informed consent will presuppose a general warning by the surgeon of a significant risk of the surgery'. His Lordship approved Lord Woolf MR's dictum in *Pearce v United Bristol Healthcare NHS Trust*, that '... if there is a significant risk which would affect the judgment of a reasonable patient, then in the normal course it is the responsibility of a doctor to inform the patient of that significant risk'.

For his part, Lord Hope, who was the only other member of the House to address the issue in detail, was more cautious, and preferred to see in the *Sidaway* decision itself an approach aleady sufficiently protective of patient autonomy. As he noted [at para 54]:

> Lord Templeman said [in *Sidaway*] that he did not subscribe to the theory that the patient is entitled to know everything. Some information might confuse and other information might alarm the patient. So it was for the doctor to decide in the light of his training and experience what needed to be said, and how it should be said. But he went on to add these words ...: 'At the same time the doctor is not entitled to make the final decision with regard to treatment which may have disadvantages or dangers. Where the patient's health and future are at stake, the patient must make the final decision.'

Lord Hope went on to suggest [at para 55] that, 'the right to make the final decision and the duty of the doctor to inform the patient if the treatment may have special disadvantages or dangers go hand in hand'.

Significantly, as the House of Lords recognised, nowadays good practice guidelines promulgated by doctors' own professional organisations make clear the rights of patients to be informed of significant treatment risks. In the light of this, it could be argued that the dichotomy previously identified, between the *Sidaway* 'prudent doctor' and US-style 'informed consent' approaches, has disappeared. This is because, on the logic of the *Bolam* test itself, if responsible accepted practice generally is to disclose risks that a reasonable patient would wish to know about, the failure of a particular doctor to do so in a given case will be a straightforward breach of duty.

In other words, the effect of the doctors' own professional guidance, which now increasingly recognises the patient's right to be told of treatment risks, is that 'informed consent' in the US sense (or something close to it) has been transformed via the *Bolam* test into a legal requirement: the doctor who failed to respect the patient's informational needs would not be acting in accordance with accepted medical practice, and would thus be in breach of duty.

The latest Department of Health guidance to health professionals which accompanies the NHS consent form states:

> The courts have stated that patients should be told about 'significant risks which would affect the judgement of a reasonable patient'. 'Significant' has not been legally

defined, but the GMC requires doctors to tell patients about 'serious or frequently occurring' risks. In addition if patients make clear they have particular concerns about certain kinds of risk, you should make sure they are informed about these risks, even if they are very small or rare. You should always answer questions honestly.

As the DoH notes in its *Reference Guide to Consent* (March 2001), the General Medical Council has gone further. In the latter's guidance, *Seeking Consent: the Ethical Considerations* (November 1998), doctors are enjoined to 'find out about the patient's individual needs and priorities when providing information about treatment options'.

Therapeutic privilege

The issue of therapeutic privilege was considered in *Canterbury v Spence* 464 F 2d 772 (1972), where it was stated that where the patient is likely to become so distraught by medical information that he is incapable of making a rational decision, information may be withheld on the grounds of the doctor's privilege.

In the days when the English courts held to the 'prudent doctor' approach, this issue could be regarded as part of the doctor's general discretion not to disclose risks where this accorded with his clinical instincts. However, now that the informational needs of the reasonable patient increasingly provide the yardstick, recourse to 'therapeutic privilege' to justify non-disclosure in specific instances may become more common. In his minority speech in *Sidaway*, Lord Scarman addressed the scope of this 'defence' and stressed that the burden of proof is on the doctor: '... there is the need that the doctor should have the opportunity of proving that he reasonably believed that disclosure of the risk would be damaging to his patient or contrary to his best interests.'

In *Pearce v United Bristol Healthcare NHS Trust* [1999] PIQR P53, Lord Woolf MR can be seen as endorsing the existence of such a privilege in the following passage:

> **Lord Woolf MR:** [23] Obviously the doctor, in determining what to tell a patient, has to take into account all the relevant considerations, which include the ability of the patient to comprehend what he has to say to him or her and the state of the patient at the particular time, both from the physical point of view and an emotional point of view. There can often be situations where a course different from the normal has to be employed.

Similarly, in *Chester v Afshar* [2004] UKHL 41, Lord Steyn remarked:

> **Lord Steyn:** [16] A surgeon owes a legal duty to a patient to warn him or her in general terms of possible serious risks involved in the procedure. The only qualification is that there may be wholly exceptional cases where objectively in the best interests of the patient the surgeon may be excused from giving a warning.

Would it be preferable to remove all question of 'best interests' and limit therapeutic privilege to the avoidance of positive damage to the patient? Otherwise there is perhaps a danger that doctors might rely on the defence generally to avoid telling patients of risks to treatment they feel is in the patient's interests to have. Moreover, such positive damage should arguably be of such a magnitude as would render the patient incapable of making a decision. In other words, therapeutic privilege would be inextricably linked to capacity.

Disclosure of 'success rates'

What about the need for more general matters to be disclosed? For example, should a doctor tell a patient that he has never performed this operation before? It may be thought that the training of surgeons is such, that they will always have assisted and observed before carrying out a surgical procedure, and therefore, they will always have 'done' the operation in various ways before taking responsibility for it. However, this will not be the case when new procedures and techniques are developed, for example, keyhole surgery. What sort of disclosure should be made then? It is likely that many patients would be very interested to know that their surgeons had never done this before, particularly if there was alternative treatment (that is, conventional surgery), but what would a responsible body of medical opinion decide? This point is considered further in Chapter 6 in relation to innovative treatment.

It is also a moot point as to whether there is any obligation to disclose matters such as success or, crucially, failure rates for the type of treatment proposed. This is particularly pertinent in the light of the GMC proceedings against three doctors at the United Bristol Healthcare Trust (see *GMC v Wisheart and others* (Decision of the GMC's PCC, 18 June 1998). The doctors were found to be in breach of professional standards in continuing to carry out heart operations on babies in the knowledge that the death rates of the children they were treating were well above the average for such operations.

The subsequent inquiry into the events chaired by Professor Ian Kennedy, *Learning from Bristol: The Report of the Public Inquiry into Children's Heart Surgery at the Bristol Royal Infirmary 1984–1995* (Command Paper: Cm 5207), recommended, *inter alia*, that:

> 102 Patients are always entitled to know the extent to which a procedure which they are about to undergo is innovative or experimental. They are also entitled to be informed about the experience of the clinician who is to carry out the procedure'.

The second part of this may be thought controversial, in that it could lead to patients refusing care from less experienced clinicians (preventing them from gaining experience, and posing logistical problems for the hospital). Also problematic is the Inquiry's recommendation (no 155), that 'patients and the public must be able to obtain information as to the relative performance of the trust and the services and consultant units within the trust'. It is true that many patients would probably regard such knowledge as of considerable interest and value. However, leaving aside arguments over the interpretation of statistics, the information could potentially be highly sensitive politically (in terms of highlighting geographical inequalities). It might, although perhaps this is fanciful, even raise the prospect of patients refusing to be treated in certain hospitals altogether.

Battery, negligence and capacity

An interesting problem arises, lastly, as to the amount of information to be disclosed to patients of impaired or partial capacity. Does the test of capacity differ in deciding whether the patient is capable of consenting (thereby avoiding an action in battery), from the test in relation to the amount of information that should be given to avoid an action in negligence? If so, might a doctor find that he must accept the consent of a patient of only limited understanding, only to find that he will almost certainly be negligent in not having warned of risks which he thinks the patient would not understand? Or would the *Bolam* test here let him off the hook? Further, would the prudent patient test also let him off the hook because the patient would not wish for further information, or because therapeutic privilege would be used to justify the lack of information given?

Causation

General principles

An important consequence of the fact that the law deals with the failure to disclose treatment risks in negligence is that, to succeed in a claim, the patient, besides showing that a given non-disclosure was a breach of duty, must go on to prove causation of damage. (By contrast, causation does not have to be proven in cases of battery, because trespass to the person is actionable *per se* – ie without the need for damage: see *Chatterton v Gerson* [1981] QB 432, *per* Bristow J at 442.)

As we shall see, when we discuss causation in Chapter 6, the first aspect of this – the so called *factual causation* element – requires that, if the defendant had behaved properly (ie not been in breach), the claimant would not have suffered the injury: this is known as the 'but for test'. In the particular context we are addressing here, ie a breach by a doctor of the duty to warn the patient of risks, the latter must establish that, if he had been properly warned, he would not have gone ahead and had the (injurious) treatment. Generally, this will require the court to determine the truth of assertions by the patient in relation to his own hypothetical conduct.

The question of how far it will be guided here by what an objective 'reasonable patient' would have chosen to do in similar circumstances was addressed in *Smith v Barking, Havering and Brentwood HA* [1994] 5 Med LR 285:

Smith v Barking, Havering and Brentwood HA [1994] 5 Med LR 285, QB (Hutchison J)

The plaintiff was a young woman with a serious spinal condition. Without surgery straightaway she would inevitably develop tetraplegia within a matter of months. However, the surgeon who treated her failed to warn her of the 25% risk of immediate tetraplegia attendant on the operation, which unfortunately materialised:

> Hutchison J: There was some discussion as to whether the issue of causation should be approached on what was called the objective or the subjective basis – ie, was the question to be resolved by deciding what a reasonable person in the plaintiff's position would have chosen to do, or by deciding what the plaintiff herself would have chosen to do. In support of the former approach I was referred to the Canadian authority of *Reibl v Robert A Hughes* [1980] 2 SCR 880 and in support of the latter to the decision of Hirst J in *Hills v Potter* [1984] 1 WLR 641. Both counsel invited me to accept that in the end the matter must be one for decision on a subjective basis. This must plainly as a matter of principle be right, because the question must be: 'If this plaintiff had been given the advice that she should have been given, would she have decided to undergo the operation or not?'
>
> However, there is a peculiar difficulty involved in this sort of case – not least for the plaintiff herself – in giving, after the adverse outcome of the operation is known, reliable answers as to what she would have decided before the operation had she

been given proper advice as to the risks inherent in it. Accordingly, it would, in my judgment, be right in the ordinary case to give particular weight to the objective assessment. If everything points to the fact that a reasonable plaintiff, properly informed, would have assented to the operation, the assertion from the witness box, made after the adverse outcome is known, in a wholly artificial situation and in the knowledge that the outcome of the case depends upon that assertion being maintained, does not carry great weight unless there are extraneous or additional factors to substantiate it. By extraneous or additional factors I mean, and I am not doing more than giving examples, religious or some other firmly held convictions; particular social or domestic considerations justifying a decision not in accordance with what, objectively, seems the right one; assertions in the immediate aftermath of the operation made in a context other than that of a possible claim for damages; in other words, some particular factor which suggests that the plaintiff had grounds for not doing what a reasonable person in her situation might be expected to have done. Of course, the less confidently the judge reaches the conclusion as to what objectively the reasonable patient might be expected to have decided, the more readily will he be persuaded by her subjective evidence.

I should make it clear that nothing I have said is intended to reflect adversely on the plaintiff or to suggest that I have any doubts as to her honesty; but, as I listened to her grappling with the different hypothetical questions which were put to her, I felt the greatest sympathy for her and reflected that one would need almost to be a saint to answer such questions objectively – ie without allowing one's reaction to be influenced by the knowledge of what had, in fact, happened and appreciation of the vital significance of the question. Hence the importance of giving proper weight to an objective assessment of what a reasonable patient could be expected to decide in the light of such proper advice as should have been given.

This subjective approach (looking to what the *particular* patient would have done), which, nevertheless, takes account of objective 'reasonableness' for evidential purposes was approved in *Chester v Afshar* at the Court of Appeal stage: see [2002] 3 All ER 552, at para 25. It was also accepted as the correct approach by the Australian High Court in *Rosenberg v Percival* (2001) 75 ALJR 734.

In the latter case, the patient underwent a form of oral surgery, known as an osteotomy, as a result of which she suffered complications which included a chronic disabling pain in the jaw. It was accepted that she was not warned about this (inherent) risk, but there was some controversy about the likelihood of the risk materialising, and also the likelihood of the severity of the problems. In 1993, when the surgery took place, a reasonable practitioner could only be expected to give a warning that jaw problems could occur, the likelihood was about 10%, and the likely symptoms were temporary and non-serious. The trial judge's decision to dismiss the claim was based on both the medical evidence which he preferred and the fact that he did not believe the patient when she said that she would not have gone ahead with the surgery if she had known about the risk. The High Court upheld the judge's decision, but also took the opportunity to confirm that the correct test as far as disclosure of information is concerned, is the subjective one, albeit that, when faced with deciding what this particular patient needed to know, what a reasonable person would or would not have wanted in the patient's circumstances will be an important factor in determining whether the court will accept or reject the patient's evidence (*per* McHugh J).

The subjective approach may, however, be contrasted with the US and Canadian approach, which is to focus simply on how an objective reasonable patient would have behaved: see, eg, the Canadian Supreme Court's decision in *Arndt v Smith* [1997] 2 SCR 539. The latter approach, whose effect is that a patient may lose even if able to prove that he, individually, would have refused the treatment, is hard to justify.

The problem of legal *causation*

As noted previously, to establish factual causation the patient must show that, had he known of the risk, he would have declined the course of treatment. However, should this fact also be *sufficient* to justify the recovery of damages? What of a case where the patient can show they would have initially refused treatment, and hence would have avoided the (random) risk of the injury that occurred, but would ultimately have required that treatment (and, hence, been exposed to the self-same risk) in the future? Such a case creates a problem in terms of so called *legal* causation.

The Australian High Court was confronted with this problem in *Chappel v Hart* (1998) 72 ALJR 1344, in which the respondent, Mrs Hart, suffered damage to her vocal cord in the course of throat surgery – a risk that the appellant, in breach of duty, had failed to disclose. The respondent accepted that, had she been warned, she would still have had the surgery, but at a later date:

Stauch, M, 'Taking the consequences for failure to warn of medical risks: *Chappel v Hart*' (2000) 63 MLR 261:

To understand the peculiar difficulties that the facts of the case presented for the Court, one should begin with the generally accepted proposition that, in order for legal causation to be satisfied, and thus to be liable for the damage suffered by the plaintiff, the defendant's conduct must have created or added to the risk of the type of damage that subsequently occurred. In contrast, as McHugh J forcefully expressed the matter:

If ... the defendant's conduct does not increase the risk of injury to the plaintiff, the defendant cannot be said to have materially contributed to the injury suffered by the plaintiff ... [I]f the act or omission of the defendant has done no more than expose the plaintiff to a class of risk to which the plaintiff would have been exposed irrespective of the defendant's act or omission, the law of torts should not require the defendant to pay damages.

Both McHugh and Hayne JJ were of the view that Mrs Hart's case was one in which, even if Dr Chappel had warned her, 'the risk of her suffering the consequences that in fact befell her would, for all practical purposes have been the same'. Instead, Dr Chappel had simply altered the time and place at which Mrs Hart was exposed to the risk of the injury occurring. In Hayne J's words:

Of course, the respondent did suffer a perforated oesophagus, she did suffer an infection, she did suffer paralysis of the laryngeal nerve. But if she had not attended the hospital on that day, the probabilities are that none of this would have happened. And if the appellant had told her of the risk to her voice, she would not have had the operation when she did. But precisely the same argument would be open if, instead of suffering damage to her voice, as she has, the operating theatre in which her procedure was performed had been struck by lightning, or a runaway truck, and she had been injured. But for the negligent failure to warn she would not have been in harm's way.

However, a majority of the High Court found Dr Chappel liable. Broadly, and without resolving the conceptual problem posed by the minority, it appears to have felt that, since Mrs Hart's injury would almost certainly not otherwise have occurred (ie *factual* causation was clearly present), such injury should as a matter of 'common sense' also be attributed to Dr Chappel's failure as a matter of *legal* causation.

Recently, in *Chester v Afshar* [2004] UKHL 41, the House of Lords was required to address exactly the same problem as had vexed the Australian High Court:

Chester v Afshar [2004] UKHL 41, HL (Lords Bingham, Steyn, Hoffmann, Hope and Walker)

Miss Chester had suffered from progressively worsening back pain for a number of years, and was referred to Mr Afshar, a distinguished consultant neurosurgeon. Although she was apprehensive about operations in general, at consultation the defendant swiftly persuaded her as to the merits of surgery, which he carried out a few days later. Unfortunately, despite being performed with due care, a risk of such surgery, 'cauda equina syndrome' (assessed at around 1–2%), materialised, leaving Miss Chester with serious disabilities. The trial judge (Robert Taylor J) found that the defendant had failed to disclose this risk, and that this constituted a breach of duty.

As to causation, the judge found that Miss Chester, if warned, would not have undergone the operation when she did (as she would have wished to seek further medical opinions as to the need for the surgery), albeit she may well have submitted to it in the future. He noted that, 'had she been adequately warned, the operation in question would not have taken place and she would not have suffered damage. In these circumstances, and without more, it seems to me that the necessary causal link is sufficiently established. I do not see how the fact that the claimant cannot prove that at no future time would she have undergone such an operation can break the causal link thus established'.

The judge accordingly found in favour of Miss Chester, and this was upheld by the Court of Appeal. The defendant appealed to the House of Lords:

> **Lord Steyn:** [13] Counsel for the surgeon submitted that it is contrary to general principles of tort law to award damages when a defendant's wrong has not been proved to have increased the claimant's exposure to risk. He argued that in order to establish causation in a case of a surgeon's failure to warn a patient of a significant risk of injury, the patient must prove both that she would not have consented to run the relevant risk then and there, and that she would not, ultimately, have consented to run the relevant risk. The only qualification was the case where a claimant could prove an accelerated onset of injury. That the claimant could not do on the facts of the case. On analysis it was an all or nothing case. Counsel said that the injury that the claimant sustained was just a coincidence, a piece of abominable bad luck, like lightning striking a person. This was a powerful argument and persuasively presented.
>
> ... [18] [I]n the context of attributing legal responsibility, it is necessary to identify precisely the protected legal interests at stake. A rule requiring a doctor to abstain from performing an operation without the informed consent of a patient serves two purposes. It tends to avoid the occurrence of the particular physical injury the risk of which a patient is not prepared to accept ...
>
> [19] [I]t is a distinctive feature of the present case that but for the surgeon's negligent failure to warn the claimant of the small risk of serious injury the actual injury would not have occurred when it did and the chance of it occurring on a subsequent

occasion was very small. It could therefore be said that the breach of the surgeon resulted in the very injury about which the claimant was entitled to be warned.

Lord Hope agreed:

Lord Hope: [86] I start with the proposition that the law which imposed the duty to warn on the doctor has at its heart the right of the patient to make an informed choice as to whether, and if so when and by whom, to be operated on. Patients may have, and are entitled to have, different views about these matters. All sorts of factors may be at work here – the patient's hopes and fears and personal circumstances, the nature of the condition that has to be treated and, above all, the patient's own views about whether the risk is worth running for the benefits that may come if the operation is carried out. For some the choice may be easy – simply to agree to or to decline the operation. But for many the choice will be a difficult one, requiring time to think, to take advice and to weigh up the alternatives. The duty is owed as much to the patient who, if warned, would find the decision difficult as to the patient who would find it simple and could give a clear answer to the doctor one way or the other immediately.

[87] To leave the patient who would find the decision difficult without a remedy, as the normal approach to causation would indicate, would render the duty useless in the cases where it may be needed most. This would discriminate against those who cannot honestly say that they would have declined the operation once and for all if they had been warned. I would find that result unacceptable. The function of the law is to enable rights to be vindicated and to provide remedies when duties have been breached. Unless this is done the duty is a hollow one, stripped of all practical force and devoid of all content. It will have lost its ability to protect the patient and thus to fulfil the only purpose which brought it into existence. On policy grounds therefore I would hold that the test of causation is satisfied in this case. The injury was intimately involved with the duty to warn.

Lord Walker agreed with Lords Steyn and Hope in dismissing Mr Afshar's appeal. However, Lords Bingham and Hoffmann dissented:

Lord Hoffmann: [28] My Lords, the purpose of a duty to warn someone against the risk involved in what he proposes to do, or allow to be done to him, is to give him the opportunity to avoid or reduce that risk. If he would have been unable or unwilling to take that opportunity and the risk eventuates, the failure to warn has not caused the damage. It would have happened anyway.

[29] The burden is on a claimant to prove that the defendant's breach of duty caused him damage. Where the breach of duty is a failure to warn of a risk, he must prove that he would have taken the opportunity to avoid or reduce that risk. In the context of the present case, that means proving that she would not have had the operation.

[30] The judge made no finding that she would not have had the operation. He was not invited by the claimant to make such a finding. The claimant argued that as a matter of law it was sufficient that she would not have had the operation at that time or by that surgeon, even though the evidence was that the risk could have been precisely the same if she had it at another time or by another surgeon. A similar argument has been advanced before this House.

[31] In my opinion this argument is about as logical as saying that if one had been told, on entering a casino, that the odds on the number 7 coming up at roulette were only 1 in 37, one would have gone away and come back next week or gone to a different casino. The question is whether one would have taken the opportunity to avoid or reduce the risk, not whether one would have changed the scenario in some irrelevant detail. The judge found as a fact that the risk would have been precisely the same whether it was done then or later or by that competent surgeon or by another.

[32] It follows that the claimant failed to prove that the defendant's breach of duty caused her loss. On ordinary principles of tort law, the defendant is not liable.

Their Lordships appeared to believe that, allowing recovery by the claimant involved a special departure from the ordinary rules of causation (the disagreement centring on the propriety of such a departure). With respect, it is unfortunate in this regard that the House of Lords failed to distinguish more carefully between *factual* and *legal* causation. Had it done so, it would have been clearer that no radically new principle was involved. There was merely a modest (and justifiable) relaxation of legal causation:

Stauch, M, 'Causation and confusion in respect of medical non-disclosure: *Chester v Afshar'* **(2005) 14 Nott LJ 66:**

It ought to be clear that, in *Chester, factual* causation was present: Mr Afshar's breach, in failing to advise of the risk, had changed the course of events and led to the claimant being injured when, otherwise, she would almost certainly have escaped such injury. As Lord Steyn commented, ' ... but for the surgeon's negligent failure to warn the claimant of the small risk of serious injury the actual injury would not have occurred when it did and the chance of it occurring on a subsequent occasion was very small' ...

... The reason why, once established, factual causation is significant is two-fold. First it prevents the claimant from getting a windfall. It seems right (as the minority in *Chester* suggested, while failing to see that the claimant fulfilled the relevant condition) to reserve substantial damages for cases where the doctor's conduct has altered the course of events and resulted in injury (when otherwise there would very likely have been no injury). Indeed, this is merely an instance of the general requirement, foundational in the tort of negligence, that the claimant must show 'damage' ... [T]he second, more positive reason why proof of factual causation is significant is that it gives rise to a powerful *prima facie* case for compensation: 'if you had behaved properly, I would not have been injured!' Qualifications on liability based upon remoteness/legal causation points are relatively unusual. This is all the more so in cases where the injury intrudes in close temporal proximity to the wrongful act, and was readily foreseeable (both of which were true here) ...

The further question, as to how far the normal legal causation requirement that the defendant's breach created or added to the risk, should be relaxed in this type of case had been exhaustively discussed in *Chappel v Hart*, a recent case from the High Court of Australia with similar facts, as well as in the meticulous judgment of the Court of Appeal in *Chester* itself. In fact there would seem to be good reasons for such a relaxation. Most importantly, as the majority in the House of Lords recognised, the doctor's duty to inform patients of risks would otherwise be very much attenuated ...

At a more general level, we should recall the reason for normally insisting, at the legal causation stage, that the defendant's conduct increased the risk of the claimant's injury. This is so as to rule out liability for coincidences of the sort canvassed by Lord Walker in his speech, such as where a passenger in a speeding taxi is injured by a falling tree. In such cases it is true that, had the defendant behaved properly, the injury would have been avoided. Nonetheless, the rationale for the rule wrongfully breached by the defendant (namely, to reduce the risk of injury over a range of similar cases) is confounded by the particular circumstances at hand: the injury would here have been just as likely to occur if the rule had been respected.

Importantly, the above point has only limited force in medical non-disclosure cases: here the rule of conduct (requiring disclosure of significant treatment risks) is designed not principally to reduce the risk of injury from treatment: in many cases –including *Chester*- the risk in question cannot be reduced. Rather, the main function of the rule is to promote the distinct goal of the patient's autonomy. The patient should be told that there is an inevitable risk to the proposed treatment precisely so that he can decide if he wishes to submit to it and, if he does so decide, make contingency plans in case it should materialise.

As mentioned earlier, we shall consider further issues of causation – both factual and legal, in Chapter 6. We shall also advert there to the problem of quantifying damages, which can sometimes present difficulty in non-disclosure of risk cases.

CHAPTER 4

TREATING THE INCOMPETENT PATIENT

There can be no doubt that patients who lack capacity should nevertheless receive medical treatment. The difficulties arise when considering the legal framework in which treatment decisions are made, and the criteria used to decide on the suitability of treatment.

The treatment of the incompetent patient will be considered in later chapters in relation to particular forms of treatment (for example, organ donation – Chapter 11; medical research – Chapter 10; and – where the patient is terminally ill or gravely incapacitated – Chapter 12). In this chapter we will concentrate on the basic legal framework and general principles, making particular reference to so called non-therapeutic areas relating to the control of fertility by sterilisation and abortion.

THE LEGAL FRAMEWORK

A doctor who treats without a valid consent may still not be liable in an action in battery if he can raise the defence of necessity and has treated the patient in the patient's best interests. Although the defence of necessity must be equated with acting in the best interests of the patient, the defence of necessity is frequently used to refer to emergency treatment carried out on unconscious patients, whilst the best interests defence tends to be referred to when dealing with patients who are permanently lacking in capacity, whether emergency cases or not. It must be stressed, however, that there is no strict dichotomy and, arguably, the distinction is meaningless.

The temporarily incompetent – necessity

As indicated in the previous chapter, there have been attempts to argue that, for example, when faced with an unconscious patient, a doctor can assume that there is an implied consent to treatment. These attempts, however, have not been successful and the favoured view is that, in such circumstances, the doctor treats without any consent, but can raise the defence of necessity:

Mason, JK and Laurie, GT, *Law and Medical Ethics*, 7th edn, 2006, Oxford: OUP, 351:

It is widely recognised in both criminal and civil law that there are times when acting out of necessity legitimates an otherwise wrongful act ...

Necessity will be a viable defence to any proceedings for non-consensual treatment where an unconscious patient is involved and there is no known objection to treatment. The treatment undertaken, however, must not be more extensive than is required by the exigencies of the situation ... A doctor cannot, therefore, 'take advantage' of unconsciousness to perform procedures which are not essential for the patient's survival or well-being.

The defence of necessity, therefore, must necessarily entail the doctor acting in the best interests of the patient. The difference lies in the nature of the treatment. In an emergency, the treatment must be confined to that which is necessary to preserve life and limb, when it is impossible to obtain consent. However, as we shall see, the best interests test will apply to all forms of medical treatment carried out on permanently incompetent patients.

The nature of necessity was examined in the case of *Re F (Mental Patient: Sterilisation)* [1990] 2 AC 1:

Re F (Mental Patient: Sterilisation) [1990] 2 AC 1:

Lord Goff (p 73): Upon what principle can medical treatment be justified when given without consent? We are searching for a principle upon which, in limited circumstances, recognition may be given to a need, in the interests of the patient, that treatment should be given to him in circumstances where he is (temporarily or permanently) disabled from consenting to it. It is this criterion of a need which points to the principle of necessity as providing justification ...

We are concerned here with action taken to preserve the life, health or well being of another who is unable to consent to it. Such action is sometimes said to be justified as arising from an emergency; in Prosser and Keeton, *Handbook on Torts*, 5th edn, 1984, p 117, the action is said to be privileged by the emergency. Doubtless, in the case of a person of sound mind, there will ordinarily have to be an emergency before such action taken without consent can be lawful; for otherwise there would be an opportunity to communicate with the assisted person and to seek his consent. But this is not always so ...

We can derive some guidance as to the nature of the principle of necessity from the cases on agency of necessity in mercantile law. When reading those cases, however, we have to bear in mind that it was there considered that (since there was a pre-existing relationship between the parties) there was a duty on the part of the agent to act on his principal's behalf in an emergency. From these cases it appears that the principle of necessity connotes that circumstances have arisen in which there is a necessity for the agent to act on his principal's behalf at a time when it is in practice not possible for him to obtain his principal's instructions so to do. In such cases, it has been said that the agent must act bona fide in the interests of his principal: see *Prager v Blatspiel Stamp and Heacock Ltd* [1924] 1 KB 566, p 572, *per* McCardie J. A broader statement of the principle is to be found in the advice of the Privy Council delivered by Sir Montague Smith in *Australasian Steam Navigation Co v Morse* (1872) LR 4 PC 222, p 230, in which he said:

> ... when by the force of circumstances a man has the duty cast upon him of taking some action for another, and under that obligation, adopts the course which, to the judgment of a wise and prudent man, is apparently the best for the interest of the persons for whom he acts in a given emergency, it may properly be said of the course so taken, that it was, in a mercantile sense, necessary to take it.

In a sense, these statements overlap. But from them can be derived the basic requirements, applicable in these cases of necessity, that, to fall within the principle, not only (1) must there be a necessity to act when it is not practicable to communicate with the assisted person, but also (2) the action taken must be such as a reasonable person would in all the circumstances take acting in the best interests of the assisted person.

On this statement of principle, I wish to observe that officious intervention cannot be justified by the principle of necessity. So intervention cannot be justified when another more appropriate person is available and willing to act; nor can it be justified when it is contrary to the known wishes of the assisted person, to the extent that he is capable of rationally forming such a wish. On the second limb of the principle, the introduction of the standard of a reasonable man should not in the present context be regarded as materially different from that of Sir Montague Smith's 'wise and prudent man', because a reasonable man would, in the time available to him, proceed with wisdom and prudence before taking action in relation to another man's person or property without his consent. I shall have more to say on this point later. Subject to that, I hesitate at present to indulge in any greater refinement of the principle, being well aware of many problems which may arise in its application – problems which it is not necessary, for present purposes, to examine. But as a general rule, if the above criteria are fulfilled, interference with the assisted person's person or property (as the case may be) will not be unlawful. Take the example of a railway accident, in which injured passengers are trapped in the wreckage. It is this principle which may render lawful the actions of other citizens – railway staff, passengers or outsiders – who rush to give aid and comfort to the victims: the surgeon who amputates the limb of an unconscious passenger to free him from the wreckage; the ambulance man who conveys him to hospital; the doctors and nurses who treat him and care for him while he is still unconscious. Take the example of an elderly person who suffers a stroke which renders him incapable of speech or movement. It is by virtue of this principle that the doctor who treats him, the nurse who cares for him, even the relative or friend or neighbour who comes in to look after him, will commit no wrong when he or she touches his body. The two examples I have given illustrate, in the one case, an emergency, and in the other, a permanent or semi-permanent state of affairs. Another example of the latter kind is that of a mentally disordered person who is disabled from giving consent. I can see no good reason why the principle of necessity should not be applicable in his case as it is in the case of the victim of a stroke. Furthermore, in the case of a mentally disordered person, as in the case of a stroke victim, the permanent state of affairs calls for a wider range of care than may be requisite in an emergency which arises from accidental injury. When the state of affairs is permanent, or semi-permanent, action properly taken to preserve the life, health or well being of the assisted person may well transcend such measures as surgical operation or substantial medical treatment and may extend to include such humdrum matters as routine medical or dental treatment, even simple care such as dressing and undressing and putting to bed.

The distinction I have drawn between cases of emergency, and cases where the state of affairs is (more or less) permanent, is relevant in another respect. We are here concerned with medical treatment, and I limit myself to cases of that kind. Where, for example, a surgeon performs an operation without his consent on a patient temporarily rendered unconscious in an accident, he should do no more than is reasonably required, in the best interests of the patient, before he recovers consciousness. I can see no practical difficulty arising from this requirement, which derives from the fact that the patient is expected before long to regain consciousness and can then be consulted about longer term measures. The point has, however, arisen in a more acute form where a surgeon, in the course of an operation, discovers some other condition which, in his opinion, requires operative treatment for which he has not received the patient's consent. In what circumstances he should operate forthwith, and in what circumstances he should postpone the further treatment until he has received the patient's consent, is a difficult matter which has troubled the Canadian courts (see *Marshall v Curry* (1933) 3 DLR 260; and *Murray v McMurchy* (1949) 2 DLR 442), but which it is not necessary for your Lordships to consider in the present case.

But where the state of affairs is permanent or semi-permanent, as may be so in the case of a mentally disordered person, there is no point in waiting to obtain the patient's consent. The need to care for him is obvious; and the doctor must then act in the best interests of his patient, just as if he had received his patient's consent so to do. Were this not so, much useful treatment and care could, in theory at least, be denied to the unfortunate. It follows that, on this point, I am unable to accept the view expressed by Neill LJ in the Court of Appeal ... that the treatment must be shown to have been necessary.

Lord Goff referred to the Canadian case of *Marshall v Curry* (1933) 3 DLR 260, where a patient brought an action in battery against a surgeon who had removed a diseased testicle during the course of a hernia operation. The surgeon tried to argue that it was necessary to remove the testicle because it seriously threatened the health of the patient. In other words, though couched in terms of necessity, the defence, in reality, was that it was in the best interests of the patient to perform this operation. The court held that the removal of the testicle was necessary and that it would have been unreasonable to put the procedure off to a later date. This is a somewhat troubling decision, and was not followed in a later Canadian case. In *Murray v McMurchy* (1949) 2 DLR 442, the patient was a woman who had been sterilised without her consent in the course of a Caesarean section. The defence was that the condition of her uterus was such as to make it dangerous for her to go through another pregnancy. The court held that it would have been reasonable to postpone this operation in order to seek her consent.

Children

Consent to treatment

Although the English age of majority is 18 years, and up until that date minors are still subject to the jurisdiction of the courts, the Family Law Reform Act 1969 provides that minors who have attained the age of 16 may give a valid consent to medical treatment:

Family Law Reform Act 1969:

8(1) -The consent of a minor who has attained the age of 16 years to any surgical, medical or dental treatment which, in the absence of consent, would constitute a trespass to his person, shall be as effective as it would be if he were of full age; and where a minor has by virtue of this section given an effective consent to any treatment it shall not be necessary to obtain any consent for it from his parent or guardian.

Just as mental illness without more will not remove capacity, neither will tender years. The case of *Gillick v West Norfolk and Wisbech AHA* [1986] 1 AC 112 had to consider the capacity of children to consent to treatment. In *Gillick*, it was acknowledged that there was no magic in the age of 16, and that younger children may be able to consent to medical treatment, depending on their level of understanding, that is, what is generally known as '*Gillick* competence'.

Gillick v West Norfolk and Wisbech AHA [1986] 1 AC 112, HL (Lords Fraser, Scarman, Bridge, Brandon, and Templeman)

Following concern about the number of under age pregnancies, the Department of Health and Social Security issued guidance to area health authorities on family planning services containing particular provisions relating to young people. Although it stressed the importance of the parents of children under 16 being involved in the consultation, it went on to say that, in exceptional cases, it was for a doctor to decide whether to prescribe contraception without informing the parents of the child. Mrs Gillick, who had a number of daughters under the age of 16, sought a declaration that the guidance gave advice which was unlawful and which adversely affected parental rights and duties. Woolf J refused the declaration. Mrs Gillick succeeded before the Court of Appeal (Eveleigh, Fox and Parker LJJ). The House of Lords allowed the Department of Health and Social Security's appeal by a majority of 3:2:

> **Lord Fraser**: It would, therefore, appear that, if the inference which Mrs Gillick's advisers seek to draw from the provisions [of the FLRA 1969] is justified, a minor under the age of 16 has no capacity to authorise any kind of medical advice or treatment or examination of his own body. That seems to me so surprising that I cannot accept it in the absence of clear provisions to that effect. It seems to me verging on the absurd to suggest that a girl or a boy aged 15 could not effectively consent, for example, to have a medical examination of some trivial injury to his body or even to have a broken arm set. Of course the consent of the parents should normally be asked, but they may not be immediately available. Provided the patient, whether a boy or a girl, is capable of understanding what is proposed, and of expressing his or her own wishes, I see no good reason for holding that he or she lacks the capacity to express them validly and effectively and to authorise the medical man to make the examination or give the treatment which he advises. After all, a minor under the age of 16 can, within certain limits, enter into a contract. He or she can also sue and be sued, and can give evidence on oath. Moreover, a girl under 16 can give sufficiently effective consent to sexual intercourse to lead to the legal result that the man involved does not commit the crime of rape – see *R v Howard* [1966] 1 WLR 13, p 15, when Lord Parker CJ said:
>
> > ... in the case of a girl under 16, the prosecution, in order to prove rape, must prove either that she physically resisted, or if she did not, that her understanding and knowledge were such that she was not in a position to decide whether to consent or resist ... there are many girls under 16 who know full well what it is all about and can properly consent.
>
> Accordingly, I am not disposed to hold now, for the first time, that a girl aged less than 16 lacks the power to give valid consent to contraceptive advice or treatment, merely on account of her age.

Lord Fraser suggested a five point test for doctors contemplating whether to provide such a girl with contraceptive advice and treatment without reference to her parents:

> **Lord Fraser**: ... [T]he doctor will, in my opinion, be justified in proceeding without the parents' consent or even knowledge provided he is satisfied on the following matters: (1) that the girl (although under 16 years of age) will understand his advice; (2) that he cannot persuade her to inform her parents or to allow him to inform the parents that she is seeking contraceptive advice; (3) that she is very likely to begin or to continue having sexual intercourse with or without contraceptive treatment; (4) that unless she receives contraceptive advice or treatment her physical or mental health or both are likely to suffer; (5) that her best interests require him to give her contraceptive advice, treatment or both without the parental consent.

Lord Scarman, in his judgment, emphasised the increasing autonomy of minors as they approach adulthood:

> **Lord Scarman**: ... I would hold that as a matter of law the parental right to determine whether or not their minor child below the age of 16 will have medical treatment

terminates if and when the child achieves sufficient understanding and intelligence to enable him or her to understand fully what is proposed. It will be a question of fact whether a child seeking advice has sufficient understanding of what is involved to give a consent valid in law. Until the child achieves the capacity to consent, the parental right to make the decision continues save only in exceptional circumstances. Emergency, parental neglect, abandonment of the child or inability to find the parent are examples of exceptional situations justifying the doctor proceeding to treat the child without parental knowledge and consent; but there will arise, no doubt, other exceptional situations in which it will be reasonable for the doctor to proceed without the parent's consent.

When applying these conclusions to contraceptive advice and treatment it has to be borne in mind that there is much that has to be understood by a girl under 16 if she is to have legal capacity to consent to such treatment. It is not enough that she should understand the nature of the advice which is being given: she must also have a sufficient maturity to understand what is involved. There are moral and family questions, especially her relationship with her parents; long term problems associated with the emotional impact of pregnancy and its termination; and there are the risks to health of sexual intercourse at her age, risks which contraception may diminish but cannot eliminate. It follows that a doctor will have to satisfy himself that she is able to appraise these factors before he can safely proceed on the basis that she has capacity at law to consent to contraceptive advice and treatment. And it further follows that ordinarily the proper course will be for him, as the guidance lays down, first to seek to persuade the girl to bring her parents into consultation, and, if she refuses, not to prescribe contraceptive advice and treatment unless he is satisfied that her circumstances are such that he ought to proceed without parental knowledge and consent.

Lord Bridge agreed with Lords Fraser and Scarman. Dissenting judgments were given by Lords Brandon and Templeman. Lord Templeman accepted the general principle that consent is a function of understanding, not status, but dissented on the specific matter of contraceptive advice and treatment:

Lord Templeman: The effect of the consent of the infant depends on the nature of the treatment and the age and understanding of the infant. For example, a doctor with the consent of an intelligent boy or girl of 15 could, in my opinion, safely remove tonsils or a troublesome appendix. But any decision on the part of a girl to practise sex and contraception requires not only knowledge of the facts of life and of the dangers of pregnancy and disease but also an understanding of the emotional and other consequences to her family, her male partner and to herself. I doubt whether a girl under the age of 16 is capable of a balanced judgment to embark on frequent, regular or casual sexual intercourse fortified by the illusion that medical science can protect her in mind and body and ignoring the danger of leaping from childhood to adulthood without the difficult formative transitional experiences of adolescence. There are many things which a girl under 16 needs to practise but sex is not one of them. Parliament could declare this view to be out of date. But in my opinion the statutory provisions discussed in the speech of my noble and learned friend, Lord Fraser of Tullybelton, and the provisions of s 6 of the Sexual Offences Act 1956, indicate that as the law now stands an unmarried girl under 16 is not competent to decide to practise sex and contraception ...

The position seems to me to be as follows. A doctor is not entitled to decide whether a girl under the age of 16 shall be provided with contraceptive facilities if a parent who is in charge of the girl is ready and willing to make that decision in exercise of parental rights. The doctor is entitled in exceptional circumstances and in emergencies to make provision, normally temporary provision, for contraception but in most cases would be bound to inform the parent of the treatment. The court would not hold the doctor liable for providing contraceptive facilities if the doctor had reasonable grounds for believing that the parent had abandoned or abused parental rights or that there was no parent immediately available for consultation or that there was no parent who was responsible for the girl. But exceptional circumstances and emergencies cannot be expanded into a general discretion for the doctor to provide contraceptive facilities without the knowledge of the parent because of the possibility that a girl to whom contraceptive facilities are not available may irresponsibly court the risk of pregnancy. Such a discretion would enable any girl to obtain contraception on request by threatening to sleep with a man.

Lord Brandon relied on public policy arguments based upon the criminalisation of acts of sex with girls under the age of 16:

> **Lord Brandon**: The Sexual Offences Act 1956 represents the latest pronouncement of parliament on these matters. Sections 5 and 6 provide, so far as material:
>
> > 5 -It is a felony for a man to have unlawful sexual intercourse with a girl under the age of 13.
> >
> > 6(1) -It is an offence … for a man to have unlawful sexual intercourse with a girl not under the age of 13 but under the age of 16.
>
> Further, by s 37 and Sched 2, the maximum punishment for an offence under s 5 is imprisonment for life, and that for an offence under s 6 imprisonment for two years. Since the passing of the Act of 1956 the distinction between felonies and misdemeanours has been abolished. For the purposes of this case, however, nothing turns on this change of terminology.
>
> My Lords, the inescapable inference from the statutory provisions of the Acts of 1885 and 1956 to which I have referred is that parliament has for the past century regarded, and still regards today, sexual intercourse between a man and a girl under 16 as a serious criminal offence so far as the man who has such intercourse is concerned. So far as the girl is concerned, she does not commit any criminal offence, even if she aids, abets or incites the having of such intercourse. The reason for this, as explained earlier, is that the relevant statutory provisions have been enacted by parliament for the purpose of protecting the girl from herself. The having of such intercourse is, however, unlawful, and the circumstance that the man is guilty of a criminal offence, while the girl is not, cannot alter that situation.
>
> On the footing that the having of sexual intercourse by a man with a girl under 16 is an unlawful act, it follows necessarily that for any person to promote, encourage or facilitate the commission of such an act may itself be a criminal offence, and must, in any event, be contrary to public policy. Nor can it make any difference that the person who promotes, encourages or facilitates the commission of such an act is a parent or a doctor or a social worker.
>
> [T]o give such a girl advice about contraception, to examine her with a view to her using one or more forms of protection, and finally to prescribe contraceptive treatment for her, necessarily involves promoting, encouraging or facilitating the having of sexual intercourse, contrary to public policy, by that girl with a man.

However, as Lord Brandon himself observed, on this logic Mrs Gillick's desire to have the girl's parents involved would also be problematic, since they too would become accessories to an offence. Moreover, it is interesting to reflect upon the earlier judgment of Lord Brandon in the case of *R v D* [1984] AC 778, which was cited with approval by both Lords Fraser and Scarman. That judgment clearly implied that a mature child could make decisions about medical treatment. It seems that the nature of the treatment in *Gillick* influenced Lord Brandon to take a restrictive approach.

Refusals of treatment

Although *Gillick* makes it clear that, depending on the nature of the treatment, a child may have the capacity to consent, the case has been interpreted subsequently by the Court of Appeal as relating only to consent and not *refusal*, so that a child's refusal of treatment can still be overridden by his parents or others *in loco parentis*.

Re R (A Minor) (Wardship: Consent to Treatment) [1991] 4 All ER 177, CA (Lord Donaldson MR, Staughton and Farquharson LJJ)

The mental health of a 15 year old girl in the care of the local authority deteriorated and she was placed in an adolescent psychiatric unit. Her condition fluctuated between periods of lucidity and, what was described as 'florid psychotic behaviour'. However, she objected to receiving antipsychotic drugs, and the local authority applied under the wardship jurisdiction for leave to administer the drugs regardless of her lack of consent. The judge at first instance (Waite J) decided that if she had the necessary capacity, then her refusal could not be overridden, but, on the facts, decided that she lacked capacity. The Court of Appeal accepted that she was not mentally competent due to the fluctuating nature of her mental illness, but went on to assert, *obiter*, that the wardship jurisdiction could not in any event be ousted by the decision of a Gillick competent child. The basis of the *Gillick* decision was interpreted by Lord Donaldson (p 184):

> **Lord Donaldson MR:** ... [C]onsent by itself creates no obligation to treat. It is merely a key which unlocks a door. Furthermore, whilst in the case of an adult of full capacity there will usually only be one keyholder, namely the patient, in the ordinary family unit where a young child is the patient there will be two keyholders, namely the parents, with a several as well as a joint right to turn the key and unlock the door. If the parents disagree, one consenting and the other refusing, the doctor will be presented with a professional and ethical, but not with a legal, problem because, if he has the consent of one authorised person, treatment will not without more constitute a trespass or a criminal assault.
>
> If Mrs Gillick was to succeed in her claim to a declaration that the memorandum of guidance issued by the department was unlawful, she had to show that no child under the age of 16 could be a keyholder in respect of contraception advice and treatment or that the parents' key overrode the child's. As Lord Fraser put it ([1985] 3 All ER 402, p 412; [1986] AC 112, p 173): 'She has to justify the absolute right of veto in a parent.' If she was to succeed in her claim against the area health authority, she had also to show that it was under a duty to inform all medical staff employed by it that Mrs Gillick was exercising that right of veto, but in the light of the House's finding that there was no such right, this additional factor can be ignored.
>
> In the instant appeal Mr James Munby QC, appearing for the Official Solicitor, submits that: (a) if the child has the right to give consent to medical treatment, the parents' right to give or refuse consent is terminated; and (b) the court in the exercise of its wardship jurisdiction is only entitled to step into the shoes of the parents and thus itself has no right to give or refuse consent. Whilst it is true that he seeks to modify the effect of this rather startling submission by suggesting that, if the child's

consent or refusal of consent is irrational or misguided, the court will readily infer that in the particular context that individual child is not competent to give or withhold consent, it is necessary to look very carefully at the *Gillick* decision to see whether it supports his argument and, if it does, whether it is binding upon this court.

The key passages upon which Mr Munby relies are to be found in the speech of Lord Scarman ([1985] 3 All ER 402, pp 423–24):

> ... as a matter of law the parental right to determine whether or not their minor child below the age of 16 will have medical treatment terminates if and when the child achieves a sufficient understanding and intelligence to enable him or her to understand fully what is proposed. It will be a question of fact whether a child seeking advice has sufficient understanding of what is involved to give a consent valid in law ...

... What Mr Munby's argument overlooks is that Lord Scarman was discussing the parents' right *'to determine* whether or not their minor child below the age of 16 will have medical treatment' (my emphasis) and this is the 'parental right' to which he was referring in the latter passage. A right of determination is wider than a right to consent. The parents can only have a right of determination if either the child has no right to consent, ie, is not a keyholder, or the parents hold a master key which could nullify the child's consent. I do not understand Lord Scarman to be saying that, if a child was '*Gillick* competent', to adopt the convenient phrase used in argument, the parents ceased to have an independent right of consent as contrasted with ceasing to have a right of determination, ie, a veto. In a case in which the '*Gillick* competent' child refuses treatment, but the parents consent, that consent enables treatment to be undertaken lawfully, but in no way determines that the child shall be so treated. In a case in which the positions are reversed, it is the child's consent which is the enabling factor and again the parents' refusal of consent is not determinative. If Lord Scarman intended to go further than this and to say that in the case of a '*Gillick* competent' child, a parent has no right either to consent or to refuse consent, his remarks were *obiter*, because the only question in issue was Mrs Gillick's alleged right of veto. Furthermore I consider that they would have been wrong.

One glance at the consequences suffices to show that Lord Scarman cannot have been intending to say that the parental right to consent terminates with the achievement by the child of '*Gillick* competence'. It is fundamental to the speeches of the majority that the capacity to consent will vary from child to child and according to the treatment under consideration, depending upon the sufficiency of his or her intelligence and understanding of that treatment. If the position in law is that upon the achievement of '*Gillick* competence' there is a transfer of the right of consent from parents to child and there can never be a concurrent right in both, doctors would be faced with an intolerable dilemma, particularly when the child was nearing the age of 16, if the parents consented, but the child did not. On pain, if they got it wrong, of being sued for trespass to the person or possibly being charged with a criminal assault, they would have to determine as a matter of law in whom the right of consent resided at the particular time in relation to the particular treatment. I do not believe that that is the law.

The Court of Appeal subsequently considered the status of consent under s 8 of the Family Law Reform Act 1969 in relation to a 16 year old child's refusal of treatment. It will be seen from the section (see p 160, above) that it merely states that there is no need to obtain the consent of a parent or guardian if a child gives consent. However, on the face of it, there is no *obligation* on a doctor to obtain the consent of the child in preference to that of the parent or guardian:

Re W (A Minor) (Medical Treatment) [1992] 4 All ER 627, CA (Lord Donaldson MR, Balcombe and Nolan LJJ)

A 16 year old girl was suffering from anorexia nervosa and was in the care of the local authority in an adolescent residential unit. Her condition deteriorated and the local authority sought authorisation from the court for removal of the girl to a specialist unit for treatment without her consent. As she had attained the age of 16, she resisted the application on the ground that s 8 of the Family Law Reform Act 1969 conferred on her the same right as an adult to refuse treatment without her consent. Although there is some suggestion in the judgments that, because of her condition, Miss W may not have been competent, the essence of the Court of Appeal's decision was that s 8 did not in any event confer an absolute right upon a child, and could be overridden by the court exercising its inherent jurisdiction:

Lord Donaldson MR:

Is s 8 ambiguous?

The wording of sub-s (1) shows quite clearly that it is addressed to the legal purpose and legal effect of consent to treatment, namely, to prevent such treatment constituting in law a trespass to the person, and that it does so by making the consent of a 16 or 17 year old as effective as if he were 'of full age'. No question of 'Gillick competence' in common law terms arises. The 16 or 17 year old is conclusively presumed to be 'Gillick competent' or, alternatively, the test of 'Gillick competence' is bypassed and has no relevance. The argument that W or any other 16 or 17 year old can, by refusing to consent to treatment, veto the treatment notwithstanding that the doctor has the consent of someone who has parental responsibilities, involves the proposition that s 8 has the further effect of depriving such a person of the power to consent. It certainly does not say so. Indeed if this were its intended effect, it is difficult to see why the sub-section goes on to say that it is not necessary to obtain the parents' consent, rather than providing that such consent, if obtained, should be ineffective. Furthermore, such a construction does not sit easily with sub-s (3), which preserves the common law as it existed immediately before the Act which undoubtedly gave parents an effective power of consent for all children up to the age of 21, the then existing age of consent ...

The most promising argument in favour of W having an exclusive right to consent to treatment and thus, by refusing consent, to attract the protection of the law on trespass to the person, lies in concentrating upon the words 'as effective as it would be if he were of full age'. If she were of full age her ability to consent would have two separate effects. First, her consent would be fully effective as such. Second, a failure or refusal to give consent would be fully effective as a veto, but only *because no one else would be in a position to consent*. If it is a possible view that s 8 is intended to put a 16 or 17 year old in exactly the same position as an adult and there is thus some ambiguity, although I do not think that there is, it is a permissible aid to construction to seek to ascertain the mischief at which the section is directed.

The Latey Committee Report

It is common ground that the Family Law Reform Act 1969 was parliament's response to the *Report of the Committee on the Age of Majority*, Cmnd 3342, 1967. The relevant part is contained in paras 474–84. These show that the mischief aimed at was twofold. First, cases were occurring in which young people between 16 and 21 (the then age of majority) were living away from home and wished and needed urgent medical treatment which had not yet reached the emergency stage. Doctors were unable to treat them unless and until their parents had been traced and this could cause unnecessary suffering. Second, difficulties were arising concerning:

> ... operations whose implications bring up the question of a girl's right to privacy about her sexual life. A particularly difficult situation arises in the case of a girl who is sent to hospital in need of a therapeutic abortion and refuses point blank to enter the hospital unless a guarantee is given that her parents shall not be told about it.

The committee had recommended that the age of majority be reduced to 18 generally. The report, in para 480, records that all the professional bodies which gave evidence recommended that patients aged between 16 and 18 should be able to give an effective consent to treatment and all but the Medical Protection Society recommended that they should also be able to give an effective refusal. The point with which we are concerned was therefore well in the mind of the committee. It did not so recommend. It recommended that:

> ... *without prejudice to any consent that may otherwise be lawful*, the consent of young persons aged 16 and over to medical or dental treatment shall be as valid as the consent of a person of full age. (Original emphasis.)

Conclusion on s 8

I am quite unable to accept that parliament in adopting somewhat more prolix language was intending to achieve a result which differed from that recommended by the committee.

On reflection I regret my use in *Re R* ... of the keyholder analogy because keys can lock as well as unlock. I now prefer the analogy of the legal 'flak jacket' which protects the doctor from claims by the litigious whether he acquires it from his patient who may be a minor over the age of 16, or a '*Gillick* competent' child under that age or from another person having parental responsibilities which include a right to consent to treatment of the minor. Anyone who gives him a flak jacket (that is, consent) may take it back, but the doctor only needs one and so long as he continues to have one he has the legal right to proceed.

It is interesting to compare Lord Donaldson's interpretation of s 8(3) of the 1969 Act with that of Lord Scarman in *Gillick*. The latter said that 'sub-s (3) leaves open the question whether the consent of a minor under 16 could be an effective consent' (see p 161, above), whereas Lord Donaldson interprets it as safeguarding parental rights in cases of minors over 16. In the light of this conflict, it should be noted that in Scottish law a child under the age of 16 has legal capacity to consent to medical treatment if 'he is capable of understanding the nature and possible consequences of the procedure or treatment' (s 2(4) of the Age of Legal Capacity (Scotland) Act 1991), and in *Houston, Applicant* (see [1997] 5 Med LR 237), the Sheriff's Court confirmed that the child's power to consent could not be overridden by a guardian, even though s 5(1) of the Act provides that the guardian of a person under 16 has the same powers after the passing of the Act as before. It was said that it would be illogical to grant a power to consent to medical treatment if this decision could be overridden by a guardian.

Certainly *Re R* and *Re W* sit rather uneasily with the *Gillick* decision. It is hard to see how, for example, Lord Scarman's wide ranging approach to the issue of understanding and the gradual attainment of the age of discretion can simply have been constructed to provide the doctor with protection from legal action. On the other hand, the recommendation of the Latey Committee does appear to support

Lord Donaldson's view. However, could it not be argued that the committee was leaving the question open, and that the *Gillick* decision has since decided the position? Not surprisingly, the cases have drawn a large amount of critical comment:

Bainham, A, 'The judge and the competent minor' (1992) 108 LQR 194:

[In *Re R*] Lord Donaldson sought to draw a distinction between 'determination' and 'consent', the former being a wider concept than the latter, since it implied a right of veto. In his view, Lord Scarman in *Gillick* was referring to the parent's right to determine whether or not a child should receive medical treatment. This right of determination, which amounted to a definitive right to decide, would be removed where the child also had a capacity to consent. But, according to Lord Donaldson, Lord Scarman was not saying that the parent's independent right to consent would be lost in these circumstances. There would, according to this interpretation, be concurrent independent rights in parent and child and it would be open to a doctor to act on either consent ...

There are fundamental objections to this position. It can only work on the assumption that a doctor is dealing solely with the parent or solely with the child and is unaware of any disagreement between them. Where he is aware of a disagreement then, in the absence of judicial intervention, he must choose between the conflicting views. This is so where the parent is proposing action and the child is objecting, or conversely, where the child is in favour of action and the parent is objecting. If the doctor decides to proceed, or not to proceed, on the basis of the parent's view, he is in reality giving effect to a parental veto over the child's view. He is allowing the parent to 'determine' the matter, and the suggested distinction between 'determination' and 'consent' falls apart. And it is difficult to see how medical personnel seeking to administer drugs with the consent of a parent (or, as here, someone else with parental responsibility) could possibly be unaware of the child's objection. The dilemma referred to by Lord Donaldson of choosing between two potentially valid consents (either of which might subsequently be held invalid) is inevitable in the absence of a mandatory judicial procedure.

However Lord Donaldson did not stop there. Surprisingly, he took the view that the same principles governed the situation of a young person over 16. Section 8(1) of the Family Law Reform Act 1969 provides that where this age has been attained, the child's consent 'to any surgical, medical or dental treatment ... shall be as effective as it would be if he were of full age' and that 'it shall not be necessary to obtain any consent for it from his parent or guardian'. He adopted a literal interpretation to the effect that, while it was unnecessary for a doctor to secure parental consent in relation to a 16 year old, there was nothing to preclude him from acting on a parent's consent alone. This flies in the face of the settled interpretation of this provision that it was intended to confer complete autonomy on a young person of this age and that by implication this must outweigh any parental claim to decide.

The majority in *Gillick* were clearly aware of the potential for conflict between two independently valid consents and gave precedence to the views of the competent child. Lord Scarman could hardly have been more definite about this. Even Lord Fraser, who was anxious to ensure that the parental contribution was properly explored, also supported a doctor's right in specified circumstances to act on the child's consent alone. There is nothing in either speech which gives the remotest hint that a parent's view could lawfully be allowed to prevail over that of the mature child. Lord Donaldson's remarks, if accepted, would have the effect of turning the clocks back on *Gillick* and would surely be unlikely to survive the scrutiny of the House of Lords.

However, there has also been support for the Court of Appeal's interpretation:

Lowe, N and Juss, S, 'Medical treatment – pragmatism and the search for principle' (1993) 56 MLR 865:

Whether one uses Lord Donaldson MR's 'keyholder analogy' or his 'flak jacket' approach, the effect is the same. It enables the court to prevent, in the words of the Latey Committee, 'permanent disability' or 'unnecessary pain and suffering'.

In our view, the decision in *Re W* should not be reversed by the House of Lords. Similarly, we would support the outcome in *Re R* and in *Re E* … [T]hese decisions establish two grounds upon which a child's refusal can be overridden: namely (1) the inability to make an informed judgment, in which case the refusal carries no weight; and (2) where the child is capable of making an informed view, that preference is balanced against the harm to the child's welfare which will ensue if these wishes are observed.

We would support the decisions on either basis because it seems to us wrong for the court to allow a child to refuse treatment that would do him or her irreparable harm. After all, it is perhaps all too easily forgotten that, in the final analysis, a child is still only a child. Moreover, the entire thesis based on the premise of Lord Scarman's child of 'sufficient understanding and intelligence' who is able 'to understand fully what is proposed' is, it is submitted, in one sense open to question. Is a child of sufficient understanding and intelligence if he or she acts irrationally? Is autonomy meaningful if it is irrational? The point is well illustrated by Re W itself. At first instance, Thorpe J, with support from W's consultant psychiatrist who specialised in anorexia nervosa, had 'no doubt at all' that she was '*Gillick* competent'. Lord Donaldson MR, however, had serious doubts, contending 'it is a feature of anorexia nervosa that it is capable of destroying the ability to make an informed choice' being 'an illness which is not the fault of the sufferer' but which in its clinical manifestations contains 'a firm wish not to be cured'. Balcombe LJ recognised that if W's refusal not to take solid food was not shortly reversed 'she would be likely to suffer permanent damage to her brain and reproductive organs and not be able to bear children'. Can it humanely be argued, in these circumstances, that the court ought not to have intervened? We agree with Ward J [in *Re E*] that a court should be slow to let a child martyr himself. To those who question how a child can be held able to give a valid consent yet be unable to exercise a power of veto, we would reply that there is a rational distinction to be made between giving consent and withholding it. We must start with the assumption that a doctor will act in the best interests of his patient. Hence, if the doctor believes that a particular treatment is necessary for his patient, it is perfectly rational for the law to facilitate this as easily as possible and hence allow a '*Gillick* competent' child to give a valid consent, and also to protect the child against parents opposed to what is professionally considered to be in its best medical interests. In contrast, it is surely right for the law to be reluctant to allow a child of whatever age to be able to veto treatment designed for his or her benefit, particularly if a refusal would lead to the child's death or permanent damage. In other words, the clear and consistent policy of the law is to protect the child against wrong-headed parents and against itself with the final safeguard, as *Re W* unequivocally establishes, of giving the court the last word in cases of dispute.

On this view, a child may be deemed to be *Gillick* competent, but still lacking the necessary capacity that an adult would enjoy, to the extent that the outcome of its decision is not deemed to be in its own best interests. However, the support Lowe and Juss seek to derive from the Latey Committee report – that it sought to prevent 'unnecessary pain and suffering' – is in our view not justified. The pain and suffering at issue was caused, not by 'unacceptable' treatment decisions by minors, but by the fact that – pre-*Gillick* – they had no legal power to make any decisions. The Court of Appeal seems to be substituting the functional view of capacity (at the heart of the later adult case of *Re C (Adult: Refusal of Treatment)* [1994] 1 WLR 290) with a bare 'all or nothing' test: either under or over 18 years of age, either competent or incompetent. Whatever view is taken it can be seen that the effect of *Re W*, so far as refusals of treatment are concerned, is to re-establish the very 'status' approach which the House of Lords were at pains to reject in *Gillick* in relation to consent. The 'all or nothing' aspect is illustrated by the train of events during and after the case of *Re E (A Minor) (Wardship: Medical Treatment)* [1993] 1 FLR 386, referred to in the Lowe and Juss article. The patient was 15 and, like his parents, a devout Jehovah's Witness. He was suffering from leukaemia, the treatment of which included blood transfusions. Ward J ordered the carrying out of the treatment, which continued until the boy reached 18. At this point he refused further medical treatment and died.

Re L (Medical Treatment: Gillick Competency) [1998] 2 FLR 810 concerned a 14 year old girl who had suffered extensive burns and in the course of the essential surgery to treat them, would require blood transfusions. Without treatment she would die an unpleasant death. She was a Jehovah's Witness and refused consent to the transfusions. Sir Stephen Brown, President (as he then was), whilst noting that counsel's submissions had included a reference to Lord Donaldson's analysis of *Gillick* competence, made his decision on the basis of lack of capacity, as she had limited experience of life and that limited her understanding of 'matters which are as grave as her own present situation'. Arguably, this is just another way of saying that she lacks capacity because she is a child. However, it refers to the grave matters under consideration, and, therefore, she might have sufficient understanding in a less serious situation. Nevertheless, the suggestion might be that, in cases where a religious or similar belief is involved, a child might form views which s/he rejects in adulthood. The difficulty with this approach, however, is that the same argument could be advanced for young adults, or, arguably, all adults.

The incapacitated and proxy decision-making

Here we are considering children who are not Gillick competent, and adults who are temporarily or permanently incompetent, but in situations where the treatment concerned is not emergency treatment. Aside from those patients compulsorily detained under the Mental Health Act (MHA) 1983 who can be treated for the mental disorder itself without consent (s 63), the presumption is that consent is necessary. In cases where there is a lawful proxy or surrogate decision maker, consent may, and sometimes must, be obtained from that source. The test, however, is that the treatment must be in the best interests of the patient.

If an adult patient is permanently incompetent, then medical procedures may be carried out without consent. However, it will be seen that the law at present is significantly different in respect of adults than it is with regard to children (although there will be few divergences when the Mental Capacity Act 2005 comes into force in 2007). Having said that, however, it must be noted that, although the court's jurisdiction in respect of children is much wider, in the case of both adults and children, dubious treatment decisions can only be challenged if there is an interested party willing to bring the matter before the courts. In cases where the patient's family and the patient's doctors agree a course of action there may be no such interested party. In the case of *Re D (A Minor) (Wardship: Sterilisation)* [1976] 1 All ER 326 (considered in detail at p 201, below), the proposed sterilisation of a child only came before the court because of the chance intervention by an educational psychologist at the child's school.

Children and the rights of parents

In *Gillick*, on the subject of parental rights Lord Fraser said:

Gillick v West Norfolk and Wisbech AHA [1986] AC 112

Lord Fraser (p 171): In practice most wise parents relax their control gradually as the child develops and encourage him or her to become increasingly independent. Moreover, the degree of parental control actually exercised over a particular child does in practice vary considerably according to his understanding and intelligence and it would, in my opinion, be unrealistic for the courts not to recognise these facts. Social customs change, and the law ought to, and does in fact, have regard to such changes when they are of major importance ...

In times gone by the father had almost absolute authority over his children until they attained majority. A rather remarkable example of such authority being upheld by the court was *In re Agar-Ellis* (1883) 24 Ch D 317 which was much relied on by the Court of Appeal. The father in that case restricted the communication which his daughter aged 17 was allowed to have with her mother, against whose moral character nothing was alleged, to an extent that would be universally condemned today as quite unreasonable. The case has been much criticised in recent years and, in my opinion, with good reason ...

... In *J v C* [1970] AC 668 Lord Guest and Lord MacDermott referred to the decision in *Agar-Ellis* (1883) 24 Ch D 317 as an example of the almost absolute power asserted by the father over his children before the Judicature Act 1873 and plainly thought such an assertion was out of place at the present time: see Lord MacDermott, pp 703–04. In *Reg v D* [1984] AC 778 Lord Brandon of Oakbrook cited *Agar-Ellis* as an example of the older view of a father's authority which his Lordship and the other members of the House rejected. In my opinion, the view of absolute paternal authority continuing until a child attains majority which was applied in *Agar-Ellis* is so out of line with present day views that it should no longer be treated as having any authority. I regard it as a historical curiosity ...

Once the rule of the parents' absolute authority over minor children is abandoned, the solution to the problem in this appeal can no longer be found by referring to rigid parental rights at any particular age. The solution depends upon a judgment of what is best for the welfare of the particular child. Nobody doubts, certainly I do not doubt, that in the overwhelming majority of cases the best judges of a child's welfare are his or her parents. Nor do I doubt that any important medical treatment of a child under 16 would normally only be carried out with the parents' approval. That is why it would and should be 'most unusual' for a doctor to advise a child without the knowledge and consent of the parents on contraceptive matters. But, as I have already pointed out, Mrs Gillick has to go further if she is to obtain the first declaration that she seeks. She has to justify the absolute right of veto in a parent. But there may be circumstances in which a doctor is a better judge of the medical advice and treatment which will conduce to a girl's welfare than her parents. It is notorious that children of both sexes are often reluctant to confide in their parents about sexual matters, and the DHSS guidance under consideration shows that to abandon the principle of confidentiality for contraceptive advice to girls under 16 might cause some of them not to seek professional advice at all, with the consequence of exposing them to 'the immediate risks of pregnancy and of sexually transmitted diseases'. No doubt the risk could be avoided if the patient were to abstain from sexual intercourse, and one of the doctor's responsibilities will be to decide whether a particular patient can reasonably be expected to act upon advice to abstain. We were told that in a significant number of cases such abstinence could not reasonably be expected ...

... the doctor will, in my opinion, be justified in proceeding without the parents' consent or even knowledge provided he is satisfied on the following matters: (1) that the girl (although under 16 years of age) will understand his advice; (2) that he cannot persuade her to inform her parents or to allow him to inform the parents that she is seeking contraceptive advice; (3) that she is very likely to begin or to continue having sexual intercourse with or without contraceptive treatment; (4) that unless she receives contraceptive advice or treatment her physical or mental health or both are likely to suffer; (5) that her best interests require him to give her contraceptive advice, treatment or both without the parental consent.

Lord Scarman took a similar view (p 182):

Lord Scarman: Mrs Gillick relies on both the statute law and the case law to establish her proposition that parental consent is in all other circumstances necessary. The only statutory provision directly in point is s 8 of the Family Law Reform Act 1969. Sub-section (1) of the section provides that the consent of a minor who has attained the age of 16 to any surgical, mental or dental treatment which in the absence of consent would constitute a trespass to his person shall be as effective as if he were of full age and that the consent of his parent or guardian need not be obtained. Sub-section (3) of the section provides:

Nothing in this section shall be construed as making ineffective any consent which would have been effective if this section had not been enacted.

I cannot accept the submission made on Mrs Gillick's behalf that sub-s (1) necessarily implies that prior to its enactment the consent of a minor to medical treatment could not be effective in law. Sub-section (3) leaves open the question whether the consent of a minor under 16 could be an effective consent. Like my noble and learned friend Lord Fraser of Tullybelton, I read the section as clarifying the law without conveying any indication as to what the law was before it was enacted. So far as minors under 16 are concerned, the law today is as it was before the enactment of the section ...

The law has, therefore, to be found by a search in the judge-made law for the true principle. The legal difficulty is that in our search we find ourselves in a field of medical practice where parental right and a doctor's may point us in different directions. This is not surprising. Three features have emerged in today's society which were not known to our predecessors: (1) contraception as a subject for medical advice and treatment; (2) the increasing independence of young people; and (3) the changed status of women. In times past contraception was rarely a matter for the doctor: but with the development of the contraceptive pill for women it has become part and parcel of everyday medical practice, as it made clear by the department's *Handbook of Contraceptive Practice*, 1984 revision, particularly para 1.2. Family planning services are now available under statutory powers to all without any express limitation as to age or marital status. Young people, once they have attained the age of 16, are capable of consenting to contraceptive treatment, since it is medical treatment: and, however extensive be parental right in the care and upbringing of children, it cannot prevail so as to nullify the 16 year old's capacity to consent which is now conferred by statute. Furthermore, women have obtained by the availability of the pill a choice of lifestyle with a degree of independence and of opportunity undreamed of until this generation and greater, I would add, than any law of equal opportunity could by itself effect.

The law ignores these developments at its peril ...

... The principle of the law, as I shall endeavour to show, is that parental rights are derived from parental duty and exist only so long as they are needed for the protection of the person and property of the child. The principle has been subjected to certain age limits set by statute for certain purposes: and in some cases the courts have declared an age of discretion at which a child acquires before the age of majority the right to make his (or her) own decision. But these limitations in no way undermine the principle of the law, and should not be allowed to obscure it.

Let me make good, quite shortly, the proposition of principle ...

... It is abundantly plain that the law recognises that there is a right and a duty of parents to determine whether or not to seek medical advice in respect of their child, and, having received advice, to give or withhold consent to medical treatment. The question in the appeal is as to the extent, and duration, of the right and the circumstances in which, outside the two admitted exceptions to which I have earlier referred, it can be overridden by the exercise of medical judgment ...

Although statute has intervened in respect of a child's capacity to consent to medical treatment from the age of 16 onwards, neither statute nor the case law has ruled on the extent and duration of parental right in respect of children under the age of 16. More specifically, there is no rule yet applied to contraceptive treatment, which has special problems of its own and is a latecomer in medical practice. It is open, therefore, to the House to formulate a rule. The Court of Appeal favoured a fixed age limit of 16, basing themselves on a view of the statute law which I do not share and upon their view of the effect of the older case law which for the reasons already given I cannot accept. They sought to justify the limit by the public interest in the law being certain. Certainty is always an advantage in the law, and in some breaches of the law it is a necessity. But it brings with it an inflexibility and a rigidity which in some branches of the law can obstruct justice, impede the law's development, and stamp upon the law the mark of obsolescence where what is needed is the capacity for development. The law relating to parent and child is concerned with the problems of the growth and maturity of the human personality. If the law should impose upon the process of 'growing up' fixed limits, where nature knows only a continuous process, the price would be artificiality and a lack of realism in an area where the law must be sensitive to human development and social change. If certainty be thought desirable, it is better that the rigid demarcations necessary to achieve it should be laid down by legislation after a full consideration of all the relevant factors than by the courts, confined as they are by the forensic process to the evidence adduced by the parties and to whatever may properly fall within the judicial notice of judges. Unless and until Parliament should think fit to intervene, the courts should establish a principle flexible enough to enable justice to be achieved by its application to the particular circumstances proved by the evidence placed before them ...

The modern law governing parental right and a child's capacity to make his own decisions was considered in *Reg v D* [1984] AC 778. The House must, in my view, be understood as having in that case accepted that, save where statute otherwise provides, a minor's capacity to make his or her own decision depends upon the minor having sufficient understanding and intelligence to make the decision and is not to be determined by reference to any judicially fixed age limit ...

In the light of the foregoing I would hold that as a matter of law the parental right to determine whether or not their minor child below the age of 16 will have medical treatment terminates if and when the child achieves a sufficient understanding and intelligence to enable him or her to understand fully what is proposed. It will be a question of fact whether a child seeking advice has sufficient understanding of what is involved to give a consent valid in law. Until the child achieves the capacity to consent, the parental right to make the decision continues save only in exceptional circumstances. Emergency, parental neglect, abandonment of the child, or inability to find the parent are examples of exceptional situations justifying the doctor proceeding to treat the child without parental knowledge and consent: but there will arise, no doubt, other exceptional situations in which it will be reasonable for the doctor to proceed without the parent's consent.

When applying these conclusions to contraceptive advice and treatment it has to be borne in mind that there is much that has to be understood by a girl under the age of 16 if she is to have legal capacity to consent to such treatment. It is not enough that she should understand the nature of the advice which is being given: she must also have a sufficient maturity to understand what is involved. There are moral and family questions, especially her relationship with her parents; long term problems associated with the emotional impact of pregnancy and its termination; and there are the risks to health of sexual intercourse at her age, risks which contraception may diminish but cannot eliminate. It follows that a doctor will have to satisfy himself that she is able to appraise these factors before he can safely proceed upon the basis that she has at law capacity to consent to contraceptive treatment. And it further follows that ordinarily the proper course will be for him, as the guidance lays down, first to seek to persuade the girl to bring her parents into consultation, and if she refuses, not to prescribe contraceptive treatment unless he is satisfied that her circumstances are such that he ought to proceed without parental knowledge and consent.

Most medical decisions made by parents on behalf of their children will be uncontroversial. However, in certain areas, such as the control of fertility, there can be a real conflict between parental wishes and the interests of the child. Bernard M Dickens examines the concept of parental rights:

Dickens, BM, 'Function and limits of parental rights' (1981) 97 LQR 462:

The modern function of parental rights, it is proposed, is not to enforce duties children owe their parents, or simply to enforce against third parties powers of custody and control parents enjoy over their children. It is to permit parents to discharge their duties to their children. These duties are not positively to do good, but to avoid harm. It is obvious that to the extent that ill health and, for instance, illiteracy are considered harm, parents are bound by positive duties to provide health care and education. This proposition may be derived from an abundance of case law and legislation. The duty to avoid harm is more elastic, however, since it affords licence to control a child not for its benefit, but in non-beneficial and non-therapeutic ways falling short of causing or risking harm. The issue to be critically addressed is the point at which an exercise of parental choice over a child's management and future is so potentially harmful to the welfare or interests of the child as to require State intervention and possibly a countermanding of parental choice.

Not surprisingly, the courts recognise that there are limits to the rights of a parent. The case of *Re S (A Minor) (Medical Treatment)* [1993] 1 FLR 376 is a clear illustration of this. The patient was a young child suffering from T-cell leukaemia, treatable only by chemotherapy which necessitated blood transfusions. The parents of the child were devout Jehovah's Witnesses and therefore were fundamentally opposed to blood transfusions. The local authority invoked the inherent jurisdiction of the court under s 100 of the Children Act 1989, and sought an order permitting such treatment to be given:

> **Thorpe J**: ... [T]he test must remain the welfare of the child as the paramount consideration. Specifically, in this case, the choice is not between two medical procedures with similar, if differing, prospects of success. Here the stark choice is between one medical procedure with no prospect of success and one medical treatment with a prospect of success which is put at even.
>
> So, as I put to Mr Daniel in argument: are the religious convictions of the parents to deny their child a 50% chance of survival? Are those convictions to deny him that 50% chance and condemn him to inevitable and early death? Mr Daniel realistically saw that this was an extreme case and one in which it is difficult to pursue the argument that the religious convictions of the parents should deny the child the chance of treatment.
>
> Finally, Mr Daniel invites the court to look ahead to the later years of childhood. If this treatment is applied in the face of parental opposition what would be the difficulties and stresses for S in years to come – parented by parents who believe that his life was prolonged by an ungodly act? Well, that consideration seems to me one that has little foundation in reality. The reality seems to me to be that family reaction will recognise that the responsibility for consent was taken from them and, as a judicial act, absolved their conscience of responsibility.

Parental opposition to clinical decisions was considered in the case of *Re C (A Minor)* [1998] 1 Lloyd's Rep Med 1. The patient was a 16 month old baby, suffering from spinal muscular atrophy, and said to be seriously disabled and severely emaciated. For a few weeks before the case came before the court, the child had been ventilated to support her own breathing. The opinion of the consultant paediatric neurologist in charge of the child's care was that no further ventilation should take place, and if, following withdrawal of the ventilation, the child should undergo further respiratory arrest, she should not be resuscitated. The evidence was that further respiratory arrest would mean long term ventilator dependency. The parents of the child, who were religious orthodox Jews, were opposed to this. They agreed that ventilation should be withdrawn, but would not agree that no attempt at resuscitation be made. A second medical opinion was obtained which supported the opinion of the treating doctor. Sir Stephen Brown P held that support of the parents' view would be tantamount to requiring doctors to undertake a course of treatment which they were unwilling to do, and no order would be made to this effect. Clinical judgment, however, will not always prevail, as will be seen from the case of *Re T (A Minor) (Wardship: Medical Treatment)* [1997] 1 All ER 906.

In the case of *Re S*, above, Thorpe J was considering a case where the treatment objected to (the blood transfusion) carried virtually no risk, and nothing more than inconvenience to the child. What about the case of a parent who refuses to agree to a difficult form of treatment which may be lengthy and painful? This was considered in the case of *Re T*. The child was born with a serious liver defect and underwent surgery at the age of three and a half weeks. The operation caused pain and distress and was unsuccessful. The medical prognosis was that without a liver transplant the child would not live more than a couple of years. The mother refused consent to a transplant. The child's father (to whom she was not married) agreed with her. Both parents were described as 'health care professionals' with experience of caring for sick children. The mother had moved out of the country at the time of the hearing of the local authority's application for permission for the operation to be carried out.

The application had been brought at the behest of the consultants who had treated the child. The judge at first instance granted the application on the basis that it was in the child's best interests for it to be carried out and that the mother was being 'unreasonable'. The Court of Appeal allowed the mother's appeal:

Re T (A minor) (Wardship: Medical Treatment) [1997] 1 All ER 906

Waite LJ: The law's insistence that the welfare of a child shall be paramount is easily stated and universally applauded, but the present case illustrates, poignantly and dramatically, the difficulties that are encountered when trying to put it into practice. Throughout his clear and able judgment, the judge demonstrated his appreciation of the dilemma to which the case gives rise. Loving and devoted parents have taken, after anxious consideration, a decision to withhold consent to operative transplant treatment. Although it is relatively novel treatment, still unavailable in many countries, doctors of the highest expertise have unanimously recommended it for this child on clinical grounds, taking the view that it involves a relatively minor level of risk which they regard as well worth taking in the child's long term interests (which in this instance include an extension of life itself). The parents' opposition is partly instinctive and (being based on their own awareness of the procedures involved) partly practical. It has sufficient cogency to have led one of the principal medical experts in the field of this operation to say that his team would decline to operate without the mother's committed support.

What is the court to do in such a situation? It is not an occasion – even in an age preoccupied with 'rights' – to talk of the rights of a child, or the rights of a parent, or the rights of the court. The cases cited by Butler-Sloss LJ are uncompromising in their assertion that the sole yardstick must be the need to give effect to the demands of paramountcy for the welfare of the child. They establish that there are bound to be occasions when such paramountcy will compel the court, acting as a judicial parent, to substitute the judge's own views as to the claims of child welfare over those of natural parents – even in a case where the views of the latter are supported by qualities of devotion, commitment, love and reason. The judge, after anxious consideration, reached the conclusion that this case provides such an occasion. Was he right to do so?

Of course if his decision was founded on a correct application of legal principle, it is unassailable, however tempted individual members of an appellate court might be to substitute a judgment of our own. These decisions, not least because they are so difficult and finely balanced, are best left to the discretion of the experienced judges who have the task, often a lonely and worrying one, of weighing the numerous delicate elements (including the view taken of the parties and witnesses) which enable a cumulative picture to be formed of the demands of welfare in a particular case, and taking the momentous decision which the child patient cannot take for himself.

In this instance, however, in agreement with Butler-Sloss LJ, I consider that the judge was betrayed into an error of law by his concern with the need to form a judgment about the reasonableness of the mother's approach. An appraisal of parental reasonableness may be appropriate in other areas of family law (in adoption, for example, where it is enjoined by statute), but when it comes to an assessment of the demands of the child patient's welfare, the starting point – and the finishing point too – must always be the judge's own independent assessment of the balance of advantage or disadvantage of the particular medical step under consideration.

In striking that balance, the judge will of course take into account as a relevant, often highly relevant, factor the attitude taken by a natural parent, and that may require examination of his or her motives. But the result of such an inquiry must never be allowed to prove determinative. It is a mistake to view the issue as one in which the clinical advice of doctors is placed in one scale and the reasonableness of the parent's view in the other. Had the judge viewed the evidence more broadly from the standpoint of his own perception of the child's welfare when appraised in all its aspects, he would have been bound, in my view, to take significant account of other elements in the case. Those include the parents' ties in country AB, and – crucially – the evidence of Dr P.

No one disputes that in the aftermath of the operation the child would remain in the primary care of the mother. Dr P maintained a very clear view that – even assuming that the operation proved wholly successful in surgical terms – the child's subsequent development could be injuriously affected if his day to day care depended upon the commitment of a mother who had suffered the turmoil of having her child being compelled against her will to undergo, as a result of a coercive order from the court, a major operation against which her own medical and maternal judgment wholeheartedly rebelled.

All these cases depend on their own facts and render generalisations – tempting though they may be to the legal or social analyst – wholly out of place. It can only be said safely that there is a scale, at one end of which lies the clear case where parental opposition to medical intervention is prompted by scruple or is of a kind which is patently irreconcilable with principles of child health and welfare widely accepted by the generality of mankind; and that at the other end lie highly problematic cases where there is genuine scope for a difference of view between parent and judge. In both situations it is the duty of the judge to allow the court's own opinion to prevail in the perceived paramount interests of the child concerned, but in cases at the latter end of the scale, there must be a likelihood (though never of course a certainty) that the greater the scope for genuine debate between one view and another the stronger will be the inclination of the court to be influenced by a reflection that in the last analysis the best interests of every child include an expectation that difficult decisions affecting the length and quality of its life will be taken for it by the parent to whom its care has been entrusted by nature. I too would allow this appeal.

Is the distinction between the 'welfare of the child' approach and the 'reasonableness of the parent' approach one of semantics only? In other words, was the first instance decision that the mother was being unreasonable only another way of saying that she was not acting in the best interests of the child, and that the Court of Appeal was wrong to disturb the decision?

It is also of some concern that the Court of Appeal was relying too heavily upon the judgment of the mother to whom the child's care 'has been entrusted by nature'. Marie Fox and Jean McHale, referring to Butler-Sloss LJ's judgment, comment as follows:

Fox, M and McHale, J, 'In whose best interests?' (1997) 60 MLR 700:

... a significant feature is the emphasis in the Court of Appeal judgments on the parents' status as health care professionals, with experience of paediatric care. However it is questionable whether such significance should have been attributed to the parents' profession. It should be noted that, in the context of medical treatment, there is some evidence that health care professionals are actively discouraged from treating their families. However, amongst the professional bodies there appears to be uncertainty about the ethics of the practice. While the General Medical Council and United Kingdom Council for Nursing, Midwifery and Health Visiting do not censure health professionals who treat themselves or their family members, the British Medical Association regards such practice as unethical. In *Re T*, however, the Court of Appeal drew an implicit distinction between medical treatment on the one hand and 'caring' on the other. This calls into question whether the same objections apply when health professionals are involved in caring for their own children, and what weight their views should carry in this context. Pinpointing the divide between treatment and care is a process fraught with difficulties, especially since caring may be entrusted to either professionals or lay persons. Such difficulties become particularly acute where parents are also health practitioners. Significantly, this policy issue was not addressed in *Re T*. In part, the Court of Appeal was able to avoid the issue by downplaying the importance of medical opinion. A striking feature of the judgments is that there is virtually no reference to medical evidence. This is in stark contrast to earlier cases, such as *Re C* and *Re J*, where a wealth of expert evidence was cited. Indeed, in *Re T*, greater weight appeared to be placed on a fact sheet published by the Children's Liver Disease Foundation (which highlighted the general complications of liver transplantation, thus endorsing the parental reservations about treatment) than on the specific medical evidence pertaining to this child. Thus, rather than focusing on the evidence which would have justified treatment, the judges focused on the implications for the carers should treatment be authorised against their will. A further point is that the judgments do not clarify whether the significance of the parents' occupations lies simply in their status as health professionals or is derived from their greater competence as decision makers.

Since the legitimacy of according carers an enhanced decision-making role by virtue solely of their status as health care professionals is questionable, we need to explore whether other special features of this case justify the weight accorded to the position of the carers. In this regard Butler-Sloss LJ noted that:

> Some of the objections of the mother, such as the difficulties of the operation itself, turned out ... to be less important than the mother believed. Underlying those less important objections by the mother was deep-seated concern of the mother as to the benefits to her son of the major invasive surgery and post-operative treatment, the dangers of failure long term as well as short term, the possibility of the need for further transplants, the likely length of life and the impact upon her son of all these concerns.

Thus, the mother's opposition to the procedure is represented as rooted in caring attitudes. Butler-Sloss LJ also refers to 'the enormous significance of the close attachment between the mother and baby'. Yet there are unresolved tensions in this portrayal of the mother. We are given little evidence to support the court's opinion that this mother was exceptionally devoted. Furthermore, even assuming that this representation is accurate, two troublesome issues arise. First, if we accept the court's depiction of her as especially caring, it was surely incumbent upon the judges to examine why she was so reluctant to undertake the care of her son following a procedure which could save his life, particularly in view of her professional expertise in this area. Secondly, there is no exploration of the relationship between caring and reasonableness. It must be doubted whether the decisions of an exceptionally caring parent, even one who is a health professional herself, may automatically be deemed reasonable ones ...

A further noteworthy point is the manner in which caring was construed as the mother's responsibility rather than that of both the parents. Nowhere in the judgments was the role of the father clearly articulated. In the circumstances this may have been largely because the parents were unmarried so that parental responsibility was vested in the mother alone. Certainly, the effect of the relative marginality of the father was to make it easier for the court to depict the mother as sole carer and then to conflate the interests of mother and child. This occurs most strikingly in the following passage of Butler-Sloss LJ's judgment:

> This mother and child are one for the purpose of this unusual case and the decision of the court to consent to the operation jointly affects the mother and

son and it also affects the father. The welfare of this child depends upon his mother.

… It may be questioned what the broader implications of this line of reasoning are for the autonomy of the mother in cases where no clinical support exists for her views, with the result that they are not upheld by the court.

Nevertheless, in this case, construing the mother and child as one permitted the Court of Appeal to minimise the potential conflict between the interests of the woman and child. It effectively allowed the court to encompass within the best interests test the interests of the mother as carer as well as the interests of the child. The problem of disentangling the determination of best interests from the question of who decides is rendered still more intractable by the court's reasoning in this case. Thus, it is significant that when Butler-Sloss LJ considered the consequences of upholding the judge's original order that the child should be returned to England for treatment, her emphasis was upon the difficulties and inconvenience of such an outcome for the mother:

> She will have to comply with the court order; return to this country and present the child to one of the hospitals. She will have to arrange to stay in this country for the foreseeable future … If [the father] does not come she will have to manage unaided. How will the mother cope? Can her professionalism overcome her view that her son should not be subjected this distressing procedure? Will she break down? How will the child be affected by the conflict with which the mother may have to cope?

… surely the Court of Appeal's approach in this case is exceptional, given that in the Jehovah's Witness cases cited above doctors were prepared to undertake treatment in the face of intransigent parental opposition?

Certainly, there is cause for concern in intertwining the interests of a child and its mother, or indeed a child and its parents. It is difficult to see the difference between *Re T (A Minor) (Wardship: Medical Treatment)* [1997] 1 All ER 906 and cases where sincere religious views of caring parents are overridden in the best interests of the child.

In the case of *Re T*, the parents purported to care for their child, despite the potentially tragic consequences of their views holding sway. In a case where the parents simply do not want the child to live, judicial decision-making is more clear cut. The case of *Re B (A Minor) (Wardship: Medical Treatment)* [1981] 1 WLR 1421 may have been such a case. The child was a newly born Down's syndrome baby who also had an intestinal complaint that required surgery in order for the child to survive. The parents refused consent. Their view was that the child would be better off dead. This may have been because they anticipated a poor life ahead for the child, or it may have been the fact that they did not want a Down's syndrome child. In that case, the Court of Appeal authorised the treatment. Templeman LJ described the choice as a stark one between authorising the operation so that the child may live for 20 or 30 years as a mongoloid, or terminating the life of a mongoloid child because she also has an intestinal complaint. (See Chapter 12 for further discussion of this and other cases of gravely incapacitated children.)

An interesting contrast to this case is *Re SL (Adult Patient) (Medical Treatment)* [2000] 2 FCR 452. The mother of a 29 year old woman, with severe learning difficulties, made an application to the court for a declaration in respect of the lawfulness of a proposed sterilisation/hysterectomy. It was anticipated that before long the mother would not be able to continue to care for her daughter and that she would have to go and live in local authority sheltered accommodation. The mother feared that, as her daughter was an attractive woman, she might become pregnant, and also that she was distressed by 'heavy' menstrual bleeding. Three medical options were available. The first was a total hysterectomy (this would render her incapable of bearing children and eliminate menstruation); the second, a sterilisation by clipping of the fallopian tubes (a contraceptive measure, but it would do nothing about menstruation); the third by the fitting of a Mirena coil (contraceptive, with the possibility of reducing or even eliminating menstruation). The mother favoured the first option. The medical evidence all pointed to trying the Mirena coil as a first attempt, but one of the experts stated that, in his opinion, a hysterectomy could be justified even if undertaken at the outset. This seemed to influence the judge, Wall J, who decided that it would be in the woman's best interests, even if it was not the doctors' first choice because, first, the court should decide the best interests question and, secondly, the decision satisfied the *Bolam* test because there was a body of opinion that would undertake the hysterectomy at this, the first stage. The judge then said that as both treatments (the sterilisation was not favoured by anyone) were *Bolam* compliant, he would make a declaration to this effect and leave the mother to discuss with the doctors what was best. This aspect of the case is considered further at p 216, below, but, here, the issue is the view taken by the Court of Appeal of the mother's wishes. These were based upon the fact that her daughter became very distressed at the time of her periods, regarding herself as being dirty, and the Mirena coil would not necessarily have any effect upon this. Further, the coil itself had to be inserted under general anaesthetic, and had to be replaced every five years, or more frequently if it became dislodged. The woman had a horror of hospitals and much of this would take place when her mother would not be there to help her. These were understandable concerns, but they did not sway the Court of Appeal. As it happens, in this case, the coil could be tried first and the more invasive method tried later if it did not work. This is unfortunate because, otherwise, the court could have made it more explicit that the interests of this woman and her mother could not be conflated and that might have been an embarrassing contrast with the decision in *Re T (A Minor) (Wardship: Medical Treatment)* [1997] 1 All ER 906.

The question of parental rights was considered in the case of *Re P (A Minor)* (1982) 80 LGR 301, when Butler-Sloss J (as she then was) made an order for the termination of a 15 year old girl's pregnancy in the face of her parents' opposition. The girl already had a baby and resided in a special mother and baby unit. Her parents wanted to care for the second child she was carrying, and her father objected to abortion on religious grounds:

> **Butler-Sloss J**: I would not like it to be thought that because she says she does not want the child her wishes should be given such paramount importance as to mean that for that reason only she should have an abortion. But where her wishes coincide with the facts that she is in danger of injury to her mental health; that she is undoubtedly – when I consider her interests, as I do, as the first and paramount consideration – unable to fulfil her own growing up as a child at her schooling as a consequence of this second pregnancy; where she is endangering the future of her current child; and where I take into account all the aspects of her actual and reasonably foreseeable environment, I have no doubt that this case comes within s 1(a) of the Abortion Act 1967 ...
>
> I must take into account in considering the welfare of Shirley – and her welfare is what is paramount in my mind because she is a ward of court – and through her the

effect on her son of having this unwanted child, the important aspect of her parents. I was helpfully reminded of what had been said in the House of Lords in *J v C* [1970] AC 668 about the rights and obligations of parents. These parents are in certain difficulties in that they do not have the day to day care of Shirley since she is in care, and they are not able to offer to take over the day to day care of Shirley. In the circumstances, although I must give weight to their feelings as a factor in the case to be taken into consideration, and I must take into account their deeply and sincerely held religious objection, in considering the best interest of the minor as to whether she should have her pregnancy terminated I draw to some extent an analogy with Jehovah's Witnesses and blood transfusions ... I am satisfied ... that there is a risk of injury to the mental health of this minor, the factors raised by the grandfather on behalf of himself and his wife – which I have taken into account – cannot weigh in the balance against the needs of this girl so as to prevent the termination which I have decided is necessary in her best interests.

This may be thought to be in stark contrast with the views expressed by Butler-Sloss LJ in the much later case of *Re T*, p 171, above. However, even if it had been in issue, the closeness of the parent/child relationship, which was regarded as so important in *Re T*, would not have been relevant here as, unlike the case of a young, sick child, there was no question of this child needing her parents to care for her.

Note that, in *Re P*, the judge had to take into account the provisions of the Abortion Act 1967, where, *inter alia*, there has to be a risk to the health of the pregnant woman (see Chapter 8). There were, therefore, objective factors that had to be satisfied regardless of the wishes of the child and her parents. However, in abortion cases, it is always arguable that a child who does not want to continue with her pregnancy is going to be mentally damaged if she is compelled to continue it. In the context of other areas of medicine and surgery, however, there have been a number of recent cases where there have been disagreements between the parents, either among themselves or, more often, with the doctors, as to what is the appropriate medical treatment for their children.

In *Re J (Child's Religious Upbringing and Circumcision)* (1999) 52 BMLR 82, the Court of Appeal refused an application by a child's father that the child be circumcised. The child's parents had separated when he was two and a half and the mother had custody. The father applied for a specific issue order under the Children Act 1989. The Turkish father, who was permanently resident in the UK was a Muslim, but non-practising. Similarly, the child's mother was described as non-practising Church of England. The child went to a secular school. The Court of Appeal upheld the first instance decision that it would not be in the child's best interests, as a non-practising Muslim, to undergo irreversible, non-therapeutic surgery which carried with it pain and the small risk of psychological harm. On the other hand, the same surgery, if agreed by both parents, for religious or cultural reasons, would be lawful.

In *C (HIV Test)* [1999] 2 FLR 1004, both parents were agreed that they did not wish their baby to be tested for HIV. The mother was HIV positive and had resisted any form of intervention to prevent transmission of the virus to the child, both during pregnancy and afterwards. The clinical view was that, if the child was infected, there were measures which could be taken to manage the condition and that, if the child was not infected, then immediate cessation of breast feeding would be recommended. The local authority made an application for a specific issue order that the child be tested and this was supported by the Official Solicitor on behalf of the child. The judge at first instance granted the order on the basis that it was in the child's best interests and the Court of Appeal refused leave to appeal, confirming that the wishes of parents could be overruled and approving the judge's evaluation of the medical evidence.

The case of *Re MM (A Child) (Medical Treatment)* [2000] 1 FLR 224 concerned a child's treatment for immunodeficiency by immunoglobin, which doctors recommended. The parents were not prepared to consent to this because treatment received in Russia before the family moved to the UK had been working well and because there had been an early misdiagnosis by the English doctors which had shaken their confidence. In the event, an order was agreed that the immunoglobin treatment be continued, but with the parents closely involved in the decision-making, with liberty for either party to apply to the court for further directions.

The joined cases in *Re C (Welfare of Child: Immunisation)* [2003] EWCA Civ 1148, concerned disputes between parents as to whether children should receive the MMR injection which immunised against multiple infectious diseases. There has been some controversy about the safety of the MMR immunisation, and the mothers alleged that it presented unacceptable risks, whereas the fathers argued that there was convincing medical evidence that the benefits outweighed any risks. At first instance the judge made a declaration ordering immunisation of the children. The Court of Appeal upheld the decision on the basis that the judge had properly weighed up the medical evidence, and the court confirmed that there was no general proposition of law that a court would not order non-essential invasive medical treatment in the face of stong opposition from a child's primary carer (in both these cases, the children lived with their mothers).

The extraordinary circumstances which brought the case of *R v Portsmouth Hospital NHS Trust ex p Glass* [1999] Lloyd's Law Reports 367 before the courts, came about through such a total breakdown of relationships between the doctors and the patient's relatives, that a fight broke out in which medical staff were punched, kicked and bitten, and three of the patient's relatives were prosecuted and received prison sentences. The patient, David, aged 12, was severely disabled, both mentally and physically, but his family cared for him devotedly and wanted him to live as long as possible. He was hospitalised several times during the summer of 1998, suffering from breathing and digestive problems. The doctors believed he was dying. In October, they wanted to administer diamorphine to relieve distress, but the child's mother refused to consent to this, fearing that sedation was a prelude to death. The doctors went ahead anyway, and a 'Do Not Resuscitate' order was placed on his medical records without consulting his mother. Visiting relatives made strenuous attempts to revive the child, in the course of which the assaults upon the medical staff took place. The child eventually went home and was successfully treated by the family GP. The trust wrote to the child's mother indicating that any future care should be administered by a hospital in Southampton and that it would only deal with him as an emergency admission. The mother sought judicial review of the trust's decision to administer diamorphine in the face of her refusal. Scott-Baker J dismissed the application for judicial review on the basis that the situation which gave rise to the application had now passed; the child was to be admitted to a different hospital and the judicial review mechanism was too blunt a tool for the sensitive and ongoing problems of the type thrown up in such a case. The Court of Appeal agreed and refused leave to appeal, stating that, if future conflicts of 'a grave nature' arose, then declarations could be sought from the court at the appropriate time, rather than trying to anticipate the 'almost infinite' considerations that might arise in the future. The judgment of the court, given by Lord Woolf MR, whilst peppered with reminders that these cases give rise to sensitive issues, declined to comment on the fact that, in the face of total breakdown of confidence, the trust did not see fit to bring the matter before the court, when the only course of action which seemed open to the family at that crucial time was, literally, to fight for the child's life.

The case went before the European Court of Human Rights and the decision of that Court (*Glass v United Kingdom* (2004) 39 EHRR 15) was that the decision to impose treatment on David in defiance of his mother's objections gave rise to an interference with the child's Article 8 rights, and in particular his right to physical integrity. Obviously, there are circumstances in which it is right to impose treatment on a child in the face of a parental refusal of consent, as evidenced by the cases above and, under such circumstances, save in emergency situations, UK law requires doctors to seek the intervention of the courts. In the *Glass* case failure to do this meant that there had been a breach of Article 8. See also *Royal Wolverhampton Hospitals NHS Trust v E and RB and Others* [2000] 1 FLR 953, where, it was assumed by the judge that, in circumstances of parental/medical disagreement, an application to the court by the trust was in the best interests of the child patient.

In *Re O (A Minor) (Blood Tests: Constraint) and Re J (A Minor)* [2000] 1 FLR 418, it was held that the Family Law Reform Act 1969, which required the consent of the custodial parent to the taking of blood tests to determine paternity, ousted the inherent jurisdiction of the courts to determine whether blood tests should be taken on the welfare of the child principle. (The effect of this decision, however, has been reversed by s 82(3) of the Child Support, Pensions and Social Security Act 2000 which amends s 21(3) of the 1969 Act and allows the court to order the taking of a blood sample for the purposes of resolving paternity disputes where the custodial parent objects.) See the case of *Re Z (A Minor) (Freedom of Publication)* [1995] 4 All ER 961. See also the case of *In re S(FC)* [2004] UKHL on the balancing exercise which must take place when competing Articles of the European Convention are engaged.

Children and the role of the court

Decisions concerning the treatment of children can come before the court via the Children Act 1989 (specific issue orders under s 8), or via the jurisdiction of the High Court. The wardship jurisdiction must be distinguished from the inherent jurisdiction of the High Court. In the former case parental authority is vested in the court; in the latter the court is dealing only with the particular treatment issue put before it. The inherent jurisdiction of the court may be invoked by local authorities, as the wardship jurisdiction is unavailable to them. Regardless of the nature of the judicial proceedings, the welfare of the child is paramount.

Adults and the rights of others

In a number of the sterilisation cases we are about to consider, it was argued that the views of the close relatives of the patients were relevant to the final outcome of the cases. However, though taken into account by the courts, as they were in the case of *Re P*, the case concerning a child, the argument that a close relative's views could in any way be determinative has been rejected. In the Canadian case of *Re Eve* [1986] 2 SCR 388, La Forest J stated:

> **La Forest J**: One may sympathise with Mrs E [the adult patient's mother]. To use Heilbron J's phrase, it is easy to understand the natural feelings of a parent's heart. But the *parens patriae* jurisdiction cannot be used for her benefit. Its exercise is confined to doing what is necessary for the benefit and protection of persons under disability like Eve. And a court ... must exercise great caution to avoid being misled by this all too human mixture of emotions and motives.

(See below, for explanation of the *parens patriae* jurisdiction.)

Commenting upon the use of surrogate decision-makers, Pellegrino and Thomasma state:

> **Pellegrino, ED and Thomasma, DC, *For the Patient's Good*, 1988, Oxford: OUP, p 164:**
>
> Some have argued that the family is almost always the best surrogate because of the family member's 'bonding' to the patient. This may not always be the case. The physician's first responsibility ... is to ascertain the moral validity – that is to say, the moral acceptability – of the surrogate decision maker. This is the only way the physician can fulfil his or her own responsibility as steward of the patient's interests.
>
> The criteria for a morally valid surrogate decision are as follows:
>
> (1) First, the surrogate must provide some evidence that he or she really knows the patient and his or her values. This is not necessarily the case even with families. In our mobile society parents and children are often separated geographically; they may be estranged from each other, or may not have seen each other for a long time. Friends may have a closer, or more recent, knowledge of what the patient would want. Nurses may know more about a patient in a long term care setting than does the patient's family.
>
> (2) Further, the surrogate or proxy must not have a conflict of interest with the patient's best interests. The desire for gain – settlement of an estate, inheritance of property, changing a will, and so on – can impel surrogates, consciously or not, to hasten a patient's death by undertreatment.
>
> (3) Also to be guarded against is the deleterious effect of psychological antipathies – the unconscious desire to overtreat a patient whom one has neglected or maltreated for many years, or, conversely, the motivation to undertreat and thus act vindictively to settle old scores.

The relevance of blood ties was considered by the Court of Appeal in the case of *Re S (Hospital Order: Court's Jurisdiction)* [1995] 3 All ER 290. The plaintiff was the patient's cohabitee and the defendant, his son. Hale J held, at first instance, (approved in the Court of Appeal, p 295) as follows:

> **Hale J**: Yet although his relationship to the patient is a close one, and his wishes are of course worthy of respect, he has no more legal right to decide the patient's future than has the plaintiff. Indeed, were this to be a Mental Health Act case, the facts might be such that the plaintiff (rather than the wife) would be the patient's nearest relative for the purposes of s 26 of the Mental Health Act 1983.

Adults and the role of the court

It may seem odd, but in English law, until the enactment of the Mental Capacity Act 2005 there was no mechanism whereby someone may be sanctioned to make decisions about medical treatment on behalf of an adult patient, and this legislation does not come into force until 2007. Incompetent adults once had protection: there was an inherent power in the courts (known as the *parens patriae* jurisdiction) to act on behalf of the incapacitated adult in very much the same way as minors are still protected today. This is the jurisdiction extant in the Canadian legal process referred to by La Forest J in the judgment in *Re Eve*, p 200, below. However, the royal warrant by which this power was delegated to the courts was revoked shortly after the Mental Health Act (MHA) 1959 came into force because it was believed that the Act made all necessary provision for mental patients. However, whilst the current MHA 1983 provides for the appointment of a guardian in respect of the patient's financial affairs, who is then overseen by the Court of Protection, no such power was provided for in respect of the personal welfare or health of the patient. At present doctors make decisions about medical treatment and the incompetent purely on the basis of what they, the doctors, believe to be best for the patient. The great majority of these decisions will be uncontroversial, but some can have huge ethical significance and, in those circumstances, although doctors would be wise to seek the appropriate declaration from the court, they are under no obligation to do so. The case of *In re F (Mental Patient: Sterilisation)* [1990] 2 AC 1 concerned the sterilisation of a mentally impaired woman aged 36, but said to have an overall mental age of four or five. The case is considered in further detail at p 158, but on the subject of the court's role, only Lord Griffiths dissented from the view that an application to the court remains within the discretion of the doctors concerned (p 70):

> **Lord Griffiths**: I cannot agree that it is satisfactory to leave this grave decision with all its social implications in the hands of those having the care of the patient with only the expectation that they will have the wisdom to obtain a declaration of lawfulness before the operation is performed. In my view the law ought to be that they must obtain the approval of the court before they sterilise a woman incapable of giving consent and that it is unlawful to sterilise without that consent. I believe that it is open to your Lordships to develop a common law rule to this effect ...

Similarly, in the earlier case of *Re B (A Minor) (Wardship: Sterilisation)* [1988] AC 199, only Lord Templeman took the view that court approval should always be obtained. However, in the Australian High Court's decision in *Department of Health v JWB and SMB* (1992) 66 ALJR 300, although the judges did not express the view that it is mandatory to apply to the court in the case of a therapeutic sterilisation, in the case of a non-therapeutic sterilisation (that is, a sterilisation carried out where the physical health of the patient does not demand it), the court held that it required prior court approval. Although this case and the case of *Re B* concerned children, it is arguable that exactly the same view should be taken in the case of an incompetent adult.

Most of the cases using the declaratory jurisdiction have been brought by the health carers involved with the patient. However, it was used in the case of *Re S (Hospital Order: Court's Jurisdiction)* [1995] 3 All ER 290 to decide a dispute between the wife and the mistress of a elderly Norwegian who had become incompetent following a stroke. Both wife and mistress wanted to care for him. The court held that the declaratory jurisdiction could be used by anyone with a genuine and legitimate interest in obtaining a decision on a serious justiciable issue. The dispute in this case was found to be such an issue. (See also *Re S (Adult's Lack of Capacity: Carer and Residence)* [2003] EWHC 1909.)

In *Re GF (Medical Treatment)* [1992] 1 FLR 293, Sir Stephen Brown (when President) had said that no application to the court would be necessary if: (1) the procedure was necessary for therapeutic purposes; (2) was in the best interests of the patient; and (3) that there is no practicable, less intrusive means of treating the condition. In *Re SL (Adult Patient) (Medical Treatment)* [2000] 2 FCR 452, the Court of Appeal said that these criteria should be strictly and cautiously interpreted and applied.

In *Re F (Adult: Court's Jurisdiction)* [2000] 2 FLR 512, the facts concerned a mentally impaired 18 year old woman (T). It was agreed that she lacked capacity to make decisions, particularly about the place where she should live. She had been in local authority care, initially with the consent of her parents, but consent to further placement was withdrawn. The local authority sought declarations that it could keep her in similar accommodation and restrict and supervise her contact with her family (previously, she had been neglected and sexually exploited when she had been living at home). An application for guardianship under the MHA 1983 had already been rejected by the Court of Appeal on the basis that she did not satisfy the definition of mental impairment under the Act (see further, Chapter 9, p 470) – *Re F (Mental Health Act: Guardianship)* [2000] 1 FLR 192). However, having reached the age of 18, the wardship jurisdiction was no longer available to the court. The Court of Appeal (*Re F (Mental Health Act: Guardianship)* [2000] 1 FLR 512) held that the common law could 'plug the gap' in the statutory framework, but went on to lament the fact that there was not a clearly defined framework of protection for vulnerable, mentally incapacitated adults. This had been proposed by the Law Commission in its report, *Mental Incapacity*, Report No 231, 1995, London: HMSO. In December 1997, the government published a Green Paper, *Who Decides?*, which was closely based upon the Law Commission's report. In 1999 the *White Paper, Making Decisions: The Government's Proposals for Making Decisions on Behalf of Mentally Incapacitated Adults*, Cm 4465, 1999, London: HMSO, was published. Subsequently there was the draft Mental Incapacity Bill, the draft Mental Capacity Bill (no doubt the change of emphasis reflecting the presumption of capacity) and, finally, this resulted in the passing of the Mental Capacity Act 2005. This is not due to come into force until 2007.

The new Act abolishes the existing Court of Protection and introduces a new court (confusingly this will also be called the Court of Protection) which will have jurisdiction to deal with all aspects of decision-making on behalf of mentally incapacitated people. Although the Act is primarily about incapacitated adults it will have the jurisdiction to deal with children if the court considers that it is likely that they will not gain capacity at the age of 18 – see ss 18 and 21 of the Act.

The Court of Protection, in its new form, will (*inter alia*) make declarations as to whether or not a person has the capacity to make a decision relating to, in our context, a particular form of medical treatment, to appoint what is described as a 'deputy' to make decisions in relation to those matters in which the person lacks capacity, to make decisions about advance treatment decisions (see Chapter 12), and to make declarations as to the lawfulness or otherwise of acts done or proposed to be done to a patient who lacks capacity (see ss 15 to 23). The Act also makes provision for the appointment of a new office-holder to be known as the Public Guardian who will carry out a variety of administrative functions, will be responsible for supervising deputies and will report on various matters to the court (see ss 57 to 60).

Note should be taken of the current guidance from the Official Solicitor on dealing with adults who lack capacity: *Practice Note (Official Solicitor: Declaratory Proceedings: Medical and Welfare Proceedings for Adults Who Lack Capacity)* [2001] 2 FLR 158. This states that declarations should be sought where there are disputes as to the patient's capacity or their best interests. The courts have given guidance in relation to sterilisation in *Re B (A Minor) (Wardship: Sterilisation)* [1988] AC 199 and *Re F (Mental Patient: Sterilisation)* [1990] 2 AC 1, in relation to withdrawal of nutrition for those in vegetative states in *Airedale NHS Trust v Bland* [1993] AC 789, and as to the general jurisdiction of the High Court in *Re F (Adult: Court's Jurisdiction)*, [2001] Fam 38. Issues involving the medical treatment or welfare of children are to be dealt with under the Children Act 1989 or the inherent jurisdiction. Applications for the Official Solicitor's involvement are to be on the basis that the applicant lacks capacity, and treatment, or its discontinuation, is required. Evidence as to capacity and best interests is to be submitted with the application and the claimant should be the appropriate NHS trust with the patient as the defendant. The note also sets a timetable for dealing with such cases and gives guidance as to the matters to which the Official Solicitor should have regard.

DECISION-MAKING CRITERIA

The therapeutic/non-therapeutic distinction

Most medical procedures performed on mentally incompetent patients will be carried out to cure or ameliorate the effects of disease and disorder. However, this will not always be the case. In the case of medical research on healthy volunteers (see Chapter 10), and the control of fertility (see p 197, below), there is no physical or mental disorder which is being treated. It is common to refer to these latter cases as instances of non-therapeutic 'treatment'. Of course, they are not really 'treatment' cases at all. However, when the patient is incompetent and the procedure is being carried out on the basis of his 'best interests', the English courts have questioned whether the distinction has any useful purpose.

The validity of making such a distinction was accepted by the Australian High Court in the case of *Secretary, Department of Health and Community Services v JWB and SMB* (1992) 66 ALJR 300. However, although accepting that there is a distinction, all seven judges acknowledged that it was not easy to draw the line. Brennan J suggests the following distinguishing factors:

> **Brennan J**: It is necessary to define what is meant by therapeutic medical treatment. I would define treatment (including surgery) as therapeutic when it is administered for the chief purpose of preventing, removing or ameliorating a cosmetic deformity, a pathological condition or a psychiatric disorder, provided the treatment is appropriate for and proportionate to the purpose for which it is administered. 'Non-therapeutic' medical treatment is descriptive of treatment which is inappropriate or disproportionate having regard to the cosmetic deformity, pathological condition or psychiatric disorder for which the treatment is administered and of treatment which is administered chiefly for other purposes.

In the Canadian case of *Re Eve* [1986] 2 SCR 388, the distinction was crucial to the decision of the court. The case concerned a 24 year old woman suffering from extreme expressive aphasia, which is a condition inhibiting the patient from communicating thoughts and feelings. She was described as being mildly to moderately retarded. It was accepted that she may be able to carry out the physical aspects of child care, but due to her severe lack of communication skills she would not make a suitable mother in the wider sense. As a result of what was described as a close relationship with a male student at the school for retarded adults that she attended, her mother became concerned and wished her daughter to be sterilised:

> **La Forest J**: ... [I]t is difficult to imagine a case in which non-therapeutic sterilisation could possibly be of benefit to the person on behalf of whom a court purports to act, let alone one for in which that procedure is necessary in his or her best interest. And how are we to weigh the best interests of a person in this troublesome area, keeping in mind that an error is irreversible? Unlike other cases involving the use of the *parens patriae* jurisdiction, an error cannot be corrected by the subsequent exercise of judicial discretion. That being so, one need only recall Lord Eldon's remark ... that 'it has always been the principle of this court, not to risk damage to children which it cannot repair' to conclude that non-therapeutic sterilisation may not be authorised in the exercise of the parens patriae jurisdiction.
>
> McQuaid J was, therefore, right in concluding that he had no authority or jurisdiction to grant the application.

In the case of *Re B (A Minor) (Wardship: Sterilisation)* [1988] AC 199, the distinction was rejected. The child in this case was 17 years old and described as having the mental age of a five or six year old. She was in the care of the local authority, and, when it was thought that she was exhibiting signs of some sexual appetite, it applied to the High Court for leave for her to be sterilised. The case eventually reached the House of Lords:

> **Lord Hailsham of St Marylebone LC:** We were also properly referred to the Canadian case of *Re Eve* ... I find, with great respect [La Forest J's] conclusions ... that the procedure of sterilisation 'should never be authorised for non-therapeutic purposes' (my emphasis) totally unconvincing and in startling contradiction to the welfare principle which should be the first and paramount consideration in wardship cases. Moreover, for the purposes of the present appeal I find the distinction he purposes to draw between 'therapeutic' and 'non-therapeutic' purposes of this operation in relation to the facts of the present case above as totally meaningless, and, if meaningful, quite irrelevant to the correct application of the welfare principle.
>
> ... To say that the court can never authorise sterilisation of a ward as being in her best interests would be patently wrong. To say that it can only do so if the operation is 'therapeutic' as opposed to 'non-therapeutic' is to divert attention from the true issue, which is whether the operation is in the ward's best interests, and remove it to an area of arid semantic debate as to where the line is to be drawn between 'therapeutic' and 'non-therapeutic' treatment.

Kennedy and Grubb comment as follows on the rejection of the distinction by the English courts:

> **Kennedy, I and Grubb, A, *Medical Law*, 2nd edn, 1994, London: Butterworths, pp 316–17:**
>
> In the light of the views expressed by the Canadian Supreme Court and Australian High Court, it could therefore be argued that the House of Lords' rejection of the distinction is out of step. It could be said that the distinction is rejected out of a misunderstanding of its true basis. It is not entirely a descriptive distinction to be applied or not mechanistically to any particular intervention. This is because the

distinction is also, in part, normative, reflecting prior value judgments as to what types of medical interventions are legitimate and acceptable to society. A differing set of values are at the heart of the different results in *Re B* and *Re Eve*. The misunderstanding of the House of Lords in *Re B* is that they applied the simplistic 'best interests' approach, instead of proceeding in two stages. First, the court must determine in general terms the permissible limits of medical interventions. Secondly, the court must then determine whether the particular doctor did what he did with the intention of producing those permissible ends. The value of the distinction between therapeutic and non-therapeutic interventions is that ordinarily, *ex hypothesi*, the court will regard a therapeutic intervention as legitimate. By contrast the court will need to be persuaded that an intervention which has no therapeutic purpose is legitimate ...

It may be that the insistence of the Australian High Court on the distinction need not in fact produce any different result in any particular case from an application of the 'best interests' test. This is because the 'best interests' test also proceeds from judicial and societal values. The question then has to be put, if the result may be the same why should we be concerned? The answer is that the criterion of 'best interests' contains within it, as Brennan J is anxious to point out, virtually no explicit guidelines as to the values it embraces and thereby allows the court free rein and provides no guidance to proxy decision makers. By contrast, the distinction between therapeutic and non-therapeutic causes the court to identify the values underlying the notion of treatment and then places a not inconsiderable burden on those who would engage in a non-therapeutic intervention to justify it. Finally, we may speculate that the true reason for the House of Lords' preference for the 'best interests' test rested on pragmatic rather than theoretical grounds. It may well be that their Lordships thought that the therapeutic/non-therapeutic distinction limited them to a consideration of medical matters whereas the 'best interests' test allowed a consideration of wider matters. Wanting the freedom to take account of non-medical factors, their Lordships opted for the 'best interests' approach.

Does this interpretation suggest that the Law Lords were rejecting the distinction because it worked against the interests of the person concerned? Clearly, there is a good argument that the courts should not be fettered by having no discretion to consider 'wider' issues, but, by implication, adopting the therapeutic/non-therapeutic distinction means that these wider issues can be considered, even though, as, in *Re Eve*, non-therapeutic treatment of a certain nature is rejected.

The case of *R v Human Fertilisation and Embryology Authority ex p Blood* [1997] 2 WLR 806 concerned the legality of using the sperm of the woman's deceased husband after his death (see further Chapter 7). The argument before the court was about the application of the Human Fertilisation and Embryology Act 1990. However, it was accepted that at least some of the sperm was taken from the man before his death (see Chapter 11 for a discussion of the rights anyone may have when tissue is removed from a dead body). Surprisingly, the Court of Appeal passed little comment on the common law, despite the fact that the procedure was non-therapeutic, carried out without consent and, therefore, probably constituted a battery. However, consider the position if the patient would have wished for his sperm to be taken in this way and used after his death (as his widow tried to argue): would it mean that the 'battery' would be transformed into something done in his best interests? Consider also the 'substituted judgment' test, dealt with at p 194, below.

The case of *S v S* [1972] AC 24 concerned two disputed cases of paternity. The parents of the children had agreed that blood samples be taken from the children in question for the appropriate tests to be carried out. The Official Solicitor had argued that the blood tests could not be carried out unless it was in the interests of the children. The House of Lords considered the matter:

> **Lord MacDermott:** In exercising what I have called the ancillary jurisdiction in relation to infants the court must also observe and, if need be, exercise its protective jurisdiction. For instance, if the court were satisfied that – as might possibly be the case on rare occasions – a blood test would prejudicially affect the health of the infant it would, no doubt, exercise its discretion against ordering the test. And, again, if the court had reason to believe that the application for a blood test was of a fishing nature, designed for some ulterior motive to call in question the legitimacy, otherwise unimpeached, of a child who had enjoyed a legitimate status, it would be justified in refusing the application. I need not, however, pursue such instances as they do not arise on these appeals. The point to be made is that the protective jurisdiction, if of the nature I have described, would not ordinarily afford ground for refusing a blood test merely because it might, in revealing the truth, prove the infant's illegitimacy in duly constituted paternity proceedings.

The implications of this are considered further below, but would it be possible to argue that the child has an interest in knowing the identity of his father, and therefore, this 'procedure' would be 'therapeutic' in the sense that it would have psychological benefits for the child? Arguably it would not. It is pure speculation as to the outcome of the paternity dispute and its effect upon the child, and therefore whether it would make him *feel* better is unascertainable. However, this raises a crucial factor in the concept of the 'therapeutic' – the making life better for the person concerned. It must be remembered that we are not talking here about patients. The healthy volunteer in a research programme is not a patient. The mentally handicapped person whom it is proposed to sterilise because she may become pregnant is not a patient (she may or may not live in a hospital, but her residence there would not be because of gynaecological disorder). That is not to say that these procedures may never be carried out, but the decision is not a medical decision. It is arguable that it is important to label the procedure as 'non-therapeutic' so as not to lose sight of this.

However, might the converse be the case? We consider at p 197, below, a number of cases where sterilisations have been carried out on women for the purposes of 'managing menstruation'. These have been regarded as 'therapeutic' because the purpose was not to render the women sterile. By describing them thus, it could be said that the distinction might be used to mask a real 'non-therapeutic' intention.

The 'best interests' test

The Mental Capacity Act 2005 states that one of the principles of the Act is that 'an act done, or a decision made under this Act for or on behalf of a person who lacks capcity must be done, or made, in his best interests' (s 1(5)). Section 4 of the Act deals with the way in which 'best interests' must be determined. The concept of 'best interests' is not new to the law regarding medical treatment decisions and incapacitated persons and has been used extensively in case law (see eg *Re F (Mental Patient: Sterilisation)* [1990] 2 AC 1). What does 'best interests' mean?

Mental Capacity Act 2005

4 Best interests

(1) In determining for the purposes of this Act what is in a person's best interests, the person making the determination must not make it merely on the basis of–

   (a) the person's age or appearance, or

   (b) a condition of his, or an aspect of his behaviour, which might lead others to make unjustified assumptions about what might be in his best interests.

(2) The person making the determination must consider all the relevant circumstances and, in particular, take the following steps.

(3) He must consider–

   (a) whether it is likely that the person will at some time have capacity in relation to the matter in question, and

   (b) if it appears likely that he will, when that is likely to be.

(4) He must, so far as reasonably practicable, permit and encourage the person to participate, or to improve his ability to participate, as fully as possible in any act done for him and any decision affecting him.

(5) Where the determination relates to life-sustaining treatment he must not, in considering whether the treatment is in the best interests of the person concerned, be motivated by a desire to bring about his death.

(6) He must consider, so far as is reasonably ascertainable–

   (a) the person's past and present wishes and feelings (and, in particular, any relevant written statement made by him when he had capacity),

   (b) the beliefs and values that would be likely to influence his decision if he had capacity, and

   (c) the other factors that he would be likely to consider if he were able to do so.

(7) He must take into account, if it is practicable and appropriate to consult them, the views of–

   (a) anyone named by the person as someone to be consulted on the matter in question or on matters of that kind,

   (b) anyone engaged in caring for the person or interested in his welfare,

   (c) any donee of a lasting power of attorney granted by the person, and

   (d) any deputy appointed for the person by the court,

   as to what would be in the person's best interests and, in particular, as to the matters mentioned in subsection (6).

(8) The duties imposed by subsections (1) to (7) also apply in relation to the exercise of any powers which–

   (a) are exercisable under a lasting power of attorney, or

   (b) are exercisable by a person under this Act where he reasonably believes that another person lacks capacity.

(9) In the case of an act done, or a decision made, by a person other than the court, there is sufficient compliance with this section if (having complied with the requirements of subsections (1) to (7)) he reasonably believes that what he does or decides is in the best interests of the person concerned.

(10) 'Life-sustaining treatment' means treatment which in the view of a person providing health care for the person concerned is necessary to sustain life.

(11) 'Relevant circumstances' are those–

　　(a) of which the person making the determination is aware, and

　　(b) which it would be reasonable to regard as relevant.

Cases on the common law application of 'best interests' will of course continue to provide guidance on the concept after the Act comes into force in 2007.

Consider, once again, the case of *S v S* (see p 190, above). Here, it was found that there were no reasons why the tests should not be carried out, as opposed to there being positive reasons in favour. However, Kennedy and Grubb (*Medical Law*, 2nd edn, 1994, London: Butterworths, p 258) suggest that this decision, that is, that the carrying out of blood tests was not against the interests of the child, may be interpreted as being special on the facts, that is, it relates to the ancillary jurisdiction of the court to make orders to ensure a fair trial. Any other interpretation would mean that the emphasis would change. Instead of examining the reasons for the treatment and how these may be for the positive benefit of the patient, the court would be left to decide whether there was any likelihood of detriment to the patient. In practice, might such a change of emphasis be disadvantageous to the patient?

The House of Lords in *Re F* gave no definition of 'best interests', dealing with the case on its particular facts. The lack of judicial guidance has been criticised:

Kennedy, I, 'Patients, doctors and human rights', in Blackburn, R and Taylor, J (eds), 1991, *Human Rights for the 1990s*, London: Mansell, p 90:

... [the best interests test] allows lawyers and courts to persuade themselves and others that theirs is a principled approach to law. Meanwhile, they engage in what to others is clearly a form of '*ad hocery*'. The best interests approach of family law allows the courts to atomise the law, to claim that each case depends on its own facts. The court can then respond intuitively to each case while seeking to legitimate its conclusion by asserting that it is derived from the general principle contained in the best interests formula. In fact, of course, there is no general principle other than the empty rhetoric of best interests; or rather, there is some principle (or principles) but the court is not telling. Obviously the court must be following some principles, otherwise a toss of a coin could decide cases. But these principles, which serve as pointers to what amounts to the best interests, are not articulated by the court. Only the conclusion is set out. The opportunity for reasoned analysis and scrutiny is lost.

This view was supported by Brennan J in his dissenting judgment in the Australian case of *Department of Health v JWB and SMB* (1992) 66 ALJR 300:

Brennan J:

14 ... the best interests approach offers no hierarchy of values which might guide the exercise of a discretionary power to authorise sterilisation, much less any general legal principle which might direct the difficult decisions to be made in this area by parents, guardians, the medical profession and courts. It is arguable that, in a field where the law has not developed, where ethical principles remain controversial and where each case turns on its own facts, the law should not pretend to too great a precision. Better, it might be said, that authority and power be conferred on a suitable repository – whether it be parents or guardians, doctors or the court – to decide these difficult questions according to the repository's view as to the best interests of the child in the particular circumstances of the case. In that way, it can be said, the blunt instrument of legal power will be sharpened according to the exigencies of the occasion. The absence of a community consensus on ethical principles may be thought to support this approach. But it must be remembered that, in the absence of legal rules or a hierarchy of values, the best interests approach depends upon the value system of

the decision maker. Absent any rule or guideline, that approach simply creates an unexaminable discretion in the repository of the power.

15 Of course the variable circumstances of each case require evaluation and judicial evaluations of circumstances vary, but the power to authorise sterilisation is so awesome, its exercise is so open to abuse, and the consequences of its exercise are generally so irreversible, that guidelines if not rules should be prescribed to govern it. The courts must attempt the task in the course of, and as a necessary incident in, the exercise of their jurisdiction. That is not to say that the courts should arrogate to themselves the power to authorise sterilisations of intellectually disabled children, but it is to say that it has become the duty of the courts – and, in the present case, specifically the duty of this court – to define the scope of the power to authorise sterilisations of intellectually disabled children and the conditions of exercise of the power, and to determine the repository of the power. The power cannot be left in a state so amorphous that it can be exercised according to the idiosyncratic views of the repository as to the 'best interests' of the child. That approach provides an insubstantial protection of the human dignity of children; it wraps no cloak of protective principle around the intellectually disabled child.

The potentially broad scope of the best interests test is illustrated in the organ transplant cases, where it has been argued that it may be in the best interests of the donor to be treated as an altruistic member of the wider community (see Chapter 11).

In *Re M (Child: Refusal of Medical Treatment)* (1999) 52 BMLR 124, the patient was a girl of 15 and a half who did not want a heart transplant because she did not want someone else's heart inside her, believing that this would make her 'different'. Dying from heart failure, which was the certain outcome without such a transplant, would not have this effect. Johnson J held that it would be in her best interests to have the operation, notwithstanding that there were risks attached to the operation itself and thereafter, in terms of rejection in the medical sense and rejection by M of further treatment. There was also the risk that she would, for the rest of her life, resent having had the operation imposed upon her. However, balancing these matters against the certainty of death meant that the best interests test was satisfied.

As has been seen above, *Re SL (Adult Patient) (Medical Treatment)* [2000] 2 FCR 452 concerned a conflict between medical opinion and the opinion of the mother of the incompetent adult patient in her care. There were two concerns: that the woman would be become pregnant and that she had heavy periods which caused her distress. The two relevant alternatives were the use of a Mirena coil which would be contraceptive and which would, at the least, reduce menstrual bleeding, and a hysterectomy which would eliminate all bleeding and render the woman permanently incapable of bearing children. The decision of Wall J was that, although medical opinion favoured the less invasive procedure to be tried first, as the hysterectomy, the procedure favoured by the mother and other relatives, was not ruled out by at least one of the experts, that satisfied the *Bolam* test, and could be carried out in the woman's best interests. Wall J said: '... in my judgment the court is entitled to declare lawful a particular course of treatment if that treatment itself is proper and in the interests of the patient, even if it is not the doctor's first choice.' Furthermore, the *Bolam* test, said the judge, should take into account wider social and emotional factors. These statements, without more, are to be welcomed. Unfortunately, the result in this case was that the judge did not sufficiently take into account the medical evidence. What might be described as a bold resistance to being overly influenced by medical opinion, in the event resulted in him endorsing the most medically invasive option, whilst, at the same time, saying that, since both options satisfied the *Bolam* test, he would make a declaration to that effect and leave the mother to discuss with the doctors what option was to be preferred. The Court of Appeal, whilst upholding the appeal (not least because it appears that the judge misunderstood some of the medical evidence), endorsed the view that, in considering best interests, the *Bolam* test is incorrect, as a number of medical options can satisfy the *Bolam* test, but the best interests test means that the best option must be chosen. The court also stated that it is for the court to declare what that best option is and not to refer it back to the parties concerned, which must surely be correct, as such cases come before the courts in the first place because of a disagreement between the parties, not on whether treatments are objectively '*Bolam* compatible', but on subjective concerns about the incapacitated person.

In *Simms v Simms and Another* [2003] Fam 83 the High Court had to consider the case of two people, aged 18 and 16 respectively, who were suffering from probable variant CJD. Their parents sought a delaration that they lacked capacity and that the proposed treatment was lawful. This treatment was new and untested on human beings. It involved the giving of an infusion surgically under a general anaesthetic. There was no doubt that the patients lacked capacity, but as the treatment was untested, Dame Butler-Sloss was required to consider the application of the *Bolam* test (see Chapter 6) and whether the treatment was in the patients' best interests. She held that a wider view of best interests should be taken in such as case and that the views of the parents and the effect upon them of a refusal to permit the treatment should be taken into account. The declarations were granted. Clearly in this case there was no alternative treatment available and there was no other hope of ameliorating the affects of this progressive and fatal disease. The experts, however, saw the treatment as offering only a very slim chance of improvement. Nevertheless, it must be right not to deny the patients this opportunity on the basis that it was not in their best interests because it could not be shown to have a good chance of success.

The 'substituted judgment' test

Is it possible to look at the situation from the point of view of the patient, and to make medical decisions on the basis of what he would have wanted, regardless of what may be thought by others to be good for him? The English courts have not adopted the 'substituted judgment' test used by some American courts (see *Re Eve* [1986] 2 SCR 388). In any event, the test cannot be used when the patient has never had sufficient understanding to form genuine personal opinions on such matters, but is relevant to the status of Advance Directives (see further Chapter 12).

The 'substituted judgment' test was considered, and rejected, in *Airedale NHS Trust v Bland* [1993] 1 All ER 821, p 872:

> **Lord Goff**: I wish however to refer at this stage to the approach adopted in most American courts under which the court seeks, in a case in which the patient is incapacitated from expressing any view on the question whether life-prolonging

treatment should be withheld in the relevant circumstances, to determine what decision the patient himself would have made had he been able to do so. This is called the substituted judgment test, and it generally involves a detailed inquiry into the patient's views and preferences: see, for example, *Re Quinlan* 70 NJ 10 (1976) and *Belchertown State School Superintendent v Saikewicz* 373 Mass 728 (1977). In later cases concerned with PVS patients it has been held that, in the absence of clear and convincing evidence of the patient's wishes, the surrogate decision maker has to implement as far as possible the decision which the incompetent patient would make if he was competent. However, accepting on this point the submission of Mr Lester, I do not consider that any such test forms part of English law in relation to incompetent adults, on whose behalf nobody has power to give consent to medical treatment. Certainly, in *F v West Berkshire HA* your Lordships' House adopted a straightforward test based on the best interests of the patient ... Of course, consistent with the best interests test, anything relevant to the application of the test may be taken into account; and, if the personality of the patient is relevant to the application of the test (as it may be in cases where the various relevant factors have to be weighed), it may be taken into account, as was done in *Re J (A Minor) (Wardship: Medical Treatment)* [1990] 3 All ER 930; [1991] Fam 33.

It is reasonable to conclude that the views of a patient will not be taken into account if he has never been capable of making an anticipatory decision: his views will be subsumed under the 'best interests' test, as indicated in the Law Commission's Report *Mental Incapacity*, Report No 231, 1995 (see Chapter 12).

The *Bolam* test

The test set down in *Bolam v Friern Hospital Management Committee* [1957] 1 WLR 582 provides that a doctor will not be negligent if he follows a medical practice which is supported by a responsible body of medical opinion, and recent case law indicates that the 'body' of opinion to support the actions of the doctor can be small (see *Defreitas v O'Brien and Another* [1995] 4 Med LR 108). This test has been subjected to much criticism on the basis that it results in judicial abstentionism, leaving the standard of care to be set exclusively by a single faction within the medical profession (see Chapter 6). In the case of *Re F (Mental Patient: Sterilisation)* [1990] 2 AC 1, which concerned a non-therapeutic sterilisation, it was held that decisions by doctors in respect of incompetent patients should be judged by the *Bolam* test:

> **Lord Bridge**: The common law should be readily intelligible to and applicable by all those who undertake the care of persons lacking the capacity to consent to treatment. It would be intolerable for members of the medical, nursing and other professions devoted to the care of the sick that, in caring for those lacking the capacity to consent to treatment they should be put in the dilemma that, if they administer the treatment which they believe to be in the patient's best interests, acting with due skill and care, they run the risk of being held guilty of trespass to the person, but if they withhold that treatment, they may be in breach of a duty of care owed to the patient. If those who undertake responsibility for the care of incompetent or unconscious patients administer curative or prophylactic treatment which they believe to be appropriate to the patient's existing condition of disease, injury or bodily malfunction or susceptibility to such a condition in the future, the lawfulness of that treatment should be judged by one standard, not two. It follows that if the professionals in question have acted with due skill and care, judged by the well known test laid down in *Bolam v Friern Hospital Management Committee* [1957] 1 WLR 582, they should be immune from liability in trespass, just as they are immune from liability in negligence. The

special considerations which apply in the case of the sterilisation of a woman who is physically perfectly healthy or of an operation upon an organ transplant donor arise only because such treatment cannot be considered either curative or prophylactic.

In the Court of Appeal, the *Bolam* test had been rejected by Neill LJ, with whom Butler-Sloss LJ agreed:

> **Neill LJ**: A doctor may defeat a claim in negligence if he establishes that he acted in accordance with a practice accepted at the time as proper by a responsible body of medical opinion skilled in the particular form of treatment in question. This is the test laid down in *Bolam* ... But to say that it is not negligent to carry out a particular form of treatment does not mean that that treatment is necessary. I would define necessary in this context as that which the general body of medical opinion in the particular speciality would consider to be in the best interests of the patient in order to maintain the health and to secure the well being of the patient. One cannot expect unanimity but it should be possible to say of an operation which is necessary in the relevant sense that it would be unreasonable in the opinion of most experts in the field not to make the operation available to the patient. One must consider the alternatives to an operation and the dangers or disadvantages to which the patient may be exposed if no action is taken. The question becomes: what action does the patient's health and welfare require?

Commenting upon this in the House of Lords, Lord Brandon stated (p 68):

> **Lord Brandon**: With respect to the Court of Appeal, I do not agree that the *Bolam* test is inapplicable to cases of performing operations on, or giving other treatment to, adults incompetent to give consent. In order that the performance of such operations on, and the giving of such other treatment to, such adults should be lawful, they must be in their best interests. If doctors were to be required, in deciding whether an operation or other treatment was in the best interests of adults incompetent to give consent, to apply some test more stringent than the *Bolam* test, the result would be that such adults would, in some circumstances at least, be deprived of the benefit of medical treatment which adults competent to give consent would enjoy. In my opinion it would be wrong for the law, in its concern to protect such adults, to produce such a result.

Whilst in the context of, say, diagnosis, there is much force in the argument that there should be the same standard of care regardless of whether the patient is competent or incompetent, in the context of non-therapeutic treatment the *Bolam* test is not sufficiently rigorous. By its very nature, the decision can only be made on *non-medical* grounds and there is no reason why a doctor should be privileged to make such decisions. Clearly, as we shall see, in cases such as *Re F*, the best interests of the patient will be concerned with her best 'social' or 'personal' interests, and the *Bolam* test is far too weak to safeguard these. Josephine Shaw comments as follows:

> **Shaw, J, 'Sterilisation of mentally handicapped people: judges rule OK' (1990) 53 MLR 91:**
>
> It is unfortunate, but not surprising, that the *Bolam* test, which attaches great weight to clinical freedom, should have penetrated still further into the realm of consent to treatment. The construction of decision-making concerning mental disability within the courtroom as an aspect of the doctor–patient relationship in which the doctor's word is paramount fits in with a general pattern which devalues the power of patient autonomy in medical decision-making generally. Yet the *Bolam* test has never been either academically or judicially uncontroversial and Lord Scarman, for one, has argued vehemently against its application in the realm of consent, preferring a more

patient-centred approach to the disclosure of the risks of medical treatment which places weight on the factors which a reasonable patient, rather than a reasonable doctor would consider significant.

It is not insignificant that English law should have been criticised for failure to give adequate weight to both patient autonomy in the field of informed consent and the rights of mentally handicapped people in the field of reproduction. It cannot be correct entirely to equate the standard of care to which a doctor must adhere if he or she is not to run the risk of paying compensation for damage caused and the standard which governs the application of a strictly limited exception to the consent principle encapsulating a fundamental right to self-determination. In the latter case there is an overriding public interest in ensuring that the fundamental rights of a class of person not able to operate autonomously in society are respected and that other interests will only prevail where there is a clear and precise benefit thereby to be gained. The application of the *Bolam* test provides no guarantee that this goal will be realised.

The Law Commission considered the relationship of best interests and negligence:

Law Commission, *Mental Incapacity*, Report No 231, 1995, London: HMSO:

3.27 It should be made clear beyond any shadow of a doubt that acting in a person's best interests amounts to something more than not treating that person in a negligent manner. Decisions taken on behalf of a person lacking capacity require a careful, focused consideration of that person as an individual. Judgments as to whether a professional has acted negligently, on the other hand, require a careful, focused consideration of how that particular professional acted as compared with the way in which other reasonably competent professionals would have acted. Lord Mustill, who was both a member of the appellate committee of the House of Lords which decided the case of *Airedale NHS Trust v Bland* and a member of the House of Lords Select Committee on Medical Ethics, said during oral evidence to the latter committee that:

> ... one of the things that is not very good is that the phrase 'best interests' has been put into play without any description of what it means. This, I think, actually increases the difficulties for the doctors rather than helps to solve them. What is at the back of my mind is whether perhaps Parliament could give some more specific definition of ... what are the relevant factors ...

However, it must be noted that the *Bolam* test was not considered in the case of *Re T*, where the Court of Appeal said that the welfare of the child was better served by overriding majority medical opinion (see p 175, above). Was this because the *parental* views in the case of a very young child were of greater importance? In the case of an incapacitated adult, would the decision be the same? It is also important to note that, in *Re F*, best interests were rolled up with necessity. It is arguable that this implies a more stringent test than *Bolam* (see now also *Re SL (Adult Patient: Medical Treatment)* [2000] 2 FCR 452).

THE CONTROL OF FERTILITY AND THE INCOMPETENT

Introduction

The sterilisation of incompetent patients raises profound ethical issues. Furthermore, these procedures are inevitably associated with the practice of eugenics carried out by the Nazis during the 1930s and 1940s. However, as Davies points out, the practice was by no means unknown before this:

Davies, M, *Medical Law*, 1996, London: Blackstone, p 262:

13.3.1 Historical development of sterilisation

The debate on sterilising the mentally handicapped has been a long, and as the case law will show, a vociferous one. The debate has as its emotive backdrop the history of late 19th and early 20th centuries. The case law will show that the judiciary of a number of common law jurisdictions are aware of the dark side of this history. Sterilisation for eugenic purposes was not a product of Nazi Germany, although that regime was the most horrific expression of the perversion of the concept of eugenics. The theory that the species could be improved or perfected by a cleansing of the gene pool through selective breeding was introduced by Sir Francis Galton at University College London in 1869. It was not long before a number of US State reformatories were using the concept to justify the sterilisation of what were deemed to be those carrying undesirable traits within society ... One of the best known, and to some most frightening, judicial justifications for the performance of these irreversible operations was found in *Buck v Bell* 274 US 200 (1927). Carrie Buck was described as the 'feeble-minded' daughter of a mother who was herself described (among other things) as 'feeble-minded'. Her proposed sterilisation was challenged on 'due process' as a 'cruel and unusual punishment' grounds under the US Constitution. The Supreme Court's view was that it was not going to be done as a punishment, but as a means to facilitate her freedom within the community. One of the most chilling quotes comes from Mr Justice Oliver Wendell Holmes (p 207):

> We have seen more than once that the public welfare may call upon the best citizens for their lives. It would be strange if it could not call upon those who already sap the strength of the State for these lesser sacrifices, often not felt to be such by those concerned, in order to prevent our being swamped with incompetents. It is better for all the world, if instead of waiting to execute degenerate offspring for crime, or to let them starve for their imbecility, society can prevent those who are manifestly unfit from continuing their kind. The principle that sustains compulsory vaccination is broad enough to cover cutting the fallopian tubes. Three generations of imbeciles are enough.

Freeman charts the American experience after *Buck v Bell* 274 US 200 (1927):

Freeman, MD, 'Sterilising the mentally handicapped', in *Medicine, Ethics and the Law*, 1988, London: Stevens, p 57:

There have been a number of significant cases in the USA since *Buck v Bell*. There have been attempts to reverse the decision. That this has not happened is in part attributable to the fact that the line of argument has changed. Eugenics (or rather negative eugenics) is out of fashion: instead, the appeal is grounded on the burden placed on society by the need to care for the handicapped. The most interesting of the recent cases is *North Carolina Association for Retarded Children v State of North Carolina* in 1976. The statute challenged authorised both voluntary and involuntary sterilisations. There was a duty to institute sterilisation proceedings when the relevant official felt it was either in (i) the best interests of the retarded person, or (ii) the public at large, or (iii) where the retarded person would be likely, unless sterilised, to procreate children with a tendency to serious physical, mental or nervous disease or deficiency or would be unable to care for the child, or (iv) when the next of kin or legal guardian of the retarded person 'requests' that he file the petition. The court found (iv) irrational and irreconcilable with (i), (ii) and (iii). But it thought the first three provisions made out 'a complete and sensible scheme'. The fourth, however, granted to the retarded person's next of kin or legal guardian 'the power of a tyrant'. The scheme was thus found constitutional with the exception of the fourth provision. The language and ideology of Holmes' 'incantation' was rejected. 'Medical and genetical experts', the court noted, 'are no longer sold on sterilisation to benefit either retarded patients or the future of the Republic'. The case is also significant for containing a number of general propositions about the origins of mental retardation, about expression of sexuality, about the ability of the handicapped to use contraceptive methods. Finally, the opinion holds that in rare unusual cases it can be medically determined that involuntary sterilisation is in the best interests of either the mentally retarded persons, or the State, or both.

A lot of people have been sterilised in the USA pursuant upon the compulsory programmes depicted here. By 1964, by which time the programmes had long passed their peak, 63,678 such sterilisations had taken place. Those sterilised were mainly young women and for the large part they were poor and came from socio-economically and culturally deprived environments. Whether it was, as Gonzales indicates, a popular way of controlling reproduction, it certainly was a convenient method for controlling the reproductive urges of the populace. Given the population concerned and the imperfections of classification, the dangers of labelling with sterilisation merely an incident of stigmatisation were difficult to overcome. The evidence suggests they were not surmounted.

It is not surprising, therefore, that the case of *Re B (A Minor)* [1988] 1 AC 199, which concerned the sterilisation of a mentally handicapped girl, caused a considerable amount of controversy. Freeman, in a BBC interview, had described the approval of the sterilisation by the Court of Appeal as 'Nazi-like'. In the House of Lords, Lord Hailsham, no doubt bearing in mind this reaction, had sought from the outset to distinguish this case from the practice of eugenics (p 202):

Lord Hailsham: There is no doubt that, in the exercise of its wardship jurisdiction, the first and paramount consideration is the well being, welfare, or interests (each expression occasionally used, but each, for this purpose, synonymous) of the human being concerned, that is the ward herself or himself. In this case I believe it to be the only consideration involved. In particular there is no issue of public policy other than the application of the above principle which can conceivably be taken into account, least of all (since the opposite appears to have been considered in some quarters) any question of eugenics.

When the case of *Re F (Mental Patient: Sterilisation)* [1990] 2 AC 1 was in the Court of Appeal, Lord Donaldson had taken the view that sterilisation operations were special cases (p 19):

Lord Donaldson MR:

Is sterilisation in a special category?

... Mr Munby seeks to persuade us that it is in a special category and in this I think he is right, although I would include in the same category abortion and surgical intervention to enable an incompetent adult to donate an organ during lifetime. However, there is a real distinction between medical treatment undertaken with a view to securing abortion or sterilisation and that undertaken for a different purpose, for example the excision of a malignant tumour, which has this incidental result. It is only the former type of treatment which the law regards as being in a special category, probably because of its irreversible and emotive character in the light of the history of our times.

As stated by Lord Donaldson, sterilisation operations can be carried out for exclusively therapeutic purposes, for example, when the ovaries or uterus are damaged or diseased. Those operations do not concern us here. The cases we will examine fall into two categories. First, 'social' sterilisations, where it is proposed to render sterile those who, it is said, are simply incapable of understanding parenthood and caring for a child. Secondly, there have been a number of cases where young women have been sterilised to avoid difficulties with menstruation. The question arises as to whether these can properly be called 'therapeutic'.

Non-therapeutic sterilisations

We have considered at p 187, above, whether there is any meaningful distinction between a therapeutic and a non-therapeutic procedure, and saw that La Forest J in the case of *Re Eve* [1986] 2 SCR 388 favoured such a distinction. (See p 187, above, for the facts of the case.) In the following extract, the court considers issues raised by the proposed 'non-therapeutic' sterilisation, that is, for social reasons:

> **La Forest J**: Another factor merits attention. Unlike most surgical procedures, sterilisation is not one that is ordinarily performed for the purpose of medical treatment. The Law Reform Commission of Canada tells us this in *Sterilisation*, Working Paper [No] 24, 1979, a publication to which I shall frequently refer as providing a convenient summary of much of the work in the field. It says at p 3:
>
>> Sterilisation as a medical procedure is distinct, because except in rare cases, if the operation is not performed, the physical health of the person involved is not in danger, necessity or emergency not normally being factors in the decision to undertake the procedure. In addition to its being elective, it is for all intents and purposes irreversible.
>
> As well, there is considerable evidence that non-consensual sterilisation has a significant negative psychological impact on the mentally handicapped; see *Sterilisation* ... pp 49–52. The Commission has this to say at p 50:
>
>> It has been found that, like anyone else, the mentally handicapped have individually varying reactions to sterilisation. Sex and parenthood hold the same significance for them as for other people and their misconceptions and misunderstandings are also similar. Rosen maintains that the removal of an individual's procreative powers is a matter of major importance and that no amount of reforming zeal can remove the significance of sterilisation and its effect on the individual psyche.
>
>> In a study by Sabagh and Edgerton, it was found that sterilised mentally retarded persons tend to perceive sterilisation as a symbol of reduced or degraded status. Their attempts to pass for normal were hindered by negative self-perceptions and resulted in withdrawal and isolation rather than striving to conform ...
>
> The psychological impact of sterilisation is likely to be particularly damaging in cases where it is a result of coercion and when the mentally handicapped have had no children:
>
>> In the present case, there is no evidence to indicate that failure to perform the operation would have any detrimental effect on Eve's physical or mental health. The purposes of the operation, as far as Eve's welfare is concerned, are to protect her from possible trauma in giving birth and from the assumed difficulties she would have in fulfilling her duties as a parent. As well, one must assume from the fact that hysterectomy was ordered, that the operation

was intended to relieve her of the hygienic tasks associated with menstruation ...

The justifications advanced are the ones commonly proposed in support of non-therapeutic sterilisation (see *Sterilisation*). Many are demonstrably weak. The Commission dismisses the argument about the trauma of birth by observing at p 60:

> For this argument to be held valid would require that it could be demonstrated that the stress of delivery was greater in the case of mentally handicapped persons than it is for others. The generally known wide range of *post-partum* response would likely render this a difficult cause to prove.

The argument relating to fitness as a parent involves many value-loaded questions. Studies conclude that mentally incompetent parents show as much fondness and concern for their children as other people; see *Sterilisation* ... pp 33 *et seq*, pp 63–64. Many, it is true, may have difficulty in coping, particularly with the financial burdens involved. But this issue does not relate to the benefit of the incompetent; it is a social problem, and one, moreover, that is not limited to incompetents. Above all it is not an issue that comes within the limited powers of the courts, under the *parens patriae* jurisdiction, to do what is necessary for the benefit of persons who are unable to care for themselves. Indeed, there are human rights considerations that should make a court extremely hesitant about attempting to resolve a social problem by this means. It is worth noting that in dealing with such issues, provincial sterilisation boards have revealed serious differences in their attitudes as between men and women, the poor and the rich, and people of different ethnic backgrounds; see *Sterilisation* ... at p 44.

As far as the hygienic problems are concerned, the following view of the Law Reform Commission (p 34) is obviously sound:

> ... if a person requires a great deal of assistance in managing their own menstruation, they are also likely to require assistance with urinary and faecal control, problems which are much more troublesome in terms of personal hygiene.

The grave intrusion on a person's rights and the certain physical damage that ensues from non-therapeutic sterilisation without consent, when compared to the highly questionable advantages that can result from it, have persuaded me that it can never safely be determined that such a procedure is for the benefit of that person ...

One of the first English cases to examine the issue was *Re D (A Minor) (Wardship: Sterilisation)* [1976] 1 All ER 326. The case concerned an 11 year old child, who suffered from Sotos syndrome, a condition characterised by epilepsy, clumsiness, unusual facial appearance, behavioural problems such as emotional instability and aggression and impairment of mental function. She was described as having an IQ of 80 (described as 'dull normal'), some reading and writing skills, good conversational skills and the understanding of a nine or nine and a half year old. An application was made to the court under the wardship jurisdiction for authorisation of a sterilisation. The reasons are outlined in the judgment of Heilbron J (p 330):

Re D (A Minor) (Wardship: Sterilisation) [1976] 1 All ER 326
Heilbron J:

The background to the decision to operate

When Mrs B first realised that she had given birth to a handicapped child, she recalled with deep concern that, many years before, she had lived near a family who had the misfortune to have three mentally retarded children, and their plight and their troubled lives had deeply affected her. She and her husband not unnaturally were extremely worried about D's future, as at that time they thought D could never improve, and so even when D was a very young child they decided that when she reached the age of about 18 they would take the necessary steps to prevent her from having any children, and would apply to have her sterilised. From the decision made in those early days Mrs B has never resiled, and she has in consequence, over the years, had several discussions about this operation with Dr Gordon. When D reached puberty by the age of 10 Mrs B's concern increased, and so she discussed the operation once again with Dr Gordon on 7 January 1975. Mrs B said, and I accept, that when she reiterated to Dr Gordon that she would like D sterilised when she was older, the doctor said: 'We can do it now.' This is indeed confirmed by the doctor in his affidavit when he says that rather than wait any longer the decision could be taken then. Mrs B agreed that the operation should be performed. She was very worried lest D might be seduced and possibly give birth to a baby, which might also be abnormal. She had always believed that D would not, or should not, marry and in any event would be incapable of bringing up a child. Her anxieties are genuine and understandable.

Dr Gordon took the view that there was a real risk that D might give birth to an abnormal foetus. I have already referred to some of his other anxieties. As to the possibility of producing an abnormal child, the evidence of Dr Snodgrass and Dr Newton, the well known consultant psychiatrist called on behalf of the Official Solicitor, confirmed that there was, as Dr Gordon stated, an increased risk of such an eventuality. On the other hand, they pointed out that no one with this particular syndrome had ever been known to have a baby, and it is not therefore possible to make any precise predictions whether or not they are able to do so.

At that consultation in January Dr Gordon, with Mrs B's agreement, came to a decision provided that Miss Duncan, the consultant gynaecologist, who is a senior lecturer and gynaecologist to the Sheffield and Northern General Hospital, to whom he referred, concurred in his recommendation that the operation should be performed. Miss Duncan saw and interviewed both D and Mrs B on 7 February 1975, but she did not examine the child, and I think there is little doubt that Miss Duncan did not give very much independent consideration to the wider implications of this operation, but was content in large measure to rely on Dr Gordon's recommendation and assessment of the situation. She did, however, agree to perform the sterilisation, namely a hysterectomy, and I am satisfied that D was booked to enter hospital on 4 May for that operation to be carried out on 6 May. No one else was consulted prior to that decision. It is surprising that Dr T, the child psychiatrist, was not, for, prior to the date of the recommendation, he had on a number of occasions interviewed and examined the child, and his views, as Dr Gordon later agreed in evidence, must have been of considerable importance in evaluating the numerous problems, medical, social, educational and psychiatric, which such a vital decision involved.

Dr Gordon maintains, however, that his recommendation was one which was based on clinical judgment as a doctor, and that he and the gynaecologist should be the sole judges whether or not it should be performed, provided of course that they had the parent's consent.

Despite Dr Gordon's assertion that his decision should be upheld because it was based on his clinical judgment, he nevertheless, in putting forward his grounds for recommending this operation, stated that such reasons or such grounds were of a twofold character, ie, that they were both medical and social. The medical reasons included the possibility that she might give birth to an abnormal child, that her epilepsy might cause her to harm a child, and that the only satisfactory method of birth control was this operation. The social reasons included his opinion that D would be unable in the future to maintain herself save in a sheltered environment, her inability due to epilepsy and other handicaps to cope with a family if she were to marry, without substantial support, the deterioration in her behaviour for which he said there was no known method of improvement and the possibility that she might have to enter an institution as he alleged for social or criminal reasons in the future. Certain persons concerned with D's welfare, however, took a different view. They were the former and present headmaster of her school, Mrs Hamidi and the social worker involved with the family. They believed that an operation for sterilisation in the case of a minor, particularly a girl of 11, being irreversible and permanent, was a matter of grave concern, and so on 26 March Mrs Hamidi wrote on their behalf and on her own to the senior school medical officer, pointing out in detail the conflict between Mrs B and the school and the welfare services in regard to D's attainments and their concern in regard to the proposed operation, which they pointed out could affect the whole of her future.

On 21 April there was a meeting between Dr Gordon and those professionals working with the child and her family, at which Dr Gordon's social and behavioural reasons for performing this operation were seriously challenged. Dr Gordon, however, refused to acknowledge that these views could possibly be wrong or exaggerated or premature. I think Dr Gordon, whose sincerity cannot be challenged, was persuaded by his emotional involvement with Mrs B's considerable problems and anxieties, and his strong personal views in favour of sterilisation – as he stated in his affidavit, 'Sterilisation is now an emotive word, and we must try to change its image' – to form a less than detached opinion in regard to a number of matters which were not in my view in reality matters of clinical judgment, but which were concerned, to a large extent, with grounds which were other than medical. I feel it is a pity that he was not prepared to accept that others, whose duties, training and skills were directed to the assessment and amelioration of many of these problems, had much to contribute in the formulation of a decision of this gravity.

In my judgment Dr Gordon's views as to D's present and future social and behavioural problems were somewhat exaggerated and mistaken. I think in this area his views were clouded by his resentment at what he considered unjustified interference.

In the event Dr Gordon did not accept the alternative views, and he and Miss Duncan refused to defer the operation despite the grave implications for the child. Mrs Hamidi and the others, therefore, wrote to the area administrator of the health authority requesting an urgent and independent review of this decision. The area administrator consulted the local authority's specialist in community medicine (child health) and he later replied saying that she had made a very careful appraisal of the case, but could not interfere. Mrs Hamidi and her colleagues, however, were not daunted and they thereupon consulted solicitors, and in due course these proceedings got under way. It is only right that I should pay tribute to their courage, persistence and humane concern for this young girl.

... I am dealing here with the case of this particular young girl, but the evidence, including that which disclosed that Dr Gordon has recommended and Miss Duncan has performed two prior operations of this nature on handicapped children in Sheffield, indicates the possibility that further consideration may need to be given to this topic, consideration which would involve extensive consultation and debate elsewhere.

Dr Gordon's reason for wishing this operation to be performed was, of course, to prevent D ever having a child. He recognised, as did Mrs B, that there are other methods of achieving that objective, but his view was that D could not satisfactorily manage any form of contraception. Mrs B was concerned lest D might be seduced and become pregnant ...

Mrs B's genuine concern ... cannot be disregarded. A body of evidence was produced, therefore, to indicate the advantages and disadvantages of various forms of contraception. I shall not, however, burden this judgment with any detailed examination of it, save to say that I do not accept on the evidence Dr Gordon's contention that this young girl, if and when the time arrived, would not be a suitable subject for one of the various methods described by the doctors ...

It was common ground that D had sufficient intellectual capacity to marry, in the future of course, and that many people of a like kind are capable of, and do so. Dr Gordon agreed that this being so, she and her future husband would then be the persons most concerned in a question of sterilisation, and such an operation might have a serious and material bearing on a future marriage and its consequences.

The purpose of performing this operation is permanently to prevent the possibility of reproduction. The evidence of Professor Huntingford, consultant and professor of obstetrics and gynaecology at the University of London and at St Bartholomew's Hospital and the London Hospital Medical Colleges, was that in his view such an operation was normally only appropriate for a woman who consented to it, possibly at the conclusion of child-bearing, and then only after careful and anxious consideration by her and her husband of many factors and, what is most important, with full knowledge of all its implications.

Professor Huntingford, Dr Snodgrass and Dr Newton were all agreed that such an operation was not medically indicated in this case, and should not be performed. Dr Snodgrass said he was firmly of the view that it was wrong to perform this operation on an 11 year old, on the pretext that it would benefit her in the future. Dr Newton said:

> In my opinion sterilisation of a child before the age of consent can only be justified if it is the treatment for some present or inevitable disease. In this case, sterilisation is not a treatment for any of the signs or symptoms of Sotos syndrome, from which she suffers. I am totally against this operation being performed on D.

... Dr Gordon, however, maintained that, provided the parent or parents consented, the decision was one made pursuant to the exercise of his clinical judgment, and that no interference could be tolerated in his clinical freedom.

The other consultants did not agree. Their opinion was that a decision to sterilise a child was not entirely within a doctor's clinical judgment, save only when sterilisation was the treatment of choice for some disease, as, for instance, when in order to treat a child and to ensure her direct physical well being, it might be necessary to perform a hysterectomy to remove a malignant uterus. Whilst the side effect of such an operation would be to sterilise, the operation would be performed solely for therapeutic purposes. I entirely accept their opinions. I cannot believe, and the evidence does not warrant the view, that a decision to carry out an operation of this nature performed for non-therapeutic purposes on a minor, can be held to be within the doctor's sole clinical judgment ...

A review of the whole of the evidence leads me to the conclusion that in a case of a child of 11 years of age, where the evidence shows that her mental and physical condition and attainments have already improved, and where her future prospects are as yet unpredictable, where the evidence also shows that she is unable as yet to understand and appreciate the implications of this operation and could not give a valid or informed consent, but the likelihood is that in later years she will be able to make her own choice, where, I believe, the frustration and resentment of realising (as she would one day) what had happened, could be devastating, an operation of this nature is, in my view, contra-indicated.

Three things in particular are noteworthy: first, the apparent lack of concern by the gynaecologist; secondly, the intransigence of Dr Gordon; and, thirdly, the chance way in which the case came before the court. As far as the first two are concerned, would the combined opinions of Miss Duncan and Dr Gordon have constituted a responsible body of medical opinion for the purposes of the *Bolam* test? Even if two opinions were deemed insufficient, it is likely that, if necessary, other doctors could have been found to endorse their views. On an application of the *Bolam* test, would Heilbron J have been able, nevertheless, to reject these opinions on the ground that they were not 'responsible' or that they were 'illogical'? Or would the 'welfare of the child' principle relegate the *Bolam* test to a secondary position (see *Re T (A Minor) (Wardship: Medical Treatment)* [1997] 1 All ER 906, above)? Consider this and the other sterilisation cases when looking at the application of the *Bolam* test in Chapter 6.

Commenting on the way in which this case reached the court, Freeman writes as follows:

Freeman, MD, 'Sterilising the mentally handicapped', in *Medicine, Ethics and the Law*, 1988, London: Stevens, p 57:

... the Sheffield girl in *Re D* was not the first English victim, or even the first in Sheffield. The chance intervention by an educational psychologist and the financial support of the NCCL for once converted a private matter into a public concern. Just how many young persons have been sterilised in Britain is something that will never be known. Dr David Owen in 1975 said the Ministry of Health kept no comprehensive statistics. He quoted figures from two out of 14 regional health authorities. According to *The Sun* in September 1975, the DHSS believed that in 1973 and 1974 11 girls and four boys under 16 had been sterilised and 29 girls and 34 boys of between 16 and 18. Figures in the *Journal of Medical Ethics* do not tally with these. It is indicated there (by Sir George Porter) that at least 14 sterilisations were performed in this period on under 16 year olds and another 22 on those in the age range 16 to 18. According to the *Birmingham Evening Mail* (in January 1976), one West Midlands leading child psychiatrist had himself recommended 12 adolescents under 16 for sterilisation. In *Re D* there is reference to two sterilisations having been carried out in Sheffield. Figures released by the Department of Health in March 1987 indicate that about 90 sterilisations are performed a year in England on females under 19. The department is unable to break the figures down into those aged under 18, and those who have reached the age of majority, nor to give the reasons for the sterilisations.

The case of *Re B (A Minor) (Wardship: Sterilisation)* [1988] 1 AC 199 (the case of 'Jeanette') concerned a 17 year old girl. She was a voluntary patient in a local authority residential unit. The facts are outlined in the judgment of Lord Oliver (p 207):

Lord Oliver: ... [Jeanette] suffers from what is described as a 'moderate' degree of mental handicap but has a very limited intellectual development. Her ability to understand speech is that of a six year old, but her ability to express herself has been described as comparable to that of a two year old child. No cause for her mental handicap has been established but the report of Dr Berney, a consultant psychiatrist who gave evidence before the judge, indicates that her epilepsy and the degree of her mental incapacity suggest an underlying abnormality of the brain. It is not envisaged that she will ever be capable of caring for herself in the community or reach a stage where she could return permanently to her mother's care. She is capable of finding her way round a limited locality, of dressing and bathing herself and performing simple household tasks under supervision and she has been taught to cope with menstruation; but the evidence is that she is unlikely to show an improvement in mental capacity beyond that of a six year old child. She has, in the past, shown evidence of extremes of mood and can become violent and aggressive, a phenomenon associated with premenstrual tension. Since the middle of 1986 there has been prescribed for her a drug known as Danazol to help in controlling her irregular periods and relieving premenstrual tension, whilst her epilepsy is controlled by anti-convulsant drugs. She suffers from obesity and an earlier attempt to treat her outbursts of violence with Microgynon 30 (a combined oral contraceptive) had to be abandoned because it produced a significant increase in weight. Another behavioural feature of significance is her high tolerance of pain. There is evidence that she bites her arm and that if injured she interferes with the process of healing by opening and probing the wounds.

What prompted the application to the court was the consciousness on the part of her mother and officers of the council responsible for her care that she was beginning to show recognisable signs of sexual awareness and sexual drive exemplified by provocative approaches to male members of the staff and other residents and by touching herself in the genital area. There was thus brought to their attention the obvious risk of pregnancy and the desirability of taking urgent and effective contraceptive measures. Although at present she is subject to effective supervision, her degree of incapacity is not such that it would be thought right that she should, effectively, be institutionalised all her life. The current approach to persons of her degree of incapacity is to allow them as much freedom as is consistent with their own safety and that of other people and although the likelihood is that she will, for the foreseeable future, continue to live at the residential institution, she visits her mother and her siblings at weekends and will, inevitably, be much less susceptible to supervision when she goes to an adult training centre. At the same time the risks involved in her becoming pregnant are formidable. The evidence of Dr Berney is that there is no prospect of her being capable of forming a long term adult relationship, such as marriage, which is within the capacity of some less mentally handicapped persons. She has displayed no maternal feelings and indeed has an antipathy to small children. Such skills as she has been able to develop are limited to those necessary for caring for herself at the simplest level and there is no prospect of her being capable of raising or caring for a child of her own. If she did give birth to a child it would be essential that it be taken from her for fostering or adoption although her attitude towards children is such that this would not cause her distress. So far as her awareness of her own sexuality is concerned, she has, as has already been mentioned, been taught to manage for herself the necessary hygienic mechanics of menstruation, but it has not been possible to teach her about sexuality in any abstract form. She understands the link between pregnancy and a baby but is unaware of sexual intercourse and its relationship to pregnancy. It is not feasible to discuss contraception with her and even if there should come a time when she becomes capable of understanding the need for contraception, there is no likelihood of her being able to develop the capacity to weigh up the merits of different types of contraception or to make an informed choice in the matter. Should she become pregnant, it would be desirable that the pregnancy should be terminated, but because of her obesity and the irregularity of her periods there is an obvious danger that her condition might not be noticed until it was too late for an abortion to take place safely. On the other hand, the risks if she were permitted to go to full term are serious, for although it is

Dr Berney's opinion that she would tolerate the condition of pregnancy without undue distress, the process of delivery would be likely to be traumatic and would cause her to panic. Normal delivery would be likely to require heavy sedation, which could be injurious to the child, so that it might be more appropriate to deliver her by Caesarean section. If this course were adopted, however, past experience of her reaction to injuries suggests that it would be very difficult to prevent her from repeatedly opening up the wound and thus preventing the healing of the post-operative scar. It was against this background and in the light of the increasing freedom which must be allowed her as she grows older and the consequent difficulty of maintaining effective supervision that those having the care of the minor concluded that it was essential in her interests that effective contraceptive measures be taken. Almost all drugs appear to have a bad effect upon her and the view was formed, in which her mother concurred, that the only appropriate course offering complete protection was for her to undergo sterilisation by occluding the fallopian tubes, a relatively minor operation carrying a very small degree of risk to the patient, a very high degree of protection and minimal side effects. There is, however, no possibility that the minor, even if of full age, would herself have the mental capacity to consent to such an operation. Hence the application to the court.

... Your Lordships' attention has, quite properly, been directed to the decision of Heilbron J in *In re D (A Minor) (Wardship: Sterilisation)* [1976] Fam 185, a case very different from the instant case, where the evidence indicated that the ward was of an intellectual capacity to marry and would in the future be able to make her own choice. In those circumstances, Heilbron J declined to sanction an operation which involved depriving her of her right to reproduce. That, if I may say so respectfully, was plainly a right decision. But the right to reproduce is of value only if accompanied by the ability to make a choice and in the instant case there is no question of the minor ever being able to make such a choice or indeed to appreciate the need to make one. All the evidence indicates that she will never desire a child and that reproduction would in fact be positively harmful to her.

Was this operation in Jeanette's best interests? Much of the reasoning behind the court's decision was that the operation was necessary to protect her. Lord Oliver said (p 210):

Lord Oliver: My Lords, I have thought it right to set out in some detail the background of fact in which this appeal has come before your Lordships' House because it is, in my judgment, essential to appreciate, in considering the welfare of this young woman which it is the duty of the court to protect, the degree of her vulnerability, the urgency of the need to take protective measures and the impossibility of her ever being able at this age or any later age either to consent to any form of operative treatment or to exercise for herself the right of making any informed decision in matters which, in the case of a person less heavily handicapped, would rightly be thought to be matters purely of personal and subjective choice.

Note that, in the judgment of Lord Oliver, he moves from reference to 'provocative gestures' to the 'risk of pregnancy' without pausing to consider that there is no inevitable progression from one to the other. The somewhat hollow ring of the efficacy of this procedure as a protective measure may be, at least in part, related to the fact that it is at odds with much of the evidence. If Jeanette was so limited in her understanding, and this was stressed by carers and judges alike, then the operation was arguably unnecessary *for precisely this very reason*. She would simply never have the opportunity to have sexual intercourse. The concern that she would not be supervised sufficiently at the adult training centre which she was shortly due to attend is not entirely consistent with the negative assertions about her uncontrolled behaviour:

De Cruz, SP, 'Sterilisation, wardship and human rights' [1988] Fam Law 6:

... since Jeanette could not even be allowed on the streets unsupervised, as she could not understand traffic, she would certainly need close and constant attention for a great deal of the time. Admittedly, provided she was indoors, the supervision need not be quite so intensive or intrusive, once this alarming prospect of pregnancy no longer existed. Yet given the prospect of sexual exploitation, of course, sterilisation would give no protection against rape or sexual abuse. Furthermore, the operation would certainly not free her, as Lord Hailsham seemed to imply, from 'incarceration', nor give her the liberty to satisfy the sexual desires she was experiencing, when she would certainly experience difficulties in relationships with the opposite sex. If anything, the ruling accentuates her vulnerability and, tragically, results in her being treated very differently from 'normal' people, which would undermine all the advances made in the last decade or so in the achievements of mental health groups in their efforts to integrate people with mental disabilities into the community at large.

The lack of consistency in the evidence and the conclusions drawn from the statements made about Jeanette's abilities and difficulties were highlighted by Lee and Morgan:

Lee, R and Morgan, D, 'Sterilisation and mental handicap: sapping the strength of the State?' (1988) 15 JLS 229:

... a curious pattern emerges. It is of a girl who can manage 'the necessary hygienic mechanics of menstruation', but could not cope with contraception; who can understand the link between pregnancy and babies, but 'is unaware of sexual intercourse and its relationship to pregnancy'. No information is offered about Jeanette's sex education and why it has failed to overcome her ignorance of one of the outcomes of sexual intercourse. Nothing explains why her carers are able successfully to manage the regime of medication necessary to control her epilepsy, but would be unable to supervise the use of an oral contraceptive because 'it would not be possible in the light of her swings of mood and considerable physical strength to ensure the administration of the necessary daily doses'.

Lord Oliver had said that the concern of the court had been about 'what is in the best interests of this unfortunate young woman and how best she can be given the protection which is essential to her future well being so that she may lead as full a life as her intellectual capacity allows' (p 212). It is tempting, however, to conclude that the 'full life' was a life which relieved her carers of many of their duties to protect her.

Might someone in Jeanette's position be in need of protection from exploitation from those responsible for her safety? Freeman comments upon this as follows:

Freeman, MD, 'Sterilising the mentally handicapped', in *Medicine, Ethics and the Law,* **1988, London: Stevens, p 68:**

If it was really unlikely that Jeanette would become pregnant, was sterilisation the right answer? If she understood as little as the law report seems to indicate, she certainly needed (and needs) protection, in particular from exploitation. It is noticeable how many parents of mentally handicapped daughters complain about their daughters being 'raped' by employees of institutions, for example, drivers employed to take them back and forth. One right that the mentally handicapped undoubtedly have is the right not to be sexually abused. Sterilisation does nothing to protect them from sexual exploitation. Saner employment policies (for example the employment of female drivers) and better sex education might achieve rather more.

In this regard, see the case of *Re LC (Medical Treatment: Sterilisation)* [1997] 2 FLR 258, where an application for authority to perform a sterilisation operation on a 25 year old mentally impaired woman, came before the court because of her mother's anxiety following an indecent assault upon her by a member of staff at her former residential home. In the event, the operation was not authorised, as the woman was now resident in a home where the care was described as 'of exceptionally high quality', and, on balance, the operation was not justified. Whilst not disputing the correctness of this decision, is it right for the outcome to depend upon the quality of care? If this woman had been in a home where the quality of care was poor, would the operation have been authorised? If so, the woman would have been exposed to a double jeopardy: the imposition of major, invasive and irreversible surgery, together with risk of sexual abuse and exploitation.

It is also questionable that there was any significant likelihood that Jeanette would have become pregnant. Freeman (Freeman, MD, 'Sterilising the mentally handicapped', in *Medicine, Ethics and the Law*, 1988, London: Stevens, p 68) cites evidence that the majority of those with serious impairment do not have effective fertility. Furthermore, as De Cruz says ('Sterilisation, wardship and human rights' [1988] Fam Law 6) 'mere provocative gestures are not necessarily to be equated with an invitation to have sex':

> **Lee, R and Morgan, D, 'Sterilisation and mental handicap: sapping the strength of the State?' (1988) 15 JLS 229:**
>
> The fears of undetected pregnancy, abortion, and traumatic childbirth must all be subject to some real likelihood of Jeanette's becoming pregnant. Moreover, had Jeanette been sexually active, pregnancy is not the only risk she would face; the hazards of AIDS and other sexually transmitted diseases are ignored.

It is, of course, possible that an incompetent patient may not be suited to pregnancy and motherhood. Likewise, in the case of a competent woman there may be circumstances which would mean that pregnancy and motherhood would be similarly undesirable. In such a case would sterilisation be thought to be the only solution, particularly when she was not sexually active, was aged only 17 and her future development was uncertain? Surely, it is highly unlikely that sterilisation would even be considered at that stage in her life. However, it is essential to compare Jeanette with a competent woman, otherwise Jeanette is being treated differently *because of her mental impairment*. The comparison with 'normal' people was made in the dissenting judgment of Brennan J in *Department of Health v JWB and SMB* (1992) 66 ALJR 300, where the majority of the High Court of Australia sanctioned a 'non-therapeutic' sterilisation on a 14 year old girl:

> **Brennan J:**
>
> 22 ... a variety of different purposes may appear which many would regard as of significant value in assessing the 'best interests' of an intellectually disabled child. The purposes which fall into this category can be gathered under the broad description of 'preventative': to prevent the risk of a pregnancy which the child could not properly understand and the concomitant risk of parenthood with responsibilities beyond the capacity of the child to discharge. These risks are an understandable source of anxiety

to parents, guardians and others who have a genuine concern for the welfare of an intellectually disabled child. These are risks which create an understandable anxiety in many parents, guardians and others who have a genuine concern for the welfare of a normal child. In the case of a normal female child, it would be wholly unacceptable to permit sterilisation in order to prevent pregnancy or parenthood, though those events might be thought to be tragedies in particular circumstances by reasonable persons concerned with the welfare of the child. Depending on the circumstances, the use – or, *a fortiori*, the exploitation – of the sexual attributes of a female child may entail tragic consequences, yet the risk or even the likelihood of tragic consequences affords no justification for her sterilisation. What difference does it make that the risk is occasioned by an intellectual disability? The answer to this question depends on the view taken of the proposition earlier set out in the Declaration on the Rights of Mentally Retarded Persons: they are entitled to the same rights as other humans to the maximum degree of feasibility. To accord in full measure the human dignity that is the due of every intellectually disabled girl, her right to retain her capacity to bear a child cannot be made contingent on her imposing no further burdens, causing no more anxiety or creating no further demands. If the law were to adopt a policy of permitting sterilisation in order to avoid the imposition of burdens, the causing of anxiety and the creating of demands, the human rights which foster and protect human dignity in the powerless would lie in the gift of those who are empowered and the law would fail in its function of protecting the weak.

23 ... In any event, though pregnancy be a possibility, sterilisation, once performed, is a certainty. If a non-therapeutic sterilisation could be justified at all, it could be justified only by the need to avoid a tragedy that is imminent and certain. Such a situation bespeaks a failure of care, and sterilisation is not the remedy for the failure. Nor should it be forgotten that pregnancy and motherhood may have a significance for some intellectually disabled girls quite different from the significance attributed by other people. Though others may see her pregnancy and motherhood as a tragedy, she, in her world, may find in those events an enrichment of her life.

Were the alternatives properly explored by the court, and, indeed, by Jeanette's carers? Most forms of contraceptive pill were thought to be unsuitable because of her obesity, although it was argued by the Official Solicitor that insufficient consideration had been given to the use of a progestogen contraceptive pill less likely to have that effect. The prospect of a *daily* dose, however, was daunting to Jeanette's carers, although other drugs were administered to her for her epilepsy, apparently without undue difficulty. In addition, it was thought undesirable for the contraceptive drug to be administered to her for 30 years or more. Why should this have been regarded as a foregone conclusion? Again, it is instructive to consider the comparison with a competent woman.

The possibility of Jeanette making progress, socially, was considered by Lee and Morgan:

Lee, R and Morgan, D, 'Sterilisation and mental handicap: sapping the strength of the State?' (1988) 15 JLS 229:

The certainty of the sterilisation operation, compared with Jeanette's developmental prognosis, is striking. All the judges seem prepared to accept that from her present position she will never be able to develop, either on her own or in the company of a sympathetic and supportive partner or community, into a woman who might just be able to form the affective links with children which would enable her meaningfully to exercise her procreative capacities. And yet the evidence surveyed by the House of Lords indicates that she has already developed from the age of four, when she was first received into care, from being a 'wild animal' to someone who will in a short time be going to an adult training centre ... To arrest Jeanette's metamorphosis at the age of 17 and to treat her as though she will never become 27, 37 or 40 abandons 25 years of potential reproductive capacity, affinitive development, and emotional maturing to expert evidence which is necessarily speculative in nature, imprecise, and heavily opinionated. It is used to justify a procedure which is certain in its consequences, definite, and irreversible.

De Cruz suggests that the decision may have been made in something approaching indecent haste:

De Cruz, SP, 'Sterilisation, wardship and human rights' [1988] Fam Law 6:

Should the Law Lords have deferred the decision, pending further investigation and observation? The Canadian courts took nearly seven years to decide Eve's case, and it took 16 months for the Supreme Court to produce its judgment, after studying a very wide range of expert opinions and the exhaustive research of the Canadian Law Commission. In their desire not to be faced with a jurisdictional problem once Jeanette reached the age of 18, the English Law Lords only took 28 days to decide the case, but their assumptions about her future conduct may well have led them to discount other possibilities too readily.

As far as adult patients are concerned, the leading case is *Re F (Mental Patient: Sterilisation)* [1990] 2 AC 1. The facts of that case concerned a female mental patient, a woman in her thirties, who had been assessed as having a mental age of a four to five year old. She was a voluntary in-patient in a mental hospital where she had formed what was described as a sexual relationship with a male patient. Both hospital staff, and the patient's mother, felt that she would not be able to cope with childbirth, nor with the subsequent rearing of a child, and that it would, therefore, be in her best interests to be sterilised. A declaration was sought from the court that the proposed sterilisation would be lawful. The unanimous decision of the Court of Appeal and the House of Lords was that the operation was in her best interests.

In both this case and the case of Jeanette, the mental age of the women concerned was a crucial factor. The crude application of intelligence assessments to social and emotional development is questionable:

Lee, R and Morgan, D, 'Sterilisation and mental handicap: sapping the strength of the State?' (1988) 15 JLS 229:

The problem of mental age

If the Law Lords appear to have been woefully uninformed as to the reality of the present life for mentally handicapped women, they are also less than convincing in showing an understanding of their capacities. One of the most persistent criticisms of the decision in the professional press concerned the emphasis ascribed to the criteria of mental age, and the use to which this was put. Having stated that Jeanette had a mental age of five or six, the judgments in *Re B* seem to treat Jeanette as if she were simply a child of that age. Jeanette, like all other handicapped people, would be expected to demonstrate different functional abilities across a whole range of skills. Intelligence testing offers little information as to many of these abilities, and in so far as it leads to labels such as 'mental age of five', it misdescribes the mentally handicapped person in a discriminatory fashion. Jeanette may not read at all, unlike many six year olds, but she may consistently outperform most children of that age in terms of socialisation or self-help. In addition, the criterion of 'mental age' was treated as static. Yet, as Woolrych has observed ... the use of the discredited concept of 'mental age' is disturbing, since current experiences indicate learning potential is dependent on the quality and variety of services available in developing an understanding of issues such as the connection between sex and having babies.

Nor will the concept of mental age shed much light upon Jeanette's biological and emotional state as a 17 year old woman. While it may be difficult to grapple with the concept of a physically mature woman manifesting childlike intelligence in some respects, we must be careful that we do not discount and become repulsed by the notion that this person manifests adult sexual desires. This is a problem facing many parents of mentally handicapped young women.

Can we expect judges to be aware of the controversy which surrounds the notion of mental age? It is used, in part, to justify an irreversible surgical procedure. This procedure eliminates reproductive capacities, infringing what some would claim to be a basic human right. If the courts are to be used to channel issues of controversial ethical dilemmas, and if they are to legitimate their authority to resolve them, then informed judgment is a starting point.

It was stated in *Re B* that the case was about removing the 'right to reproduce'. Is there such a right? It is often stated that there is: for example, Article 12 of the European Convention on Human Rights enshrines the 'right to marry and found a family':

Freeman, MD (ed), *Medicine, Ethics and the Law*, 1988, London: Stevens, p 72:

Why do we have the rights we have and do we have the right to reproduce? One common answer links rights with interests. Such a view was implicit in Bentham and Ihering and is found in such contemporary writers as Feinberg and McCloskey. Thus, Feinberg writes that 'the sort of beings who can have rights are precisely those who have (or can have) interests'. It is an argument often employed by those who believe that animals have rights. It is also one of the arguments employed by Carby-Hall to demonstrate the Jeanette did not have the right to reproduce. She writes: 'A being can truly be said to have an interest in x, the subject of a potential right, if and only if x will benefit him in the sense of furthering some or all of his present or future desires.' She argues that a necessary condition of possession of a right is at least the capacity to possess the relevant concepts and a desire for that right. Jeanette clearly lacked the former and almost certainly the latter. But is this association of rights and interests justifiable? I think not. What this does not answer is how the having of interests establishes the grounds for having rights. Animals have interests. I have an interest in Middlesex winning the County Cricket Championship. In neither would it make sense to talk of rights. Human beings do not have the same interests. Surely this does not justify an unequal distribution of human rights. I agree with Alan White that 'no valid argument can be given either for including or for excluding children, imbeciles (*inter alia*) ... as holders of rights on the ground that being capable of having a right ensures or necessitates being capable either of having something in one's interest or of being interested in something. Hence, he concludes, 'the question whether animals, etc ... can or cannot have interests, either in the sense of something being in their interest or in the sense of their being interested in something, is irrelevant to the question whether they can have rights'.

Before we pursue the justifying principle any further it may be as well to ponder the Carby-Hall claim. Can it be right that a necessary condition for the possession of a right is the capacity to possess relevant concepts and a desire for the right in question? Carby-Hall is far from being alone in thinking that it is. In *Causing Death and Saving Lives*, Glover puts the case as follows:

> Desires do not presuppose words, but they do presuppose concepts. A baby can want to be fed, or be changed, or go to his mother, although he does not speak. Innumerable signs of recognition and pleasure show us that he has these concepts. But a baby cannot want to escape from death any more than he can want to escape the fate of being a chartered accountant when grown up. He has no idea of either.

> Glover goes on to argue that the autonomy argument is no objection to infanticide. 'In killing a baby, someone is overriding the baby's autonomy to no greater extent than he would be if he prevented the mother from coming home that day.' Or, in the language of *Re B*: 'In sterilising Jeanette, we are overriding her autonomy to no greater extent than we would be doing if we prevented her seeing her boyfriend this evening (by, for example, arranging for him to be elsewhere).' I do not find this very convincing. The fact that a baby has no awareness of, or desire for, life cannot mean that it does not have a right to life. It may be difficult, if not impossible, to exercise a right if one is unaware of its existence or one lacks the concepts or the desire, but this cannot mean that one lacks the right in question.

Freeman is trying to resist the argument that Jeanette had no right to reproduce as long as she was unaware of that so called right. Is awareness of such a right relevant to its existence? If you are deliberately locked in a room and are unaware of this, does it mean that up until the point that you wish to leave you have no right to leave the room? Of course, in the cases of Jeanette and F, it was assumed that they would never wish to leave the room, but it is questionable whether that assumption is justified. Further, the assertion that the right to reproduce meant nothing to her belongs to a dangerous species of argument, that is, 'you have no rights because you are incapable of exercising them, or incapable of exercising them in your own best interests'.

It could be said that there is no *right* to reproduce because such a right is unenforceable. It might be better to say that one has a right to *attempt* to reproduce. However, viewed in this language, would it make sense to say that in the cases of Jeanette and F, they had no right to attempt, because that presupposes a decision-making capacity which they may not have had? It is doubtful whether this is correct. Many children are produced unintentionally. If one was only endorsing a right to attempt to reproduce, it may be argued that such an unintentional pregnancy was less valuable than others. Might the better view be that of Raanan Gillon who argues that there is a *prima facie* right not to be prevented? (See 'On sterilising severely mentally handicapped people' (1987) 13 JME 59.) The right may not be absolute, but it is arguable that it should only be overridden, in the words of Brennan J, 'to avoid a tragedy that is imminent and certain'.

Is it even necessary to consider the issue in the language of rights? It must be the case that a woman, even if mentally impaired, is entitled to the same amount of respect for her human dignity and physical integrity as any other person. There is a strong argument that subjecting her to invasive surgery on the off-chance that she may become pregnant and 'pregnancy does not mean anything to her', is flouting respect for her dignity as a human being.

The cases of Jeanette and F are very different in at least one important respect. In the case of Jeanette, there was no suggestion that she was sexually active, or indeed, that she wished to be (it does not necessarily follow that she did, despite the so called provocative gestures – again consider her in comparison with a competent woman). In the case of F, however, it was said that she was having a sexual relationship (in the Court of Appeal, p 9):

> **Lord Donaldson MR**: The particular problem in this case arises out of a relationship F has formed with another patient, P. This is of a sexual nature and probably involves sexual intercourse or something close to it on about two occasions a month ... There is no evidence of distress or distaste on the part of F. It is probable that she obtains some physical enjoyment. When asked what has happened she replies, 'Nice'. Dr McDonald does not regard P as having the state of mind to make him criminally liable and Dr McDonald certainly does not regard what is happening as sexual molestation. Professor Bicknell made the point that F is quite strong willed and if she does not want something she will not have it. Therefore, whilst there is no direct evidence whether F is a purely passive participant or obtains active enjoyment, I incline to the latter view. There is also evidence that F enjoys a cuddle with those with whom she has some bond. The attitude of F's carers to her relationship with P has been neither to encourage nor discourage it. Although there has been some criticism that this is equivocal, it is, in my judgment, entirely understandable and appropriate.

Some may argue that F needed protecting from this just as much as Jeanette may have needed protecting from sexual exploitation. However, too much 'protection' may interfere with the right to a private life, which, for example, is protected by Article 8 of the European Convention on Human Rights. Many legal mechanisms and social conventions allow competent individuals a considerable measure of privacy. It is generally accepted that mentally impaired people should be afforded similar access to privacy and the means to enjoy pleasurable intimate activities as far as is possible (see, for example, O'Brien, J and Tyne, A, *The Principle of Normalisation*, 1981, London: Campaign for Mentally Handicapped People). At least, this is accepted in principle, the practical considerations of providing the necessary facilities are less well worked out. This was acknowledged in *Re F* by Lord Donaldson MR, p 9:

> There has been a shift from the paternalistic to a much freer approach. Mentally handicapped people have the same needs, feelings and longings as other people, and this is much more frequently acknowledged nowadays than years ago.

It was argued by the Official Solicitor that the proper course of action was to put an end to the relationship with P, but surely it would have been wrong to deny F the opportunity of sexual enjoyment simply as a contraceptive measure, as this would have been treating her differently from people deemed to have capacity. The desirability of sterilisation as opposed to other forms of contraception, however, does not follow from the desirability of allowing this woman a degree of sexual freedom. What does follow from the case of *Re F* is that there was a real risk of pregnancy from a sexual relationship which, it appeared, was pleasurable and non-exploitative. The question of obtaining the consent of P (on the assumption that he may have been able to give consent) to the use of contraception, or even vasectomy, was not raised. If P was not capable of consenting, would sterilisation of him have been in his best interests? The decision in *Re A (Mental Patient Sterilisation)* [2000] 1 FLR 549 was anticipated by Douglas, G, in *Law, Fertility and Reproduction*, 1991, London: Sweet & Maxwell.

The case concerned A, a 28 year old Down's syndrome man, who was described as being on the borderline of significant and severe impairment. Although he was supervised by his mother at the time of the application to the court, she was concerned that if her ill health meant that he had to go and live in local authority accommodation, he might have a sexual relationship and would not be able to understand the possible consequences, or cope with them if and when they occurred. The mother applied for a declaration that a vasectomy was in his best interests. There was evidence that the man was sexually aware, but the judge refused the declaration. The Court of Appeal rejected the appeal, holding that male sterilisation on non-therapeutic grounds was not in his best interests. The fact of the birth of a child or disapproval of his conduct would have little effect on him. A further application could be made if he was moved to local authority accommodation and his freedom was unacceptably curtailed to avoid the risk of him fathering a child. However, it was said that, in such circumstances, the likely outcome would be that the female concerned would be subject to extra supervision, rather than him. The Court of Appeal might have gone on to say that the female concerned would probably find herself the subject of court proceedings relating to her own sterilisation. From the point of view of sexual equality, the contrast between this and the female sterilisation cases might give rise to an accusation of unfairness, but doubtless on the application of the best interests test, the decision in *Re A* is correct.

A difficulty which does arise in this context is that, under s 7 of the Sexual Offences Act 1956, it is an offence to have sexual intercourse with a mental defective (defined as someone with severe impairment of intelligence and social functioning). This may well place obstacles in the way of the sexual liberation of mentally impaired people. It is suggested that the offence, codified nearly 50 years ago, does not reflect the changes in attitude towards the 'normalisation' of impaired people alluded to above.

Some other sterilisation cases merit attention. In *Re W (A Mental Patient) (Sterilisation)* [1993] 1 FLR 381 Hollis J authorised a sterilisation operation in circumstances where there was no evidence that the woman was involved in any sexual activity. In *Re P (A Minor) (Wardship: Sterilisation)* [1989] 1 FLR 182, the application was in respect of a 17 year old girl, who was described as having the intellectual development of a six year old, but with 'normal' sexual libido. Evidence suggested that she was likely to improve in the development of her 'social' skills. It was also said that pregnancy would be disastrous for her because she would be unlikely agree to an abortion, and to take the child away from her would cause her great distress as she had some maternal feelings. Similarly, in *Re X (Adult Patient: Sterilisation)* [1998] 2 FLR 1124, in the case of a severely mentally disabled 31 year old woman, it was found to be in her best interests to be sterilised when she expressed her desire to have a baby, and had a boyfriend. In *B*, it will be recalled, the fact that Jeanette had *no* maternal feelings was of some importance. We are now faced with a situation where the *presence* of maternal feelings is still disastrous. The question again arises: were these two women being treated the same as women with capacity? An important factor in the case of *P* was that the type of operation proposed was considered to be reversible. If it was clear that pregnancy would be a disaster, what was the significance of reversibility, if it was not to regard the surgical procedure in the same light as contraceptive measures?

In *Re S (Medical Treatment: Adult Sterilisation)* [1998] 1 FLR 944, Johnson J refused to grant a declaration that it would be lawful to sterilise a 22 year old woman. Although it was contended that she was vulnerable to sexual exploitation, the judge regarded this as a 'speculative' risk. The invasive procedure of sterilisation with its attendant risk of fatality could not be justified without an identifiable risk of pregnancy. In *Re SL (Adult Patient) (Medical Treatment)* [2000] 2 FCR 452, (p 180, above), the Court of Appeal upheld an appeal against a declaration that it would be lawful to carry out a hysterectomy on a patient when there was a less invasive alternative available. It should also be noted in this case that, although the trial judge had found that there was an identifiable risk of pregnancy, in the Court of Appeal this was doubted by Dame Butler-Sloss P. Certainly, the risk in *SL* was 'speculative' and not identifiable, as the woman concerned was still living at home with her mother who carefully supervised her, and whose concerns were all about what might happen in the future.

In *Re F*, Lord Bridge had suggested (at p 52) that doctors may be under a *duty* to carry out a sterilisation operation, even for what we have described as 'non-therapeutic' reasons, if it was in the best interests of the patient. What is to be made of this suggestion? It is arguable that this could never be the case in respect of non-therapeutic sterilisations, in that the doctor's duty arises from the therapeutic context only.

However, *Re F* brings us face to face with the *Bolam* test in interpreting 'best interests'. In the Canadian case of *Re Eberhardy's Guardianship* (1981) 307 NW 2d 881 it was stated:

> **Heffernan J**: While courts are always dependent upon the opinions of expert witnesses, it would appear that the exercise of judicial discretion unguided by well thought out policy determination reflecting the interests of society, as well as of the person to be sterilised, are hazardous indeed. Moreover, all seriously mentally retarded persons may not *ipso facto* be incapable of giving birth without serious trauma, and some may be good parents. Also there has been a discernible and laudable tendency to 'mainstream' the developmentally disabled and retarded. A properly thought out public policy on sterilisation or alternative contraceptive methods could well facilitate the entry of these persons into a more nearly normal relationship with society.

The 'interests of society' can be interpreted in two ways. First, these interests can be used to legitimise eugenic sterilisations. The second interpretation, and it is submitted that this is preferred in the light of Heffernan J's other remarks, is that the '*ad hoc*' approach to best interests is open to substantial criticism. Although other issues were said to be relevant to best interests in *Re SL (Adult Patient) (Medical Treatment)* [2000] 2 FCR 452, it is not clear from that case that 'policing' issues should be considered, as opposed to the wider, for example, social, implications for the individual concerned.

At the moment, although there is no legal obligation to bring these cases before the court (although it may be a matter of 'good practice', see *Re F* above), the Official Solicitor has issued a Practice Note stating that the sanction of a High Court judge will be required in 'almost all circumstances'. There is also some guidance as to what should be evidenced before the court:

> *Practice Note (Official Solicitor: Declaratory Proceedings: Medical and Welfare Proceedings for Adults Who Lack Capacity)* [2001] 2 FLR 158:

> [1] If a sterilisation procedure is necessary for therapeutic as opposed to contraceptive purposes then there may be no need for an application to court: *Re GF (A Patient)* [1991] FCR 786: *sub nom Re GF (Medical Treatment)* [1992] 1 FLR 293. If, however, any case lies anywhere near the boundary line it should be referred to the court: *Re SL (Adult Patient) (Medical Treatment)* [2000] 2 FCR 452 at 469; *sub nom Re S (Sterilisation: Patient's Best Interests)* [2000] 2 FLR 389 at 405.

The claim

[2] The relief sought in relation to an adult should be declarations that:

(1) [The patient] lacks capacity to consent to an operation of ... [specify procedure proposed, eg, 'tubal occlusion by Filshie clips', or 'laparoscopic sub-total hysterectomy', or 'vasectomy']. (2) It is in the existing circumstances in the best interest of [the patient] for her/him to undergo an operation of ... [specify procedure as above].

The evidence

[3] The court must be satisfied that the patient lacks capacity and that the operation will promote the best interests of the patient, rather than the interests or convenience of the claimant, carers or public. In sterilisation cases, the best interests test has at least three particular components.

(1) Likelihood of pregnancy

An operation must address a current real need. It must be shown that the patient is capable of conception and is having or is likely to have full sexual intercourse. In relation to a young woman who has no interest in human relationships with any sexual ingredient a high level of supervision is an appropriate protection: *Re LC (Medical Treatment) (Sterilisation)* [1997] 2 FLR 258. Any risk of pregnancy should be identifiable rather than speculative: *Re S (Adult: Sterilisation)* [1999] 1 FCR 277; *sub nom Re S (Medical Treatment: Adult Sterilisation)* [1998] 1 FLR 944.

(2) Damage deriving from conception and/or menstruation

The physical and psychological consequences of pregnancy and childbirth for the patient should be analysed by obstetric and psychiatric experts. In the case of a male, these considerations will be different: *Re A (Medical Treatment: Male Sterilisation)* [2000] 1 FCR 193 at 202–03; *sub nom Re A (Male Sterilisation)* [2000] 1 FLR 549 at 557. Psychiatric evidence as to the patient's likely ability to care for and/or have a fulfilling relationship with a child should be adduced. Evidence as to any child having a disability is likely to be irrelevant: *Re X (Adult Sterilisation)* [1999] 3 FCR 426 at 431; [1998] 2 FLR 1124 at 1129. If the proposed procedure is intended to affect the patient's menstruation, then evidence about any detriment caused by her current menstrual cycle must also be adduced.

(3) Medical and surgical techniques

The court will require a detailed analysis of all available and relevant methods of addressing any problems found to be substantiated under (1) and (2) above. This analysis should be performed by a doctor or doctors with expertise in the full range of available methods. The expert should explain the nature of each relevant method and then list its advantages and disadvantages (in particular, morbidity rates, mortality rates and failure rates) for the individual patient, taking into account any relevant aspects of her physical and psychological health. The Royal College of Obstetrics and Gynaecology has published relevant evidence-based clinical guidelines (No 4: *Male and Female Sterilisation*, April 1999 and No 5: *The Management of Menorrhagia in Secondary Care*, July 1999).

It is important to consider non-therapeutic sterilisation cases in the light of the Human Rights Act 1998 and the European Convention on Human Rights and how Articles 8 (right to a private life) and 12 (right to marry and found a family).

Finally, it should be noted that failure to consider whether hysterectomies performed on two mentally incapacitated patients were in their best interests has resulted in a finding of serious misconduct by the General Medical Council: *Pembrey v GMC* [2003] UKPC 60.

Sterilisation to manage menstruation – therapeutic or non-therapeutic?

In *Re Eve* [1986] 2 SCR 388 it was said:

> **La Forest J**: I should perhaps add … that sterilisation may, on occasion, be necessary as an adjunct to treatment of a serious malady, but I would underline that this, of course, does not allow for subterfuge or for treatment of some marginal medical problem … The recent British Columbia case of *Re K* (1985) 19 DLR (4th) 255, is at best dangerously close to the limits of the permissible.

The case of *Re K* concerned the authorisation of a sterilisation operation on a child to prevent menstruation occurring because the child had an aversion to blood. There have been several other cases where sterilisation has been advocated as a suitable way of managing menstruation. For example in *Re E (A Minor) (Medical Treatment)* [1991] 2 FLR 585 and *Re GF (Medical Treatment)* [1992] 1 FLR 293 hysterectomies were authorised in both cases where the women, described as severely handicapped, suffered from excessively heavy periods. In *Re E*, the proposed sterilisation was in respect of a 17 year old girl. Sir Stephen Brown P held that since it was for therapeutic reasons and not to achieve sterilisation, the parents could consent to the operation, and there was no need for the intervention of the court. In *Re GF*, the woman was an adult. Again, Sir Stephen Brown referred to the therapeutic nature of the procedure, stating that, because of this, there was no need for a declaration as to its lawfulness. It is submitted that the removal of court protection in this way is wrong. It was suggested earlier in this chapter that the therapeutic/non-therapeutic distinction may not always protect the person lacking capacity. Sterilisations carried out for the purposes of 'menstrual management' do achieve sterilisation, even if this was not the purpose. To remove the need for an order of the court is to deny the person valuable protection from non-therapeutic sterilisations being carried out under the guise of 'therapeutic' purposes.

The dangers of such operations being used for non-medical reasons have been considered by Natasha Cica:

Cica, N, 'Sterilising the intellectually disabled' (1993) 1 Med L Rev 186, p 198:

Care must … be taken in defining when performing a hysterectomy to prevent menstruation may be considered to be 'therapeutic'. It is submitted that four broad principles should govern this category of sterilisation.

1 The procedure should only be described as therapeutic if performed to alleviate or prevent a recognised clinical condition. Merely 'hygienic' purposes should, for the reasons discussed above, be classified as non-therapeutic. The recognised clinical condition may be a physical condition such as a disorder whose symptoms include excessively heavy or painful periods. Or it may be a psychiatric or psychological condition, in which case 'mere' distress or embarrassment would seem to be insufficient. The distress or disturbance suffered by the woman must be sufficiently serious to pose an identifiable danger to her mental health. Again this is necessary to ensure that the woman's best social interests are not confused with her best medical interests. This requirement that a clinically recognised psychiatric or psychological condition be present was imposed by Brennan J in *Department of*

Health v JWB and SMB (1992) 66 ALJR 300 when he referred to the need for 'a psychiatric disorder' of sufficient severity before suppression of menstruation via hysterectomy may be justified. The requirement was arguably also implicit in Deane J's description of his second category of permissible sterilisations [in *Department of Health v JWB and SMB*]. As described above, this category was based upon the facts of the New Zealand case of *Re X* (1992), in which the intellectually disabled 15 year old's reaction to menstrual pain would have been fits of uncomprehending irritability, violence towards others and self-mutilation. For a case to fall within Deane J's second category, menstruation must entail 'grave and unusual problems and suffering ... pain and extraordinary behavioural and personal problems'. Deane J specified that these grave, unusual and extraordinary problems may arise from, *inter alia*, an inability to comprehend or cope with pain; a phobic aversion to blood; or a complete inability to cope with problems of hygiene with *psychiatric or psychological consequences*.

2 Such a procedure will only be 'therapeutic' if the clinically recognised condition is already present or is virtually certain to arise in the near future. There must be a 'real possibility' that the condition will arise. The less imminent the clinical condition whose treatment is sought by hysterectomy, the more likely the physical, psychiatric or psychological state of the intellectually disabled woman will change and that hysterectomy will not be required.

3 A hysterectomy will only be 'therapeutic' if it is *necessary* for the above purposes, in that it is a treatment of 'last resort'. There must be no alternative, less invasive treatment which would effectively alleviate the condition. The harm done must be proportionate to the risk of harm avoided. Brennan J's notion of 'proportionality' is clearly the guiding principle here.

4 There must be advice from appropriately qualified medical experts that the above conditions are satisfied. Where the health-threatening condition is psychiatric or psychological, expert advice must be given by an appropriately qualified psychiatrist or psychologist. The expert opinions of general practitioners and gynaecologists alone would be insufficient in such cases.

The Law Commission has not thought it necessary to require court authorisation for such procedures, but the report goes on to say:

Law Commission, *Mental Incapacity*, Report No 231, 1995, London: HMSO, para 6.9:

... many of our respondents expressed concern about operations being labelled 'for menstrual management', with the result that no independent supervision at all is required. A consultant in developmental psychiatry who has made a special study of sterilisation of people with learning disabilities suggested that the level of menstrual distress is often misrepresented, and that further investigation can reveal less drastic means of coping with the problem than a sterilisation operation.

The Commission goes on to recommend that such procedures should require a certificate from an independent medical practitioner where it is for relieving the existing detrimental effects of menstruation. Is this a safeguard? It is submitted that it is not. There is no suggestion that the certificate should specify whether the 'detrimental' effects are medical or social; it does not impose a requirement as to the gravity of the detrimental effects, and no mention is made of alternative measures that could be taken.

A proposed hysterectomy was declared to be lawful in the case of *Re ZM and OS (Sterilisation: Patient's Best Interests)* [2000] 1 FLR 523, where it was required to be carried out for both contraceptive purposes and for the elimination of menstruation which was painful and caused her great embarrassment. The woman was aged 19, born with Down's syndrome and about to move into a residential unit to achieve more independence. She also had a boyfriend. The procedure was said to be in her best interests, as her periods brought her nothing but pain and discomfort, she would be incapable of looking after a child, and pregnancy and childbirth and the removal of the child would be a catastrophe, as would the emotional and psychological consequences of an abortion.

Abortion

It was stated in *Re SG (A Patient)* [1993] 4 Med LR 75 that the provisions of the Abortion Act 1967 as amended are an adequate safeguard for an incompetent woman, and there is no need of court authorisation. It is submitted that they are not (see Chapter 8). In addition, assuming that the woman (although incompetent) has expressed a wish to have the child, there is something highly distasteful about forcing her to submit to an abortion. Whilst there may be many occasions when an abortion will be the best course of action for an incompetent woman, it is suggested that the vigilance necessary in cases of sterilisation should be present when considering the performance of an abortion (see, for example, the remarks of Lord Donaldson MR in the Court of Appeal in *Re F*, p 19).

In *Re SS (Adult: Medical Treatment)* [2002] 1 FCR 73, the court had to consider the case of an adult woman who suffered from schizophrenia and who was detained under the MHA 1983. She was 24 weeks pregnant. Her application to the court sought two declarations: first, that she lacked the capacity to make a decision about the termination of her pregnancy; and, secondly, that it was in her best interests. It was accepted by the Official Solicitor, on her behalf, that she lacked decision-making capacity. As will be seen in Chapter 8, 24 weeks is a significant time in the duration of a pregnancy. Unless certain special conditions apply, terminations cannot take place after this time. Having a termination at such a late time entailed going into labour and giving birth to the unviable foetus. Other factors which were considered relevant by the court were: the woman had already had four children, three of whom lived with the father, the fourth had been given up for adoption; the child would be of mixed race and therefore more difficult to place for adoption; she had expressed a desire for a termination and believed the child to be dead. One psychiatrist who had examined her had to consider the provisions of the Abortion Act 1967 (as amended) and weigh up the likely effect of the baby being removed at birth against the termination of the pregnancy, and concluded that it was not clear that a termination was in her best interests. Another psychiatrist, instructed by the Official Solicitor reported that the woman had said that she would kill herself if she did not have a termination. The woman's responsible medical officer (under the MHA 1983) considered the matter to be so finely balanced that he did not feel he could express an opinion one way or the other. Wall J held that the correct approach was to assess the various risks but, in this case, because the evidence of the medical experts did not come down on one side or another, then it followed that it could not be said that a termination was in her best interests. It was also said that, because the problem of terminating late pregnancies could arise frequently in psychiatric hospitals, each hospital should have a protocol for dealing with them. Two observations can be made. First, it would have been a late termination, that is, later than 24 weeks, and, therefore, different considerations apply as far as complying with the Abortion Act is concerned (see Chapter 8). Secondly, the woman had decided that she wanted a termination. Although lacking capacity, her views should be taken into account. If the other matters are finely balanced, there is some merit in saying that her wishes should tilt the balance.

CHAPTER 5

CONFIDENTIALITY, PRIVACY AND ACCESS TO MEDICAL RECORDS

CONFIDENTIALITY – THE DUTY

The ethical obligation

It is not only of academic interest to look at the ethical justifications for the obligation of confidence, it is also important to keep them in mind when examining the circumstances in which the obligation can be lawfully breached, and to consider whether the breaches in question can also be justified on ethical grounds.

As we have seen, the doctrine of utilitarianism assesses the ethics of a course of action on the basis that it will result in the best consequences overall. In the context of confidentiality, therefore, the obligation is justified by the utility of doctors keeping medical information secret. The argument is that if there no assurance of secrecy, then patients would be reluctant to seek medical advice and treatment, or would be less than frank when doing so. This would, it is argued, have an adverse effect on the health of society. The argument is described by Raanan Gillon:

Gillon, R, *Philosophical Medical Ethics*, 1986, Chichester: John Wiley, p 108:

Why should doctors from the time of Hippocrates to the present have promised to keep their patients' secrets? If confidentiality is not a moral good in itself what moral good does it serve? The commonest justification for the duty of medical confidentiality is undoubtedly consequentialist: people's better health, welfare, the general good, and overall happiness are more likely to be attained if doctors are fully informed by their patients, and this is more likely if doctors undertake not to disclose their patients' secrets. Conversely, if patients did not believe that doctors would keep their secrets then either they would not divulge embarrassing but potentially medically important information, thus reducing their chances of getting the best medical care, or they would disclose such information and feel anxious and unhappy at the prospect of their secrets being made known.

The utilitarian view is particularly appropriate to confidentiality as it will readily admit that the duty is not absolute and can be breached in certain circumstances. It would be argued that the breach is justified when the utility of disclosure outweighs the utility produced by keeping the confidences. As will be seen, the only legal justification at common law for disclosure is either that the patient has consented, or that it is in the public interest to disclose. The language of the public interest defence has a strong utilitarian flavour: *AG v Guardian Newspapers (No 2)* [1990] AC 109, p 282, *per* Lord Goff:

Lord Goff: ... although the basis of the law's protection of confidence is that there is a public interest that confidences should be preserved and protected by the law, nevertheless that public interest may be outweighed by some other countervailing public interest which favours disclosure.

Gurry, F, *In Breach of Confidence*, 1984, Oxford: Clarendon, p 5:

The public interest is a reincarnation of the older common law principle of public policy, which was described by Winfield as 'a principle of judicial legislation or interpretation founded on the current needs of the community'. Its function in the enforcement of confidences is the same as the role played by public policy in the formulation of contract law. It provides a starting point for the courts' intervention and circumscribes the scope of that intervention.

As we have already seen, utilitarianism can be contrasted with deontological theories in which duty rather than purpose is the fundamental concept of ethics. Gillon states:

Gillon, R, *Philosophical Medical Ethics*, 1986, Chichester: John Wiley, p 108:

Deontologists ... are likely to base their arguments for confidentiality not just (if at all) on welfare considerations but also on the moral principle of respect for autonomy or sometimes on a putatively independent principle of respect for privacy, which is seen as a fundamental moral requirement in itself. Thus, while the principle of medical confidentiality is not defended as a moral end in itself, it is defended by utilitarians and deontologists alike as a means to some morally desirable end [such as] the general welfare, respect for people's autonomy, or respect for their privacy.

Beauchamp and Childress suggest an approach based upon autonomy:

Beauchamp, TL and Childress, JF, *Principles of Biomedical Ethics*, 5th edn, 2001, Oxford: OUP, p 308:

A second approach to the justification of rules and rights of confidentiality looks to respect for autonomy and privacy. The argument for privacy ... can here be extended to confidentiality, breaches of which have often been viewed as primarily violations of privacy and personal integrity ...

These concerns are reflected in the various ethical codes referred to in Chapter 1. The Hippocratic Oath states: '... all that may come to my knowledge in the exercise of my profession or outside of my profession or in daily commerce with men, which ought not to be spread abroad, I will keep secret and will never reveal.' The Declaration of Geneva contains a similar statement.

The General Medical Council's guidance

It must be remembered that the following guidance issued by the General Medical Council (GMC) does not have the force of law, and cannot be taken to be co-extensive with the law. However, there is no doubt that the guidance has persuasive authority (see the reference thereto in *W v Edgell* [1990] 1 All ER 835, p 843):

General Medical Council, *Confidentiality: Protecting and Providing Information*, 2004, London: GMC:

Being registered with the GMC gives you rights and privileges. In return, you have a duty to meet the standards of competence, care and conduct set by the GMC.

Doctors hold information about patients which is private and sensitive. This information must not be given to others unless the patient consents or you can jusitfy the disclosure.

When you are satisfied that information should be released, all relevant information should be disclosed promptly. This is often essential to the best interests of the patient, or to safeguard the well-being of others.

Disclosing information about patients

9. You must respect patients' confidentiality. Seeking patients' consent to disclosure of information is part of good communication between doctors and patients. When

asked to provide information you must follow the guidance in paragraph 1 of this booklet.

Circumstances where patients may give implied consent to disclosure

Sharing information in the health care team or with others providing care

10. Most people understand and accept that information must be shared within the health care team in order to provide their care. You should make sure that patients are aware that personal information about them will be shared within the health care team, unless they object, and of the reasons for this. It is particularly important to check that patients understand what will be disclosed if you need to share identifiable information with anyone employed by another organisation or agency who is contributing to their care. You must respect the wishes of any patient who objects to particular information being shared with others providing care, except where this would put others at risk of death or serious harm.

11. You must make sure that anyone to whom you disclose personal information understands that it is given to them in confidence, which they must respect. All staff members receiving personal information in order to provide or support care are bound by a legal duty of confidence, whether or not they have contractual or professional obligations to protect confidentiality.

12. Circumstances may arise where a patient cannot be informed about the sharing of information, for example because of a medical emergency. In these cases you must pass relevant information promptly to those providing the patient's care.

Disclosing information for clinical audit

13. Clinical audit is essential to the provision of good care. All doctors in clinical practice have a duty to participate in clinical audit. Where an audit is to be undertaken by the team which provided care, or those working to support them, such as clinical audit staff, you may disclose identifiable information, provided you are satisfied that patients:

- have been informed that their data may be disclosed for clinical audit, and their right to object to the disclosure; and

- have not objected.

14. If a patient does object you should explain why information is needed and how this may benefit their care. If it is not possible to provide safe care without disclosing information for audit, you should explain this to the patient and the options open to them.

15. Where clinical audit is to be undertaken by another organisation, information should be anonymised wherever that is practicable. In any case where it is not practicable to anonymise data, or anonymised data will not fulfil the requirements of the audit, express consent must be obtained before identifiable data is disclosed.

Disclosures where express consent must be sought

16. Express consent is usually needed before the disclosure of identifiable information for purposes such as research, epidemiology, financial audit or administration. When seeking express consent to disclosure you must make sure that patients are given enough information on which to base their decision, the reasons for the disclosure and the likely consequences of the disclosure. You should also explain how much information will be disclosed and to whom it will

be given. If the patient withholds consent, or consent cannot be obtained, disclosures may be made only where they are required by law or can be justified in the public interest. Where the purpose is covered by a regulation made under s 60 of the Health and Social Care Act 2001, disclosures may also be made without patients' consent. You should make a record of the patient's decision, and whether and why you have disclosed information.

17. Where doctors have contractual obligations to third parties, such as companies or organisations, they must obtain patients' consent before undertaking any examination or writing a report for that organisation. Before seeking consent they must explain the purpose of the examination or report and the scope of the disclosure. Doctors should offer to show patients the report, or give them copies, whether or not this is required by law.

Disclosures in the public interest

22. Personal information may be disclosed in the public interest, without the patient's consent, and in exceptional cases where patients have withheld consent, where the benefits to an individual or to society of the disclosure outweigh the public and the patient's interest in keeping the information confidential. In all cases where you consider disclosing information without consent from the patient, you must weigh the possible harm (both to the patient, and the overall trust between doctors and patients) against the benefits which are likely to arise from the release of information.

23. Before considering whether a disclosure of personal information 'in the public interest' would be justified, you must be satisfied that identifiable data are necessary for the purpose, or that it is not practicable to anonymise the data. In such cases you should still try to seek patients' consent, unless it is not practicable to do so, for example because:

   • the patients are not competent to give consent (see paragraphs 28 and 29); or

   • the records are of such age and/or number that reasonable efforts to trace patients are unlikely to be successful; or

   • the patient has been, or may be violent; or obtaining consent would undermine the purpose of the disclosure (eg disclosures in relation to crime); or

   • action must be taken quickly (for example in the detection or control of outbreaks of some communicable diseases) and there is insufficient time to contact patients.

24. In cases where there is a serious risk to the patient or others, disclosures may be justified even where patients have been asked to agree to a disclosure, but have withheld consent (for further advice see paragraph 27).

25. You should inform patients that a disclosure will be made, wherever it is practicable to do so. You must document in the patient's record any steps you have taken to seek or obtain consent and your reasons for disclosing information without consent.

26. Ultimately, the 'public interest' can be determined only by the courts; but the GMC may also require you to justify your actions if a complaint is made about the disclosure of identifiable information without a patient's consent. The potential benefits and harms of disclosures made without consent are also considered by the Patient Information Advisory Group in considering applications for Regulations under the Health and Social Care Act 2001. Disclosures of data covered by a Regulation are not in breach of the common law duty of confidentiality.

Disclosures to protect the patient or others

27. Disclosure of personal information without consent may be justified in the public interest where failure to do so may expose the patient or others to risk of death or serious harm. Where the patient or others are exposed to a risk so serious that it outweighs the patient's privacy interest, you should seek consent to disclosure where practicable. If it is not practicable to seek consent, you should disclose information promptly to an appropriate person or authority. You should generally inform the patient before disclosing the information. If you seek consent and the patient withholds it you should consider the reasons for this, if any are provided by the patient. If you remain of the view that disclosure is necessary to protect a third party from death or serious harm, you should disclose information promptly to an appropriate person or authority. Such situations arise, for example, where a disclosure may assist in the prevention, detection or prosecution of a serious crime, especially crimes against the person, such as abuse of children.

Disclosures where a patient may be a victim of neglect or abuse

29. If you believe a patient to be a victim of neglect or physical, sexual or emotional abuse and that the patient cannot give or withhold consent to disclosure, you must give information promptly to an appropriate responsible person or statutory agency, where you believe that the disclosure is in the patient's best interests. If, for any reason, you believe that disclosure of information is not in the best interests of an abused or neglected patient, you should discuss the issues with an experienced colleague. If you decide not to disclose information, you must be prepared to justify your decision.

The guidance, *inter alia*, also deals with disclosure in connection with teaching, and during the course of court proceedings.

Consider whether disclosure within the family is acceptable. It is here that the interface between law and pragmatism reflects many of the essential difficulties of medical law. What is a doctor to do, say, when faced with a distressed spouse of a terminally ill patient? If the patient has informed the doctor that he does not wish any form of disclosure to the spouse, then although any subsequent conversations with that spouse may be difficult, it is quite clear that the doctor must refuse to discuss his patient's medical condition. However, in the absence of that express request on the part of the patient, under what principle does the doctor justify discussing the patient's medical condition with relatives of the patient? In the case of *Re S (Hospital Orders: Court's Jurisdiction)* [1995] 3 All ER 290, it was held that blood ties conferred no right to determine the course of treatment or care, and this would surely extend to the acquisition of confidential information. It seems that the law does not sanction such disclosure, unless one can argue that there is some form of implied or tacit consent.

Consider also that the guidelines state there is still an obligation of confidentiality after the death of the patient (para 30). Although the law lacks clarity on this point, it may be that the legal obligation of confidence will not remain after the death of the patient (see further p 263, below).

The issues raised by this guidance are considered under the appropriate headings below.

The legal obligations of confidentiality and privacy

A rights-based approach might regard the duty of keeping confidences as a respect for the right to privacy. There is no right to privacy in English law, although in practice much that is private can be protected in other ways, for example, the tort of trespass, nuisance and so on. Furthermore, the European Convention on Human Rights (ECHR), incorporated into English law by the Human Rights Act 1998, protects the right to a 'private life' (Art 8).

The right to privacy

What is the difference between a right to privacy and a right to have confidential information protected? The law imposes a number of requirements in order for a cause of action to arise for breach of confidence, and these criteria mean that, for example, press photographers owe no duty of confidence unless the photography takes place in 'confidential circumstances', or there had been a prior agreement not to publish. If neither of these apply, only a right to privacy can offer protection from publication.

Article 8 of the ECHR states:

1 Everyone has the right to respect for his private and family life, his home and his correspondence.

2 There shall be no interference by a public authority with the exercise of this right except such as is in accordance with the law and is necessary in a democratic society in the interest of national, security, public safety or the economic well being of the country, for the prevention of disorder or crime, for the protection of health or morals, or for the protection of the rights and freedoms of others.

In *Z v Finland* (1998) 25 EHRR 371, the European Court of Human Rights stated:

The protection of personal data, not least medical data, is of fundamental importance to a person's enjoyment of his or her right to respect for private and family life as guaranteed by Article 8 of the Convention ... Without such protection, those in need of medical assistance may be deterred from revealing such information of a personal and intimate nature as may be necessary in order to receive appropriate treatment and, even, from seeking such assistance, thereby endangering their own health and in the case of transmissible diseases, that of the community.

The facts were as follows. Mrs Z was the wife of a man who had been accused of attempted manslaughter by raping his victims and knowingly infecting them with the HIV virus. For evidential purposes, it was necessary to obtain evidence from Mrs Z's doctors and to obtain her medical records. The court limited the confidentiality of the trial record to 10 years, and in its judgment the court disclosed Mrs Z's identity. It was common ground that there had been a violation of Mrs Z's rights under Art 8; the issue for the European Court to decide was whether this could be justified under Art 8(2). It was accepted that the court action was 'in accordance with the law' so the issue was whether it was 'necessary in a democratic society'. The taking of evidence from the doctors and the obtaining of the medical records was held not to breach Article 8(2). However, limiting confidentiality of the trial record to 10 years was a disproportionate interference with her right and the disclosure of her identity was not justified at all.

In *MS v Sweden* (1997) 45 BMLR 133, medical records relating to a woman's gynaecological condition held by a clinic had been requested by, and disclosed to, the social security department dealing with a claim of hers for state industrial injury benefit. She had not been consulted about this, and the European Court held that this clear breach under Article 8(1) was, nevertheless, justified under Article 8(2) on the basis that the needs of the state (to avoid paying funds from the public purse to undeserving cases) were for the economic well being of the country. It is arguable, however, that it is disproportionate to obtain medical records in this way, without prior reference to the claimant. A more appropriate way of achieving the same end would have been for such claims to be subject to the consent of the claimant to the disclosure of all relevant medical records (the case of *MS* had, at least in part, given rise to the court action because the records disclosed had contained information about a wholly irrelevant abortion).

It might be argued that, given the protection of Article 8, the obligation of confidence is redundant. However, the language of confidentiality is still used by the courts (see eg *A Health Authority v X and others* [2001] EWCA Civ 2014). Further, the limitation placed upon Article 8 by Article 8(2) means that there will be circumstances when there can be justification for breaching Article 8 and these circumstances will frequently be analogous to the justification for breaching confidences so that the legal framework is still pertinent. In *Rose and Another v Secretary of State for Health* (2003) 69 BMLR 83 the claimaints, who had been conceived by artificial insemination, were seeking disclosure of of non-identifying information about sperm donors and, where possible, information that would actually identify such donors. They had requested such information from the Secretary of State who had declined to provide it, and they had commenced an action for judicial review. They argued, first, that the state had an obligation to provide non-identifying information and, secondly, that the state had an obligation to establish a voluntary contact register similar to the contact register available to adopted to children. Scott Baker J held that this information engaged Article 8 because such information went to the heart of their identity, and allowed the case to go forward. However, he declined to make a declaration of incompatibility under the Human Rights Act 1998, leaving it open to a court to decide on the basis of the specific facts before it. He did, however, hint strongly that because the donor semen would have been obtained under circumstances of confidentiality, Article 8(2) limitations would weigh heavily in the balance. A further example is the case of *R (on the application of John Wooder) v Dr Graham Fegetter and the Mental Health Act Commission* [2002] EWCA Civ 554 where Potter LJ stated that, on the question of the patient's right to information regarding s 58 treatment under the Mental Health Act (MHA) 1983 (see Chapter 9), there was no need to invoke Article 8 as the common law provides the necessary protection.

The obligation of confidence

The law of the obligation to keep confidences is not easy to categorise. It is sometimes regarded as an application of equitable principles, sometimes as belonging to the law of tort and/or contract. There is no doubt that the obligation may arise under the law of contract, either expressly or impliedly, but it is clear that it is wider than that. Certainly, as far as medicine is concerned, if it were contract-based only, there would be no legal obligation to keep confidences within the context of National Health Service treatment (see *Pfizer Corp v Ministry of Health* [1965] AC 512). There has been much academic debate on the subject:

Gurry, F, *In Breach of Confidence*, 1984, Oxford: Clarendon, p 25:

> The jurisdictional basis of the action for breach of confidence has been a source of lingering uncertainty and controversy. Contract, equity and property have at different times each provided the basis on which the courts have granted relief. In some cases, a mixture of these bases has been relied on. Thus, in *Alperton Rubber Co v Manning* Peterson J referred to the defendant's conduct as 'a breach of trust or confidence, and … a breach of the implied provision in all contracts of service that the employee will observe the rules of honesty'; and, in *Prince Albert v Strange*, the court founded the defendants' liability first on property, secondly on a 'breach of trust, confidence or contract'.

The lack of clarity in the law led to a Law Commission inquiry which reported in 1981 (Law Commission, *Breach of Confidence*, Report No 110, Cmnd 8388, 1981, London: HMSO). The Commission made a number of recommendations, the principal one being that there be a new statutory tort of breach of confidence. No government action has ever been taken on this.

The obligation of confidence, whatever its origin, although not absolute, is free standing, in that the preservation of confidence itself is in the public interest and therefore an end in itself. However, it can conflict with other matters of public interest. It is important to stress that when conflicts arise, they are conflicts between two competing *public* interests, not between private and public interests:

Scott, R, 'Introduction', in Clarke, L (ed), *Confidentiality and the Law*, 1990, London: LLP, p xxii:

> The law of confidentiality, like the law of negligence and the law of nuisance, requires a balance to be struck. The balance will, on both sides, involve public and private interests. The newspapers that wanted to publish extracts from *Spycatcher* had private commercial interest in doing so. But there was also a public interest in freedom of speech. On the other side there was a public interest in the protection of the secrets of the security service (no private interest since the litigant was the Government). In the *Francome* case, the plaintiff had a private interest in maintaining the privacy of his telephone conversations but, ranged on the same side, there was a public interest that private telephone conversations should not be the subject of eavesdropping. On the other side, the *Daily Mirror* could rely, in aid of its own private interest, on the public interest in the disclosure of alleged wrongdoing. These are examples to make the point that every case where the law of confidentiality is invoked requires the judge to strike a balance between competing interests.

The elements of an action for breach of confidence

The essential elements of the law can be summarised by the statement in *AG v Guardian Newspapers (No 2)* [1990] AC 109, pp 281–82, *per* Lord Goff:

> **Lord Goff:** I start with the broad general principle (which I do not intend in any way to be definitive) that a duty of confidence arises when confidential information comes to the knowledge of a person (the confidant) in circumstances where he has notice, or is held to have agreed, that the information is confidential, with the effect that it would be just in all the circumstances that he should be precluded from disclosing the information to others …

[In addition to] this broad general principle, there are three limiting principles to which I wish to refer. The first limiting principle (which is rather an expression of the scope of the duty) is highly relevant to this appeal. It is that the principle of confidentiality only applies to information to the extent that it is confidential. In particular, once it has entered what is usually called the public domain (which means no more than that the information in question is so generally accessible that, in all the circumstances, it cannot be regarded as confidential) then, as a. general rule, the principle of confidentiality can have no application to it ...

The second limiting principle is that the duty of confidence applies neither to useless information, nor to trivia ...

The third limiting principle is of far greater importance. It is that, although the basis of the law's protection of confidence is that there is a public interest that confidences should be preserved and protected by the law, nevertheless that public interest may be outweighed by some other countervailing public interest which favours disclosure.

There can be no doubt that the doctor–patient relationship gives rise to an obligation of confidence which fits clearly into the criteria applied generally in the law.

Hunter v Mann [1974] 1 QB 767 confirmed such an obligation which was reiterated in *AG v Guardian Newspapers (No 2)* [1990] AC 109, p 255, *per* Lord Keith:

Lord Keith: The law has long recognised that an obligation of confidence can arise out of particular relationships. Examples are the relationships of doctor and patient, priest and penitent, solicitor and client, banker and customer.

The uncontroversial nature of the obligation, therefore, means that generally problems will only arise when decisions have to be made which will breach the obligation and whether the breach can be justified. Indeed, it may be said that the doctor's duty of confidence is over-determined in that it stems both from the quality of the information and from the circumstances in which it is acquired, each of which is independently sufficient. It follows that, although not usually the subject of litigation, there may be difficulties, first, if the information is not *medical* information and, secondly, if it has been imparted in circumstances other than a doctor–patient consultation.

The confidential information

The law on confidentiality will protect a variety of types of information, imparted in a variety of different situations. Information acquired in the confidential circumstances of an employment relationship, for example, will be protected, as will that acquired in the course of an intimate domestic relationship. The latter need not be a marriage, nor even a heterosexual relationship. This was examined in the case of *Stephens v Avery* [1988] 1 Ch 449, where it was held that information relating to sexual conduct (in that case, a lesbian relationship) could be the subject of a legally enforceable duty of confidentiality.

On this basis, therefore, information concerning the sexual conduct of a patient, if imparted to a doctor in circumstances of confidentiality, will be protected, even though it is not medical information. The Court of Appeal decision in *R v Wilson* [1996] 3 WLR 125 raises this issue. In that case, the defendant appealed against a conviction for actual bodily harm under s 47 of the Offences Against the Person Act 1861. He had been charged as a result of marking his wife's buttocks with his initials by use of a hot knife. This was done with her consent and, it appeared from the case reports, at her specific request. Although the appeal was concerned with the applicability of the decision in *R v Brown* [1993] 2 All ER 75, the implications for medical confidentiality arise from the fact that the matter appears to have come to the attention of the police from a report made to them by her doctor, who became aware of the marks during the course of a medical examination (see (1996) *The Times*, 5 March and (1996) *The Guardian*, 1 March, p 5).

If the police were informed of this by the doctor, without the consent of the woman concerned, then here was a potential breach of confidentiality. The fact that the information was not strictly medical would not protect the doctor because, first, on the basis of *Stephens v Avery*, it has the necessary quality of confidence and, secondly, it was imparted in the circumstances of a medical consultation.

In *R v Department of Health ex p Source Informatics Ltd* [2000] 1 All ER 786, the Court of Appeal had to decide whether disclosure of patient information which had been anonymised breached the obligation of confidence. The company had obtained anonymised patient data from pharmacists and doctors which had been extracted from prescription forms. The information was used to create a database for the use of pharmaceutical companies. The Department of Health produced guidance which stated that disclosure of anonymised patient information still amounted to a breach of confidence. Source Informatics challenged this by way of judicial review. The judge at first instance took the view that the Department of Health was correct. However, the Court of Appeal allowed the appeal, stating that the touchstone as to whether there has been a breach of confidence is the 'conscience' of the discloser. Arguably, as Fennell points out ((2000) 8 Med L Rev 155), it is correct that there is no breach, but the reason is that it is not against the patients' interests and not something to do with the good faith on the part of the discloser.

Note that, in 1997, the Department of Health published *On the Review of Patient-Identifiable Information* (the 'Caldicott Report'), 1997, London: Department of Health, which made a number of recommendations on how to safeguard confidentiality by the anonymisation of the information, and which provides for so called 'Caldicott guardians' within the NHS to supervise and take responsibility for information systems. See further below, on the application of the Data Protection Act 1998 to such situations, and see also the reference to anonymised patient information in the Health Service (Control of Patient Information) Regulations 2002, p 253, below.

The circumstances in which the information is acquired

It may be that it is not clear that the circumstances are such as to amount to 'confidential' circumstances. The inadvertent acquisition of information which clearly has the necessary quality of confidence about it, binds the recipient, as was suggested by Lord Goff in *AG v Guardian Newspapers (No 2)* [1990] AC 109, p 282:

> **Lord Goff**: I realise that, in the vast majority of cases, in particular those concerned with trade secrets, the duty of confidence will arise from a transaction or relationship between the parties – often a contract, in which event the duty may arise by reason of either an express or an implied term of that contract. It is in such cases as these that the expressions 'confider' and 'confidant' are perhaps most aptly employed. But it is well settled that a duty of confidence may arise in equity, independently of such cases; and I have expressed the circumstances in which the duty arises in broad terms, not merely to embrace those cases where a third party receives information from a person

who is under a duty of confidence in respect of it, knowing that it has been disclosed by that person to him in breach of his duty of confidence, but also to include certain situations, beloved of law teachers, where an obviously confidential document is wafted by an electric fan out of a window into a crowded street, or where an obviously confidential document, such as a private diary, is dropped in a public place, and is then picked up by a passer-by.

The case of *R v Wilson* is, again, interesting in relation to this point, as it raises the possibility of a doctor being obliged towards a third party when he acquires confidential information in the context of a medical consultation:

Wheat, K, 'Can paternalism ever justify a breach of confidence?' (1997) 3(3) Health Care Risk Report 12:

Extension of duty

Another difficult question raised to which there is no clear answer is the position of the husband of the patient in this case. Could it be argued that the doctor owed him a duty of confidence? Further, would it make any difference if he were also a patient of the doctor? To look at the latter question first, if the doctor–patient relationship is to make any difference, then it must be the case that the duty extends to any information obtained about a patient which has the necessary quality of confidence.

It cannot be said with any degree of certainty that this reflects the legal position. Gurry, for example, says that, although the duty is not limited to information acquired directly from the patient but extends to information from other sources, that further information must have been picked up by the doctor by way of his or her position as the patient's doctor. Kennedy and Grubb interpret this as extending to information obtained from third parties who know of the doctor–patient relationship, but pass no comment as to whether it would extend to non-medical information.

Here, the information would not have been obtained by the doctor by virtue of his status as the patient's doctor, but as another patient's doctor, and, although the third party here, namely the wife, would have known about the doctor–patient relationship, the information was not of a medical nature. Given the difficulties, therefore, in arguing that the duty owed is a duty owed *qua* doctor, perhaps it is open to the husband to rely upon the general law of confidentiality and a duty owed to him regardless of him being a patient of the doctor concerned.

...

Elements of a breach of confidence action

[Referring to the *Guardian* criteria] [t]here is no difficulty in satisfying the first limb of the test as the information concerned intimate details of a sexual relationship, which will possess the necessary quality of confidence. As to the second limb, although a consultation between doctor and patient will usually impart an obligation of confidence, it is arguable that the circumstances only impart the obligation by the doctor towards the patient ...

If it is clear from its nature that information is confidential, then a third party should be bound by it (see *Saltman Engineering v Campbell Engineering* [1963] 3 All ER 413), so it is hard to see how the fact that it is not acquired by chance, but in the context of another, different set of confidential circumstances should make any difference.

See also *Douglas v Hello! Ltd* [2000] 2 All ER 389, where the law of confidentiality was applied to photographs taken at a private party.

Statutory obligations of confidence

Good, utilitarian, public health arguments can sometimes justify a specific emphasis on confidentiality via statutory means. An example of this is contained within the National Health Service (Venereal Disease) Regulations 1974 SI 1974/29:

The NHS Trusts and Primary Care Trusts (Sexually Transmitted Diseases) Regulations 2000 SI 1974/29:

Confidentiality of information

2 Every NHS Trust and every Primary Care Trust shall take all necessary steps to secure that any information capable of identifying an individual obtained by any of their members or employees with respect to persons examined or treated for any sexually transmitted disease shall not be disclosed except:

    (a) for the purpose of communicating that information to a medical practitioner or to a person employed under the direction of a medical practitioner in connection with the treatment of persons suffering from such disease or the prevention of the spread thereof; and

    (b) for the purpose of such treatment or prevention.

Referring to earlier but identical provisions Kennedy and Grubb comment as follows:

Kennedy, I and Grubb, A, *Medical Law*, 3rd edn, 2000, London: Butterworths, p 1127:

This regulation was introduced so as to give statutory emphasis to the obligation of confidence in this area of medical practice.

…

The reasons are obvious: thus, the circumstances under which disclosure can be made are carefully circumscribed. Curiously, the Regulations have not been amended to apply to NHS trusts (but see NHS Trust (Venereal Disease) Directions 1991). Although it is often said that reg 2 creates a duty of confidentiality, strictly speaking it does not. Rather, it imposes a statutory duty upon a Health Authority *to enforce* a duty of confidentiality that arises by virtue of the common law (or statute) between the patient and the doctor or Health Authority. It could be argued that the wording of the provision is such as to allow a patient's GP to be informed by those working in a genito-urinary clinic without the consent of, and even in the face of the refusal of, the patient. This has particular significance in the context of HIV infection where some have argued for the right of the GP to be informed of a patient's HIV status, allegedly in the interests of the patient so as to ensure any future care is medically optimal but, in the case of some doctors at least, in their own perceived interests.

A careful reading of the words of the Regulation suggests that it is only information relating to treatment for venereal disease and only when the GP himself is also treating for the disease that the exception comes into play. In essence it is merely an example of sharing information in the context of team care.

Even if this is wrong, a further point can be made. The notion of treatment entails the need for the patient's consent which itself entails agreement to share information about his condition. Arguably, reg 2(b) can have no application in the absence of the patient's agreement to the transfer of the information to his GP.

A small, but important, point to notice is that the obligation of confidence under the Regulations applies to any disease which is 'sexually transmitted'. If this is so, a patient who is HIV positive may need to look to the common law for protection of his confidence if he became infected by some other means as, for example, if he is a haemophiliac or has otherwise become HIV positive as a result of an infected blood donation. Alternatively a 'sexually transmitted disease' within the Regulations could be said to be one usually transmitted through sexual contact but which may be transmitted by other means. Blood, for example, may be infected with syphilis and transfused into someone who then develops the disease. The disease remains a 'sexually transmitted disease'. On this analysis HIV infection would be within the Regulations regardless of the means of infection. (See *X v Y* [1988] 2 All ER 648, in which Rose J assumes the latter to be the case.)

Incompetent patients and confidentiality

Are patients who lack capacity to make decisions about medical treatment owed the same duty of confidentiality?

Children

The ability of children to consent to medical treatment was dealt with in Chapter 4. The leading case is *Gillick v West Norfolk and Wisbech AHA* [1986] AC 112, and it is important to remember that this case was about confidentiality as well as consent. It will be recalled that Mrs Gillick objected to a DHSS circular which stated that a doctor, acting in good faith, would not be acting unlawfully if he prescribed contraceptives to a girl under the age of 16 and that, exceptionally, this could be done without informing the child's parents, as the principle of confidentiality applied between a doctor and a patient under the age of 16.

As we have seen, the *Gillick* case has been subject to a number of interpretations by the Court of Appeal which have sought to limit its application to one of protection for doctors acting in good faith, rather than an assertion of a child's right to self-determination when he has the necessary capacity. Although these later cases (*Re R (A Minor) (Wardship: Medical Treatment)* [1991] 4 All ER 177 and *Re W (A Minor) (Medical Treatment)* [1992] 4 All ER 627) were not about confidentiality, they have implications for this area of medical law. In *Re R*, Lord Donaldson said at p 186:

> **Lord Donaldson MR:** ... the judges treated *Gillick*'s case as deciding that a '*Gillick* competent' child has a right to refuse treatment. In this I consider that they were in error. Such a child can consent, but if he or she declines to do so or refuses, consent can be given by someone else who has parental rights or responsibilities. The failure or refusal of the '*Gillick* competent' child is a very important factor in the doctor's decision whether or not to treat, but does not prevent the necessary consent being obtained from another competent source.

The clear implication of this interpretation is that a doctor, faced with a refusal of medical treatment by a child, is entitled to seek consent from a parent or someone *in loco parentis*. Suppose, however, the child consents to treatment, but requests that his parents are not informed? Two views can be taken of the implications for confidentiality of Lord Donaldson's interpretation of *Gillick*. The doctor is protected if, in good faith, he respects the child's confidence, and he cannot have a duty to disclose. If, however, the doctor discloses the matter to the child's parents (let us say, in the course of another consultation), then, one view of Lord Donaldson's interpretation is that he will not be in breach of any duty of confidence owed to the child, because the child's consent to treatment was not based on child autonomy, but on the provision of a 'flak jacket' of legal immunity for the doctor. In other words, the obligation of confidence would be modified in exactly the same way as is the requirement that there be a valid consent. The second view would be that the doctor should respect the child's request, as breaching confidentiality serves no purpose in relation to securing treatment. The latter view is to be preferred, being more consistent with the ethic of confidentiality.

However, if one takes a true autonomy view of *Gillick*, that is, that a child may be capable of making decisions about medical treatment so that he can refuse rather than consent, then it must be the case that he is entitled to respect of his medical confidences. It may be argued that the doctor is still under an obligation to inform his parents of what is happening because, although the parents will not be responsible for the consequences of medical treatment which they may have opposed if they had been given the opportunity, they will still have general parental responsibility for the child. On the other hand, it was clear from *Gillick* that some duty of confidentiality was owed. It is no explanation to say, without more, that it depends on the nature of the treatment, because capacity to consent depends upon the understanding by the child of that particular treatment. However, the nature of the treatment may mean there are circumstances where a child is deemed to have sufficient understanding to, say, consent to an abortion. In consequence, even if this conflicts with parental opinion it may be necessary for the parents to be informed of the refusal, and the reasons for it, to enable them to continue to act as parents.

In the context of confidentiality, it is tempting to take the view that *Gillick* was special on its facts, that is, contraceptive advice, and that there was a strong element of policy in the decision, to avoid teenage pregnancies, and that the *Gillick* view on consent to other forms of medical treatment and advice would not usually involve a co-extensive view on confidentiality. Jonathan Montgomery comments on the situation in the USA:

Montgomery, J, 'Confidentiality and the immature minor' [1987] Fam Law 10:

The American position

American litigation in the field of birth control and abortion for minors proceeds by considering the extent of constitutional rights to privacy. In *Bellotti v Baird* 443 US 662 (1979) the court was asked to strike down a statute requiring parental consent before a minor was entitled to an abortion. Such a statute, said Powell J in giving the judgment of the court, could not be constitutional because it allowed an agency external to the minor herself to have a veto. A permissible system could be built around the 'mature minor rule'. Under that rule, a girl could go to court in order to have the abortion authorised. If she can prove herself sufficiently mature to take the decision herself, the court will automatically uphold her autonomy. If she cannot prove this, but can show that it would be in her best interests to have the abortion, the court must authorise the procedure. Otherwise the court has a discretion. In these latter circumstances the court may decide that it will be in the best interests of the child to inform her parents.

This position is similar to that which now prevails in English law. It differs in that the person who must decide whether the minor is sufficiently mature to take her own decision is, in this country, a doctor and not a judge. Powell J also considered the issue of confidentiality for the immature minor. He held that the Massachusetts statute before him was only constitutionally valid because under it 'every pregnant minor is entitled in the first instance to go directly to the court for a judicial determination without prior parental notice, consultation or consent' (443 US 662, p 649). Translated into the English context, this would mean that a minor is entitled to approach his or her doctor to have that person determine her capacity to consent to the medical procedures without her parents being informed. If she is found not to have that capacity, she must choose between not receiving the treatment or telling her parents, but that is 'her choice, not the doctor's'.

The GMC's guidance is as follows:

General Medical Council, *Confidentiality: Protecting and Providing Information*, 2004, London: GMC:

Children and other patients who may lack competence to give consent

Disclosures in relation to the treatment sought by children or others who lack capacity to give consent

28. Problems may arise if you consider that a patient lacks capacity to give consent to treatment or disclosure[5]. If such patients ask you not to disclose information about their condition or treatment to a third party, you should try to persuade them to allow an appropriate person to be involved in the consultation[6]. If they refuse and you are convinced that it is essential, in their medical interests, you may disclose relevant information to an appropriate person or authority. In such cases you should tell the patient before disclosing any information, and where appropriate, seek and carefully consider the views of an advocate or carer. You should document in the patient's record your discussions with the patient and the reasons for deciding to disclose information.

Disclosures where a patient may be a victim of neglect or abuse

29. If you believe a patient to be a victim of neglect or physical, sexual or emotional abuse and that the patient cannot give or withhold consent to disclosure, you must give information promptly to an appropriate responsible person or statutory agency, where you believe that the disclosure is in the patient's best interests. If, for any reason, you believe that disclosure of information is not in the best interests of an abused or neglected patient, you should discuss the issues with an experienced colleague. If you decide not to disclose information, you must be prepared to justify your decision.

Incompetent adults

The sensitive issues surrounding medical decision-making on behalf of incompetent adults have been examined in Chapter 4. Generally, decisions can be taken, and treatment administered if these are in the patient's best interests. It is arguable that it will always be in the patient's best interests to respect his confidences, unless one or more of the circumstances exist in which confidence can be breached lawfully in respect of a competent adult patient.

CONFIDENTIALITY – BREACHING CONFIDENCES

The duty of confidence is not absolute and there are circumstances in which medical information can be divulged. This part of the chapter will examine these circumstances.

Consent

It may seem trite to say that confidence can be breached with the consent of the patient, but this fell to be considered by the court in the case of *C v C* [1946] 1 All ER 562. A doctor had refused to disclose details of the respondent's venereal disease on the basis that it would have been in breach of his duty of confidentiality, despite the fact that both the divorcing petitioner and the respondent (that is, the patient) had requested this:

> **Lewis J**: The question which arises out of these circumstances is: is a doctor, when asked by his patient to give him or her particulars of his or her condition and illness to be used in a court of law, when those particulars are vital to the success or failure of the case, entitled to refuse and in effect to say, 'Go on with your case in the dark and I will tell you in court when I am subpoenaed what my conclusions are'? In the present case the patient asked the doctor to give her this information and asked him also to give the petitioner that same information, with the object of their being placed in a position which would enable them to know whether or not the petitioner had a case against the respondent, in other words, to assist the course of justice. It is, of course, of the greatest importance from every point of view that proper secrecy should be observed in connection with venereal disease clinics, and that nothing should be done to diminish their efficiency or to infringe the confidential relationship existing between doctor and patient. But, in my opinion, those considerations do not justify a doctor in refusing to divulge confidential information to a patient or to any named person or persons when asked by the patient so to do. In the circumstances of this case the information should have been given, and in all cases where the circumstances are similar the doctor is not guilty of any breach of confidence in giving the information asked for.

It is also important to remember that consent must be validly obtained. Given the powerful position of a doctor in the doctor–patient relationship, it is of considerable importance that the patient's consent is obtained scrupulously.

Public interest

> **Gurry, F,** *In Breach of Confidence*, **1984, Oxford: Clarendon, p 324:**
>
> The influence of principles based on the public interest is predominant in the action for breach of confidence. The public interest has two principal roles in the action. In the first place, since it is the law of the land that confidences are enforceable obligations, it is, of course, 'in the public interest that when information is received in confidence – for a limited and restricted purpose, as it always is – it should not be used for other purposes'. The public interest requires that confidences, like contracts, 'be held sacrosanct'. In this role, the public interest operates not only in the private sector, to enforce a confider's right to preserve the confidentiality of information which he entrusts to another, but also in the public sphere, where the public interest in national security or joint ministerial responsibility may require a public official or a Cabinet minister to keep confidential information secret.
>
> But the public interest also has an opposing role which sometimes requires that confidences be broken, and that information which the courts would otherwise protect from disclosure be released for various purposes. The opposing public interests which call for the release of confidential information may be the interests of justice itself, or the disclosure of iniquity, and, wherever such a judicially recognised

opposing interest is identified it must 'be put into the scales against the public interest in preserving privacy and protecting confidential information'.

The philosopher, Richard Hare, sums up the picture as follows:

Hare, RM, 'The philosophical basis of psychiatric ethics', in *Essays on Bioethics*, **1993, Oxford: Clarendon, p 23:**

If, for example [a psychiatrist] has as a patient somebody who he knows will be a great deal of trouble to anybody who is so unwise as to employ him, has he any duty to reveal the fact when asked for a medical certificate? Here, as before, it is obviously no use treating the duty of confidentiality to the patient and the duty of candour to the employer as duties on the same level but ranked in order of priority; for it may depend on the case which duty should have precedence. If the patient is an airline pilot and his condition will cause him to lose control of the plane, we may think the public interest paramount; if he is a bank clerk and is merely going to turn up late to work from time to time, we may think that his condition should be concealed.

... At the critical level of moral thinking we are bound to be impartial between the interests of all those affected by our own actions. So at this level, we shall have to give no special edge to our patients, but simply ask, in each case we consider, what action would produce the best results for all those affected, treated impartially ...

The following are examples of public interests which may outweigh the competing public interest in maintaining confidences.

Disclosure to maintain the freedom of the press

There is a public interest in the freedom of the press and other forms of media to investigate and report on matters of legitimate public concern. This was examined in the case of *X v Y* [1988] 2 All ER 648, where the court was unsympathetic to the interests of press freedom, in the face of the protection of the anonymity of patients being treated for AIDS. A health authority sought an injunction restraining a newspaper from publishing the names of two practising doctors who were also being treated for AIDS. The names of the doctors had been given to the newspaper by an employee within the health authority. The issue of freedom of the press was dealt with by Rose J, p 661:

X v Y [1988] 2 All ER 648:

Rose J: I keep in the forefront of my mind the very important public interest in freedom of the press. And I accept that there is some public interest in knowing that which the defendants seek to publish (in whichever version). But in my judgment those public interests are substantially outweighed when measured against the public interests in relation to loyalty and confidentiality both generally and with particular reference to AIDS patients' hospital records ... The deprivation of the public of the information sought to be published will be of minimal significance if the injunction is granted; for, without it, all the evidence before me shows that a wide ranging public debate about AIDS generally and about its effect on doctors is taking place among doctors of widely differing views, within and without the BMA, in medical journals and in many newspapers, including *The Observer*, *The Sunday Times* and the *Daily Express*. Indeed, the sterility of the defendants' argument is demonstrated by the edition of the second defendant's own newspaper dated 22 March 1987. It is there expressly stated, purportedly quoting a Mr Milligan, that three general practitioners, two of whom are practising (impliedly in Britain), have AIDS. Paraphrasing

Templeman LJ in the *Schering* case, the facts, in the most limited version now sought to be published, have already been made available and may again be made available if they are known otherwise than through the medium of the informer. The risk of identification is only one factor in assessing whether to permit the use of confidential information. In my judgment, to allow publication in the recently suggested restricted form would be to enable both defendants to procure breaches of confidence and then to make their own selection for publication. This would make a mockery of the law's protection of confidentiality when no justifying public interest has been shown.

The authority succeeded on the basis that the doctors needed protection just as any other patient did. Rose J said at p 665:

> **Rose J**: The public in general and patients in particular are entitled to expect hospital records to be confidential and it is not for any individual to take it upon himself or herself to breach that confidence whether induced by a journalist or otherwise.

In *H (A Healthcare Worker) v Associated Newspapers Ltd and N (A Health Authority)* [2002] EWCA Civ 195, a health care worker had been diagnosed as HIV positive and, in injunction proceedings, his former employer, a health authority, was permitted to be named in newspaper reports. The judge had concluded that the risk of identification of the worker did not justify preserving the anonymity of the health authority. The Court of Appeal held that disclosure of the identity of the health authority would enable the worker to be identified and that part of the judge's order was set aside. It was also said, however, that to disclose the particular speciality of the worker did not run such a high risk, and to restrain publication of that would be an unnecessary fetter on the freedom of the press.

Disclosure to prevent crime

In the case of *X v Y*, the health authority unsuccessfully tried to obtain disclosure of the name of the person within the authority who had criminally sold the medical records of the doctors concerned (ie contrary to the Public Bodies Corrupt Practices Act 1889 and the Prevention of Corruption Act 1906). The argument of the authority was based on its alleged duty to prevent crime. The court held that it had no public duty to prosecute crime, and that its real purpose had been to prevent publication which was prevented on other grounds. Rose J considered the wording of s 10 of the Contempt of Court Act 1981 which states that, *inter alia*, the information required must be *necessary* for the prevention of crime (p 664):

> **Rose J**: I accept that it is right to stress that the word used in the section is 'necessary' and I am unable to accept the submission of counsel for the plaintiffs that the effect of Slade LJ's judgment is of general application in construing the word 'necessary' as 'likely to be of substantial assistance', for such an approach would not only be contrary to the word in the 1981 Act but would be at variance with what was said in the House of Lords in the *Guardian* case in the speeches of Lord Diplock, Lord Fraser and Lord Roskill to which I have earlier referred. What I understand Slade LJ to be saying is that, in the circumstances of that case (and necessity is a question of fact in each case: see per Lord Diplock in the *Guardian* case [1984] 3 All ER 601, p 607; [1985] 1 AC 339, p 350), disclosure was necessary if it was likely to be of substantial assistance to the inspectors. It was central to that decision that those seeking disclosure were specifically charged with investigating and hence preventing criminal offences.
>
> The position of a health authority is entirely different and the question for me is whether the evidence proves necessity in this case on the balance of probability. I am

unable to accept the submission of counsel for the second defendants based on *Gouriet v Union of Post Office Workers* [[1978] AC 435]; s 10 refers to prevention, not prosecution, and it is not, in my judgment, a prerequisite for success that the plaintiffs should adduce evidence from a prosecuting arm of the Crown, whether the Attorney General, police officers, investigating inspectors or otherwise. Every citizen has an interest in the prevention of crime and satisfaction as to necessity is, by the terms of the section, a matter for the court, not some other body. But there must, in my judgment, be clear evidence in relation to necessity ... I accept, contrary to the submission of counsel for the second defendants, that the plaintiffs' motive is not merely curiosity or a desire to punish or threaten the culprit. They do not want such a breach to happen again, whether for payment of money (which may be crucial to the occurrence of a criminal offence) or otherwise. But the prevention of crime is not one of their tasks and the physician neither said nor, in my view, implied that criminal investigation was the intended or likely consequence of disclosure. He did not suggest that the matter had been referred to the police and there was no evidence as to what security procedures existed or what inquiries had been made to identify the source. Appropriate deterrent action could take a variety of forms, from warning the culprit to dismissal, and might well not, for policy reasons, extend to criminal investigation. There was no clear evidence as to how few or how many of the plaintiffs' servants had access to the hospital records, but he said that security procedures had been improved since the breaches in question. The evidence in relation to the offer of money to a nurse was, in my judgment, too vague to support an inference of necessity. Accordingly, though I bear in mind that the plaintiffs do not have to show that there is no other means of identification available or that all other possible means of identification have been exhausted, the evidence in this case falls short of proving that disclosure of the source is necessary for the prevention of crime. The matter can be tested by the use of Lloyd LJ's two questions. As to the first, disclosure would no doubt be of real importance to the plaintiffs in carrying out their inquiry. But, as to the second, it cannot be said that the purpose of their inquiry is the prevention of crime.

The protection of the public from crime was considered in *W v Edgell* [1990] 1 All ER 835. The patient was a prisoner in a secure hospital following conviction for a number of killings and woundings, and had made an application to a mental health review tribunal with a view to being transferred to a regional unit. Such a step would be a step towards discharge, and, therefore, the question arose as to whether the patient was still a danger to the public. His legal advisers sought the opinion of an independent psychiatrist, which, it was hoped, could be produced in support of the application. Dr Edgell, however, formed the view that the patient was still dangerous. In the light of this, the patient's application was withdrawn. However, his case was due to be reviewed under the automatic review process, under s 79(1) of the MHA 1983, and Dr Edgell, realising that his report, commissioned confidentially and independently by the patient's legal advisers, would not be included in the notes, sent a copy to the medical director of the hospital and a further copy to the Home Office. The patient brought an action alleging breach of confidence, but the court upheld the breach on the grounds of the public interest, that is, the protection of the public from dangerous criminal acts. The patient failed in his action at first instance and appealed. The Court of Appeal stated (*per* Bingham LJ, p 851):

W v Egdell [1990] 1 All ER 835, CA:

Bingham LJ: The parties were agreed, as I think rightly, that the crucial question was how, on the special facts of the case, the balance should be struck between the public interest in maintaining professional confidences and the public interest in protecting the public against possible violence. Counsel for W submitted that on the facts here the public interest in maintaining confidences was shown to be clearly preponderant. In support of that submission he drew our attention to a number of features of the case, of which the most weighty were perhaps these:

(1) Section 76 of the Mental Health Act 1983 shows a clear parliamentary intention that a restricted patient should be free to seek advice and evidence for the specified purposes from a medical source outside the prison and secure hospital system. Section 129 ensures that the independent doctor may make a full examination and see all relevant documents. The examination may be in private, so that the authorities do not learn what passes between doctor and patient.

(2) The proper functioning of s 76 requires that a patient should feel free to bare his soul and open his mind without reserve to the independent doctor he has retained. This he will not do if a doctor is free, on forming an adverse opinion, to communicate it to those empowered to prevent the patient's release from hospital.

(3) Although the present situation is not one in which W can assert legal professional privilege, and although tribunal proceedings are not strictly adversarial, the considerations which have given rise to legal professional privilege underpin the public interest in preserving confidence in a situation such as the present. A party to a forthcoming application to a tribunal should be free to unburden himself to an adviser he has retained without fearing that any material damaging to his application will find its way without his consent into the hands of a party with interests adverse to his.

(4) Preservation of confidence would be conducive to the public safety: patients would be candid, so that problems such as those highlighted by Dr Edgell would become known, and steps could be taken to explore and if necessary treat the problems without disclosing the report.

(5) It is contrary to the public interest that patients such as W should enjoy rights less extensive than those enjoyed by other members of the public, a result of his judgment which the judge expressly accepted (see [1989] 2 WLR 689, p 714; and [1989] 1 All ER 1089, p 1105).

Of these considerations, I accept (1) as a powerful consideration in W's favour. A restricted patient who believes himself unnecessarily confined has, of all members of society, perhaps the greatest need for a professional adviser who is truly independent and reliably discreet. (2) I also, in some measure, accept, subject to the comment that if the patient is unforthcoming, the doctor is bound to be guarded in his opinion. If the patient wishes to enlist the doctor's wholehearted support for his application, he has little choice but to be (or at least convince an expert interviewer that he is being) frank. I see great force in (3). Only the most compelling circumstances could justify a doctor in acting in a way which would injure the immediate interests of his patient, as the patient perceived them, without obtaining his consent. Point (4), if I correctly understand it, did not impress me. Counsel's submissions appeared to suggest that the problems highlighted by Dr Edgell could be explored and if necessary treated without the hospital authorities being told what the problems were thought to be. I do not think this would be very satisfactory. As to (5), I agree that restricted patients should not enjoy rights of confidence less valuable than those enjoyed by other patients save in so far as any breach of confidence can be justified under the stringent terms of r 81(g).

Counsel for Dr Edgell justified his client's disclosure of his report by relying on the risk to the safety of the public if the report were not disclosed. The steps of his argument, briefly summarised, were these:

(1) As a result of his examination Dr Edgell believed that W had a long standing and abnormal interest in dangerous explosives dating from well before his period of acute illness.

(2) Dr Edgell believed that this interest had been overlooked or insufficiently appreciated by those with clinical responsibility for W.

(3) Dr Edgell believed that this interest could throw additional light on W's interest, also long standing and in this instance well documented, in guns and shooting.

(4) Dr Edgell believed that exploration of W's interest in explosives and further exploration of W's interest in guns and shooting might lead to a different and more sinister diagnosis of W's mental condition.

(5) Dr Edgell believed that these explorations could best be conducted in the secure hospital where W was.

(6) Dr Edgell believed that W might possibly be a future danger to members of the public if his interest in firearms and explosives continued after his discharge.

(7) Dr Edgell believed that these matters should be brought to the attention of those responsible for W's care and treatment and for making decisions concerning his transfer and release.

Dr Edgell's good faith was not in issue. Nor were his professional standing and competence. His opinions summarised in (1), (2), (3) and (4) (although not accepted) were not criticised as ill-founded or irrational. Dr Edgell deferred to the greater knowledge of another medical expert relied on by W concerning the regime in a regional secure unit but did not (as I understood) modify his view that the explorations he favoured should take place before transfer ...

There is one consideration which, in my judgment, as in that of the judge, weighs the balance of public interest decisively in favour of disclosure. It may be shortly put. Where a man has committed multiple killings under the disability of serious mental illness, decisions which may lead directly or indirectly to his release from hospital should not be made unless a responsible authority is properly able to make an informed judgment that the risk of repetition is so small as to be acceptable. A consultant psychiatrist who becomes aware, even in the course of a confidential relationship, of information which leads him, in the exercise of what the court considers a sound professional judgment, to fear that such decisions may be made on the basis of inadequate information and with a real risk of consequent danger to the public is entitled to take such steps as are reasonable in all the circumstances to communicate the grounds of his concern to the responsible authorities. I have no doubt that the judge's decision in favour of Dr Edgell was right on the facts of this case.

The question arises whether this case is different from a case where a dangerous criminal is *at large* and a doctor breaches medical confidentiality to enable him to be taken into custody. It is arguable that there is an important difference. After all, in the *Edgell* case the patient was already the subject of expert medical scrutiny by the doctors at the hospital where he was detained; if those doctors had formed the view that the patient was no longer dangerous (that is, a view contrary to that of Dr Edgell), does not this difference of professional opinion considerably weaken the public interest defence to disclosure? Grubb (*Medical Law*, 3rd edn, 2000, London: Butterworths, p 1101), suggests that it may turn on whether the breaching doctor is basing his view on new facts of which he is aware, and which, without breaching confidence, are not known by the other doctor. If it is merely a difference of opinion based on the same set of facts, then there is a good argument against disclosure.

The public interest defence in the prevention of crime was upheld by the Court of Appeal in the case of *R v Crozier* (1990) *The Independent*, 11 May, where a psychiatrist, instructed by the defendant in an attempted murder case, disclosed his report to the prosecution when he realised that the defence had not produced it in court, when sentence was passed. As a result, the Crown informed the judge of the contents of the report, and the judge quashed the sentence of imprisonment and made a hospital order instead.

There is no doubt that the patient in *W v Edgell* [1990] 1 All ER 835 had committed very grave criminal offences. Would fear of less serious offences justify disclosure? Although case law in non-medical areas of confidentiality appears to put all crimes in the same basket (see *Initial Services Ltd v Putterill* [1968] 1 QB 396 and *Malone v Commissioner of Police of the Metropolis (No 2)* [1979] 2 All ER 620), in the Edgell case, the repeated references to the safety of the public – 'In this case the number and nature of the killings by W must inevitably give rise to the gravest concern for the safety of the public' (*per* Sir Stephen Brown P, p 846) – strongly suggests that the risk of minor crimes being committed would not sway the court in the same way. Furthermore, the non-medical cases generally concern issues of fraud upon the general public (see *British Steel Corp v Granada Television Ltd* [1981] 1 All ER 417). The GMC guidance on this subject is illuminating:

> 18 Disclosures may be necessary in the public interest where a failure to disclose information may expose the patient or others to risk of death or *serious* harm. [Emphasis added.]

An example given is disclosure being necessary to prevent or detect a *serious* crime (again, emphasis added).

It should also be noted that in the *Edgell* case, it was said that the risk must be 'real, immediate and serious' (*per* Sir Stephen Brown P, p 845). This is important, as it must mean that a doctor acting in good faith and in the genuine belief that there is such a risk, will be in breach of confidence if it transpires that the risk did not amount to one that was real, immediate and serious. Should all three of these requirements be satisfied: what of a risk which is real and serious, but unlikely to materialise for some time?

What of past, undetected criminal offences? Again, the GMC guidance should be noted, and the implications of the judgments in *Edgell*. However, the *risk* of a crime being committed is different to a past crime gone unpunished, the former only a perceived likelihood of criminal activity, the latter a certainty (on the assumption that the doctor is certain). Nevertheless, clearly the GMC does not consider it desirable that non-serious crime should be reported to the police, and, it is submitted, that is the correct view on the basis that the counterveiling public interest in maintaining medical confidences outweighs disclosure, as, we suggest, was the case in *Wilson*.

Disclosure to prevent civil wrongs

Gurry, *In Breach of Confidence*, 1984, Oxford: Clarendon, p 334, reviews the case law, and concludes that disclosure of a *proposed* civil wrong would be in the public interest, but doubts whether the disclosure of a past civil wrong would satisfy this, as 'this would serve only to raise quibbling enmities and thus destroy, rather than advance, the public welfare', whilst in the context of commercial confidences it may be the case that proposed civil wrongs may justify a breach. However, it is hard to envisage the circumstances in which past or future civil wrongs would justify a breach of medical confidences. Medical confidentiality would always override the prevention of civil wrongs because of weightier public interest arguments. In any event, what might be an example of a situation where a doctor would consider breaching confidence to prevent a proposed civil wrong? Perhaps a doctor may consider reporting a patient to his employer if, for example, he has failed to disclose a medical condition on a job application form, for example, psychiatric history (see *O'Brien v Prudential Assurance Co* [1979] IRLR 140). It is submitted that this sort of medical busybodying would be swiftly condemned by the courts and the GMC. Although paragraph 19 of the GMC's guidance gives the example of disclosure to the DVLC in the case of a patient who is driving against medical advice as a justification for breach of confidentiality, it is submitted that this would not be an example of a civil wrong justifying disclosure, but a case in which the protection of third parties would be at issue.

Disclosure for the public good

It might be argued that if no wrong, criminal or civil, has been, or is likely to be committed, then disclosure could not possibly be justified. However, there is clear authority for the fact that 'the public good' can be sufficient. The Court of Appeal in *Lion Laboratories v Evans and Express Newspapers* [1985] QB 526, authorised the publication of internal documents from the manufacturer of the intoximeter that cast doubt upon the accuracy of the machine, which was widely used in the convictions for drink-driving offences. The court held that the possibility of future wrongful convictions raised a matter of legitimate public interest despite the fact that no wrongdoing was involved.

It is possible to envisage countless examples of revelation of medical information for the public good, for example, the publication of information about new drugs and treatments and breakthroughs in medical research may be in the public good. Release of information about the dangers to public health, for example, an outbreak of illness caused by contaminated materials, would, of course, always be in the public good (indeed, the public health authorities would be under a positive duty to do this). However, in most of these cases, there would be no need to name identifiable individuals, so there would be no breach of confidentiality. Nevertheless, if circumstances were such that individuals had to be named, for example, a patient at large suffering from a highly dangerous and contagious disease, identification may be necessary. Consider the facts of the case of *Distillers Co (Biochemicals) Ltd v Times Newspapers Ltd* [1975] QB 613, p 250, below, and whether similar facts, giving rise to a breach of medical confidentiality, would be justified for the public good.

In *Woolgar v Chief Constable of Sussex Police* [1999] Lloyd's Rep Med 335, the Court of Appeal had to decide whether police records could be disclosed to a regulatory body. The appellant was a registered nurse and the former matron of a nursing home. She had been investigated by the police following the death of a patient at the home. There were no criminal charges brought, but this, and other matters, were referred to the United Kingdom Central Council for Nursing, Midwifery and Health Visiting (UKCC), which was the regulatory and disciplinary body for the nursing, midwifery and health visiting professions. The normal practice was, that if there has been a police investigation before the UKCC became involved, the UKCC would contact the police, and with the consent of those who have made statements, obtain copies of those statements. The nurse refused permission for her statement to be released. The court accepted that the statement was confidential on the basis that, if no charges were brought, the person making it is entitled to rely upon it remaining undisclosed. However, the court also decided that there was a sufficiently strong countervailing interest in the release of the statement. (Note that the UKCC has now been replaced by the Nursing and Midwifery Council (NMC).)

Woolgar v Chief Constable of Sussex Police [1999] Lloyd's Rep Med 335, CA (Kennedy, Otton and Waller LJJ)

Kennedy LJ: ... where a regulatory body such as the UKCC, operating in the field of public health and safety, seeks access to confidential material in the possession of the police, being material which the police are reasonably persuaded is of some relevance to the subject matter of an enquiry being conducted by the regulatory body, then a countervailing public interest is shown to exist which, as in this case, entitles the police to release the material to the regulatory body on the basis that save in so far as it may be used by the regulatory body for the purposes of its own enquiry, the confidentiality which already attaches to the material will be maintained. As Mr Horan said in ... his skeleton argument:

> A properly and efficiently regulated nursing profession is necessary in the interest of the medical welfare of the country, to keep the public safe, and to protect the rights and freedoms of those vulnerable individuals in need of nursing care.

Putting the matter in Convention terms Lord Lester submitted, and I would accept, that disclosure is necessary in a democratic society in the interests of ... public safety ... or ... for the protection of health or morals, or for the protection of the rights and freedoms of others.

Disclosure for the protection of third parties

It might be thought that the protection of third parties would come within the ambit of preventing either a criminal or a civil wrong. However, it may be necessary to disclose medical information when neither of these apply. The case of *Re C (A Minor) (Evidence: Confidential Information)* (1991) 7 BMLR 138, concerned the proposed adoption of a one year old baby. A day before the hearing, the mother withdrew her consent to the adoption. At an adjourned hearing, the adopting parents' solicitor produced an affidavit sworn voluntarily by the mother's GP, containing evidence of her medical condition and fitness to bring up a child. The mother objected to the admissibility of this evidence as it was a breach of medical confidentiality. She was unsuccessful at first instance, and the case went to the Court of Appeal. Sir Stephen Brown said, p 143:

> **Sir Stephen Brown**: It is in fact an unusual case. There is no previous authority which is directly in point, and all the cases which have been cited to the court refer to very different situations. The court is concerned with the proposed adoption of a little child. That is, of course, a very serious matter for the child, as well as being a serious decision for the court to have to make when the mother is withholding her consent.

The court should have before it all relevant and significant information which will assist it to make a right decision.

In this case, it is clear that the doctor's affidavit is highly relevant. If it can properly be placed before the judge, then it should be admitted. I consider that this case rests on its own very special facts. Moreover, I have considerable hesitation in reaching a conclusion that there was, in fact, any breach of confidence by the doctor in this case. I observe that it was apparently conceded before the judge that, *prima facie*, there was a breach of confidence. However that may be, in my judgment in this case the doctor was justified in making available her evidence. It may be that it could have been made available to the mother's advisers at an earlier stage, or in some other way, but that is not the issue before this court. In any event, I believe that a judge, if carrying out any balancing exercise, would be fully justified in coming down clearly in favour of admitting this evidence.

It should also be recognised that the disclosure of the material contained in this affidavit was the subject of a restricted disclosure. It was not being made available to the public at large. It was being made available only to the judge who had to decide the application, and to those who were also bound by the confidentiality of the hearing in chambers.

Accordingly, I have no hesitation in reaching the conclusion that the judge was correct to rule that this evidence was admissible and that it should be admitted.

What is of particular interest is the suggestion that the finding at first instance that there had been a breach of confidence, albeit a justified breach, may not have been correct. This was a view supported by both the other appeal judges. This was on the basis that the child was also (or had been) a patient of the doctor. However, in our view this is the wrong approach. To hold that there is no breach is tantamount to saying there was no duty in the first place.

Of course, in all these cases we are looking at *competing* public interests, and the protection of children will frequently justify a refusal of disclosure. In *D v National Society for the Prevention of Cruelty to Children* [1977] 1 All ER 589, the mother of a child who, it had been alleged, had been abused by her, brought proceedings in negligence against the NSPCC, following the shock-induced illness she had suffered as a result of the society's inspector's call to her home. She alleged that the society had failed to investigate properly the complaint made against her. The society denied negligence and made an application to the court for an order that there should be no discovery of documents which might reveal the identity of the complainant. The House of Lords held that in the interests of the proper functioning of a body such as the NSPCC, charged with the duty of protecting children against ill-treatment, they should have immunity from disclosure, analogously to the guaranteed anonymity of police informers. The case also upheld the principle of disclosure in the interests of the administration of justice.

Confidentiality and HIV and AIDS

It will be recalled that the case of *X v Y* concerned the difficulties that can arise in relation to information relating to HIV and AIDS. Such is the concern about this sensitive area that the GMC have issued special guidance to doctors on dealing with such patients. A patient who is HIV positive is not, of course, ill. The patient is merely carrying the virus, which, it is thought, will almost always develop into the

Acquired Immunity Deficiency Syndrome, a condition characterised by an extremely distressing variety of symptoms.

Both HIV and AIDS attract huge stigma. This is partly because there is no cure for AIDS, and although it is too soon to say with any certainty, it is still assumed that an HIV positive person will become ill with AIDS sooner or later. However, many other incurable conditions exist, with prognoses far worse than that of someone recently discovered to be HIV positive, who could well live for over 10 years with no sign of AIDS, with the prospect of a cure becoming available in the meantime. It is suggested that the stigma is as a result of two things: first, the fact that it may be transmitted through sexual activity; and, secondly, the fact that someone with no outward manifestations of illness may nevertheless be carrying a lethal virus about which very little is known. It also carries some stigma because of the erroneous belief, amongst some, that it is exclusive to, or caused by homosexual activities and/or drug use. Commenting upon the stigmatisation, Robert Lee states:

Lee, R, 'Disclosure of medical records: a confidence trick?', in Clarke, L (ed), *Confidentiality and the Law,* **1990, London: LLP, p 40:**

Even though the law seems to give relatively limited rights to patients regarding information about themselves, that body of law nonetheless proceeds from the basis that information relating to health and health status generally is a private matter. However, in one field this is particularly true, as the regulations governing disclosure of information relating to communicable diseases tend to illustrate. The rationale is presumably that persons can be stigmatised by the fact that they are suffering from a communicable disease. Often this has to do with methods of contraction of that disease. In the case of AIDS, methods of contraction may include homosexual practices and intravenous drug usage so that those suffering from AIDS may also be members of social groups who already suffer from various forms of stigma or engage in criminal activities. On the other hand, it seems relatively clear that the virus is unlikely to be spread by most forms of casual or everyday contact. Nonetheless we have seen that persons who are HIV positive are shunned in schools, hospitals and work places.

In this context confidentiality has a clear public health purpose. Medical confidence will encourage persons to come forward for testing, education, counselling, examination and treatment. Indeed co-operation in relation to medical practices may depend on confidentiality. If it is to be made widely known that certain persons who have volunteered for blood transfusions have been rejected for unspecified reasons, then people may draw their own (perhaps wrong) conclusions. This may lead to persons refusing to volunteer blood or come forward for blood testing.

This problem has been identified for some time, as the practices in relation to venereal diseases show. The National Health Service (Venereal Diseases) Regulations 1974 confine the communication of information on this subject to medical practitioners alone and for the treatment and prevention of the diseases in question. However AIDS is not included within the 1974 Regulations notwithstanding the fact that it is primarily sexually transmitted. The AIDS (Control) Act 1987, on the other hand, requires a mass of statistical information, but to no stated or obvious purpose. Finally AIDS is not a notifiable disease under the Public Health (Control of Disease) Act 1984, but the Secretary of State does have the power to hospitalise, and if necessary detain persons under the Public Health (Infectious Diseases) Regulations 1988.

Insurance problems are also thought to be one of the special aspects of HIV and AIDS disclosure. Lee goes on to consider this:

Lee, R, 'Disclosure of medical records: a confidence trick?', in Clarke, L (ed), *Confidentiality and the Law,* **1990, London: LLP, p 40:**

The other area in which AIDS-related information creates difficulties of medical confidence is insurance. The problem here, from the perspective of the life insurance company, is that younger males are usually a low premium group, but if HIV positive, will undergo prolonged illness which will prove fatal. On the other hand the risk to the insurance companies may be over-emphasised, given that the persons most likely to become HIV positive are not likely to be strong purchasers of life insurance, being either homosexuals with a lack of dependants, or young drug users who have perhaps not given much thought to life insurance purchase. Insurance companies might counter that, given the long latency period of HIV, it is not always possible to look at the present lifestyle of an individual in order to assess that individual for insurance purposes.

Nonetheless, one option for insurance companies in this area is to isolate a target population for whom life insurance is regularly refused. This would include perhaps single males aged between 20 years and 50 years with no insurable interests and whose lifestyle might be indicated by such questions as residence, or leisure activity. The alternative is simply to use AIDS antibody testing. The problem here is that false positive results run at something like one in every 20,000 tests. The stigmatisation which may result from a false positive, in addition to the difficulties that will then face that person in relation to obtaining insurance and employment, are of sufficient concern that a number of the States legislatures have banned or restricted the use of blood tests in order to determine insurability.

The GMC has provided specific guidance on serious communicable diseases:

General Medical Council, *Serious Communicable Diseases,* **1998, London: GMC:**

Informing other health care professionals

18 If you diagnose a patient as having a serious communicable disease, you should explain to the patient:

- the nature of the disease and its medical, social and occupational implications, as appropriate;

- ways of protecting others from infection;

- the importance of giving the professionals who will be providing care information which they need to know about the patient's disease or condition. In particular, you must make sure the patient understands that general practitioners cannot provide adequate clinical management and care without knowledge of their patients' conditions.

19 If patients still refuse to allow other health care workers to be informed, you must respect the patients' wishes except where you judge that failure to disclose the information would put a health care worker or other patient at serious risk of death or serious harm. Such situations may arise, for example, when dealing with violent patients with severe mental illness or disability. If you are in doubt about whether disclosure is appropriate, you should seek advice from an experienced colleague. You should inform patients before disclosing information. Such occasions are likely to arise rarely and you must be prepared to justify a decision to disclose information against a patient's wishes.

Disclosures to others

20 You must disclose information about serious communicable diseases in accordance with the law. For example, the appropriate authority must be informed where a notifiable disease is diagnosed. Where a communicable disease has contributed to the cause of death, this must be recorded on the death certificate. You should also pass information about serious communicable diseases to the relevant authorities for the purpose of communicable disease control and surveillance.

21 ...

Giving information to close contacts

22 You may disclose information about a patient, whether living or dead, in order to protect a person from risk of death or serious harm. For example, you may disclose information to a known sexual contact of a patient with HIV where you have reason to think that the patient has not informed that person, and cannot be persuaded to do so. In such circumstances you should tell the patient before you make the disclosure, and you must be prepared to justify a decision to disclose information.

23 You must not disclose information to others, for example relatives, who have not been, and are not, at risk of infection.

It will be seen, therefore, that if there is a serious and identifiable risk to a specific individual, such as a spouse or other sexual partner, then disclosure can be made. Recalling the case of *Re C (A Minor) (Evidence: Confidential Information)* (1991) 7 BMLR 138, if the partner is also the patient of the doctor, the Court of Appeal suggested there may be no breach (see p 246, above).

The administration of justice

Francis Gurry has commented upon this:

Gurry, F, *In Breach of Confidence*, 1984, Oxford: Clarendon, p 346:

In litigation, two competing aspects of the public interest often come into conflict: the administration of justice, which requires the full disclosure of all relevant evidence to assist the courts in their judicial functions; and the maintenance of the privacy of confidential communications, which militates against the disclosure of information which has been received under an obligation of confidence. Where a party or witness is required to give evidence which relates to information received in confidence, the conflict arises. In general, the administration of justice has been regarded as paramount ...

Generally speaking, litigants have a right to obtain and present evidence in the course of court proceedings. For a very detailed account of this, see McHale, J, *Medical Confidentiality and Legal Privilege*, 1993, London: Routledge.

In the course of civil proceedings, ss 33 and 34 of the Supreme Court Act 1981 provide for the discovery of documents during the course of a court action (s 34), and, where appropriate, prior to the commencement of proceedings (s 33). The question as to how far documents discovered in the course of legal proceedings may subsequently be published was considered in *Distillers (Biochemicals) Ltd v Times Newspapers Ltd* [1975] QB 613. The case concerned the drug thalidomide, and in proceedings brought by those injured by the drug, certain documents were ordered to be disclosed. One of the claimants' expert advisers entered into an agreement with the defendants to sell them the documentary information. The claimant company sought an injunction to prevent publication. The injunction was granted on the basis that those who disclosed documents were entitled to the court's protection against any use of the documents otherwise than in the action in which they were disclosed. Talbot J said, p 625:

> **Talbot J**: Whilst, as I have said, the public have a great interest in the thalidomide story (and it is a matter of public interest), and any light thrown onto this matter to obviate any such thing happening again is welcome, nevertheless the defendants have not persuaded me that such use as they proposed to make of the documents which they possess is of greater advantage to the public than the public's interest in the need for the proper administration of justice, to protect the confidentiality of discovery of documents. I would go further and say that I doubt very much whether there is sufficient in the use which the defendants have proposed to raise a public interest which overcomes the plaintiffs' private right to the confidentiality of their documents. In any event I consider that the plaintiffs have established their right (this is not really disputed) and have an arguable case for its protection by an injunction.

To refer back to the 'public good' justification, it is clear from this case that the court found that the proper administration of justice outweighed any public interest in knowing about the history of the drug thalidomide. Although it is clear that doctors have no immunity from the normal processes of disclosure in court proceedings, in *Hunter v Mann* [1974] 1 QB 767 it was said by Lord Widgery that a doctor who did not wish to answer a question in court because it would involve confidential issues, may point this out to the judge, who should advise as to whether it is necessary to answer the question. See also the Canadian Supreme Court case *M(A) v Ryan* [1997] SCR 157, in which it was confirmed that communications between psychiatrist and patient are not absolutely privileged. Limited disclosure could be sufficient protection.

Disclosure in the interests of national security

It is highly unlikely that this could apply to medical information. It is enough to note it as a legitimate area of public interest.

Medical research

It might be thought that there are no special considerations in the case of disclosure in research, but it is different, in that it could be argued that by consenting to take part in research, particularly non-therapeutic research, there was an altruistic motive on the part of the research subject which changes the nature of confidentiality.

However, the GMC guidance (para 31) stresses the importance of consent, so it appears that the only special aspect of research and confidentiality is that information may well be disclosed, but anonymously.

Exchange of information amongst health care workers

This is a grey area. Although it is included here as a particular example of the way in which confidences may be breached, unauthorised exchange of information amongst health care workers may fall foul of the law unless it can be argued that the patient has impliedly consented to this because he knows that he is being cared for by a team of people. This is reflected in the GMC guidance (see paras 10–12 reproduced at p 225, above). See also the Health Service (Control of Patient Information) Regulations 2002, p 253, below).

It is instructive, however, to consider into how many pairs of hands medical information may fall. Gillon refers to the investigation by a doctor of a patient's complaint:

Gillon, R, *Philosophical Medical Ethics*, 1986, Chichester: John Wiley, p 109:

Dr Siegler was 'astonished to learn that at least 25 and possibly as many as 100 health professionals and administrative personnel at our university hospital had access to the patient's record and that all of them had a legitimate need, indeed a professional responsibility, to open and use that chart'.

Is it arguable that the larger these numbers become, the less significant the concept of medical confidentiality becomes?

Breaches of confidence justified by statute law

A number of statutory provisions provide for the disclosure of information, and doctors generally are not exempt.

The Health Act of 1999, which created the Commission for Health Improvement (CHI), which can be authorised to inspect NHS premises and take copies of documents, includes authorisation in respect of patient records. Section 23(2) limits the obtaining of such information as follows:

Health Act 1999, s 23(2):

Regulations under this section may not make provision with respect to the disclosure of confidential information, which relates to and identifies a living individual unless one or more of the following conditions is satisfied:

(a) the information is disclosed in a form in which the identity of the individual cannot be ascertained;

(b) the individual consents to the information being disclosed;

(c) the individual cannot be traced despite the taking of all reasonable steps;

(d) in a case where the Commission is exercising its functions under section 20(1)(c) (the section which relates to the Commission's function of carrying out investigations into, and making reports on, the management, provision or quality of health care for the Health Authorities, Primary Care Trusts or NHS Trusts):

    (i) it is not practicable to disclose the information in a form in which the identity of the individual cannot be ascertained;

    (ii) the Commission considers that there is a serious risk to the health or safety of patients arising out of the matters which are the subject of the exercise of those functions; and

    (iii) having regard to that risk and the urgency of the exercise of those functions, the Commission considers that the information should be disclosed without the consent of the individual.

Similar restrictions are imposed upon the powers of the Health Service Ombudsman in respect of information obtained in the course of that function (see the Health Service Commissioners Act 1993). The Health and Social Care Act 2001 provides in very wide, some might say unacceptably wide, terms for the Secretary of State for Health to make regulations as follows:

Health and Social Care Act 2001, s 60:

Control of patient information

(1) The Secretary of State may by regulations make such provision for and in connection with requiring or regulating the processing of prescribed patient information for medical purposes as he considers necessary or expedient:

    (a) in the interests of improving patient care; or

    (b) in the public interest.

Regulations may not make provision requiring the processing of confidential patient information for any purpose if it would be reasonably practicable to achieve that purpose otherwise than pursuant to such regulations, having regard to the cost of and the technology available for achieving that purpose, and neither may they make provision for requiring the processing of confidential patient information solely or principally for the purpose of determining the care and treatment to be given to particular individuals. There is provision for the Secretary of State to consult with appropriate bodies (sub-section 7), and the provisions of this section are subject to the Data Protection Act 1998 (c 29).

The Secretary of State has issued regulations (the Health Service (Control of Patient Information) Regulations 2002) which provide for the creation of databases for the purposes of surveillance and analysis of health and disease, public health, occupational health and safety, and other medical purposes such as medical research. As required, the Secretary of State has stated that the regulations are compatible with the Human Rights Act 1998, but the regulations are controversial as they do make provision for disclosure of patient information which would otherwise be unlawful and where consent cannot be obtained. Although reg 6(2) provides that, in so far as it is practical to do so, such records should be anonymised, there is no absolute requirement to do this. As the Department of Health's Explanatory Notes suggest, there is concern about this, stating that they seek to balance the need for medical research and public health measures to be undertaken and the importance of not undermining patients' rights to confidentiality. It should be noted that the Secretary of State has given approval for the processing of such information. This would be amenable to judicial review.

It should be noted that s 18 of the Prevention of Terrorism Act 1989 created a criminal offence in respect of failure to disclose information which might be of material assistance in preventing acts of terrorism or in apprehending or securing a prosecution or conviction. When the 1989 Act was replaced with the Terrorism Act 2000, this measure was not re-enacted.

Note the provisions of the Road Traffic Act 1988:

Road Traffic Act 1988, s 172:

(2) -Where the driver of a vehicle is alleged to be guilty of an offence to which this section applies–

    (a) the person keeping the vehicle shall give such information as to the identity of the driver as he may be required to give by or on behalf of a chief officer of police; and

(b) any other person shall if required as stated above give any information which it is in his power to give and may lead to identification of the driver.

In this sub-section references to the driver of a vehicle include references to the person riding a cycle.

(3) A person who fails to comply with the requirement of sub-s (2)(a) above is guilty of an offence unless he shows to the satisfaction of the court that he did not know and could not with reasonable diligence have ascertained who the driver of the vehicle or, as the case may be, the rider of the cycle was.

(4) A person who fails to comply with the requirement of sub-s (2)(b) above is guilty of an offence.

The case of *Hunter v Mann* [1974] 1 QB 766 examined the extent to which this requirement was applicable to doctors in relation to the forerunner of the 1988 provision, s 168 of the Road Traffic Act 1972. The relevant part of the provision is identical to the 1988 Act. The question to be answered by the Divisional Court was whether a doctor who failed to comply with the provision under s 172(2)(b), above, in respect of information brought to his knowledge in the course of his professional relationship with a patient, was guilty of an offence under s 172(3). The argument on the part of the doctor was that the relevant words should be given a restricted meaning, so as to exclude confidential information, and those in a special position of confidence such as doctors. Boreham J stated (p 774):

Boreham J: For my part I cannot find any ground for saying that a restricted meaning should be given. I find the words clear and unequivocal. I accept, as Mr Bingham has suggested, that one should assume that Parliament has passed this Act, and this section in particular, with the existing law in mind. Accepting that, then it seems to me that Parliament must have been conscious of the use of very wide words here and if it had been intended to create exceptions, why then it would have been easy enough to do so. It has not been done. Moreover I ask myself the question: if there is to be a restriction how far is it to go? Where is it to stop? I find it impossible to provide an answer to that question.

In these circumstances I am driven to the conclusion that a doctor acting within his professional capacity, and carrying out his professional duties and responsibilities, is within the words 'any other person' in s 168(2)(b).

The next limb of Mr Bingham's argument was directed at the words in the expression 'information which it is in his power to give'. He contends that power must include a legal right, that there is no legal right or power to disclose so far as a doctor is concerned and, therefore, that he is not caught by those words.

I am not going to attempt to define 'power'. It seems to me a word of fairly common understanding and reading it in its ordinary way I have no difficulty in coming to the conclusion that a doctor in the circumstances in which the defendant found himself had the power. It may be that but for the section in the Act he would not have exercised that power because of his duty to his patient, but that seems to me to beg the question, for that would have been in accordance with his duty not to make voluntary disclosure. Once it is decided that the defendant is a person to whom the statutory duty imposed by s 168(2)(b) applies, then I have no doubt that he had the power. I think that it would be no injustice to Mr Bingham to say that this is the least strenuously argued of his points and I find it a point without substance …

In my view it is important when one is considering this section to have in mind that on many occasions serious accidents are caused by people who take away, without consent, other people's motor cars and who have no hesitation in leaving the scene as quickly as they possibly can so as to avoid detection. I, therefore, find it a comfort to think that the section gives the police a wide power for the purpose of detecting people who may cause damage to others.

May I say, before leaving this case, that I appreciate the concern of a responsible medical practitioner who feels that he is faced with a conflict of duty. That the defendant was conscious of a conflict and realised his duty, both to society and to his patient, is clear from the finding of the justices, but he may find comfort, although the decision goes against him, from the following. First, that he has only to disclose information which may lead to identification and not other confidential matters; secondly, that the result, in my judgment, is entirely consistent with the rules that the British Medical Association have laid down and from which I have quoted in the course of this judgment.

In the result I have come to the conclusion that the justices were correct and that this appeal, therefore, must be dismissed.

Information must also be disclosed pursuant to the Abortion Regulations 1991 SI 1991/499:

5 (a) for the purposes of carrying out their duties–

    (i) to an officer of the Department of Health authorised by the Chief Medical Officer of that Department, or to an officer of the Welsh Office authorised by the Chief Medical Officer of that Office, as the case may be; or

    (ii) to the Registrar General or a member of his staff authorised by him; or

(b) for the purposes of carrying out his duties in relation to offences under the Act or the law relating to abortion, to the Director of Public Prosecutions or a member of his staff authorised by him; or

(c) for the purposes of investigating whether an offence has been committed under the Act or the law relating to abortion, to a police officer not below the rank of superintendent or a person authorised by him; or

(d) pursuant to a court order, for the purposes of proceedings which have begun; or

(e) for the purposes of *bona fide* scientific research; or

(f) to the practitioner who terminated the pregnancy; or

(g) to a practitioner, with the consent in writing of the woman whose pregnancy was terminated; or

(h) when requested by the President of the General Medical Council for the purpose of investigating whether there has been serious professional misconduct by a practitioner, to the President of the General Medical Council or a member of its staff authorised by him.

In the interests of public health, disclosure of serious infectious diseases can be made pursuant to the Public Health (Control of Disease) Act 1984:

Public Health (Control of Disease) Act 1984:

10 Notifiable diseases

In this Act, 'notifiable disease' means any of the following diseases–

(a) cholera;

(b) plague;

(c) relapsing fever;

(d) smallpox; and

(e) typhus.

11 Cases of notifiable disease and food poisoning to be reported

(1) If a registered medical practitioner becomes aware, or suspects, that a patient whom he is attending within the district of a local authority is suffering from a notifiable disease or from food poisoning, he shall, unless he believes, and has reasonable grounds for believing, that some other registered medical practitioner has complied with this sub-section with respect to the patient, forthwith send to the proper officer of the local authority for that district a certificate stating–

   (a) the name, age and sex of the patient and the address of the premises where the patient is;

   (b) the disease or, as the case may be, particulars of the poisoning from which the patient is, or is suspected to be, suffering and the date, or approximate date, of its onset ...

Under s 31 of the Human Fertilisation and Embryology Act 1990 there is provision for regulations to be made to allow children conceived as a result of infertility treatment to obtain certain genetic information about their origins. At the moment there are no such regulations.

Although the Police and Criminal Evidence Act 1984 empowers the police to search for and seize materials, these do not include 'excluded material', and medical records and human tissue or tissue fluid would normally fall within the definition of 'excluded material' under ss 11 and 12 of the Act.

Note the provisions of ss 33 and 34 of the Supreme Court Act 1981, which provide for disclosure of documents during the course of litigation considered above.

Might there be a common law duty to disclose?

As we have seen in *Hunter v Mann* [1974] 1 QB 766, a doctor may have a statutory duty to disclose certain information about a patient. However, might there be circumstances in which a common law duty may arise, as opposed to the common law defence which gives a doctor a *discretion* to disclose? This is illustrated by the case of *Tarasoff v Regents of the University of California* 17 Cal 3d 425 (1976). A patient of a psychologist confided that he intended to kill a girl. The psychologist informed the campus police who briefly detained the man, releasing him on the basis that he appeared to be rational. He subsequently killed the girl, and her parents sued the University for failing to warn them that their daughter was in danger. By a majority the California Supreme Court upheld their claim:

> **Tobriner J**: We shall explain that defendant therapists cannot escape liability merely because Tatiana herself was not their patient. When a therapist determines, or pursuant to the standards of his profession should determine, that his patient presents a serious danger of violence to another, he incurs an obligation to use reasonable care to protect the intended victim against such danger. The discharge of this duty may require the therapist to take one or more of various steps, depending upon the nature of the case. Thus it may call for him to warn the intended victim or others likely to apprise the victim of the danger, to notify the police, or to take whatever other steps are reasonably necessary under the circumstances ...
>
> In each instance the adequacy of the therapist's conduct must be measured against the traditional negligence standard of the rendition of reasonable care under the circumstances ... In sum, the therapist owes a legal duty not only to his patient, but

also to his patient's would-be victim and is subject in both respects to scrutiny by judge and jury ... Some of the alternatives open to the therapist, such as warning the victim, will not result in the drastic consequences of depriving the patient of his liberty. Weighing the uncertain and conjectural character of the alleged damage done to the patient by such a warning against the peril to the victim's life, we conclude that professional inaccuracy in predicting violence cannot negate the therapist's duty to protect the threatened victim ...

Justice Clark, dissenting, stated:

Clark J: Until today's majority opinion, both legal and medical authorities have agreed that confidentiality is essential to effectively treat the mentally ill, and that imposing a duty on doctors to disclose patient threats to potential victims would greatly impair treatment ... Policy generally determines duty. Principal policy considerations include foreseeability of harm, certainty of the plaintiff's injury, proximity of the defendant's conduct to the plaintiff's injury, moral blame attributable to defendant's conduct, prevention of future harm, burden on the defendant, and consequences to the community.

Overwhelming policy considerations weigh against imposing a duty on psychotherapists to warn a potential victim against harm. While offering virtually no benefit to society, such a duty will frustrate psychiatric treatment, invade fundamental patient rights and increase violence. The importance of psychiatric treatment and its need for confidentiality have been recognised by this court. It is clearly recognised that the very practice of psychiatry vitally depends upon the reputation in the community that the psychiatrist will not tell ... Assurance of confidentiality is important for three reasons:

Deterrence from treatment

First, without substantial assurance of confidentiality, those requiring treatment will be deterred from seeking assistance. It remains an unfortunate fact in our society that people seeking psychiatric guidance tend to become stigmatised. Apprehension of such stigma apparently increased by the propensity of people considering treatment to see themselves in the worst possible light creates a well recognised reluctance to seek aid. This reluctance is alleviated by the psychiatrist's assurance of confidentiality.

Full disclosure

Second, the guarantee of confidentiality is essential in eliciting the full disclosure necessary for effective treatment. The psychiatric patient approaches treatment with conscious and unconscious inhibitions against revealing his innermost thoughts ...

Successful treatment

Third, even if the patient fully discloses his thoughts, assurance that the confidential relationship will not be breached is necessary to maintain his trust in his psychiatrist – the very means by which treatment is effected ...

Given the importance of confidentiality to the practice of psychiatry, it becomes clear that the duty to warn imposed by the majority will cripple the use and effectiveness of psychiatry. Many people, potentially violent – yet susceptible to treatment – will be deterred from seeking it; those seeking it will be inhibited from making revelations necessary to effective treatment; and, forcing the psychiatrist to violate the patient's trust will destroy the interpersonal relationship by which treatment is effected.

Violence and civil commitment

By imposing a duty to warn, the majority contributes to the danger to society of violence by the mentally ill and greatly increases the risk of civil commitment – the total deprivation of liberty – of those who should not be confined. The impairment of treatment and risk of improper commitment resulting from the new duty to warn will not be limited to a few patients but will extend to a large number of the mentally ill. Although under existing psychiatric procedures only a relatively few receiving treatment will ever present a risk of violence, the number making threats is huge, and it is the latter group – not just the former – whose treatment will be impaired and whose risk of commitment will be increased.

Michael Jones examines the issue in relation to the case of *W v Edgell* [1990] 1 All ER 835 (see p 241, above):

Jones, M, 'Medical confidentiality and the public interest' (1990) 6 Professional Negligence 16:

The question arises whether, if Dr Edgell had not disclosed his report and W had been released and had shot someone else, the psychiatrist would have owed a duty of care to the victim? W had made no specific threats, though Dr Edgell clearly regarded him as a potential danger 'to the public'. In these circumstances the courts would probably not impose a duty of care, on the basis that the victim was merely a member of a large unascertained class. Although, in the final analysis, the public is comprised of individuals, in *Hill v Chief Constable of West Yorkshire* the House of Lords held that the police owed no duty of care to the victim of a notorious serial murderer for allegedly negligently failing to apprehend him, partly on the ground that the victim 'was one of a vast number of the female general public who might be at risk from his activities but was at no special distinctive risk'. This would be consistent with the approach of the American courts.

On the other hand, in *Holgate v Lancashire Mental Hospitals Board* (1937) a hospital was held liable for negligently releasing on licence a dangerous patient who had been compulsorily detained following convictions for violent offences. The patient entered the plaintiff's home and assaulted her. The judge seemed to assume that a duty of care existed and the report deals largely with the question of whether there had been negligence. The case may be justified on the basis of the degree of control exercised by the defendants over the dangerous patient, a control analogous to the relationship between gaoler and prisoner which may give rise to a duty of care. The independent psychiatrist does not exercise this degree of control, and so some alternative basis for a duty of care would have to be established. It has been argued that this is to be found in the doctor's unique capacity to influence the patient's behaviour, whether through treatment or advice. But this is questionable, given that the doctor's ability to influence the patient may be limited, and in the circumstances which arose in *W v Edgell* it may be virtually non-existent. The basis of any potential duty of care, it is submitted, is the foreseeability of harm to the victim. It is unfashionable these days to rest a duty of care on foreseeability alone. There must also be a sufficiently proximate relationship between plaintiff and defendant, and it must be just and reasonable in the circumstances to impose a duty. But the more foreseeable the harm, the more likely it is that a court will find the relationship between the parties to be proximate. Thus, if a patient made genuine threats of serious injury to an identified third person and there was a real risk that the threats would be carried out, it is arguable that a doctor would come under a duty of care to the potential victim. It is difficult, however, to see how this duty can be based on the doctor–patient relationship *per se*. If, for example, the patient had made the same statement to a friend, there would be no obvious reason for distinguishing between the obligations of the friend and the doctor to the potential victim, apart from the purely practical point that the doctor may be in a better position to assess whether the threats are genuine. The duty, if any, arises from the defendant's knowledge of the foreseeable danger of serious physical harm to the third party.

There are difficulties, however, with imposing such a duty. The first is conceptual, and stems from the 'mere omissions' rule, namely that there is no general obligation in tort to take positive steps to confer a benefit on others by preventing harm befalling them. So, for example, there is no obligation to rescue someone in danger, even if rescue would involve little or no effort and involves no danger to the rescuer (for example, shouting a warning to a blind man about to walk over the edge of a cliff). The rule has been criticised, but it will be applied in the absence of special circumstances giving rise to a duty to intervene, such as a special relationship between the plaintiff and defendant or some degree of control by the defendant over the conduct of a third party who caused damage to the plaintiff. If, it might be argued, the doctor's relationship with the patient is not sufficient to give him 'control' over the patient's conduct, then there is nothing (other than mere foreseeability of harm) on which to base a duty to intervene. Possession of knowledge, which, if not passed on in the form of a warning, may result in harm to the 'victim', does not in itself constitute control, otherwise the observer of the blind man walking off the cliff would owe a duty of care.

A further difficulty which might militate against the imposition of a duty of care (probably as part of the assessment of whether it was just and reasonable) is that the doctor could be placed on the horns of a dilemma. If he overestimates the danger presented by the patient he is open to an action for breach of confidence by the patient. On the other hand, if he underestimates the danger and the patient harms a third party, the doctor may be liable in negligence. Moreover, although the risk of an action for breach of confidence exists in any event where the doctor has miscalculated the 'public interest', a duty of care to potential victims would tend to push the balance towards disclosure rather than non-disclosure. This problem may be more apparent than real, given that a doctor need only act with reasonable care to avoid liability for negligence, and the *Bolam* test gives the profession considerable discretion in setting the boundaries of what is reasonable. It is true that where the imposition of a duty of care might lead to a defendant being subject to conflicting duties the courts may be reluctant to find a duty of care, but where the public interest defence applies there is no duty to maintain confidentiality and so no conflict with a possible duty of care. Indeed, in Scott J's view in *W v Edgell* the public interest may require a doctor to disclose the information ... a situation which can hardly involve a conflict with a potential duty of care. Thus if, as seems likely, the circumstances in which a duty of care would be imposed are narrower (or at least, not broader) than the circumstances in which the public interest defence applies there could never be such a conflict ...

This discussion of the doctor's possible duty of care to third parties has concentrated on the position of the psychiatrist and his patient. Another obvious situation in which, arguably, a duty of care would arise is that of the patient with AIDS. Would a practitioner owe a duty to the patient's sexual partner(s) to inform them of the patient's condition and the potential risk to their health if the patient refused consent to the disclosure? If the sexual partner was also the doctor's patient there would probably be little difficulty in finding a duty of care, since a 'duty to inform' could be seen as part and parcel of the doctor's more general duty to exercise reasonable care to safeguard the health of his patient. It might be thought somewhat arbitrary, however, if the doctor's liability in this situation turned upon whether the sexual partner happened also to be one of his patients. Arguably, the duty would arise irrespective of the sexual partner's status, on the basis that serious physical harm was foreseeable as a real risk.

An analogy could be drawn here with cases where it is alleged that a doctor has negligently permitted a person to come into contact with a contagious disease. For example, in *Lindsey County Council v Marshall* the House of Lords held the defendants liable for negligently failing to warn the plaintiff of the risk of infection by puerperal fever when she was admitted to their maternity home, following a recent outbreak of the disease. In this case the plaintiff was a patient, but the result should not differ if she were not. If, for example, a doctor was negligent in discharging an infectious patient from hospital, and as a result a third party contracted the disease, the third party would surely have a claim against the doctor.

This view was confirmed in the Californian case of *Reisner v Regents of the University of California* (see (1997) Med L Rev 250), where a doctor was found to have been in breach of a duty of care owed to the sexual partner of a patient who had contracted HIV after receiving a contaminated blood transfusion, which information had been concealed by the doctor concerned. It was said that the patient would have been likely to have warned her sexual partner. However, it was said that third parties who might have become infected by contact with the sexual partner would not be owed a duty of care on remoteness principles. (On the doctor's duty to third parties generally, see further *Palmer v Tees HA* [1999] Lloyd's Rep Med 351, discussed in Chapter 6.)

To whom should disclosure be made and what should be the extent of that disclosure?

It is well established that even if a breach of confidence may be justified, it may still be actionable if the disclosure goes further than that which is necessary. If, for example, as was alluded to by Bingham LJ, p 848, in *W v Edgell* [1990] 1 All ER 835, Dr Edgell had disclosed his report to a newspaper, or commented upon it in a journal article, then this would have been going further than was necessary in the public interest of prevention of crime. The defence of public interest was only available to him in the disclosure to the hospital treating the patient, and the Home Office. Similarly, a doctor who is justified in revealing one aspect of the patient's condition is not thereby justified in revealing other medical information. For example, the revelation that a woman is HIV positive, as we have seen, may occasionally be justified. A doctor who, at the same time, points out that this was discovered in the course of an abortion procedure will be in breach of confidence. However, additional information may be revealed if it is necessary by way of explanation. This point was dealt with in *Edgell*, p 853:

> **Bingham LJ**: Counsel for W argued that even if Dr Edgell was entitled to make some disclosure he should have disclosed only the crucial paragraph of his report and his opinion. I do not agree. An opinion, even from an eminent source, cannot be evaluated unless its factual premise is known, and a detailed 10 page report cannot be reliably assessed by perusing a brief extract.

The extent of disclosure was the subject of *A Health Authority v X and Others* [2001] EWCA Civ 2014. The case concerned the release of papers which resulted from a case brought under the Children Act 1989. The health authority sought an order for production of case papers and GP records of two people involved in the case. Munby J had ordered disclosure, subject to express conditions to limit the extent of the disclosure. The health authority appealed against such conditions. One argument advanced on behalf of the health authority was that the NHS would grind to a halt if there were not 'free internal exchange of confidential information'. The Court of Appeal rejected this:

A Health Authority v X and Others [2001] EWCA Civ 2014, CA (Thorpe and Laws LJJ, Harrison J)

Thorpe LJ: ... the only real issue in the present appeal is whether the conflict between the private/public interest in the confidentiality of medical records and some other public interest should be decided by the health authority or a judge ... I accept Mr Pannick's submission that the importance of the resolution of such a conflict requires the independence of a judge. I conclude that the spectres developed by Mr Havers, cost and delay and administrative overload, are no more than speculations which good sense and management can contain.

... I conclude that [there was no] error of law or principle that would justify our intervention ... The judge elected for a cautious approach. In my opinion he was not only entitled but wise to do so.

CONFIDENTIALITY – REMEDIES

Detriment

In *AG v Guardian Newspapers (No 2)* [1990] AC 109, there was no clear stance as to whether there is a need for detriment to be shown in private actions for breach of confidence. Lord Goff, for example, left the question open (pp 281–82). Although there are instances where a patient would suffer pecuniary loss as a result of that breach (for example, disclosure of a medical condition to an employer which results in dismissal), in many cases no quantifiable loss would result. It is arguable that breach of confidence should be actionable *per se*, or that, if detriment is required, the breach itself is a detriment to the patient in the sense that he has been betrayed.

An interesting point arises if we consider inadvertent disclosure. Up until now we have assumed that the act of disclosure has been deliberate. However, if a confidential medical report were to be carelessly lost in a public place, does the patient have to show that damage has resulted from this? In other words would the negligence criterion be applied, that is, that damage must have resulted from the non-deliberate act? This will be examined further in relation to damages.

Damages

The rather curious New Zealand case of *Furniss v Fitchett* [1958] NZLR 396 was decided on negligence principles. The facts were as follows. The marriage of a Mr and Mrs Furniss was under a great deal of strain. Both were patients of Dr Fitchett. Mr Furniss asked the doctor to provide him with a letter detailing his wife's psychiatric problems, which he did. It was not marked 'confidential' and the doctor did not know how it was to be used. Just over a year later, it was produced in the course of a court hearing – the first time Mrs Furniss had heard of it. She suffered what is oddly described in the law report as 'shock to the injury of her health'. Leaving aside the difficult issue of what sort of injury this is (the judge referred to it as 'physical' injury), the general negligence criteria were applied. Barrowclough CJ said, p 404:

> **Barrowclough CJ**: I find that the defendant doctor was aware that the opinion which he expressed ... would, if it should come to the knowledge of his patient, be likely to injure her in her health. I find also that in the circumstances in which he issued that certificate – handing it to the patient's husband to be given to his solicitor, knowing that the husband and wife were then estranged, and without marking it as confidential or otherwise restricting its use – he ought reasonably to have foreseen that the certificate or its contents would be likely to come to the knowledge of his patient. I conclude, therefore, that in the circumstances to which I have referred, the doctor owed to his patient at common law a duty to take reasonable care to ensure that no expression of his opinion as to her mental condition should come to her knowledge. The doctor did not take any precautions in that respect ...

The last point is an odd one. If this letter had been disclosed to a number of people, but in circumstances which Mrs Furniss would not know about, the implication is that the doctor would be off the hook. Indeed, the judge seemed to doubt whether the ethical duty of confidentiality was reflected in the law at all. However, the case resulted in the award to Mrs Furniss of the sum of A$3,250 in damages.

In *Cornelius v De Taranto* [2002] EMLR 6, the Court of Appeal upheld the decision of the trial judge that a consultant psychiatrist had breached client confidentiality in disclosing a medico-legal report to the patient's GP and another psychiatrist without first obtaining her consent. The report contained defamatory and hurtful material relating to her mental state. Damages of £3,750 were awarded for injury to feelings.

Although it is probably the case that actual loss does not have to be shown, as a general principle, damages should reflect the degree of loss suffered. Unjustifiable disclosure of HIV or AIDS may well result in considerable and long standing distress. Given that we are not here considering a strict application of negligence criteria, it is submitted that ordinary distress, as opposed to psychiatric illness, would attract damages. The Law Commission, *Breach of Confidence*, Report No 110, Cmnd 8388, 1981, London: HMSO, paras 4.79–4.82, examined the issue of damages for mental distress, and concluded that there is no basis for the award of damages for mental distress for a non-contractual breach of confidence, that is, for our purposes, when we are considering NHS treatment. However, it recommended that damages should be awarded for mental distress, if a person of reasonable fortitude would so suffer.

The Law Commission also considered whether punitive damages might be available for breach of confidence, but decided it was wrong to look at the issue in isolation. Under the present criteria set down by *Rookes v Barnard* [1964] AC 1129 and *AB v South West Water Services Ltd* [1992] 4 All ER 574, punitive damages would not be available.

Injunctions

It is important to remember that the injunction is a discretionary remedy and, in the context of breach of confidence, if the information is already in the public domain, there will be no purpose served by an order preventing further publication: see *AG v Guardian Newspapers (No 2)* [1990] AC 109.

An injunction at the final trial of the action will rarely be granted if there has been no interim injunction when the proceedings are first issued, because if there has been no prior prevention of publication, then by the time of trial, the information will either be well and truly in the public domain, or no longer worth suppressing.

The interim injunction, therefore, is the key weapon in a breach of confidence action. It means that publication will be prevented for what may be a long time before trial. The basis upon which such relief would be granted was set out in *American Cyanamid Co v Ethicon Ltd* [1975] AC 396, and is generally known as 'the balance of convenience test', where the court has to decide whether either party will suffer irreparable harm and, if both will suffer, who will suffer the most.

The dead

As we have seen, the Hippocratic Oath binds a doctor to keep medical confidences after death, and the GMC guidance reflects this. However, it is not clear whether there is any legal obligation to keep confidences after the death of the person to whom the duty is owed, that is, in medicine, after the death of the patient.

Referring to the GMC guidance which states that there is still an obligation of confidence after the patient's death, Grubb states:

Kennedy, I and Grubb, A, *Medical Law*, 3rd edn, 2000, London: Butterworths, p 1081:

Is this the legal position? We are not considering here the separate and equally difficult question of whether an action for a breach of confidence which occurred during the life of a patient survives his death ... Instead, we are concerned with an action by a patient's estate for disclosures after the death of the patient. Such a claim could only be brought if the estate had itself suffered a legal wrong. Arguably, the estate can only be legally wronged in this context if it inherits a right of the deceased which is unlawfully interfered with after death. So, for example, the right to sue on a contract passes to the estate. Similarly, where property passes to the estate on death any unlawful dealing with it by others will give the estate a right of action. Thus the crucial question is whether the right to have confidences observed is a right which passes as a chose in action to the estate. There is no clear answer. It could be argued that since what is at stake is the deceased's feelings and reputation, the analogy with the law of defamation is persuasive (ie, the cause of action does not survive death). Of course, in relation to defamation, the position is governed by statute. In our view the courts would reflect this policy in the case of breach of medical confidence.

Davies, M, *Medical Law*, 1996, London: Blackstone, pp 45–46:

2.10 Confidence and death

A brief mention should be made of confidences that endure after death. Why? Simply because of the ethical notion of respecting the memory of the deceased but also because medical revelations can harm the living. The declaration of Geneva, it will be recalled, could not be clearer on the matter. Strangely, there is little confidential about the death itself because the death certificate itself is a public document. Mason and McCall Smith pertinently note the stigma of AIDS following victims to the grave. To be strictly accurate on the death certificate, the doctor should correctly indicate the cause of death. If 'AIDS' is placed on the certificate, then ill-informed rumour might well attach to living partners, friends and relatives. The key to the issue of death and confidentiality in medical law takes one back to the beginning: upon what is it based? If it is the reciprocity of the doctor–patient relationship, then that has ceased to exist. If it is the doctor's duty to society as a whole, then this 'public' duty might include an enduring duty of overall medical confidence.

CONFIDENTIALITY AND THE DATA PROTECTION ACT 1998

The Act was passed to give effect to the European Directive 95/46/EC which requires Member States to implement legislation to protect the right of individuals to privacy with respect to the processing of personal data. As far as medical records are concerned, the Act gives patients the right of access to their medical records, subject to exclusions. It also gives patients the right to ask for necessary corrections to be made to those records. Data will be processed in adherence to the 'Data Protection Principles':

1 Personal data shall be processed fairly and lawfully.

2 Personal data shall be obtained only for one or more specified lawful purposes.

3 Personal data shall be adequate, relevant and not excessive.

4 Personal data shall be accurate and up to date.

5 Personal data shall not be kept for longer than necessary.

6 Personal data shall be processed in accordance with rights of data subjects.

7 Measures shall be taken against unauthorised or unlawful processing and accidental loss or destruction.

David Stone outlines the application of the Act to medical records:

> **Stone, D, 'Confidentiality, access to health records and the Human Rights Act 1998', in Garwood-Gowers et al, Healthcare: The Impact of the Human Rights Act 1998, 2001, London: Cavendish Publishing, pp 137–44:**
>
> The first main purpose of the DPA 1998 is to control the way in which such data are 'processed'. This is a comprehensive term covering almost every conceivable activity in relation to such information. Under s 1(12), processing includes the 'obtaining, recording or holding ... organisation, adaptation or alteration ... retrieval, consultation or use ... disclosure ... alignment, combination, blocking, erasure or destruction' of data.
>
> A 'data processor' is anybody who does one of these things. It will therefore include hospital staff, GPs and their staff; while a 'data controller' is anybody who determines the purpose for which, or manner in which, the data are processed. This will include NHS organisations and GPs alike. Almost everyone who reads or uses patient records in any way – even putting copies in the post or reading them on screen – will be 'processing' data and will therefore be bound by the provisions of the DPA 1998. This will include not only professional staff but, for example, hospital managers and GP receptionists.
>
> ... [referring to the first data protection principle] To be 'fair' the data must, in general terms, have been obtained from the patient honestly or in accordance with a legal obligation; the patient must have been told the purposes for which the information is to be processed; and the rules for providing access to the data subject must also have been observed (Sched 1, Pt 2).

The word 'lawfully' is not defined. However, it implies that the processing must not be in breach of any other existing legal restrictions, for example, the common law duty of confidence. This emphasises the point that the DPA 1998 does not replace the common law framework of confidentiality and access, but is an addition to it – albeit a dominant one.

Most importantly, it should be noted that, to be considered fair and lawful, the processing of patient records (as 'sensitive personal data') must meet at least one detailed specific criterion from Sched 2 and at least one from Sched 3. In summary these are:

(a) that the patient has given 'explicit consent' to the processing ('explicit' is not defined, but Guidance from the Data Protection Commissioner suggests that it means that the patient's consent must be absolutely clear, that is, that it should cover the specific purpose of the processing); or

(b) that the processing is necessary for the purposes of exercising or performing a right or obligation imposed by law; or

(c) that it is necessary to protect the vital interests of the patient or another person where consent cannot be given by or on behalf of the patient, or where the data controller cannot reasonably be expected to obtain it or it has been unreasonably withheld; or

(d) that the information has already been deliberately made public by the patient; or

(e) that the processing is necessary for the purpose of actual or prospective legal proceedings, or for obtaining legal advice, or for the purpose of establishing, exercising or defending legal rights; or

(f) that it is necessary for the purposes of 'legitimate interests' pursued by the data controller or the third party to whom the data are to be disclosed, unless disclosure would be unwarranted because it would prejudice the data subject; or

(g) that it is necessary for the administration of justice, or for the exercise of statutory functions; or

(h) that it is necessary for medical purposes (including preventative medicine, diagnosis, research, care, treatment and management of healthcare services), and is carried out by a healthcare professional (as defined in s 69) or by a person who owes the patient an equivalent duty of confidentiality; or

(i) that it is authorised by an Order of the Secretary of State.

For the most part, the processing of patient records will be necessary for medical purposes (Sched 3, para 8), so one can avoid the need for consent in that way. However, one can see areas of uncertainty where important tissues will arise.

...

Potential problems

In practical terms, there are a wide range of every day situations in a hospital or surgery in which the legal rights and duties of NHS data controllers may not be clear ... one example would be where a trust has the opportunity to generate income by selling prescribing data to a data collection company. Will the court necessarily agree with the Court of Appeal's view in the *Source Informatics* case [see above, p 246] that anonymisation is sufficient to dispel any common law duty of confidentiality? Or should the process of anonymising prescriptions be deemed 'processing' for the purposes of the DPA 1998, as the Department of Health seemed to be arguing in that case? If so, what would be the position if the patient had explicitly indicated his/her opposition to such a process? Would Art 8 enable a GP to rely on the legitimate interests exception under Sched 2 to the DPA 1998, where the sole purpose of the exercise was commercial and contractual?

Again, the issue of disclosing information capable of identifying the patient has caused difficulties. The increasing sophistication of information technology has facilitated the production of group studies and the creation of national databases to assist with the treatment and prevention of conditions such as cancer. However, with rare conditions such as CJD, the possibility of a patient being identified even by anonymised information can never be completely eliminated as the GMC's guidance recognises. It is likely that where a legitimate public health purpose can be shown here (for example, under the Public Health (Control of Diseases) Act 1984), the conditions of Art 8 will be adjudged to have been met. However, that is not to say that patients will not challenge the disclosure.

Another possible difficulty might arise from relying on an exemption under Scheds 2 and 3 of the DPA 1998 based on a legal obligation. For instance, under s 35A of the Medical Act 1983, the GMC is entitled to demand disclosure of information from any person in order to assist with the performance of the GMC's functions. But what if the patient is specifically asked first, for example, as a matter of courtesy, and explicitly refuses disclosure out of loyalty to the doctor: does the exemption available to the data controller override the a patient's views, or would disclosure be unlawful in the terms of the First Data Protection Principle and Art 8?

Similarly, the Secretary of State is empowered by the DPA 1998 to make Orders in respect of disclosure in a variety of circumstances without the date subject's consent. For example, the Data Protection (Processing of Sensitive Personal Data) Order 2000 [SI 2000/417] allows disclosure of patient records without consent for a range of purposes 'in the substantial public interest', including for the prevention and detection of crime or protecting the public against incompetence or misconduct. The Order falls squarely within Scheds 2 and 3 of the DPA 1998 allowing the disclosure of health records without the a patient's consent; but will such blanket authorisations be considered consistent with the specific reservations set out in Art 8, or will patients be able to challenge them successfully as illegitimate encroachments on the basic principle of right to private and family life?

ACCESS TO MEDICAL RECORDS – ETHICAL CONSIDERATIONS

As a corollary to the duty of confidentiality owed by a doctor to a patient, one could be forgiven for assuming that a patient should have an unfettered right to see his medical records. After all, if a doctor is to be privy to intimate medical information which he has a duty to keep quiet about, but not an absolute duty, then the accuracy of that information should be verifiable at least by the patient concerned. At first sight, it might seem that here there are two discrete patient rights, that is, the right to respect for privacy and the right to know what the doctor is placing in the medical records. However, in practice they are intertwined. The patient's right to protection of confidences must surely extend to the right to know that the information concerned is accurate. Further, the utilitarian argument that the patient will be more candid if confidentiality is protected and that such candour is necessary for the patient's health and that of society generally, also sustains the proposition that a patient should have a right to check the accuracy of that information. (Interestingly, it has been argued that, in order to preserve confidentiality, patients should keep their own medical records. See 'Editorial' (1991) 17 JME 115, and the article in the same edition by Gilhooly, M and McGhee, S, 'Medical records: practicalities and principles of patient possession' (1991) 17 JME 235.)

On the other hand, if the patient has only a discretionary right (or, indeed, no right at all), then this would usually be justified on paternalistic principles. The types of arguments that are advanced in the cause of paternalism, are, for example, that the patient would not understand the records, that they may frighten or confuse him, the doctor would not be able to make 'frank' comments about the patient and so on. However, are paternalistic principles justifiable in certain circumstances where revelation of the contents of records may damage the patient or others? It will be seen that both common law and statute favour the paternalistic approach.

ACCESS TO MEDICAL RECORDS – THE LAW

Statutory provisions

The Access to Health Records Act 1990 was passed as a result of the case of *Gaskin v United Kingdom* (1990) 12 EHRR 36, where the European Court of Human Rights held that the UK's refusal to grant a right of access by a patient to his health records was in breach of Article 8 of the European Convention. This has now been replaced by the Data Protection Act 1998.

The Data Protection Act 1998 enables data subjects to have access to data held about them:

Data Protection Act 1998, Part II:

Rights of data subjects and others

7–

(1) Subject to the following provisions of this section and to sections 8 and 9, an individual is entitled–

    (a) to be informed by any data controller whether personal data of which that individual is the data subject are being processed by or on behalf of that data controller;

    (b) if that is the case, to be given by the data controller a description of–

        (i)   the personal data of which that individual is the data subject;

        (ii) the purposes for which they are being or are to be processed; and

        (iii) the recipients or classes of recipients to whom they are or may be disclosed;

    (c) to have communicated to him in an intelligible form–

        (i)   the information constituting any personal data of which that individual is the data subject; and

        (ii) any information available to the data controller as to the source of those data; and

    (d) where the processing by automatic means of personal data of which that individual is the data subject for the purpose of evaluating matters relating to him such as, for example, his performance at work, his creditworthiness, his reliability or his conduct, has constituted or is likely to constitute the sole basis for any decision significantly affecting him, to be informed by the data controller of the logic involved in that decision-taking.

(2) A data controller is not obliged to supply any information under subsection (1) unless he has received–

(a) a request in writing; and

(b) except in prescribed cases, such fee (not exceeding the prescribed maximum) as he may require.

(3) A data controller is not obliged to comply with a request under this section unless he is supplied with such information as he may reasonably require in order to satisfy himself as to the identity of the person making the request and to locate the information which that person seeks.

(4) Where a data controller cannot comply with the request without disclosing information relating to another individual who can be identified from that information, he is not obliged to comply with the request unless–

(a) the other individual has consented to the disclosure of the information to the person making the request; or

(b) it is reasonable in all the circumstances to comply with the request without the consent of the other individual.

(5) In subsection (4) the reference to information relating to another individual includes a reference to information identifying that individual as the source of the information sought by the request; and that subsection is not to be construed as excusing a data controller from communicating so much of the information sought by the request as can be communicated without disclosing the identity of the other individual concerned, whether by the omission of names or other identifying particulars or otherwise.

(6) In determining for the purposes of subsection (4)(b) whether it is reasonable in all the circumstances to comply with the request without the consent of the other individual concerned, regard shall be had, in particular, to–

(a) any duty of confidentiality owed to the other individual;

(b) any steps taken by the data controller with a view to seeking the consent of the other individual;

(c) whether the other individual is capable of giving consent; and

(d) any express refusal of consent by the other individual.

(7) An individual making a request under this section may, in such cases as may be prescribed, specify that his request is limited to personal data of any prescribed description.

(8) Subject to subsection (4), a data controller shall comply with a request under this section promptly and in any event before the end of the prescribed period beginning with the relevant day.

(9) If a court is satisfied on the application of any person who has made a request under the foregoing provisions of this section that the data controller in question has failed to comply with the request in contravention of those provisions, the court may order him to comply with the request.

(10) In this section–

'prescribed' means prescribed by the Secretary of State by regulations;

'the prescribed maximum' means such amount as may be prescribed;

-'the prescribed period' means forty days or such other period as may be prescribed;

-'the relevant day', in relation to a request under this section, means the day on which the data controller receives the request or, if later, the first day on which the data controller has both the required fee and the information referred to in subsection (3).

Section 14 entitles the data subject to correct inaccurate information.

The Data Protection (Subject Access Modification) (Health) Order 2000 SI 2000/413 also provides that someone with parental responsibility or appointed by a court to manage someone's affairs cannot obtain access to records if the patient does not wish that information to be disclosed. In addition, access cannot be provided if it identifies another person, other than a health care professional, who has not consented to the disclosure, unless it is reasonable to comply with the request without the consent of that other individual. This provision has been inserted to comply with the European Court decision in *Gaskin v United Kingdom* (1990) 12 EHRR 36, where records where withheld on the ground that the social workers objected or could not be traced. The court found that an absolute prohibition on disclosure was in breach of Article 8. As will be seen, s 7(6) sets out those matters to be considered in relation to 'reasonableness'.

The Access to Health Records Act 1990 and the Data Protection Act 1984, both contained exemptions, enabling data/record holders to withhold access to medical records in certain circumstances. There are now some exemptions within the 1998 Act itself (for example, relating to the detection of crime). The main medical record exemption in respect of the Data Protection Act 1998 is contained within The Data Protection (Subject Access Modification) (Health) Order 2000 SI 2000/413. Basically, this entitles the health professional concerned to withhold patient records if they consider that disclosure would be likely to cause serious harm to the physical or mental health or condition of the data subject or any other person (Art 5(1)). Before deciding whether this exemption applies, a data controller who is not a health care professional is obliged to consult the health professional responsible for the clinical care of the data subject, or if there is not such a person, someone with the necessary qualifications or experience. Unlike the Access to Health Records Act 1990, there is no specific provision in the Data Protection Act 1998 for applications by, or on behalf of child patients, nor for incompetent adults, although it is assumed by the Data Protection (Subject Access Modification) (Health) Order 2000 SI 2000/413 that these applications can be made.

If the record holder forms the opinion that the information may cause serious harm to the health of the patient or another, access may be excluded to the relevant part of the records. Yet again, this reflects medical paternalism. Further, it is makes no sense that access should be refused because it may seriously harm the patient. If the patient is refused access on this ground, is not the refusal itself likely to cause harm? Speculation as to what the records may contain could, and probably would, cause considerable anxiety. Even if one accepts the argument that many patients do not want to know about risks of treatment before consent is given, the same argument cannot apply to access. Patients of sound mind, who have gone to the trouble of making an application, should have their requests respected. Harm caused to third parties raises different issues, which would depend upon the identity of the third party, the type and magnitude of the harm and so on.

Access to Medical Reports Act 1988

This Act confers a right of access to medical reports obtained for employment or insurance purposes:

3 Consent to applications for medical reports for employment or insurance purposes

(1) A person shall not apply to a medical practitioner for a medical report relating to any individual to be supplied to him for employment or insurance purposes unless–

   (a) that person ('the applicant') has notified the individual that he proposes to make the application; and

   (b) the individual has notified the applicant that he consents to the making of the application.

(2) Any notification given under sub-s (1)(a) above must inform the individual of his right to withhold his consent to the making of the application, and of the following rights under this Act, namely–

   (a) the rights arising under sub-ss 4(1)–(3) and 6(2) below with respect to access to the report before or after it is supplied;

   (b) the right to withhold consent under sub-s (1) of sub-s 5 below; and

   (c) the right to request the amendment of the report under sub-s (2) of that section, as well as of the effect of sub-s 7 below.

The Act also gives a right for the individual to have access to the report before it is supplied, and provides for the correction by the patient of matters contained in the report.

It is interesting to note the provision of s 3(1). Clearly, this adds nothing to the common law, as a doctor could not provide a medical report to a third party without consent if he is the patient's own doctor, and it is important to note that the Act only applies to reports prepared by a medical practitioner who is, or has been, responsible for the clinical care of the individual (s 2(1)). What of the situation where the doctor is nominated by an insurance company or employer, to whom the Act does not apply? Would an obligation of confidence arise? It is submitted that, once the doctor had examined the patient and obtained medical information, without express or implied consent that it would be disclosed, the doctor would owe a duty of confidence. However, would it be easier to conclude that implied consent had been given by attending the medical appointment in the first place?

The right under the Act is qualified in the same way as it is under the Data Protection Act 1998.

There is a right to apply to the court if access is refused (sub-s (8)).

Common law

As has been seen above, there is now a qualified, statutory right of access to medical records, but this does not apply to non-computerised records made prior to 1 November 1991. The common law is still, therefore, of considerable importance. The issue was examined by the Court of Appeal in the case of *R v Mid Glamorgan Family Health Services Authority and Another ex p Martin* [1995] 1 WLR 110. The facts were as follows. As a young man, the applicant had received psychiatric treatment from doctors employed by the respondents. He had also received assistance from a female social worker, with whom he became infatuated. She was taken off his case, and for some years he had sought access to his medical records, to find out why the social worker had been removed and why he had subsequently been committed under the 1959 Mental Health Act. Access had been refused, on the basis that they were the property of the relevant authority and that disclosure would be damaging to the applicant and to third parties. The applicant's lawyers had responded to the effect that these doctors were in no position to judge whether the applicant would be damaged. Clearly, this was a forceful argument, and it resulted in a compromise offer: the respondents would agree to disclose the records to a medical adviser nominated by him, for that person to decide whether they may be damaging. The offer was refused. The judge at first instance dismissed the application for unmediated disclosure. In the Court of Appeal, the appeal was dismissed:

> **Nourse LJ** (p 116): ... a public body, in fulfilment of its duty to administer its property in accordance with its public purposes, is bound to deal with medical records in the same way as a private doctor. In that regard the observations of Lord Templeman in *Sidaway* [1985] 1 AC 871, p 904, are pertinent:
>
>> I do not subscribe to the theory that the patient is entitled to know everything nor to the theory that the doctor is entitled to decide everything. The relationship between doctor and patient is contractual in origin, the doctor performing services in consideration for fees payable by the patient. The doctor, obedient to the high standards set by the medical profession, impliedly contracts to act at all times in the best interests of the patient. No doctor in his senses would impliedly contract at the same time to give to the patient all the information available to the doctor as a result of the doctor's training and experience and as a result of the doctor's diagnosis of the patient. An obligation to give a patient all the information available to the doctor would often be inconsistent with the doctor's contractual obligation to have regard to the patient's best interests. Some information might confuse, other information might alarm a particular patient. Whenever the occasion arises for the doctor to tell the patient the results of the doctor's diagnosis, the possible methods of treatment and the advantages and disadvantages of the recommended treatment, the doctor must decide in the light of his training and experience and in the light of his knowledge of the patient what should be said and how it should be said.
>
> These observations provide a sensible basis for holding that a doctor, likewise a health authority, as the owner of a patient's medical records, may deny the patient access to them if it is in his best interests to do so, for example if their disclosure would be detrimental to his health. In the light of the offer made in the respondents' solicitor's letter of 24 March 1993, that is a complete answer to the applicant's application. I agree with Popplewell J that the respondents have offered all that is necessary to comply with their duty to the applicant. The judge was entitled, in the exercise of his discretion, to refuse the applicant the relief that he sought and I would affirm his decision on that ground. Although the respondents have not taken this point, it might also, as a matter of discretion, have been affirmed on the ground that the applicant did nothing effective to pursue his rights against either of the respondents between 1981 and 1990.
>
> It is inherent in the views above expressed that I do not accept that a health authority, any more than a private doctor, has an absolute right to deal with medical records in any way that it chooses. As Lord Templeman makes clear, the doctor's general duty,

likewise the health authority's, is to act at all times in the best interests of the patient. Those interests would usually require that a patient's medical records should not be disclosed to third parties; conversely, that they should usually, for example, be handed on by one doctor to the next or made available to the patient's legal advisers if they are reasonably required for the purposes of legal proceedings in which he is involved. The respondents' position seems to be that no practical difficulty could arise in such circumstances, but that they would act voluntarily and not because they were under a legal duty to do so. If it ever became necessary for the legal position to be tested, it is inconceivable that this extreme position would be vindicated. On all the other points taken by the applicant I agree with Popplewell J. I would dismiss this appeal.

The court also relied on the fact that, although there were a number of statutory rights to access, these were not absolute, and could be wholly or partially excluded in appropriate circumstances. Some commentators, such as Dermot Feenan, have found this an unsatisfactory decision:

Feenan, D, 'Common law access to medical records' (1996) 59 MLR 101:

Detriment to patient – insufficient

The framing of the exception in terms only of detriment to the patient seems insufficient protection of a patient's interests in personal health information. The sufficiency of the exception may be tested by reference to analogous law, comprising persuasive Commonwealth and American *dicta* and British legislation. In the leading American authority on informed consent, *Canterbury v Spence*, the court held that a doctor is not obliged to disclose where disclosure poses *such a threat of detriment* to the patient as to become unfeasible or contraindicated from a medical point of view. It is recognised that patients may become *so emotionally distraught* on disclosure as to *foreclose a rational decision*, or complicate or hinder the treatment, or perhaps even pose psychological damage to the patient. Where that is so, the cases have generally held that the physician is armed with a privilege to keep the information from the patient, and we think it clear that portents of that type may justify the physician in action he deems medically warranted.

Here harm alone was insufficient. There had to be harm of the type envisaged by the court. Similarly, in the South Australian Supreme Court, King CJ approved his *dictum* in a previous case to the effect that a doctor is justified in withholding information 'when he judges on reasonable grounds that the patient's physical or mental, might be seriously harmed by the information'. Here, the court imposes two qualifications on the prospect of harm. First, that there must be reasonable grounds for establishing such a prospect, and, second, that the harm must be serious.

It is easy to understand why these courts require more than simply the doctor's view of potential detriment. There appears to be an implicit acknowledgment by them of the danger of paternalistic bias by the doctor regarding information disclosure. Aside from judicial precedent, mounting empirical evidence undermines doctors' assertions designed to restrict or obstruct information disclosure on the basis that patients would be unable to deal with harmful information. In 1982 the United States President's Commission for the Study of Ethical Problems in Medicine and Biomedical and Behavioural Research stated:

Despite all the anecdotes about patients who committed suicide, suffered heart attacks, or plunged into prolonged depression upon being told 'bad news', little documentation exists for claims that informing patients is more dangerous to their health than not informing them, particularly when the informing is done in a sensitive and tactful fashion.

Similar findings exist in relation to medical records. It is also acknowledged that unless the exception is carefully circumscribed it may swallow up the primary principle of information disclosure. Arguably, similar considerations apply to access to medical records.

The exception in Martin also falls short of similar policy encapsulated in British freedom of information legislation. In the Access to Health Records Act 1990, which gives a statutory right of access to health records, sub-s 5(1)(a) provides that access shall not be given where in the opinion of the holder of the record … information is '*likely* to cause *serious harm* to the physical or mental health of the patient'. This section makes clear the gravity of harm and its likelihood. These criteria reflect the fact that the purpose of the legislation, which was to establish a right of access to health records, was not to be circumscribed too easily. Identical wording, and similar policy considerations, are found in the relevant legislative provisions exempting disclosure made under the Data Protection Act 1984 and in the Access to Medical Reports Act 1988.

It seems that the Court of Appeal in *Martin* simply accepted the opinion of the consultant psychiatrist and, thence, the respondents' solicitors, that disclosure would be detrimental to the patient. As the above common law *dicta* and legislation show, detriment alone ought to be insufficient.

Is it not the case that the 'serious harm' exception in relation to *the patient*, however stringently applied, is contrary to patient autonomy? Surely if the patient is competent and suitably warned, he should be entitled to run the risk?

A paternalistic approach was taken by the Australian Supreme Court of New South Wales in the case of *Breen v Williams* (1995) 6 Med LR 385, where the doctor's right to decide what it would be good for a patient to know was upheld:

Mahoney JA (p 427): Subject to what I shall say, the documents are created for the purpose of such diagnosis and treatment and they are merely what the doctor uses to achieve those purposes. Accordingly, in my opinion, *prima facie*, a medical file kept by a doctor is the property of the doctor.

However, the position is, of course, more complicated. It is necessary to examine the circumstances surrounding the creation of each document. Documents created merely for the purposes of the doctor, for example, as records of his practice, as material from which to assess charges and the like, will be the property of the doctor. On the other hand, some documents created for the purpose of enabling the doctor to diagnose and to determine the treatment to be recommended may be the property of the patient. Thus, a document, though held by the doctor, may be the property of the patient because it was procured by or for the patient and has been paid for by her. X-rays, pathology reports and some reports by consultant specialists may be such: cf as to the case of a solicitor *Wentworth v de Montfort*, p 356B. Correspondence with consultant specialists or with treating hospitals may, if of this kind, be the property of the patient.

More difficult questions arise in relation to matters such as those particularly referred to by Dr Cashman in the present case, namely, notes taken by the doctor to record the patient's medical history and her signs and symptoms. In one sense such records are made for the purposes of the patient, the making of them is one of the things which the doctor, by his engagement, may undertake to do. In this sense, the document is created so that there may be a record of what the patient has told the doctor and her signs and symptoms at the time. The record may not merely help in the instant diagnosis and a selection of treatment, it may provide a valuable resource for future purposes. Considered in isolation, a record of this kind, if it were contained in a separate document, would, I think, be the property of the patient.

> On the other hand, the doctor may – as Dr Williams has said he ordinarily will – include with the record of the history and the signs and symptoms of the patient, comments and observations which are made and recorded for the purpose of helping the doctor form the diagnosis and the opinion to be formed as to treatment. There may be observations – Dr Williams used the term 'musings' – which, if standing alone, would ordinarily be the property of the doctor and not of the patient. It is the fact that these things are combined in the documents which illustrates the nature of the problem in a case such as this.
>
> The combination of such things: the history, signs and symptoms on the one hand and the 'musings' and other things on the other hand, may be accidental in the sense that the combination of the two in the one record is not inherent in the process of medical knowledge. But the thrust of Dr Williams' evidence is, I think, that such a combination is not accidental. His evidence suggests that the combination of these two things is inherent in the way medical practice is conducted or, at least in the way he conducts his practice. The trial judge accepted this portion of the doctor's evidence.
>
> If the records kept by the doctor be in this form, then, in my opinion, the records remain the property of the doctor ...

This decision does not deny that a patient has a right to know the main contents of his records, what it denies to him is the right to look through them and discover his doctor's comments. The reason given for this is that the doctor will be inhibited when making his notes, and that may not be in the patient's interest. It is easy to see that a doctor may feel restrained from making adverse comments relating to, say, genuineness of symptoms, when, for example, referring a patient to another doctor, if he thought that the patient may see this. However, the suspicions must be based upon factual matters such as an inconsistent history of symptoms, and physical examination failing to accord with alleged symptoms, and surely these are matters which the doctor should discuss openly with his patient. Or is it arguable that there is a risk of losing the patient's trust?

However, in *Breen v Williams*, there was a dissenting judgment, by Kirby P, in favour of disclosure, which relied on there being a fiduciary duty owed to the patient. This was following the Canadian Supreme Court decision of *McInerney v MacDonald* (1992) 93 DLR (4th) 415. In this case comment was made as follows:

> **La Forest J** (p 421): Information about oneself revealed to a doctor acting in a professional capacity remains, in a fundamental sense, one's own. The doctor's position is one of trust and confidence. The information conveyed is held in a fashion somewhat akin to a trust. While the doctor is the owner of the actual record, the information is to be used by the physician for the benefit of the patient. The confiding of the information to the physician for medical purposes gives rise to an expectation that the patient's interest in and control of the information will continue. The trust-like 'beneficial interest' of the patient in the information indicates that, as a general rule, he or she should have a right of access to the information and that the physician should have a corresponding obligation to provide it.

How might the fiduciary duty argument have changed the decision of the Court of Appeal in *Martin*?

Supreme Court Act 1981

As mentioned previously, ss 33 and 34 of the Supreme Court Act permit disclosure of documents, both prior to commencement of proceedings, and during the course of those legal proceedings. Not only is this an exception to the principle of confidentiality; it may also provide an opportunity for a patient to acquire knowledge of his medical records. The provisions of the Act permit disclosure to the applicant's legal and medical advisers only. However, does this prevent the adviser disclosing the contents of the documents to the patient? It is submitted that it does not. If the adviser, either medical or legal, is to advise, then a discussion of the medical history is inevitable, and for this purpose the contents of the notes will be revealed. However, this perhaps may not extend to giving the patient photocopies of the notes, as it could be interpreted as a circumvention of the provisions of ss 33 and 34.

CHAPTER 6

MEDICAL MALPRACTICE

INTRODUCTION

Medical malpractice may be defined, broadly, as any unjustified act or failure to act upon the part of a doctor or other health care worker which results in harm to the patient. In this chapter we shall be considering the means, under the civil law, by which a victim of such malpractice may pursue a claim for redress, and the difficulties that lie in his way. (The rare instances in which the doctor may also be the subject of criminal liability have been noted already in Chapter 2.)

First, what form might the patient's claim take? On the face of it, there would seem to be three possibilities – to sue in tort, either in battery or negligence, or to mount an action for breach of contract. In practice, however, it is the second of these, a negligence action, which offers the only appropriate channel for the vast majority of malpractice claims. The first option, battery, which forms the civil analogue to the crime of assault, generally only arises as a possibility in those rare cases where treatment is carried out without any consent at all (see Chapter 3). It is no use to the patient who, having given such consent, suffers injury, however poor the execution of the treatment subsequently turns out to be.

As for the third option, breach of contract, the first thing to note is that this will not assist patients treated under the NHS scheme (that is, the majority of patients in this country), who provide no consideration in return for the services they receive: see *Appleby v Sleep* [1968] 2 All ER 265. Equally, it was confirmed by the High Court in *Reynolds v The Health First Medical Group* [2000] Lloyd's Rep Med 240, that the relationship between a GP and his patient is not a contractual one.

What, though, of the growing numbers of patients treated in the private sector? Whilst it is true that the latter may sue for breach of contract instead of (or as well as) in negligence, in proving a breach they normally have exactly the same task as their NHS counterparts. This is because it is most unlikely that the doctor will have promised expressly to achieve a specific desired outcome (although for an exceptional Canadian case in point, see *LaFleur v Cornelis* (1979) 28 NBR (2d) 569). And otherwise, in implying the terms which govern such contracts, the courts have held the standard of skill and care warranted by the private doctor to be identical to the standard of care required to avoid a claim in negligence. In *Thake v Maurice* [1986] QB 644, a case in which a patient treated privately sued following the failure of his vasectomy, Neill LJ in the Court of Appeal commented:

> **Neill LJ**: I do not consider that a reasonable person would have expected a responsible medical man to be intending to give a guarantee. Medicine, though a highly skilled profession, is not, and is not generally regarded as being, an exact science. The reasonable man would have expected the defendant to exercise all the special care and skill of a surgeon in that speciality; he would not in my view have expected the defendant to give a guarantee of 100% success.

This common law standard of care is also echoed in s 13 of the Supply of Goods and Services Act 1982, which provides that a person who supplies services in the course of a business must carry them out with reasonable care and skill.

Accordingly, in the remainder of this chapter we shall be focusing upon actions in medical negligence. In order for such actions to succeed, a number of basic elements (familiar from the general tort of negligence) must be made out, that is, the existence of a duty of care, the fact of its breach, and that legally recognised damage was thereby caused, and we shall consider these various requirements in turn. It is, of course, notorious that medical negligence claims are, by their nature, often very hard to prove (as well as being costly, time consuming and traumatic for those involved), and we shall conclude by considering the case for legal reforms in this area.

THE DUTY OF CARE

The duty to the patient

The patient must establish that the defendant, who may be a doctor, nurse, NHS trust, or a health authority, owed him a legal duty of care. This is generally speaking the easiest element to show. As Michael Jones comments:

Jones, M, *Medical Negligence*, 1996, London: Sweet & Maxwell, p 29:

Normally, there will be no difficulty in finding a duty of care owed by the doctor to his patient, at least where the claim is in respect of personal injuries, and this is true even where there is a contractual relationship. The practitioner may also owe a duty of care to the patient in respect of pure financial loss. In addition, there are a number of circumstances where a doctor may also owe a duty of care to a third party arising out of the treatment given to the patient, but the incident and extent of such duties is more problematic.

The well known case of *Barnett v Chelsea and Kensington Hospital Management Committee* [1969] 1 QB 428 is authority for the proposition that an open accident and emergency unit has a duty to treat or at least assess the patient. The facts arose after three nightwatchmen, who were taken ill after drinking some tea, went to their local hospital's casualty department, but were sent away without being seen by a doctor. Nield J stated:

Nield J: I turn to consider the nature of the duty which the law imposes on persons in the position of the defendants and their servants and agents. The authorities deal in the main with the duties of doctors, surgeons, consultants, nurses and staff when a person is treated either by a doctor at his surgery or the patient's home or when the patient is treated in or at a hospital. In *Cassidy v Ministry of Health* [1951] 2 KB 343, Denning LJ dealt with the duties of hospital authorities and said:

In my opinion, authorities who run a hospital, be they local authorities, government boards, or any other corporation, are in law under the self-same duty as the humblest doctor. Whenever they accept a patient for treatment, they must use reasonable care and skill to cure him of his ailment. The hospital authorities cannot, of course, do it by themselves. They have no ears to listen through the stethoscope, and no hands to hold the knife. They must do it by the staff which they employ, and, if their staff are negligent in giving the treatment, they are just as liable for that negligence as is anyone else who employs others to do his duties for him. Is there any possible difference in law, I ask, can there be, between hospital authorities who accept a patient for treatment and railway or shipping authorities who accept a passenger for carriage? None whatever.

> Once they undertake the task, they come under a duty to use care in the doing of it, and that is so whether they do it for reward or not.

Here the problem is different and no authority bearing directly on it has been cited to me. It is to determine the duty of those who provide and run a casualty department when a person presents himself at that department complaining of illness or injury and before he is treated and received into the hospital wards. This is not a case of a casualty department which closes its doors and says that no patients can be received. The three watchmen entered the defendants' hospital without hindrance, they made complaints to the nurse who received them and she in turn passed those complaints on to the medical casualty officer, and he sent a message through the nurse purporting to advise the three men. Is there, on these facts, shown to be created a relationship between the three watchmen and the hospital staff such as gives rise to a duty of care in the defendants which they owe to the three men?

... In my judgment, there was here such a close and direct relationship between the hospital and the watchmen that there was imposed on the hospital a duty of care which they owed to the watchmen. Thus, I have no doubt that Nurse Corbett and Dr Banerjee were under a duty to the deceased to exercise that skill and care which is to be expected of persons in such positions acting reasonably, or, as it is, I think very helpfully, put by the learned author of *Winfield on Torts*, 7th edn, 1963, p 183:

> Where one is engaged in a transaction in which he holds himself out as having professional skill, the law expects him to show the average amount of competence associated with the proper discharge of the duties of that profession or trade or calling, and if he falls short of that and injures someone in consequence, he is not behaving reasonably.

In relation to general practitioners, who operate outside hospitals, these clearly owe a duty of care to their own patients, that is, those who are registered with them. Moreover, by virtue of the National Health Service (General Medical Services) Regulations 1992 SI 1992/635, Schedule 2, paragraph 4(1)(h), such a practitioner is required, pursuant to his statutory contract with the area Family Health Services Authority, to treat:

> (h) persons to whom he may be requested to give treatment which is immediately required owing to an accident or other emergency at any place in his practice area, provided that–
>
> (i) he is not, at time of the request, relieved of liability to give treatment under para 5; and
>
> (ii) he is not, at the time of the request, relieved, under para 19(2), of his obligation to give treatment personally; and
>
> (iii) he is available to provide such treatment,
>
> and any persons by whom he is requested, and agrees, to give treatment which is immediately required owing to an accident or other emergency at any place in the locality of any FHSA in whose medical list he is included, provided there is no doctor who, at the time of the request, is under an obligation otherwise than under this head to give treatment to that person, or there is such a doctor but, after being requested to attend, he is unable to attend and give treatment immediately required ...

(Paragraphs 5 and 19(2) of the Schedule relieve the doctor of liability to treat, respectively, in cases where he is elderly or infirm, or another doctor is already present.)

The nature of the duty of care owed in such cases by the practitioner to the patient was considered *obiter* by Stuart-Smith LJ in *Capital and Counties v Hants CC* [1997] 2 All ER 865:

> **Stuart-Smith LJ**: As a general rule a sufficient relationship of proximity will exist when someone possessed of special skill undertakes to apply that skill for the assistance of another person who relies upon such skill and there is direct and substantial reliance by the plaintiff on the defendant's skill (see *Hedley Byrne and Co Ltd v Heller and Partners* and *Henderson v Merrett Syndicates Ltd*). There are many instances of this. The plaintiffs submit that that which is most closely analogous is that of doctor and patient or health authority and patient. There is no doubt that once the relationship of doctor and patient or hospital authority and admitted patient exists, the doctor or the hospital owe a duty to take reasonable care to effect a cure, not merely to prevent further harm. The undertaking is to use the special skills which the doctor and hospital authorities have to treat the patient. In *Cassidy v Ministry of Health (Fahrni, Third Party)* [1951] 1 All ER 574, p 588, Denning LJ said:
>
> > In my opinion, authorities who run a hospital, be they local authorities, government boards, or any other corporation, are in law under the self-same duty as the humblest doctor. Whenever they accept a patient for treatment, they must use reasonable care and skill to cure him of his ailment.
>
> In *Barnett v Chelsea and Kensington Hospital Management Committee* [1968] 1 All ER 1068, Nield J drew a distinction between a casualty department of a hospital that closes its doors and says no patients can be received, in which case he would by inference have held there was no duty of care, and the case before him where the three watchmen who had taken poison entered the hospital and were given erroneous advice, where a duty of care arose.
>
> Likewise, a doctor who happened to witness a road accident will very likely go to the assistance of anyone injured, but he is not under any legal obligation to do so (save in certain limited circumstances which are not relevant) and the relationship of doctor and patient does not arise. If he volunteers his assistance, his only duty as a matter of law is not to make the victim's condition worse.

Subsequently, however, the decision in *Capital and Counties* was distinguished by Lord Woolf MR in *Kent v Griffiths (No 3)* [2001] QB 36, in the context of an ambulance's failure to respond expeditiously to a 999 call made on behalf of a woman who had suffered a serious asthma attack. (The ambulance took nearly 40 minutes to complete a journey that should have taken no more than 20 minutes, and the patient in the meantime suffered a cardiac arrest.) In holding that a duty of care was owed by the ambulance service, his Lordship commented as follows:

> **Lord Woolf MR**: Here what was being provided was a health service. In the case of health services under the 1977 Act the conventional situation is that there is a duty of care. Why should the position of the ambulance staff be different from that of doctors or nurses? In addition the arguments based on public policy are much weaker in the case of the ambulance service than they are in the case of the police or the fire service. The police and fire services' primary obligation is to the public at large. In protecting a particular victim of crime, the police are performing their more general role of maintaining public order and reducing crime. In the case of fire the fire service will normally be concerned not only to protect a particular property where a fire breaks out but also to prevent fire spreading. In the case of both services, there is therefore a concern to protect the public generally ... Situations could arise where there is a conflict between the interests of a particular individual and the public at large. But, in the case of the ambulance service in this particular case, the only member of the

public who could be adversely affected was the claimant. It was the claimant alone for whom the ambulance had been called.

It remains uncertain how far a similar affirmative duty of rescue (requiring him to assist an ill or injured stranger whom he happens to come across outside his practice) would be imposed upon an individual doctor. This question must now be considered in the light of the courts' obligation, under the Human Rights Act 1998, to develop the common law in line with rights under the European Convention on Human Rights, and in this context, Article 2, safeguarding the right to life may well be relevant. In particular, the person who suffers avoidable injury through the doctor's non-assistance might argue that the law's failure to impose liability upon the latter itself amounts to an infringement of his Article 2 right. (For an instructive Australian decision, in which a doctor, who was in his surgery at the time, was held liable in tort for failing to answer a summons for help from a stranger, see *Lowns v Woods* [1996] Aust Torts Rep 81–376.)

Another difficulty with Stuart-Smith LJ's approach in *Capital and Counties* is his suggestion (repeated in *Powell v Boldaz* (1997) 39 BMLR 35) that the extent of any volunteer doctor's duty, insofar as he does intervene, will be limited to not making the victim's condition worse than it was before. By stopping and assisting, the doctor is treating the injured person and has voluntarily assumed a responsibility for him; the victim has become the doctor's patient and the *Bolam* standard of care (see p 296, below) will govern his actions. The latter standard will, of course, be situation specific and equate to whatever the reasonable 'Good Samaritan' doctor would do in the circumstances. Surely a reasonable doctor would try to stabilise and improve the accident victim's condition and, hence, (save for the most pressing reasons) is not entitled in law simply to 'wash his hands' of the patient. (See also in this regard the decision of the Supreme Court of South Australia in *Goode v Nash* (1979) 21 SASR 419.)

Similar questions arise in relation to examinations carried out by doctors upon persons at the behest of third parties, such as employers or insurance companies. Here the examinee does not become the patient of the doctor in the strict sense: nonetheless, should the latter be placed under a positive duty carefully to diagnose and inform him of any abnormalities (as opposed to having a merely negative duty not to cause him injury during the examination)? In *X (Minors) v Bedfordshire County Council* [1995] 2 AC 633, Lord Browne-Wilkinson suggested *obiter* that only the negative duty would arise, and this was applied by the Court of Appeal in *Kapfunde v Abbey National* (1998) 46 BMLR 176. The latter case, however, was one of purely economic loss, suffered by a job-applicant who failed to get a job in the light of an unfavourable medical report. By contrast, in the context of physical injury related to a condition negligently overlooked by the examining doctor, it is likely that a duty would be found. As Andrew Grubb writes:

Grubb, A, (ed), *Principles of Medical Law*, 2nd edn, 2004, Oxford: OUP, p 365:

5.119 … [I]n principle, applying the well-known *Caparo* test, there is no difficulty in holding the doctor liable for *all* the immediate consequences of a failure to exercise reasonable care and skill in the course of the examination. Consequently, he could be liable for failing (carelessly) to diagnose a medical condition which could have been treated or its symptons alleviated if it had been diagnosed earlier. Injury to the person would be foreseeable and there would be a proximate relationship based upon an implied assumption of responsibility by the doctor. The expectation of both examinee and doctor will usually be that the doctor will perform his professional obligation to the person which would include alerting the person to anything untoward.

The duty in 'wrongful conception/birth' cases

Until a few years ago, English law was prepared, in principle, to award damages to parents for the costs of bringing up healthy children who would not have been born but for negligence on the part of a doctor: see, for example, the Court of Appeal's decision in *Thake v Maurice* [1986] QB 644, where the defendant failed to advise a husband that the vasectomy that he had been given was liable to reverse spontaneously. However, this area of the law was dramatically altered by the decision of the House of Lords in *McFarlane v Tayside Health Board* [2000] 2 AC 59:

McFarlane v Tayside Health Board [2000] 2 AC 59, HL (Lords Slynn, Steyn, Hope, Clyde and Millett)

Mr McFarlane, who was married with four children, underwent a vasectomy operation at the defendant's hospital and was told that it had been a success and that he and his wife need no longer use contraception. Subsequently, his wife became pregnant by him again and gave birth to a fifth child. In their negligence action against the board, the couple claimed damages both for the physical discomfort suffered by Mrs McFarlane during her pregnancy, and for the financial costs of bringing up the child:

> **Lord Slynn of Hadley**: My Lords, I do not find real difficulty in deciding the claim for damages in respect of the pregnancy and birth itself. The parents did not want another child for justifiable economic and family reasons; they already had four children. They were entitled lawfully to take steps to make sure that that did not happen, one possible such step being a vasectomy of the husband. It was plainly foreseeable that if the operation did not succeed, or recanalisation of the vas took place, but the husband was told that contraceptive measures were not necessary, the wife might become pregnant. It does not seem to me to be necessary to consider the events of an unwanted conception and birth in terms of 'harm' or 'injury' in its ordinary sense of the words. They were unwanted and known by the health board to be unwanted events. The object of the vasectomy was to prevent them happening. It seems to me that in consequence the wife, if there was negligence, is entitled by way of general damages to be compensated for the pain and discomfort and inconvenience of the unwanted pregnancy and birth and she is also entitled to special damages associated with both – extra medical expenses, clothes for herself and equipment on the birth of the baby ...

> The question remains whether as a matter of legal principle the damages should include, for a child by then loved, loving and fully integrated into the family the cost of shoes at 14 and a dress at 17 and everything that can reasonably be described as necessary for the upbringing of the child until the end of school, university, independence, maturity? ...

> The doctor undertakes a duty of care in regard to the prevention of pregnancy: it does not follow that the duty includes also avoiding the costs of rearing the child if born and accepted into the family. Whereas I have no doubt that there should be compensation for the physical effects of the pregnancy and birth, including of course solatium for consequential suffering by the mother immediately following the birth, I consider that it is not fair, just or reasonable to impose on the doctor or his employer liability for the consequential responsibilities, imposed on or accepted by the parents

to bring up a child. The doctor does not assume responsibility for those economic losses. If a client wants to be able to recover such costs he or she must do so by an appropriate contract.

Lord Steyn: It is possible to view the case simply from the perspective of corrective justice. It requires somebody who has harmed another without justification to indemnify the other. On this approach the parents' claim for the cost of bringing up Catherine must succeed. But one may also approach the case from the vantage point of distributive justice. It requires a focus on the just distribution of burdens and losses among members of a society. If the matter is approached in this way, it may become relevant to ask commuters on the Underground the following question: 'Should the parents of an unwanted but healthy child be able to sue the doctor or hospital for compensation equivalent to the cost of bringing up the child for the years of his or her minority, ie until about 18 years?' My Lords, I am firmly of the view that an overwhelming number of ordinary men and women would answer the question with an emphatic 'No'. And the reason for such a response would be an inarticulate premise as to what is morally acceptable and what is not. Like Ognall J in *Jones v Berkshire AHA*, 2 July 1986, they will have in mind that many couples cannot have children and others have the sorrow and burden of looking after a disabled child. The realisation that compensation for financial loss in respect of the upbringing of a child would necessarily have to discriminate between rich and poor would, surely appear unseemly to them. It would also worry them that parents may be put in a position of arguing in court that the unwanted child, which they accepted and care for, is more trouble than it is worth. Instinctively, the traveller on the Underground would consider that the law of tort has no business to provide legal remedies consequent upon the birth of a healthy child, which all of us regard as a valuable and good thing.

Lord Millett: ... I am persuaded that the costs of bringing Catherine up are not recoverable. I accept the thrust of both the main arguments in favour of dismissing such a claim. In my opinion the law must take the birth of a normal, healthy baby to be a blessing, not a detriment. In truth it is a mixed blessing. It brings joy and sorrow, blessing and responsibility. The advantages and the disadvantages are inseparable. Individuals may choose to regard the balance as unfavourable and take steps to forgo the pleasures as well as the responsibilities of parenthood. They are entitled to decide for themselves where their own interests lie. But society itself must regard the balance as beneficial. It would be repugnant to its own sense of values to do otherwise. It is morally offensive to regard a normal, healthy baby as more trouble and expense than it is worth.

Although the Law Lords did not speak with one voice in *McFarlane*, it is apparent that, where a healthy child is born, damages will be limited to the physical pain and discomfort suffered by the mother during pregnancy. By contrast, no duty of care is owed to the parents in respect of the subsequent costs of maintaining a healthy child. Given both the incalculable benefits to the parents involved, and the policy factors adverted to by Lord Steyn, it was felt that such a birth should simply not sound in damages in tort (see also the subsequent decision of the Court of Appeal in *Greenfield v Irwin (A Firm)* [2001] 1 WLR 1279).

An issue left unresolved by *McFarlane* concerned the problem of parents who, in similar circumstances, end up with a disabled child. This matter was subsequently considered in *Parkinson v St James and Seacroft University Hospital NHS Trust* [2001] 3 WLR 376, in which, after usefully analysing the diverse speeches in *McFarlane*, the Court of Appeal concluded that the additional costs associated with the child's disability were recoverable. As Brooke LJ commented:

Brooke LJ: (i) For the reasons given by Waller LJ in *Emeh*, the birth of a child with congenital abnormalities was a foreseeable consequence of the surgeon's careless failure to clip a Fallopian tube effectively; (ii) There was a very limited group of people who might be affected by this negligence: viz Mrs P and her husband (and, in theory, any other man with whom she had had sexual intercourse before she realised that she had not been effectively sterilised); (iii) There is no difficulty in principle in accepting the proposition that the surgeon should be deemed to have assumed responsibility for the foreseeable and disastrous economic consequences of performing his services negligently; (iv) The purpose of the operation was to prevent Mrs P from conceiving any more children, including children with congenital abnormalities, and the surgeon's duty of care is strictly related to the proper fulfilment of that purpose; (v) Parents in Mrs P's position were entitled to recover damages in these circumstances for 15 years between the decisions in *Emeh* and *McFarlane*, so that this is not a radical step forward into the unknown; (vi) For the reasons set out in (i) and (ii) above, Lord Bridge's tests of foreseeability and proximity are satisfied, and for the reasons given by the Supreme Court of Florida in *Fassoulas [v Ramey* (1984) 450 So 2d 822], an award of compensation which is limited to the special upbringing costs associated with rearing a child with a serious disability would be fair, just and reasonable; (vii) If principles of distributive justice are called in aid, I believe that ordinary people would consider that it would be fair for the law to make an award in such a case, provided that it is limited to the extra expenses associated with the child's disability. I can see nothing in any majority reasoning in *McFarlane* to deflect this court from adopting this course, which in my judgment both logic and justice demands.

(The case of *Emeh v Kensington and Chelsea AHA*, referred to by Brooke LJ, is discussed below in Chapter 8.)

In another case following *McFarlane*, that of *Rees v Darlington Memorial Hospital NHS Trust* [2002] 2 All ER 177, a majority of the Court of Appeal (Robert Walker and Hale LJJ, Waller LJ dissenting) held that, similarly, a *disabled mother* who gave birth to a healthy child was entitled to recover the extra costs of child care arising out of her disability. This decision was subsequently taken on appeal by the NHS trust to a specially constituted seven-judge House of Lords.

Rees v Darlington Memorial Hospital NHS Trust [2003] UKHL 52, HL (Lords Bingham, Nicholls, Steyn, Hope, Hutton, Millett and Scott)

Ms Rees underwent a sterilisation, due, *inter alia*, to her concern that her severe visual disability would prevent her from being able to care for a child. The operation was performed negligently and she subsequently became pregnant and gave birth to a healthy son. Essentially, the House of Lords was required to consider three points: (i) should it affirm the the principle it had laid down four years before in *McFarlane* that damages would not lie for the maintenance of (healthy) children? If so: (iia) did a case, such as this one, involving a disabled parent, comprise an exception to that principle, as *per* the decision of the majority of the Court of Appeal? And, albeit an *obiter* issue: (iib) had the Court of Appeal been right, in the *Parkinson* case, to treat cases of disabled children as an exception to the *McFarlane* principle?

As to the first point, all seven Law Lords upheld the correctness of the decision in *McFarlane*. In his speech Lord Bingham commented on this aspect as follows:

Lord Bingham: [15] In *McFarlane*'s case, your Lordships' House held unanimously that a negligent doctor is not required to meet the cost of bringing up a healthy child born in these circumstances. The language, and to some extent the legal reasoning, employed by each of their Lordships differed. But, however expressed, the underlying perception of all their Lordships was that fairness and reasonableness do not require that the damages payable by a negligent doctor should extend so far. The approach usually adopted in measuring recoverable financial loss is not appropriate when the subject of the legal wrong is the birth of an unintended healthy child and the head of claim is the cost of the whole of the child's upbringing.

[16] I have heard nothing in the submissions advanced on the present appeal to persuade me that this decision by the House was wrong and ought to be revisited. On the contrary, that the negligent doctor or, in most cases, the National Health Service should pay all the costs of bringing up the child seems to me a disproportionate response to the doctor's wrong. It would accord ill with the values society attaches to human life and to parenthood. The birth of a child should not be treated as comparable to a parent suffering a personal injury, with the cost of rearing the child being treated as special damages akin to the financially adverse consequences flowing from the onset of a chronic medical condition.

On the other hand, a 'gloss' on *McFarlane* was approved by a majority of their Lordships (over the dissents of Lords Steyn and Hope), in the form of permitting a 'conventional award' of £15,000 in such cases to reflect the legal wrong done to claimants in having their wishes to stay childless thwarted.

As to the other issues, the House of Lords reversed, by a bare majority (Lords Steyn, Hope and Hutton dissenting), the decision of the Court of Appeal to award Ms Rees the extra costs of maintaining her healthy child in this case: in short, she was entitled to the £15,000 conventional sum, but nothing more. As to the final, *obiter* question of the position in relation to disabled children, this was left unresolved. Lords Bingham and Nicholls were of the view that here too only the conventional sum should lie, and disapproved the contrary decision of the Court of Appeal in *Parkinson*. By contrast, Lords Steyn, Hope and Hutton supported the recovery of extra costs attributable to maintaining a disabled child (albeit in the context of their dissenting view that a disabled parent should also recover). The two remaining Law Lords, Millett and Scott, left the question open.

In his speech, the latter Law Lord addressed the various points as follows:

Lord Scott: [139] In my opinion ... it is important to recognise that the conclusion [in the *McFarlane* case] is not that which the normal application of established tortious damages principles would lead to. It is an exception based upon a recognition of the unique nature of human life, a uniqueness that our culture and society recognise and that the law, too, should recognise ...

[143] The majority in the Court of Appeal treated [the present] case as justifying, on account of the mother's blindness, an exception to *McFarlane*'s case. An exception to an exception is apt to produce messy jurisprudence and for all the reasons so cogently expressed by Waller LJ in his dissenting judgment in the Court of Appeal, the creation of an exception in the present case would lead to further exceptions. The exception that *McFarlane*'s case constitutes is based on a recognition of the uniqueness of a human being. The principle on which *McFarlane*'s case is based cannot be limited to the particular circumstances peculiar to that particular case and I do not think the mother's disability in the present case can justify a departure from the basis on which *McFarlane*'s case was decided. I suspect that underlying the majority decision in the Court of Appeal lies the thought that *McFarlane*'s case was wrong and a desire to limit its effect as much as possible. In my opinion, however, *McFarlane*'s case was correctly decided and the basis of the decision should be applied in the present case.

[144] I should mention *Parkinson v St James and Seacroft University Hospital NHS Trust* [2001] EWCA Civ 530, [2001] 3 All ER 97, [2002] QB 266. In Parkinson's case a

sterilisation operation on the claimant was negligently performed. As a result the claimant conceived when she thought, and hoped, she was unable to do so. She declined to have her pregnancy terminated although warned that the child might be born with a disability. The child was born with severe disabilities. The claimant claimed damages for negligence. The Court of Appeal, following *McFarlane*'s case up to a point, held that she was entitled to recover damages for the costs of providing for her child's special needs relating to his disabilities but was not entitled to recover the basic costs of his ordinary maintenance.

[145] The question how the *McFarlane* principle should be applied to a case in which the mother is healthy but the child is born with a disability is not one which needs to be resolved on this appeal. In my opinion, however, a distinction may need to be drawn between a case where the avoidance of the birth of a child with a disability is the very reason why the parent or parents sought the medical treatment or services to avoid conception that, in the event, were negligently provided and a case where the medical treatment or services were sought simply to avoid conception. *Parkinson*'s case was a case in the latter category. In such a case, where the parents have had no particular reason to fear that if a child is born to them it will suffer from a disability, I do not think there is any sufficient basis for treating the expenses occasioned by the disability as falling outside the principles underlying *McFarlane*'s case. The striking of the balance between the burden of rearing the disabled child and the benefit to the parents of the child as a member of their family seems to me as invidious and impossible as in the case of the child born without any disability.

As Lord Scott points out, the disability suffered by the child in the *Parkinson* case was incidental to the hospital's negligence – the medical procedure there was designed to render the claimant sterile, not because she was at any special risk of having a disabled child, but simply for family planning purposes. However, as his Lordship recognises, another possible scenario is that the specific purpose of the procedure, whose negligent performance is the subject of a claim, was to avoid the birth of a disabled child. An example is *Hardman v Amin* [2000] Lloyd's Rep Med 498, where the defendant negligently failed to diagnose the claimant's rubella, thereby depriving her of the opportunity to have an abortion (which, it was accepted, she would have taken).

It is submitted that recovery should be permitted in the latter type of ('direct disability') case. In this regard it is interesting to note that, in several such cases, the lower courts have awarded quite generous damages to cover the child's maintenance, not simply the extra costs attendant upon its disability (besides *Hardman*, see *Nunnerley v Warrington HA* [2000] PIQR Q69 and *Lee v Taunton and Somerset NHS Trust* [2001] 1 FLR 419; but cf *Rand v East Dorset HA* [2000] Lloyd's Rep Med 181). The issue in relation to 'incidental disability' is by contrast more finely balanced.

The duty to third parties

Interesting questions arise as to how far a doctor will owe a duty to third parties to whom he personally offers no medical care at all. Two broad types of scenario require to be considered. The first ('dangerous patient cases') is where the third party is injured in a foreseeable way through subsequent contact with one of the doctor's patients. The second ('injured patient cases') is where the third party – typically a close relative – suffers secondary harm through the negligence of the doctor in harming the patient.

Dangerous patient cases

Suppose that a doctor fails to spot that one of his patients is carrying a contagious disease, and the latter subsequently passes on the infection: does the person he infects have any right of action against the doctor? As a general rule, and in accordance with established principles of tort, a person (A)'s liability for injury caused by another (B) to a third party (C) has tended to depend upon two factors: first, the extent to which B is an involuntary agent in the events which lead to C's injury; and, secondly, the ability on A's part to foresee C's presence in relation to B. Both factors appear to have played a part in the rejection by the Court of Appeal of the claimant's action in the case of *Palmer v Tees HA* [1999] Lloyd's Rep Med 351:

Palmer v Tees HA [1999] Lloyd's Rep Med 351, CA (Stuart-Smith, Pill and Thorpe LJJ)

Mrs Palmer, whose four year old daughter, Rosie, was murdered by a psychopath called Armstrong, brought an action against the defendant health authority both in her own name (in respect of the psychiatric illness she suffered) and on behalf of Rosie's estate. Some months prior to committing the murder Armstrong had been treated as an outpatient at the defendant's psychiatric hospital, where he had allegedly told staff that he would kill a child:

> **Stuart-Smith LJ**: Was the judge right to hold that on the facts there was no proximity between the defendants and Rosie or the claimant? Basing himself on the *Dorset Yacht* case and *Hill*'s case the judge held that:
>
>> ... in cases where it is alleged that a defendant by his negligence is responsible for the actions of a third party it must be shown that the victim or injured person was one who came into a special or exceptional or distinctive category of risk from the activities of the third party. It is not sufficient to show that the victim or injured party was one of a wide category of members of the general public.
>
> He held that the potential victim was not identified or identifiable. In the court below Mr Sherman argued that the fact that Rosie and the claimant lived in the same street as Armstrong was sufficient to establish proximity. But he did not rely on this argument before us. Instead he challenged the judge's conclusion stated in the last paragraph. He submitted that in cases of personal injury, it was sufficient that the injury was foreseeable. He relied upon the two passages already cited in paragraphs 16 and 17 above from Lord Oliver's speech in *Caparo* [[1990] 2 AC 605] and Lord Steyn's speech in *Marc Rich* [[1996] AC 211] approving Saville LJ. But in my opinion the judges, in making those statements, did not have in mind the situation which exists here where there is the interposition of the conscious and voluntary act of a third party ...
>
> [T]he critical decision is that of *Hill v Chief Constable of West Yorkshire* [1989] 1 AC 53 which is a case concerned with personal injury ...
>
> While there are of course differences between *Hill*'s case and the present, that was a case of the police and not psychiatrists, and the identity of the offender was unknown, the crucial point is that there is no relationship between the defendant and the victim. Mr Sherman relied on the case of *Holgate v Lancashire Mental Hospital Board* [1937] 4 All ER 19. The facts bear a striking resemblance to those in the present case. L was a defective who had been convicted of serious crimes and sentenced to detention during His Majesty's pleasure. In due course he was transferred to the defendant's

institution. He was allowed out on licence without any proper inquiry being made, and the licence was subsequently extended. During the period of his extended licence L visited the plaintiff's house and savagely assaulted her. The action was tried by a jury and the report contains the summing-up of Lewis J. It appears to have been assumed that the defendant owed a duty of care to the claimant. The summing-up is concerned only with the issue of want of care. It can be said that this decision received some qualified support from Lord Morris in the *Dorset Yacht* case (see [[1970] AC 1004], 1040–41) and even more qualified support from Lord Reid (1031H). But Lord Diplock reserved his opinion as to its correctness. The other two members of the House did not mention it. The case occurred at a time when the essential elements of a duty of care were much less clearly defined than is the position today. In my judgment the case cannot be reconciled with *Hill* on the question of proximity. Mr Sherman referred to a number of American cases. In *Peterson v State of Washington* (1983) 671 Pacific Reports 2nd Series 230, the Supreme Court of Washington held in somewhat similar circumstances that a duty was owed to an unidentified and unidentifiable victim. But the case proceeds on the premise that it is sufficient that there is a special relationship between the defendant and either the third party or the foreseeable victims. In English law it is plainly not sufficient that this relationship exists only between the defendant and third party, Armstrong in this case ...

An additional reason why in my judgment in this case it is at least necessary for the victim to be identifiable (though as I have indicated it may not be sufficient) to establish proximity, is that it seems to me that the most effective way of providing protection would be to give warning to the victim, his or her parents or social services so that some protective measure can be made. As Mr Moon pointed out, the ability to restrict and restrain a psychiatric patient is subject to considerable restriction under the Mental Health Act 1983 (see particularly section 3) and are not unlimited in time. Moreover treatment, especially drug treatment of the patient, depends on his or her co-operation when an out-patient, and is limited when an in-patient. It may be a somewhat novel approach to the question of proximity, but it seems to me to be a relevant consideration to ask what the defendant have done to avoid the danger, if the suggested precautions, *ie* committal under section 3 of the Mental Health Act or treatment are likely to be of doubtful effectiveness, and the most effective precaution cannot be taken because the defendant does not know who to warn.

Injured patient cases

It is readily apparent that, where a patient is injured or dies as a result of a doctor's negligence, this will have a knock-on effect upon others, in particular the patient's next of kin. The question of the duty of care in the context of breaking bad news to relatives was one of the issues considered by the Court of Appeal in *Powell and Another v Boldaz and Others* (1997) 39 BMLR 35, where a young boy died after a failure to diagnose Addison's disease:

Stuart-Smith LJ: I turn then to consider whether the pleaded post-death matters can give rise to an action for negligence ... Mr Powers submits that the duty of care arises under the principles enunciated by Lord Bridge of Harwich in *Caparo Industries plc v Dickman* [1990] 2 AC 605, pp 616E–18F, namely where the following three elements are present:

(a) foreseeability of damage arising from the relevant act or omission;

(b) a sufficient relationship of proximity between the parties;

(c) as a matter of legal policy it is fair, just and reasonable that a duty of care should exist.

I propose to consider first whether a sufficient relationship of proximity existed. It must be appreciated that prior to 17 April 1990, although the plaintiffs were patients of the defendants in the sense that they were on their register, the only patient who was seeking medical advice and treatment was Robert. It was to him that the defendants owed a duty of care. The discharge of that duty in the case of a young child will often involve giving advice and instruction to the parents so that they can administer the appropriate medication, observe relevant symptoms and seek further medical assistance if need be. In giving such advice, the doctor obviously owes a duty to be careful. But the duty is owed to the child, not to the parents. As Lord Diplock said in *Sidaway v Governors of Bethlem Royal Hospital* [1985] AC 871, p 890:

> ... a doctor's duty of care, whether he be a general practitioner or consulting surgeon or physician, is owed to that patient and none other, idiosyncrasies and all.

> ... I do not think that a doctor who has been treating a patient who has died, who tells relatives what has happened, thereby undertakes the doctor-patient relationship towards the relatives. It is a situation that calls for sensitivity, tact and discretion, but the mere fact that the communicator is a doctor, does not, without more, mean that he undertakes the doctor-patient relationship. It is of course possible that the doctor in such a situation may realise that the shock has been so great that some immediate therapy is needed, but even so this situation is probably more akin to the doctor giving emergency treatment to an accident victim, though no doubt it will be a question of fact and degree in each case whether doctor-patient relationships came into existence by the doctor undertaking to treat and heal the person as a patient.

Nonetheless, it is apparent that, where they actually witness the harm occur, relatives may claim as secondary victims of psychiatric injury, subject to satisfying the control mechanisms laid down by the House of Lords in *Alcock v Chief Constable of South Yorkshire Police* [1992] 1 AC 310. In *Allin v City and Hackney HA* [1996] 7 Med LR 167, a woman recovered damages for post-traumatic stress disorder caused by being told (falsely) that her baby was dead. More recently, in *North Glamorgan NHS Trust v Walters* [2002] EWCA 1792, a series of events, which began when the respondent awoke to find her 10-month-old son suffering a seizure and ended with his life-support being terminated some 36 hours later, was held to be a single 'shocking event', entitling her to recover for her pathological grief reaction. Ward LJ held:

> **Ward LJ:** [34] In my judgment the law as presently formulated does permit a realistic view being taken from case to case of what constitutes the necessary 'event'. Our task is not to construe the word as if it had appeared in legislation but to gather the sense of the word in order to inform the principle to be drawn from the various authorities ... It is a matter of judgment from case to case depending on the facts and circumstance of each case. In my judgment on the facts of this case there was an inexorable progression from the moment when the fit occurred as a result of the failure of the hospital properly to diagnose and then to treat the baby, the fit causing the brain damage which shortly thereafter made termination of this child's life inevitable and the dreadful climax when the child died in her arms. It is a seamless tale with an obvious beginning and an equally obvious end. It was played out over a period of 36 hours, which for her both at the time and as subsequently recollected was undoubtedly one drawn-out experience.

By contrast, recovery has been denied in cases where, rather than a shock, there is a 'dawning realisation' that one's next of kin will die. Thus, in *Sion v Hampstead HA* [1994] 5 Med LR 170, the court rejected the claim of a father whose psychiatric injury was caused by watching his son die over a two-week period (see also *Ward v Leeds Teaching Hospitals NHS Trust* [2004] Lloyd's Rep Med 530).

Finally, albeit in a rather different context, it should be noted that, on grounds of public policy, a doctor will not owe a duty of care to parents in cases where he mistakenly diagnoses child abuse on their part (leading, for example, to the child's temporary removal). As the House of Lords recently held in *JD v East Berkshire Community Health NHS Trust* [2005] UKHL 23, the doctor, provided he acts in good faith, should not be inhibited in the course of his investigations by the prospect of such possible liability: his duty is owed to the child alone.

Who to sue?

Individual doctors (with the exception of GPs) and nurses are unlikely to be sued directly by the injured patient. A legal claim will normally be made against the health professional's employer, who will be vicariously liable. This assumes that the negligent doctor or nurse was an employee and was acting in the course of his or her employment. The Department of Health has produced special guidance on handling clinical negligence claims against NHS staff:

> **Department of Health, *NHS Indemnity – Arrangements for Negligence Claims in the NHS*, Catalogue No 96 HR 0024, 1996, London: DoH:**
>
> **Purpose of this document**
>
> This document describes the arrangements which apply to handling clinical negligence claims against NHS staff (NHS Indemnity). It updates the guidance given in Health Circular HC (89) 34 ...
>
> **Clinical negligence**
>
> Clinical negligence is defined as:
>
>> ... a breach of duty of care by members of the health care professions employed by NHS bodies or by others consequent on decisions or judgments made by members of those professions acting in their professional capacity in the course of their employment, and which are admitted as negligent by the employer or are determined as such through the legal process.
>
> The term health care professional includes hospital doctors, dentists, nurses, midwives, health visitors, pharmacy practitioners, registered ophthalmic or dispensing opticians (working in a hospital setting), members of professions allied to medicine and dentistry, ambulance personnel, laboratory staff and relevant technicians.
>
> **Main principles**
>
> NHS bodies are vicariously liable for the negligent acts and omissions of their employees and should have arrangements for meeting this liability.
>
> NHS Indemnity applies where:
>
> (a) the negligent health care professional was:
>
>> (i) working under a contract of employment and the negligence occurred in the course of that employment;
>>
>> (ii) not working under a contract of employment but was contracted to an NHS body to provide services to persons to whom that NHS body owed a duty of care;
>>
>> (iii) neither of the above but otherwise owed a duty of care to the persons injured;

(b) persons, not employed under a contract of employment and who may or may not be a health care professional, who owe a duty of care to the persons injured. These include locums; medical academic staff with honorary contracts; students; those conducting clinical trials; charitable volunteers; persons undergoing further professional education, training and examinations; students and staff working on income generation projects.

Where these principles apply, NHS bodies should accept full financial liability where negligent harm has occurred, and not seek to recover their costs from the health care professional involved.

Who is not covered

NHS Indemnity does not apply to family health service practitioners working under contracts for services, for example: GPs (including fundholders), general dental practitioners, family dentists, pharmacists or optometrists; other self-employed health care professionals, for example, independent midwives; employees of FHS practices; employees of private hospitals; local education authorities; voluntary agencies ...

Circumstances covered

NHS Indemnity covers negligent harm caused to patients or healthy volunteers in the following circumstances: whenever they are receiving an established treatment, whether or not in accordance with an agreed guideline or protocol; whenever they are receiving a novel or unusual treatment which, in the judgment of the health care professional, is appropriate for that particular patient; whenever they are subjects as patients or healthy volunteers of clinical research aimed at benefiting patients now or in the future.

In the case of a patient whose treatment is 'farmed out' to a private hospital (an increasing expedient in the drive to cut waiting lists), it is apparent, following *M v Calderdale and Kirklees HA* [1998] Lloyd's Rep 157, that the referring NHS institution remains under a non-delegable duty of care in respect of such treatment.

In certain circumstances the hospital or health authority may be directly liable to the patient in negligence; in *Wilsher v Essex AHA* [1986] 3 All ER 801, the Court of Appeal suggested that such liability would arise if it were shown that the hospital authorities had filled treatment positions with staff who were unable (through inexperience or otherwise) to cope with the demands made upon them. Direct liability will also arise where the claimant's injury is attributable to some overall failure, of an organisational nature, to provide a safe environment for carrying out treatment. In *Bull v Devon AHA* [1993] 4 Med LR 117, one of the claimant's twins was born brain damaged due to the delay in getting the registrar to attend her. The defendants maintained maternity services on two sites and the system for calling him over to effect delivery had broken down.

Liability of the Department of Health

Could the Department of Health and the Secretary of State be held to owe a duty of care to an injured claimant, in so far as the injury is alleged to be the consequence of some failure at the level of national policy making? Clearly, given the nature of the discretion given to the Secretary of State in fulfilling his duties under s 3 of the National Health Services Act 1977, it will be very hard to sustain an action in negligence. Indeed, if any action is to lie, it might be thought to do so only in judicial review (on the latter, see Chapter 2). Nevertheless, in the case of *Re HIV Haemophiliac*

Litigation [1990] NLJR 1349, the Court of Appeal was not prepared to reject the possibility of a negligence action out of hand. The claimants were a group of haemophiliacs who were infected with the HIV virus after being treated with infected blood products from the USA. They claimed that the failure by the Secretary of State to provide for UK self-sufficiency in blood supplies had been negligent. The action only concerned the preliminary question of whether discovery (requiring the Department of Health to make its internal documents available to the claimants) should be ordered:

> **Bingham LJ**: Mr Andrew Collins QC for the Department ... pointed out, relying on recent authority, that there is no close precedent for such a claim as the present, which differs in nature and scale from the negligence actions with which the courts customarily deal. Furthermore, he argued, the plaintiffs' complaints relate to matters within areas of political and administrative discretion which the courts are incompetent to evaluate (save, where *vires* are in issue, on applications for judicial review). There were, he said, by analogy with *Hill v Chief Constable of West Yorkshire* [1989] AC 53, strong reasons of public policy (or justice and reasonableness) for not holding a minister and department exercising public functions for the benefit of the community as a whole to owe a duty of care towards individual members of the public.
>
> These are points properly and responsibly argued and they may ultimately prevail, but on the necessarily brief arguments which we have heard at this stage I am not at present satisfied that they must do so.

Latterly, in *Danns and Another v Department of Health* [1998] PIQR P226, the Department of Health was sued for not passing on the risks of late recanalisation of the vas in male sterilisation to a patient whose partner became pregnant after the operation. The Department was aware of this risk after a reported academic study but decided not to publicise the findings generally in the media. The plaintiff alleged that it was negligent in not doing so. However, the action failed *inter alia* on the ground that there was, in fact, no duty of care owed by the Department:

> **Leggatt LJ**: Mr Cartwright sought to support his submission that the Department was negligent, by looking to the component parts of the tort and contending that there was foreseeability, because it must have been obvious that there could be health consequences from an unexpected pregnancy, as well as proximity on the basis that the reliance of the general public on the Department was also obvious. He sought to reinforce that aspect by inviting attention to the recent case of *Munroe Ltd v London Fire Authority* [1996] 4 All ER 318 ... in which (p 329) Rougier J was contrasting the position of the London Fire Authority with a hospital. He said, p 329D:
>
> > I consider that against the background of the highly personal element involved in 'adequate medical care', proximity has effectively been imposed upon hospital authorities by the statute. In obedience to that statute, they hold themselves out as being prepared to assume responsibility for the sick and injured. Patients are invited in, whether to the ward or the casualty department, and are entitled to rely upon the hospital assuming responsibility for them.
>
> It seems to me that that kind of proximity is itself to be contrasted in the present context with the position of the Department, which is, indisputably, incomparably more remote from the patient than is the casualty department of a hospital.

See also *Smith v Secretary of State for Health (On Behalf of the Committee on Safety of Medicines)* [2002] EWHC 200, in which Morland J held that the Committee's decision to delay issuing a public warning on the possible link between aspirin and Reye's Syndrome in children was not justiciable in negligence.

THE BREACH OF DUTY

The standard of care

The ordinary professional

The first point to note is that the standard of care against which the doctor will be judged is not going to be that of the ordinary reasonable man who enjoys no medical expertise. Instead, in holding himself out as possessing the special skills of his profession, the doctor is under a duty to conform to the ordinary standards of that profession. In *Bolam v Friern Hospital Management Committee* [1957] 1 WLR 582, McNair J put this point as follows:

> **McNair J**: How do you test whether [an] act or failure is negligent? In an ordinary case it is generally said that you judge that by the action of the man in the street. He is the ordinary man. In one case it has been said that you judge it by the conduct of the man on the top of a Clapham omnibus. He is the ordinary man. But where you get a situation which involves the use of some special skill or competence, then the test whether there has been negligence or not is not the test of the man on the top of the Clapham omnibus, because he has not got this special skill. The test is the standard of the ordinary skilled man exercising and professing to have that special skill. A man need not possess the highest expert skill at the risk of being found negligent. It is well established law that it is sufficient if he exercises the ordinary skill of an ordinary competent man exercising that particular art.

It is further apparent, however, that doctors will not be treated as an homogenous group in this context. Referring to the case of *Hunter v Hanley* (1955) SC 200, Lord Bridge stated in *Sidaway v Governors of Bethlem Royal Hospital* [1985] 1 All ER 1018:

> **Lord Bridge:** The language of the *Bolam* test clearly requires a different degree of skill from a specialist in his own special field than from a general practitioner. In the field of neuro-surgery it would be necessary to substitute for Lord President Clyde's phrase 'no doctor of ordinary skill', the phrase 'no neuro-surgeon of ordinary skill'.

What does 'ordinary skill' mean here? Might the case be difficult, so that a neuro-surgeon of special skill might be needed? If so, would there be negligence if such a neuro-surgeon were not used, and, would the negligence be in breach of the health authority's primary duty of care, or would the 'ordinary' neuro-surgeon be in breach?

The ordinary professional will be expected to keep his knowledge reasonably up-to-date. What counts as 'reasonable' in this context will again vary with the doctor's degree of specialisation. The doctor is not required to read every article in the medical press. In *Crawford v Board of Governors of Charing Cross Hospital* (1953) *The Times*, 8 December, the Court of Appeal found that there had been no breach of duty when an operative procedure was performed resulting in paralysis, which some months previously had been the subject of an isolated report in *The Lancet*. Nonetheless, the doctor should certainly keep abreast of the most significant developments in his field: see *Gascoine v Ian Sheridan and Co (A Firm) and Latham* [1994] 5 Med LR 437.

Junior doctors

A particular difficulty arises in relation to the level of skill expected of junior medical staff who, *ex hypothesi*, will lack the experience of the ordinary competent doctor. Here, the courts have felt obliged to follow the reasoning in *Nettleship v Weston* [1971] 3 All ER 581, in which a learner driver was held to be subject to the same standard of care as the reasonably competent and experienced driver. This principle was stated in the early medical negligence case of *Jones v Manchester Corp* [1952] 2 All ER 125, where a patient died after the maladministration of anaesthetic by a doctor qualified for only five months. It was said that 'errors due to inexperience are no defence'.

There is an understandably pragmatic aspect to this approach. Courts do not want to apply a sliding scale of standards of care depending upon the subjective attributes of the particular defendant. The liability of junior doctors was one of the issues that fell to be considered by the Court of Appeal in *Wilsher v Essex AHA* [1987] QB 730.

Wilsher v Essex AHA [1987] QB 730, CA (Sir Nicolas Browne-Wilkinson VC, Glidewell and Mustill LJJ)

The plaintiff was a premature baby who was treated in the defendant's ante-natal unit. He was given oxygen by two doctors, both inexperienced. They inserted the catheter through which the oxygen was to be administered, into a vein rather than an artery. This is, apparently, a common mistake and was not due to negligence. The position of the catheter can be checked by use of an x-ray. The doctors, however, failed to notice the mistake, and the senior registrar checking their work also failed to notice. The majority of the Court of Appeal confirmed that there should be a uniform standard of care:

> **Glidewell LJ**: In my view, the law requires the trainee or learner to be judged by the same standard as his more experienced colleagues. If it did not, inexperience would frequently be urged as a defence to an action for professional negligence.
>
> If this test appears unduly harsh in relation to the inexperienced, I should add that, in my view, the inexperienced doctor called upon to exercise a specialist skill will, as part of that skill, seek the advice and help of his superiors when he does or may need it. If he does seek such help, he will often have satisfied the test, even though he may himself have made a mistake. It is for this reason that I agree that Dr Wiles was not negligent. He made a mistake in inserting the catheter into a vein, and a second mistake in not recognising the signs that he had done so on the x-ray. But, having done what he thought right, he asked Dr Kawa, the senior registrar, to check what he had done, and Dr Kawa did so. Dr Kawa failed to recognise the indication on the x-ray ...

As this makes clear, junior doctors are entitled to expect their work to be checked, and, on the facts of the case, were found not to be liable (although the registrar was); indeed, the court suggested that a hospital could be primarily liable if it failed to have a proper system for inspecting the work of junior staff.

Mustill LJ commented as follows on the argument that there should be a subjective standard of care dependent upon the doctor's experience:

> **Mustill LJ**: To my mind, this notion of a duty tailored to the actor, rather than to the act which he elects to perform, has no place in the law of tort. Indeed, the defendants

did not contend that it could be justified by any reported authority on the general law of tort. Instead, it was suggested that the medical profession is a special case. Public hospital medicine has always been organised so that young doctors and nurses learn on the job. If the hospitals abstained from using inexperienced people, they could not staff their wards and theatres, and the junior staff could never learn. The longer term interests of patients as a whole are best served by maintaining the present system, even if this may diminish the legal rights of the individual patient: for, after all, medicine is about curing, not litigation.

I acknowledge the appeal of this argument, and recognise that a young hospital doctor, who must get on to the wards in order to qualify without necessarily being able to decide what kind of patient he is going to meet, is not in the same position as another professional man who has a real choice whether or not to practise in a particular field. Nevertheless, I cannot accept that there should be a special rule for doctors in public hospitals – I emphasise public, since presumably those employed in private hospitals would be in a different category. Doctors are not the only people who gain their experience, not only from lectures or from watching others perform, but from tackling live clients or customers, and no case was cited to us which suggested that any such variable duty of care was imposed on others in a similar position. To my mind, it would be a false step to subordinate the legitimate expectation of the patient that he will receive from each person concerned with his care a degree of skill appropriate to the task which he undertakes, to an understandable wish to minimise the psychological and financial pressures on hard-pressed young doctors.

However, his Lordship arguably muddied the waters by introducing the notion that one could ascertain the standard of care by reference to the 'post' that the doctor held:

Mustill LJ: For my part, I prefer [the proposition which] relates the duty of care not to the individual, but to the post which he occupies. I would differentiate 'post' from 'rank' or 'status'. In a case such as the present, the standard is not just that of the averagely competent and well informed junior houseman (or whatever the position of the doctor) but of such a person who fills a post in a unit offering a highly specialised service. But, even so, it must be recognised that different posts make different demands. If it is borne in mind that the structure of hospital medicine envisages that the lower ranks will be occupied by those of whom it would be wrong to expect too much, the risk of abuse by litigious patients can be mitigated, if not entirely eliminated.

What is the difference between this and the assessment (which the court will refuse to undertake) of junior doctors by reference to reasonable doctors with the same limited experience? The answer would seem to lie in the existence of a minimum standard attaching to each 'post', below which no doctor, however new to the job, can fall.

For his part, Sir Nicolas Browne-Wilkinson VC, who dissented from the majority view, stated:

Browne-Wilkinson VC: ... one of the chief hazards of inexperience is that one does not always know the risks which exist. In my judgment, so long as the English law rests liability on personal fault, a doctor who has properly accepted a post in a hospital in order to gain necessary experience should only be held liable for acts or omissions which a careful doctor with his qualifications and experience would not have done or omitted.

(The case subsequently went to the House of Lords on the issue of causation: see further p 314, below.)

Emergencies

An exception to the principle, that a doctor will be judged according to the standard of reasonably experienced doctors in their field, is provided by emergency treatment. Michael Jones has commented as follows on the level of experience expected in the latter context:

Jones, M, *Medical Negligence*, 1996, London: Sweet & Maxwell, p 135:

In an emergency it may well be reasonable for a practitioner inexperienced in a particular treatment to intervene, or indeed for someone lacking medical qualifications to undertake some forms of treatment. For example, a bystander who renders assistance at a road accident does not necessarily hold himself out as qualified to do so. He would be expected to achieve only the standard that could reasonably be expected in the circumstances, which would probably be very low. This approach is clearly borne of the emergency since if there was no urgency, the unqualified person who undertakes treatment which is beyond his competence would be held to the standard to be expected of the reasonably competent and experienced practitioner. A person who holds himself out as trained in first aid must conform to the standards of 'the ordinary skilled first aider exercising and professing to have that special skill of a first aider'.

Secondly, in relation to treatment decisions taken in an emergency, a doctor will not be found negligent simply because the reasonably competent doctor would have made a different decision, given more time and information. In the case of *Wilson v Swanson* (1956) 5 DLR (2d) 113, the Supreme Court of Canada held that there was no negligence when a surgeon had to make an immediate decision whether to operate, and the operation was subsequently found to have been unnecessary. Moreover, the skill itself required in the execution of treatment may be somewhat lower. As Mustill LJ commented in the *Wilsher* case:

Mustill LJ: An emergency may overburden the available resources, and, if an individual is forced by circumstances to do too many things at once, the fact that he does one of them incorrectly should not lightly be taken as negligence.

Accepted practice – the *Bolam* test

Development and rationale

In determining whether, in a particular case, a doctor has satisfied the appropriate standard of care, the courts will look in the first place to accepted practice within the profession: has the doctor conducted himself in the manner in which other doctors would have conducted themselves in the same circumstances? Of course, medicine is a developing science and new schools of thought as to how best to carry out treatments are constantly emerging. For this reason, the courts do not expect to find uniformity of standard medical practice in any given case. Rather, they ask whether the doctor has conformed with *an* (note the use of the indefinite article) accepted practice within the profession. This approach informed McNair J's direction to the jury in the famous (or infamous) case of *Bolam v Friern Hospital Management Committee* [1957] 1 WLR 582:

Bolam v Friern Hospital Management Committee [1957] 1 WLR 582 (McNair J)

The plaintiff suffered from clinical depression and it was decided to treat him with electro-convulsive therapy (ECT), which involves passing an electric current through the patient's brain to induce a fit. In the 1950s this was fairly novel treatment and doctors differed as to how best to minimise the risk of the patient suffering bone fractures during the fit. At the hospital where Mr Bolam was treated, a system of manual restraint in which nurses held the patient down, but only by the chin, was in use (two other practices adopted elsewhere involved the use of rigid restraint, and relaxant drugs administered following a general anaesthetic, respectively). Unfortunately, in the plaintiff's case the manual restraint was ineffective and he suffered serious pelvic injuries during treatment:

> McNair J (directing the jury): Counsel for the plaintiff put it in this way, that in the case of a medical man, negligence means failure to act in accordance with the standards of reasonably competent medical men at the time. That is a perfectly accurate statement, as long as it is remembered that there may be one or more perfectly proper standards; and if a medical man confirms with one of those proper standards then he is not negligent. Counsel for the plaintiff was also right, in my judgment, in saying that a mere personal belief that a particular technique is best is no defence unless that belief is based on reasonable grounds. That again is unexceptional. But the emphasis which is laid by counsel for the defendants is on this aspect of negligence: he submitted to you that the real question on which you have to make up your mind on each of the three major points to be considered is whether the defendants, in acting in the way in which they did, were acting in accordance with a practice of competent respected professional opinion ... I myself would ... put it this way: a doctor is not guilty of negligence if he has acted in accordance with a practice accepted as proper by a responsible body of medical men skilled in that particular art.

One factor which appears to have influenced the courts to take a deferential attitude towards accepted medical practice is the fear of otherwise encouraging an explosion of malpractice litigation and an uncongenial climate for doctors to go about their business of treating patients: as Mustill LJ commented in *Wilsher v Essex* AHA [1987] QB 730, 'medicine is about curing, not litigation'. This attitude found its most notorious expression in Lord Denning's suggestion (repeated in a number of cases over the years), that an 'error of clinical judgment' could not amount to negligence, a view finally laid to rest in 1981 in the case of *Whitehouse v Jordan* [1981] 1 All ER 267:

Whitehouse v Jordan [1981] 1 All ER 267, HL (Lords Wilberforce, Edmund-Davies, Fraser, Russell, Bridge)

The plaintiff was born brain damaged, allegedly as a result of the defendant obstetrician's negligence. The latter had made prolonged attempts at normal delivery using forceps before realising this was impossible. The plaintiff, suing by his mother as next friend, argued that the defendant should have moved more quickly to delivery by Caesarean section:

> Lord Edmund-Davies: ... [T]he principal questions calling for decision are: (a) in what manner did Mr Jordan use the forceps? And (b) was that manner consistent with the degree of care which a member of his profession is required by law to exercise? Surprising though it is at this late stage in the development of the law of negligence, counsel for Mr Jordan persisted in submitting that his client should be completely exculpated were the answer to question (b), 'Well, at worst he was guilty of an error of clinical judgment'. My Lords, it is high time that the unacceptability of such an answer be fully exposed. To say that a surgeon committed an error of clinical judgment is wholly ambiguous, for, while some such errors may be completely consistent with the due exercise of professional skill, other acts or omissions in the

course of exercising 'clinical judgment' may be so glaringly below proper standards as to make a finding of negligence inevitable. Indeed, I should have regarded this as a truism were it not that, despite the exposure of the 'false antithesis' by Donaldson LJ in his dissenting judgment in the Court of Appeal, counsel for the defendants adhered to it before your Lordships.

But doctors and surgeons fall into no special category, and, to avoid any future disputation of a similar kind, I would have it accepted that the true doctrine was enunciated, and by no means for the first time, by McNair J in *Bolam v Friern Hospital Management Committee* in the following words, which were applied by the Privy Council in *Chin Keow v Government of Malaysia* [1967] 1 WLR 813:

> ... where you get a situation which involves the use of some special skill or competence, then the test as to whether there has been negligence or not is not the test of the man on the top of a Clapham omnibus because he has not got this special skill. The test is the standard of the ordinary skilled man exercising and professing to have that special skill.

If a surgeon fails to measure up to that standard in any respect ('clinical judgment' or otherwise), he has been negligent and should be so adjudged.

Nevertheless, before finding a negligent error of clinical judgement, the court must be satisfied – on the basis of the opinions of other doctors (acting as expert witnesses) – that no reasonable doctor would have acted as the defendant doctor. Of particular interest in this regard is the judgment of Lord Scarman in another leading case from the 1980s, *Maynard v West Midlands RHA* [1984] 1 WLR 634.

Maynard v West Midlands RHA [1984] 1 WLR 634, HL (Lords Fraser, Elwyn-Jones, Scarman, Roskill, Templeman)

The plaintiff was being treated for a chest complaint. Her consultants believed her probably to be suffering from tuberculosis, but, given also the slight chance that she might have Hodgkin's disease, decided to carry out an exploratory operation, to reach a concluded diagnosis. This confirmed that the plaintiff had tuberculosis, but also (through an inevitable risk materialising without fault on the defendants' part) left her paralysed in one of her vocal cords. At trial, the expert witnesses were divided over whether the decision to perform the operation had been an appropriate one in the circumstances. The trial judge preferred the view of the plaintiff's experts that the risk inherent in it had not been worth taking, and awarded damages. The defendants' appeal was allowed by the Court of Appeal and the matter reached the House of Lords:

> **Lord Scarman:** The present case may be classifiable as one of clinical judgment. Two distinguished consultants, a physician and a surgeon experienced in the treatment of chest diseases, formed a judgment as to what was, in their opinion, in the best interests of their patient. They recommended that tuberculosis was the most likely diagnosis. But in their opinion, there was an unusual factor, viz, swollen glands in the mediastinum unaccompanied by any evidence of lesion in the lungs. Hodgkin's disease, carcinoma, and sarcoidosis were, therefore, possibilities. The danger they thought was Hodgkin's disease; though unlikely, it was, if present, a killer (as treatment was understood in 1970) unless remedial steps were taken in its early stage. They therefore decided on mediastinoscopy, an operative procedure which would provide them with a biopsy from the swollen gland which could be subjected to immediate microscopic examination. It is said that the evidence of tuberculosis was so strong that it was unreasonable and wrong to defer diagnosis and to put their patient to the risks of the operation. The case against them is not mistake or carelessness in

performing the operation which is admitted was properly carried out, but an error of judgment in requiring the operation to be undertaken.

A case which is based on an allegation that a fully considered decision of two consultants in the field of their special skill was negligent clearly presents certain difficulties of proof. It is not enough to show that there is a body of competent professional opinion which considered that theirs was a wrong decision, if there also exists a body of professional opinion, equally competent, which supports the decision as reasonable in the circumstances. It is not enough to show that subsequent events show that the operation need never have been performed, if at the time the decision to operate was taken it was reasonable in the sense that a responsible body of medical opinion would have accepted it as proper.

It may well be wondered if there was not an easier way in which the doctors in *Maynard* could have avoided litigation. In particular, what did they *tell* the patient before they decided to operate? This is not known, because the patient's medical notes were missing for the period during which the doctors made their decision. However, there was no argument advanced that the doctors had discussed the treatment with the patient in terms of risks and alternatives, which would perhaps have resulted in the patient deciding against undergoing what might well prove to be unnecessary surgery.

Subsequently, in *Sidaway v Governors of Bethlem Royal Hospital* [1985] 1 All ER 1018, Lord Scarman articulated the *Bolam* test in the following terms:

Lord Scarman: The *Bolam* principle may be formulated as a rule that a doctor is not negligent if he acts in accordance with a practice accepted at the time as proper by a responsible body of medical opinion even though other doctors adopt a different practice. In short, the law imposes the duty of care, but the standard of care is a matter of medical judgment.

What are the reasons that the courts have for using the *Bolam* test in cases of medical negligence? One has already been mentioned: medicine is recognised as not being an exact science; there may, at any given moment, be two or more perfectly respectable ways of dealing with a particular problem. Indeed one could go further and cite the possibility of competition between different accepted practices as a key element in allowing progress in treatment to be made. *Bolam* itself provides an illustration of this: in the 1950s only one of three schools of thought administered ECT following a general anaesthetic, but nowadays it is invariably done this way. Despite the risks associated with anaesthesia itself, experience ultimately has shown this to be preferable to running the risks of bone fracture associated with either rigid or manual restraint.

Application and scope

Whilst initially confined to assessing matters of diagnosis and treatment, the *Bolam* test became ubiquitous in defining the courts' approach to allegations of malpractice against medical professionals. It will be recalled from Chapter 3 that, in *Sidaway v Governors of Royal Bethlem and Maudsley Hospital* [1985] 1 All ER 1018, the majority of the House of Lords used it as the starting point for determining the standard of care owed by doctor to patient in respect of disclosing risks. Just as controversial was the extension of *Bolam* into areas in which the nature of decision-making by doctors is predominantly ethical rather than medical. These have included, in particular, determinations as to when treatment has been in the best interests of patients who are incompetent. The use of the test for resolving such issues is the subject of further discussion elsewhere (see Chapters 4 and 10–12).

In the past, the highly technical nature of some of the information seemed of itself to provide sufficient warrant for deferring to schools of expert opinion in medical cases. Thus, in the Court of Appeal case of *Dwyer v Roderick* (1983) 127 SJ 805, May LJ stated:

> **May LJ**: It would be to shut one's eyes to the obvious if one denied that the burden of achieving something more than the mere balance of probabilities was greater when one was investigating the complicated and sophisticated actions of a qualified and experienced doctor than when one was inquiring into the inattention of the driver in a simple running down action.

However, it could be argued that the courts were tending too readily to mystify medical matters. As Michael Jones comments:

> **Jones, M, *Medical Negligence*, 1996, London: Sweet & Maxwell, p 106:**
>
> Where the case does not involve difficult or uncertain questions of medical or surgical treatment, or abstruse or highly technical scientific issues, but is concerned with whether obvious and simple precautions could have been taken, the question of the practice of experts should be largely irrelevant. The courts do not rely on expert rally drivers, for example, to say whether a motorist was negligent.
>
> Moreover, before any question of complying with accepted practice can arise the court must be satisfied on the evidence presented to it that there is a responsible body of professional opinion which supports the practice. It is always open to the court to reject expert evidence applying the ordinary principles of credibility that would be applied in any courtroom, for example, that the evidence is internally contradictory, or that the witness was acting as an advocate rather than an impartial and objective expert.

In fact, recently the courts have begun to pay greater attention to the proper circumstances for the application of the test. In the case of *Penney v East Kent HA* [2000] Lloyd's Rep Med 41, it was accepted that where the dispute between the expert witnesses is factual in nature (here whether cervical smear slides showed significant abnormalities), the *Bolam* test in fact has no part to play. As Lord Woolf MR commented:

> **Lord Woolf MR**: ... the *Bolam* test has no application where what the judge is required to do is to make findings of fact. This is so, even where those findings of fact are the subject of conflicting expert evidence. Thus in this case there were three questions which the judge had to answer: What was to be seen in the slides? At the relevant time could a screener exercising reasonable care fail to see what was on the slide? Could a reasonably competent screener, aware of what a screener exercising reasonable care would observe on the slide, treat the slide as negative? Thus, logically the starting point for the experts reasoning was what was on the slides. Except in relation to the slide known as Palmer 2, as to which there was a striking conflict, as a result of a meeting which took place between the experts they were in substantial but by no means total agreement. In so far as they were not in agreement, the judge had the unenviable task of deciding as a matter of fact which of the experts were correct as to what the slides showed. This was a task which required expert evidence. However the evidence having been given, the judge had to make his own finding on the balance of probabilities on this issue of fact in order to proceed to the next step in answering the question of negligence or no negligence. Having come to his own

conclusion as to what the slides showed, the judge had, therefore, then to answer the 2nd and 3rd questions in order to decide whether the screener was in breach of duty in giving a negative report. Whether the screener was in breach of duty would depend on the training and the amount of knowledge a screener should have had in order to properly perform his or her task at that time and how easy it was to discern what the judge had found was on the slide. These issues involved both questions of fact and questions of opinion as to the standards of care which the screeners should have exercised.

(See also *Marriott v West Midlands HA* [1999] Lloyd's Rep Med 23, discussed at p 304, below.)

This more critical approach can be seen as part of a general sea change that has occurred in the courts' attitude towards the *Bolam* test in the past few years. This development is discussed further in the next section.

Impugning accepted practice – 'new Bolam'

In Lord Scarman's judgments in the cases of *Maynard* and *Sidaway* (see p 299, above), the *Bolam* test appeared to be framed in such a way as to make compliance with an accepted practice a complete defence: that is to say, provided a doctor could show that what he had done complied with such a practice, he could never be found negligent. However, this was never regarded universally as the correct interpretation of the test, and it was one rejected especially vociferously by Commonwealth courts. In the case of *F v R* (1983) SASR 189, Bollen J, in the Supreme Court of South Australia, commented as follows:

> **Bollen J:** Many cases require the calling of expert evidence. These experts frequently express opinions on matters within their field. Sometimes they speak of what is usually done in any activity within that field. Why is the evidence received? It is received to guide or help the court. A court cannot be expected to know the correct procedure for performing a surgical operation. The court cannot be expected to know why a manufacturer should guard against metal fatigue. A court cannot be expected to know how to mix chemicals. And so on. Expert evidence will assist the court. But in the end it is the court which must say whether there was a duty owed and a breach of it. The court will have been guided and assisted by the expert evidence. It will not produce an answer merely at the dictation of the expert evidence. It will afford great weight to the expert evidence ... But the court does not merely follow expert evidence slavishly to a decision ... If the court did merely follow the path apparently pointed by expert evidence with no critical consideration of it and the other evidence, it would abdicate its duty to decide, on the evidence, whether in law a duty existed and had not been discharged ...

> ... I can find nothing in *Bolam v Friern Hospital Management Committee* which justifies any suggestion that evidence of the practice obtaining in the medical profession is automatically decisive of any issue in an action against a surgeon for damages in negligence ...

> ... I respectfully think that some of the cases in England have concentrated rather too heavily on the practice of the medical profession.

Note what is said here about deciding on the evidence whether the duty had been breached. It is pointing up what has always been the case: that courts *evaluate* the evidence they hear. The uncritical acceptance of the defendant's evidence alone, even when it is given by the appropriate experts, is the unacceptable interpretation of the *Bolam* test which denies that there is an obligation to evaluate. That English courts, too, ultimately have the power to review an accepted practice and find it wanting, was confirmed by the House of Lords in *Bolitho v City and Hackney HA* [1997] 4 All ER 771, the leading modern authority on the application of the *Bolam* test in relation to medical negligence:

Bolitho v City and Hackney HA [1997] 4 All ER 771, HL (Lords Browne-Wilkinson, Slynn, Nolan, Hoffmann, and Clyde)

The plaintiff two year old was readmitted to hospital on 16 January 1984 after suffering a serious bout of the croup. He had been experiencing breathing difficulties following his earlier discharge on 15 January but, following further treatment, appeared to be progressing satisfactorily. On 17 January he suffered two acute episodes in which his breathing was temporarily obstructed, and on both occasions the nurse observing him summoned the senior paediatric registrar. However, neither the latter nor her senior house officer responded to the calls and the plaintiff subsequently suffered a third episode, which led to cardiac arrest and brain damage.

It was accepted for the defendant that the failure of its doctors to attend the plaintiff amounted to a breach of duty. However, it claimed that, even if they had attended, they would not have instigated the one procedure – intubation – which would have saved him. Although this was a defence based essentially on lack of causation (see further the discussion at p 322, below), to succeed it required the court to accept that the hypothetical failure to intubate in such a case would not itself have been a breach of duty. In this regard, the defendant adduced evidence from a number of expert witnesses to the effect that, faced with a patient exhibiting the plaintiff's history and symptoms, they too would not intubate:

> **Lord Browne-Wilkinson:** ... [I]n my view, the court is not bound to hold that a defendant doctor escapes liability for negligent treatment or diagnosis just because he leads evidence from a number of medical experts who are genuinely of the opinion that the defendant's treatment or diagnosis accorded with sound medical practice. In the *Bolam* case itself, McNair J stated ... that the defendant had to have acted in accordance with the practice accepted as proper by a 'responsible body of medical men'. Later ... he referred to 'a standard of practice recognised as proper by a competent *reasonable* body of opinion'. Again, in the passage which I have cited from *Maynard*'s case, Lord Scarman refers to a 'respectable' body of professional opinion. The use of these adjectives – responsible, reasonable and respectable – all show that the court has to be satisfied that the exponents of the body of opinion relied upon can demonstrate that such opinion has a logical basis. In particular in cases involving, as they so often do, the weighing of risks against benefits, the judge before accepting a body of opinion as being responsible, reasonable or respectable, will need to be satisfied that, in forming their views, the experts have directed their minds to the question of comparative risks and benefits and have reached a defensible conclusion on the matter.

> There are decisions which demonstrate that the judge is entitled to approach expert professional opinion on this basis. For example, in *Hucks v Cole* [1993] 4 Med LR 393 (a case from 1968), a doctor failed to treat with penicillin a patient who was suffering from septic spots on her skin though he knew them to contain organisms capable of leading to puerperal fever. A number of distinguished doctors gave evidence that they would not, in the circumstances, have treated with penicillin. The Court of Appeal found the defendant to have been negligent. Sachs LJ said, at p 397:

When the evidence shows that a lacuna in professional practice exists by which risks of grave danger are knowingly taken, then, however small the risk, the court must anxiously examine that lacuna – particularly if the risk can be easily and inexpensively avoided. If the court finds, on an analysis of the reasons given for not taking those precautions that, in the light of current professional knowledge, there is no proper basis for the lacuna, and that it is definitely not reasonable that those risks should have been taken, its function is to state that fact and where necessary to state that it constitutes negligence. In such a case the practice will no doubt thereafter be altered to the benefit of patients. On such occasions the fact that other practitioners would have done the same thing as the defendant practitioner is a very weighty matter to be put on the scales on his behalf; but it is not, as Mr Webster readily conceded, conclusive. The court must be vigilant to see whether the reasons given for putting a patient at risk are valid in the light of any well-known advance in medical knowledge, or whether they stem from a residual adherence to out-of-date ideas.

Again, in *Edward Wong Finance Co Ltd v Johnson Stokes and Master* [1984] 1 AC 296, the defendant's solicitors had conducted the completion of a mortgage transaction in 'Hong Kong style' rather than in the old fashioned English style. Completion in Hong Kong style provides for money to be paid over against an undertaking by the solicitors for the borrowers subsequently to hand over the executed documents. This practice opened the gateway through which a dishonest solicitor for the borrower absconded with the loan money without providing the security for such loan. The Privy Council held that even though completion in Hong Kong style was almost universally adopted in Hong Kong and was therefore in accordance with a body of professional opinion there, the defendant's solicitors were liable for negligence because there was an obvious risk that could be guarded against. Thus, the body of professional opinion, though almost universally held, was not reasonable or responsible.

These decisions demonstrate that in cases of diagnosis or treatment there are cases where, despite a body of professional opinion sanctioning the defendant's conduct, the defendant can properly be held liable for negligence (I am not here considering questions of disclosure of risk). In my judgment that is because, in some cases, it cannot be demonstrated to the judge's satisfaction that the body of opinion relied upon is reasonable or responsible. In the vast majority of cases the fact that distinguished experts in the field are of a particular opinion will demonstrate the reasonableness of that opinion. In particular, where there are questions of assessment of the relative risks and benefits of adopting a particular medical practice, a reasonable view necessarily presupposes that the relative risks and benefits have been weighed by the experts in forming their opinions. But if, in a rare case, it can be demonstrated that the professional opinion is not capable of withstanding logical analysis, the judge is entitled to hold that the body of opinion is not reasonable or responsible.

On the facts, his Lordship (with whose judgment the rest of the House of Lords agreed) held that the hypothetical decision not to intubate the plaintiff would have been in accord with responsible medical practice:

Lord Browne-Wilkinson: According to the accounts of Sister Sallabank and Nurse Newbold, although Patrick had had two severe respiratory crises, he had recovered quickly from both and for the rest presented as a child who was active and running about. Dr Dinwiddie's view was that these symptoms did not show a progressive respiratory collapse and that there was only a small risk of total respiratory failure. Intubation is not a routine, risk-free process. Dr Roberton described it as 'a major undertaking – an invasive procedure with mortality and morbidity attached – it was an assault'. It involves anaesthetising and ventilating the child. A young child does not tolerate a tube easily 'at any rate for a day or two' and the child unless sedated tends to remove it. In those circumstances it cannot be suggested that it was illogical for Dr Dinwiddie, a most distinguished expert, to favour running what, in his view, was a very small risk of total respiratory collapse rather than to submit Patrick to the invasive procedure of intubation.

It is apparent that, in requiring 'responsible practice' to stand up to logical analysis, Lord Browne-Wilkinson has in mind some form of risk-benefit analysis: the risks inherent in a given procedure must be justified by the benefit it may bring (including the amelioration of any greater risk). However, whilst this may lead to rejection of practices which entail quite unnecessary risks (that is, those where negligible or no benefit is to be gained from running them, as in *Hucks v Cole* and *Edward Wong*), it remains unclear what a judge is to do when faced with evidence of a practice which, say, exposes the patient to a 1% risk of total paralysis but carries a 90% chance of curing the patient's stiff neck. Is such a practice 'illogical'?

In the Court of Appeal in *Bolitho*, Dillon LJ had suggested that before impugning an accepted practice, the court should be satisfied that it was '*Wednesbury* unreasonable'. As we saw in Chapter 2, this test is employed in judicial review proceedings and requires a very high degree of unreasonableness (the practice in question must be perverse or irrational). In so doing, it reflects the courts' reluctance to second guess the decisions of public bodies, which are entrusted with a discretion over how best to implement policy (often involving considerations of finite resources). Such a test would seem an inappropriate basis on which to assess the individual treatment decisions made by doctors, and indeed it finds no place in Lord Browne-Wilkinson's judgment. Nevertheless, arguably the latter's approach is scarcely more favourable to the plaintiff:

> **Lord Browne-Wilkinson**: I emphasise that in my view it will very seldom be right for a judge to reach the conclusion that views genuinely held by a competent medical expert are unreasonable. The assessment of medical risks and benefits is a matter of clinical judgment which a judge would not normally be able to make without expert evidence. As the quotation from Lord Scarman [from *Maynard v W Midlands RHA*] makes clear, it would be wrong to allow such assessment to deteriorate into seeking to persuade the judge to prefer one of two views, both of which are capable of being logically supported. It is only where a judge can be satisfied that the body of expert opinion cannot be logically supported at all that such opinion will not provide the bench mark by reference to which the defendant's conduct falls to be assessed.

To date, judges applying the approach to *Bolam* endorsed by Lord Browne-Wilkinson in *Bolitho* have been cautious. Thus, decisions where a doctor's conduct has been held negligent notwithstanding its compliance with accepted practice remain rare. Nevertheless, one case that seems to have been decided on this basis is *Marriott v West Midlands HA* [1999] Lloyd's Rep Med 23, in which the trial judge found that, given the risk of neurological deficit, a GP's failure to refer a head injury patient back to hospital for further tests was negligent. As Beldam LJ commented in the Court of Appeal:

> **Beldam LJ**: Having read the evidence of both doctors, I think it is questionable whether either Dr Fell or Dr La Frenais had given evidence from which it was reasonable to infer that their individual approaches were shared by a responsible body of others in their profession. Rather it seems that each was saying what his own

approach would have been in the circumstances. It is true that each of them gave evidence of discussing the question with their partners, who (perhaps understandably) did in neither case disagree with their approach. But such evidence fell short of establishing that their views of the appropriate course for Dr Patel to have taken were shared by a body of professional colleagues. However, the judge treated this evidence as if it were evidence of that kind, and she correctly directed herself that it was not open to her simply to prefer the expert evidence of one body of competent professional opinion over that of another where there was a conflict between the experts called by the parties ... She then subjected that body of opinion to analysis to see whether it can properly be regarded as reasonable. In my view, she was entitled to do so.

It may be, as suggested by Beldam LJ, that the defendant's expert, whose evidence was impugned by the trial judge here, was not testifying to the existence of any accepted practice, but merely offering a personal opinion. In that case, the *Bolam* test should arguably have had little role in the first place (see the discussion at p 300, above).

A recent example of a court finding a breach of duty, notwithstanding the defendant's compliance with accepted medical practice, is the decision of Gage J in *AB v Leeds Teaching Hospital NHS Trust* [2004] EWHC 644. The case centred upon the failure of doctors to inform parents that tissue removed from their deceased children for post mortem examinations might subsequently be retained by the hospital. In this unusual fact constellation, the very universality of the practice was regarded as counting against its reasonableness. As his Lordship commented:

> **Gage J**: [237] ... [T]he evidence shows that the practice adopted was blanket practice carried out by virtually all clinicians. In so far as it involved the exercise of a therapeutic judgment it was one which does not appear to have been exercised on a case by case basis. The general view was that such information was unnecessary and likely to be distressing to parents. But there is no evidence that clinicians considered the matter individually with each parent or family. To take an example from the lead claims, although the issue does not arise in their claim, Mr and Mrs Carpenter would, in my judgment, have been quite capable of coping with this information at the time of Daniel's death. In any event, in my opinion, there was very little risk of parents being caused greater distress by being given the additional information. It would have been very simple and easy for a clinician to have provided this information and generally they ought to have done so. If the clinician did not know what was involved in a post-mortem, in my opinion, as Dr Moore said, he ought to have known. In the circumstances, my conclusion is that the practice of not warning parents and in particular a mother that a post-mortem might involve the removal and subsequent retention of an organ cannot be justified as a practice to be adopted in all cases.

For further discussion of the *AB* case, see Chapter 11, at p 594, below.

Departures from approved practice

Normally, where there is only a single course of treatment recognised by the medical profession (an increasing possibility given the work of the National Institute for Clinical Excellence in disseminating 'best practice' clinical guidelines: see Chapter 2), it will be practically impossible to demonstrate that the practice is illogical and, hence, not reasonable. (Arguably, it could be said, even then, that judges might consider practices in other jurisdictions and find that these were superior and should have been adopted by the medical profession here, but this approach was rejected in *Whiteford v Hunter* (1950) 94 SJ 758.)

However, how far does the converse apply? That is, will deviation from such practice automatically be regarded as negligent? This issue was addressed in the case of *Clark v MacLennan* [1983] 1 All ER 416:

Clark v MacLennan [1983] 1 All ER 416, HC (Peter Pain J)

The plaintiff was a woman who had recently given birth and was suffering from stress incontinence. The gynaecologist performed a corrective operation one month after the birth of the child. The normal practice was not to perform such operations until at least three months after birth, as the condition often spontaneously resolved itself and there would be less likelihood of haemorrhage. A haemorrhage did, in fact, take place, and despite further surgery, the plaintiff's condition became permanent. Although evidence was that in very special circumstances the operation might be performed early, this was not an exceptional case. In fact, none of the witnesses knew of a case where the operation had taken place earlier than three months. Contrasting this situation where there is more than one approved practice, Peter Pain J stated:

> **Peter Pain J**: Where ... there is but one orthodox course of treatment and the doctor chooses to depart from that, his position is different. It is not enough for him to say as to his decision simply that it was based on his clinical judgment. One has to inquire whether he took all proper factors into account which he knew or should have known, and whether his departure from the orthodox course can be justified on the basis of these factors.
>
> The burden of proof lies on the plaintiff. To succeed she must show, first, that there was a breach of duty and, second, that her damages flowed from that breach ...
>
> ... [C]ounsel for the plaintiff contended that, if the plaintiff could show: (1) that there was a general practice not to perform an anterior colporrhaphy until at least three months after birth; (2) that one of the reasons for this practice was to protect the patient from the risk of haemorrhage and a breakdown of the repair; (3) that an operation was performed within four weeks; and (4) that haemorrhage occurred and the repair broke down, then the burden of showing that he was not in breach of duty shifted to the defendants.
>
> It must be correct on the basis of *McGhee v National Coal Board* [1973] 1 WLR 1 to say that the burden shifts so far as damages are concerned. But does the burden shift so far as the duty is concerned? Must the medical practitioner justify his departure from the usual practice?
>
> It is very difficult to draw a distinction between the damage and the duty where the duty arises only because of a need to guard against the damage. In *McGhee's* case it was accepted that there was a breach of duty. In the present case the question of whether there was a breach remains in issue.
>
> It seems to me that it follows from *McGhee* that where there is a situation in which a general duty of care arises and there is a failure to take a precaution, and that very damage occurs against which the precaution is designed to be a protection, then the burden lies on the defendant to show that he was not in breach of duty as well as to show that the damage did not result from his breach of duty.

Peter Pain J's view that, in cases of departure from approved practice, the burden shifts to the defence to prove absence of negligence was subsequently doubted, however, by Mustill LJ in the Court of Appeal in *Wilsher v Essex AHA* [1986] 3 All ER 801:

> **Mustill LJ**: ... [A]lthough the judge [in *Clark v MacLennan*] indicated that he proposed to decide the case on burden of proof ... this could be understood as an example of the forensic commonplace that, where one party has, in the course of the trial, hit the ball into the other's court, it is for that other to return it. But the prominence given in the judgment to *McGhee* and the citation from *Clark* in the present case suggest that the judge may have set out to assert a wider proposition, to the effect that in certain kinds of case of which *Clark* and the present action form examples, there is a general burden of proof on the defendant. If this is so, then I must respectfully say that I find nothing in ... general principle to support it.

In the light of this, it may be more accurate to speak in terms of evidential presumptions: the fact, if it is established, that the defendant failed to act in accordance with accepted practice supports a *prima facie* inference of negligence, which it is then up to the defendant to rebut. Such rebuttal will be more difficult if the accepted practice is universal and is specifically directed against the risk that the defendant, in failing to comply, allowed to materialise. A case in point is that of *Chin Keow v Government of Malaysia* [1967] 1 WLR 813 in which a patient died after the doctor gave her penicillin without checking for the possibility of an allergic reaction. The doctor was unable to give any satisfactory explanation of his failure to observe accepted practice in this regard.

On other occasions, however, the doctor may be able to provide cogent reasons for departing from normal practice. In fact, the importance of giving doctors a certain degree of latitude to try out 'innovative' forms of treatment was noted by Lord Clyde in the pre-*Bolam*, Scottish decision of *Hunter v Hanley* (1955) SC 200:

> **Lord President Clyde**: ... [I]n regard to allegations of deviation from ordinary professional practice ... such a deviation is not necessarily evidence of negligence. Indeed it would be disastrous if this were so, for all inducement to progress in medical science would then be destroyed. Even a substantial deviation from normal practice may be warranted by the particular circumstances. To establish liability by a doctor where deviation from normal practice is alleged, three facts require to be established. First of all it must be proved that there is a usual and normal practice; secondly it must be proved that the defender has not adopted that practice; and thirdly (and this is of crucial importance) it must be established that the course the doctor adopted is one which no professional man of ordinary skill would have taken if he had been acting with ordinary care.

It is important to distinguish here between medical research, which is a planned exercise designed specifically to test a new form of treatment, using control groups and almost always approved by a local ethics committee (see further Chapter 10), and a 'one off' treatment for a particular patient. We are only concerned at present with the latter situation. There is no doubt that there would be no *automatic* finding of negligence, if the treatment was innovative. In *Sidaway* Lord Diplock stated:

> **Lord Diplock**: Those members of the public who seek medical or surgical aid would be badly served by the adoption of any legal principle that would confine the doctor to some long-established, well tried method of treatment only, although its past record of success might be small, if he wanted to be confident that he would not run the risk of being held liable in negligence simply because he tried some more modern treatment, and by some unavoidable mischance it failed to heal but did some harm to the patient. This would encourage 'defensive medicine' with a vengeance.

More recently, in *Simms v Simms and Another* [2003] Fam 83, which concerned the lawfulness of experimental treatment on two young patients dying from variant CJD, Butler-Sloss P commented that, '[t]he *Bolam* test ought not to be allowed to inhibit medical progress'. In short, doctors should not be afraid to try new treatments when existing ones are not working. Such a constraint would inhibit the development of better treatments, contrary to important utilitarian considerations, and would be contrary to trying to do the best for the individual patient (both of these limbs must be satisfied as utility without more would involve using the patient merely as a means to an end).

There are two important issues here. First (subject to a possible defence of therapeutic privilege), it is suggested that the patient should be fully apprised of the fact that the treatment is innovative and, accordingly, that there may be side effects or other risks that the doctor does not know about. Secondly, the context in which the treatment is given must be considered. In some cases, established treatments may not have been successful, and the patient will, perhaps, agree to accept a 'long shot' chance of success as a last resort. However, what of the situation where other conventional treatments exist and have not been tried? Certainly, in such a case, the patient should be fully informed about these alternatives, associated risks, likely outcomes and so on, but the question must be raised as to whether novel treatment should be given at all. When would such treatment be in the best interests of *this* patient?

A case in which unjustified 'experimentation' on the part of a doctor was at issue is that of *Hepworth v Kerr* [1995] 6 Med LR 139. The plaintiff was admitted to hospital in 1979 for a mastoid operation. During the course of the operation, the anaesthetist reduced the patient's blood pressure to a very low level for a period of one and a half hours. The purpose was to create a relatively blood-free operating field in the middle ear. The anaesthetist had been using this technique for some years and had used it in around 1,500 cases. However, in the case of this patient the level to which he reduced the blood pressure was 40 mm Hg, when a minimum of 60 mm Hg was strongly indicated in the medical literature. McKinnon J described the defendant as 'plainly negligent':

> **McKinnon J**: As I find, the defendant adopted a new hypotensive anaesthetic technique which, as he knew, had never been attempted routinely before. Other anaesthetists had never gone to such low levels over such long periods. The defendant, as he accepted, was to begin with, at least, plainly experimenting. He expected serious complications such as cerebral or cardiac thrombosis to occur. He was surprised when they did not. He never, however, attempted to embark upon any proper scientific validation of his technique in some 1,500 patients by the time of the plaintiff's operation ...
>
> I simply cannot, and do not, accept that the defendant was justified in doing what he did without proper scientific validation of his technique.

Proving the breach

In every case it is for the claimant to demonstrate that the defendant was negligent on the *balance of probabilities* (that is, according to the usual civil burden of proof). As we have seen, this makes things very awkward for claimants in cases where medical opinion is divided as to whether the defendant's conduct accorded with responsible medical practice: see *Maynard v W Midlands RHA* [1984] 1 WLR 634 and *Ashcroft v Mersey RHA* [1983] 2 All ER 245. Following *Bolitho*, it may be said that the onus is squarely on the claimant to show that the conduct in question 'cannot be logically supported at all'.

On other occasions, though, where, as a matter of evidence, it is not clear what such conduct actually consisted of, a claimant may be able to bypass these difficulties by entering a plea of *res ipsa loquitur*. A claimant who enters such a plea (literally 'the thing speaks for itself') alleges that the injury could not have happened *without* negligence and, therefore, throws the ball into the doctor's court to show otherwise. To get this far, he must establish three elements: first, the defendant (either primarily or vicariously) must be in control of the situation prior to injury; secondly, in the ordinary course of events, such injury does not occur; and, finally, the claimant does not have all the facts to show what actually happened. (It is the third aspect which gave rise to the principle in the first place, so as to allow a claimant to sue in circumstances where he cannot properly plead specific allegations of negligence.)

Tort lawyers have long debated whether the principle means, in effect, that the burden of proof is reversed. The favoured view is that it is not. In the Privy Council decision of *Ng Chun Pui v Lee Chuen Tat* [1988] RTR 298, it was said that *res ipsa loquitur* is no more than the use of a Latin maxim to describe the state of the evidence from which it is proper to draw an inference of negligence. In other words, if the claimant asserts that such an accident would not normally happen without negligence, he is merely inviting a finding of negligence earlier in the proceedings than usual.

Two relatively early medical negligence cases in which the principle was invoked are *Roe v Minister of Health* [1954] 2 QB 66 and *Cassidy v Ministry of Health* [1951] 2 KB 343. In *Roe*, the plaintiffs were paralysed during the course of surgery due to the contamination of their anaesthetic by phenol: the latter had seeped through invisible fissures in the glass storage vessels in which the anaesthetic was stored:

> **Denning LJ:** The judge [at first instance] has said that those facts do not speak for themselves, but I think that they do. They certainly call for an explanation. Each of these men is entitled to say to the hospital: 'While I was in your hands something has been done to me which has wrecked my life. Please explain how this has come to pass.' ... I approach this case, therefore, on the footing that the hospital authorities and Dr Graham were called on to give an explanation of what has happened.

(The defendant was eventually able to establish that, at that time, the danger of such contamination was unknown to science.) In *Cassidy*, the plaintiff was admitted for surgery to correct Dupuytren's syndrome which had resulted in the contraction of the third and fourth fingers of his left hand. After surgery the contraction had spread to his two other fingers. The Court of Appeal held that *res ipsa loquitur* applied. It was Denning LJ again who stated:

> **Denning LJ:** If the plaintiff had to prove that some particular doctor or nurse was negligent, he would not be able to do it. But he was not put to that impossible task: he says:
>
> > I went into the hospital to be cured of two stiff fingers. I have come out with four stiff fingers, and my hand is useless. That should not have happened if due care had been used. Explain it, if you can.

Nevertheless, in subsequent cases the courts have tended to vacillate on the question of how far, and in what circumstances, the principle should apply in medical negligence cases. The issue has recently been exhaustively reconsidered by the Court of Appeal in *Ratcliffe v Plymouth and Torbay HA* [1998] Lloyd's Rep Med 162:

Ratcliffe v Plymouth and Torbay HA [1998] Lloyd's Rep Med 162, CA (Brooke and Hobhouse LJJ, and Sir John Vinelott)

In September 1989, the plaintiff underwent a triple arthrodesis of his right ankle, in one of the defendants' hospitals. He received a spinal anaesthetic to relieve post-operative pain. Although the operation itself was a success, he was left with a serious neurological defect on the right side from his waist downwards:

Brooke LJ [*after reviewing the authorities*]: It is now possible to draw some threads out of all this material, by way of explanation of the relevance of the maxim *res ipsa loquitur* to medical negligence cases: (1) In its purest form, the maxim applies where the plaintiff relies on the 'res' (the thing itself) to raise the inference of negligence, which is supported by ordinary human experience, with no need for expert evidence. (2) In principle, the maxim can be applied in that form in simple situations in the medical negligence field (surgeon cuts off right foot instead of left: swab left in operation site; patient wakes up in the course of surgical operation despite general anaesthetic). (3) In practice, in contested medical negligence cases the evidence of the plaintiff, which establishes the 'res', is likely to be buttressed by expert evidence to the effect that the matter complained does not ordinarily occur in the absence of negligence. (4) The position may then be reached at the close of the plaintiff's case that the judge would be entitled to infer negligence on the defendant's part unless the defendant adduces evidence which discharges this inference. (5) This evidence may be to the effect that there is a plausible explanation of what may have happened which does not connote any negligence on the defendant's part. The explanation must be a plausible one and not a theoretically or remotely possible one, but the defendant certainly does not have to prove that his explanation is more likely to be correct than any other. If the plaintiff has no other evidence of negligence to rely on, his claim will then fail. (6) Alternatively, the defendant's evidence may satisfy the judge on the balance of probabilities that he did exercise proper care. If the untoward outcome is extremely rare, or is impossible to explain in the light of the current state of medical knowledge, the judge will be bound to exercise great care in evaluating the evidence before making such a finding, but he does so, the *prima facie* inference of negligence is rebutted and the plaintiff's claim will fail. The reason why the courts are willing to adopt this approach, particularly in very complex cases, is to be found in the judgments of Stuart-Smith and Dillon LJJ in *Delaney v Southmead HA* [1995] 6 Med LR 355. (7) It follows from all this that, although in very simple situations the 'res' may speak for itself at the end of the lay evidence adduced on behalf of the plaintiff, in practice the inference is then buttressed by expert evidence adduced on his behalf, and if the defendant were to call no evidence, the judge would be deciding the case on inferences he was entitled to draw from the whole of the evidence (including the expert evidence), and not on the application of the maxim in its purest form.

Hobhouse LJ: Medical negligence cases have the potential to give rise to considerations whether the plaintiff has made out a *prima facie* case and whether or not the defendant has provided an adequate answer to displace the inference to be drawn from the plaintiff's *prima facie* case. Further, it is commonplace that the plaintiff will not, himself or herself, have fully known what occurred, particularly if the relevant procedure was an operation carried out under anaesthetic. The procedures were under the control of the defendant and what the defendant did or did not do is exclusively within the direct knowledge of the defendant. But, in practical terms, few, if any, medical negligence cases are brought to trial without full discovery having been given, particulars having been obtained where necessary of the defendant's pleading, witness statements having been exchanged and experts' reports lodged. Therefore, the trial opens not in the vacuum of available evidence and explanation as sometimes occurs in road traffic accident cases, but with expert evidence on both sides and defined battlelines drawn. The aspects of the facts and aetiology which can and cannot be explained with reasonable certainty will have been identified and the rival explanations marshalled. The viable allegations or inferences of negligence will have been identified, and the parties and the trial judge will have a reasonable idea of the specific factual issues which are going to have to be investigated and determined at the trial.

CAUSATION

Assuming that the claimant manages to establish that the defendant doctor was 'negligent' (in the sense of having breached his duty of care), it does not follow that he will succeed in his claim in *negligence*. A further, and in this context often very troublesome, hurdle remains for him to negotiate in the form of proving causation. Analytically, causation subdivides into two main stages: first, it must be shown that the defendant's breach of duty was a *factual cause* of the claimant's harm; if so, the law must then also deem it to be the *legal cause* (ie the harm must not be so distant from the defendant's breach or unexpected in nature to qualify as 'too remote'). As we shall see, in the context of medical negligence the first of these aspects, especially, may give rise to great difficulty.

Factual causation: causal necessity and the 'but for' test

A framework for analysis

For the purposes of the tort of negligence, the crucial question is whether the defendant's breach of duty made a difference to the harmful outcome suffered by the claimant. This is generally resolved by means of the so-called 'but for' test. In the well-known words of Denning LJ in the (non-medical negligence) case of *Cork v Kirby Maclean Ltd* [1952] 2 All ER 402, '[i]f the damage would not have happened but for a particular fault then that fault is the cause of the damage; if it would have happened just the same, fault or no fault, the fault is not the cause of the damage'.

A good illustration of the test's application, in the context of medical negligence, is provided by the case of *Barnett v Chelsea and Kensington Hospital Management Committee* [1969] 1 QB 428:

Barnett v Chelsea & Kensington Hospital Management Committee [1969] 1 QB 428, QBD (Nield J)

Three nightwatchmen attended the defendant's casualty department complaining of being violently sick after drinking some tea. The casualty doctor on duty negligently failed to see the men and they were sent away untreated. One of them later died from what it transpired were the effects of arsenic poisoning. In the subsequent action brought by the man's widow, the judge, after holding that the defendant owed a duty of care to the deceased and was in breach, continued as follows:

> **Nield J**: It remains to consider whether it is shown that the deceased's death was caused by that negligence or whether, as the defendants have said, the deceased must have died in any event. In his concluding submission Mr Pain submitted that the casualty officer should have examined the deceased and had he done so he would have caused tests to be made which would have indicated the treatment required and that, since the defendants were at fault in these respects, therefore the onus of proof passed to the defendants to show that the appropriate treatment would have failed, and authorities were cited to me. I find myself unable to accept that argument, and I am of the view that the onus of proof remains upon the plaintiff, and I have in mind (without quoting it) the decision cited by Mr Wilmers in *Bonnington Castings Ltd v Wardlaw* [1956] AC 613 ... However, were it otherwise and the onus did pass to the defendants, then I would find that they have discharged it, as I would proceed to show. There has been put before me a timetable which I think is of much importance. The deceased attended at the casualty department at five or 10 minutes past eight in the morning. If the casualty officer had got up and dressed and come to see the three men and examined them and decided to admit them, the deceased (and Dr Lockett agreed with this) could not have been in bed in a ward before 11 am. I accept Dr Goulding's evidence that an intravenous drip would not have been set up before 12 noon, and if potassium loss was suspected it could not have been discovered until 12.30 pm. Dr Lockett, dealing with this, said: 'If this man had not been treated until after 12 noon the chances of survival were not good.' Without going in detail into the considerable volume of technical evidence which has been put before me, it seems to me to be the case that when death results from arsenical poisoning it is brought about by two conditions; on the one hand dehydration and on the other disturbance of the enzyme processes. If the principal condition is one of enzyme disturbance – as I am of the view it was here – then the only method of treatment which is likely to succeed is the use of the specific antidote which is commonly called BAL. Dr Goulding said in the course of his evidence: 'The only way to deal with this is to use the specific BAL I see no reasonable prospect of the deceased being given BAL before the time at which he died' – and at a later point in his evidence – 'I feel that even if fluid loss had been discovered death would have been caused by the enzyme disturbance. Death might have occurred later.' I regard that evidence as very moderate, and it might be a true assessment of the situation to say that there was no chance of BAL being administered before the death of the deceased. For those reasons, I find that the plaintiff has failed to establish, on the balance of probabilities, that the defendants' negligence caused the death of the deceased.

The *Barnett* case is instructive for a number of reasons. First, it emphasises that, for the purposes of attributing liability in negligence, the law's focus – as embodied in the 'but for' test – is upon causal *necessity* ('if not c, then not e'), not causal *sufficiency* ('if c, then e'). In other words, it is enough that the defendant, by his fault, contributed just one of several conditions jointly required to produce the harmful outcome: here, the fact that Mr Barnett would not have died if someone had not poisoned his tea was irrelevant in terms of considering the hospital's liability. Secondly, the case also illustrates the inevitably *hypothetical* nature of the factual causation enquiry: the court is required to construct a counter-factual parallel series – ie to speculate as to how things *would have turned out* if the defendant had properly performed his duty.

In the third place, however, *Barnett* provides a powerful hint as to why it is that factual causation is often difficult to prove in the specific context of medical negligence. This is because, in such cases, the claimant – at the time of the doctor's breach – was normally already at risk of suffering an adverse outcome (as a result of the ailment that led him to seek the doctor's assistance). Thus, in principle, it is always open to the doctor to argue that his admitted breach of duty made no difference; that the patient's injury was due to the progress of the illness, which, even with all due medical care, could not have been arrested: if the patient's illness was indeed untreatable, it alone will have been a sufficient condition for the patient's injury; the risk posed by the doctor's failure to offer treatment will remain just that – it will not have materialised in the sense of playing a necessary part in (ie *causing*) the harm.

As we have seen, it was just this type of argument that Nield J accepted in *Barnett* itself. (It is useful here to contrast the position of defendants in most other negligence scenarios: thus a negligent motorist is highly unlikely to be able to suggest that the pedestrian whose leg he crushed would have lost the leg in any event through an independent risk materialising.)

Evidential problems in applying the 'but for' test

The fact that, in medical negligence cases, the court must normally consider the respective role in the patient's injury of two or more independent risks (the doctor's breach of duty *and* the patient's underlying illness) may generate significant evidential uncertainty. The scientific evidence may be unable to distinguish between the respective risks and determine which of them actually materialised.

On the face of it, given that it is for the claimant to show, on the balance of probabilities (the civil standard of proof) that the breach positively made the difference, it would seem that in such cases his claim must fail. However, at least where it is clear that the defendant's conduct has exposed the claimant to an added risk of harm, the courts have on occasion been prepared to allow recovery without the latter having to show that it actually materialised and caused the harm, as in the non-medical negligence case of *McGhee v National Coal Board* [1972] 3 All ER 1008. In that case an employee of the coal board brought an action alleging that his dermatitis had come about due to its failure to provide him with proper washing facilities. This meant that he had to cycle home with the brick dust, to which his work unavoidably exposed him, still caked to his skin. Here, there was no doubt that brick dust caused the claimant's injury. The difficulty lay in determining whether the 'guilty' dust (that is, that which continued to adhere to the claimant on his journey home) had played any causative role. The House of Lords' solution was to assert that, in this type of case, it was open to a court simply to infer, as a question of fact, that the defendant's breach had materially contributed to the injury. Indeed, in one of the judgments, Lord Wilberforce appeared to go further and suggest that once the claimant has shown that the defendant's breach of duty created a risk of harm, the burden of proving that it did *not* materialise and materially contribute to the harm passed to the defendant.

The question of how far the claimant-friendly approach to resolving such difficulties in *McGhee* should continue to apply in the field of medical negligence was faced by the House of Lords in *Wilsher v Essex AHA* [1988] 1 All ER 871.

Wilsher v Essex AHA [1988] 1 All ER 871, HL (Lords Bridge, Fraser, Lowry, Griffiths and Ackner)

The plaintiff baby was found to be suffering from retrolental fibroplasia (RLF), rendering him virtually blind, following treatment in the defendant's post-natal unit. Owing to a breach of duty by hospital staff, the baby had been over-saturated with oxygen in the first weeks of his life (see p 294, above). However, whilst this might, according to some of the evidence, have caused or contributed to the RLF, there were four other natural conditions, all of which had afflicted the baby, and which could equally have had the same effect. The majority of the Court of Appeal found for the plaintiff on causation on the basis of Lord Wilberforce's speech in *McGhee*; the defendant appealed:

> **Lord Bridge**: The Court of Appeal, although it felt unable to resolve the primary conflict in the expert evidence as to the causation of Martin's RLF, did make a finding that the levels of PO2 which Martin experienced in consequence of the misplacement of the catheter were of a kind capable of causing RLF. Mustill LJ expressed his anxiety whether 'by making a further finding on an issue where there was a sharp conflict between the expert witnesses, we are going too far in the effort to avoid a retrial' (see [1986] 3 All ER 801, p 825). But he concluded that it was 'legitimate, after rereading the evidence', to make this finding based on 'the weight of the expert evidence'. This finding by the Court of Appeal is challenged by counsel for the authority as one which it was not open to it to make ... But assuming, as I do for the present, that the finding was properly made, it carried the plaintiff's case no further than to establish that oxygen administered to Martin as a consequence of the negligent failure to detect the misplacement of the catheter was one of a number of possible causes of Martin's RLF.

> Mustill LJ subjected the speeches in *McGhee v National Coal Board* [1972] 3 All ER 1008 ... to a careful scrutiny and analysis and concluded that they established a principle of law which he expressed in the following terms:

>> If it is an established fact that conduct of a particular kind creates a risk that injury will be caused to another or increases an existing risk that injury will ensue, and if the two parties stand in such a relationship that the one party owes a duty not to conduct himself in that way, and if the first party does conduct himself in that way, and if the other party does suffer injury of the kind to which the risk related, then the first party is taken to have caused the injury by his breach of duty, even though the existence and extent of the contribution made by the breach cannot be ascertained.

> Applying this principle to the finding that the authority's negligence was one of the possible causes of Martin's RLF, he held that this was sufficient to enable the court to conclude that the negligence was 'taken to have caused the injury'. Glidewell LJ reached the same conclusion by substantially the same process of reasoning. Sir Nicolas Browne-Wilkinson VC took the opposite view ...

> Much of the academic discussion to which [*McGhee*] has given rise has focused on the speech of Lord Wilberforce, particularly on two paragraphs. He said:

>> ... First, it is a sound principle that where a person has, by breach of duty of care, created a risk, and injury occurs within the area of that risk, the loss should be borne by him *unless he shows that it had some other cause*. Secondly, from the evidential point of view, one may ask, why should a man who is able to show that his employer should have taken certain precautions, because without them there is a risk, or an added risk, of injury or disease, and who in fact sustains exactly that injury or disease, have to assume the

burden of proving more: namely, that it was the addition to the risk, caused by the breach of duty, which caused or materially contributed to the injury? In many cases of which the present is typical, this is impossible to prove, just because honest medical opinion cannot segregate the causes of an illness between compound causes. And if one asks which of the parties, the workman or the employers should suffer from this inherent evidential difficulty, the answer as a matter in policy or justice should be that it is the creator of the risk who, *ex hypothesi*, must be taken to have foreseen the possibility of damage, who should bear its consequences. (My emphasis.)

He then referred to *Bonnington Castings Ltd v Wardlaw and Nicholson v Atlas Steel Foundry and Engineering Co Ltd* and added:

I must say that, at least in the present case, to bridge the evidential gap by inference seems to me something of a fiction, since it was precisely this inference which the medical expert declined to make. But I find in the cases quoted an analogy which suggests the conclusion that, *in the absence of proof that the culpable condition had, in the result, no effect*, the employers should be liable for an injury, squarely within the risk which they created and that they, not the pursuer, should suffer the consequence of the impossibility, foreseeably inherent in the nature of his injury, of segregating the precise consequence of their default. (My emphasis.)

My Lords, it seems to me that both these paragraphs, particularly in the words I have emphasised, amount to saying that, in the circumstances, the burden of proof of causation is reversed and thereby to run counter to the unanimous and emphatic opinions expressed in *Bonnington Castings Ltd v Wardlaw* [1956] 1 All ER 615 ... to the contrary effect. I find no support in any of the other speeches for the view that the burden of proof is reversed and, in this respect, I think Lord Wilberforce's reasoning must be regarded as expressing a minority opinion.

The conclusion I draw ... is that *McGhee v National Coal Board* laid down no new principle of law whatever. On the contrary, it affirmed the principle that the onus of proving causation lies on the pursuer or plaintiff. Adopting a robust and pragmatic approach to the undisputed primary facts of the case, the majority concluded that it was a legitimate inference of fact that the defenders' negligence had materially contributed to the pursuer's injury. The decision, in my opinion, is of no greater significance than that and the attempt to extract from it some esoteric principle which in some way modifies, as a matter of law, the nature of the burden of proof of causation which a plaintiff or pursuer must discharge once he has established a relevant breach of duty is a fruitless one.

In the Court of Appeal in the instant case Sir Nicolas Browne-Wilkinson VC, being in a minority, expressed his view on causation with understandable caution. But I am quite unable to find any fault with the following passage in his dissenting judgment:

To my mind, the occurrence of RLF following a failure to take a necessary precaution to prevent excess oxygen causing RLF provides no evidence and raises no presumption that it was excess oxygen rather than one or more of the four other possible agents which caused or contributed to RLF in this case. The position, to my mind, is wholly different from that in *McGhee*, where there was only one candidate (brick dust) which could have caused the dermatitis, and the failure to take a precaution against brick dust causing dermatitis was followed by dermatitis caused by brick dust. In such a case, I can see the common sense, if not the logic, of holding that, in the absence of any other evidence, the failure to take the precaution caused or contributed to the dermatitis. To the extent that certain members of the House of Lords decided the question on inferences from evidence or presumptions, I do not consider that the present case falls within their reasoning. A failure to take preventive measures against one out of five possible causes is no evidence as to which of those five caused the injury.

More recently, in *Fairchild v Glenhaven Funeral Services* [2002] 3 WLR 89, the view taken of *McGhee* by Lord Bridge in *Wilsher* was itself the subject of reappraisal. In *Fairchild*, which like *McGhee* was a negligence action brought by an employee, the evidential problem in relation to causation was that of multiple possible tortfeasors. The claimant was suffering from mesolethemia, which it was accepted had been caused by inhaling asbestos fibres during his employment. However, he had worked for a number of different companies, each of whom had negligently exposed him to asbestos, and it was not possible now to say, of any particular one, that the fatal inhalation took place while the claimant was working there.

In allowing recovery, the House of Lords regarded *McGhee* as authority for departing from the normal need to satisfy the 'but for' test on the balance of probabilities on the basis of special policy considerations. Where these applied, the proven creation of a significant risk of harm (rather than proof that the risk actually materialised) should be treated as sufficient for liability. Nonetheless, their Lordships affirmed the correctness of *Wilsher* on its facts. In his speech in *Fairchild*, Lord Hoffmann was anxious to emphasise that a similar relaxation of causation would not apply in the context of medical negligence:

> **Lord Hoffmann**: [68] The Court of Appeal [in *Wilsher*] treated the causal requirement rule applied in *McGhee* as being of general application ...
>
> [69] The House of Lords, in a speech by Lord Bridge of Harwich with which all other noble Lords concurred, rejected this broad principle. I would respectfully agree. The principle in *McGhee's* case is far narrower and I have tried to indicate what its limits are likely to be. It is true that actions for clinical negligence notoriously give rise to difficult questions of causation. But it cannot possibly be said that the duty to take reasonable care in treating patients would be virtually drained of content unless the creation of a material risk of injury were accepted as sufficient to satisfy the causal requirements for liability. And the political and economic arguments involved in the massive increase in the liability of the National Health Service which would have been a consequence of the broad rule favoured by the Court of Appeal in *Wilsher's* case are far more complicated than the reasons given by Lord Wilberforce [in *McGhee*] for imposing liability upon an employer who has failed to take simple precautions.

Claims for 'loss of chance'

In *Wilsher* we saw that, due to the over-complexity and lack of clarity of the available evidence, the plaintiff was unable to show that the defendant's breach of duty had played a causative role in his injury. However, in many instances, notably where a doctor's failure to make a prompt or proper diagnosis of a given illness is at issue, the plaintiff *will* have evidence as to the effect this has had upon him. Such evidence takes the form of class statistics which record the chances of recovery for patients who *are* diagnosed with the relevant condition at a similar stage of progression.

The courts were required to decide whether a claim founded upon such statistical evidence was admissible in the case of *Hotson v East Berkshire AHA* [1987]

1 AC 750 in which the claimant schoolboy attended the defendant's casualty department after falling from a tree and injuring his hip. The defendant failed, in breach of duty, to carry out an x-ray of the hip and by the time the true extent of the injury was discovered (when the boy returned to hospital several days later) permanent disability was unavoidable. However, the medical evidence was to the effect that, even with immediate diagnosis, 75% of patients with such an injury went on to develop the same disability anyway.

Rather than suing on the basis that the defendant had caused the disability itself (clearly an impossible task, given the need to satisfy the civil standard of proof by showing *on the balance of probabilities* that the failed diagnosis had played a necessary part in it), the plaintiff restricted his claim to the loss of the residual 25% chance that proper diagnosis would have resulted in successful treatment. At first instance, Simon Brown J accepted that the loss of a substantial chance of this kind was actionable and awarded damages assessed at 25% of the full quantum in respect of such an injury, and this approach was upheld in the Court of Appeal:

> **Sir John Donaldson MR:** ... Mr Whitfield, for the defendants, submits that no causal connection between the negligence and the development of avascular necrosis and consequent disability has been established, since a 25% likelihood fails to achieve the requisite standard of proof. Without that causal connection, there can be no liability in damages based upon that development. In more concrete terms, it is all, ie, £46,000, or nothing – £46,000 if the likelihood of the connection exceeds 50% and otherwise nothing. In the instant case it is nothing ...

> As a matter of common sense, it is unjust that there should be no liability for failure to treat a patient, simply because the chances of a successful cure by that treatment were less than 50%. Nor, by the same token, can it be just that if the chances of a successful cure only marginally exceed 50%, the doctor or his employer should be liable to the same extent as if the treatment could be guaranteed to cure. If this is the law, it is high time that it was changed, assuming that this court has power to do so.

However, the health authority appealed successfully to the House of Lords:

> **Lord Bridge:** The plaintiff's claim was for damages for physical injury and consequential loss alleged to have been caused by the authority's breach of their duty of care. In some cases, perhaps particularly medical negligence cases, causation may be so shrouded in mystery that the court can only measure statistical chances. But that was not so here. On the evidence there was a clear conflict as to what had caused the avascular necrosis. The authority's evidence was that the sole cause was the original traumatic injury to the hip. The plaintiff's evidence, at its highest, was that the delay in treatment was a material contributory cause. This was a conflict, like any other about some relevant past event, which the judge could not avoid resolving on a balance of probabilities. Unless the plaintiff proved on a balance of probabilities that the delayed treatment was at least a material contributory cause of the avascular necrosis he failed on the issue of causation and no question of quantification could arise. But the judge's findings of fact ... are unmistakably to the effect that on a balance of probabilities the injury caused by the plaintiff's fall left insufficient blood vessels intact to keep the epiphysis alive. This amounts to a finding of fact that the fall was the sole cause of the avascular necrosis.

> The upshot is that the appeal must be allowed ...

Although in *Hotson* their Lordships stopped short of saying that there could never be recovery in medical negligence for loss of chance, they gave little clue as to when it might be allowed. Recently, in *Gregg v Scott* [2005] UKHL 2, the House of Lords had another opportunity to consider the merits of a claim framed in this way:

Gregg v Scott [2005] UKHL 2 (Lords Nicholls, Hoffmann, Hope and Phillips, Baroness Hale)

The claimant, Mr Gregg, consulted Dr Scott in November 1994 about a lump under his arm. The latter assumed it was benign and negligently failed to refer the claimant to hospital for tests. The claimant was subsequently admitted to hospital in January 1996 where it was found that he was suffering from non-Hodgkin's lymphoma. The effect of the 14-month delay in diagnosis was that the cancer had spread and, statistically, Mr Gregg's chance of a 'cure' (defined, medically, as 10-year disease-free survival) had diminished from 42 to 25%.

In his negligence action against the doctor, the claimant advanced two separate arguments. First, it was argued that the spread of the tumour was itself cognisable damage and, in quantifying its worth, account should (in accordance with general principles of *quantum*) be taken of the increased possibility that it would result it his premature death: we shall consider this point under 'Damages', at p 327ff below. Secondly, as in the *Hotson* case, it was proposed that the lost (or here, more accurately, *reduced*) statistical chance of a cure should itself be compensated for. This second basis of the claim would have been allowed by Lord Nicholls:

> **Lord Nicholls**: [20] ... [H]ow should the loss suffered by a patient in Mr Gregg's position be identified? The Defendant says 'loss' is confined to an outcome which is shown, on balance of probability, to be worse than it otherwise would have been. Mr Gregg must prove that, on balance of probability, his medical condition after the negligence was worse than it would have been in the absence of the negligence. Mr Gregg says his 'loss' includes proved diminution in the prospects of a favourable outcome. Dr Scott's negligence deprived him of a worthwhile chance that his medical condition would not have deteriorated as it did.
>
> [21] Of primary relevance on this important issue is an evaluation of what, in practice, a patient suffering from a progressive illness loses when the treatment he needs is delayed because of a negligent diagnosis. What the patient loses depends, of course, on the circumstances of the individual case. No doubt in some cases medical opinion will be that, given his pre-existing condition, the patient lost nothing by the delay in treatment because he never had any realistic prospect of recovery. The doctor's misdiagnosis made no significant difference to the patient's prospects of recovery. In other cases medical opinion may be that the patient lost everything. Barring unforeseen complications he would have made a complete recovery had his condition been diagnosed properly and had he then received appropriate treatment.
>
> [22] These two types of case are, in the present context, straightforward. But there are also many cases of serious illness or injury where a patient's existing chances of recovery fall between these extremes. There are occasions where medical opinion will be that, given prompt and appropriate treatment, the outcome was uncertain but the patient's prospects of recovery were appreciable, sometimes exceeding 50%, sometimes not ...
>
> [24] Given this uncertainty of outcome, the appropriate characterisation of a patient's loss in this type of case must surely be that it comprises the loss of the chance of a favourable outcome, rather than the loss of the outcome itself. Justice so requires, because this matches medical reality. This recognises what in practice a patient had before the doctor's negligence occurred. It recognises what in practice the patient lost

by reason of that negligence. The doctor's negligence diminished the patient's prospects of recovery. And this analysis of a patient's loss accords with the purpose of the legal duty of which the doctor was in breach. In short, the purpose of the duty is to promote the patient's prospects of recovery by exercising due skill and care in diagnosing and treating the patient's condition.

[25] This approach also achieves a basic objective of the law of tort. The common law imposes duties and seeks to provide appropriate remedies in the event of a breach of duty. If negligent diagnosis or treatment diminishes a patient's prospects of recovery, a law which does not recognise this as a wrong calling for redress would be seriously deficient today. In respect of the doctors' breach of duty the law would not have provided an appropriate remedy.

However, Lord Hoffmann was in the opposite camp. As foreshadowed in his speech in *Fairchild*, one of his Lordship's concerns related to the effect of permitting such claims upon scarce health care resources:

Lord Hoffmann: [84] Academic writers have suggested that in cases of clinical negligence, the need to prove causation is too restrictive of liability. This argument has appealed to judges in some jurisdictions; in some, but not all, of the states of the United States and most recently in New South Wales and Ireland: *Rufo v Hosking* ... 2004] NSWCA 391); *Philp v Ryan* ... [2004] 1 IESC 105. In the present case it is urged that Mr Gregg has suffered a wrong and ought to have a remedy. Living for more than 10 years is something of great value to him and he should be compensated for the possibility that the delay in diagnosis may have reduced his chances of doing so. In effect, the Appellant submits that the exceptional rule in *Fairchild* should be generalised and damages awarded in all cases in which the defendant may have caused an injury and has increased the likelihood of the injury being suffered. In the present case, it is alleged that Dr Scott may have caused a reduction in Mr Gregg's expectation of life and that he increased the likelihood that his life would be shortened by the disease.

[85] It should first be noted that adopting such a rule would involve abandoning a good deal of authority. The rule which the House is asked to adopt is the very rule which it rejected in *Wilsher's* case [1988] AC 1074. Yet *Wilsher's* case was expressly approved by the House in *Fairchild* [2003] 1 AC 32. *Hotson* [1987] AC 750 too would have to be overruled. Furthermore, the House would be dismantling all the qualifications and restrictions with which it so recently hedged the *Fairchild* exception. There seem to me to be no new arguments or change of circumstances which could justify such a radical departure from precedent ...

[90] ... [A] wholesale adoption of possible rather than probable causation as the criterion of liability would be so radical a change in our law as to amount to a legislative act. It would have enormous consequences for insurance companies and the National Health Service.

Lord Phillips and Baroness Hale agreed with Lord Hoffmann in dismissing the claimant's appeal. However, they appear to have been swayed more by the particular factual complexities of the case at hand, and a distrust of the statistical evidence on offer. As the former commented:

Lord Phillips: [189] There are no doubt cases where it is possible to adopt the simple approach of asking to what extent the negligent treatment has reduced the prospects of curing the patient. There are other cases, and this is one, where that simple question is almost impossible to answer ... The likelihood seems to be that Dr Scott's negligence has not prevented Mr Gregg's cure, but has made that cure more painful.

[190] The complications of this case have persuaded me that it is not a suitable vehicle for introducing into the law of clinical negligence the right to recover damages for the loss of a chance of a cure. Awarding damages for the reduction of the prospect of a cure, when the long term result of treatment is still uncertain, is not a satisfactory exercise. Where medical treatment has resulted in an adverse outcome and negligence has increased the chance of that outcome, there may be a case for permitting a recovery of damages that is proportionate to the increase in the chance of the adverse outcome. That is not a case that has been made out on the present appeal. I would uphold the conventional approach to causation ...

For his part, Lord Hope would have allowed the appeal, but the focus of his speech is not upon 'loss of chance', but rather the first, 'quantification-based' argument of the claimant.

Gregg v Scott is undoubtedly a complex and difficult case, and one may well agree with Lord Phillips' assessment that it did not provide a suitable vehicle for recognising 'loss of chance' claims in medical negligence. A fundamental problem, as their Lordships noted, was that the claimant was still alive nearly 10 years after the original misdiagnosis. Thus (ignoring, for present purposes, the more painful treatment he had to undergo and his increased mental suffering) he had quite possibly lost nothing, not even a chance. Although statistically it made a difference for 17% of patients with a similar condition whether diagnosis took place at the earlier stage (when it should have occurred here) or only later on, it appeared increasing likely that the claimant was not in that group. Instead, his case was akin to that of someone who is exposed to a hazardous substance, known to increase the risk of a given harm, but where as yet no harm has materialised and no one knows whether it will or not (and where it is generally acknowledged that – except, possibly, for mental distress – no recovery can lie in tort law).

Reverting to the classical 'loss of chance' scenario illustrated by *Hotson* – where the claimant's injury has already occurred, it is submitted that such claims, based upon statistical evidence as to the typical progress of the condition that led up to it, should be permitted. Just as in the *Barnett* case, the basic question is whether or not the claimant's medical condition was untreatable *ab initio*. Would the risk it posed have sufficed by itself – despite proper treatment – for the injury the claimant suffered? Or did the lack of timeous treatment also play a necessary part? In such cases, empirically derived statistics (where available) serve to bring us significantly closer to the truth than adherence to the balance of probabilities standard of proof:

Stauch, M, 'Causation, risk and loss of chance in medical negligence' (1997) 17 OJLS 205:

... [T]he causal laws by reference to which particular assertions of cause and effect are justified are typically incomplete in form. Given both the state of our knowledge and the nature of our motivation we are rarely either able or willing to specify every member of the antecedent causal set upon which a given result invariably follows. Instead, we generally make do with causal generalisations which make reference to just a few of the set's elements. Such generalisations take the form of 'If (C, B, ??), then E', where 'C' is a [known risk], 'B' a bundle of more obvious background conditions, and '??' stands for the presence of further, unknown conditions. The corollary of the incompleteness in such causal statements is that, given the antecedent, C, alone, we cannot predict for certain that E will follow: it may be that on this particular occasion, the '??' are absent. What we can do, however, by employing statistics which record the previous occasions when E has been observed to follow C, is state with a high degree of accuracy the probability that E will follow this time ...

Such matters seem at first sight to be remote from the concerns of the lawyer. As already noted, the latter conducts his causal inquiry from a point in time when the effect is known to have come about. Accordingly, when on a given occasion E follows upon C and B, the presence of other unknown conditions can normally be taken on trust. Nevertheless, it is precisely the incompleteness in our causal laws which is the basis of the peculiar evidentiary difficulties created by multiple causation cases. In such cases, our inability to specify fully the relevant causal sets means that, even where a given [risk], C1, is followed by E, we cannot be sure whether C1 featured in an operative set: it may be that, on this occasion, the unknown further conditions required to complete the set were absent, and that E instead came about through the working of a different set containing a rival [risk], C2. Even in the simpler causal scenario in *Hotson*, where only a single causal set was present, it was impossible to say on the evidence whether the patient's non-treatment had featured in it ... [I]t might simply have contained the original fall, background conditions, plus further unknown conditions. The use of statistics, however, minimises such uncertainty by telling us over a range of similar cases how frequently the unknown conditions appear: in *Hotson*, 75% of the time (or on 75 out of every 100 occasions). Conversely, on the other 25% of occasions, when the unknown conditions are absent, non-treatment does feature in the set (ie, treatment will benefit the patient).

Statistics and the balance of probabilities

Given the *prima facie* interest and utility of these statistics, why was the House of Lords in fact so hostile to their use in *Hotson*? A number of reasons may be suggested.

First, their Lordships almost certainly distrusted the fact that, as just noted, statistical statements assert a connection between types of event over a range or 'class' rather than in respect of an individual case. Paradoxically this misgiving was best expressed in Croom-Johnson LJ's judgment in the Court of Appeal (which was ultimately favourable to the plaintiff):

> If it is proved statistically that 25% of the population have a chance of recovery from a certain injury and 75% do not, it does not mean that someone who suffers that injury and does not recover from it has lost a 25% chance. He may have lost nothing at all. What he has to do is prove that he was one of the 25% and his loss was caused by the defendant's negligence. To be a figure in a statistic does not itself give him a cause of action.

Instead, the House of Lords felt that, in line with established authority, the question of causation that the case raised was to be determined, like any other issue of past (as opposed to hypothetical) fact, on the balance of probabilities ...

[However], the idea that in a case of 'past fact' the balance of probabilities standard of proof could provide a more satisfactory means of resolving the issue of causal uncertainty than the use of statistics, shows a general failure to understand the epistemological relationship between the two approaches. As already noted, in multiple causation cases, the inherent incompleteness of our causal laws means that we are often unable to allocate causal responsibility between rival [risks]. However, whereas statistics derived systematically from our previous experience of similar cases, provide us with a very accurate probability-weighting for each [risk], the balance of probabilities test attempts to perform the same operation by appealing crudely to what we *feel* the likely cause to have been. The relevant feeling must, once again, derive from our previous experience of similar cases, but this time in its rawest form. [Reprinted by permission of Oxford University Press.]

Human agency in the causal chain

Complications of a different kind arise in cases in which resolving the causal inquiry requires us to decide how a human agent would have behaved in the hypothetical circumstances of no original breach of duty. In contrast to the cases considered previously, in which the causal chain consists only of physical events, such as the progress of an untreated disease, it may well be felt that the balance of probabilities standard of proof remains the most acceptable one here. (To assert that because, in a given situation, X per cent of persons are observed to do A, a particular individual, P, is X% likely to do A, would be to take an unduly mechanistic view of human agency.)

As we saw in Chapter 3, a common type of case, which requires us to assess the impact of human agency in the causal chain, is where the doctor fails to advise the patient of a given risk attached to treatment. Here the patient, in order to succeed in his claim, must show that, on the balance of probabilities, he would not have agreed to the treatment had he been properly advised. However, in other cases it is the defendant's hypothetical conduct that will be at issue: this is true in particular where a doctor negligently fails to attend the patient. Assuming that treatment is available which would benefit the patient, would the doctor have administered it? If not, so the doctor might argue, the failure by him to attend made no difference.

Here (as with the analogous claim by a patient that, had he known of a risk, he would have refused treatment), the court must first accept the veracity of the doctor's assertion that he would not have given treatment. In *Wisniewski v Central Manchester Health Authority* [1998] PIQR P324, the court, in holding that the necessary treatment would probably have been carried out, drew an adverse inference from the doctor's non-appearance in the witness box to back up his contrary assertion. If, though, the doctor's testimony is accepted, then, as Lord Browne-Wilkinson made clear in *Bolitho v City and Hackney HA* [1997] 4 All ER 771, that is not the end of the matter. There is a second question that the court must resolve:

> **Lord Browne-Wilkinson**: Where, as in the present case, a breach of a duty of care is proved or admitted, the burden still lies on the plaintiff to prove that such breach caused the injury suffered: *Bonnington Castings Ltd v Wardlaw* [1956] AC 613; *Wilsher v Essex AHA* [1988] AC 1074. In all cases the primary question is one of fact: did the wrongful act cause the injury? ... In a case of non-attendance by a doctor, there may be cases in which there is a doubt as to which doctor would have attended if the duty had been fulfilled. But in this case there was no doubt: if the duty had been carried out it would have either been Dr Horn or Dr Rodger, the only two doctors at St Bartholomew's who had responsibility for Patrick and were on duty. Therefore in the present case, the first relevant question is 'what would Dr Horn or Dr Rodger have done if they had attended?' As to Dr Horn, the judge accepted her evidence that she would not have intubated. By inference, although not expressly, the judge must have accepted that Dr Rodger also would not have intubated: as a senior house officer she would not have intubated without the approval of her senior registrar, Dr Horn ...

> However in the present case the answer to the question 'what would have happened?' is not determinative of the issue of causation. At the trial the defendants accepted that if the professional standard of care required any doctor who attended to intubate Patrick, Patrick's claim must succeed. Dr Horn could not escape liability by proving that she would have failed to take the course which any competent doctor would have adopted. A defendant cannot escape liability by saying that the damage would have occurred in any event because he would have committed some other breach of duty thereafter. I

have no doubt that this concession was rightly made by the defendants. But there is some difficulty in analysing why it was correct. I adopt the analysis of Hobhouse LJ in *Joyce v Merton, Sutton and Wandsworth HA* [1996] 7 Med LR 1. In commenting on the decision of the Court of Appeal in the present case, he said, p 20:

> Thus a plaintiff can discharge the burden of proof on causation by satisfying the court *either* that the relevant person would in fact have taken the requisite action (although she would not have been at fault if she had not), or that the proper discharge of the relevant person's duty towards the plaintiff required that she take that action. The former alternative calls for no explanation since it is simply the factual proof of the causative effect of the original fault. The latter is slightly more sophisticated: it involves the factual situation that the original fault did not itself cause the injury but that this was because there would have been some further fault on the part of the defendants; the plaintiff proves his case by proving that his injuries would have been avoided if proper care had continued to be taken. In the *Bolitho* case the plaintiff had to prove that the continuing exercise of proper care would have resulted in his being intubated.

There were, therefore, two questions for the judge to decide on causation: (1) 'What would Dr Horn have done, or authorised to be done, if she had attended Patrick?' And: (2) 'If she would not have intubated, would that have been negligent?' The *Bolam* test has no relevance to the first of those questions but is central to the second.

There can be no doubt that, as the majority of the Court of Appeal held, the judge directed himself correctly in accordance with that approach ... The dissenting judgment of Simon Brown LJ in the Court of Appeal is based on a misreading of the judge's judgment. He treats the judge as having only asked himself one question, namely, the second question. To the extent that the Lord Justice noticed the first question – would Dr Horn have intubated? – he said that the judge was wrong to accept Dr Horn's evidence that she would not have intubated. In my judgment it was for the judge to assess the truth of her evidence on this issue.

Importantly, as this judgment makes clear, where the agent whose hypothetical conduct is called into question is the defendant, such conduct – if it is to be accepted as negativing causation – must in any event fall within the bounds of the non-negligent.

Legal causation/remoteness of damage

Legal causation, or 'remoteness', operates as a further limiting device, which may exclude liability even where the defendant's conduct clearly *did* play a necessary part in the claimant's injury (ie the factual causation requirement of the 'but for' test has been satisfied). In negligence, the dominant approach of the courts, following the decision of the Privy Council in *The Wagon Mound (No 1)* [1961] AC 388, is to begin by considering the nature of the harm in suit (that is, the damage that actually materialised) and ask if it was reasonably foreseeable. In other words, was it the risk of *that* harm occurring that made the defendant's conduct faulty?

It is often said that, once the broad 'type' of harm suffered by the claimant was reasonably foreseeable, the fact that its precise manner of upshot or extent may not have been is immaterial. On the other hand, as cases since *The Wagon Mound* demonstrate, given that any harmful outcome can be described at different levels of abstraction, the question of its foreseeability – and, hence, the defendant's liability – will turn on the specificity of the description applied by the court in a particular case. This point has led some commentators to regard the whole remoteness enquiry as merely a cover for the concealed policy choices of judges. Arguably a more principled solution would be to focus not so much on the 'type' of harm that has occurred, but rather on the further necessary conditions that (together with the defendant's conduct) completed the causal set for harm in the particular case. Was the possible completion of a causal set that included those further conditions a reason for regarding the conduct as a breach of duty? (See generally Stauch, M, 'Risk and remoteness of damage in negligence' (2001) 64 MLR 191.)

In principle, remoteness principles may apply in medical negligence (just as in other negligence cases) to defeat the claimant's action. In *Brown v Lewisham and North Southwark HA* [1999] Lloyd's Rep Med 110 the claimant, who had undergone heart surgery was negligently discharged from hospital while suffering from a chest infection. Later he was found to have an unsuspected thrombosis, which led to the loss of his leg. The court did not accept that, had he remained in hospital, the leg would have been saved (ie it denied factual causation). However, as Beldam LJ noted in the Court of Appeal, the claimant's action would in any event have failed on remoteness grounds:

> **Beldam LJ**: The public policy of limiting the liability of tortfeasors by the control mechanism of foreseeability seems to me as necessary in cases of medical as in any other type of negligence. I do not see on what policy ground it would be fair or just to hold a doctor to be in breach of duty who failed to diagnose an asymptomatic and undetectable illness merely because he was at fault in the management of a correctly diagnosed but unrelated condition. In short, it must be shown that the injury suffered by the patient is within the risk from which it was the doctor's duty to protect him.

(See also the case of *R v Croydon HA* [1998] Lloyd's Rep Med 44, CA.)

In practice, however, a patient's claim will seldom fail on this basis. Generally, the courts will refuse to make fine distinctions between the risk which ought to have been foreseen and that which actually materialised. Thus, in *Hepworth v Kerr* (1995) 6 Med LR 139, a doctor was held liable for using an experimental anaesthetic technique on a patient which resulted in a spinal stroke. The risk of inducing a spinal stroke was, in fact not known about, but the risk of a cerebral stroke (thus, making the procedure's use negligent) was. Similarly, in *Wisniewski v Manchester HA* [1998] PIQR P324, the defendant sought to deny liability on the basis that, although the claimant's hypoxia during birth – which he had negligently failed to manage – had been foreseeable, the mechanics of it in the particular case (involving a rare instance of a knot in the umbilical cord) had not been. In the Court of Appeal, Brooke LJ commented that to make such a distinction would be an 'affront to common sense, and the law would look an ass'.

As we saw in Chapter 3, the requirement of legal causation may also be relaxed in the context of 'non-disclosure' cases (leading exceptionally to liability for risks over which the doctor ultimately had no control at all).

DEFENCES AND LIMITATIONS OF ACTIONS

Defences

It must be said that the usual tortious defences are rarely used in medical cases, and, for that reason, are dealt with briefly.

Contributory negligence

Contributory negligence involves the claim by the doctor/hospital that the patient has also been at fault in his conduct, in relation to the management of his own condition, and that this has contributed to the injury he suffered, or to its severity. If this is accepted, the court may reduce the damages awarded in accordance with the Law Reform (Contributory Negligence) Act 1945. However, as Grubb and Jones note, this defence has an unattractive feel in the context of medical negligence and will seldom be argued:

Grubb, A, (ed), *Principles of Medical Law,* **2nd edn, 2004, Oxford: OUP, p 465:**

7.55 Although, in theory, there is no reason why contributory negligence should not apply in a claim for medical negligence, in practice the defence is rarely invoked successfully, and this is reflected in a comparative dearth of cases. It may be that the plea is considered to be inappropriate, given the inequality between the respective positions of doctor and patient. Patients do not generally question the advice or conduct of their doctors, even when they are aware that their condition is deteriorating or not improving. If the patient has ignored the doctor's advice (for example by discharging himself from hospital or failing to return for further treatment) it may be easier to establish the defence. It would have to be shown that a reasonable person would have been aware of the significance of the advice, which will depend on the nature of the advice and whether it was clear to the patient …

7.57 The one English reported case in which the claimant's conduct was held to be negligent is *Pidgeon v Doncaster HA* [[2002] Lloyd's Rep Med 130 (Doncaster County Ct)] where a claimant who developed cervical cancer, having been told that the results of a smear test were negative, was held to have been two-thirds contributory negligent in failing to have a further smear test despite frequent reminders. It would also be possible for a plea of contributory negligence to apply in cases where the claimant attempts suicide and a claim is brought against medical staff on the basis of a negligent failure to prevent the suicide attempt …

Consent or volenti non fit injuria

This is where the defendant argues that the patient had consented to the risk. In a Scottish medical negligence decision, *Sabri-Tabrizi v Lothian Health Board* (1997) 43 BMLR 190, it was said that such consent must normally have occurred prior to, and certainly cannot come after, the defendant's breach of duty. It is arguable that this condition would never be satisfied in the context of medical treatment, and there would appear to be no cases where the defence has been argued successfully.

Illegality or ex turpi causa

The defence of *ex turpi causa*, or illegality, potentially applies when the background events relied on by the claimant in his negligence action disclose criminal wrongdoing on his part. In such cases, the defendant may persuade the court that, as a matter of public policy, it would not be seemly to allow the action. The doctrine will seldom be of any relevance in the medical negligence context. However, the Court of Appeal had recourse to it in *Clunis v Camden and Islington HA* [1998] 3 All

ER 180, where the claimant, a mentally ill man imprisoned for manslaughter, alleged that the defendant authority had negligently failed to detain him in time under the Mental Health Act 1983.

Limitation of actions

There are good pragmatic reasons for imposing time limits upon litigants, beyond which they cannot pursue their cause of action. These include the evidential difficulties which may arise when relevant documentation may have been destroyed, and memories have faded, and the fact that both plaintiffs and defendants need to know when an action is no longer possible. However, the common law imposes no limitation. This is governed entirely by statute law, the most recent statute being the Limitation Act 1980 (as amended).

The Act imposes time limits for different causes of action. The provisions which concern us in medical malpractice are those relating to contract where the limitation period is six years, from the date on which the cause of action accrued (s 5), and personal injury claims, dealt with in s 11:

> 11 Special time limit for actions in respect of personal injuries
>
> (1) This section applies to any action for damages for negligence, nuisance or breach of duty (whether the duty exists by virtue of a contract or of provision made by or under a statute or independently of any contract or any such provision) where the damages claimed by the plaintiff for the negligence, nuisance or breach of duty consist of or include damages in respect of personal injuries to the plaintiff or any other person.
>
> ...
>
> (3) An action to which this section applies shall not be brought after the expiration of the period applicable in accordance with sub-s (4) or (5) below.
>
> (4) Except where sub-s (5) below applies, the period applicable is three years from–
>
> (a) the date on which the cause of action accrued; or
>
> (b) the date of knowledge (if later) of the person injured.
>
> (5) If the injured person dies before the expiration of the period mentioned in sub-s (4) above, the period applicable as respects the cause of action surviving for the benefit of his estate by virtue of s 1 of the Law Reform (Miscellaneous Provisions) Act 1934 shall be three years from–
>
> (a) the date of death; or
>
> (b) the date of the personal representative's knowledge; whichever is the later.

The time limit of three years (in the case of medical negligence) is calculated from the date the damage occurred. This will usually be the date on which the breach occurred, but if the claimant was unaware of significant aspects of his treatment, or the injury did not develop until a later date, then the provision of s 11(4)(b) will apply, that is, the date of his knowledge. What is entailed by 'knowledge' is defined further in s 14 of the Act, and has generated a complex case law of its own: see *Rowbottom v Royal Masonic Hospital* [2003] PIQR P1 (CA). However, a discretion is retained by the court under s 33 of the Act to allow out-of-time claims if, in all the circumstances, it appears to it equitable to do so.

In relation to persons under a disability (minors, or adults who are of unsound mind so as to be incapable of managing their own affairs), s 28 provides that time will not start to run until the disability ends or the person dies. In consequence, if the action accrued when the patient was a child, he will have until the age of 21 to bring proceedings. A person of unsound mind, who never achieves mental competency, will not be subject to any limitation period. In such a case, a very long delay makes no difference to his right to issue proceedings at any time. In *Headford v Bristol and DHA* [1995] 6 Med LR 1, the claimant issued proceedings 28 years after the event. The defendant sought to deal with this by an application to have the proceedings struck out as being an abuse of legal process. The defendant was unsuccessful. The Court of Appeal held that, if the proceedings were within the open ended time limit envisaged by Parliament in s 28, then they could hardly be said to be an abuse of legal process.

DAMAGES

Principles governing awards

The general principles applying to damages apply to all personal injury cases, and there is no special body of law which applies to medical malpractice cases. In view of this, readers are referred to the specialist personal injury texts for a detailed analysis (for example, Kemp & Kemp, *The Quantum of Damages in Personal Injury and Fatal Accident Claims*, 1992, London: Sweet & Maxwell). However, general principles and heads of damage are here considered in outline.

The general compensatory principle underlying tort is that a successful claimant should receive damages to restore him to the position he would have been in, had the tort never occurred. The law distinguishes here between general damages (for non-pecuniary loss) and special damages (for pecuniary loss).

Damages for non-pecuniary loss

Damages in battery

Even if the claimant has sustained no loss, damages, albeit of a nominal amount, can be recovered. The other important point to note is that, in battery, there is no place for the concept of foreseeability; damages can be recovered for all direct consequences of the battery. For example, in *Allan v New Mount Sinai Hospital* (1980) 109 DLR (3d) 634, an anaesthetist, although not negligent, was liable for a highly unusual and unforeseeable reaction, when the action was brought in battery.

Pain and suffering and loss of amenity

According to McGregor (*McGregor on Damages*, 17th edn, 2003, London: Sweet & Maxwell), 'pain' is the immediately felt effect on the nerves and brain, while 'suffering' is distress not directly connected with any bodily condition, and would include fear of future incapacity (in relation to health, sanity or the ability to make a living), and humiliation, sadness and embarrassment caused by disfigurement. This may also include a sum for the anguish caused by reduced life expectancy (s 1(1)(b) of the Administration of Justice Act 1982). It must be stressed that there are no damages for ordinary mental distress such as shock or fear, but if, say, shock or grief has exacerbated the claimant's physical injury, then damages may be increased accordingly: *Kralj v McGrath* [1986] 1 All ER 54.

Damages for loss of amenity are to compensate for things like injuries to the senses, sexual dysfunction, loss of marriage prospects, loss of enjoyment of family life and loss of enjoyment of work. An interesting question arises as to whether the claimant who is unconscious should receive damages for these losses when he is not aware of them. The House of Lords had to consider this in the medical negligence case of *Lim Poh Choo v Camden and Islington AHA* [1980] AC 174, where, following an anaesthetic error, the patient was rendered almost completely unconscious so as to be unaware of her condition. It was argued by the defendant that her lack of awareness precluded an award of damages for loss of amenity. The court rejected this argument, relying upon the case of *H West and Son Ltd v Shepherd* [1964] AC 326, where it was said (*per* Lord Morris):

> **Lord Morris**: Certain particular questions have been raised. How are general damages affected, if at all, by the fact that the sufferer is unconscious? How are they affected, if at all, if it be the fact that the sufferer will not be able to make use of any money which is awarded?
>
> The first of these questions may be largely answered if it is remembered that damages are designed to compensate for such results as have actually been caused. If someone has been caused pain, then damages to compensate for the enduring of it may be awarded. If, however, by reason of an injury, someone is made unconscious either for a short or for a prolonged period with the result that he does not feel pain, then he needs no monetary compensation in respect of pain because he will not have suffered it ... An unconscious person will be spared pain and suffering ... The fact of unconsciousness is therefore relevant in respect of and will eliminate those heads or elements of damage which can only exist by being felt or thought or experienced. The fact of unconsciousness does not, however, eliminate the actuality of the deprivations of the ordinary experiences and amenities of life which may be the inevitable result of some physical injury.

In other words, damages for pain and suffering have to relate to actual experiences, whereas damages for loss of amenity can be assessed without reference to the claimant's experience.

Another question concerns how far damages for 'pure' mental distress (ie arising in the absence of any physical injury suffered by the claimant) may be compensated for. Traditionally, tort law has been chary in making such awards. On the other hand, as noted at p 289 above, an exception is recognised in relation to persons who suffer psychiatric harm due to witnessing death or serious injury to their loved ones, where this occurred in a shocking manner. In fact, the categories of psychiatric harm are expanding and now include the so-called 'worried well', ie persons whose psychiatric harm results from knowing that they are at a significant risk of harm (due to their exposure to a hazardous agent or event), but it is not certain that they will actually suffer the harm: see *Re Creutzfeldt-Jakob Litigation (No 9)* (2000) 54 BMLR 111. However, in every case the claimant's injury must take the form of a recognised psychiatric illness: mental distress below this will not attract any damages.

Progress of disease and loss of a chance

As we saw in *Gregg v Scott* [2005] UKHL 2 (see p 318, above), the claimant's first argument was that the progress of his disease – the enlargement of the tumour that had occurred during the 14-month period of non-diagnosis – should itself be characterised as 'damage', and that it should be quantified by reference to his increased risk of dying. This approach was accepted by Lord Hope, but rejected by the other Law Lords. In his speech, Lord Hoffmann commented as follows:

Lord Hoffmann: [70] [In the Court of Appeal] Latham LJ, who accepted the quantification argument, put the matter in this way (para 41):

'In the present case, the evidence clearly established that the cancer had spread, on the findings of the judge, by reason of the negligence of the respondent. That was all that was necessary to found his claim in negligence. Once that had been established, the question for the court was the extent to which the consequences, which included the reduced prospects of successful treatment, could themselves be established as an issue of quantification of damage.'

[71] I respectfully think that this formulation begs more than one question. It is true that the delay caused an early spread of the cancer and that this reduced his percentage chance of survival for more than 10 years. But to say that the claimant can therefore obtain damages for the reduction in his chances of survival assumes in his favour that a reduction in the chance of survival is a recoverable head of damage; an issue raised by the claimant's second argument which Latham LJ said (at para 41) that he did not need to decide. On the other hand, if the claim is for actually depriving him of survival for more than 10 years, the question is whether the spread of the cancer caused it. The judge's finding was that it did not. It was likely that his life would have been shortened to less than 10 years anyway.

The rejection of the notion that progression of disease *per se* should be regarded as damage is, with respect, compelling. If it were not so, then, in every case where the defendant negligently delays in abating the progress of a natural condition affecting the claimant, damages would lie (the latter could always argue that the possible, ultimate negative outcome has drawn closer). That is not to say that the claimant should not recover – on ordinary principles – for proven additional setbacks to his interests (including more invasive therapy that would not have been needed if the disease had been diagnosed earlier). In *Gregg*, both Lord Phillips and Baroness Hale voiced regret that the claimant had not pleaded this latter head of damages. Arguably, an award may also lie in respect of the claimant's increased mental suffering.

As noted, in *Gregg* the majority of the House of Lords also refused – at least in the context of that case – to recognise the possibility of claiming for 'loss of chance' in medical negligence. However, as suggested earlier, such claims (which, properly, arise only where the claimant's disease has already culminated in identifiable harm, ie a permanent set-back to his interests), have in our view much to commend them. As in *Hotson*, the issue here relates to the appropriateness of using statistical evidence to assess the role played by the defendant's negligence in past, actual harm to the claimant. It is clear that damages in such cases are readily quantifiable on the basis adopted by the lower courts in *Hotson* itself, that is, the full award for the relevant damage is divided by the statistical chance of avoiding it lost as a result of the defendant's negligence.

What is perhaps not so obvious is that, equally, in cases in which the claimant currently receives the full quantum (under the 'all or nothing' balance of probabilities approach), a discount should be made where empirical statistics show that the claimant's chance of avoiding injury would in any event have been less than 100%.

This approach (representing the *quid pro quo* from the defendant's point of view) was taken at first instance in *Clark v MacLennan* [1983] 1 All ER 416, *Bagley v North Herts HA* (1986) 136 NLJ 1014, and *Judge v Huntingdon HA* [1995] 6 Med LR 223 (although cf Baroness Hale's disapproval of it in *Gregg*). It is submitted that such discounting is consonant with legal principle: as Sir John Donaldson MR remarked in *Hotson*, why should a patient receive 100% damages in respect of negligent late treatment, if he was 49% likely to have suffered the same harm even if treated promptly? Moreover, it would draw much of the sting from Lord Hoffmann's concern in *Gregg*, as to the impact on NHS finances of allowing loss of chance claims in this area.

Non-disclosure cases

Interesting quantum issues arise in the wake of the House of Lords' recognition, in *Chester v Afshar* [2004] UKHL 41, that for causation to be present in 'non-disclosure' cases, the claimant need show only that, if he had known of the risk, he would have delayed the injurious treatment, not rejected it for all time (see Chapter 3, at p 152, above). In such cases, how far should the fact that the claimant would later have been exposed to the same risk of injury be reflected by a reduction in damages?

> **Stauch, M, 'Causation and confusion in respect of medical non-disclosure: *Chester v Afshar*' (2005) 14 Nott LJ 66**
>
> Suppose, first of all that, though identifiable in advance only as a small risk, it subsequently becomes clear that the factors that, together with (carefully executed) surgery, led to the patient's injury were inherent in the latter's constitution: ie he was predisposed to suffer that injury. In such a case, the doctor's wrongful failure to advise of the risk, which brought forward the surgery, has simply accelerated an injury that would have occurred later in any event. It is true that factual 'but for' causation is still present: the patient would not have suffered the injury *when he did*, if the doctor had given the warning. Nevertheless, his loss –apart from mental distress- only extends to a short period of freedom from the injury in question. This fact should be recognised, in accordance with normal quantum principles, by a reduced award of damages.
>
> In *Chester*, the above issue did not arise: the risk of caudal equine syndrome appears to have been 'free-floating' – as liable to strike one patient as the next. However, the second quantum problem does so, albeit in a relatively minor form. The problem is this: to what extent should the fact that the claimant would ultimately have run the same risk of injury also be reflected in discounted damages? In *Chester* itself, any such discount would only be in the order of 1–2 per cent. However, another case could quite easily arise in which the risk attached to the hypothetical delayed surgery is very much greater, say 30 per cent. Here, it seems right for damages to be reduced to take account of the substantial chance that the patient would later have suffered the same injury anyway.

Fatal accidents

Section 1(1) of the Fatal Accidents Act 1976 gives a right to certain dependants to recover for their loss of dependency. In addition to this a fixed sum of 'bereavement' damages is recoverable (s 1A) by the spouse of the deceased or the parents of a deceased unmarried minor child.

Damages for pecuniary loss

Such damages include loss of earnings, medical expenses and the cost of care. There is also the possibility of the claimant recovering what is known as a '*Smith v*

Manchester' award to compensate for disadvantage on the labour market, that is, the claimant has been able to return to work but, due to the injury, would be disadvantaged in finding another job in the event of the present one ending (*Smith v Manchester Corp* (1974) 17 KIR 1).

LIABILITY FOR DEFECTIVE MEDICINES

Frequently patients may allege that they were injured, not through negligence on a doctor's part, but by medicinal drugs that they were (properly) given during treatment.

Before they are made available for prescription, medicines are subject to comprehensive licensing requirements pursuant to the Medicines Act 1968. However, the fact that such drugs may sometimes give rise to unpredictable and harmful metabolic reactions was brought poignantly to the public consciousness by the Thalidomide tragedy of the late 1960s and, given the difficulty in proving fault on the part of manufacturers (even the most thorough testing may fail to reveal a particular reaction in advance), provoked calls from both the Law Commission (Report 82, Cmnd 6831, 1977) and the Pearson Committee (Cmnd 7054, 1978 (the Pearson Report)) for 'no fault' compensation to be introduced for such injury.

In the event, the emergence of a no fault scheme had to await initiatives at EC level in relation to defective consumer products generally. As a result of Directive 85/374/EEC, the Government passed Pt I of the Consumer Protection Act 1987, which imposes strict liability upon manufacturers in respect of products put into circulation after 1 March 1988:

Product liability

1 Purpose and construction of Part I

This Part shall have effect for the purpose of making such provision as is necessary in order to comply with the product liability Directive and shall be construed accordingly.

2 Liability for defective products

(1) Subject to the following provisions of this Part, where any damage is caused wholly or partly by a defect in a product, every person to whom sub-s (2) below applies shall be liable for the damage.

(2) This sub-section applies to–

(a) the producer of the product;

(b) any person who, by putting his name on the product or using a trade mark or other distinguishing mark in relation to the product, has held himself out to be the producer of the product;

(c) any person who has imported the product into a Member State from a place outside the Member States in order, in the course of any business of his, to supply it to another.

...

(5) Where two or more persons are liable by virtue of this Part for the same damage, their liability shall be joint and several.

(6) This section shall be without prejudice to any liability arising otherwise than by virtue of this Part.

3 Meaning of 'defect'

(1) Subject to the following provisions of this section, there is a defect in a product for the purposes of this Part if the safety of the product is not such as persons generally are entitled to expect, and for those purposes 'safety', in relation to a product, shall include safety with respect to products comprised in that product and safety in the context of risks of damage to property, as well as in the context of risks of death or personal injury.

(2) In determining for the purposes of sub-s (1) above what persons generally are entitled to expect in relation to a product, all the circumstances shall be taken into account, including–

   (a) the manner in which, and purposes for which, the product has been marketed, its get-up, the use of any mark in relation to the product and any instructions for, or warnings with respect to, doing or refraining from doing anything with or in relation to the product;

   (b) what might reasonably be expected to be done with or in relation to the product; and

   (c) the time when the product was supplied by its producer to another,

   and nothing in this section shall require a defect to be inferred from the fact alone that the safety of a product which is supplied after that time is greater than the safety of the product in question.

4 Defences

(1) In any civil proceedings by virtue of this Part against any person ('the person proceeded against') in respect of a defect in a product it shall be a defence for him to show–

   (a) that the defect is attributable to compliance with any requirement imposed by or under any enactment or with any Community obligation; or

   (b) that the person proceeded against did not at any time supply the product to another; or

   (c) that the following conditions are satisfied, that is to say–

      (i) that the only supply of the product to another by the person proceeded against was otherwise than in the course of a business of that person's; and

      (ii) that s 2(2) above does not apply to that person or applies to him by virtue only of things done otherwise than with a view to profit; or

   (d) that the defect did not exist in the product at the relevant time; or

   (e) that the state of scientific and technical knowledge at the relevant time was not such that a producer of products of the same description as the product in question might be expected to have discovered the defect if it had existed in his products while they were under his control; or

   (f) that the defect–

      (i) constituted a defect in a product ('the subsequent product') in which the product in question had been comprised; and

      (ii) was wholly attributable to the design of the subsequent product or to compliance by the producer of the product in question with instructions given by the producer of the subsequent product ...

For a number of years there were very few cases on the Act, but latterly several claims have been brought under it in respect of matters as diverse as a torn condom, resulting in pregnancy (*Richardson v LRC Products* [2000] Lloyd's Rep Med 280), and an elasticated buckle on a sleeping bag, which hit a child in the eye (*Abouzaid v Mothercare* (2001) *The Times*, 20 February). The two main issues that the courts have had to wrestle with are the meaning of 'defect' within s 3 of the Act, and the scope of the so called 'development risk' defence afforded to manufacturers under s 4(1)(e). Both these matters were recently at the heart of the important High Court ruling in *A and Others v National Blood Authority* [2001] 3 All ER 289, a class action brought by 114 people who contracted Hepatitis C from contaminated blood supplies. In finding for the claimants, Burton J took the view that, for a 'defect' to arise under s 3, it was enough that the risk of infection was not one that was known and accepted by society generally. As Deards and Twigg-Flesner comment:

Deards, E and Twigg-Flesner, C, 'The Consumer Protection Act 1987: proof at last that it is protecting consumers' (2001) 10(2) Nott LJ 1:

The High Court drew a distinction between 'standard' and 'non-standard' products. 'Standard' products were those that met the design and standard of safety intended by the manufacturer. A 'non-standard' product was a particular unit of the product that did not meet the standard. In *A and Others*, the court stated that the infected blood products were non-standard, that is to say, differed from the standard product intended by the manufacturer. The standard blood products were not inherently defective. In the case of blood transfusions, it was only 1% of the product that 'failed' in that it had been contaminated with the Hepatitis C virus. The court suggested that it might be easier to prove a defect where the product was non-standard, since it would fall to be compared with the standard product. The problem with this argument is that a product is only non-standard if it is defective, but whether it is defective could be affected by whether it is non-standard. Admittedly the court envisaged that a non-standard product was one that was defective in a non-technical, non-Act sense, but there could be cases where even this was disputed, and then a circular argument would result. In respect of non-standard products, the court stated that the consumers' expectations as to safety depended on whether they accepted the non-standard nature of the product.

The High Court confirmed that the factors for assessing the defectiveness listed in section 3 of the Act were not exclusive, and that all relevant circumstances were to be considered. However, it ruled that avoidability of the risk of infection was not a relevant factor. The possibility of avoiding the harmful characteristics by taking precautionary measures, the impracticality, cost and difficulty of taking such measures and the benefit to society of the product were therefore not relevant. On the facts, the risk was known by doctors but was not known and accepted by society generally. The risk of infected blood could therefore not have been accepted by consumers unless they were warned, which they had not been. The infected blood products were therefore defective.

Equally significant was the judge's approach to the 'development risk' defence under s 4(1)(e). Previously, the general view had been that the defence provided a broad escape for manufacturers of products, such as new drugs, whose research and development occurs at the frontiers of scientific knowledge, and where the occasional defect may be regarded as inevitable. Indeed, it was lobbying from the pharmaceutical industry (who argued that, without such a provision, drugs companies would be deterred from developing new products) that led to its inclusion in the EC Directive in the first place. However, in *A and Others*, Burton J interpreted the defence narrowly, holding that it could not be invoked once the risk was known to the defendant (or should have been known in the light of information then accessible to it). The fact that here there was no available test for detecting the presence of Hepatitis C in any specific batch of blood was held to be irrelevant. It remains to be seen whether the case, with its robust assertion of true strict liability in this area, will be followed in the higher courts.

Finally, it should be noted that the payment of compensation under the act remains in any event contingent upon causation being shown between the medicinal product and injury. Given the frequently opaque nature of causal processes in this area (with plausible causal chains between phenomena often hard to find) this may remain a serious obstacle for many claimants. This is especially so in respect of idiosyncratic reactions to a drug on the part of a small minority of users where, *ex hypothesi*, the degree of regularity between cause (ingesting the drug) and effect (injury) which generally ground causal inferences will be absent. In two cases brought in negligence at common law, the courts indeed held that the claimants had failed to show that the drugs they were given (an overdose of penicillin and the pertussis vaccine, respectively) were even capable of causing their injuries: see *Kay v Ayrshire and Arran Health Board* [1987] 2 All ER 417 and *Loveday v Renton* [1990] 1 Med LR 117.

REFORMING THE LAW

Problems with the medical litigation system

Medical negligence cases are often very expensive to bring, because of the technical and complex nature of the litigation. Moreover, statistically, far fewer such claims succeed – 17% – than the average for negligence actions generally (around 80%). Nevertheless, this has not prevented a major upsurge in such claims over the last 20 years or so, with the public generally appearing less deferential, more aware of their rights, and holding higher expectations of what can and should be achieved on their behalf.

The Woolf Report, July 1996, looked critically at medical negligence litigation and found some major problems:

Lord Woolf MR, *Access to Justice: The Final Report to the Lord Chancellor on the Civil Justice System in England and Wales, 1996,* **London: HMSO:**

Chapter 15: Medical Negligence

Reasons for looking at medical negligence

1 Why have I singled out medical negligence for the most intensive examination during Stage 2 of my Inquiry? (I am using the term 'medical negligence' in this report to refer to any litigation involving allegations of negligence in the delivery of health care, whether by doctors, nurses or other health professionals.) It may appear a surprising choice, because medical negligence cases have no special procedures or rules of court. They are a sub-species of professional negligence actions, and they also belong to what is numerically the largest category of cases proceeding to trial, personal injury. Neither of these is singled out for special attention.

2 The answer is that early in the Inquiry it became increasingly obvious that it was in the area of medical negligence that the civil justice system was failing most conspicuously to meet the needs of litigants in a number of respects:

(a) The disproportion between costs and damages in medical negligence is particularly excessive, especially in lower value cases.

(b) The delay in resolving claims is more often unacceptable.

(c) Unmeritorious cases are often pursued, and clear-cut claims defended, for too long.

(d) The success rate is lower than in other personal injury litigation.

(e) The suspicion between the parties is more intense and the lack of co-operation frequently greater than in many other areas of litigation.

... 5   The difficulty of proving both causation and negligence, which arises more acutely in medical negligence than in other personal injury cases, accounts for much of the excessive cost. The root of the problem, however, lies less in the complexity of the law or procedure than in the climate of mutual suspicion and defensiveness which is still all too prevalent in this area of litigation. Patients feel let down when treatment goes wrong, sometimes because of unrealistic expectations as to what could be achieved. Doctors feel they are under attack from aggrieved patients and react defensively. The patients' disappointment is then heightened by what they perceive to be a refusal to acknowledge fault and an attempt to cover up.

...   **change of culture**

21   The extent of patients' mistrust of doctors and other hospital staff is illustrated by the submission I have received from Action for Victims of Medical Accidents (AVMA). They argue that the real reason for defendants' reluctance to investigate complaints where there is a possibility of legal action is a concern that such an investigation might indeed disclose negligence:

       [The defendants] do not in fact want a relatively simple and cheap way of investigating a complaint which might expose that there has been negligence.

22   If that mistrust is to be removed, the medical profession and the NHS administration must demonstrate their commitment to patients' well being by adopting a constructive approach to claims handling. It must be clearly accepted that injured patients are entitled to redress, and that professional solidarity or individual self-esteem are not sufficient reasons for resisting or obstructing valid claims.

23   Patients and their representatives, for their part, must recognise that some degree of risk is inherent in all medical treatment, and that even the best practitioners do sometimes make mistakes. They should not pursue unrealistic claims, and should make every effort to resolve disputes without recourse to litigation.

24   It is fundamental to my approach to civil litigation in general that legal proceedings should be treated as a last resort, to be used only when other means of resolving a dispute are inappropriate or have failed. When someone has a potential negligence claim against a doctor or hospital, the first essential step is to find out what the patient wants to achieve. If his or her main need is for substantial financial compensation to cover future loss of earnings or the cost of continuing care, then litigation may be (but is not always) the best way to proceed. If the patient is chiefly concerned to get an explanation or apology for what went wrong, or to ensure that procedures are changed so that future accidents can be avoided, then litigation is less likely to be the best course. Recourse to the NHS complaints procedures and, if necessary, the Health Service Ombudsman, may offer a more appropriate means of redress.

... 28   ... Effective communication ... needs to start before things go wrong. All patients who are about to undergo treatment should understand that the outcome of medical treatment can be uncertain, and should be told about the range of possible outcomes in their particular case. Wherever practicable, the advice should be confirmed in writing. Doctors and hospitals should encourage patients to report any unsatisfactory outcome as soon as possible, and to seek an explanation direct from the individual doctor or hospital before going to a solicitor.

The Woolf reforms, along with the reduction proposed by the Lord Chancellor in civil legal aid (although for the time being medical negligence cases remain exempt), have attracted a great deal of controversy. However, it is generally accepted that reform to medical negligence litigation is inevitable. The possibility, adverted to by Lord Woolf of greater use of mediation, as an alternative to recourse to the courts, was piloted in two NHS regions from 1995–98. However, as the NHS Executive noted in its subsequent report, the scheme's success remained equivocal:

NHS Executive, *Mediating Medical Negligence Claims: An Option for the Future?*, Report of the NHS Executive, 2000, London: DoH:

The pilot scheme was launched in two NHS regions – Anglia and Oxford and Northern and Yorkshire – and two regional coordinators were appointed. It was anticipated that up to 40 cases would be mediated over a two-year period but the scheme was extended for an additional year when the number of referrals remained low. By the end of the third year a total of 12 cases had been mediated and settlement reached in 11 of them. In addition, there were 44 other cases identified by the research team in which mediation had been suggested to the opposing side, 14 of these are on-going referrals at the close of the scheme ...

Concerns about low take-up of the scheme were also associated with reticence amongst solicitors to refer cases. Although support for mediation was given in principle, and benefits over the traditional litigation system identified, solicitors seemed reluctant to refer their cases to the pilot scheme. Despite this, they saw the introduction of mediation as an inevitable part of civil justice reform.

A number of criticisms were also made of practices adopted in the mediated cases. These included concerns about the role of medics in mediation; how the decision whether or not to mediate was made; last-minute ambushes with information and experts; unnecessarily defensive stances adopted by solicitors; the intensity of the day; and perceptions of mediator bias.

... The costs of mediation

Proponents of mediation do not base their call for greater use of this method on financial considerations but prefer to stress the ways in which the process can lead to more constructive consideration and settlement of disputes. But, debate over the merits of mediation cannot be divorced from considerations about costs. However, it has been difficult to obtain objective information about the costs of introducing mediation and it has not been possible in this report to be definitive about the likely financial implications of the widespread use of this technique ...

When traditionally managed cases with a similar profile to the 12 mediated cases are compared, it becomes clear that mediation has the potential to increase the costs of the settlement process. Additional costs included those of mediators, of accommodation and the loss to the NHS of having doctors present. However, these findings are tentative as the number of mediated cases was very small and other models of mediation are available which would not be so cost-intensive.

Moving to a 'no fault' system?

A more radical solution, that has been proposed frequently over the years, and was reiterated by Professor Ian Kennedy in his conclusions to the Bristol Royal Infirmary

Inquiry (*Learning from Bristol: the report of the public inquiry into children's heart surgery at the Bristol Royal Infirmary 1984–1995*, Cm 5207, July 2001), is that we should move away from the common law of tort altogether towards a statutory 'no fault' based system of liability for medical negligence.

In this regard, the New Zealand experience of no fault compensation is sometimes cited as a way forward for the UK. However, on close examination, significant problems in the implementation of such schemes reveal themselves. As Ken Oliphant notes:

Oliphant, K, 'Defining "medical misadventures" – lessons from New Zealand' (1996) 4 Med L Rev 1:

The New Zealand experience of no fault compensation for medical accidents provides cause for alarm for tort law reformers in the UK. New Zealand's Accident Compensation Scheme encompasses claims arising out of accidental injuries of all sorts, not just those which can be attributable to 'medical misadventure'. The latter, in fact, represent only a tiny fraction of the scheme's case-load, yet they have given rise to difficulties disproportionate to their frequency. These difficulties raise doubts as to the practicality of developing and maintaining a scheme of no fault compensation that deals exclusively with medical accidents, as some have urged for the UK. Had compensation for 'medical misadventure' in New Zealand been free standing – had it not been possible to draw on the credit earned by the successes of the Accident Compensation Scheme as a whole – then it is no exaggeration to suggest that the no fault experiment in that country might have failed.

This is not to say that ideas of a no fault compensation scheme for medical accidents should be consigned to the scrap heap. It may be possible to learn from the New Zealand experience and thereby to avoid certain of the difficulties that have afflicted the operation of the 'medical misadventure' provisions of that country's Accident Compensation Scheme. But no fault reformers will have to pay more attention to the definition of the core concept of 'medical accident' or 'medical misadventure' than they have hitherto. To date, there has been a wholly unwarranted complacency on this matter, most notably in two recent private members' Bills which sought to introduce no fault compensation for medical accidents. As Margaret Brazier comments, 'both Bills were flawed. Neither proposal adequately tackled the task of defining medical accident, and so patient eligibility for compensation' ... Absent a clearly defined set of qualifying conditions, it will be impossible to adhere to the sound accounting practices which are essential to the scheme's long term survival.

The need for clarity and precision on this matter is intensified by the special problems of causal attribution raised by the concept of 'medical misadventure'. The patient who suffers an adverse outcome of medical treatment has undergone that treatment for a reason: as a result of disease or personal injury, perhaps, or of some other condition such as pregnancy. The outcome of treatment may be viewed as adverse in that a pre-existing condition has been allowed to run its course, or in that the treatment has had certain harmful effects of its own. In both types of case, the question arises: on what basis is the adverse outcome to be attributed to 'medical misadventure' rather than to the pre-existing condition? Where tort law can rely upon the notion of 'fault', and the New Zealand Accident Compensation Scheme – by and large – on that of 'accident', those who advocate a no fault compensation scheme for 'medical misadventure' cannot draw upon common parlance and generally accepted standards to determine the boundaries of their proposed scheme. Yet these boundaries must be clearly drawn, lest the scheme be inundated, and overwhelmed, by claims more properly analysed as flowing from disease, personal injury by accident, and so on.

As this suggests, the difficulties for the claimant associated with proving causation will in any event remain, and his ability to overcome them will determine whether he comes within the no fault scheme at all. Moreover, it may well be asked just what the moral basis of such a scheme is supposed to be. Once we abandon the principle of corrective justice associated, however imperfectly, with the tort system (the idea that it is right for the injurer to compensate his victim), why pay out only to those injured by 'misadventure' rather than to everyone who becomes ill according to need?

In 2001, the Department of Health launched a wide-ranging review by the Chief Medical Officer, Sir Liam Donaldson, into the way the law functions in practice in this area, and options for its reform. The CMO's Report, *Making Amends*, was published in June 2003:

Chief Medical Officer, *Making Amends: A consultation paper setting out proposals for reforming the approach to clinical negligence in the NHS*, 2003, London: Department of Health: Summary:

The case for reform: key issues

- I have considered whether recent reforms and those currently in train are sufficient to improve the response to clinical negligence cases, as some commentators have argued. However even with those reforms, the present system warrants further action because:

  – it is complex;

  – it is unfair – apparently similar cases may reach different outcomes;

  – it is slow – cases can take up to four years from the time of claim to settlement – though timescales have decreased in recent years;

  – it is costly in legal fees; diversion of clinical staff time from clinical care; staff morale; and public confidence;

  – patients are dissatisfied with the lack of explanations and apologies or reassurance that action has been taken to prevent repetition;

  – it encourages defensiveness and secrecy and stands in the way of learning and improvement in the health service.

A vision for a successful alternative to the present system

- Any new system should create a climate where:

  – risks of care are reduced and patient safety improves because medical errors and near misses are readily reported, successfully analysed and effective corrective action takes place and is sustained;

  – remedial treatment, care and rehabilitation are available to redress harm and injuries arising from healthcare;

  – any financial compensation is provided fairly and efficiently;

  – payments of compensation act as financial incentives on healthcare organisations and their staff to improve quality and patient safety;

  – the process of compensation does not undermine the strength of the relationship between patient and healthcare professional;

  – different entry points to expressing complaints and concerns about standards of care are well co-ordinated and well understood by the public and healthcare professionals;

- the system of compensation is affordable and reasonably predictable in the way it operates.

... The case for no fault compensation

- The main arguments in favour of 'no fault' compensation are:

  - fairness;

  - speedier resolution of cases;

  - lower administrative and legal costs than court action;

  - increased certainty for claimants on the circumstances in which compensation is payable and increased consistency between claimants;

  - reduced tension between clinicians and claimants;

  - greater willingness by clinicians to report errors and adverse events.

The case against no fault compensation

- Critics of no fault compensation schemes argue that:

  - overall costs will be higher than under a tort system;

  - it will open the floodgates to compensation payments and fuel a compensation culture;

  - disputes about causation remain, even if 'fault' is removed;

  - disputes about the amount of damages remain, unless there is a tariff-based approach;

  - it is difficult to distinguish injury from the natural progression of the disease in some cases;

  - explanations and apologies are not necessarily provided in a system which focuses on financial recompense alone;

  - a no fault scheme, in itself, does not improve accountability or ensure learning from adverse events.

- The review specifically considered the option of a comprehensive no-fault compensation system. This was rejected because:

  - a true 'no-fault' scheme would lead to a potentially huge increase in claims and overall costs would be far higher than under the present tort system. Initial estimates suggest that the annual bill could reach £4 billion.

  - to be affordable, compensation would need to be set at a substantially lower level than current tort awards and would not necessarily meet the needs of the harmed patient;

  - it would be difficult to distinguish harm to a patient from the natural progression of a disease;

  - no-fault schemes, of themselves, do not improve processes for learning from error or reduction of harm to patients.

The CMO's preferred solution is for the establishment of a so called 'NHS Redress Scheme', involving no-fault compensation in two limited, but key areas. The first comprises lower-value claims against the NHS (of up to £30,000). Secondly, compensation without fault should be available to babies who suffer neurolgical impairment in the course of their birth: as the CMO noted, the latter type of claim accounted, in 2002/2003 for just over 5% of claims where damages were paid, but over 60% of total expenditure on medical litigation. As part of the Redress Scheme, the NHS would also offer an additional package of ongoing care to those within it:

Chief Medical Officer, *Making Amends: A consultation paper setting out proposals for reforming the approach to clinical negligence in the NHS*, 2003, London: Department of Health: Summary:

... New NHS-based system of redress

- The establishment of a new system of providing redress for patients who have been harmed as a result of seriously substandard NHS hospital care is proposed (The NHS Redress Scheme). The new arrangements would have four main elements:

  - *an investigation of the incident* which is alleged to have caused harm and of the harm that has resulted;

  - *provision of an explanation* to the patient and of the action proposed to prevent repetition;

  - *development and delivery of a package of care* providing remedial treatment, therapy and arrangements for continuing care where needed;

  - *payments* for pain and suffering, out of pocket expenses and care or treatment that the NHS could not provide.

- Patients would be eligible for payment for serious shortcomings in NHS care if the harm could have been avoided and if the adverse outcome was not the result of the natural progression of the illness. Payment would be made:

  - by a local NHS Trust for reimbursement of the cost of the care leading to harm (or similar amount)

  - by a national body for amounts up to £30,000.

- Families of neurologically impaired babies would also be eligible for the new NHS Redress Scheme if:

  - the birth was under NHS care;

  - the impairment was birth-related;

  - severe neurological impairment (including cerebral palsy) was evident at birth or within eight years. Genetic or congenital abnormality would be excluded.

- A package of compensation would be provided in cash or kind according to the severity of the impairment, judged according to the ability to perform the tasks of daily living, and would comprise:

  - a managed care package;

  - a monthly payment for the costs of care (at home or in a residential setting) which cannot be provided through a care package (in the most severe cases this could be up to £100,000 per annum);

  - one-off lump sum payments for home adaptations and equipment at intervals throughout the child's life (in the most severe cases, this could be up to £50,000);

  - an initial payment in compensation for pain, suffering and loss of amenity capped at £50,000.

The CMO's proposals have received a cautious welcome from healthcare professionals and lawyers active in the medical litigation field. Significant doubts remain as to the true financial costs of even the more modest no-fault provisions of the Redress Scheme, and concerns have also been voiced about the impact on the morale and reputation of doctors in allowing liability despite treatment and care being entirely professional and responsible (in accordance with the *Bolam* test). However, other aspects of the Report (including the introduction of a 'duty of candour' – ie doctors should tell patients when mistakes are made – and the proposal that the NHS may offer an ongoing 'care package' partly in lieu of damages) have attracted a broad level of support.

It was announced in the 2005 Queen's speech that the Government intends to introduce an NHS Redress Bill, based upon the CMO's proposals, at some point during the life of the new Parliament.

PART II

SPECIFIC AREAS IN MEDICAL TREATMENT

CHAPTER 7

ASSISTED REPRODUCTION

INTRODUCTION

In the last 25 years, medical science has made significant strides in an area previously largely 'off limits', that of human reproduction. The law, in attempting to regulate these developments, has had to balance many competing interests and viewpoints in an area of particular ethical sensitivity. Four years after the birth, in Britain, of the world's first 'test tube baby', the Government established a Committee of Inquiry led by the moral philosopher, Dame Mary Warnock, to recommend an appropriate legislative response. The Warnock Committee, which reported in 1984, was well aware of the unprecedented and controversial nature of its remit:

Warnock Committee, *Report of the Committee of Inquiry into Human Fertilisation and Embryology,* **Cmnd 9314, 1984, London: HMSO (the Warnock Report):**

1.1 The birth of the first child resulting from the technique of *in vitro* fertilisation in July 1978 was a considerable achievement. The technique, long sought, at last successful, opened up new horizons in the alleviation of infertility and in the science of embryology. It was now possible to observe the very earliest stages of human development, and with these discoveries came the hope of remedying defects at this very early stage. However, there were also anxieties. There was a sense that events were moving too fast for their implications to be assimilated. Society's views on the new techniques were divided between pride in the technological achievement, pleasure at the new-found means to relieve, at least for some, the unhappiness of infertility, and unease at the apparently uncontrolled advance of science, bringing with it new possibilities for manipulating the early stages of human development.

1.2 Against this background of public excitement and concern, this Inquiry was established in July 1982, with the following terms of reference:

To consider recent and potential developments in medicine and science related to human fertilisation and embryology; to consider what policies and safeguards should be applied, including consideration of the social, ethical and legal implications of these developments; and to make recommendations.

In the introduction to her 1985 book, *A Question of Life* (incorporating the report), Mary Warnock noted the stormy reception accorded to the report, and a key problem faced by the Committee:

Warnock, M, *A Question of Life,* **1985, Oxford: Blackwells, p viii:**

The Times, on 15 December 1984, carried a dramatic headline. It read 'Warnock: Ethics Undermined'. What followed was a denunciation of the Report of the Committee of Inquiry into Human Embryology ascribed to the Chief Rabbi which was, in fact, moderate in tone compared with some of the abuse to which members of the Inquiry had been, and are still, subjected both collectively and individually, since the publication of our report in July 1984. None of the members of the Inquiry had any doubt that they were concerned with moral issues. But we were not perhaps all of us certain how such issues ought to be approached, and especially how they should be approached by a body set up by Parliament to make recommendations which might lead to legislation. Many of our critics (including, I believe, the Chief Rabbi) have not really addressed themselves to this problem either: the problem of legislation, and its relation to morality, in such controversial fields.

The question of how far, and in what manner, legal regulation of human procreation should occur is undoubtedly one of great complexity. In what follows we shall first consider the principal parties whose interests stand to be affected, before looking at broader considerations which bear upon the issue.

The key interests at stake

Potential parents

People who wish to be parents and would otherwise be infertile are the most obvious beneficiaries of infertility treatment. As the Warnock Committee commented:

Warnock Committee, *Report of the Committee of Inquiry into Human Fertilisation and Embryology*, Cmnd 9314, 1984, London: HMSO (the Warnock Report):

2.1 In the past, there was considerable public ignorance of the causes and extent of infertility, as well as ignorance of possible remedies. At one time, if a couple were childless, there was very little they could do about it. Generally the cause of infertility was thought to be something in the woman which made her childless; only occasionally was it thought that there might be something wrong with the man. Even today, there is very little factual information about the prevalence of infertility. A commonly quoted figure is that one couple in 10 is childless, but accurate statistics are not available, nor is it known what proportion of this figure relates to couples who choose not to have children. In certain religious and cultural traditions, infertility was, and still is, considered sufficient grounds for divorce. In our own society, childless couples used to be advised to adopt a child. Now, as a result of improved contraception, the wider availability of legal abortion and changed attitudes towards the single mother, far fewer babies are placed for adoption.

2.2 Childlessness can be a source of stress even to those who have deliberately chosen it. Family and friends often expect a couple to start a family, and express their expectations, either openly or by implication. The family is a valued institution within our present society: within it the human infant receives nurture and protection during its prolonged period of dependence. It is also the place where social behaviour is learnt and where the child develops its own identity and feeling of self-value. Parents likewise feel their identity in society enhanced and confirmed by their role in the family unit. For those who long for children, the realisation that they are unable to found a family can be shattering. It can disrupt their picture of the whole of their future lives. They may feel that they will be unable to fulfil their own and other people's expectations. They may feel themselves excluded from a whole range of human activity and particularly the activities of their child-rearing contemporaries. In addition to social pressures to have children there is, for many, a powerful urge to perpetuate their genes through a new generation. This desire cannot be assuaged by adoption.

Gamete providers/surrogates

The success of many infertility treatments depends upon the use of gametes (sperm and eggs) and embryos or, in the case of surrogacy, gestational capacity, provided by third parties, that is, persons who, it is envisaged, will not subsequently be responsible for rearing the children born as a result of treatment. A key problem for the law in such cases is to determine how best to regulate the involvement of such third parties. Should such third parties (who are the genetic or gestational parents) receive money in return for their services? Should they be screened? How should they be counselled? In addition, in so far as a child results, what sort of claims should it have on such third parties? Should the latter be protected, for example, by absolute anonymity?

Potential children

The answers we give to these last questions clearly have a direct impact on the interests of children who result from infertility treatment involving third party providers. For example, giving gamete providers anonymity will be to deny the child's interest in knowing who one (at least) of its genetic or gestational parents is. In other cases, there may be a conflict between the interests of the potential child and its potential rearing parent(s). A more recent inquiry into reproductive technologies, led by the moral philosopher, Jonathan Glover, and sponsored by the European Commission, commented as follows:

> **Glover, J et al, Report to the European Commission on Reproductive Technologies, Fertility and the Family, 1989, London: Fourth Estate (the Glover Report), p 48:**
>
> The children are those most deeply affected. Their family circumstances may be unusually complicated: like adopted children, they may have to get used to the fact that at least one of their social parents is not their biological parent. Much more importantly, their very existence results from reproductive help. If they are glad to be alive, they are perhaps the greatest beneficiaries. They are the people who have no say at the time the decisions are taken, and their needs and interests have to be given great weight. Their central need is for a certain kind of home and family ...

Embryos

So far we have been assuming that a child is born following treatment. The position is complicated when we introduce the human embryo (as a separate entity) into the equation. The procedure of *in vitro* fertilisation (IVF), in particular, involves the manipulation of the early human embryo. To work effectively, the procedure habitually requires the creation of more embryos than can ever be implanted in the uterus of the woman receiving treatment. There is therefore the question of what to do with such 'spare' embryos; must we simply let them perish? This in itself may be seen as a bad thing. Alternatively should we store them (there are techniques available for freezing early embryos) and, if so, for how long? Alternatively, is it permissible to use them for research purposes? Indeed, is there any reason not to employ IVF technology specifically to create embryos for research?

These last questions are hugely contentious because they turn partly on a debate of a metaphysical character, viz, do early embryos have any interests in the first place? We shall return to this question at p 360 *et seq*, below.

The response of the law

In the light of the interests and putative interests just outlined, how should the law respond? In a liberal democratic state, such as the UK, the autonomous activity of individual citizens, each pursuing their own ends, is regarded as of central importance, and this gives rise to a strong presumption in favour of respecting procreative liberty. In A *Question of Life*, Mary Warnock had the following to say about the extent to which the law may intrude into the area of assisted reproduction:

Warnock, M, *A Question of Life*, 1985, Oxford: Blackwells, pp x–xii:

The relation between morality and the law has been a central issue in jurisprudence for very many years … If the question is what measures to remedy infertility should be permitted in this country, the problem may be put in the following form: why should the law intervene to prevent people using whatever methods are possible to enable them to have children? Why should not everybody be entitled to whatever is currently the best and most efficient treatment for infertility? The issues here are quite closely parallel to the issues raised in the 1960s by the Wolfenden Report on homosexuality between consenting males. Ought the law to intervene to make such conduct criminal or ought it not? The famous view of Lord Devlin (*The Enforcement of Morals*, 1959) was that where there is a consensus of opinion against a certain practice among members of the general public (exemplified by the notorious 'man on the Clapham omnibus') then the law must intervene to prevent conduct which is repellent to that public. A shared moral view, Lord Devlin argued, was the cement that bound society together. If such shared views were not reflected in law, if law did not enforce what society held to be morally right and wrong, then society itself would disintegrate. A society is characterised by a shared moral view; without it there would be no society. Therefore to act against such a shared view would be tantamount to treason. The law could no more permit acts contrary to the shared morality than it could permit treason.

The drawback with Devlin's view is that, increasingly, we are compelled to accept that 'common morality' is a myth. There is no agreed set of principles which everyone, or the majority, or any representative person, believes to be absolutely binding, and especially is this so in areas of moral concern which are radically and genuinely new. We saw that the concept of a 'rule' breaks down, in novel and hitherto unthought-of cases, and the notion that there is a consensus morality in such cases is equally untenable. The question must be recast: In situations where people disagree with each other as to the rights and wrongs of a specific form of behaviour, how do we decide whether or not the law is to intervene?

HLA Hart (*Law, Liberty and Morality*, 1963) identified two moral problems, one 'primary' and the other 'critical'. At the first level the question is whether a certain practice (homosexual acts between consenting males, or AID [Artificial Insemination by Donor]) is morally right or wrong; at the second level the question is whether, if the law intervened on this matter, the infringement of liberty involved would itself be morally right or wrong. If we consider a case that concerned the Inquiry, the case of AID, it is plain that moral opinions about it vary through the whole spectrum, from those who think it absolutely wrong (like members of the Jewish community, who think that it is 'bringing orphans into the world', and therefore necessarily wrong) through those who are doubtful, because of the possible risks to AID children, to those who regard it as an absolute right that anyone should have access to AID, whether they are married or single, hetero- or homosexual.

Furthermore, any law enacted to render AID a criminal offence, besides going against the moral views of a fair number of the community, would involve, in itself, a disagreeable intrusiveness, for AID is something that can relatively easily be carried out at home, without any medical intervention. For a law to be enforceable, there would need to be a band of snoopers or people ready to pry into the private lives of others, which might well itself constitute a moral wrong …

The Human Fertilisation and Embryology Act 1990 scheme

In 1990, Parliament enacted the Human Fertilisation and Embryology Act (HFEA). The Act followed many of the recommendations of the Warnock Report; perhaps most importantly, it accepted the need to establish a statutory regulatory authority to oversee continuing developments in this area. Some barriers in the form of absolute prohibitions – backed by criminal sanctions – were established. However, the Act is more notable for its flexibility and its willingness to entrust the new regulatory authority, the Human Fertilisation and Embryology (HFE) Authority, with large amounts of discretion. Jonathan Montgomery, in assessing the impact of the 1990 Act and the tasks entrusted to the new Authority, has noted the way in which 'pragmatism' rather than 'principle' seems to have been the driving force behind the new legal regime:

Montgomery, J, 'Rights, restraints and pragmatism' (1991) 54 MLR 524:

The nature of the forum in which the debates about infertility treatment and embryo research are to be carried out is structured by a complex web of discretion, restraints control and accountability. The Human Fertilisation and Embryology Authority is to be given powers to oversee the activities of individual health practitioners, and will not be limited to applying standards established by parliament or government. It will be able, indeed required, to develop its own standards of what is acceptable and proper. The authority will thus have considerable autonomy. It will not be left entirely to its own devices, however, and a series of checks will exist to supervise the exercise of its power ...

Having conferred this considerable flexibility upon the licensing authority, the Government has also reserved a number of powers to reduce it. The boundaries of the power to license may be contracted and expanded by regulations. By requiring annual reports to the Secretary of State, detailing both past activities and those projected for the following 12 months, the Act seeks to ensure that the Authority's practice can be monitored (s 7). The reports are to be laid before parliament by the minister. Nevertheless, pending the exercise of the power to make regulations, considerable trust is placed in the members of the Authority.

The Act permits the Authority to exercise a high degree of control over practitioners. In addition to the power to grant or withhold licences, the Authority will be able to issue mandatory directions (ss 23 and 24). Failure to comply with these directions will sometimes constitute an offence (s 41(2)), but will always empower the Authority to revoke a licence (s 18(1)(c)). Secondly, a code of practice is to be drawn up to provide guidance as to the proper conduct of licensees. This is less coercive than the power to give directions in that disobedience will not in itself constitute an offence, but it may be taken into account by the Authority when considering revocation (s 25).

In practice, this will make it difficult for practitioners to resist the power of the Authority to make policy on controversial matters ... This will represent a considerable inroad into such people's clinical autonomy ...

The final issue in relation to the Authority concerns its membership. Very different conclusions could be drawn about the framework which the Act establishes depending on the composition of the licensing body. On one model the purpose of the Authority might be to provide a forum for the resolution of the fundamental ethical disagreements. In this case one would expect the membership to reflect a range of views. This would leave fundamental issues open and make the creation of the Authority an exercise in democratic accountability. Such an authority would be intended to provide a forum for informed discussion and compromise. On the other hand, the aim of the selection process might be to facilitate the collective exercise of responsibility by the medical profession. This would be the model provided by the voluntary Licensing Authority set up by the profession following the Warnock Report. It would make the involvement of non-doctors a way of informing the profession of the views of the public rather than an exercise in external scrutiny. A glance at the membership list seems to reveal that the latter model is the more accurate.

The statute ensures that between one-third and half of the members will be drawn from medical professions and interested researchers ... Some 'non-professionals' will also be on the Authority: a television producer, a well known actress, and a senior bank official. There will be a nearly exact equal representation of the sexes.

In summary, the Human Fertilisation and Embryology Authority has been entrusted with considerable powers to determine what embryo research and infertility treatment will be carried out. A system of checks and balances has been created which will allow for the Authority to be accountable to parliament, but many of the normative principles to be applied will be established neither by the law nor by democratic discussion. In essence, the creation of the Authority is a pragmatic exercise in facilitating medical advances rather than a principled approach to the vindication of rights.

Recently, in his speech in *R (On the Application of Quintavalle) v Secretary of State for Health* [2003] UKHL 13, Lord Bingham distinguished three levels of control provided for by the 1990 Act:

Lord Bingham of Cornhill: [4] The Act imposes three levels of control. The highest is that contained in the Act itself. As is apparent, for example from section 3(2) and (3), the Act prohibits certain activities absolutely, a prohibition fortified by a potential penalty of up to ten years' imprisonment (section 41(1)). The next level of control is provided by the Secretary of State, who is empowered to make regulations for certain purposes subject (so far as relevant here) to an affirmative resolution of both Houses of Parliament (section 45(1), (4)). Pursuant to section 3(3)(c) the Secretary of State may make regulations prohibiting the keeping or use of an embryo in specified circumstances. The third level of control is that exercised by the Authority. Section 3(1) prohibits the creation, keeping or use of an embryo except in pursuance of a licence, and the Act contains very detailed provisions governing the grant, revocation and suspension of licences and the conditions to which they may be subject: see, among other references, sections 11–22 of and Schedule 2 to the Act. A power is also conferred on the Authority to give binding directions: sections 23–24.

Much of the day-to-day supervision exercised by the HFE Authority over fertility clinics up and down the country (currently around 100, most within the private sector) occurs by means of the Code of Practice, which it promulgates. This is currently in its sixth edition (January 2004) and provides detailed guidance on all aspects of the treatment that clinics might wish to provide. Breaches of the Code by a clinic may result in the Authority revoking its licence.

However, it is important to note that not all types of infertility treatment are regulated by the 1990 Act. In fact, to fall within the statutory licensing scheme, such treatment must either involve the creation of an embryo *ex vivo* (that is, outside the woman's body), or the use of genetic material which has been donated and/or stored: see ss 3 and 4 of the Act. The principal treatments that, thus, remain unlicensed are Artificial Insemination by Husband (AIH), provided that the woman is inseminated with sperm *freshly* obtained from her husband/partner; Gamete

Intra-Fallopian Transfer (GIFT), in which fertilisation occurs *in vivo* and the product is then removed and placed directly in the woman's womb (to bypass blocked or damaged fallopian tubes); and the use of 'fertility drugs' to increase ovulation.

In the rest of this chapter, we shall be exploring in more detail the specific solutions adopted in relation to the key areas of licensed infertility treatment. We shall focus next upon IVF treatment involving the creation of an embryo *ex vivo*. Although IVF obviously has wide potential applications (it may be used in conjunction with forms of collaborative reproduction involving donated gametes and surrogacy), at this stage the assumption will be that the recipient couple are also the gamete providers. We will then address the additional complexities that arise when third party gamete providers are introduced into the picture by procedures such as Artificial Insemination by Donor (AID – often also termed 'DI') and egg donation. Here, the law must regulate not only the conditions subject to which donation occurs, but provide for the legitimacy of any resultant children. Finally, we look at one area where such third party involvement in reproduction has aroused particular controversy, namely, surrogacy.

IN VITRO FERTILISATION

Background

In its report, the Warnock Committee explained the process of *in vitro* fertilisation (IVF) in the following terms:

> **Warnock Committee, *Report of the Committee of Inquiry into Human Fertilisation and Embryology*, Cmnd 9314, 1984, London: HMSO (the Warnock Report):**
>
> 5.2 -The concept of IVF is simple. A ripe human egg is extracted from the ovary, shortly before it would have been released naturally. Next, the egg is mixed with the semen of the husband or partner, so that fertilisation can occur. The fertilised egg, once it has started to divide, is then transferred back to the mother's uterus. In practice the technique for recovery of the eggs, their culture outside the mother's body, and the transfer of the developing embryo to the uterus has to be carried out under very carefully controlled conditions. The development of laparoscopic techniques during the 1960s made the collection of the egg, in cases where the ovaries were accessible, relatively easy. (Another technique for egg recovery based on ultrasound identification has now been developed.) It was not particularly difficult to fertilise the human egg *in vitro*. The real difficulty related to the implantation of the embryo in the uterus after transfer. A pregnancy achieved in this way must not only survive the normal hazards of implantation of *in vivo* conception, but also the additional problems of IVF and embryo transfer. More is now known about how best to replicate the natural sequence of events, but undoubtedly achieving a successful implantation is still the most uncertain part of the procedure.

Pursuant to s 3(1) of the HFEA 1990, IVF is a treatment which may only be carried out under licence from the HFE Authority:

3 Prohibitions in connection with embryos

(1) No person shall–

    (a) bring about the creation of an embryo; or

    (b) keep or use an embryo, except in pursuance of a licence.

The conditions that the authority may attach to such a licence are elaborated upon in Schedule 2, paragraph 1 of the Act:

Schedule 2

Activities for which licences may be granted

Licences for treatment

1 (1) A licence under this paragraph may authorise any of the following in the course of providing treatment services–

   (a) bringing about the creation of embryos *in vitro*;

   (b) keeping embryos;

   (c) using gametes;

   (d) practices designed to secure that embryos are in a suitable condition to be placed in a woman or to determine whether embryos are suitable for that purpose;

   (e) placing any embryo in a woman;

   (f) mixing sperm with the egg of a hamster, or other animal specified in directions, for the purpose of testing the fertility or normality of the sperm, but only where anything which forms is destroyed when the test is complete and, in any event, not later than the two cell stage; and

   (g) such other practices as may be specified in, or determined in accordance with, regulations.

(2) Subject to the provisions of this Act, a licence under this paragraph may be granted subject to such conditions as may be specified in the licence and may authorise the performance of any of the activities referred to in sub-para (1) above in such manner as may be so specified.

(3) A licence under this paragraph cannot authorise any activity unless it appears to the Authority to be necessary or desirable for the purpose of providing treatment services.

(4) A licence under this paragraph cannot authorise altering the genetic structure of any cell while it forms part of an embryo.

(5) A licence under this paragraph shall be granted for such period not exceeding five years as may be specified in the licence.

Broadly, there are, in relation to IVF treatment services, three principal matters that the 1990 legislation has been required to determine. First, what rights, in respect of obtaining treatment, receiving adequate information in relation to such treatment, and controlling the use/disposition of their gametes and any *ex vivo* embryos created with them, are enjoyed by a couple seeking parenthood by such means? Secondly, what is the legal status – and what use may lawfully be made – of the *ex vivo* embryo? Thirdly, how should the law regulate embryonic manipulations that may have consequences for a future child? We shall look at each issue in turn.

The potential parents

Access to treatment

In so far as a heterosexual couple seeks treatment with IVF, matters are left very much up to the discretion of individual fertility clinics acting pursuant to the Code of Practice promulgated by the HFE Authority. Where a couple are refused treatment, paragraph 3.24 of the Code (6th Revision, January 2004) makes it clear that reasons should be given.

There are two main reasons why treatment might be refused. First, the couple may be medically unsuitable. Secondly, and far more controversially, they may be deemed socially unsuitable as parents. In the latter case, the decision essentially turns on the potential welfare of any child born as a result of treatment. The Glover Report addressed the key arguments in this regard, as follows:

> **Glover, J et al, Report to the European Commission on Reproductive Technologies, Fertility and the Family, 1989, London: Fourth Estate (the Glover Report), pp 48–50:**
>
> It is hard to know who will be a good or bad parent. But children need warmth and love. Some of the worst cases of cruelty to children would make any humane person wish that those parents stayed childless. It is surely unthinkable that anyone would have wished to help them have children. Of course we cannot easily predict such disasters. But, where there seems a risk, there is a strong reason not to help.
>
> Some other cases are much more controversial. Is it a disadvantage for a child to grow up with only one parent? (This often happens through death or separation, but should it be seen as a situation we ought deliberately to bring about for a child?) Is it a disadvantage to be brought up by a lesbian couple rather than by a mother and father? What about parents with severe psychological problems, say where one parent is an alcoholic or a drug addict? What about parents who are severely mentally handicapped?
>
> ... But a distinction has to be drawn between two very different types of case. If it is a question of giving a child to people who will behave with horrifying cruelty, it may be 'a mercy if the child is not born'. On the other hand, perhaps a child with only one parent suffers some disadvantage relative to other children, but few such children would feel life was anywhere near so bad as to wish they had not been born.
>
> A parallel can be drawn with handicap. Some handicaps are so terrible that death can seem a mercy, and it is possible to think it would have been better if the person had not been born. But many handicaps are mild or only moderately severe. No one would think that colour blindness made it better for someone not to have been born. No one would think it wrong to help a couple have a child who would be at risk of colour blindness.
>
> Just as there are degrees of handicap, so there are degrees of social disadvantage, and having only one parent perhaps comes towards the mild end of the spectrum. In the case of mild or only moderately severe social disadvantage, it may be misleading to say there is a conflict of interest between the future child and its potential parents. If the disadvantage is only relative, and the child will come nowhere near regretting having been born, it is hard to see how it can be in the interests of the future child for the potential parents to be denied help.

Although, as Glover notes, it seems far fetched (save in the most extreme cases) to suppose that the interests of the child could dictate that it never exist at all, the HFEA 1990 clearly requires such an assessment to be made. Section 13(5) provides as follows:

> 13(5) A woman shall not be provided with treatment services unless account has been taken of the welfare of any child who may be born as a result of the treatment (including the need of that child for a father), and of any other child who may be affected by the birth.

The HFE Authority's Code (6th edn, January 2004) elaborates on this requirement in paragraph 3.12. Among the factors to which clinics should have regard in deciding whether to provide treatment are the patients' commitment to having a child and their ability to provide a stable and supportive environment for it.

In so far as infertility treatment is in fact denied to a couple, what, if any, form of legal redress is available to them? In respect of IVF provided by an NHS funded clinic, a case predating the 1990 Act, that of *R v Ethical Committee of St Mary's Hospital (Manchester) ex p Harriott* [1988] 1 FLR 512, suggests that an action may lie in judicial review.

R v Ethical Committee of St Mary's Hospital (Manchester) ex p Harriott [1988] 1 FLR 512, HC (Schiemann J)

The applicant applied for judicial review after being refused IVF treatment as a result of advice given to her consultant by the hospital's ethical committee. The committee was unhappy with the fact that she and her husband had already been rejected as foster parents on the basis of her past convictions for offences relating to prostitution:

Schiemann J: The applicant wishes to have a child. Unfortunately she has difficulty in conceiving one. She has applied a number of times to Manchester City's social services department to be allowed to foster or adopt children. These applications have been uniformly unsuccessful, the authority taking the view that the applicant's criminal record (which includes allowing premises to be used as a brothel and soliciting for prostitution), and her allegedly poor understanding of the role of a foster parent and the social services department, precluded them from approving her applications.

Frustrated in her desire to foster and adopt and to conceive by normal means, the applicant wishes to be considered for *in vitro* fertilisation ... under the National Health Service. The Health Service – to use an imprecise term for the moment – decided to refuse to give her this treatment. In this application for judicial review she complains of that decision essentially alleging that it was reached by the wrong body: alternatively that she was not given an adequate opportunity to make representations to the decision maker before the decision was taken.

This, I believe, is the first occasion when a decision to refuse treatment for an illness – and for present purposes infertility may be regarded as an illness – has been the subject of an application for judicial review. The respondents submit that the courts will not investigate the reasons behind a decision by the Health Service to refuse treatment nor, submit the respondents, will the courts investigate the procedures which have been followed in the decision making process. It will be obvious that this case potentially raises issues of the widest social and legal significance ...

Mr Bell, for the committee, submitted that judicial review does not lie to review any advice given by the committee. As at present advised, I would be doubtful about accepting that submission in its full breadth. If the committee had advised, for instance, that the IVF unit should in principle refuse all such treatment to anyone who was a Jew or coloured, then I think the courts might well grant a declaration that such a policy was illegal: see in this context, *R v Takeover Panel ex p Datafin plc* [1977] 2 WLR 699 in the Court of Appeal and *Gillick v W Norfolk and Wisbech AHA and Another* [1986] 1 FLR 224 in the House of Lords. But I do not need to consider that situation in this case. Here the complaint is that the committee's advice was that the consultant must make up her own mind as to whether the treatment should be given. That advice was, in my judgment, unobjectionable.

Subsequently, a 37 year old woman failed to persuade the High Court to quash a health authority's decision to exclude her from its IVF programme on the basis of her age. The judge held that, in view of its limited resources and the lower success rates achieved with older women, the Authority's policy only to treat women below the age of 35 was not irrational: see *R v Sheffield HA ex p Seale* (1994) 25 BMLR 1.

A somewhat different issue arose in the more recent case of *R v Human Fertilisation and Embryology Authority ex p Assisted Reproduction and Gynaecology Centre and H* [2002] EWCA Civ 20. Here the applicants – a 46 year old woman and the clinic treating her – challenged the form her treatment was required to take. In particular, they claimed that the HFE Authority's policy of only allowing a maximum of three embryos to be placed in women during a single treatment cycle (so as to reduce the risk of multiple pregnancy) was irrational: the clinic would have wished to transfer five embryos into the patient in this case. However, the Court of Appeal, in upholding Ousely J's dismissal of the action, took the view that the court had no part to play in the scientific debate and no power to intervene. (In its latest Code of Practice, the Authority has reduced the permitted number of multiple embryo transfers to two for women under 40, while still allowing a maximum of three for women over 40: see the Code, 6th edn, at para 8.20.)

Protection through counselling and informed consent

A problem which can be underestimated is the need for adequate counselling on treatment to be given to the couple being treated with IVF. This is necessary so that they can make an informed decision regarding ethically sensitive aspects of the procedure, such as the creation of surplus embryos with little chance of ever developing into fully fledged human beings, and the potential need for 'selective reduction' (see Chapter 8). Equally, they should be warned of the substantial risk that the treatment will fail: it has been estimated that less than 20% of IVF procedures will result in a successful live birth.

Such counselling requirements are outlined in s 13(6) of the HFEA 1990:

13 (6) A woman shall not be provided with any treatment services involving–

(a) the use of any gametes of any person, if that person's consent is required under para 5 of Sched 3 to this Act for the use in question;

(b) the use of any embryo the creation of which was brought about *in vitro*; or

(c) the use of any embryo taken from a woman, if the consent of the woman from whom it was taken is required under para 7 of that Schedule for the use in question,

unless the woman being treated and, where she is being treated together with a man, the man have been given a suitable opportunity to receive proper counselling about the implications of taking the proposed steps, and have been provided with such relevant information as is proper.

The various forms of counselling that should be offered to people seeking treatment are spelt out in detail in Part 7 of the HFE Authority's Code of Practice (6th edn, January 2004).

Control over the use/disposition of embryos/gametes

One of the cornerstones of the HFEA 1990 consists in the great weight accorded to the consents of the gamete providers in determining what may be done with those gametes and/or any embryos created with them. In establishing a regime in which the providers are invited, following proper counselling, to specify the uses to which the material may be put, including in a range of hypothetical circumstances (for example, in the event of the death of a provider or the dissolution of the relationship between a pair of providers) the Act reflects a commitment to the autonomy of such providers. The key consent provisions are contained in Schedule 3 to the Act:

Consents to use of gametes or embryos

Consent

1   A consent under this Schedule must be given in writing and, in this Schedule, 'effective consent' means a consent under this Schedule which has not been withdrawn.

2 (1) A consent to the use of any embryo must specify one or more of the following purposes–

(a) use in providing treatment services to the person giving consent, or that person and another specified person together;

(b) use in providing treatment services to persons not including the person giving consent; or

(c) use for the purposes of any project of research,

and may specify conditions subject to which the embryo may be so used.

(2)   A consent to the storage of any gametes or any embryo must–

(a) specify the maximum period of storage (if less than the statutory storage period); and

(b) state what is to be done with the gametes or embryo if the person who gave the consent dies or is unable because of incapacity to vary the terms of the consent or to revoke it,

and may specify conditions subject to which the gametes or embryo may remain in storage.

(3)   A consent under this Schedule must provide for such other matters as the Authority may specify in directions.

(4)   A consent under this Schedule may apply–

(a) to the use or storage of a particular embryo; or

(b) in the case of a person providing gametes, to the use or storage of any embryo whose creation may be brought about using those gametes,

and in the para (b) case the terms of the consent may be varied, or the consent may be withdrawn, in accordance with this Schedule either generally or in relation to a particular embryo or particular embryos ...

In vitro **fertilisation and subsequent use of embryo**

6 (1) A person's gametes must not be used to bring about the creation of any embryo in vitro unless there is an effective consent by that person to any embryo the creation of which may be brought about with the use of those gametes being used for one or more of the purposes mentioned in para 2(1) above.

(2) An embryo the creation of which was brought about *in vitro* must not be received by any person unless there is an effective consent by each person whose gametes were used to bring about the creation of the embryo to the use for one or more of the purposes mentioned in para 2(1) above of the embryo.

(3) An embryo the creation of which was brought about *in vitro* must not be used for any purpose unless there is an effective consent by each person whose gametes were used to bring about the creation of the embryo to the use for that purpose of the embryo and the embryo is used in accordance with those consents ...

Storage of gametes and embryos

8 (1) A person's gametes must not be kept in storage unless there is an effective consent by that person to their storage and they are stored in accordance with the consent.

(2) An embryo the creation of which was brought about *in vitro* must not be kept in storage unless there is an effective consent, by each person whose gametes were used to bring about the creation of the embryo, to the storage of the embryo and the embryo is stored in accordance with those consents.

(3) An embryo taken from a woman must not be kept in storage unless there is an effective consent by her to its storage and it is stored in accordance with the consent.

The requirement, pursuant to Schedule 3, paragraph 1, of an effective consent in writing to the use or storage of gametes was at issue in the well-known case of *R v Human Fertilisation and Embryology Authority ex p Blood* [1997] 2 WLR 806, which concerned the posthumous use of sperm taken from a dying patient.

R v Human Fertilisation and Embryology Authority ex p Blood [1997] 2 WLR 806, CA (Lord Woolf MR, Henry and Waite LJJ)

Mrs Blood sought judicial review of the HFE Authority's refusal to license infertility treatment of her with her dead husband's sperm. The sperm had been taken from Mr Blood as he lay in a coma shortly before his death from meningitis and, consequently, none of the written consents to its storage or use (stipulated in the 1990 Act) had been obtained:

Lord Woolf MR: As to storage, s 4(1) makes it clear that it must always be pursuant to a licence. That means that storage can only take place lawfully in accordance with the requirements of the licence which for the present purposes are those contained in Sched 3. This means that there must be a consent in writing (para 1 and para 8) which complies with para 2(2) and para 3 before the storage can lawfully take place.

The position as to storage

Sperm can be used fresh or after it has been preserved. Its life, if not preserved, is extremely limited, a matter of a few hours. If it is preserved then it is being stored for the purposes of the Act and therefore is subject to the requirements of a licence. This is made clear by the definition of keeping or preserving sperm contained in s 2(2). The Act therefore takes the preservation process as the beginning of storage. This is understandable, since preservation involves the processing of gametes, and parliament has required that this should be done subject to the control of the licensing process. The result is that in the ordinary way no preservation can take place unless the required written consents exist. This would also apply in the case of the preservation of sperm intended for export unless a particular direction was obtained prior to preservation which permitted the storage to take place notwithstanding that there were not the requisite consents.

It follows that Mr Blood's sperm should not in fact have been preserved and stored. Technically therefore an offence was committed by the licence holder as a result of the storage under s 41(2)(b) of the 1990 Act by the licensee. There is however no question of any prosecution being brought in the circumstances of this case and no possible criticism can be made of the fact that storage has taken place because Professor Cook of IRT was acting throughout in close consultation with the Authority in a perfectly *bona fide* manner, in an unexplored legal situation where humanity dictated that the sperm was taken and preserved first, and the legal argument followed. From now on, however, the position will be different, as these proceedings will clarify the legal position. Because this judgment makes it clear that the sperm of Mr Blood has been preserved and stored when it should not have been, this case raises issues as to the lawfulness of the use and export of sperm which should never arise again.

In the special circumstances, it was held that, although Mrs Blood could not be lawfully treated with the sperm in this country, she was entitled to export it and receive treatment in Belgium pursuant to her rights under Article 59 (now Article 49) of the EC Treaty. She has since had two children as a result.

In the wake of this case, the Government commissioned an inquiry, led by Professor Sheila McLean, into whether the consent provisions in the 1990 Act should be modified. The inquiry concluded, however, that the provisions, in particular the need for written consent, should generally remain as they are (see *Review of the Common Law Provisions Relating to the Removal of Gametes and of the Consent Provisions in the Human Fertilisation and Embryology Act 1990*, 1998, London: DoH). The only exception would be the (rare) situation in which the incompetent patient was likely to recover his or her competence but have been rendered sterile in the meantime. In such a case, it was suggested that the law should permit storage to occur in the patient's best interests, and that Schedule 3 of the HFEA 1990 be amended accordingly (see paragraph 2.6 of the Review). To date, however, this last recommendation has not been implemented.

To the extent that requisite consents were obtained at the outset, it is apparent from paragraph 2 of Schedule 3 that they remain inherently revocable. Thus, either gamete provider remains at liberty to vary those terms. A case in point is that of *Centre for Reproductive Medicine v Mrs U* [2002] EWCA Civ 565, where the respondent widow's husband, after initially agreeing to the posthumous use of his sperm to treat his wife, later revoked this consent. The Court of Appeal, having rejected the respondent's argument that the clinic had unduly influenced her husband's change of mind, held that she was not entitled to use the sperm.

On the face the 1990 Act, exactly the same consequences apply in relation to a 'frozen embryo': that is to say, the withdrawal of the consent of either provider to the continued storage of any embryo formed with their gametes, for example following a divorce, will entail that further storage (and *a fortiori* use in IVF treatment) are impermissible: see Schedule 3, paragraph 6(3). The validity of these statutory provisions, and in particular their compatibility with the Human Rights Act 1998, was recently the subject of legal challenge in *Evans v Amicus Healthcare Ltd* [2004] EWCA Civ 727:

Evans v Amicus Healthcare Ltd [2004] EWCA Civ 727, CA (Thorpe, Sedley and Arden LJJ)

The claimant, Ms Evans, had a number of eggs harvested from her at the defendant clinic in October 2001 following the diagnosis of ovarian cancer. These were mixed with the sperm of her then partner, Mr Johnston, and the resulting embryos stored by the defendant. In May 2002, the relationship between the claimant and Mr Johnston broke down, whereupon the latter wrote to the defendant revoking his consent to the embryos' further storage or use. The claimant attempted to resist the embryos' destruction by arguing, *inter alia*, that Mr Johnston was estopped from revoking his consent:

> **Thorpe and Sedley LJJ:** [35] In relation to his estoppel ground ... Mr Tolson [counsel for Ms Evans] sought to develop the submission that Mr Johnston had concealed his ambivalence, thereby inducing Ms Evans to go forward with him into couple treatment. Mr Tolson submitted that had she known his true state of mind and feeling she would have appreciated the risks of his withdrawing consent and, perhaps, elected for fertilisation of her eggs with donor sperm.
>
> ... [37] [T]he clear policy of the Act is to ensure continuing consent from the commencement of treatment to the point of implant. Consent may be given subject to conditions. Consent may be varied. Consent may be withdrawn. Against that background the court should be extremely slow to recognise or to create a principle of waiver that would conflict with the Parliamentary scheme.
>
> ... [41] In our judgment therefore, Mr Johnston was entitled by the terms of the Act to withdraw his consent as and when he did. The effect of his withdrawal of consent is to prevent both the use and the continued storage of the embryo fertilised with his sperm. Future treatment of the appellant would not be 'treatment together' with Mr Johnston.

In the alternative, Ms Evans contended that the HFEA 1990, by permitting such revocation, was incompatible with her rights under Article 8 of the European Convention on Human Rights (ECHR):

> **Arden LJ:**
>
> *Article 8*
>
> [108] It is common ground that Article 8, which has already been set out by Thorpe and Sedley LJJ, is engaged because Ms Evans' bodily integrity (private life) is affected. I do not consider that she could assert any right to family life with a future child whose embryo has yet been transferred to her ... The assumption made by all parties is that Article 8 is engaged to the extent that the 1990 Act purports to regulate any right they would otherwise have to use an embryo ...
>
> [109] The next question is whether the interference is justified under Article 8(2). In the 1990 Act Parliament has taken the view that each genetic parent should have the right to withdraw their consent for as long as possible. It was not inevitable that Parliament should take that view. Subject to the possible effect of the Convention, Parliament could have taken the view that, as in sexual intercourse, a man's procreative liberty should end with the donation of sperm but that, in the light of the woman's unique role in making the embryo a child, she should have the right to determine the fate of the embryo. But Parliament did not take that view. Nor did Parliament take the view that the court should have any power to dispense with the requirement for consent of both parties, even when circumstances occur which were not envisaged when the original arrangements were made.
>
> [110] Like Thorpe and Sedley LJJ, I consider that the imposition of an invariable and ongoing requirement for consent in the 1990 Act in the present type of situation satisfies Article 8(2) of the Convention. ... As this is a sensitive area of ethical judgment, the balance to be struck between the parties must primarily be a matter for Parliament: see the passage from the speech of Lord Nicholls in *Wilson v First County Trust Ltd (No 2)* [2004] AC 816 [70] ... Parliament has taken the view that no-one

should have power to override the need for a genetic parent's consent. The wisdom of not having such a power is, in my judgment, illustrated by the facts of this case. The personal circumstances of the parties are different from what they were at the outset of treatment, and it would be difficult for a court to judge whether the effect of Mr Johnston's withdrawal of his consent on Ms Evans is greater than the effect that the invalidation of that withdrawal of consent would have on Mr Johnston. The court has no point of reference by which to make that sort of evaluation. The fact is that each person has a right to be protected against interference with their private life. That is an aspect of the principle of self-determination or personal autonomy ...

[111] The interference with Ms Evans's private life is also justified under Article 8(2) because, if Ms Evans's argument succeeded, it would amount to interference with the genetic father's right to decide not to become a parent. Motherhood could surely not be forced on Ms Evans and likewise fatherhood cannot be forced on Mr Johnston, especially as in the present case it will probably involve financial responsibility in law for the child as well.

Accordingly, the Court of Appeal dismissed the claimant's appeal.

The embryo

What is its status?

From what has been said above, in relation to the primacy granted to the wishes of gamete providers in determining what may be done with resulting embryos, it might appear that the embryo's own status is an entirely subordinate one. This is partly true; as we have just seen, the consequence of a gamete provider withdrawing consent to storage of an embryo is the latter's inevitable destruction. Nevertheless, there are important limits on the freedom of action of both gamete providers and others (in particular, researchers) so far as the treatment of embryos is concerned. The ambivalence of the law on the early embryo was foreshadowed in the Warnock Report. After describing the initial stages of embryonic development, the report notoriously ducked the question of what moral inferences were to be drawn:

Warnock Committee, *Report of the Committee of Inquiry into Human Fertilisation and Embryology*, Cmnd 9314, 1984, London: HMSO (the Warnock Report):

11.6 Once fertilisation has occurred, the subsequent developmental processes follow one another in a systematic and structured order, leading in turn through cleavage, to the morula, the blastocyst, development of the embryonic disc, and then to identifiable features within the embryonic disc such as the primitive streak, neural folds and neural tube. Until the blastocyst stage has been reached the embryo in vivo is unattached, floating first in the fallopian tube and then in the uterine cavity. From the sixth to the 12th or 13th day, internal development proceeds within the blastocyst while during the same period implantation is taking place. Both the internal and external processes of development are crucial to the future of the embryo. If the inner cell mass does not form within the blastocyst, there is no further embryonic development; while if implantation does not occur, the blastocyst is lost at or before the next menstrual period ...

The starting point for discussion

11.8 It was the development of IVF that, for the first time, gave rise to the possibility that human embryos might be brought into existence which might have no chance to implant because they were not transferred to a uterus and hence no chance to be born as human beings. This inevitably led to an examination of the moral rights of the embryo.

11.9 Some people hold that if an embryo is human and alive, it follows that it should not be deprived of a chance for development, and therefore it should not be used for research. They would give moral approval to IVF if, and only if, each embryo produced were to be transferred to a uterus. Others, while in no way denying that human embryos are alive (and they would concede that eggs and sperm are also alive), hold that embryos are not yet human persons and that if it could be decided when an embryo becomes a person, it could also be decided when it might, or might not, be permissible for research to be undertaken. Although the questions of when life or personhood begin appear to be questions of fact susceptible of straightforward answers, we hold that the answers to such questions in fact are complex amalgams of factual and moral judgments. Instead of trying to answer these questions directly we have therefore gone straight to the question of how it is right to treat the human embryo. We have considered what status ought to be accorded to the human embryo, and the answer we give must necessarily be in terms of ethical or moral principles.

In the American case of *Davis v Davis* 842 SW 2d 588 (1992), which involved a custody battle over frozen embryos, the Tennessee Supreme Court was concerned with the question of whether embryos should be categorised as 'persons' or 'property' or as having an interim, *sui generis* legal status. In his judgment, Daughtrey J discussed the position as follows:

Daughtrey J: To our way of thinking, the most helpful discussion on this point is found not in the minuscule number of legal opinions that have involved 'frozen embryos', but in the ethical standards set by the American Fertility Society, as follows:

Three major ethical positions have been articulated in the debate over pre-embryo status. At one extreme is the view of the pre-embryo as a human subject after fertilisation, which requires that it be accorded the rights of a person. This position entails an obligation to provide an opportunity for implantation to occur and tends to ban any action before transfer that might harm the pre-embryo or that is not immediately therapeutic, such as freezing and some pre-embryo research.

At the opposite extreme is the view that the pre-embryo has a status no different from any other human tissue. With the consent of those who have decision making authority over the pre-embryo, no limits should be imposed on actions taken with pre-embryos.

A third view – one that is most widely held – takes an intermediate position between the other two. It holds that the pre-embryo deserves respect greater than that accorded to human tissue but not the respect accorded to actual persons. The pre-embryo is due greater respect than other human tissue because of its potential to become a person and because of its symbolic meaning for many people. Yet, it should not be treated as a person, because it has not yet developed the features of personhood, is not yet established as developmentally individual, and may never realise its biologic potential ...

... In its report, the Ethics Committee then calls upon those in charge of IVF programs to establish policies in keeping with the 'special respect' due pre-embryos and suggests:

Within the limits set by institutional policies, decision making authority regarding pre-embryos should reside with the persons who have provided the gametes ... As a matter of law, it is reasonable to assume that the gamete providers have primary decision making authority regarding pre-embryos in the absence of specific legislation on the subject. A person's liberty to procreate or to avoid procreation is directly involved in most decisions involving pre-embryos.

We conclude that pre-embryos are not, strictly speaking, either 'persons' or 'property', but occupy an interim category that entitles them to special respect because of their potential for human life.

Recently, in the English frozen embryos case of *Evans v Amicus Healthcare Ltd* (see p 358, above) the Court of Appeal similarly rejected the notion that the embryo was a legal person for the purposes of Article 2 of the ECHR (see also the discussion of the status of the foetus in Chapter 8).

While, as we have seen, the Warnock Committee had earlier declined to commit itself to a definite position, it took the view that 'the status of the embryo is a matter of fundamental principle which should be enshrined in legislation' (para 11.17). This recommendation was largely followed in the HFEA 1990; the Act omits mention of embryos enjoying any particular status, but in s 3 lays down a number of important restrictions and prohibitions in respect of them:

Activities governed by the Act

3 Prohibitions in connection with embryos

(1) No person shall–

   (a) bring about the creation of an embryo; or

   (b) keep or use an embryo, except in pursuance of a licence.

(2) No person shall place in a woman–

   (a) a live embryo other than a human embryo; or

   (b) any live gametes other than human gametes.

(3) A licence cannot authorise–

   (a) keeping or using an embryo after the appearance of the primitive streak;

   (b) placing an embryo in any animal;

   (c) keeping or using an embryo in any circumstances in which regulations prohibit its keeping or use; or

   (d) replacing a nucleus of a cell of an embryo with a nucleus taken from a cell of any person, embryo or subsequent development of an embryo.

(4) For the purposes of sub-s (3)(a) above, the primitive streak is to be taken to have appeared in an embryo not later than the end of the period of 14 days beginning with the day when the gametes are mixed, not counting any time during which the embryo is stored.

The Act, thus, adopts a 'two tier' approach to protecting the *ex vivo* embryo: in relation to the embryo's creation and use, either for IVF treatment of persons or for research prior to the formation of the primitive streak, this is sanctioned by licence with the additional proviso that the consents of the gamete providers be obtained. Activities falling outside this sphere of the permissible (for example, research after the primitive streak forms, placing embryos in animals, and cloning) are straightforwardly prohibited. Indeed, such activities are, by virtue of s 41 of the Act, punishable by imprisonment of up to 10 years.

As the Warnock Report notes, the formation of the primitive streak marks that stage in embryonic development when a new individual entity is first discernible:

Warnock Committee, *Report of the Committee of Inquiry into Human Fertilisation and Embryology*, Cmnd 9314, 1984, London: HMSO (the Warnock Report):

11.5 The first of these features is the primitive streak, which appears as a heaping up of cells at one end of the embryonic disc on the 14th or 15th day after fertilisation. Two primitive streaks may form in a single embryonic disc. This is the latest stage at which identical twins can occur. The primitive streak is the first of several identifiable features which develop in and from the embryonic disc during the succeeding days, a period of very rapid change in the embryonic configuration. By the 17th day the neural groove appears and by the 22nd to 23rd day this has developed to become the neural folds, which in turn start to fuse and form the recognisable antecedent of the spinal cord.

The storage of embryos and gametes

As we have already seen, the consent of gamete providers must be obtained in order to continue to store their gametes/embryos in accordance with the Act. Such storage, in relation to both embryos and gametes is possible by means of 'cryopreservation' (freezing). Nevertheless (assuming that valid consents are in force), should there be any absolute time limit beyond which the material in question may in any event not be kept?

The Warnock Committee recommended the need for an upper time limit to storage, on grounds both of the possible (albeit speculative) risk of physical harm to children born from embryos after extended storage, and the increased risk of gamete providers dying or falling into disagreement over the period in question. The HFEA 1990 reflected these concerns in stipulating in s 14(4)) maximum storage periods of 10 years for gametes and five years for embryos. More recently, however, following a report by the HFE Authority, it was felt desirable to relax this limit in respect of embryos. This was especially so in cases where gametes were taken from a female provider prior to therapy for cancer, where it is medically preferable to wait for as long as possible after such therapy before implanting her with any embryo formed with them.

The Government accordingly passed the Human Fertilisation and Embryology (Statutory Storage Period for Embryos) Regulations 1996 SI 1996/375. The regulations replace the absolute limit on storage of embryos for longer than five years with a weak *presumption* that normally embryos will not be kept longer than this; in nearly every case this can be rebutted in favour of a 10-year limit (reg 2(4)(b)). Exceptionally, the latter limit itself may be exceeded, notably in cases where a woman is due to undergo some other treatment, for example, radiotherapy, interfering with her fertility (see reg 2(2)(c)). Here, the only limit still operative is that implantation must be carried out on the woman in question before she attains the age of 55 (reg 2(1)).

In relation to embryos whose storage had begun prior to the passing of the regulations, an obligation was imposed on the clinics storing them to obtain confirmation in writing from the providers that they had no objection to extending storage beyond five years. Whilst this ensured respect for the autonomy of such providers (the legal matrix in which their original consents had been given had changed), it had the unfortunate consequence that, in cases where the providers could not be traced, their embryos had to be allowed to perish.

Embryo research

The creation of human embryos *ex vivo* opens up significant opportunities for the conduct of medical research. As we have seen, subject to licence and to the gamete providers' approval, such research is currently permitted until the formation of the embryo's primitive streak. Nevertheless, for many people the possibility of such research is undoubtedly the most troubling aspect of IVF treatment, significantly more so than, for example, simply allowing spare or unwanted embryos to perish. Why this should be so is a complex question, which is inextricably linked to our attitudes towards unborn human life in general. In *A Question of Life*, Mary Warnock commented as follows:

Warnock, M, *A Question of Life*, 1985, Oxford: Blackwells, pp xii–xiii:

There was, however, a more testing kind of question [than the issue of regulating fertility treatment], infinitely more important, in my opinion.

This was the question of research using human embryos ... Utilitarianism could ... by itself, provide no solution, simply because the very question at issue was whether or not embryos count as those whose harms and benefits, pleasures and pains, have to be thrown into the balance to be weighed against the benefits or harms to society as a whole. But here we had, it seemed, an issue on which legislation must be foreseen, and must be enacted quickly. No one felt inclined to argue that the decision whether or not to embark on research with the use of human embryos was a matter of personal conscience, as they might in the case of AID, surrogacy, or, for that matter, homosexuality between adults. Everyone agreed that this was a matter on which there must be legislation, and that whether and to what extent embryos should be used must be a decision for the law.

It is certainly true that the moral permissibility of embryo research turns upon the issue of the embryo's moral status in a particularly direct way. This is because, unlike the cases of 'spare embryos' allowed to perish in the course of IVF or of embryos/foetuses destroyed through abortion (see Chapter 8), the rights/interests of identifiable, fully fledged individuals are not directly implicated. To the extent that the view of embryo-as-person is rejected, such research may appear acceptable in principle. On the other hand, as argued by John Robertson, other problems – notably the symbolic damage it may cause – remain:

Robertson, JA, *Children of Choice*, 1994, Ewing, New Jersey: Princeton UP, p 201:

... creating embryos for research and then discard deserves protection only if other important interests are served that justify whatever symbolic costs deliberate creation and discard of embryos entails. The purpose here is to increase knowledge of how to treat infertility, improve contraception, and treat or prevent cancer or birth defects. With cryopreservation of extra embryos limiting the number donated for research, a policy against creating embryos solely for research and discard could greatly limit the amount of embryo research. Research with embryos would then occur only with spare embryos created as a byproduct of IVF treatment of infertility, which may be too few to meet all research needs, with the result that important research across a range of fields is lost. The symbolic benefits of protecting embryos from being created solely for research purposes does not appear to justify this loss. If the embryo is so rudimentary that research on excess, discarded embryos does not harm them and is permissible, there would appear to be no additional harm to embryos from creating them for this purpose only. In both cases research will occur at the same stage of development, and thus no added harm would occur from deliberate creation of embryos for research purposes.

Opponents, however, would argue that additional symbolic harm arises from creating embryos solely to be vehicles of research and then discarded. Additional symbolic harm results because creating embryos with the intent to discard them demonstrates a profound disrespect for the earliest stages of human life. This practice permits human life to be created, manipulated, and discarded for utilitarian purposes, without regard to the embryo's own interests or potential. The deliberateness of the act – creating new human life only to destroy it – is thus viewed as symbolically more offensive than research on excess embryos created as a byproduct of the IVF process of treating infertility.

The various purposes for which the HFE Authority may license a clinic to carry out embryo research are enumerated in Schedule 2, paragraph 3, to the 1990 Act, and originally included promoting infertility treatment, increasing knowledge about congenital diseases, and improving techniques of contraception. Recently, however, three new purposes have been added to the paragraph by the Human Fertilisation and Embryology (Research Purposes) Regulations 2001 SI 2001/188. Regulation 2(2) provides that:

A licence may be issued for the purposes of–

(a) increasing knowledge about the development of embryos;

(b) increasing knowledge about serious disease; or

(c) enabling any such knowledge to be applied in developing treatments for serious disease.

The reason for this amendment (which followed a report by the Chief Medical Officer's Expert Group, *Stem Cell Research: Medical Progress with Responsibility*, 2000, London: DoH) is to allow research into embryonic stem cells, including those generated by the technique of CNR (Cell Nuclear Transfer). The latter is a form of cloning in which a nucleus taken from an adult human is introduced into an egg that has not been fertilised. The egg is then stimulated artificially to begin the process of division and embryo-formation. Possibly, in the future, embryonic cells could be used, in conjunction with cells taken from particular patients, to clone replacement organs and tissue. As the Human Genetics Advisory Commission (HGAC) and the HFE Authority commented in their report, *Cloning Issues in Reproduction, Science and Medicine*:

HGAC and HFE Authority, *Cloning Issues in Reproduction, Science and Medicine*, December 1998

5.3 The most likely objective of a research project involving the use of CNR would be to create a cultured cell line for the purposes of cell or tissue therapy. People who have tissues or organs damaged by injury or disease (eg, skin, heart muscle, nervous tissue) could provide their own somatic nuclei and, by using these to replace nuclei in their own or donated eggs, individual stem cells (not embryos) could be produced in culture. These cells could then be induced (by exposure to appropriate growth factors) to form whichever type of cell or tissue was required for therapeutic purposes with no risk of tissue rejection and no need for treatment of the patient with immunosuppressive drugs.

The approach taken in the HGAC/HFE Authority report (and reflected in the 2001 Regulations) was that CNR is permissible under the HFEA 1990, since the prohibition on cloning found in s 3(3)(d) of the Act (see p 362, above) is directed only against the replacement of 'a nucleus of a cell *of an embryo* with a nucleus of any person' – an older form of cloning known as 'nucleus substitution'. As just noted, in CNR it is not a nucleus from an embryonic cell that is replaced, but rather the nucleus of an unfertilised egg. Accordingly, research on embryos resulting from CNR could take place subject to licensing by the HFE Authority (under s 3(1) of the 1990 Act). However, the view that CNR was regulated at all under the Act was challenged by the pressure group Pro-Life in *R (On the Application of Bruno Quintavalle on Behalf of Pro-Life Alliance) v Secretary of State for Health* [2003] UKHL 13.

R (On the Application of Bruno Quintavalle on Behalf of Pro-Life Alliance) v Secretary of State for Health [2003] UKHL 13, HL (Lords Bingham, Steyn, Hoffmann, Millett and Scott)

Pro-Life sought a declaration in judicial review that human embryos produced by CNR fell outside the terms of the 1990 Act, and hence research on them could not be regulated by the HFE Authority. In doing so, it hoped to provoke a parliamentary debate on the subject, that might lead to the prohibition of the practice. Pro-Life's argument was based on the fact that, in defining 'embryo', s 1(1)(a), of the Act appears to treat the embryo's coming into being through a process of fertilisation as essential. In contrast, the 'embryos' that result from CNR (that is, once the egg whose nucleus has been replaced is stimulated and starts to divide) have never been fertilised. At first instance, Crane J accepted this argument, and granted Pro-Life's declaration: see [2001] EWHC Admin 918. However, the Court of Appeal allowed the Secretary of State's appeal. Subsequently the matter reached the House of Lords.

Lord Bingham of Cornhill:

The background to the [1990] Act

... [12] There is no doubting the sensitivity of the issues. There were those who considered the creation of embryos, and thus of life, in vitro to be either sacrilegious or ethically repugnant and wished to ban such activities altogether. There were others who considered that these new techniques, by offering means of enabling the infertile to have children and increasing knowledge of congenital disease, had the potential to improve the human condition, and this view also did not lack religious and moral arguments to support it. Nor can one doubt the difficulty of legislating against a background of fast-moving medical and scientific development. It is not often that Parliament has to frame legislation apt to apply to developments at the advanced cutting edge of science.

[13] The solution recommended and embodied in the 1990 Act was not to ban all creation and subsequent use of live human embryos produced in vitro but instead, and subject to certain express prohibitions of which some have been noted above, to permit such creation and use subject to specified conditions, restrictions and time limits and subject to the regimes of control briefly described in paragraph 4 above. The merits of this solution are not a matter for the House in its judicial capacity. It is, however, plain that while Parliament outlawed certain grotesque possibilities (such as placing a live animal embryo in a woman or a live human embryo in an animal), it otherwise opted for a strict regime of control. No activity within this field was left unregulated. There was to be no free for all.

Section 1(1)(a)

[14] It is against this background that one comes to interpret section 1(1)(a) … The crucial point, strongly relied on by Mr Parker QC in his compelling argument [for the Secretary of State], is that this was an Act passed for the protection of live human embryos created outside the human body. The essential thrust of section 1(1)(a) was directed to such embryos, not to the manner of their creation, which Parliament (entirely understandably on the then current state of scientific knowledge) took for granted.

[15] Bearing in mind the constitutional imperative that the courts stick to their interpretative role and do not assume the mantle of legislators, however, I would not leave the matter there but would seek to apply the guidance of Lord Wilberforce [from *Royal College of Nursing v DHSS* [1981] AC 800]:

(1) Does the creation of live human embryos by CNR fall within the same genus of facts as those to which the expressed policy of Parliament has been formulated? In my opinion, it plainly does. An embryo created by in vitro fertilisation and one created by CNR are very similar organisms. The difference between them as organisms is that the CNR embryo, if allowed to develop, will grow into a clone of the donor of the replacement nucleus which the embryo produced by fertilisation will not. But this is a difference which plainly points towards the need for regulation, not against it.

(2) Is the operation of the 1990 Act to be regarded as liberal and permissive in its operation or restrictive and circumscribed? This is not an entirely simple question. The Act intended to permit certain activities but to circumscribe the freedom to pursue them which had previously been enjoyed. Loyalty to the evident purpose of the Act would require regulation of activities not distinguishable in any significant respect from those regulated by the Act, unless the wording or policy of the Act shows that they should be prohibited.

(3) Is the embryo created by CNR different in kind or dimension from that for which the Act was passed? Plainly not: as already pointed out, the organisms in question are, as organisms, very similar.

While it is impermissible to ask what Parliament would have done if the facts had been before it, there is one important question which may permissibly be asked: it is whether Parliament, faced with the taxing task of enacting a legislative solution to the difficult religious, moral and scientific issues mentioned above, could rationally have intended to leave live human embryos created by CNR outside the scope of regulation had it known of them as a scientific possibility. There is only one possible answer to this question and it is negative.

The other Law Lords delivered concurring judgments rejecting Pro-Life's argument.

In the alternative, Pro-Life contended that if the HFEA 1990 does apply to embryos resulting from CNR, then, just as it prohibits cloning by nucleus substitution, s 3(3)(d) should be read as prohibiting CNR cloning too. However, the House of Lords rejected this suggestion (as indeed the lower courts had done). The upshot is that, as scientists advising the Government had been hoping, stem cell research on embryos produced by CNR cloning may lawfully be carried out under licence from the HFE Authority.

The House of Lords Select Committee on *Stem Cell Research*, which reported in 2002, in the meantime gave the HFE Authority the 'green light' to begin the licensing of such research, while stressing the need for fully informed consent from the donors of the genetic material, and that the 14-day time limit on all forms of research involving human embryos should remain. In February 2005, the Authority granted the second such licence to the Roslin Institute near Edinburgh (responsible for cloning 'Dolly' the Sheep) to allow the use of CNR-derived stem-cells for research into the causes of motor neurone disease.

On the other hand, it is important not to confuse the above developments in the field of 'therapeutic cloning' with the rather more contentious possibility of 'reproductive cloning', of which more shortly.

Embryonic manipulations that will affect a future child

In addition to the 'pure' embryo research just looked at, there are further concerns, shared by the public and those in government, which arise where technological advances in assisted reproduction could allow manipulations of the embryo so as to affect the attributes of a future child. Three key areas of debate will be looked at in turn, namely reproductive cloning, genetic engineering, and the selection of embryos for implantation on grounds of sex.

Reproductive cloning

This form of cloning requires, first, that an embryo is created which is a genetic copy of an existing individual (through nucleus substitution or cell nuclear replacement) and, secondly, that the embryo is implanted into a uterus to be gestated to term. Although in its infancy, such cloning has already successfully been carried out on some mammals. Most famously, 'Dolly' the sheep was produced by CNR cloning in 1997, and in February 2002 it was announced in Texas that a kitten had been cloned in the same way.

The notion that human beings might also be deliberately cloned in this fashion undoubtedly evokes widespread fear and repugnance. Whilst some of the concerns surrounding reproductive cloning are directly consequentialist in form (relating to the potential well being, physical or psychological, of the individuals who result from cloning), others are of a more intuitive character, and not so easy to rationalise. Nevertheless, an important aspect is probably the foreboding that, if people were 'manufactured' in this way, deep-rooted notions of human dignity (and perhaps the sanctity of human life itself) might be placed in jeopardy. For an exhaustive and scholarly account of the issues involved, the reader is directed to John Robertson's article 'Liberty, identity, and human cloning' (1998) 76 Texas Law Review 1371.

As regards the law, it has already been noted (see p 362, above) that the creation of an embryonic human clone by nucleus substitution is prohibited by s 3(3)(d) of the HFEA 1990. However, the parliamentary draftsman did not foresee the emergence of the newer CNR form of cloning, and the wording of the sub-section does not catch the latter. Indeed, as noted above, in the light of Crane J's decision (later reversed by the higher courts) in *R (On the Application of Bruno Quintavalle on Behalf of Pro-Life Alliance) v Secretary of State for Health* [2001] EWHC Admin 918, CNR cloning seemed to fall outside the terms of the 1990 Act altogether. In response to that decision, Parliament immediately passed a short Act, the Human Reproductive Cloning Act 2001, providing as follows:

Human Reproductive Cloning Act 2001:

1 The offence

(1) A person who places in a woman a human embryo which has been created otherwise than by fertilisation is guilty of an offence.

(2) A person who is guilty of the offence is liable on conviction on indictment to imprisonment for a term not exceeding 10 years or a fine or both.

(3) No proceedings for the offence may be instituted–

   (a) in England and Wales, except with the consent of the Director of Public Prosecutions;

   (b) in Northern Ireland, except with the consent of the Director of Public Prosecutions for Northern Ireland.

The effect of this statute is to prohibit the second and decisive step in reproductive cloning, ie placing a CNR-cloned embryo in a woman's uterus. It does not prevent the creation of cloned embryos by CNR for research purposes (that is, the therapeutic cloning discussed at pp 365–67, above).

Genetic engineering

The term 'genetic engineering' is used here in a wide sense to cover any manipulation of an early embryo (including testing its genetic traits and deciding whether to implant it), with consequences for the characteristics possessed by the child subsequently born. In this regard, an important (albeit potentially slippery) distinction may be drawn between positive and negative forms of such engineering.

Negative genetic engineering is aimed at eliminating disabilities associated with genetic defects. At present, it requires that couples at risk of passing on genetic diseases to their children undergo IVF treatment, and the embryos produced are subjected to 'pre-implantation genetic diagnosis' (PGD). Only those embryos free of the genes associated with the disease will be implanted, while the other ones are discarded. (In the future 'gene-therapy', involving the removal of defective genes from affected embryos and avoiding the need for embryo discard, may well become technically feasible. Its practice would nonetheless remain unlawful – pending statutory amendment – by virtue of Schedule 2, paragraph 1(4) to the HFEA 1990, which provides that a treatment licence from the HFE Authority 'cannot authorise the alteration of the genetic structure of any cell while it forms part of an embryo'.)

In 1999, the HFE Authority and Advisory Committee on Genetic Testing published a report, *Pre-Implantation Genetic Diagnosis*, which concluded that PGD was ethically sound, at least in the case of serious genetic diseases such as cystic fibrosis. An analogy can be invoked here with abortion on grounds of serious foetal handicap, which is also widely regarded as permissible (see Chapter 8). Indeed, in terms of the implications for the 'sanctity of life', not to mention the health of the putative mother, the discard of an embryo prior to implantation may well be thought preferable to the termination an already existing pregnancy. Nonetheless, the practice's lawfulness has recently been the subject of legal challenge in the context of its use – together with tissue typing – to try to create a so called 'saviour sibling' (ie a new child whose tissue is compatible with that of an existing sick child of the same parents). Specifically, in the case of *R (On the Application of Josephine Quintavalle on Behalf of CORE) v HFEA* [2005] UKHL 28, the pressure group CORE ('Comment on Reproductive Ethics') argued that the HFE Authority had no power to license such a procedure.

R (On the Application of Josephine Quintavalle on Behalf of CORE)
v HFEA **[2005] UKHL 28, HL (Lords Steyn, Hoffmann, Scott, Walker**
and Brown)

In February 2002, the Authority granted a licence to a clinic in Nottingham to carry out treatment designed to enable a couple, Mr and Mrs Hashmi, to produce a child who would be a compatible tissue donor for one of their children, Zain, who suffered from beta-thalassaemia, a potentially fatal genetic blood disorder. The treatment involved the creation of a number of embryos by IVF, and subsequent PGD (plus HLA-tissue-typing) to determine their genetic status. Only those which provided a potential donor-match for Zain, and were themselves free of beta-thalassaemia, would be implanted.

In its challenge, CORE argued that testing the embryos in this way fell outside the scope of the Authority's licensing powers. It relied on the wording of Schedule 2, paragraph 1(3) of the 1990 Act, which provides that a licensed activity must be necessary or desirable for the purpose of providing 'treatment services'. Under paragraph 1(1)(d) of the Schedule, an activity in this context may be 'designed to secure that embryos are in a suitable condition to be placed in a woman or to determine whether embryos are suitable for that purpose'. According to CORE, these provisions ought to be construed narrowly as assisting a woman physically to carry a child, not a child (as in this case) with specific genetic attributes. This argument succeeded before Maurice Kay J, who quashed the treatment licence, but his decision was reversed by the Court of Appeal (Lord Phillips MR, Schiemann and Mance LJJ). CORE appealed to the House of Lords:

> **Lord Hoffmann:** [24] ... Paragraph 1(1) of Schedule 2 enables [the authority] to authorise a variety of activities (with the possibility of others being added by regulation) provided only that they are done 'in the course of' providing IVF services to the public and appear to the authority 'necessary or desirable' for the purpose of providing those services. Thus, if the concept of suitability in sub-paragraph (d) of 1(1) is broad enough to include suitability for the purposes of the particular mother, it seems to me clear enough that the activity of determining the genetic characteristics of the embryo by way of PGD or HLA typing would be 'in the course of' providing the mother with IVF services and that the authority would be entitled to take the view that it was necessary or desirable for the purpose of providing such services.
>
> [25] The chief argument of Lord Brennan [Counsel for CORE] against interpreting suitability in this sense was that, once one allowed the mother's choice to be a legitimate ground for selection, one could not stop short of allowing it to be based upon such frivolous reasons as eye or hair colour as well as more sinister eugenic practices. It was, he said, inconceivable that Parliament could have contemplated the possibility of this happening.
>
> [26] Let it be accepted that a broad interpretation of the concept of suitability would include activities highly unlikely to be acceptable to majority public opinion. It could nevertheless be more sensible for Parliament to confine itself to a few prohibitions which could be clearly defined but otherwise to leave the authority to decide what should be acceptable. The fact that these decisions might raise difficult ethical questions is no objection. The membership of the authority and the proposals of the Warnock Committee and the White Paper make it clear that it was intended to grapple with such issues ...
>
> [29] Perhaps the most telling indication that Parliament did not intend to confine the authority's powers to unsuitability on grounds of genetic defects is, as Mance LJ

pointed out [2004] QB 168, 209, para 143, the absence of any reference in the Act to selection on grounds of sex. It could be said that the Act made no reference to HLA typing because neither the Warnock Committee nor Parliament in 1990 foresaw it as a possibility. But there was intense discussion, both in the report and in Parliament, about selection for sex on social grounds. If ever there was a dog which did not bark in the night, this was it. It is hard to imagine that the reason why the Act said nothing on the subject was because Parliament thought it was clearly prohibited by the use of the word 'suitable' or because it wanted to leave the question over for later primary legislation. In my opinion the only reasonable inference is that Parliament intended to leave the matter to the authority to decide. And once one says that the concept of suitability can include gender selection on social grounds, it is impossible to say that selection on the grounds of any other characteristics which the mother might desire was positively excluded from the discretion of the authority, however unlikely it might be that the authority would actually allow selection on that ground.

The rest of their Lordships concurred in the dismissal of CORE's appeal.

In fact, the circumstances in which the HFE Authority will consider granting a treatment licence in such cases remain tightly controlled: *inter alia*, the condition of the existing, child should be serious or life-threatening and all other possibilities of treatment and sources of tissue have been exhausted (see HFE Authority press release, 13 December 2001).

Originally, a further requirement imposed by the Authority was that the tested embryos should themselves be at risk of developing the condition affecting the existing child. For this reason it refused, in the summer of 2002, to grant a licence to carry out PGD and tissue-typing in the case of a couple, the Whitakers, who wanted a child to provide a tissue match for their three-year-old son, who had Diamond Blackfan anaemia. (The crucial difference between their case and the Hashmis' was that the anaemia was sporadic rather than congenital, so that any further embryos produced by them were not at special risk of having it.) However, this requirement – which the Authority attempted to justify by reference to the speculative risk to embryos from PGD itself – was much criticised and has since been abandoned (see HFE Authority press release, 21 July 2004).

'Saviour sibling' cases are on one view not far from the borderline with 'positive genetic engineering'. It is of course true that there is no active interference with the genetic makeup of any embryo. Rather, as with the longer-standing use of PGD to screen out genetic diseases, embryonic testing serves as a basis for deciding which, out of a number of possible embryos, to implant. However, whereas in the earlier cases, the embryos chosen for implantation were free from a negative attribute (serious genetic defects), in cases such as Hashmi any implanted embryo will possess a positive attribute, namely tissue-compatibility with its existing sibling.

Turning to the stricter form of positive genetic engineering, which aims to introduce into the embryo genetic elements not naturally present, so as to produce a child with specific attributes, this is generally perceived to be ethically problematic. The Glover Report commented on this issue as follows:

Glover, J *et al*, *Report to the European Commission on Reproductive Technologies, Fertility and the Family*, 1989, London: Fourth Estate (the Glover Report), pp 138–41:

Safe gene therapy is not yet with us. But it is better to start thinking about the implications of likely technological developments before they arrive. The stage when a technology seems too remote to be worth thinking about has been followed so often by abrupt transition to the stage when it is already out of control. If ... 'negative' gene therapy does come, one worry is that it may be part of a slide towards other, non-medical interventions of a 'positive' kind, designed to make 'improvements' in people. The technology for this is even further off. But the eventual mapping and sequencing of the human genome, together with knowledge of how genes affect characteristics, may one day make positive genetic engineering possible. One view is that, just as a child can benefit from an upbringing which makes him or her more intelligent, more musical, or better at making friends, so a child could equally benefit from genetic changes which are found to have the same effects.

The other view is that it is in the interests of the child not to be genetically the product of other people's decisions. As the European Parliament put it (Recommendation 934/1982), there is a 'right to genetic inheritance which has not been artificially interfered with, except for therapeutic purposes'.

Positive genetic engineering is in many ways an extremely disturbing prospect. But it is debatable whether the issue is best seen in terms of violating the rights of those whose genes would be altered ... [A] particular problem about this right is how far people would in fact feel that their interests had been overridden. Some people might greatly dislike the fact that their genes had been chosen for them; but others might feel that they had gained from having genes making them more intelligent or more amiable, and be glad that their genes were not left to the natural lottery.

It might be hard to convince people in this second category that a right of theirs had been violated. Perhaps the fact that some might be glad of the intervention is not enough to justify it. But there are complex issues here, and there is a suspicion that the 'right' has been plucked out of the air to settle a difficult issue at great speed.

There are real causes for concern about positive genetic engineering, and it is worth bringing them into sharper focus.

One concern is perhaps obvious to any late 20th century European. This is the danger of giving new technological powers to a government with a programme of racist eugenics, or perhaps to one which had some other, not 'race' linked, category of people it regarded as less than fully human. In our countries there is nearly universal revulsion against this kind of outlook. But technology once developed is always available, and it is hard to be sure that such an outlook will never return.

Another cause for concern is not the deliberate use of genetic engineering for perverted ends, but the accidental side effects of well intentioned uses. One problem is that we may overlook some genetic linkage between different characteristics. In choosing, say, genes for high intelligence, we may find we have inadvertently also chosen genes for high levels of aggression or depression. All technology carries with it the risk of mistakes and unwanted side effects. Here the 'mistakes' will be human beings. There is also the risk of disasters which are irreversible: 'mistaken' genes would be passed on to future generations.

Another problem is that if certain characteristics were frequently selected, those who did not have them might come to be seen as inferior. It may be hard to keep the decent reluctance to see people in terms of some competitive rank ordering, when, in another part of our mind, we are ranking characteristics which may be available for our children.

There are also enormous problems about who would take the decisions. These problems are sometimes gestured at by describing the choice as 'playing God', with the implication that it would take a great deal of presumption to put oneself forward as qualified to choose the genes of another person.

Perhaps, if there were great benefits, we would overcome our reluctance to play God in this way. But there would remain the question of whose decision it should be. Many shudder at the idea of some central government committee taking such decisions. The alternative of parents choosing for their children is much more attractive. But that too has huge unsolved problems. Could parents not sometimes choose disastrously for their children? And suppose too many parents chose the same characteristics? What social limits to their choice would be set, and by what means?

... This adds up to a case for saying that positive human genetic engineering is unethical now (or when it becomes available) and will remain so at least until policies have been worked out to cope with the huge problems it raises.

Under the law as it stands (just as with the removal of defective genes) any such interventions to enhance an embryo's genetic makeup – assuming they became scientifically feasible – could not be licensed by the HFE Authority (see Schedule 2, paragraph 1(4) to the HFEA 1990) and would, thus, be unlawful.

Sex selection

The potential selection, by way of IVF treatment and pre-implantation genetic diagnosis, of embryos for implantation on the basis of their sex has caused unease for a number of years. How far should this practice be permitted for merely social (as opposed to medical) reasons? The Warnock Report had the following to say:

Warnock Committee, *Report of the Committee of Inquiry into Human Fertilisation and Embryology*, Cmnd 9314, 1984, London: HMSO (the Warnock Report):

Other reasons for sex selection

9.11 -So far we have discussed the use of sex selection in a clinical context, where it would be practised solely for the purpose of avoiding hereditary sex-linked disorders. We see no reason why, if a method of selecting the sex of a child before fertilisation is developed, this should not be offered to couples who have good medical reasons for choosing the sex of their child. But if an efficient and easy method of ensuring the conception of a child of a particular sex became available, it is likely that some couples would wish to make use of it for purely social reasons. Such a practice would obviously affect the individual family and the children involved, and would also have implications for society as a whole. It is impossible to predict, either in the long or the short term, the likely effects of such a practice on the ratio of males to females within society. It is often suggested that a majority of couples would choose that their first child was male, and if this happened, it could have important social implications, since there is considerable evidence that the first born sibling may enjoy certain advantages over younger siblings. It would have particular implications for the role of women in society, although some would argue that these effects would today be less damaging than they might have been a hundred years ago. These important considerations make the Inquiry dubious about the use of sex selection techniques on a wide scale, but because of the difficulty of predicting the outcome of any such trend we have not found it possible to make any positive recommendations on this issue. Nevertheless, we consider that the whole question of the acceptability of sex selection should be kept under review.

As Lord Hoffmann noted in his speech in *Quintavalle v HFEA* [2005] UKHL 28, the possibility of licensing sex selection has been left to the discretion of the HFE Authority. In 1993, following a process of consultation, the Authority decided that such selection for non-medical reasons was unethical and should not be carried out, a stance recently reaffirmed in its report, *Sex Selection: Options for Reform* (London: HFEA 2003). In October 2000, it was reported that a Scottish couple, Mr and Mrs Masterton, who were desperate to have a girl to replace their daughter who had died in an accident, were preparing to challenge the HFE Authority in judicial review over its refusal to grant their fertility clinic the requisite licence to perform sex selection on their embryos. However, it appears that the case has not progressed.

It is now possible simply through testing sperm to determine the sex of a subsequent child with a high degree of accuracy. However, paragraph 14.10 of the Authority's Code of Practice (6th edn, January 2004) is intended to foreclose any form of testing: it states that 'Centres may not use any information derived from tests on an embryo, or from any material removed from it or the gametes that produced it, to select embryos of a particular sex for social reasons'. Interestingly, a different approach was recently advocated by the House of Commons Select Committee on Science and Technology in its report, *Reproductive Technologies* (March 2005): it stated that it could find no adequate justification for prohibiting sex selection on social grounds, and that the onus of showing possible harm should be on those opposing its use.

COLLABORATIVE REPRODUCTION

Background

The term 'collaborative reproduction' (borrowed from JA Robertson) is used to describe situations in which a third party (who will have no parenting role once the child is born) assists in the production of the child. Such assistance may come either through the donation of gametes and embryos, or (in the case of a woman) the provision of her uterus to gestate the child. The latter practice, known as surrogacy, raises particular problems and will accordingly be dealt with separately at p 388ff, below. For the time being we shall restrict our discussion to issues centring on gamete/embryo donation; useful summaries of the key techniques can be found in the Warnock Report:

> **Warnock Committee,** *Report of the Committee of Inquiry into Human Fertilisation and Embryology,* **Cmnd 9314, 1984, London: HMSO (the Warnock Report):**
>
> **I Artificial insemination**
>
> 4.1 The term artificial insemination (AI) is used to refer to the placing of semen inside a woman's vagina or uterus by means other than sexual intercourse. The principle of this technique has been known for centuries in the veterinary context. The simplicity of artificial insemination contrasts sharply with the technical complexity of more recent developments such as *in vitro* fertilisation. It begins with the collection of semen from the husband or a donor, through masturbation. The semen is either placed in the upper part of the vagina next to the cervix or injected into the uterus through a fine catheter. Insemination is undertaken near the predicted time of ovulation, the time in a woman's menstrual cycle when she has the highest chance of conceiving. The semen used may be fresh or it may have been previously frozen and thawed before use ...
>
> ...

II Artificial insemination by donor (AID)

4.6 Artificial insemination by donor (AID) may be used when investigations
have shown the husband to be sterile or to have significantly reduced fertility, or
it may be used for the avoidance of hereditary diseases when these are carried
by the male ... In this procedure the woman is inseminated with semen from a
donor.

...

III Egg donation

6.1 Egg donation has been attempted in the United States of America and in
Australia, where there has been one live birth. This procedure may help those
women who cannot themselves produce an egg. It may also help those who
would be candidates for IVF except that in their case egg collection is impossible
because their ovaries are inaccessible. About 5% of infertile couples might benefit
from the technique. A mature egg is recovered from a fertile woman donor, for
example, during sterilisation, and is fertilised *in vitro*, using the semen of the
husband of the infertile woman. The resulting embryo is then transferred to the
patient's uterus. If it implants she may then carry the pregnancy to term. There
are other situations where eggs might be donated. When a woman is herself
undergoing infertility treatment and several eggs have been recovered from her,
she may be prepared to donate one or more eggs to another woman whose
infertility can be treated only by egg donation.

...

IV Embryo donation

7.1 Embryo donation would help the same groups of women who might benefit
from egg donation and, more particularly, the even smaller number whose
husbands are also infertile. Embryo donation may take two forms. One
involves the donation of both egg and semen. The donated egg is fertilised *in
vitro* with donated semen and the resulting embryo transferred to a woman
who is unable to produce an egg herself and whose husband is infertile.
The second method, known as lavage, does not involve removing the egg
by surgical intervention. Instead the egg is released naturally from the ovary at
the normal time in the donor's menstrual cycle. At the predicted time of
ovulation she is artificially inseminated with semen from the husband of
the infertile woman (or from a donor if the husband is also infertile). Some
three to four days later, before the start of implantation, the donor's uterus is
'washed out' and any embryo retrieved is then transferred to the uterus of
the infertile woman. If the embryo implants successfully the recipient carries
the pregnancy to term. Embryo donation by lavage is, according to its
advocates, much safer for the donor as it does not require general anaesthesia,
and a simple and safer procedure is involved; moreover, for the embryo, there is
the advantage of a shorter interval *in vitro* during which time it might deteriorate.
When semen from the husband is used, the child is genetically his, though not
his wife's.

To date such donor-assisted conception has been responsible for the births of over
37,000 children in the UK (see HFE Authority press release, 11 November 2004).
While the potential use of such techniques to assist single women, or those in
lesbian relationships, to conceive has occasioned much political debate, more often
the persons relying on them will be a heterosexual couple where one (or possibly

both) of them is infertile. Nonetheless, as Robertson writes, even here various difficulties may arise:

Robertson, JA, *Children of Choice*, 1994, Ewing, New Jersey: Princeton UP, pp 119–20:

Resort to donor gametes or surrogates is not an easy choice for infertile couples. The decision arises after previous efforts at pregnancy have failed, thus confronting the couple with the fact of one or both partners' infertility. A collaborative technique is chosen because it offers an opportunity to have a child who is the biologic offspring of one or, in the case of egg donation and gestational surrogacy, both partners. Yet collaborative reproduction occurs in an uncertain ethical, legal, and social milieu, where social practices and legal rules are still largely unclear.

A basic commitment to procreative liberty – to the freedom to have and rear offspring – should presumptively protect most forms of collaborative reproduction. After all, collaborative reproduction occurs for the same reason as IVF: the couple is infertile and cannot produce offspring. They need donor or surrogate assistance if they are to have children. Even if both rearing partners are not reproducing in the strict genetic sense, at least one partner will have a genetic or gestational relationship with their child. The same techniques may also be sought by a single woman or a same-sex couple that wishes to have offspring. In a few cases, donor gametes are used to avoid genetic handicap in offspring.

Despite its clear link to procreative choice, collaborative reproduction often generates controversy and even calls for prohibition. Collaborative reproduction is problematic because it intrudes a third party a donor or surrogate – into the usual situation of two party parenthood, and separates or deconstructs the traditional genetic, gestational, and social unity of reproduction. A child could in theory end up with three different biologic parents (a genetic mother, a gestational mother, a genetic father) and two separate rearing parents, with various combinations among them. Such collaboration risks confusing offspring about who their 'true' parent is and creating conflict about parental rights and duties.

What, then, are the current legal implications of gamete/embryo donation for the immediate parties to such an enterprise? In addressing this issue, we may distinguish between the interests of the potential rearing parent(s), the gamete provider(s), and any child who is born as a result. In practice, however, the weight attached by the law to the interests of one party will inevitably affect those of the others.

The potential rearing parent(s)

Access to treatment

Pursuant to s 4(1) of HFEA 1990, infertility treatment involving the use of third party gametes may only be carried out under licence. (The same condition applies to donated embryos by virtue of s 3 of the Act.) The first major issue is who should be eligible for such treatment. In particular, should it be limited to those in a traditional heterosexual marriage who are unable to reproduce by reason of medical infertility, or may it be given also to single persons or homosexual couples whose 'infertility' is a product of their chosen lifestyle? The Warnock Committee had the following to say on the matter:

Warnock Committee, *Report of the Committee of Inquiry into Human Fertilisation and Embryology*, Cmnd 9314, 1984, London: HMSO (the Warnock Report):

2.9 - ... the various techniques for assisted reproduction offer not only a remedy for infertility, but also offer the fertile single woman or lesbian couple the chance of parenthood without the direct involvement of a male partner. To judge from the evidence, many believe that the interests of the child dictate that it should be born into a home where there is a loving, stable, heterosexual relationship and that, therefore, the *deliberate* creation of a child for a woman who is not a partner in such a relationship is morally wrong. On the other side some expressed the view that a single woman or lesbian couple have a right under the European Convention to have children even though those children may have no legal father. It is further argued that it is already accepted that a single person, whether man or woman, can in certain circumstances provide a suitable environment for a child, since the existence of single adoptive parents is specifically provided for in the Children Act 1975.

2.10 In the same way that a single woman may believe she has a right to motherhood, so a single man may feel he has a right to fatherhood. Though the feminist position is perhaps more frequently publicised, we were told of a group of single, mainly homosexual, men who were campaigning for the right to bring up a child. Their primary aim at present is to obtain in practice equal rights in the adoption field, but they are also well aware of the potential of surrogacy for providing a single man with a child that is genetically his. There have been cases in other countries of surrogacy in such circumstances. It can be argued that, as a matter of sex equality, if single women are not totally barred from parenthood, then neither should single men be so barred.

2.11 We have considered these arguments, but, nevertheless, we believe that as a general rule it is better for children to be born into a two-parent family, with both father and mother, although we recognise that it is impossible to predict with any certainty how lasting such a relationship will be.

Although the Warnock Committee stopped short of making specific recommendations on this point, its attitudes were reflected by the insertion into the HFEA 1990 of s 13(5). We have already discussed some of the difficulties of this provision (see p 353, above). In this context, the parenthetical clause in s 13(5), which directs the treatment provider to consider the child's need for a father, is of especial relevance.

As was suggested earlier, in respect of a couple seeking treatment, an action in judicial review may lie against refusal of treatment by an NHS clinic: *Ex p Harriott* (1988). However, on the face of it, no such action could be maintained in respect of a refusal to treat a single person or homosexual couple, since such a use of discretion is expressly legitimated by the Act. Might it be possible to challenge the validity of the Act itself, though under the ECHR? In particular, it might perhaps be argued that the extra obstacle for non-heterosexual parties represented by s 13(5) breaches their right to respect for their private and family life under Article 8 of the ECHR (together with Article 14, which provides that Convention rights should be secured without discrimination on grounds of sex, etc).

However, following the judgment of the European Court of Human Rights (ECtHR) in *Sheffield and Horsham v United Kingdom* (1998) 27 EHRR 163, the success of any such challenge seems unlikely. In that case, the Strasbourg Court asserted that in deciding if a positive right (for example, to a particular medical treatment) exists under Article 8, 'regard must be had to the fair balance that has to be struck between the general interests of the community and the interests of the individual'. In this regard, the direction given to treatment-providers by s 13(5), which does not after all mandate a refusal in any particular case, would appear unobjectionable. In any event, in the context of NHS treatment, the main concern of clinics presented with, for example, a single woman desiring fertility treatment, is likely to be whether their limited resources should be expended on those who are 'socially' as opposed to 'medically' infertile.

Counselling requirements

As in the case of a couple seeking IVF treatment, those seeking treatment involving donated gametes are required to be offered counselling pursuant to s 13(6) of the 1990 Act (see p 355). Arguably, the need for potential rearing parents to receive counselling in such a case is particularly pressing. As noted by Robertson, they must of necessity accept the fact of their infertility as a couple and, where the infertility is specifically attributable to one partner, the latter's possible reaction to rearing a child not genetically his or her own must be canvassed. Infertility is still a problem attracting a significant degree of stigma in our society and how well the rearing parents adjust to it will clearly have an impact on the subsequent well being of any child.

Legal status vis à vis child

It is self-evident that a couple (or, indeed, a single person) who seek infertility treatment, involving the use of third party gametes/embryos, will be concerned about the legitimacy of any child born as a result. Indeed, the attitude of the law towards this issue may be one of the most significant factors taken into account by would-be rearing parents when deciding whether to opt for treatment in the first place. The response of the legislature is found in ss 27–28 of the HFEA 1990:

27 **Meaning of 'mother'**

    (1) The woman who is carrying or has carried a child as a result of the placing in her of an embryo or of sperm and eggs, and no other woman, is to be treated as the mother of the child.

    (2) Sub-section (1) above does not apply to any child to the extent that the child is treated by virtue of adoption as not being the child of any person other than the adopter or adopters.

    (3) Sub-section (1) above applies whether the woman was in the United Kingdom or elsewhere at the time of the placing in her of the embryo or the sperm and eggs.

28 **Meaning of 'father'**

    (1) This section applies in the case of a child who is being or has been carried by a woman as the result of the placing in her of an embryo or of sperm and eggs or her artificial insemination.

    (2) If–

        (a) at the time of the placing in her of the embryo or the sperm and eggs or of her insemination, the woman was a party to a marriage; and

        (b) the creation of the embryo carried by her was not brought about with the sperm of the other party to the marriage, then, subject to sub-s (5) below, the other party to the marriage shall be treated as the father of the child unless it is shown that he did not consent to the placing in her of the embryo or the sperm and eggs or to her insemination (as the case may be).

(3) If no man is treated, by virtue of sub-s (2) above, as the father of the child but–

(a) the embryo or the sperm and eggs were placed in the woman, or she was artificially inseminated, in the course of treatment services provided for her and a man together by a person to whom a licence applies; and

(b) the creation of the embryo carried by her was not brought about with the sperm of that man, then, subject to sub-s (5) below, that man shall be treated as the father of the child.

(4) Where a person is treated as the father of the child by virtue of sub-s (2) or (3) above, no other person is to be treated as the father of the child.

(5) Sub-sections (2) and (3) above do not apply–

(a) in relation to England and Wales and Northern Ireland, to any child who, by virtue of the rules of common law, is treated as the legitimate child of the parties to marriage;

(b) in relation to Scotland, to any child who, by virtue of any enactment or other rule of law, is treated as the child of the parties to a marriage; or

(c) to any child to the extent that the child is treated by virtue of adoption as not being the child of any person other than the adopter or adopters.

...

(6) Where–

(a) the sperm of a man who had given such consent as is required by para 5 of Sched 3 to this Act was used for a purpose for which such consent was required; or

(b) the sperm of a man, or any embryo the creation of which was brought about with his sperm, was used after his death,

he is not to be treated as the father of the child ...

The effect of section 27 is that, in every case, the woman who receives donated gametes (sperm or eggs), or a donated embryo, and gestates the child to term, is the legal mother of that child. Conversely, in no case will the egg or embryo donor be regarded as the mother.

As regards the legal father, the position is more complex. First, in the case of sperm donated to a woman who is married, s 28(2) applies the presumption of legitimacy, so that her husband will be the child's legal father unless it is shown that he did not consent to his wife receiving such treatment. Recently, in *The Leeds Teaching Hospitals NHS Trust v Mr A, Mrs A et al* [2003] EWHC QB 259, the High Court was required to determine the effect of this provision in circumstances (scarcely foreseeable by the parliamentary draftsman) of a mistake at a fertility clinic, which led to a woman, Mrs A, receiving sperm not as planned from Mr A, her husband, but from a Mr B. For his part, Mr B had given his sperm for the treatment of his wife, Mrs B. In determining the paternity of the resulting twins, Butler-Sloss P held that the mistake as to the identity of the embryos vitiated Mr A's consent so that he was not the father under s 28(2). Instead, Mr B was their father at common law (it would have been otherwise if Mr B had been a sperm donor – there s 28(6)(a) would have removed his paternity; however, he had not consented to the use of his sperm to treat anyone but Mrs B).

Secondly, in respect of unmarried women, sub-section 28(3) applies. Here, there is no presumption of legitimacy, but in so far as the woman received infertility treatment together with a male partner, the latter will be the legal father. In *Evans v Amicus Healthcare Ltd* [2004] EWCA Civ 727, paragraph 29, Thorpe and Sedley LJJ held that treatment together meant 'the couple are united in their pursuit of treatment, whatever may otherwise be the nature of the relationship between them'. In this regard, the 1990 Act may be seen as encouraging couples to obtain treatment at licensed clinics (in contrast to relying on 'DIY' methods of donation where the legal father would remain the sperm provider). However, it is apparent that, as a result of this policy, situations may arise where the child is legally fatherless.

One example is where an unmarried couple seeks treatment abroad: thus in *U v W (AG Intervening)* [1997] 2 FLR 282, the partner of a woman who received IVF treatment in Italy (using donated embryos) was held not to be the legal father of the resulting twins, even though he had been present with her at the clinic when it was administered. Another unusual case is that of *Re R (A Child)* [2003] EWCA Civ 182. Here, a woman received IVF treatment, involving donor sperm at a licensed fertility clinic after she and her partner had provided the requisite consents under Schedule 3. The treatment was unsuccessful and she later returned to the clinic for a further course of treatment, accompanied by a man whom the clinic took to be the original partner (and did not ask to consent), but was in fact a different man. When the further treatment resulted in the birth of a child, the original partner sought to argue that, as the consent-provider, he was the baby's legal father under s 28(3). In rejecting this contention, Hale LJ (speaking for the Court of Appeal) commented:

> **Hale LJ:** [22] ... Section 28(3) cannot mean that the man is to be treated as the legal father if at any time during the provision of treatment services for the woman they were provided for them together. Gametes and embryos can be stored for up to ten years or even longer in some circumstances. There must be a point in time when the question has to be judged. The simple answer is that the embryo must be placed in the mother at a time when treatment services are being provided for the woman and the man together.

(This has recently been upheld by the House of Lords: see *In re D* [2005] UKHL 33.)

Finally, mention should be made of the effect of s 28(6)(b), which makes clear that, in cases of posthumous use of sperm or implantation of an embryo, the deceased male provider is not to be treated as the father. This provision was inserted, *inter alia*, to avoid the difficulties that would otherwise arise in winding up the man's estate. Nonetheless, following the *ex p Blood* case (see p 357, above), Mrs Blood successfully campaigned for an amendment to this provision so that, where the man was the woman's husband or partner, his name could at least be registered on the child's birth certificate. This has been achieved by the HFE (Deceased Fathers) Act 2003, which inserts a number of new sub-sections, ss (5)(A) – (I), into s 28 of the HFEA 1990.

The gamete providers

The ethical and legal issues in relation to the third party 'collaborators' who contribute their gametes in order for others to be treated may conveniently be divided into two parts. First, how should they be treated at the initial point of recruitment and screening; secondly, what role, if any, should they be accorded after the birth of any child which, genetically, is theirs?

Recruitment and screening issues

Up until now, the recruitment of gamete providers in the UK has occurred under a shroud of secrecy. This is particularly true as regard sperm donation, whose main source hitherto has apparently been students in medical schools. As we shall see below, there are reasons to think this situation may be about to change. However, even at the time of the Warnock Report, other approaches to recruitment were canvassed: the Committee was clearly impressed with the system operative in France:

Warnock Committee, *Report of the Committee of Inquiry into Human Fertilisation and Embryology*, Cmnd 9314, 1984, London: HMSO (the Warnock Report):

4.27 We have heard from many sources about the difficulty of finding semen donors. It is our hope that this problem will diminish with growing public acceptance of AID, and with the legal changes we have recommended. We were however interested to hear of the way in which the French AID system recruits new donors. Prospective recipients of AID are asked to approach married couples among their friends with a view to persuading them to make a donation, not for the use of any particular recipient, to the semen bank. This approach seems to us to have several benefits: it spreads the appeal for donors to a broader section of the community; it emphasises the donation aspect, and couples rather than individuals are party to the donation. We heard of a strong dependence in some UK clinics on students for donations and we are concerned that a young man may in later years find the fact that he has made donations difficult to discuss with his wife and children. An argument has also been put to us that the only way to attract sufficient donors in this country is to offer a fee. The practice of the payment of donors varies considerably at the moment. It is something about which we are uneasy, given the atmosphere in which AID is practised. We are concerned that the offer of a fee may tempt some men to withhold from the doctor details that would, if known, make them unacceptable as donors.

Although Warnock was unhappy about payment in return for gamete and embryo donations, s 12(e) of the 1990 Act contemplates that such payment may occur pursuant to directions issued by the HFE Authority. At present, the Authority allows clinics to offer a modest fee of £15 plus reasonable expenses for gametes, the fear being that otherwise their supply would diminish (see the Code of Practice, 6th edn, para 4.26 and Appendix G).

The evidence as regards egg donation (which entails some discomfort and risk) is that the donor is likely to be someone known to the infertile woman, such as a sister, who wishes to help her for altruistic reasons. In fact, eggs generally remain in short supply, which has given rise to various suggestions as to how to remedy the shortfall. One possibility would be significantly to increase payments to donors. However, the concern here is that some women may thereby be financially pressured into donating, a process – as noted – not without risk to her. In this regard, there are parallels with organ donation, in respect of which payments are prohibited by criminal statute (see further Chapter 11). Until recently, 'compensated egg sharing', in which a woman's own IVF treatment is subsidised in return for the donation of some of her eggs, was regarded as permissible. However, this practice was rejected by the HFE Authority in December 2003, after a review, because of the increased medical risks to the donor.

In 1993 a more radical solution to the problem was mooted, namely the harvesting of aborted female foetuses for their eggs (these, albeit in undeveloped form, are already present in the foetus and future technology could make their use possible). The suggestion, predictably, excited controversy, not only because of the practice's dependency on abortion (see, generally, the discussion of the use foetal tissue transplants in Chapter 11), but because of anxieties over the psychological well being of any child who might result. Accordingly, the Government asked the HFE Authority to prepare a report on the practice. Nevertheless, by the time the Authority reported in July 1994 (against it), Parliament had already legislated on the matter. Section 3A of the HFEA 1990 (as inserted by the Criminal Justice and Public Order Act 1994) provides that:

3A Prohibition in connection with germ cells

(1) No person shall, for the purpose of providing fertility services for any woman, use female germ cells taken or derived from an embryo or a foetus or use embryos created by using such cells.

(2) In this section 'female germ cells' means cells of the female germ line and includes such cells at any stage of maturity and accordingly includes eggs; and 'fertility services' means medical, surgical or obstetric services provided for the purpose of assisting women to carry children.

Two points are noteworthy here. First, the provision appears to leave open the possibility that such eggs could be used for the purpose of creating embryos solely for research purposes. Secondly, whilst one may agree in principle with Parliament's conclusion, the manner in which it proceeded seems, in this case, significantly to have usurped the role of the HFE Authority of leading debate in this area.

The second main issue concerns the screening of donors. The need for testing, so as to reduce the risk (to the recipient woman and/or potential children) from infectious disease or genetic defects is obvious and is the subject of detailed guidance in the Code of Practice (6th edn, 2004) at paragraphs 4.10–4.21. However, matters are more problematic when it comes to the screening/selection of donors for their *positive* attributes. This arguably enhances the autonomy of would-be parents. However, Warnock commented unfavourably upon the practice, in parts of the USA, of offering the latter a choice of donors:

Warnock Committee, *Report of the Committee of Inquiry into Human Fertilisation and Embryology*, Cmnd 9314, 1984, London: HMSO (the Warnock Report):

4.19 It is the practice of some clinics in the USA to provide detailed descriptions of donors, and to permit couples to exercise choice as to the donor they would prefer. In the evidence there was some support for the use of such descriptions. It is argued that they would provide information and reassurance for the parents and, at a later date, for the child. They might also be of benefit to the donor, as an indication that he is valued for his own sake. A detailed description also offers some choice to the woman who is to have the child, and lack of such choice can be said to diminish the importance of the woman's right to choose the father of her child.

4.20 The contrary view, also expressed in the evidence, is that detailed donor profiles would introduce the donor as a person in his own right. It is also argued that the use of profiles devalues the child who may seem to be wanted only if certain specifications are met, and this may become a source of disappointment to the parents if their expectations are unfulfilled.

Warnock, instead, felt that information provided to the rearing parent(s) should be limited to that needed for their reassurance, such as the donor's ethnic group and genetic health (para 4.21). In fact, the current Code of Practice operated by the HFE Authority appears to be rather more liberal: it suggests that donors should be 'encouraged to provide as much other non-identifying biographical information about themselves as they wish, so that it may be available to prospective parents and future children' (6th edn, 2004, para 4.4). However, the danger of 'runs' on attractive donors is largely pre-empted by paras 8.30–8.31, which impose a normal limit of 10 live births *per* gamete provider.

In relation to the need for counselling of donors (eg as to the possibility that screening may reveal them to be suffering from a condition such as HIV) this is provided for under Schedule 3, paragraphs 1, 3 and 5 of the 1990 Act. Such an offer of counselling is a precondition for valid consent to the disposition of one's gametes.

Status vis à vis resulting children

As we have already seen, the HFEA 1990 (ss 27–28) makes it clear that, in relation to children born through treatment involving gamete donation, all parental powers and obligations inhere in the recipient(s) of such gametes, not the donor(s). Nonetheless, a very important question is how far the identity of donors should also be protected. As the Glover Report discusses, by reference to example of Sweden (where open gamete donation has been practised since the 1980s), the donor's right to anonymity as against his future genetic offspring, may be essential to his willingness to donate in the first place:

> **Glover, J et al, Report to the European Commission on Reproductive Technologies, Fertility and the Family, 1989, London: Fourth Estate (the Glover Report), pp 36–38:**
>
> The effect of abolishing anonymity in Sweden seems to have been an initial decline in numbers of donors. This may suggest that many donors prefer to be anonymous, quite apart from fear of paternity suits. But this must be linked to two other effects of the new law. There was a decline in demand: couples felt less comfortable at the thought that the child might eventually wish to contact the donor. And physicians in some AID centres refused to continue offering AID under the new law. In the centres still continuing with AID, the numbers of donors have returned to normal, although they are now more often older and more often married ...
>
> In a system without anonymity, donors need not themselves be hugely disadvantaged. As in Sweden, their legal position can be protected. There may be some disadvantages in later contact by their offspring. But no one need become a donor if they think this possibility is a terrible one. Perhaps the interests of the children count for more than the possible disadvantages to the donors.
>
> But the case for anonymity does not here simply rest on a direct appeal to the interests of the donors. The fear is that, through putting off potential donors, abolition of anonymity will damage the whole programme. The losers will be infertile couples who will no longer be able to have this help in having children because potential donors have voted with their feet.
>
> The extreme views are, on the one hand, that knowledge of the donor is an inviolable right, and, on the other hand, that anonymity should always be guaranteed. Perhaps a reasonable middle course can be found.

We suggest that the child's interests create a strong *presumption* in favour of openness, but with protection for the various parties involved. As in the Swedish model, the social parents should be protected from intrusion when the 'child' still is a child, and the donor should be protected from paternity claims. But, although we favour openness, this is a presumption rather than an absolute right. There is a case for adopting a Swedish-type law for an experimental period, and seeing what happens to donor recruitment. If it slumps disastrously, public appeals could be tried to counteract the effects of the new system. If none of this worked, there would then be a case for abandoning the experiment.

The Warnock Report adopted a cautious approach and recommended that the anonymity of sperm donors be guaranteed (para 4.22). Its position was subsequently reflected in the 1990 Act: although the HFE Authority has been required from the outset to maintain a register linking gamete providers with resulting children, the latter's access to this information has until now been strictly controlled:

Human Fertilisation and Embryology Act 1990:

Information

31 The Authority's register of information

    (1) The Authority shall keep a register which shall contain any information obtained by the Authority which falls within sub-s (2) below.

    (2) Information falls within this subsection if it relates to–

        (a) the provision of treatment services for any identifiable individual; or

        (b) the keeping or use of the gametes of any identifiable individual or of an embryo taken from any identifiable woman, or if it shows that any identifiable individual was, or may have been, born in consequence of treatment services.

    (3) A person who has attained the age of 18 ('the applicant') may by notice to the Authority require the Authority to comply with a request under sub-s (4) below, and the Authority shall do so if–

        (a) the information contained in the register shows that the applicant was, or may have been, born in consequence of treatment services; and

        (b) the applicant has been given a suitable opportunity to receive proper counselling about the implications of compliance with the request.

    (4) The applicant may request the Authority to give the applicant notice stating whether or not the information contained in the register shows that a person other than a parent of the applicant would or might, but for ss 27–29 of this Act, be a parent of the applicant and, if it does show that–

        (a) giving the applicant so much of that information as relates to the person concerned as the Authority is required by regulations to give (but no other information); or

        (b) stating whether or not that information shows that, but for ss 27–29 of this Act, the applicant, and a person specified in the request as a person whom the applicant proposes to marry, would or might be related.

    (5) Regulations cannot require the Authority to give any information as to the identity of a person whose gametes have been used or from whom an embryo has been taken if a person to whom a licence applied was provided with the information at a time when the Authority could not have been required to give information of the kind in question …

As is apparent from the terms of s 31(3) and (4)(a), it was contemplated that in the future regulations would be passed requiring the Authority to divulge information about the donor to their genetic offspring who have attained the age of 18 and been offered suitable counselling. In fact, regulations of this form have just recently come into effect, namely the HFE (Disclosure of Donor Information) Regulations 2004 (SI 2004/1511).

These provide, in regulation 2(2), that, as regards gamete dononations prior to April 2005, detailed information about the donor shall be provided to the child, but not such as to identify the former: this is in accord with s 31(5) of the 1990 Act, which stipulates that regulations may not retrospectively require a donor's identity to be divulged (ie where he had donated under the assumption of anonymity). By contrast, under regulation 2(3) of the 2004 Regulations, children born from gametes that were donated after 31 March 2005, will have the right, when they are 18, also to discover the identity of the donor. In other words, gamete donation is now no longer anonymous.

In November 2004, the HFE Authority announced a wide-ranging public consulation and review, *The Regulation of Donor Assisted Conception*, to consider, *inter alia*, the implications of this legal change. In fact, its practical effect upon collaborative reproduction in the UK remains to be seen: while the previous policy of anonymity may be viewed partly in terms of encouraging unencumbered donation, also significant were/are the attitudes of the rearing parents. The continued stigma surrounding infertility means that at least some parents may prefer not to tell the child that it was produced by collaborative reproduction (in which case the child is likely to remain unaware that it is the subject of any new right in the first place).

The child

It is apparent from the foregoing discussion that, while since 1990 the law has given a nod to the interests of prospective children (in s 13(5) of the HFEA 1990), these were until recently largely subordinated to those of the other key players in the collaborative reproductive process, that is, the gamete providers and the rearing parents. In particular, the interests of the latter in preserving anonymity/ confidentiality have been allowed to prevail over any interest the child may have in knowledge as to its provenance. Nonethetheless, as the Glover Report discussed in 1989, the potentially deleterious psychological consequences of such a policy for the child are real:

Glover, J et al, *Report to the European Commission on Reproductive Technologies, Fertility and the Family*, 1989, London: Fourth Estate (the Glover Report), p 37:

Our sense of who we are is bound up with the story we tell about ourselves. A life where the biological parents are unknown is like a novel with the first chapter missing. Also there are the marked similarities between children and their biological parents. The child may wonder who is the person, perhaps among those passed in the street, who has that degree of closeness.

On the other hand, for young children who know who the semen donor was, there may be problems about their identity. They may see neither person as being unambiguously their father. This suggests that it may not be in the children's interest to be told who the donor is at an early age, but is not a point against a system of the

Swedish type, setting the right to know at the age of 18. And, since the legal right to know need not be exercised, no child loses anything by it. Since some people care so much about their origins, seeing them as an important part of their identity, the interests of the children count strongly in favour of the right to know ...

Some of us were inclined to see knowledge of one's origin as so central to identity as to be a right. We all accept that ignorance of it can be a severe psychological disadvantage, and we give this great weight in thinking about policy. But the claim that this knowledge is an absolute right suggests, for instance, that it should always outweigh any degree of unwillingness by donors to discard the protection of anonymity. Is this plausible?

As the Report hints, there is a philosophical point here that prima facie favours a policy of donor anonymity/rearing parent confidentiality: this is that, without such protection for these other parties, the child would, perhaps, never have existed at all, and that its existence, albeit with the relative disadvantage of not knowing who one (or, rarely, either) of its genetic parents is, is surely preferable from its own point of view. On the other hand, it is not clear that a blanket policy of anonymity is defensible on this basis (there may, after all, be significant numbers of donors who would be quite happy to have contact with their genetic offspring when they reach 18, and arguably the state should do more to promote this, eg by establishing voluntary contact registers, as in the case of adoption.

As noted earlier, the HFE Authority has since its inception maintained a register linking gamete providers and offspring. Nonetheless the register remains strictly confidential: it is thus specifically exempted from the access provisions of the Data Protection Act 1998 (see Chapter 5) by the Data Protection (Miscellaneous Subject Access Exemptions) Order 2000 SI 2000/419. On the other hand, the more general question of the state's obligations in this field after the Human Rights Act 1998 was at issue in the recent case of *Rose and Another v Secretary of State for Health* [2002] EWHC Admin 1593. In *Rose*, the applicants, two AID children, sought a declaration that their interest in obtaining information about the sperm donor engaged Article 8 of the ECHR. In granting the declaration, Scott Baker J commented that:

Scott Baker J: [47] It is to my mind entirely understandable that A.I.D. children should wish to know about their origins and in particular to learn what they can about their biological father or, in the case of egg donation, their biological mother. The extent to which this matters will vary from individual to individual. In some instances, as in the case of the Claimant Joanna Rose, the information will be of massive importance. I do not find this at all surprising bearing in mind the lessons that have been learnt from adoption. A human being is a human being whatever the circumstances of his conception and an A.I.D. child is entitled to establish a picture of his identity as much as anyone else. We live in a much more open society than even 20 years ago. Secrecy nowadays has to be justified where previously it did not. The distinction between identifying and non-identifying information is not relevant at the engagement stage of Article 8, but it is likely to become very relevant when one comes to the important balancing exercise of the other considerations in Article 8(2).

Here, the applicants were not seeking information that would have actually identified the donors. If they had been, the judge implies that such information could have been legitimately withheld in accordance with the donor's interests under Article 8(2) ECHR (a view that now gains strong support from the decision of the ECtHR in *Odièvre v France* [2003] 1 FCR 621). As we saw earlier, the UK legal position has subsequently changed, with the enactment of the HFE (Disclosure of

Donor Information) Regulations 2004. As noted, children aged 18 or over may now request detailed non-identifying information about the donor held by the HFE Authority. For children born using gametes donated after 31 March 2005, the donor's identity itself can be revealed (although naturally this will not begin to happen until around the year 2024).

Even before the 2004 Regulations, there were, however, two specific exceptions allowed for by the HFEA 1990 where the child had a right to discover information about its genetic antecedence. First, as provided for by s 31(4)(b), non-identifying information bearing on the applicant's genetic relationship with a third party is allowed for in contemplation of their marriage. Indeed, given that a person may marry at 16, s 31(6)–(7) specifically extends this right to those aged between 16 and 18, as follows:

31 The Authority's register of information

(6) A person who has not attained the age of 18 ('the minor') may by notice to the Authority specifying another person ('the intended spouse') as a person whom the minor proposes to marry require the Authority to comply with a request under sub-s (7) below, and the Authority shall do so if–

(a) the information contained in the register shows that the minor was, or may have been, born in consequence of treatment services; and

(b) the minor has been given a suitable opportunity to receive proper counselling about the implications of compliance with the request.

(7) The minor may request the Authority to give the minor notice stating whether or not the information contained in the register shows that, but for ss 27–29 of this Act, the minor and the intended spouse would or might be related.

It is apparent that these provisions are designed to reduce the risk of children born from the same donated gametes from entering into an incestuous marriage with each other.

Secondly, full disclosure (that is, which identifies the individual gamete provider) may occur in accordance with s 35 of the Act:

35 Disclosure in interests of justice: congenital disabilities, etc

(1) Where for the purpose of instituting proceedings under s 1 of the Congenital Disabilities (Civil Liability) Act 1976 (civil liability to child born disabled) it is necessary to identify a person who would or might be the parent of a child but for ss 27–29 of this Act, the court may, on the application of the child, make an order requiring the Authority to disclose any information contained in the register kept in pursuance of s 31 of this Act identifying that person ...

Such disclosure is part of a cluster of provisions designed to afford remedies to children injured prenatally in the course of fertility treatment provided to one or both of their parents. Gillian Douglas explains the logic and potential effect of these provisions as follows:

Douglas, G, *Law, Fertility and Reproduction*, 1991, London: Sweet & Maxwell, pp 137–38:

English law does not usually permit a child to bring an action for 'wrongful life' which is a claim that he or she should never have been born. However, a handicapped child who claims that his or her birth resulted from defective gametes being used, or a defective embryo being wrongly transferred, has now been given a right of action under the Congenital Disabilities (Civil Liability) Act 1976, which was originally enacted to deal with cases concerning prenatal injury.

That legislation was amended by the 1990 Act, to make clear that a child may sue under it where he or she is born disabled, and the disability results from an act or omission in course of the selection, or the keeping or use outside the body, of the embryo ... or of the gametes used to bring about the creation of the embryo.

While this will cover damage caused by cryopreservation, for example, it also encompasses selection of gametes or an embryo, and is therefore akin to the wrongful life action, because the plaintiff will be arguing that the particular gametes or embryo should never have been transferred and the plaintiff should therefore never have been born.

The new section is obviously directed towards the medical staff who carry out the treatment. Under s 1A(3), they are liable if, at the time of the embryo transfer, placement of the sperm and eggs in the woman, or insemination, either or both parents knew the risk of the child being born disabled as a result of the act or omission. This is an added incentive to ensure that patients are aware of the risks they run, and it also means that it will be rare that a child will be able to succeed under the Act.

Where the *donor* of the gametes fails to reveal infection or genetic disease, it will be more difficult for the child to bring a claim. Of course, in most cases, there would be no advantage to the child to sue the donor rather than the doctor, who will carry insurance. But where a condition cannot be revealed by testing, so that the doctor would not be at fault, the child might wish to seek redress from the donor. The anonymity of the donor may in such a case be overridden, by the child applying to the court for an order under s 35 of the 1990 Act requiring the Authority to disclose identifying information, so that the child may sue under the 1976 Act. The child would have to rely on s 1 of that Act, which requires that an 'occurrence' ... 'affected either parent of the child in his or her ability to have a normal healthy child'. Section 4(4A) now provides that 'parent' includes a person who would be a parent, but for the operation of ss 27–29 of the 1990 Act, so a child could claim where, for example, the sperm donor had been exposed to radiation, leading to genetic aberrations which may cause childhood leukaemia. However, where a donor carries a genetic disease such as cystic fibrosis, there would not seem to have been an 'occurrence' which has affected his ability to have a normal healthy child, for he was born with the gene. A child who suffers from the disease may not therefore be able to claim against him.

As Douglas notes, the need for 'an occurrence' makes the precise scope of s 35 somewhat uncertain. Moreover, it can be argued that the very extension of protection to a child who, but for the negligent conduct in question, would not have been conceived, is (unless the child's life is a truly awful one) vulnerable to philosophical objections of the type noted above by the Glover Report. It also appears to run counter to established case law (see the discussion of *Mackay v Essex AHA* [1982] QB 1166 in Chapter 8).

SURROGACY

Background

The concept of surrogacy, the possible motivations behind its practice, and the variety of forms it may take, are described by Gillian Douglas:

Douglas, G, *Law, Fertility and Reproduction*, 1991, London: Sweet & Maxwell, pp 141–44:

Surrogacy has received more adverse criticism than any of the other 'new' reproductive techniques. It was the first to receive legislative attention, in 1985 ... The true incidence of surrogacy is unknown, though it seems likely that the amount of emotion expended upon it is out of all proportion to the extent to which people would and do resort to it in order to have children. But surrogacy, together with abortion, raises in perhaps starkest form the questions of (a) the extent to which women should be free to exploit and control their reproductive capacity, even when they have no wish to raise a child themselves, and (b) the degree to which others should be able to call upon that reproductive capacity to fulfil their own needs.

Our stereotyped images of motherhood and of the appropriate circumstances in which children should be born are particularly challenged here. Additionally, the conflict between the potential of surrogacy to enhance female reproductive freedom, and its potential to allow exploitation and control by others of women's bodies, has been responsible for considerably divided opinions among feminists on the desirability of its practice.

(a) Definition of surrogacy

Surrogacy was defined by the Warnock Committee as the 'practice whereby one woman carries a child for another with the intention that the child should be handed over after birth'. This implies that the carrying woman acts *at the request of another woman* who is usually unable to have a child herself. While this may be so in some cases, the impression gleaned from the few cases which have arisen in this country, and the greater number in the United States of America, suggests rather that the inspiration and driving force for the arrangement often comes from the husband or partner (the 'commissioning father') of the infertile woman. It is the man's desire to have a child genetically related to himself which appears the prime motivation for many surrogacy arrangements. However, it is certainly right to stress that the essence of surrogacy is that the woman who bears the child gives it to someone else to be raised.

Some confusion surrounds the definition of surrogate arrangements. The carrying woman may or may not be the genetic mother. In the more common type of surrogate arrangement at present, she provides the ovum, and the commissioning father provides the sperm. This type of arrangement has been called partial surrogate motherhood. As IVF and embryo technology become surer, and now that the Human Fertilisation and Embryology Act 1990 caters for, and perhaps encourages, such treatments, a different type of surrogacy can be expected to become more common. In this version, the commissioning mother provides the ovum, which is fertilised *in vitro* with her husband's sperm, then gestated in the surrogate's uterus. This full surrogacy may also be described as womb-leasing. The carrying woman is not genetically related to the child she carries.

Since the general aim of these reproductive techniques is to maximise the possibility of having a child who is genetically related to the intended parents, it is to be expected that womb-leasing would offer a 'better' bargain to the commissioning parents because the child would be genetically theirs.

In English law, the only statutory definition of surrogacy is contained in the Surrogacy Arrangements Act 1985. Under s 1(2), a surrogate mother:

> ... means a woman who carries a child in pursuance of an arrangement:
>
> (a) made before she began to carry the child; and
>
> (b) made with a view to any child carried in pursuance of it being handed over to, and the parental rights being exercised (so far as practicable) by, another person or other persons.

By s 1(3):

> An arrangement is a surrogacy arrangement if, were a woman to whom the arrangement relates to carry a child in pursuance of it, she would be a surrogate mother.

It has been the prospect of a woman bearing a child for money which has generated most heat in the surrogacy debate, and indeed, evidence suggests that few women are likely to enter into surrogacy for altruistic reasons.

(b) When might surrogacy be used?

Partial surrogacy could be used where the commissioning mother is unable either to produce eggs or to gestate them. Full surrogacy could be utilised where the woman ovulates, but may lack a uterus, or where carrying a child could be dangerous for her health, or for that of the child. For example, the commissioning mother might have kidney disease or high blood pressure, or she might have a history of miscarriages or ectopic pregnancies ... Surrogacy could also be used as a less high-tech strategy where one or other of the commissioning parents carries a genetic disorder which might be passed on to offspring. The Warnock Committee noted that surrogacy could theoretically be used for 'convenience', where the commissioning mother is physically able to bear a child, but wishes to avoid doing so, perhaps in order not to interrupt her career, or not to affect her appearance. Surrogacy could also be utilised by lesbian women, and by single men and male homosexuals who want to bring up children.

Ethical considerations

As Douglas hints, the Warnock Report was generally hostile to surrogacy. Its principal objection seems to have taken a deontological form, ie 'that people should treat others as a means to their own ends, however desirable the consequences, must always be liable to moral objection' (para 8.17). Glover, reporting to the EC Commission in 1989, summarised the main arguments for and against the practice as follows:

Glover, J et al, Report to the European Commission on Reproductive Technologies, Fertility and the Family, 1989, London: Fourth Estate (the Glover Report), pp 74–76:

1 The case for surrogacy

Part of the case is straightforward. Surrogacy relieves childlessness. For women who have had repeated miscarriages, or who suffer from conditions making pregnancy dangerous, surrogacy may be the only hope of having a child.

Another, more problematic, argument appeals to the interests of the child who would not have existed without surrogacy.

Another argument appeals to liberty. Some strong justification is needed for preventing people from bearing children to help their sisters or friends. And a similar strong justification is needed for preventing people freely contracting to do this for someone for money. This argument relates to the legality of surrogacy, but does nothing to show that surrogacy is a good thing in itself. The central case for that has to rest on relieving the burden of childlessness.

2 The case against surrogacy

(a) *The children*: One line of thought appeals to the rights of the child. It appears in the Catholic document issued by the Congregation for the Doctrine of the Faith, which says that surrogacy 'offends the dignity and the right of the child to be conceived, carried in the womb, brought into the world and brought up by his own parents'.

This case seems to us not overwhelming. Even if the child has a strong interest in being created sexually, to call this a right is to claim that it trumps any interests of the childless couple. This requires that being the child of a surrogate is such an indignity that, by comparison, relieving any degree of the potential parents' misery is to count for nothing. We have not found the powerful supporting argument this would need.

The objection is made even weaker by a further problem. For the potential child, the alternative to surrogacy may be non-existence. It seems unlikely that the child will see surrogacy as so bad as to wish he or she had not been born at all. The 'right' looks like one the child will later be glad was not respected. It is hard to see the case for giving this supposed interest any weight at all, let alone for saying that it justifies leaving people unwillingly childless.

Another argument appeals to the psychological effects of surrogacy on the child. If the surrogacy is paid for there is a danger that the child will think he or she has been bought. Also, it is sometimes suggested that surrogacy breaks a bond formed by the time of birth. Dr John Marks, the chairman of the British Medical Association, has said: 'By the time a baby is born there is a bond between the mother and the child. With surrogacy you break that bond. You are depriving the child of one natural parent. We think that is wrong.' ((1987) *The Guardian*, 8 May). It is reported that the General Medical Council may ban doctors from involvement in surrogacy. This step has already been taken in West Germany.

The surrogate mother may well feel a bond between herself and the child. But is there reason to believe in any bond in the other direction before birth? Or could this be an illusion created by projecting the mother's feelings on to the foetus? If the child's feelings are a reason against surrogacy, the baby has to have, by the time of birth, highly specific feelings towards the particular woman who bears him. The evidence for this can charitably be described as slight.

Suppose, for the sake of argument, that there is such a bond. It is then undesirable to break it. But, where it is broken, is the child so harmed that it would have been better if he or she had not been born? For this is what banning surrogacy on these grounds seems to imply. We do not have such drastic thoughts about people who are adopted. The British Medical Association's Board of Science is quoted as saying that while adoption may be 'the next best thing' for a child facing an uncertain future, any arrangement where a surrogate mother hands over the child 'dooms it to second best from the start' ((1987) *The Independent*, 8 May). But is it obvious here that no life at all is preferable to 'second best'?

(b) *Conflicts*: The conflicts sometimes arising between the potential parents and the surrogate mother may harm the child, and this is part of the case against surrogacy.

(c) *Effects on the family*: Perhaps introducing a third party so intimately into the process of having children may weaken the institution of the family ...

(d) *The surrogate mother*: The position of the surrogate mother varies, according to whether she is bearing a child to help a sister or friend, or has made a commercial arrangement. There is the criticism that surrogacy is an invasion of her bodily integrity. This criticism may be weaker if she willingly agreed than if she was forced into it by money problems. Sometimes she may bitterly regret having agreed to give away the baby. As we have seen, there is a danger of her being exploited. Financial pressures may put her in a weak position to resist contractual conditions which give little weight to her interests.

Another important motive for volunteering to act as a surrogate seems to be the desire for friendship with the parents-to-be. As this is usually exactly what the parents-to-be do not want, it is an illusory objective. She wants friendship: she is treated as a provider of a service, and afterwards dismissed ...

The response of the law

It is important that the questions of the moral and legal permissibility of surrogacy are kept separate. In particular, the law must distinguish in its response between two different moments in time; it must first determine how far it is legitimate to discourage, or indeed prohibit, the formation of surrogacy arrangements in the first place. Secondly, however, in so far as its strictures at this earlier stage are ignored and a surrogacy arrangement results in pregnancy, the law must attribute rights and duties to the participants and, if they are in dispute, adjudicate between them. In doing so, of course, the position of any resulting child must be resolved. These two distinct stages were recognised by Latey J in one of the first surrogacy cases to reach the English courts:

Re C (A Minor) (Wardship: Surrogacy) [1985] FLR 846, HC (Latey J)

A partial surrogacy arrangement, negotiated by an agency, was entered into between an American commissioning couple and a British woman, Kim Cotton (who was married with three children of her own). Following the successful birth of a child, it was clear that Mrs Cotton was happy to relinquish all parental rights in respect of it. The commissioning father issued a wardship summons in order to obtain custody, which was duly granted:

Latey J: First and foremost, and at the heart of the prerogative jurisdiction in wardship, is what is best for the child or children concerned. That and nothing else. Plainly the methods used to produce a child, as this baby has been, and the commercial aspects of it, raise difficult and delicate problems of ethics, morality and social desirability. These problems are under active consideration elsewhere.

Are they relevant in arriving at a decision on what now and, so far as one can tell, in the future is best for this child? If they are relevant, it is incumbent on the court to do its best to evaluate and balance them.

In my judgment, however, they are not relevant. The baby is here. All that matters is what is best for her now that she is here and not how she arrived. If it be said (though it has not been said during these hearings) that because the father and his wife entered into these arrangements it is some indication of their unsuitability as parents, I should reject any such suggestion. If what they did was wrong (and I am not saying that it was), they did it in total innocence.

It follows that the moral, ethical and social considerations are for others and not for this court in its wardship jurisdiction.

So, what is best for this baby? Her natural mother does not ask for her. Should she go into Mr and Mrs A's care and be brought up by them? Or should some other arrangement be made for her, such as long term fostering with or without adoption as an end?

The factors can be briefly stated. Mr A is the baby's father and he wants her, as does his wife. The baby's mother does not want her. Mr and Mrs A are a couple in their 30s. They are devoted to each other. They are both professional people, highly qualified. They have a very nice home in the country and another in a town. Materially they can give the baby a very good upbringing. But, far more importantly, they are both excellently equipped to meet the baby's emotional needs. They are most warm, caring, sensible people, as well as highly intelligent. When the time comes to answer the child's questions, they will be able to do so with professional advice if they feel they need it. Looking at this child's well being, physical and emotional, who better to have her care? No one.

Clearly, the two stages are often not separate in practice: the anticipated response of the law at the second stage will almost certainly have an impact on the parties' decision to risk entering into the arrangement in the first place. Nevertheless, in conceptual terms, it is useful to look at each in turn.

Entering into the surrogacy arrangement

Following adverse media reaction to the *Re C* case, and in the light of the recommendations of the Warnock Committee, Parliament enacted the Surrogacy Arrangements Act (SAA) 1985. After defining such arrangements (see the extract from Douglas, p 389, above) the Act went on, in s 2, to make the negotiation of surrogacy arrangements on a commercial basis a criminal offence:

2 Negotiating surrogacy arrangements on a commercial basis, etc

(1) No person shall on a commercial basis do any of the following acts in the United Kingdom, that is–

(a) initiate or take part in any negotiations with a view to the making of a surrogacy arrangement;

(b) offer or agree to negotiate the making of a surrogacy arrangement; or

(c) compile any information with a view to its use in making, or negotiating the making of, surrogacy arrangements,

and no person shall in the United Kingdom knowingly cause another to do any of those acts on a commercial basis.

(2) A person who contravenes sub-s (1) above is guilty of an offence; but it is not a contravention of that sub-section–

(a) for a woman, with a view to becoming a surrogate mother herself, to do any act mentioned in that sub-section or to cause such an act to he done; or

(b) for any person, with a view to a surrogate mother carrying a child for him, to do such an act or to cause such an act to be done.

(3) For the purposes of this section, a person does an act on a commercial basis (subject to sub-s (4) below) if–

(a) any payment is at any time received by himself or another in respect of it; or

(b) he does it with a view to any payment being received by himself or another in respect of making, or negotiating or facilitating the making of, any surrogacy arrangement.

In this sub-section 'payment' does not include payment to or for the benefit of a surrogate mother or prospective surrogate mother.

As is apparent, the thrust of the legislation is against the facilitators of commercial surrogacy arrangements, notably agencies which make a profit from mediating between a would-be commissioning couple and a potential surrogate. Similarly, s 3 of the SAA 1985 imposes criminal liability on those involved in the advertising of such arrangements. In respect of s 2, it is important to note that s 2(2) expressly confers an immunity from criminal liability upon the immediate participants: s 2(2)(a) protects the surrogate and s 2(2)(b) the commissioning couple (in accordance with established principles of statutory interpretation, the reference to 'him' in the latter clause includes 'her'). This reflected the view of the Warnock Committee that it would be undesirable for the birth of a child to a surrogate to be tainted with criminality.

The section is not aimed to catch a doctor (or his clinic) who receives a fee for medically facilitating a surrogate pregnancy, ie by carrying out IVF or AID treatment on the surrogate. Accordingly (assuming that he has the appropriate licence to carry out such treatment under the HFEA 1990), he would not be liable for any offence. Nonetheless, a relatively cautious approach has been taken both by the BMA (in its report, *Changing Conceptions of Motherhood, The Practice of Surrogacy in Britain*, 1996) and by the HFE Authority in its Code of Practice. The latter provides that clinics should only consider providing medical assistance where 'the commissioning mother is unable for physical or other medical reasons to carry a child or her health may be impaired by doing so' (6th edn, 2004, para 3.17).

In *Briody v St Helen's and Knowsley AHA* [2001] EWCA Civ 1010, the Court of Appeal was required to consider whether damages for medical negligence, which resulted in the loss of the claimant's womb, might include a sum to allow her to fund a surrogacy arrangement. While rejecting this on the facts (given the claimant's very slim chance of successfully so having a child), the court demonstrated an open-minded approach to surrogacy in general. In her judgment, Hale LJ commented as follows:

> **Hale LJ:** [14] ... [W]hile there is general agreement that commercial agencies and advertising should be banned, that surrogacy for convenience or social rather than medical reasons is unacceptable, and that the agreement should be unenforceable, there is little discernible consensus on anything else. Lord Winston's view was that opinion was turning against surrogacy, and that was certainly his experience at his hospital, but if anything the tone of official publications since Warnock has been more sympathetic. Professor Craft's view was certainly different. The British Medical Association has published guidelines for health professionals: see Changing Conceptions of Motherhood, The Practice of Surrogacy in Britain (BMA, 1996). These begin:
>
> > '... surrogacy is an acceptable option of last resort in cases where it is impossible or highly undesirable for medical reasons for the intended mother to carry a child herself. In all cases the interests of the potential child must be paramount and the risks to the surrogate mother must be kept to a minimum.'
>
> [16] ... I find it impossible to say that the proposals which the claimant now wishes to pursue are contrary to public policy ... She fulfils the criteria for permissible surrogacy laid down both by the Human Fertilisation and Embryology Authority and the BMA: she has no other way of having a baby because she has no womb. She has found a surrogate mother through perfectly lawful means with whom she proposes to make a lawful, although unenforceable, arrangement. She is being treated through a clinic which is licensed to provide these treatments by the Human Fertilisation and Embryology Authority, which has arranged the counselling required under the HFEA Code of Practice, and has presumably made its assessment of the welfare of the child (and of the surrogate mother's children) in accordance with that code.

Resolving surrogacy arrangements

We must now consider the second stage at which the law may need to become involved in surrogacy, namely when an arrangement results in pregnancy (and the birth of a child). Two possibilities need to be considered. First, the parties to a surrogacy arrangement may have fallen into dispute. Secondly, in so far as there is no dispute (that is, the surrogate is willing to hand over the child and the commissioning parents are happy to accept it and to pay the agreed fee), there remains the need to legitimate the child.

Where the parties are in dispute

Sometimes the surrogate, during the course of her pregnancy, may decide that she is not, after all, prepared to go through with the agreement to hand over the child over after birth. In an early case, *A v C* [1985] FLR 445 (decided in 1978), the Court of Appeal upheld the trial judge's ruling that the surrogacy agreement providing, *inter alia*, for this handing over, was void on grounds of public policy. Parliament subsequently chose (when enacting the HFEA 1990) to amend the SAA 1985 so as to reinforce the point that surrogacy contracts will be void and of no effect:

1A Surrogacy arrangements unenforceable

No surrogacy arrangement is enforceable by or against any of the persons making it

...

Nevertheless, the unenforceability of the arrangement will not, in itself, be determinative of the outcome in a surrogacy dispute. This is because what is generally at issue is the future of a child: is it to be brought up by the surrogate who gestated it or the couple who commissioned it (and to whom it may be partly or wholly genetically related)? Thus, in principle, and notwithstanding the voidness of their contractual rights, it might seem that the commissioning parents could win custody.

An analogy could be drawn here with cases of marital break-up in which the custody of a child is at issue. The courts, in dealing with such matters as residence and contact, will, in accordance with the provisions of the Children Act 1989, regard the welfare of the child as paramount. This approach can indeed already be seen at work in the pre-Children Act case of *Re P (Minors)* [1987] 2 FLR 421:

Re P (Minors) [1987] 2 FLR 421, HC (Sir John Arnold P)

Mrs P, a divorcée with one son of her own, entered into an arrangement with Mr B to bear his child and hand it over to him and his wife, Mrs B. As her pregnancy progressed, she began to have doubts about honouring the agreement and these hardened following the birth of twins. Although upset about disappointing Mr and Mrs B, she ultimately refused to hand the twins over. The latter were made wards of court:

Sir John Arnold P: In this, as in any other wardship dispute, the welfare of the children, or child, concerned is the first and paramount consideration which the court must, by statute, take into account, and that is what I do.

These children have been, up to their present age of approximately five months, with, quite consistently, their mother and in those circumstances there must necessarily have been some bonding of those children with their mother and that is undoubtedly coupled with the fact that she is their mother, a matter which weighs predominantly in the balance in favour of leaving the children with their mother, but there are other factors which weigh in the opposite balance and which, as is said by Mr B through his counsel, outweigh the advantages of leaving the children with their mother, and it is that balancing exercise which the court is required to perform ...

What then are the factors which the court should take into account? I have already mentioned on the side of Mrs P the matters which weigh heavily in the balance are the fact of her maternity, that she bore the children and carried them for the term of their gestation and that ever since she has conferred upon them the maternal care which they have enjoyed and has done so successfully. The key social worker in the case who has given evidence testifies to the satisfactory nature of the care which Mrs P has conferred upon the children and this assessment is specifically accepted by Mr B as being an accurate one. I start, therefore, from the position that these babies have bonded with their mother in a state of domestic care by her of a satisfactory nature and I now turn to the factors which are said to outweigh those advantages, so as to guide the court upon the proper exercise of the balancing function to the conclusion that the children ought to be taken away from Mrs P, and passed over, under suitable arrangements, to Mr and Mrs B. They are principally as follows. It is said, and said quite correctly, that the shape of the B family is the better shape of a family in which these children might be brought up, because it contains a father as well as a mother and that is undoubtedly true. Next, it is said that the material circumstances of the B family are such that they exhibit a far larger degree of affluence than can be demonstrated by Mrs P. That, also, is undoubtedly true. Then it is said that the intellectual quality of the environment of the B's home and the stimulus which would be afforded to these babies, if they were to grow up in that home, would be greater than the corresponding features in the home of Mrs P ... Then it is said that the religious comfort and support which the B's derive from their Church is greater than anything of that sort available to Mrs P. How far that is true, I simply do not know. I do know that the B's are practising Christians and do derive advantages from that circumstance, but nobody asked Mrs P about this and I am not disposed to assume that she lacks that sort of comfort and support in the absence of any investigation by way of cross-examination to lay the foundations for such a conclusion. Then it is said, and there is something in this, that the problems which might arise from the circumstance that these children who are, of course, congenitally derived from the semen of Mr B and bear traces of Mr B's Asiatic origin would be more easily understood and discussed and reconciled in the household of Mr and Mrs B, a household with an Asiatic ethnic background, than they would be if they arose in relation to these children while they were situated in the home of Mrs P, which is in an English village and which has no non-English connections ...

As regards [these] factors, they are, in the aggregate, weighty, but I do not think, having given my very best effort to the evaluation of the case dispassionately on both sides, that they ought to be taken to outweigh the advantages to these children of preserving the link with the mother to whom they are bonded and who has, as is amply testified, exercised over them a satisfactory level of maternal care, and accordingly it is, I think, the duty of the court to award the care and control of these babies to their mother.

This case suggests that there is a strong presumption that the welfare of the child is best served by leaving it with the surrogate mother. This is especially so, given the inevitable delay, following the birth of the child, in such disputes coming before the courts. The position might well be different where the surrogate initially surrenders custody of the child and subsequently tries to reclaim it from the commissioning couple. This is borne out by the decision of the New Jersey Supreme Court in the well known American case, *In the Matter of Baby M* 537 A 2d 1227 (1988). Whilst holding the agreement void, the court allowed custody to remain with the commissioning couple who, by the time of the final hearing, had been caring for the child for 18 months (but cf the recent Australian case of *Re Evelyn* (1998) 23 Fam LR 53).

Are there any other circumstances in which the commissioning couple might win out? In particular, might the fact of a particular surrogacy being 'total' in nature make a difference? (All the cases considered so far have been ones of partial surrogacy, that is, the surrogate has also been the genetic mother.) The first point to remember is that, whether the surrogacy is total or partial, the surrogate remains the mother at law: see s 27 of the HFEA 1990. Having said that, it might be felt that the commissioning couple should have more rights in cases where they both are the child's genetic parents and the surrogate 'merely' gestated it.

In a Californian case, *Johnson v Calvert* 851 P 2d 776 (1993), the court, in awarding custody in a total surrogacy case to the genetic parents saw genetic, rather than gestational, parenthood as the locus of parental rights, at least where the parties' original intention had been that the genetic/commissioning parents should raise the child. Significantly, however, the commissioning/genetic parents in that case (as in the *Baby M* case) were already caring for the child. Where this is not so, it is suggested that the courts – at least in the UK – may well prefer to allow the child to remain with the surrogate. For one thing, they would be reluctant to send out a signal to future surrogate mothers who, while pregnant, change their minds about handing over the child that, where it is not genetically their own, it could be taken from them against their will. As the Glover Report argues, this could be bad for the child. Instead, the report suggests that 'the possibility of the surrogate mother changing her mind should be accepted by the couple as one of the risks of this way of trying to overcome childlessness'.

Where the parties are agreed

Fewer problems arise where there is consensus between the surrogate and commissioning couple that the child be handed over.

Indeed, s 30 of the HFEA 1990 expressly allows for application to the court by the commissioning parents to obtain a parental order in respect of the child (a special procedure, with similarities to adoption). This section, which was brought into effect on 1 November 1994 by the Parental Order (Human Fertilisation and Embryology) Regulations 1994 SI 1994/2767, provides that:

30 Parental orders in favour of gamete donors

(1) The court may make an order providing for a child to be treated in law as the child of the parties to a marriage (referred to in this section as 'the husband' and 'the wife') if–

    (a) the child has been carried by a woman other than the wife as the result of the placing in her of an embryo or sperm and eggs or her artificial insemination;

    (b) the gametes of the husband or the wife, or both, were used to bring about the creation of the embryo; and

    (c) the conditions in sub-ss (2)–(7) below are satisfied.

(2) The husband and the wife must apply for the order within six months of the birth of the child or, in the case of a child born before the coming into force of this Act, within six months of such coming into force.

(3) At the time of the application and of the making of the order–

    (a) the child's home must be with the husband and the wife; and

    (b) the husband or the wife, or both of them, must be domiciled in a part of the United Kingdom or in the Channel Islands or the Isle of Man.

(4) At the time of the making of the order both the husband and the wife must have attained the age of 18.

(5) The court must be satisfied that both the father of the child (including a person who is the father by virtue of s 28 of this Act), where he is not the husband, and the woman who carried the child have freely, and with full understanding of what is involved, agreed unconditionally to the making of the order.

(6) Sub-section (5) above does not require the agreement of a person who cannot be found or is incapable of giving agreement and the agreement of the woman who carried the child is ineffective for the purposes of that sub-section if given by her less than six weeks after the child's birth.

(7) The court must be satisfied that no money or other benefit (other than for expenses reasonably incurred) has been given or received by the husband or the wife for or in consideration of–

    (a) the making of the order;

    (b) any agreement required by sub-s (5) above;

    (c) the handing over of the child to the husband and the wife; or

    (d) the making of any arrangements with a view to the making of the order;

unless authorised by the court.

The requirement that the surrogate must consent to the order, and that such consent is not valid where given less than six weeks after the birth of the child, is clearly there to protect the surrogate's position. Less obviously defensible is the underlying condition that the commissioning parents should be married: it may plausibly be argued that this amounts to unjustified discrimination against couples in long term heterosexual relationships, who are unmarried. *A fortiori* it will also prevent those in homosexual relationships from utilising the section. Instead, such couples will be forced back to using other, less favourable methods of adoption under the Adoption Act 1976. It is also noteworthy that responsibility for registering a child's birth remains with the surrogate. Because the child will ultimately have access to the Register of Births, it is apparent that, in contrast to gamete donation, the surrogacy process cannot remain anonymous.

The High Court was required to consider the effect of s 30, including the possibility of authorising payment thereunder to the surrogate, in the case of *Re Q (Parental Order)* [1996] 1 FLR 369:

Re Q (Parental Order) [1996] 1 FLR 369, HC (Johnson J)

Baby Q was born in the summer of 1995 as a result of a total surrogacy arrangement. The unmarried surrogate, who received IVF treatment at a licensed clinic, was paid

£8,280 to cover her expenses and loss of earnings. The commissioning couple applied for a parental order under s 30:

Johnson J: Turning belatedly to the particular application made to me, I am satisfied that the statutory requirements are all complied with, but I mention three.

The first relates to the consent of the carrying mother. She had entered into the procedure with the best of intentions, but when the time came to relinquish the child that she had carried so devotedly, she was overcome with doubt and at first declined to give her consent. This reaction is natural and was contemplated by parliament in stipulating that the carrying mother is to be given at least six weeks after the birth to make her decision before she can give a binding consent. One of the duties of the guardian *ad litem* under the Family Proceedings Courts (Children Act 1989) (Amendment) Rules 1994 is to investigate the circumstance of the carrying mother's consent.

It may be of interest if I quote *verbatim* from the guardian's report:

I have visited Miss A twice in order to ascertain her wishes in this matter and to try and clarify the issues around her agreement to the order. Miss A explained how she came to offer herself as a surrogate mother due to seeing the anguish of infertile friends and how she had never thought she would have difficulty parting with the baby she bore. When she received details of Mr and Mrs B she immediately warmed to them and these first good impressions were confirmed when she met them. Miss A has two children of her own and they are both aware of this child's whereabouts. They met Mr and Mrs B numerous times prior to the child's birth, staying at the house both with their mother and alone. They have been told that Mrs B could not grow the baby in her own tummy so Miss A did it for her and they always knew that the baby would not be living with them. At about 28 weeks Miss A experienced some bleeding and was admitted to hospital. She questioned for the first time what she was doing and feels that it was only at this stage that the baby began to feel like a real person to her and that she began to bond with her. Notwithstanding this first period of questioning she decided to carry through handing over the baby to Mr and Mrs B and remained of this view until after the birth. She left hospital without the baby but unfortunately when she decided a few days later to go in and visit the baby the hospital refused her access. Miss A was very upset and although the refusal was due to a misunderstanding and she later saw the baby, she then visited her solicitor with a view to securing the baby's placement with her. This was the position until late July 1995, but Miss A then thought deeply about what she could give the baby versus Mr and Mrs B. At no time had her decision to withdraw her agreement had anything to do with dissatisfaction with Mr and Mrs B as parents and she gradually decided that it was right for the baby to remain with them. In talking to Miss A, it is clear that the depth of feeling she experienced towards her baby took her by surprise. She said that she felt no different toward this baby at her birth than she had felt towards her other children and had not really been prepared for this. It is clear that Miss A felt emotionally torn in half by the separation from the baby. With time, however, and as her own body settled after the birth, so she was able to think more clearly about the issues and this is why she decided to give her agreement. I prepared an agreement form for her to sign on my second visit and she did this willingly and in a positive and definite manner. She fully understands the effects of a parental order, understanding that she loses all parental responsibility, and wishes the order to be made as soon as possible. She does not now wish to attend court herself for the hearing.

This account of the feelings of this carrying mother shows the sensitivity and, indeed, difficulty of the task of the guardian *ad litem* in these cases. This is obviously a demanding role and I was greatly heartened by the obvious care, fairness and understanding with which this guardian had performed her function.

Secondly, I had to consider whether or not I should authorise payments totalling £8,280 which had been made to Miss A by Mr and Mrs B.

I hold that such authorisation can be given retrospectively. In so doing I follow the decision of Latey J in *Re Adoption Application (Payment for Adoption)* [1987] Fam 81 ... which was concerned with a similar provision in the Adoption Act 1976.

The guardian told me that she had at first thought that this amount seemed rather high but on further inquiry she concluded that the payments were understandable. £3,280 was made up of payments to cover clothes, daily trips to the doctor for injections, child care provision of her own children during some of those visits and similar related expenses. A further £5,000 was a payment to compensate Miss A for loss of earnings. Given the circumstances of the pregnancy and her potential earnings of £15,000 [per annum], I joined with the guardian in concluding that the payment was reasonable and, retrospectively, I gave authority for it. Finally, in the course of the guardian's investigation, the consultant who had carried out the medical procedures insisted that in his view and in the view of his hospital, Mr B was to be treated as the legal father of the child. The guardian told me that in her experience this is a frequent misunderstanding of the legislation and it was for this reason that I was asked to give a formal ruling. Certainly on my application of the Act to the circumstances of this case, there was no man who was to be 'treated as the father' and whose consent was necessary to the making of the order. I hope that this judgment will draw attention to the working of this important new statutory provision and will help to resolve the problems that are raised by s 30 concerning who is to be treated as the father for the purpose of giving consent to the making of this new form of order.

This case shows the degree of attachment that the surrogate may develop towards the child she carries, even in the case of total surrogacy. It also suggests that, at least where the sum is in no way extortionate, a court will be fairly relaxed about authorising payment retrospectively to the surrogate under s 30(7) of the HFEA 1990. Indeed, recently, in *Re C (A Child)* [2002] 1 FLR 1008, a payment of £12,000 was authorised by the High Court in similar circumstances. On the other hand, as regards, the last issue mentioned by Johnston J, that of Mr B's legal paternity, *Re Q* can no longer be regarded as authoritative. Provided that the surrogate is unmarried, then, as noted at p 380, 'treatment together' (conferring paternity under s 28(3) of the 1990 Act) means simply that a man and woman 'are united in their pursuit of treatment'. This would presumably be satisfied in relation to the surrogate and commissioning father, making the latter the child's legal father from the outset. (Rather anomalously, if the surrogate is married, *her* husband – assuming he assented to the surrogacy arrangement – will be the legal father under s 28(2).)

In October 1997, following further adverse media publicity accorded to the practice of surrogacy, the Government commissioned an inquiry (headed by Professor Margaret Brazier) into the arrangements for payments and regulation under the 1985 Act. The ensuing report, *Surrogacy: Review for Health Ministers of Current Arrangements for Payment and Regulation*, Cm 4068, 1998, London: DoH, recommended a number of changes to the existing law. In particular, it felt that payment to surrogate mothers should be more closely controlled to ensure that only genuine expenses were covered and that the (charitable) agencies involved in negotiating surrogacy arrangements should be required to operate in accordance with a Code of Practice drawn up by the Department of Health. To achieve these changes, the report proposed that both the SAA 1985 and s 30 of the HFEA 1990 should be repealed, and a new Surrogacy Act passed to consolidate the law in the UK.

As yet the Government has not acted upon these recommendations.

CHAPTER 8

PREGNANCY AND ABORTION

INTRODUCTION

By contrast with the issues examined in Chapter 7, in which the law has had, in the main, to respond to novel problems created by recent advances in medical technology, abortion as a procedure has existed for centuries. Nevertheless, it remains one of the most intractable and emotive topics within the province of medical law. Broadly speaking, 'abortion' denotes the practice of terminating a pregnancy in such a way as to destroy the life of the foetus being carried by the pregnant woman. In the case of abortions carried out early in pregnancy on non-viable foetuses, the fact that the foetus is expelled from the womb is sufficient for its death. In other cases, where the foetus is more mature (and capable of surviving outside the womb), additional steps will be taken to ensure that it dies prior to delivery. Either way, it is apparent that the practice stands in direct opposition to the major forms of fertility treatment considered in the last chapter. There, the intention is normally to produce a pregnancy resulting in a successful live birth. Here, the intention is to bring an existing pregnancy to an end without the live birth of the child. In another sense, however, there is a close relationship between the practices in that they both implicate (albeit in opposing ways) reproductive freedom. As John Robertson notes:

Robertson, JA, *Children of Choice*, 1994, Ewing, NJ: Princeton UP, p 26:

An essential distinction is between the freedom to avoid reproduction and the freedom to reproduce. When people talk of reproductive rights, they usually have one or the other aspect in mind. Because different interests and justifications underlie each, and countervailing interests for limiting each aspect vary, recognition of one aspect does not necessarily mean that the other will also be respected; nor does limitation of one mean that the other can also be denied.

However, there is a mirroring or reciprocal relationship here. Denial of one type of reproductive liberty necessarily implicates the other. If a woman is not able to avoid reproduction through contraception or abortion, she may end up reproducing, with all the burdens that unwanted reproduction entails. Similarly, if one is denied the liberty to reproduce ... one is forced to avoid reproduction, thus experiencing the loss that absence of progeny brings. By extending reproductive options, new reproductive technologies present challenges to both aspects of procreative choice.

Gillian Douglas has explored the background to the right to avoid reproduction claimed for individuals as follows:

Douglas, G, *Law, Fertility and Reproduction*, 1991, London: Sweet & Maxwell, p 15:

Methods, effective or not, for avoiding conception or childbirth are probably as old as civilisation itself, and various remedies to alleviate childlessness are probably of equal antiquity. To what extent have individuals been at liberty to make use of these? The former, certainly, have always been forthrightly condemned by the Roman Catholic Church, drawing originally upon the Jewish view that the duty to procreate through marriage is the first of all commandments. Sex became associated by St Augustine with sin, and could only be justified by procreation. Aquinas considered that to dissociate sex from procreation was to act against nature and therefore to sin.

The breaking down of this religious influence and the rise of a rights-based political philosophy in the West during the 18th and 19th centuries, utilised first by men and then by women, enabled individuals to challenge these old ideas and control of sexual behaviour. Since women are the central actors in reproduction, it is not surprising to find that the first wave of feminism in the 19th century was in part characterised by a desire to enable women to restrict their childbearing, albeit mainly to ensure that they could be better mothers to a few children, rather than poor mothers to too many. The possibility of a right to control one's reproductive capacity through contraception is more likely to be a female than a male concern because of the consequences for the woman where such a possibility is not permitted. In this century, the modern wave of feminism has demanded such a freedom directly, as an aspect of a general desire to gain autonomy and control over one's own body.

In this chapter, we shall first consider the principal moral arguments for and against abortion, together with the additional factors which influence the legal response to what many regard as an ethical impasse. Next, the present state of the law will be analysed, including the implications for the parties most directly affected by the practice. The final part of the chapter then takes the discussion beyond the question of abortion to address the legal position in relation to other forms of avoidable pre-natal harm.

The morality of abortion

Traditionally, the debate as to the rights and wrongs of abortion has been couched in terms of the 'right to life' of the foetus versus the pregnant woman's 'right to choose' whether or not to bear a child. In many cases, the position a person takes in this debate will depend upon the underlying moral status they accord to the human foetus. As Rosalind Hursthouse writes:

Hursthouse, R, *Beginning Lives*, Oxford: Blackwells, 1987, pp 27–28:

The simplest view on the issue of abortion, the one often expressed explicitly or implicitly by non-philosophers in letters to newspapers, discussions on the wireless and so on, is that the moral rights and wrongs of abortion can be unproblematically settled by determining the moral status of the foetus. Hence it is common to find people on the conservative side insisting that the foetus is an unborn baby and hence that abortion is infanticide or murder and absolutely wrong, while people on the opposite side insist that the foetus is just a clump of living cells and hence that abortion is merely an operation which removes some part of one's body and hence is morally innocuous.

Now it is certainly true that the question of the moral status of the foetus is important, for according to what its status is, different arguments will bear upon the rights and wrongs of abortion. If, as conservatives believe, the foetus has the same moral status as a baby, then the mother's moral right to abortion is, to say the least, problematic; if there were any such right, a quite particular case would have to be made out for it. If, on the other hand, the foetus has the same moral status as, say, a kidney, then the argument for the mother's moral right to abortion could proceed, quite generally, as an argument concerning the right, of both women and men, to decide what happens to their own bodies.

The physical attributes of the foetus and the developmental process that it undergoes during pregnancy are, as we saw in the previous chapter, agreed upon. What is controverted is the moral inferences as to its status that should be drawn from the physical facts. The two key contrasting views, the 'theological' and 'personhood' approaches, are discussed by Jane Fortin in the following extract, along with a middle position put forward by Michael Lockwood:

Fortin, J, 'Legal protection for the unborn child' (1988) 51 MLR 54:

1 The concept of 'personhood'

... most philosophers argue that the point in time when human life begins is quite distinct from and less relevant than when a human 'person' comes into existence. The advantage of this approach is that it avoids the 'speciesism' involved in maintaining that all human life automatically has a greater intrinsic value and right to protection than that of any other species. Instead, it concentrates on those aspects of human life that merit such preferment. Thus whilst few would claim that a human sperm or unfertilised egg merits greater protection than a 10 week old kitten, most would accept without question the automatic right to life of a 10 year old child. This is because the child has become a person and as such, his life has an intrinsic value both to himself and others. Arguably then, there is little reason for extending legal protection to human life until 'a person' comes into existence. If this argument is accepted, it becomes vital to establish a clear definition of 'personhood'; no easy matter when moral philosophers show little accord in their choice of essential attributes to be displayed by a 'person'.

Perhaps the most widely known to the general public is the traditional Roman Catholic approach to the question. This is a metaphysical one which, in its strictest form, maintains that a human person comes into existence at the moment of the ovum being fertilised. At this moment of 'ensoulment', the fertilised ovum becomes infused with a rational soul of its own and this theory of immediate animation is widely believed to embody the official teaching of the Roman Catholic Church ...

Some Roman Catholic philosophers adopt the less extreme theory of 'delayed animation'. This was developed by the theologian, Thomas Aquinas, who maintained that there were a number of stages in human generation and that ensoulment did not take place until a later stage, some time after conception. The more modern explanation is that a human soul can only infuse a human form which is sufficiently well developed to exhibit essentially human characteristics; clearly this does not occur until some time after conception.

Many moral philosophers reject the metaphysical approach to personhood which is so often associated with the Roman Catholic Church. In their view personhood is not defined by reference to the presence or otherwise of an immaterial human soul but by reference to a complicated combination of mental and or physical properties. There seems to be little agreement over which properties are essential, although many maintain that to be a person, a human being or entity must, *inter alia*, possess rationality and self-consciousness, be capable of action and be the subject of non-momentary goals or interests. Inevitably, many proponents of such a combination of properties, find it impossible to accept that a human foetus can be deemed a person and worthy of protection; consequently, in their view, there can be no moral objection to abortion, however late. Indeed, Michael Tooley lucidly presents the argument that since even a newly born child lacks these properties, infanticide is not morally objectionable.

2 Human organisms, human beings and persons

Although many would find Tooley's conclusion distasteful, its logic cannot be denied. A possible way of avoiding some, but not all, of these problems is to maintain three clear distinctions. Thus Michael Lockwood distinguishes between human organisms, human beings and persons. In this way, depending on the definition of 'human being', a newly born infant might be classified as such, with certain consequential rights, despite its not having attained the status of personhood. Lockwood uses the term 'human being' to describe what 'you and I are essentially, what we can neither become nor cease to be, without ceasing to exist'. Thus, in his view, this concept revolves round that of personal identity, which underlies 'certain discernible continuities' such as memory and personality – those unchanging elements in a human being which establishes his own unique blueprint. Accordingly, the concept of identity is established not by the continuities themselves but by those elements underlying them ...

In his view, it is only when the brain develops to this extent, that a human embryo can be said to have become a human being. Only then does it become able to sustain distinctively mental processes, thereby justifying certain protection. Lockwood himself feels that it is impossible to be precise over the point in time when this occurs. Nevertheless, on the basis of the existing, albeit sparse, scientific evidence, he suggests that an appropriate marker might be 10 weeks' gestation. Lockwood's analysis is attractively clear and less cold blooded than that of Tooley. Moreover, it has the advantage of allowing both the unborn and the newly born child to have a measure of protection as human beings, without claiming either to be a fully fledged person.

However, it is apparent that all three views described by Fortin require some commitment to unprovable 'metaphysical' premises. As Margaret Brazier has noted:

Brazier, M, 'The challenge for Parliament', in Dyson, A and Harris, J (eds), *Experiments on Embryos*, 1990, London: Routledge, p 134:

The difficulty is that the dispute is itself incapable of any conclusive resolution. Perception of the status of the embryo derives in many cases from the presence or absence of religious belief. Most, but not all, proponents of the belief that the embryo is from fertilisation a genetically unique individual as fully human as you or I, rest that belief, at least in part, on the embryo's potential possession of an immortal, immaterial soul ... Many, but again by no means all, proponents of allowing research on embryos deny or doubt the existence of the soul.

Thus the argument on abortion becomes for opponents: 'How can the law permit the wanton destruction of human life?' And supporters of liberal abortion laws respond: 'By what right do you seek to impose your personal unprovable claims about God and the soul on others?' The dispute reaches stalemate ... The humanity of the embryo is unproven and unprovable. But that acts both ways. Just as I cannot prove that humanity was divinely created and that each and every one of us possesses an immortal soul, so it cannot be proved that it is not so. Admitting the possibility of the soul, the moment of ensoulment cannot be proved. Nothing more or less can be concluded about the full humanity of the embryo save to say that the cases for and against are, to borrow a Scottish term, not proven.

Rather than attempting to found the moral status of the foetus on any particular attribute it possesses as it now is, an increasingly popular approach is to stress the potential (understood in terms of how it would develop naturally, other things equal) that the foetus has to become a person in the future. However, this concept stands in need of significant clarification if it is to bear any real moral weight. As Glover notes:

Glover, J *et al*, *Report to the European Commission on Reproductive Technologies, Fertility and the Family*, **1989, London: Fourth Estate (the Glover Report), p 97:**

Perhaps what matters is not some property an embryo now has, but what it has the potential to become. This claim seems to imply that disposing of an embryo is wrong because it prevents the existence of a particular developed person, namely the one the embryo would have become. But this argument rules out contraception. You are a particular developed person, and contraception would have prevented your existence. The apparently innocuous word 'potential' turns out to be very slippery.

To avoid ruling out contraception, potentiality has to be interpreted differently. Perhaps the destruction of potential is not just a matter of the loss of a future developed person, but also the loss of something that has got a certain distance on the way there: the programme is already in existence, as all the genes are present. But this leaves some unanswered questions. If the properties an embryo now has do not generate a right to life, and the argument about one less future person does not do so either, why should combining the two considerations give the desired result? Of course a compound can have properties not possessed by its individual ingredients, but in this case some account is needed of the moral chemistry involved ...

It is accordingly important to consider whether there may be alternative ways to understand the debate which allow conclusions about the morality of abortion which do not depend on views about the status of the foetus. Two very different, but equally bold, attempts to recouch the abortion debate to precisely this end have been made, respectively, by Judith Jarvis Thomson and Ronald Dworkin. Taking Thomson's argument first, in a celebrated article 'A defense of abortion', she suggested that, even if, for the sake of argument, we were to grant the foetus equal moral status to adult human persons, abortion would remain morally permissible in a large number of circumstances, given the prior right of the pregnant woman to exercise control over her body:

Thomson, JJ, 'A defense of abortion' (1971) 1 Philosophy and Public Affairs 1:

Most opposition to abortion relies on the premise that the foetus is a human being, a person, from the moment of conception. The premise is argued for, but, as I think, not well. Take, for example, the most common argument. We are asked to notice that the development of a human being from conception through birth into childhood is continuous; then it is said that to draw a line, to choose a point in this development and say 'before this point the thing is not a person, after this point it is a person' is to make an arbitrary choice, a choice for which in the nature of things no good reason can be given. It is concluded that the foetus is, or anyway that we had better say it is, a person from the moment of conception. But this conclusion does not follow. Similar things might be said about the development of an acorn into an oak tree, and it does not follow that acorns are oak trees, or that we had better say they are. Arguments of this form are sometimes called 'slippery slope arguments' – the phrase is perhaps self-explanatory – and it is dismaying that opponents of abortion rely on them so heavily and uncritically.

I am inclined to agree, however, that the prospects for 'drawing a line' in the development of the foetus look dim. I am inclined to think also that we shall probably have to agree that the foetus has already become a human person well before birth. Indeed, it comes as a surprise when one first learns how early in its life it begins to acquire human characteristics. By the 10th week, for example, it already has a face, arms and legs, fingers and toes; it has internal organs, and brain activity is detectable. On the other hand, I think that the premise is false, that the foetus is not a person from the moment of conception. A newly fertilised ovum, a newly implanted clump of cells, is no more a person than an acorn is an oak tree. But I shall not discuss any of this. For it seems to me to be of great interest to ask what happens if, for the sake of argument, we allow the premise. How, precisely, are we supposed to get from there to the conclusion that abortion is morally impermissible? Opponents of abortion commonly spend most of their time establishing that the foetus is a person, and hardly any time explaining the step from there to the impermissibility of abortion. Perhaps they think the step too simple and obvious to require much comment. Or perhaps instead they are simply being economical in argument. Many of those who defend abortion rely on the premise that the foetus is not a person, but only a bit of tissue that will become a person at birth; and why pay out more arguments than you have to? Whatever the explanation, I suggest that the step they take is neither easy nor obvious, that it calls for closer examination than it is commonly given, and that when we do give it this closer examination we shall feel inclined to reject it.

I propose, then, that we grant that the foetus is a person from the moment of conception. How does the argument go from here? Something like this, I take it. Every person has a right to life. So the foetus has a right to life. No doubt the mother has a right to decide what shall happen in and to her body; everyone would grant that. But surely a person's right to life is stronger and more stringent than the mother's right to decide what happens in and to her body, and so outweighs it. So the foetus may not be killed; an abortion may not be performed.

It sounds plausible. But now let me ask you to imagine this. You wake up in the morning and find yourself back to back in bed with an unconscious violinist. A famous unconscious violinist. He has been found to have a fatal kidney ailment, and the Society of Music Lovers has canvassed all the available medical records and found that you alone have the right blood type to help. They have therefore kidnapped you, and last night the violinist's circulatory system was plugged into yours, so that your kidneys can be used to extract poisons from his blood as well as your own. The director of the hospital now tells you: 'Look, we're sorry the Society of Music Lovers did this to you – we would never have permitted it if we had known. But still, they did it, and the violinist now is plugged into you. To unplug you would be to kill him. But never mind, it's only for nine months. By then he will have recovered from his ailment, and can safely be unplugged from you.' Is it morally incumbent on you to accede to this situation? No doubt it would be very nice of you if you did, a great kindness. But do you have to accede to it? What if it were not nine months, but nine years? Or longer still? What if the director of the hospital says: 'Tough luck, I agree, but you've now got to stay in bed, with the violinist plugged into you, for the rest of your life. Because remember this. All persons have a right to life, and violinists are persons. Granted you have a right to decide what happens in and to your body, but a person's right to life outweighs your right to decide what happens in and to your body. So you cannot ever be unplugged from him.' I imagine you would regard this as outrageous, which suggests that something really is wrong with that plausible-sounding argument I mentioned a moment ago.

In this case, of course, you were kidnapped; you didn't volunteer for the operation that plugged the violinist into your kidneys. Can those who oppose abortion on the ground I mentioned make an exception for a pregnancy due to rape? Certainly. They can say that persons have a right to life only if they didn't come into existence because of rape; or they can say that all persons have a right to life, but that some have less of a right to life than others, in particular, that those who came into existence because of rape have less. But these statements have a rather unpleasant sound. Surely the question of whether you have a right to life at all, or how much of it you have, shouldn't turn on the question of whether or not you are the product of a rape. And in fact the people who oppose abortion on the ground I mentioned do not make this distinction, and hence do not make an exception in case of rape ...

Despite its ingenuity, there are a number of difficulties with Thomson's argument. First, whilst it may well permit abortion in cases of rape (where the woman has not given the foetus a 'right' to the use of her body), it is not clear that it can be extended to pregnancy which results from consensual sex. As Hursthouse notes:

Hursthouse, R, *Beginning Lives,* **1987, Oxford: Blackwells, pp 187–89:**

Thomson asserts it as a premise that a woman cannot be said to have given the foetus the right to use her body if she is pregnant because of rape. Plausibly the pregnancy must result from voluntary intercourse ... However this still leaves a very large number of cases; does Thomson agree that in all cases of pregnancy due to voluntary intercourse in full knowledge of the facts of life the mother could be said to have given the foetus the right to use her body – that the intercourse, as it were, amounts to an offer to have one's body thus used?

She clearly does not, but her argument at this point depends on two rather unsatisfactory analogies. In one she imagines that children come about by people-seeds taking root in one's carpet; this may happen even if one has gone to great trouble to try to prevent it by putting fine mesh screens over one's windows. In the other analogy, she does not consider children, but how people might acquire a right to use my house, and says it would be absurd to suppose that someone had acquired it by just blundering in, through a window I had happened to open, behind bars I had installed to keep people out which happened to have a defect. In each case I go to some trouble to try to keep people-seeds or people out; in each case there is supposed to be a way that would guarantee keeping them out, say with sealed windows, but it cannot be said that I am responsible for their being in my house and that hence they have a right to it simply because I do not go in for this extreme measure.

These analogies are obviously supposed to be with contraception; despite the woman's efforts not to become pregnant, she does. Given that she was trying not to, her voluntary intercourse cannot count as an offer, conferring a right, to have her body used by the foetus. But the difficulty with the people-seed analogy is that, because it is so far-fetched, it lacks all the background that enables one (sometimes) to make up one's mind. Do these people-seeds just root for nine months? What are the available alternatives to uprooting and killing them – can they be transplanted, can you swap your house for nine months with someone who wants children ... ? The difficulty with the other analogy is that it misses out the crucial aspect of the foetus being dependent on the use of the woman's body for its survival ...

Secondly, there remains the problem that abortions are typically carried out by a third party, the doctor, and it may be argued that conceiving of abortion in terms of a conflict of maternal–foetal rights cannot settle the question of what would be an appropriate moral response on the part of such a third party. Finally, and more generally, Thomson's narrow focus on rights may be felt to obscure other ways in which an action is morally problematic. In particular, it does not follow, from the mere fact that the foetus lacks a right to use the woman's body, that abortion is morally innocuous. This is apparently recognised by Thomson herself:

Thomson, JJ, 'A defense of abortion' (1971) 1 Philosophy and Public Affairs 1:

We surely must all grant that there may be cases in which it would be morally indecent to detach a person from your body at the cost of his life. Suppose you learn that what the violinist needs is not nine years of your life, but only one hour: all you need do to save his life is to spend one hour in that bed with him. Suppose also that letting him use your kidneys for that one hour would not affect your health in the slightest. Admittedly you were kidnapped. Admittedly you did not give anyone permission to plug him into you. Nevertheless it seems to me plain you *ought* to allow him to use your kidneys for that hour – it would be indecent to refuse.

Again, suppose pregnancy lasted only an hour, and constituted no threat to life or health. And suppose that a woman becomes pregnant as a result of rape. Admittedly she did not voluntarily do anything to bring about the existence of a child. Admittedly she did nothing at all which would give the unborn person a right to the use of her body. All the same it might well be said, as in the newly amended violinist story, that she *ought* to allow it to remain for that hour – that it would be indecent in her to refuse.

In a telling recent contribution to the abortion debate, Ronald Dworkin has attempted to bridge the gap between the 'pro-life' and 'pro-choice' positions by identifying an important piece of common ground between the two camps. In particular, he argues that both conservatives and liberals share a common commitment to the sanctity of human life:

Dworkin, R, *Life's Dominion: An Argument About Abortion and Euthanasia*, 1993, London: HarperCollins, pp 88–90:

Both conservatives and liberals assume that in some circumstances abortion is more serious and more likely to be unjustifiable than in others. Notably, both agree that a late term abortion is graver than an early term one. We cannot explain this shared conviction simply on the ground that foetuses more closely resemble infants as pregnancy continues. People believe that abortion is not just emotionally more difficult but morally worse the later in pregnancy it occurs, and increasing resemblance alone has no moral significance. Nor can we explain the shared conviction by noticing that at some point in pregnancy a foetus becomes sentient. Most people think that abortion is morally worse early in the second trimester – well before sentience is possible – than early in the first one … Foetal development is a continuing creative process, a process that has barely begun at the instant of conception. Indeed, since genetic individuation is not yet complete at that point, we might say that the development of a unique human being has not started until approximately 14 days later, at implantation. But after implantation, as foetal growth continues, the natural investment that would be wasted in an abortion grows steadily larger and more significant.

Human and divine

So our sense that frustration rather than just loss compromises the inviolability of human life does seem helpful in explaining what unites most people about abortion. The more difficult question is whether it also helps in explaining what divides them …

Suppose parents discover, early in the mother's pregnancy, that the foetus is genetically so deformed that the life it would lead after birth will inevitably be both short and sharply limited. They must decide whether it is a worse frustration of life if the gravely deformed foetus were to die at once – wasting the miracle of its creation and its development so far – or if it were to continue to grow in utero, to be born, and to live only a short and crippled life. We know that people divide about that question, and we now have a way to describe the division. On one view, immediate death of the foetus, even in a case like this one, is a more terrible frustration of the miracle of life than even a sharply diminished and brief infant life would be, for the latter would at least redeem some small part, however limited, of the natural investment. On the rival view, it would be a worse frustration of life to allow this foetal life to continue, because that would add, to the sad waste of a deformed human's biological creation, the further, heartbreaking waste of personal emotional investments made in that life by others, but principally by the child himself, before his inevitable early death.

We should therefore consider this hypothesis: though almost everyone accepts the abstract principle that it is intrinsically bad when human life, once begun, is frustrated, people disagree about the best answer to the question of whether avoidable premature death is always or invariably the most serious possible frustration of life. Very conservative opinion, on this hypothesis, is grounded in the conviction that immediate death is inevitably a more serious frustration than any option that postpones death, even at the cost of greater frustration in other respects. Liberal opinion, on the same hypothesis, is grounded in the opposite conviction: that in some cases, at least, a choice for premature death minimises the frustration of life and is therefore not a compromise of the principle that human life is sacred but, on the contrary, best respects that principle ...

Although enlightening, Dworkin's inclusive strategy is not likely to satisfy everybody. In particular, in the metaphysical assumptions he makes about the foetus he appears to be far closer to the liberal than the conservative position. Even if he is right that some conservatives oppose abortion on the 'detached' ground that it frustrates life in the abstract, there will inevitably remain others whose opposition is derived from specific beliefs about foetuses which are not amenable to any compromise. Equally, it is likely that some adherents of a liberal-feminist persuasion will not be convinced that the foetus is to be regarded as any more sacred than other parts of the woman's body tissue. Nevertheless, it is probable that Dworkin's view is one that, empirically speaking, accurately reflects a broad consensus of opinion in our society today.

Abortion and legislation

The point that questions as to the morality of a practice must be distinguished from the rightness of legislating against the same was noted in Chapter 7. In relation to abortion, the salient arguments are well put by Rosalind Hursthouse:

Hursthouse, R, *Beginning Lives*, Oxford: Blackwells, 1987, pp 15–16:

The confusion of questions about morality and legislation is particularly common in arguments about abortion ... One reason why the questions become readily confused in debate is because of the tactics of opposition. Many people, particularly women, do think there is something wrong about having an abortion, that it is not a morally innocuous matter, but also think that the current abortion laws are if anything still too restrictive, and find it difficult to articulate their position on the morality of abortion without, apparently betraying the feminist campaign concerning legislation. To give an inch on 'a woman's right to choose', to suggest even for a moment that having an abortion is not only 'exercising that right' (which sounds fine) but also 'ending a human life' (which sounds like homicide) or even 'ending a potential human life' (which sounds at least serious) is to play into the hands of the conservatives.

What happens to the conservative and the liberal sides of the debate once the distinction between questions of morality and questions of legislation is drawn? In theory, drawing the distinction opens up the possibility of four different positions.

Morality of abortion	Laws on abortion	Position
Wrong	Restrictive	Conservative
Innocuous	Restrictive	'Totalitarian'
Innocuous	Liberal	Liberal/radical
Wrong	Liberal	Liberal/moderate

The 'totalitarian' position is of merely theoretical interest. (It might be occupied by someone in an underpopulated country, indifferent both to women's rights and to appeals to the sanctity of life, who thought it was necessary to increase the population quickly.) The first position is a familiar one. It is well known that the conservative position on legislation about abortion is based on a corresponding conservative position about its morality. According to the conservative view, abortion is morally wrong because it is the taking of human life, and hence, like any other case of homicide, justifiable in only a restricted range of circumstances, which should be laid down by law.

It is the possibility of two distinct liberal positions, which for want of better labels I will henceforth distinguish as the 'radical' and the 'moderate', which is not so familiar, and much that is said on the liberal side about women's rights leaves it quite unclear which of two views about the morality of abortion its supporters hold. Do they hold that abortion is morally quite innocuous – and hence that to have laws restricting women's access is as absurd and punitive as having laws which decreed, say, that women (though not men) were forbidden to cut their hair or smoke? Or do they agree with the conservatives that it is a morally very serious matter but hold that nevertheless the suffering and lack of freedom that women must at present undergo when abortion is not legally available not only justify but require our having laws which permit this wrong to be done whenever the woman wishes it? Is abortion a necessary evil as things are at present, or not an evil at all?

As this suggests, at a pragmatic level any lawmaker must consider the likely *effect* of laws which (for whatever reason) straightforwardly prohibited abortion. Experience, in both this country as well as in many others, has indeed tended to show that, rather than curtailing the practice, abortion will simply be driven underground.

THE LEGAL POSITION

Criminal law provisions

Abortion in the UK remains *prima facie* a criminal offence. Historically, the influence of the canon law of the Christian Church played an important part in the emergent common law on the subject. John Keown has charted this influence as follows:

Keown, J, *Abortion, Doctors and the Law*, 1988, Cambridge: CUP, pp 3–4:

... the weight of available authority supports the view that the common law prohibited abortion, at the latest, after the foetus had become 'quick' or 'animated'. Animation was believed to occur when the foetus 'quickened' in the womb. An incident of the second trimester of pregnancy, quickening marks the first maternal perception of foetal movement. In associating the origin of life with quickening, the law betrayed both pragmatic and metaphysical influences. The former concerned the need to prove, in any prosecution for abortion, that the woman had been pregnant and that the foetus had been killed by the abortifacient act. Evidence of quickening would clearly facilitate prosecution. The metaphysical influence upon the law was the popular theory, originated by Aristotle and perpetuated by Galen, that human life began at the point of 'animation'. This theory was espoused by the canon law of the Christian Church and thence it found its way into the developing common law.

The criminal law of abortion achieved its modern form only in the mid-19th century. As JK Mason has written:

Mason, JK, *Medico-Legal Aspects of Reproduction and Parenthood*, 2nd edn, 1998, Aldershot: Dartmouth, p 111:

The recognition of variable foetal rights has fluctuated in English law. The influence of medieval teaching was still apparent in 1803 when procuring the miscarriage of a woman who was 'quick with child' was a statutory offence subject to capital punishment. Abortion at an earlier state of gestation carried a lesser penalty, albeit a sentence of up to 14 years' transportation. The law remained the same until 1861 when the Offences Against the Person Act came into being. This introduced two major changes: firstly, the death penalty was replaced by potential penal servitude for life and, secondly, any distinction as to fetal age was abolished. The 1861 Act remains the definitive law in England, Wales and Northern Ireland ...

Section 58 of the Offences Against the Person Act (OAPA) 1861 provides as follows:

Attempts to procure abortion

58 Administering drugs or using instruments to procure abortion

Every woman, being with child, who, with intent to procure her own miscarriage, shall administer to herself any poison or other noxious thing, or shall unlawfully use any instrument or other means whatsoever with the like intent, and whosoever, with intent to procure the miscarriage of any woman, whether she be or be not with child, shall unlawfully administer to her or cause to be taken by her any poison or other noxious thing, or shall unlawfully use any instrument or other means whatsoever with the like intent, shall be guilty of felony, and being convicted thereof shall be liable to be kept in penal servitude for life.

Furthermore, s 59 of the Act prohibits various ancillary acts designed to facilitate the commission of the offence:

59 Procuring drugs, etc, to cause abortion

Whosoever shall unlawfully supply or procure any poison or other noxious thing, or any instrument or thing whatsoever, knowing that the same is intended to be unlawfully used or employed with intent to procure the miscarriage of any woman, whether she be or be not with child, shall be guilty of a misdemeanour, and being convicted thereof shall be liable to be kept in penal servitude.

It will be noted that the Act does not speak in terms of 'carrying out an abortion', but rather of 'procuring a miscarriage'. This (although it remains undefined) is arguably a narrower concept, which would apparently leave certain forms of foetal killing lawful, namely those where the woman does not 'miscarry' as a result of the procedure. The most startling example would be a situation in which the foetus is destroyed once the woman is already in labour: no miscarriage occurs here, but equally the foetus, even one which has partially emerged from the womb, does not yet enjoy the protection of the criminal law against homicide. The existence of such a legal *lacuna* was deplored by Talbot J in charging a jury at Liverpool in 1928, and his comments led to the passing of a further piece of legislation, the Infant Life (Preservation) Act (ILPA) 1929. Section 1(1) of the 1929 Act created a new offence of 'child destruction':

1 Punishment for child destruction

(1) Subject as hereinafter in this sub-section provided, any person who, with intent to destroy the life of a child capable of being born alive, by any wilful act causes a child to die before it has an existence independent of its mother, shall be guilty of felony, to wit, of child destruction, and shall be liable on conviction thereof on indictment to penal servitude for life:

> Provided that no person shall be found guilty of an offence under this section unless it is proved that the act which caused the death of the child was not done in good faith for the purpose only of preserving the life of the mother.

Although, as noted, the primary purpose of this provision was the protection of the foetus during the course of its birth, it is apparent that its effect goes further by extending such protection back in time to the point in the pregnancy at which the foetus became 'capable of being born alive'. By virtue of s 1(2) of the Act, this is rebuttably presumed to be at 28 weeks' gestation:

> 1(2)-For the purposes of this Act, evidence that a woman had at any material time been pregnant for a period of 28 weeks or more shall be *prima facie* proof that she was at that time pregnant of a child capable of being born alive.

Thus, the 1861 and 1929 Acts operate to some extent in overlap: a termination carried out on a foetus capable of being born alive will, in so far as it occurs by way of a miscarriage, be an offence under both statutes. By contrast, only the 1861 Act applies to the younger, non-viable foetus and, conversely, only the 1929 Act to a foetus already in the course of its birth.

Defences to abortion prior to 1967

Section 1(1) of the ILPA 1929 contains an express proviso to the effect that no offence is committed by a person who causes the death of the foetus in order to save the life of the pregnant woman. This provision was included because, before the development of modern Caesarean sections, the craniotomy (crushing the foetus's skull) was a standard medical procedure to deal with cases where normal delivery was not medically possible. It is apparent, however, that no similar defence was provided for in the OAPA 1861 in relation to procuring a miscarriage. A question that long remained open, therefore, was whether a doctor who terminated a pregnancy at this earlier stage in order to save the pregnant woman's life was necessarily guilty of an offence under the 1861 Act. The issue finally came before a court in 1938 in the case of *R v Bourne* [1939] 1 KB 687.

R v Bourne [1939] 1 KB 687 (Macnaghten J)

A 14 year old girl became pregnant as a result of a brutal rape. Mr Bourne, an eminent gynaecologist, made public his intention to perform an abortion on the girl and, having obtained the consent of her parents, duly did so. He was charged with procuring a miscarriage contrary to s 58 of the OAPA 1861. In his defence, could a similar proviso to that found in the ILPA 1929 be read into the section and, if so, what was its scope?

> **Macnaghten J**: No such proviso is in fact set out in s 58 of the Offences Against the Person Act 1861; but the words of that section are that any person who 'unlawfully' uses an instrument with intent to procure miscarriage shall be guilty of felony. In my opinion the word 'unlawfully' is not, in that section, a meaningless word. I think it imports the meaning expressed by the proviso in s 1, sub-s (1) of the Infant Life (Preservation) Act 1929, and that s 58 of the Offences Against the Person Act 1861 must be read as if the words making it an offence to use an instrument with intent to procure a miscarriage were qualified by a similar proviso.
>
> In this case, therefore, my direction to you in law is this – that the burden rests on the Crown to satisfy you beyond reasonable doubt that the defendant did not procure the miscarriage of the girl in good faith for the purpose only of preserving her life ...
>
> What then is the meaning to be given to the words 'for the purpose of preserving the life of the mother'? There has been much discussion in this case as to the difference between danger to life and danger to health. It may be that you are more fortunate than I am, but I confess that I have found it difficult to understand what the discussion really meant, since life depends upon health, and it may be that health is so gravely impaired that death results. A question was asked by the learned Attorney General in the course of his cross-examination of Mr Bourne. 'I suggest to you, Mr Bourne,' said the Attorney General, 'that there is a perfectly clear line – there may be border-line cases – there is a clear line of distinction between danger to health and danger to life'. The answer of Mr Bourne was: 'I cannot agree without qualifying it; I cannot say just yes or no. I can say there is a large group whose health may be damaged, but whose life almost certainly will not be sacrificed. There is another group at the other end whose life will be definitely in very great danger.' And then he adds:
>
> > There is a large body of material between those two extremes in which it is not really possible to say how far life will be in danger, but we find, of course, that the health is depressed to such an extent that life is shortened, such as in cardiac cases, so that you may say that their life is in danger, because death might occur within measurable distance of the time of their labour.
>
> If that view commends itself to you, you will not accept the suggestion that there is a clear line of distinction between danger to health and danger to life. Mr Oliver wanted you to give what he called a wide and liberal meaning to the words 'for the purpose of preserving the life of the mother'. I should prefer the word 'reasonable' to the words 'wide and liberal'. I think you should take a reasonable view of those words.
>
> It is not contended that those words mean merely for the purpose of saving the mother from instant death. There are cases, we are told, where it is reasonably certain that a pregnant woman will not be able to deliver the child which is in her womb and survive. In such a case where the doctor anticipates, basing his opinion upon the experience of the profession, that the child cannot be delivered without the death of the mother, it is obvious that the sooner the operation is performed the better. The law does not require the doctor to wait until the unfortunate woman is in peril of immediate death. In such a case he is not only entitled, but it is his duty to perform the operation with a view to saving her life.

Mr Bourne was acquitted by the jury. Nevertheless, although an important decision, the law continued to remain in a state of some uncertainty. Margaret Brazier has described how pressure gradually built up in favour of legislative reform, culminating in the passing of a new Act, the Abortion Act of 1967:

Brazier, M, *Medicine, Patients and the Law*, 2nd edn, 1992, Harmondsworth: Penguin, p 290:

The law embodied in the 1861 Act was applied rigorously up to 1967. In one case in 1927, a girl of 13 was prosecuted for attempting to induce an abortion on herself by taking laxative tablets and sitting in a hot bath. The rigour of the law was tempered by a defence to a charge of criminal abortion by a doctor, that he acted to preserve the life or health of the mother. At no time in England was abortion absolutely prohibited so as to require the mother to be sacrificed for her unborn child ... But the extent of the defence available to doctors was unclear. Some doctors interpreted this defence liberally as including the mother's mental health and even happiness. Others would intervene only to prevent a life-threatening complication of pregnancy endangering the woman. Illegal abortion flourished. And several thousand women were admitted to hospital for treatment after backstreet abortions. The Abortion Act 1967 was introduced to bring uniformity into the law, to clarify the law for the doctors, and to stem the misery and injury resulting from unhygienic, risky illegal abortions.

The effect of the Abortion Act 1967 as originally enacted

It is important to state at the outset that the Abortion Act 1967 has not replaced the pre-existing criminal law statutes on abortion. Rather, its effect is to provide a medical practitioner who carries out an abortion within its terms with a statutory immunity. As originally passed in 1967, the relevant terms were set out in s 1 of the Act as follows:

1 Medical termination of pregnancy

(1) Subject to the provisions of this section, a person shall not be guilty of an offence under the law relating to abortion when a pregnancy is terminated by a registered medical practitioner if two registered medical practitioners are of the opinion, formed in good faith–

    (a) that the continuance of the pregnancy would involve risk to the life of the pregnant woman, or of injury to the physical or mental health of the pregnant woman or any existing children of her family, greater than if the pregnancy were terminated; or

    (b) that there is a substantial risk that if the child were born it would suffer from such physical or mental abnormalities as to be seriously handicapped.

(2) In determining whether the continuance of a pregnancy would involve such risk of injury to health as is mentioned in para (a) of sub-s (1) of this section, account may be taken of the pregnant woman's actual or reasonably foreseeable environment.

(3) Except as provided by sub-s (4) of this section, any treatment for the termination of pregnancy must be carried out in a hospital vested in the Secretary of State for the purposes of his functions under the National Health Service Act 1977 or the National Health Service (Scotland) Act 1978 or in a place approved for the purposes of this section by the Secretary of State.

(4) Sub-section (3) of this section, and so much of sub-s (1) as relates to the opinion of two registered medical practitioners, shall not apply to the termination of a pregnancy by a registered medical practitioner in a case where he is of the opinion, formed in good faith, that the termination is immediately necessary to

save the life or to prevent grave permanent injury to the physical or mental health of the pregnant woman.

Importantly, the 1967 Act gave immunity only in relation to the offence of procuring a miscarriage under ss 58 and 59 of the OAPA 1861. So far as the offence of child destruction was concerned, s 5(1) of the Act expressly provided that:

5 Supplementary provisions

(1) Nothing in this Act shall affect the provisions of the Infant Life (Preservation) Act 1929 (protecting the life of the viable foetus).

This meant that the 1929 Act continued to impose an upper time limit beyond which terminations (apart from those necessary to preserve the pregnant woman's life) could not lawfully take place. Unfortunately, the precise position of this upper time limit remained uncertain. This is because, although the 1929 Act mentions a gestational age of 28 weeks as amounting to *'prima facie* proof' that a foetus is capable of being born alive, this is merely a presumption. Thus, in principle, evidence could be led that a particular foetus, even after 28 weeks, was not yet capable of being born alive, or conversely (and more likely, given advances in neonatal care since 1929) that one of under 28 weeks was so capable. In this regard, the Court of Appeal was required to define the concept 'capable of being born alive' in the case of *C v S* [1988] 1 All ER 1230.

C v S [1988] 1 All ER 1230, CA (Sir John Donaldson MR, Stephen Brown and Russell LJJ)

Mr C, whose ex-girlfriend was pregnant with a 18–21 week old foetus, sought an injunction to restrain her from having an abortion on the ground, *inter alia*, that the foetus at this age was capable of being born alive and hence fell within the protection of the ILPA 1929:

> **Sir John Donaldson MR:** We have received affidavit evidence from three doctors, none of whom has examined the first defendant. Their evidence is thus necessarily directed at the stage in the development of a foetus which can normally be expected to have been reached by the 18th to 21st week. On this, as one would expect, they are in substantial agreement. At that stage the cardiac muscle is contracting and a primitive circulation is developing. Thus the foetus could be said to demonstrate real and discernible signs of life. On the other hand, the foetus, even if then delivered by hysterotomy, would be incapable ever of breathing either naturally or with the aid of a ventilator. It is not a case of the foetus requiring a stimulus or assistance. It cannot and will never be able to breathe. Where the doctors disagree is as to whether a foetus, at this stage of development, can properly be described as 'a child capable of being born alive' within the meaning of the Act of 1929. That essentially depends upon the interpretation of the statute and is a matter for the courts.

> We have no evidence of the state of the foetus being carried by the first defendant, but if it has reached the normal stage of development and so is incapable ever of breathing, it is not in our judgment 'a child capable of being born alive' within the meaning of the Act and accordingly the termination of this pregnancy would not constitute an offence under the Infant Life (Preservation) Act 1929.

The notion that an ability to draw breath is central to the capacity to be born alive was subsequently followed by the High Court in the case of *Rance v Mid-Downs HA* [1991] 1 QB 587. However, in holding that a 26 week old foetus was protected under the ILPA 1929 (the case's facts arose in 1983), Brooke J rejected the plaintiff's contention that 'viability', in the sense of enjoying longer term survival prospects, was also a necessary part of the concept.

The Abortion Act 1967 as amended

Since 1990, concerns as to the precise scope of the protection that the ILPA 1929 affords to the older foetus have assumed much less importance. This is because, although the Act remains on the statute book, its effect upon abortions carried out within the terms of the 1967 Abortion Act has been removed. The major reason for this step seems to have been a desire to clarify the law. As the House of Lords Select Committee on the Infant Life (Preservation) Bill reported in 1988:

> **House of Lords Select Committee,** *Report of the Select Committee on the Infant Life (Preservation) Bill*, **HL Paper No 50, 1987–88, London: HMSO:**
>
> 58 The Committee also recommend that the 1967 Act should be totally disengaged from the 1929 Act and that the s 5 proviso should be removed from the 1967 Act, with the consequence that the existing 28-week gestational limit for lawful abortions derived from the 1929 Act will cease to apply; and that the 1967 Act should specifically enact that a medical practitioner, acting in good faith and in full compliance with the other provisions of the 1967 Act, should not be liable to prosecution under the 1929 Act ... One of the unfortunate effects of the s 5 proviso, as has already been mentioned, is that many practitioners, and possibly most practitioners, wishing to avoid the possibility of a prosecution under the 1929 Act, approach the request for an abortion on the basis that the woman is two weeks later in her pregnancy than she is estimated to be. The Committee consider that this example of defensive medicine, though understandable as the law now stands, is highly undesirable. Medical practitioners who act in good faith should not stand in fear of the criminal law.

Ultimately, the changes were achieved by inserting amendments into the 1967 Act during the course of enacting the Human Fertilisation and Embryology Act (HFEA) 1990. In particular, s 5(1) of the Abortion Act 1967 (as amended by s 37 of the HFEA 1990) now reads as follows:

5 Supplementary provisions

(1) No offence under the Infant Life (Preservation) Act 1929 shall be committed by a registered medical practitioner who terminates a pregnancy in accordance with the provisions of this Act.

At the same time, parliament inserted a new s 1(1) into the Abortion Act 1967. This sub-section now spells out the grounds on which a lawful termination may be carried out as follows:

1 Medical termination of pregnancy

(1) Subject to the provisions of this section, a person shall not be guilty of an offence under the law relating to abortion when a pregnancy is terminated by a registered medical practitioner if two registered medical practitioners are of the opinion, formed in good faith–

   (a) that the pregnancy has not exceeded its 24th week and that the continuance of the pregnancy would involve risk, greater than if the pregnancy were terminated, of injury to the physical or mental health of the pregnant woman or any existing children of her family; or

(b) that the termination is necessary to prevent grave permanent injury to the physical or mental health of the pregnant woman; or

(c) that the continuance of the pregnancy would involve risk to the life of the pregnant woman, greater than if the pregnancy were terminated; or

(d) that there is a substantial risk that if the child were born it would suffer from such physical or mental abnormalities as to be seriously handicapped.

In terms purely of content, the changes to the s 1(1) grounds are largely cosmetic. Their true impact (which undoubtedly amounts to a liberalising of the law) consists in the new time limits – or absence thereof – within which abortion may now take place. We shall consider each of the four grounds for termination provided for in the amended s 1(1) in turn:

(a) ... risk ... of injury to the physical or mental health of the pregnant woman or any existing children of her family

This ground is used to justify the great majority of abortions carried out in Britain. It is widest in scope and the suggestion that it permits abortions on 'social' as well as strictly 'medical' grounds is given weight by the terms of s 1(2) of the Act, which provides:

(2) In determining whether the continuance of a pregnancy would involve such risk of injury to health as is mentioned in para (a) or (b) of sub-s (1) of this section, account may be taken of the pregnant woman's actual or reasonably foreseeable environment.

It is apparent that the risk in question need not be a substantial one; it is enough that it exceeds the risk to the woman of carrying out the termination. This has led to an argument that since, statistically, an abortion carried out in the first 12 weeks of pregnancy poses fewer health risks to the woman than carrying the foetus to term, the Act will invariably permit such early terminations. Jonathan Montgomery has commented upon the operation of ground (a) as follows:

Montgomery, J, _Health Care Law_, 1997, Oxford: OUP, p 365:

The first ground for termination is only available up to the 25th week. It applies where the two doctors have formed the opinion, in good faith, that the pregnancy has not exceeded its 24th week and that the continuance of the pregnancy would involve risk, greater than if the pregnancy were terminated, of injury to the physical or mental health of the pregnant woman or any existing children of her family.

While this ground clearly refers to health matters, it has been described as a 'social' ground, because doctors may take account of the woman's actual or foreseeable environment when they assess the risks involved. This means that the inconvenience of having a child may provide a basis for an abortion. It has been argued that this makes it lawful to terminate a pregnancy on the basis of the sex of the foetus where the social and cultural pressures upon a woman to produce a child of a particular sex are strong.

The majority of induced abortions are performed under s 1(1)(a). In 1993 there were 157,846 abortions to women resident in England and Wales. Approximately 1.2% of these were performed on the basis of foetal abnormality. Just over 96% were recorded as justified on the 'social grounds'. This overwhelming pattern of 'social' abortions has led to the 1967 Act being criticised for allowing abortion on demand. This assertion is based on the practice of some doctors who argue that there is statistical evidence that carrying a foetus to term is more dangerous to the woman than terminating the pregnancy in its early stages. This enables them to hold that s 1(1)(a) is made out whenever a woman is pregnant. This argument has never been tested in the courts, but it appears that doctors have given 'pregnancy' as the sole reason for believing that termination is less risky than continuing without being prosecuted.

However, it is apparent that the fact that proceeding to term poses some risk to the woman is not, in itself, a sufficient reason for termination. Rather, the doctor must perform a balancing operation in respect of the patient and determine that termination itself carries a *lower* risk: it is after all possible that, in a particular case, the risks of termination may in fact be greater than those attached to continuance, for example, where the woman may subsequently suffer some form of psychological reaction. This need to identify the risks running both ways suggests that the doctor's role requires him to engage in more than mere statistical 'rubber stamping'.

Importantly, unlike the other grounds under s 1(1), ground (a) contains a time limit: it may only be invoked in so far as the pregnancy has not exceeded its 24th week. This limit was introduced in the 1990 amendments to compensate for the fact that, as already noted, the same amendments removed the effect of the ILPA 1929, which had previously supplied a rough upper time limit to lawful abortions. The uncertainty over when, exactly, this limit used to apply has been commented on above: see *C v S* [1988] 1 All ER 1230 and *Rance v Mid-Downs HA* [1991] 1 QB 587, p 417, above. Nevertheless, the introduction of a specific time period has brought with it its own difficulties. As Andrew Grubb has noted:

Grubb, A, 'The new law of abortion: clarification or ambiguity' [1991] Crim LR 659:

Section 1(1)(a) does not specify the point in time which starts the clock running in calculating the 24 weeks. There are four possibilities: (A) the first day of the woman's last period; (B) the date of conception (up to 14 days later); (C) the date of implantation (up to 10 days later); and (D) the first day of the woman's first missed period (about four weeks after (A)).

In England the medical profession calculates the length of gestation of a baby on the basis of (A) because it is the most certain date of any of these alternatives. Options (B) and (C), namely the date of conception and the date the fertilised egg implants into the woman, by contrast, cannot be known for certain. But there are difficulties with option (D), because although the first day of the woman's first missed period is certain, it may be quite misleading to indicate length of pregnancy where, for example, following conception during the last week of a cycle the woman does not miss the next period but only the one that follows. The date calculated on the basis of (D) could be about five weeks after conception has actually occurred.

Consequently, when does time start to run? The law might accept the medical profession's approach because of the certainty it would achieve. More importantly, however, it might be accepted because it is the basis upon which parliament introduced the 24 week time limit in s 1(1)(a). The 24 week limit (as calculated by the medical profession) represents parliament's view of the stage of development when a foetus is capable of surviving. At this point the legislative intent is that the foetus should not be aborted except under the more restrictive grounds set out in the remainder of s 1(1). If any of the other options for starting time to run were accepted, this premise would be nullified. On that basis, in order to conform to the underlying premise that a foetus which is capable of surviving should not be aborted on the ground in s 1(1)(a), the time limit should actually be 22 weeks or even less.

On the other hand, there are a number of arguments which suggest that options (B) or (C) are more appropriate interpretations of s 1(1)(a). First, it is wrong to adopt an interpretation which leads to the absurd conclusion that a woman is pregnant in the 14 days (approximately) between the first day of her last period and the time of conception when this is patently not the case. Secondly, the medical profession's approach exemplified in option (A) could act to the detriment of a defendant, since it results in the shortest possible time for the 24 week period to run. A pregnancy calculated on the basis of (A) at 25 weeks is likely, in fact, to be a case where conception and implantation will have occurred less than 24 weeks before the abortion. Ambiguities in criminal statutes should be construed in a defendant's favour and not against him, particularly when interpreting a section providing a defence to a criminal offence ...

(b) ... termination necessary to prevent grave permanent injury to the physical or mental health of the pregnant woman

This ground contains no time limit and, by virtue of s 1(4), may be invoked in an emergency by a single doctor without waiting for a second certificate. Arguably, it simply codifies the common law defence available to the doctor who performs a therapeutic abortion designed to avoid serious harm to the woman, as established in *R v Bourne*. There is, however, one oddity. In speaking of the termination being 'necessary', the ground appears to require foresight by the doctor of such harm as a practical certainty, yet s 1(2) (which applies to this ground as well as (a) above) implies that a mere 'risk' of such injury will be sufficient. Whilst, doubtless, at some point a high enough risk may be treated, analytically, as forming a practical certainty, the term usually denotes something rather less than this.

(c) ... risk to the life of the pregnant woman, greater than if the pregnancy were terminated

Like ground (b) above, this ground may be used in an emergency by a single doctor. Although ground (c) specifically refers to risk to 'life', in practice a large measure of overlap may be expected between the two grounds. This is because, as was apparent in *R v Bourne*, it may be difficult to say, as a matter of evidence, where grave injury to health ceases and risk to life begins. Moreover, given that – as in the case of ground (a) – the doctor is required to conduct a simple balancing of risks to determine whether a termination is justified, ground (c) may actually be easier to employ: the risk to the woman's life in continuing to term need not be substantial provided that it exceeds the risk involved in abortion. Ironically, the risks at issue are likely to be more readily quantifiable than the somewhat diffuse harms contemplated under ground (a), so it may be here that a 'statistical argument' would have the greatest purchase. For example, suppose that a doctor assesses the risk to the life of the woman in giving birth at one in 8,000. Provided the risk attached to termination is even lower, say, one in 10,000, an abortion would apparently be justified here. Since, in contrast with ground (a), no time limit is placed on terminations under this ground, it appears that an abortion in the circumstances just described could, in theory, take place until birth.

(d) ... substantial risk that if the child were born it would suffer from such physical or mental abnormalities as to be seriously handicapped

In common with the first three grounds, there are significant difficulties in interpreting the precise application and scope of this ground. On the face of it, however, it differs from the others in being directed to the welfare of the foetus rather than that of the pregnant woman. Derek Morgan has argued for a strict interpretation of the ground, allowing its use only in cases of 'foetal euthanasia', that is to say where termination is in the foetus' best interests:

Morgan, D, 'Abortion: the unexamined ground' [1990] Crim LR 687:

Section 1(1)[(d)] requires that the physician decide that there is a 'substantial' risk that the physical or mental abnormalities are such that the child if born would be 'seriously' handicapped ...

One immediate analogy which could be drawn is that of the severely handicapped neonate who if its condition had been known, might have been aborted under s 1(1)[(d)]. In two recent cases, the Court of Appeal has had to consider in what, if any, circumstances a severely handicapped infant might be allowed to die. In *In Re C* the court was concerned with a baby born with an unusually severe form of hydrocephalus and with a poorly formed brain structure. She was physically handicapped, including generalised spastic cerebral palsy of all limbs, probable blindness and deafness and an inability to absorb food. In the first judgment of its kind, the High Court acknowledged and condoned the paediatric practice of managing some neonates towards their death rather than striving with heroic interventions to save or treat at all costs ...

Re C amplified the earlier judgment of the Court of Appeal in *Re B*. There, the court had established, first, that these cases could only proceed under a 'best interests' test (in that case of the ward). And secondly, the court held that only in a case where the prognosis established that the child's life was going to be 'demonstrably ... so awful', and where there was no lingering doubt about that future, could a non-treatment order be contemplated. Lords Justices Templeman and Dunn observed that this would include cases of severe proved damage such that the court would be driven to conclude that non-treatment was appropriate. This would not be the case, however, where the prognosis or information about the damage was 'still so imponderable' that it would be wrong for the baby to be allowed to die.

The attempt to invoke an analogy between the severely disabled foetus (even at term) and the similarly afflicted neonate is weakened, however, by the fact that, in another crucial respect, the law clearly regards the two situations as very different. In particular, whereas the foetus remains vulnerable to active measures to destroy it, the most that is permitted in relation to the neonate is the passive withholding of measures that would otherwise prolong its life (see, further, Chapter 12). The view that this ground, like the others, in fact goes principally to the mother's interests, is supported by the history behind the 1990 amendments, which removed the time limits restricting the abortion of handicapped foetuses 'capable of being born alive'. The 1988 Select Committee of the House of Lords had the following to say on the issue:

House of Lords Select Committee, *Report of the Select Committee on the Infant Life (Preservation) Bill*, HL Paper No 50, 1987–88, London: HMSO:

41 Although abortions on ground 4, that is to say, a substantial risk that the child if born would suffer from such abnormalities as to be seriously handicapped, are

only a small proportion of the total abortions, they comprise most of the abortions performed after 24 weeks ... It is these late abortions which would be made more difficult to obtain if an upper limit of 24 weeks were to be imposed, and they represent in the opinion of the Committee a highly important factor. Whether an abortion is desired or justified in such a case will depend to a large extent on the degree of abnormality which is diagnosed and the circumstances and attitude of the parents. Although a severely handicapped child is often the cause of crisis and disaster, there are other cases where even severe handicap has been the means of inspiring love and care within the family, and even the strengthening of character and family ties. At its worst, a child severely affected by spina bifida may be not only mentally retarded, but also severely paralysed so as to be unable to walk, doubly incontinent, deaf and blind. It is obvious that the birth of such a child will constitute an immediate crisis for parents and doctors. Although some women elect nevertheless to have severely handicapped children, the Committee have received evidence that the cumulative effect on families of years of caring for a totally dependent child can be devastating, and when the parents die the child must all too often be institutionalised, with traumatic effects. Ante-natal care is rightly directed to the detection of mothers who are subject to these risks, and counselling must always be available, though the choice will be the mother's.

As we have seen, s 1(1)(d) speaks of the foetus suffering from 'such mental or physical abnormalities as to be seriously handicapped'. This undoubted vagueness is compounded by the fact that the section requires only 'a substantial risk' of such abnormalities. Gillian Douglas has commented on the application of the latter concept as follows:

Douglas, G, _Law, Fertility and Reproduction_, 1991, London: Sweet & Maxwell, p 94:

A further problem is in deciding what amounts to a 'substantial' risk. The Royal College of Physicians describe a risk of more than 10% of producing a seriously abnormal child as a 'high' risk. Presumably, where the abnormality is less severe, a greater degree of probability would be classed as high. A one in 10 chance of a foetus carrying spina bifida may indeed be regarded as a substantial risk, but a further complication is that it is not generally possible to determine from pre-natal screening the degree of handicap an affected foetus may suffer. Parents may therefore be faced with the possibility of aborting a normal, or mildly affected foetus.

It would be preferable if the ground were ... clearly expressed to be based on the consequences for the _parents_, or subsumed under s 1(1)(a) and s 1(2). This would be a more justifiable rationale for aborting a potentially handicapped foetus, and it would also avoid overt reliance on eugenic factors. In any case, it would only need to be resorted to in a small number of cases, if current practice is indicative. At present, the detection of abnormalities is rarely relied upon as the sole ground for termination. This may be due to the delay inherent in current screening procedures making abortion less safe, and also more complicated and distressing when eventually carried out. If a doctor suspects abnormality, perhaps from the woman's prior history of child-bearing, or exposure to rubella, it may be preferable to perform the abortion earlier than to wait for confirmation which might still prove in error. Reliance may then be placed on another ground, such as injury to the woman's mental health.

Douglas suggests here that the severity of abnormality is relevant in deciding when a risk is 'substantial'. Arguably, however, Kennedy and Grubb's view, that the latter term goes primarily to the _probability_ of the risk materialising (and should be kept separate from the question of what the _magnitude_ of harm will be in so far as it does materialise), is preferable.

In December 2003, an abortion carried out under section 1(1)(d) upon a more than 24-week term foetus with a cleft palate was the subject of legal challenge in *Jepson v Chief Constable of West Mercia Police* [2003] EWHC 3318. In her action the claimant, a Church of England curate, sought judicial review of the police's decision not to prosecute the doctors involved, as well as a declaration that a cleft palate was not capable of constituting a serious handicap within the section. The High Court gave leave to proceed, but so far the case does not appear to have been heard further.

IMPLICATIONS OF THE LAW

The interested parties

Given the legal framework sketched above, what rights are enjoyed by the key actors in the abortion process? We begin by considering the position of the foetus itself.

The foetus

Self-evidently, the existence of the regime under the 1967 Abortion Act, permitting legal abortion in a large number of circumstances, means that the foetus has no legal right to life. In this regard, Jane Fortin has written as follows:

Fortin, J, 'Legal protection for the unborn child' (1988) 51 MLR 54:

... the abortion legislation has contrived a situation whereby a decision to terminate the life of the foetus can be reached by two doctors in consultation only with the mother. There is thus no possibility of anyone intervening on behalf of the foetus, to ensure that adequate consideration has been given to its particular stage of physical and mental development, in order to assess the precise degree of its increasing 'humanness' and whether it warrants protection against its mother's desire for an abortion.

In this context, there is a stark contrast between the legal protection accorded to the unborn and to the newly born. In relation to the latter, however premature, the wardship jurisdiction can be used to cast an immediate cloak of protection over the child, thereby ensuring that fundamentally important decisions relating to the child's future can be considered dispassionately by the High Court. Thus, in the case of *Re B*, the Court of Appeal authorised a life-giving operation on a Down's syndrome child, against the wishes of its parents who had rejected it. By contrast, it is clear from the decisions in *Paton* and *C v S* that although an abortion has a fatal effect on the unborn child, intervention by a third party would be impossible even if in his view the abortion decision has been reached erroneously ...

Despite the heavy responsibility for interpreting the 1967 Act imposed on the medical profession, it is surprising that the Act contains no guidance to them as to the factors to consider when deciding whether to approve an abortion. The omission of any direction specifically requiring the doctors to consider the interests of the foetus itself, when deciding whether to approve the abortion, implies that the abortion is a purely medical matter relating only to the mother herself and devoid of any moral implications relating to the foetus.

As Fortin notes elsewhere, the perceived need to safeguard the interests of the pregnant woman has led the courts to deny that the foetus, *in utero*, enjoys any legal personality. This important point lay behind the decision of the High Court in the case of *Paton v Trustees of British Pregnancy Advisory Services* [1979] QB 276.

Paton v Trustees of British Pregnancy Advisory Services [1979] QB 276, HC (Sir George Baker P)

The plaintiff sought an injunction restraining his wife from having an abortion under the Abortion Act 1967. Although she had obtained the required certificates from two doctors that she satisfied one of the statutory grounds, the plaintiff alleged that she was in fact acting in *male fides*. As a starting point, the plaintiff needed to establish *locus standi* to bring his action, either in his own right or as 'next friend' of the foetus:

> **Sir George Baker P**: The first question is whether this plaintiff has a right at all. The foetus cannot, in English law, in my view, have a right of its own at least until it is born and has a separate existence from its mother. That permeates the whole of the civil law of this country (I except the criminal law, which is now irrelevant), and is, indeed, the basis of the decisions in those countries where law is founded on the common law, that is to say, in America, Canada, Australia and, I have no doubt, in others.
>
> For a long time there was great controversy whether, after birth, a child could have a right of action in respect of pre-natal injury ... but it was universally accepted, and has since been accepted, that in order to have a right the foetus must be born and be a child. There was only one known possible exception ... an American case, *White v Yup* 458 P 2d 617 (1969), where a wrongful 'death' of an eight month old viable foetus, stillborn as a consequence of injury, led an American court to allow a cause of action, but there can be no doubt, in my view, that in England and Wales the foetus has no right of action, no right at all, until birth. The succession cases have been mentioned. There is no difference. From conception the child may have succession rights by what has been called a 'fictional construction', but the child must be subsequently born alive: see per Lord Russell of Killowen in *Elliot v Lord Joicey* [1935] AC 209, p 233.

The approach of the High Court in *Paton* was subsequently endorsed by the Court of Appeal, outside the context of abortion, in the case of *Re F (In Utero)* [1988] Fam 122.

Re F (In Utero) [1988] Fam 122, CA (May, Balcombe and Staughton LJJ)

A woman with a history of psychiatric problems was 38 weeks pregnant when she absconded from the residential care home in which she lived. Her local authority, which was responsible for her care, sought to make her unborn child a ward of court as a preliminary to further measures to protect its health at this late stage in the pregnancy:

> **May LJ**: Even though this is a case in which, on its facts, I would exercise the [wardship] jurisdiction if I had it, in the absence of authority I am driven to the conclusion that the court does not have the jurisdiction contended for. I respectfully agree with the dictum from the judgment of Sir George Baker P in the *Paton* case ...
>
> Secondly, I respectfully agree with the judge below in this case that to accept such jurisdiction and yet to apply the principle that it is the interest of the child which is to be predominant is bound to create conflict between the existing legal interests of the mother and those of the unborn child, and that it is most undesirable that this should occur ...

Staughton LJ: I agree that this appeal should be dismissed. In their notice of appeal the local authority seek orders as follows:

(1) The tipstaff do seek and detain in a suitable place the defendant and do report her whereabouts to the plaintiffs and the court.

(2) The defendant do not leave the jurisdiction so long as she remains pregnant and further following the birth of the said child do not remove the said child from the jurisdiction.

(3) The defendant do forthwith surrender her passport or other travel document to the court.

(4) The defendant do attend forthwith such hospital suitable for the delivery of the said unborn child as the plaintiffs in their discretion direct.

It will be observed that all are orders directed at the mother, as in the nature of things they must be until the child is born.

When the wardship jurisdiction of the High Court is exercised, the rights, duties and powers of the natural parents are taken over or superseded by the orders of the court. Until a child is delivered it is not, in my judgment, possible for that to happen. The court cannot care for a child, or order that others should do so, until the child is born; only the mother can. The orders sought by the local authority are not by their nature such as the court can make in caring for the child; they are orders which seek directly to control the life of both mother and child. As was said by the European Commission of Human Rights in *Paton v United Kingdom* ... p 415, 'the 'life' of the foetus is intimately connected with, and cannot be regarded in isolation from, the life of the pregnant woman' ...

In the wake of the decision in *Paton v BPAS*, Mr Paton took his case to Strasbourg; however, he failed to persuade the European Commission on Human Rights that the foetus's right to life is protected under Article 2 of the European Convention on Human Rights (ECHR) (see *Paton v UK* (1980) 3 EHRR 408). The Commission's view was that, given the intimate connection between the foetus's life and that of the pregnant woman, any such right must in any event be limited in cases where the latter's life and health are at stake. Recently, in *Vo v France* (2004) 2 FCR 577, the European Court of Human Rights (ECtHR), after noting the lack of consensus in ECHR signatory states as to the nature and status of the foetus, held that unborn life need not be treated as within the ambit of Article 2 of the ECHR. Thus, the degree of legal protection to be accorded to the foetus (in particular by criminal law) was a matter for each individual state.

On the other hand, it should not be concluded – in relation to the UK – that a foetus enjoys no protection at all at law. It is rather that its interests are subordinated to those of full legal subjects – ie persons already born. Especially in the context of abortion, where there is a conflict between its interests and those of the pregnant woman, the law will accord priority to the latter. (The degree to which the foetus is protected in other circumstances is explored at p 443 *et seq*, below.)

An opposing, and on the face of it rather fanciful, issue concerns the degree to which the foetus has a right *to be* aborted. This question, nevertheless, has lain behind actions for so called 'wrongful life'. The leading English authority in point is *Mackay v Essex AHA* [1982] QB 1166:

Mackay v Essex AHA [1982] QB 1166, CA (Stephenson, Griffiths and Ackner LJJ)

The plaintiff's mother was infected with German measles while pregnant with the plaintiff. The latter claimed, *inter alia*, that the defendant doctor had negligently failed to advise her mother of the desirability of an abortion, and (given that her mother would have accepted such advice) she had consequently suffered damage by 'entry into a life in which her injuries are highly debilitating, and distress, loss and damage':

Stephenson LJ: There is no doubt that this child could legally have been deprived of life by the mother's undergoing an abortion with the doctor's advice and help. So the law recognises a difference between the life of a foetus and the life of those who have been born. But because a doctor can lawfully by statute do to a foetus what he cannot lawfully do to a person who has been born, it does not follow that he is under a legal obligation to a foetus to do it and terminate its life, or that the foetus has a legal right to die ...

To impose such a duty towards the child would, in my opinion, make a further inroad on the sanctity of human life which would be contrary to public policy. It would mean regarding the life of a handicapped child as not only less valuable than the life of a normal child, but so much less valuable that it was not worth preserving, and it would even mean that a doctor would be obliged to pay damages to a child infected with rubella before birth who was in fact born with some mercifully trivial abnormality. These are the consequences of the necessary basic assumption that a child has a right to be born whole or not at all, not to be born unless it can be born perfect or 'normal', whatever that may mean. Added to that objection must be the opening of the courts to claims by children born handicapped against their mothers for not having an abortion ...

Finally, there is the nature of the injury and damage which the court is being asked to ascertain and evaluate.

The only duty of care which courts of law can recognise and enforce are duties owed to those who can be compensated for loss by those who owe the duties, in most cases, including cases of personal injury, by money damages which will as far as possible put the injured party in the condition in which he or she was before being injured. The only way in which a child injured in the womb can be compensated in damages is by measuring what it has lost, which is the difference between the value of its life as a whole and healthy normal child and the value of its life as an injured child. But to make those who have not injured the child pay for that difference is to treat them as if they have injured the child, when all they have done is not having taken steps to prevent its being born injured by another cause.

The only loss for which those who have not injured the child can be held liable to compensate the child is the difference between its condition as a result of their allowing it to be born alive and injured and its condition if its embryonic life had been ended before its life in the world had begun. But how can a court of law evaluate that second condition and so measure the loss to the child? Even if a court were competent to decide between the conflicting views of theologians and philosophers and to assume an 'after life' or non-existence as the basis for the comparison, how can a judge put a value on the one or the other, compare either alternative with the injured child's life in this world and determine that the child has lost anything, without the means of knowing what, if anything, it has gained?

Griffiths LJ: To my mind, the most compelling reason to reject this cause of action is the intolerable and insoluble problem it would create in the assessment of damage. The basis of damages for personal injury is the comparison between the state of the plaintiff before he was injured and his condition after he was injured. This is often a hard enough task in all conscience and it has an element of artificiality about it, for who can say that there is any sensible correlation between pain and money? Nevertheless, the courts have been able to produce a broad tariff that appears at the moment to be acceptable to society as doing rough justice. But the whole exercise, difficult as it is, is anchored in the first place to the condition of the plaintiff before the injury which the court can comprehend and evaluate. In a claim for wrongful life how does the court begin to make an assessment? The plaintiff does not say, 'But for your negligence I would have been born uninjured'. The plaintiff says, 'But for your negligence I would never have been born'. The court then has to compare the state of the plaintiff with non-existence, of which the court can know nothing; this I regard as an impossible task.

The pregnant woman

The general view is that the 1967 Act gives the pregnant woman no right to demand an abortion. As Jonathan Montgomery notes:

Montgomery, J, *Health Care Law*, 1997, Oxford: OUP, pp 365–66:

... it does not follow from the fact that doctors are in practice usually immune from prosecution that the Abortion Act 1967 provides for abortion on demand. The Act does not provide women with rights to terminate their pregnancy. Instead, it leaves them dependent upon finding a doctor who will co-operate with their wishes. This means that women who can afford to go to private clinics will usually have little difficulty obtaining a legal abortion. Those reliant on NHS provision, however, are faced with considerable variation between the practice of different doctors. Consequently, there is considerable disparity in the degree to which abortions are readily available both between and within different areas of the country. Official statistics showed that in 1973 only 10% of those seeking an abortion in Walsall were able to get one through the NHS, while in Oxford the figure was 79%.

It is therefore doctors who control access to abortions. Women's access to abortions is dependent on the ethical position of individual doctors and is vulnerable to prejudices of an essentially white middle class profession. Norrie has pointed out that terminations sought because the child is the 'wrong' sex are as justifiable under the Act as those because the pregnancy is inconvenient for economic or career reasons. However, the former is far less likely to be accepted by the medical profession. The Abortion Act 1967 may allow doctors to offer abortion on demand in the early stages of pregnancy, but it does not secure it for women.

It is certainly true that nowhere in the Abortion Act 1967 is there to be found any express right to an abortion and, in this omission, it could be argued that it is a less liberal measure than similar laws in many other jurisdictions. In the USA, for example, the effect of the decisions of the Supreme Court in *Roe v Wade* 410 US 113 (1976) and *Planned Parenthood v Casey* 112 S Ct 2791 (1992) is that, until viability, state laws placing undue obstacles in the path of abortion will infringe the woman's constitutionally protected right to privacy. However, although English law, thus, inhibits (at least in symbolic terms) a woman's freedom to terminate her pregnancy, it could be asked whether abortion differs in this respect from any other form of medical treatment available in this country. After all, it is well established that a patient cannot insist upon a particular procedure if the doctor does not believe it to be medically indicated as in the patient's best interests: see *R v Cambridge HA ex p B* (1995) 23 BMLR 1. In similar fashion, the general remedy for the patient who can show that they were improperly denied treatment is to bring an *ex post facto* action in negligence, and in this regard, too, abortion arguably is no different. Indeed, a number of successful cases have been brought by women who have argued that they should have been given the opportunity to have an abortion on the ground of foetal handicap contained in the 1967 Act. A notable example is the case of *Mackay v Essex AHA* considered at p 426, above. Although the child lost its claim for 'wrongful life', the mother's action in 'wrongful birth' was allowed to proceed. In his speech, Griffiths LJ expressly suggested that the medical profession is under a duty to advise the pregnant woman of 'her right to have an abortion and the pros and cons of doing so'.

By contrast, in so far as a pregnant woman, who is a competent adult, chooses not to abort her foetus, it is clear that the law will not make her do so. At first glance, this assertion may seem to be a straightforward application of the principle that competent adults must always consent to medical procedures carried out upon them. However, this is to ignore the possible use of indirect legal means to pressurise women to opt for terminations in certain cases. For example, in the context of an action for wrongful birth, might a woman be denied compensation for the costs of raising a handicapped child on the basis that her failure to have a termination was 'unreasonable'? This question was at the heart of the case of *Emeh v Kensington and Chelsea AHA* [1985] QB 1012:

Emeh v Kensington and Chelsea AHA [1985] QB 1012, CA (Slade, Waller and Purchas LJJ)

The plaintiff, who already had four children, underwent a voluntary sterilisation at the defendant's hospital. The operation was negligently performed and the plaintiff subsequently became pregnant, only discovering this fact when her foetus was of 17–20 weeks' gestation. She refused the defendant's offer of an abortion and later gave birth to a handicapped child. At first instance, Park J denied her claim for the costs of raising the child, finding that her failure to have the abortion amounted to a *novus actus interveniens*, which eclipsed the defendant's earlier negligence and made her the author of her loss. The plaintiff appealed:

> **Waller LJ**: In my opinion, on the findings of the judge, even as they were, I would be disposed to say that this conduct on the part of the plaintiff was not so unreasonable as to eclipse the defendants' wrongdoing. But ... when one sees no reference was made by the judge to the difference between a 20 week pregnancy and an eight week pregnancy, it would seem that when the plaintiff decided to have the baby and, having made that decision, she then decided to sue the defendants, her conduct could not be described as utterly unreasonable. Especially when one bears in mind that she had an argument with her husband about it – he apparently wanted her to have an abortion; and the judge accepted that evidence – that makes her decision all the more understandable. I would therefore come to the conclusion that that finding of the judge, namely her failure to undergo an abortion was so unreasonable as to eclipse the defendants' wrongdoing, is incorrect, and that the plea of novus actus, or the failure to take steps to minimise the damage – in whatever way the matter is put – fails.
>
> **Slade LJ**: The judge, in saying that her failure to obtain an abortion was so unreasonable as to eclipse the defendants' wrongdoing, was, I think, really saying that the defendants had the right to expect that, if they had not performed the operation properly, she would procure an abortion, even if she did not become aware of its existence until nearly 20 weeks of her pregnancy had elapsed.
>
> I do not, for my part, think that the defendants had the right to expect any such thing. By their own negligence, they faced her with the very dilemma which she had sought to avoid by having herself sterilised.

For the reasons which I have attempted to give, I think that they could and should have reasonably foreseen that if, as a consequence of the negligent performance of the operation she should find herself pregnant again, particularly after some months of pregnancy, she might well decide to keep the child. Indeed, for my part I would go even a little further. Save in the most exceptional circumstances, I cannot think it right that the court should ever declare it unreasonable for a woman to decline to have an abortion in a case where there is no evidence that there were any medical or psychiatric grounds for terminating the particular pregnancy. And no such evidence has been drawn to our attention relating to this particular pregnancy of the plaintiff in the present case.

However, following the new, more restrictive approach to the duty of care in wrongful birth cases, signalled by the House of Lords in *McFarlane v Tayside Health Board* [2000] 2 AC 59, it is apparent that if the facts of *Emeh* were to occur today only a conventional sum, plus the extra costs associated with the child's disability, would be recoverable in any event: see Chapter 6.

The father

It is well established that, under English law, the father of a foetus cannot prevent a pregnant woman from having an abortion and, indeed, has no right even to be consulted over her proposed course of action. As we have seen, this was made clear in *Paton v Trustees of British Pregnancy Advisory Services* [1979] QB 276:

> **Sir George Baker P**: The father's case must ... depend upon a right which he has himself. I would say a word about the illegitimate, usually called the putative, but I prefer myself to refer to the illegitimate father. Although American decisions to which I have been referred concern illegitimate fathers, and statutory provisions about them, it seems to me that in this country the illegitimate father can have no rights whatsoever except those given to him by statute. That was clearly the common law. One provision which makes an inroad into this is s 14 of the Guardianship of Minors Act 1971, s 9(1) and some other sections of that Act which apply to illegitimate children, giving the illegitimate father or mother the right to apply for the custody of or access to an illegitimate child. But the equality of parental rights provision in s 1(1) of the Guardianship Act 1973 expressly does not apply in relation to a minor who is illegitimate: see s 1(7).

> ... [T]his plaintiff must, in my opinion, bring his case, if he can, squarely within the framework of the fact that he is a husband. It is, of course, very common for spouses to seek injunctions for personal protection in the matrimonial courts during the pendency of or, indeed, after divorce actions, but the basic reason for the non-molestation injunction often granted in the family courts is to protect the other spouse or the living children, and to ensure that no undue pressure is put upon one or other of the spouses during the pendency of the case and during the breaking up of the marriage ...

> The law is that the court cannot and would not seek to enforce or restrain by injunction matrimonial obligations, if they be obligations, such as sexual intercourse or contraception (a non-molestation injunction given during the pendency of divorce proceedings could, of course, cover attempted intercourse). No court would ever grant an injunction to stop sterilisation or vasectomy. Personal family relationships in marriage cannot be enforced by the order of a court. An injunction in such circumstances was described by Judge Mager in *Jones v Smith* (1973) 278 So 2d 339 in the District Court of Appeal of Florida as 'ludicrous'.

I ask the question, 'If an injunction were ordered, what could be the remedy?' and I do not think I need say any more than that no judge could even consider sending a husband or wife to prison for breaking such an order. That, of itself, seems to me to cover the application here; this husband cannot by law stop his wife by injunction from having what is now accepted to be a lawful abortion within the terms of the Abortion Act 1967.

In his action before the European Commission of Human Rights (see p 426, above), Mr Paton argued that his right to 'respect for family life' under Article 8 of the ECHR had been infringed. In dismissing this claim, however, the Commission noted that Article 8(2) specifically limits that right in so far as necessary to protect the rights of another person (here the pregnant woman). The view taken in *Paton* as to the father's status was endorsed by the Court of Appeal in *C v S* [1988] QB 135, and recently led a Scottish court to reject a husband's application for an injunction to restrain his wife from having an abortion: see *Kelly v Kelly* 1997 SLT 896.

The doctor/health care worker

As will have been apparent in the discussion of s 1(1) of the Abortion Act 1967 above, the Act gives doctors a very wide discretion in determining whether the one of the grounds for lawful termination has been met. Writing in *The Lancet* in 1971, IM Ingram suggested that the wording of the Act is indeed so wide as to be meaningless, and, though the 1990 amendments to the Act have moved the key provisions around, it is apparent that they have not introduced any greater precision. What safeguards are there, then, to prevent an unscrupulous doctor from abusing his discretion? John Keown has discussed this issue as follows:

Keown, J, *Abortion, Doctors and the Law*, 1988, Cambridge: CUP, pp 130–32:

During the parliamentary debates on his Bill, Mr Steel [the Act's sponsor] said that it was necessary for such a measure as his to contain 'safeguards' against abuse, and he pointed to three 'essential and new' safeguards in his Bill: the requirements of certification of opinions, notification of abortions, and approval of premises where the operations were to be performed. To what extent have these safeguards, which he said would prevent abuse of the Act, operated as a check on excessively permissive interpretation of s 1?

The Abortion Regulations 1968–80

The Abortion Regulations 1968 came into effect on the same day as the Abortion Act in discharge of the statutory duty placed on the minister by s 2(1) of the Act. Section 3 of the Regulations deals with the certification of the practitioner's opinions. Section 3(2) requires the two opinions to be certified on 'Certificate A' before treatment is begun.

This Regulation undoubtedly represents a restriction on the practitioner's freedom in that it introduces a formality which he must observe, on pain of a fine. However, certification hardly restricts the exercise of medical discretion, for although it ensures a second opinion it requires neither the second practitioner to be of a particular status nor limits the number of practitioners who may be approached for a second opinion. It does not even require the second practitioner to see the patient. Indeed, it was concern at the failure of some doctors to do just this that led to the amendment of the Regulations, at the recommendation of Lane, to require the certifying practitioners to state whether they had seen or examined the patient. However, the Regulations as amended do not require either of the practitioners to see the patient and it is difficult to see how they might do so without being *ultra vires*.

As a safeguard against abuse of medical discretion, therefore, certification is only of limited effectiveness. Its main virtue is in ensuring a second opinion, but this had been standard practice well before the enactment of the Regulations, among both reputable and disreputable practitioners. Although the ostensible function of certification is the protection of the patient, it also serves the interests of the practitioner by helping to protect him from suspicion of impropriety.

If certification is only a limited safeguard against abuse of the Act, what of notification? This safeguard was built into the Act in the form of s 2(1)(b), and its requirements are specified in s 4 of the Regulations. Section 4(1) requires the operating practitioner to notify the abortion to the CMO [Chief Medical Officer] within seven days, including in the notification form such information as is specified in Sched 2 to the Regulations.

Unlike certification, notification did represent a significant innovation in this area of medical practice, for whereas it had long been usual to obtain a second opinion, practitioners had not previously reported the operation to a third party. Moreover, failure to notify might, like failure to certify, involve the practitioner in liability under s 2(3) of the Act, and also in suspicion of illegal abortion.

However, the effectiveness of notification as a safeguard is also limited, for, just as a practitioner could certify an illegal abortion as falling within the terms of the Act, so too could he notify such an operation as having been performed within the Act, and it would be extremely difficult to prove the absence of good faith. Moreover, if a practitioner fails to notify, his offence will be difficult to detect for, *ex hypothesi*, the CMO will not have been informed that an abortion has been performed.

The procedure for certification under the Act as amended is now dealt with in the Abortion Regulations 1991, made under s 2 of the Act. The Regulations provide, in reg 3, as follows:

Certificate of opinion

3 (1) Any opinion to which s 1 of the Act refers shall be certified–

    (a) in the case of a pregnancy terminated in accordance with s 1(1) of the Act, in the form set out in Part I of Sched 1 to these Regulations; and

    (b) in the case of a pregnancy terminated in accordance with s 1(4) of the Act, in the form set out in Part II of that Schedule.

(2) Any certificate of an opinion referred to in s 1(1) of the Act shall be given before the commencement of the treatment for the termination of the pregnancy to which it relates.

(3) Any certificate of an opinion referred to in s 1(4) of the Act shall be given before the commencement of the treatment for the termination of the pregnancy to which it relates or, if that is not reasonably practicable, not later than 24 hours after such termination.

(4) Any such certificate as is referred to in paras (2) and (3) of this Regulation shall be preserved by the practitioner who terminated the pregnancy to which it relates for a period of not less than three years beginning with the date of the termination.

(5) A certificate which is no longer to be preserved shall be destroyed by the person in whose custody it then is.

A rare case in which a doctor's performance of an abortion was impugned, on the basis that he had not formed the view in good faith that the termination came within one of the grounds under the 1967 Act, was that of *R v Smith (John)* [1974] 1 All ER 376:

R v Smith (John) [1974] 1 All ER 376, CA (Scarman LJ, Mackenna and Mocatta JJ)

Dr Smith performed an abortion on a young woman without, apparently, either satisfying himself that continuance of her pregnancy would involve a risk greater than termination to her mental or physical health, or obtaining the requisite second opinion. The matter came to light because, following the operation, the patient became ill, and it was she who subsequently acted as the main prosecution witness. After his conviction by a jury of procuring a miscarriage contrary to s 58 of the OAPA 1861, Dr Smith appealed:

> **Scarman LJ**: The [1967] Act, though it renders lawful abortions that before its enactment would not have been lawful, does not depart from the basic principle of the common law as declared in *R v Bourne*, namely that the legality of an abortion depends on the opinion of a doctor. It has introduced the safeguard of two opinions: but, if they are formed in good faith by the time the operation is undertaken, the abortion is lawful. Thus, a great social responsibility is firmly placed by the law on the shoulders of the medical profession ...
>
> On 28 April 1970 at the Hayward Nursing Home a Miss Rodgers underwent an operation performed by the appellant, the initial purpose of which was to terminate her pregnancy. The prosecution's case is that he was not acting in good faith; he had not formed a *bona fide* opinion as to the balance of risk between termination and continuation of her pregnancy, that is to say, that the continuance would involve risk to her physical or mental health greater than if it were terminated. The appellant's defence was twofold: he said that he formed an honest opinion as to the need for an abortion, but that when he had the girl on the operating table, he found she was starting an inevitable abortion. Thus according to him, his operation became not a termination, but a facilitating and tidying up of an inevitable abortion – a natural process which had already begun. If this be the truth, the prosecution concedes that the operation would be lawful without the need of recourse to the Abortion Act 1967.
>
> In arguing the appeal, counsel for the appellant directed the greater part of his argument not to the issue of inevitable abortion but to that of his client's good faith in deciding to terminate Miss Rodgers' pregnancy. But the course of the trial was somewhat different. The presence of an inevitable abortion already beginning when he operated was at the forefront of the doctor's defence. Professor Fairweather, the specialist called for the Crown, directed most of his evidence to this issue. No doubt both the Crown and the defence appreciated – correctly, we think – that, if the appellant was disbelieved when he said he found an inevitable abortion, his credit would be so undermined that he was unlikely to be believed when he asserted that his decision to terminate was taken only after he had formed an opinion in good faith as to the balance of risk. Nevertheless the two lines of defence merited, as indeed at trial they received, separate attention ...
>
> The case against the appellant relied on the evidence of Miss Rodgers and of police officers who interviewed the appellant in November and December 1970 and March 1971. Professor Fairweather, a distinguished gynaecologist, gave evidence on the question as to the likelihood of an inevitable abortion when there had been no history of pain or bleeding; he thought it unusual but possible. In reply to the recorder he emphasised the need for careful inquiry when the reason for abortion was injury to

mental health and agreed that the 1967 Act could be abused. Both defendants and Dr Davis gave evidence. The trial was a long one and culminated in a lengthy summing up.

Was the verdict unsafe? Counsel for the appellant took a great number of detailed points in his attack on the trial and the summing up. But, as he put it, his central submission was that a finding of bad faith against a doctor, when it relates to the forming of a medical opinion, cannot be safe or satisfactory unless supported by medical evidence pointing overwhelmingly to the lack of good faith ...

The question of good faith is essentially one for the jury to determine on the totality of the evidence. A medical view put forward in evidence by one or more doctors as to the good faith of another doctor's opinion is no substitute for the verdict of the jury. An opinion may be absurd professionally and yet formed in good faith; conversely an opinion may be one which a doctor could have entertained and yet in the particular circumstances of a case may be found either to have been formed in bad faith or not to have been formed at all. Although the 1967 Act has imposed a great responsibility on doctors, it has not ousted the function of the jury. If a case is brought to trial which calls in question the *bona fides* of a doctor, the jury, not the medical profession, must decide the issue. The risk of abuse, by some, of the protection afforded by the Act was recognised as a genuine risk by Professor Fairweather. In the instant case it was for the jury to determine whether the appellant had or had not abused the protection afforded him by the Act. By leaving the ultimate question to a jury, the law retains its ability to protect society from an abuse of the Act.

This case, which is undoubtedly an unusual one, appears, on the face of it, to be at odds with subsequent judicial reluctance (evident in Sir George Baker P's comments in *Paton v British Pregnancy Advisory Services* [1979] QB 276) to scrutinise the doctor's *bona fides* in applying the terms of the Abortion Act 1967:

Sir George Baker P: The case which was first put forward to me a week ago, and indeed is to be found in the writ, is that the wife had no proper legal grounds for seeking a termination of her pregnancy and that, indeed, not to mince words, she was being spiteful, vindictive and utterly unreasonable in seeking so to do. It now appears I need not go into the evidence in the affidavits because it is accepted and common ground that the provisions of the Act have been complied with, the necessary certificate has been given by two doctors and everything is lawfully set for the abortion ...

The case put to me finally by Mr Rankin ... is that while he cannot say here that there is any suggestion of a criminal abortion, nevertheless if doctors did not hold their views, or come to their conclusions in good faith, which would be an issue triable by a jury (see *R v Smith (John)* [1973] 1 WLR 1510), then this plaintiff might recover an injunction. That is not accepted by Mr Denny. It is unnecessary for me to decide that academic question because it does not arise in this case. My own view is that it would be quite impossible for the courts in any event to supervise the operation of the Abortion Act 1967. The great social responsibility is firmly placed by the law upon the shoulders of the medical profession: see per Scarman LJ in *R v Smith (John)* [1973] 1 WLR 1510, p 1512.

... The two doctors have given a certificate. It is not and cannot be suggested that the certificate was given in other than good faith and it seems to me that there is the end of the matter in English law.

More recently, a doctor who continued with a hysterectomy upon a patient whose pregnancy only came to light during the operation, was similarly charged with an offence under s 58 of the OAPA 1861. On this occasion, the doctor's defence that he had acted in good faith to preserve the woman from grave permanent injury to her mental health (within s 1(1)(b) of the Abortion Act 1967) was accepted by the jury: see *R v Dixon (Reginald)* (1995) (unreported). While the doctor's evidence may appear flimsy ('in view of this lady's age, her very recent history of deliberate suicide attempt by overdose ... and her express wish for hysterectomy, we felt an emergency termination of pregnancy would be justified'), the case undoubtedly highlights the reluctance of juries to criminalise the practice of the modern abortion doctor.

An opposing, and ironically perhaps more effective, brake upon a doctor's discretion under the 1967 Act may consist in the potential ability of the pregnant woman to sue in negligence in so far as the doctor *fails* to assist her in having an abortion. As we have seen above, a claim of this sort was allowed in relation to the foetal handicap ground in *Mackay v Essex AHA* [1982] QB 1166 and it is almost certain that, where continued pregnancy causes reasonably foreseeable harm of a serious nature to the pregnant woman, the doctor's failure to authorise and/or carry out a termination under s 1(1)(b) or (c) of the Act would likewise be actionable. On the other hand, it may be doubted that a similar claim could be maintained in respect of s 1(1)(a), since the harms contemplated under that ground are arguably too amorphous to form the basis of a legal remedy.

A final issue in relation to the doctor is how far he may in fact refuse to participate in an abortion. This question is dealt with in s 4 of the Abortion Act 1967:

4 Conscientious objection to participation in treatment

(1) Subject to sub-s (2) of this section, no person shall be under any duty, whether by contract or by any statutory or other legal requirement, to participate in any treatment authorised by this Act to which he has a conscientious objection,

provided that in any legal proceedings the burden of proof of conscientious objection shall rest on the person claiming to rely on it.

(2) Nothing in sub-s (1) of this section shall affect any duty to participate in treatment which is necessary to save the life or to prevent grave permanent injury to the physical or mental health of a pregnant woman.

As is apparent from s 4(2) above, this provision cannot be relied upon by a doctor called upon to perform an abortion in an emergency. The question (in non-emergency situations) of who, apart from the treating doctor, may rely on the conscientious objection clause, came before the House of Lords in *Janaway v Salford HA* [1989] AC 537:

Janaway v Salford HA [1989] AC 537, HL (Lords Keith, Brandon, Griffiths, Goff and Lowry)

The plaintiff, a Roman Catholic, lost her job working as a secretary for the defendant health authority after refusing to type a letter of referral in respect of an abortion patient. She brought an action for unfair dismissal on the basis that her refusal was protected under s 4(1) of the Abortion Act 1967:

Lord Keith: The applicant claims the protection of s 4(1). The issue in the case turns on the true construction of the words in that sub-section 'participate in any treatment authorised by this Act'. For the applicant it is maintained that the words cover taking part in any arrangements preliminary to and intended to bring about medical or surgical measures aimed at terminating a pregnancy, including the typing of letters referring a patient to a consultant. The health authority argues that the meaning of the words is limited to taking part in the actual procedures undertaken at the hospital or other approved place with a view to the termination of a pregnancy ...

The argument for the applicant proceeds on the lines that the acts attracting the protection afforded by s 4(1) are intended to be co-extensive with those which are authorised by s 1(1) and which in the absence of that provision would be criminal. The criminal law about accessories treats one who aids and abets, counsels or procures a criminal act as liable to the same extent as a principal actor. In the absence of s 1(1) the applicant by typing a letter of referral would be counselling or procuring an abortion, or at least helping to do so, and subject to a possible defence on the principle of *R v Bourne* [1939] 1 KB 687 would be criminally liable. Therefore any requirement to type such a letter is relieved, in the face of a conscientious objection, by s 4(1).

The majority of the Court of Appeal (Slade and Stocker LJJ) accepted the main thrust of the applicant's argument, to the effect that s 1(1) and s 4(1) are co-extensive, but decided against her on the ground that her intention in typing a letter of referral would not be to assist in procuring an abortion but merely to carry out the obligations of her employment. In their view the typing of such a letter by the applicant would not be a criminal offence in the absence of s 1(1).

Nolan J, however, and Balcombe LJ in the Court of Appeal rejected the applicant's main argument. They accepted the argument for the health authority that on a proper construction the word 'participate' in s 4(1) did not import the whole concept of principal and accessory residing in the criminal law, but in its ordinary and natural meaning referred to actually taking part in treatment administered in a hospital or other approved place in accordance with s 1(3), for the purpose of terminating a pregnancy.

In my opinion Nolan J and Balcombe LJ were right to reach the conclusion they did. I agree entirely with their view about the natural meaning of the word 'participate' in this context. Although the word is commonly used to describe the activities of accessories in the criminal law field, it is not a term of art there. It is in any event not being used in a criminal context in s 4(1). *Ex hypothesi* treatment for termination of a pregnancy under s 1 is not criminal. I do not consider that parliament can reasonably have intended by its use to import all the technicalities of the criminal law about principal and accessory, which can on occasion raise very nice questions about whether someone is guilty as an accessory. Such niceties would be very difficult of solution for an ordinary health authority. If parliament had intended the result contended for by the applicant, it could have procured it very clearly and easily by referring to participation 'in anything authorised by this Act' instead of 'in any treatment [so] authorised'. It is to be observed that s 4 appears to represent something of a compromise in relation to conscientious objection. One who believes all abortion to be morally wrong would conscientiously object even to such treatment as is mentioned in sub-s (2), yet the sub-section would not allow the objection to receive effect.

Whilst it was thus made clear that Mrs Janaway's actions were too ancillary to the abortion procedure to bring her within the scope of the conscientious objection clause, the position of other facilitative agents, in particular the GP who might be asked to provide a second certificate as to an abortion falling within one of the statutory grounds, was left open. As Lord Keith continued:

Lord Keith: A certain amount of argument was addressed to the Abortion Regulations 1968 SI 1968/390, which, *inter alia*, set out the form of certificate, known as the 'Green

Form', to be signed by two registered medical practitioners in pursuance of s 1(1)(a) of the Act, and to the position in relation to s 4(1) of practitioners who might be required to sign such a certificate. The Regulations do not appear to contemplate that the signing of the certificate would form part of treatment for the termination of pregnancy, since reg 3(2) provides:

> Any certificate of an opinion referred to in s 1(1) of the Act shall be given before the commencement of the treatment for the termination of the pregnancy to which it relates.

It does not appear whether or not there are any circumstances under which a doctor might be under any legal duty to sign a green form, so as to place in difficulties one who had a conscientious objection to doing so. The fact that during the 20 years that the Act of 1967 has been in force no problem seems to have surfaced in this connection may indicate that in practice none exists. So I do not think it appropriate to express any opinion on the matter.

Recently, in *Barr v Matthews* (1999) 52 BMLR 217, Alliott J expressed the view that 'once a termination of pregnancy is recognised as an option, the doctor invoking the conscientious objection clause should refer the patient to a colleague at once'.

Forms of termination raising special issues

We conclude our examination of abortion by considering a number of procedures, in relation to the practice, that have generated particular legal or ethical concern.

Pre-implantation terminations

What is the legality of a measure which prevents a newly formed embryo from implanting in the woman's uterus in the first place? In particular, is it the case here that a 'miscarriage' is procured contrary to the terms of the OAPA 1861? Margaret Brazier has commented on this question as follows:

Brazier, M, *Medicine, Patients and the Law*, 2nd edn, 1992, Harmondsworth: Penguin, pp 293–94:

The 1967 Act envisaged that once a diagnosis of pregnancy had been made, the doctor faced with a request for an abortion would then consider and weigh any risk to the woman or the child. But there is a drug approved for general use which will, if taken by a woman within 72 hours of intercourse, ensure that any fertilised ovum will not implant in the womb. This, inaptly named, 'morning after' pill is not the only means by which a fertilised ovum (egg) may be disposed of at a stage before pregnancy can be confirmed. An intra-uterine device (IUD) fitted within a similar time after intercourse will have the same effect. And finally, if more than 72 hours elapse after unprotected intercourse before the woman seeks help, menstrual extraction can be used at or just after the due date of her next period. By this technique, an instrument attached to a vacuum is used to remove the whole of a woman's monthly period within a few minutes, including, if it exists, the product of any unwanted conception.

Are such methods lawful? They raise the question of where the line is to be drawn between contraception and abortion. A distinction must be made between the 'morning after' pill and the IUD on the one hand, and menstrual extraction on the other. The first two operate at a time before the fertilised ovum can implant in the womb. By the time menstrual extraction is utilised, the ovum will have become an implanted embryo. The action taken to remove that embryo by the vacuum clearly constitutes an induced abortion. The crucial legal issue then, in relation to the use of the 'morning after' pill and the IUD, is whether a procedure which prevents implantation is an act done to procure a miscarriage so as to make the doctor liable for criminal abortion. The woman herself will not be able to be proved to be with child. She will thus not be guilty of an offence herself, but could, as we have seen, be prosecuted for conspiracy with her doctor. The argument that prevention of implantation is no offence runs thus. There is no carriage of a child by a woman before implantation takes place, and so to prevent that event even occurring cannot be an act done to procure a miscarriage. Many fertilised ova fail to implant naturally and no one then suggests that a miscarriage has occurred. The opponents of post-coital birth control reply that the fertilised ovum is present within the body of the woman; she carries it within her. Therefore there is carriage of a child, and any act removing that child from her womb is an act done to procure a miscarriage. Up to 40% of implanted embryos also abort spontaneously. Thus arguments based on spontaneous loss of fertilised ova are irrelevant.

No successful prosecution has ever been brought in respect of either the 'morning after' pill, or the use of an IUD, as means of post-coital birth control. In 1983 the Attorney General expressed his opinion that prior to implantation there is no pregnancy and so means used to prevent implantation do not constitute procuring miscarriage. In 1991 a judge dismissed a prosecution for criminal abortion based on the insertion of an IUD agreeing with the Attorney General that until implantation there is no pregnancy. The Attorney General's ruling is persuasive, but not binding on his successors. The matter remains unresolved by higher judicial authority. In practice, however, doctors are prescribing the 'morning after' pill without any pretence of applying the criteria laid down in the Abortion Act.

In spring 2002, the Society for the Protection of the Unborn Child brought judicial review proceedings against the decision by the Secretary of State for Health to allow the sale of the morning after pill in chemists, without prescription. In dismissing the application, Munby J held that 'the prescription, supply, administration or use of the morning after pill does not – cannot – involve the commission of any offence under either s 58 or s 59 of the 1861 Act': see *R v Secretary of State for Health ex p Smeaton* [2002] EWHC 610.

Selective reduction

As we saw above, in Chapter 7, certain forms of fertility treatment, IVF or (more often) the use of super-ovulatory drugs, may result in a multiple pregnancy in which the woman carries more foetuses than can safely be brought to term. The term 'selective reduction' refers to the practice, in such a pregnancy, of deliberately terminating the lives of some of the foetuses in order to improve the survival chances of those that remain. Andrew Grubb has discussed the legal problems posed by the practice as follows:

Grubb, A, 'The new law of abortion: clarification or ambiguity' (1991) Crim LR 659:

Modern medicine has developed techniques whereby a multiple pregnancy may be reduced by killing one or more foetuses *in utero*. This has become particularly important in cases where infertility treatment has led to a multiple pregnancy. The greater the number of foetuses carried by a woman, the greater is risk to her health during pregnancy and at delivery. Equally, in these circumstances there is the risk of foetal mortality and of foetal handicap, including cerebral palsy, blindness and mental retardation.

Consequently, it is often desirable out of the interests of the mother and/or the foetuses that the pregnancy should be reduced in number. This is usually done in the first 14 weeks of the pregnancy by either injecting potassium chloride into the amniotic sac or into the heart of the foetus or by aspiration. Foetus(es) will die and may be spontaneously expelled or, more likely, will remain in the mother, wither and what remains will be expelled at the time the remaining healthy foetuses are delivered. This procedure is known as selective reduction.

In addition, a similar procedure may be used later in pregnancy when one of a number of foetuses (usually twins) is discovered to be seriously handicapped. Because of the slightly differing circumstances when it is used, it is sometimes distinguished from selective reduction and is known as selective foeticide ...

Legal position pre-[HFEA 1990]

It was not clear under the law prior to 1 April 1991 whether selective reduction and selective foeticide were covered by the abortion legislation. It could be argued that in cases where the 'reduced' foetus(es) is not expelled there is not a 'miscarriage' within the terms of s 58 of the Offences Against the Person Act 1861. The better view is, however, that the term 'miscarriage' does not require expulsion of the contents of the womb but merely that some or all of the contents cease to be carried alive within it. This would bring both procedures within s 58 of the 1861 Act. In any event, the argument overlooks the fact that ultimately, the withered and dead products of the foetus will be expelled at the time the remaining foetuses are delivered.

A further complication was raised as to whether selective reduction was a 'termination of pregnancy' within the Abortion Act 1967 because the woman is still pregnant in the sense that one or more of the healthy foetuses remains after the procedure. If there was no termination of pregnancy, then the procedure could never be lawful, because what was being done would not fall within the wording of the Abortion Act. There would be a crime but no possible defence.

In the light of these uncertainties, when Parliament came to amend the Abortion Act in 1990 a new s 5(2) was introduced specifically to deal with the practice:

5 (2) -For the purposes of the law relating to abortion, anything done with intent to procure a woman's miscarriage (or, in the case of a woman carrying more than one foetus, her miscarriage of any foetus) is unlawfully done unless authorised by s 1 of this Act and, in the case of a woman carrying more than one foetus, anything done with intent to procure her miscarriage of any foetus is authorised by that section if–

(a) the ground for termination of the pregnancy specified in sub-s (1)(d) of that section applies in relation to any foetus and the thing is done for the purpose of procuring the miscarriage of that foetus; or

(b) any of the other grounds for termination of the pregnancy specified in that section applies.

It is apparent that the effect of this provision is that selective reduction will be lawful either to protect the health or life of the pregnant woman (in which case the foetus(es) for destruction may be randomly chosen) or to terminate the life of a particular foetus on the s 1(1)(d) ground of foetal handicap.

Drug-induced abortions

When the Abortion Act 1967 was first enacted, medical abortion invariably necessitated the surgical removal of the foetus by a qualified doctor. For this reason, s 1(1) confers immunity from criminal liability only where abortion is carried out by 'a registered medical practitioner'. Developments in abortion techniques since then, particularly the availability of new 'abortifacient' drugs, now allow others, besides doctors, to take a much more direct role in terminating pregnancy. How far will they be protected by the terms of the 1967 Act? The issue, in relation to nursing staff, was considered by the House of Lords in the case of *Royal College of Nursing of UK v DHSS* [1981] AC 800:

Royal College of Nursing of United Kingdom v DHSS [1981] AC 800, HL (Lords Wilberforce, Diplock, Edmund-Davies, Keith and Roskill)

The RCN became concerned over the potential liability of its members in relation to the practice of using the drug Prostaglandin to carry out many abortions. The drug acts by stimulating contractions in the uterus, leading to the expulsion of the foetus. Here, whilst a doctor will perform the initial insertion of a catheter into the pregnant woman's uterus, the drug itself is later fed through the catheter by a nurse. The College sought a declaration that a DHSS circular authorising the practice was wrong in law:

> **Lord Keith**: Section 1(1) of the Act of 1967 can operate to relieve a person from guilt of an offence under the law relating to abortion only 'when a pregnancy is terminated by a registered medical practitioner'. Certain other conditions must also be satisfied, but no question about these arises in the present case. The sole issue is whether the words I have quoted cover the situation where abortion has been brought about as a result of the procedure under consideration.
>
> The argument for the respondents is, in essence, that the words of the sub-section do not apply because the pregnancy has not been terminated by any registered medical practitioner, but by the nurse who did the act or acts which directly resulted in the administration to the pregnant woman of the abortifacient drugs.
>
> In my opinion this argument involves placing an unduly restricted and unintended meaning on the words 'when a pregnancy is terminated'. It seems to me that these words, in their context, are not referring to the mere physical occurrence of termination. The sidenote to s 1 is 'Medical termination of pregnancy'. 'Termination of pregnancy' is an expression commonly used, perhaps rather more by medical people than by laymen, to describe in neutral and unemotive terms the bringing about of an abortion. So used, it is capable of covering the whole process designed to lead to that result, and in my view it does so in the present context. Other provisions of the Act make it clear that termination of pregnancy is envisaged as being a process of treatment. Section 1(3) provides that, subject to an exception for cases of emergency, 'treatment for the termination of pregnancy' must be carried out in a National Health Service hospital or a place for the time being approved by the minister. There are similar references to treatment for the termination of pregnancy in s 3, which governs the application of the Act to visiting forces. Then by s 4(1) it is provided that no person shall be under any duty 'to participate in any treatment authorised by this Act to which he has a conscientious objection'. This appears clearly to recognise that what is authorised by s 1(1) in relation to the termination of pregnancy is a process of treatment leading to that result. Section 5(2) is also of some importance. It provides that: 'For the purposes of the law relating to abortion, anything done

with intent to procure the miscarriage of a woman is unlawfully done unless authorised by s 1 of this Act.' This indicates a contemplation that a wide range of acts done when a pregnancy is terminated under the given conditions are authorised by s 1, and leads to the inference that, since all that s 1 authorises is the termination of pregnancy by a registered medical practitioner, all such acts must be embraced in the termination.

Given that the termination of pregnancy under contemplation in s 1(1) includes the whole process of treatment involved therein, it remains to consider whether, on the facts of this case, the termination can properly be regarded as being 'by a registered medical practitioner'. In my opinion this question is to be answered affirmatively. The doctor has responsibility for the whole process and is in charge of it throughout. It is he who decides that it is to be carried out. He personally performs essential parts of it which are such as to necessitate the application of his particular skill. The nurse's actions are done under his direct written instructions. In the circumstances I find it impossible to hold that the doctor's role is other than that of a principal, and I think he would be very surprised to hear that the nurse was the principal and he himself only an accessory. It is true that it is the nurse's action which leads directly to the introduction of abortifacient drugs into the system of the patient, but that action is done in a ministerial capacity and on the doctor's orders. Even if it were right to regard the nurse as a principal, it seems to me inevitable that the doctor should also be so regarded. If both the doctor and the nurse were principals, the provisions of the sub-section would be still satisfied, because the pregnancy would have been terminated by the doctor notwithstanding that it had also been terminated by the nurse.

I therefore conclude that termination of pregnancy by means of the procedures under consideration is authorised by the terms of s 1(1). This conclusion is the more satisfactory as it appears to me to be fully in accordance with that part of the policy and purpose of the Act which was directed to securing that socially acceptable abortions should be carried out under the safest conditions attainable. One may also feel some relief that it is unnecessary to reach a decision involving that the very large numbers of medical practitioners and others who have participated in the relevant procedures over several years past should now be revealed as guilty of criminal offences.

Lord Roskill: Learned counsel for the respondents did not shrink from the anomalies which would necessarily flow from the acceptance of his submission and the construction adopted by the majority of the Court of Appeal. There was, he said, only a limited qualification engrafted upon an otherwise unchanged criminal law and in 1967 parliament had legislated by reference to the surgical techniques of abortion as they then were and not for other techniques of abortion as they might subsequently be evolved. Pressed to say whether a new method must not be adopted which involved less risk to the patient, he replied that any such new method would only be lawful if the doctor were present throughout, a view which would seemingly make unrealistic demands upon medical manpower since no one suggested that each of the seven steps taken by the nurse, to which I have already referred, was not well within the capacity of someone possessed of the qualifications and experience which such a nurse would necessarily possess.

Whilst the decision of the House of Lords (by a narrow 3:2 majority) means that nursing staff involved in abortions enjoy the same statutory protection as doctors, the problem of who else might benefit has now arisen following the development of a further abortifacient drug, RU-486 or Mifepristone. This drug is similar in its operation to Prostaglandin but is significantly easier to administer. Indeed, the drug could, in principle, be made available on prescription in tablet form to be taken by pregnant women who remain out-patients. A new s 1(3A) was specifically introduced into the Abortion Act in 1990 to allow for Mifepristone to be taken, in the future, at GPs' surgeries (previously, under s 1(3), treatment to terminate a pregnancy could only be given at NHS or other hospitals approved by the Secretary of State). Nevertheless, as Kennedy and Grubb point out, a real difficulty remains:

Kennedy, I and Grubb, A, *Medical Law*, 2nd edn, 1994, London: Butterworths, pp 916–17:

[Mifepristone] is prescribed by a doctor, dispensed by a pharmacist, but administered to herself by the pregnant woman. In this situation who terminates the pregnancy?

There are two possible situations which might arise. First, the termination is only completed after the woman has returned to the hospital some 36 to 48 hours later after the Prostaglandin pessary has been inserted. Here, undoubtedly the termination would be by the doctor even if the Prostaglandin were given by a nurse under his supervision (*Royal College of Nursing* case). This is not problematic for the law. However, the alternative situation that might arise is.

Suppose, instead, the effects of Mifepristone occur before the woman returns to the hospital for the Prostaglandin pessary. In 55% of cases bleeding (and therefore, the potential for a 'miscarriage') occur within 48 hours of administering Mifepristone. In a proportion of cases (about 3%) termination will occur before readmission. In our view, in this situation it must be the pregnant woman and not the doctor who terminates the pregnancy. It is she who does the last voluntary act necessary to effect the termination. Legally, the situation is analogous to a case where a doctor provides the means (eg, pills) for a patient to kill himself. It is the patient who commits suicide. The doctor is guilty of assisting suicide, if anything. It cannot be said that he is guilty of murder since the law regards the patient's actions as the cause of death. Mutatis mutandis, here the woman causes her own termination. The provisions of the Abortion Act 1967 would not be complied with. Clearly, Parliament overlooked this fundamental point when it sought to bring Mifepristone within the framework of the Abortion Act.

However, an argument which would challenge this view could be mounted on the basis of the *Royal College of Nursing* case. There, the House of Lords ... extended 'medical practitioner' to include all acts performed by the medical team for whom the doctor is responsible ...

Could this wider notion of 'termination by a registered medical practitioner covering all action for which the doctor takes responsibility' (or 'charge') help in the case of Mifepristone? In one sense, a doctor does have responsibility for the patient throughout the treatment. However, it is a different kind of responsibility from that contemplated in the *Royal College of Nursing* case. In that case the responsibility denoted the right to control those who acted on his behalf in a professional capacity. In the case of Mifepristone, the responsibility relates to the doctor's ethical and legal duty to his patient. The relationship is neither one of control nor one where the patient (in administering the drug to herself) can be said to act on the doctor's behalf or be in his charge. It is unlikely that a future court would further expand the meaning of the 1967 Act to cover the use of Mifepristone.

At present, the use of Mifepristone in this country is restricted, in any event, to its administration by nursing staff in hospitals, in the same manner as Prostaglandin.

Late abortion and the living abortus

As noted, the 1990 amendments to the Abortion Act 1967 permit termination of pregnancy right up until birth under grounds (b), (c) and (d). Such late terminations are extremely rare and, due to restrictions in the licences granted to private abortion clinics (imposed by the Secretary of State pursuant to s 1(3) of the Act), may only be carried out in NHS hospitals. In practice, it is the last of the grounds, foetal handicap, which is almost always invoked in such circumstances.

By contrast with early abortions, where abortifacient drugs may be used, late abortions invariably require surgical intervention. Of course, the intention of the doctor is that the foetus will not survive the abortion process; however, unless measures are taken to kill the foetus while still inside the womb, there is a real chance that it will be born alive. What is the legal position of the doctor, in such circumstances, where the foetus only dies some time after delivery? In *AG's Reference (No 3 of 1994)* [1997] 3 WLR 421 the House of Lords considered a reference in respect of the acquittal for murder (on the directions of the trial judge) of a man who had stabbed his pregnant girlfriend in the abdomen. (The woman went into labour soon after the attack and, although the child was delivered alive, it died 120 days later due to its severe prematurity.) In reversing the decision of the Court of Appeal that a murder charge could lie in such circumstances, their Lordships were nevertheless extremely cautious to limit their response to the facts in hand (involving an intention by the respondent to harm the pregnant woman). Lord Mustill commented that he 'would wish to proceed with particular care in relation to allegations of murder stemming from an injury to the foetus unaccompanied by any causative injury to the mother'. Given this present lack of certainty in the law, the doctor responsible for a late abortion would be well advised to take the greatest care that the foetus dies while it is still inside the womb.

PRE-NATAL HARM BEYOND THE ABORTION CONTEXT

General principles

Beyond the context of abortion, it is readily apparent that injuries may be caused to a foetus *in utero* which subsequently lead to it being born disabled. The question of whether a child damaged in this way can, after it is born, bring an action against the person responsible has created a surprising amount of difficulty for the common law. Nevertheless, in respect of children born after 21 July 1976, such a child has been given a statutory right to recover damages under the Congenital Disabilities (Civil Liability) Act 1976. Section 1 of this Act provides as follows:

1 Civil liability to child born disabled

(1) If a child is born disabled as the result of such an occurrence before its birth as is mentioned in sub-s (2) below, and a person (other than the child's own mother) is under this section answerable to the child in respect of the occurrence, the child's disabilities are to be regarded as damage resulting from the wrongful act of that person and actionable accordingly at the suit of the child.

(2) An occurrence to which this section applies is one which–

(a) affected either parent of the child in his or her ability to have a normal, healthy child; or

(b) affected the mother during her pregnancy, or affected her or the child in the course of its birth, so that the child is born with disabilities which would not otherwise have been present.

(3) Subject to the following sub-sections, a person (here referred to as 'the defendant') is answerable to the child if he was liable in tort to the parent or would, if sued in due time have been so; and it is no answer that there could not have been such liability because the parent suffered no actionable injury, if there was a breach of legal duty which, accompanied by injury, would have given rise to the liability.

(4) In the case of an occurrence preceding the time of conception, the defendant is not answerable to the child if at that time either or both of the parents knew the risk of their child being born disabled (that it to say, the particular risk created by the occurrence); but should it be the child's father who is the defendant, this sub-section does not apply if he knew of the risk and the mother did not.

(5) The defendant is not answerable to the child, for anything he did or omitted to do when responsible in a professional capacity for treating or advising the parent, if he took reasonable care having due regard to then received professional opinion applicable to the particular class of case; but this does not mean that he is answerable only because he departed from received opinion.

(6) Liability to the child under this section may be treated as having been excluded or limited by contract made with the parent affected, to the same extent and subject to the same restrictions as liability in the parent's own case; and a contract term which could have been set up by the defendant in an action by the parent, so as to exclude or limit his liability to him or her, operates in the defendant's favour to the same, but no greater, extent in an action under this section by the child.

(7) If in the child's action under this section it is shown that the parent affected shared the responsibility for the child being born disabled, the damages are to be reduced to such extent as the court thinks just and equitable having regard to the extent of the parent's responsibility.

The effect of s 1(3) above is to found the child's action upon the concept of 'derivative liability', ie, it may only bring a claim in so far as the occurrence which caused its injuries involved a breach of duty by the tortfeasor to one of its parents. More recently, in two cases whose facts arose prior to 1976, *Burton v Islington HA* [1992] 3 All ER 833; and *De Martell v Merton and Sutton HA* [1992] 3 All ER 833, the Court of Appeal had to tackle head on the problem at common law of how it is that a duty in tort can be owed to an entity which has no legal personality. In finding for the plaintiffs, Dillon LJ relied extensively upon Commonwealth authority, in particular the decision of the Supreme Court of Victoria in *Watt v Rama* (1972) VR 353:

Burton v Islington HA [1992] 3 All ER 833

Dillon LJ: The main Commonwealth case from a country with a common law jurisdiction is *Watt v Rama* ... which has since been accepted by other appellate courts in Australia as a correct statement of the law, that is to say the common law of Australia. That was a case which arose out of injuries in a motor accident. The leading judgment is that of Winneke CJ and Pape J. It is founded on an analysis – in my judgment, correct – of the tort of negligence by reference to decisions of the House of Lords and the Privy Council and certain Australian decisions, and it is founded also on the Montreal Tramways decision. I can take up that judgment, at pp 358–59:

The real question posed for our decision is not whether an action lies in respect of pre-natal injuries but whether a plaintiff born with injuries caused by the pre-natal neglect of the defendant has a cause of action in negligence against him in respect of such injuries. To this question the defendant answers 'No', because at the time of his neglect the plaintiff was not in existence as a living person, had no separate existence apart from her mother, was not capable of suing to assert a legal right, and was not a legal person to whom he could be under a duty.

There is then reference to well known authorities like *Donoghue v Stevenson* [1932] AC 562; *Dorset Yacht Co Ltd v Home Office* [1970] AC 1004; *Bourhill (Hay) v Young* [1943] AC 92; *Watson v Fram Reinforced Concrete Co (Scotland) Ltd* (1960) SC (HL) 92; and *Grant v Australian Knitting Mills Ltd* [1936] AC 85, and then to a South African decision which followed *Montreal Tramways v Leveille* (1933) 4 DLR 337 and to the *Montreal Tramways* case itself. After the citations the judgment continues, at pp 360–61:

> Those circumstances, accordingly, constituted a potential relationship capable of imposing a duty on the defendant in relation to the child if and when born. On the birth the relationship crystallised and out of it arose a duty on the defendant in relation to the child. On the facts which for present purposes must be assumed, the child was born with injuries caused by the act or neglect of the defendant in the driving of his car. But as the child could not in the very nature of things acquire rights correlative to a duty until it became by birth a living person, and as it was not until then that it could sustain injuries as a living person, it was, we think, at that stage that the duty arising out of the relationship was attached to the defendant, and it was at that stage that the defendant was, on the assumption that his act or omission in the driving of the car constituted a failure to take reasonable care, in breach of the duty to take reasonable care to avoid injury to the child ...

With respect, the analysis endorsed by his Lordship appears to confuse breach of duty with the damage which is thereby caused. It might be simpler to accept that legal duties can be owed to the unborn child, as a potential person, even though the corresponding right of such an entity to bring a claim remains contingent upon its subsequent birth. Though this approach may violate strict Hohfeldian logic (see Chapter 1, p 13, above), it seems to have been an unspoken assumption in many medical negligence claims: see, for example, *Whitehouse v Jordan* [1981] 1 All ER 267.

Ultimately, all that is being allowed in these cases is that a damaged child may recover damages where, but for the defendant's negligence, it would have been born undamaged. A claim, on the other hand, by such a child who, but for the defendant's negligence would never have been born at all, would, at least if the judgment of the Court of Appeal in *Mackay v Essex AHA* [1982] 1 QB 1166 is followed, form an inadmissible 'wrongful life' action. Recently, however, this area of law has been thrown into some confusion by changes made to the Congenital Disabilities (Civil Liability) Act by the HFEA 1990 (see Chapter 7, p 388, above).

Harm caused by the child's mother

It is important to note that, except in the case of negligent driving (allowed for in s 2 of the Act) no action will lie under the 1976 Act where the pre-natal injuries arose through the negligence of the child's mother. The policy grounds underlying this immunity are discussed by Jane Fortin as follows:

Fortin, J, 'Legal protection for the unborn child' (1988) 51 MLR 54:

By making liability to the child depend on liability to the parent, th[e] formula [of derivative liability] excludes a wide range of negligent acts and omissions on the part of the mother. Some would say that circumstances like those arising in the *Berkshire* case indicate quite clearly that the existence of maternal tortious liability would be a useful means of controlling the mother's ante-natal behaviour. Nevertheless, the Law Commission rejected the proposition that a child might sue its mother for pre-natal injuries caused by her negligence, largely on the social policy grounds that the existence of such a right of action would have deleterious effects on family cohesion. In particular, the mother might become vulnerable to litigation brought on behalf of her child, claiming that it was her failure to give up cigarette smoking or alcohol or to follow the latest dietary ante-natal regime that had caused the child's disablement. Moreover, the existence of such a cause of action might well fuel a matrimonial or parental conflict. Despite the undoubted sense grounding these fears, the Law Commission's acceptance of this social policy argument is inconsistent with their earlier claim that the unborn child could have no legal existence; surely the answer to the question whether the child could sue his mother in respect of pre-natal negligence, should have been that she could not, in any event, owe a duty to a legal nonentity. Nevertheless, the Law Commission was satisfied that different considerations applied to cases of pre-natal injury caused by a road accident, where the existence of third party insurance would prevent any risk of a child's claim against its mother causing family conflicts. Consequently, despite the unborn child's lack of legal personality, the 1976 Act does impose on the pregnant mother a duty of care in relation to it, but only in the context of driving a motor vehicle. The illogicality of such a provision can hardly be justified by the existence of ample insurance funds to meet any liability.

Despite the inconsistency of the exception relating to maternal liability for negligent driving, the 1976 Act maintains the general principle of the civil law that the unborn child has no legal personality. It is arguable that this principle is acquiring an element of unreality, particularly when the 1976 Act itself and now the Berkshire case, clearly adhere to the proposition that a child's development is a continuing process that commences at conception not birth.

In the case of *D v Berkshire CC* [1987] 1 All ER 20, referred to by Fortin, the House of Lords held that events prior to a child's birth (which led to it being born with drug withdrawal symptoms) could properly be taken into account by magistrates when making a care order.

In general, it might seem paradoxical, given the relative ease with which the pregnant woman may dispose of her foetus altogether through abortion, that the law should concern itself with 'lesser harms' it may suffer as a result of her behaviour while pregnant. However, the point is, of course, that in the latter case alone there will be an existing person whose interests have been adversely affected by her conduct. The highly contentious question of whether, in cases of this sort, the criminal law might be invoked to afford protection to the foetus, is addressed by John Robertson:

Robertson, JA, *Children of Choice*, 1994, Ewing, New Jersey: Princeton UP, pp 180–85:

Given the foreseeable impact of certain pre-natal acts or omissions on the welfare of offspring, one cannot reasonably argue that women and men have no pre-natal obligation to avoid harm to children they choose to bring into the world. The more contested question is what public policies and legal options should be pursued to prevent pre-natal harm to offspring. The choice ranges from education and access to treatment to post-birth sanctions and pre-natal imposition of treatment on pregnant women. Because procreative liberty is not involved, and because the conduct in question poses serious harm to offspring, coercive sanctions are not in principle excluded. However, as we shall see, the better policy in most cases will be to rely on information, education, and access to treatment ...

Opponents of prosecution also see a grave threat to personal privacy and civil liberties. If illegal drug use during pregnancy is independently punishable, then anything with the slightest pre-natal risk to offspring could be punished as pre-natal child abuse. Women could be prosecuted for smoking or drinking even moderate amounts of alcohol at any time during pregnancy, because even a few drinks might lower IQ points, and smoking increases the risk of prematurity and low birth weight. In the worst-case scenario, special pregnancy police will be commissioned to monitor women for pregnancies, and then surveil their behaviour; if they err, they are then stigmatised, shamed, fined, or incarcerated. Margaret Atwood's *The Handmaid's Tale*, a chilling novel of women forced to serve the needs of a repressive dictatorship, starts sounding much less fanciful than it appears to be ...

All these points deserve considered attention. They explain why prosecutions have been largely unsuccessful, are widely opposed, and are unlikely to be a key factor in preventing pre-natal harm. They also show why education, treatment, and services are the more desirable and most effective avenue for public policy.

Despite the drawbacks of a criminal approach, however, these criticisms do not establish that criminal sanctions should never be imposed on persons who culpably harm offspring by pre-natal conduct. When culpability is established, criminal law theory easily includes pre-natal as well as post-natal conduct that harms offspring. For example, Lord Coke in the 17th century recognised criminal liability for pre-natal actions that caused post-natal death ...

But will criminal prosecution do any good? This is a pragmatic policy judgment over which reasonable people may well differ. At the very least, prosecution will fulfil the law's function of enunciating minimum acceptable standards of conduct to which all citizens of the State, regardless of cultural affiliation, must conform. In this case, the standards are enunciated for conduct during pregnancy that risks avoidable harm to offspring. In denouncing unacceptable conduct, legal proscription and prosecution might encourage women to refrain from harmful pre-natal conduct, or to seek help, if they know that they are at risk of causing harm to offspring. In any event, it will announce the community's condemnation of such conduct, deter some injuries to offspring and generally contribute to community norms of acceptable behaviour.

Refusals of obstetric intervention

Perhaps even more controversial are cases in which, rather than doing anything active to harm her foetus, the pregnant woman passively declines medical intervention which her doctors tell her is necessary to prevent serious harm occurring to it. What should the law's approach be here? In *Re T (Adult: Refusal of Treatment)* [1992] 4 All ER 649, Lord Donaldson MR expressly left the question open as to whether the presence of a viable foetus could oust the normal principle that a competent adult patient has a right to refuse treatment:

> **Lord Donaldson MR:** An adult patient who ... suffers from no mental incapacity has an absolute right to choose whether to consent to medical treatment, to refuse it or to choose one rather than another of the treatments being offered. The only possible qualification is where the choice may lead to the death of a viable foetus. That is not the case here and if and when it arises, the court will be presented with a novel problem of considerable legal and ethical complexity.

Then, very soon afterwards, the issue came squarely before the High Court in the case of *Re S (Adult: Refusal of Treatment)* [1992] 4 All ER 671:

Re S (Adult: Refusal of Treatment) [1992] 4 All ER 671, Fam Div
(Sir Stephen Brown P)

Mrs S was a 30 year old 'born-again Christian' in labour with her third child. Her foetus was in a position of 'transverse lie' and it was a practical certainty that, unless an immediate Caesarean section was carried out, her uterus would rupture, killing the child and, very possibly, Mrs S herself. The latter refused the operation, however, on religious grounds:

> **Sir Stephen Brown P**: I have heard the evidence of P, a Fellow of the Royal College of Surgeons, who is in charge of this patient at the hospital. He has given, succinctly and graphically, a description of the condition of this patient. Her situation is desperately serious, as is also the situation of the as yet unborn child. The child is in what is described as a position of 'transverse lie', with the elbow projecting through the cervix and the head being on the right side. There is the gravest risk of a rupture of the uterus if the section is not carried out and the natural labour process is permitted to continue. The evidence of P is that we are concerned with 'minutes rather than hours' and that it is a 'life and death' situation. He has done his best, as have other surgeons and doctors at the hospital, to persuade the mother that the only means of saving her life, and also I emphasise the life of her unborn child, is to carry out a Caesarean section operation. P is emphatic. He says it is absolutely the case that the baby cannot be born alive if a Caesarean operation is not carried out. He has described the medical condition. I am not going to go into it in detail because of the pressure of time.
>
> I have been assisted by Mr Munby QC appearing for the Official Solicitor as *amicus curiae*. The Official Solicitor answered the call of the court within minutes and, although this application only came to the notice of the court officials at 1.30 pm, it has come on for hearing just before 2 o'clock and now at 2.18 pm I propose to make the declaration which is sought. I do so in the knowledge that the fundamental question appears to have been left open by Lord Donaldson MR in *Re T (Adult: Refusal of Medical Treatment)* [1992] 4 All ER 649, heard earlier this year in the Court of Appeal, and in the knowledge that there is no English authority which is directly in point. There is, however, some American authority which suggests that if this case were being heard in the American courts the answer would be likely to be in favour of granting a declaration in these circumstances: see *Re AC* (1990) 573 A 2d 1235, pp 1240, 1246–48, and 1252. I do not propose to say more at this stage, except that I wholly accept the evidence of P as to the desperate nature of this situation, and that I grant the declaration as sought.

The President referred in his judgment to the American decision of *Re AC*. This was undoubtedly an unfortunate choice of authority. Ian Kennedy has charted the history of that case as follows:

> **Kennedy, I, *Treat Me Right*, 1991, Oxford: OUP, pp 367–68:**
>
> On 10 November 1987, the Court of Appeals of the District of Columbia, in the case of Angela C, approved the lower court's order that a Caesarean section be carried out on a terminally ill woman with hours or days to live, despite her apparent refusal of permission. The child was in its 26th week of gestation. The mother was heavily sedated and in extremis suffering from a metastatic oxygenic carcinoma in her lung. The operation was performed. The child died two hours thereafter. The mother died two days later. The court in upholding the order held that 'the trial judge did not err in subordinating AC's right against bodily intrusion to the interests of the unborn,

[but potentially viable] child'. This was particularly so, the court held, because 'Caesarean section would not significantly affect AC's condition because she had, at best, two days left of sedated life'.

Obviously, 'significantly' assumes great significance here ...

[Footnote:] *Re AC* was subsequently reheard *en banc* and the Court of Appeals issued a second judgment on 26 April 1990, No 87-609 ... The court vacated its prior order on the grounds that there had not been a proper finding of fact whether AC was competent, or, if she was not, how 'substituted judgment' was to be applied. The court did, however, decide that the decision of a competent patient or substituted judgment should prevail, even if surgery was refused, in 'virtually all cases' unless there are 'truly extraordinary or compelling reasons to override them', by taking account, for example, of the State's interest in protecting life. At the same time the court did not dissent from, or overrule, a previous decision (1986) of the Superior Court in *Re Madyun* (unreported: published as Appendix to *Re AC*). In *Madyun*, the court authorised surgery on a woman who objected for religious reasons. 'All that stood between the *Madyun* foetus and its independent existence was, put simply, a doctor's scalpel [*sic*]. In these circumstances, the life of the infant inside its mother's womb was entitled to be protected.'

The issue of whether a court should authorise a Caesarean section against the wishes of the pregnant woman gives rise to considerable ethical and legal dilemmas. On the one hand, a situation in which the doctors stood idly by and allowed a mature foetus to rupture its mother's womb would arguably do serious symbolic damage to the concept of the sanctity of life, which any society must maintain. On the other, the thought of doctors carrying out invasive, and potentially risky, therapy upon unwilling patients is deeply troubling to the concept of individual autonomy, another of liberal society's fundamental values. Moreover, the fact that the patients whose rights are infringed in this way are invariably women, opens up the spectre of gender inequality and domination, a problem exacerbated by the time constraints operating which often mean that the women in question lack adequate legal representation.

In 1996 a spate of further Caesarean cases came before the English courts. In every case, it was declared that the treatment would be lawful. Almost without exception, though, the judges involved based their decisions on a prior determination of fact that the women in question were incompetent and could accordingly be treated in their best interests. In the first such case, *Tameside and Glossop Acute Services Trust v CH* [1996] 1 FLR 762, Wall J declared that a Caesarean could be performed without consent as treatment 'for mental disorder' within the terms of the Mental Health Act 1983: see Chapter 9. Subsequently, Johnson J granted a declaration authorising intervention at common law in *Norfolk and Norwich (NHS) Trust v W* [1996] 2 FLR 613:

Johnson J: On Friday 21 June 1996 an application was made to me for an order relating to a proposed medical procedure upon a patient in a hospital in Norwich. The application began at 4.45 pm and was made by Mr John Grace QC. The patient was not represented, but the hospital's solicitors had communicated with the Official Solicitor and Mr James Munby QC was present with Mr Hinchcliffe of the Official Solicitor's office. Mr Munby made submissions as *amicus curiae*. No one else was present, there were no affidavits or statements and the information upon which I had to base my decision came from Mr Grace and Mr Hinchcliffe who had both spoken by telephone to the consultants in Norwich caring for the patient.

The information available to the court

Miss W, a woman aged 32, had arrived at the hospital's accident and emergency department at 9 am that day. She was in the last stages of pregnancy, apparently having had no ante-natal treatment. She was in labour, fully dilated and ready to deliver her baby. She was said to be in a state of arrested labour. Throughout the day, despite the obvious indications to the contrary, she continued to deny that she was even pregnant. The hospital was able to ascertain that she had a history of psychiatric treatment, marked by non-co-operation by her with those seeking to help her. She had had three previous pregnancies all terminating by Caesarean section. There were two risks to the patient. In layman's terms, the first was that unless the foetus was delivered by 6 pm, it would suffocate within the patient; and the presence of a dead foetus in the patient would have serious, and indeed life-threatening, consequences for the health of the patient herself. The second risk was that the patient's old Caesarean scars would reopen and this too would lead to the life of the foetus being at risk with consequent risk to the patient herself ...

... In the *Tameside* case ... Wall J specifically left open the question whether the court has the power at common law to authorise the use of reasonable force as a necessary incident of treatment or whether the power was limited to cases which fell within s 63 of the Mental Health Act 1983. That section reads:

> The consent of a patient shall not be required for any medical treatment given to him for the mental disorder from which he is suffering ... if the treatment is given by or under the direction of the responsible medical officer.

In the present case in the opinion of the psychiatrist the patient was not suffering from a mental disorder within the meaning of this section and so, if the power exists, it has to be found in the common law.

I held that in circumstances such as the present the court does have a power at common law to authorise the use of reasonable force. I reject the line of argument which had been put to Wall J in the *Tameside* case (p 770–74), preferring the submissions made to me by Mr Munby QC. I seek to apply the principle enunciated by Lord Goff of Chieveley in *Re F*, namely that there must be a necessity to act and:

> ... the action taken must be such as a reasonable person would in all the circumstances take, acting in the best interests of the assisted person.

Conclusion

In reliance upon the opinion of the consultant psychiatrist and taking account of the information I had about the statements made by the patient during the course of the day, I held that although she was not suffering from a mental disorder within the meaning of the statute, she lacked the mental competence to make a decision about the treatment that was proposed because she was incapable of weighing up the considerations that were involved. She was called upon to make that decision at a time of acute emotional stress and physical pain in the ordinary course of labour made even more difficult for her because of her own particular mental history.

I held that termination of this labour would be in the best interests of the patient. I was satisfied that unless the patient was delivered of the foetus which she was carrying, whether by way of forceps delivery or by Caesarean section, then her own physical health would be put at risk. This risk would arise if the foetus died because of rupture of the patient's old Caesarean scar or by suffocation in the birth canal. The death of the foetus would have immediate and increasing deleterious effects upon the patient herself leading to serious physical damage and possible death. Termination would end the stress and the pain of her labour, it would avoid the likelihood of damage to her physical health which might have potentially life-threatening consequences and, despite her present view about the foetus, would avoid her feeling any feeling of guilt in the future were she, by her refusal of consent, to cause the death of the foetus.

Throughout this judgment I have referred to 'the foetus' because I wish to emphasise that the focus of my judicial attention was upon the interests of the patient herself and not upon the interests of the foetus which she bore. However, the reality was that the foetus was a fully formed child, capable of normal life if only it could be delivered from the mother ...

In this case, the view that the patient was incompetent appears to have been fully justified (see generally, on the question of establishing competence, Chapter 3). However, as Johnson J was hearing it, another emergency *ex parte* application was brought before him by Rochdale Healthcare NHS Trust in respect of Mrs C, a woman in labour who was similarly refusing to undergo a Caesarean. In finding her incompetent (in the course of a two minute hearing) the judge held that she was unable to 'make any valid decision about anything of even the most trivial kind' owing to the emotional stress and pain of labour. This was despite the evidence from Mrs C's obstetrician that she was, in the latter's opinion, competent: see *Rochdale NHS Trust v C* [1997] 1 FCR 274.

The preference in these decisions for intervention to be authorised on grounds of the woman's incompetence left the principle in *Re S (Adult: Refusal of Treatment)* [1992] 4 All ER 671 isolated and doubtful. As we have seen, Sir Stephen Brown P in that case adverted to *dicta* in Lord Donaldson MR's judgment in *Re T* as to the effect the presence of a viable foetus could have upon refusals of treatment. However, when the House of Lords in *Airedale NHS Trust v Bland* came to restate the general treatment-refusal principle, they did not mention any qualification in such a case. The issue has now been addressed once again at appellate level by the Court of Appeal in *Re MB (An Adult: Medical Treatment)* [1997] 2 FLR 426:

Re MB (An Adult: Medical Treatment) [1997] 2 FLR 426, CA (Butler-Sloss, Saville and Ward LJJ)

Miss MB required a Caesarean section in order to save her foetus from death or serious handicap. However, although she agreed to the operation, her 'needle phobia' caused her to panic in the operating theatre and refuse the preliminary anaesthetic. Hollis J granted a declaration that, in these circumstances, it would be lawful to provide her with the treatment in her own best interests and this was upheld, the same evening, by the Court of Appeal. Five weeks later, their Lordships handed down a reserved judgment:

Butler-Sloss LJ (delivering the judgment of the court): All the decisions made in the Caesarean section cases to which we have referred arose in circumstances of urgency or extreme urgency. The evidence was in general limited in scope and the mother was not always represented as a party. With the exception of *Re S* ... in all the cases the court decided that the mother did not have the capacity to make the decision. In these extremely worrying situations, it is important to keep in mind the basic principles we have outlined, and the court should approach the crucial question of competence bearing the following considerations in mind. They are not intended to be determinative in every case, for the decision must inevitably depend upon the particular facts before the court:

(1) Every person is presumed to have the capacity to consent to or to refuse medical treatment unless and until that presumption is rebutted.

(2) A competent woman who has the capacity to decide may, for religious reasons, other reasons, for rational or irrational reasons or for no reason at all, choose not to have medical intervention, even though the consequence may be the death or serious handicap of the child she bears, or her own death. In that event the courts do not have the jurisdiction to declare medical intervention lawful and the question of her own best interests, objectively considered, does not arise ...

... Applying these principles to the facts of this case we find:

(1) Miss MB consented to a Caesarean section.

(2) What she refused to accept was not the incision by the surgeon's scalpel but only the prick of the anaesthetist's needle. Capacity is commensurate with the gravity of the decision to be taken.

(3) She could not bring herself to undergo the Caesarean section she desired because, as the evidence established:

> ... a fear of needles ... has got in the way of proceeding with the operation ... At the moment of panic ... her fear dominated all ... at the actual point she was not capable of making a decision at all ... at that moment the needle or mask dominated her thinking and made her quite unable to consider anything else.

On that evidence she was incapable of making a decision at all. She was at that moment suffering an impairment of her mental functioning which disabled her. She was temporarily incompetent. In the emergency the doctors would be free to administer the anaesthetic if that were in her best interests.

A feature of some of the cases to which we have referred has been the favourable reaction of the patient who refused treatment to the subsequent medical intervention and the successful outcome. Having noted that, we are none the less sure that however desirable it may be for the mother to be delivered of a live and healthy baby, on this aspect of the appeal it is not a strictly relevant consideration. If therefore the competent mother refuses to have the medical intervention, the doctors may not lawfully do more than attempt to persuade her. If that persuasion is unsuccessful, there are no further steps towards medical intervention to be taken. We recognise that the effect of these conclusions is that there will be situations in which the child may die or may be seriously handicapped because the mother said no and the obstetrician was not able to take the necessary steps to avoid the death or handicap. The mother may indeed later regret the outcome, but the alternative would be an unwarranted invasion of the right of the woman to make the decision.

It is apparent that, though couched in strong terms, the Court of Appeal's endorsement of the principle that, where competent, the woman's autonomy must prevail over her own best interests and those of the foetus, is only *obiter*. On the facts, as we have seen, the court accepted Hollis J's finding that MB herself was not competent and thus treatment had been lawful. However, their Lordships' decision to disapprove the decision in *Re S (Adult: Refusal of Treatment)* [1992] 4 All ER 671 on the basis that, where the woman is competent, the court has no jurisdiction to intervene, is open to criticism:

Stauch, M, 'Court-authorised Caesareans and the principle of patient autonomy' (1997) 6 Nott LJ 74:

As their Lordships noted, it is a well established principle of English law that the foetus, until born, lacks legal personality. One reason, quite simply, is that the foetus' physical location within the pregnant woman would, if such personality were granted, lead to insoluble conflicts in cases where the interests of the woman and foetus were opposed. In this regard, the court referred, inter alia, to its own previous judgment in *Re F (In Utero)* which concerned the attempt by a local authority to ward the foetus of a mentally unstable woman who had absconded from her place of care. It endorsed the concern of Balcombe LJ in that case, that '[s]ince an unborn child has, *ex hypothesi*, no existence independent of its mother, the only purpose of extending the [wardship] jurisdiction to include a foetus is to enable the mother's actions to be controlled'. This, he felt, should, if appropriate at all, be a matter for Parliament.

After considering statutes which deal with the protection of unborn life, together with a number of ECHR and US authorities, the Court of Appeal in *Re MB* concluded:

> The foetus up to the moment of birth does not have any separate interests capable of being taken into account when a court has to consider an application for a declaration in respect of a Caesarean section operation. The court does not have the jurisdiction to declare that such medical intervention is lawful *to protect the interests of the unborn child* even at the point of birth. [Emphasis added.]

This, it is submitted, is correct so far as it goes. However, at most it follows that the interests of the foetus *per se* are not a sufficient warrant for intervention. Where the court appears, with respect, to have erred is in assuming that a court will therefore never have jurisdiction to declare treatment lawful in such a case, ie, on other grounds. Such a narrow reading of its own powers is contrary to other recent authorities in which doubts over medical treatment have been at issue. In fact, as a judicial tool, declaratory relief has been developed precisely to provide assistance to those, such as doctors, who are faced with urgent ethical dilemmas in situations of legal uncertainty ... [I]n *Re S (Hospital Order: Court's Jurisdiction)* ... Sir Thomas Bingham MR suggested that for such relief to be invoked, it was enough that there was 'a serious justiciable issue' before the court. As his Lordship commented, '[t]his is pre-eminently an area in which the common law should respond to social needs as they are manifested, case by case'.

Overriding an autonomous refusal?

Assuming that a court does, in principle, have the requisite jurisdiction to authorise treatment, should it do so against the competent and autonomous refusal of a pregnant woman to permit obstetric intervention? One might think the answer should always be in the negative. After all, an autonomous choice represents a considered value-ordering by the woman of her interests, and recognition of her integrity as an individual implies that we should not second-guess them. This is the more so, given that imposing intervention, while advancing some of her interests, will inevitably set back others.

A good illustration is provided by the case of *[Baby Boy Doe (A Fetus) v Mother Doe* 510 US 1032 (1993); 114 S Ct 652 (1993)] a ruling by the Illinois Supreme Court on the legitimacy of court-authorised Caesarean sections. Tabita Bricci was a Pentecostal Christian, whose faith forbade surgical intervention which would bring her pregnancy to an end before full term. In fact, a few weeks prior to birth, doctors determined that her foetus was receiving an inadequate oxygen supply and advised her that, unless delivery were carried out by immediate Caesarean section, her foetus would almost certainly die or suffer severe brain damage. In upholding Mrs Bricci's right to refuse the operation, the Supreme Court endorsed the ruling of the Illinois Supreme Court in a previous case, where it had held:

> Even though we may consider appellant's beliefs unwise, foolish or ridiculous, in the absence of an overriding danger to society we may not

permit interference therewith ... for the sole purpose of compelling her to accept medical treatment forbidden by her religious principles and previously refused by her with full knowledge of the probable consequences.

Here, if compulsory intervention had been authorised, it would have advanced the patient's interests in having a healthy live birth (which she clearly desired). On the other hand, it would clearly have damaged both her relationship with her faith and her general sense of herself as an autonomous agent. Moreover, forced surgical intervention would also have exposed her to attendant physical harm and risk of harm.

It is important to note, however, that in this last case the patient's refusal did not carry implications for her own somatic well being. What of a situation where the refusal of intervention will lead not only to death or serious harm to the foetus but also to the pregnant woman? That, after all, was the situation confronting the English High Court in Re S. In general, the courts, while recognising the force of the sanctity of life principle, which is directly implicated here, have given the impression that it is ultimately subordinate to the principle of patient autonomy ...

Nevertheless, it does not follow that a person enjoys an unlimited choice over the *manner* of their death, in so far as additional insult to the sanctity of life principle will be entailed. It is, for instance, generally accepted ... that a doctor is entitled to override a patient's refusal of treatment following a suicide attempt ... Arguably, a case where a pregnant woman will die without obstetric intervention also possesses features which set it apart from other cases in which life-saving treatment is refused. Most obviously, not only the woman but also her foetus, which (whatever its other attributes) is a potent symbol of life, stands to die. (Indeed, in cases where, without intervention, the woman's womb will rupture there is a sense in which the foetus operates as the instrument of death.) There is, perhaps, also the consideration that such deaths, if allowed, would take place in the maternity wards of hospitals.

For further discussion of the issues arising from the refusal of life-saving treatment, see Chapter 3.

Despite the failure to address the important substantive issue identified in the last extract, the Court of Appeal did enunciate a number of useful procedural guidelines to be followed in Caesarean cases:

Butler-Sloss LJ: It might be helpful to make some comments on the practice to be followed when the medical profession feel it necessary to seek declarations from the courts:

(1) The court is unlikely to entertain an application for a declaration unless the capacity of the patient to consent to or refuse the medical intervention is in issue.

(2) For the time being, at least, the doctors ought to seek a ruling from the High Court on the issue of competence.

(3) Those in charge should identify a potential problem as early as possible so that both the hospital and the patient can obtain legal advice.

In this case, for instance, the problem was identified at the ante-natal clinic.

(4) It is highly desirable that, in any case where it is not an emergency, steps are taken to bring it before the court, before it becomes an emergency, to remove the extra pressure from the parties and the court and to enable proper instructions to be taken, particularly from the patient and where possible give the opportunity for the court to hear oral evidence, if appropriate.

(5)   The hearing should be *inter partes*.

(6)   The mother should be represented in all cases, unless, exceptionally, she does not wish to be. If she is unconscious she should have a guardian *ad litem*.

(7)   The Official Solicitor should be notified of all applications to the High Court. It would be helpful if, at least for the time being, the Official Solicitor was prepared to continue to act as amicus curiae, in cases where he is not asked to be the guardian *ad litem*. He will build up a body of expertise which will be most helpful to the judge hearing the application.

(8)   There should in general be some evidence, preferably but not necessarily from a psychiatrist, as to the competence of the patient, if competence is in issue.

(9)   Where time permits, the person identified to give the evidence as to capacity to consent to or refuse treatment should be made aware of the observations we have made in this judgment.

(10) In order to be in a position to assess a patient's best interests the judge should be provided, where possible and if time allows, with information about the circumstances of and relevant background material about the patient.

These guidelines have since been incorporated in Department of Health Circular EL (97) 32, issued in June 1997.

Subsequently, in *St George's Health Care NHS Trust v S* [1999] Fam 26, the Court of Appeal dealt with an action in judicial review by a woman who had been sectioned under the Mental Health Act 1983 and then subjected to an enforced Caesarean. The latter was authorised by a trial judge who was misled by the trust into thinking that the patient was already in labour. In ruling that the latter had been subjected to an unlawful battery, the court reiterated many of the principles it had outlined in the *Re MB* case.

CHAPTER 9

MENTAL HEALTH LAW

BACKGROUND

Introduction

At first sight it may be thought that mental illness should be treated like any other form of medical disorder. However, there are special difficulties involved in deciding precisely what we mean when we say that someone is mentally ill. Perhaps this is inevitable, given the nebulous nature of mental illness and its overlap with antisocial behaviour, the holding of bizarre beliefs, and eccentric lifestyles. In addition, the mentally ill are often stigmatised and misunderstood. Furthermore, the Mental Health Act (MHA) 1983 provides for the compulsory detention of both criminal offenders and non-offenders if they are mentally ill and satisfy a number of other conditions. It is clear, therefore, that mental health law raises distinct ethical and legal issues.

Leaving aside the special problems that can arise when dealing with the mentally ill criminal offender, it is generally accepted that compulsorily detaining someone who has committed no offence is probably the most serious interference with civil liberties that a state can impose. In consequence, its ethical underpinning must be beyond reproach, and the mechanism which allows this to be done should be open to the most searching scrutiny. We are concerned here with balancing, on the one hand, the rights of the individual, and, on the other hand, both the utilitarian desire to protect the community at large, and the paternalistic impulse to protect the individual from harming himself. This is reflected in the MHA 1983, by which compulsory civil detention, either for assessment or treatment, is permitted when the patient is suffering from certain forms of mental disorder and ought to be detained either to protect himself or others (the latter being a mixture of paternalism and community protection).

Although in most areas of medical law the Human Rights Act (HRA) 1998 might be used to some effect, it is particularly pertinent to mental health law because of the power of the State to detain, without consent, people who have been diagnosed as suffering from a number of forms of mental disorder. Article 5 is particularly relevant.

Article 5 (right to liberty and security) provides that:

1 ... No one shall be deprived of his liberty save in the following cases and in accordance with a procedure prescribed by law:

...

(e) the lawful detention of persons for the prevention of the spreading of infectious diseases, of persons of unsound mind, alcoholics or drug addicts or vagrants

...

4 Everyone who is deprived of his liberty by arrest or detention shall be entitled to take proceedings by which the lawfulness of his detention shall be decided speedily by a court and his release ordered if the detention is not lawful.

The European Court of Human Rights, in *Winterwerp v Netherlands* (1979) 2 EHRR 387, set out the conditions which a national government has to satisfy in order for detention on the ground of 'unsoundness of mind' to apply:

1 except in emergency cases, a true mental disorder has been established by objective medical expertise;

2 the detention must be effected in accordance with a procedure prescribed by law;

3 the mental disorder is of a kind or degree warranting compulsory confinement;

4 the validity of continued confinement depends upon the persistence of such a disorder.

In *Aerts v Belgium* (2000) 29 EHRR 50, the European Court held that the detention of a mentally disordered person will only be lawful in terms of Article 5 if effected in a hospital, clinic or other appropriate institution.

Article 6 (right to a fair trial) has some application if a patient is claiming that his rights have been contravened, for example, under Article 5, and he has not been given the opportunity of putting his case before a court. Article 3 (the prohibition on torture or inhuman or degrading treatment or punishment) has been used successfully in the context of treatment in prison of a suicidal prisoner who was deemed to be vulnerable and who was not given the appropriate care in a medical, as opposed to a penal, context (*Keenan v United Kingdom* (2001) 33 EHRR 38. Articles of the Convention will be referred to, where appropriate, below.

What is mental illness?

There have been a number of writers who have questioned the existence of mental illness, or at least, questioned whether it is a *medical* condition. Interestingly, these views have been harnessed to both right and left wing perspectives. The American doctor and writer, Thomas Szasz, is one of the most well known proponents and approaches it from a libertarian analysis. His view is that *all* illness has a *physical* pathology, and the psychiatrist must be either a malevolent meddler or a benevolent, but misguided healer, and as he sees psychiatry as a study of personal conduct, and maintains that psychiatric interventions are directed at moral, rather than medical problems, the view he takes is that of the psychiatrist as malevolent meddler. Szasz's pithy summary of his thesis is uncompromising:

Szasz, T, *The Myth of Mental Illness: Foundations of a Theory of Personal Conduct*, revised edition, 1974, New York: Harper and Row, p 267:

Summary

The principal arguments advanced in this book and their implications may be summarised as follows.

1 Strictly speaking, disease or illness can affect only the body; hence, there can be no mental illness.

2 'Mental illness' is a metaphor. Minds can be 'sick' only in the sense that jokes are 'sick' or economies are 'sick'.

3 Psychiatric diagnoses are stigmatising labels, phrased to resemble medical diagnoses and applied to persons whose behaviour annoys or offends others.

4   Those who suffer from and complain of their own behaviour are usually classified as 'neurotic'; those whose behaviour makes others suffer, and about whom others complain, are usually classified as 'psychotic'.

5   Mental illness is not something a person has, but is something he does or is.

6   If there is no mental illness there can be no hospitalisation, treatment, or cure for it. Of course, people may change their behaviour or personality, with or without psychiatric intervention. Such intervention is nowadays called 'treatment', and the change, if it proceeds in a direction approved by society, 'recovery' or 'cure'.

7   The introduction of psychiatric considerations into the administration of the criminal law – for example, the insanity plea and verdict, diagnoses of mental incompetence to stand trial, and so forth, corrupt the law and victimise the subject on whose behalf they are ostensibly employed.

8   Personal conduct is always rule-following, strategic, meaningful. Patterns of interpersonal and social relations may be regarded and analysed as if they were games, the behaviour of the players being governed by explicit or tacit game rules.

9   In most types of voluntary psychotherapy, the therapist tries to elucidate the inexplicit game rules by which the client conducts himself; and to help the client scrutinise the goals and values of the life games he plays.

10   There is no medical, moral, or legal justification for involuntary psychiatric interventions. They are crimes against humanity.

Szasz has continued to maintain his basic contentions:

Szasz, T, 'Psychiatric diagnosis, psychiatric power and psychiatric abuse' (1994) 20 JME 135–38:

Psychiatric practice, as the term implies, is a practical, not a theoretical, enterprise. Accordingly, so long as psychiatrists continue to assign the role of mental patient to persons against their will, that fact will remain a fundamental characteristic of psychiatric practice ...

Art historians, drama critics, musicologists, and many other scholars also make subjective classifications. However, lacking State-sanctioned power over persons, their classifications do not lead to anyone's being deprived of life, liberty, or property. Surely, the plastic surgeon's classification of beauty is subjective. But because the plastic surgeon cannot treat his or her patient without the patient's consent, there cannot be any political abuse of plastic surgery. It is as simple, and inconvenient, as that.

Whilst not doubting the sincerity of Szasz's views, it is easy to see how they might be attractive to those who wish to reduce public spending on the care of those diagnosed as being mentally ill.

The British psychoanalyst, the late RD Laing, whose most well known publication is *The Divided Self*, first published in 1959 (reissued 1990, Harmondsworth: Penguin), took a different approach, and did not deny the existence of mental 'illness', but saw it as the reaction of a normal person to abnormal social pressures, for example, oppressive family situations. He related the experience of mental illness very much to being out of kilter with the social norm. It is not difficult to see how this approach might be used in libertarian and even anarchistic arguments against traditional social organisations. It must, however, be said that, interesting though theories such as those of Szasz and Laing are, they were never brought into the mainstream of psychiatry.

However, although most people would not dispute the existence of mental illness, there is an inevitable difference between patients who are physically ill, and patients who are mentally ill, in that it is by no means agreed what is meant by *mental* illness. Although there may be some dispute about areas of physical illness, generally, it is acknowledged that one can point to examples of physical 'normality', but clearly it would be futile to attempt to define a psychologically normal person. Whilst it is accepted that there can be desirable deviations from the physical norm (for example, athletic prowess), we are used to thinking of most significant deviations from the physical 'norm' as being undesirable. However, significant deviations from the psychological 'norm' can be *much better* than the norm, for example, in intellectual ability or capacity for forgiveness and compassion. Furthermore, in the case of physical characteristics, it is easier to decide whether the deviation is desirable or not, not least because mental qualities are essentially part of personal identity.

Unfortunately, as will be seen from the following, the MHA 1983, whilst referring to a number of 'mental' conditions, does nothing to clarify the difficulties in defining mental illness. There is no definition of mental illness in the Act, nor is there any guidance in the Code of Practice produced to assist those using the provisions of the Act; it is simply a matter of clinical judgment in each case. Similarly, there has been little in the way of judicial consideration of the concept. One of the few cases is *W v L* [1974] QB 711, in which the Court of Appeal considered whether a young man was mentally ill following a series of acts of violence and cruelty. He had hanged a puppy, strangled a terrier with wire, made a cat inhale ammonia and then cut its throat, and had put another cat in the gas oven. When he turned his attention away from family pets, and threatened his wife with a knife and offered other forms of violence towards her, he was admitted as an emergency under the provisions of the Mental Health Act (MHA) 1959. Both Denning MR and Orr LJ accepted the medical evidence that the patient was psychotic, and did not consider the meaning of the expression 'mentally ill'. However, Lawton LJ made these observations (pp 718–19):

> **Lawton LJ:** The facts of this case show how difficult the fitting of particular instances into the statutory classification can be. Lord Denning MR and Orr LJ have pointed out that there is no definition of 'mental illness'. The words are ordinary words of the English language. They have no particular medical significance. They have no particular legal significance. How should the court construe them? The answer in my judgment is to be found in the advice which Lord Reid recently gave in *Cozens v Brutus* [1973] AC 854, p 861 namely, that ordinary words of the English language should be construed in the way that ordinary sensible people would construe them. That being, in my judgment, the right test, then I ask myself, what would the ordinary sensible person have said about the patient's condition in this case if he had been informed of his behaviour to the dogs, the cat and his wife? In my judgment such a person would have said: 'Well, the fellow is obviously mentally ill'. If that be right, then, although the case may fall within the definition of 'psychopathic disorder' in s 4(4), it also falls within the classification of 'mental illness'; and there is the added medical fact that when the EEG was taken there were indications of a clinical character showing some abnormality of the brain. It is that application of the sensible person's assessment of the condition, plus the medical indication, which in my

judgment brought the case within the classification of mental illness, and justified the finding of the county court judge.

If it is the case that the words 'mental illness' are ordinary words and *have no particular medical significance*, what are the implications of this? In some ways this is an extraordinary conclusion, because if it has no medical significance, what significance does it have? The 'any normal person can see he's ill' definition of mental illness is a worrying one, and it adds fuel to the arguments of people such as Szasz.

On the difficulty of making precise medical classifications of mental disorders, see the House of Lords case of *R v (On the Application of B) v Ashworth Hospital Authority* [2005] UKHL 20.

The DHSS Consultative Document on the MHA 1959 in 1976 considered a closed definition of mental illness which would have required one or more of the following characteristics:

DHSS, *DHSS Consultative Document*, 1976, London: HMSO, Appendix II:

(i)   more than temporary impairment of intellectual functions shown by a failure of memory, orientation, comprehension and learning capacity;

(ii) more than temporary alteration of mood of such degree as to give rise to the patient having a delusional appraisal of his situation, his past or his future, or that of others, or to the lack of any appraisal;

(iii) delusional beliefs, persecutory, jealous or grandiose;

(iv) abnormal perceptions associated with delusional misinterpretations of events;

(v)   thinking so disordered as to prevent the patient making a reasonable appraisal of his situation or having reasonable communication with others.

In the event, a closed definition was not adopted, for reasons stated in the 1978 Review of the Act:

Department of Health and Social Security, *Review of the 1959 Mental Health Act*, Cmnd 7320, 1978, London: HMSO, para 1.17:

There have been a few suggestions as to how mental illness might be defined, but comments have underlined the difficulties of producing a definition which would be likely to stand the test of time. Nor has there been much evidence that the present lack of definition of mental illness leads to any particular problems; the Government therefore proposes to leave it undefined.

The objection based on 'standing the test of time' illustrates the curious nature of our concept of mental illness: the notion that it will change with the passage of time. Whilst it is doubtless true that attitudes change (homosexuality was, until 1974, classified by the American Psychiatric Association as a mental disorder (see Kennedy, I, *The Unmasking of Medicine*, 1981, London: Allen & Unwin, Chapter 1)), it is worrying that a less volatile attitude to mental illness cannot be reflected in a workable definition.

There are a number of different ways of attempting to define the essential ingredient(s) of mental illness. Some consider it helpful to use lack of insight into one's own condition, for example, as an essential element of mental illness for the purpose of compulsory detention. It may be thought that this would certainly be in accordance with traditional views that psychoses, which are the most serious psychiatric illnesses, are characterised by lack of insight, but some psychiatrists would argue that many psychotic patients have considerable insight, whilst many suffering from neurotic conditions have little (see, for example, Gelder *et al*, *Oxford Textbook of Psychiatry*, 1996, Oxford: OUP). Some commentators argue that by encouraging patients to have 'insight', psychiatrists are manipulating them into co-operating with treatment regimes, perhaps as voluntary patients. Michael Cavadino has summarised the process by which patients may become manipulated:

> **Cavadino, M, *Mental Health Law in Context*, 1989, Aldershot: Dartmouth, p 30:**
>
> It is usually thought in psychiatry that 'lack of insight' is a bad sign, while the acquisition of insight shows that the patient is on the road to recovery. Its social significance is this: patients with 'insight' conform to sick role etiquette by acknowledging that their present state is undesirable, that they are ill, and that they should try to get well, typically by co-operating with the doctor ...
>
> (This, of course, can put some people who do not believe that they are mentally ill in a classic 'Catch 22' situation: if they deny that they are ill, this may not be seen as a sign of health, but as a sign that they are in a particularly bad way, and particularly in need of drastic, perhaps compulsory intervention.)

Another approach is to define the illness by the presence of suffering. However, as Gelder *et al* say, it cannot be applied to everyone who would usually be regarded as ill, so, for example, 'patients with mania may feel unusually well and not experience suffering, though most people would regard them as mentally ill'. Although some mental illness has an organic origin, this is not often possible to locate, so defining mental illness by reference to the pathological process will not do.

If one looks at the two main psychiatric diagnostic manuals published by the American Psychiatric Association and the World Health Organisation (*Diagnostic and Statistical Manual of Mental Disorders*, 4th edn, 1994, Washington DC: American Psychiatric Press and *The Classification of Mental and Behavioural Disorders*, 1992, Geneva: World Health Organisation, known as DSM IV and ICD–10, respectively), it will be seen that the symptoms of all known psychiatric disorders are described in some detail, but, not surprisingly, 'mental illness' as such is not considered.

It should be noted that the category for admission for assessment is much wider than that for treatment. Under previous legislation (MHA 1959), this was known as admission for observation, and there was doubt whether it included treating the patient (surprisingly, the Act made no provision for treatment, so it was left to the clinical judgment of the doctors concerned). However, under the 1983 Act it is possible to treat the patient admitted for assessment (s 56(1)). Of particular relevance in this regard is the fact that it has been held that there is power to admit a patient for assessment under s 2, if he appears to be suffering from mental disorder, even though it turns out on assessment that the patient is not: *R v Kirklees Metropolitan BC ex p C* [1993] 2 FLR 187, p 190:

> **Lloyd LJ**: In passing, I should say that I do not, as at present advised, accept Mr Spencer's argument that s 2 is also confined to cases where the patient is in fact suffering from mental disorder. Having regard to the definition of patient in s 145 there is, in my view, power to admit a patient for assessment under s 2, if he appears to be suffering from mental disorder, on the ground that he or she is so suffering, even

though it turns out on assessment that she is not. Any other construction would unnecessarily emasculate the beneficial power under s 2 and confine assessment to choice of treatment.

Given these conclusions, it can be argued that if it is really for assessment, then treatment should not be possible without a patient's genuine consent.

Justifying detention

The Percy Commission, which reported before the MHA 1959, stated that it was wrong to detain someone compulsorily, before they had committed any criminal offence:

> **Lord Percy of Newcastle,** *Report of the Royal Commission on the Law relating to Mental Illness and Mental Deficiency,* **Cmd 169, 1954–57, London: HMSO (the Percy Commission), para 348:**
>
> Preventive detention under the ordinary criminal law may only be applied to offenders over a certain age who have a definite criminal record of a certain number of convictions for serious offences; and even preventive detention lasts only for a fixed period, after which the prisoner must be released even if it is almost certain that he will then commit further crimes. If one is to apply preventive control to psychopathic patients under wider conditions than these, one is in effect applying to them preventive detention in hospital in circumstances which would not justify preventive detention in prison under the criminal law. Whether or not special forms of control are justified on these grounds depends on how accurate the diagnosis of the patient's condition and the prognosis of his future behaviour is likely to be, and on the extent to which it is fair to assume that the risks to society from persons suffering from these forms of mental abnormality are greater than the risks which society runs from criminals who are not considered to be mentally abnormal.

Apart from having to be suffering from some form of mental disorder, the person compulsorily detained under the Act for assessment 'ought to be so detained in the interests of his own health or safety or with a view to the protection of other persons' (s 2(2)(b)), and in the case of a person compulsorily detained for treatment, it must be *'necessary* for the health or safety of the patient or for the protection of other persons that he should receive such treatment and it cannot be provided unless he is detained under this section' (s 3(2)(c)). It will be seen that, as with the type of mental disorder concerned, the 'protection' condition is wider in the case of admission for assessment, being 'ought to be so detained in the interests of' as opposed to 'necessary for' and this is hardly surprising. However, it is not clear as to what sort of risks must be involved for patients and/or third parties.

The Code of Practice contains no guidance on the safety of the patient; perhaps it is thought to be self-evident, but the assessment of the risk and the probability of the risk turning into reality must surely be of central importance. There is guidance on health risk which states:

> **Department of Health and Welsh Office,** *Mental Health Act 1983, Code of Practice,* **London: HMSO, para 2.9:**
>
> ... those assessing patients must consider any evidence suggesting that the patient's mental health will deteriorate if he does not receive treatment; the reliability of such evidence which may include the known history of the individual's mental

disorder; the views of the patient and of any relatives or close friends, especially those living with the patient, about the likely course of his illness and the possibility of its improving; the impact that any future deterioration or lack of improvement would have on relatives or close friends, especially those living with the patient, including an assessment of his ability and willingness to cope; and whether there are other methods of coping with the expected deterioration or lack of improvement.

Is the desire to protect from self-harm paternalistic and unsustainable? It has been argued that there is no interference with the positive freedom of the individual because there is a competing right held by the patient himself. The argument states that a person in ill health has reduced capacities to act and therefore less ability to make effective choices. In other words the patient will be *more free* as a result of the paternalistic intervention. Cavadino gives a good account of the civil libertarian, and other issues raised by the treatment of the mentally ill.

Cavadino, M, *Mental Health Law in Context*, 1989, Aldershot: Dartmouth, pp 138–41:

... liberal thinkers such as Isaiah Berlin (1969) have usually adopted the 'negative concept of freedom'. Negative freedom is defined as the absence of coercion or constraint imposed on the individual by other people. (I use the word 'liberty' to mean freedom in this negative sense.) In this sense, everyone who is not prevented from doing so by other people is equally free to run a mile in under four minutes or to dine at the Ritz Hotel, although only some people (those fast enough, or rich enough) actually can.

There is, however, a rival concept of freedom which also has its adherents. 'Freedom in the positive sense' may be defined as 'the ability to make effective choices about one's own life'. In this positive sense, I am not free to run a mile in under four minutes, or to dine at the Ritz in my present financial circumstances. For to be 'positively free' is to be actually able to perform the action in question, not simply to be unconstrained by other people or by the law. To be sure, negative freedom (absence of constraint) is necessary in order to have positive freedom; but to be positively free additionally requires, first, the physical and psychological capacities to carry out the action or course of action in question; and second, access to any material resources necessary to perform the action. So I am not free to dine at the Ritz if I cannot physically get there or cannot afford it.

Surely liberal theory of any kind – even those which emphasise the importance of 'negative freedom' – must presuppose that 'positive freedom' is of value. For what else is the point of valuing negative freedom (as liberalism does) if this negative freedom does not actually enable people to make real, effective choices? For all that some liberals vehemently insist on employing the negative definition of freedom, it must be 'positive freedom' which is the intrinsically valuable commodity to human beings, with 'negative freedom' only of instrumental value in so far as it is conducive to real ability to choose. In short, if negative freedom is to be valued, this can only be because positive freedom is of more fundamental value.

If we accept that positive freedom is of value, and necessarily is of value to every human being, then any defensible philosophy of morality must accept as a basic principle that every individual has an equal right to maximum positive freedom. This is the 'positive freedom principle' (PFP). I suggest that this principle provides a much more consistent and coherent approach than liberal theories typically do ...

The presumption in favour of liberty must be a strong one. For as is generally accepted over a wide spectrum of political views, States and other powerful authorities have a distressing tendency to restrict liberty excessively (thereby depriving people of the positive freedom to which they are entitled). Given this, there are good reasons for holding (as liberalism does) that people should not be deprived of substantial liberty without strong justification being adduced. Thus it is indeed right that laws should be framed to protect negative freedom with clear criteria and adequate procedural safeguards.

What should the criteria for deprivation of liberty be? First, it is clear that the protection of others can in principle be a valid justification for deprivation of liberty. The potential victims of violent assault have a right to personal safety which comes into competition with the right to liberty of the potential detainee, since the infliction of injury represents an unjustified diminution of the positive freedom of the victim. The injured person's real abilities to act are diminished by injury and totally extinguished by death, because injury and death reduce or remove a person's physical capacities.

This is not to say, however, that people may be justly deprived of liberty without further ado if there is any evidence or belief, however slight, that they might be dangerous to others. The nature of the risk to others must be assessed together with its likelihood of eventuating. As Dworkin has suggested, we 'should treat a man against his will only when the danger he presents is vivid' [Dworkin, R, *Taking Rights Seriously*, 1978, London: Duckworth, p 11]. It also follows from the strength of the presumption in favour of liberty that cogent evidence of the patient's dangerousness should normally be adduced under conditions of due process before detention can be justified. (And incidentally, as we saw in Chapter 8, a psychiatrist's assessment that a patient is dangerous is by no means always 'cogent evidence'; due process requires that such evidence should be carefully scrutinised to assess its validity.)

What about parentalism [paternalism]? Here again a case can be made for interfering with the individual's (negative) liberty on the ground that there is a more important competing right to be protected. In this case, however, the competing right is not one owned by some other individual, but by the patient, the same person who has the right to liberty. If the intervention results in the preservation or promotion of the health of the patient, this could result overall in the maximisation of the patient's positive freedom. For a person in ill health has reduced capacities to act, and consequently less ability to make effective choices ...

(Note that this argument is not a utilitarian one. It does not rest on the contention that the patient will be happier or will suffer less if the intervention occurs. It argues that the patient will be more free overall if parentalism is allowed.)

This is a persuasive justification, but it depends upon much sharper definitions of self-harm, and the possibility of accurate diagnoses which at present we do not have.

As to the protection of others, it may be accepted even on strong libertarian grounds that detention of someone who, for example violently assaults others, is consistent with the concept of the freedom of the individual as the patient will be seriously interfering with their liberty. However, there are grave difficulties in the concept of 'dangerousness':

Price, DPT, 'Civil commitment of the mentally ill: compelling arguments for reform' (1994) 2 Med L Rev 321:

It would certainly be unfair to suppose that mentally disordered persons could be involuntarily admitted to hospital because they as a class are more likely to be dangerous to others than non-mentally disordered persons, as there is no convincing evidence to support this assumption ...

If dangerousness is to be a criteria [*sic*] justifying commitment, some individual assessment of dangerous is required in each case. [Reprinted by permission of Oxford University Press.]

In the Act itself (see p 463, above), the requirement regarding harm to others is weak: there is no suggestion that the severity of the harm, and likelihood of the risk are relevant.

The Code of Practice deals with the protection of others, and it is clear from this that, whilst it includes the protection of others from psychological as well as physical harm, risk to property is not enough:

Department of Health and Welsh Office, *Mental Health Act 1983, Code of Practice*, London: HMSO, para 2.9:

In considering 'the protection of other persons' (see ss 2(2)(b) and 3(2)(c)) it is essential to assess both the nature and likelihood of risk and the level of risk others are entitled to be protected from taking into account:

• reliability of evidence including any relevant details of the patient's clinical history and past behaviour including contact with other agencies;

• any relevant details of the patient's medical history and past behaviour;

• the degree of risk and its nature. A risk of physical harm, or serious persistent psychological harm, to others is an indicator of the need for compulsory admission;

• the willingness and ability to cope with the risk, by those with whom the patient lives and whether there are alternative options available for managing the risk.

Referring to the sort of individual assessment envisaged by the Code, Price goes on to say:

Price, DPT, 'Civil commitment of the mentally ill: compelling arguments for reform' (1994) 2 Med L Rev 321:

However, even allowing for this, the difficulties are just beginning. Dangerousness is a social construct, it is not a psychiatric phenomenon and thus not peculiarly within the competence of psychiatrists to assess in individual cases. In any event, the problems in predicting dangerousness are immense. Almost all studies of predictive accuracy show that there are likely to be more false positives than true positives in any defined population. This is hardly surprising in view of the (relative) rarity of violent conduct and the fact that violent or dangerous conduct is at least partly a product of a person's environment (in other words it is situation specific). Some studies have shown very substantial overpredictions of dangerousness by psychiatrists, which is partially due to the understandable tendency to err on what can be considered from on perspective as 'the safe side'. The potential for erosion of civil liberties through the unwarranted removal of liberty is then clear. [Reprinted by permission of Oxford University Press.]

In 2000, government proposals for reform of the 1983 Act envisaged more draconian measures for 'dangerous' patients (*Reforming the Mental Health Act*, Cm 5016–1, 2000, London: DoH and the Home Office), and the Draft Mental Health Bill of 2002 repeated such proposals, and although the 2004 Bill contained modifications it has still given cause for concern (see below, Proposals for Reform).

Statutory control

History

Brenda Hoggett sets out the development of the law relating to the control of mentally disordered people. After describing the provisions of the Lunacy Act 1890 and the Mental Treatment Act 1930, she goes on:

Hoggett, B, *Mental Health Law*, 4th edn, 1996, London: Sweet & Maxwell, pp 6–7:

Until the 1959 Act, then, there were three different types of patient in mental illness hospitals – voluntary and temporary patients under the 1930 Act and patients certified under the various procedures in the 1890 Act. For mental 'defectives' there was a totally different, if rather less complex, set of procedures under the Mental Deficiency Acts of 1913 and 1927. These did not include a voluntary status, but the institutions were not expressly prohibited from taking patients without formality. After 1952, this was officially encouraged for short stays, and the Percy Commission recommended that it could be extended to long stay patients without waiting for legislation. In the Commission's report, and in the 1959 Act which implemented it, a determined effort was made to break down the rigid legal boundaries and integrate the separate legal systems relating to 'lunacy' and 'mental deficiency'.

Two developments lay behind much of the Percy Commission's thinking. First was the introduction of the National Health Service in 1948. This had led to most hospitals of any type being vested in the then Ministry of Health, and to some rearrangement of the functions of the Board of Control, but nothing had been done to remove the rigid and antiquated categorisation of mental hospitals. The Commission believed that there was no longer any need for strict legal control over public hospitals. Further, as improvements depend upon the availability of resources, full responsibility should rest with the government department which controlled the allocation of resources within the health service as a whole. The Board of Control could safely be abolished, and with it the legal segregation of mental hospitals from the main stream of hospital development.

Second was the great optimism about the advances in medical treatment for the major mental illnesses, through psycho-surgery, electro-convulsive therapy and above all the new breed of psychotropic drugs, the major tranquillisers. These made it possible for increasing numbers of seriously disordered patients to be discharged into the community or treated on clinical wards in ordinary hospital conditions. It no longer seemed necessary for the law to assume that these patients were inevitably different from the physically sick or injured. For the most part, they could be admitted to hospital in just the same way. Compulsory procedures could be kept only for those for whom they were absolutely necessary. Once in hospital, their treatment and care could be left in the hands of the medical profession. As many as possible would be discharged back into the community just like other patients.

Hence, removing the legal controls over mental patients was inextricably linked with removing the legal controls over their doctors. The 1983 Act was mainly concerned to reimpose some of the latter.

It is interesting that there has been a steady decline in the number of compulsorily detained patients:

Hoggett, B, *Mental Health Law*, 4th edn, 1996, London: Sweet & Maxwell, p 8:

More significant still was the decline in the proportion of patients in hospital at any one time who were liable to be detained. In 1955, 7% of those in mental illness hospitals were certified, because most voluntary patients stayed for only a short time and compulsion was still used for the long stay chronically ill; and virtually all mentally handicapped patients were detained. By 1986, fewer than 5% of all resident patients in NHS mental illness or mental handicap hospitals were detained. Figures for resident patients are no longer published, perhaps because the aim is to phase out the use of hospital as a place of permanent residence, and so the turnover is such that it would be misleading to give a snapshot on one particular day. The total number of detained residents is now thought to be around 11,500.

Although, as Hoggett points out, the apparent reduction in the number of compulsorily detained patients, is largely because before the 1983 Act there was no statutory 'voluntary' status, but it can also be argued that during an admission for assessment, the patient can be 'stabilised' in such a way as they will remain as a voluntary patient, rather than be detained further for treatment. This raises the concerns expressed above in relation to the potential for manipulation of patients.

Current scheme under the Mental Health Act 1983

We saw in Chapters 3 and 4 that the Mental Capacity Act 2005 provides for treatment of those who lack capacity to make medical treatment decisions. The relationship of that Act with the MHA 1983 and any statutory replacement has been the subject of debate and concern. This, and some of the proposed reforms are considered at the end of this chapter but, at the present time, the current legislation is the MHA 1983 (the Act). This will be examined in some detail later in this chapter, but it may be helpful to summarise the main provisions here, as these will be referred to when considering some of the fundamental issues raised by the care and control of the mentally disordered. It should also be noted that, pursuant to s 118 of the Act, the Secretary of State must issue a Code of Practice for the guidance of those formally involved in invoking the provisions of the Act and the latest edition was issued in 1999.

   Although some of the most contentious aspects of the Act have been considered above, the formal requirements for detention should also be noted. For a detailed and exhaustive examination of the statutory provisions, readers are advised to consult Richard Jones's excellent guide to the Act (*Mental Health Act Manual*, 8th edn, 2003, London: Sweet & Maxwell).

Detention

Admission for assessment is dealt with in s 2 of the Act, and provides for compulsory admission for a period of up to 28 days. The patient can be treated during this time.

   Under s 3 of the Act, patients can be admitted for longer periods. Admission under this section is for six months and renewable. The requirements that must be satisfied are somewhat more stringent than under s 2.

   Under both ss 2 and 3, two doctors must make the appropriate recommendations for admission; if, however, it is a case of urgent necessity, one doctor's recommendation will suffice to justify admission for up to 72 hours (s 4). Section 136 also empowers police officers to remove someone who appears to be suffering from a mental disorder to a place of safety for up to 72 hours. Compulsory detention of patients who entered hospital on a voluntary basis is dealt with in s 5 of the Act.

The Act also provides for patients to be received into the guardianship of the local social services authority or of a person approved by the authority (s 7). The guardian is empowered to impose residence and treatment requirements.

Treatment

Under s 63 of the Act, the consent of a compulsorily detained patient is not required for treatment for the mental disorder from which he is suffering. As we shall see below, this has given rise to conceptual and ethical difficulties. However, certain types of treatment, such as psychosurgery, have more stringent requirements attached to their administration, and ss 57 and 58 impose additional conditions upon such treatments being given.

Safeguards for the patient

Patients compulsorily admitted have a right to appeal to a Mental Health Review tribunal, in addition to a number of common law rights.

DETENTION

Mental disorder

Brief and somewhat unhelpful definitions of mental disorder and the other conditions referred to in the Act are contained within s 1:

1 Application of Act: 'mental disorder'

(1) The provisions of this Act shall have effect with respect to the reception, care and treatment of mentally disordered patients, the management of their property and other related matters ...

(2) In this Act–

'mental disorder' means mental illness, arrested or incomplete development of mind, psychopathic disorder and any other disorder or disability of mind and 'mentally disordered' shall be construed accordingly ...

Under s 1(3) of the Act, definitions exclude promiscuity, immoral conduct, sexual deviancy, alcohol or drug dependency without more. The *Review of the Mental Health Act 1959*, carried out by the Department of Health and Social Security (Cmnd 7320, 1978, London: HMSO) concluded that it was inappropriate to regard such problems as mental disorders. Note that Art 5 of the European Convention provides for detention of persons who are alcoholic or addicted to drugs, although the Act does not permit this, without more. It has been recognised that, where there is a 'dual diagnosis' of people with both mental illness and either drug or alcohol problems, there is a risk that they can fall between the mental health services, and substance misuse services. The Department of Health has issued guidance for both providers on 'dual diagnosis'.

The issue of sexual deviancy was considered in *R v Mental Health Act Commission ex p W* (1988) *The Times*, 27 May. The case concerned the administration of a drug known as Goserelin, a synthesis of hormones designed to reduce the male sex drive, and was primarily concerned with whether there was a need for the patient's consent to treatment, but the court also had to consider whether the treatment was for mental disorder at all, because of the provisions of s 1(3):

> **Stuart Smith LJ**: Where the mental disorder was quite distinct from the sexual deviancy referred to in s 1(3) of the Act, and the proposed treatment was solely for the purpose of dealing with the sexual deviancy condition, it was difficult to see how that could be treatment for mental disorder, although in practice it seemed likely that the sexual problem would, as here, be inextricably linked with the mental disorder and the treatment for one would be the treatment for the other.

In *St George's Healthcare NHS Trust v S* [1998] 3 All ER 673, there had been an attempt to use the provisions of the Act to detain a pregnant woman and perform a non-consensual Caesarean section. She had attended a GP practice when 36 weeks pregnant, not having previously sought antenatal care. She had pre-eclampsia and was advised that she should be admitted to hospital for an induced delivery. She refused this, wanting her baby to be born naturally. A social worker became involved and an application was made under s 2 of the Act (compulsory detention in hospital for 'assessment'). The Court of Appeal was highly critical of the way in which the case was handled from both the point of view of the law and medicine (even the way in which the court procedure was used was flawed). For example, the hospital sought legal advice because it was erroneously believed that treatment could not be given under a s 2 admission. The doctor assessing the patient found her to have capacity, although subsequently reconsidered this and amended her note to say that her mental state may be affecting her capacity. The mental state referred to was diagnosed as moderate depression. After approval by the court (the judge having been erroneously informed that it was a 'life and death situation' with only minutes to spare), the child was delivered by Caesarean section. The following day the woman was examined again, and the consultant found 'no current abnormalities in her mental state'. The s 2 order was discharged. The Court of Appeal granted judicial review and stated that someone not suffering from mental disorder could not be detained under the MHA 1983 against his will merely because his thinking process was unusual and contrary to the views of the overwhelming majority of the community. It was clear that the purpose of detention was to manage her pregnancy and confinement and not to assess and treat a mental condition.

Mental impairment

1 ...

    (2) ... 'Mental impairment' means a state of arrested or incomplete development of mind (not amounting to severe mental impairment) which includes significant impairment of intelligence and social functioning and is associated with abnormally aggressive or seriously irresponsible conduct on the part of the person concerned ...

Note that the arrested or incomplete development must be accompanied by the defined conduct. 'Severe mental impairment' is defined in the same way with the additional requirement that the intelligence and social functioning must be severely impaired. The mentally impaired are, therefore, those who would at one time have been described as mentally handicapped or mentally retarded, and who, in more politically correct parlance, are now often referred to as having learning difficulties.

However, it must be noted that, in order to be compulsorily detained under the Act for anything longer than 28 days for assessment, the impairment must be associated with antisocial behaviour of an 'abnormal' nature.

The question of what constitutes 'seriously irresponsible conduct' was raised in *Re F (Mental Health Act: Guardianship)* [2000] 1 FLR 192. The Court of Appeal held that a 17 year old's desire to return to her home where she had been severely neglected and sexually exploited was not 'seriously irresponsible'. It was said that the expression should be interpreted as relating to a significant risk of harm to self or others.

Psychopathic disorder

1 ...

    (2) ... 'psychopathic disorder' means a persistent disorder or disability of mind (whether or not including significant impairment of intelligence) which results in abnormally aggressive or seriously irresponsible conduct on the part of the person concerned ...

This is a difficult concept, and has caused a great deal of agonising by those who have considered mental health law reform. It causes difficulty for two main reasons. First, the expression 'psychopathic' has no place in the psychiatric diagnostic manuals. Secondly, it is defined in the Act by reference to behaviour only: '... a persistent disorder or disability of mind ... which results in abnormally aggressive or seriously irresponsible conduct.' Clearly, this implies that there has to be a disorder or disability in the first place, otherwise all criminal offenders would fall into this category, but how, in practice, is the disorder distinguished from its behavioural manifestations?

The Butler Committee which reported on mentally abnormal offenders (Cmnd 6244, 1975, London: HMSO) considered replacing the term 'psychopathic disorder' with 'personality disorder', as the term 'psychopathic' stigmatised those concerned.

Personality disorders are dealt with in the diagnostic manuals. DSM IV, 301.7 and ICD–10, F60.2 deal with the types of personality disorder related to, for example, reckless disregard for safety of self or others, consistent irresponsibility, lack of remorse and so on. The diagnostic criteria in DSM IV are summarised as follows:

DSM IV

Diagnostic criteria for 301.7 – antisocial personality disorder

A There is a pervasive pattern of disregard for and violation of the rights of others occurring since age 15 years, as indicated by three (or more) of the following:

    (1) failure to conform to social norms with respect to lawful behaviours as indicated by repeatedly performing acts that are grounds for arrest;

    (2) deceitfulness, as indicated by repeated use of aliases, or conning others for personal profit or pleasure;

    (3) impulsivity, or failure to plan ahead;

    (4) irritability and aggressiveness, as indicated by repeated physical fights or assaults;

    (5) reckless disregard for safety of self or others;

    (6) consistent irresponsibility, as indicated by repeated failure to sustain consistent work behaviour or honour financial obligations;

    (7) lack of remorse, as indicated by being indifferent to or rationalising having hurt, mistreated or stolen from another …

The difficulty, of course, is that whilst it is accepted that personality disorders have long been recognised by the medical profession, there is an uncomfortable blurring of distinction between those diagnosed as suffering from a psychopathic disorder and those persistent offenders who have not been so diagnosed.

The Butler Committee (*Report of the Committee on Mentally Abnormal Offenders*, Cmnd 6244, 1975, London: HMSO), whilst dissatisfied about the use of the term 'psychopathic', expressed some reservations about replacing this with 'personality disorder', because of its potentially wide interpretation (para 5.25).

The recent White Paper, *Reforming the Mental Health Act*, 2000, Cm 5016–1, London: DoH and the Home Office, proposes that the term 'psychopathic disorder' no longer be used and proposes a new category of 'dangerous people with severe personality disorder' (DSPD). This corresponds with the psychiatric diagnostic classification.

Treatability

This is an interesting concept: in order to be admitted for treatment under s 3, if the patient is suffering from either non-severe mental impairment or a psychopathic disorder, then the treatability condition must also be satisfied, ie, such treatment is likely to alleviate or prevent a deterioration of his condition. What is the purpose behind the treatability test? The *Report of the Royal Commission on the Law relating to Mental Illness and Mental Deficiency* (Cmd 169, 1954–57, London: HMSO) chaired by Lord Percy (the Percy Commission), suggested that 'treatability' be applied to all categories of mental disorder, apart from cases where protection of other people required detention of the patient.

However, the treatability requirement has been restricted to those suffering from non-severe mental impairment and psychopathy. Given the definitions of these conditions, which both contain the requirement that the patient be unable to avoid abnormally aggressive or seriously irresponsible behaviour, it is not surprising that, if there is no treatment for the conditions, hospitals would prefer not to have them as patients. The concern of the Percy Commission, however, was that the potential for abuse of civil liberties should be avoided, ie we are here considering *civil* detention, and it is undesirable that people with antisocial tendencies should be detained *before* committing any offence. As far as psychopathic disorder is concerned, it is generally thought not to be treatable, and detention of the psychopath under s 3 will not often be possible:

Gunn, J and Taylor, P, *Forensic Psychiatry: Clinical, Legal and Ethical Issues*, 1993, Oxford: Butterworth Heinemann, p 397:

Treatability is in England a crucial issue as far as the personality disordered patient is concerned. The MHA 1983 says that compulsory treatment can only be given to the psychopathically disordered if 'such treatment is likely to alleviate or prevent a deterioration of his condition'. At first sight a not unreasonable criterion, but then it will be noticed that such a barrier is not placed in the way of the 'mentally ill' or those suffering from severe mental impairment. Such blatant legal discrimination between categories of patients is unusual, but it is heuristic. It illustrates what the stigmatised patient is up against and, in practice, very few such patients get into hospital under compulsory arrangements unless they are sent there by courts or unless they are temporarily redesignated as 'ill', for example, after a suicide attempt.

A recent 23-year follow-up of mentally disordered offenders (Robertson, 1987) has shown that for the group as a whole, they have a very high risk of 'unnatural death', ie, death from accidents, suicide, or homicide. At the age of 40 years, when violent death accounts for about 12% of deaths in the general population, it accounts for 50% of deaths among the mentally disordered; suicide, for example, is five times more common than in the general population for the third decade of life. The point of considerable interest here is that these trends occur across all diagnostic groups, the personality disordered were just as vulnerable to premature death as those with schizophrenia, affective disorder, and mental handicap. This information is unlikely to impress those who wish to define and reject the personality disordered patient as 'not ill' or not suffering from 'formal mental illness' ... but it should impress the thoughtful psychiatrist.

How then should we deal with the treatability criterion? Quite simply on clinical grounds after as thorough an assessment as possible. Treatability is not synonymous with curability. If a patient has renal failure, the only effective treatment available may be renal dialysis – this has to be done frequently and will not cure him. Such treatment keeps the patient alive and ameliorates his distress. For the personality disordered patient, his lifeline may be weekly support, a group, or even in-patient care. The fact that he may relapse when the treatment is stopped is not a reason for not providing it. For a patient to be deemed 'untreatable', he would need to be so resistant to treatment as to be unaffected by nursing, or support, or counselling, so unaffected as to make these techniques completely irrelevant to his management; a rare case ...

The Butler Committee saw prison as the proper place for the psychopath (after all, the definition of psychopathic disorder is little more than the description of criminal, or potentially criminal, behaviour), but that would be after the commission of a non-trivial offence.

The issue of treatability had to be considered recently by the Court of Appeal in connection with the discharge of a s 3 patient. In *R v Canons Park Mental Health Review Tribunal ex p A* [1994] 2 All ER 659, the patient had been diagnosed as suffering from a psychopathic disorder, the treatment for which was, in her case, group therapy. The Mental Health Review Tribunal which considered her case found that as she was refusing to co-operate with the therapy, she was untreatable, but should nevertheless be detained in the interests of her own health and safety and for the protection of others. The patient applied for judicial review of the decision on the basis that she had an absolute right to be discharged:

R v Canons Park Mental Health Review Tribunal ex p A [1994] 2 All ER 659 (Roch, Kennedy and Nourse LJJ)

Roch LJ (pp 678–80):

Scope of the treatability test

The final matter is the question of the scope of the treatability rest. This court heard submissions on that issue. Mr Gordon on behalf of the applicant pointed out that arguments on the scope and meaning of the treatability test had not been deployed by counsel for the Tribunal before the Divisional Court. Mr Gordon went on to submit that this was not a live issue in this case because both Dr James and Dr Frank agreed that the only form of treatment for the applicant which was likely to alleviate or prevent a deterioration of her psychopathic disorder was that of group therapy, and that treatment to be effective required the willing co-operation of the patient. Mr Gordon accepted that medical treatment was, by reason of the terms of s 145 of the 1983 Act, wider than drugs, therapies or other treatment prescribed by doctors. He said:

> I accept that nursing care could be a step in the treatment of a mental disorder. But that was not the Tribunal's finding in this case.

The Tribunal's finding had been that group therapy was the only form of treatment likely to alleviate or prevent deterioration of the applicant's condition; that it required the applicant's willing co-operation in order to be likely to alleviate or prevent deterioration of her condition and that the applicant was unwilling to co-operate. Mr Gordon pointed out that the applicant would have co-operated with one to one therapy, but that the doctors were agreed that such therapy would have lead to a worsening of the applicant's condition and made her more dangerous.

Mr Richards' submissions were that the treatability test is concerned with the likely effect of treatment if such treatment were given, and is not concerned with the likelihood of the patient refusing such treatment. In this case there was a known treatment which was likely to alleviate or prevent deterioration of the applicant's condition, namely group therapy. Parliament could not have intended that a patient should be deemed untreatable simply because the patient withheld co-operation. That would place the key to the patient's being detained in hospital in the patient's own hands, and this would apply to cases where the patient was in hospital pursuant to an order of the Crown Court as well as to cases where the patient had been admitted under s 3 of the 1983 Act; s 37 of the Act also containing the treatability test. Further, such an interpretation would place a hitherto unnoticed constraint on the Secretary of State's discretion to make a transfer direction in respect of a prisoner under s 47 of that Act. Mr Richards' further submission was that the Divisional Court's conclusion on the meaning of treatability was not in accordance with medical experience of the treatment of those with psychopathic disorders. Here Mr Richards, in addition to passages in the reports and evidence of Dr James, relied on para 4 of Dr Raymond's affidavit. In such cases there may be an initial deterioration in the patient's condition, but detention in a secure environment with nursing care and medical supervision (medical treatment within the 1983 Act) can lead to the patient gaining an insight into his condition and the overcoming of the patient's initial refusal to co-operate. One of the skills of nurses and doctors in hospitals for the mentally disordered is to persuade their patients to accept treatment. A period of detention with nursing care and medical supervision is frequently a necessary prelude to treatment by way of therapy. If during such a period the patient is likely to gain an insight into his problem or is likely to change to being co-operative then that in itself is an alleviation of the patient's condition.

The Divisional Court, in my judgment, no doubt for the reason it did not have the advantage of the submissions addressed to this court on this aspect of the case, took too narrow a view of what could constitute medical treatment in hospital likely to alleviate or prevent a deterioration of the applicant's condition. I would suggest the following principles. First, if a Tribunal were to be satisfied that the patient's detention in hospital was simply an attempt to coerce the patient into participating in group therapy, then the Tribunal would be under a duty to direct discharge. Second, treatment in hospital will satisfy the treatability test although it is unlikely to alleviate the patient's condition, provided that it is likely to prevent a deterioration. Third, treatment in hospital will satisfy the treatability test although it will not immediately alleviate or prevent deterioration in the patient's condition provided that alleviation or stabilisation is likely in due course. Fourth, the treatability test can still be met although initially there may be some deterioration in the patient's condition, due, for example, to the patient's initial anger at being detained. Fifth, it must be remembered that medical treatment in hospital covers nursing and also includes care, habilation and rehabilitation under medical supervision. Sixth, the treatability test is satisfied if nursing care, etc, are likely to lead to an alleviation of the patient's condition in that the patient is likely to gain an insight into his problem or cease to be unco-operative in his attitude towards treatment which would potentially have a lasting benefit.

If the treatability test is given the wider scope which in my judgment it should be given, then it becomes clear that the Tribunal was deciding that their duty to direct the discharge of the applicant did not arise because they were not satisfied that medical treatment in hospital was likely to alleviate or prevent a deterioration of the applicant's condition. Such a finding is not surprising when it is appreciated that the applicant's detention in the secure unit for medical treatment had eliminated the symptoms in the diagnosis of her condition on her first admission to St Luke's Hospital of deliberate self-harm and alcohol abuse and reduced those of reactive depression and suicidal ideation.

The Court of Appeal finding that medical treatment should not be narrowly construed in this context, and that she was not to be considered untreatable because of her refusal to co-operate is fraught with difficulties. Whilst this might be reasonable in relation to, say, drug treatment, there is something ironic about holding that a disorder is still treatable when the treatment consists of participation in group therapy (an essential element of which must be co-operation), and the patient refuses to co-operate. It is hard not to conclude that this is an example of judicial sleight of hand: the clinicians wanted to detain the patient, and therefore the 'treatability' condition had to be satisfied one way or the other.

The concept of treatability was considered in the case of *Reid v Secretary of State* [1999] 1 All ER 481, where the House of Lords held that the term 'medical treatment' was wide enough to include treatment which alleviates or prevents a deterioration of the symptoms of the disorder, not the disorder itself which gives rise to them. It was said that anger management of an in-patient in a supervised environment which resulted in him being less physically aggressive, satisfied the treatability test. This case went to the European Court of Human Rights and in the decision of that court (*Hutchison Reid v United Kingdom* (2003) 37 EHRR 9) confirmed that detention was justified under Article 5(1)(e) ie it can reliably be shown that he or she suffers from a mental disorder sufficiently serious to warrant detention. This did not depend upon the condition being amenable to medical treatment. (There had been, however, procedural breaches of Article 5(4) which related to the burden of proof and speediness of the review procedure.) See also *R (On the Application of Weldon) v Rampton Hospital Authority* [2001] EWHC Admin 134, where it was said that the concept of treatability was a very wide one, depending upon the opinion of the responsible medical officer. Arguably, this gives clinicians an unacceptably wide discretion. One concern might be that patients are detained when strictly speaking they should not be, because of too wide an interpretation of treatability, but another concern might be that a dangerous patient who is found not to be treatable must be discharged.

Concern about the treatability test and the release into the community of dangerous patients who are deemed to be untreatable is illustrated by the *Report of the Committee of Inquiry into the Personality Disorder Unit at Ashworth Special Hospital*, Cm 4194 and 4195, 1999, London: Stationery Office (the Fallon Report), in which it was recommended that criminal sentences be extended when untreatable psychopathic patients were still dangerous. The recent draft Mental Health Bills have reflected this concern and the treatability test was not retained, and is unlikely to be in future reform proposals.

Key parties involved

The Act refers to a number of key personnel who are empowered to take action in respect of patients liable to be detained. Under s 11 of the Act, applications for compulsory admission may be made either by an approved social worker, or by the patient's nearest relative.

Approved social worker

Under s 114 of the Act, the local authority must appoint a 'sufficient number of approved social workers for the purpose of discharging the functions conferred upon them'. Under the 1959 Act the same functions were carried out by mental welfare officers. It will be seen from the following (s 13) that the approved social worker's duty is described as being personal to them and not as a functionary of the local authority which has appointed them:

> **13 -Duties of approved social workers to make applications for admission or guardianship**
>
> (1) It shall be the duty of an approved social worker to make an application for admission to hospital or a guardianship application in respect of a patient within the area of the local social services authority by which that officer is appointed in any case where he is satisfied that such an application ought to be made and is of the opinion having regard to any wishes expressed by relatives of the patient or any other relevant circumstances, that it is necessary or proper for the application to be made by him.
>
> (2) Before making an application for the admission of a patient to hospital an approved social worker shall interview the patient in a suitable manner and satisfy himself that detention in a hospital is in all the circumstances of the case the most appropriate way of providing the care and medical treatment of which the patient stands in need.
>
> (3) An application under this section by an approved social worker may be made outside the area of the local social services authority by which he is appointed.
>
> (4) It shall be the duty of a local social services authority, if so required by the nearest relative of a patient residing in their area, to direct an approved social worker as soon as practicable to take the patient's case into consideration under sub-s (1) above with a view to making an application for his admission to hospital; and

if in any such case that approved social worker decides not to make an application he shall inform the nearest relative of his reasons in writing.

Cavadino comments on the role of the approved social worker as follows:

Cavadino, M, *Mental Health Law in Context*, 1989, Aldershot: Dartmouth, pp 111–13:

Applications: social workers and relatives

The Percy Commission, whose recommendations were embodied in the Mental Health Act 1959, envisaged that the application for compulsory admission should 'ideally' be made by the patient's nearest relative, with a Mental Welfare Officer of the local authority on hand to explain the procedure, arrange the patient's transport to hospital, and so on. If the MWO did make the application, this would be a second-best procedure, for use in situations when the relative was not available, unreasonably refused to make the application, or preferred the MWO to do the 'dirty work' (Percy, 1957, para 403). Thus the MWO's role was basically to act as the relative's agent, or else as a surrogate for an absent or inadequate relative. Certainly, the MWO was not expected to assume a judicial role corresponding to the magistrate under the Lunacy Act.

In practice the vast majority of applications for compulsory admission to hospital under the 1959 and 1983 Acts have always been made by social workers (MWOs under the 1959 Act and Approved Social Workers since 1983). This was certainly true of admissions to Fardale: out of 50 compulsory admissions in surveys A and B, relatives made the application in only three cases (6%). Even in the three cases where the relative did make the application, a social worker (approved as an MWO) was involved in the admission.

There was one case in which the social worker had taken the highly dubious course of asking the nearest relative (the patient's daughter) to make the application 'as a safeguard for myself' because the social worker 'wasn't 100% happy about doing a section on her'. Probably more typical, however, was the following case. The social worker explained the meaning of compulsory admission to the patient's wife, who agreed that it was necessary. The social worker considered asking the wife to make the application, but decided it would not be fair on her, and so made the application himself. Many social workers believe that it could damage the relationship between relatives if one relative signs the application to 'put away' the other. (In cases of compulsory admission there can be a strong sense of betrayal and of collusion between relatives and professionals even if this does not happen.) They also feel that relatives are not appropriate people to make applications because they are not in a position to take a detached view on whether the admission is justified, and may indeed have self-interested reasons for wanting to have the patient detained. And doubtless there is also a less lofty motivation here; professionals do tend to try to aggregate power to themselves and resist sharing it with lay people. In any event it is the usual policy of social workers that they and not the patients' relatives should make any application for admission, and it seems to be rare even to inform relatives of their power to apply. This policy is not forbidden or discouraged by the Mental Health Act, but it is quite the opposite of that envisaged by the Percy Commission.

(The reference here to 'Fardale' is reference to a study carried out by Cavadino between 1976 and 1978 at an NHS psychiatric hospital, to which he gave the fictional name of 'Fardale'.)

Nearest relative

The nearest relative is defined by s 26 of the Act:

26 Definition of 'relative' and 'nearest relatives'

(1) In this Part of this Act 'relative' means any of the following persons–

   (a) husband or wife;

   (b) son or daughter;

   (c) father or mother;

   (d) brother or sister;

   (e) grandparent;

   (f) grandchild;

   (g) uncle or aunt;

   (h) nephew or niece.

(2) In deducing relationships for the purposes of this section, any relationship of the half-blood shall be treated as a relationship of the whole blood, and an illegitimate person shall be treated as the legitimate child of his mother. ...

(3) In this Part of this Act, subject to the provisions of this section and to the following provisions of this Part of this Act, the 'nearest relative' means the person first described in sub-s (1) above who is for the time being surviving, relatives of the whole blood being preferred to relatives of the same description of the half-blood and the elder or eldest of two or more relatives described in any paragraph of that sub-section being preferred to the other or others of those relatives, regardless of sex.

(4) Subject to the provisions of this section and to the following provisions of this Part of this Act, where the patient ordinarily resides with or is cared for by one or more of his relatives (or, if he is for the time being an in-patient in a hospital, he last ordinarily resided with or was cared for by one or more of his relatives) his nearest relative shall be determined–

   (a) by giving preference to that relative or those relatives over the other or others; and

   (b) as between two or more such relatives, in accordance with sub-s (3) above.

The definition does not include spouses who are separated and provision is also made for cohabitees and other persons with whom the patient has been residing to be treated as relatives (sub-ss (5)–(7)). It is possible for persons who do not come within the ambit of s 26 nevertheless still to act in the capacity of a nearest relative. The nearest relative may forfeit status, and can authorise another person to act under reg 14 of the Mental Health (Hospital, Guardianship and Consent to Treatment) Regulations 1983, or that person can be appointed by the county court to be the patient's nearest relative, under s 29:

29 ...

(2) An order under this section may be made on the application of–

   (a) any relative of the patient;

   (b) any other person with whom the patient is residing (or, if the patient is then an in-patient in a hospital, was last residing before he was admitted); or

   (c) an approved social worker,

but in relation to an application made by such a social worker, sub-s (1) above shall have effect as if for the words 'the applicant' there were substituted the words 'the local social services authority'.

(3) An application for an order under this section may be made upon any of the following grounds, that is to say–

(a) that the patient has no nearest relative within the meaning of this Act, or that it is not reasonably practicable to ascertain whether he has such a relative, or who that relative is;

(b) that the nearest relative of the patient is incapable of acting as such by reason of mental disorder or other illness;

(c) that the nearest relative of the patient unreasonably objects to the making of an application for admission for treatment or a guardianship application in respect of the patient; or

(d) that the nearest relative of the patient has exercised without due regard to the welfare of the patient or the interests of the public his power to discharge the patient from hospital or guardianship under this Part of this Act, or is likely to do so.

In *W v L* [1974] QB 711, the Court of Appeal had to consider the meaning of s 29(3)(c), that is, when does a nearest relative *unreasonably* object?

Lord Denning MR (p 717): This brings me to the final question: is the wife unreasonable in objecting to the making of an application for the husband's detention? This is a difficult question. One can see that she is pulled both ways: on the one hand, she is devoted to her husband and wants him to be with her, on the other hand, she is devoted to her baby and wants the baby to be with her too. No doubt she feels that she can cope. She says she knows her husband better than anyone else does; she will see that he takes his tablets; she is quite satisfied that neither she nor the baby will be in danger. So if you look at it from her own point of view, she may not be unreasonable. But I do not think it correct to look at it from her own point of view. The proper test is to ask what a reasonable woman in her place would do in all the circumstances of the case. It is similar to the test in adoption cases in which the House of Lords have approved this statement:

… in considering whether she is reasonable or unreasonable we must take into account the welfare of the child. A reasonable mother surely gives great weight to what is better for the child. Her anguish of mind is quite understandable; but still it may be unreasonable for her to withhold consent. (*In re W (An Infant)* [1971] AC 682, p 698.)

So we come to this: looking at it objectively, what would a reasonable woman in her place do when faced with this wife's problem? It seems to me that a reasonable woman would say: my husband ought to go in for treatment and he ought to be detained until he is cured. It is too great a risk to have him home whilst the baby is so small. Her objection is therefore unreasonable. I think that the county court judge was quite right in so holding.

This view is confirmed by what has happened since. It appears that the wife has made statements which have caused much concern to those in the case. So much so that a medical report says:

… it is becoming even clearer that the liability to compulsory detention is an essential factor in keeping any control over this harrowing situation.

The right course is therefore for the mental welfare officer to make an application for the detention of the husband on the ground that the wife unreasonably objects to doing so. I would dismiss the appeal accordingly.

Under s 14, in the case of admission by a nearest relative, the hospital managers may request a report on the patient from the local social services authority.

Under recent reform proposals the nearest relative provisions would be abolished in favour of a nominated person, the identity of whom being, to some extent, under the control of the patient. In the European Court case of *JT v United Kingdom* [2000] 1 FLR 909, where the patient alleged that there was an infringement of her Article 8 right as the legislation did not provide for her to 'change' her nearest relative, the UK government responded (to the satisfaction of the court) that this would be reformed. The same point was taken in the case of *R (On the Application of M) v Secretary of State for Health* [2003] EMHC 1094, where the nearest relative provisions (not open to challenge by the patient) were decalred to be incompatible with the HRA 1998, Article 8. See also the House of Lords decision in *MH v Secretary of State for the Department of Health* [2005] UKHL 60.

Doctors

Applications must, of course, be supported by medical recommendations. An application under s 2 (admission for assessment), s 3 (admission for treatment) and s 7 (reception into guardianship) require two medical recommendations. An application under s 4 (emergency) needs only one recommendation. When two are required, one of them must be an approved doctor under s 12(2) of the Act. Each Regional Health Authority must approve, on behalf of the Secretary of State, a number of medical practitioners 'having special experience in the diagnosis or treatment of mental disorder'. Some might argue that both doctors should be so approved, and some commentators have questioned the fact that, even within the requirement that only one doctor need be approved under s 12(2), not all those doctors are psychiatrists (see Hoggett, B, *Mental Health Law*, 4th edn, 1996, London: Sweet & Maxwell, p 67).

The doctors must each have personally examined the patient, and, if the examination is not joint, no more than five days must have elapsed between the two examinations.

The literature often makes reference to 'RMOs'. The RMO is the responsible medical officer, and is defined by s 34(1) as the doctor in charge of the patient's treatment.

The categories of admission

Admission for assessment – s 2

Section 2 of the MHA 1983 states as follows:

2 Admission for assessment

(2) An application for admission for assessment may be made in respect of a patient on the grounds that–

  (a) he is suffering from mental disorder of a nature or degree which warrants the detention of the patient in a hospital for assessment (or for assessment followed by medical treatment) for at least a limited period; and

  (b) he ought to be so detained in the interests of his own health or safety or with a view to the protection of other persons.

...

(4) Subject to the provisions of s 29(4) below, a patient admitted to hospital in pursuance of an application for admission for assessment may be detained for a period not exceeding 28 days beginning with the day on which he is admitted, but shall not be detained after the expiration of that period unless before it has expired he has become liable to be detained by virtue of a subsequent application, order or direction under the following provisions of this Act.

It should be noted that, under s 11(3) if the application is made by an approved social worker, he must inform the nearest relative that an application is to be made. There is no requirement in respect of a s 2 admission for the approved social worker to have *consulted* with the relative (see s 11(4)), but under s 13(1), the social worker must have regard to any wishes expressed by the relative when deciding whether to make the application.

It should also be noted that, under s 2 admissions, the definition of the patient's condition is wide. The patient need only be suffering from 'mental disorder', which means mental illness, arrested or incomplete development of mind, psychopathic disorder and *any other disorder or disability of mind*. It will also be recalled that there is no illegality if it subsequently transpires that the patient is not suffering from mental disorder at all (*R v Kirklees Metropolitan BC ex p C* [1993] 2 FLR 187).

Admission under s 2 is for 28 days only, and s 2(4) states that the patient 'shall not be detained after the expiration of that period unless before it has expired he has become liable to be detained by virtue of a subsequent application, order or direction under the following provisions of this Act'. Clearly, this means that it is not renewable, and it may be argued that no subsequent s 2 application could be made. However, in *R v South Western Hospital Managers ex p M* [1994] 1 All ER 161, it was held that the discretion of an approved social worker could not be fettered by the earlier decision of a Mental Health Review Tribunal to discharge a s 2 patient, albeit in this case, to pursue a subsequent application under s 3 (admission for treatment). Laws J stated that such decisions by the social workers, doctors and hospital managers would be amenable to applications for judicial review. It seems therefore that a further s 2 application, made immediately after the expiry of an earlier one, would be judicially reviewable, but, on the reasoning employed by Laws J would not be automatically regarded as unlawful on the face of the statute.

A similar issue came up in *R v East London and City Mental Health NHS Trust ex p Brandenburg* [2001] EWCA Civ 239, in relation to the discharge of a patient by a Mental Health Tribunal following a s 2 admission. The patient was redetained on the day before the discharge was due to take place. The Court of Appeal held that there did not have to be a change of circumstances to justify this under the Act, but the decision to discharge must be given great weight. A decision to redetain where there was no change of circumstances, would have to be made in the light of facts known to the doctors and not to the tribunal, otherwise the decision of the tribunal would prevail. The House of Lords rejected an appeal, but it was stated by Lord Bingham that an ASW may not lawfully apply for the admission of a patient whose discharge has been ordered by a tribunal unless s/he has formed the reasonable and *bona fide* opinion that s/he has information not known to the tribunal which puts a signficantly different complexion on the case as compared with that which was before the tribunal (*R v East London and City Mental Health NHS Trust ex p Brandenburg* [2004] 1 All ER 400). See also *R (On the Application of Wirral Health Authority and Wirral BC) v Dr Finnegan and DE* [2001] EWCA Admin 312.

A related point is the question of 'assessment' and when it is appropriate to admit for that reason. In *B v Barking Havering and Brentwood Community Healthcare NHS Trust* [1999] 1 FLR 106, it was said that assessment could be an important part of evaluating treatment. This would mean that a patient could be admitted for assessment under s 2 where a diagnosis of his condition had already been made. Admitting someone under s 2, however, and then failing to undertake any form of assessment would be unlawful (see *St George's Healthcare NHS Trust v S* [1999] Fam 26).

Admission for treatment – s 3

Long-term admission is sanctioned under s 3 of the Act.

3 Admission for treatment

...

   (2) An application for admission for treatment may be made in respect of a patient on the grounds that–

   (a) he is suffering from mental illness, severe mental impairment, psychopathic disorder or mental impairment and his mental disorder is of a nature or degree which makes it appropriate for him to receive medical treatment in a hospital; and

   (b) in the case of psychopathic disorder or mental impairment, such treatment is likely to alleviate or prevent a deterioration of his condition; and

   (c) it is necessary for the health or safety of the patient or for the protection of other persons that he should receive such treatment and it cannot be provided unless he is detained under this section ...

It can be argued that applications under s 3 are, more often than not, unnecessary. Why should this be the case? Although there is no obligation to do so, an application in respect of a patient who has not been formally sectioned before, will be under s 2 of the Act. As has been acknowledged already, an application under s 2 can be in respect of someone who is suffering from 'mental disorder', a wide category of persons who need not be more specifically diagnosed, and who are not necessarily treatable. However, not only does this make a s 2 admission more attractive, it also means that for up to 28 days a patient can be observed, and, if necessary, treated. After the lapse of this period of time, therefore, the patient may be a lot 'better' than when first admitted, and therefore more amenable to remaining as a voluntary patient, rather than by invoking the provisions of s 3. This 'labelling' process is considered further below. Phil Fennell points out the dangers of sedation of patients:

Fennell, P, *Treatment Without Consent*, 1996, London: Routledge, p 218:

In recent years concern has grown about the use of antipsychotic drugs as major tranquillisers for emergency sedation, and for behaviour control where patients have no psychotic symptoms. Some [doctors in a Mental Health Act Commission (MHAC) study] described antipsychotic medication for mentally impaired patients as being for 'behaviour control'. In January 1994 it was alleged that in Ashworth Hospital, patients diagnosed as personality disordered or mentally impaired were being given antipsychotic medication not as a treatment for illness but as a means of controlling behaviour by keeping them sedated. These cases were drawn to the attention of the authorities by a team of MHAC visitors to the hospital. An independent consultant forensic psychiatrist brought in by the hospital recommended reduction in the drug doses. Nursing staff said that the patients' behaviour on high doses of medication had been aggressive and violent. When the medication was reduced, patients suffered severe withdrawal symptoms and became even more aggressive, suggesting that these are drugs of dependence.

The use – or abuse – of the wording of s 3 was considered in the case of *R v Hallstrom and Another ex p W (No 2)* [1986] 2 All ER 306. In that case, an admission under s 3 was made, and almost immediately the patient was discharged under s 17 (a provision of the Act which enables the RMO to grant leave of absence to any patient liable to be detained). The purpose was to allow compulsory treatment within the community. McCullough J said (p 315):

> **McCullough J**: It stretches the concept of 'admission for treatment' too far to say that it covers admission for only so long as it is necessary to enable leave of absence to be granted after which the necessary treatment will begin. 'Admission for treatment' under s 3 is intended for those whose condition is believed to require a period of treatment as an in-patient. It may be that such patients will also be thought to require a period of out-patient treatment thereafter, but the concept of 'admission for treatment' has no applicability to those whom it is intended to admit and detain for a purely nominal period, during which no necessary treatment will be given.

This principle was, in the words of Phil Fennell, distinguished almost to the point of extinction in the case of *R (On the Application of DR) v Merseycare NHS Trust* [2002] All ER(D) 28 (see Commentary Med L Rev [2003] 382). In that case, the claimant alleged that the renewal of her detention under s 20(2) of the Act was only appropriate when a patient's treatment plan was for treatment as an 'in patient'. In her case, the proposal was that she be treated as an 'out patient'. He application for judicial review was rejected on the basis that 'any distinction between treatment at a hospital and in a hospital was too subtle'. (It should be noted that there is a procedure for 'supervised discharge' under s 25, but this is complex and little used). It is also important to note here that, since the 1983 Act was passed, there has been a move away from treatment in hospital to treatment in the community, a change based upon a desire to avoid the institutionalisation of patients and to allow an appropriate degree of autonomy.

The interpretation of 'the nature or degree' of the disorder warranting hospital treatment was considered in *R v The Mental Health Review Tribunal for the South Thames Region ex p Smith* [1999] COD 148. It was said that this would be satisfied in the case of a patient whose symptoms are adequately controlled by medication, but who has stopped taking medication and whose history is such that a significant deterioration can be expected as a result of this. This not uncommon scenario (and results in what is often described as the 'revolving door' of admission/ discharge/admission), was considered by the Court of Appeal in relation to the application of the HRA 1998 in the case of *R (On the Application of H) v Mental Health Review Tribunal, North and North East London Region* [2001] EWCA Civ 415. It was said that the continued detention of such a patient was not contrary to Article 5(1)(e) of the ECHR (no one shall be deprived of his liberty save in (*inter alia*) the lawful detention of persons of unsound mind and in accordance with a procedure prescribed by law). There was no contravention as long as the detention was a proportionate response having regard to the risks that would be involved in discharge.

Admission for assessment in emergencies – s 4

Section 4 of the Act states as follows:

4 Admission for assessment in cases of emergency

(1) In any case of urgent necessity, an application for admission for assessment may be made in respect of a patient in accordance with the following provisions of this section, and any application so made is in this Act referred to as 'an emergency application'.

(2) An emergency application may be made either by an approved social worker or by the nearest relative of the patient; and every such application shall include a statement that it is of urgent necessity for the patient to be admitted and detained under s 2 above, and that compliance with the provisions of this Part of this Act relating to applications under that section would involve undesirable delay.

(3) An emergency application shall be sufficient in the first instance if founded on one of the medical recommendations required by s 2 above, given, if practicable, by a practitioner who has previous acquaintance with the patient and otherwise complying with the requirements of s 12 below so far as applicable to a single recommendation, and verifying the statement referred to in sub-s (2) above.

(4) An emergency application shall cease to have effect on the expiration of a period of 72 hours from the time when the patient is admitted to the hospital unless–

(a) the second medical recommendation required by s 2 above is given and received by the managers within that period; and

(b) that recommendation and the recommendation referred to in sub-s (3) above together comply with all the requirements of s 12 below (other than the requirement as to the time of signature of the second recommendation).

Although it may be accepted that there will be cases which are genuine emergencies and where a streamlined admission procedure is necessary, some may find cause for concern if such a procedure is used frequently. Further, it is important to keep in mind the wording of the section: it should not be used where it is simply more convenient to admit in this way, and obtain a second recommendation once the patient is in hospital so that the patient can then be admitted under s 2 or s 3. These concerns were considered in the 1978 *Review of the 1959 Mental Health Act*:

Review of the 1959 Mental Health Act, Cmnd 7320, 1978, London: HMSO, para 1.17:

Emergency admission for observation (s 29)

2.3 -Section 29 provides, in a case of urgent necessity, for the compulsory admission to hospital of a patient for observation. Twelve thousand people were admitted in this way in 1976. An application can be made by any relative (as defined by the Act) or by a Mental Welfare Officer, on the basis of a recommendation by any doctor. The section authorises detention for up to 72 hours only, unless the second medical recommendation which is required … is obtained within that period. The intention of the 1959 Act was that … s 29 should be used only in emergencies when there was not enough time to obtain the second medical recommendation. Section 29 has however been invoked more frequently than originally envisaged, and it has become the most widely used form of compulsory admission. There is also wide regional variation in its use. The Government hopes that the increasing development of the 24 hour crisis intervention services envisaged in the White

Paper 'Better Services for the Mentally Ill' will in time reduce the need for such admissions, by enabling some emergencies to be contained without the need for compulsory admission to hospital or alternatively for two medical assessments to be provided. However, given the present constraints on manpower and resources, it is accepted that there is a continuing need for a statutory emergency procedure. While there is a good deal of support in comments on the Consultative Document for developing 24 hour crisis intervention services and for the view that these would reduce the use of s 29, it was also argued that, however fully developed, crisis intervention services could never adequately replace s 29 powers, particularly in rural areas. Comments included the point that s 29 allows for a short assessment or 'cooling off' period which can often lead to discharge within 72 hours or to the person staying in hospital as an informal patient.

2.4 The extent of regional variation in the use of s 29 powers attracted a good deal of comment. Community Health Councils were particularly critical that the powers are sometimes used to suit administrative expediency. Cases were cited where hospitals had made a rule that no informal admission should be accepted after 5 pm with the result that any admission after this time had to be a compulsory admission, usually under s 29. Any such rule still in being should clearly be discontinued, and hospital managers should ensure that adequate arrangements exist for the emergency admission of both voluntary and compulsory patients.

It should also be noted that treatment cannot be given to a patient admitted under this section under Part IV of the Act (that is, without his consent) so the patient is in the same position as a voluntary patient.

These emergency powers do not contravene the HRA 1998, because the ECHR's procedural safeguards to not apply in emergency situations (*Winterwerp v Netherlands* (1979) 2 EHRR 387).

Guardianship – s 7

The requirements of s 7 are such that a patient over the age of 16 can be made the subject of a guardianship order if he is suffering from mental illness, psychopathic disorder, severe mental impairment or mental impairment, of a nature or degree which warrants his reception into guardianship. There is no treatability requirement. It must also be necessary in the interests of the welfare of the patient, or for the protection of others, although, as Hoggett points out, the latter is unlikely to arise very often, as the guardian's powers are unlikely to be effective in this respect. The powers of the guardian are to require specified residence; to require attendance for medical treatment, education and training, and to require access to the patient.

Guardianship is used infrequently (see the House of Commons Health Committee, *Report on Community Supervision Orders*, 1992–93, London: HMSO), and, given that substantial resources would be necessary to 'police' the system successfully, there must be doubts as to its usefulness. Mike Fisher, referring to the Social Services Research Group Study, carried out 1985–86, notes that during that 12-month period, the 63 incidents of guardianship constituted less than 1% of all detentions under the Act. (See Fisher, M, 'Guardianship under the mental health legislation: a review' (1988) J Soc Wel L 316.)

A person received into guardianship is not a person who is 'liable to be detained' for the purposes of s 56, and therefore the Part IV provisions as to treatment do not apply, that is, the patient cannot be treated for the mental disorder against his will (see p 492, below).

Whilst it is outside the scope of this book, it should be mentioned that the provisions of the National Health Service and Community Care Act 1990 were implemented, following the Griffiths Report of 1988, to ensure the identification of individual community care needs, the construction of community care packages and the co-ordination of these services.

Both Article 5 (right to liberty) and Article 6 (right to a fair trial) apply to guardianship. There is no contravention of Article 6 because there is a right to appeal to a Mental Health Review tribunal. As far as Article 5 is concerned, this applies even though the patient is not directly physically restrained. Restrictions as to dwelling place, etc, are also capable of contravening Article 5 (*Ashingdane v United Kingdom* (1985) 7 EHRR 528).

See below, Proposals for Reform, which refers to the recent proposals to provide compulsory treatment in the community.

The detention of inpatients – s 5

5 Application in respect of patient already in hospital

(1) An application for the admission of a patient to a hospital may be made under this Part of this Act notwithstanding that the patient is already an in-patient in that hospital or, in the case of an application for admission for treatment that the patient is for the time being liable to be detained in the hospital in pursuance of an application for admission for assessment; and where an application is so made the patient shall be treated for the purposes of this Part of this Act as if he had been admitted to the hospital at the time when that application was received by the managers.

(2) If, in the case of a patient who is an in-patient in a hospital, it appears to the registered medical practitioner in charge of the treatment of the patient that an application ought to be made under this Part of this Act for the admission of the patient to hospital, he may furnish to the managers a report in writing to that effect; and in any such case the patient may be detained in the hospital for a period of 72 hours from the time when the report is so furnished.

...

The purpose of s 5 is to enable a hospital to detain a voluntary patient who decides that he is going to leave the hospital. Hoggett summarises the provisions and concerns, thus:

Hoggett, B, *Mental Health Law*, 4th edn, 1996, London: Sweet & Maxwell, p 10:

Section 5(1) makes it clear that an application for compulsory 'admission' may be made in respect of a patient who has already been informally admitted to hospital. Indeed, a substantial proportion of applications relate to patients in hospital, most of them informal (Barnes, Bowl and Fisher, 1990; Department of Health, 1995). An application cannot be made in respect of a patient already detained under an application, except that an application for long term admission for treatment may be made while a patient is detained short term for assessment (s 5(1) and (6)). But if the authorities are not immediately able to complete an application, perhaps because a relative or social worker is not available, s 5 provides two procedures for keeping an informal patient in the hospital for a short time. Neither can be used to prolong the detention of a patient whose 'section' is about to expire (s 5(6)), and neither gives any statutory power to impose treatment without consent (s 56(1)(b)).

Both powers apply only to someone who is already an 'in-patient', a term which is not defined. In ordinary language, it is usual to distinguish between an out-patient, who attends for an appointment with a specialist or for emergency treatment in casualty, and an in-patient, who has been allocated a bed in a ward. The Code of Practice (Department of Health and Welsh Office, 1993) defines an informal in-patient as someone 'who has understood and accepted the offer of a bed, who has freely appeared on the ward and who has co-operated in the admission procedure' (para 8.4). Thus, these powers should not be used as a way of preventing a would-be suicide from leaving casualty when he comes round after having been 'washed out', or to convert a day patient into an in-patient.

Where the provisions of s 5(2) and (4) are used, the patient cannot be treated without consent, that is, the patient is specifically excluded from the provisions of Part IV by s 56 of the Act.

Informal admission – s 131

Patients can be informally admitted under the Act, that is, they are voluntary patients, and, as such are free to leave at any time. Informal admission fell to be considered by the House of Lords in the case of *R v Bournewood Community and Mental Health NHS Trust ex p L* [1998] 3 All ER 289. An autistic patient had been 'informally' admitted to a mental health unit. The psychiatrist felt that formal detention was unnecessary unless the patient resisted treatment. The trust argued that he was an informal patient under s 131 because he had chosen not to leave the hospital. The House of Lords held that it had clearly been intended that patients lacking the capacity to consent could be admitted under s 131. Their Lordships relied heavily on the findings of the Percy Commission, which reported prior to the 1959 Mental Health Act and which had envisaged such admissions as avoiding the stigmatisation of such patients with the label of having been 'sectioned'. Such patients would be admitted for treatment 'in their own best interests' (see generally Chapter 4). The House of Lords was therefore suggesting that the doctrine of necessity would apply. The case was brought before the European Court of Human Rights. The court held that the patient has been detained, and that therefore he was entitled to safeguards that were Article 5 compatible:

HL v United Kingdom (2005) 40 EHRR 32, European Court of Justice

.... .

Alleged violation of Article 5(1) of the Convention

...

89 It is not disputed that in order to determine whether there has been a deprivation of liberty, the starting point must be the specific situation of the individual concerned and account must be taken of a whole range of factors arising in a particular case such as the type, duration, effects and manner of implementation of the measure in question. The distinction between a deprivation of, and restriction upon, liberty is merely one of degree or intensity and not one of nature or substance.

90 The Court observes that the High Court and the majority of the House of Lords found that the applicant had not been detained during this period while the Court of Appeal and a minority of the House of Lords found that he had. Although this Court will have regard to the domestic courts' related findings of fact, it does not consider itself constrained by their legal conclusions as to whether the applicant was detained or not, not least because the House of Lords considered the question from the point of view of the tort of false imprisonment rather than the Convention concept of 'deprivation of liberty' in Art.5(1), the criteria for assessing those domestic and Convention issues being different.

In this latter respect, considerable emphasis was placed by the domestic courts, and by the Government, on the fact that the applicant was compliant and never attempted, or expressed the wish, to leave. The majority of the House of Lords specifically distinguished actual restraint of a person (which would amount to false imprisonment) and restraint which was conditional upon his seeking to leave (which would not constitute false imprisonment). The Court does not consider such a distinction to be of central importance under the Convention. Nor, for the same reason, can the Court accept as determinative the fact relied on by the Government that the regime applied to the applicant (as a compliant incapacitated patient) did not materially differ from that applied to a person who had the capacity to consent to hospital treatment, neither objecting to their admission to hospital. The Court recalls that the right to liberty is too important in a democratic society for a person to lose the benefit of Convention protection for the single reason that he may have given himself up to be taken into detention, especially when it is not disputed that that person is legally incapable of consenting to, or disagreeing with, the proposed action.

91 Turning therefore to the concrete situation as required by the Ashingdane judgment, the Court considers the key factor in the present case to be that the health care professionals treating and managing the applicant exercised complete and effective control over his care and movements from the moment he presented acute behavioural problems on July 22, 1997 to the date he was compulsorily detained on October 29, 1997.

More particularly, the applicant had been resident with his carers for over three years. On July 22, 1997, following a further incident of violent behaviour and self-harm in his day-care centre, the applicant was sedated before being brought to the hospital and subsequently to the IBU, in the latter case supported by two persons. His responsible medical officer (Dr M) was clear that, had the applicant resisted admission or tried to leave thereafter, she would have prevented him from doing so and would have considered his involuntarily committal under s.3 of the 1983 Act: indeed, as soon as the Court of Appeal indicated that his appeal would be allowed, he was compulsorily detained under the 1983 Act. The correspondence between the applicant's carers and Dr M reflects both the carer's wish to have the applicant immediately released to their care and, equally, the clear intention of Dr M and the other relevant health-care professionals to exercise strict control over his assessment, treatment, contacts and, notably, movement and residence: the applicant would only be released from the hospital to the care of Mr and Mrs E as and when those professionals considered it appropriate. While the Government suggested that 'there was evidence' that the applicant had not been denied access to his carers, it is clear from the above-noted correspondence that the applicant's contact with his carers was directed and controlled by the hospital, his carers visiting him for the first time after his admission on November 2, 1997.

Accordingly, the concrete situation was that the applicant was under continuous supervision and control and was not free to leave. Any suggestion to the contrary was, in the Court's view, fairly described by Lord Steyn as 'stretching credulity to breaking point' and as a 'fairy tale'.

92 The Court would therefore agree with the applicant that it is not determinative whether the ward was 'locked' or 'lockable' (the evidence before the House of Lords and the Commissioner appearing to differ in this respect). In this regard, it recalls that the applicant in the Ashingdane case was considered to have been 'detained' for the purposes of Art.5(1)(e) even during a period when he was in an open ward with regular unescorted access to the unsecured hospital grounds and unescorted leave outside the hospital. [FN46]

93 Considerable reliance was placed by the Government on the above-cited HM v Switzerland judgment, in which it was held that the placing of an elderly applicant in a foster home, to ensure necessary medical care as well as satisfactory living conditions and hygiene, did not amount to a deprivation of liberty within the meaning of Art.5 of the Convention. However, each case has to be decided on its own particular 'range of factors' and, while there may be similarities between the present and the HM case, there are also distinguishing features. In particular, it was not established that HM was legally incapable of expressing a view on her position, she had often stated that she was willing to enter the nursing home and, within weeks of being there, she had agreed to stay. This combined with a regime entirely different to that applied to the present applicant (the foster home was an open institution which allowed freedom of movement and encouraged contacts with the outside world) allows a conclusion that the facts of the HM case were not of a 'degree' or 'intensity' sufficiently serious to justify the conclusion that she was detained.

The Court also finds a conclusion that the present applicant was detained consistent with the above-cited judgment on which the Government also relied. That case turned on the specific fact that the mother had committed the applicant minor to an institution in the exercise of her parental rights, [FN48] pursuant to which rights she could have removed the applicant from the hospital at any time. Although the Government noted that the hospital retained responsibility for the present applicant following his release in 1994, the fact that the hospital had to rely on the doctrine of necessity and, subsequently, on the involuntary detention provisions of the 1983 Act demonstrates that the hospital did not have legal authority to act on the applicant's behalf in the same way as Mr Nielsen's mother.

94 The Court therefore concludes that the applicant was 'deprived of his liberty' within the meaning of Art.5(1) of the Convention from July 22, 1997 to October 29, 1997.

The court did state that whether someone was detained had to be decided on the basis of the specific situation under consideration. This is important because the decision has serious implications for those mentally incapacitated patients and their carers where the patient is not in a place which is registered to take detained patients but in, say, a residential care home. As far as those informal patients in psychiatric hospitals are concerned who lack capacity it is possible that they will be formally detained or discharged.

In order to retrieve the Bournewood situation, the Government suggested amending the then Mental Health Bill to create a new category of patient, ie one who lacked capacity but was detained in 'protective care' rather than in the Mental Health Act regime. The proposal was to make provision for this to be dealt with by way of delegated legislation authorised by the Mental Capacity Act 2005. However, in the light of the seriousness of such a proposal on 17 March 2005 the Parliamentary Delegated Powers and Regulatory Reform Committee ruled that such serious proposals should be dealt with in primary, not secondary legislation.

Miscellaneous powers

Under s 17 of the Act, a detained patient may be granted leave of absence subject to such conditions as the responsible medical officer thinks necessary in the interests of the patient or for the protection of others. It should be noted that such a person is still liable to be detained, so that both the consent to treatment provisions of the Act and the HRA 1998 apply.

Finally, it must be noted that there are a number of powers under the Act conferred upon the police and social workers. Under s 115, an approved social worker may enter and inspect any premises if he has reasonable cause to believe that a mentally disordered person living there is not under proper care. Under s 136, a police officer may remove a person to a place of safety if he finds, in a public place, a person who appears to be suffering from mental disorder and to be in immediate need of care or control. Such a person can be detained to a maximum period of 72 hours to enable him to be examined by a doctor and interviewed by an approved social worker. Section 135 provides for the issue of warrants to search for and remove patients to a place of safety, so that persons believed to be suffering from mental disorder can be removed from private premises too. The power given to approved social workers under s 115 does not enable them to force entry, and in such circumstances it would be necessary to obtain a warrant under s 135.

Detention via the criminal justice system

A detailed examination of this area would involve consideration of criminological matters and penal policy which are outside the scope of this book. However, it is important to remember that many patients compulsorily detained have arrived in that state via criminal sentences. A good, brief summary of the provisions which govern them, can be found in Hoggett, B, *Mental Health Law*, 4th edn, 1996, London: Sweet & Maxwell, pp 14–16, which also contains a more detailed analysis. See also Bartlett, P and Sandland, R, *Mental Health Law: Policy and Practice*, 2003, Oxford: OUP, Chapter 6.

NON-MEDICAL TREATMENT

Part IV of the Act deals specifically with medical treatment. However, the Act is silent on issues such as the management of difficult patients, the extent to which they can be physically restrained, secluded and searched. The Code of Practice (March 1999) provides guidance on restraint and seclusion in paras 19.1–34. Generally, the advice is that restraint and seclusion are measures of last resort. In *Pountney v Griffiths* [1976] AC 314, the House of Lords said that detention under the Act (the 1959 Act at that time), necessarily involves the exercise of control and discipline. See further Bartlett, P and Sandland, R, *Mental Health Law: Policy and Practice*, 2003, Oxford: OUP, pp 351–52, 392–95.

As far as searches are concerned, these are dealt with in paragraphs 25.1–3 of the Code:

> 25.3 The [search] policy may extend to routine and random searching without cause but only in exceptional circumstances, for example, where the dangerous or violent

criminal propensities of patients create a self evident and pressing need for additional security.

This approved use of routine and random searching for no particular reason was considered by the Court of Appeal in *R v Broadmoor Special Hospital Authority and Another ex p S and Others* [1998] COD 199. Prior to 1997, Broadmoor's policy had been to search patients only when there had been a reason to do so. However, the policy was changed after a patient had attacked a priest with a heavy object which he had hidden on his person. In consequence, the search policy was amended to permit random searches, without consent or cause and, if necessary, overriding medical opinion against its exercise (presumably such opinion would be based upon the issue of 'trust'). The Court of Appeal confirmed the lawfulness of the policy on the basis that prisoners held in a special hospital such as Broadmoor were there because of their dangerous, violent or criminal propensities (s 145(1) of the Act and s 4 of the National Health Service Act 1977), and the policy was necessary in order to maintain a safe therapeutic environment.

Seclusion was considered by the House of Lords in *Colonel Munjaz v Mersey Care NHS Trust (1) The Secretary of State for Health and (2) The National Association for Mental Health (MIND), and S v Airedale NHS Trust and (1) The Secretary of State for Health and (2) The National Association for Mental Health (MIND)* [2005] UKHL 58. The majority held that Code of Practice issued by the Secretary of State in respect of the implementation of the Mental Health Act 1983 should only be departed from if there are cogent reasons for doing so. The hospital here had been entitled to do so because the Code had not addressed the special problems of high security hospitals. There was no breach of Articles 3, 5 and 8 of the Convention if a patient was secluded for more than seven days as long as there was adherence to the hospital policy of reviewing seclusions.

Section 134 of the Act permits inspection and withholding of a detained patient's outgoing and incoming mail (para 22.15 of the Code advises that there should be a specific policy on this). Article 8 of the ECHR, which protects the right to respect for private life, specifically refers to protection of correspondence, so would it be possible to use the HRA 1998 to challenge this? First, it must be said that, under the Act, the restrictions on mail are not unqualified. Except in cases where the addressee has requested that communications from the patient to him should be withheld, the restrictions apply only to hospitals at which high security psychiatric services are provided and, secondly, they can only be imposed if it is necessary to do so in the interests of the safety of the patient or for the protection of other persons. This is likely to be proportionate and to satisfy Article 8(2), that is, 'to be necessary in a democratic society in the interests of public safety ... for the prevention of disorder or crime, for the protection of heath or morals, or for the protection of the rights and freedoms of others'. Furthermore, the restriction does not apply to mail sent (*inter alia*) to 'any legally qualified persons instructed by the patient to act as his legal adviser' (see *Valle v Finland* (2000) unreported, 16 March, where restrictions on telephone calls to a psychiatric patient's legal adviser were found to be unjustified). Further, this exception should also have the effect of avoiding any potential breach of Article 6, which protects the right to a fair trial.

Article 8 was considered in *R v Ashworth Hospital Authority ex p E* [2002] QBD, Admin Court, Richards J, 19 December 2001, where it was held that the decision to refuse the request of a male patient to dress as a woman was lawful. The restrictions on dress were justified in terms of a pressing social need (the risk of disguise to facilitate abscondment was one reason) and it was proportionate.

MEDICAL TREATMENT

Consent to treatment

As we saw in Chapter 3, adult patients in possession of the necessary decision making capacity have the right to refuse even life-saving medical treatment for any physical condition from which they may be suffering. However, in the case of patients detained under the Act, treatment for the mental disorder itself requires neither their express nor their implied consent (s 63). This is subject to exceptions contained within ss 57 and 58, for certain types of treatment, and subject to s 62 which deals with urgent treatment. Consent, however, is required of voluntary patients (s 56(1) and (2)). These exceptions are examined in detail below but, first, the nature of treatment for mental disorder must be considered.

Treatment not needing the patient's consent

63 Treatment not requiring consent

The consent of a patient shall not be required for any medical treatment given to him for the mental disorder from which he is suffering, not being treatment falling within ss 57 and 58 above, if the treatment is given by or under the direction of the responsible medical officer.

The implication is that treatment for other purposes, ie, the patient's physical disorders, remains governed by the common law. The interpretation of what constitutes the medical treatment for the mental disorder from which the patient is suffering has recently been given a very wide interpretation by the courts. The Act defines medical treatment as including 'nursing, and also includes care, habilitation and rehabilitation under medical supervision' (s 145(1)), but there is no guidance as to how this should relate to the mental disorder from which the patient is suffering, and in the case of *B v Croydon HA* [1994] 2 WLR 294, the Court of Appeal interpreted this so as to permit a wide range of acts ancillary to the core treatment. The case concerned a s 3 patient, suffering from a psychopathic disorder, which, it was found, was treatable only by psychoanalytical psychotherapy. The patient made various attempts to harm herself, and when these were discovered and prevented, she decided that she would refuse to eat. The health authority decided to force feed her without her consent, and she applied to the court for an injunction to restrain them. At first instance the court refused this on the basis that it was treatment for the mental disorder and therefore, by reason of s 63, did not require her consent. The Court of Appeal upheld this.

It was accepted that, because of the 'treatability' requirement in s 3 (see p 472, above), it would not have been lawful to detain her unless her condition was treatable. However, it was held that it did not follow that every act which formed part of treatment as defined by s 145(1) must, *in itself*, be likely to alleviate or prevent a deterioration of the disorder. The nasogastric feeding would be a form of concurrent care. Hoffmann LJ said, p 297:

Hoffmann LJ: Mr Gordon says that food is a medicine. He draws our attention to the fact that some special foods (for example, gluten-free rice cookies for coeliacs) may be obtained on prescription. In my view, however, this is not relevant to whether food is a medicine within the meaning of s 58. The section is concerned with medicines administered as treatment for mental disorder. The words 'by any means' in the opening phrase show that one identifies a medicine by its chemical composition and not by whether it is administered to the patient through a tube down his throat or by being put before him on a plate. Even gluten-free rice cookies are not administered for mental disorder and in my judgment ordinary food in liquid form, such as would be used in tube feeding, is not a medicine within the meaning of s 58.

That brings one back to the question of whether tube feeding would have been treatment for the mental disorder from which Ms B was suffering. My initial reaction was that it could not be. Ms B suffers from a psychopathic disorder which, according to the evidence, is incapable of treatment except by psychoanalytical psychotherapy. How can giving her food be treatment for that disorder? Mr Gordon says that it cannot. It may be a prerequisite to a treatment for mental disorder or it may be treatment for a consequence of the mental disorder, but it is not treatment of the disorder itself. He draws attention to s 3 of the Act, which specifies the grounds upon which a person suffering from a psychopathic disorder may be detained. It is not enough that the disorder must be 'of a nature or degree which makes it appropriate for him to receive medical treatment in a hospital' (sub-s (2)(a)). The proposed treatment must be 'likely to alleviate or prevent a deterioration of his condition' (sub-s (2)(b)) and it must be 'necessary for the health or safety of the patient or for the protection of other persons that he should receive such treatment' (sub-s (2)(c)). So Mr Gordon says that the patient cannot lawfully be detained unless the proposed treatment will alleviate or prevent a deterioration of his condition. No less should be required of the treatment which can be given without his consent under s 63.

This is a powerful submission. But I have come to the conclusion that it is too atomistic. It requires every individual element of the treatment being given to the patient to be directed to his mental condition. But in my view this test applies only to the treatment as a whole. Section 145(1) gives a wide definition to the term 'medical treatment'. It includes 'nursing, and also includes care, habilitation and rehabilitation under medical supervision'. So a range of acts ancillary to the core treatment fall within the definition. I accept that by virtue of s 3(2)(b) a patient with a psychopathic disorder cannot be detained unless the proposed treatment, taken as a whole, is 'likely to alleviate or prevent a deterioration of his condition'. In my view, contrary to the submission of Mr Francis, 'condition' in this paragraph means the mental disorder on grounds of which the application for his admission and detention has been made. It follows that if there was no proposed treatment for Ms B's psychopathic disorder, s 63 could not have been invoked to justify feeding her by nasogastric tube. Indeed, it would not be lawful to detain her at all.

It does not however follow that every act which forms part of that treatment within the wide definition in s 145(1) must in itself be likely to alleviate or prevent a deterioration of that disorder. Nursing and care concurrent with the core treatment or as a necessary prerequisite to such treatment or to prevent the patient from causing harm to himself or to alleviate the consequences of the disorder are in my view all capable of being ancillary to a treatment calculated to alleviate or prevent a deterioration of the psychopathic disorder. It would seem to me strange if a hospital could, without the patient's consent, give him treatment directed to alleviating a psychopathic disorder showing itself in suicidal tendencies, but not without such consent be able to treat the consequences of a suicide attempt. In my judgment the term 'medical treatment ... for the mental disorder' in s 63 includes such ancillary acts.

Mr Francis was, I think, right to draw our attention to s 62 as throwing some light upon the question. Sections 57 and 58 place special restrictions upon the use of particular 'forms of medical treatment for mental disorder', surgical operations for destroying brain tissue or implanting hormones (s 57), electro-convulsive therapy and drugs (s 58). There are special procedures which must be followed before these treatments can be given. But s 62(1) says that in certain specified cases of emergency, these special rules need not be complied with. They include:

... any treatment–

(a) which is immediately necessary to save the patient's life; or

(b) ...

(c) which (not being irreversible or hazardous) is immediately necessary to alleviate serious suffering by the patient; or

(d) which (not being irreversible or hazardous) is immediately necessary and represents the minimum interference necessary to prevent the patient from behaving violently or being a danger to himself or to others.

Mr Francis says, in my view rightly, that these emergency cases are not primarily concerned with a direct alleviation or the prevention of a deterioration of the mental disorder. The danger to the patient's life or the likelihood of serious suffering or the patient being a danger to himself or others are more likely to be the results of symptoms of the disorder. Nevertheless, the treatment of such symptoms is assumed by s 62 to be a 'form of medical treatment for mental disorder', since otherwise it would not have come within ss 57 or 58 in the first place.

I therefore agree with Ewbank J in *In re KB (An Adult) (Mental Patient: Medical Treatment)* (1994) 19 BMLR 144, p 146 when he said of the tube feeding of an anorexic: '... relieving symptoms is just as much a part of treatment as relieving the underlying cause.' To similar effect is the judgment of Stuart-White J, quoted by Sir Stephen Brown P in *Riverside Mental Health NHS Trust v Fox* [1994] 1 FLR 614, p 619. The decision in *In re C (Adult: Refusal of Treatment)* [1994] 1 WLR 290, in which a schizophrenic was held entitled to refuse treatment for gangrene, is distinguishable. The gangrene was entirely unconnected with the mental disorder.

Mr Gordon said that if the meaning of 'medical treatment for mental disorder' was wide enough to include ancillary forms of treatment, s 63 would involve a breach of the Convention for the Protection of Human Rights and Fundamental Freedoms, Cmnd 8969, 1953. He referred us to *Herczegfalvy v Austria* (1992) 15 EHRR 437 in which the court said, p 485, that a measure constituting an interference with private life and therefore *prima facie* contrary to Art 8(1) (like involuntary tube feeding) can only be justified under Art 8(2) if, among the other requirements of that article, its terms are sufficiently precise to enable the individual 'to foresee its consequences for him'. This requirement is necessary to prevent such measures from being a source of arbitrary official power, contrary to the rule of law. In my judgment s 63 amply satisfies this test. There is no conceptual vagueness about the notion of treating the symptoms or consequences of a mental disorder, although naturally there will be borderline cases. But there is no question of an exercise of arbitrary power.

This is arguably a disturbing decision, widening as it does the ambit of non-consensual treatment. Note, also, that this case has been followed in *Re VS (Adult: Mental Disorder)* [1995] 3 Med LR 292, and, even more controversially, in the case of *Tameside and Glossop Acute Services Trust v CH* [1996] 1 FLR 762, where it was held that the performance of a Caesarean section was treatment for mental disorder under s 63 (p 773):

Wall J: Is the question of inducing the defendant's labour and/or causing her to be delivered of her child by Caesarean section 'entirely unconnected' with her mental disorder? At first blush, it might appear difficult to say that performance of a

Caesarean section is medical treatment for the defendant's mental disorder: I am, however, satisfied that on the facts of this case so to hold would be 'too atomistic a view', to use Hoffmann LJ's phrase in the passage from *B v Croydon HA* which I have cited and the reasoning of which I respectfully adopt.

There are several strands in the evidence which, in my judgment, bring the proposed treatment within s 63 of the Act. First, there is the proposition that an ancillary reason for the induction and, if necessary, the birth by Caesarean section is to prevent a deterioration in the defendant's mental state. Secondly, there is the clear evidence of Dr M that in order for the treatment of her schizophrenia to be effective, it is necessary for her to give birth to a live baby. Thirdly, the overall structure of her treatment requires her to receive strong antipsychotic medication. The administration of that treatment has been necessarily interrupted by her pregnancy and cannot be resumed until her child is born. It is not, therefore, I think, stretching language unduly to say that achievement of a successful outcome of her pregnancy is a necessary part of the overall treatment of her mental disorder. Treatment of C's gangrene was not likely to affect his mental condition: the manner in which the delivery of the defendant's child is treated is likely to have a direct effect on her mental state.

However, the Court of Appeal confirmed in *St George's Healthcare NHS Trust v S* [1998] 3 All ER 673 that s 63 cannot be used to force upon patients medical procedures that are totally unconnected with mental disorder. Nevertheless, it was said that s 63 may apply to the treatment of any condition which is integral to the mental disorder which means that it does not specifically overrule the *Tameside* case. It is arguable that it is still possible for virtually any form of treatment to be given for mental disorder and that the *St George's* case failed from the point of view of s 63, largely because of inadequate diagnosis and assessment of mental disorder, which, in turn, stemmed from the fact that the real purpose of the action was management of the pregnancy.

Treatment under s 63 was considered in the case of *R v Collins and Ashworth Hospital Authority ex p Brady* [2000] Lloyd's Rep Med 355. It was found that force feeding was treatment under s 63 because the hunger strike was a manifestation or symptom of the patient's personality disorder (the patient was also found to lack capacity so could, in any event, be treated in his best interests, see Chapter 3, p 125, above). The responsible medical officer had formed the view that the hunger strike was 'a florid example of his psychopathology in action' which stemmed from aspects of his personality such as self-importance and desire to control. The judge was also required to consider the appropriate test for the lawfulness of treatment under s 63. The argument on behalf of Brady had been that the court must be satisfied that the treatment actually was treatment for mental disorder and not just that the doctor had reasonable grounds for considering it to be, that is, the test in *Khawaja v Secretary of State for the Home Department* [1984] 1 AC 74, rather than 'Wednesbury unreasonableness' (*Associated Provincial Picture House v Wednesbury Corp* [1947] 2 All ER 680). The court rejected this argument and held that the correct test was the 'super-*Wednesbury*' test, that is, the more substantial the interference with human rights, the more the court would require by way of justification (*R v Ministry of Defence ex p Smith* [1996] QB 517). However, the judge went on to say:

Maurice Kay J: I am entirely satisfied that [the doctor's diagnosis] satisfies both tests. On any view, and to a high degree of probability, section 63 was triggered because what arose was the need to medical treatment for the mental disorder from which the applicant was and is suffering. The hunger strike is a manifestation or symptom of the personality disorder. The fact (if such it be) that a person without mental disorder could reach the same decision on a rational basis in similar circumstances does not avail the applicant because he reached and persists in his decision because of his personality disorder.

The issue was examined in a slightly different context (where the patient had been detained under the criminal provisions of the Act and was subject to a Hospital and Restriction Order under ss 37 and 41) in the case of *R (On the Application of B) v Ashworth Hospital Authority* [2005] UKHL 20. The House of Lords held that it was not unlawful for the patient to receive treatment under s 63 for a 'mental disorder' in respect of which he had not been 'classified'. A contrary decision would certainly have sat uneasily alongside the case of *B v Croydon HA* [1994] 2 WLR 294.

Exceptional treatment not covered by s 63

Section 57 – consent and a second opinion

This section covers the most drastic forms of treatment for mental disorder. It covers psychosurgery and any other form of treatment specified by the Secretary of State. At present, the only other form is surgical implantation of hormones for the purposes of reducing the male sex drive (pursuant to reg 16 of the Mental Health (Hospital, Guardianship and Consent to Treatment) Regulations 1983).

The question of surgical implantation to reduce the male sex drive was considered in *R v Mental Health Act Commission ex p W* (1988) 9 BMLR 77:

Stuart-Smith LJ: Mr Fitzgerald initially argued that the treatment in question was not 'treatment for mental disorder' within the opening words of s 57, but was treatment for sexual deviancy, which is expressly excluded by s 1(3) of the Act from the definition of mental disorder. But it became clear in the course of the hearing that Dr Silverman did consider that the treatment was for the applicant's mental disorder as well as for his sexual deviancy, and this point was therefore not pursued. It is not therefore necessary to decide the question of construction whether, as Mr Fitzgerald submits, in order to found their jurisdiction in a case involving reg 16 the commissioners have to be satisfied that the treatment is for the mental disorder and not merely excessive or deviant male drive. The alternative argument is that reg 16 has to be read into s 57(1) and that once a person is a mental patient and the treatment proposed is the surgical implantation of the hormones for the purpose of reducing male sexual drive, Parliament has in effect decreed the treatment to be for mental disorder. While I see the attraction of this argument, since Parliament no doubt intended to protect mental patients who may not be able to consent, where the mental disorder is quite distinct from the sexual deviancy or other matter referred to in s 1(3) of the Act, and the proposed treatment is solely for the purpose of dealing with the sexual deviancy or other s 1(3) condition, it is difficult to see how this can be treatment for mental disorder. In practice, however, it seems likely that the sexual problem will be inextricably linked with the mental disorder, so that the treatment for the one is treatment for the other, as in this case.

The Code of Practice's guidance on s 57 treatment states:

Treatments requiring consent and a second opinion (s 57)

16.7 -Before the RMO or doctor in charge of treatment refers the case to the Mental Health Act Commission:

(a) the referring doctor should personally satisfy himself that the patient is capable of giving valid consent and has consented;

(b) the patient and if the patient agrees his close relatives and carers should be told that the patient's willingness to undergo treatment does not necessarily mean that the treatment will be given. The patient should be made fully aware of the provisions of s 57;

(c) for psychosurgery, the consultant considering the patient's case should have fully assessed the patient as suitable for psychosurgery;

(d) for psychosurgery, the case should be referred to the Commission prior to the patient being transferred to the neuro-surgical centre for the operation. The Commission organises the attendance of two appointed persons and a doctor. The appointed persons and the doctor will usually visit and interview the patient at the referring hospital at an early stage in the procedure;

(e) for surgical implantation of hormones for the purpose of reducing male sexual drive, the relationship of the sexual disorder to mental disorder, the nature of treatment, the likely effects and benefits of treatment and knowledge about possible long term effects require considerable care and caution should be observed.

16.8 -Section 57 refers to the surgical implantation of hormones for the reduction of male sexual drive where it is administered as a medical treatment for mental disorder. If there is any doubt as to whether it is a mental disorder which is being treated, independent legal and medical advice must be sought. The advice of the Mental Health Act Commission should also be obtained about arrangements for implementing s 57 where necessary.

Section 58 – consent or a second opinion

Section 58 specifies treatment which requires consent or a second opinion. The treatment covered by s 58 is the controversial electro-convulsive therapy (ECT), and medicines administered over a period of three months or more.

It must be noted that this section does little to protect the patient's right to refuse treatment; it merely adds a safeguard by requiring that, in so far as the patient refuses, two doctors must recommend a course of treatment rather than one. Phil Fennell reports the results of a survey of second opinions carried out in 1992 (note that SOAD means Second Opinion Appointed Doctor):

Fennell, P, *Treatment Without Consent*, 1996, London: Routledge, pp 282–83:

Concerns of the 1970s and early 1980s led to the introduction of express legal provision for treatment without consent, which had previously been so much taken for granted as part of clinical authority that mentioning it did not even occur to legislators. By the 1980s it was necessary to spell it out. Part IV upheld the position of the RMO as in charge of a detained patient's treatment, and defined powers to treat without consent, subject to a second opinion procedure. If the personnel with power to decide whether or not to treat without consent had changed, did Part IV result in a change in the substance of these decisions? One clear incursion on clinical authority was that psychosurgery would no longer be allowed without valid consent. Another was that the decision of the SOAD to refuse permission was binding on the RMO and there was no appeal to the MHAC. Set against this is the fact that the second opinion is medical. Although there is a duty on the SOAD to consult other professionals, on occasion these are staff in occupations with little to do with patient care, and often nurses and others were brought in to 'get to know' the patient before being consulted. The test for giving the treatment, likelihood of benefit or prevention of deterioration, used in combination with the *Bolam* test, creates a presumption in favour of the RMO's judgment. Not surprisingly, the concordance rate for s 58 opinions is high. The 1992 survey showed that the main cases where authority was withheld for clinical reasons involved ECT or the 'new' antipsychotic Clozaril, because it was felt that other less drastic treatments should be given time to work. There was even one case, the Pimozide case, where the second opinion may have been a life saver. The survey also shows the extent of psychiatry's continued reliance on ECT, and in particular the strikingly high numbers of middle aged and elderly women who have the treatment. In this the pattern of the past is being followed, for women have traditionally been in the majority of those receiving radical treatment, whether it be clitoridectomy, ovariotomy, lobotomy, chemical shock, comas or ECT.

Perhaps the most important indicator of the effect on the substance of clinical decisions, and of the resilience of the experimental spirit, is the extent to which SOADs authorised high dose medication. The BNF recommended dose levels, used loosely as a yardstick in the second opinion process, are viewed by some psychiatrists as too low, and resistance to central prescription remains strong. The fact that 12% of medicine second opinions involved doses above [British National Formulary – BNF] limits does not suggest a significant interference with clinical authority. A poignant reminder of psychiatry's limitations were the numbers of patients in the MHAC 1 survey who had been on high doses of medication for years and who showed no improvement, remaining totally inaccessible (61 out of 232). Could it be that their medication contributed to their poor mental state?

Since s 58 offers no real protection to the patient, no real purpose of this provision is discernible.

The Code of Practice states:

Treatments requiring consent or a second opinion (s 58)

...

16.10 -Patients treated with ECT should be given a leaflet which helps them to understand and remember, both during and after the course of ECT, the advice given about its nature, purpose and likely effects.

Medication before three months

16.12 -This three month period starts on the occasion when medication for mental disorder was first administered by any means during a period of continuing detention ... The medication does not necessarily have to be administered continuously throughout the three months. The definition of this period is not affected by renewal of the patient's detention, withdrawal of consent, leave of absence or change in or discontinuance of the treatment. A fresh period will only begin if there is a break in the patient's liability for detention. Detention should never be allowed to expire as a means of enabling a fresh three month period to start.

Medication after three months (s 58)

16.13 -At the end of the three month period referred to above the patient's RMO should personally seek the patient's consent to continuing medication, and such consent should be sought for any subsequent administration of medication. If the patient consents the RMO most certify accordingly (Form 38). On the certificate the RMO should indicate all drugs proposed including medication 'as required'.

...

Withdrawal of consent

16.19 -A patient being treated in accordance with section 58 may withdraw consent at any time. Fresh consent or the implementing of s 58 procedures is then required before further treatment can be carried out or reinstated. Where the patient withdraws consent he should receive a clear explanation which should be recorded in the patient's records:

- of the likely consequences of not receiving the treatment;

- that a second medical opinion under Part IV of the Act may or will be sought, where applicable, in order to authorise treatment in the continuing absence of the patient's consent;

- of the doctor's power to begin or continue treatment under s 62 until a second medical opinion has been obtained, if applicable.

In *R v Feggetter and Another ex p Wooder* [2002] EWCA Civ 554, the Court of Appeal said that a SOAD should give adequate reasons when certifying s 58 treatment and these should be communicated to the patient unless this would be likely to cause serious harm to the physical or mental health of the patient or any other person. In *R (On the Application of Wilkinson) v RMO Broadmoor Hospital, the Mental Health Act Commission SOAD Doctor and the Secretary of State for Health* [2002] 1 WLR 419 the Court of Appeal held that a patient who was opposed to treatment under section 58 could apply for judicial review on the question as to whether his rights under Articles 2, 3 and 8 of the Convention were violated, or could raise an action in tort for assault against the Special Health Authority. In order for the court to reach a decision it would be necessary for the doctors concerned to give evidence and be subjected to cross-examination.

Urgent treatment under s 62

Under s 62 urgent treatment, normally subject to the additional requirements of ss 57 and 58, may be given without satisfying those conditions, and if it is a form of treatment for which consent was required and that consent is subsequently withdrawn, treatment can continue under these provisions if it is thought that discontinuance of the treatment would cause serious suffering to the patient:

62 Urgent treatment

(1) Sections 57 and 58 above shall not apply to any treatment–

    (a) which is immediately necessary to save the patient's life; or

    (b) which (not being irreversible) is immediately necessary to prevent a serious deterioration of his condition; or

    (c) which (not being irreversible or hazardous) is immediately necessary to alleviate serious suffering by the patient; or

    (d) which (not being irreversible or hazardous) is immediately necessary and represents the minimum interference necessary to prevent the patient from behaving violently or being a danger to himself or to others.

(2) Sections 60 and 61(3) above shall not preclude the continuation of any treatment or of treatment under any plan pending compliance with s 57 or 58 above if the responsible medical officer considers that the discontinuance of the treatment or of treatment under the plan would cause serious suffering to the patient.

(3) For the purposes of this section treatment is irreversible if it has unfavourable irreversible physical or psychological consequences and hazardous if it entails significant physical hazard.

It must be noted that it is only to ss 57 and 58 that s 62 applies. In practice, it will only be treatment under s 58 to which this section will apply, as the nature of s 57 treatments (at present, psychosurgery and surgical implantation of hormones to reduce the male sex drive) are unlikely to comply with sub-s (1)(a)–(d) in terms of hazard and/or irreversibility. The section would therefore be most likely to be used in the administration of medicine under s 58, when the three month period was about to elapse, and a second opinion could not be obtained. These occasions should be rare, genuine emergencies. However, in practice the situation may be very different. Fennell points out (*Treatment without Consent*, 1996, London: Routledge, Chapter 13) that ECT is given under s 62 and 'urgent treatment' is given under the *common law* to, for example, s 4 patients (that is, emergency admissions where one medical opinion only is needed), and to whom s 62 does not apply. We have already seen in Chapter 4 that the common law will permit treatment to be given without consent to a patient *lacking capacity* when that treatment is in his best interests. The assumption must be, therefore, that when treatment is given to a s 4 patient, lack of capacity is presumed. Fennell says:

Fennell, P, *Treatment Without Consent*, 1996, London: Routledge, p 223:

The limits on hazardous treatments in s 62 do not offer adequate protection for patients for three principal reasons. First, there appears to be a tendency on the part of doctors to see it as permissive rather than restrictive. Second, the section does not apply to patients who are detained under powers authorising detention for 72 hours or less, such as the doctor's holding power or the emergency admission for assessment under s 4. In such cases, the Code of Practice suggests that authority for emergency treatment may be found in common law: on rare occasions involving emergencies where it is not possible immediately to apply the provisions of the ... Act the common law authorises such treatment as represents the minimum necessary to avert behaviour by the patient that is an immediate serious danger to self or to other people. On this view, where patients are treated under common law, the prohibition on hazardous treatments does not appear to apply. The third weakness of s 62 in medicine cases is that, where patients are detained under longer term powers, medicines may be given without consent during the three month stabilising period at the direction of the RMO, and without the need for a second opinion. Only four of the 116 uses of s 62 in the MHAC 2 sample were for medicines; three by men and one by a woman. Two occurred because the three month stabilising period had elapsed and the RMO had not requested a second opinion in time, and in the other two the patients had withdrawn consent. Very often emergency sedation is given in the period immediately following admission. After three months, the MHAC view is that PRN medication for which the patient's consent cannot be anticipated should be included by the SOAD on the Form 39. Since Form 39 certificates are widely drafted to authorise treatment in terms of BNF categories of drug, this is not an effective safeguard. Once there has been a second opinion which includes the PRN medication, s 58 has been complied with and there is no need for recourse to s 62.

Is it right to give any form of treatment without consent?

Psychiatrists, as it has been seen, have very wide powers to treat without consent. The interests of the wider community may be able to justify detention, but can they justify treatment? It is arguable that most treatment will be consented to because after the initial treatment, the patient is compliant and will therefore consent to subsequent treatment. But in the case of a refusal, why should we make treatment compulsory?

Given that a patient can refuse life-sustaining treatment for physical illness if mentally competent, what is the argument for saying that the mentally ill patient cannot refuse treatment of mental illness? The 1959 Mental Health Act did not deal with the issue of consent to treatment, and it was thought that detention was sufficient to suspend the need to obtain a patient's consent.

During the passage of the 1983 Mental Health Act through Parliament, a justification for being able to treat without consent was given by the Minister of Health in the debate on the proposal in parliamentary committee:

Special Standing Committee on the Mental Health (Amendment) Bill (Parliamentary Session 1981–82), 29 June 1982

... those who looked after them (those forcibly detained) would have to gaze on them knowing perfectly well that some treatment could be given to alleviate their suffering and distress and enable them eventually to recover their liberty. Hospitals are places of treatment ...

This reasoning relies upon the fact that, by detaining someone against their will on the ground that they are ill, means that it is in the interests of them regaining their liberty that they receive treatment to enable them to do just this. It has to be admitted that this argument has a certain force. What is clear is that the reason cannot be that, *by definition*, the mental patient is incompetent because of the vagueness of the definition of mental illness, and indeed, case law confirms that a long term mental patient can refuse life-sustaining treatment for a physical condition (see Chapter 3). The question is whether the patient has the capacity to understand the particular form of treatment.

The White Paper, *Reforming the Mental Health Act*, Cm 5016–1, 2000, London: DoH and the Home Office, does not propose any reforms as far as compulsory treatment is concerned, although there are some minor refinements to what is now s 57.

Is competence treated differently when the patient is suffering from a mental disorder?

The case of *Re C (Adult: Refusal of Treatment)* [1994] WLR 290, as was seen in Chapter 3, dealt with capacity to consent to medical treatment, and that case was about a mentally disordered patient. In that enlightened judgment, the patient's mental capacity was considered in an objective and unpatronising manner. Thorpe J said, p 294:

Thorpe J: C himself, throughout the hours that he spent in the proceedings, seemed ordinarily engaged and concerned. His answers to questions seemed measured and generally sensible. He was not always easy to understand and the grandiose delusions were manifest, but there was no sign of inappropriate emotional expression. His rejection of amputation seemed to result from sincerely held conviction. He had a certain dignity of manner that I respect.

We have already seen above from the case of *B v Croydon HA* [1994] 2 WLR 294 that a woman who refused to be fed by nasogastric tube could not, in law, do so because it was treatment for the mental disorder from which she was suffering and therefore her consent was not necessary. There was a finding at first instance (questioned by the Court of Appeal) that she had the capacity to refuse medical treatment. If the court had decided that she lacked capacity then the case would not have been controversial because a decision to feed her could have been made in her 'best interests' (see Chapter 4). The consequence of that decision appears to be that incidental care which is not for the treatment of the disorder *per se* but which is part of the general management of the patient can be given without consent. Of course, in some ways this will, on a pragmatic level, be inevitable, despite civil libertarian objections: a disruptive patient may be subjected to some form of restraint which does nothing to treat his condition but merely to keep him quiet and make life better for other patients. It is perhaps the controversial nature of force feeding that focuses attention here, and gives rise to the question as to the precise nature of 'treatment'. Under the Act it includes nursing, care, habilitation and rehabilitation (s 145(1), and note that 'habilitation' is included for reasons of semantics, that is, a severely disabled child, say, may never have had skills, so cannot be said to be *rehabilitated*), and in the context of treatment for physical illness, treatment has been held to cover counselling and advice (see *Gillick v West Norfolk and Wisbech AHA* [1986] AC 112). The difficulty in the case of patients compulsorily detained under the Act is the fact that their consent is dispensed with, and therefore, this wide definition of 'treatment' means that the patient can be physically managed non-consensually in ways which have no effect whatsoever on their progress towards cure or amelioration of the mental disorder from which they are suffering. The justification for treating such patients without consent clearly does not address this point, nor, arguably, can it justify these peripheral forms of treatment.

The case of *R v Ashworth Hospital Authority ex p Brady* [2000] Lloyd's Rep Med 355 illustrates the way in which different approaches may be made to competence in cases of mental patients and non-mental patients. Brady's competence was called into question because he had engaged in a 'battle of wills' with the hospital authority. Although medical evidence was given to relate this to his 'personality disorder', it referred to his narcissism, self-importance and need for control, all traits which are easily recognisable in the non-mentally disordered. It is arguable that, if there was to be a battle of wills, then for political and social reasons, Brady was not going to be allowed to win it, regardless of the subtleties (or lack of) of psychiatric diagnosis.

It is generally acknowledged that, if possible, it is always preferable to obtain the consent of a patient, even if treatment can be given without it. The Code of Practice states (para 16.4):

> A detained patient is not necessarily incapable of giving consent. The patient's consent should be sought for all proposed treatments which may be lawfully given under the Act. It is the personal responsibility of the patient's current RMO to ensure that valid consent has been sought. The interview at which such consent was sought should be properly recorded in the medical notes.

This clearly envisages that, regardless of the provisions of s 63, initially the consent of the patient to treatment for the mental disorder should be sought.

The Mental Capacity Act 2005 is discussed in Chapter 4 in relation to incapable patients generally and, some such patients may be psychiatric patients. The interrelationship of the 2005 Act with current proposals for reform of the mental health legislation is at present unclear.

SAFEGUARDING THE PATIENT

Discharge of the patient under s 23

Section 23 states:

23 Discharge of patients

...

(2) An order for discharge may be made in respect of a patient–

  (a) where the patient is liable to be detained in a hospital in pursuance of an application for admission for assessment or for treatment by the responsible medical officer, by the managers or by the nearest relative of the patient;

  (b) where the patient is subject to guardianship, by the responsible medical officer, by the responsible local social services authority or by the nearest relative of the patient.

It should be noted that, under s 23, these are powers, and not duties, and therefore a patient cannot claim that, for example, once he ceased to be a danger to self, or others, he should be discharged under s 23.

In *Johnson v United Kingdom* (1997) 27 EHRR 296, the European Court of Human Rights held that, even if there is no longer justification under the Act for detention, this does not mean that the patient must be discharged immediately if he still poses a risk to others. Discharge can be delayed until after-care facilities have been put in place. But, see *R v Camden and Islington HA ex p K* [2001] EWCA Civ 240, and s 117 of the Act, p 509, below. (See also *R v Nottinghamshire Healthcare NHS Trust and Others ex p IH* [2001] EWHC Admin 1037 and *R v Mental Health Review Tribunal, North and East London Region ex p H* (2001) unreported, 28 March.)

There can be no doubt that the powers of civil detention under the Act have great potential for abuse. The importance of protective procedures, therefore, cannot be over-estimated.

The Mental Health Act Commission

Section 120 of the Act deals with the general protection of detained patients:

120 General protection of detained patients

(1) The Secretary of State shall keep under review the exercise of the powers and the discharge of the duties conferred or imposed by this Act so far as relating to the detention of patients or to patients liable to be detained under this Act and shall make arrangements for persons authorised by him in that behalf–

  (a) to visit and interview in private patients detained under this Act in hospitals and mental nursing homes; and

  (b) to investigate:

    (i) -any complaint made by a person in respect of a matter that occurred while he was detained under this Act in a hospital or mental nursing home and which he considers has not been satisfactorily dealt with by the managers of that hospital or mental nursing home; and

    (ii) -any other complaint as to the exercise of the powers or the discharge of the duties conferred or imposed by this Act in respect of a person who is or has been so detained.

The Commission carries out the functions under s 120(1) and (4), together with functions under s 61 of the Act (review of treatment given under s 57(2) and s 58(3)(b)). The Commission was established under s 11 of the National Health Service Act 1977, and s 121 of the MHA 1983 provides for its continuance. In addition to the above, the Commission appoints medical practitioners and other persons for the purposes of providing second opinions and verifying consent to treatment under Part IV of the Act and examines reports on that treatment; submits proposals for inclusion in the Code of Practice; submits proposals in relation to s 57 treatments, and produces a biennial report on its activities. There are about 90 commissioners, made up of doctors, nurses, social workers and lawyers.

It is important to note that the Commission's powers do not extend to voluntary patients, but only to those who are formally detained under the Act. This is regrettable: as we have seen, a large number of in-patients are not formally detained and, in particular, note the decision in *R v Bournewood Community and Mental Health NHS Trust ex p L* [1998] 3 All ER 289.

Challenging detention

The powers of the Commission are not designed to provide a mechanism for challenging the validity of the compulsory admission itself. There are, however, a number of ways in which a compulsorily detained patient may gain his liberty, both under the Act itself, and by the use of the common law.

Mental Health Review tribunals

A statutory framework for challenging compulsory admissions was first introduced by the 1959 Act following the recommendations made by the Royal Commission (the Percy Commission, see para 438). Under s 66, patients, including those admitted for assessment, can apply to a Tribunal for a review of their case. The nearest relative also has a right to apply. There is also an automatic review process, under s 68, whereby hospital managers must refer to a Tribunal any patient admitted for treatment who has not exercised his right to apply within the first six months. They must also refer any patient admitted for treatment if his detention is renewed and three years have gone by since the case was last considered by a tribunal.

Mental Health Review tribunals consist of at least one 'legal member', one 'medical member' and the third must be neither a legal nor a medical member. Procedures are governed by the Mental Health Review Tribunals Rules. A useful summary of the entitlement to apply to a tribunal is contained in Eldergill, A, *Mental Health Review Tribunals Law and Practice*, 1997, London: Sweet & Maxwell.

Decisions of Mental Health Review tribunals are susceptible to the judicial review test if no reasonable tribunal would come to such a decision (*R v Mental Health Review Tribunal for West Midlands and North West ex p Ashworth Hospital Authority and Others* [2001] EWHC Admin 901).

Habeas corpus

It may be thought that, since the introduction of the right to apply to a Mental Health Review tribunal, this ancient remedy would have little application. However, it has continued to be used, and was given approval as, in certain circumstances, *the* only remedy for an unlawfully detained patient (see *Re S-C (Mental Patient: Habeas Corpus)* [1996] 1 FLR 548). Nevertheless, challenges are more likely to be made by way of judicial review, paarticularly since the enactment of the HRA 1998.

Judicial review

Judicial review was considered in the following article with reference to the cases of *R v Hallstrom and Another ex p W* [1986] 2 All ER 306, and *R v Gardner and Another ex p L* [1986] 1 QB 1090:

> **Gunn, M, 'Judicial review of hospital admissions and treatment in the community under the Mental Health Act 1983' [1986] J Soc Wel L 290:**
>
> **Miss W**
>
> Miss W had been admitted to a hospital for treatment under s 3 of the Mental Health Act 1983 (hereafter, the Act) on the basis of medical recommendations provided by Dr Hallstrom, a consultant psychiatrist with 'special experience in the diagnosis and treatment of mental disorder' (s 12(2)), and Miss W's general practitioner. It would seem that the application was made by the hospital social worker, who was presumably an approved social worker. The day after being admitted to hospital, Miss W was given leave of absence, subject to treatment conditions, under s 17.
>
> She applied to a Mental Health Review Tribunal, which refused to direct her discharge from the effects of s 3. Thereafter, Miss W did not request a case stated by the Tribunal for consideration by the High Court under s 78(8), which would have allowed the court to consider simply the role of the Tribunal. Instead she went to the High Court for leave to apply for judicial review of the admission to hospital, which would allow wider consideration of the relevant issues. She sought an order for certiorari so that the admission would be quashed and regarded as though it had never been, or, in the alternative, a declaration that the admission was unlawful in the sense that the doctors did not have the power to do what they had done: they had acted *ultra vires* ...
>
> There are three heads under which decisions and actions of doctors, approved social workers and nearest relatives are subject to control by judicial review: 'illegality, irrationality and procedural impropriety'. The major concern in the instant cases is with 'illegality'. Before considering it, it is worth noting that the irrationality ground also could be important. For example, if a nearest relative used the power of application for an improper purpose, such as getting the patient out of the house in order to make it easier to obtain control of his/her premises, that application could be quashed by the court. Indeed damages might now have to be paid to the 'patient'. It is unlikely that the principles of procedural impropriety will have much of a role to play because an extensive procedure complying with these principles is clearly laid down in the Act and if it is not fulfilled, the admission is illegal.
>
> The right to apply for judicial review forms, along with an application for a writ of habeas corpus, a vital way in which the patient can complain about the original admission. Indeed, they form the only way, if it is right that a Mental Health Review Tribunal cannot consider the validity of the initial admission to hospital, as one member of the Court of Appeal, Ackner LJ, said in passing. It is important, therefore, to emphasise that a Mental Health Review Tribunal apparently can only decide whether a person should continue to be detained in hospital by considering whether the conditions justifying detention exist at the time the Tribunal sees the patient.

Although judicial review and habeas corpus do permit consideration of the original admission decision, neither provide a form of appeal on the merits of the decision: neither can question whether the decision was right or wrong. Instead they concentrate on whether the doctors, social workers and nearest relatives had the legal power to admit the patient; they consider whether the discretion that the professionals have was exercised in a proper manner; for example, did they take all relevant factors into account?

In *R v Ashworth Hospital Authority ex p Brady* [2000] Lloyd's Rep Med 355, the validity of the *Wednesbury* unreasonableness test was upheld, subject to what was said in *R v Ministry of Defence ex p Smith* [1996] QB 517, which had introduced what have come to be known as the super-*Wednesbury* principles that take into account the provisions of the Human Rights Act 1998.

In *R v Mental Health Review Tribunal and Another ex p KB and Others* (2002) 152 NLJ 672, it was held that commonplace delays in hearings before the Mental Health Review tribunal breached the right to a speedy hearing under Article 5(4) of the ECHR. See also *R v Mental Health Review Tribunal South West Region ex p C* [2002] 1 WLR 176.

One of the issues in the 'Bournewood' case was the adequacy or otherwise of the judicial review (and habeas corpus) procedures to safeguard the patient's Article 5 rights:

HL v United Kingdom (2005) 40 EHRR 32, European Court of Human Rights

…

Lawfulness and protection against arbitrary detention

…

136 The Government mainly argued that an application for leave to apply for judicial review of the decision to admit and detain, including a writ of habeas corpus, constituted a review fulfilling the requirements of Art.5(4) of the Convention. The applicant disagreed.

137 The Court considers that the starting-point must be the above-cited X v United Kingdom judgment where the Court found that the review conducted in habeas corpus proceedings was insufficient for the purposes of Art.5(4) as not being wide enough to bear on those conditions which were essential for the 'lawful' detention of a person on the basis of unsoundness of mind since it did not allow a determination of the merits of the question as to whether the mental disorder persisted. The Court is not persuaded by the Government's argument that the X case can be distinguished because it concerned detention pursuant to a statutory power: no authority has been cited and no other material adduced to indicate that the courts' review of detention based on the common law doctrine of necessity would indeed have been more intrusive.

138 Nor does the Court find convincing the Government's reliance on the development of the 'super- Wednesbury' principles of judicial review prior to the entry into force of the Human Rights Act 1998 in October 2000. Those principles were outlined and applied in the domestic judgment in the above-cited case of R. v Ministry of Defence Ex p. Smith. In the subsequent application to this Court by the same applicant, it was found that, even if his essential complaints under Art.8 of *805 the Convention had been considered by the domestic courts, the threshold at which those courts could have found to be irrational the impugned policy prohibiting homosexuals from the armed forces had been placed so high that it effectively

excluded any consideration by the domestic courts of the question whether the interference with the applicants' rights answered a pressing social need or was proportionate to the national security and public order aims pursued, principles which lay at the heart of the Court's analysis of complaints under Art.8 of the Convention. The Court concluded that the remedy of judicial review, even on a 'super- Wednesbury' basis, could not therefore constitute an effective remedy (within the meaning of Art.13) for a breach of Mr Smith's rights under Art.8.

139 The Court considers that it can be equally concluded for the purposes of Art.5(4) (the lex specialis vis-à-vis Art.13 in terms of entitlement to a review of the lawfulness of detention) that, even with the application of the 'super- Wednesbury' principles on judicial review, the bar of unreasonableness would at the time of the applicant's domestic proceedings have been placed so high as effectively to exclude any adequate examination of the merits of the clinical views as to the persistence of mental illness justifying detention. This is indeed confirmed by the decision of the Court of Appeal, in a case where the necessity of medical treatment was contested by the patient, that pre-incorporation judicial review of necessity in accordance with 'the super- Wednesbury' criteria was not sufficiently intrusive to constitute an adequate examination of the merits of the relevant medical decisions.

140 For these reasons, the Court finds that the requirements of Art.5(4) were not satisfied, as suggested by the Government, by judicial review and habeas corpus proceedings. It is not necessary therefore to examine the applicant's additional submissions that those proceedings did not satisfy the requirements of that Article because, inter alia, the burden of proof was on the detainee or because such proceedings did not provide 'speedy' and 'periodic control' at 'reasonable intervals'.

141 The Government also contended, without elaboration, that a dissatisfied patient could bring a civil claim for damages for negligence, false imprisonment and for trespass to the person (technical assault consequent on detention for treatment) which actions would be 'likely' to cause the hospital to justify its treatment of the patient without consent. The Government then proposed, without further detail, that the applicant could have invoked the declaratory jurisdiction of the High Court. However, the applicant did not allege that the relevant health professionals were negligent but rather that they had been incorrect in their diagnoses. His own action in false imprisonment and assault did not involve the submission of expert evidence by each of the parties or any assessment by the courts of that expertise and no case, decided at or around the relevant time, has been cited where such expertise was requested or such a merits review was carried out. As to seeking declaratory relief from the High Court, the Government has not cited any case decided around the relevant time where the High Court accepted that there was a 'serious justiciable issue' to be examined by it in a case such as the present one where the patient was readmitted and detained for assessment and treatment (which treatment was not of an exceptional nature) on the basis of a consensus amongst the health professionals that admission was necessary.

142 In such circumstances, the Court concludes that it has not been demonstrated that the applicant had available to him a procedure which satisfied the requirements of Art.5(4) of the Convention. There has been therefore a violation of this provision.

Reform of the MHA 1983, together with the provisions of the Mental Capacity Act 2005 will, preumably, deal with the inadequacy of the present regime.

For general comments as to judicial review and Human Rights Act challenges, see *R v Responsible Medical Officer Broadmoor Hospital and Others ex p Wilkinson* [2002] 1 WLR 419. Judicial review also applies to private psychiatric hospitals: *R v Partnerships in Care Ltd ex p A* [2002] EWHC 529.

A RIGHT TO TREATMENT FOR MENTAL DISORDER?

Because of the civil liberty issues that it raises, much of the concern surrounding patient rights is to do with the patient's right to liberty unless there are compelling reasons to the contrary. However, it can also be asked whether a mentally ill patient has a right to be treated.

In terms of medical treatment generally, there have been a number of attempts over the years to persuade courts to intervene when limited health care resources within the UK National Health Service have resulted in the denial of treatment to physically ill patients (see Chapter 2 and, for example, the cases of *R v Secretary of State for Social Services ex p Hincks* (1980) 1 BMLR 93; *R v Central Birmingham HA ex p Walker* (1987) 3 BMLR 32; and *R v Cambridge HA ex p B* [1995] 2 All ER 129). The conclusion to be drawn from these cases is that unless there is irrationality or procedural impropriety, the courts will not intervene. There is, therefore, very limited scope in making a challenge, and none in respect of *clinical* judgment.

However, the element of public protection in mental health law means that treatment for physical illness and treatment for psychiatric illness are not exactly comparable. There have been a number of recent incidents when members of the public have been injured and even killed by ex-psychiatric patients, and there has been something of an outcry that the persons concerned were not receiving treatment, or not receiving in-patient treatment (see, for example, newspaper reports in (1994) *The Independent*, 16 September; and (1995) *The Guardian*, 28 July; and (1997) *The Guardian*, 30 May). However, in this regard, note the case of *Clunis v Camden and Islington HA* [1998] 2 WLR 902, where the Court of Appeal held that there was no liability of a discharging health authority towards a patient who subsequently killed a member of the public (the *Jonathan Zito* case). This was based upon the fact that the action was grounded in the patient's own illegal act, so that *ex turpi causa non oritur actio* applied, and upon the court's decision that the obligation under s 117 of the Act to provide patient after care did not give rise to an obligation at common law. See Jones, MA, 'The violent mentally disordered patient: who cares?', *Professional Negligence*, Vol 14, No 2, 1998, p 99.

Judicial review was brought to allege a violation of the patient's rights under Article 5 in the case of *R v Secretary of State for the Home Department and another ex parte IH* [2003] UKHL 59. A Mental Health Review tribunal had been satisfied that the patient should be discharged, but subject to suitable s117 supervision within the community. There were difficulties in finding suitable supervision and discharge was deferred. The patient made an application for judicial review and, at the suggestion of the court, the case went before another tribunal. The decision of this tribunal was that it was appropriate for the patient to be detained in hospital. The allegations of the patient were twofold: first that his rights under Article 5(4) had been violated (this requires a speedy review of lawfulness of detention). He succeeded in this respect. However, the more interesting aspect of his application concerned Article 5(1)(e), which provides for detention of patients of unsound mind. The patient argued that this should be interpreted as providing for detention *only in circumstances in which the level of security represents a proportionate response to the risk posed by the patient*. In other words, he was asking for a gloss to be placed on the provision to reflect the European law concept of proportionality. The House of Lords rejected this, and distinguished the ECtHR case of *Johnson v UK* (1997) 27 EHRR 296, where an applicant's discharge had been delayed because suitable accommodation could not be found and, in circumstances where there was no doubt that the patient was no longer ill. Here, the difficulty in finding suitable aftercare was based upon the fact that the psychiatric services who would have been responsible for aftercare disagreed with discharge into the community as 'being clinically inappropriate'.

A patient is unlikely to request to be compulsorily detained under the Act, but could request to be informally admitted (s 131). For the purposes of this, the patient would have no more rights than a patient who demanded to be admitted to hospital for the treatment of physical illness. The decision would be based upon clinical judgment, and in the absence of judicially reviewable procedural irregularity, the courts would not intervene.

After the discharge of a patient detained under s 3 (or under certain criminal provisions, under ss 37, 47 or 48 of the Act, for detention), there is a duty on both the local health authority and the local social services authority to provide, in co-operation with the relevant voluntary agencies, after-care services until both are satisfied that the patient no longer needs them (s 117):

117 After-care

(1) This section applies to persons who are detained under s 3 above, or admitted to a hospital in pursuance of a hospital order make under s 37 above, or transferred to a hospital in pursuance of a transfer direction made under ss 47 or 48 above, and then cease to be detained and leave hospital.

(2) It shall be the duty of the District Health Authority and of the local social services authority to provide, in co-operation with relevant voluntary agencies, after-care services for any person to whom this sub-section applies until such time as the District Health Authority and the local social services authority are satisfied that the person concerned is no longer in need of such services.

This is a duty in respect of the individual patient rather than to the mentally disordered generally who are owed a similar duty under the National Health Service Act 1977 (Sched 8, para 2(1)).

Given the concern about the discharge of potentially dangerous patients mentioned above, it is interesting to speculate on the nature of this duty and whether it does impose a heavier onus on health care providers in the field of mental health than on their counterparts who are providing treatment for physical illnesses. This was considered in the case of *R v Ealing District HA ex p Fox* [1993] 3 All ER 170, where a health authority refused to provide psychiatric supervision for a patient who had been conditionally discharged by a Mental Health Review Tribunal subject to receiving psychiatric supervision in the community. In this case, the judge held that the health authority had erred in law in not attempting with all reasonable expedition and diligence to make arrangements so as to enable the patient to comply with arrangements *'required by a Mental Health Review Tribunal'* (*per* Otton J, emphasis added). However, does this mean that if Tribunals are prepared to attach such conditions to discharge orders that they will be enforceable? The answer to this is in the negative. In *Fox*, it was said that there should have been a reference back to the Tribunal, presumably with a view to amendment, and that duties owed to the patient could only be enforced by alleging procedural defectiveness through the mechanism of judicial review, which, as we have seen, are important, but limited in scope. In *R v Mental Health Review Tribunal ex p H* [2000] 1 WLR 1323, the Court of Appeal confirmed that a tribunal does not have the power to make orders against local and health authorities compelling them to implement any particular s 117 after care plan.

Furthermore, in *R v Camden and Islington HA ex p K* [2001] EWCA Civ 240, the Court of Appeal confirmed that s 117 does not impose an absolute obligation on authorities to satisfy any conditions imposed by a tribunal on the discharge of a patient.

In other words, as with treatment for physical illness, the courts will defer to clinical judgment and will not compel treatment to be given, as long as the decision to refuse to treat has been taken in a procedurally sound way. In this particular case the authority's consultant psychiatrist was doubtful that supervision in the community would work. However, the judge said that the health authority is bound to continue to seek to provide the necessary treatment, either from its own resources or from elsewhere, and if it cannot do so, then the matter should be referred back to the Mental Health Review Tribunal to reconsider the discharge condition. However, suppose there was not clinical doubt, but simply lack of the appropriate resources to provide the treatment? After all, the reason for the failure to provide medical treatment is more likely to be lack of financial resources than anything else (although in the case of *R v Cambridge HA ex p B* [1995] 2 All ER 129, resources were in issue, but the stress was upon the likelihood of success of the treatment). The question of resources was raised in the case of *R v Hertfordshire CC ex p Three Rivers DC* (1992) 90 LGR 526. This was about the level of provision in the community under the National Health Service and Community Care Act 1990, which imposes a duty upon the local social services authority to assess the needs of, *inter alia*, discharged mental patients. It was held in that case that identifying the level and nature of the service to be provided may be constrained by available resources and that these constraints could properly be taken into account when identifying the appropriate level of service provision.

The conclusion is, therefore, that ultimately there is no 'right' to treatment for the psychiatrically ill any more than there is for the physically ill. The only right is to be considered for treatment and given the appropriate clinical assessment.

LIABILITY TOWARDS PATIENTS

Criminal liability

Although the commission of common law or statutory offences against mental patients is rare, mention should be made of the specific statutory provisions which create criminal liability in respect of health care workers.

First, anomalously, s 128 of the 1959 Act remains in force. This makes it a criminal offence for a man on the staff of a hospital or mental nursing home, to have sexual intercourse with a female mental patient. Interestingly, it makes no reference to female staff having sexual relationships with patients, nor to male staff and male patients engaging in such activities. There is, under s 127 of the 1983 Act, a specific statutory offence of ill-treatment or wilful neglect of a mental patient, and under s 126, the offence of falsification of documents for the purposes of the Act.

Civil liability

False imprisonment

In addition to the remedies discussed above, a patient unlawfully detained may pursue a civil claim for false imprisonment, and, if successful, obtain an award of damages. In the case of *Furber v Kratter* (1988) *The Times*, 21 July, the patient succeeded despite the fact that the original detention was lawful. It was held that the substitution of a harsher regime than at first prescribed could constitute false imprisonment.

Battery and negligence

The same principles of common law negligence apply to the treatment of psychiatric patients. If it can be shown that those treating a potentially suicidal patient failed to supervise and treat in accordance with the appropriate standard of care, then the claimant will succeed: see *Selfe v Ilford and District Hospital Management Committee* (1970) 114 SJ 935. *Kirkham v The Chief Constable of the Greater Manchester Police* [1990] 2 QB 283 concerned a successful suicide in police custody. The widow of the person concerned succeeded in her claim. The Court of Appeal rejected the argument that the defence of *volenti* could apply: it was held that, as the person was clinically depressed, his judgment was too impaired in order for this to succeed. The latter point is of some interest: it is accepted that mental disorder itself does not mean that a patient is incompetent as far as medical decision making is concerned. Refusal of life-saving treatment by such a patient, unless it can be shown that the treatment is for the mental disorder *itself* (see the case of *B v Croydon HA* [1994] 2 WLR 294, p 492, above), is acceptable. However, a positive act of suicide in *Kirkham* should have been prevented on the basis of clinical impairment of judgment. Is there an illogicality here, or are we simply back to the distinction between positive acts, and omissions to take certain courses of action?

The liability of doctors and nurses to supervise suicidal patients was considered in the case of *Selfe v Ilford Hospital Management Committee* (1970) 119 SJ 935, where damages were awarded when there was found to be an unacceptable level of supervision. The clinical judgment of a psychiatrist was examined by the Supreme Court of Canada in the case of *Villemure v l'Hopital Notre-Dame et al* (1972) 31 DLR (3d) 454, where a '*Bolam*' argument as to what other doctors would have done was rejected. The majority decision approved the following finding of the trial judge:

> **Villemure v l'Hopital Notre-Dame et al (1972) 31 DLR (3d) 454:**
>
> The court is unable to accept the opinion of Drs Fortin and Saucier. It may be that they would have done exactly what Dr Turcot did. Had they done so, in the opinion of the court they would have been wrong and negligent. It is no answer to say it is impossible absolutely to prevent a person from committing suicide unless he is placed in a straitjacket. This of course is obvious. But it is surely possible to prevent him from committing suicide for 30 hours and until a sufficient investigation has been made into his condition to be able more accurately to diagnose his true situation. The court also rejects Dr Saucier's view that there were many factors which indicated that the patient's condition was not nearly as serious as might at first have been thought. The facts as proven of what happened prior to the entry into the hospital, coupled with the incidents in the hospital, indicate to the court rather a situation which should have made both Dr Turcot and the nurses take particular care of the deceased.

In the context of civil liability, mention must be made of a form of statutory immunity contained within s 139(1) of the Act:

> 139 (1) -No person shall be liable, whether on the ground of want of jurisdiction or on any other ground, to any civil or criminal proceedings to which he would have been

liable apart from this section in respect of any act purporting to be done in pursuance of this Act or any regulations or rules made under this Act, or in, or in pursuance of anything done in, the discharge of functions conferred by any other enactment on the authority having jurisdiction under Part VII of this Act, unless the act was done in bad faith or without reasonable care.

It will be seen that the reference to 'without reasonable care' means that this section gives no immunity against an action in negligence. However, under s 139(2), leave of a High Court judge is required to bring an action in the first place. Gunn considered the effect of s 139 on an application for judicial review:

Gunn, M, 'Judicial review of hospital admissions and treatment in the community under the Mental Health Act 1983' [1986] J Soc Wel L 290:

Section 139 of the Mental Health Act 1983

The decision of the Court of Appeal on these preliminary issues is of major importance to people compulsorily admitted to hospital. The court decided that s 139 does not operate as an additional barrier that patients as applicants for judicial review have to overcome beyond the requirements of RSC Ord 53, which apply to applicants for judicial review whatever the circumstances.

As has been stated s 139(2) requires a patient to obtain the leave of the High Court before being able to take civil proceedings. In *Winch v Jones*, the Court of Appeal decided that this leave should be granted when the court decides that 'on the materials available ... the applicant's complaint appears to be such that it deserves the fuller investigation which will be possible if the intended applicant is allowed to proceed'. This is similar to the ground upon which leave will be granted for an application for judicial review. *Hallstrom (No 1)* avoids the unnecessary confusion that would have arisen if leave had been required to be obtained both under s 139 of the Act and RSC Ord 53.

Section 139 and judicial review

Section 139(1) provides care staff with a defence when civil or criminal proceedings are taken against them. The decision of the Court of Appeal also means that this defence does not apply to applications for judicial review. This is a very significant decision because hearing a case on judicial review will allow the High Court to question the legality of many decisions taken in relation to patients in hospital and otherwise affected by the Act. In particular, it permits the High Court to question whether, for example, all the relevant factors were taken into account when the decision to admit the patient to hospital was made.

The decision in *Hallstrom (No 1)* means that the applicant for judicial review does not have to allege either bad faith or lack of reasonable care on the part of the person, for example, a doctor, whose action is being considered. Indeed, no such allegation was made by Miss W. A requirement to establish bad faith or lack of reasonable care would have been a major, often insuperable, obstacle for a patient to overcome.

PROPOSALS FOR REFORM

In 1998, the Government set up a 'scoping study review committee' to examine the current provisions of the 1983 Act, to take soundings from experts and interested parties and to prepare a report, outlining recommendations for reform (at least in part this was prompted by the implications for mental health of the newly enacted HRA 1998, see above illustrations of the conflicts that have arisen between the current legislation and the ECHR). The committee reported in July 1999 and, in November 1999, the Government issued a Green Paper, *Reform of the Mental Health Act 1983: Proposals for Reform*, 1999, Cm 4480, London: DoH. In 1999, another consultation document was issued by the Department of Health and the Home Office, *Managing Dangerous People with Severe Personality Disorder*. This was caused largely by the public outcry following the murders committed by Michael Stone, an allegedly 'untreatable' personality disordered patient who had been released into the community. Subsequently, a White Paper was issued, *Reforming The Mental Health Act*, 2000, Cm 5016–1, London: Department of Health and the Home Office. In 2002 a draft Mental Health Bill was issued, which gave rise to much criticism that it was too draconian in its measures to deal with people who were classified as personality disordered and dangerous.

In September 2004, the Government issued another draft Mental Health Bill. It contains a broad definition of mental disorder that is identical to that contained in s 2 of the Mental Capacity Act 2005. The Bill does not include a treatability requirement (one of the most controversial aspects of the current legislation, see above). This is to meet the public concern about severely disturbed patients being released from detention because they are untreatable, yet there is much dispute about how many people have what is defined as 'severe personality disorder'. Some argue that there are no more than around 12 people who meet the criteria and remain in the community, yet the proposed new law could affect around 50,000 people (see *Guardian Unlimited* 29 March 2005, http//society.guardian.co.uk/ mentalhealth/story/0,8150,836476,00.html). The Bill also provides for compulsory treatment in the community which is an attempt to avoid the 'revolving door' syndrome whereby patients are detained under the Act, treated successfully, released into the community, only to suffer relapse when they fail to take stabilising medication. However, as has been demonstrated above (see *R (On the Application of DR) v Merseycare NHS Trust* [2002] All ER (D)28 (Aug)), in effect, the interpretation of the requirement under the present legislation that the patient's condition 'warrants the detention of him in a hospital' has included hospital out patient treatment, so that treatment can effectively be carried out in the community under the current regime.

The draft Bill seeks to provide more safeguards for detained patients. Unlike the current admission regime, under the draft Bill there can be no compulsory detention beyond 28 days unless this is authorised by a new form of mental health tribunal. The draft Bill also provides for an independent advocacy scheme so that detained people are properly represented. There are also new provisions to protect the rights of children so that at the ages of 16 and 17 they can refuse treatment and this refusal cannot be overriden by their parents.

Pre-legislative scrutiny has been carried about by a specially appointed Joint Committee, whose first report was published on 23 March 2005 (http:///www. publications.parliament.uk/pa/jt200405/jtselect/jtment/79/7903.htm). The report is highly critical of the Bill, not least because the Committee found it difficult to read. One of the most controversial of its recommendations is that a treatability test be retained. Other criticisms are that the provisions for treatment in the community are too wide and should only be for a small group of patients that are explicitly clinically identified in the legislation, and that there are not enough safeguards for patients, eg the Bill makes no provision for the current 'second opinion appointed doctor' scheme. The Committee makes 30 recommendations in respect of safeguards. Furthermore, the Committee is extremely doubtful about the estimated extra resources necessary for the new mental health tribunal scheme.

Mental health legislation was expressly mentioned in the Queen's Speech in May 2005, so there can be little doubt that a new piece of legislation will hit the statute books in the next year or so (perhaps having taken on board at least some of the Committee's recommendations) and it may be that the aim will be for this to come into force in 2007 alongside the Mental Capacity Act 2005. It is to be hoped that the legislation will contain some provisions to show how the legislation will interact with the Mental Capacity Act 2005, as the lack of clarity in this respect was one of the Committee's concerns. This is particularly so because the definition of people who lack capacity in s 2 of the Act is that they are unable to make a decision because of 'an impairment of, or a disturbance in the functioning of the mind or brain' which is the same as the definition of mental disorder in the draft Bill (cl 85). Under s 28 of the Mental Capacity Act 2005 authorisation of treatment for mental disorder is expressly excluded if the treatment is regulated by the MHA 1983. What is needed is some criteria that sets out under which legislation treatment will be so regulated. The Joint Committee has recommended that this be dealt with in the codes of practice governing each of the pieces of legislation.

CHAPTER 10

MEDICAL RESEARCH

INTRODUCTION

Background

It is self-evident that medical science is not standing still. New therapies are constantly being developed in an ongoing battle against sickness and disease, and advances are not merely desired, but expected by society at large. However, their achievement inevitably involves carrying out previously untried treatment upon human subjects, with attendant uncertainty as to the treatment's capacity to harm rather than benefit the subjects in question.

In this chapter, we are concerned with the legal and ethical issues presented by medical research. To this end, we look first at the scientific methodology of research, and examine the key ethical dilemmas raised by such practices. The remaining sections then consider the legal and quasi-legal constraints that operate upon the researcher: the requirement that the subject consent to research; the various voluntary codes which seek to impose further safeguards in this field; and the issue of *ex post facto* compensation for those injured during the course of research.

Defining 'research'

Scientific research may be defined, very broadly, as any systematic inquiry aimed at discovering new facts about the way things in the world around us behave. In the case of medical research, the object of such inquiry is new methods of treatment: what effects do they have upon human subjects?

It is important to emphasise the deliberate and systematic nature of the research enterprise. Otherwise, one might be inclined to regard all medical treatment as constituting 'research', given that our store of knowledge will inevitably increase in the course of providing it. As John Marshall comments:

Marshall, J, 'The case against experimentation', in Dyson, A and Harris, J (eds), *Experiments on Embryos*, 1989, London: Routledge, pp 55–56:

… [In] one sense any medical intervention is research. Giving an aspirin to a patient, though done thousands and thousands of times, may on the thousand-and-oneth [*sic*] occasion produce some unexpected, unpredictable result because of idiosyncrasies in that patient. Therefore, when people talk on the one hand about certain orthodox procedures which they do without thinking and, on the other hand, about unorthodox procedures, it is clear that there is a difference in degree but never a difference in kind. Anything that is done, any intervention in another person, can have unexpected and unpredictable results. But it is not about that that we are really talking in this context.

The other area which ought to be distinguished is that of improving therapy. Again, people think that there is a certain standard way of doing appendectomies, or coronary bypass procedures, that there is a certain standard way of treating people with respiratory failure. But medicine is always engaged in the business of improving therapy, and improving therapy is often on a research basis. When you try to modify some procedure because you think it might work better in a different way, you are engaged in a form of research, a form of inquiry.

It is generally accepted that, in scientific terms, randomised clinical trials (RCTs) represent the ideal form of medical research. The basic idea is that subjects are randomly divided into different groups. One will be offered the treatment under research, and another (the 'control group') will not. As is evident from the following extract written by Charles Fried in 1974, many therapies that are considered standard today were once the subject of RCTs to establish their efficacy:

Fried, C, *Medical Experimentation – Personal Integrity and Social Policy*, 1974, Amsterdam: North-Holland Publishing, pp 146–47:

Coronary bypass surgery

In recent years techniques have been developed for bypassing regions of serious atherosclerotic blockage in the major coronary arteries, and thus permitting increased blood supply to the heart muscle below these blockages. There have, however, been serious questions raised regarding the efficacy of this technique in certain cases of coronary artery disease, and some responsible persons have questioned whether in certain situations the more traditional 'best' therapies and regimens might not be as good if not better. Moreover, the incidence of surgical mortality itself is far from negligible, and the operation is extremely costly in terms of time, technical resources and blood needed for transfusion. If the claims of the more enthusiastic proponents of this technique were valid there would be many hundreds of thousands of good candidates for this surgery each year at staggering social cost.

In order to evaluate the claims for coronary bypass surgery in various categories of disease, a number of hospitals throughout the country have instituted randomised clinical trials. In one trial, participants are referred by their physician to cardiologists in the participating hospital. The participants are told that a study is being conducted in which they are involved, that they will receive the best available treatment for their case, and that they are free not to join in or stay in the study. Although they know of the alternative therapies, only if they ask are they told that the choice is determined by a randomising scheme.

The scientific utility of RCTs is derived from the elimination, through the randomisation process, of potential bias (either on the part of researcher or research subject) in observing and interpreting the results of the treatment. However, as Sarah Hewlett notes, from the point of view of participants, a measure of inconvenience, and indeed risk, will be entailed:

Hewlett, S, 'Consent to clinical research – adequately voluntary or substantially influenced?' (1996) 22 JME 232:

Clinical research is necessary to establish the safety and efficacy of a therapy. It may include, for example, the testing of nursing or physiotherapy techniques, as well as the testing of new drugs …

Clinical testing of a new drug is required by the Medicines Control Agency (MCA) before a product licence for that drug can be given. As the drug is being tested for safety and efficacy, patients taking part will be put at risk of unknown side effects and may also be randomised to receive either the unproven drug or a placebo. When we enter a patient into such a clinical trial we are normally testing a drug appropriate to his or her condition. However, because of randomisation we may not always be selecting a particular drug for a particular patient's needs. If the comparator drug is a placebo then we may not be acting in that patient's best interests. In some cases the patient is being used as a means to an end: establishing the safety and efficacy of a new drug for the benefit of future patients. The justification for this is that the only way to establish the most effective and safe treatments to improve health (desired by most members of society) is by clinical research. By consenting, the patient knowingly agrees to this goal and makes it his own, becoming an active participant in the research so that it cannot then be said that the patient is being used as a means to an end. Clearly the quality of that consent is therefore vital.

What does clinical research mean for the patient?

The scientific gold standard for clinical research is the randomised controlled trial (RCT) which attempts to establish statistically the risk-benefit ratio of the drug by reducing bias and controlling for variables. This it does by controlling the selection of well characterised groups of patients, randomising them into treatment groups, using standardised outcome measurements performed by blinded assessors, and stipulating a population size powerful enough to answer the question being asked. Although not without criticisms the RCT is a credible test of safety and efficacy within the medical world and some would say it would be unethical to introduce a new drug without RCT data.

Patients participating in an RCT will usually need to attend hospital regularly for safety and efficacy assessments – perhaps clinical examination, blood and urine samples, and possibly x-rays. Such visits may take several hours and their frequency varies from every few days to every month, as does the duration of the RCT (from a few days to several years). Neither the safety nor the efficacy of the drug is yet proven and in addition the patient may receive a placebo during the course of the study. When taken together these are not inconsiderable inconveniences for the patient and although hopefully kept to minimum impact, there is sometimes an element of risk.

(The term 'placebo' used here refers to an inert substance, such as a 'dummy' pill, which is given to a subject so that he is unaware that he is in the control group not receiving the therapy under research.) We shall consider further the particular ethical dilemmas generated by the use of RCTs as a research tool, see p 525, below.

Therapeutic and non-therapeutic research

The distinction between therapeutic and non-therapeutic research is central to any discussion of the ethical and legal issues surrounding medical research. This does not go to the methodology of the research process (RCTs may equally be used for both), but derives from the two main classes of research subject on whom research may be carried out, and to what end.

Therapeutic

This type of research is defined as that which is carried out on patients with the direct potential for beneficial results in respect of their illness. The researcher (who is in a doctor–patient relationship with the subject) will commonly be attempting to establish whether a new treatment is more effective than existing therapy available for that condition. It is significant here, that the doctor/researcher, has what is termed a 'dual-intention': he desires both the attainment of new knowledge *and* benefits for the individual patient/subject.

Non-therapeutic

In contrast to the therapeutic form, non-therapeutic research denotes that which is carried out on volunteers (either drawn from the public or, perhaps, those hospitalised with unrelated conditions) and offers no hope of benefiting them personally. It often takes place in relation to new drug treatments in order to establish toxicity levels or any side effects. Here, the researcher is in the position of scientist alone: he does not owe duties to the research subject *qua* patient, and intends only the gaining of knowledge.

Although these two categories may admit of some blurring, they have been recognised for legal and ethical purposes as distinct and are addressed separately in Codes such as the Declaration of Helsinki (see p 521, below).

Innovative therapy

Both of the above forms of research may usefully be distinguished from the concept of innovative therapy: the latter denotes the use of novel treatment on a 'one off' basis. Although it is true that experience with such treatment may subsequently form the 'jumping off point' for proper research (especially if it turns out to be highly effective), it lacks the necessary systematic and repetitive quality to count as such itself; equally its level of scientific probity remains fairly low.

Significantly, from the doctor's point of view, the desire in such cases is solely to benefit the individual patient being treated in this way. Of course, he may foresee the likelihood of gaining new knowledge in the process, but this merely equates to a wide intention on his part to have it (contrast therapeutic research where it is part of his desire). The upshot is that there is no conflict between the doctor *qua* doctor and *qua* scientist: he acts as the former alone. In such a case, it is also submitted that (subject to gaining proper consent) the doctor may also run higher risks on the patient's behalf than those permissible in the context of research. This is because the intended beneficiary of the treatment is the patient alone; he is not being used as a means to any further end.

The concept of risk

As already mentioned, medical research, at least where its focus is invasive forms of therapy, exposes the human research subject to a degree of *additional* risk. Additional, that is to say, to the risks attendant upon receiving treatment where no research is being carried out. Why is this, and what meaning may be ascribed to the concept of risk itself, in this context?

We may begin by recognising, with Marshall, p 515, above, that there is always a residual uncertainty, when carrying out any invasive medical procedure, as to whether the patient may in fact be harmed in the process. Given the complexity of each individual human metabolism, we can never be 100% sure in advance that, say, a particular drug will not react with some feature (perhaps of a highly idiosyncratic order) in that metabolism, perhaps with disastrous consequences. Nevertheless, the more often we give the treatment in question, the better the picture we build up of the drug's causal properties, including any such propensity to do harm and, if so, with what frequency and magnitude.

Clearly, in the case of research involving novel treatment, we will lack this (relative) certainty: the very fact that a particular treatment is untried means that we have no databank of experience as to how the treatment in question has acted upon patients in the past. Although, by the very nature of things, the precise degree of risk presented to a research subject through their participation is thus difficult to quantify, the following rough categories have been proposed:

Nicholson, RH (ed), *Research on Children*, 1986, Oxford: OUP, p 119:

Table 5.6 Risk equivalents

	Negligible	Minimal minimal	More than
British definition	Negligible	Minimal minimal	More than
American definition	Minimal	Minor increase over minimal	Greater than minor increase over minimal
Risk of death	Less than 1 per million	1 to 100 per million	Greater than 100 per million
Risk of major complication	Less than 10 per million	10 to 1,000 per million	Greater than 1,000 per million
Risk of minor complication	Less than 1 per thousand	1 to 100 per thousand	Greater than 100 per thousand

Despite their tentative character, as we shall see (pp 544–45, below), these categories are often considered ethically significant in furnishing acceptable parameters within which research may take place.

THE ETHICS OF GOOD RESEARCH PRACTICE

Background

Although, as we have seen, nearly all medical research involves some extra degree of risk to the research subject, without it medical science would be unable to progress properly. This raises a classic dilemma (similar to that in relation to the use of body tissue and organs from live donors, see Chapter 11): under what conditions and to what extent is it permissible to treat a person (the research subject) as a means to an end (here greater medical knowledge)?

The need for some form of response, at an international level, to this question became dramatically apparent in the wake of the Second World War when, at the Nuremberg Trials, Nazi doctors were revealed to have performed a catalogue of horrific medical experiments on inmates of concentration camps causing terrible suffering and death.

In the course of their judgment, the judges at Nuremberg articulated a set of parameters within which they felt research might acceptably take place. This has become known as the Nuremberg Code:

Katz, J, *Experimentation with Human Beings*, 1972, Bognor Regis: Russell Sage Foundation, pp 305–06:

Judgment

Beals, Sebring, Crawford JJ: The great weight of the evidence before us is to the effect that certain types of medical experiments on human beings, when kept within reasonably well defined bounds, conform to the ethics of the medical profession generally. The protagonists of the practice of human experimentation justify their views on the basis that such experiments yield results for the good of society that are unprocurable by other methods or means of study. All agree, however, that certain basic principles must be observed in order to satisfy moral, ethical, and legal concepts:

(1) The voluntary consent of the human subject is absolutely essential.

    This means that the person involved should have legal capacity to give consent; should be so situated as to be able to exercise free power of choice, without the intervention of any element of force, fraud, deceit, duress, over-reaching, or other ulterior form of constraint or coercion; and should have sufficient knowledge and comprehension of the element of the subject matter involved as to enable him to make an understanding and enlightened decision. This latter element requires that before the acceptance of an affirmative by the experimental subject there should be made known to him the nature, duration, and purpose of the experiment; the method and means by which it is to be conducted; all inconveniences and hazards reasonably to be expected; and the effects upon his health or person which may possibly come from his participation in the experiment.

    The duty and responsibility for ascertaining the quality of the consent rests upon each individual who initiates, directs, or engages in the experiment. It is a personal duty and responsibility which may not be delegated to another with impunity.

(2) The experiment should be such as to yield fruitful results for the good of society, unprocurable by other methods or means of study, and not random and unnecessary in nature.

(3) The experiment should be so designed and based on the results of animal experimentation and a knowledge of the natural history of the disease or other problem under study that the anticipated results will justify the performance of the experiment.

(4) The experiment should be so conducted as to avoid all unnecessary physical and mental suffering and injury.

(5) No experiment should be conducted where there is an a priori reason to believe that death or disabling injury will occur; except, perhaps, in those experiments where the experimental physicians also serve as subjects.

(6) The degree of risk to be taken should never exceed that determined by the humanitarian importance of the problem to be solved by the experiment.

(7) Proper preparations should be made and adequate facilities provided to protect the experimental subject against even remote possibilities of injury, disability, or death.

(8) The experiment should be conducted only by scientifically qualified persons. The highest degree of skill and care should be required through all stages of the experiment of those who conduct or engage in the experiment.

(9) During the course of the experiment the human subject should be at liberty to bring the experiment to an end if he has reached the physical or mental state where continuation of the experiment seems to him to be impossible.

(10) During the course of the experiment the scientist in charge must be prepared to terminate the experiment at any stage, if he has probable cause to believe, in the exercise of the good faith, superior skill, and careful judgment required of him that a continuation of the experiment is likely to result in injury, disability, or death to the experimental subject.

This was followed, in 1964, by the World Medical Association's Declaration of Helsinki, which deals with the issues in a lengthier and more systematic fashion. As will be seen, the Declaration consists of a preamble followed by two parts: Part B sets out basic principles which apply to all forms of medical research and Part C applies specifically to medical research combined with medical care, that is, therapeutic research. Three themes dominate: the research must be scientifically sound, it must satisfy the proportionality test (that is, risks to the subject should be commensurate with the expected benefits of carrying the research out), and there must be the greatest possible respect at all times for the integrity of the research subject:

Declaration of Helsinki (1964) (as amended – most recently in Scotland, October 2000)

A *Introduction*

1 The World Medical Association has developed the Declaration of Helsinki as a statement of ethical principles to provide guidance to physicians and other participants in medical research involving human subjects. Medical research involving human subjects includes research on identifiable human material or identifiable data.

2 It is the duty of the physician to promote and safeguard the health of the people. The physician's knowledge and conscience are dedicated to the fulfillment of this duty.

3 The Declaration of Geneva of the World Medical Association binds the physician with the words, 'The health of my patient will be my first consideration,' and the International Code of Medical Ethics declares that, 'A physician shall act only in the patient's interest when providing medical care which might have the effect of weakening the physical and mental condition of the patient'.

4 Medical progress is based on research which ultimately must rest in part on experimentation involving human subjects.

5 In medical research on human subjects, considerations related to the well being of the human subject should take precedence over the interests of science and society.

6 The primary purpose of medical research involving human subjects is to improve prophylactic, diagnostic and therapeutic procedures and the understanding of the aetiology and pathogenesis of disease. Even the best proven prophylactic, diagnostic, and therapeutic methods must continuously be challenged through research for their effectiveness, efficiency, accessibility and quality.

7 In current medical practice and in medical research, most prophylactic, diagnostic and therapeutic procedures involve risks and burdens.

8 Medical research is subject to ethical standards that promote respect for all human beings and protect their health and rights. Some research populations are vulnerable and need special protection. The particular needs of the economically and medically disadvantaged must be recognized. Special attention is also required for those who cannot give or refuse consent for themselves, for those who may be subject to giving consent under duress, for those who will not benefit personally from the research and for those for whom the research is combined with care.

9 Research Investigators should be aware of the ethical, legal and regulatory requirements for research on human subjects in their own countries as well as applicable international requirements. No national ethical, legal or regulatory requirement should be allowed to reduce or eliminate any of the protections for human subjects set forth in this Declaration.

B BASIC PRINCIPLES FOR ALL MEDICAL RESEARCH

10 It is the duty of the physician in medical research to protect the life, health, privacy, and dignity of the human subject.

11 Medical research involving human subjects must conform to generally accepted scientific principles, be based on a thorough knowledge of the scientific literature, other relevant sources of information, and on adequate laboratory and, where appropriate, animal experimentation.

12 Appropriate caution must be exercised in the conduct of research which may affect the environment, and the welfare of animals used for research must be respected.

13 The design and performance of each experimental procedure involving human subjects should be clearly formulated in an experimental protocol. This protocol should be submitted for consideration, comment, guidance, and where appropriate, approval to a specially appointed ethical review committee, which must be independent of the investigator, the sponsor or any other kind of undue influence. This independent committee should be in conformity with the laws and regulations of the country in which the research experiment is performed. The committee has the right to monitor ongoing trials. The researcher has the obligation to provide monitoring information to the committee, especially any serious adverse events. The researcher should also submit to the committee, for review, information regarding funding, sponsors, institutional affiliations, other potential conflicts of interest and incentives for subjects.

14 The research protocol should always contain a statement of the ethical considerations involved and should indicate that there is compliance with the principles enunciated in this Declaration.

15 Medical research involving human subjects should be conducted only by scientifically qualified persons and under the supervision of a clinically competent medical person. The responsibility for the human subject must always rest with a medically qualified person and never rest on the subject of the research, even though the subject has given consent.

16 Every medical research project involving human subjects should be preceded by careful assessment of predictable risks and burdens in comparison with foreseeable benefits to the subject or to others. This does not preclude the participation of healthy volunteers in medical research. The design of all studies should be publicly available.

17 Physicians should abstain from engaging in research projects involving human subjects unless they are confident that the risks involved have been adequately assessed and can be satisfactorily managed. Physicians should cease any investigation if the risks are found to outweigh the potential benefits or if there is conclusive proof of positive and beneficial results.

18 Medical research involving human subjects should only be conducted if the importance of the objective outweighs the inherent risks and burdens to the subject. This is especially important when the human subjects are healthy volunteers.

19 Medical research is only justified if there is a reasonable likelihood that the populations in which the research is carried out stand to benefit from the results of the research.

20 The subjects must be volunteers and informed participants in the research project.

21 The right of research subjects to safeguard their integrity must always be respected. Every precaution should be taken to respect the privacy of the subject, the confidentiality of the patient's information and to minimize the impact of the study on the subject's physical and mental integrity and on the personality of the subject.

22 In any research on human beings, each potential subject must be adequately informed of the aims, methods, sources of funding, any possible conflicts of interest, institutional affiliations of the researcher, the anticipated benefits and potential risks of the study and the discomfort it may entail. The subject should be informed of the right to abstain from participation in the study or to withdraw consent to participate at any time without reprisal. After ensuring that the subject has understood the information, the physician should then obtain the subject's freely-given informed consent, preferably in writing. If the consent cannot be obtained in writing, the non-written consent must be formally documented and witnessed.

23 When obtaining informed consent for the research project the physician should be particularly cautious if the subject is in a dependent relationship with the physician or may consent under duress. In that case the informed consent should be obtained by a well-informed physician who is not engaged in the investigation and who is completely independent of this relationship.

24 For a research subject who is legally incompetent, physically or mentally incapable of giving consent or is a legally incompetent minor, the investigator must obtain informed consent from the legally authorized representative in accordance with applicable law. These groups should not be included in research unless the research is necessary to promote the health of the population represented and this research cannot instead be performed on legally competent persons.

25 When a subject deemed legally incompetent, such as a minor child, is able to give assent to decisions about participation in research, the investigator must obtain that assent in addition to the consent of the legally authorized representative.

26 Research on individuals from whom it is not possible to obtain consent, including proxy or advance consent, should be done only if the physical/mental condition that prevents obtaining informed consent is a necessary characteristic of the research population. The specific reasons for involving research subjects with a condition that renders them unable to give informed consent should be stated in the experimental protocol for consideration and approval of the review committee.

The protocol should state that consent to remain in the research should be obtained as soon as possible from the individual or a legally authorized surrogate.

27 Both authors and publishers have ethical obligations. In publication of the results of research, the investigators are obliged to preserve the accuracy of the results. Negative as well as positive results should be published or otherwise publicly available. Sources of funding, institutional affiliations and any possible conflicts of interest should be declared in the publication. Reports of experimentation not in accordance with the principles laid down in this Declaration should not be accepted for publication.

C ADDITIONAL PRINCIPLES FOR MEDICAL RESEARCH COMBINED WITH MEDICAL CARE

28 The physician may combine medical research with medical care, only to the extent that the research is justified by its potential prophylactic, diagnostic or therapeutic value. When medical research is combined with medical care, additional standards apply to protect the patients who are research subjects.

29 The benefits, risks, burdens and effectiveness of a new method should be tested against those of the best current prophylactic, diagnostic, and therapeutic methods. This does not exclude the use of placebo, or no treatment, in studies where no proven prophylactic, diagnostic or therapeutic method exists.

30 At the conclusion of the study, every patient entered into the study should be assured of access to the best proven prophylactic, diagnostic and therapeutic methods identified by the study.

31 The physician should fully inform the patient which aspects of the care are related to the research. The refusal of a patient to participate in a study must never interfere with the patient-physician relationship.

32 In the treatment of a patient, where proven prophylactic, diagnostic and therapeutic methods do not exist or have been ineffective, the physician, with informed consent from the patient, must be free to use unproven or new prophylactic, diagnostic and therapeutic measures, if in the physician's judgement it offers hope of saving life, re-establishing health or alleviating suffering. Where possible, these measures should be made the object of research, designed to evaluate their safety and efficacy. In all cases, new information should be recorded and, where appropriate, published. The other relevant guidelines of this Declaration should be followed.

It should be noted that there was some confusion following the insertion of paragraph 29 by the meeting of the World Medical Association in 2000. As a result, the WMA has issued the following note of clarification:

[The World Medical Association] hereby reaffirms its position that extreme care must be taken in making use of a placebo-controlled trial and that in general this methodology should only be used in the absence of existing proven therapy. However, a placebo-controlled trial may be ethically acceptable, even if proven therapy is available, under the following circumstances:

– where for compelling and scientifically sound methodological reasons its use is necessary to determine the efficacy or safety of a prophylactic, diagnostic or therapeutic method; or

– where a prophylactic, diagnostic or therapeutic method is being investigated for a minor condition and the patients who receive placebo will not be subject to any additional risk of serious or irreversible harm.

All other provisions of the Declaration of Helsinki must be adhered to, especially the need for appropriate ethical and scientific review.

At its 2004 meeting in Tokyo, the WMA calirified paragraph 30 by stating: 'Post-trial access arrangements or other care must be described in the study protocol so the ethical review committee may consider such arrangments duting the review.

As will be apparent, pp 561 *et seq*, below, the Helsinki Declaration has acted as a template for the various domestic codes, which have subsequently been drafted in respect of particular areas of research practice in the UK.

The duty of doctor/researcher

Our concern in this section is the duties of an *ethical* nature that the doctor/researcher may be held to owe to the research subject. (Consideration of duties imposed by the law is left until later in this chapter, pp 546 *et seq*, below). In accordance with the central distinction, outlined above, between therapeutic and non-therapeutic research, we shall deal separately with the duties which exist in each case.

Duties to patients

Can therapeutic research, and the additional risks it entails, be reconciled (and if so, how far) with the doctor's pledge under the Hippocratic Oath to do the best for each of his patients? In itself, this question admits of an affirmative answer: the higher risks can be balanced against the hope that a new therapy will bring increased benefits for the patients so treated. However, matters are complicated by the use, in RCTs, of randomisation to determine the treatment given to each patient. For here it might well be argued that the doctor has abdicated his duty to tailor the treatment he provides to the latter's individual needs. The ethical conflict here, and the question of how far the patient's fully informed consent could provide a justification, is analysed by Charles Fried:

> **Fried, C, *Medical Experimentation – Personal Integrity and Social Policy*, 1974, Amsterdam: North-Holland Publishing, pp 51–56:**
>
> In the RCT a physician (or group of physicians) determines each individual's precise therapy by considering not only that individual's need, but also by considering the needs of the experimental design, that is the needs of the wider social group that will be benefited by a more definitive evaluation of the therapies concerned. Concretely, the actual therapy the patient receives is determined by a randomising scheme. Does this not, then, clearly pose the dilemma of the physician's duty to the individual and his interest in serving a wider group that would be benefited by the results of the trial? Is this not a case in which that conflict is resolved at least in part by sacrificing the interests and claims of the individual to those of the wider group? Now some would seek to short-circuit this philosophical inquiry at the outset by denying that any conflict exists and that the individual's interests have in any way been sacrificed.
>
> The argument is frequently made that where the balance of opinion is truly in equipoise, there is no sense to the accusation that the prescribing of one or the other of the equally eligible treatments can constitute a withholding of anything or can constitute doing less than one's best (the alternative being no better). And so no one sacrifices anybody to anything. Surely, this is the strongest defence that can be made in favour of the RCT. Yet, this defence is unsatisfactory at least in so far as it seeks to show that there is in fact not even any problem to be resolved, no difficulty of conscience, of ethics and philosophy.

First, one might admit to a certain scepticism about whether the facts often, if ever, correspond to those which are needed to dissolve so handily the dilemma. Is it ever likely to be the case that in a complex medical situation the balance of harms and benefits discounted by their appropriate probabilities really does appear on the then available evidence to be in equipoise? Or even approximately enough in equipoise to make the argument go through? I would concede that as to a particular medical condition, even quite carefully defined, viewed across a general population there might be a number of cases where the balance between treatments was equal; but I would suppose that in many of these situations this equipoise would not exist in respect to a particular patient. Consider, for instance, the choice between medical and surgical intervention for acute unstable angina pectoris. I would suppose that a group of patients could be so defined that the risks and benefits of the two available courses of action were quite evenly balanced. But, when a particular patient is involved, with a particular set of symptoms, a particular diagnostic picture and a particular set of values and preferences (this last is an issue on which more must be said later), then one may doubt how often a physician carefully going into all of these particularities would conclude that the risks and benefits are truly equal.

Perhaps, after all, this may happen, and may happen often enough to justify a significant number of RCTs. But before one concludes that the dilemma has really been dissolved in these cases, one must be quite careful to determine whether the condition of equipoise obtains just because it has been previously decided not to inquire too closely into the particular circumstances of the particular patient, proceeding rather on the balance of risks and benefits as they pertain to a larger group. One must be careful of this, because if the equipoise appears as a result of this failure of inquiry, then the sacrifice has indeed taken place, but only at another level, in a different way. One might say that the individual patient has perhaps not been sacrificed in the crude sense that the best available treatment has been withheld from him, but he has been sacrificed in that for the sake of the experimental design his interest in having his particular circumstances investigated has been sacrificed. But this amounts to the same thing.

The RCT raises a further conflict between the interest of the individual and that of the experiment: what should the patient be told? Should he be told that he is receiving that therapy which in the judgment of his physicians is the best available in his case, or should he be told more fully that his therapy is being determined by some randomising device in furtherance of a medical experiment? In the case where the choice between the two treatments is not in equipoise, the failure to disclose the existence of the RCT adds insult to injury since it plainly withholds information which any patient should find relevant and indeed the basis for considering a change of doctors. The non-disclosure is deceptive because it fails to reveal that the patient's interests are, to some extent, being sacrificed for the sake of the experimental design and thus, the wider social good. That sacrifice might be the overt one of exposing the patient to the risk of a treatment which in the present state of knowledge is somewhat less favoured, or the less overt one of not inquiring fully into his particular circumstances (including his particular value system) in order to determine whether the balance of probabilities is in equipoise in his particular case. There are two justifications for non-disclosure frequently offered: (1) that the distress this would cause the patient would be therapeutically undesirable; and (2) that the disclosure would endanger the experiment by introducing a disturbing element or even by causing the patient to withhold his consent. Both justifications are inadequate to show that non-disclosure does not sacrifice some interest of the subject. Both justifications beg this question, since they assume that the choice by randomisation is proper, and thus they assume that limiting disclosure in order to facilitate this kind of experimentation is proper.

Finally, the failure to make full disclosure is problematic even in the case where the two treatments are really in equipoise for the particular patient, with his particular life plan and physical characteristics. That there is a real problem even here is suggested by the high probability that many patients would surely want to know or would feel deceived if they had not been told ... I shall argue that the patient has an interest in knowing and thus participating in processes that touch some of his most vital interests, even if we are sure that there is only one rational choice for him to make. Thus, whatever the compensating benefits to the participant in the RCT or to society as a whole, it seems pretty clear that the experimental subject has something to lose, and it is his doctor who is imposing these burdens on him. This does seem to conflict with the conception of a physician as bearing an obligation of undivided loyalty to his patient.

Clearly, these problems are particularly acute in the context of serious life-saving therapy, where one group of patients may end up with inferior treatment (or possibly no treatment at all) and where doctors may stand upon their 'therapeutic privilege' to avoid disclosure. Nor, as Graham Thorpe notes, are they diminished merely because the patient's condition is thought to be incurable:

Thorpe, G, 'Experiments on the dying', in Williams, CJ (ed), *Introducing New Treatments for Cancer: Practical, Ethical and Legal Problems,* **1992, Chichester: John Wiley, pp 217–19:**

In 1967 the debate concerning the medical ethics of research on patients was fuelled dramatically by the publication in Britain of a book, *Human Guinea Pigs,* by MH Pappworth. He drew attention to the fact that the human being was the only animal that doctors could experiment upon without a licence, and demonstrated a wide gap between the doctor's care of the patient and his pursuit of knowledge. A chapter was devoted to each of the following vulnerable groups: infants and children, pregnant women, mental detectives and mentally sick, prison inmates, the dying and the old, and patients awaiting or undergoing operations.

Looking back 25 years, much of the research cited involved puncture and catheterisation of blood and other vessels, an indication of the frontier of medical progress at that time. Numerous examples of exploitation and abuse were given. With respect to the dying and the old, Pappworth lists the new techniques of splenic puncture to measure blood pressure in the splenic vein in patients with liver disease and percutaneous splenoportography, percutaneous transhepatic cannulation of a hepatic or portal vein, arterial and cardiac catheterisation, and cannulation of the thoracic duct.

Other research involved the production of temporary anuria by the injection of large volumes of water intravenously to induce haemolysis, the measurement of oxygen consumption in paralysed men exposed to cold, and rib puncture with the injection of contrast medium to outline the azygos veins.

In some of the patients, many of whom had advanced cancer, there were complications ranging from minor to serious, and several died as a direct result of the experiments. In a number of instances a new investigational procedure was first practised on cadavers and then on an ill patient with a poor prognosis. If he should die in the course of perfecting the technique or improving the operator's technical skill, then that would be unfortunate, but a lesser loss than a fitter patient or normal subject.

All this research was non-therapeutic and of no benefit to the persons concerned and Pappworth argued that patients seriously ill with advanced disease should not be treated as expendable, but they were entitled to the best possible palliative care. As for experiments and research, they should be regarded as prohibited subjects. To this end acknowledged and observed safeguards should be introduced, otherwise abuses would inevitably continue.

A secret trial

Fourteen years later in 1981 an anterior resection of a carcinoma of the rectum was performed on an 84 year old widow who had previously enjoyed good health. She died 15 days later from acute bone marrow depression induced by 5-fluorouracil (5-FU). At the inquest it emerged that the patient had been an unwitting participant in a randomised controlled trial ...

Following earlier work which suggested that the infusion of 5-FU into the portal vein would reduce the incidence of liver metastasis, a new multi-centre study had been set up. After an operation to remove a primary carcinoma of rectum had been performed, patients with no evidence of metastatic disease were allocated randomly into three groups. In one there was no further treatment. In the second group, as heparin had been given with the 5-FU in the previous study to determine whether this drug alone had any effect, a heparin infusion was given via the portal vein twice daily for seven days. In the third group 500 mg of 5-FU was infused with heparin as in the second group.

Careful consideration had been given by ethical committees as to whether patients and their relatives should be informed of the existence and details of the trial, and it had been decided that they should not be informed and therefore their consent was not sought.

Writing about this case in *The Lancet*, the barrister Diana Brahams stated:

> I find the concept of secret random control trials wholly unacceptable, and the reasons offered to justify them both unconvincing and unsatisfactory. It is usual to tell patients and obtain their consent apparently, but where the end measure is death and cancer is involved, the doctor thinks he knows best.

At the inquest, evidence showed that the trial protocol which required blood counts every other day after operation had not been followed and therefore the bone marrow depression which had occurred was not detected at an early stage. The coroner brought in a verdict of misadventure and stated that the whole idea of concealed controlled trials should be brought to the public notice so that proper discussion could take place.

On the other hand, it may be felt that to insist upon fully informed consent in this context may be counterproductive, not only from the point of view of hindering medical progress (in so far as one were prepared to recognise utilitarian trade-offs here) but in terms of the individual patient's own interests. An argument to this effect is put forward by Tobias and Souhani:

Tobias, J and Souhani, R, 'Fully informed consent can be needlessly cruel' (1993) 307 BMJ 1199:

Cruelty to patients

After many years of experience as committed trialists and believers in the statistical and clinical value of the randomised clinical trial, we feel that uniform recommendation for full written informed consent, as outlined, for example, by the Royal College of Physicians, may be not only bad for clinical trials but, far more important, unnecessarily cruel to patients.

Consider for example the case of cancer of the cervix. Since we now have, for the first time, several cytotoxic agents with activity in patients with advanced disease, it is of critical importance to establish whether or not this new approach combined with the conventional treatment (radiotherapy), offers an improvement in overall cure rate. If it does, this would be the first step forward in this tumour since radiotherapy was introduced as standard treatment over 50 years ago. The issue can be settled only by clinical trials of sufficient size to quantify any possible benefit but the difficulty that many trialists have with the informed consent consultation with these patients has made this kind of study extremely problematic.

It is neither faintheartedness nor a disinclination to be questioned that discourages the clinician; rather, it is the overwhelming difficulty of describing the details of a potentially valuable (but as yet unproved) new remedy, gaining the patient's assent, and later having to inform her that she has been randomised to receive radiotherapy alone. However carefully the pros and cons of chemotherapy may have been explained, the result of the randomisation often leads the doctor towards a rather shabby display of back pedalling, in which the possible advantages of the chemotherapy are 'talked down' and perhaps the side effects 'talked up'. The patient may become extremely distressed, which is not only counterproductive (with refusal to participate) but also alarming for the doctor and by no means easily resolved.

It does not take many such consultations to change a well intentioned and committed trialist into a disgruntled clinician who no longer feels that the game is worth the candle. It can be extremely difficult to sustain the doctor-patient relationship through such a harrowing discussion, and particularly unfortunate for patients such as those in the example above whose treatment by radiotherapy (that is, the control group) would be regarded as entirely conventional and proper. Both the support and reassurance of the doctor, and the patient's trust and confidence in the medical advice, may have been irretrievably lost. Too frank an explanation, with patient overload from too much information, can have most serious consequences.

A way forward

The ethical double standard is obvious. If doctors are sure they know which is the correct general policy of management, and if they recommend treatment according to their judgment or preference, they are excused any ethical criticism on the grounds of freedom of clinical judgment. All would agree that a clinician must be able to advise according to the particular circumstances (medical, social, psychological) of the patient, but what if the doctor is ill informed or dogmatic? Why should the clinician who shares with expert colleagues a genuine doubt about the best treatment be subject to the difficulties outlined above? ...

In ordinary clinical practice (outside clinical trials) it is essential that doctors judge how quickly to impart information and to what degree they will spell out the medical facts, especially if they are frightening or unpalatable. The move towards full disclosure of all details of diagnosis, treatment, and prognosis is a major change in social perception in the United Kingdom and the United States – one by no means found in all countries to the same degree. However, no sensible doctor makes full disclosure to every patient. This would be a recipe for needless cruelty and distress. Although in most branches of medicine an honest and candid approach is generally desirable, one of the challenges of clinical medicine is to know how quickly to proceed and how to judge the amount of information which should be given at a particular moment. Informing a patient is a continuous process.

We suggest that the process of informed consent should be viewed as another straightforward instance in which the clinical judgment of the doctor is paramount.

Clearly, for a patient who wishes to know what underlies all aspects of decision making, there is no doubt that full explanation should be given, together with all the necessary information about the trial. At the other extreme a distraught patient, possibly within days of diagnosis of a potentially lethal illness, may be unable to take in any but the most basic details. Often in desperate need of reassurance, patients such as this can hardly be expected to cope with a full discussion of options to be decided at random. In between there will be more complex judgments in which the outlines of alternative treatments must be explained and the patient reassured that the treatment policy decided on will always be in his or her best interests. The crucial point here may sometimes include the question of whether to disclose that this decision is based on a randomisation in which the physician plays no direct part. This may be very unnerving for patients, and in some situations – for example, in discussion with parents of a child with cancer (in which age group randomised trials are usual) – it may be extremely difficult.

Duties to volunteers

As previously noted, the researcher who carries out non-therapeutic research on volunteers has no doctor–patient relationship with his subject. Nevertheless, this does not entail the absence of ethical duties on his part towards the latter. In some ways, indeed, it may heighten his obligations. As Charles Fried writes:

Fried, C, *Medical Experimentation – Personal Integrity and Social Policy*, 1974, Amsterdam: North-Holland Publishing, pp 26–27:

Non-therapeutic experimentation

No special doctrines apply to non-therapeutic experimentation. Indeed, to the extent that the experimentation is non-therapeutic, the fact that it is being carried out by doctors should be entirely irrelevant. The usual privileges under which doctors work, and the usual special doctrines according to which the liabilities of doctors are judged, should not be applicable, since they proceed from the premise that the doctor must be given considerable latitude as he works in the presumed interests of his patient. But that is not the case in non-therapeutic research. The doctor confronts his subject simply as a scientist.

In general, the law imposes a strict duty of disclosure, wherever an individual with a great deal to lose is exposed to a risk or is asked to relinquish rights by someone with considerably greater knowledge. And this is true, whether the relation is one of buyer and seller or involves some public interest. Persons selling cosmetics, automobiles or pharmaceuticals are required to make full disclosures of all the hazards involved in the products they sell. But policemen seeking damaging admissions from suspects are also required to issue a warning of constitutional rights and to offer legal assistance before those rights are waived. There is no reason why the case should be any different where a researcher asks an experimental subject to risk his health.

Exceptionally a doctor may rely on the doctrine of 'therapeutic privilege' – see Chapter 3 and below at p 536 – to avoid informing a patient of his participation in therapeutic research, no such argument is admissible in relation to volunteers. (We shall consider at p 541, below, how far this increased duty of candour in cases of non-therapeutic research forms part of English law.)

CONSENT TO RESEARCH

Whereas research upon embryos may only be carried out under licence pursuant to the Human Fertilisation and Embryology Act 1990 (see Chapter 7), and that upon animals is regulated by the Animals (Scientific Procedures) Act 1968, there are no similar statutory safeguards operative in respect of research upon (full) human beings. Perhaps the major reason for this is that the human research subject is thought able to protect himself adequately against abuse by the researcher through the mechanism of consent at common law. How far is this really so? Although we have examined consent to treatment in some detail (see Chapter 3), medical research gives rise to some special considerations. For example, in relation to general treatment, consent may sometimes simply be inferred from the surrounding circumstances, as when a patient submits to a medical examination. In the context of therapeutic research, the additional (and cloaked) intention of the doctor/researcher means that the subject's consent cannot be so inferred.

It will be recalled that the three elements to a valid consent are capacity, voluntariness and information, and each will be examined in relation to therapeutic and non-therapeutic research, respectively.

Therapeutic research

The competent patient

The first issue here is to determine whether the subject has genuine capacity to consent. In this regard, could it be argued that the latter must possess a more sophisticated understanding than someone who is receiving 'ordinary' medical treatment? In one sense, the answer is 'yes', because the issues in a research project may be quite complex, but there is no real difference of criteria. Consent to general treatment requires an ability to understand the nature of the treatment and this general principle applies equally to therapeutic research.

More problematic, however, may be the requirement for such consent to be free from coercion. This is because there is a danger that pressure (real or perceived) may be placed upon a patient to agree to participate in a clinical trial for fear of not receiving the best treatment in the face of a refusal. Sarah Hewlett comments on this problem as follows:

Hewlett, S, 'Consent to clinical research – adequately voluntary or substantially influenced?' (1996) 22 JME 232:

Influences or controlling influences?

Whilst circumstances and people will always influence any decision we make, it is the responsibility of the researcher to ensure that in clinical research, these are not so strong as to be controlling. Unlike healthy volunteers, many patients invited to participate in clinical research will have an illness and the experience of illness (which may at times include pain, disability, fear of deterioration or death, physical or emotional dependence) and the accompanying psychological response (possibly depression, mourning, denial, anger, anxiety, passivity and regression to an invalid role) may well reduce autonomy. In addition, a request to enter a research trial may of necessity come at the time of, or soon after, the shock of diagnosis. Furthermore, some patients in hospital feel vulnerable – unaware of the normal routine or what is expected of them, and reduced, as they are, to wearing night clothes. Is it possible to make a reflective decision, free of strong influences in such a situation?

The doctor-patient relationship is centred around patients' trust that doctors act in their best interests. Thus even though the doctor has explained that treatment in the research trial is randomised and according to a strict protocol, patients often still believe that the doctor will only act in their best interests. In a recent trial 41% of patients believed there were no risks in a Phase II trial of a new anti-inflammatory agent, despite being told it was unlicensed and being tested for safety. So strong is this trust that patients may agree to anything the doctor suggests and even the invitation to participate may be viewed as a recommendation rather than a request. Patients may feel flattered by the request and under an obligation to help because of past care received.

For many patients the relationship is an unequal one, with the doctor being perceived as a powerful figure on whom they depend, making it difficult for them to take an unnaturally dominant role and refuse the doctor's request. Patients may fear that if they do so, the doctor will be displeased and their future care will be jeopardised. Patients may view clinical research as a means of access to care (which may be true for patients in countries where many people do not have health care insurance) and may also equate the frequent safety visits with improved care.

External pressures may be brought to bear on the patient: the patient may be asked to decide immediately, without time to reflect; family and friends may suggest the patient 'ought' to participate; the facts we give the patient will be laden with our beliefs; we may use closed questions or statistics which are loaded in a persuasive fashion (for example 75% of patients do well rather than 25% do badly); doctors may be under pressure to reach target numbers, with academic and financial kudos resulting from a completed trial. Thus the influences on the patient are multiple and complex.

She proposes several practical strategies for dealing with these problems:

Hewlett, S, 'Consent to clinical research – adequately voluntary or substantially influenced?' (1996) 22 JME 232:

Reducing influences on consent to clinical research

Whilst it could be argued that the adequately autonomous patient is the best person to decide if his or her decision is adequately voluntary, as health care professionals we have a professional responsibility to try and promote adequately voluntary consent by the manner in which we obtain it. This is similar to our responsibilities in trying to ensure adequately informed consent by the manner in which we inform patients. Areas where influences could be reduced include the doctor–patient relationship, selection of patients, education of the researcher and information given during recruitment.

The doctor–patient relationship

Interventions here might allow the patient to step back from the relationship and consider the proposal in a more detached manner. This could be done by using a researcher/doctor as well as a carer/doctor, by using a patient advocate or by recruiting patients in groups. Separating the doctors into researcher/doctors and carer/doctors may allow patients to feel less anxious about future care if they refuse. However, the doctors are likely to be, or to become, close colleagues; the carer/doctor will have to be responsible for recruitment, which involves him in the research; the researcher/doctor will need to know about the patient's care; and both doctors will need to deal with clinical problems as they arise, thus causing practical problems as a result of creating this split. In therapeutic research, care and research are so closely interlinked that it is impractical and impossible not to mix the two.

A patient advocate might ask questions on the patient's behalf, act as an impartial sounding board, and deter the doctor from pressurising or hurrying the patient. A lay advocate (friend or relative) might not be able to interpret technical details any better than the patient, might also be in awe of the perceived power of the doctor, and might influence the patient by the strength of their own relationship. A non-doctor health care professional might be well suited to advocacy because of his or her familiarity with the health care system, rapport with patients and ability to interpret technical data. However, such a professional may be seen as part of the doctor's team and may well be employed by the doctor so that he or she has a vested interest in encouraging recruitment. However, a trained advocate, perhaps funded by the health authority or trust, could be specifically trained and supervised by the research ethics committee. Such posts, separate from any research or care team, have the potential to develop into an independent advocacy system.

Talking to patients about clinical research in groups rather than individually may reduce pressure on patients – more outspoken patients may ask questions which others are reluctant to voice. However, patients may also find it difficult to go against the group decision if they do not agree with it.

Selection of patients

It has been suggested that we should first approach patients who are best able to understand the research, and who are most highly motivated and least captive, such as health care professionals who have the particular disease in question. The numbers in this group are likely to be so small as to make research impractical and where there is a link between educational level and disease, selecting highly educated subjects might bias the study.

Education of researchers

Education of health care professionals in research ethics and obtaining consent should ease pressure on patients by increasing the researchers' awareness. This is gradually happening as nursing and medical schools include medical ethics in their curricula.

Information to patients

Specific trial information sheets are vital and patients must have time to read and discuss them. However, as they are written by the researchers who wish the patient to consent there is the real possibility that they will be biased. Consumers for Ethics in Research (CERES) produce a standard leaflet on medical research which is not written in relation to specific projects. Having seen this leaflet and following our own research into consent, we have developed a Patient's Guide to Medical Research ... which is given to all rheumatology patients as they are invited to participate in clinical research, alongside the specific trial information sheets. It is independent of any single researcher or research trial, is designed to cover many of the issues raised in this article and has an 'easy' readability level.

We have made other changes to the consent process, including giving the responsibility for information-giving and initial interview and consent to the research nurses, who are perhaps seen as less powerful figures than the doctor. We give patients at least 48 hours to reflect on the proposal and encourage them to discuss it with family, friends and GP, before telephoning them to discuss the trial, answer questions and take their decision, which is passed on to the doctor on their behalf. We believe that these strategies reduce the difficulty patients experience in deciding to take part in research and we will be assessing this in future trials.

The Royal College of Physicians confirms in its Guidance (*Research Involving Patients*, 1990, London: RCP) that patients must feel free to decline to participate and assured that the refusal will not put them at a disadvantage, (paras 7.4 *et seq*). Note, below, the provisions of s 33 of the Mental Capacity Act 2005 which reflects this as do the Medicines for Human Use (Clinical Trials) Regulations 2004 (below p 547).

There is concern that certain groups in particular may be vulnerable to exploitation in the field of research. It will be recalled that this was examined in Chapter 3 (see the cases of *Freeman v Home Office* [1984] 1 All ER 1036 and *Kaimowitz v Michigan Department of Mental Health* 42 USLW 2063 (1973)). Mason and McCall comment as follows:

Royal College of Physicians, *Research Involving Patients*, 1990, London: RCP:

7.48 It has been suggested that involuntary detention of any sort invalidates consent and hence makes participation in research impossible. We reject this view and consider that research into medical and psychological disturbances affecting prisoners may be beneficial. Furthermore, there is evidence that prisoners may not wish to be excluded from participation in worthwhile research. For example, we see no reason to exclude those patients who are imprisoned from a study involving patients with hepatitis merely because of their imprisonment.

7.49 We recommend that research should not be undertaken solely in prisoners who are patients as defined in s 2.1 unless the fact of being imprisoned is itself an essential component of the research.

7.50 In the case of research in which it is considered that the participation of an independent informed individual or patient's friend is helpful (see 7.22), the prison officer may not always be appropriate and another person such as a prison visitor should then be considered.

Mason, JK and Laurie, GT, *Law and Medical Ethics*, 7th edn, 2006, Oxford: OUP, p 664:

[We come] to the problems of the use of specific populations who are special because of their easy access, malleability and the like. Students, and particulary medical students, provide an example about whom there is little difficulty; they are of an age to make legally valid decisions, they may well have an active interest in the trial and most, if not all, educational establishments have very stringently controlling ethics committees to protect against, say, repititive use. [Can this be said of] the armed forces, who may be particularly vulnerable to improper research in war or when war threatens – even in 1990, non-consensual trials were allowed on American troops engaged in the Gulf War ...[?]

... The use of prisoners, however, exposes many ethical issues that are based, essentially, on the arguments that some advantage, even if only imagined, must accrue to the prisoner participating in a trial; that advantage may be so great as to induce the prisoner to volunteer for research which involves greater discomfort or risk than would be accepted by a free man and, in particular, it may compromise his inalienable right to withdraw from the trial. The arguments are not, however, entirely one way – it is possible to be paternalistic in an attempt to preserve peoples' autonomy. Thus, prisoners could well resent protective attitudes on the grounds that it is their right to dispose of their bodies and to take such risks as they please that is being compromised. This could be the subject of lengthy debate, but we suggest that the conditions in today's prisons are such that any process which provides some relief deserves, at least, a sympathetic evaluation and, secondly, that many prisoners might be benefited therapeutically through helping society. But it is also felt that experiments on prisoners should be particularly rigidly controlled by ethical committees which should always contain lay members with experience in criminology ...

The Central Office for Research Ethics Committees (see p 560 below) states that research involving prisoners and young offenders should relate directly to prisoners' health care and be of such a nature that it could only be conducted in this population; official guidance has, therefore, favoured a paternalistic approach.

A further major issue in respect of therapeutic research carried out upon competent patients concerns the amount of information to which they are legally entitled. We have seen that a battery will be committed if the patient is not informed of the broad nature of an intended medical procedure. Kennedy and Grubb comment as follows:

Kennedy, I and Grubb, A, *Medical Law*, 3rd edn, 2000, London: Butterworths, pp 1710–11:

One view, and it is ours, is that where there is a dual intention on the part of the doctor, ie, to treat and to conduct research, any failure to inform the patient concerning *both* of these intentions and their possible consequences would amount in law to a battery. This is because in the absence of such knowledge the patient will have assented to a procedure which is materially different in its nature from that which the doctor intends to carry out. To put it another way, research adds a further component to the quality of the consent that the law requires.

The law does not require people to volunteer and will provide a remedy to the patient against the doctor who conscripts him, the remedy being in battery to demonstrate the law's concern for the rights of the patient. Indeed, arguably the failure to disclose the intention to conduct research would amount to fraud sufficient to vitiate any consent which might otherwise be valid. If this is the law, that failure to inform is a battery, then what must the doctor do to act lawfully? In short, the answer must be that the doctor must make explicit his intention to carry out research. A court may insist on the patient being informed of three particular matters in addition to this generalised intention. Each of them is an aspect of those interests of the patient which the law of battery seeks to protect. The patient must be informed: (1) that he may refuse to take part in the research project or may at any time withdraw from the research and that in either case if he does so he will suffer no adverse consequences in terms of the treatment he will then receive; (2) that the nature of the research may be such that he may be a member of a control group in a trial which is intended to evaluate the efficacy of a new therapy; (3) that the trial is a randomised controlled trial (RCT) if it be such.

As regards (2), one consequence of being a member of a control group could be that the patient does not receive the form of treatment which subsequently proves to be the more efficacious. To meet this ethical difficulty researchers ordinarily would be expected to provide for periodic examination of the emerging data. It is our view that a patient's consent is not informed for the purpose of the tort of battery unless he is made aware of this periodic review.

As regards (3), randomisation means that a treatment regime is assigned to a patient randomly without regard to the particular circumstances of that patient, his needs, his preferences or the preferences of his doctor. Again, it is our view that a patient may volunteer for such a trial but his consent is only valid if he is given the opportunity of knowing it is randomised and he is aware of what this means.

Since its redrafting in 2000, the Declaration of Helsinki has placed greater emphasis upon informed consent (see paras 31 and 32) than it did in the 1964 version which provided for circumstances in which the physician might consider it essential not to obtain informed consent (para II(5).), but even so the 2000 version does not expressly refer to disclosure of the precise nature and use of a RCT. Furthermore, the Royal College of Physicians, in *Guidelines on the Practice of Ethics Committees in Medical Research Involving Human Subjects*, 1996, London: RCP cite the Tobias and Souhani article (extracted at p 528, above), to support its view that, where it would cause distress to reveal the nature of the investigation but it is in the clinical interest of the patient, information can be withheld in 'exceptional circumstances'. These guidelines are in the process of being redrafted and should be available at the end of 2005. It will be interesting to see whether this will be removed in the new version. As Kennedy and Grubb point out (*Medical Law*, 3rd edn, 2000, London: Butterworths, p 1711), if the patient would be caused distress by the knowledge that he is in a clinical trial, this is an argument for excluding him from the trial, not for including him without his knowledge. As yet, however, the position has not been tested in the courts. The cases of *Sidaway v Board of Governors of the Bethlem Royal Hospital and the Maudsley Hospital* [1985] AC 871 and *Chester v Afshar* [2004] UKHL 41 are pertinent here. As we have seen (see Chapter 3) *Chester* confirmed that the patient has a right to be informed of any risks that would have affected the decision of the reasonable patient in his/her circumstances. The same conclusion must be drawn, even more forceably, in a case where there is an objective (here, research) other than the well being of the patient. However, even in *Chester* it was acknowledged that there could be circumstances where therapeutic privilege might apply, and in *Sidaway* Lord Scarman had stated the same thing. In the USA, where there is Federal law that regulates medical research, the doctrine of therapeutic privilege is acknowledged (see Myers, D, *The Human Body and the Law*, 1990, Edinburgh: Edinburgh UP). Given that, at least in part, the purpose of therapeutic research is to offer some benefit to the patient, is it not inevitable that something akin to therapeutic privilege will exist? A report from Peter Hamilton, the Sheriff in Aberdeen, however, highlights a case where the patient had been positively misled:

Hamilton, P (Sheriff), 'Sheriff's Report, Aberdeen' (1997) Bulletin of Medical Ethics 22:

28 January 1997

In 1993, while recovering from a fractured hip, Mrs Phyllis Moffit was recruited into a clinical trial after receiving the following revised patient information sheet:

> Dear …
>
> We are asking patients who have had a hip fracture in the past if they will take part in a research project. The aim is to try to prevent their unaffected hip from breaking at a later date.
>
> In order to do this, we would like to have the opportunity to inject your unaffected hip (the one you have not broken) with a material which we think would actually strengthen the bone. It is composed of crystals of calcium, very like bone, and a protein which is known to stimulate bone growth.
>
> We know there is a one in five chance that you might break the other hip within four years, and therefore there would be great benefits if the injection

were to be successful. We are not aware of any significant risks associated with this injection.

If you agree to this injection, you will be admitted to Woodend Hospital. It will be done under a local anaesthetic in the operating theatre. It will involve having a small cut (about half an inch) made in your unaffected hip and the material being injected into your hip bone. This is not a painful procedure and should not inconvenience or incapacitate you in any way. This will not affect your mobility ...

Mrs Moffit died in August 1994 of heart failure while under sedation for the experimental hip surgery. The heart failure was caused by an unsuspected aneurysm of the coronary artery.In this case, the statistic quoted in the information sheet as to the likelihood of a second hip fracture was based upon inconclusive evidence and had indeed been changed from an earlier sheet in which the chance was described as 'one in 10 over two years'. The victim's daughter gave evidence that the alarm her mother had felt on reading this was the chief reason she had agreed to participate in the research. Moreover, the research proposal approved by the local research ethics committee (LREC) had not mentioned the need for sedation of subjects as initially it had not been thought that the procedure would be painful. Whilst the researchers had become aware that this would in fact be required some time prior to recruiting Mrs Moffit, they failed either to amend the information sheet or to inform the LREC. Finally, although the patient here was recovering from a fractured hip, it may be queried whether this was really *therapeutic* research at all.

The incompetent patient

Children

First, does s 8 of the Family Law Reform Act 1969 (see Chapter 4) apply to research? The section refers to 'any surgical, medical or dental treatment', and it has been argued (by, for example, Kennedy and Grubb in *Medical Law*, 3rd edn, 2000, London: Butterworths) that this does not cover treatment which includes a research component. This would mean that the age of 16 would have no significance as far as consent of the child is concerned, but presumably the concept of *Gillick* competence would apply. Some might take the simplistic view that there is no need to consider the problem of carrying out research on children because such research can easily be outlawed. However, the implicit assumption behind this is that adults can just as eaily be used as research subjects. Unfortunately, this is not the case, as there are conditions that affect only children, and in other cases it is not possible to use with any degree of accuracy, the outcome of research on adults to predict the outcome in children Mason and Laurie comment as follows:

Mason, JK and Laurie, GT, *Law and Medical Ethics*, 7th edn, 2006, Oxford: OUP, p 685:

Children respond differently to drugs, as they do to a number of other treatments, and it is impossible to say that the effect of a particular therapy on an adult will be mirrored when applied to a child. Medical research on children is, therefore, necessary before a treatment can be approved for paediatric use ... Research involving children has lowered the rate of infant mortality considerably; for example, research on vitamin A deficiency in children in developing countries has made it possible to lower mortality rates among those affected by measles. Similarly, research on mother/child transmission of HIV has reduced the incidence of infection in the children of infected mothers – an important matter in the control of the global pandemic. At the same time, numerous surveys also indicate that there is a worrying dearth of well-conducted research involving children. One study by community paediatricians, for example, found that quality research to support their clinical decisions only existed in 40 per cent cases.

As we have seen (in Chapter 4) in the House of Lords case of *S v S* [1970] 3 All ER 107 the 'not against the interests of the child' test was endorsed. The implication for therapeutic research appears to be that the therapeutic aspect of the treatment means that it would not be contrary to the child's interests. However, if we consider randomised control tests, where the child may be getting no treatment at all, and where the choice as to whether the child is treated is not made on clinical grounds, can it still be argued that this is not contrary to the interests of the child?

Incompetent adults

As we have seen, until the enactment of the Mental Capacity Act 2005, due to come into force 2007) there was no provision in English law for proxy decision-making in medical and personal welfare matters. However, the new legislation not only applies to *bona fide* medical treatment but also extends to providing for medical research to be carried out on incompetent adults. The Law Commission had recommended that research on incompetent adults should be permitted (Law Commission Report 231 (1995)), but this recommendation was not followed up in the Mental Incapacity Bill. It was, however, taken up again when the Mental Capacity Bill was drafted following the pre-legislative scrutiny of the Joint Committee (Reports HL Paper 189–I & HC 1983–I).

Mental Capacity Act 2005:

30 Research

(1) Intrusive research carried out on, or in relation to, a person who lacks capacity to consent to it is unlawful unless it is carried out–

    (a) as part of a research project which is for the time being approved by the appropriate body for the purposes of this Act in accordance with section 31, and

    (b) in accordance with sections 32 and 33.

(2) Research is intrusive if it is of a kind that would be unlawful if it was carried out–

    (a) on or in relation to a person who had capacity to consent to it, but

    (b) without his consent.

(3) A clinical trial which is subject to the provisions of clinical trials regulations is not to be treated as research for the purposes of this section.

(4) 'Appropriate body', in relation to a research project, means the person, committee or other body specified in regulations made by the appropriate authority as the appropriate body in relation to a project of the kind in question.

(5) 'Clinical trials regulations' means–

    (a) the Medicines for Human Use (Clinical Trials) Regulations 2004 (S.I. 2004/1031) and any other regulations replacing those regulations or amending them, and

    (b) any other regulations relating to clinical trials and designated by the Secretary of State as clinical trials regulations for the purposes of this section.

(6) In this section, section 32 and section 34, 'appropriate authority' means–

   (a) in relation to the carrying out of research in England, the Secretary of State, and

   (b) in relation to the carrying out of research in Wales, the National Assembly for Wales.

31 Requirements for approval

(1) The appropriate body may not approve a research project for the purposes of this Act unless satisfied that the following requirements will be met in relation to research carried out as part of the project on, or in relation to, a person who lacks capacity to consent to taking part in the project ('P').

(2) The research must be connected with–

   (a) an impairing condition affecting P, or

   (b) its treatment.

(3) 'Impairing condition' means a condition which is (or may be) attributable to, or which causes or contributes to (or may cause or contribute to), the impairment of, or disturbance in the functioning of, the mind or brain.

(4) There must be reasonable grounds for believing that research of comparable effectiveness cannot be carried out if the project has to be confined to, or relate only to, persons who have capacity to consent to taking part in it.

(5) The research must–

   (a) have the potential to benefit P without imposing on P a burden that is disproportionate to the potential benefit to P, or

   (b) be intended to provide knowledge of the causes or treatment of, or of the care of persons affected by, the same or a similar condition.

(6) If the research falls within paragraph (b) of subsection (5) but not within paragraph (a), there must be reasonable grounds for believing–

   (a) that the risk to P from taking part in the project is likely to be negligible, and

   (b) that anything done to, or in relation to, P will not–

      (i) interfere with P's freedom of action or privacy in a significant way, or

      (ii) be unduly invasive or restrictive.

(7) There must be reasonable arrangements in place for ensuring that the requirements of sections 32 and 33 will be met.

Section 32 provides for consultation with carers.

The following are some observations on these provisions. First, the Act does not apply to clinical trials as these are covered by the Medicines for Human Use (Clinical Trials) Regulations 2004 (see below). Secondly, the key provisions of s 31(1) to (4) should be carefully noted. The research must be connected with either an impairing condition which affects the incompetent patient, or its treatment, and the condition must be one which causes some impairment or functioning of the mind or brain. In other words, the research could not be on a physical condition that affects the patient, as such a physical condition might affect those who are competent to provide the necessary consent. Nevertheless although we are referring to patients here, there is no requirement that the 'patient' is 'suffering' or acutely ill, merely that he has an impairment, so it is not strictly speaking correct to think of these people as 'patients'. Interestingly, this neatly conflates the patient/healthy volunteer distinction, arguably to the detriment of the research subject, whether described as a patient or not.

Further, under s 31(5), the research must either have the potential to benefit the patient (without imposing a disproportion burden), or to be beneficial to other persons affected by the same or similar conditions. It is arguable that the second part of the justification is unethical as it means that research which is not of benefit to the incompetent person can be carried out. However, this might be countered by s 31(6), which states that in these circumstances there must be reasonable grounds for believing that the risk is negligible and that it will not interfere with the patient's 'freedom of action or privacy in a significant way' or 'be unduly invasive or restrictive'. The key ethical point here is whether these provisions are sufficient to justify actions which might well constitute a battery upon a competent person who refused consent. For the protection of the patient it is important that s 31(6)(b) is construed so that neither (i) nor (ii) can pertain, and not be construed as justifiable alternatives. The explanatory notes to the Bill indicated that the type of research typical to s 31(6) might include indirect research on medical notes, or on human tissue already taken for other purposes, or may include interviews or questionnaires about health or social-care with the patient or his carers or limited observation of him. This is interesting given the views expressed by the Law Commission: see paragraph 6.30 on p 545, below, and the Commission's acknowledgment of the risk to the dignity and privacy of the research participants when they were incompetent and the research was non-therapeutic. Here we have a situation where provision is made quite clearly for this sort of research to be carried out on participants when it is not of benefit to them, ie it is non-therapeutic.

Section 33 provides additional safeguards and s 34 deals with loss of capacity during a research project:

33 Additional safeguards

(1) This section applies in relation to a person who is taking part in an approved research project even though he lacks capacity to consent to taking part.

(2) Nothing may be done to, or in relation to, him in the course of the research–

    (a) to which he appears to object (whether by showing signs of resistance or otherwise) except where what is being done is intended to protect him from harm or to reduce or prevent pain or discomfort, or

    (b) which would be contrary to–

        (i) an advance decision of his which has effect, or

        (ii) any other form of statement made by him and not subsequently withdrawn, of which R is aware.

(3) The interests of the person must be assumed to outweigh those of science and society.

(4) If he indicates (in any way) that he wishes to be withdrawn from the project he must be withdrawn without delay.

(5) P must be withdrawn from the project, without delay, if at any time the person conducting the research has reasonable grounds for believing that one or more of the requirements set out in section 31(2) to (7) is no longer met in relation to research being carried out on, or in relation to, P.

(6) But neither subsection (4) nor subsection (5) requires treatment that P has been receiving as part of the project to be discontinued if R has reasonable grounds for believing that there would be a significant risk to P's health if it were discontinued.

34 Loss of capacity during research project

(1) This section applies where a person ('P')-

   (a) has consented to take part in a research project begun before the commencement of section 30, but

   (b) before the conclusion of the project, loses capacity to consent to continue to take part in it.

(2) The appropriate authority may by regulations provide that, despite P's loss of capacity, research of a prescribed kind may be carried out on, or in relation to, P if-

   (a) the project satisfies prescribed requirements,

   (b) any information or material relating to P which is used in the research is of a prescribed description and was obtained before P's loss of capacity, and

   (c) the person conducting the project takes in relation to P such steps as may be prescribed for the purpose of protecting him.

(3) The regulations may, in particular,-

   (a) make provision about when, for the purposes of the regulations, a project is to be treated as having begun;

   (b) include provision similar to any made by section 31, 32 or 33.

Non-therapeutic research

The competent volunteer

Given that we are not considering *treatment* at all, should the test of capacity to consent be different in this context? The test, it is suggested, will be the same. The volunteer will still be required to understand the nature of the procedure and any risks involved, and weigh up the risks of the procedure with the advantage of participating (either financial, or psychological well being because of the potential benefits to others).

However, just as there may be a temptation for a doctor, who wishes to treat a refusing patient in the latter's own interests, to regard such a patient as *incompetent*, here, where a researcher needs healthy volunteers to assist in what he believes to be valuable research, the opposite temptation may arise: that is to say, the researcher may be over-ready to find an assenting volunteer competent. It is clear that vigilance is needed to protect individuals from physical interference in both cases.

Difficulties also arise in the context of ensuring that consent to participate is truly voluntary. This is especially true of volunteers, who are already in hospital for unrelated treatment, and who may feel unable to refuse 'secondment' into a trial if approached by their doctor. Another potential group of research subjects, vulnerable in a somewhat different way, are the poor. Although the financial inducements are relatively modest, the sums may tempt those on low incomes. For example, advertisements in *The Big Issue* (a publication sold on the streets by the homeless) invite volunteers for medical research (stating that they are 'all approved by ethics committees'), for £100. The Royal College of Physicians, albeit in the context of research on patients, states:

Royal College of Physicians, *Research Involving Patients*, 1990, London: RCP, p 27:

... many studies, particularly in pharmacology, are lengthy and tedious, and may involve urine collection, multiple venepunctures or other procedures associated with some discomfort. It is reasonable that volunteers in this type of research should be paid, over and above reimbursement of expenses incurred. These payments are for inconvenience or discomfort and increased payments may be reasonable for procedures requiring extra care on the part of the subject or involving more discomfort.

Payments should never be for undergoing risk

Payments should not be such as to persuade people to volunteer against their better judgment, nor to induce them to volunteer more frequently than is advisable for their own good. While appreciating that any given sum would be viewed differently by a student or person who is unemployed than by a person in full paid employment, we suggest that payment should range somewhere between rates equivalent to current student grants and a daily rate equivalent to the average wage, but time involved and inconvenience incurred should be taken into consideration. All payments to volunteers should be approved by the ethics committee.

The next requirement, once again, is that the research subject be properly informed of the risks attendant upon participating in the research. Clearly, therapeutic privilege can have no part to play in research on healthy volunteers. In the Canadian case of *Halushka v University of Saskatchewan* (1965) 52 WWR 608 it was stated:

Hall JA: The example of risks being properly hidden from a patient when it is important that he should not worry can have no application in the field of research. The subject of medical experimentation is entitled to a full and frank disclosure of all the facts, probabilities and opinions which a reasonable man might be expected to consider before giving his consent.

To what extent would the English courts similarly distinguish non-therapeutic from therapeutic research in this context? In the post-*Sidaway* case of *Gold v Haringey HA* [1987] 2 All ER 888, the Court of Appeal held that disclosure, in the context of non-therapeutic treatment, was just as much governed by the *Bolam* test as advice given in the course of therapy. However, it is probable that this question is of theoretical interest only since, as noted earlier in our discussion of therapeutic research, the *Bolam* test itself would surely impose the duty to obtain fully informed consent upon the researcher (all guidance, including the Declaration of Helsinki, is unanimously to this effect).

The incompetent volunteer

The expression 'incompetent volunteer' is, of course, a contradiction in terms. If the person is incompetent, then, by definition, he is unable to volunteer. However, others may 'volunteer' on his behalf, and this undoubtedly generates some of the most contentious ethical and legal issues in medical research. Indeed it may be felt that there is an argument for prohibiting any form of non-therapeutic research on those who lack the capacity to consent.

Children

It is generally thought ethically acceptable, in certain circumstances, to carry out non-therapeutic research upon children. That is certainly the view taken by such bodies as the Royal College of Paediatricians and the Royal College of Physicians, whose guidelines offer very similar advice here to that covering therapeutic research on patients. In the case of mature minors, there is an assumption that *Gillick* competence will apply. (Clearly, s 8 of the Family Law Reform Act 1969 will not apply to 16 and 17 year olds in this context: see Chapter 4.) However, should children really be able to consent at all to non-therapeutic measures on *Gillick* principles? It is suggested here that the answer is 'yes', at least where the risks involved are negligible or minimal. After all, mature minors are capable of giving consent to major medical interventions, such as surgery, which may require them to comprehend and balance much higher risks.

Interesting issues arise when the child is incapable of consenting, and the parent consents on the child's behalf. Robert Redmon tackles arguments which state that children in such research are being used merely as 'ends' and sees participation as part of the child's wider development as a moral being, even though the research is not for the benefit of the child's immediate health:

Redmon, R, 'How children can be respected as 'ends' yet still be used as subjects in non-therapeutic research' (1986) 12 JME 77:

If the child is old enough, she may enjoy seeing how this aspect of science functions, and her participation may aid her education. Also, this participation can be seen as part of her moral education. We certainly encourage our children to perform acts of benevolence when there is little chance of harm (walking down the road to take an invalid some food), and if the purposes of the research are *understood* well enough by the child, her participation might be viewed in the same way.

But if a child is an infant and too young to assent, much less consent, to such an experiment, then none of these benefits are possible. And, more importantly, what is required is a Kantian solution to this problem. Otherwise, the weighing of benefits can lead very easily to the misuse of the child.

However, these particular benefits – scientific and moral education – are of a different nature from most others (money, health, prestige, etc). To aid in the development of intellectual and, especially, moral abilities (or sensitivities) is to aid in the development of the individual's autonomy. For Kant, a person was only free when she was doing the morally praiseworthy thing (acting from 'a good will'). A development of a 'good will' (notwithstanding Kant's view that such a will is 'non-empirical' and thus, in some sense, innate) is a step towards being an ultimate 'end'.

Citing a piece by Hans Jonas ('Philosophical reflections on experimenting with human subjects' (1969) Daedalus (Spring) 219), Redmon favours the approach whereby, if the goals of the subject are the same as the researcher, then the subject is not being merely used. This he refers to as an 'identification of interests':

Redmon, R, 'How children can be respected as 'ends' yet still be used as subjects in non-therapeutic research' (1986) 12 JME 77:

Thus in allowing such experiments with 'minimal risk' (no more risk than can be expected in the normal, protective environment of a child), we are wagering that the child will 'identify' and approve of such experiments. This 'hypothetical consent' cannot be judged on the 'reasonable person' hypothesis since, as has been shown, it is difficult to predict how altruistic the 'reasonable person' would be in a moral situation. It does make sense, however, to ask how a person with a particular moral outlook, particular values, virtues and vices, would act. Thus the prediction of how the child will later view his participation must be made by those in the child's family, in particular by his parents. Their consent should be based upon their own values and the expectation that the child will share, to some extent, in them. They might reasonably expect, for example, that their child may later, as an adult, have an interest in the welfare of children whom the research may benefit. Their child will probably be a parent himself. They should also, as the National Commission for the Protection of Human Subjects recommended, be present during all stages of the research, and be involved in it as much as possible. This will help confirm their judgment that their child will later 'identify' with the research project.

My 'Kantian deliberations' thus lead to a tentative conclusion: if we can reasonably expect this child to 'identify' (in Jonas' sense) with the goals of the research when she is an adult, and that the identification will be strong enough to outweigh the harm of the knowledge of being used by her parents, and if the child (if old enough) assents, and if the possibility of harm is slight ('minimal risk'), then such research is permissible.

Could it be argued, in the light of this (and echoing the approach taken in the case of *S v S* [1970] 3 All ER 107), that parental consent to enter their child into non-therapeutic research involving minimal risk is not contrary to the child's best interests? In the US case of *Curran v Bosze* 566 NE 2d 1319 (1990), it was suggested that 'individual altruism in an abstract theoretical sense' was an insufficient basis for regarding a non-therapeutic procedure as in a child's best interests (see Chapter 11). Significantly, in that case, however, the children's mother opposed the procedure in issue.

For their part, both the British Paediatric Association, in its 1992 Guidelines, *The Ethical Conduct of Research Involving Children*, and the Medical Research Council in similarly titled guidance from 1991, suggest that non-therapeutic research on young, incompetent children is permissible with parental consent, provided that this is the only means of procuring the knowledge in question, and that the child is exposed to no more than minimal risk.

Adults

It is arguable that non-therapeutic research on the incompetent adult is always wrong, both morally, and in law, as it constitutes a battery. (Contrast the position of children, where at least a parent may (and must) consent on their behalf.) At the very least, additional safeguards should be necessary. The Law Commission in its report, *Mental Incapacity*, commented as follows:

Law Commission, *Mental Incapacity*, Report No 231, 1995, London: HMSO:

6.29 'Non-therapeutic' research ... does not claim to offer any direct or immediate benefit to the participant. Such procedures may well be scientifically and ethically acceptable to those who are qualified to decide such matters. If, however, the participant lacks capacity to consent to his or her participation, and the procedure cannot be justified under the doctrine of necessity, then any person who touches or restrains that participant is committing an unlawful battery. The simple fact is that the researcher is making no claim to be acting in the best interests of that individual person and does not therefore come within the rules of law set out in *Re F*. It was made abundantly clear to us on consultation, however, that non-therapeutic research projects of this nature are regularly taking place. We were told of a research project into the organic manifestations of Alzheimer's disease which involves the administration of radioactive isotopes to sufferers, followed by extensive testing of blood and bodily functions. Another project was said to involve the examination of written patients' records, although they are unable to consent to this examination. In some cases relatives are asked to 'consent' to what is proposed, and do so. It appears that some funding bodies and ethics committees stipulate for consent by a relative where the research participant cannot consent. As a matter of law, such 'consent' is meaningless. It appears that the question of the legality of non-therapeutic research procedures is regularly misunderstood or ignored by those who design, fund and approve the projects.

6.30 A number of our respondents expressed concern about non-invasive research based on observations, photography or videoing of participants (sometimes covertly). We accept that questions of dignity and privacy arise in such situations where the project is not designed to benefit the research participant.

6.31 We suggested in our consultation paper that the balance of expert opinion favours the participation of people unable to consent in even non-therapeutic research projects, subject to strict criteria. The majority of our consultees argued that there is an ethical case for such participation. This case turns on the desirability of eradicating painful and distressing disabilities, where progress can be achieved without harming research subjects ...

We recommend that research which is unlikely to benefit a participant, or whose benefit is likely to be long delayed, should be lawful in relation to a person without capacity to consent if (1) the research is into an incapacitating condition with which the participant is or may be affected and (2) certain statutory procedures are complied with. (Draft Bill, cl 11(1).)

The Commission, therefore, took the view that one of the essential conditions of non-therapeutic research taking place on an incompetent person is that the person suffers from the condition which the research is seeking to alleviate. Arguably, this has not been followed in the Mental Capacity Act 2005, where therapeutic and non-therapeutic research are both provided for, as outlined above (see p 540). Nevertheless, as the Law Commission's report noted, non-therapeutic research on incompetent patients does occur and, indeed, the Medical Research Council's guidelines, *The Ethical Conduct of Research on the Mentally Incapacitated*, 1991, in this respect mirror its Guidance on incompetent minors: such research may be carried out provided the hoped-for knowledge is unprocurable by other means and risk to the subject is no more than minimal. Furthermore, paragraph 24 of the Declaration of Helsinki (see above) expressly acknowledges that this may take place as it is contained within section B, which is not restricted to therapeutic research. It is also anticipated by Article 17(2) of the European Convention on Human Rights and Biomedicine which states that, exceptionally, and under conditionas that are protectible by law, non-therapeutic research can be carrried out on incompetent adults. However, whether this position is plausible or not in ethical terms, it is now provided for by the Mental Capacity Act 2005. Nevertheless, it is still pertinent to ask how such research can satisfy the 'best interests' requirement laid down in *Re F*. Admittedly, the courts have been prepared to construe best interests quite widely in some cases (see especially the discussion of *Re Y (An Adult Patient) (Transplant: Bone Marrow)* (1996) BMLR 111 in Chapter 11), but only to the extent that some form of benefit can be shown to accrue directly to the individual concerned.

THE REGULATION OF RESEARCH IN THE UK

Until recently, medical research has been subject to the common law, and clinical trials have been subject to the Medicines Act 1968. However, the enactment of the European Directive has prompted the government to issue regulations to govern the conduct of clinical trials (ie trials concerned with the investigation of medical products). Research that lies outside this ambit will still be governed by a mixture of the common law, any constraints imposed by ethics committees, and any quasi-statutory guidance from the relevant bodies (see below).

Common law

Contract

There are two contractual relations that are relevant to medical research. First, there is the contract between the research subject and the researcher, and secondly, the contract between the sponsor of the research (usually a drug manufacturer), and the researcher, or investigator. Ian Dodds-Smith comments as follows:

> **Dodds-Smith, I, 'Clinical research', in Dyer, C (ed), *Doctors, Patients and the Law*, 1992, Oxford: Blackwell Science, p 146:**
>
> **The sponsor's obligations to the investigator**
>
> The contract between the sponsor/manufacturer and the investigator will govern the legal relationship between them. Ideally, to avoid uncertainty and possible unnecessary dispute, the agreement should be in writing and clearly expressed. There is no model format for such contracts – they may be and often are contained in a letter. The overriding concern, however, is that they should be unambiguous and contain all the crucial details relating to the protocol to be adopted, information to be made available about the test product, reporting of adverse drug reactions, the duration of the study, the maintenance of patient confidentiality, the publication of results, liability for injury to subjects and the fee for the study. Under English law, certain conditions are implied additionally into any contract for services. These include that the service will be performed with reasonable care and skill and in a reasonable period. There are also rules under statute which may restrict the ability of the parties to exclude their liability for damages for personal injury caused by negligence.
>
> **The sponsor's obligations to the research subject**
>
> *Contract*
>
> The Declaration of Helsinki does not address the matter of how the subject/sponsor relationship might be structured or recorded. In general, the sponsor and a patient subject do not enter into a direct contractual arrangement. However, where studies are to be conducted upon healthy volunteers, a form of contract may and usually will exist. In 1970 the Association of the British Pharmaceutical Industry (ABPI) published a report to which a simple form of written contract was appended. In 1986 the Royal College of Physicians issued a report on healthy volunteer studies in which it advocated the use of a 'simple form of contract' mainly to ensure that the subject would be compensated for any injury occurring during a trial. In the appendix to the report the college provided a checklist of matters which should be considered when drawing up such a contract. In 1988, the ABPI published revised Guidelines for medical experiments in non-patient human volunteers which contained both a model

patient information form and draft provisions for a volunteer agreement and consent form and stated that all volunteers 'must sign a simple form of agreement' (recording the basis upon which they agreed to participate and dealing with four other basic matters) with the sponsor or outside research establishment (depending upon who had the responsibility for recruitment and supervision).

As Dodds-Smith states, in relation to the contract between sponsor and investigator, certain terms are implied into the contract. These terms will also apply to any contract between sponsor and research subject. Although when the patient is receiving NHS treatment, there will not be a contract, a contractual situation must arise, within the NHS as well as elsewhere, in the case of healthy volunteers (in the context of non-therapeutic research), as they are not being treated pursuant to a statutory obligation. Clearly, the Unfair Contract Terms Act 1977 would prevent any such contract excluding liability for damages for negligently caused personal injury, and there would be an implied term that the research would be carried out with reasonable skill and care.

Although, for the purposes of the research subject bringing an action for injuries suffered, the contents of the contract may well be important, in the context of the research subject failing to participate, or withdrawing part way through the research, would a court enforce such a contract? The answer must surely be that it is unenforceable from the point of view of the researcher. Damages would be unquantifiable, and an order for specific performance repugnant.

Tort

The torts of battery and negligence will apply to those who participate in medical research. These have already been considered in relation to consent, and will be looked at again, in the context of recovering compensation for injuries, p 561, below.

Criminal law

It is important to recall (see Chapter 3) that battery is a crime as well as a tort, and that statutory criminal offences may apply in the appropriate circumstances. Whilst, in the normal course of medical research, the criminal law would be unlikely to be invoked, note the US case of *Hyman v Jewish Chronic Disease Hospital* 251 NYS 2d 818 (1964), where doctors injected live cancer cells into 22 patients, not only without their consent, but by leading them to believe that the injections were part of their normal treatment. The Medical Association Review Board found the doctors guilty of fraudulent and deceitful conduct, but no criminal proceedings were taken. There is some precedent in English law in the case of *R v Burdee* (1916) 25 Cox 598, where a doctor who had prescribed cold water foot baths and a three day fast for a sick patient who subsequently died, was convicted of manslaughter. (As has previously been noted, however, something which is experimentation at best, and quackery at worst, is not research in the accepted sense of the term.)

Statutory provisions in relation to clinical trials

The European Clinical Trials Directive 2001/20 EC governs the regulation of clinical trials of medicines and has been transposed into UK law by the Medicines for

Human Use (Clinical Trials) Regulations 2004 which replace the current clinical trial provisions of the Medicines Act 1968 and regulations made thereunder. These came into force on 1 May 2004. The Medicines and Healthcare Products Regulatory Agency is the regulatory body that oversees the operation of the Regulations.

The aim of the Directive is to simplify and harmonise the regulation of clinical trials. There are two main aspects to this: the establishment of a clear procedure for dealing with clinical trials and the facilitation of effective co-ordination of clinical trials throughout Europe. Whilst the protection of trial participants is given importance it seems that the advancement of medical research and the promotion of the internal market in medicinal products are key to the impetus behind the Directive. As well as the regulation of research it also deals with manufacturing standards. For our purposes the important part of the Regulations is Schedule 1 (implementing Article 3(2) of the Directive) and this deals with consent to participation. As far as capable adults are concerned, the conditons are: that the subject has had an interview with the investigator, or another member of the investigating team, in which he has been given the opportunity to understand the objectives, risks and inconveniences of the trial and conditions under which it is to be conducted; that he has been informed of his right to withdraw from the trial at any time; that he has given his 'informed consent' to participating and that this can be withdrawn at any time without resulting in detriment; and that he has been given a contact point for further information.

As far as children are concerned, the Schedule provides for a hierarchy of consent on behalf of the child, commencing with a parent or person with parental responsibility. The others are personal legal representatives and professional legal representatives (ie someone nominated by the relevant health care provider) but consent can only be taken from these in emergencies. There are similar provisions for incompetent adults. Obviously a parent has no relevance in the latter case, *qua* parent, but the personal legal representative is someone suitable to act as the legal representative by virtue of his or her relationship with the adult concerned, and who is not connected with the conduct of the trial. The following provisions contained within Schedule 1 relate to the principles of good clinical practice and the protection of clinical trial subjects:

PART 2

CONDITIONS AND PRINCIPLES WHICH APPLY TO ALL CLINICAL TRIALS

Principles based on International Conference on Harmonisation GCP Guideline

1. Clinical trials shall be conducted in accordance with the ethical principles that have their origin in the Declaration of Helsinki, and that are consistent with good clinical practice and the requirements of these Regulations.

2. Before the trial is initiated, foreseeable risks and inconveniences have been weighed against the anticipated benefit for the individual trial subject and other present and future patients. A trial should be initiated and continued only if the anticipated benefits justify the risks.

3. The rights, safety, and well-being of the trial subjects are the most important considerations and shall prevail over interests of science and society.

4. The available non-clinical and clinical information on an investigational medicinal product shall be adequate to support the clinical trial.

5. Clinical trials shall be scientifically sound, and described in a clear, detailed protocol.

6. A trial shall be conducted in compliance with the protocol that has a favourable opinion from an ethics committee.

7. The medical care given to, and medical decisions made on behalf of, subjects shall always be the responsibility of an appropriately qualified doctor or, when appropriate, of a qualified dentist.

8. Each individual involved in conducting a trial shall be qualified by education, training, and experience to perform his or her respective task(s).

9. Subject to the other provisions of this Schedule relating to consent, freely given informed consent shall be obtained from every subject prior to clinical trial participation.

10. All clinical trial information shall be recorded, handled, and stored in a way that allows its accurate reporting, interpretation and verification.

11. The confidentiality of records that could identify subjects shall be protected, respecting the privacy and confidentiality rules in accordance with the requirements of the Data Protection Act 1998 and the law relating to confidentiality.

12. Investigational medicinal products used in the trial shall be –

    (a) manufactured or imported, and handled and stored, in accordance with the principles and guidelines of good manufacturing practice, and

    (b) used in accordance with the approved protocol.

13. Systems with procedures that assure the quality of every aspect of the trial shall be implemented.

Conditions based on Article 3 of the Directive

14. A trial shall be initiated only if an ethics committee and the licensing authority comes to the conclusion that the anticipated therapeutic and public health benefits justify the risks and may be continued only if compliance with this requirement is permanently monitored.

15. The rights of each subject to physical and mental integrity, to privacy and to the protection of the data concerning him in accordance with the Data Protection Act 1998 are safeguarded.

16. Provision has been made for insurance or indemnity to cover the liability of the investigator and sponsor which may arise in relation to the clinical trial.

PART 3

CONDITIONS WHICH APPLY IN RELATION TO AN ADULT ABLE TO CONSENT OR WHO HAS GIVEN CONSENT PRIOR TO THE ONSET OF INCAPACITY

1. The subject has had an interview with the investigator, or another member of the investigating team, in which he has been given the opportunity to understand the objectives, risks and inconveniences of the trial and the conditions under which it is to be conducted.

2. The subject has been informed of his right to withdraw from the trial at any time.

3. The subject has given his informed consent to taking part in the trial.

4. The subject may, without being subject to any resulting detriment, withdraw from the clinical trial at any time by revoking his informed consent.

5. The subject has been provided with a contact point where he may obtain further information about the trial.

PART 4

CONDITIONS AND PRINCIPLES WHICH APPLY IN RELATION TO A MINOR

Conditions

1. Subject to paragraph 6, a person with parental responsibility for the minor or, if by reason of the emergency nature of the treatment provided as part of the trial no such person can be contacted prior to the proposed inclusion of the subject in the trial, a legal representative for the minor has had an interview with the investigator, or another member of the investigating team, in which he has been given the opportunity to understand the objectives, risks and inconveniences of the trial and the conditions under which it is to be conducted.

2. That person or legal representative has been provided with a contact point where he may obtain further information about the trial.

3. That person or legal representative has been informed of the right to withdraw the minor from the trial at any time.

4. That person or legal representative has given his informed consent to the minor taking part in the trial.

5. That person with parental responsibility or the legal representative may, without the minor being subject to any resulting detriment, withdraw the minor from the trial at any time by revoking his informed consent.

6. The minor has received information according to his capacity of understanding, from staff with experience with minors, regarding the trial, its risks and its benefits.

7. The explicit wish of a minor who is capable of forming an opinion and assessing the information referred to in the previous paragraph to refuse participation in, or to be withdrawn from, the clinical trial at any time is considered by the investigator.

8. No incentives or financial inducements are given –

   (a) to the minor; or

   (b) to a person with parental responsibility for that minor or, as the case may be, the minor's legal representative, except provision for compensation in the event of injury or loss.

9. The clinical trial relates directly to a clinical condition from which the minor suffers or is of such a nature that it can only be carried out on minors.

10. Some direct benefit for the group of patients involved in the clinical trial is to be obtained from that trial.

11. The clinical trial is necessary to validate data obtained –

   (a) in other clinical trials involving persons able to give informed consent, or

   (b) by other research methods.

12. The corresponding scientific guidelines of the European Medicines Agency are followed.

Principles

13. Informed consent given by a person with parental responsibility or a legal representative to a minor taking part in a clinical trial shall represent the minor's presumed will.

14. The clinical trial has been designed to minimise pain, discomfort, fear and any other foreseeable risk in relation to the disease and the minor's stage of development.

15. The risk threshold and the degree of distress have to be specially defined and constantly monitored.

16. The interests of the patient always prevail over those of science and society.

PART 5

CONDITIONS AND PRINCIPLES WHICH APPLY IN RELATION TO AN INCAPACITATED ADULT

Conditions

1. The subject's legal representative has had an interview with the investigator, or another member of the investigating team, in which he has been given the opportunity to understand the objectives, risks and inconveniences of the trial and the conditions under which it is to be conducted.

2. The legal representative has been provided with a contact point where he may obtain further information about the trial.

3. The legal representative has been informed of the right to withdraw the subject from the trial at any time.

4. The legal representative has given his informed consent to the subject taking part in the trial.

5. The legal representative may, without the subject being subject to any resulting detriment, withdraw the subject from the trial at any time by revoking his informed consent.

6. The subject has received information according to his capacity of understanding regarding the trial, its risks and its benefits.

7. The explicit wish of a subject who is capable of forming an opinion and assessing the information referred to in the previous paragraph to refuse participation in, or to be withdrawn from, the clinical trial at any time is considered by the investigator.

8. No incentives or financial inducements are given to the subject or their legal representative, except provision for compensation in the event of injury or loss.

9. There are grounds for expecting that administering the medicinal product to be tested in the trial will produce a benefit to the subject outweighing the risks or produce no risk at all.

10. The clinical trial is essential to validate data obtained –

   (a) in other clinical trials involving persons able to give informed consent, or

   (b) by other research methods.

11. The clinical trial relates directly to a life-threatening or debilitating clinical condition from which the subject suffers.

Principles

12. Informed consent given by a legal representative to an incapacitated adult in a clinical trial shall represent that adult's presumed will.

13. The clinical trial has been designed to minimise pain, discomfort, fear and any other foreseeable risk in relation to the disease and the cognitive abilities of the patient.

14. The risk threshold and the degree of distress have to be specially defined and constantly monitored.

15. The interests of the patient always prevail over those of science and society.

A comparison should be made between the conditions placed upon clinical trials (of medicinal products) in relation to adults who lack capacity and the more general conditions that are contained in the Mental Capacity Act 2005. Put simply, conditions are much more stringent in relation to clinical trials, notably in the case of clinical trials the requirement that the trial relates directly to a 'life-threatening or debilitating clinical condition from which the subject suffers' (see para 11 above). Whilst conditions such as Alzheimer's disease would be covered by this, mere mental impairment would not.

The Ethics Committee System

As we saw at p 521, above, the Declaration of Helsinki states as one of its basic principles that the design and performance of all research trials should be subject to scrutiny by 'a specially appointed ethical review committee which must be independent of the investigator, the sponsor or any other kind of undue influence' (para 13). The Royal College of Physicians made recommendations to the same effect in both 1967 and 1973, and in 1975 the Department of Health issued instructions to health authorities to implement them. The current NHS guidelines were formulated in 2001. The Medicines for Human Use (Clinical Trials) Regulations 2004 establish (Regulation 5) the United Kingdom Ethics Committees Authority which is responsible for establishing, recognising and monitoring those ethics committees that give opinions on clinical trials on medicines under those Regulations.

The 2001 guidance deals with the composition of an LREC as follows:

Department of Health, *Governance Arrangements for NHS Research Ethics Committees,* **2001, London: DoH:**

6 Composition of an REC

6.1 An REC should have sufficient members to guarantee the presence of a quorum (*see* 6.11) at each meeting. The maximum should be 18 members. This should allow for a sufficiently broad range of experience and expertise, so that the scientific, clinical and methodological aspects of a research proposal can be reconciled with the welfare of research participants, and with broader ethical implications.

6.2 Overall the REC should have a balanced age and gender distribution. Members should be drawn from both sexes and from a wide range of age groups. Every effort should also be made to recruit members from black and ethnic minority backgrounds, as well as people with disabilities. This should apply to both expert and lay members.

6.3 RECs should be constituted to contain a mixture of 'expert' and 'lay' members. At least three members must be independent of any organisation where research under ethical review is likely to take place.

Expert members

6.4 The 'expert' members of the committee shall be chosen to ensure that the REC has the following expertise:

relevant methodological and ethical expertise in:

– clinical research;

– non-clinical research;

– qualitative or other research methods applicable to health services, social science and social care research,

clinical practice including:

– hospital and community staff (medical, nursing and other);

– general practice,

statistics relevant to research.

Lay members

6.5 At least one third of the membership shall be 'lay' members who are independent of the NHS, either as employees or in a non-executive role, and whose primary personal or professional interest is not in a research area.

6.6 The 'lay' membership can include non-medical clinical staff who have not practised their profession for a period of at least five years.

6.7 At least half of the 'lay' members must be persons who are not, and never have been, either health or social care professionals, and who have never been involved in carrying out research involving human participants, their tissue or data.

However, the lack of the relevant experience was highlighted in a review of the role of LRECs carried out in 1992:

Neuberger, J, *Ethics and Health Care: The Role of Research Ethics Committees in the United Kingdom*, 1992, London: King's Fund Institute (the Neuberger Report), p 28:

Vetting the research

The DoH guidelines say that the [L]REC will need to know whether the scientific merit of a proposal has been properly assessed. It is not clear whether this should extend to the REC satisfying itself that the research is well designed. Several of the RECs visited regarded it as part of their function to examine the protocol design, claiming that 'bad research is unethical research'. They have to assess whether the expected benefits from the research are likely to justify the demands made on the human subjects. It is debatable whether they can do this without making, some assessment of the research itself. The issue becomes particularly acute when the applicant may be motivated by other concerns than the advancement of medical knowledge, for example where he is receiving substantial funds for carrying out the research, or is carrying it out as part of his training.

Against this it can be argued that the RECs do not have the skills or expertise to make such an assessment. They may also reflect their own personal biases; a case in point is nursing research. Much nursing research concerns patients' attitudes and views rather than the objective evaluation of different treatments. Some RECs view such research very positively, while others feel it is non-scientific, as well as unduly intrusive for patients, and should not be permitted.

Scientific assessment of research

There was no objective definition of 'scientific' and 'non-scientific' research. The tendency was for any research involving the use of questionnaires, and submitted by whatever discipline, to be regarded as 'non-scientific'. Those RECs which were largely medically dominated thus tended to class as 'non-scientific' a great deal of research that was submitted by nurses, psychologists, medical students and psychiatrists. Discussion often focused on the delivery of 'soft data' and on the poor design of questionnaires. It was clear that those who took that view thought the research methods used by other disciplines were inadequate and that the data were not to be trusted. It was therefore remarkable to see other RECs welcome non-medical research, and, in two cases, discuss ways of encouraging more qualitative research on the effects of certain treatments on patients.

One possible solution to the unsatisfactory nature of debate about the quality of the research is to ensure a wider spread of interest on the committee, as the DoH and RCP guidelines both suggest. For the technically complex scientific and medical research there is also an argument for a separate research methods committee, as exists in many US institutions and is under active discussion at a few UK institutions as well, to ensure that the research is vetted properly for its scientific validity before the REC sees it. Alternatively, members could be co-opted to the REC as necessity arose to discuss the complex issues, though lengthy technical discussion of very specialist issues might be difficult for lay and other non-specialist members. The solution followed by each REC and DHS might depend on the quantity of such complex and technical research that takes place in the institution. It is, however, clear that a confusion of roles exists, so that the RECs often act as both research and research ethics committees, often beyond their capabilities.

It can be questioned as to exactly what sort of experience is required of an LREC member, as it raises the question of the very function of the committee. The Department of Health guidance states baldly that the purpose of the committee is 'to consider the ethics of proposed research projects within the NHS'. Matters that the committee should have regard to, as a minimum, in doing so are as follows:

Department of Health, *Governance Arrangements for NHS Research Ethics Committees,* **2001, London: DoH:**

Requirements for a favourable opinion

9.12 Before giving a favourable opinion, the REC should be adequately reassured about the following issues as applicable:

9.13 *Scientific design and conduct of the study*

a the appropriateness of the study design in relation to the objectives of the study, the statistical methodology (including sample size calculation where appropriate), and the potential for reaching sound conclusions with the smallest number of research participants

b the justification of predictable risks and inconveniences weighed against the anticipated benefits for the research participants, other present and future patients, and the concerned communities

c the justification for use of control arms in trials, (whether placebo or active comparator), and the randomisation process to be used

d criteria for prematurely withdrawing research participants e criteria for suspending or terminating the research as a whole

    f the adequacy of provisions made for monitoring and auditing the conduct of the research, including the constitution of a data safety monitoring committee (DSMC)

    g the adequacy of the research site, including the supporting staff, available facilities, and emergency procedures. For multi-centre research, these locality issues will be considered separately from the ethical review of the research proposal itself

    h the manner in which the results of the research will be reported and published.

9.14 *Recruitment of research participants*

    a the characteristics of the population from which the participants will be drawn (including gender, age, literacy, culture, economic status and ethnicity) and the justification for any decisions made in this respect

    b the means by which initial contact and recruitment is to be conducted

    c the means by which full information is to be conveyed to potential research participants or their representatives

    d inclusion criteria for research participants

    e exclusion criteria for research participants.

9.15 *Care and protection of research participants*

    a the safety of any intervention to be used in the proposed research

    b the suitability of the investigator(s)'s qualifications and experience for ensuring good conduct of the proposed study

    c any plans to withdraw or withhold standard therapies or clinical management protocols for the purpose of the research, and the justification for such action

    d the health and social care to be provided to research participants during and after the course of the research

    e the adequacy of health and social supervision and psychosocial support for the research participants

    f steps to be taken if research participants voluntarily withdraw during the course of the research

    g the criteria for extended access to, the emergency use of, and/or the compassionate use of study products

    h the arrangements, if appropriate, for informing the research participant's general practitioner, including procedures for seeking the participant's consent to do so

    i a description of any plans to make the study product available to the research participants following the research

    j a description of any financial costs to research participants

    k the rewards and compensations (if any) for research participants (including money, services and/or gifts)

    l whether there is provision in proportion to the risk for compensation/treatment in the case of injury/disability/death of a research participant attributable to participation in the research; the insurance and indemnity arrangements

    m the nature and size of any grants, payments or other reward to be made to any researchers or research hosts n circumstances that might lead to conflicts of interest that may affect the independent judgement of the researcher(s).

9.16 *Protection of research participants' confidentiality*

    a a description of the persons who will have access to personal data of the research participants, including medical records and biological samples

    b the measures taken to ensure the confidentiality and security of personal information concerning research participants

    c the extent to which the information will be anonymised

    d how the data/samples will be obtained, and the purposes for which they will be used

    e how long the data/samples will be kept

    f to which countries, if any, the data/samples will be sent

    g the adequacy of the process for obtaining consent for the above.

9.17 *Informed consent process*

    a a full description of the process for obtaining informed consent, including the identification of those responsible for obtaining consent, the time-frame in which it will occur, and the process for ensuring consent has not been withdrawn

    b the adequacy, completeness and understandability of written and oral information to be given to the research participants, and, when appropriate, their legally acceptable representatives

    c clear justification for the intention to include in the research individuals who cannot consent, and a full account of the arrangements for obtaining consent or authorization for the participation of such individuals

    d assurances that research participants will receive information that becomes available during the course of the research relevant to their participation (including their rights, safety and well being)

    e the provisions made for receiving and responding to queries and complaints from research participants or their representatives during the course of a research project.

9.18 *Community considerations*

    a the impact and relevance of the research on the local community and on the concerned communities from which the research participants are drawn

    b the steps which had been taken to consult with the concerned communities during the course of designing the research

    c the extent to which the research contributes to capacity building, such as the enhancement of local healthcare, research, and the ability to respond to public health needs

    d a description of the availability and affordability of any successful study product to the concerned communities following the research

    e the manner in which the results of the research will be made available to the research participants and the concerned communities.

However, as suggested in the Neuberger Report, there is argument that the scientific and ethical aspects of a committee's work should be separated. Paul McNeill surveys the issues in the following extract:

McNeill, PM, *The Ethics and Politics of Human Experimentation,* **1993, Cambridge: Press Syndicate of the University of Cambridge, pp 185–87:**

Research ethics committees fall between the interdisciplinary professional review model and the jury model in that they are composed of some members who are there because of their expertise and other members who are there as representatives of the community without special expertise. For Veatch, this mixture represented a conflict in the premises underlying these committees.

... Originally, committees were 'peer review' panels rather than interdisciplinary committees in that most of the members were medically trained or were biomedical researchers. In most countries the membership of peer review panels has been expanded to include members of other professions (notably lawyers and the clergy) and, in some cases, members of the community. It is in this broadening of the membership of committees to include both those with professional expertise and those who are representative of the community that Veatch identified a basic schism in the committee structure. In his view, this split reflects the lack of any clear rationale 'of what these committees are supposed to be able to do, of what purposes they are to serve [and] of what skills their members ought to have'. He considered that there was a need for a theory to clarify the ambiguities and for structural changes to be made to committees to make them consistent with that theory. Without these changes he believed it would be impossible for research ethics committees to fulfil their task successfully, although he acknowledged that subjects were better protected by committees, even as presently constituted, than by reliance on a researcher's judgment alone.

In my view, the schism described by Veatch is still apparent in committees all over the world. Interviews with members of committees in Australia and the United States have indicated that it is not clear to members whether their committee should function as a panel of experts (as in the interdisciplinary professional review model) or as committees expressing a community morality on the desirability of particular research projects (as in a jury model). In the main, committees appear to function as panels of experts with some small input from the lay members. The only countries to give equal representation to lay and professional members are New Zealand and Denmark ...

Our study of Australian committees and a study in the United States ... together show that the medical and research members participate more actively on committees and are generally regarded by all members of committees as more important in the decision making process. The non-medical and non-professional members become marginal in a number of ways. The use of language and technical terms which presume medical (and other technical) knowledge is one of the factors edging them to the margins (Glantz, 1984). Lay members may feel comfortable in offering an opinion on matters within their comprehension (such as the understandability of the consent form) but seldom speak on other issues. I suggest that this is one of the reasons why invasive, high risk research may be passed without question while relatively harmless research may consume a great deal of the committee's time and be disapproved by a committee (Shannon and Ockene, 1985). For example, many committees spend time on the wording of questionnaires (which have relatively low risks of harm) and relatively little time on technical protocols that are difficult to understand by members without the relevant expertise. Yet the technical and difficult studies are more likely to involve invasive procedures or drug research which have a higher risk of harm ...

Veatch considered that a 'dominance of the committee by scientific professionals' would produce a risk shift in the direction of the researchers' values – normally in favour of research. 'Risk shift' is based on the observation that groups make riskier decisions than individuals (Douglas, 1985). The presence of community members is not likely to overcome the shift toward accepting risky proposals – at best it can dilute it. Veatch goes further in suggesting that 'even a feisty member of a minority will find it extremely difficult to withstand the psychological pressure to co-operate in forming a consensus'. He argued that as long as one researcher was on the committee it would still be influenced in the direction of research values compared with a committee composed on a 'jury model' ...

Veatch's solution to the conflict between the 'professional review model' and the 'jury model' was to have two committees. One of these would be composed entirely of professional members and would consider the acceptability of research proposals on the basis of scientific and professional criteria. The other committee would be composed entirely of community representatives who would consider the acceptability of research proposals in terms of community morality ...

McNeill sets out the different experiences of lay members, and health care workers other than doctors:

McNeill, PM, *The Ethics and Politics of Human Experimentation*, 1993, Cambridge: Press Syndicate of the University of Cambridge, pp 93–94:

Table 4.2 -Typical quotes from interviews with committee members about their perception of their performance:

Lay person

Initially I found it very hard in the meetings. Being a lay person, you sit there and think all these other people know so much more than me about the protocols: the lawyers, and the ministers, and the doctors are from high up in medical things. But then you realise that you have to put your two cents worth in when it's there because they often forget how the little people feel ... The main problem in the meetings is thinking how to say what I want to say and make it sound important. Really, the best way is to say what you feel, but it often appears unimportant compared to the other issues.

Minister of religion

My role in the committee meetings is from the back seat. I would only speak if I had problems after the science and drug aspects were explained. The discussion is largely up to the medical people ... There have been protocols where I seriously questioned the infringement on patients, but I've never opposed them on these grounds. I've always been convinced by the medical argument that the research had to be done.

Lawyer

There's six medical type people as against myself, a minister of religion, a lay man and a lay woman. And then you find the lay man and the lay woman more often than not are intimidated by the doctors, so they won't disagree with them because there's not the knowledge, there's not the confidence in having a view ... to stand up to them. And without the confidence I suppose that you have from being a fellow professional ... it's a bit terrifying for them. I have the confidence to express my views, but the other people just sit there and say nothing.

Medical graduate

The routine protocol that has no problems about it, is presented, usually by a medical man, and the others understand it, and we all come to a very quick decision and there's no problem. When there's a problem, where ethical issues as opposed to scientific issues are at stake, then the other people come into it.

Administrator

The number one thing that concerns me is that they [research proposals] are properly presented, because many of our committee now don't have medical training and they don't necessarily have scientific training ... My prime concern is to get a protocol to the committee in a form in which it can be understood by almost everyone present. The second thing is to get it through and to see that there are no obvious gaps.

Nurse

The nurse is a subservient role, she's still calling all the doctors 'Doctor'. So even though she might be quite active it's never going to be an active that actually challenges what is going on.

A lawyer's comment about the nurse

The nurse is very much subservient to the specialist doctors in the hospital. And it's difficult to change that. Always I feel that it was a conditioned response on the nurse's part that one didn't challenge, or shouldn't challenge, the specialist view, which for medical things is fair enough but these were not necessarily just medical things. So, the area in which she was conditioned to do what she was told tended to spill over into the non-medical and ethical issues.

The lack of training of members was highlighted in the Neuberger Report, and, perhaps in a belated response to this, the Department of Health have issued a briefing pack for research ethics committee members, although it is stated that it is aimed mainly at new and prospective members of research ethics committees. The first part considers general ethical issues, and the second leads the reader through eight different types of research, such as epidemiological studies and psychological research.

Regulation 12 of the Medicines for Human Use (Clinical Trials) Regulations 2004 prohibits anyone from commencing or conducting a clinical trial, recruiting subjects or advertising to recruit subjects to be in a trial unless certain contitions are met. Specifically, such a trial can only be started or conducted if it has been authorised by the Medicines and Healthcare Products Regulatory Agency and approved by an ethics committee. As far as all research proposals that involve NHS patients are concerned the 2001 Guidelines state as follows:

Department of Health, *Governance Arrangements for NHS Research Ethics Committees*, 2001, London: DoH:

3   The remit of an NHS REC

3.1 Ethical advice from the appropriate NHS REC is required for any research proposal involving:

a Patients and users of the NHS. This includes all potential research participants recruited by virtue of the patient or user's past or present treatment by, or use of, the NHS. It includes NHS patients treated under contracts with private sector institutions.

b Individuals identified as potential research participants because of their status as relatives or carers of patients and users of the NHS, as defined above.

c Access to data, organs or other bodily material of past and present NHS patients.

d Fetal material and IVF involving NHS patients.

e The recently dead in NHS premises.

f The use of, or potential access to, NHS premises or facilities.

g NHS staff – recruited as research participants by virtue of their professional role.

What would be the legal consequences of a breach of the above guidelines? Certainly, any researcher employed by the NHS who was in breach would be liable to dismissal or other form of discipline, but would a patient or healthy volunteer have any right of redress? It is likely that the breach would be akin to a breach of statutory duty, in the sense that it would not necessarily give rise to a private law right in itself. However, if the patient suffered injury, then failure to obtain LREC approval might point towards negligence, although the problem of causation would remain. Another problem, highlighted by the case involving Mrs Moffit (see p 536, above), arises where, although initially obtaining approval in the proper way, a researcher fails to keep the Committee apprised of changes in the execution of a project. However, now that the Central Office for Research Ethics Committees is part of the National Patient Safety Agency, recent regulatory development points to increased centralised control.

As will be seen from paragraph 3.1, ethical advice for non-NHS research is not specifically required. However, even if the private sector can, in theory, ignore LRECs, in practice, because of the effect upon insurance and legal liability generally (not to mention publication), researchers will want to obtain approval of their projects, and paragraph 3.2 makes provision for this. Furthermore, as far as clinical trials are concerned, Regulation 12 of the Medicines for Human Use (Clinical Trials) Regulations 2004 applies to non-NHS trials.

Multi-centre trials

There has been concern about consistency of approach when the same research protocol comes before a number of different LRECs (see, for example, Neuberger). In consequence, the Department of Health has set up a system of multi-centre research ethics committees (MRECs), one in each of the English regions and one each in Wales, Scotland and Northern Ireland. The Department of Health guidelines, *Governance Arrangements for NHS Research Ethics Committees*, 2001, states as follows:

8 Multi-centre Research

8.1 For the purposes of ethical review of research, a research 'site' is defined as the geographical area covered by a single Health Authority, and includes all the research institutions and localities within it.

8.2 For the present, multi-centre research will continue to be defined as research carried out within five or more 'sites, ie the area covered by five or more Health Authority boundaries, irrespective of the number of LRECs within each Authority.

8.3 For research taking place in from two to four sites, application should be made to one LREC within each of the Health Authority boundaries. However, when a favourable opinion has been obtained from the first Health Authority's LREC, the second, third and fourth Health Authorities may, on the advice of their own LRECs, accept that opinion with further review by their own LREC only of the 'locality issues' ...

Quasi-statutory guidance

A number of bodies have issued guidelines, not only for researchers, but also for local research ethics committees, which amount to what is often described as 'soft law', in as much as, in litigation, departure from such guidance may provide strong evidence of malpractice.

We have already encountered some of this guidance. Other examples include Royal College of Physicians, *Guidelines on the Practice of Ethics Committees in Research Involving Human Subjects*, 1996, London: RCP; the European Commission, *Guidelines for Good Clinical Practice for Trials on Medicinal Products in the European Community*, Committee for Proprietary Medicinal Products III/3976/88-EN; and Association of the British Pharmaceutical Industry, *Guidelines for Medical Experiments in Non-Patient Human Volunteers*, 1988, London: ABPI.

COMPENSATION FOR INJURIES ARISING FROM RESEARCH

Compensation at common law

As we saw at pp 525 *et seq*, a patient who is entered in a clinical trial without giving his properly informed consent may arguably have an action against the doctor in battery; this would perhaps be most likely in the case of a volunteer involved in non-therapeutic research. Failing an action in battery, however, an action in negligence may lie and could arise in two main ways, albeit in both cases the subject must show some tangible injury. In the first case, the trial itself may be properly conducted, but the doctor/researcher (whilst providing enough basic facts to escape an action in battery) fall below his duty of care in the amount of information he divulges to his subject, and the latter is able to show that, if properly informed, he would not have participated in the trial.

In the second case, the trial itself, in terms of design or execution, may turn out to be defective in some way. An additional issue which arises here is whether, to the extent that the defect was something which the LREC, in approving the trial, should have noticed, the members of that committee could be joined as defendants in any action. This matter was of sufficient concern to be addressed directly by Department of Health Guidelines in 1991:

Department of Health, *Guidelines on LRECs*, 1991, London: DoH:

2.11 Concern has been expressed by some LREC members that they may be legally liable for injury caused to patients participating in research projects. DHAs will wish to advise appointees on these matters. Legal advice available to the Department of Health is that there is little prospect of a successful claim against a LREC member for a mishap arising from research approved as ethical by the LREC. Any such claim would lie principally against the researcher concerned and against the NHS body under the auspices of which the research took place. The principal defendants should seek to have any claim against an LREC member struck out. Those members of an LREC who are employees of an NHS body are already covered by NHS indemnity arrangements. The DHA should also bear any costs in the case of other LREC members unless the member concerned is guilty of misconduct or gross lack of care in the performance of his or her duties and provided that, if any claim is threatened or made, the member notifies the DHA and assists it in all reasonable ways. If necessary the DHA may give the following undertaking to this effect to LREC members who are not employees of an NHS body:

We confirm that the DHA will take full responsibility for all actions in the course of the performance of your duties as a member of the LREC other than those involving bad faith, wilful default or gross negligence; you should, however, notify the DHA if any action or claim is threatened or made, and in such an event be ready to assist the authority as required.

'No fault' compensation?

Whatever form his action takes, the injured research subject (like his 'pure' patient counterpart) will have substantial hurdles to overcome, both in relation to the breach of duty question and causation. However, an ethical argument for treating research subjects more favourably than other patients injured in the course of treatment is that, just as society at large stands to benefit from any advances in medical knowledge that the research may secure, so it should bear the costs of mishaps along the way. Accordingly, it has frequently been urged that those injured in the course of medical research should be compensated on a 'no fault' basis. A direct analogy can be invoked here with persons injured in the course of a community-wide vaccination programme, who are entitled to 'no fault' compensation under the Vaccine Damage Payments Act 1979:

1 Payments to persons severely disabled by vaccination

(1) If, on consideration of a claim, the Secretary of State is satisfied–

(a) that a person is, or was immediately before his death, severely disabled as a result of vaccination against any of the diseases to which this Act applies; and

(b) that the conditions of entitlement which are applicable in accordance with s 2 below are fulfilled,

he shall in accordance with this Act make a payment of the relevant statutory sum to or for the benefit of that person or to his personal representatives.

(1A) -In sub-s (1) above 'statutory sum' means £100,000 or such other sum as is specified by the Secretary of State for the purposes of this Act by order made by statutory instrument with the consent of the Treasury; and the relevant statutory sum for the purposes of that subsection is the statutory sum at the time when a claim for payment is first made.

(2) The diseases to which this Act applies are–

(a) diphtheria;

(b) tetanus;

(c) whooping cough;

(d) poliomyelitis;

(e) measles;

(f) rubella;

(h) tuberculosis;

(i) smallpox; and

(j) any other disease which is specified by the Secretary of State for the purposes of this Act by order made by statutory instrument.

(3) Subject to s 2(3) below, this Act has effect with respect to a person who is severely disabled as a result of a vaccination given to his mother before he was born as if the vaccination had been given directly to him and, in such circumstances as may be prescribed by regulations under this Act, this Act has effect with respect to a person who is severely disabled as a result of

contracting a disease through contact with a third person who was vaccinated against it as if the vaccination had been given to him and the disablement resulted from it.

(4) For the purposes of this Act, a person is severely disabled if he suffers disablement to the extent of 80% or more, assessed as for the purposes of s 103 of the Social Security Contributions and Benefits Act 1992 or the Social Security Contributions and Benefits (Northern Ireland) Act 1992 (disablement gratuity and pension) ...

In its 1978 Report, the Royal Commission on Civil Liability and Compensation for Personal Injury (the Pearson Committee), recommended that a similar scheme of compensation be established for injuries in the course of medical research. Whilst this recommendation has not been acted upon by Parliament, the DoH's LREC Guidelines mention the existence of provision for *ex gratia* compensation as a relevant factor in the sanctioning of trials (para 9.15(1)).

In every case, of course, it remains necessary for the research subject to demonstrate that his injuries were caused by participation in the trial. This may be by no means easy to do: after all, research will be taking place precisely because the causal properties of the new treatment (including its propensity to do harm) are unclear. Sometimes, to be sure, the claimant's case will be a strong one, for example where everyone in the trial is similarly affected. However, where the claimant's injury is a more isolated occurrence, a court may well take the view that some unknown, independent cause was, just as likely, at work. (See, in this regard, the case of *Loveday v Renton* [1990] 1 Med LR 117 referred to in Chapter 6, above.)

Drug-induced injury

One area in which the use of research subjects has attracted particular attention is in relation to the testing of new drugs and pharmaceutical products. There is a heightened sense here (engendered both by the power imbalance between subject and drug company and by the latter's pre-eminently economic motivation), that volunteers and patients participating in such trials require protection. As Soutar and McLean write:

Soutar, D and McLean, S, 'Medical progress and the law', in McLean, S (ed), *Legal Issues in Medicine*, 1981, Aldershot: Gower, pp 116–17:

There is available a wide variety of clinical trials, using healthy volunteers or patients, in both therapeutic and non-therapeutic clinical research programmes. Trials may be randomised, or controlled, and the most valid clinical results are obtained in 'blind' and 'double blind' trials. The most helpful information, when trying to justify a new treatment, comes from comparative trials where one method of therapy is evaluated against another, but unfortunately such trials are rarely, if ever, performed prior to marketing a new product.

Further, most manufacturers retain control over publication of the results of their clinical trials. This protects them from competitors by preventing premature release of information and, in the event that the product proves of little or no value, avoids public and professional humiliation. Not surprisingly, there is considerable concern as to the advisability of permitting the manufacturing industry this freedom in controlling the only sources of clinical data concerning a new medical product, and the recent controversy over the clinical information presented by the company in the marketing of Debendox/Bendectin is a case in point. This is not to suggest that all, or even many, companies will deliberately disguise unfavourable information regarding a new product, and in recent times at least one major company has accepted significant financial loss rather than market a product concerning whose safety there were serious doubts.

However, as in any industry, economic factors are of prime importance to companies, which invest a considerable proportion of their substantial income in researching and developing new drugs ...

Direct or indirect financial assistance to those performing clinical trials, is an additional moral and ethical problem. Such assistance can be used to persuade doctors to carry out clinical trials or to 'try out' the product following market release and here society is totally dependent on the moral and ethical codes of the individual manufacturers and doctors concerned. It could be argued that it is immoral for a manufacturer to finance or 'buy' a clinical trial, but should analysis and investigation require expensive and sophisticated equipment or specialised technical help, then perhaps the manufacturing industry should be responsible for providing these, even although this may amount indirectly at least to financing the project. Since often, in such cases, the specialised knowledge and equipment remain available for the medical staff concerned and thus benefit the National Health Service, it may be felt that the overall benefits of this practice outweigh the potential disadvantages.

Certainly, if doctors apply their ethical codes to the expected high standard, then problems should be minimised, although it has been suggested that the pressures on doctors are such that 'events ... have diminished an honourable profession [medicine] to the level of a junior partner in an immensely powerful industrial-medical complex' ...

In fact, the Association of the British Pharmaceutical Industry, in its Guidelines, has recommended that *ex gratia* compensation should be paid in cases where injury results. As Christopher Hodges writes:

Hodges, C, 'Harmonisation of European controls over research: ethics committees, consent, compensation and indemnity', in Goldberg, A and Dodds-Smith, I (eds), *Pharmaceutical Medicine and the Law*, 1991, London: RCP, pp 80–82:

The [ABPI] ... guidelines were revised in 1991 in the light of developing considerations, especially the 1990 report of the RCP's working party, *Research Involving Patients*. The relationship between the sponsor and subject is, in the case of [therapeutic research], not contractual and the guidelines state that the sponsor's assurance to abide by them is 'without legal commitment':

1.2 Compensation should be paid when, on the balance of probabilities, the injury was attributable to the administration of a medicinal product under trial or any clinical intervention or procedure provided for by the protocol that would not have occurred but for the inclusion of the patient in the trial.

1.3 Compensation should be paid to a child injured in utero through the participation of the subject's mother in a clinical trial as if the child were a patient-volunteer with the full benefit of these guidelines.

1.4 Compensation should only be paid for the more serious injury of an enduring and disabling character (including exacerbation of an existing condition) and not for temporary pain or discomfort or less serious or curable complaints.

1.5 Where there is an adverse reaction to a medicinal product under trial and injury is caused by a procedure adopted to deal with that adverse reaction, compensation should be paid for such injury as if it were caused directly by the medicinal product under trial.

1.6 Neither the fact that the adverse reaction causing the injury was foreseeable or predictable, nor the fact that the patient has freely consented (whether in writing or otherwise) to participate in the trial, should exclude a patient from consideration for compensation under these guidelines, although compensation may be abated or excluded in the light of the factors described in para 4.2, below.

1.7 For the avoidance of doubt, compensation should be paid regardless of whether the patient is able to prove that the company has been negligent in relation to research or development of the medicinal product under trial or that the product is defective and therefore, as the producer, the company is subject to strict liability in respect of injuries caused by it ...

4.1 The amount of compensation paid should be appropriate to the nature, severity and persistence of the injury and should in general terms be consistent with the quantum of damages commonly awarded for similar injuries by an English court in cases where legal liability is admitted.

4.2 Compensation may be abated, or in certain circumstances excluded, in the light of the following factors (on which will depend the level of risk the patient can reasonably be expected to accept):

4.2.1 -the seriousness of the disease being treated, the degree of probability that adverse reactions will occur and any warnings given;

4.2.2 -the risks and benefits of established treatments relative to those known or suspected of the trial medicine.

This reflects the fact that flexibility is required given the particular patient's circumstances. As an extreme example, there may be a patient suffering from a serious or life-threatening disease who is warned of a certain defined risk of adverse reaction. Participation in the trial is then based on an expectation that the benefit-risk ratio associated with participation may be better than that associated with alternative treatment. It is, therefore, reasonable that the patient accepts the high risk and should not expect compensation for the occurrence of the adverse reaction of which he or she was told.

There is provision for arbitration by an independent expert in the event of any difference of opinion.

Compensation is excluded, however, where:

1 The product failed to have its intended effect.

2 The injury was caused by another licensed medicinal product which was administered as a comparison with the product under trial.

3 A placebo has failed to provide a therapeutic benefit.

Compensation should not be paid, or should be abated, to the extent that the injury has arisen through:

1 A significant departure from the agreed protocol.

2 -The wrongful act or default of a third party, including a doctor's failure to deal adequately with an adverse reaction.

3 Contributory negligence by the patient.

These Guidelines are echoed by guidance at EC level (*Guidelines on Good Clinical Practice for Trials on Medicinal Products in the EC*, CPMP of the EC, 1990, Brussels: EC Commission), which further stresses the weight to be accorded to the research subject, including the need, at least in the context of non-therapeutic research upon healthy volunteers, for fully informed consent.

Finally, in cases of drug-induced injury, the subject may also wish to bring an action under the Consumer Protection Act 1987. The issues in relation to the use of this Act have previously been addressed in Chapter 6.

CHAPTER 11

ORGAN TRANSPLANTATION

INTRODUCTION

Organ transplantation is undoubtedly one of the triumphs of modern medicine. The procedure has become increasingly routine as a means of saving and improving the quality of the lives of thousands of people each year. The history of this programme, and the manner in which it has expanded to encompass an increasing variety of organs and other body tissue, has been chronicled by David Lamb:

Lamb, D, *Organ Transplants and Ethics*, 1990, London: Routledge, pp 7–9:

The idea of taking bone, skin, or organs from one person and transplanting them into another has been a subject of fascination and intrigue since earliest times. Yet until the 20th century the dream of creating a healthy whole person by transplantation remained in the realm of mythology and the miraculous. Early attempts at blood transfusion met with no success until knowledge of different blood types and their mutual compatibility or incompatibility was discovered. This meant that many attempts at blood transfusion during the 18th century resulted in charges of homicide before several European courts outlawed the practice. However, blood transfusion was widely used in the 1914–18 war when blood banks were created to store blood. This, perhaps, was one of the most important features in the early stages of the history of transplantation.

But blood is self-replaceable, and although there have been considerable ethical discussions about the policies for collection and distribution of blood, they do not address the kind of ethical and philosophical problems associated with the transplantation of non-regenerating solid organs, such as kidneys, hearts, lungs, pancreases, and livers.

Transplantation of non-vital organs has steadily increased during the 20th century. Skin grafts began in the late 1920s. This procedure is usually applied as a temporary measure in cases of burns. Recent experiments with cultured skin, however, suggest that procurement from donors may one day be unnecessary. Under appropriate conditions skin can be stored and there are now skin and bone banks, where bone is stored for treatment of the skeletal system.

Corneal transplants actually began in 1905, although the operation did not become routine until the 1940s. In 1983 a corneal transplant service was set up in the UK to encourage corneal donation. Improvements in storage techniques now allow corneas to be stored for up to 30 days. The Corneal Tissue Act of 1986 greatly enhanced cadaveric procurement in the UK by allowing non-medical personnel to remove corneas. Since 1944, when the world's first eye bank was opened in the Manhattan Eye, Ear and Throat Hospital, eye banks have become an integral part of most countries' health care systems ...

The modern transplant era, however, began with the transplantation of non-regenerating vital organs in the 1950s, but its antecedents can be traced back to the turn of the century when Dr Alexis Carrel and Dr Charles C Guthrie developed the technique of suturing blood vessels. Then, in 1902, an Austrian surgeon, Dr Emmerick Ullman, removed a kidney from a dog and kept it functioning in the body of another dog for a few days. The eventual failure of this transplant revealed the problem of rejection, and it was discovered in further experiments that successful transplants depend on a close genetic resemblance between donor and recipient ...

The major breakthrough in understanding rejection had to wait until Dr Peter Medawar, winner of the 1960 Nobel Prize, explained how the body's immunisation system recognises foreign bodies that enter it by means of markers or antigens, and then rejects foreign matter by means of the production of antibodies. This knowledge led to the development of tissue-typing, where the donor's and recipient's tissues are examined with a view to compatibility, such that the antigens of both tissues are sufficiently similar to prevent recognition as alien bodies and thus avoid exciting the destructive immune system response. In recent years great efforts have been made to overcome the rejection problem, without which surgical technique would be insufficient. Throughout the 1960s and 1970s drugs were developed which lessened the organism's ability to develop antibodies. But many of these had the unfortunate effect of weakening the recipient's immune system. However, a major breakthrough occurred in 1983 when a Swiss pharmaceutical company produced Cyclosporin, which selectively inhibits the rejection of foreign tissues without damaging their ability to combat viruses and bacteria. The ability to control tissue rejection marks the transition from the era of transplantation as an experimental therapy to the era of organ transplantation as routine therapy.

However, despite compelling evidence that such transplants are not only of significant therapeutic benefit to the majority of recipients but highly cost effective (in allowing savings in other, more expensive forms of treatment, for example, dialysis), this is an area which remains fraught with ethical difficulty. This is especially so as the demand for donor organs continues markedly to outstrip supply. As New *et al* note:

New, B, Solomon, M, Dingwall, R and McHale, J, *A Question of Give and Take*, 1994, London: Kings Fund Institute, p 9:

The transplanting of organs from one human to another is a medical intervention which 50 years ago would have seemed a suitable topic for a science fiction novel. And yet, in the 1990s, kidney transplants are the treatment of choice for end-stage renal disease, and heart and liver transplants offer the only chance of life for thousands of people across the world with chronic heart or liver failure. It is an operation which attracts intense media attention, particularly when children's lives are at stake. However, the reason for such attention is often particularly poignant, involving a race against time for a suitable donor.

The legal framework within which transplantation takes place – the general law as to the removal, retention and use of human materials – has recently been subject to important review and change in the form of the Human Tissue Act 2004, most of whose provisions are due to enter force in April 2006. The background to the Act, which illustrates once again the sensitivity of this whole area of medical activity, is set out in the explanatory notes issued by the Department of Health:

Department of Health, *Explanatory Notes to the Human Tissue Act*, 2004, London: DoH, Crown Copyright:

4. The purpose of the Act is to provide a consistent legislative framework for issues relating to whole body donation and the taking, storage and use of human organs and tissue. It will make consent the fundamental principle underpinning the lawful storage and use of human bodies, body parts, organs and tissue and the removal of material from the bodies of deceased persons. It will set up an over-arching

authority which is intended to rationalise existing regulation of activities like transplantation and anatomical examination, and will introduce regulation of other activities like *post mortem* examinations, and the storage of human material for education, training and research. It is intended to achieve a balance between the rights and expectations of individuals and families, and broader considerations, such as the importance of research, education, training, pathology and public health surveillance to the population as a whole.

5. The Act arose from concern raised by events at Bristol Royal Infirmary and the Royal Liverpool Children's Hospital (Alder Hey) 1999–2000. The *Kennedy* and *Redfern* inquiries at these hospitals established that organs and tissue from children who had died had often been removed, stored and used without proper consent. A subsequent census by the Chief Medical Officer for England (2000) and the *Isaacs Report* (2003) showed that storage and use of organs and tissue from both adults and children without proper consent has been widespread in the past. It also became clear that the current law in this area was not comprehensive, nor as clear and consistent as it might be for professionals or for the families involved ...

In this chapter our main focus will remain the law as it pertains to organ transplants (although at times we shall touch upon wider issues arising from the use of human material). We shall examine next the different sources from which organs for transplantation may be obtained, and the legal and ethical issues raised in each case. We then consider the (relatively novel) legal problem of what status to accord to extracted body parts, before addressing the rights of the donee of such material. The chapter concludes by analysing possible measures of law reform aimed to increase the number of organs available for transplantation.

EXTRACTION OF MATERIAL

The live donor

The world's first successful kidney transplant, which took place in Boston in 1954, involved a live donation between identical twins. Indeed, until the development of powerful new immuno-suppressant drugs in the early 1980s, live donation between close relatives was preferred in order to reduce the chance of organ rejection by the donee. Although, since then, live donations have decreased as a proportion of total organ transplants (2004 statistics, from 'UK Transplant' – formerly the UK Transplants Support Service Authority, show that in the UK live donors accounted for around a quarter of kidney transplants), the numbers have been rising in actual terms. Moreover, certain tissues, namely bone marrow, skin and blood, are invariably obtained from live donors. (In what follows, unless the context indicates otherwise, the terms 'organ donor' and its correlates are used to encompass tissue donation as well.)

Ethical considerations

The major ethical issue here is similar to that considered in the last chapter in relation to medical research, ie how far is it permissible to expose a person to harm, or the risk of harm, in order to benefit another? Just as in the case of research, the question exposes a conflict between two differing systems of moral philosophy. As Price and Garwood-Gowers note:

Price, DPT and Garwood-Gowers, A, 'Transplantation from minors: are children other people's medicine?' (1995) 1 Contemporary Issues in the Law 1:

By virtue of the fact that removal of the material from the donor is primarily for the prospective benefit of another individual, the whole issue of living donation of body materials for transplantation raises starkly the conflict between the two fundamental philosophical theories, deontological theory and consequentialist theory. Few areas of law highlight this conflict as keenly as deontological theory, of which Immanuel Kant is the prime exponent, which seeks to guide our actions by reference to overriding moral imperatives and insists that as part of a respect for persons their intrinsic moral worth dictates that they should not be used merely as a means to another's ends. By contrast, consequentialist approaches, of which utilitarianism is the pre-eminent example, attempt to judge the rightness or wrongness of an action according to the consequences which flow from it. The action which maximises happiness and minimises suffering is the preferred one. Clearly, on a utilitarian calculus the pendulum swings further in favour of donation than on a deontological approach in so far as the risks from donating even a paired organ are generally fairly modest, whereas transplanting such an organ has the potential to improve the quality (and duration) of life of the recipient dramatically.

The Kantian approach, with its emphasis on the primacy of human autonomy, may well be preferred here. On the other hand, as suggested in Chapter 1, the conflict between the two systems largely disappears once it is realised that any plausible form of utilitarianism must also accord great weight to individual autonomy (albeit as an instrumental rather than intrinsic value): a society in which persons could have their organs forcibly extracted for the benefit of others would be a perilous and miserable one indeed.

That having been said, an interesting question concerns how far autonomy in this area should be completely unfettered. This is relevant where a person actively wishes to donate an organ even though the consequences to them will be serious harm or death. The Nuffield Council on Bioethics has expressed its conclusions on this matter as follows:

Nuffield Council on Bioethics, *Human Tissue: Ethical and Legal Issues*, 1995, London: Nuffield Council on Bioethics:

6.4 We identify the avoidance and limitation of injury as a basic requirement for any type of use of human tissue to be ethically acceptable. Avoidance and limitation of injury can be seen as expressing a central element of the undefined, yet widely endorsed, demand for respect for the human body and for respect for human dignity. In paras 6.7–6.16 we identify and elaborate this basic requirement which makes types of use of human tissue ethically acceptable.

6.5 We note, however, that the avoidance and limitation of injury is a complex requirement, and that in certain circumstances, injury can be avoided or limited only by inflicting injury. In our view, the only circumstance in which inflicting injury is acceptable is when it is done to avoid greater injury. It is this that justifies much medical treatment, and action taken in self defence and in other situations. This principle is also useful in evaluating proposed uses of human tissue.

6.6 Although we identify the avoidance and limitation of injury as basic to acceptable use of human tissue, there are other important considerations. For example, consent of those from whom tissue is taken (patient, donor) or of relatives (post mortem) is important. Consent, however, is not the primary consideration. In particular, consent cannot justify injury: for example, killing or maiming cannot be justified by the victim being willing ...

Avoidance and limitation of injury

6.7 It is not easy to state the underlying rationale for viewing these and other sorts of action as unacceptable. The difficulty is in part that many people see these actions as wrong, repugnant or repellent for multiple reasons, about some of which there is no agreement. The most widely accepted reasons, however, often stress that these sorts of action fail to respect others or to accord them dignity, that they injure human beings by treating them as things, as less than human, as objects for use. Although all these phrases are vague, there is considerable agreement about a central range of injurious activity that would constitute disrespect for human beings and for human dignity ...

A related issue, touched upon at p 610, below, is how far a person should be entitled to benefit financially from the provision of his or her body parts.

The legal position at common law

The competent donor and consent

As a minimum, the donor must, where adult and competent, always consent to the removal of an organ. This is simply an application of the general rule that the consent of such a person is needed to any medical procedure (see Chapter 3). In this context, however, there may well be doubts about one of the preconditions for valid consent being present, namely freedom from coercion or undue influence. This is especially so in the vast majority of cases where the donation is between two members of the same family. As we saw in relation to consent, the Court of Appeal was obliged to consider the effect of institutionalised power relationships upon the reality of consent in the case of *Freeman v Home Office (No 2)* [1984] 1 All ER 1036. Nevertheless, there is a suspicion that, in the case of related live transplants, the courts do not wish to get involved in determining such matters, and are instead leaving the question very much to the doctors.

The law of assault

A question long unresolved at judicial level was whether the removal of an organ for transplant by a surgeon would qualify as an assault *notwithstanding* the donor's consent. Writing in 1970, Gerald Dworkin commented on this issue as follows:

Dworkin, G, 'The law relating to organ transplantation in England' (1970) 33 MLR 353:

To determine the legality of live donor transplantations it is first necessary to examine the legal basis for surgical operations generally. Under medieval law, a person committed the crime of mayhem (maim) if he so injured another as to make him less able to fight or to defend himself or to annoy an adversary. To amputate a limb, even with the victim's consent was, on the face of it, an unlawful act, since it deprived the king of a fighting man. In early Victorian times when soldiers, as part of their training, had to bite cartridges, a soldier got a dentist to pull out his front teeth to enable him to avoid training and it was thought that both were guilty of a crime. The modern law is obscure but the crime, to some extent, turns on two interconnected factors. The first is the nature of the physical harm: one person does not have a licence to mutilate or cause bodily harm to another for any purpose merely because that person has consented. The degree of bodily harm is, of course, important: the test is no longer whether it impairs or may impair the victim's ability to fight for his country, but presumably the seriousness of the harm must be of that order … The second factor involves questions of public policy. The law may permit some kinds of assault and battery but not others: the dividing line between the permissible and the impermissible is not clear but the courts have accepted and still accept the burden of safeguarding individuals even against themselves.

The relevance of this aspect of the criminal law is that it provides a basis for saying that many surgical operations are *prima facie* unlawful. Without further justification not only would operations be criminal acts, but they would also be unlawful in the civil law and surgeons might be liable to pay compensation for the consequences of their acts, even though they had exercised all reasonable care. What are the criteria, then, which convert unlawful acts into lawful surgical operations? In some countries the criminal codes absolve from responsibility persons who perform in good faith and with reasonable care and skill a surgical operation upon another person, with his consent and for his benefit, if the performance of the operation is reasonable in the circumstances. No such provision appears in any United Kingdom legislation but it is clear, of course, that surgery, within limits, is a perfectly legal activity. Sir James Fitzjames Stephen formulated the general proposition that 'everyone has a right to consent to the infliction of any bodily injury in the nature of a surgical operation upon himself' and stated that although he knew of no authority for this, the existence of surgery as a profession assumed its truth.

Dworkin suggested four conditions that would need to be satisfied for surgery in general, and donor-organ removal in particular, to be lawful:

(i) *The patient must give a full, free and informed consent.* The importance of consent cannot be overemphasised … It is clear that, in any common law jurisdiction, the general principle is that a patient should be informed of all the material facts relating to the operation which would enable a reasonable person to weigh up the risks and benefits and arrive at a rational decision whether or not to undergo the operation. Also, there should be no unfair pressure upon the patient which induces him to give his consent in spite of all the risks.

(ii) *The operation must be therapeutic: it must be expressly for the patient's benefit.* The major distinguishing feature between surgical operations and unlawful mutilation is, of course, that all surgical operations are allegedly in the medical interests of the patient. Coke refers to a case in 1603 where 'a young and lustie rogue prevailed upon a friend to cut off his left hand, so that he might be better able to beg'. Both were found guilty of the crime of maim; today, they would also be criminally liable. In the criminal codes of some countries, the provisions concerning surgical operations expressly state that they must be for the patient's benefit; in other countries this, until recently, has been accepted as being obvious.

(iii) *There must be lawful justification.* This is a relatively unexplored and open ended requirement. Ethical and social questions are more relevant here and the courts may occasionally use this rubric to extend the law to meet new circumstances. Most surgical operations are lawful … There are other surgical operations, only arguably of therapeutic benefit to the patient, where the courts nevertheless may be tempted to emphasise their lawful justification. It is unlikely that the courts would condemn circumcision as unlawful. No doubt the ritual circumcision of Jewish infants could be upheld on grounds of religious toleration, although circumcision for non-religious reasons would have to be accepted on wider public policy grounds.

(iv) Generally, the operation must be performed by a person with appropriate medical skills ...

It is suggested that, rather than each being necessary in its own right, condition (ii) would tend now to be regarded as a particular application of the more general principle contained in (iii). In the present context (as opposed to therapeutic surgery), it is all-important to look at the reason why the operation is taking place: removal for transplantation is a socially recognised good and is lawfully justified; removal for other purposes, for example, because the person whose organ it was wanted to taste it, would remain a battery. A further requirement, given that no therapeutic benefit will accrue to the donor, appears to be that such removal not expose the donor to an unreasonable amount of harm (or a significant risk thereof). In this regard, the media reported in February 1996 that doctors had refused the request of a father that his remaining kidney be transplanted into his chronically ill son and he be placed on dialysis instead. He had previously given up his first kidney to his other son.

The law of homicide

It follows *a fortiori* from what has just been said that the law will not sanction the removal of vital organs where the consequence for the donor will be death. Gerald Dworkin ('The law relating to organ transplantation in England' (1970) 33 MLR 353) cites the comment, made extra-judicially by Edmund-Davies LJ (as he then was) to the effect that he would:

... be surprised if a surgeon were successfully sued for trespass to the person or convicted of causing bodily harm to one of full age and intelligence who freely consented to act as donor always provided that the operation did not present unreasonable risk to the donor's life or health. That proviso is essential. A man may declare himself ready to die for another, but the surgeon must not take him at his word.

In such a case, the surgeon would be guilty of murder (or, at the very least, manslaughter). For this reason, transplants involving live donors are generally limited to tissues such as bone marrow, blood, and (now) liver lobes (which are all capable of regenerating) or kidneys, of which most people have a 'spare'. The only exception relates to so called 'domino transplants' of hearts which may occur following the donor's own receipt of a heart-lung transplant.

The incompetent donor

Adults

The legal position, until recently, was less clear in relation to the lawfulness of using incompetent adults as donors. Such persons are by definition incapable of giving their consent; rather, as we saw from the House of Lords decision in *Re F (Mental Patient: Sterilisation)* [1990] 2 AC 1 (see Chapter 4), they may be subjected to medical intervention only in so far as the procedure is in their best interests. Can donating an organ be regarded as in the donor's (as opposed to the donee's) best interests? An important US case in point is *Strunk v Strunk* 445 SW 2d 145 (1969) (Kentucky CA), where an affirmative answer was given. The court authorised a kidney transplant from Jerry, a 27 year old man with a mental age of six, to his 28 year old brother after hearing psychiatric evidence of the 'extremely traumatic effect' that his brother's death would have upon him.

The question finally arose for determination by an English court in the case of *Re Y (An Adult Patient) (Transplant: Bone Marrow)* (1996) 35 BMLR 111:

Re Y (Adult Patient) (Transplant: Bone Marrow) (1996) 35 BMLR 111, Fam Div (Connell J)

Miss Y was 25 years old and had been severely mentally and physically disabled from birth. She had lived in care since the age of 10. Her sister, aged 36, who suffered from pre-leukaemic bone marrow disorder, sought a declaration that it would be lawful to perform blood tests and possible bone marrow extraction upon Miss Y, despite the latter's inability to consent:

Connell J: The taking of blood tests and the harvesting of bone marrow from the defendant who is incapable of giving informed consent would amount to assaults upon the defendant and would therefore be illegal unless shown to be in the best interests of the defendant and therefore lawful.

The test to be applied in a case such as this is to ask whether the evidence shows that it is in the best interests of the defendant for such procedures to take place. The fact that such a process would obviously benefit the plaintiff is not relevant unless, as a result of the defendant helping the plaintiff in that way, the best interests of the defendant are served.

The approach is as set out in the case of *Re F (Mental Patient: Sterilisation)* [1990] 2 AC 1 ... a non-therapeutic sterilisation case. Thus, the giving of medical treatment to mentally disordered adult patients is, save as to treatment for their mental disorder under the Mental Health Act 1983, governed by common law. The lawfulness of the action depends upon whether the treatment is in the best interests of the patient ...

This case is different from the case of *Re F* because it involves the concept of donation of bone marrow by a donor who is incapable of giving consent where a significant benefit will flow to another person. There was no other person in *Re F* who would have benefited directly as a result of the declaration sought, the benefits of sterilisation attaching solely to the mentally incapacitated subject of the application.

Nonetheless, I am satisfied that the root question remains the same, namely, whether the procedures here envisaged will benefit the defendant and accordingly benefits which may flow to the plaintiff are relevant only in so far as they have a positive effect upon the best interests of the defendant ...

The information provided by those who now care for the defendant in the residential home make it apparent that the defendant benefits from the visits which she receives from her family and from her occasional involvement in family events, for example, the wedding of one of her sisters, particularly because these visits maintain for her a link with the outside world which is helpful to her and which would otherwise be lost to her.

In addition, the Official Solicitor's representative observed affection between mother and daughter during a recent visit which demonstrated that her mother holds a special place in the defendant's world even if the defendant does not appreciate that this lady is in fact her mother.

If this application is not successful, the chances that the plaintiff will not survive are materially increased. She might be able to receive bone marrow from one of the two unrelated donors but evidence to me shows that the recipient's chances of survival for 18 months following transplant from a sibling are at least 40%, whereas those chances after donation from a stranger in the case of the plaintiff s illness are at best 30%. The match from strangers is never quite as good as the match from a sibling.

Further, if the plaintiff survives the first six months post-transplant then the prospects for survival semi-indefinitely are good. On the other hand, without any transplant her prospects of survival are very poor and are deteriorating fast. If the plaintiff dies, this is bound to have an adverse effect upon her mother who already suffers from significant ill health. One lay witness took the gloomy view that this event would prove fatal to the mother, but in any event her ability to visit the defendant would be handicapped significantly, not only by a likely deterioration in her health, but also by the need which would then arise for her to look after her only grandchild, E.

In this situation, the defendant would clearly be harmed by the reduction in or loss of contact to her mother. Accordingly, it is to the benefit of the defendant that she should act as donor to her sister, because in this way her positive relationship with her mother is most likely to be prolonged. Further, if the transplant occurs, this is likely to improve the defendant's relationship with her mother who in her heart clearly wishes it to take place and also to improve her relationship with the plaintiff who will be eternally grateful to her.

This case shows the court adopting a wide interpretation of 'best interests'; it is not somatic health alone which is relevant, but the wider interests a person has as part of the social community. (This approach is also in line with decisions relating to sterilisation discussed in Chapter 4.) Nevertheless, there are important limits on invoking the test in order to justify organ extraction, especially where the organ is non-regenerative. As Andrew Grubb has commented:

Grubb, A, 'Commentary on *Re Y'* (1996) 4 Med L Rev 204:

Of course, the judge recognised that it was insufficient for him merely to identify a 'benefit' to Miss Y without weighing against this any detriment that she might suffer by undergoing the procedures. However, the risks inherent in the procedures – the general anaesthetic and the removal of two pints of bone marrow – were regarded as 'very small' (one in 10,000 risk of death) and non-existent (as bone marrow is regenerative) respectively. Further any pain that might arise from the harvesting could be controlled by morphine. And, of course, there could be a detriment by not undergoing the procedure ... In *Re Y*, Connell J referred to the 'harm' Miss Y would suffer (directly and indirectly) from the death of her sister although the evidence never elevated this to the level of psychiatric injury.

Limitations in future cases. Given the weaknesses in the evidence which have been suggested above, *Re Y* could be seen as giving a 'green light' to support donations by incompetent adults and children in the future. This would, I think, be a misreading of the case and not Connell J's intention for a number of reasons.

First, the case is probably an unusual one in that it concerned a procedure which does have minimal risks for the donor. Given the need to weigh the benefits of the procedure against the risks of doing it, it is not likely that a court would contemplate donation of non-regenerative tissue such as a kidney. Connell J suggested as much when he remarked that his decision should not be considered 'a useful precedent in cases where the surgery involved is more intrusive'. While the long term risks of having one kidney are not great, they do exist and the nature of the procedure suggests that it would be difficult to satisfy the 'best interests' test ...

Secondly, the courts will undoubtedly look for evidence of a 'close relationship' which will be damaged if the donee patient dies. It is most unlikely, therefore, that the court would contemplate even a minimally risky procedure if the donor's mental disability or if the child's age prevented them forming such a relationship. Donations by babies and the severely mentally disabled may thus be out of court. Also, the court will look for immediate psychological benefit and would reject as too tenuous evidence of the long term future benefit of not 'living in a family under the shadow of avoidable, premature death' ...

Thirdly, the court might well as a rule-of-thumb look for the 'agreement' (though obviously not the consent) of the donor as a condition to allowing the donation. This would also exclude donations from the very young or severely disabled. Also, it is unthinkable that the 'best interests' test could be satisfied if the donor objected to the donation.

Fourthly, there is no suggestion in Connell J's judgment that purely altruistic benefit will satisfy the 'best interests' test. He restricted himself to situations of 'psychological benefit' ... There is no support, therefore, in his judgment for permitting non-therapeutic research upon incompetent adults or children even though this does have strong professional support in exceptional cases of 'minimal risk' ...

Fifthly, at the invitation of the Official Solicitor, Connell J indicated that cases involving donation by an incompetent adult fell into the 'special category' of case where it was desirable that the court should be involved ...

Children

In contrast to the position with incompetent adults, there is no English authority directly on the question of live organ donation by minors. Moreover, this issue raises a number of further complications. First, in the case of older children who satisfy the test of 'Gillick competence', can they consent in their own right to act as donors? The answer, in principle, would appear to be yes. As Lord Donaldson MR noted, obiter, in Re W (A Minor) (Medical Treatment) [1992] 4 All ER 627:

Lord Donaldson MR: [Section 8 of the Family Law Reform Act 1969 establishing the presumption that a minor of 16 years can consent to medical treatment] extends not only to treatment, but also to diagnostic procedures (see sub-s (2)). It does not, however, extend to the donation of organs or blood since, so far as the donor is concerned, these do not constitute either treatment or diagnosis. I cannot remember to what extent organ donation was common in 1967, but the Latey Committee expressly recommended that only 18 year olds and older should be authorised by statute to consent to giving blood (see paras 485–89). It seems that parliament accepted this recommendation, although I doubt whether blood donation will create any problem as a 'Gillick competent' minor of any age would be able to give consent under the common law.

Organ transplants are quite different and, as a matter of law, doctors would have to secure the consent of someone with the right to consent on behalf of a donor under the age of 18 or, if they relied upon the consent of the minor himself or herself, be satisfied that the minor was 'Gillick competent' in the context of so serious a procedure which would not benefit the minor. This would be a highly improbable conclusion. But this is only to look at the question as a matter of law. Medical ethics also enter into the question. The doctor has a professional duty to act in the best interests of his patient and to advise accordingly. It is inconceivable that he should proceed in reliance solely upon the consent of an under-age patient, however 'Gillick competent', in the absence of supporting parental consent and equally inconceivable that he should proceed in the absence of the patient's consent. In any event he will need to seek the opinions of other doctors and may be well advised to apply to the court for guidance, as recommended by Lord Templeman in a different context in *Re B (A Minor) (Wardship: Sterilisation)* [1987] 2 All ER 206, pp 214–15 ...

Lord Donaldson MR suggests here that it would be 'inconceivable' both that extraction would go ahead without parental consent *and* that it could occur solely on the basis of the latter (a necessary caveat in the light of his Lordship's 'flak jacket' approach to consent in his decision in the case (see Chapter 4)).

In the case of children who lack capacity, it is apparent that the parents must normally give proxy consent to any form of medical intervention upon them. Indeed, in the American case of *Bonner v Moran* 126 F 2d 121 (1941) (USCA DC) a doctor who failed to obtain parental consent was held liable in battery after taking skin grafts from a 15 year old boy to treat the latter's badly burnt cousin. On the other hand, it is clear that parental authorisation of such an intervention will not guarantee that it is lawful. Rather, as Lord Scarman suggested in *Gillick v W Norfolk and Wisbech HA* [1986] 1 AC 112, the parent's power here is one that they should exercise exclusively for the child's protection.

In fact, it appears that bone marrow donation between minor siblings is widely practised. Indeed, it is apparent that parents are sometimes conceiving children with a view to them acting as marrow donors to sick siblings (recall the case, referred to in Chapter 7, in which the Human Fertilisation and Embryology Authority licensed pre-implantation genetic diagnosis to identify IVF embryos that could later provide compatible tissue for a couple's existing child). In relation to more intrusive and risky procedures, such as organ donation, it is much less likely that parental consent alone would suffice. Rather, as in the case of non-therapeutic procedures upon incompetent adults, the matter would almost certainly come before the court for a declaration of lawfulness. In the USA, whilst such declarations have been granted in several cases (see, for example, *Hart v Brown* 289 A 3d 386 (1972) which concerned a kidney transplant between seven year old identical twins), the court refused to make one in a more recent case, *Curran v Bosze* 566 2d 1319 (1990):

Curran v Bosze 566 NE 2d 1319 (1990), Illinois Sup Ct

The plaintiff was the former wife of the defendant and mother of three and a half year old twins by him. The defendant's 12 year old son from a previous marriage was dying from leukaemia and the defendant brought a petition requiring her to submit the twins to a blood test to establish compatibility with the 12 year old with a view to a subsequent bone marrow transplant:

> **Calvo J**: In each of the foregoing cases where consent to the kidney transplant was authorised, regardless whether the authority to consent was to be exercised by the court, a parent or a guardian, the key inquiry was the presence or absence of a benefit to the potential donor. Notwithstanding the language used by the courts in reaching their determination that a transplant may or may not occur, the standard by which the determination was made was whether the transplant would be in the best interest of the child or incompetent person.
>
> The primary benefit to the donor in these cases arises from the relationship existing between the donor and recipient. In *Strunk [v Strunk]*, the donor lived in a State institution. The recipient was a brother who served as the donor's only connection with the outside world. In both *Hart [v Brown]* and *Little [v Little* 576 SW 2d 493 (1979)], there was evidence that the sibling relationship between the

donor and recipient was close. In each of these cases, both parents had given their consent ...

We hold that a parent or guardian may give consent on behalf of a minor daughter or son for the child to donate bone marrow to a sibling, only when to do so would be in the minor's best interest.

The evidence reveals three critical factors which are necessary to a determination that it will be in the best interests of a child to donate bone marrow to a sibling. First, the parent who consents on behalf of the child must be informed of the risks and benefits inherent in the bone marrow harvesting procedure to the child.

Second, there must be emotional support available to the child from the person or persons who take care of the child. The testimony reveals that a child who is to undergo general anaesthesia and the bone marrow harvesting procedure needs the emotional support of a person whom the child loves and trusts. A child who is to donate bone marrow is required to go to an unfamiliar place and meet with unfamiliar people. Depending upon the age of the child, he or she may or may not understand what is to happen. The evidence establishes that the presence and emotional support by the child's caretaker is important to ease the fears associated with such an unfamiliar procedure.

Third, there must be an existing, close relationship between the donor and recipient. The evidence clearly shows that there is no physical benefit to a donor child. If there is any benefit to a child who donates bone marrow to a sibling it will be a psychological benefit. According to the evidence, the psychological benefit is not simply one of personal, individual altruism in an abstract theoretical sense, although that may be a factor.

The psychological benefit is grounded firmly in the fact that the donor and recipient are known to each other as family. Only where there is an existing relationship between a healthy child and his or her ill sister or brother may a psychological benefit to the child from donating bone marrow to a sibling realistically be found to exist. The evidence establishes that it is the existing sibling relationship, as well as the potential for a continuing sibling relationship, which forms the context in which it may be determined that it will be in the best interests of the child to undergo a bone marrow harvesting procedure for a sibling ...

Ms Curran has refused consent on behalf of the twins to the bone marrow transplant because she does not think it is in their best interests to subject them to the risks and pains involved in undergoing general anaesthesia and the harvesting procedure. While Ms Curran is aware that the risks involved in donating bone marrow and undergoing general anaesthesia are small, she also is aware that when such risk occurs, it may be life-threatening ...

This court shares the opinion of the circuit court that Jean Pierre's situation evokes sympathy from all who've heard [it]. No matter how small the hope that a bone marrow transplant will cure Jean Pierre, the fact remains that without the transplant, Jean Pierre will almost certainly die. The sympathy felt by this court, the circuit court, and all those who have learned of Jean Pierre's tragic situation cannot, however, obscure the fact that, under the circumstances presented in the case at bar, it neither would be proper under existing law nor in the best interests of the three and a half year old twins for the twins to participate in the bone marrow harvesting procedure.

Actions by donors in negligence

Whilst no special issues arise in respect of the duty of care owed by extracting surgeon to donor, interesting questions are posed by the negligence of third parties.

Suppose A requires a kidney transplant because of negligent conduct by B; if C comes forward and donates one of his kidneys to A, can he then claim compensation from B? A Canadian case in which recovery was allowed in these circumstances is analysed by Gerald Robertson:

Robertson, G, 'A new application of the rescue principle' (1980) 96 LQR 19:

The recent decision of the Manitoba Queen's Bench in *Urbanski v Patel* (1978) 84 DLR (3d) 650 is further evidence of the significant contribution which Canadian courts have made in relation to 'rescue' cases in the law of tort (see, for example, *Linden* (1971) 34 MLR 241). In the instant case, the plaintiff's daughter underwent a sterilisation operation performed by the defendant surgeon. During the course of the operation, the defendant mistakenly removed the patient's only kidney, believing it to be an ovarian cyst. The patient was immediately linked to a dialysis machine and the long process of waiting for a suitable kidney donor began. After almost 12 months of fruitless search, the plaintiff volunteered to have one of his own kidneys removed for transplantation to his daughter. This was done (unfortunately the transplant proved to be unsuccessful) and thereafter the plaintiff raised an action against the defendant claiming damages for the loss of his kidney. The plaintiff's claim was successful and he was awarded $8,650 in damages.

Not surprisingly, the court tackled this fact situation from the standpoint of 'foreseeability'. It concluded that it was reasonably foreseeable that if the defendant's negligence resulted in the removal of the patient's only kidney, 'one of her family would be invited, and would agree, to donate a kidney for transplant'. Thus the plaintiff's altruistic act was to be regarded as a natural and probable consequence of the defendant's negligence and therefore did not constitute a *novus actus interveniens*.

The only other case to have considered this question was that of *Sirianni v Anna* 285 NYS 2d 709 (1967), in which a New York court, dealing with an identical fact situation, dismissed the plaintiff's action on the grounds that the kidney donation was not a foreseeable consequence of the defendant's negligence. The court in *Urbanski* distinguished this decision on the basis that in 1967 kidney transplantation was still in its infancy, whereas by 1976 it had become accepted medical practice and was therefore 'entirely foreseeable'.

This treatment of the foreseeability question is, however, open to criticism. In regarding the issue of foreseeability as being relevant only to the question of remoteness, the court failed to consider whether or not the defendant owed the plaintiff a duty of care. The defendant was unaware, until after the operation, that the patient had only one kidney, and thus he could not be expected to have foreseen, at the time of the operation, that removal of the patient's kidney would result in the need for transplantation. It follows, therefore, that since injury to the plaintiff was not reasonably foreseeable at the time of the negligent act, no duty of care was owed to him by the defendant.

However, *Urbanski* is far from unique in failing to consider this question. Indeed, the decision is consistent with the approach adopted in many other rescue cases, in which courts have tended to gloss over the question of duty of care by concentrating on the foreseeability of the initial injury to the rescuee, rather than on the foreseeability of the rescue attempt ...

The significance of *Urbanski* lies in the fact that it extends the basis for recovery in rescue cases to an entirely new type of situation. In previous cases, the rescue attempt has involved a risk of physical injury to the rescuer, which he has chosen, either consciously or instinctively, to ignore in going to the assistance of the person in danger. In the *Urbanski* situation, physical injury is inevitable, and it is the rescuer's conscious decision to submit to such injury that forms the basis of the rescue attempt.

Despite this distinction, the court regarded the plaintiff's claim as falling within the established 'rescue principle', and it is submitted that an English court would be likely to do the same. There is no reason why the plaintiff's claim should be prejudiced merely because the sustaining of physical injury is a necessary part, and not merely an incidental consequence, of the rescue attempt ...

The court also concluded that the defence of volenti should be rejected, and once again it is thought that an English court would reach a similar conclusion. Cases such as *Haynes v Harwood* [1935] 1 KB 146 and *Baker v Hopkins* [1959] 1 WLR 966 demonstrate a firm reluctance on the part of English courts to uphold the defence of *volenti* in rescue cases. The plaintiff in *Urbanski* can scarcely be said to have voluntarily assumed the risk of injury, notwithstanding that he realised that such injury was inevitable, given the dilemma in which he had been placed by the defendant's negligent act. The plaintiff's parental feelings towards his daughter, coupled with an understandable sense of moral obligation, left him without any real choice in the matter.

Subsequently, however, in the case of *Moore v Shah* 458 NYS 2d 33 (1982), a New York court refused to award compensation similar circumstances. Weiss J commented as follows:

Weiss J: In order to recover, a plaintiff must be one within the 'zone of danger' (*Tobin v Grossman* 24 NY 2d 609 (1969) ... *Palsgraf v Long Is RR Co* 248 NY 339 (1928) ...). It is difficult to charge a physician with the responsibility to foresee each and every person other than his patient who might conceivably be affected by his negligence ...

Our research has disclosed but one reported case in which the plaintiff was an actual organ donor. In *Sirianni v Anna* 55 Misc 2d 553 (1967) ... where a similar factual pattern to the instant case existed, Special Term granted defendant's motion to dismiss the complaint. While this court is not bound by *stare decisis* to follow that decision, we are persuaded by subsequent cases that it was correct. Only one year ago, the Court of Appeals held that where there is no allegation that the defendant was negligent with respect to the plaintiff as opposed to the patient, the case does not fall within recognised limits to the rescue doctrine and it declined to extend existing principles of law so as to include third parties who suffer (shock) as a result of direct injury to others. (*Tobin v Grossman*) ... There are serious policy considerations which militate against the recovery sought here. Our decision may best be summarised in the words of then Associate Judge Breitel in *Tobin v Grossman* ... 'Every injury has ramifying consequences, like the ripplings of the waters, without end. The problem for the law is to limit the legal consequences of wrongs to a controllable degree' ... We decline here to extend the common law to create a remedy for these plaintiffs.

It is submitted that an English court would be more likely to favour the cautious approach adopted in *Moore* to that in *Urbanski*.

Statutory limitations upon live organ donation

The need for 'appropriate consent' to the storage and use of organs and tissue

The Human Tissue Act 2004 will introduce a new statutory regime of consent (termed by the Act 'appropriate consent') needed before human organs and tissue may be used and/or stored, including for transplantation. Nominally, the Act leaves it to the common law to determine the lawfulness of the prior *removal* of such material from live donors. However, in practice the new regime will already operate – in duplication with the common law – at the point of removal. Not only does removal here precede the material's use for transplantation but, as noted earlier, in legal terms such an intended use is essential. In other words, the failure to have obtained statutory consent (to subsequent use and/or storage) before removing an organ will render the removal itself unlawful at common law.

The relevant consent provisions of the 2004 Act, so far as they relate to live donors, are as follows:

Human Tissue Act 2004

2 'Appropriate consent': children

(1) This section makes provision for the interpretation of 'appropriate consent' in section 1 in relation to an activity involving the body, or material from the body, of a person who is a child or has died a child ('the child concerned').

(2) Subject to subsection (3), where the child concerned is alive, 'appropriate consent' means his consent.

(3) Where–

    (a) the child concerned is alive,

    (b) neither a decision of his to consent to the activity, nor a decision of his not to consent to it, is in force, and

    (c) either he is not competent to deal with the issue of consent in relation to the activity or, though he is competent to deal with that issue, he fails to do so,

'appropriate consent' means the consent of a person who has parental responsibility for him. ...

3 'Appropriate consent': adults

(1) This section makes provision for the interpretation of 'appropriate consent' in section 1 in relation to an activity involving the body, or material from the body, of a person who is an adult or has died an adult ('the person concerned').

(2) Where the person concerned is alive, 'appropriate consent' means his consent. ...

6 Activities involving material from adults who lack capacity to consent

Where–

    (a) an activity of a kind mentioned in section 1(1)(d) or (f) involves material from the body of a person who-

        (i) is an adult, and

        (ii) lacks capacity to consent to the activity, and

    (b) neither a decision of his to consent to the activity, nor a decision of his not to consent to it, is in force,

there shall for the purposes of this Part be deemed to be consent of his to the activity if it is done in circumstances of a kind specified by regulations made by the Secretary of State.

As previously noted, these provisions will operate on top of the existing common law requirements in relation to the lawful removal of material. Thus, for example, as regards the use of material from an incompetent child, s 2(3), providing for consent by a person with parental responsibility, is simply a further safeguard: it will not detract from the need for a determination at common law that the removal procedure is also in the child's best interests. In this context, were a situation to arise where two parents (each with parental responsibility) disagreed as to whether one of their children should act as a donor to its sick sibling, the lack of agreement would itself be a factor relevant in assessing such interests.

Section 6 of the Act provides for the Health Secretary to introduce regulations to address the issue of consent in relation to incompetent adults. The Department of Health's explanatory notes comment upon this section and the need to dovetail the law here with the new Mental Capacity Act, as follows:

> **Department of Health, *Explanatory Notes to the Human Tissue Act*, 2004, London: DoH, Crown Copyright**
>
> **Section 6: Activities involving material from adults who lack capacity**
>
> 22. This section enables the Secretary of State to specify in regulations the circumstances in which there is to be deemed to be consent to activities regulated by the Act in relation to adults who lack capacity to consent for themselves, where a decision of theirs about such matters is not already in force. It is envisaged that the regulations will provide for consent to be deemed to be in place where the activity would be in the adult's best interests – for example, it could be in their best interests to donate tissue to a close relative for transplantation. The regulations will also be able to provide that where consent has been given by a proxy in accordance with Schedule 1 to the Medicines For Human Use (Clinical Trials) Regulations 2004/1031, storage and use of material from the adult lacking capacity as part of the trial should be treated as done with consent. The regulations will also be able to take account of the Mental Capacity Bill, introduced in the House of Commons on 17 June 2004, in particular in relation to research involving those who lack capacity to consent, which will be regulated by that Bill.

The prohibition on organ (and tissue) trafficking

Following a well publicised scandal in the late 1980s, in which it was revealed that a Harley Street clinic was paying impoverished Turkish donors up to £3,000 for their spare kidneys, Parliament enacted the Human Organ Transplants Act 1989. This statute prohibited commercial dealings in organs (which were defined by the Act to include non-regenerative body parts, such as kidneys, but not regenerative tissues such as bone marrow or blood). The 1989 Act will be repealed by the 2004 Human Tissue Act once it enters into force in 2006. However, the salient prohibitions are re-enacted by the new Act, which indeed extends them to cover other forms of human tissue. Section 32 provides as follows:

> **Human Tissue Act 2004:**
>
> *Trafficking*
>
> **32 Prohibition of commercial dealings in human material for transplantation**
>
> (1) A person commits an offence if he–
>
>   (a) gives or receives a reward for the supply of, or for an offer to supply, any controlled material;
>
>   (b) seeks to find a person willing to supply any controlled material for reward;
>
>   (c) offers to supply any controlled material for reward;
>
>   (d) initiates or negotiates any arrangement involving the giving of a reward for the supply of, or for an offer to supply, any controlled material;

(e) takes part in the management or control of a body of persons corporate or unincorporate whose activities consist of or include the initiation or negotiation of such arrangements.

(2) Without prejudice to subsection (1)(b) and (c), a person commits an offence if he causes to be published or distributed, or knowingly publishes or distributes, an advertisement–

    (a) inviting persons to supply, or offering to supply, any controlled material for reward, or

    (b) indicating that the advertiser is willing to initiate or negotiate any such arrangement as is mentioned in subsection (1)(d).

(3) A person who engages in an activity to which subsection (1) or (2) applies does not commit an offence under that subsection if he is designated by the Authority as a person who may lawfully engage in the activity ...

(6) For the purposes of subsections (1) and (2), payment in money or money's worth to the holder of a licence shall be treated as not being a reward where–

    (a) it is in consideration for transporting, removing, preparing, preserving or storing controlled material, and

    (b) its receipt by the holder of the licence is not expressly prohibited by the terms of the licence.

(7) References in subsections (1) and (2) to reward, in relation to the supply of any controlled material, do not include payment in money or money's worth for defraying or reimbursing–

    (a) any expenses incurred in, or in connection with, transporting, removing, preparing, preserving or storing the material,

    (b) any liability incurred in respect of–

        (i) expenses incurred by a third party in, or in connection with, any of the activities mentioned in paragraph (a), or

        (ii) a payment in relation to which subsection (6) has effect, or

    (c) any expenses or loss of earnings incurred by the person from whose body the material comes so far as reasonably and directly attributable to his supplying the material from his body.

(8) For the purposes of this section, controlled material is any material which–

    (a) consists of or includes human cells,

    (b) is, or is intended to be removed, from a human body,

    (c) is intended to be used for the purpose of transplantation, and

    (d) is not of a kind excepted under subsection (9).

(9) The following kinds of material are excepted–

    (a) gametes,

    (b) embryos, and

    (c) material which is the subject of property because of an application of human skill ...

Gametes and embryos are excepted on the basis that they are subject to their own regulatory regime under the Human Fertilisation and Embryology Act 1990 (see further Chapter 7). However, otherwise it is apparent that the definition of controlled material under the Act is very wide, and will potentially also include blood used for transfusions. It is for this reason that s32(3) allows 'the Authority' – a reference to the new Human Tissue Authority (see further, the discussion at p 604 below) – to designate persons who may lawfully trade in human material: as the DoH Explanatory Notes to the Act suggest, 'the National Blood Service will continue to be allowed to purchase blood from abroad'.

Sub-sections 32(4) and (5) provide for offences under the section to be punishable by stiff penalties, including (in the case of a breach of sub-section (1)) by a term of imprisonment of up to three years.

Further restrictions upon live donations

In addition to prohibiting commercial dealings, Parliament, in passing the 1989 Human Organ Transplants Act, evinced a general concern about live donations between persons not genetically related. Accordingly, it created a special authority, the Unrelated Live Transplants Regulatory Authority (ULTRA), and provided that, to be lawful, such transplants had first to be approved by this authority. In this regard, ULTRA was directed by statutory instrument to satisfy itself of the following matters:

Human Organ Transplants (Unrelated Persons) Regulations 1989 SI 1989/2480:

3 Transplants between persons who are not genetically related

(1) The prohibition in s 2(1) of the [1989] Act (restriction on transplants between persons not genetically related) shall not apply in cases where a registered medical practitioner has caused the matter to be referred to the Authority and where the Authority is satisfied–

   (a) that no payment has been, or is to be, made in contravention of s 1 of the Act;

   (b) that the registered medical practitioner who has caused the matter to be referred to the Authority has clinical responsibility for the donor; and

   (c) except in a case where the primary purpose of removal of an organ from a donor is the medical treatment of that donor, that the conditions specified in para (2) of this regulation are satisfied.

(2) The conditions referred to in para (1)(c) of this regulation are–

   (a) that a registered medical practitioner has given the donor an explanation of the nature of the medical procedure for, and the risk involved in, the removal of the organ in question;

   (b) that the donor understands the nature of the medical procedure and the risks, as explained by the registered medical practitioner, and consents to the removal of the organ in question;

   (c) that the donor's consent to the removal of the organ in question was not obtained by coercion or the offer of an inducement;

   (d) that the donor understands that he is entitled to withdraw his consent if he wishes, but has not done so;

   (e) that the donor and the recipient have both been interviewed by a person who appears to the Authority to have been suitably qualified to conduct such interviews and who has reported to the Authority on the conditions contained in sub-paras (a)–(d) above and has included in his report an account of any difficulties of communication with the donor or the recipient and an explanation of how those difficulties were overcome.

However, the basis for singling out the unrelated donor for special protection in this way was never entirely convincing: arguably it is, if anyone, the related donor who may be vulnerable to illicit pressure to donate. As Kennedy and Grubb pointed out in their analysis of the 1989 legislation:

Kennedy, I and Grubb, A, *Medical Law*, 2nd edn, 1994, London: Butterworths, p 1092:

... Parliament was concerned that the donation be entirely altruistic and presumes that this will be so in the case of those who are 'genetically related' whereas it may not be otherwise. It is fair to ask, however, if the key to altruism is close family ties, why should a spouse be treated as a stranger? Furthermore, grandparents and grandchildren are genetically related and may surely be presumed to act as altruistically as those included within the Act, yet they too are excluded as if they were strangers. It cannot be that a grandparent is necessarily too old to be a donor because someone may be a grandparent at 40!

By contrast, if altruism is the key, why should parliament restrict unregulated donation to the genetically related? It could be said that intrafamily donations may well be the product of severe social pressure ('coercion') rather than altruism ... In some jurisdictions, consequently, legislation prohibits the removal of non-regenerative tissue from a minor for the purpose of transplantation, recognising the danger of pressure within the family (see, for example, s 14(1) of the Human Tissue Act 1982 in Victoria, Australia).

Under the new Human Tissue Act, while special safeguards in relation to live transplants will remain, the distinction between genetically related and unrelated donors is removed from the face of the legislation. Instead, all proposed transplants – related and unrelated – must be referred to the new Human Tissue Authority (which will supersede ULTRA). The relevant provision of the 2004 Act, s 33, is as follows:

Human Tissue Act 2004:

Transplants

33 Restriction on transplants involving a live donor

(1) Subject to subsections (3) and (5), a person commits an offence if–

    (a) he removes any transplantable material from the body of a living person intending that the material be used for the purpose of transplantation, and

    (b) when he removes the material, he knows, or might reasonably be expected to know, that the person from whose body he removes the material is alive.

(2) Subject to subsections (3) and (5), a person commits an offence if–

    (a) he uses for the purpose of transplantation any transplantable material which has come from the body of a living person, and

    (b) when he does so, he knows, or might reasonably be expected to know, that the transplantable material has come from the body of a living person.

(3) The Secretary of State may by regulations provide that subsection (1) or (2) shall not apply in a case where–

    (a) the Authority is satisfied–

        (i) that no reward has been or is to be given in contravention of section 32, and

        (ii) that such other conditions as are specified in the regulations are satisfied, and

    (b) such other requirements as are specified in the regulations are complied with.

(4) Regulations under subsection (3) shall include provision for decisions of the Authority in relation to matters which fall to be decided by it under the regulations to be subject, in such circumstances as the regulations may provide, to reconsideration in accordance with such procedure as the regulations may provide.

(5) Where under subsection (3) an exception from subsection (1) or (2) is in force, a person does not commit an offence under that subsection if he reasonably believes that the exception applies. ...

(7) In this section–

... 'transplantable material' means material of a description specified by regulations made by the Secretary of State.

The regulations in question should be made by April 2006, ready for the Act's expected commencement, and it remains to be seen if they will reintroduce any distinction between related and unrelated donors. In general, the kind of factors for the Human Tissue Authority to consider when approving a transplant are likely to resemble those found (for unrelated transplants) in the corresponding 1989 regulations (see p 584 above).

The dead donor

As noted earlier, the development of new immuno-suppressant drugs within the last 20 years has diminished the importance of donor-donee compatibility and permitted the increased use of cadaveric transplants. Currently, around three-quarters of kidneys transplanted in the UK are obtained in this way and the practice enjoys a number of practical advantages. Most obviously, there is no difficulty in terms of exposing the dead donor to harm (or the risk of harm) and a total harvesting of organs is therefore possible, including the heart, lungs, pancreas, liver and eyes. On the other hand, some distinct problems are also created, notably the need for the organs to be removed fairly rapidly after death, if they are to be of any use. This raises the issue not only of who may authorise such removal, but also the larger question of how it is proper to treat the recently deceased human corpse. David Lamb has commented on this latter issue as follows:

Lamb, D, *Organ Transplants and Ethics*, 1990, London: Routledge, pp 122–24:

Although respect for the deceased takes different forms in different cultures, for the most part violation of the body's integrity for therapeutic purposes, such as organ transplantation, is not regarded as disrespect. At least no Western Church has adopted an unfavourable stance towards organ removal. Jewish, Christian, and Buddhist countries, despite prohibitions on the mutilation of corpses, permit cadaveric transplants provided prior consent of the deceased – or family consent – has been obtained.

The respect accorded to dead bodies in the Muslim faith rules out the study of anatomy on indigenous corpses. Post mortems are rare in Islamic countries. But in 1982 organ donation after death was declared *halal* (permissible) by the Senior 'Ulama' Commission, the highest religious authority in such matters, in Saudi Arabia ...

Nevertheless, there are sources of resistance to organ transplantation which deserve consideration. An important aspect of resistance to routine harvesting of cadaveric organs is the symbolic role which is assigned to the dead body. This role should not be underestimated, even though the interests of the living may outweigh those of the dead. Joel Feinberg ... cites a case which brings out the importance of such symbolism. In 1978 the Department of Transport in the USA contracted with several university laboratories to test designs for automobiles in actual crashes at varying velocities. Dummies had proven unsatisfactory. Some researchers – with the consent of the relatives – had substituted human cadavers. After a public outcry the tests were stopped, despite the Department of Transport's protest that such a decision would set back progress on safety protection for years. The grounds for the prohibition of these tests were that 'the use of human cadavers for vehicle safety research violated fundamental notions of morality and human dignity' ...

It should be stressed that no coercive measures were employed. Research workers were not coerced and the tests were conducted in private. Relatives had expressed consent and prior consent to donation for experimental purposes had been indicated by the deceased. What then, is the difference between this project, designed to save lives, and the use of cadavers for laboratory or transplantation purposes?

The only difference is the violent 'assault' on the cadavers during the car crashes. But the violence was not experienced violence. No pain or discomfort could possibly have been inflicted upon the 'victims'. The issue at stake appears to concern the symbolic role of the human cadaver. Violent assault on a cadaver is an assault on the important symbolic role assigned to the newly dead.

According to Feinberg, symbolic fears of this kind, though culturally significant, should not outweigh the imperative to save lives. Certainly objections to the routine salvaging of cadaveric organs based on symbolic fears should not impede research to improve life expectancy. To drive home this point Feinberg draws an analogy with William James' story of a Russian aristocrat who wept over a fictional tragedy in a theatre while her coachman froze to death outside in her carriage. In such cases the symbolic has outweighed the real.

There is merit in Feinberg's argument. But in reply it must be stressed that symbols are important to the very fabric of society. A society with no symbolic values for the dead is little short of savagery. Moreover, a body is not just a symbol. The newly dead continue as a presence, which is why they are referred to as deceased. The absence of the life that once existed has a very real presence ...

Arguably, such symbolic concerns contributed to the furore in the wake of the revelations at Bristol and Alder Hey as to the non-consensual retention of organs from deceased children. As noted earlier, a result of these scandals has been the Human Tissue Act 2004, which aims to clarify the law governing the treatment of human materials generally. We shall look at the effect of the new Act in relation to cadaveric organ transplants shortly. However, first there is a residual matter of common law that remains important.

Establishing death

Traditionally, death was defined in terms of cessation of cardiovascular function, that is, the person had no pulse, was not breathing, etc. Advances in medical technology have rendered this approach obsolete: the features in question, though closely aligned with death, are no longer either sufficient or necessary for it (a person may be revived from the above state or, conversely, have the relevant functions sustained mechanically in the absence of all brain activity). Accordingly, a new definition of death was put forward in Guidelines issued by the Medical Royal Colleges in 1976 ((1976) 2 BMJ 1187). Death is now equated with irreversible loss of brainstem function: the brainstem, which is the last part of the brain to die off, is necessary both for any possibility of awareness (the upper brainstem) and for spontaneous reflexes such as respiration (lower brainstem).

Although this new concept of death (referred to interchangeably as 'brainstem death' or simply 'brain death') has not been incorporated into legislation, it is accepted by the courts. A leading case in point is that of *Re A* [1992] 3 Med LR 303:

Re A [1992] 3 Med LR 303, Fam Div (Johnson J)

A was a 19 month old infant who was admitted to hospital with serious head injuries following a domestic incident. He was placed upon a ventilator but showed no signs of recovery. The hospital, after carrying out the diagnostic tests laid down by the MRC Guidelines, was satisfied that A was dead and applied for a declaration allowing his removal from the ventilator:

> **Johnson J**: On 20 January – that is last Monday – the consultant removed A briefly from the ventilator to see whether he was capable of supporting himself without the ventilator. When she did so she heard slight gasping noises which led her to believe that A was not brainstem dead according to criteria now generally accepted in medical circles.
>
> The precise definition of death has been the subject of recommendations by both the Royal College of Surgeons and the Royal College of Physicians and a working party of the British Paediatric Association. Applying the criteria laid down by her profession the consultant concluded on 20 January that A was not then brainstem dead. On the following day she again carried out the tests which are necessary to determine whether the necessary criteria are satisfied. The consultant described those tests to me and she explained to me that each one was satisfied. The tests lasted overall about half an hour.
>
> Describing the criteria and her observations of A, and expressing myself in lay terms, her evidence was to the following effect. A's pupils were fixed and dilated. On movement of the head his eyes moved with his head. What is called the 'doll's eye response' was absent. On his eye being touched with a piece of cotton wool there was no response. On cold water being passed into his ear there was no eye movement in response. On steps being taken, in effect, to cause him to 'gag' there was no reflex reaction, neither was there reaction to pain being applied to his central nervous system. Finally, on his temporary removal from the ventilator to enable the carbon dioxide content of his body to increase there was no respiratory response. All in all, the consultant was satisfied that A was brainstem dead ...
>
> On the same day the consultant had arranged for a colleague consultant paediatric neurologist to carry out the same tests that she had, herself, carried out the previous day with a view to confirming or otherwise the validity of her own professional conclusion. Under professional guidelines it was not necessary for her to seek a second opinion in that way, but she decided that in the particular circumstances of the case it would be a wise thing for her to do. Accordingly, the tests were carried out again on Wednesday of last week, 22 January, by this colleague who reached the same conclusion as had been reached by the first consultant. Both doctors were at pains to exclude other possibilities for A's state, including the possibility of his suffering from extreme hypothermia or some abnormality of his biochemistry. Moreover, they tested

for drugs, lest his brainstem function should have been suppressed by the administration of some drug of which they had not been aware ...

Both doctors concluded that A was brainstem dead ...

It is now Monday 27 January. I have no hesitation at all in holding that A has been dead since Tuesday of last week, 21 January.

The current DoH Code of Practice in relation to diagnosing brain stem death, issued in March 1998, reiterates the earlier Medical Royal Colleges guidance.

Elective ventilation?

The ability to establish the fact of death swiftly, but nevertheless with an appropriate degree of certainty, is important in the context of transplanting organs where, to maximise the chances of success, removal should generally take place as soon as possible. Before death is positively verified, the removal cannot of course come into question; even so, once the doctors are certain that a patient will not survive, there are other steps they might wish to take in order to preserve his organs pending their removal after death has been confirmed.

The problem here is that the patient will be – if not already dead – in an irreversible coma, and thus can, as an incompetent person, only be treated in his own best interests. Concerns as to the legality of medical interventions upon patients in this situation led to the halting of a technique for organ retrieval previously deployed in the South West of England with some success. The background to the procedure in question, known as 'elective ventilation', and the debate it aroused, are described by David Price:

Price, DPT, 'Organ transplant initiatives: the twilight zone' (1997) 23 JME 170:

In 1988 the Royal Devon and Exeter Hospital became the first British hospital to develop an E[lective] V[entilation] protocol. Patients in deep irreversible coma and believed to be dying imminently of intracranial haemorrhage were transferred to intensive care, with relatives' consent, so that artificial ventilation could be commenced immediately respiratory arrest occurred and until brain (stem) death tests could be satisfied. However, in October 1994, the Health Departments of England and Wales issued guidelines stating that EV for transplantation purposes constituted an unlawful battery – being non-therapeutic and not done in the best interests of the individual. This mirrored the conclusion of the 1994 King's Fund Institute Report (which none the less endorsed EV as an ethically acceptable practice, as incidentally have the BMA and the British Transplantation Society), and is probably an accurate perception of the present common law. Although an alternative 'not against the interests of the individual' test has been occasionally employed in relation to non-therapeutic procedures performed on minors, such a standard has yet to be legally employed in respect of a mentally incompetent adult person in a similar context ...

The meaning of death

By contrast with the majority view across all disciplines, the clinicians who developed the Exeter protocol argue that the process of dying is not prolonged by EV, as the patient is already dead – one is ventilating a corpse ... Riad, from Exeter, has said, 'The procedure causes no harm to the patient as ventilation is instituted at the time of respiratory arrest *which is the consequence of brain death* ... Therefore it is important not to institute EV before respiratory arrest'. Such a sequence of events is explicitly referred to in the Memorandum on the Diagnosis of Death attached to Cadaveric Organs for Transplantation (1983) issued by the Conference of the Medical Royal Colleges:

> In a minority of cases, brain death does not occur as a result of the failure of other organs or systems but as a direct result of severe damage to the brain itself from, perhaps, a head injury or a spontaneous intracranial haemorrhage. Here the order of events is reversed: instead of the failure of such vital functions as heart beat and respiration eventually resulting in brain death, brain death results in the cessation of spontaneous respiration: this is normally followed within minutes by cardiac arrest due to hypoxia. If, however, oxygenation is maintained by artificial ventilation, the heart beat can continue for some days, and haemoperfusion will for a time be adequate to maintain function in other organs, such as the liver and kidneys.

Supporters of the Exeter protocol argue that cessation of respiration is (necessary and sufficient) evidence that the patient has already succumbed to brain death – the question is whether this is so ...

Judicial acceptance

... although there is no definition of death in English law, brain stem death established in accordance with the agreed criteria incorporated in the code of practice of the medical royal colleges has been accepted as establishing legal as well as 'medical' death. However, whilst this constitutes judicial acceptance of these tests, it does not necessarily indicate that this is the sole criterion for the determination of death in law. But what, if any, other evidence of (brain) death would satisfy a court of law? In *Re A* ... two sets of tests were carried out to confirm [brain death], the first on 21 January and the second on 22 January. Johnson J stated: 'I have no hesitation at all in holding that A has been dead since Tuesday of last week, 21 January.' In other words, the *time* of death was *before* the second sets of tests were performed to confirm lack of brainstem responses. However, the code of practice states that the time of death should be recorded as the time when death was conclusively established and that 'Death is only conclusively established when the criteria have been satisfied on two successive occasions'. It appears therefore that the code was not fully adhered to in this instance, nor were the recommendations of the British Paediatric Association, which stipulate that in children older than two months, two sets of tests should be conducted separately by two experienced clinicians 12–24 hours apart. *Re A* illustrates that death can be legally declared to have occurred according to brain death criteria before two sets of tests have been completed and death has been confirmed ... Despite certain views to the contrary, it seems that there is no mandatory legal requirement at present that a person cannot be declared brain (stem) dead unless the recommendations of the report of the medical royal colleges – ie, the code of practice – have been complied with in their entirety. The code of practice, although highly influential, does not have the force of law ...

The DoH's 1998 Code of Practice on Brain Stem Death commented upon the practice of elective ventilation as follows:

> **Department of Health,** *Code of Practice for the Diagnosis of Brain Stem Death – Including Guidelines for the Identification and Management of Potential Organ and Tissue Donors,* **HSC 1998/035, 1998, London: DoH:**
>
> 4.3 *Elective Ventilation.* Very occasionally it may be considered certain that death will inevitably occur shortly, as in the case of gross cerebral trauma or cerebral haemorrhage, but brain stem death has not yet been established. In these cases artificial ventilation of the patient should not be undertaken solely to preserve

organ function. The Health Departments have advised that ventilation in these circumstances is unlawful. It cannot be demonstrated to be for the benefit of the patient (and may indeed run the risk of causing serious harm) and thus is not in the best interests of the patient. The agreement of the relatives to elective ventilation does not alter the legal position.

As noted by Price, proponents of the Exeter protocol argued that, in some cases (ie where patients had received direct injury to the brainstem), brain stem death should be recognised as preceding – and causing – cessation of respiration, rather than vice versa. However, if contrary to this analysis, the law insisted upon awaiting the completion of full diagnostic tests before acknowledging death, might not an argument still be made that ventilation could be in such a patient's best interests? Admittedly, he will not benefit medically, but recent judicial *dicta* make clear that 'best interests' are wider than purely medical interests: see, for example *Re A* (*Male Sterilisation*) [2000] 1 FLR 549.

At least where the patient had made a prior request to act as a donor, an argument that elective ventilation were lawful might thus have a chance of success. On the other hand, there is some evidence that the procedure carries a risk for a few patients of them entering a permanent vegetative state (this presumably is the 'serious harm' referred to parenthetically in the DoH Code). The condition of PVS, and the vexed problem of assessing the interests of patients who survive in this state – including whether they thereby suffer any harm – are examined further in Chapter 12.

As regards the Human Tissue Act 2004, this specifically allows, in s 43, for doctors to take steps to preserve cadaveric organs for transplantation. However, this provision is directed to potential donors whose death has *already* been confirmed (it relates to the legality of measures taken after this point, but before 'appropriate consent' has been obtained to the organs' removal and use: see further, p 594 below).

Authorising the removal and use of organs

Historical background

Gerald Dworkin has commented upon the shortcomings in previous law in this area, and the consequent need for more recent statutory intervention, as follows:

Dworkin, G, 'The law relating to organ transplantation in England' (1970) 33 MLR 353:

The existing law

(a) *Common law*. The common law position concerning corpses is curious but relatively well established. A corpse cannot ordinarily be the subject of ownership. Usually the executor or next of kin will have lawful possession of the body and there is a duty to arrange for burial at the earliest opportunity. It follows that, at common law, a man cannot by his will, or otherwise, legally determine what shall happen with his body after his death, although in most cases his wishes concerning the disposal of his body will be observed. That does not, of itself, authorise organs to be taken from corpses for the purpose of transplantation.

(b) *Statute*. The need for human bodies for medical purposes is not new: bodies have always been required for anatomical teaching and research. But any attempt on the part of persons in possession of a body to sell it, even for the purpose of dissection, was unlawful; the bodies of persons convicted of murder were alone capable of being used for dissection. The scandals of body snatching and the publicity of the murder trial of Burke and Hare led to the passing of the Anatomy Act 1832, which enabled bodies to be supplied legally to medical schools for the purpose of anatomical examination. The demand for corpses was then successfully met for over a century.

It is only in recent times that the medical profession realised that the law relating to cadavers was far too restrictive. The successful development of the corneal graft operation focused attention on the lack of supply of eyes and the inability of potential donors to bequeath their eyes for such purposes. In a little debated, but carefully prepared, piece of legislation the Corneal Grafting Act 1952 (the wording of which to some extent followed the Anatomy Act 1832) was passed authorising the use of eyes of deceased persons for therapeutic purposes. This Act quickly proved to be too narrow, for it did not enable any other part of the body to be removed. However, once this kind of provision was on the statute book, it was much easier to extend it. The Human Tissue Act 1961 replaced the 1952 Act and authorised, in certain circumstances, *'the use of the body or any specified part of the body after death for therapeutic purposes or for purposes of medical education or research'*. This Act, which provided a model for many other jurisdictions, at present governs the English law relating to cadaver transplantation.

The 1961 Act was designed to increase the ability of persons to donate their organs for therapeutic purposes after their death. It provides in s 1 as follows:

Human Tissue Act 1961:

1 Removal of parts of bodies for medical purposes

(1) If any person, either in writing at any time or orally in the presence of two or more witnesses during his last illness, has expressed a request that his body or any specified part of his body be used after his death for therapeutic purposes or for purposes of medical education or research, the person lawfully in possession of his body after his death may, unless he has reason to believe that the request was subsequently withdrawn, authorise the removal from the body of any part or, as the case may be, the specified part, for use in accordance with the request.

(2) Without prejudice to the foregoing sub-section, the person lawfully in possession of the body of a deceased person may authorise the removal of any part from the body for use for the said purposes if, having made such reasonable inquiry as may be practicable, he has no reason to believe–

(a) that the deceased had expressed an objection to his body being so dealt with after his death, and had not withdrawn it; or

(b) that the surviving spouse or any surviving relative of the deceased objects to the body being so dealt with.

...

The effect of this provision is to allow organs to be removed for transplant in two main situations: either where the deceased has made an express request to that effect (s 1(1)); or, in the absence of such a request, where reasonable inquiry reveals no objection to the same either by the deceased or by his spouse/surviving relatives (s 1(2)). In these circumstances, 'the person in lawful possession of the body' – usually the hospital where death occurred – is empowered to authorise removal, and charged with making the relevant inquiries.

The 1961 Act is due to be repealed by the Human Tissue Act 2004, when the latter enters into force in 2006. The new Act is intended to address certain difficulties that emerged in respect of the earlier statute.

Problems with the 1961 Act

As noted, the effect of s 1(2)(b) of the 1961 Act is to give the deceased's spouse and surviving relatives the opportunity to object to the transplant of the organs, in so far as the deceased has not expressed any wishes in the matter. It is apparent that this amounts to a conditional power of veto as opposed to a requirement that such persons must actively consent, since if they cannot be traced by reasonable inquiry, donation may simply proceed in their absence.

Nonetheless, there are significant vagaries in the provision, both as to the meaning of 'any surviving relative' and with regard to what amounted to the making by the hospital of 'such reasonable inquiry as may be practicable'. More seriously, even if a breach of the statute could clearly be demonstrated – eg the parents of the deceased were present but simply not asked if they objected to organ removal – the Act failed to provide for any offence to be committed. Although it was once thought that liability might arise at common law for the residual offence of breaching a statute (see *R v Lennox-Wright* [1973] Crim LR 529), this view was subsequently repudiated by the Court of Appeal in *R v Horseferry Road Justices ex p IBA* [1986] 2 All ER 666. There, it was stated that there is a general presumption, in modern statutory interpretation, that no offence will lie in a statute's contravention unless it expressly says so.

The lack of effective legal penalties for taking cadaveric organs without reference to the relatives may well have contributed to the Alder Hey scandal. Indeed, the subsequent public inquiry into those events recommended urgent amendment of the 1961 Act to provide for criminal, and possibly also civil law sanctions:

The Royal Liverpool Children's Inquiry Report, 2001, London: HMSO:

We respectfully recommend that:

- The Department of Health, the Royal Colleges and medical schools shall instruct members of the medical profession in the precise terms and provisions of the Human Tissue Act 1961, on the basis of our analysis, and the need for strict compliance.

- The Human Tissue Act 1961 shall be amended to provide a test of fully informed consent for the lawful post mortem examination and retention of parts of the bodies of deceased persons. While we have concluded that there has been little difference between 'lack of objection' and 'informed consent' in practical terms for the next of kin, it is important that the law and future practice are brought into line and updated.

- The class of persons relevant to the obtaining of fully informed consent shall be defined as the 'next of kin'.

- The class of 'any surviving relative' shall no longer be relevant to post mortem examination.

- There shall be a programme of health education for the public relevant to the medical need for continued post mortem examination and access to organs and samples for therapeutic, educational and research purposes.

- The Department of Health, the Royal Colleges and medical schools shall provide training for all those involved in obtaining fully informed consent.

- The Human Tissue Act 1961 shall be amended to impose a criminal penalty by way of fine for breach of its provisions in order to encourage future compliance.

- Guidelines relating to the requirements of the Human Tissue Act 1961 and the obtaining of fully informed consent shall be drawn up and provision made for breach to result in disciplinary proceedings which could lead to suspension, dismissal or financial penalty.

The Human Rights Act 1998 makes provision for an effective remedy other than in criminal proceedings. If breaches of the Human Tissue Act 1961 amount to breaches of the Human Rights Act 1998 consideration shall be given to incorporating a financial remedy with the Human Tissue Act 1961 itself. If necessary, reference should be made to the Law Commission.

In fact, following the Alder Hey inquiry, a number of parents, whose deceased children's organs had been retained (after post mortem examinations) without their consent, brought a class action in civil law for damages from the hospitals involved: see *AB v Leeds Teaching Hospital NHS Trust* [2004] EWHC 644. The claims were based, *inter alia*, on the causation of psychiatric harm in negligence. In his judgment, Gage J held that, in the particular circumstances, the claimants could be regarded as primary victims of such harm: accordingly they did not need to satisfy the restrictive control mechanisms from *Alcock v Chief Constable of South Yorkshire Police* [1991] 4 All ER 907. However, only in one case (involving the mother of a full-term still born baby) was such injury – caused by the revelations several years after the event as to retention having occurred – reasonably foreseeable. He awarded modest damages in the sum of £2,750.

The effect of the Human Tissue Act 2004

As already stated, a direct result of the Alder Hey scandal has been the enactment of the Human Tissue Act 2004, which will shortly repeal the 1961 Act. It should be emphasised that the new consent regime established in relation to the removal, storage and/or use of human tissue has wider implications than for transplantation alone (indeed, Alder Hey itself did not involve any issues of transplantation). However, transplantation is one of the scheduled purposes caught by the Act, in respect of which 'appropriate consent' will now be required. We have already examined the relevant sections as they bear upon live donors (see p 581, above). As regards cadaveric donors, the salient terms of the Act are as follows:

Human Tissue Act 2004:

2 'Appropriate consent': children

(1) This section makes provision for the interpretation of 'appropriate consent' in section 1 in relation to an activity involving the body, or material from the body, of a person who is a child or has died a child ('the child concerned') …

(7) Where the child concerned has died … 'appropriate consent' means–

    (a) if a decision of his to consent to the activity, or a decision of his not to consent to it, was in force immediately before he died, his consent;

    (b) if paragraph (a) does not apply–

        (i) the consent of a person who had parental responsibility for him immediately before he died, or

        (ii) where no person had parental responsibility for him immediately before he died, the consent of a person who stood in a qualifying relationship to him at that time.

3 'Appropriate consent': adults

(1) This section makes provision for the interpretation of 'appropriate consent' in section 1 in relation to an activity involving the body, or material from the body, of a person who is an adult or has died an adult ('the person concerned') ...

(6) Where the person concerned has died ... 'appropriate consent' means–

    (a) if a decision of his to consent to the activity, or a decision of his not to consent to it, was in force immediately before he died, his consent;

    (b) if–

        (i) paragraph (a) does not apply, and

        (ii) he has appointed a person or persons under section 4 to deal after his death with the issue of consent in relation to the activity,

    consent given under the appointment;

    (c) if neither paragraph (a) nor paragraph (b) applies, the consent of a person who stood in a qualifying relationship to him immediately before he died.

(7) Where the person concerned has appointed a person or persons under section 4 to deal after his death with the issue of consent in relation to the activity, the appointment shall be disregarded for the purposes of subsection (6) if no one is able to give consent under it.

(8) If it is not reasonably practicable to communicate with a person appointed under section 4 within the time available if consent in relation to the activity is to be acted on, he shall be treated for the purposes of subsection (7) as not able to give consent under the appointment in relation to it.

4 Nominated representatives

(1) An adult may appoint one or more persons to represent him after his death in relation to consent for the purposes of section 1.

(2) An appointment under this section may be general or limited to consent in relation to such one or more activities as may be specified in the appointment.

(3) An appointment under this section may be made orally or in writing ...

The intended effect of these provisions is described in the explanatory notes issued by the Department of Health as follows:

Department of Health, *Explanatory Notes to the Human Tissue Act*, 2004, London: DoH, Crown Copyright

Section 2: 'Appropriate consent': children

... 17. Where a child has died, if he or she was competent and made an advance decision (to give or refuse consent), that will apply. *Subsections (4) to (6)* provide that consent of a competent child to have his or her body used for anatomical examination or public display must be in writing and witnessed. No-one other than a competent child may give consent to the use of his or her own body for purposes of anatomical examination or public display ... For other scheduled purposes, such as the carrying out of a *post mortem* examination or the use of organs for transplantation, the consent of someone with parental responsibility will be appropriate consent, but only if the child did not deal with the issue of consent. *Subsection (7)* provides that if a child has died and there is no-one with parental responsibility, someone in a 'qualifying relationship' may give consent to removal, storage or use of the child's body or material from the body ...

Section 3: 'Appropriate consent': adults

18. Section 3 sets out the meaning of 'appropriate consent', in relation to activities concerning the body of a deceased adult ... *Subsections (3) to (5)* provide that after death, the adult's consent, given in advance in writing and witnessed, is required for purposes of anatomical examination or public display ... For other scheduled purposes, if the adult made no prior decision, a person nominated by him in accordance with section 4 to make decisions after his death or, failing that, someone in a 'qualifying relationship' ... may give consent.

Section 4: Nominated Representatives

19. This section sets out how an adult aged 18 or over can make a valid appointment of one or more 'nominated representative(s)', who may give consent after the adult's death to storage or use of his or her body, or removal, storage and use of relevant material from his or her body for scheduled purposes. *Subsection (6)* says that where two or more people are appointed as nominated representative, they will be assumed to be able to act alone unless the appointment says they must act jointly. Unless they have been appointed to act jointly, the consent of one of several nominated representatives is sufficient to make the activity lawful, even if the others object.

It will be recalled that, under section 1(1) of the Human Tissue Act 1961, the wish of a person that his body be used after his death for therapeutic or other purposes had either to be in writing, or expressed orally during his last illness in the presence of at least two witnesses. By contrast, the 2004 Act does not make clear exactly what will qualify in terms of the deceased's own consent (apart from the special requirements it imposes in relation to anatomical examination or public display). Presumably, this issue will be dealt with by the Human Tissue Authority in its Code of Practice (see below).

As the DoH explanatory notes make clear, ultimately, in the case of deceased adults as well as children, consent for the purpose of transplantation may fall to be given by someone in a 'qualifying relationship'. Such persons are defined in s 54(9) as 'spouse, partner, parent, child, brother, sister, grandparent, grandchild, child of a brother or sister, stepfather, stepmother, half-brother, half-sister and friend of long standing'. In practice a ranking will be applied: in particular, the Act enjoins the Human Tissue Authority (established by the Act) to provide in its Code of Practice as follows:

Human Tissue Act 2004:

27 Provision with respect to consent

(1) The duty under section 26(3) [*viz, to deal with consent issues in its Code of Practice*] shall have effect, in particular, to require the Authority to lay down the standards expected in relation to the obtaining of consent where consent falls by virtue of section 2(7)(b)(ii) or 3(6)(c) to be obtained from a person in a qualifying relationship ...

(4) The qualifying relationships for the purpose of sections 2(7)(b)(ii) and 3(6)(c) should be ranked in the following order–

   (a) spouse or partner;

   (b) parent or child;

   (c) brother or sister;

   (d) grandparent or grandchild;

   (e) child of a person falling within paragraph (c);

(f) stepfather or stepmother;

(g) half-brother or half-sister;

(h) friend of longstanding.

(5) Relationships in the same paragraph of subsection (4) should be accorded equal ranking.

(6) Consent should be obtained from the person whose relationship to the person concerned is accorded the highest ranking in accordance with subsections (4) and (5) ...

The Act makes clear in s 28 that the breach of the Code of Practice will not by itself render the party in breach liable to any proceedings. Thus if, in a given case, a hospital obtained consent from the 'wrong person' (ie lower down the ranking than someone else it could have asked) there would be no offence. This contrasts with the position if no one at all is asked to consent, in which case the material will have been taken without 'appropriate consent'. In the latter case criminal liability is provided for in section 5, as follows:

Human Tissue Act 2004:

5 Prohibition of activities without consent etc

(1) A person commits an offence if, without appropriate consent, he does an activity to which subsection (1), (2) or (3) of section 1 applies, unless he reasonably believes–

(a) that he does the activity with appropriate consent, or

(b) that what he does is not an activity to which the subsection applies ...

(7) A person guilty of an offence under this section shall be liable-

(a) on summary conviction to a fine not exceeding the statutory maximum;

(b) on conviction on indictment–

(i) to imprisonment for a term not exceeding 3 years, or

(ii) to a fine, or

(iii) to both.

Residual concerns

In general, it should be noted that, under s 1(1) of the 2004 Act, the presence of 'appropriate consent' merely makes it lawful for the hospital to remove material from the deceased and use it for a stipulated scheduled purpose, including for transplantation. There is, however, no obligation upon it to do so. Experience in relation to the 1961 Act (whose effect is materially the same in this respect) shows that, as a matter of clinical practice, the hospital will not proceed in the face of objection by relatives, even where the deceased had expressed the desire to donate, eg by carrying a donor card. As the Department of Health's 1998 Guidelines suggest:

Department of Health, *Code of Practice for the Diagnosis of Brain Stem Death – Including Guidelines for the Identification and Management of Potential Organ and Tissue Donors*, HSC 1998/035, 1998, London: DoH:

8.2 *The donor card.* If a patient carries a signed donor card or has otherwise recorded his or her wishes, for example, by inclusion in the NHS Organ Donor Register, there is no legal requirement to establish lack of objection on the part of relatives, although it is good practice to take account of the views of close relatives. If a relative objects, despite the known request by the patient, staff will need to judge, according to the circumstances of the case, whether it is wise to proceed with organ removal. Staff need to consider the feelings of relatives, who may be under great stress, so that in practice any objections raised by relatives usually take priority over donor's wishes.

A few years ago, media reports into an incident in the North of England highlighted a somewhat different concern, namely the practice of 'conditional donation' in which the relatives, or indeed the deceased, have sought to impose conditions upon the donation of the deceased's organs – in that case that they should only go to a white person. In its subsequent report into the incident, the Department of Health rejected as unethical the possibility of any such conditional donation:

> **Department of Health, *An Investigation into Conditional Organ Donation: The Report of the Panel*, 2000, London: DoH:**
>
> 6.1 This was a very unfortunate incident. It should not have happened. In the Panel's view to attach any condition to a donation is unacceptable, because it offends against the fundamental principle that organs are donated altruistically and should go to patients in the greatest need. The Panel consider that racist conditions are completely abhorrent, as well as being unacceptable under the Race Relations Act ...
>
> 6.4 In saying this, the Panel are conscious that one consequence of a decision not to accept organs might be that seriously ill potential recipients might die before other organs become available. This is therefore a hard judgement to make. The Panel are, however, convinced that it is the right one, morally as well as legally. The Panel have been interested to discover that the vast majority of those they have talked to in the course of their investigation, patient groups as well as clinicians, take the same view.
>
> 6.5 This is not true of everyone, however. Some very strongly believe that the overriding principle should be the saving of lives. In their view any conditions should be accepted if the consequence is that more organs become available than would otherwise be the case. The Panel do not accept this argument.

Other sources of organs/tissue

Before leaving this area, a number of other possible sources of supply of organs and tissue need to be considered. As transplant technology continues to advance, some of these may be expected to assume increasing importance in the future.

Foetal tissue transplants

Recent developments in medical science have revealed the possibility of using live brain cells, harvested from aborted foetuses of 10–14 weeks' gestation, to treat certain degenerative brain disorders, notably Parkinson's and Alzheimer's disease. In the future, foetal pancreatic cells may also be used in the treatment of some forms of diabetes. In contrast to the issue of embryo research looked at in Chapter 7, the focus here is on the usage of *in vivo* foetuses. The ethical difficulty that this gives rise to, and the entanglement of this issue with the abortion debate, is explored by David Lamb:

> **Lamb, D, *Organ Transplants and Ethics*, 1990, London: Routledge, pp 74–76:**
>
> What are the chief ethical objections to foetal tissue research and transplants? There are three closely related objections. First, it is argued that killing and then dissecting a

foetus is an abuse to the developing human being. The second objection is that engaging in such practices will brutalise those who perform this work, and the third objection is that it will encourage abortions and even motivate conceptions with the express intention to abort ... In addition to these objections are ethical problems concerning the authorisation of embryo tissue research and transplantation.

The ... objections are so closely related that they can be dealt with together. The issue they relate to is the morality of voluntary termination of pregnancy. The morality of elected abortions has been widely discussed in learned journals, the popular media, and various legislative assemblies. Strong views have been expressed and the general standpoints are so familiar that they need not be repeated here. At present, however, voluntary termination of pregnancy, subject to certain conditions, is legally permissible in the USA, the UK, and several other European countries. If the opponents of voluntary termination are correct in stating that it is immoral, then it might be argued that performing an abortion is an abuse to the developing human being, and that those who perform this work are likely to become brutalised, and that any steps likely to increase the number of terminations should be resisted. In short, if voluntary termination is wrong, then so are actions which depend on it, and at least some degree of guilt by association is incurred by those who seek to benefit from the killing of a foetus. Moreover, an assurance that no foetus is ever dissected prior to death would be of no consequence. For on these terms the issue turns on the rightness or wrongness of killing the foetus in the first place ...

On these terms, it would seem that if the arguments against voluntary terminations are persuasive, then the only scope for ethical discussion on foetal tissue transplantation is whether it is morally acceptable to use material from spontaneous abortions. The problem is that material from the latter is less reliable than from voluntary abortions. This is because the possibility of foetal abnormality is too high, and because of various problems concerning the time lag between the actual death of the foetus and its expulsion from the uterus. In any case, most miscarriages occur too early for viable transplantation.

But given the obvious benefits of foetal cadaver research and transplantation, can these virtues be separated from what some people see as the immorality of elected abortion? According to the foregoing discussion the rights and wrongs of abortion and foetal tissue research and transplantation stand or fall together. Yet despite an obvious causal relationship between them, this is not necessarily the case. It could be argued that even if abortion is regarded as wrong, discussions concerning the ethical status of research on embryos and possible transplantation of foetal tissue are an independent issue. The UK Committee, chaired by John Polkinghorne (1989), outlined a 'separation principle' according to which there must be 'a separation of the supply of foetal tissue from its use'. This is to ensure that the need for foetal tissue does not influence decisions to have abortions. One consequence of this principle was the recommendation that whilst informed maternal consent is required for the use of foetal tissue, the woman concerned should have no knowledge of what happens to it.

What is the ethical basis of a separation principle? [John] Robertson, who maintains that the abortion issue and the ethics of foetal research can be treated separately, suggests an analogy with transplant organs taken from homicide victims. If consent is obtained, then the victim's organs can be retrieved and distributed to recipients without any suggestion that the surgeon who has received the heart, lung, or kidneys, was an accomplice to murder, even if he or she was aware of the source. By the same token medical students, who use cadavers of murder victims in anatomy, cannot be associated with a crime. Moreover, research on legally obtained cadavers of murder victims cannot, in any way, be said to be responsible for the brutalisation of the researchers or contribute to an increase in the homicide rate. 'One may benefit from another's evil act without applauding or approving of that evil', says Robertson ...

The Polkinghorne Report referred to here was presented in 1989 by a Committee of Inquiry, chaired by the Revd John Polkinghorne, into the research use of such foetuses. It set out its 'separation principle' as follows:

Polkinghorne Committee, *Review of Guidance on the Research Use of Foetuses and Foetal Tissue*, Cm 762, 1989, London: HMSO (the Polkinghorne Report):

4.1 We have taken the view that, whatever one's ethical opinion about abortion itself, it does not follow that morally there is an absolute prohibition on the ethical use of foetuses or foetal tissue from lawful abortion. We have argued that the termination of pregnancy and the subsequent use of foetal tissue should be recognised as separate moral questions and we regard it as of great importance that the separation of these moral issues should be reflected in the procedures employed. Accordingly, we have recommended that great care should be taken to separate the decisions relating to abortion and to the subsequent use of foetal material. The prior decision to carry out an abortion should be reached without consideration of the benefits of subsequent use. The generation or termination of pregnancy to produce material for research or therapy is unethical.

4.2 It has been argued that knowledge of the use of foetal tissue could influence mothers' decisions to have their pregnancies terminated. It has been suggested that the use of foetal tissue could place women under pressure when reaching a decision or result in more abortions taking place. It has even been put to us that someone could become pregnant in order to make a foetus available for medical use. In our view, pregnancy undertaken to such an end would be an ethically unacceptable use of the foetus as an instrument (treating it as a 'thing'). It is not possible fully to discern people's motivations, but it is possible to limit the degree to which morally dubious wishes can be implemented. To this end we recommend, not only the separation of the decisions relating to abortion and the subsequent use of foetal tissue, but also procedures which will make it impossible for a mother to specify that foetal tissue, which she makes available, should be used in a particular way.

A related question is whether the consent of the mother of the foetus should in fact be sought in these circumstances. David Lamb comments on this as follows:

Lamb, D, *Organ Transplants and Ethics*, 1990, London: Routledge, pp 78–79:

It might be argued that having decided to terminate her pregnancy, she has foregone any rights concerning the foetal disposal. [John] Harris argues that there is no moral basis for seeking the mother's consent over what happens to an aborted foetus. 'Has she not already abdicated responsibility for the foetus by opting for abortion?' asks Harris ... Moreover, when the aborted foetus cannot live, or is already dead, Harris sees no moral requirement to seek maternal consent:

If experimenters ask her for, and are given, permission to experiment on the foetus this permission will not absolve them from the responsibility of deciding for themselves whether such a course of action is ethically sound. And if she withholds permission, we must ask what gives her the right to decide that others should not benefit from the research or from transplantation ...

Harris is equally dismissive of the view that the mother has quasi property rights by virtue of the fact that the foetus is growing inside her. Deadly and infectious viruses may grow in someone's body without any claim that they are in some way 'owned' by the being who plays host to them. Furthermore, if it were established that a foetus were a person, then prohibitions against slavery would rule out property rights over the foetus ...

In contrast Robertson argues that the case for denying the mother's control is not persuasive: 'As a product of her body and potential heir that she has for her own compelling reasons chosen to abort, she may care deeply about whether foetal remains are contributed to research or therapy to help others' ... Thus, although:

> ... she cannot insist that foetal remains be used for transplant because no donor has the right to require that intended donees accept anatomical gifts, but she should retain the existing legal right to veto use of foetal remains for transplant research or therapy. Her consent to donation of foetal tissue should be routinely sought.

Now the case for giving the woman control, on Robertson's terms, seems to rest on the analogy with organ donation, such as live kidney donation. But this analogy is complicated by the suggestion that, by undergoing voluntary termination for family planning purposes, her interest in the foetus ceases with its removal. In electing an abortion, she is, on these terms, expressing an overriding interest in a premature separation from the foetus, consequently terminating any potential interest which could apply to the foetus. Having fulfilled her primary interest, further interest in the foetus would be foregone ...

For its part, the Polkinghorne Committee took the view that the woman's informed consent should always be obtained:

Polkinghorne Committee, *Review of Guidance on the Research Use of Foetuses and Foetal Tissue*, Cm 762, 1989, London: HMSO (the Polkinghorne Report):

2.8 ... The use of foetal tissue from terminations of pregnancy has been justified by analogy with the use of human organs which have become available as a result of morally questionable circumstances, such as careless accident or even murder. However, it has been suggested that this analogy is imperfect, since in the case of abortions the one who consents to the use of the material (the mother) is also the one who has brought about its availability by her decision to seek the termination of the existence of her foetus. Some have argued that this decision abrogates the mother's subsequent rights in relation to her foetus. Again, this is an opinion to which the Committee has given careful consideration, but once more it is one that we are unable to accept. Because abortion is a decision of moral ambiguity and perplexity for many, reached only through a conflict of considerations, it seems too harsh a judgment of the mother's relation to her foetus to suppose that she is no longer in a special position with regard to it, following an abortion.

Xenotransplantation

Recently, much research effort has gone into the possibility of xenografting, literally the use of organs and tissue taken from non-human animals. Previously, though such transplants were occasionally tried (a well known case from 1984 concerned a Californian infant, baby Fae, who survived for three weeks with a baboon's heart) there was a formidable difficulty in the way of lasting success in the form of inevitable tissue rejection by the donee. However, there now seem real prospects of overcoming this problem by genetically engineering certain breeds of animals specifically for transplant purposes.

The Nuffield Council of Bioethics, in its report *Animal to Human Transplants: The Ethics of Xenotransplantation*, charted some of the obstacles that remain in the way of carrying out such transplants on a wide scale:

Nuffield Council on Bioethics, *Animal to Human Transplants: The Ethics of Xenotransplantation*, 1996, London: Nuffield Council on Bioethics:

10.9   Even if some use of animals for medical purposes can be justified in principle, their use for xenotransplantation raises specific issues that need further consideration. Particular concerns are raised by the use of primates, such as baboons ... The high degree of evolutionary relatedness between human beings and primates both suggests that xenotransplantation of primate organs and tissue might be successful and also raises questions about whether it is ethical to use primates in ways that it is not considered acceptable to use human beings. Certainly, any harm suffered by primates should be given great weight. This position is reflected in the principles underlying current practice in the UK. *The Working Party endorses the special protection afforded to primates used for medical and scientific purposes.*

10.10 The Working Party would accept the use of very small numbers of primates *as recipients of organs* during research to develop xenotransplantation of organs and tissue from non-primates. In this case, using a small number of primates for research, while undesirable, can be justified by the potential benefits if xenotransplantation were to become a successful procedure ...

10.11 The routine use of higher primates to supply organs for xenotransplantation on a scale sufficient to meet the organ shortage would represent a new use of primates in the UK. In addition to the special weight given to the harm suffered by primates, other concerns must be taken into account. The endangered status of chimpanzees rules out their use for xenotransplantation. The potential risk of extinction, even to a species like the baboon that is not currently endangered, must be taken seriously. Xenotransplantation using primate organs or tissue may pose particular risks of disease transmission ...

10.12 Given the ethical concerns raised by the use of primates for xenotransplantation, attention has turned to developing the pig as an alternative source of organs and tissue. As discussed below, in the view of the Working Party, the use of pigs for xenotransplantation raises fewer ethical concerns. To develop the use of primates for xenotransplantation, when there is an ethically acceptable alternative, would not be justifiable. *The Working Party recommends that non-primate species should be regarded as the source animals of choice for xenotransplantation.* However, possibilities for alleviating the organ shortage which do not involve the use of animals, such as increased donation of human organs, and the development of artificial organs and tissue, should be actively pursued ...

...

10.23 Important [animal] welfare implications are raised by the breeding of transgenic animals; producing animals free from infectious organisms; and removing organs and tissue from animals for xenotransplantation ... In view of [these] implications ... *the Working Party recommends that the Home Office should require that all animals use xenotransplantation are protected under the Animals (Scientific Procedures) Act 1986.* Any reputable company producing animals in order to supply organs and tissue for xenotransplantation would, in any case, wish to be licensed under the 1986 Act in order to reassure the public that their activities were meeting the highest standards of animal welfare. The Working

Party recommends that the standards set by the 1986 Act become the minimum for the industry ...

Transmission of infectious diseases

10.24 -Xenotransplantation of animal organs and tissue carries with it the potential risk that diseases will be transmitted from animals to xenograft recipients and to the wider human population ... It is difficult to assess this risk, since it is impossible to predict whether infectious organisms that are harmless in their animal host will cause disease in human xenograft recipients or whether the disease will spread into the wider human population. There are certain to be infectious organisms of both primates and pigs that are currently unknown, and some of these might cause disease in human beings. There is evidence that infectious organisms of primates, notably viruses, can pass into the human population and cause disease. This supports the recommendation that non-primate species should be regarded as the source animals of choice for xenotransplantation. The possible risk of disease transmission from pigs, however, also requires careful consideration ...

10.25 -It is not possible to predict or quantify the risk that xenotransplantation will result in the emergence of new human diseases. But in the worst case, the consequences could be far-reaching and difficult to control. The principle of precaution requires that action is taken to avoid risks in advance of certainty about their nature. It suggests that the burden of proof should lie with those developing the technology to demonstrate that it will not cause serious harm. *The Working Party concluded that the risks associated with possible transmission of infectious diseases as a consequence of xenotransplantation have not been adequately dealt with. It would not be ethical therefore to begin clinical trials of xenotransplantation involving human beings ...*

In January 1997 a government inquiry, chaired by Professor Ian Kennedy, also took the view that, because of the unknown risks associated with infectious diseases passing from animal to human, clinical trials should be delayed. In the meantime, a new body, the Xenotransplantation Interim Regulatory Authority, has been set up to keep the situation under review.

Mechanical organs

Although artificial implants and other devices have long been a mainstay of modern medical science (for example, hip replacements, pacemakers, etc) in terms of organs, the only real candidate at present for such manufacture is the heart. David Lamb chronicles the history of such devices, and the ethical problems to which their use gives rise, as follows:

Lamb, D, *Organ Transplants and Ethics*, 1990, London: Routledge, pp 114–15:

The idea of a totally implantable artificial heart was first mooted in 1964, when the USA National Heart Institute drew up a plan for the construction of a prototype and obtained financial support from Congress for the project. The researchers were unrealistically optimistic, for they looked forward to the mass production and implantation of artificial hearts by 1970 ... Despite some limited success with animals, artificial implants into humans did not achieve any significant results. One major problem is the high incidence of strokes and chronic infections, which has not been overcome. The first human implantation of an artificial heart was performed in Texas in 1969 on a dying patient, Haskelle Karp, who survived for a further 65 hours with it before receiving a human heart. He died shortly after. In 1977 a woman in Zurich survived for two days with an artificial heart ... The initial belief that an artificial heart might function as a permanent replacement has given way to more realistic therapy. Artificial hearts are presently used, in a limited sense, as 'bridges' to assist survival until a donor becomes available. As of January 1987, some 17 US transplant centres were using artificial heart 'bridges', and 63 patients had been implanted with such a device ... The number of artificial hearts and ventricular assistance devices currently functioning as bridges is 200 worldwide ...

The deeper ethical and philosophical aspects of artificial heart implants surfaced in the widely discussed case of Dr Barney Clark, a retired American dentist who received an artificial heart in 1982. Dr Clark's own defective heart was replaced with a device made of polyurethane. The motor driving the heart was too large to be implanted, so it was placed in a cart which the patient had to push around. He lived for 112 days, and his death was caused by the failure of most of his other organs, but not by the failure of the heart, which went on pumping blood to a mass of dead organs, thus demonstrating the separability of the heart function from the mechanism of death. The longest survivor with an artificial heart was William Schroeder, who lived for 620 days, but during that time he suffered four strokes and developed chronic infections which sapped his strength ...

The suffering endured by Barney Clark and William Schroeder and their families certainly raises ethical problems concerning the extent to which doctors should strive to maintain life. But this limited success may bring hope for the future; hope that an artificial heart is not an impossible dream, and that with sufficient technological improvements artificial implants could reduce waiting lists for human organs.

Although they continue to be refined and developed and, in the long term, may be expected to offer very real benefits, the use of artificial organs remains in its nascent stages.

THE STATUS OF EXTRACTED MATERIAL

The requirements of the Human Tissue Act 2004

The 2004 Act establishes a new authority, the Human Tissue Authority, which will be responsible for licensing various activities in relation to extracted human material (whether taken from the living or the deceased). Section 16 provides as follows:

Human Tissue Act 2004:

Licensing

16 Licence requirement

(1) No person shall do an activity to which this section applies otherwise than under the authority of a licence granted for the purposes of this section.

(2) This section applies to the following activities–

    (a) the carrying-out of an anatomical examination;

    (b) the making of a post-mortem examination;

    (c) the removal from the body of a deceased person (otherwise than in the course of an activity mentioned in paragraph (a) or (b)) of relevant material of which the body consists or which it contains, for use for a scheduled purpose other than transplantation;

(d) the storage of an anatomical specimen;

(e) the storage (in any case not falling within paragraph (d)) of–

   (i) the body of a deceased person, or

   (ii) relevant material which has come from a human body,

   for use for a scheduled purpose;

(f) the use, for the purpose of public display, of–

   (i) the body of a deceased person, or

   (ii) relevant material which has come from the body of a deceased person ...

(7) In subsection (2)–

(a) references to storage do not include storage which is incidental to transportation, and

(b) 'relevant material', in relation to use for the scheduled purpose of transplantation, does not include blood or anything derived from blood.

Organ transplantation is a scheduled purpose (under Schedule 1 of the Act). The effect of this provision, so far as relevant to that purpose, is that, while the organs' removal need not be licensed, their storage will need to be (although this excludes storage in the course of transportation). This will admittedly have little impact in relation to 'organs' in the narrower sense of solid matter, such as kidneys, etc, which are not presently capable of storage in any event, but will affect holdings of tissue including bone marrow. Licensees will be required to adhere to good practice guidelines issued by the Human Tissue Authority, which will in due course incorporate EU-wide standards of quality assurance and safety, as laid down in the EC Tissues and Cells Directive (2004/23/EC). The storage of blood for transfusion is excluded, and will be subject to its own regulatory regime pursuant to a separate EC Directive (2002/98/EC).

The framework of regulation instituted by the 2004 Act, and especially its creation of a special authority with responsibility for licensing and disseminating codes of practice, is clearly modelled upon the regime established in relation to reproductive medicine by the Human Fertilisation and Embryology Act 1990 (see Chapter 7). In fact, the Government has already announced plans for the merger by 2008 of the Human Tissue Authority with the Human Fertilisation and Embryology Authority into a new entity to be known as 'RAFT' (the Regulatory Authority for Fertility and Tissues).

The question of property rights

The phenomenon of organ and tissue transplantation, and the practice of removing tissue for medical purposes including donation, give rise to interesting questions as to the status of such material. Is it susceptible of ownership, and, if so, who enjoys the relevant property rights? It is convenient to look at the position in relation to deceased persons first, and then move on to look at ownership of body parts taken from living persons.

Rights in the body of a deceased person (or parts taken therefrom)

Gerald Dworkin and Ian Kennedy have analysed this issue as follows:

Dworkin, G and Kennedy, I, 'Human tissue: rights in the body and its parts' (1993) 1 Med L Rev 291:

B Rights of the deceased in his/her own body after death?

... There are many dicta going back through the centuries proclaiming that there can be no property in a corpse. Thus, where a person by will had directed that his body should be cremated after death, it was held that such a request, though it might be honoured in practice, could not be imposed as a legal obligation upon his executors since he lacked any property rights in his body.

C Rights of third parties in corpses

Nor do any third parties acquire any property interests in a corpse. At most, there are obligations on the next of kin or others in possession of a body to dispose of it decently and it may be a criminal offence at common law to neglect to carry out these duties or in any other way interfere with a corpse. Modern writers maintain that such well established rules survive and limit the modern law of theft (which involves the taking of property), at least to the extent that there could be no theft of a buried corpse.

D Changing characteristics

The situation appears to change, however, after a period of time. If the law did not recognise any property rights in a cadaver, or in body parts, problems could arise at a later stage about the status of any physical material which remains. Thus, if the law is not prepared to recognise property rights in skeletons possessed by medical institutions or students, or in the embalmed body of Jeremy Bentham (which has been taken from University College London from time to time by enterprising students from other colleges), or in Egyptian mummies, then those who take them may not be committing any theft, nor, possibly, any legally redressible wrong against those from whom they have been taken.

The common law has occasionally grappled with this situation. If, after some time, the characteristics of the body, or the body parts, have changed in some way so that one is no longer concerned with a corpse awaiting burial, the law may look upon it as property and confer upon owners the usual rights to protect it from interference and to deal with it commercially. Thus, in *Doodeward v Spence* an Australian court appears to have held that a stillborn two-headed foetus, which had been preserved with spirits in a bottle by the doctor some 40 years earlier, was now an item of property in the hands of its present owner. In that case it was said that:

> ... when a person has by the lawful exercise of work or skill so dealt with a human body or part of a human body in his lawful possession that it has acquired some attributes differentiating it from a mere corpse awaiting burial, he acquires a right to retain possession of it, at least as against any person not entitled to have it delivered to him for the purposes of burial ...

In this case it was said that work and skill had been bestowed by the plaintiff's predecessor in title upon the body and it had acquired actual pecuniary value.

This approach was endorsed, *obiter*, by the Court of Appeal in *Dobson v North Tyneside HA and Another* [1996] 4 All ER 474:

Dobson and Another v North Tyneside HA and Another [1996] 4 All ER 474, CA (Butler-Sloss, Peter Gibson and Thorpe LJJ)

The family of a woman, who had died as a result of an undiagnosed brain tumour, brought a claim in conversion against the health authority for allowing the destruction of the woman's brain after it had been removed, and briefly stored in a jar of paraffin, for the purposes of a post mortem. The plaintiffs would have wished to use the same as evidence in their main action in medical negligence against the authority:

> **Peter Gibson LJ**: Mr Hone ... submitted that the present case raises an important question of law ... whether it remains established law that there is no property in a dead body or part of a dead body so that personal representatives of a deceased cannot maintain a cause of action in respect of human tissue. That was modified before us ... and on the primary way in which he put his case, viz, in conversion, it is trite law that a person has title to sue if and only if he has at the time of conversion either actual possession or the immediate right to possession ...
>
> As the question of law as framed by Mr Hone indicates, in the present state of the English authorities there is no property in a corpse (see *Williams v Williams* (1880) 20 Ch D 659, p 662–63 and *Clerk and Lindsell on Torts*, 17th edn, 1995, para 13–50). However that bare statement needs some qualification. First, as is stated in *Clerk and Lindsell*, 'the executors or administrators or other persons charged by the law with the duty of interring the body have a right to the custody and possession of it until it is properly buried'. In the present case there were no executors and there was no administratrix until ... long after the body of the deceased was buried ... I am not aware that there is any authority that there is such a duty on the next of kin as such. If there is no duty, there is no legal right to possession of the corpse. However, even if that is wrong and the next of kin do have some right to possession of the body, there is no authority that right is otherwise than for the interment or other proper disposition of the body. The second qualification is also to be found in *Clerk and Lindsell* where it is said: 'Once a body has undergone a process or other application of human skill, such as stuffing or embalming, it seems it can be the subject of property in the ordinary way; hence it is submitted that conversion will lie for a skeleton or cadaver used for research or exhibition, and the same goes for parts of, and substances produced by, a living person.' Mr Hone relies on the tentatively expressed proposition in the first part of that statement, the authority for which is said to be *Doodeward v Spence* (1908) 6 CLR 406 ... *Doodeward v Spence* is ... not a decision establishing the proposition in Clerk and Lindsell. However I am prepared to accept that proposition is properly arguable, particularly in the light of the academic writings to which Mr Hone referred us (Matthews, P, 'Whose body? People as property' (1983) CLP 193, pp 193 *et seq*, *Palmer on Bailment*, 2nd edn, 1991, pp 9 *et seq* and Magnusson, R, in Palmer and McKendrick (eds), *Proprietary Rights in Human Tissue in Interests in Goods*, 1993, pp 237 *et seq*).
>
> Does this mean that it is arguable that when Dr Perry fixed the brain in paraffin, he thereby transformed it into an item the right to possession of which or the property in which belonged to the plaintiffs? For my part, I do not think so. The removal of the brain was lawfully performed in the course of the post mortem which at the coroner's request Dr Perry had undertaken to determine the cause of the deceased's death. Dr Perry was under an obligation imposed by r 9 of the Coroners Rules 1984 to make provision for the preservation of material which in his opinion bore upon the cause of death, but only for such period as the coroner thought fit ... I do not see how the fact that the brain was so fixed rendered it an item to possession of which the plaintiffs ever became entitled for the purpose of interment or any other purpose, still less that the plaintiffs ever acquired the property in it ...

The principle that property rights in material from a deceased person may be acquired by third parties in lawful possession, such as medical personnel, where the remains have been transformed in some way through human skill, was subsequently applied by the Criminal Court of Appeal in *R v Kelly* [1998] 3 All ER 741. It has now received statutory recognition in s 32(9)(c) Human Tissue Act 2004, which excludes from the prohibition on commercial dealings, 'material which is the subject of property because of an application of human skill'.

Rights in body parts taken from the living

We now need to consider the problem of body parts taken from a living person; the issue is complicated here by the fact that the latter, himself, may be felt to have a *prima facie* claim upon such material. The question, which is now of huge practical import given the scope for the commercial exploitation of DNA, was recently addressed by the Nuffield Council in its 1995 Report:

Nuffield Council on Bioethics, *Human Tissue: Ethical and Legal Issues,* **1995, London: Nuffield Council on Bioethics:**

9.4 At common law the issue has not been tested in English law. It is instructive to inquire why the question of a claim over tissue once removed has not received legal attention. The answer seems simple. In the general run of things a person from whom tissue is removed has not the slightest interest in making any claim to it once it is removed. This is obviously the case as regards tissue removed as a consequence of treatment. It is equally true in the case of donation of tissue whether, for example, blood, bone marrow or an organ. The word donation clearly indicates that what is involved is a gift.

9.5 It is certainly true, of course, that an appendix or gallstone may be returned to a patient who may refer to it as her appendix or gallstone. But this says nothing about any legal claim that she may have to the appendix. In fact, in the case of the returned appendix, one view of the legal position may be as follows: the patient consents to the operation which involves the removal of her appendix: by her consent to the operation she abandons any claims to the appendix, on removal the appendix acquires the status of a res (a thing) and comes into the possession of the hospital authority prior to disposal; in response by a request of the patient that it can be returned the hospital gives the appendix to the patient as a gift; the appendix then becomes the property of the patient.

...

9.7 But there are other circumstances in which ... it could be argued, and has been by a number of commentators, that tissue once removed becomes the property of the person from whom it is removed. This is to say that consent to removal does not *entail* an intent to abandon. The tissue may well, in fact, be abandoned or donated, but these imply a prior coming into existence of a res and the exercise of rights over it. Indeed, such an analysis is logically essential, it is argued, even if the resulting property (ie, a person's assertion of a property right over the new res) exists merely for the moment (a *scintilla temporis*). On this view the person from whom tissue is removed must have a property right in the tissue which expressly or by implication he could waive on the removal so that the property passes to another. The consequence is, of course, that if the property right were not waived, it would be retained. To return to the example in para 9.5, the appendix would have become (and remained) the patient's property had she not by implication waived any right to it.

9.8 The case of *Venner v State of Maryland* decided by the Court of Special Appeals in Maryland, USA, may be of assistance. Powers J held that, 'By the force of social custom ... when a person does nothing and says nothing to indicate an intent to assert his rights of ownership, possession and control over [bodily] material, the only rational inference is that he intends to abandon the material'. The emphasis of this approach is clear:

1 The legal presumption is in favour of abandonment.

2 Abandonment may be prospective.

3 Where, however, the circumstances are such that abandonment may not be presumed, it must follow that if no consent were given, or a consent expressed to be 'on terms' were given, property rights over the tissue would not necessarily pass but would be retained by the person from whom the property was removed.

9.9 It is fair to say that some support for this approach can be derived from various statutes already referred to ... While the Human Tissue Act 1961 is of no assistance, both the Human Organ Transplants Act 1989 and the Human Fertilisation and Embryology Act 1990 appear to endorse a property approach. Indeed the latter, though relying upon a scheme of consents so as to avoid the need to decide the issue of property, contemplates that the control and disposal of gametes and embryos rests with the donor(s) and allows for the transfer of the reproductive material between those with a licence to deal with them. A final statutory provision, s 25 of the National Health Service Act 1977, also seems implicitly to adopt a property approach. The section provides that:

... where the Secretary of State has acquired:

(a) supplies of human blood; ... or

(b) any part of a human body; ...

he may arrange to make such supplies or that part available (on such terms, including terms as to charges as he thinks fit) to any person ...

...

9.11 ... A further legal approach is to argue that tissue once removed becomes property, but at the time of its removal it is *res nullis*, ie, that it belongs to no one until it is brought under dominion (the traditional legal example is the wild animal or plant). This would reflect the traditional view of 'no property in the body'. It would also mean that a person could not prospectively donate 'his' tissue once removed from the body. All he could do would be to consent to the removal. If this analysis were adopted, the tissue would be the property of the person who removed it or subsequently came into possession of it. The person from whom it was removed would not, however, have any property claim to it.

9.12 The current state of English law makes it unclear (at best) which of these approaches (or another) represents the law. Interest in the validity of property claims over removed tissue has, however, been rekindled because of the awareness of circumstances in which tissue has been removed and then developed in some way so as to serve as the basis for a commercial product. The *locus classicus* is the well known *Moore* case. In *Moore* the Supreme Court of California, trying a preliminary point of law, decided that Moore had no property right over the tissue taken from his body. Although not expressed in such a way, if we impose the language that we have employed, the court appears to have found that Moore's consent to the operation entailed an abandonment of any claim to the removed tissue. Thus, he could not assert a claim in property as the basis either for objecting to the removal of his tissue or for having a share in whatever profit was gained through its use. The issue of the validity of the consent he gave to the operation and subsequent procedures then becomes the focus of the case.

The case of *Moore v Regents of University of California* 793 Pd 479 (1990), referred to in the last paragraph, arose after the plaintiff had his spleen removed during treatment for leukaemia. Unknown to him, the doctors used the spleen to generate a cell line from which a highly lucrative drug was produced. Paul Matthews ('The man of property' (1995) 3 Med L Rev 251) has in fact criticised the Nuffield Report for suggesting that Moore, in consenting to the operation, was held to have 'abandoned' any property claims over the spleen; the majority of the court instead appears to have taken the view that Moore never had any such claims in the first place.

Would an English court perhaps take a more favourable view of the property rights enjoyed by a claimant in such a case? There would seem to be two related reasons why someone might wish to assert the existence of such rights. First, the living donor would acquire the ability to exclude or restrict use or dealings by others with the tissue in question. However, it was precisely this possibility (potentially allowing the donor to hamper research of great value to medical science) which provided the decisive policy argument *against* such rights in *Moore*. Secondly, possessing rights of this nature could at least allow the donor to share in any commercial profits arising from the exploitation of his tissue. However, even if such apportionment were practicable, we may legitimately ask *why* individual donors should be entitled to benefit in this way?

In rejecting commercial rewards for donors in the context of stem cell lines deriving from donated embryos, the House of Lords Select Committee on Stem Cell Research suggested that 'any commercial benefits will have come about as a result of the research and subsequent development rather than any intrinsic quality of a particular embryo donated' (see para 8.32 of its report published in February 2002). This in itself seems dubious: in a case such as *Moore*, there clearly was something 'intrinsic' about the material taken from the patient, which made it potentially of especial value. On the other hand, it was blind chance that the material happened to be in Moore (as opposed to anybody else). Here, any reward to the patient may well seem wrong. After all, a fundamental aim of any equitable system of health care is to even out, not encourage, inequalities that arise from the 'natural lottery'.

Intellectual property rights

If the above arguments are accepted for not conferring property rights in body parts upon the donor, it does not follow that such rights should not be enjoyed by third parties. Indeed, the ability of researchers to safeguard discoveries and inventions achieved with human tissue through patenting may provide an important incentive for such research. This was acknowledged implicitly in the *Moore* case, where the doctors' right to patent the cell line created with Moore's tissue was left unchallenged. In the UK, the Human Tissue Act 2004 is intended to exclude cell lines from the prohibtion on commercial dealings and other regulatory provisions in relation to human tissue. In s 54(7) it is stated that, 'for the purposes of this Act, material shall not be regarded as from a human body if it is created outside the human body'.

Nevertheless, as discussed by Bently and Sherman in the following extract, the issue of patenting in relation to biotechnological inventions remains a controversial one:

Bently, L and Sherman, B, 'The ethics of patenting: towards a transgenic patent system' (1995) 3 Med L Rev 275:

Article 53(a) [of the European Patent Convention] states that patents are not to be granted for inventions, the publication or exploitation of which would be contrary to *ordre public* or morality. Section 1(3)(a) of the Patents Act (UK) 1977 is in similar terms, stating that a patent will not be granted for 'an invention the publication or exploitation of which would be generally expected to encourage offensive, immoral or antisocial behaviour'.

The first occasion on which Art 53(a) was discussed at the [European Patent Office] was in the *Onco Mouse* case. In this case, the Technical Board of Appeal was asked to consider whether it was necessary to apply Art 53(a) when deciding the patentability of a mouse which had been genetically modified so that the mouse would suffer from cancer. The applicant hoped that such altered mice would be useful in cancer research. Reversing the findings of the Examining Division, the Technical Board of Appeal stated that ethical concerns needed to be taken into account in deciding issues of patentability. In particular, it held that:

> The genetic manipulation of mammalian animals is undeniably problematical in various respects, particularly where activated onco genes are inserted to make an animal abnormally sensitive to carcinogenic substances and stimuli and consequently prone to develop tumours, which necessarily cause suffering. There is also a danger that genetically manipulated animals, if released into the environment, might entail unforeseeable and irreversible adverse effects ... The decision as to whether or not Art 53(a) EPC is a bar to patenting the present invention would seem to depend mainly on a careful weighing up of the suffering of animals and possible risks to the environment on the one hand, and the invention's usefulness to mankind on the other.

On reconsideration by the Examining Division, it was held that the usefulness of the invention in cancer research outweighed any suffering that might be caused to the animal and, as such, that it was not an immoral invention and therefore was *prima facie* patentable.

The utilitarian approach adopted in *Onco Mouse* was applied in 1991, when the EPO warned the pharmaceutical company, Upjohn, that it would not accept an application to patent a mouse into which a gene had been introduced such that the mouse would lose its hair. In considering the benefit which flowed from the invention (the usefulness of the mice in experiments to cure hair loss), as against the harm suffered by the mice, the EPO asserted that the invention was immoral and thus would not be patentable.

The next occasion on which the application of Art 53(a) was considered was in *Greenpeace UK v Plant Genetic Systems NV* (1995). In this case, the opponents objected to the patent, which had been granted for a genetically engineered plant, on the grounds that it was inherently immoral and that it created environmental risks. Following the cost-benefit test suggested in *Onco Mouse*, the opponents argued that these concerns and risks should be balanced against the benefits likely to accrue from the invention. The Opposition Division refused to apply the utilitarian test, on the basis that it was only necessary to consider the exclusion where the invention would be universally regarded as outrageous, and an overwhelming consensus would exist to the effect that no patent should be granted. The upshot of this was that in most cases it would not be necessary to consider the morality of particular patents ...

The approach advocated in *Greenpeace* was adopted by the Opposition Division in the *Relaxin* case. This decision concerned an opposition by the Green Party to the Howard Florey Institute's patent for the DNA sequences of a naturally occurring substance, which relaxes the uterus during childbirth, and which had been obtained from the human ovary. There were three grounds of objection: first, that the use of pregnancy for profit was offensive to human dignity; secondly, that the applicant was involved in 'patenting life', an activity that was intrinsically immoral; thirdly, that such patenting was equivalent to slavery. In rejecting the Green Party's objections, the EPO noted that the tissue used in the research was donated during the course of necessary gynaecological operations and thus the procedures had not offended 'human dignity'. Moreover, the Opposition Division characterised DNA not as 'life' but rather as a 'chemical substance which carries genetic code'. The argument that the applicant was 'patenting life' was thus misconceived. Finally, it rejected the Green Party's assertion that such patenting was equivalent to slavery on the grounds that such an assertion misunderstood the nature of a patent. This was because, according to the Opposition Division, a patent does not give the proprietor any rights over a human being: all a patent monopoly provides is the right to prevent someone from practising the same invention *outside the human body*.

As with the Greenpeace decision, the Opposition Division's decision in *Relaxin* further highlights the problems that confront patent law in accommodating ethical considerations. This fact was explicitly acknowledged by the Opposition Division in *Relaxin* when it commented that '[w]hether or not human genes should be patented is a controversial issue on which many persons have strong opinions ... the EPO is not the right institution to decide on fundamental ethical questions'. Furthermore, the case reveals the difficulty involved in translating the ethical concerns of the objectors into the language of patent law. Faced with a choice between a scientific understanding of DNA as chemicals, and the social understanding of DNA as life, the former interpretation was preferred by the Opposition Division. This prioritisation of the scientific view of genetic process over the Green Party's approach illustrates the depth of the conflict between the logic of ethical objections and those of patenting, at least as currently understood.

The patenting of inventions in the field of biotechnology is now regulated at European Union level pursuant to Directive 98/44/EC on the protection of biotechnological inventions.

Genetic privacy and the use of DNA

A final topic, which we shall briefly consider in this part of the chapter, concerns the use of human DNA for genetic testing. This is an area of greatly increasing significance in the light of advances in scientific knowledge about the human genome, and brings with it questions of daunting ethical and legal complexity. As Loane Skene suggests in the following extract, it may be that traditional legal categories will require reshaping – away from an individualistic towards a family-oriented perspective – to deal with some of the scenarios that are starting to arise:

Skene, L, 'Genetic Secrets and the Family: A Response to Bell and Bennett' (2001) 9 Med L Rev 162

... If a pregnant woman asks for a genetic test for Huntington Disease (HD) on her fetus *in utero*, can that be done without her husband's consent? Say, for example, that the husband is aware of his genetic risk of HD because one of his parents has it (this is the reason why the mother wants the fetus to be tested). His risk is 1:2 and the child's risk is 1:4. If the child tests positive, the child has the mutation and will develop HD later in life (usually after the age of 40). Also, however, a positive test on the fetus will indicate that the father has the mutation and will later develop the condition. This is knowledge that many people do not wish to have and he may not wish to risk finding out by allowing a test on the fetus. Should a test be permitted if the mother wants it but the father will not agree?

The practice of clinicians throughout the world is apparently not to allow the test without the father's participation and consent. Their view is that the role of a clinician or a counsellor is to inform and support both parties. International guidelines have been published to this effect. The reason for this approach is that 'Counselling [should explore] present and potential future issues, with attention to family dynamics'. Clearly there may be serious problems within the family if the father later discovers that the mother has overridden his wishes, lied to him or misled him. Also if the mother suddenly reveals his genetic status to him when he does not know that a test has been undertaken, he will receive that devastating news without the counselling or support that is recommended by counsellors before testing for HD. Even if the mother acts altruistically, hoping to protect the father from bad news, the burden of that knowledge may be heavy for her in the future.

Thus clinicians and counsellors focus on situations that they face in day-to-day practice as the starting point in developing guidelines on how they should behave. They do not start with legal principles. In contrast, when I am asked as a lawyer to advise or offer policy suggestions, I naturally respond as I have been trained to do, looking for the legal categories and principles into which to slot the question. In the HD case, for example, why, in law, should the husband be informed and his consent obtained? The doctor's duty to inform is imposed by the law of negligence but the duty is not generally owed to third parties, such as the husband. The need to obtain consent is imposed by the law of battery but the husband's body will not be touched, so his consent id not needed ... An alternative approach is to start where the clinicians and counsellors do and think what rules are needed to achieve the best result for the family. The current law is that doctors have duties towards patients. It *could*, however, be that doctors and counsellors undertaking genetic testing and counselling have duties towards *families*.

In the UK, following recommendations by the Human Genetics Commission, the Government published a White Paper, *Our Inheritance, Our Future: Realising the potential of genetics in the NHS*, which, *inter alia*, proposed a new offence of non-consensual genetic testing. This has now been enacted in s 45 of the Human Tissue Act 2004, which provides as follows:

Human Tissue Act 2004:

45 Non-consensual analysis of DNA

(1) A person commits an offence if–

    (a) he has any bodily material intending–

        (i) that any human DNA in the material be analysed without qualifying consent, and

        (ii) that the results of the analysis be used otherwise than for an excepted purpose,

    (b) the material is not of a kind excepted under subsection (2), and

    (c) he does not reasonably believe the material to be of a kind so excepted.

(2) Bodily material is excepted if–

    (a) it is material which has come from the body of a person who died before the day on which this section comes into force and at least one hundred years have elapsed since the date of the person's death,

    (b) it is an existing holding and the person who has it is not in possession, and not likely to come into possession, of information from which the individual from whose body the material has come can be identified, or

    (c) it is an embryo outside the human body …

(4) Schedule 4 (which makes provision for the interpretation of 'qualifying consent' and 'use for an excepted purpose' in subsection (1)(a)) has effect.

Schedule 4, Part 1, provides that 'qualifying consent' will be the consent of the person from whom the material came, or someone with parental responsibility if the person is a child. Where the person has died, consent may be given by anyone who stood in a qualifying relationship with the deceased (as listed in s 54(9)). In this context, the ranking system in s 27(4) – see p 596 above – will not apply.

The main thrust of this provision will be to prevent the taking and testing of samples containing a person's DNA in order surreptitiously to assess his insurance or employment risk. It does not, and is not intended to, address the question (alluded to in the article by Skene) of how far close relatives should be involved in a decision to test one of their number for a given genetic condition, where the result would have implications for the rest of them.

IMPLANTATION OF MATERIAL

The interests of the putative donee

Could someone, desperately in need of a transplant, legally compel another person to submit to the extraction of the necessary material if the latter is found to be a suitable donor? The answer, unsurprisingly in the light of what has been noted at p 571, in respect of the need for the donor's consent, is a clear 'no'.

A well known case in point is that of *McFall v Shimp* 10 Pa D & C (3d) 90 (1978), in which an American court refused to compel a man to undergo a bone-marrow transplant in order to save his dying cousin. While Flaherty J took the view that the man's refusal to submit voluntarily to the extraction was *morally* indefensible, he was not prepared to recognise a legal duty to donate, which would fly in the face of the stress placed by liberal society on the inviolability of the individual (see further, the extract from his judgment cited in Chapter 3, p 95–96, above). It is virtually certain that an English court, faced with a similar predicament, would come to the same conclusion.

The rights of the actual donee

Against the surgeon

As we have seen, much organ transplant therapy (especially that involving animal or artificial implants) remains highly experimental in nature. It has been suggested by JK Mason (in Dyer, C (ed), *Doctors, Patients and the Law*, 1992, Oxford: Blackwells, p 122) that, just as the donor cannot consent to the extraction of an organ if it is likely to cause them serious harm, 'it is equally unlawful to consent to accept an organ in the certainty or near certainty that it would be fatal to do so'. We respectfully doubt whether, so far as a 'near certainty' is involved, this is correct: a one in a thousand chance of life is surely better – other things equal – than no chance at all.

More generally, it is clear that if a transplant surgeon performs the operation without due care and, in so doing causes harm to the donee, the standard principles of negligence will apply to afford the latter a remedy (see Chapter 6).

Against the procurement agency

An allegation of negligence may also be framed against the agency or authority which procured the organ for transplantation. This will be so if the organ itself turns out to be defective in some way, notably if the donee is exposed to a virus, such as HIV or hepatitis, that the donor was carrying. The Nuffield Council on Bioethics considered some of the special problems that might face a donee claimant in such a case in its 1995 report as follows:

Nuffield Council on Bioethics, *Human Tissue: Ethical and Legal Issues*, 1995, London: Nuffield Council on Bioethics:

12.53 -Standards of care change from time to time: what was not negligence in 1990 may well be negligence in 1995. As knowledge, and the perception of risks and their avoidance, improve, so too do the obligations imposed upon those who work in these areas. For example, at one time far less was known than today about the various contaminants in blood products: HIV, hepatitis, syphilis, malaria and toxoplasmosis; and methods of screening or heat treating blood products were not so prevalent. There may have been no negligence liability on the supplier of defective blood had a person then been contaminated with an HIV virus. The situation would be different today, when the norm is to test for such viruses. But what of other viruses? Does an obligation to screen for all known viruses arise as soon as the risk of their presence becomes known? The view has been expressed that as:

> ... more and more minor contaminants of recombinant DNA derived human growth hormone are being identified which are biologically active and pose no safety problem ... the effort and expense in identifying them and then measuring them on a batch-to-batch basis may be out of proportion to the public health risk.

-As long as no adverse consequences follow, that argument may appear to be sound. But what happens if a virus which is deliberately neglected turns out to be far more potent than was anticipated? This has been an issue with hepatitis C: could it be said to be negligent to take a professional, and considered, decision not to screen for this virus even when its presence but not its full potency were known? And what of such bodies as the Committee on the Safety of Medicines and the Licensing Authority ... should they be liable for failure to act earlier to impose higher standards of care? In the last resort, it will be for the courts to weigh up all the factors and decide whether the balance struck was reasonable ...

The Nuffield Council also considered whether a claimant might be able to bring an action under the Consumer Protection Act 1987:

12.57 -A product is 'defective' when it does not provide the safety which a person is entitled to expect, taking all the circumstances into account. Thus, instructions for use, contraindications and warnings and supplied information in one form or another may in some cases assist in determining whether the product was 'defective'. Contaminated blood supplied to patients, or a defective organ used for transplantation, are likely to be regarded as 'defective products' regardless of the information which is given to patients.

12.58 -Liability is imposed upon producers, including manufacturers, importers and suppliers of such products. It is likely that human tissue would be regarded as 'products' for these purposes. This was recommended by the Pearson Royal Commission in 1978. Human tissue used for medical purposes, although not strictly manufactured, would possess the 'essential characteristics attributable to an industrial or other process'.

12.59 -Although these strict liability provisions are an improvement on the negligence action, there are still many difficult hurdles which an injured person has to face before liability can be established. The two most difficult are the so called 'development-risk' defence and, once again, causation.

With regard to the residual hurdles under the 1987 Act mentioned in 12.59, the development risk defence may no longer pose such an obstacle to claimants in the light of the recent ruling in *A and Others v National Blood Authority* [2001] 3 All ER 289, which arose out of the supply of blood contaminated with the Hepatitis C virus: see further Chapter 6.

Lastly, it should be noted that other forms of action, besides those just mentioned, may be available against the procurement agency in appropriate cases. In *Ashcraft v King* 278 Cal Rptr 900 (1991), an American case, the plaintiff recovered in battery after receiving HIV infected blood from an anonymous donor; she had stipulated that she wanted blood obtained only from members of her immediate family. Equally, in France the director of a procurement agency was charged with manslaughter after a patient, who had received an infected corneal graft, died of rabies.

Against the donor

Because of limitations in current screening techniques, it is possible for infected tissue to fail to be identified even though the procurement agency took all reasonable precautions. In such a case a donee, injured through the use of such tissue, would have an action, if at all, only against the original donor of the material: it may be that the latter was (or should have been) aware of their infected status and/or failed to reply honestly to the inquiries of the procurement agency.

In a number of US and Commonwealth cases, the courts have been unsympathetic to the donee's cause. In *Rasmussen v South Florida Blood Service* 500 So 2d 533 (1987), a case in which the plaintiff became infected with HIV following a blood transfusion, public policy in favour of the preservation of donor anonymity was said to outweigh the donee's rights in the matter:

Barkett J: As the district court recognised, petitioner needs more than just the names and addresses of the donors. His interest is in establishing that one or more of the donors has AIDS or is in a high risk group. Petitioner argues that his inquiry may never go beyond comparing the donors' names against a list of known AIDS victims, or against other public records (for example, conviction records in order to determine whether any of the donors is a known drug user). He contends that because a limited inquiry may reveal the information he seeks, with no invasion of privacy, the donors' privacy rights are not yet at issue. We find this argument disingenuous. As we have already noted, the discovery rules allow a trial judge upon good cause shown to set conditions under which discovery will be given. Some method could be formulated to verify the Blood Service's report that none of the donors is a known AIDS victim while preserving the confidentiality of the donors' identities. However, the subpoena in question gives petitioner access to the names and addresses of the blood donors with no restrictions on their use. There is nothing to prohibit petitioner from conducting an investigation without the knowledge of the persons in question. We cannot ignore, therefore, the consequences of disclosure to non-parties, including the possibility that a donor's co-workers, friends, employers, and others may be queried as to the donor's sexual preferences, drug use, or general lifestyle.

The threat posed by the disclosure of the donors' identities goes far beyond the immediate discomfort occasioned by a third party probing into sensitive areas of the donors' lives. Disclosure of donor identities in any context involving AIDS could be extremely disruptive and even devastating to the individual donor. If the requested information is released, and petitioner queries the donors' friends and fellow employees, it will be functionally impossible to prevent occasional references to AIDS ...

We wish to emphasise that although the importance of protecting the privacy of donor information does not depend on the special stigma associated with AIDS, public response to the disease does make this a more critical matter. By the very nature of this case, disclosure of donor identities is disclosure in a damaging context. We conclude, therefore, that the disclosure sought here implicates constitutionally protected privacy interests.

Our analysis of the interests to be served by denying discovery does not end with the effects of disclosure on the private lives of the 51 donors implicated in this case. Society has a vital interest in maintaining a strong volunteer blood supply, a task that has become more difficult with the emergence of AIDS. The donor population has been reduced by the necessary exclusion of potential blood donors through AIDS screening and testing procedures as well as by the unnecessary reduction in the donor population as a result of the widespread fear that donation itself can transmit the disease. In light of this, it is clearly 'in the public interest to discourage any serious disincentive to volunteer blood donation'. Because there is little doubt that the prospect of inquiry into one's private life and potential association with AIDS will deter blood donation, we conclude that society's interest in a strong and healthy blood supply will be furthered by the denial of discovery in this case.

A similar conclusion was reached in the Scottish case of *AB v Scottish National Blood Transfusion Service* 1993 SLT 36. However, in other cases some relaxation of this strict anonymity requirement has been allowed in favour of a rule of 'cloaked disclosure': see *Snyder v Mekhjian* 593 A 2d 318 (1991) and *PD v Australian Red Cross Society* (NSW Div) (1993) 30 NSWLR 376. Nevertheless, the point of doing this is to assist a plaintiff where there is a suspicion that the procurement agency may have been negligent in allowing the blood through. Indeed, as one of the conditions for receiving such information, the plaintiff has had to undertake not to sue the donor directly.

TACKLING THE SHORTAGE IN ORGANS

Transplant activity is increasingly constrained by the shortage of organs, a phenomenon affecting every country which has developed the ability to undertake this form of surgery. Quite possibly uniquely, doctors and surgeons are prevented from alleviating suffering and avoiding death by the shortage of a particular physical resource – a human organ. As at the end of 2004, there were, for example, a total of 5,206 persons on the National Transplant 'active' waiting list for a kidney transplant in the UK (the active list only includes persons with a reasonable chance of receiving an organ; the overall number of persons who could benefit from the procedure is much higher). Given the poignant consequence of a significant number of avoidable deaths, often of quite young people, it is natural that much attention has been focused on the possibility of remedying this shortfall through legal reform. In terms of the possible sources of organs and tissue identified above, cadaveric transplants seem *prima facie* to be the type where such reform may have the greatest chance of achieving positive results.

Addressing the shortfall in cadaveric organs

The system, shortly to be superseded, of organ procurement under the 1961 Act, with its emphasis on the deceased's desire to donate (usually expressed in the form of a donor card) was often described as an 'opt in' scheme. This was in fact not quite accurate; the failure to express such a desire would not automatically preclude the use of one's organs, it merely meant that one's relatives – in so far as they could reasonably be found – had the right to object to such use. However, the Human Tissue Act 2004 is a stronger candidate for such a description: in default of 'appropriate consent', either from the deceased or someone else empowered by the Act to give it, material cannot be taken or used.

The reason for this stricter approach may be understood in the context of the scandals that formed the background to the 2004 Act. Although transplantation was not implicated in those scandals, the Act's effect is to make it more difficult to salvage and use organs for this purpose, as well. In fact, during the passage of the Act, a number of MPs pressed for an amendment to apply special exemptions in relation to the taking and use of human material for transplantation. Indeed, they wished to use the legislative opportunity to introduce a more radical 'opt out' approach to organ donation, based upon the presumed consent of the donor unless he made known his objections while alive. This proposal was rejected by the Government, but is at present the subject of a Private Member's Bill to amend the 2004 Act (see the Human Tissue Act 2004 (Amendment) Bill, introduced in January 2005).

The possibility of changing the law in the direction of presumed consent, and its potential impact upon organ donation, has been explored by New *et al* by reference to experience in other jurisdictions:

New, B, Solomon, M, Dingwall, R and McHale, J, *A Question of Give and Take,* **1994, London: King's Fund Institute, pp 56–58:**

Changing the law on gaining consent

Of particular interest to policy makers has been the various legal frameworks within which procurement takes place. The UK, along with Germany, the Netherlands, Italy, Canada, Australia and New Zealand, have what might broadly be termed 'opting in' legal systems. Two other systems have generated much interest in the literature: presumed consent – also known as opting out – and required request.

Presumed consent

Presumed consent schemes have been introduced into many countries, although attempts to enact such legislation in the UK have always failed, the latest being the Transplantation of Human Organs Bill 1993. The international legislation falls into several categories. The purest version of the law allows automatic removal except in a situation in which the deceased has expressed an objection during his or her lifetime. This 'strict' type of presumed consent procedure applies in Austria where organs can be removed provided in his or her life, the person concerned has not expressed an objection. The views of close relatives are not taken into account ...

A slightly less strict version of presumed consent operates in Belgium where, if there is no explicit objection by the deceased, the relatives are allowed to object but the medical profession are under no obligation to seek their views. The relatives must initiate the process under these circumstances ...

Other, still weaker, schemes allow removal unless the deceased has made an explicit or informal objection at any time. Such a formulation of the law effectively requires that the relatives are consulted in order to glean the wishes of the deceased. Although it is formally the views of the deceased whilst alive which are being sought, such schemes allow the relatives to object on the deceased's behalf. France and Spain operate presumed consent legislation of this kind ...

Finally, a scheme in operation in Singapore provides for the automatic exclusion of certain categories of potential donor, including non-citizens and Muslims ... Muslims can, however, donate their organs if they wish, by pledging their organs whilst alive or if their relatives consent ...

Does presumed consent work? Belgium

Belgium enacted presumed consent legislation in June 1986 in the middle of a period of sustained and steady growth in kidney transplantation across Europe ...

Belgium did increase the number of available kidneys by a significant margin during 1987 – a rise of 37% over the year before – and this does not seem to be simply the continuation of an earlier trend. Furthermore, neither the UK, Germany nor the Netherlands experienced a similar increase in the same year. On the other hand, Austria did experience a similar increase, drawing attention to the fact that the effect experienced in Belgium could have been as a result of other factors (Austria did not introduce similar legislation in the same year, having done so in 1982, formalising a 200 year tradition of routinely utilising the corpse for medical purposes). For instance, the publicity devoted to the organ donation issue whilst the law was being debated could itself have promoted a greater willingness to donate on the part of the public and a more informed attitude on behalf of ICU staff. It has also been noted that the number of transplant co-ordinators increased at around this time, and that the law formalised systems of reimbursement so that donating hospitals could be sure that they would receive the appropriate payment for managing the donor.

These objections are inconclusive, however. One would expect a 'publicity effect' to subside. The increase in the number of co-ordinators was likely to be as much a result of the increased number of donors as the cause of it. And the law merely formalised payment systems which operated successfully for the majority of hospitals beforehand. But perhaps the best evidence is provided by ... [comparing] the difference between centres which always asked permission, and the centre which 'followed the law'. It is clear that the influence of publicity, co-ordinators and payment systems had no effect in those centres where relatives' permission is always sought. It certainly seems as though the law had an independent effect on kidney retrieval where its provisions were adopted ...

Another option may be to introduce a system of 'required request' as is operated in the USA. As the King's Fund Institute Report continues:

New, B, Solomon, M, Dingwall, R and McHale, J, *A Question of Give and Take*, 1994, London: King's Fund Institute, pp 59–60:

Required request

Required request and routine inquiry are used extensively in the United States with the aim of increasing the supply of organs. The Uniform Anatomical Gift Act 1987, which forms the model for many State statutes, makes provision for required request and routine inquiry. The development of required request policies by hospitals was encouraged by the Omnibus (Budget) Reconciliation Act 1986. This Act provides that failure on the part of hospitals to adopt routine inquiry or required request policies will lead to the denial of Medicare and Medicaid reimbursements from the Health Care Finance Authority.

Required request is a procedure in which inquiries must be made of the families of potential donors to see whether they would allow their relatives' organs to be used. Twenty six US States have this type of policy. The legislation in some States incorporates exceptions to the general duty of inquiry where, for example, the wishes of the deceased are already known, or the medical staff are unable to locate the family in a timely manner, or where inquiry would exacerbate mental or emotional distress.

Routine inquiry is the procedure of informing individuals and families of the option of organ donation. Eighteen States have legislation of this kind. Some States do not require hospitals to approach families directly but stipulate that they must establish organ and tissue donation committees to design policies which would result in prompt identification of donors and prompt referral to the Organ Procurement Agency.

How successful have the required request and routine inquiry schemes been? While there was an initial increase in the availability of organs, over time the schemes do not appear to have had a major impact ... One reason for this, it is suggested, is the lack of institutional commitment to ensuring that the required request procedures are followed. The United States experience illustrates that simply to enact required request legislation is not enough. It is vital to have adequately trained and qualified personnel.

As one organ procurement official observed: '... if you simply ask relatives about organ donation by simply citing the law the consent rate is zero ...'

Another reason suggested for the lack of dramatic impact of required request is that doctors find organ procurement time consuming and emotionally demanding. It is questionable whether statutory enactment of required request would have a significant impact. The national audit found that only 6% of relatives in the UK are not approached when an otherwise potential donor is on a ventilator, and many of these would probably have communicated their unwillingness to consider donation by other means.

Arguably, in this area, legal change unaccompanied by any corresponding change in cultural values (notably the pre-eminence accorded to the views of relatives), or commitment of greater technical resources to organ retrieval, is unlikely to decrease appreciably the shortfall in donor organs. As Bernard Teo has observed:

Teo, B, 'Strategies of organ procurement' (1992) 6 Bioethics 113:

What strategy of organ procurement a society ought to adopt depends on its willingness to expend resources for its transplant programme(s), ie, after the requirements of social priorities have been considered. If it chooses to ration resources for these programme(s), then it is arguably wiser to adopt a less efficient but ethically preferable strategy of expressed consent or its variants. The system would most likely yield a limited quantity of organs which would probably remain comfortably within the resources allocated for the programme(s). What would be the purpose of adopting a more efficient organ procurement policy when the number of procedures capable of being performed would be constrained by limitations in other resources? Furthermore, would those involved with the procurement of organs be as eager to procure organs?

Perhaps France is a case in point. In his report on the French organ transplant and procurement programmes, Arthur Caplan noted that concerns for the rising costs of health care have created a less than enthusiastic commitment of its scarce medical resources to its transplant programmes. Restrictions in the availability of resources for transplants have placed '... severe limits both in terms of personnel and hospital space on the number of transplants of all types that can now be performed'. Its effect on medical professionals is to dampen their enthusiasm in seeking out potential organ donors. Thus, it is arguable that France ought not to have adopted presumed consent without prior consideration of the extent to which it is prepared to support its transplant programmes. Furthermore, the policy creates ethical problems that are more difficult to overcome than would be the case if it had adopted ethically preferable, but less efficient, policies.

Of course, it might be argued that a more efficient system of organ procurement would create better chances for patients to find matching tissues since the chances would increase in proportion to the number of organs the system yields. The counter-argument to this is that a more efficient system of organ procurement could also increase the possibility of a fiscal overload, and subsequently distort a society's medical priorities if it is forced to spend more resources on its transplant program than it is willing. Thus it may be legitimate to question whether every State in the USA ought to adopt the policy of required request when some States have clearly indicated that transplants are not priorities in their health delivery, and have chosen to restrict resources for their programmes.

Even if there is a commitment to meet all its transplant needs, a society should first try out such ethically preferable strategies as expressed consent or, in the event of its failure, the system of required request ...

Even as a society contemplates the adoption of presumed consent, it ought to consider another important factor: political feasibility. It seems unwise for France to have adopted the legislation without consideration of political feasibility. The French people hold a strong belief in the rights of families relative to cadaver disposal. French doctors find it 'psychologically intolerable to remove tissues from a body without obtaining the permission of the next of kin' which explains their customary practice of always asking familial consent for organ removal. In practice, France's presumed consent policy, ie, of not requiring familial consent, exists only on paper. It is the policy of required request that is being carried out. Thus it seems that France could have adopted the policy of required request which would have been more in tune with the French custom of familial consultation.

Elective ventilation – clarifying the law

The meaning of this practice and the background to the debate surrounding its legality have been described at p 589ff, above. Prior to the practice's suspension, the King's Fund Institute Report was optimistic about its potential to generate a significant number of additional donor organs:

New, B, Solomon, M, Dingwall, R and McHale, J, *A Question of Give and Take,* **1994, London: King's Fund Institute, p 56:**

... what difference would a national policy of elective ventilation make? At Exeter – and this is likely to be an over-estimate – the team found on average three donors per year from the protocol from a population of 303,000. This translates into 10 donors pmp per year. The 277 ICUs in England ... serve a population of 47.8 million, which means that, at best, there would be 478 extra donors to be found nationwide, an average of just under two per unit. Let us assume an upper limit of three per unit for the purposes of this discussion.

How long would these donors spend in an ICU bed? No electively ventilated donors should spend more than 48 hours in the ICU according to the Exeter experience, and this can be written into the protocol. Thus if donors turn out not to be suitable or do not continue to respiratory arrest, then they should be removed from the ICU. One donor in Exeter spent 127 hours in the ICU, but personal communication with staff from the hospital has confirmed that this would not be normal practice and only occurred because there was no pressure on ICU beds at the time. Indeed, all but two of the donors in the initial report of the protocol were in the ICU for less than 24 hours ... Let us estimate two bed days per donor as the highest likely average length of stay.

Thus, on the most extreme estimate, units will, on average, have to accommodate three electively ventilated donors per year spending a total of six bed days in the unit. This would be in addition to the current mean occupancy rate of 1,314 bed days – an increase of 0.46%. 478 extra donors constitutes an increase of 66% on the English donor rate for 1991, but is likely to increase ICU workload by less than one hundredth of that proportion. Whilst it is acknowledged that these average figures hide the fact that some units will be at full capacity, and therefore entirely unable to contribute to the policy, this analysis draws attention to the relatively small impact such a policy would have on the intensive care community, whilst having a potentially enormous impact on transplant activity.

If this assessment is correct, the clarification of the law in this area should arguably be undertaken as a matter of some priority.

Creating a market in organs

The shortfall in organs could probably be eradicated at one stroke if we were prepared to sanction commercial dealings in them. However, such a possibility undoubtedly arouses widespread repugnance. The main arguments for and against permitting a market in organs are explored by Wilkinson and Garrard:

Wilkinson, S and Garrard, E, 'Bodily integrity and the sale of human organs' (1996) 22 JME 334:

The case in favour of permitting organ sale

There's plenty to be said in favour of permitting a trade in human organs. Most obviously, it would generate an increased supply of a scarce and life-saving resource, as well as providing some much needed income for those who have little else to sell. Furthermore, it seems inconsistent to allow bomb disposal experts, firefighters and deep-sea divers to be paid for their dangerous (and sometimes painful) work, while preventing other people from being paid for the equally valuable contribution their kidneys would make to the well being of others. Finally, libertarian thoughts might incline us to permit people to dispose of their own body parts in whatever way they wish (we're talking about *their* body parts, after all, and so they should be allowed to do what they want with them).

In spite of these considerations, though, many still find the idea of paying a healthy person for one of her organs deeply repugnant. Given the apparent advantages of permitting organ sale, what justification might there be for this reaction?

The case against permitting organ sale

There seem to us to be four standard objections to permitting organ sale, each of which we regard as ultimately unconvincing:

Pain and risk

The first is simply that the organ seller is subjected to an extremely high level of pain and risk. This in itself, though, can't be sufficient to justify a ban on organ sale, since we don't in general think that it's wrong to pay people for doing dangerous things. (There are numerous examples of this: firefighters, astronauts, miners and divers, to name but a few.) Common forms of 'risky labour' are often more dangerous than organ sale, but are regarded as heroic, rather than condemned; it is seen as quite proper to reward those who do them. And this difference in attitude can't be justified in terms of the good consequences that 'risky labour' produces, since the consequences of an organ sale (typically, saving a life) may be just as good or better.

Exploitation and commodification

The second worry is that the relationship between the buyer and seller is likely to be exploitative and to either cause or constitute an unacceptable *commodification* of the seller and/or her body. Brecher, for example, describes trading in human kidneys (along with many other practices) as 'exploitation based on making a commodity of human beings'.

There are two problems with this objection. First, although organ sale does necessarily involve treating a human body part as a commodity, there is no reason to suppose that this is *necessarily exploitative*. Would we really regard it as exploitative if the organ seller were wealthy, educated, rational and well informed and got paid £1,000,000 for her organ? Second, we do, in fact, permit many practices which are at least as exploitative and 'commodifying' as organ sale (for example, poorly paid labour). Of course, this doesn't show that exploitation and commodification are acceptable. But it *does* show that they aren't a special problem for organ sale and that they alone can't explain why organ sale is seen as more offensive than (say) low wages. (It may, of course, be argued that the thought that organ sale is worse than low wages is simply irrational and/or false. This is, roughly, Bob Brecher's view.)

It is sometimes claimed, however, that there is an important difference between banning a proposed new practice and banning an established one, since banning an established one will be more disruptive, unpopular and costly. This might provide a reason for banning organ sale, even if it were morally no worse than other permitted exploitative practices. For we could hold that although, as an ideal, we should ban all exploitative practices, in the real world we must settle for banning just those which we can ban, or can ban without excessive disruption and cost. However, although the distinction between banning new and banning existing practices is an important one, it is not sufficient to show that organ sale is morally worse than these other exploitative practices and so won't serve to explain or justify the widespread moral intuition that there is something especially objectionable about the sale of body parts. In short, it seems that the moral difference between organ sale and poorly paid labour is not merely that one is easier to ban than the other.

Undermining the practice of free donation

Another objection to permitting organ sale is that to do so would undermine the practice of free donation. Abouna *et al*, for example, claim that there is 'considerable evidence to indicate that marketing in human organs will eventually deprecate and destroy the present willingness of members of the public to donate their organs out of altruism'. There are two distinct worries here. The first is a purely practical one. If payment is allowed, then virtually all donors will begin to expect payment and so voluntary donations will cease. The second is that allowing payment for organs would deprive people of an opportunity to participate in 'giving' relationships with one another: relationships which have some ethical or social value, independently of their practical consequences.

Taking the second worry first, it is sufficient to point out that the mere permissibility of sale doesn't itself prevent people from donating (although it might, of course, encourage them to sell rather than donate). Organ givers are at liberty to waive their fee and, in a sense, the possibility of sale allows the (free) donor to be even more generous than she could otherwise have been; for not only does she give up her organ, but she gives up her fee as well.

As regards the first worry, it seems that there's no compelling reason to believe that organ sale would undermine the practice of free donation. After all, professional social work and charitable social work co-exist. Also, if organ sale led to a significant overall increase in the supply of organs, this would more than compensate for the reduced number of free organs. But in any case, it is far from clear that there is a significant practice of free donation to be undermined. As Harvey points out, 'it is doubtful that there is a great number of willing, non-related potential organ donors who will give without payment'. Given the high level of pain and risk involved, free donation (except by relatives, who might well waive the fee, if it were offered) is very unlikely to take place anyway.

Concerns about autonomy and consent

It is generally agreed that the absence of coercion and manipulation is required for genuine consent. And the final objection we consider is that no one could ever be in a position autonomously to consent to selling an organ such as a kidney, since the process would be so unpleasant and/or dangerous that only someone who was coerced or manipulated would agree to it. One virtue of this objection is that it would explain why we're more concerned about organ selling than the selling of blood and certain other body products. In the case of the latter, the level of pain and/or risk is very low, and so the need for coercion and manipulation is much less.

This objection does, indeed, raise a serious practical worry about the possibility of organ sellers being coerced, and it is certainly true that, were organ sale to be permitted, rigorous safeguards aimed at ensuring fully informed consent in every case would be required. But does organ sale necessarily involve coercion or manipulation? It seems not, since even a wealthy, informed and rational agent might consent to it (without coercion or manipulation) if the price were high enough. Would we want to say, in such a case, that the person hadn't really consented? (Of course, with a broad enough conception of manipulation, the answer to this question might be 'yes', but we would question whether so broad a conception would be able to do any ethical work, since too many things would be counted as manipulative.)

Also, given that organ sale is less unpleasant and dangerous than many accepted forms of 'risky labour', were we to take this objection seriously, then a wide range of accepted practices should be condemned on similar grounds. What is more, the same line of reasoning might lead us to ban many cases of organ *donation*, for as Harvey points out:

> ... there is financial pressure when the potential [paid] donor is in poverty. And perhaps it may be argued that this alone is sufficient for banning all paid-for donations. But then, in consistency, the same reasoning should be applied to related donors: since some of them are open to heavy psychological and emotional pressure (for example, perhaps by being the submissive and 'guilt'-ridden offspring of an extremely domineering and now ailing parent) ...

If the possibility of (financially) pressuring the organ *seller* is sufficient to warrant a ban on organ sale, then the possibility of (emotionally) pressuring the related organ *donor* must also be sufficient to warrant a ban on organ donation. But since we clearly don't want to ban donation, the possibility of pressuring can't be a sufficient reason to ban sale.

In response to this, it might be argued that financial and emotional pressures are importantly different, in that financial pressure is more erosive of the possibility of genuine consent. This may well be true. The pressure on someone facing starvation (due to poverty) may well be such that an offer to buy her kidney is irresistible. However, a not unreasonable reply is that in those circumstances, if the potential seller's plight cannot (or will not) be relieved in any other way, then forbidding her to sell her kidney is more harmful to her than undermining her autonomous consent (by allowing her to sell it). Furthermore, the evil involved here seems to lie not in the sale itself, but in her being allowed to be in such desperate circumstances in the first instance.

Ultimately, our reluctance to treat irreplaceable bodily parts as commodities which may be the subject of buying and selling seems to be grounded both in an intrinsic sense of respect for persons as ends in themselves, and in fears as to the moral climate of any society in which organised trading in organs became the norm. As Bernard Teo writes:

Teo, B, 'Strategies of organ procurement' (1992) 6 Bioethics 113:

... the human body is not like other things. Since human bodiliness is intrinsically tied to human personality and identity, it follows that respect for the human person would also be intrinsically tied to respect for the human body and its parts. In every culture and society, the instinctive revulsion and strong moral aversion toward treating the human body as property and commodity in both religious and secular attitudes is shown by the special respect accorded to the body in elaborate ceremonies and rituals surrounding death and burial. They are signs of respect and reverence for the person who lived. There seems to be that intuitive instinct that the human body has a special moral significance that cannot be equated with other things or commodities. Leon Kass, a physician and philosopher, has warned against trivialising human embodiment. Because human dignity is intrinsically linked to human embodiment, treating the body and its parts as commodities would be to strip the human body of its proper dignity. It would be morally intolerable therefore if human body parts are treated as objects for payment and as commodities of exchange in the market place. Thus it is arguable that placing a monetary value on human body parts would be ethically unacceptable.

Furthermore, in a society where cherished communal values such as altruism and giving are encouraged and cultivated, legalising a commercial market for organs and paying for them would dissolve communal bonds and relationships based on goodwill and altruism. It would transform them into one of contractual buying and selling. Arguably, allowing payment for organs and legalising a market approach would not only dehumanise the transacting parties, but would also undermine the humanitarian character of the transplant undertaking and be an effective dissolvent of community. The wisdom of paying for organs and allowing commercialisation is therefore highly questionable even for the lofty purpose of saving lives.

As the law in the UK stands, commercial dealing in organs (both from live donors and cadavers) is a criminal offence under the Human Organ Transplants Act 1989. As discussed above, this will continue to be the position under the Human Tissue Act 2004.

CHAPTER 12

EUTHANASIA

INTRODUCTION

What is euthanasia?

Euthanasia (literally 'an easeful death', from the Greek) describes the practice of bringing about death in a manner that causes the least amount of suffering to the patient. The term is sometimes used narrowly to refer only to the taking of life by positive means, for example, the giving of a lethal injection to a patient whose life is full of unbearable pain. However, in this chapter, we employ it more widely, to encompass, in addition, cases in which a doctor, intending his patient's death, refrains from providing life-prolonging treatment: we thus distinguish between 'active' and 'passive' euthanasia. Whilst this is ultimately a matter of terminology, the reader should be alert, especially when reading judgments, as to whether the narrower or wider usage has been adopted in a particular instance. In addition to the active/passive distinction, the practice of euthanasia may also be characterised as 'voluntary' or 'non-voluntary' depending on whether the patient was mentally competent to request it or not.

The value of human life

What makes the issue of euthanasia so morally contentious is the enormous value which we place upon human life. In the following extract, Helga Kuhse charts the historical framework in which respect for individual human life attained centrality in Western thought, as well as noting the difficulties encountered by the view in an increasingly secular age:

Kuhse, H, *The Sanctity-of-Life Doctrine in Medicine*, 1987, Oxford: Clarendon, pp 16–20:

Every society known to us subscribes to some principle or principles involving respect for human life. As Georgia Harkness puts it:

> In every society there appears to be an elemental reverence for life which makes the deliberate killing of another person a punishable offence. In all societies there are exceptions ... yet aversion to murder is probably the most universal of all moral attitudes.

But if aversion to murder, or wrongful killing, is universal, there have been great variations between cultural traditions as to what constitutes wrongful killing.

If we turn to the roots of our Western tradition, we find that in Greek and Roman times not all human life was regarded as inviolable and worthy of protection. Slaves and 'barbarians' did not have a full right to life, and human sacrifices and gladiatorial combat were acceptable at different times. Spartan law required that deformed infants be put to death; for Plato, infanticide is one of the regular institutions of the ideal State; Aristotle regards abortion as a desirable option; and the Stoic philosopher Seneca writes unapologetically: 'Unnatural progeny we destroy; we drown even children who at birth are weakly and abnormal.'

Stoic and Epicurean philosophers thought that suicide and euthanasia were acceptable options when life no longer held any value. Once again to quote Seneca:

> I shall not abandon old age, if old age preserves me intact as regards the better part of myself, but if old age begins to shatter my mind, and to pull its various faculties to pieces, if it leaves me, not life, but only the breath of life, I shall rush out of a house that is crumbling and tottering. I shall not avoid illness by seeking death, as long as the illness is curable and does not impede my soul. I shall not lay violent hands upon myself just because I am in pain; for death under such circumstances is defeat. But if I find out that the pain must always be endured, I shall depart, not because of the pain, but because it will be a hindrance to me as regards all my reasons for living.

And whilst there were deviations from these views (one of which is the Hippocratic Oath, briefly to be discussed below), it is probably correct to say that such practices as abortion, infanticide, suicide, and euthanasia were less proscribed in ancient times than they are today. There has been a gradual expansion of the circle protecting human life, outlawing not only the killing of slaves or 'barbarians', gladiatorial combat, and human sacrifice, but also abortion, infanticide, and euthanasia.

Most historians of Western morals agree that the rise of Judaism and even more of Christianity contributed greatly to the general feeling that human life is valuable and worthy of respect.

WEH Lecky gives the now classical account of the sanctity of human life in his *History of European Morals*:

> Considered as immortal beings, destined for the extremes of happiness or of misery, and united to one another by a special community of redemption, the first and most manifest duty of the Christian man was to look upon his fellow men as sacred beings and from this notion grew up the eminently Christian idea of the sanctity of human life … it was one of the most important services of Christianity that besides quickening greatly our benevolent affections it definitely and dogmatically asserted the sinfulness of all destruction of human life as a matter of amusement, or of simple convenience, and thereby formed a new standard higher than any which then existed in the world … This minute and scrupulous care for human life and virtue in the humblest form, in the slave, the gladiator, the savage, or the infant, was indeed wholly foreign to the genius of Paganism. It was produced by the Christian doctrine of the inestimable value of each immortal soul.

Whilst it is true that even before the rise of Christianity some philosophical and religious schools expressed a strong respect for human life, it is generally agreed that such views were only held by a minority. For example, the Hippocratic Oath, which Ludwig Edelstein assigns to the 4th century BC, already strongly disapproves of abortion, euthanasia, and suicide – independently of Judaeo-Christian influence. However, if Edelstein is correct, this oath represented only 'a small segment of Greek opinion' and was not generally accepted until the end of antiquity when Christianity became the dominant religion. Edelstein attributes the oath to the Pythagoreans who strongly condemned suicide on the grounds that 'we are all soldiers of God, placed in an appointed post of duty, which it is a rebellion against our Maker to desert'.

Whatever the importance of the Pythagoreans in the evolution of the idea of the sanctity of human life, it would seem that at least one strand of their view, namely, the belief that we must not take our own life because God has assigned a certain post to us, is continued in the more influential Christian tradition (both Catholic and Protestant), which holds that we are God's property and must not quit our station in life wilfully. Life is, in the Christian tradition, not our own to do with as we like, but is 'entirely an ordination, a loan and a stewardship'. From such presuppositions it follows quite logically that 'only God has the right to take the life of an innocent, and that man ... must wait his appointed time till his charge cometh, till he sinks and is crushed with the weight of his own misery'.

On this view, then, it is not human life as such which is inviolable or has sanctity; it is rather the will of God which has sanctity and must not be violated. As the theologian Karl Barth puts it:

> Life itself does not create this respect. The command of God creates respect for it. It is thus not killing as such which is wrong, but it is wrong to act contrary to the will of God. In other words, killing is not an act wrong either in itself or wrong because of what it does to the victim; rather, killing is wrong simply because it is contrary to the will of God.

... There is no longer a universal acceptance of religion and of the belief that ethics consists in doing what God commands. Conventional attitudes based on these beliefs are, however, still very much with us today. During the long period when Christian beliefs moulded European thought, the sanctity-of-life view became part of an unquestioned moral tradition: it became part of medical ethics and the law. It was, for example, not until 1516 that Sir Thomas More presented the first important defence of mercy killing in the Christian era, and it was not until the 17th and 18th centuries that philosophers began to question the view that ethics requires a religious basis. From such initial philosophical questionings, however, it is a long way to a fundamental change in popular attitudes. Whilst it is today no longer generally believed that life has sanctity in the religious sense, the ethical attitudes to which these religious beliefs gave rise still find expression in the deep-seated belief that human life, irrespective of its quality or kind, is absolutely inviolable and equally valuable; and that we must never take life – either our own or that of anyone else – because life is not ours to do with as we see fit.

But now we must be clear about just what a non-theistic account of the sanctity of human life entails. While it may have made some religious sense to hold that mere bodily life has sanctity because life is a gift from God and has received its value from Him, it makes but poor philosophical sense to say that mere bodily life is intrinsically valuable and absolutely inviolable, for a secular account of the sanctity of human life will be hard put to provide a convincing reason for this view. [© Helga Kuhse 1987. Reprinted from *The Sanctity of Life Doctrine in Medicine* by Helga Kuhse (1987) by permission of Oxford University Press.]

'Sanctity of life' and 'vitalism'

Kuhse associates the 'sanctity of life' doctrine, in its strongest form, with the view that human life is of absolute value and should, where possible, be maintained at any cost, including the cost to the individual whose life it is. Thus, it is impermissible to shorten (or fail to extend) life, by however small an amount and irrespective of any suffering endured by the person concerned. However, in the following article, John Keown denies that the sanctity of life principle, properly understood, commits us to such a conclusion, which he instead ascribes to a separate doctrine, that of 'vitalism':

Keown, J, 'Restoring moral and intellectual shape to the law after *Bland*' (1997) 113 LQR 481:

The principle of the sanctity of life is often advocated but much less often understood. In Western thought, the development of the principle has owed much to the Judaeo-Christian tradition. That tradition's doctrine of the sanctity of life holds that human life is created in the image of God and is, therefore, possessed of an intrinsic dignity which entitles it to protection from unjust attack. With or without that theological underpinning, the doctrine grounds the principle that one ought never intentionally to kill an innocent human being. The 'right to life' is essentially a right not to be intentionally killed.

The dignity of human beings inheres because of the radical capacities, such as for understanding and rational choice, inherent in human nature. Some human beings, such as infants, may not yet possess the ability to exercise these radical capacities. But radical capacities must not be confused with abilities: one may have, for example, the radical capacity but not the ability to speak Swahili. All human beings possess the capacities inherent in their nature even though, because of infancy, disability or senility, they may not yet, not now, or no longer have the ability to exercise them.

As this account of human dignity might suggest, the principle can also be articulated in non-religious terms, in which 'inviolability' might be more apt than 'sanctity'. Indeed, a prohibition on killing is central to the pre-Christian fount of Western medical ethics – the Hippocratic Oath and the modern reaffirmation of that Oath by the (arguably post-Christian) Declaration of Geneva – and many non-believers recognise the right of human beings not to be intentionally killed. Lord Goff of Chieveley noted in *Bland* that the sanctity principle has long been recognised in most, if not all, civilised societies throughout the modem world, as is evidenced by its recognition by international conventions on human rights. Article 2 of the European Convention, for example, provides:

> Everyone's right to life shall be protected by law. No one shall be deprived of his life intentionally save in the execution of a sentence of a court following his conviction of a crime for which this penalty is provided by law.

The right not to be killed is enjoyed regardless of inability or disability. Rejecting any such distinctions as fundamentally arbitrary and inconsistent with a sound concept of justice, the principle (whether in its religious or secular forms) asserts that human life is not only an instrumental good, a necessary precondition of thinking or doing, but a basic good, a fundamental constituent of human flourishing. It is, in other words, not merely good as a means to an end but is, like other integral aspects of a flourishing human life, like friendship and knowledge, something worthwhile in itself. Of course some people, like those who are pictures of health in the prime of life, participate in the good of life and health to a greater extent than others, such as the terminally ill, but even the sick and the dying participate in the good to the extent they are able.

Although life is a basic good it is not an absolute good, a good to which all the other basic goods must be sacrificed in order to ensure its preservation. The sanctity doctrine is not vitalistic. The core of the doctrine is the principle prohibiting intentional killing, not an injunction requiring the preservation of life at all costs. However, although the doctrine denies that human life is an absolute good, the principle that it may never intentionally be taken is an absolute principle, that is, one which has no acceptable exceptions. Although the value of human life is not absolute, the prohibition on taking it is.

Although Keown refers here to the prohibition on 'killing' or 'taking life' as lying at the heart of the sanctity of life principle, it should not be supposed that he wishes to draw any distinction between active and passive euthanasia: in his view (although perhaps this is not the term's standard usage), it is just as possible – and *prima facie* culpable – to 'kill' by an omission as by an act. Rather, the sanctity of life principle acquires flexibility in permitting death in certain circumstances (and is, hence, saved from unacceptable 'vitalistic' consequences) through a combination of two other sub-principles: these are, respectively, the principle of 'double effect' and the distinction between 'ordinary' and 'extraordinary' treatment. Reliance on these latter principles informs the teachings on euthanasia of the Roman Catholic Church, and has been defended by natural law theorists such as JM Finnis. Nevertheless, both principles have been subjected to powerful criticism. In relation to that of double effect, John Harris has written as follows:

Harris, J, *The Value of Life*, 1985, London: Routledge & Kegan Paul, pp 43–45:

... I will take as an authoritative statement of the principle the explanation of it given in a recent Linacre Centre publication:

> ... the term 'double effect' relates to 'side effects' ... The principle of the side effect merely states a possibility: where you may not aim at someone's death, causing it does not necessarily incur guilt – it can be that there are necessities which in the circumstances are great enough or there are legitimate purposes in hand of such a kind to provide a valid excuse for risking or accepting that you cause death. Without such excuse foreseeable killing is either murder or manslaughter.

We should be clear also that you may not aim at someone's death either as an end or a means. There is an immense, and I think insoluble, problem about deciding when a death (or any other consequence) is aimed at as an end or a means and when it is merely a side effect. It all depends on how the action is described, and crucially on how to set limits to the re-description of any action. This can clearly be seen if we examine the Linacre Centre's own example in illustration of the distinction:

> Imagine a potholer stuck with people behind him and water rising to drown them. And suppose two cases: in one he can be blown up; in the other a rock can be moved to open another escape route, but it will crush him to death ...

> There might be people among them who, seeing the consequence, would move the rock, though they would not blow up the man because that would be choosing his death as the means of escape. This is a far from meaningless stance, for they thus show themselves as people who will absolutely reject any policy making the death of innocent people a means or end.

It is difficult to see how anyone could read this and not be impressed by it as an example of the most comprehensive sophistry. If this example has any plausibility, it depends on our accepting that blowing up the potholer can only be described as killing him whereas moving the rock is a complete action description, of which crushing the man is a mere side effect. It is a feature of any action that its description is almost infinitely expandable or contractable. My crooking my finger, is my pulling the trigger, is my shooting at Samson, is my hitting Delilah, is my killing the President, is my orphaning her children, etc. The problem is to set a limit to the legitimacy of characterising the action in one way rather than another. The above description of what went on in the cave could seem plausible only because the whole distinction between direct means and ends on the one hand, and side effects on the other, has already been rigged by a particular choice of action descriptions. This can easily be seen if we change the phraseology slightly:

> Suppose two cases: in one he is crushed leaving room to escape; in the other a hole can be blown in the rock at its weakest point but this will dismember the potholer ...

These descriptions are equally plausible but the impression of which course of action involves direct killing, and which involves death as a side effect of what is done, is different. The crucial point for anyone who wishes to have a realistic appreciation of what is involved in one choice rather than another is surely not: 'which description makes the most undesirable consequence a side effect?' But: 'am I justified in behaving in a way that has these consequences?'

Anyone who thinks that, in the Linacre Centre example, those who choose to save themselves by crushing the potholer rather than by blowing him up are those who 'show themselves as people who will absolutely reject any policy making the death of innocent people a means or end' is simply and comprehensively deceiving himself.

The distinction between effects and side effects, and between effects and double effects, drawn in this way is entirely without moral significance. What matters ... is how our decisions and actions affect the world, not whether that effect is direct or indirect ...

Side effects revisited

I should emphasise that there is a perfectly respectable everyday use of the term 'side effects' and I am not denying that for some purposes it may be useful to distinguish between the direct effects and the side effects of a drug or a course of treatment. But it is important to be clear that this distinction is entirely without moral significance and cannot be used to limit our responsibility for bringing about those side effects.

A usual way of drawing the distinction in medical practice is to characterise the hoped-for result of the treatment as its direct effect, and any unwanted or redundant effects as side effects. So, for example, the degree to which it diminishes pain is the direct effect of an analgesic, and any consequent drowsiness or toxicity a side effect. However, those who administer the analgesic remain responsible for the drowsiness and the toxicity, and will be justified in producing these effects along with the reduction in pain only if, all things considered, the reduction is worth having at the cost of the side effects.

Equally, Jonathan Glover has doubted the analytical and moral propriety of deciding whether to provide life-saving treatment by reference to whether it can be regarded as ordinary or extraordinary:

Glover, J, *Causing Death and Saving Lives*, 1977, Harmondsworth: Penguin, pp 195–97:

The distinction drawn between ordinary and extraordinary means of saving life is not based on the line between what is and is not medically orthodox, but on a cluster of features clearly supposed to be relevant to the question: do the likely results justify the drawbacks of the methods?

In discussions of this distinction, aspects of the means relevant to whether or not they are extraordinary are said to be the degree to which they are expensive, unusual, difficult, painful or dangerous. And the extent to which the outcome is satisfactory is also thought relevant to assessing the 'ordinariness' of the means: it is sometimes suggested that, where the means have many of the drawbacks listed, they are not ordinary if their outcome is to leave the patient severely disabled or a heavy burden on his family.

The trouble with this distinction (whatever its virtues as a rough and ready rule for doctors) is that it tries to do too much at once. The decision about the 'ordinariness' of the means involves assessing how worthwhile the life saved will be, assessing the side effects on the family and the cost in effort and money, and then in the light of all this making an overall assessment of the desirability of the life-saving project. So a stand has to be taken on a number of the largest questions about relative priorities before an answer can be given about ordinariness. It is clear both that there is much room for disagreement about answers here and that to present this cluster of questions as though they were a single one, and almost a technical one concerning 'means' at that, is highly misleading.

The confusion of thought involved in this way of presenting the questions can be seen by looking at those of the factors usually cited that really are to do with the means. We are supposed to assess the extent to which the means are expensive, unusual, difficult, painful or dangerous. The obvious question is what 'unusual' is doing in this list. It seems either redundant or undesirable. For, if the unusual treatment is expensive, difficult, painful or dangerous, we can object to it already on those grounds. But where an effective treatment is cheap, easy, painless and risk-free, only someone whose conventionality verges on dementia will object to it because of its being unusual.

Those who ask whether the outcome will be a high enough chance of a life good enough to justify the pain, or the cost in time, effort or money involved in some life-saving procedure, are asking the unavoidable and central question. What is important is to face this as involving decisions about priorities, and not to slur it over in a way which implies that the answer depends on how often the techniques are used.

Quality of life

Philosophers such as Glover and Harris argue that, in making decisions about ending life, we should be prepared to deploy overt quality of life considerations. Human life is no longer to be regarded as possessing intrinsic value *per se*; rather, what makes life valuable is, crudely, the life-holder's capacity for pleasurable states of consciousness. As Kuhse notes, this value is enhanced where the individual in question is a person with a sense of existing over time and capable of valuing their existence:

Kuhse, H, *The Sanctity-of-Life Doctrine in Medicine*, 1987, Oxford: Clarendon, pp 211–14:

… what is it that gives value to human life, but not – or not to the same degree – to the lives of other living things? Two answers are possible. The first answer is that human life has sanctity simply because it is human life, that is, because it is the life of a member of the species *Homo sapiens*. The second answer is that human life has special value because humans are self-aware, rational, autonomous, purposeful, moral beings, with hopes, ambitions, life purposes, ideals, and so on … Any of these qualities, or a combination of them, could serve as a basis for a moral distinction between human beings and lettuces or chickens. That such distinguishing qualities are needed is clear: for if the value of life were based on 'mere life', rather than on one or more of the above characteristics, then every life including the earthworm's or the lettuce's would be equally valuable.

It is not difficult to see that the second answer does point to a morally relevant difference between some lives and others. For example, it is quite plausible to hold that the life of a self-aware, rational, purposeful being that sees itself as existing over time is more valuable than the life of an entity or being who lacks these characteristics. But if one takes this approach, then one is not saying that human life has sanctity, but rather that rationality, the capacity to be self-aware, moral or purposeful, and so on, have 'sanctity'. Of course, one may still hold ... that human life has sanctity or special worth, but only in so far as it is a precondition for rationality, purposiveness, or whatever else one takes the valuable characteristic to be. One would not, on this view, be able to argue that the lives of all members of the human species have special value – for example, the lives of the irreversibly comatose, or the lives of severely brain-damaged new-born infants. The second approach, then, does not give us a reason for preserving all human lives, and cannot serve as the basis for the view that all human lives, irrespective of their quality or kind, are equally valuable ...

This conclusion should, in my view ... be applied to decision-making in the practice of medicine. What is important is not that a patient is human (and therefore should have her life sustained). Rather, we must ask questions about the quality and kind of the patient's life ...

Quality of life and interests

I start with the assumption that conscious life has value because it enables the existence of pleasurable states of consciousness. Whilst the existence of pleasurable states is not the only value to which human life gives rise, it will be agreed, I think, that it is at least a value that morality ought to take into account. In other words, I am suggesting that life is not an intrinsic good, not a good in itself, but rather a means to something else – for example, pleasurable states of consciousness.

If we were thus to agree that the value of life is not in life *qua* life ('mere life'), but rather has its locus in the value it has for the individual concerned, then it would follow that life is not an unconditional good, but good only in so far as it is of value to its possessor. This means that not all life is equally valuable, as the sanctity-of-life view suggests, nor is it, as I want to suggest, always inviolable. To the extent that we can all envisage situations where we would choose death for ourselves rather than continue living, there will also be situations where any morality based on the Golden Rule or the principle of universalisability would direct that a moral agent take the life of another rather than preserve it ...

As the last sentence of the above passage makes clear, those who take a quality of life approach to euthanasia do not distinguish, other things being equal (that is, leaving aside possible policy reasons of a consequentialist nature, see p 641, below), between active and passive measures designed to terminate life. A positive act of killing, for example, by lethal injection, is regarded as on a par with passively allowing death to occur by withholding treatment: in both cases, what is important is the quality of the life in question.

The qualified sanctity of life principle

We now turn to a position which may be regarded as a compromise between the sanctity and quality of life approaches. This 'qualified' sanctity doctrine agrees with the fully fledged sanctity approach that there is something special about human life, such that it is not reducible to the sum of the life-holder's states of consciousness. The respect due to such life is reflected in a (virtual) prohibition on active steps by third parties, including doctors, to terminate it. On the other hand, the doctrine is more relaxed about allowing quality of life considerations to determine when third parties need not act to prolong life.

It is this position which has been adopted by the English courts:

Airedale NHS Trust v Bland [1993] 1 All ER 821

Hoffmann LJ: In my view the choice which the law makes must reassure people that the courts do have full respect for life, but that they do not pursue the principle to the point at which it has become almost empty of any real content and when it involves the sacrifice of other important values such as human dignity and freedom of choice. I think that such reassurance can be provided by a decision, properly explained, to allow Anthony Bland to die ... Is this answer affected by the proposed manner of his death? Some might say that as he is going to die, it does not matter how. Why wait for him to expire for lack of food or be carried off by an untreated infection? Would it not be more humane simply to give him a lethal injection? No one in this case is suggesting that Anthony Bland should be given a lethal injection. But there is concern about ceasing to supply food as against, for example, ceasing to treat an infection with antibiotics. Is there any real distinction? In order to come to terms with our intuitive feelings about whether there is a distinction, I must start by considering why most of us would be appalled if he was given a lethal injection. It is, I think, connected with our view that the sanctity of life entails its inviolability by an outsider. Subject to exceptions like self-defence, human life is inviolate even if the person in question has consented to its violation. That is why although suicide is not a crime, assisting someone to commit suicide is. It follows that, even if we think Anthony Bland would have consented, we would not be entitled to end his life by a lethal injection.

On the other hand, we recognise that, one way or another, life must come to an end. We do not impose on outsiders an unqualified duty to do everything possible to prolong life as long as possible. I think that the principle of inviolability explains why, although we accept that in certain cases it is right to allow a person to die (and the debate so far has been over whether this is such a case) we hold without qualification that no one may introduce an external agency with the intention of causing death.

This approach was subsequently affirmed by the House of Lords in the same case, although not without a degree of soul searching:

Lord Goff: I must however stress, at this point, that the law draws a crucial distinction between cases in which a doctor decides not to provide, or to continue to provide, for his patient treatment or care which could or might prolong his life, and those in which he decides, for example by administering a lethal drug, actively to bring his patient's life to an end ... [T]he former may be lawful, either because the doctor is giving effect to his patient's wishes by withholding the treatment or care, or even in certain circumstances in which ... the patient is incapacitated from stating whether or not he gives his consent. But it is not lawful for a doctor to administer a drug to his patient to bring about his death, even though that course is prompted by a humanitarian desire to end his suffering, however great that suffering may be: see *R v Cox* (1992) unreported, 18 September [now reported at (1992) 12 BMLR 38]. So to act is to cross the Rubicon which runs between on the one hand the care of the living patient and on the other hand euthanasia – actively causing his death to avoid or to end his suffering. Euthanasia is not lawful at common law. It is of course well known that there are many responsible members of our society who believe that euthanasia should be made lawful; but that result could, I believe, only be achieved by legislation which expresses the democratic will that so fundamental a change should be made in our law, and can, if enacted, ensure that such legalised killing can only be carried out subject to appropriate supervision and control.

Lord Browne-Wilkinson: Finally, the conclusion I have reached will appear to some to be almost irrational. How can it be lawful to allow a patient to die slowly, though painlessly, over a period of weeks from lack of food but unlawful to produce his immediate death by a lethal injection, thereby saving his family from yet another ordeal to add to the tragedy that has already struck them? I find it difficult to find a moral answer to that question. But it is undoubtedly the law and nothing I have said casts doubt on the proposition that the doing of a positive act with the intention of ending life is and remains murder.

(For the full facts of the *Bland* case, and further consideration of the House of Lords' judgment, see p 675 below.)

The acts/omissions distinction

Whether the law's position is in fact coherent turns upon the tenability of the acts/omissions distinction: is there a morally significant distinction between, say, a doctor who gives a lethal injection to a neonate in his care which suffers from severe spina bifida, and a doctor who omits to give such an infant life-saving antibiotics in the face of an infection? This question was the subject of a debate between John Lorber, a Sheffield paediatrician who pioneered a policy of 'selective treatment' for such neonates in the early 1970s, and the philosopher, John Harris:

Harris, J, *The Value of Life,* **1985, London: Routledge & Kegan Paul, pp 33–39:**

Selective treatment of severely handicapped children is calculated to result in their deaths. I am thinking particularly of the management of children with severe spina bifida. Such a policy has been justified on the hypothesis that it is reasonable to conclude that the child would be better off dead. This paradoxical sounding conclusion means simply that it is judged to be in the child's best interests to die. I am assuming that the children in question are too young, or too severely handicapped, to be themselves consulted. I assume also that this sort of judgment, while difficult to make, is unproblematic in that we can all imagine many cases in which life is so intolerable, so painful, so miserable, so difficult and so utterly without reward, that we would not wish to live such a life and that it is reasonable to suppose that no one would. I assume also that severe spina bifida is such a case.

What is, however, highly problematic is the judgment that it is morally preferable to withhold treatment from such children so that they die slowly, rather than to kill them quickly and painlessly. Since 'selective treatment' in this context usually means not treating and often not feeding either, I will use the term 'selective non-treatment' to refer to this procedure ...

The tragedy is, of course, that these children or their families should suffer unnecessarily for even one month. Lorber sees this and records that 'it is painful to see such infants gradually fading away over a number of weeks or months when everybody hopes for a speedy end'. Lorber's motives are of the highest, he wants to save children and their families as much suffering as in conscience he can, and he has been courageous in pioneering selective non-treatment which is more economical of suffering and of resources than is the active treatment of severe spina bifida. It is therefore particularly poignant that he believes it right to stop short of killing and particularly worthwhile examining his arguments for so doing ...

The argument from brutalisation

This argument has two parts which are stated in two sentences, 'active euthanasia may brutalise the person who carries it out ... It would be wrong for a doctor to order his junior or his nurses to carry out such a task if he cannot bring himself to do it'. To 'brutalise' in this context is, I suppose, to render individuals more insensitive to the pain and suffering of others and more careless of or callous about the value of their lives. Evidence of brutalisation would be very hard to find and Lorber cites none. But what we have to balance here surely is a remote and imponderable danger of sensitive medical staff becoming 'brutalised' to an unknown (but perhaps insignificant) degree, against real and present pain, suffering and distress to the patients, their loving ones, and the medical staff who have to preside over their slow demise. We must also take into account the equally probable brutalising effect of taking responsibility for a slow and distressing rather than a quick and painless end. In the absence of any evidence, it is plausible to suppose that the responsibility of bringing about a slow and distressing death would be more rather than less brutalising than would a quick and merciful killing ...

The argument from lack of consent

'I strongly disagree with active euthanasia', Lorber states, 'especially for babies and children, who cannot possibly ask for it or give their considered consent'. Consent is worrying, but it is no more worrying for active euthanasia in the cases under consideration, than it is for selective non-treatment. As we have seen, selective non-treatment is intended to result in death and it does, and those who die cannot possibly ask for it or give their considered consent.

The slippery slope argument

> It would be impossible to formulate legislation, however humane are the intentions, that could not be abused by the unscrupulous. There have been plenty of examples in the past, especially in Hitler's Germany. Few just or compassionate persons would wish to give such a dangerous legal power to any individual or group of people.

There are two points that need to be made here. The first is again that Lorber and others already have this power, they decide to act so as to bring about the speedy deaths of their patients and they are very successful. Whatever the dangers of legislation are, it must surely be possible to make them less than those that already exist without specific legislation. The power is awesome but it is already exercised. The second point is about the spectre of Hitler and Nazism. By raising it, Lorber invites us to see the difference between active and passive euthanasia as the difference between humane medical practice in a civilised society and the first step on the road to the holocaust. But the Nazi euthanasia programme was nothing like the possibilities we are considering. Under the Nazis euthanasia was simply one way of exterminating those racially or politically beyond moral consideration. And the Nazis were not short of other ways to achieve the same ends. It is precisely because we care about spina bifida children, precisely because we are in no doubt that they must not suffer, that we are concerned about what it is in their best interests to do. The spectre of Nazism offers no analogy at all and so only fogs the issues.

We must again remind ourselves that doctors already take decisions which result in death with no legal or publicly debated safeguards. If we do not cry 'Nazism' it is simply because we know there is no analogy and we know that all concerned are concerned only about the welfare of their patients. But if we fear even the slimmest chance of abuse, we should take care that all decisions in these areas are taken in the open with the widest possible public debate and scrutiny.

The last door argument

The argument here is that active euthanasia closes the last door on an individual's life whereas 'No treatment with normal nursing care is a safeguard against wrong diagnosis ... If an infant's condition is not as grave as was thought, he will live and he can then be given optimal care'. But this is just not true on Lorber's own account of the treatment. If a child selected for non-treatment contracts an infection and dies because it is not given antibiotics or, if it requires resuscitation which is not given and it dies, there will be no opportunity to discover whether the diagnosis was wrong or not. So this 'safeguard' is hit and miss at best. If the child *per* almost *impossible* lives, we may find reason to say the diagnosis was wrong, but if the child dies we cannot say the diagnosis was right unless the non-treatment played no role at all in the death, for otherwise the diagnosis is self-fulfilling. Whether closing a particular door on life chances is closing the last door will be a question of fact in each case. If the child dies of an untreated infection, then the withholding of the antibiotic drugs was in fact the closing of the last door, just as the administering of a lethal injection would be ...

The argument from self-deception

One argument that is sometimes advanced is the suggestion that parents and relatives of severely handicapped children would not accept or consent to anything resembling killing, and so if doctors are to be able to recommend what they see as the most humane course, such a recommendation or, if that is too strong a term, such a possible course of treatment would be useless if it were always rejected by those whose consent is judged necessary. But this, even if true, should not prevent us from seeing clearly what the most humane course of action is and advocating its acceptance. Unless we do so those concerned will continue to deceive themselves as to the reality of what they are doing, or consenting to have done, and will continue to choose a programme which involves weeks and months of avoidable suffering. And we should be clear that it is self-deception unless it can be unequivocally demonstrated that one procedure is of different moral quality to the other. The only palpable differences demonstrated by Lorber are that non-treatment takes longer to bring about death than would active euthanasia and is minimally less certain to result in death. And both these features seem to count against rather than in favour of selective non-treatment, given the reasons which justify its being undertaken at all.

Indeed self-deception is sometimes advanced as itself constituting the moral difference between active and passive euthanasia. The argument here is that it is only because the medical staff and the relatives of the children are able to protect themselves from full awareness of what they are doing that they are able to bring themselves to do what they judge to be morally required by the circumstances. Here the idea that they are only 'letting nature take its course' allows them to distance themselves from the death of the child and fit their part in events more comfortably into their conception of the medical role.

There is a terrible irony here in that the whole practice of medicine might be described as a comprehensive attempt to frustrate the course of nature, of which disease is after all a part, and to prevent 'nature' from killing people in its usual extravagant fashion. There is undoubtedly a widespread, but equally undoubtedly an irrational, respect for what is natural or part of the course of nature. Famines, floods, droughts, storms are all natural and all disastrous. We only, and rightly, want the natural when it's good for us. What is natural is morally inert and progress-dependent. It was only natural for people to die of infected wounds before antibiotics were available and it is only natural for spina bifida children to die if their condition is inoperable, but it is not natural if they are selected for non-treatment, when with full treatment they would live.

It is also perhaps worth emphasising that if we are ever to feel confident that the right thing is for the child to die in these circumstances then we should face the decision under its most stark and 'non-distanced' description. One might say that there is a moral requirement that in matters of such importance where the lives of others are at stake, we should be absolutely sure that we have faced squarely the full import of what we are doing. Whereas if we disguise the facts from ourselves and others by various distancing strategies, we may permanently shield ourselves both from full awareness of what we are about and from the possibility of thinking through all the implications of such consequential decisions.

Equally, James Rachels has produced a pair of well known, and colourful, hypothetical cases to deny the relevance of whether death is caused by action or inaction:

Rachels, J, *The End of Life*, 1986, Oxford: OUP, p 112:

Smith stands to gain a large inheritance if anything should happen to his six year old cousin. One evening while the child is taking his bath, Smith sneaks into the bathroom and drowns the child, and then arranges things so it will look like an accident. No one is the wiser, and Smith gets his inheritance.

Jones also stands to gain if anything should happen to his six year old cousin. Like Smith, Jones sneaks in planning to drown the child in his bath. However, just as he enters the bathroom Jones sees the child slip, hit his head, and fall face down in the water. Jones is delighted; he stands by, ready to push the child's head under if necessary, but it is not necessary. With only a little thrashing about, the child drowns all by himself, 'accidentally', as Jones watches and does nothing. No one is the wiser, and Jones gets his inheritance.

It is certainly true that in many cases the intention of an agent and the consequences of his conduct, in the context of bringing about the death of another individual, will be the same whether active or passive means are adopted. However, a residual difference can be found in the causal relationship between the agent and the death:

Stauch, M, 'Causal authorship and the equality principle: a defence of the acts/omissions distinction in euthanasia' (2000) 26 JME 237:

... [G]iven their negative nature, before omissions can figure in a causal set sufficient for some harm, the risk of such harm, generally in the form of a positive cause (as distinct from mere background conditions), must already be present. The failure to provide someone with medical assistance cannot by itself cause that person's death: he must first be in need of life-saving treatment through illness or otherwise. In fact, the agent who fails, through omission, to prevent death is allowing the completion (his non-intervention is *necessary* for this) of a pre-existing causal set for that outcome. By contrast, the agent who causes death by an act, for example by administering a lethal injection, typically instigates a causal set for the same result: his act is *sufficient* to produce it in conjunction with normal background conditions alone.

Profound consequences

This difference can sometimes have profound consequences in determining the individual authorship of outcomes. In particular, in the case of failure to provide medical treatment, the 'authorship' of an omitting agent lapses in the absence of a socially imposed *duty to act*. The same is not true of an agent who acts in the absence of a *duty not to act*. For example, consider a doctor, W, whose patient, X, is being maintained on a ventilator and will die if such support is discontinued. As we have seen, if W removes the support and the patient dies, then to hold W responsible requires us to ascribe causal status to his omission, while regarding the concurrent omissions of all other agents as (collectively) a mere negative background condition. Usually this is easily done: W alone is the doctor involved with the responsibility and opportunity to keep X alive. Suppose, however, that the quality of X's life was so poor that we believed W should be released from his duty to treat. There is no longer any reason to distinguish between his omission and those of other agents: all are actual omissions, which permit the completion of causal set for X's death. Secondly, imagine that law reform occurs, such that active euthanasia becomes acceptable and normal, and that another doctor, Y thereupon gives his patient, Z (who, like X, has a very poor quality of life), a lethal injection. Let us suppose further that, if he had not done so, some other agent would have taken it upon himself to give Z the injection instead. Here, by contrast with W in the first example, Y remains the author of Z's death: his act was the only actual member of a causal set sufficient for Z's death. The 'act' of any other agent here remains only *hypothetical*.

Arguably, the causal authorship of the doctor who actively kills his patient makes his conduct problematic in a sense not shared (at least where the duty to treat has ceased) by the doctor whose non-intervention results in his patient's death. The problem resides in the first doctor's breaching of the 'equality principle':

Stauch, M, 'Causal authorship and the equality principle: a defence of the acts/omissions distinction in euthanasia' (2000) 26 JME 237:

According to [the equality principle], the life of each individual has an equal claim to a minimum respect by possessing irreducible value (ie, a value that cannot be fully cashed out in terms of the life-holder's own states of consciousness, pleasurable or otherwise). An agent who engages in active euthanasia (even at the behest of the 'victim') fails to show this respect, for, in assuming authorship over that other's death, he automatically accords his own life an ontological priority: he draws upon his own resources (for which his life is, of course, a precondition) in such a way as to extinguish the life of the other. This breaching of the equality principle amounts, it is submitted, to a prima facie reason against any killing, and one which persists even if, in all the circumstances, we are disposed morally to excuse a *particular* killing. Consider, for example, the following hypothetical case proposed by Dan Brock [in *Life and Death*, 1993, Cambridge: CUP]:

> A patient is dying from terminal cancer, undergoing great suffering that cannot be relieved without so sedating him that he is unable to relate in any way to others. This patient prepared an advance directive at an early stage of his disease indicating that in circumstances like this he wanted to have his life ended either by direct means or by withdrawing life-sustaining treatment. In a recent lucid moment he reaffirmed the directive. The attending physician and the patient's family are in agreement that the patient's desire to die ought now to be granted.

Brock offers two alternative conclusions to this case. In the first, the man's wife places a pillow over his face and asphyxiates him while he is asleep. In the second, the man develops breathing problems (while unconscious) and needs placing on a respirator to prolong his life. His wife, who is present and knows this, fails to alert the medical staff and the man dies. Brock goes on to ask if there is 'any reason why what the wife does in the first instance is morally (as opposed to legally) worse or different to what she does in the second instance?' The answer (and remember we are not being asked whether, in the first instance as well, we should not morally excuse her action) is surely simply that in the first instance, by assuming authorship over the man's death, she infringes the equality principle. In the second instance she does not.

Euthanasia and the state

Leaving aside the question of any moral difference, it is apparent that policy arguments also play an important part in the law's adherence to the acts/omissions distinction. Jonathan Glover has commented on this point as follows:

Glover, J, *Causing Death and Saving Lives*, 1977, Harmondsworth: Penguin, pp 186–88:

One [objection to abandoning the distinction] is the suggestion that, if voluntary [active] euthanasia were known to be an option, people might put pressure on their burdensome relations to volunteer. It is hard to evaluate this objection. It seems to me rather implausible, but perhaps I am being too optimistic. In advance of trying a voluntary euthanasia policy, we do not know how people would behave. (Is there any evidence of such pressures in a country where voluntary euthanasia is not illegal?)

A related objection is that, even without pressure being brought by relations, people who felt they were a burden might think that, although they had lives worth living, they ought to volunteer for euthanasia. This gains some support from the fact that there have been cases of suicide by people whose motive was a reluctance to be a burden on others. Part of the difficulty of evaluating this objection is that it is hard to predict how widespread such feelings would be. Another difficulty is the more fundamental uncertainty about whether it is right in such a case to override the person's autonomy. Where he is wrong in thinking he is a burden, he should not be given euthanasia, but should be persuaded of the truth. (It seems possible that, with so much talk of old people almost as though they were members of another species, many old people who are loved and wanted members of a family do have unnecessary fears that they are a nuisance to the others.) But there are sometimes cases where a person who is old or ill does put a great strain on a family, and where he sees this and would rather die than have the situation continue, it is not obvious that a paternalist refusal to carry out his wishes is justified.

Another possible bad side effect of voluntary euthanasia concerns the treatment of dying patients. Is there a danger that allowing such a policy would hamper the development of the kind of terminal care which would make euthanasia unnecessary? The policy of total rejection of euthanasia may have the advantage of strengthening people's commitment to developing more humane and imaginative forms of terminal care. Certainly some of the most sensitive and impressive work here, such as that of Cicely Saunders and others, has been done in the context of a principled refusal to comply with euthanasia requests. But it is not clear that voluntary euthanasia would seem an alternative rather than a supplement to better terminal care. A hospital with a voluntary euthanasia policy could still have a staff that did all they could to make euthanasia requests unnecessary. The view that voluntary euthanasia would be accepted as an easy alternative to improved care underrates the deep revulsion against killing which most people have, and which often seems especially strong among those in professions like nursing. (Perhaps this is again too optimistic. Is there any clear evidence relevant to this?)

We shall return to such policy concerns later in this chapter when we touch upon the question of law reform in this area.

ACTIVE EUTHANASIA

Background

As we have seen, the law, in holding to its 'qualified sanctity of life' position, draws a fundamental distinction between a positive act which is intended to kill ('active euthanasia') and an omission to act which, equally intentionally, allows the patient's death to occur ('passive euthanasia'). Whereas the former is prohibited in virtually all cases, the latter is permissible in a somewhat wider set of circumstances. This attitude may be roughly summed up by reference to the Victorian poet AH Clough's sardonic lines: ' … thou shalt not kill, but need'st not strive officiously to keep alive.'

An example of the law's response to active euthanasia, which also illustrates the point that, generally, the killer's motive in performing the act will be irrelevant, is provided by the case of *R v Cox* (1992) 12 BMLR 38:

R v Cox (1992) 12 BMLR 38, Winchester CC (Ognall J)

Dr Cox injected a 70 year old patient, Lillian Boyes, with the lethal poison potassium chloride, after she pleaded with him to put her out of her misery; she was *in extremis*, suffering from the terminal stages of rheumatoid arthritis, and her pain was beyond the control of analgesic drugs. He was charged only with her attempted murder on the basis that, given her condition, Mrs Boyes' death at that time could in fact have been due to her illness (thus, pre-empting the operation of the poison):

Ognall J (directing the jury): This is a sad and testing case for all of us involved. The reason is obvious. A distinguished professional man of unblemished reputation and character is now on trial, and the allegation is that he behaved in a way which is a clear repudiation of a doctor's lifelong professional duty, namely to save and not to take life.

Even the prosecution case acknowledged that he did so only because he was prompted by deep distress at Lillian Boyes' condition; by a belief that she was totally beyond recall and by an intense compassion for her fearful suffering. Nonetheless, members of the jury, if he injected her with potassium chloride for the primary purpose of killing her, of hastening her death, he is guilty of the offence charged. You are therefore tested to the utmost, members of the jury, for you must do your best to put emotion to one side. You must try this case impartially and objectively. You 12 ladies and gentlemen represent the public interest in ensuring that, where it is surely proved, no man of whatever situation or in whatever circumstance can place himself above the law …

And so to the charge, ladies and gentlemen. The prosecution allege that Dr Cox attempted to murder Lillian Boyes. They say that be deliberately injected her with potassium chloride in a quantity and in a manner which had no therapeutic purpose and no capacity to afford her any relief from pain and suffering whilst alive. They submit that Dr Cox must have known that, and that, in truth, his conduct in giving that injection was prompted solely, and certainly primarily, by the purpose of bringing her life to an immediate end …

If it is proved that Dr Cox injected Lillian Boyes with potassium chloride in circumstances which make you sure that by that act he intended to kill her, then he is guilty of the offence of attempted murder. From the earliest stage it has been admitted that he did indeed inject her intravenously with two ampoules of undiluted potassium chloride, which his note in the medical records clearly indicates …

You must understand, members of the jury, that in this highly emotional situation, neither the express wishes of the patient nor of her loving and devoted family can affect the position. Lillian Boyes was fully entitled to decline any further active medical treatment and to specify that thereafter she should only receive painkillers. She did that on 11 August. That was her absolute right and the doctors and nursing staff were obliged to respect her wishes. A young senior house officer, Dr Byrne, gave evidence before you. He told you that on that day when Lillian Boyes had said 'no more active intervention, please, only painkillers from now on', he had said to her, in effect: 'Thus far and no further. We will stop your positive medical treatment, we will confine ourselves to giving you only analgesics, only painkillers, but we cannot accede to your request that we give you something to kill you.'

Dr Cox was convicted of attempted murder.

The separation of a non-viable conjoined twin

Recently, however, an inroad was made into the distinction between active and passive euthanasia to the extent that, in one particular set of circumstances, the Court of Appeal sanctioned radical surgery whose inevitable consequence was to terminate a patient's life. This step was taken in the well known case of the conjoined twins, *Re A (Children) (Conjoined Twins: Surgical Separation)* [2001] Fam 147:

Re A (Children) (Conjoined Twins: Surgical Separation) [2001] Fam 147, CA (Ward, Brooke and Robert Walker LJJ)

Jodie and Mary were conjoined twin girls who were born joined at the pelvis. The medical evidence was that Jodie sustained the life of Mary (whose own heart and lungs did not function) by circulating oxygenated blood through a common artery, and that, if they were not separated, Jodie's heart would eventually fail and they would both die within a few months. The hospital wished to perform separation surgery, which would enable Jodie to lead a relatively normal life (though Mary would die almost immediately), but the parents refused to consent on religious grounds. In the High Court, Johnson J granted a declaration that the hospital could lawfully carry out the surgery in both twins' best interests, and suggested that the procedure (from Mary's point of view) could be likened to the withholding of hydration and nutrition. The parents appealed:

> **Robert Walker LJ**: Every member of the court has been deeply troubled by this case, but we have to decide it in accordance with the principles of existing law as we perceive them to apply to this unprecedented situation. I will summarise my conclusions as to the applicable principles as simply as I can.
>
> (i) The feelings of the twins' parents are entitled to great respect, especially so far as they are based on religious convictions. But as the matter has been referred to the court the court cannot escape the responsibility of deciding the matter to the best of its judgment as to the twins' best interests.
>
> (ii) The judge erred in law in equating the proposed surgical operation with the discontinuance of medical treatment (as by disconnecting a heart–lung machine). Therefore the Court of Appeal must form its own view.
>
> (iii) Mary has a right to life, under the common law of England (based as it is on Judaeo-Christian foundations) and under the European Convention on Human Rights. It would be unlawful to kill Mary intentionally, that is to undertake an operation with the primary purpose of killing her.

(iv)   But Jodie also has a right to life.

(v)   Every human being's right to life carries with it, as an intrinsic part of it, rights of bodily integrity and autonomy – the right to have one's own body whole and intact and (on reaching an age of understanding) to take decisions about one's own body.

(vi)   By a rare and tragic mischance, Mary and Jodie have both been deprived of the bodily integrity and autonomy which is their natural right. There is a strong presumption that an operation to separate them would be in the best interests of each of them.

(vii) In this case the purpose of the operation would be to separate the twins and so give Jodie a reasonably good prospect of a long and reasonably normal life. Mary's death would not be the purpose of the operation, although it would be its inevitable consequence. The operation would give her, even in death, bodily integrity as a human being. She would die, not because she was intentionally killed, but because her own body cannot sustain her life.

(viii) Continued life, whether long or short, would hold nothing for Mary except possible pain and discomfort, if indeed she can feel anything at all.

(ix)   The proposed operation would therefore be in the best interests of each of the twins. The decision does not require the court to value one life above another.

(x)   The proposed operation would not be unlawful. It would involve the positive act of invasive surgery and Mary's death would be foreseen as an inevitable consequence of an operation which is intended, and is necessary, to save Jodie's life. But Mary's death would not be the purpose or intention of the surgery, and she would die because tragically her body, on its own, is not and never has been viable.

I would therefore dismiss this appeal.

The Court of Appeal's judgment runs to over 100 pages in total, and the three Lord Justices, while agreeing in the result, justify their conclusions in different ways. Thus, whereas Robert Walker LJ (relying on the doctrine of 'double effect') suggested that the doctors who performed the operation would not intend Mary's death, both Ward and Brooke LJJ applied the criminal law approach to intention set out by the House of Lords in *R v Woollin* [1998] 4 All ER 103, and found that there would be intent.

For his part, Ward LJ thought that an argument based on self-defence could be used to justify the doctors' intervention on behalf of Jodie, but was not supported in this by Brooke or Robert Walker LJJ. Moreover, although all three members of the Court took the view that Mary's killing could be justified on the basis of the doctrine of necessity, they appear to have differed as to the precise ambit of this doctrine in the criminal law. Ward LJ, in particular, was careful to limit his decision to the particular circumstances of the case:

Ward LJ: In my judgment, the appeal must be dismissed. Lest it be thought that this decision could become authority for wider propositions, such as that a doctor, once he has determined that a patient cannot survive, can kill the patient, it is important to restate the unique circumstances for which this case is authority. They are that it must be impossible to preserve the life of X without bringing about the death of Y, that Y by his or her very continued existence will inevitably bring about the death of X within a short period of time, and that X is capable of living an independent life but Y is incapable under any circumstances, including all forms of medical intervention, of viable independent existence. As I said at the beginning of this judgment, this is a very unique case.

An extensive academic literature has been generated by the case. For a selection, see the special edition of the *Medical Law Review* (Vol 9, No 3, Autumn 2001).

Medicines which shorten life

Another, more longstanding exception exists, where it is accepted that a doctor may act in a manner that intentionally shortens his patient's life. This is through the administration of powerful analgesic (pain killing) drugs, such as morphine, which, if ingested in large doses, have the known side effect of accelerating death. The existence of this exception (that is, the fact that a doctor who prescribes such drugs to control pain, though foreseeing his patient's earlier death, will not be guilty of murder) was established in the case of *R v Bodkin Adams* [1957] Crim LR 365:

R v Bodkin Adams [1957] Crim LR 365 (Devlin J)

Dr Bodkin Adams was charged with murder after increasing the dosage of opiates for an elderly stroke patient, who left him a Rolls-Royce and a chest of silver in her will. Devlin J, commenting upon the doctor's defence that his primary purpose had been to dull the patient's sensation of pain, gave the following direction to the jury:

> **Devlin J**: ... [A] doctor who is aiding the sick and the dying [need not] calculate in minutes, or even in hours, and perhaps not in days or weeks, the effect upon a patient's life of the medicines which he administers or else be in peril of a charge of murder. If the first purpose of medicine, the restoration of health, can no longer be achieved there is still much for a doctor to do, and he is entitled to do all that is proper and necessary to relieve pain and suffering, even if the measures he takes may incidentally shorten life. That is not because there is any special defence for medical men; it is not because doctors are put into any category different from other citizens for this purpose. The law is the same for all, and what I have said to you rests simply upon this: no act is murder which does not cause death. 'Cause' means nothing philosophical or technical or scientific. It means what you 12 men and women sitting as a jury in the jury box would regard in a common sense way as the cause ... If, for example, because a doctor has done something or has omitted to do something death occurs, it can be scientifically proved – if it could – at 11 o'clock instead of 12 o'clock, or even on Monday instead of Tuesday, no people of common sense would say, 'Oh, the doctor caused her death'. They would say the cause of her death was the illness or the injury, or whatever it was, which brought her into hospital, and the proper medical treatment that is administered and that has an incidental effect of determining the exact moment of death, or may have, is not the cause of death in any sensible use of the term. But it remains the fact, and it remains the law, that no doctor, nor any man, no more in the case of the dying man than of the healthy, has the right deliberately to cut the thread of life.

The notion that, in such a case, the doctor may be regarded as not having caused the patient's death is, with respect, difficult to accept: after all, usually it is clear that 'but for' the administration of morphine, the patient would have lived somewhat longer, and nor will legal causation (in terms of foreseeability) be in issue. More recently, in the *Cox* case, Ognall J preferred to concentrate upon the doctor's intention as providing the key to his possible exculpation:

Ognall J: We all appreciate that some medical treatment, whether of a positive, therapeutic character or solely of an analgesic kind – by which I mean designed solely to alleviate pain and suffering – some treatment carries with it a serious risk to the health or even the life of the patient. Doctors are frequently confronted with, no doubt, distressing dilemmas. They have to make up their minds as to whether the risk, even to the life of their patient, attendant upon their contemplated form of treatment, is such that the risk is, or is not, medically justified. If a doctor genuinely believes that a certain course is beneficial to his patient, either therapeutically or analgesically, then even though he recognises that that course carries with it a risk to life, he is fully entitled, nonetheless, to pursue it. If in those circumstances the patient dies, nobody could possibly suggest that in that situation the doctor was guilty of murder or attempted murder.

The problem is obviously particularly acute in the case of those who are terminally ill and in considerable pain, if not agony. Such was the case of Lillian Boyes. It was plainly Dr Cox's duty to do all that was medically possible to alleviate her pain and suffering, even if the course adopted carried with it an obvious risk that, as a side effect of that treatment, her death would be rendered likely or even certain.

There can be no doubt that the use of drugs to reduce pain and suffering will often be fully justified notwithstanding that it will, in fact, hasten the moment of death. What can never be lawful is the use of drugs with purpose of hastening the moment of death.

And so, in deciding Dr Cox's intention, the distinction the law requires you to draw is this. Is it proved that in giving that injection, in that form and in those amounts, Dr Cox's primary purpose was to bring the life of Lillian Boyes to an end?

If it was, then he is guilty. If, on the other hand, it was, or may have been, his primary purpose in acting as he did to alleviate her pain and suffering, then he is not guilty. That is so even though he recognised that, in fulfilling that primary purpose, he might or even would hasten the moment of her death ...

Of course, members of the jury, to hasten the death not merely alleviates suffering, it bring it to an end. A dead person suffers no more. But that is not what I mean by alleviation of suffering. Alleviation of suffering means that easing of it for so long as the patient survives; not the easing of it in the throes of, and because of, deliberate purpose killing.

The apparent reliance of this way of regarding the *Bodkin Adams* defence on the principle of double effect (which, as we saw above, has the support of advocates of the full sanctity of life position, but is rejected by most other commentators), has given rise to much debate. It is suggested that the defence is best viewed as a special dispensation to the doctor engaged in the palliative care of a terminally ill patient. Provided he is exercising *bona fide* clinical judgment in easing the dying process, the law will exceptionally limit its focus to the 'narrow intention' of such a doctor, that is, the desire to relieve pain; it is prepared to overlook the fact that, in foreseeing the patient's earlier death, the doctor intends the death in the 'wide' sense sufficient to establish criminal *mens rea* in most other contexts.

In a case brought in 1997 by a woman, Annie Lindsell, dying from motor neurone disease, Sir Stephen Brown, President of the Family Division of the High Court, confirmed that in his view the same principle will protect doctors who prescribe such analgesics to ease their patients' mental torment (although this was not made the subject of a formal declaration: see *Lindsell v Holmes, The Guardian*, 29 October 1997).

Assisted suicide

In respect of patients who are not already dying, or though dying are not in pain, the doctor is clearly not permitted to do anything that directly shortens life. How far, though, may he furnish the means to allow such patients to kill themselves? It is evident that a doctor who acts thus is not guilty of murder; even one who, say, in the case of a paralysed patient, places a lethal pill in the latter's mouth will (provided the patient knows what is in the pill) at most have assisted in the patient's suicide. The reason is that the latter's voluntary and informed action of swallowing the pill operates as a *novus actus interveniens* which breaks the chain of causation between the doctor's previous act of providing the pill and the patient's death. Instead, the doctor will be guilty of an offence contrary to s 2 of the Suicide Act 1961:

> **2 Criminal liability for complicity in another's suicide**
>
> (1) A person who aids, abets, counsels or procures the suicide of another, or an attempt by another to commit suicide, shall be liable on conviction on indictment to imprisonment for a term not exceeding 14 years.
>
> (2) If on the trial of an indictment for murder or manslaughter it is proved that the accused aided, abetted, counselled or procured the suicide of the person in question, the jury may find him guilty of that offence.
>
> ...
>
> (4) No proceedings shall be instituted for an offence under this section except by or with the consent of the Director of Public Prosecutions.

The ambit of the offence under s 2 of the 1961 Act was tested in the case of *AG v Able* [1984] 1 All ER 277, in which certain members of the Voluntary Euthanasia Society were prosecuted in connection with the distribution of a suicide manual entitled 'A guide to self-deliverance'. Woolf J held that an offence would be committed if, in a particular case, it was known to the defendants that the recipient planned to use the manual to commit suicide (and the latter did so use it).

Recently, in *R (On the Application of Pretty) v DPP* [2002] 1 All ER 1, the House of Lords was required to rule on the compatibility of the provisions of the Suicide Act 1961 with the rights of the would-be suicide under the European Convention on Human Rights (ECHR):

R (On the Application of Pretty) v DPP [2002] 1 All ER 1, HL (Lords Bingham, Steyn, Hope, Hobhouse and Scott)

Dianne Pretty, aged 42, was suffering from the terminal stages of motor neurone disease. Rather than await death through suffocation or starvation (the natural outcome of the disease), she wished to commit suicide, but, due to her condition, needed help to do so. Her husband was willing to assist her, provided that the Director of Public Prosecutions undertook not to prosecute him under s 2 of the Suicide Act 1961. When the DPP refused to give any such undertaking, Mrs Pretty brought an action in judicial review proceedings, challenging the legality of the refusal in the light of the Human Rights Act (HRA) 1998:

Lord Steyn: This is the first occasion on which the House of Lords has been asked to consider the question of assisted suicide by a terminally ill individual. She suffers from motor neurone disease and she has not long to live. The specific question before the House is whether the appellant is entitled to a declaration that the Director of Public Prosecutions is obliged to undertake in advance that, if she is assisted by her husband in committing suicide, he will not be prosecuted under section 2(1) of the Suicide Act 1961. If Mrs Pretty is entitled to this relief, it follows that it may have to be granted to other terminally ill patients or patients suffering excruciating pain as a result of an incurable illness, who want to commit assisted suicide. Her case is squarely founded on the Human Rights Act 1998, which incorporated the European Convention of Human Rights into English law. For her to succeed it is not enough to show that the European Convention allows member states to legalise assisted suicide. She must establish that at least that part of section 2(1) of the 1961 Act which makes aiding or abetting suicide a crime is in conflict with her Convention rights. In other words, she must persuade the House that the European Convention compels member states of the Council of Europe to legalise assisted suicide ...

Policy grounds

If section 2 of the 1961 Act is held to be incompatible with the European Convention, a right to commit assisted suicide would not be doctor assisted and would not be subject to safeguards introduced in the Netherlands. In a valuable essay Professor Michael Freeman trenchantly observed 'A repeal of section 2 of the Suicide Act 1961, without more, would not be rational policy-making. We would need a 'Death with Dignity' Act to fill the lacuna': 'Death, dying and the Human Rights Act 1998' (1999) 52 CLP 218, at 237. That must be right. In our parliamentary democracy, and I apprehend in many member states of the Council of Europe, such a fundamental change cannot be brought about by judicial creativity. If it is to be considered at all, it requires a detailed and effective regulatory proposal. In these circumstances it is difficult to see how a process of interpretation of Convention rights can yield a result with all the necessary in-built protections. Essentially, it must be a matter for democratic debate and decision-making by legislatures.

... The specific articles

Counsel for Mrs Pretty argued that article 2 and in particular its first sentence acknowledges that it is for the individual to choose whether to live or die and that it protects her right of self-determination in relation to issues of life and death. This interpretation is not sustainable. The purpose of article 2(1) is clear. It enunciates the principle of the sanctity of life and provides a guarantee that no individual 'shall be deprived of life' by means of intentional human intervention. The interpretation now put forward is the exact opposite viz a right of Mrs Pretty to end her life by means of intentional human intervention. Nothing in the article or the jurisprudence of the European Court of Human Rights can assist Mrs Pretty's case on this article.

... The core of counsel's argument [under Art 3] is that ... the state's obligations are to take effective steps to ensure that no one shall be subjected to inhuman or degrading treatment. For my part article 3 is not engaged. The word 'treatment' must take its colour from the context in which it appears. While I would not wish to give a narrow interpretation to what may constitute degrading treatment, the concept appears singularly inapt to convey the idea that the state must guarantee to individuals a right to die with the deliberate assistance of third parties. So radical a step, infringing the sanctity of life principle, would have required far more explicit wording. But counsel argues that there is support for his argument to be found in the jurisprudence of the ECHR on the 'positive obligations' of a state to render effective the protection of article 3. For this proposition he cites the decision of the ECHR in *D v United Kingdom*

(1997) 24 EHRR 423. The case concerned the intended deportation of an individual in the final stages of an incurable disease to St Kitts where there would not be adequate treatment for the disease. The ECHR held that in the exceptional circumstances of the case the implementation of the decision to remove the individual to St Kitts would amount to inhuman treatment by the UK. Unlike *D v United Kingdom* the present case does not involve any positive action (comparable to the intended deportation) nor is there any risk of a failure to treat her properly. Instead the complaint is that the state is guilty of a failure to repeal section 2(1) of the 1961 Act. The present case plainly does not involve 'inhuman or degrading *treatment*'.

... Counsel submitted that [Art 8] explicitly recognises the principle of the personal autonomy of every individual. He argues that this principle necessarily involves a guarantee as against the state of the right to choose when and how to die. None of the decisions cited in regard to article 8 assist this argument. It must fail on the ground that the guarantee under article 8 prohibits interference with the way in which an individual leads his life and it does not relate to the manner in which he wishes to die.

... The logic of the European Convention does not justify the conclusion that the House must rule that a state is obliged to legalise assisted suicide. It does not require the state to repeal a provision such as section 2(1) of the 1961 Act. On the other hand, it is open to a democratic legislature to introduce such a measure. Our Parliament, if so minded, may therefore repeal section 2(1) and put in its place a regulated system for assisted suicide (presumably doctor assisted) with appropriate safeguards.

The European Court of Human Rights (ECtHR) in Strasbourg subsequently held that Mrs Pretty's rights under Article 8 of the ECHR were engaged (though it agreed with the House of Lords' analysis of the other Articles), but that the interference in those rights – in terms of the prohibition on assisted suicide – was justified under Article 8(2) of the ECHR. Accordingly, it dismissed her action against the UK Government: *Pretty v UK* (2002) 35 EHRR 1.

As Lord Steyn suggests, the decriminalisation of assisted suicide would have to be a matter for Parliament. However, there are few indications of political support for of such a step. The House of Lords Select Committee on Medical Ethics (1994) recommended that the current prohibition should remain, and a similar approach is evident in most other jurisdictions. In *Rodriguez v AG of British Columbia* (1993) 82 BCLR (2d) 273, Sopinka J commented on Canadian Law Reform Commission's decision to retain the crime of assisted suicide, as follows:

Sopinka J: The Law Reform Commission had discussed in the Working Paper the possibility of the decriminalisation of assisted suicide in the following terms, pp 53–54:

First of all, the prohibition in [s 241(b)] is not restricted solely to the case of the terminally ill patient, for whom we can only have sympathy, or solely to his physician or a member of his family who helps him to put an end to his suffering. The section is more general and applies to a variety of situations for which it is much more difficult to feel sympathy. Consider, for example, a recent incident, that of inciting to mass suicide. What of the person who takes advantage of another's depressed state to encourage him to commit suicide, for his own financial benefit? What of the person who, knowing an adolescent's suicidal tendencies, provides him with large enough quantities of drugs to kill him? The accomplice in these cases cannot be considered morally blameless. Nor can one conclude that the criminal law should not punish such conduct. To decriminalise completely the act of aiding, abetting or counselling suicide would therefore not be a valid legislative policy ...

It can be seen, therefore, that while the Law Reform Commission of Canada [has] great sympathy for the plight of those who wish to end their lives so as to avoid significant suffering, [it has not been] prepared to recognise that the active assistance of a third party in carrying out this desire should be condoned, even for the terminally ill. The basis for this refusal is twofold it seems – first, the active participation by one individual in the death of another is intrinsically morally and legally wrong, and second, there is no certainty that abuses can be prevented by anything less than a complete prohibition. Creating an exception for the terminally ill might therefore frustrate the purpose of the legislation of protecting the vulnerable because adequate guidelines to control abuse are difficult or impossible to develop.

Similarly, in *Washington v Glucksberg and Vacco v Quill* 117 S Ct 2258 and 2293 (1997), the US Supreme Court held that state laws prohibiting physician-assisted suicide were not unconstitutional.

Nonetheless, the issue of assisted suicide seems likely to remain current, especially given its lawfulness in certain other European countries. Recently, in *A Local Authority v Z* (2004) EWHC 2817, Hedley J discharged a local authority injunction preventing a man from taking his seriously ill and physically disabled wife to Switzerland for her suicide to be assisted there. Such an injunction, he held, was unnecessary in the light of the fact that the DPP could, if he so wished, initiate a prosecution of the husband after the event for assisting his wife's suicide. As his Lordship commented:

Hedley J: [14] ... Although it is the case that all that Mr and Mrs Z propose to do is not criminal under the law of Switzerland, it seems to me inevitable that by making arrangements and escorting Mrs Z on the flight, Mr Z will have contravened section 2(1) [of the Suicide Act 1961]. It follows that in order for Mrs Z actually to be able to carry out her decision, it will require the criminal conduct of another. That said I remind myself of sub-section (4). Although not unique, the provision is rare and is usually found where Parliament recognises that although an act may be criminal, it is not always in the public interest to prosecute in respect of it ...

[21] This case affords no basis for trying to ascertain the court's views about the rights or wrongs of suicide, assisted or otherwise. This case simply illustrates that a competent person is entitled to take their own decisions on these matters and that that person alone bears responsibility for any decision so taken. That is the essence of what some will regard as God-given freewill and what others will describe as the innate right of self-autonomy. It illustrates too that the civil court, and in this context, especially the family court, will be slow to restrain behaviour consistent with the rights of others simply because it is unlawful where adequate powers are vested in the criminal justice agencies.

PASSIVE EUTHANASIA

Background

Our concern here is with the more flexible attitude taken by the qualified sanctity of life doctrine in respect of omissions to provide life-sustaining treatment (reflected in the 'need'st not strive officiously' part of AH Clough's couplet).

A preliminary question is what conduct, in the context of providing medical care, will be regarded in law as an *omission* rather than an *act*? For example, a common means of sustaining the life of a critically ill patient in hospital is to place him on a ventilator. If, in a given case, a doctor decides that there is no hope of recovery and switches the machine off, could he not be said to have acted to bring about the patient's death? Lord Goff, however, forcefully rejected this possibility in the *Bland* case:

> **Lord Goff:** Why is it that the doctor who gives his patient a lethal injection which kills him commits an unlawful act and indeed is guilty of murder, whereas a doctor who, by discontinuing life support, allows his patient to die, may not act unlawfully – and will not do so, if he commits no breach of duty to his patient? Professor Glanville Williams has suggested (see his *Textbook of Criminal Law*, 2nd edn, 1983, p 282) that the reason is that what the doctor does when he switches off a life support machine 'is in substance not an act but an omission to struggle', and that 'the omission is not a breach of duty by the doctor, because he is not obliged to continue in a hopeless case'.
>
> I agree that the doctor's conduct in discontinuing life support can properly be categorised as an omission. It is true that it may be difficult to describe what the doctor actually does as an omission, for example where he takes some positive step to bring the life support to an end. But discontinuation of life support is, for present purposes, no different from not initiating life support in the first place. In each case, the doctor is simply allowing his patient to die in the sense that he is desisting from taking a step which might, in certain circumstances, prevent his patient from dying as a result of his pre-existing condition; and as a matter of general principle an omission such as this will not be unlawful unless it constitutes a breach of duty to the patient. I also agree that the doctor's conduct is to be differentiated from that of, for example, an interloper who maliciously switches off a life support machine because, although the interloper may perform exactly the same act as the doctor who discontinues life support, his doing so constitutes interference with the life-prolonging treatment then being administered by the doctor. Accordingly, whereas the doctor, in discontinuing life support, is simply allowing his patient to die of his pre-existing condition, the interloper is actively intervening to stop the doctor from prolonging the patient's life, and such conduct cannot possibly be categorised as an omission.

It is apparent that, for these purposes, the description of a given piece of conduct by the doctor as an *act* turns not upon a narrow criterion of voluntary physical movement, but rather upon whether what he has done amounts to an interference with the natural course of events. Whereas the doctor, in stopping life support, simply brings to a close his own previous and continuing interference in nature, the malicious interloper does interfere in (and hence 'acts' relative to) the life-sustaining regime – a sort of second 'nature' created and maintained by the doctor.

Nevertheless, it would be a serious mistake to conclude that, insofar as his conduct can be characterised as an omission, the doctor has an automatic free hand in allowing death to occur. The reason why this is not so, and the manner in which the doctor's position differs in this respect from that of the average citizen, is evident from the following passage from Lord Browne-Wilkinson's speech in *Bland*:

> **Lord Browne-Wilkinson:**
>
> **Criminal liability/murder**
>
> It is the submission of the Official Solicitor that the withdrawal of artificial feeding would constitute murder. The Official Solicitor has been criticised for using emotive language in this case. In my judgment this criticism is misplaced: much the most

difficult question is indeed whether the proposed course of action is, in law, murder notwithstanding the best motives from which everyone concerned is acting.

Murder consists of causing the death of another with intent so to do. What is proposed in the present case is to adopt a course with the intention of bringing about Anthony Bland's death. As to the element of intention or *mens rea*, in my judgment there can be no real doubt that it is present in this case: the whole purpose of stopping artificial feeding is to bring about the death of Anthony Bland.

As to the guilty act, or *actus reus*, the criminal law draws a distinction between the commission of a positive act which causes death and the omission to do an act which would have prevented death. In general an omission to prevent death is not an actus reus and cannot give rise to a conviction for murder. But where the accused was under a duty to the deceased to do the act which he omitted to do, such omission can constitute the actus reus of homicide, either murder (*R v Gibbins* (1918) 13 Cr App R 134) or manslaughter (*R v Stone* [1977] QB 354) depending upon the *mens rea* of the accused ...

It is apparent, then, that the lawfulness of passive euthanasia revolves around the question: 'When is the doctor released from his normal duty to treat?' In answering this, we shall look at the position of competent and incompetent patients in turn.

Competent patients

The patient who wishes treatment to take place

Insofar as a competent patient wishes to receive life-sustaining treatment, then it will be the doctor's duty to provide it, at least where the treatment is readily available and medically established. This principle lay at the heart of the recent case of *R (on the application of Burke) v GMC*.

R (On the Application of Burke) v GMC [2005] EWCA 1003, CA (Lord Phillips MR, Waller and Wall LJJ)

Mr Burke suffered from a cerebellar ataxia, a terminal degenerative condition that at some point would require him to receive artificial nutrition and hydration (ANH) to prolong his life: he would thereupon remain conscious and competent for a considerable time until the disease reached its final stages. He was concerned by the tenor of the GMC's Guidance to doctors (*Withholding and Withdrawing Life-prolonging Treatment: Good Practice and Decision Making*, Aug 2002), which implied that unless the patient was actively refusing ANH, its continuation was a matter of medical discretion, and challenged the Guidance's legality in relation both to the common law and his rights under the ECHR.

At first instance ([2004] EWHC 1879 (Admin)), Munby J agreed that the Guidance had attached too little weight to the patient's right, reinforced by ECHR considerations, to require life-prolonging ANH, and ruled it unlawful in a number of respects. However, this ruling was reversed by the Court of Appeal, which emphasised that the patient was amply protected by the existing common law, and that nothing in the GMC's Guidance should be read as detracting from this:

Lord Phillips MR (delivering the judgment of the Court): [32] So far as ANH is concerned, there is no need to look far for the duty to provide this. Once a patient is accepted into a hospital, the medical staff come under a positive duty at common law to care for the patient. The authorities cited by Munby J ... under the heading 'The duty to care' establish this proposition, if authority is needed. A fundamental aspect of this positive duty of care is a duty to take such steps as are reasonable to keep the patient alive. Where ANH is necessary to keep the patient alive, the duty of care will normally require the doctors to supply ANH. This duty will not, however, override the competent patient's wish not to receive ANH. Where the competent patient makes it plain that he or she wishes to be kept alive by ANH, this will not be the source of the duty to provide it. The patient's wish will merely underscore that duty.

[33] Insofar as the law has recognised that the duty to keep a patient alive by administering ANH or other life-prolonging treatment is not absolute, the exceptions have been restricted to the following situations: (1) where the competent patient refuses to receive ANH and (2) where the patient is not competent and it is not considered to be in the best interests of the patient to be artificially kept alive. It is with the second exception that the law has had most difficulty. The courts have accepted that where life involves an extreme degree of pain, discomfort or indignity to a patient, who is sentient but not competent and who has manifested no wish to be kept alive, these circumstances may absolve the doctors of the positive duty to keep the patient alive. Equally the courts have recognised that there may be no duty to keep alive a patient who is in a persistent vegetative state ('PVS'). In each of these examples the facts of the individual case may make it difficult to decide whether the duty to keep the patient alive persists.

[34] No such difficulty arises, however, in the situation that has caused Mr Burke concern, that of the competent patient who, regardless of the pain, suffering or indignity of his condition, makes it plain that he wishes to be kept alive. No authority lends the slightest countenance to the suggestion that the duty on the doctors to take reasonable steps to keep the patient alive in such circumstances may not persist. Indeed, it seems to us that for a doctor deliberately to interrupt life-prolonging treatment in the face of a competent patient's expressed wish to be kept alive, with the intention of thereby terminating the patient's life, would leave the doctor with no answer to a charge of murder.

... [64] Is the Guidance defective? Munby J declared in declaration (5) that paragraphs 13, 16, 32 and 42 were unlawful in that they failed to recognise that the decision of a competent patient on whether ANH should be provided was determinative in principle of whether or not such treatment was in the patient's best interests. We have commented that equating best interests with the expressed wishes of a competent patient is unhelpful. The question to be asked in relation to these paragraphs is whether they indicate clearly, in their context, that a doctor cannot remove ANH that is keeping a competent patient alive when this is contrary to the wishes of the patient. Paragraphs 13 and 16 are general paragraphs, not specifically directed to ANH. They make it clear that a patient is legally entitled to refuse treatment and state that doctors must 'take account' of patients' preferences when providing treatment. Taken alone, they do not state in terms that a doctor cannot discontinue ANH contrary to the wishes of a competent patient, but we consider that this is their inference. The same is true of paragraphs 32 and 42. These suggest that the wishes of the patient should be respected unless this is 'clinically inappropriate' and, as we have said, administering treatment that is necessary to keep a patient alive cannot be described as 'clinically inappropriate'.

Refusals of medical treatment

As we saw in Chapter 3, it is a cardinal principle of medical law that, in respect of a competent adult patient, treatment may generally not be administered without consent. This is so even in a situation in which, without the treatment, the patient will die. This was made clear, *obiter*, by the Court of Appeal in *Re T (Adult: Refusal of Medical Treatment)* (1992) (in which Lord Donaldson MR gave the leading judgment); and House of Lords' *dicta* to the same effect may be found both in *Sidaway v Governors of Royal Bethlem Hospital* [1985] 1 All ER 643 (*per* Lord Templeman, p 666) and in *Airedale NHS Trust v Bland* [1993] 1 All ER 821 (*per* Lord Keith, p 857; Lord Goff, p 866; and Lord Mustill, p 892).

Subsequently, the principle formed the *ratio* in the High Court decisions of Thorpe J in *Re C (Adult: Refusal of Treatment)* [1994] 1 All ER 819 and *Secretary of State v Robb* [1995] 2 WLR 722. Indeed, recently, in *Ms B v An NHS Hospital Trust* [2002] EWHC Fam 429, the President of the Family Division, Dame Elizabeth Butler-Sloss, upheld the right of a competent, paralysed woman to have her life-sustaining ventilator switched off.

On the other hand, as discussed in Chapter 3, it may be that the right to refuse treatment is tempered in certain circumstances by overriding State interests, including the prevention of suicide. In this regard, a natural question to ask is why refusals of life-saving treatment are not construed in general as attempts at suicide which doctors are entitled to thwart? This issue has been analysed by David Price as follows:

Price, DPT, 'Assisted suicide and refusing medical treatment: linguistics, morals and legal contortions' (1996) 4 Med L Rev 370:

A Intention

Does a patient intend to die when he or she refuses further medical treatment definitely resulting in death? The courts typically adopt a narrow construction of intention in this context, equating it with desire, yet seemingly then deny the self-evident truth. In *Bouvia v Superior Court*, for instance, a 28 year old mentally competent quadriplegic woman with cerebral palsy and crippling arthritis, who required others to feed her, refused to allow further food to be administered to her. The trial court said:

> It is fairly clear from the evidence and the court cannot close its eyes to the fact that [petitioner] during her stay in defendant hospital, and for some time prior thereto, had formed an intent to die. She voiced this desire to a member of staff of defendant hospital.

The California Court of Appeal, however, disagreed finding that there was no such intent to die. Similarly, in *McKay v Bergstedt* (1990), involving a 31 year old quadriplegic patient who wished to be disconnected from the life-sustaining respirator. The Nevada Supreme Court found that Kenneth Bergstedt had no intent to take his own life, and thus did not commit suicide, although he realised that death would be the effect of his decision. Yet, he wished to be removed from the respirator because he feared an agonising death and 'despaired over the prospect of life without the attentive care, companionship and love of his devoted father'. It is arguable though that Elizabeth Bouvia did intend to die, even in the sense of wanting to do so – she plainly stated her desire to starve herself to death. Likewise Kenneth Bergstedt, who could not face life without his father. In *Satz v Perlmutter* (1978) the Florida Supreme Court even held that the competent (ventilator-dependent) patient had no intention to die despite having attempted on several occasions to disconnect himself from the respirator, but having been physically prevented from so doing by hospital staff.

1 Intention: desire or more?

In some US cases the courts have rationalised their decision that a request for the removal of life-support equipment does not manifest an intention to die by declaring that the patient really wanted to live. But, even if it is not specious to argue that an individual does not intend to die despite the adoption of a preference for death over life (surely a person may desire, wish or will a result even though it is only the lesser of two evils?), this reasoning relies on the dubious doctrine of double effect. According to the doctrine, all intended, bad ends are morally wrong, and this includes all bad means chosen to achieve ends. Where a consequence is unintended it is perceived as a side effect which, if bad, can be justified according to the totality of the circumstances. The doctrine in this context appeals to the distinction between desiring death for its own sake and intending to avoid continued existence in an unacceptable condition, knowing death is the consequence of the decision. Elizabeth Bouvia wished to avoid continued existence in her quadriplegic and unbearable condition; Kenneth Bergstedt found the thought of life without his father and of experiencing an agonising death unbearable, etc. However, this distinction would lead to treating almost all rational self-killings as non-suicides because it is invariably the case that persons only choose death to avoid some other more undesirable fate, for example, continued existence in unendurable pain or indignity. Indeed, such self-killings are commonly perceived as paradigmatic instances of suicide ...

[C]ould it nevertheless be asserted that suicide is incapable of being committed by an omission? It is submitted that, contrary to the views of Glanville Williams, the fact that the patient is (on one view) merely passive and does nothing positive to cause the death is not to the point. One can seemingly commit suicide by failing to act, by deliberately failing to feed oneself for instance. In the Supreme Court of the United States in *Cruzan v Director, Missouri Health Department* (1990), Scalia J stated that:

> ... it would not make much sense to say that one may not kill oneself by walking into the sea, but may sit on the beach until submerged by the incoming tide.

He later added:

> Starving oneself to death is no different from putting a gun to one's temple as far as the common law definition of suicide is concerned; the cause of death in both cases is the suicide's conscious decision to 'put an end to his own existence'.

It is indeed difficult to see what justification could be advanced for a distinction to be drawn between acts and omissions here. The individual is clearly terminating his own life deliberately by either means – it is the ends not the means which are the essence of suicide. Thus, neither lack of intention nor the absence of a causal connection provide a proper basis for the conclusion that the refusal of life-sustaining treatment is not suicide. [Reprinted by permission of Oxford University Press.]

Despite the cogency of these arguments, the English courts have made it clear that they will not equate refusals of life-saving medical treatment with suicide (see, in this regard, Lord Goff's speech in *Bland*, p 866 and Thorpe J's judgment in *Secretary of State v Robb*). It is apparent that, in making such judgments, the courts (in accord with their 'qualified sanctity of life' approach) do in fact regard the acts/omissions distinction as crucial: the person who passively declines a life-saving opportunity is distinguished from one who actively engineers his own end. The upshot in the great majority of refusal-of-treatment cases involving competent patients is that, as Lord Goff stated in *Bland*, 'the doctor's duty to act in the best interests of his patient must likewise be qualified'.

Advance directives

A further issue, in relation to refusals of life-saving medical treatment, concerns the time at which they are made. How far will a refusal made by a competent patient at time 1 subsequently bind a doctor who wishes to treat the patient – who in the interim becomes incompetent – at time 2?

Across the Atlantic, the use of 'advance directives' (colloquially termed 'living wills') to refuse treatment has long been commonplace; a good illustration of their operation is provided by the case of *Malette v Shulman* (1990) 72 OR (2d) 417:

Malette v Shulman (1990) 72 OR (2d) 417, Ontario CA

The plaintiff was a Jehovah's Witness who was admitted to hospital unconscious following a road accident. She was found to be carrying a card which (translated from French into English) read as follows:

No blood transfusion!

As one of Jehovah's Witnesses with firm religious convictions, I request that no blood or blood products be administered to me under any circumstances. I fully realise the implications of this position, but I have resolutely decided to obey the Bible command: 'Keep abstaining ... from blood' (Acts 15:28, 29). However, I have no religious objection to the use of non-blood alternatives, such as Dextran, Haemaccel, PVP, Ringer's Lactate or saline solution.

However, the defendant doctor carried out a life-saving blood transfusion:

Robins JA: On the facts of the present case, Dr Shulman was clearly faced with an emergency. He had an unconscious, critically ill patient on his hands who, in his opinion, needed blood transfusions to save her life or preserve her health. If there were no Jehovah's Witness card he undoubtedly would have been entitled to administer blood transfusions as part of the emergency treatment and could not have been held liable for so doing. In those circumstances he would have had no indication that the transfusions would have been refused had the patient then been able to make her wishes known and, accordingly, no reason to expect that, as a reasonable person, she would not consent to the transfusions.

... Here, the patient, anticipating an emergency in which she might be unable to make decisions about her health care contemporaneous with the emergency, has given explicit instructions that blood transfusions constitute an unacceptable medical intervention and are not to be administered to her. Once the emergency arises, is the doctor nonetheless entitled to administer transfusions on the basis of his honest belief that they are needed to save a patient's life?

The answer, in my opinion, is clearly no. A doctor is not free to disregard a patient's advance instructions any more than he would be free to disregard instructions given at the time of the emergency. The law does not prohibit a patient from withholding consent to emergency medical treatment, nor does the law prohibit a doctor from following his patient's instructions. While the law may disregard the absence of consent in limited emergency circumstances, it otherwise supports the right of competent adults to make decisions concerning their own health care by imposing civil liability on those who perform medical treatment without consent.

The patient's decision to refuse blood ... was made prior to and in anticipation of the emergency. While the doctor would have had the opportunity to dissuade her on the basis of his medical advice, her refusal to accept his advice or her unwillingness to discuss or consider the subject would not relieve him of his obligation to follow her instructions. The principles of self-determination and individual autonomy compel the conclusion that the patient may reject blood transfusions even if harmful consequences may result and even if the decision is generally regarded as foolhardy. Her decision in this instance would be operative after she lapsed into unconsciousness, and the doctor's conduct would be unauthorised. To transfuse a Jehovah's Witness in the face of her explicit instructions to the contrary would, in my opinion, violate her right to control her own body and show disrespect for the religious values by which she has chosen to live her life ...

The plaintiff was awarded $20,000 in damages.

In this country, the concept of advance directives was supported by the Court of Appeal in *Re T (Adult: Refusal of Medical Treatment)* [1992] 4 All ER 649, where Lord Donaldson MR commented as follows:

Lord Donaldson MR: There seems to be a view in the medical profession that in such emergency circumstances the next of kin should be asked to consent on behalf of the patient and that, if possible, treatment should be postponed until that consent has been obtained. This is a misconception because the next of kin has no legal right either to consent or to refuse consent. This is not to say that it is an undesirable practice if the interests of the patient will not be adversely affected by any consequential delay. I say this because contact with the next of kin may reveal that the patient has made an anticipatory choice which, if clearly established and applicable in the circumstances – two major 'ifs' – would bind the practitioner.

An example of a case in which an advance directive was held no longer applicable in the circumstances that arose is that of *HE v A Hospital NHS Trust and AE* [2003] EWHC 1017 (Fam). Here, a young woman was unconscious with serious heart problems, and required surgery including the use of blood products in order to survive. She had been brought up a Muslim, but – together with her mother – subsequently became a Jehovah's Witness and at that time (in February 2001) signed an advance directive rejecting the use of blood products. Although by the time of the proposed surgery (in April 2003) all the indications were that she had reverted to the Muslim faith, her mother insisted that the hospital abide by the directive 'despite the greatly increased risk of death'. In declaring the use of blood products during surgery lawful, Munby J held that the the burden of proof was on those asserting the continued applicability of a directive and that, given that life was at stake, the evidence offered would need especially close and anxious scrutiny. Here, the decisive fact against the directive's applicability was the patient's rejection of the faith upon which it had been founded.

The cases so far discussed have involved directives from patients who were temporarily incompetent: they were unable contemporaneously to consent to or refuse life-saving treatment, but potentially (ie insofar as the treatment were provided) would regain their earlier competence. However, an interesting question is whether advance directives should apply (provided that the maker's intention is clear) to situations where the patient has become *permanently* incompetent. Despite the fact that the courts and many commentators appear to regard a positive answer as virtually self-evident, it is an approach whose justification involves accepting arguments of some philosophical complexity:

Kuczewski, MG, 'Whose will is it, anyway? A discussion of advance directives, personal identity and consensus in medical ethics' (1994) 8 Bioethics 27:

The general problem raised by [John] Robertson and [Rebecca] Dresser can be expressed very simply. They ask, by what warrant/right can we apply the judgments encoded in a living will by a competent person at one time (t1) to the incompetent patient at a later time (t2)? The employment of advance directives has become so common that the question almost seems strange. We are tempted to simply reply, 'by the patient's right of self-determination'. However, to understand the inadequacy of this answer, we need to explore their concept of 'person'.

There are two slightly different versions of the problem put forth by these authors. Robertson's version we shall call the 'weak thesis' because it is the less radical of the two. Robertson's argument rests on the assumption that both the incompetent individual at t2 and the competent person at t1 are the same person but have very different interests. The interests of a person change over the course of her life, sometimes dramatically. Living wills are attempts by the competent person to make treatment decisions for her future based upon her present, rather than future, interests. It may be wrong to base how we treat a patient on interests the person previously possessed rather than her current ones. As Robertson states, 'The values and interests of the competent person no longer are relevant to someone who has lost the rational structure on which those values and interests rested'. Robertson wishes his critique to apply only to situations that involve an incompetent conscious patient. This limitation occurs, presumably, because permanently unconscious patients do not possess significant enough interests to generate a morally weighty conflict with their previous wishes.

Dresser called attention to the fact that one can base an even more radical thesis on the philosophical conception of personal identity advanced by Derek Parfit. Parfit's 'Complex View' stipulates that personal identity is equivalent to psychological continuity. That is, our identity is based on the strength of the connectedness and continuity of our memories, intentions, beliefs, desires, etc. If the strength of this connectedness falls below a certain minimum threshold, there are philosophical grounds to claim that we are, in fact, dealing with a different person. Thus Dresser employs this background to advance the 'strong or radical thesis' that in applying living wills at t2, we are sometimes applying the directions given by one person to a different person ...

We need to keep in mind that this is not a mere abstract philosophical word game. Rather, it is exactly the warrant of the application of the person's interests at t1 to the person at t2 that is challenged by Dresser and Robertson. It is not empirically obvious why interests in dignity, the financial well being of one's family, bodily integrity, and so on, should be said to survive and be applicable to a person who either no longer exists or cannot cognise and presently appreciate these values. Although present practices regarding the use of living wills may go on despite the failure to justify their employment philosophically, such failure would mean that the consensus was forged on a fictitious account of self-determination. Thus, those who argued in the pre-consensus years for the primacy of the best interest standard as the sole standard of decision-making would actually be correct.

It may not be clear which account, that of the consensus or that of the Parfitians, should bear the burden of proof. It is perhaps best to proceed simply on the assumption that we need at least to require each to provide a coherent account in its own terms. Therefore, it is perfectly reasonable to demand from the consensus a way to make sense of the idea of the survival of interests

...

Kuczewski goes on to argue that the interests of the formerly competent person do survive, not in a personal, but rather in a communal or institutional sense:

We must make clear what it means to say that interests 'survive'. There is an easy suggestion to be made regarding the location of these interests. They survive in the memories, both personal and institutional, of the community. One's interest in his son's education survives because people remember his commitment to it; the arrangements the father made to provide for the education encode these intentions. If all who remember my commitment die and the social arrangements that bear evidence of my intent collapse, my interest cannot be said to 'survive' in any real sense. This is an uncontroversial sense of surviving interest and is operative in last wills and testaments, institutions that are commemoratively named, etc.

Likewise, an individual's interest in dignity, privacy, and bodily integrity is encoded in his living will, in the memory of others, and even in their perceptions of the situation at the time of one's incompetence. I currently remember other people and have an interest in how others remember me in the future. It is this social meaning of interests that best accounts for their survival. It is a narrative sense of interest in that I conceive of myself objectively as part of a larger group that contains a 'part' of me that transcends my individual consciousness and psychological continuity. My story is, to some degree, only complete when told from this vantage point outside of my stream of consciousness. The body that belongs to the incompetent patient at t2 is in some sense 'mine' because other persons will call it by my name and make the story of what happens to it a chapter of the story they tell about 'me'. As such, I attempt to make that chapter embody the values which are presently mine. Through the same type of act of will by which I commit to live today in accordance with dignity, so also, I commit that my final chapter shall embody those values ...

Our intuition to honour living wills is indicative or reflective of the premium our society places on the values of dignity, privacy, and bodily integrity. Thus, we feel the normative force to help individuals bind these values to their narrative identity even after conscious appreciation of them has fled the body ... The answer to the question of the same person is that it is the same person at t1 and t2 mainly because the society recognises and helps constitute this as the case. This recognition has both descriptive and normative components. The normative component is the basis of applying categories such as dignity to the incompetent individual. Society is, in part, the source of individual psychological and narrative continuity and accomplishes this in binding certain features to the individual and fostering their higher commitments. It is this same warrant that is employed in honouring the person's living will.

In its report, *Mental Incapacity* (No 231, 1995), the Law Commission recommended that the legal effect of advance directives be enshrined in legislation and this has now occurred by virtue of ss 24–26 of the Mental Capacity Act 2005. In particular, s 26 provides as follows:

Mental Capacity Act 2005:

26 Effect of advance decisions

(1) If P has made an advance decision which is-

    (a) valid, and

    (b) applicable to a treatment,

    the decision has effect as if he had made it, and had had capacity to make it, at the time when the question arises whether the treatment should be carried out or continued.

(2) A person does not incur liability for carrying out or continuing the treatment unless, at the time, he is satisfied that an advance decision exists which is valid and applicable to the treatment.

(3) A person does not incur liability for the consequences of withholding or withdrawing a treatment from P if, at the time, he reasonably believes that an advance decision exists which is valid and applicable to the treatment.

(4) The court may make a declaration as to whether an advance decision–

    (a) exists;

    (b) is valid;

    (c) is applicable to a treatment.

(5) Nothing in an apparent advance decision stops a person–

    (a) providing life-sustaining treatment, or

    (b) doing any act he reasonably believes to be necessary to prevent a serious deterioration in P's condition,

    while a decision as respects any relevant issue is sought from the court.

As can be seen, the Act uses the term 'advance decision' (rather than 'advance directive'), but nothing turns on this. Nonetheless, the new provisions are undoubtedly complex. In the explanatory notes, which accompanied the passage of the Bill that became the 2005 Act, the Department of Constitutional Affairs sought to explain their effect as follows:

Explanatory Notes to the Mental Capacity Bill, 2004, London: Dept of Constitutional Affairs, HMSO

… Advance decisions to refuse treatment

Clause 24: Advance decisions to refuse treatment: general

82. Clauses 24–26 deal with advance decisions to refuse treatment. Some people already choose to make such decisions and their legal effect has been analysed in a number of judicial decisions. It has recently been confirmed by the High Court that a competent adult patient's anticipatory refusal of consent remains binding and effective notwithstanding that the patient has subsequently become incompetent (*HE v NHS Trust A and AE* [2003] EWHC 1017 (Fam), a case concerning a refusal of blood transfusion). Broadly, the clauses seek to codify and clarify the current common law rules, integrating them into the broader scheme of the Bill. There would otherwise be a lacuna in the scheme of the Bill and the powers of the new court. Many general forms of advance statement or 'living will' will be important and relevant as 'past wishes' of the person for the purposes of the best interests checklist in clause 4. An 'advance decision' as defined in these clauses is a special type of advance statement that represents an actual decision made to refuse treatment by P, albeit at an earlier date. As now, it will therefore be decisive in certain circumstances.

83. The key characteristics of an 'advance decision' for the purposes of the Bill are set out in subsection (1) of this clause. It must be made by a person who is 18 or over and at a time when the person has capacity to make it. A qualifying advance decision must specify the treatment being refused, although this can be in lay terms, for example using 'tummy' instead of stomach. It may specify particular circumstances, again in lay terms, in which the refusal will apply. A person can change or completely withdraw the advance decision if he has capacity to do so (subsection (3)).

Clause 25: Validity and applicability of advance decisions

84. This introduces the two important safeguards of 'validity' and 'applicability' in relation to advance decisions to refuse treatment.

85. To be valid the advance decision must not have been withdrawn, nor overridden by a subsequent [Lasting Power of Attorney] giving a donee the authority to consent, or refuse consent, to the treatment (other LPAs will not override – see

subsection (6)). Also, if the person has acted in a way that is clearly inconsistent with the advance decision remaining his fixed decision, then the advance decision is invalid. An example of an inconsistent action might be a former Jehovah's Witness converting to Islam and marrying a Muslim man. Even if she had forgotten to destroy a written advance decision refusing blood transfusion, her actions could be taken into account in determining whether that earlier refusal remained her fixed decision.

86. An advance decision will not be applicable if the person actually has capacity to make the decision at the particular time. It will also not be applicable to treatments not specified in the decision or if the circumstances are not those specified in the decision. Furthermore the decision will not be applicable if there are reasonable grounds for believing that the current circumstances were not anticipated by P and, if they had been anticipated by P would have affected his decision. For example, there may be new medications available that radically change the outlook for a particular condition and make treatment much less burdensome than was previously the case.

87. Subsection (5) introduces another rule about applicability. An advance decision will not apply to life-sustaining treatment unless P specified that it should.

Clause 26: Effect of advance decisions

88. This deals with the legal effect of a qualifying advance decision. If it is both valid and applicable it has the same effect as a contemporaneous refusal of treatment by a person with capacity. That is, the treatment cannot lawfully be given. If given, the person refusing would be able to claim damages for the tort of battery and the treatment-provider might face criminal liability for assault. Subsections (2)-(3) clarify the rules about liability. A treatment-provider may safely treat unless satisfied that there is a valid and applicable qualifying advance refusal; and a treatment-provider may safely withhold or withdraw treatment as long as he has reasonable grounds for believing that there is a valid and applicable qualifying advance decision.

89. If there is doubt or a dispute about the existence, validity or applicability of an advance decision then the court can determine the issue. There is an important proviso to the general rule that an advance refusal is legally effective. There may be a doubt or dispute about whether a particular refusal is in fact one which meets all the tests (existence, validity and applicability). As with decisions by donees or deputies in clause 6(6), action may be taken to prevent the death of the person concerned, or a serious deterioration in his condition, whilst any such doubt or dispute is referred to the court.

A final issue with respect to advance directives is the form in which they are expressed: in *HE v A Hospital NHS Trust and AE* [2003] EWHC 1017, Munby J suggested that an oral directive – if established – would bind the doctors (this is arguably also implied by Lord Donaldson MR's *dictum* in *Re T (Adult: Refusal of Medical Treatment)* [1992] 4 All ER 649, extracted at p 657 above). Nonetheless, as a practical matter, unless a directive is recorded in some form it is difficult to envisage circumstances where the courts would find sufficient evidence of a clear and consistent refusal: a telling example is the recent Court of Appeal decision in *W Healthcare NHS Trust v H* [2004] EWCA 1324, discussed at p 670 below.

The matter has now been addressed by Parliament in the Mental Capacity Act 2005. Although, initially, it was not proposed to require that advance directives be in writing, this aspect of the legislation was tightened in the course of amendment at

Committee stage: as enacted, s 25(6) of the 2005 Act provides that, in order to apply to life-sustaining treatment, a directive must not only be in writing, but signed by the patient (or his nominee in his presence) and witnessed by one other person.

Incompetent patients

Background

In addressing the question of when life-saving treatment may be withheld or withdrawn from the incompetent patient, we are within the province of *non-voluntary* passive euthanasia. As already noted, the crucial issue here is the extent of the doctor's duty to employ life-prolonging measures in respect of his patient. It is clear that common sense has never regarded this duty as an absolute one. Moreover, as we have already seen – in the context of John Harris's critique of the policy of 'selective treatment' for infants with spina bifida – such euthanasia has been practised openly at least since the early 1970s. Nevertheless, the first significant English authority in point is a Court of Appeal decision from as recently as 1981:

Re B (A Minor) (Wardship: Medical Treatment) [1981] 1 WLR 1421, CA (Templeman and Dunn LJJ)

B was a baby girl born with Down's syndrome and also suffering from an intestinal blockage. Without an operation to remove the blockage, she would die within a few days. Her parents, however, refused to consent to the treatment and B was made a ward of court. The judge at first instance initially authorised treatment, but revoked his order after speaking to the parents and also hearing that the surgeon appointed to the case was unwilling to operate contrary to their wishes. The health authority appealed:

> **Templeman LJ**: The question which this court has to determine is whether it is in the interests of this child to be allowed to die within the next week or to have the operation, in which case if she lives she will be a mongoloid child, but no one can say to what extent her mental or physical defects will be apparent. No one can say whether she will suffer or whether she will be happy in part. On the one hand the probability is that she will not be a cabbage, as it is called when people's faculties are entirely destroyed. On the other hand it is certain that she will be very severely mentally and physically handicapped.
>
> On behalf of the parents Mr Gray has submitted very movingly, if I may say so, that this is a case where nature has made its own arrangements to terminate a life which would not be fruitful and nature should not be interfered with. He has also submitted that in this kind of decision the views of responsible and caring parents, as these are, should be respected, and that their decision that it is better for the child to be allowed to die should be respected. Fortunately or unfortunately, in this particular case the decision no longer lies with the parents or with the doctors, but lies with the court. It is a decision which of course must be made in the light of the evidence and views expressed by the parents and the doctors, but at the end of the day it devolves on this court in this particular instance to decide whether the life of this child is demonstrably going to be so awful that in effect the child must be condemned to die, or whether the life of this child is still so imponderable that it would be wrong for her to be condemned to die. There may be cases, I know not, of severe proved damage where the future is so certain and where the life of the child is so bound to be full of pain and suffering that the court might be driven to a different conclusion, but in the present

case the choice which lies before the court is this: whether to allow an operation to take place which may result in the child living for 20 or 30 years as a mongoloid or whether (and I think this must be brutally the result) to terminate the life of a mongoloid child because she also has an intestinal complaint. Faced with that choice I have no doubt that it is the duty of this court to decide that the child must live. The judge was much affected by the reasons given by the parents and came to the conclusion that their wishes ought to be respected. In my judgment he erred in that the duty of the court is to decide whether it is in the interests of the child that an operation should take place. The evidence in this case only goes to show that if the operation takes place and is successful then the child may live the normal span of a mongoloid child with the handicaps and defects and life of a mongol child, and it is not for this court to say that life of that description ought to be extinguished.

Accordingly the appeal must be allowed and the local authority must be authorised themselves to authorise and direct the operation to be carried out on the little girl.

This decision is an important one, not least because it renders doubtful a well known criminal case of about the same time, *R v Arthur* (1981) 12 BMLR 1, in which a doctor was acquitted of attempting to murder a Down's syndrome baby (whose parents did not wish it to live) after ordering treatment to be withheld: the effect of *Re B* is that, whatever the parents' views, doctors will generally be obliged to treat babies with the standard, albeit serious, disabilities associated with Down's syndrome. However, although Templeman LJ recognised *obiter* the possibility that, in other cases of more drastic disability, treatment could be withheld, it remained unclear in what circumstances this would be so.

Subsequently, some light was shed on this problem in *Re C (A Minor) (Wardship: Medical Treatment)* [1989] 2 All ER 782, where the Court of Appeal authorised the withdrawal of treatment from a severely brain-damaged baby said to be 'dying' in any event. The decisive step, in favour of a more open endorsement of passive euthanasia in extreme cases, came shortly afterwards in the seminal case of *Re J (A Minor) (Wardship: Medical Treatment)* [1990] 3 All ER 930:

Re J (A Minor) (Wardship: Medical Treatment) [1990] 3 All ER 930, CA (Lord Donaldson MR, Taylor and Balcombe LJJ)

J was a five month old baby who suffered severe brain damage as a result of his grossly premature birth. He was profoundly disabled, both mentally and physically, and was unlikely to develop even the most basic functions. He had collapsed on a number of occasions since his birth and the court, pursuant to its wardship jurisdiction, was asked to decide if mechanical ventilation of J should occur in the event of a further collapse:

Lord Donaldson MR: Of the three neonatalogists who have been concerned with [J's] care, the most optimistic is Dr W. His view is that J is likely to develop serious spastic quadriplegia, that is to say, paralysis of both his arms and legs. It is debatable whether he will ever be able to sit up or to hold his head upright. J appears to be blind, although there is a possibility that some degree of sight may return. He is likely to be deaf. He may be able to make sounds which reflect his mood, but he is unlikely ever to be able to speak, even to the extent of saying Mum or Dad. It is highly unlikely that he will develop even limited intellectual abilities. Most unfortunately of all, there is a likelihood that he will be able to feel pain to the same extent as a normal baby, because pain is a very basic response. It is possible that he may achieve the ability to smile and to cry. Finally, as one might expect, his life expectancy has been considerably reduced, at most into his late teens, but even Dr W would expect him to die long before then ...

The issue here is whether it would be in the best interests of the child to put him on a mechanical ventilator and subject him to all the associated processes of intensive care, if at some future time he could not continue breathing unaided ... The judge has found that the odds are about even whether the need for artificial ventilation, whether mechanical or manual, will ever arise. If it does arise, the very fact that it has arisen will mean that the more optimistic end of the range of prognoses, pessimistic though the whole range is, will have been falsified. On the other hand, the child's state of health might change at any time for the better as well as for the worse, even though there are distinct limits to what could be hoped for, let alone anticipated.

The doctors were unanimous in recommending that there should be no mechanical reventilation in the event of his stopping breathing, subject only to the qualifications injected by Dr W, and accepted by the judge, that in the event of a chest infection, short term manual ventilation would be justified, and that in the event of the child stopping breathing the provisional decision to abstain from mechanical ventilation could and should be revised, if this seemed appropriate to the doctors caring for him in the then prevailing clinical situation.

There can be no criticism of the judge for endorsing this approach on the footing that he was thereby abdicating his responsibility and leaving it to the doctors to decide. He had reviewed and considered the basis of the doctor's views and recommendations in the greatest detail and with the greatest care. Nothing could be more inimical to the interests of the child than the judge should make an order which restricted the doctors' freedom to revise their present view in favour of more active means to preserve the life of the child, if the situation changed and this then seemed to them to be appropriate.

The basis of the doctors' recommendations, approved by the judge, was that mechanical ventilation is itself an invasive procedure which, together with its essential accompaniments, such as the introduction of a nasogastric tube, drips which have to be re-sited and constant blood sampling, would cause the child distress. Furthermore, the procedures involve taking active measures which carry their own hazards, not only to life but in terms of causing even greater brain damage. This had to be balanced against what could possibly be achieved by the adoption of such active treatment. The chances of preserving the child's life might be improved, although even this was not certain, and account had to be taken of the extremely poor quality of life at present enjoyed by the child, the fact that he had already been ventilated for exceptionally long periods, the unfavourable prognosis with or without ventilation and a recognition that if the question of reventilation ever arose, his situation would have deteriorated still further.

Best interests

In the above case, the Court of Appeal invoked the 'best interests' of the infant as the justification for not prolonging his life by further mechanical ventilation. We have previously encountered the 'best interests' test in the context of decisions to provide incompetent patients with treatment of a non-life-saving nature, most notably in sterilisation cases involving mentally disabled women: see Chapter 4. In itself the test lacks substance: it is merely a direction that, in reaching the decision whether to treat, the decider should objectively weigh up the factors in favour of treatment against those which militate against it. The factors themselves, and their respective weighting, clearly stand in need of further specification.

An initial question, however, is whether a balancing exercise can be meaningfully performed at all in a context in which one of the options (non-treatment) leads to death. This point was taken by Counsel for the Official Solicitor in *Re J* [1990] 3 All ER 930:

Lord Donaldson MR: [James Munby QC's] first, or absolutist, submission is that a court is never justified in withholding consent to treatment which could enable a child to survive a life-threatening condition, whatever the pain or other side effects inherent in the treatment, and whatever the quality of the life which it would experience thereafter. In making this submission, he distinguishes a case such as that of Baby C ... where the child was dying and no amount of medical skill or care could do more than achieve a brief postponement of the moment of death. He submits, rightly, that in such a case neither the parents nor the court in deciding whether to give or to withhold consent, nor the doctors in deciding what treatment they recommend or would be prepared to administer, are balancing life against death. In such a case, death is inevitable, not in the sense that it is inevitable for all of us, but in the sense that the child is actually dying. What is being balanced is not life against death, but a marginally longer life of pain against a marginally shorter life free from pain and ending in death with dignity ...

In support of this submission, Mr Munby draws attention to the decision of this court in *McKay v Essex HA* [1982] 1 QB 1166. There a child suffered severe and irreversible damage before birth, as a result of her mother contracting rubella (German measles). She sued the health authority claiming damages under two heads. First, she claimed that if her mother had received appropriate treatment her disabilities would have been less. She, therefore, claimed damages based upon the difference between the quality of her life as it was and the quality of life which she would have enjoyed if her mother had received that treatment. That claim was allowed to proceed. However, the child also claimed damages on a different basis. This was founded upon the proposition that her mother should have been advised to seek an abortion and that, if this advice had been given and accepted, she would never have been born at all. The damages claimed under this head were necessarily based upon a comparison between her actual condition and her condition if, as a result of an abortion, she had never been born at all.

This court struck out the second claim as disclosing no cause of action, and it is upon the reasoning which underlay this decision that Mr Munby relies – Stephenson LJ said, p 1180H:

To impose such a duty towards the child [to give the child's mother an opportunity to terminate the child's life] would, in my opinion, make a further inroad on the sanctity of human life which would be contrary to public policy. It would mean regarding the life of a handicapped child as not only less valuable than the life of a normal child, but so much less valuable that it was not worth preserving.

Later he said, p 1181E:

But how can a court of law evaluate that second condition [where 'the child's embryonic life has been ended before its life in the world had begun'] and so measure the loss to the child? Even if a court were competent to decide between the conflicting views of theologians and philosophers and to assume an 'after life' or non-existence as the basis for the comparison, how can a judge put a value on the one or the other and compare either alternative with the injured child's life in this world, without the means of knowing what, if anything, it has gained?

... I do not regard this decision as providing us with either guidance or assistance in the context of the present problem. The child was claiming damages, and the decision was that no monetary comparison could be made between the two states. True it is, that it contains an assertion of the importance of the sanctity of human life, but that is not in issue.

Taylor LJ: Despite the court's inability to compare a life afflicted by the most severe disability with death, the unknown, I am of the view that there must be extreme cases in which the court is entitled to say: 'The life which this treatment would prolong would be so cruel as to be intolerable.' If, for example, a child was so damaged as to have negligible use of its faculties and the only way of preserving its life was by the continuous administration of extremely painful treatment such that the child either would be in continuous agony or would have to be so sedated continuously as to have no conscious life at all, I cannot think Mr Munby's absolute test should apply to require the treatment to be given. In those circumstances, without there being any question of deliberately ending the life or shortening it, I consider the court is entitled in the best interests of the child to say that deliberate steps should not be taken artificially to prolong its miserable lifespan.

Assuming that a balancing exercise is possible, it will nevertheless clearly be rather different in form to the comparative assessment of benefits and burdens (the patient's *life with treatment* against her *life without treatment*) familiar from decisions dealing with such matters as sterilisation. In the latter type of case, one can imagine that decisions may sometimes be finely weighted, ultimately turning on apparently marginal differences. By contrast, where without treatment death will occur, the courts will brook no such ambiguity: not only must a life be truly awful for death to seem preferable, but the residual force of the (qualified) sanctity of life principle here asserts itself:

Taylor LJ: Three preliminary principles are not in dispute. First, it is settled law that the court's prime and paramount consideration must be the best interests of the child
...

Secondly, the court's high respect for the sanctity of human life imposes a strong presumption in favour of taking all steps capable of preserving it, save in exceptional circumstances. The problem is to define those circumstances.

Thirdly, and as a corollary to the second principle, it cannot be too strongly emphasised that the court never sanctions steps to terminate life. That would be unlawful. There is no question of approving, even in a case of the most horrendous disability, a course aimed at terminating life or accelerating death. The court is concerned only with the circumstances in which steps should not be taken to prolong life.

What, then, will be the substantive factors relevant to a decision that it is not in a patient's best interests to have his or her life prolonged? In his judgment Taylor LJ addressed this issue as follows:

Taylor LJ: At what point in the scale of disability and suffering ought the court to hold that the best interests of the child do not require further endurance to be imposed by positive treatment to prolong its life? Clearly, to justify withholding treatment, the circumstances would have to be extreme. Mr Munby submitted that if the court rejected his absolute test, then at least it would have 'to be certain that the life of the child, were the treatment to be given, would be intolerably awful'.

I consider the correct approach is for the court to judge the quality of life the child would have to endure if given the treatment, and decide whether in all the circumstances such a life would be so afflicted as to be intolerable to that child. I say 'to that child' because the test should not be whether the life would be tolerable to the decider. The test must be whether the child in question, if capable of exercising sound judgment, would consider the life tolerable. This is the approach adopted by McKenzie J in *Re Superintendent of Family and Child Service and Dawson* (1983) 145 DLR (3d) 610 ... It takes account of the strong instinct to preserve one's life even in circumstances which an outsider, not himself at risk of death, might consider unacceptable. The circumstances to be considered would, in appropriate cases, include the degree of existing disability and any additional suffering or aggravation of the disability which the treatment itself would superimpose. In an accident case, as opposed to one involving disablement from birth, the child's pre-accident quality of life and its perception of what has been lost may also be factors relevant to whether the residual life would be intolerable to that child.

Mr Munby argued that, before deciding against treatment, the court would have to be certain that the circumstances of the child's future would comply with the extreme requirements to justify that decision. Certainty as to the future is beyond human judgment. The courts have not, even in the trial of capital offences, required certainty of proof. But, clearly, the court must be satisfied to a high degree of probability.

In the present case, the doctors were unanimous that in his present condition, Baby J should not be put back on to a mechanical ventilator. That condition is very grave indeed. I do not repeat the description of it given by the Master of the Rolls. In reaching his conclusion, the judge no doubt had three factors in mind. First, the severe lack of capacity of the child in all his faculties, which even without any further complication would make his existence barely sentient. Secondly, that, if further mechanical ventilation were to be required, that very fact would involve the risk of a deterioration in J's condition, because of further brain damage flowing from the interruption of breathing. Thirdly, all the doctors drew attention to the invasive nature of mechanical ventilation and the intensive care required to accompany it. They stressed the unpleasant and distressing nature of that treatment. To add such distress and the risk of further deterioration to an already appalling catalogue of disabilities was clearly capable, in my judgment, of producing a quality of life which justified the stance of the doctors and the judge's conclusion.

Subsequently, Taylor LJ's approach was followed in the High Court in *Re R (Adult: Medical Treatment)* [1996] 2 FLR 99, the first case of this type to involve an adult patient:

Re R (Adult: Medical Treatment) [1996] 2 FLR 99, HC (Sir Stephen Brown P)

R was a 23 year old man who had been born with a serious malformation of the brain and cerebral palsy. He was described as being in a 'low-awareness state' with roughly the perception and cognitive faculties of a new-born infant. During 1995 he was admitted to hospital on no fewer than five occasions and his weight dropped to five stone. The NHS trust responsible for his care sought a declaration that it would be lawful to withhold resuscitation if he collapsed and, subject to the views of his doctors and parents at the relevant time, antibiotics in the face of a life-threatening infection:

Sir Stephen Brown P: All the medical witnesses in this case support the view that CPR would not be appropriate in R's case. Dr S, the responsible consultant, has expressed that view very firmly. Dr Greenwood, a consultant neurologist, has also expressed that view in his report to be found in the documents. Dr John Morgan, a consultant psychiatrist for people with learning disability, in his report says:

> There is a danger that if cardio-pulmonary resuscitation were attempted, he might suffer further brain damage, and his body is relatively fragile and excessive pressure or enthusiasm might lead to damage to his ribs or more serious complications.

Dr Piachaud has also expressed the opinion that CPR would not be appropriate in this patient's case. The Official Solicitor on behalf of the patient R has made a report and counsel on his behalf has made it clear that the Official Solicitor in the light of his own expert's opinions and all the other evidence before the court supports the view that the procedure of CPR and ventilation would be inappropriate in this patient's case.

So far as the withholding of antibiotics is concerned Dr Andrews stated that this is a matter which can only properly be decided at the time when a potentially life-threatening situation from infection arises. There should not be, as it were, a global 'do not treat' policy. The plaintiff trust has indicated that it is content to accept that position. The decision as to the withholding of the administration of antibiotics in a potentially life-threatening situation is a matter fully within the responsibility of the consultant having the responsibility for treating the patient. It is a matter which should be considered in conjunction with the general practitioner and furthermore in the case of R, with his parents. The Official Solicitor submits that it would be appropriate for the court at this stage to make a declaration that it would be lawful to withhold the administration of antibiotics in the event of the patient developing a potentially life-threatening infection which would otherwise call for the administration of antibiotics, but only if immediately prior to withholding the same:

(a) the trust is so advised both by the general medical practitioner and by the consultant psychiatrist having the responsibility at the time of the patient's treatment and care; and

(b) one or other or both of the parents first give their consent thereto.

Such a declaration would recognise the ultimate and effective clinical responsibility of the consultant having responsibility at the time for the patient's treatment and care ...

In this case there is no question of the court being asked to approve a course aimed at terminating life or accelerating death. The court is concerned with circumstances in which steps should not be taken to prolong life. The facts are very different from those in the case of *Airedale NHS Trust v Bland* ... The principle of law to be applied in this case is that of the 'best interests of the patient' as made clear by the Court of Appeal in *Re J (A Minor) (Wardship: Medical Treatment)* ... In the course of his judgment ... Taylor LJ said:

> I consider the correct approach is for the court to judge the quality of life the child would have to endure if given the treatment, and decide whether in all the circumstances such a life would be so afflicted as to be intolerable to that child.

Although this present case concerns a handicapped adult and not a child who is a ward of court the overriding principle in my judgment is the same.

At first instance in *R (On the Application of Burke) v GMC* [2004] EWHC 1879, Munby J favoured the recognition of 'intolerability' as providing the general touchstone of best interests in the context of withdrawing medical treatment from a sentient, incompetent patient. (While the application in that case was brought by a competent patient –see p 652 above- the court was asked to rule generally upon the lawfulness of GMC Guidance on withdrawing artificial nutrition and hydration, which extended also to incompetent patients.)

However, in reversing that judgment, the Court of Appeal was critical both of the scope of Munby J's pronouncements – ranging well beyond what was necessary to deal with Mr Burke's concerns – and of the attempt to define best interests by means of a single test.

R (On the Application of Burke) v GMC [2005] EWCA 1003, CA (Lord Phillips MR, Waller and Wall LJJ)

Lord Phillips MR (delivering the judgment of the Court): [58] There are tragic cases where treatment can prolong life for an indeterminate period, but only at a cost of great suffering while life continues. Such a case was *In re J (a Minor) (Wardship: Medical Treatment)* ... There are other cases, and these are much more common, where a patient has lost competence in the final stages of life and where ANH may prolong these final stages, but at an adverse cost so far as comfort and dignity are concerned, sometimes resulting in the patient's last days being spent in a hospital ward rather than at home, with family around.

[59] It is to these situations that so much of the debate in this case has been directed. Apprehensions have been expressed by some who have intervened that those in charge of patients may too readily withdraw, or fail to provide, ANH or other life prolonging treatment on the ground that the patient's life, if prolonged, will not be worth living. As an example of the first situation described above, the Disability Rights Commission brought to our attention the disturbing story of Jane Campbell. She suffers from spinal muscular atrophy and is severely disabled. She was not expected to live beyond the age of four, but has lived a fulfilling and productive life of high achievement. In 2003 she was struck down by pneumonia. Two consultants were minded to conclude that her life was so parlous that, if she needed artificial respiration to remain alive she would not wish to receive it. Only the intervention of her husband, who showed them a photograph of her taking her degree, persuaded the consultants that her life was worth saving.

[60] Turning to the other situation described above, disturbing case reports were placed by the Medical Ethics Alliance before the Joint Committee on the draft Mental Incapacity Bill, and subsequently before us. These were cases where patients who were terminally ill appear to have been denied water and nutrition in circumstances where this was contrary to the demands of palliative care.

[61] These reports did not constitute admissible evidence, but underlined the importance of clear law and guidance in this area. After a lengthy analysis of jurisprudence under the heading 'Best interests and life-prolonging treatment', the judge set out a summary of his conclusions at paragraph 116, which included the following:

"There is a very strong presumption in favour of taking all steps which will prolong life, and save in exceptional circumstances, or where the patient is dying, the best interests of the patient will normally require such steps to be taken. In case of doubt that doubt falls to be resolved in favour of the preservation of life. But the obligation is not absolute. Important as the sanctity of life is, it may have to take second place to human dignity. *In the context of life-prolonging treatment the touchstone of best interests is intolerability. So if life-prolonging treatment is providing some benefit it should be provided unless the patient's life, if thus prolonged, would from the patient's point of view be intolerable.*"

[62] We do not think that any objection could have been taken to this summary had it not contained the final two sentences, which we have emphasised. The suggestion that the touchstone of 'best interests' is the 'intolerability' of continued life has, understandably given rise to concern. The test of whether it is in the best interests of the patient to provide or continue ANH must depend on the particular circumstances. The two situations that we have considered above are very different. As to the approach to be adopted in the former, this court dealt with that in *Re J* and we do not think that it is appropriate to review what the court there said in a context that is purely hypothetical.

[63] As to the approach to best interests where a patient is close to death, it seems to us that the judge himself recognised that 'intolerability' was not the test of best interests. At paragraph 104 he said:

"where the patient is dying, the goal may properly be to ease suffering and, where appropriate, to 'ease the passing' rather than to achieve a short prolongation of life."

We agree. We do not think it possible to attempt to define what is in the best interests of a patient by a single test, applicable in all circumstances. We would add that the disturbing cases referred to in paragraphs 59 and 60, if correctly reported, were cases where the doctors appear to have failed to observe the Guidance. They are not illustrative of any illegality in the Guidance. The Guidance expressly warns against treating the life of a disabled patient as being of less value than the life of a patient without disability, and rightly does so.

(See now also the decision of the Court of Appeal in *Wyatt v Portsmouth NHS Trust* [2005] EWCA 1181.)

In the wake of the enactment of the Human Rights Act 1998, this whole area is of course now permeated by human rights arguments. In this context, it may be asked whether submitting sentient, incompetent patients to invasive medical treatment will in certain circumstances amount to inhuman or degrading treatment contrary to Art 3 of the ECHR. This possibility was adverted to in *A NHS Trust v D* [2000] Lloyd's Rep Med 411. There, in deciding that doctors need not mechanically ventilate a severely disabled 19 month old child with incurable lung disease, Cazalet J cited Strasbourg jurisprudence (*D v UK* (1997) 24 EHRR 423) in which Art 3 was held to include the right to die with dignity. His Lordship stated that, 'It is that right … which is to be protected through the declaration that I propose to make in this case'. However, in the subsequent Court of Appeal decision in *W Healthcare NHS Trust v H*, the potential of Article 3 of the ECHR to apply in this way appears not to have been argued before the Court:

W Healthcare NHS Trust v H [2004] EWCA Civ 1324, CA (Brooke, Clarke and Kay LJJ)

The trust caring for KH, a 59 year old woman in the latter stages of multiple sclerosis, obtained a declaration that it would be lawful to reinsert her feeding tube (PEG), which had become detached. KH had been incompetent, due to the effects of her illness, for at least 20 years and was now only minimally conscious, being unable to recognise her family or to utter more than the occasional word. Physically, most of her bodily functions had ceased to work and she required 24-hour care to survive. In their appeal, KH's family presented evidence that she had made it clear, when still competent, that she would not wish to be kept alive in her present condition.

Brooke LJ: [14] In a case like this there are three tests that have to be applied. First, is the patient capable of taking an informed decision for herself? I need not pause on that test. It is agreed that KH is not so capable and has not been so capable for many years.

[15] The next question when what is being proposed amounts to a trespass is whether there is a clear exposition of the patient's wishes before she became incapable, which is capable in law of amounting to a direction as to how she wishes to be treated when no longer capable of taking decisions for herself. The logic behind this is that the important principle of personal autonomy means that each one of us, certainly when we become an adult, are capable of saying no to any infringement of our bodily integrity. The insertion of a PEG tube would certainly be an infringement of KH's bodily integrity. If we say this clearly at a time when we are capable of expressing our wishes, then that clear declaration is binding on those who would have the responsibility for our care when we are no longer competent. But the declaration has to be clear and it has to be referable to the particular circumstances.

... [21] I am of the clear view that the judge was correct in finding that there was not an advance directive which was sufficiently clear to amount to a direction that she preferred to be deprived of food and drink for a period of time which would lead to her death in all circumstances. There is no evidence that she was aware of the nature of this choice, or the unpleasantness or otherwise of death by starvation, and it would be departing from established principles of English law if one was to hold that there was an advance directive which was established and relevant in the circumstances in the present case, despite the very strong expression of her wishes which came through in the evidence.

[22] One is then left with stage 3, which is where the patient's best interests lie ...

[23] The judge was referred, and the court today has been referred, to the helpful summaries of the law included in the judgment of Mr Justice Munby in *R (on the application of Burke) v The General Medical Council* [2004] EWHC 1879 (Admin) ... If the House of Lords in 1990 had come down in favour of substituted choice so that the law of England was that the court should put itself in the shoes of the patient and do its best to make a choice now, then we would be applying a different test, and one which might well be more favourable to the family than the test which the law requires us to apply.

[24] Mr H, who has addressed us with great clarity and dignity, referred us in particular to the quotation from paragraph 1.2 of the British Medical Association's Guidance for Decision-making, quoted in paragraph 112 of Mr Justice Munby's judgment [in *Burke*], in which the British Medical Association say:

> 'Where, however, the disability is so profound that individuals have no or minimal levels of awareness of their own existence and no hope of recovering awareness ... the question arises as to whether continuing to provide treatment aimed at prolonging that life artificially would provide a benefit to them.'

He said that his sister no longer had any of the qualities which are referred to in that guidance.

[25] As Mr Justice Munby said, after referring to that guidance, the test which the law applies is 'best interests'. The touchstone of best interests in this context is intolerability ...

... [27] The way that the judge came to the conclusion was that in KH's present state he was unable to say that life prolonging treatment would provide no benefit, and that death by, in effect, starvation would be even less dignified than the death which she will face in due course if kept artificially alive for more weeks or months or possibly years.

[28] The judgment is not ours to make. This is a court of appeal. The balance is for the judge of first instance to assess, and this court can only interfere on well recognised grounds if the judge has misdirected himself in law or there are reasons why we are entitled to fault the exercise of the judgment he concluded.

[29] The judge, having rightly put on one side the question whether there was a legally binding advance directive, looked, on the one hand, at the consequences of withdrawing nutrition and the effect this would have and, on the other hand, at the continuance of a life in which there is some feeling of pain, some sensation and some slight ability to answer questions. He came to the conclusion that it was in the best interests of the patient to accede to the unanimous wish of those who are responsible for her treatment.

[30] As I have said, the Official Solicitor supports this application. These cases are always agonisingly difficult. Nobody would wish to be in the position in which the members of this family find themselves. But judges have to apply the law as they find it. English law, as it stands at present, places a very heavy burden on those who are advocating a course which would lead inevitably to the cessation of a human life. In my judgment, it is impossible for this court to interfere with the judge's judgment.

[31] Accordingly I would dismiss this appeal.

This case may be seen as an illustration of Taylor LJ's *dictum* in the *Re J* (1990) case, that 'the court's high respect for the sanctity of human life imposes a strong presumption in favour of taking all steps capable of preserving it'. In fact, the Mental Capacity Bill 2004 proposed to incorporate this presumption into the 'best interests' test: clause 4(5) stated that, '[the decision-maker] must, where the determination relates to life-sustaining treatment, begin by assuming that it will be in the person's interests for his life to continue'.

However, this clause was altered late in the day, and s 4(5) of the 2005 Act now reads rather differently:

Mental Capacity Act 2005:

4 Best interests

... (5) Where the determination relates to life-sustaining treatment [the person making the determination] must not, in considering whether the treatment is in the best interests of the person concerned, be motivated by a desire to bring about his death.

This is a peculiar provision. On the one hand it acknowledges that removal of life-sustaining treatment may sometimes be in a person's best interests. On the other, it attempts to exclude wrongly motivated determinations by the decision-maker. However, it is hard to see what one has to do with the other. (Suppose that a doctor would be very pleased if a given patient dies, as he stands to gain a fortune in her will: this is surely irrelevant to the fact (if established) that the patient's continued life would be intolerable.) It remains to be seen how the courts will interpret the sub-section.

As noted, the Court of Appeal in the *W Healthcare* case was not asked to consider the application of Article 3 of the ECHR to the facts. This is unfortunate as it could have served to clarify an important point that has already given rise to divergent views in the High Court, namely whether, to be engaged, Article 3 requires the patient to be aware of the indignity or suffering caused by his or her treatment (compare Butler-Sloss P's view in *NHS Trust A v M, NHS Trust B v H* [2001] 1 All ER

801 that awareness is required, with that of Munby J in *Burke v GMC* [2004] EWHC 1879 that it is not). In this regard, the Court would have had to decide whether the (apparently unfelt) indignity of KH's life in her present condition was more inimical to her Article 3 rights than the physical suffering that she might undergo in the process of slowly starving to death.

Substituted judgment?

In his judgment in the *W Healthcare* case, Brooke LJ alluded to an alternative to the best interests approach, which might potentially be applied in such cases (and could have favoured the views of KH's family), namely the test of substituted judgment. As noted in Chapter 4, this test directs attention to the hypothetical wishes of the incompetent person. It does so by asking whether the patient himself (were he magically restored for a split second to his former state of competence) would wish to receive treatment in his present circumstances. This approach has been used in a number of American cases involving the withdrawal of treatment from permanently insensate patients: see, for example, *Re Quinlan* 70 NJ 10 (1976) and *Re Jobes* 529 A 2d 434 (1987); however, in *Airedale NHS Trust v Bland* [1993] 1 All ER 821, the House of Lords disparaged the test's application in English law:

> **Lord Mustill**: The second method, which is adopted if the evidence is insufficient to justify an inference of what the patient chose in the past so that it can be projected to the present, involves the appointment of a surrogate to make on behalf of the patient the choice which he believes the patient would now make if able to do so. For this purpose the surrogate builds up a picture of the patient's former character, feelings, convictions and so on from which the putative choice is deduced. This process may perhaps have some justification where the patient is sentient but unable to communicate a choice, but it breaks down totally in a case such as the present. To postulate a patient who is in such a condition that he cannot know that there is a choice to be made, or indeed know anything at all, and then ask whether he would have chosen to terminate his life because that condition made it no longer worth living is surely meaningless, as is very clearly shown by the lengths to which the court was driven in *Superintendent of Belchertown State School v Saikewicz* 370 NE 2d 417. The idea is simply a fiction, which I would not be willing to adopt even if there were in the case of Anthony Bland any materials upon which a surrogate could act, which as far as I can see there are not.

(See also the judgment of Lord Goff, pp 871–72, cited in Chapter 4.)

Such disapproval is difficult to reconcile with the law's favourable attitude to advance directives, which embody the same underlying rationale of respecting a person's integrity beyond the onset of incompetence – albeit they perform this task with more formality. It may well be that, as Kennedy and Grubb have argued, their Lordships misunderstood the test as applying to those who had never been competent: the reference to the 1977 American case of *Saikewicz* – which concerned the treatment of a sensate 67 year old man who had been incompetent from birth – is revealing. In fact, a close reading of the latter case suggests that the Massachusetts Supreme Court was applying a straightforward best interests test, albeit this made reference to features peculiar to the patient's situation, in particular his inability to comprehend the purpose of (painful) treatment if given: in contrast to the substituted judgment test proper, there is no forensic inquiry into the patient's erstwhile personality here. (The same, incidentally, may be said of the English Court of Appeal's decision in *Re J (A Minor) (Wardship: Medical Treatment* [1990] 3 All ER

930 where, despite first appearances – recall Taylor LJ's *dictum* that life, following treatment, should be 'intolerable to that child' – the approach of the court was clearly an objective one.)

Prior to *Bland*, in *Re T*, Lord Donaldson MR appeared more sympathetic to substituted judgment in the case of the formerly competent, although he subsumed it within a more general 'best interests' test:

> **Lord Donaldson MR**: Consultation with the next of kin has a further advantage in that it may reveal information as to the personal circumstances of the patient and as to the choice which the patient might have made, if he or she had been in a position to make it. Neither the personal circumstances of the patient nor a speculative answer to the question 'What would the patient have chosen?' can bind the practitioner in his choice of whether or not to treat or how to treat or justify him in acting contrary to a clearly established anticipatory refusal to accept treatment but they are factors to be taken into account by him in forming a clinical judgment as to what is in the best interests of the patient. For example, if he learnt that the patient was a Jehovah's Witness, but had had no evidence of a refusal to accept blood transfusions, he would avoid or postpone any blood transfusion so long as possible.

Subsequently, the Law Commission in its report on mental incapacity endorsed a similar approach:

> **Law Commission, *Mental Incapacity*, Report No 231, 1995, London: HMSO, para 328:**
>
> We recommend that in deciding what is in a person's best interests regard should be had to:
>
> (1) the ascertainable past and present wishes and feelings of the person concerned, and the factors that person would consider if able to do so;
>
> (2) the need to permit and encourage the person to participate, or to improve his or her ability to participate, as fully as possible in anything done for and any decision affecting him or her;
>
> (3) the views of other people whom it is appropriate and practicable to consult about the person's wishes and feelings and what would be in his or her best interests;
>
> (4) whether the purpose for which any action or decision is required can be as effectively achieved in a manner less restrictive of the person's freedom of action. (Draft Bill, cl 3(2).)
>
> **Wishes, feelings and putative factors**
>
> 3.29 -This first element in the checklist establishes the importance of individual views. Realistically, the former views of a person who is without capacity cannot in every case be determinative of the decision which is now to be made. Past wishes and feelings may in any event conflict with feelings the person is still able to express in spite of incapacity. People who cannot make decisions can still experience pleasure and distress. Present wishes and feelings must therefore be taken into account, where necessary balanced with past wishes and feelings. One of the failings of a pure 'substituted judgment' model is the unhelpful idea that a person who cannot make a decision should be treated as if his or her capacity were perfect and unimpaired, and as if present emotions need not also be considered.

These recommendations are broadly reflected in the Mental Capacity Act 2005. As part of the exercise to determine an incompetent person's best interests under s 4(6), the decision-maker is required to consider, 'so far as is reasonably ascertainable

(a) the person's past and present wishes and feelings (and, in particular, any relevant written statement made by him when he had capacity), (b) the beliefs and values that would be likely to influence his decision if he had capacity, and (c) the other factors that he would be likely to consider if he were able to do so'.

Permanently insensate patients

So far our concern has been with patients who have been sentient (ie capable of experience) but severely impaired. Here it has arguably made sense to conduct a form of comparative exercise in which their (intolerable) quality of life is measured against death (conceived of as permanent unconsciousness). We must now consider a second category of patient for whom no such exercise appears possible, viz, those who, while still alive, become permanently insensate. As Jonathan Glover remarks, citing the German idealist philosopher, Arthur Schopenhauer, in subjective terms such patients are already dead:

> **Glover, J, *Causing Death and Saving Lives*, 1977, Harmondsworth: Penguin, pp 45–46:**
>
> I have no way of refuting someone who holds that being alive, even though unconscious, is intrinsically valuable. But it is a view that will seem unattractive to those of us who, in our own case, see a life of permanent coma as in no way preferable to death. From the subjective point of view, there is nothing to choose between the two. Schopenhauer saw this clearly when he said of the destruction of the body:
>
> > But actually we feel this destruction only in the evils of illness or of old age; on the other hand, for the *subject*, death itself consists merely in the moment when consciousness vanishes, since the activity of the brain ceases. The extension of the stoppage to all the other parts of the organism which follows this is really already an event after death. Therefore, in a subjective respect, death concerns only consciousness.

Legally, of course, such patients are alive: as we saw in Chapter 11, death is regarded in law as occurring only when the whole of an individual's brainstem has perished. The brainstem is divided into upper and lower parts, the former, together with the cerebral cortex, being necessary for consciousness while the latter controls the body's automatic functions such as breathing, swallowing and other basic reflexes. When the brain is starved of oxygen, the lower brainstem is the last part of it to die, a fact which may give rise to a permanently insensate condition known, medically, as a permanent (formerly 'persistent') vegetative state or 'PVS'.

The issue of whether a patient diagnosed as being in PVS should be subject to a life-sustaining regime of treatment and care fell to be decided by the House of Lords in the most famous passive euthanasia case in English law to date, *Airedale NHS Trust v Bland* [1993] 1 All ER 821:

Airedale NHS Trust v Bland [1993] 1 All ER 821, HL (Lords Keith, Goff, Browne-Wilkinson, Lowry and Mustill)

Tony Bland suffered massive and irreversible brain damage in the Hillsborough football disaster in April 1989. He had lain in a PVS for more than three years and the medical evidence was unanimous that he would never regain any form of awareness. The trust caring for him applied, with his parents' approval, for a declaration that it would be lawful to withhold further life-prolonging treatment and care (artificial nutrition and hydration as well as antibiotics) from him, thus, allowing him to die. The order was granted by Sir Stephen Brown P in the High Court and unanimously affirmed by the Court of Appeal (Sir Thomas Bingham MR, Butler-Sloss and Hoffmann LJJ). The Official Solicitor appealed:

> **Lord Keith of Kinkel**: The broad issue raised by the appeal is stated by the parties to be: 'In what circumstances, if ever, can those having a duty to feed an invalid lawfully stop doing so?' The immediate issue, however, is whether in the particular circumstances of Anthony Bland's case those in charge of it would be acting lawfully if they discontinued the particular measures, including feeding by nasogastric tube, which are now being used to maintain Anthony Bland in his existing condition ...
>
> The object of medical treatment and care is to benefit the patient. It may do so by taking steps to prevent the occurrence of illness, or, if an illness does occur, by taking steps towards curing it. Where an illness or the effects of an injury cannot be cured, then efforts are directed towards preventing deterioration or relieving pain and suffering. In Anthony Bland's case the first imperative was to prevent him from dying, as he would certainly have done in the absence of the steps that were taken. If he had died, there can be no doubt that the cause of this would have been the injuries which he had suffered. As it was, the steps taken prevented him from dying, and there was instituted the course of treatment and care which still continues. For a time, no doubt, there was some hope that he might recover sufficiently for him to be able to live a life that had some meaning. Some patients who have suffered damage to the cerebral cortex have, indeed, made a complete recovery. It all depends on the degree of damage. But sound medical opinion takes the view that if a PVS patient shows no signs of recovery after six months, or at most a year, then there is no prospect whatever of any recovery. There are techniques available which make it possible to ascertain the state of the cerebral cortex, and in Anthony Bland's case these indicate that ... it has degenerated into a mass of watery fluid. The fundamental question then comes to be whether continuance of the present regime of treatment and care, more than three years after the injuries that resulted in the PVS, would confer any benefit on Anthony Bland. It is argued for the respondents, supported by the *amicus curiae*, that his best interests favour discontinuance. I feel some doubt about this way of putting the matter. In *Re F (Mental Patient: Sterilisation)* [1990] 2 AC 1 this House held that it would be lawful to sterilise a female mental patient who was incapable of giving consent to the procedure. The ground of the decision was that sterilisation would be in the patient's best interests because her life would be fuller and more agreeable if she were sterilised than if she were not. In *Re J (A Minor) (Wardship: Medical Treatment)* [1991] Fam 33 the Court of Appeal held it to be lawful to withhold life-saving treatment from a very young child in circumstances where the child's life, if saved, would be one irredeemably racked by pain and agony. In both cases it was possible to make a value judgment, as to the consequences to a sensate being, of in the one case withholding and in the other case administering the treatment in question. In the case of a permanently insensate being, who if continuing to live would never experience the slightest actual discomfort, it is difficult, if not impossible, to make any relevant comparison between continued existence and the absence of it. It is, however, perhaps permissible to say that to an individual with no cognitive capacity whatever, and no prospect of ever recovering any such capacity in this world, it must be a matter of complete indifference whether he lives or dies.
>
> Where one individual has assumed responsibility for the care of another who cannot look after himself or herself, whether as a medical practitioner or otherwise, that responsibility cannot lawfully be shed unless arrangements are made for the responsibility to be taken over by someone else. Thus a person having charge of a

baby who fails to feed it, so that it dies, will be guilty at least of manslaughter. The same is true of one having charge of an adult who is frail and cannot look after herself: *R v Stone* [1977] QB 354. It was argued for the guardian *ad litem*, by analogy with that case, that here the doctors in charge of Anthony Bland had a continuing duty to feed him by means of the nasogastric tube and that if they failed to carry out that duty they were guilty of manslaughter, if not murder. This was coupled with the argument that feeding by means of the nasogastric tube was not medical treatment at all, but simply feeding, indistinguishable from feeding by normal means. As regards this latter argument, I am of opinion that regard should be had to the whole regime, including the artificial feeding, which at present keeps Anthony Bland alive. That regime amounts to medical treatment and care, and it is incorrect to direct attention exclusively to the fact that nourishment is being provided. In any event, the administration of nourishment by the means adopted involves the application of a medical technique. But it is, of course, true that in general it would not he lawful for a medical practitioner who assumed responsibility for the care of an unconscious patient simply to give up treatment in circumstances where continuance of it would confer some benefit on the patient. On the other hand a medical practitioner is under no duty to continue to treat such a patient where a large body of informed and responsible medical opinion is to the effect that no benefit at all would be conferred by continuance. Existence in a vegetative state with no prospect of recovery is by that opinion regarded as not being a benefit, and that, if not unarguably correct, at least forms a proper basis for the decision to discontinue treatment and care: *Bolam v Friern Hospital Management Committee* [1957] 1 WLR 582.

Given that existence in the persistent vegetative state is not a benefit to the patient, it remains to consider whether the principle of the sanctity of life, which it is the concern of the State, and the judiciary as one of the arms of the State, to maintain, requires this House to hold that the judgment of the Court of Appeal was incorrect. In my opinion it does not. The principle is not an absolute one. It does not compel a medical practitioner on pain of criminal sanctions to treat a patient, who will die if he does not, contrary to the express wishes of the patient. It does not authorise forcible feeding of prisoners on hunger strike. It does not compel the temporary keeping alive of patients who are terminally ill where to do so would merely prolong their suffering. On the other hand it forbids the taking of active measures to cut short the life of a terminally ill patient. In my judgment it does no violence to the principle to hold that it is lawful to cease to give medical treatment and care to a PVS patient who has been in that state for over three years, considering that to do so involves invasive manipulation of the patient's body to which he has not consented and which confers no benefit upon him ...

My Lords, for these reasons, which are substantially the same as those set out in the speech delivered by my noble and learned friend, Lord Goff of Chieveley, with which I agree, I would dismiss the appeal.

The rest of their Lordships delivered concurring speeches.

Best interests in PVS?

As we have seen, there is a philosophical problem in applying the best interests approach to a patient who will never again enjoy any form of experience. For such patients, rather than offering any prospect of release from suffering, death must (as Lord Keith recognised) be a matter of pure indifference. Thus, it might well be argued, it cannot be in their best interests. In the Court of Appeal in *Bland*, Hoffmann LJ, drawing on Ronald Dworkin's work, *Life's Dominion*, addressed this difficulty by suggesting that patients in PVS do in fact retain certain interests (*critical*

– as opposed to *experiential* – interests, in Dworkinian terms) and that these are served by allowing them to die:

> **Hoffmann LJ**: Counsel for the Official Solicitor argued that however vestigial Anthony Bland's life might be, one could not assume that he would choose to die. Being unconscious, he felt no pain or humiliation and therefore had no interests which suffered from his being kept alive. Anthony Bland was in fact indifferent to whether he lived or died and there was nothing to put in the balance against the intrinsic value of his life.
>
> I think that the fallacy in this argument is that it assumes that we have no interests except in those things of which we have conscious experience. But this does not accord with most people's intuitive feelings about their lives and deaths. At least a part of the reason why we honour the wishes of the dead about the distribution of their property is that we think it would wrong them not to do so, despite the fact that we believe that they will never know that their will has been ignored. Most people would like an honourable and dignified death and we think it wrong to dishonour their deaths, even when they are unconscious that this is happening. We pay respect to their dead bodies and to their memory because we think it an offence against the dead themselves if we do not. Once again I am not concerned to analyse the rationality of these feelings. It is enough that they are deeply rooted in our ways of thinking and that the law cannot possibly ignore them. Thus I think that counsel for the Official Solicitor offers a seriously incomplete picture of Anthony Bland's interests when he confines them to animal feelings of pain or pleasure. It is demeaning to the human spirit to say that, being unconscious, he can have no interest in his personal privacy and dignity, in how he lives or dies ...

This argument has a slightly metaphysical flavour and was not adopted in the House of Lords. Instead, as reflected in Lord Keith's judgment, their Lordships preferred to look at the question from the opposite direction and ask if *treatment* was a benefit to the patient. This approach found its most robust expression in the speech of Lord Mustill:

> **Lord Mustill**: [Anthony Bland] feels no pain and suffers no mental anguish. Stress was laid in argument on the damage to his personal dignity by the continuation of the present medical regime, and on the progressive erosion of the family's happy recollections by month after month of distressing and hopeless care. Considerations of this kind will no doubt carry great weight when parliament comes to consider the whole question in the round. But it seems to me to be stretching the concept of personal rights beyond breaking point to say that Anthony Bland has an interest in ending these sources of others' distress. Unlike the conscious patient he does not know what is happening to his body, and cannot be affronted by it; he does not know of his family's continuing sorrow. By ending his life the doctors will not relieve him of a burden become intolerable, for others carry the burden and he has none. What other considerations could make it better for him to die now rather than later? None that we can measure, for of death we know nothing. The distressing truth which must not be shirked is that the proposed conduct is not in the best interests of Anthony Bland, for he has no best interests of any kind.

Best interests: the termination of treatment

After much expression of negative opinions I turn to an argument which in my judgment is logically defensible and consistent with the existing law. In essence it turns the previous argument on its head by directing the inquiry to the interests of the patient, not in the termination of life but in the continuation of his treatment. It runs as follows: (i) the cessation of nourishment and hydration is an omission not an act;

(ii) accordingly, the cessation will not be a criminal act unless the doctors are under a present duty to continue the regime; (iii) at the time when Anthony Bland came into the care of the doctors, decisions had to be made about his care which he was unable to make for himself. In accordance with *Re F* [1990] 2 AC 1 these decisions were to be made in his best interests. Since the possibility that he might recover still existed his best interests required that he should be supported in the hope that this would happen. These best interests justified the application of the necessary regime without his consent; (iv) all hope of recovery has now been abandoned. Thus, although the termination of his life is not in the best interests of Anthony Bland, his best interests in being kept alive have also disappeared, taking with them the justification for the non-consensual regime and the correlative duty to keep it in being; (v) since there is no longer a duty to provide nourishment and hydration, failure to do so cannot be a criminal offence.

However, although unassailable as a matter of logic, this analysis may be thought to attach too little weight to the general presumption, underpinning the qualified sanctity of life principle, that life should be preserved unless death is unambiguously preferable.

Today, of course, such matters must also be assessed through the prism of human rights jurisprudence centred upon the ECHR. In this context it is interesting that Munby J, in his recent and compendious summary of legal principle in *R (On the Application of Burke) v GMC* [2004] EWHC 1879, expressed a clear preference for Hoffmann LJ's approach in *Bland*. As noted, he was also of the view that Article 3 of the ECHR could extend to protect the objective interest in dignity of patients with no self-awareness. However, this gives rise to the awkward question of whether such an interest might actually *require* that PVS patients be allowed to die. (It may be noted in passing that, in *Bland*, two Law Lords (Browne-Wilkinson, at p 883, and Lowry, at p 876) suggested that, if it could clearly be established that life-prolonging treatment were no longer in an incompetent patient's best interests, such treatment would become an unlawful battery.)

It must be said that, in *Burke*, the case was not directly concerned with the position of PVS patients. On the other hand, the ECHR compatibility of the common law relating to such patients was the focus of the following decision by the President of the Family Division in 2001:

NHS Trust A v M, NHS Trust B v H [2001] Fam 348, Fam Div (Butler-Sloss P)

Mrs M and Mrs H were two patients who had been in PVS for three years, and nine months, respectively. The applicant hospital trusts, supported by the women's families, applied for declarations that, notwithstanding the HRA 1998, it would be lawful to discontinue artificial nutrition and hydration in respect of each of them. In granting the declarations, Butler-Sloss P analysed the effect of the ECHR as follows:

Butler-Sloss P: If a decision to cease medical treatment in the best interests of the patient is to be characterised as intentional deprivation of life, in view of the absolute nature of the prohibition on intentional killing, [Counsel] submitted that there would be a duty in every case to take steps to keep a terminally ill patient alive by all means possible, and to continue those steps indefinitely, until the patient's body could no longer sustain treatment, irrespective of the circumstances or the prognosis. I agree with [Counsel] that such an interpretation of article 2 [the right to life] cannot be correct.

Although the intention in withdrawing artificial nutrition and hydration in PVS cases is to hasten death, in my judgment the phrase 'deprivation of life' must import a deliberate act, as opposed to an omission, by someone acting on behalf of the state, which results in death. A responsible decision by a medical team not to provide treatment at the initial stage could not amount to intentional deprivation of life by the state. Such a decision based on clinical judgment is an omission to act. The death of the patient is the result of the illness or injury from which he suffered and that cannot be described as a deprivation. It may be relevant to look at the reasons for the clinical decision in the light of the positive obligation of the state to safeguard life, but, in my judgment, it cannot be regarded as falling within the negative obligation to refrain from taking life intentionally. I cannot see the difference between that situation and a decision to discontinue treatment which is no longer in the best interests of the patient and would therefore be a violation of his autonomy, even though that discontinuance will have the effect of shortening the life of the patient.

The analysis of these issues by the House of Lords in *Bland's* case [1993] AC 789 is entirely in accordance with the Convention case law on article 2 and is applicable to the distinction between negative and positive obligations ...

However, article 2 also contains a positive obligation, to take adequate and appropriate steps to safeguard life: see *Osman v United Kingdom* (1998) 29 EHRR 245 305, para 115. [Even so] that positive obligation upon a state to protect life is not absolute ... The court held in the *Osman* case, at p 306, para 116:

> For the court, and having regard to the nature of the right protected by article 2, a right fundamental in the scheme of the Convention, it is sufficient for an applicant to show that the authorities did not do all that could be reasonably expected of them to avoid a real and immediate risk to life of which they have or ought to have knowledge. This is a question which can only be answered in the light of all the circumstances of any particular case.

The standard applied by the European Court of Human Rights bears a close resemblance to the standard adopted in the domestic law of negligence and approximates to the obligation recognised by the English courts in the *Bolam* test ...: see *Airedale NHS Trust v Bland* [1993] AC 789. In a case where a responsible clinical decision is made to withhold treatment, on the grounds that it is not in the patient's best interests, and that clinical decision is made in accordance with a respectable body of medical opinion, the state's positive obligation under article 2 is, in my view, discharged.

In *Widmer v Switzerland* (unreported) the Commission considered the claim that there was negligent failure on the part of the hospital to treat the applicant's father. The Commission rejected the petition and said that 'the idea that the right of any person to life is protected by law requires the state ... to take all reasonable steps to protect life'. It considered that Switzerland in its legislation had taken sufficient steps to carry out the duty imposed upon it by article 2. The court in *Osman v United Kingdom* 29 EHRR 245, 305, para 116 said that the positive obligation under article 2 'must be interpreted in a way which does not impose an impossible or disproportionate burden on the authorities'.

Article 2 therefore imposes a positive obligation to give life-sustaining treatment in circumstances where, according to responsible medical opinion, such treatment is in the best interests of the patient but does not impose an absolute obligation to treat if such treatment would be futile. This approach is entirely in accord with the principles laid down in *Airedale NHS Trust v Bland* ...

As regards Article 3, the President held that this had no application to patients in a state of non-awareness.

On the assumption that article 3 requires to be considered, I am satisfied that the proposed withdrawal of treatment from these two patients has been thoroughly and anxiously considered by a number of experts in the field of PVS patients and is in accordance with the practice of a responsible body of medical opinion. The withdrawal is for a benign purpose in accordance with the best interests of the patients not to continue life-saving treatment; it is legitimate and appropriate that the residual treatment be continued until death. I am, moreover, satisfied that article 3 requires the victim to be aware of the inhuman and degrading treatment which he or she is experiencing or at least to be in a state of physical or mental suffering. An insensate patient suffering from permanent vegetative state has no feelings and no comprehension of the treatment accorded to him or her. Article 3 does not in my judgment apply to these two cases.

Here, of course, the point at issue was whether Article 3 militated *against* the withdrawal of treatment, not whether it positively *required* this. Nonetheless, in view of the Article's doubled-edge quality, the President's approach, short-circuiting arguments based upon it, has the merit of simplicity. In general, her decision is strongly to the effect that the principles developed in the case law prior to the HRA 1998 remain good law.

Concerns in relation to decisions withdrawing treatment from patients in PVS

It is certainly unlikely that doctors, others (including relatives) involved in the care of patients in PVS would accept any interpretation of the law that required them to cease treatment (as opposed to sometimes permitting them to do so). As Margaret Brazier suggests in the following extract, the general concern following *Bland* has rather been that treatment has in some cases been withdrawn too readily, including in cases of so-called 'near PVS':

Brazier, M, *Medicine, Patients and the Law*, 3rd edn, 2003, Harmondsworth: Penguin, p 451:

The series of decisions that followed *Bland* indicate that it has led to radical change in the law governing the end of life. The carefully constituted limitations built into *Bland* to keep that decision within bounds have been eroded step by step. In [*Frenchay Healthcare NHS Trust v S* [1994] 2 All ER 403] the patient was said to have been in PVS for two and a half years following a drug overdose. His feeding tube was accidentally disconnected. The hospital immediately sought a declaration that it could lawfully refrain from re-inserting the tube. The Court of Appeal granted the declaration in haste and without any independent medical opinion confirming that S was irreversibly in PVS. The court recognised that the evidence as to S's condition was neither as unanimous nor as emphatic as in *Bland*. The judges found that in the emergency that had arisen because of the disconnection of the tube, there was no benefit conferred on S by reinserting the tube. Indeed following Lord Browne-Wilkinson's reasoning in *Bland* it might be construed as an assault on S to do so. In these circumstances the further inquiry necessary to take an independent medical opinion could be dispensed with. A fortuitous event affected the criteria set out in Bland to protect patients. On the facts of *S* some doubt exists as to whether S was truly in PVS. There was evidence of restlessness and distress for which S was receiving medication. The third condition set by Lord Goff in *Bland*, independent evidence confirming PVS, survived for barely a year.

Subsequent decisions erode the *Bland* limitations still further. In [*Re D (Medical Treatment)* [1998] FLR 411] the patient had suffered serious brain damage after a road accident. As in *Frenchay*, her feeding tube had become disconnected. Stephen Brown P accepted evidence that D's condition did not fully conform to guidelines for the diagnosis of PVS laid down by the Royal College of Physicians. He was satisfied that there was 'no evidence of any meaningful life whatsoever' and held that it was lawful to refrain from re-inserting the tube. In [*Re H (A Patient)* [1998] 2 FLR 36] a 43 year old woman had suffered brain injuries in a car crash. She retained some rudimentary awareness and like D did not fit squarely within the RCP definition of PVS. The President of the Family Division authorised cessation of artificial feeding. He was '... satisfied that it is in the best interests of this patient that the life sustaining treatment currently being administered should be brought to a conclusion'.

In *Bland*, *Frenchay*, *D* and *H* the patient's family fully supported the doctors' judgement to cease treatment. [*Re G (Persistent Vegetative State)* [1995] 2 FCR 46] revealed a difference of opinion among the family. G suffered serious injuries while riding his motorcycle. In the course of attempts to resuscitate him, he suffered a heart attack, which resulted in the interruption of blood flow to his brain. In 1992 he was diagnosed as being in PVS, a state in which he had lain for nearly two years at the time of the application to withdraw feeding. G's wife and mother remained devoted to him and visited regularly. G's wife somewhat reluctantly supported the application to withdraw feeding from G. His mother opposed the application. Stephen Brown P said that he was satisfied that doctors had taken into account all the views of G's family. The mother's views could not prevail against what was considered to be in the best interests of the patient. It might be argued that the wife's judgement should be preferred. This is not the basis of the finding in G. The judge seems to give relatively little weight to any relative's views. He says:

> It would indeed be an apalling burden to place on any relative to transfer as it were the responsibility for making a decision in a case of this nature to that relative. In this case, the responsibility must ultimately remain with the doctors in charge of the case, albeit taking fully into account the views of relatives.

Mason and McCall Smith [*Medical Ethics and the Law*, at p 401] comment that the '... heavy and continuing emphasis placed on medical assessment rather than on a robust and principled approach to individualised human and patients' rights may mean that an expansionist development of clinical discretion is inevitable'.

It may be thought curious that in some of these cases, the application to court was expedited after a spontaneous problem developed with the patient's feeding tube. (Another example is the recent non-PVS case of *W Healthcare NHS Trust v H* discussed earlier.) Such hasty decisions will predictably arouse public concern. Moreover, in legal terms, they are unnecessary: just as it makes no difference whether a doctor removes a patient's feeding tube or fails to reconnect it (both are omissions *per* Lord Goff in *Bland*) equally there is no reason to regard the act of reattaching the tube as any more of a battery (if that is what it is) than was previously constituted by the regime of artificial feeding.

Other bases for the withdrawal of life-sustaining medical treatment?

'Impractability'

In his judgment in *R (On the Application of Burke) v GMC* [2004] EWHC 1879, Munby J suggested that, besides the PVS type of case, where continued treatment may be said to be futile, and the class of case looked at earlier of sentient incompetentent patients whose lives with continued treatment would be 'intolerable', there may be a third category of case where it is permissible to withdraw life-sustaining treatment, namely where it is impractical to administer it. By way of illustration, he posited a case in which 'the patient, although incompetent, strongly objects and is not prepared to submit to the relevant procedure ...'.

This type of situation occurred in the case of *Re D (Medical Treatment: Mentally Disabled Patient)* [1998] 2 FLR 22, where a long term psychiatric patient required on-going dialysis treatment for renal failure. The patient was refusing to cooperate and sometimes had to be anaesthetised for the treatment to take place. In the circumstances, the High Court ruled that the continued imposition of dialysis was not in the patient's best interests. However, arguably a stricter approach may be found in the subsequent case of *A Hospital NHS Trust v S and others* [2003] EWHC 365 (Fam). Here, the question for the High Court related to the medical care of an 18 year old with serious mental disabilities, who had suffered end stage renal failure. In holding that further, invasive treatment (possibly including a kidney transplant) should not be ruled out on 'non-medical grounds', Butler-Sloss P commented as follows:

> **Butler-Sloss P:** [64] The medical situation cannot, of course, be considered in isolation. There is no doubt that S's severe learning disability militates against explanations other than the simplest. I recognise the complexity of the operation and the probability of emergency recall to hospital on more than one occasion. I recognise the real concerns about the risk of infection and the likely need for one, or possibly even several, biopsies and the added difficulties for S to have an immediate biopsy, since he is on warfarin. The very real concerns of the Hospital Trust are, however, mainly based upon the consequences of emergency surgery on an autistic boy without any preparation of any kind. However, an emergency admission to hospital followed by lifesaving surgery and treatment would be a traumatic experience for anyone. For an autistic boy, as I have set out above, it must have been extremely distressing and he reacted accordingly. I have little doubt from the evidence of Dr H as to how to manage someone suffering from autism in the hospital surroundings, supported by the evidence of Ms C that a lot could be done to prepare S for the more practical and concrete elements of a major operation. He is accustomed to having minor operations. Post-operatively, the presence of someone he knows who is able to talk to him by facilitated methods would probably help considerably. With some preparation and with the support of a person or people in whom he had trust, in my view, and despite the opposite conclusions of the medical and nursing team at the Hospital Trust, S ought to be manageable post operation. The need for blood tests, the use of needles and the likelihood of several returns to hospital post operation, do not seem to me to be insuperable obstacles. On balance, however, if the medical reasons for a kidney transplantation are in his favour, and alternative methods of dialysis are no longer viable, in my judgment, a kidney transplantation ought not to be rejected on the grounds of his inability to understand the purpose and consequences of the operation or concerns about his management.

Resource issues

The general discussion has so far ignored the fact that, in keeping alive patients who enjoy a low (or, in the case of someone in PVS, non-existent) quality of life, there is an 'opportunity cost' in the sense that scarce resources are expended which might otherwise be utilised upon people with a greater capacity to benefit from them. In *Re*

J (A Minor) (Wardship: Medical Treatment) [1992] 4 All ER 614 (not to be confused with the case of the same name and similar facts from 1990), the Court of Appeal quashed the trial judge's order that the health authority treat a severely disabled baby. Balcombe LJ stated:

> **Balcombe LJ**: I would also stress the absolute undesirability of the court making an order which may have the effect of compelling a doctor or health authority to make available scarce resources (both human and material) to a particular child, without knowing whether or not there are other patients to whom those resources might more advantageously be devoted. Lord Donaldson MR has set out in his reasons the condition of J and his very limited future prospects. The effect of the order of Waite J, had it not been immediately stayed by this court, might have been to require the health authority to put J on a ventilator in an intensive care unit, and thereby possibly to deny the benefit of those limited resources to a child who was much more likely than J to benefit from them. At the very least it would in those circumstances have required the health authority to make a further application to the court to vary or discharge the injunction.

In *Airedale NHS Trust v Bland* [1993] 1 All ER 821, the fact that resource allocation is ultimately an issue that must be faced up to was noted by Lord Mustill:

> **Lord Mustill:**
>
> **Best interests of the community**
>
> Threaded through the technical arguments addressed to the House were the strands of a much wider position, that it is in the best interests of the community at large that Anthony Bland's life should now end. The doctors have done all they can. Nothing will be gained by going on and much will be lost. The distress of the family will get steadily worse. The strain on the devotion of a medical staff charged with the care of a patient whose condition will never improve, who may live for years and who does not even recognise that he is being cared for, will continue to mount. The large resources of skill, labour and money now being devoted to Anthony Bland might in the opinion of many be more fruitfully employed in improving the condition of other patients, who if treated may have useful, healthy and enjoyable lives for years to come.
>
> This argument was never squarely put, although hinted at from time to time. In social terms it has great force, and it will have to be faced in the end. But this is not a task which the courts can possibly undertake. A social cost-benefit analysis of this kind, which would have to embrace 'mercy killing' to which exactly the same considerations apply, must be for parliament alone, and the outcome of it is at present quite impossible to foresee. Until the nettle is grasped, we must struggle on with the existing law, imperfect as it is.

(See further on the resources question the discussion in Chapter 2.)

The role of the court

A safeguard laid down in the *Bland* case in relation to patients in PVS was that the decision to withdraw treatment should invariably be subject to judicial sanction. In this regard, Lord Goff commented in his speech as follows:

> **Lord Goff:** I turn finally to the extent to which doctors should, as a matter of practice, seek the guidance of the court, by way of an application for declaratory relief, before withholding life-prolonging treatment from a PVS patient. The President considered

that the opinion of the court should be sought in all cases similar to the present. In the Court of Appeal, Sir Thomas Bingham MR expressed his agreement with Sir Stephen Brown P in the following words ... pp 815–16:

> This was in my respectful view a wise ruling, directed to the protection of patients, the protection of doctors, the reassurance of patients' families and the reassurance of the public. The practice proposed seems to me desirable. It may very well be that with the passage of time a body of experience and practice will build up which will obviate the need for application in every case, but for the time being I am satisfied that the practice which the President described should be followed.

Before the Appellate Committee, this view was supported both by Mr Munby, for the Official Solicitor, and by Mr Lester, as *amicus curiae*. For the respondents, Mr Francis suggested that an adequate safeguard would be provided if reference to the court was required in certain specific cases, ie, (1) where there was known to be a medical disagreement as to the diagnosis or prognosis, and (2) problems had arisen with the patient's relatives – disagreement by the next of kin with the medical recommendation; actual or apparent conflict of interest between the next of kin and the patient; dispute between members of the patient's family; or absence of any next of kin to give their consent. There is, I consider, much to be said for the view that an application to the court will not be needed in every case, but only in particular circumstances, such as those suggested by Mr Francis. In this connection I was impressed not only by the care being taken by the Medical Ethics Committee to provide guidance to the profession, but also by information given to the Appellate Committee about the substantial number of PVS patients in the country, and the very considerable cost of obtaining guidance from the court in cases such as the present. However, in my opinion this is a matter which would be better kept under review by the President of the Family Division than resolved now by your Lordships' House. I understand that a similar review is being undertaken in cases concerned with the sterilisation of adult women of unsound mind, with a consequent relaxation of the practice relating to applications to the court in such cases. For my part, I would therefore leave the matter as proposed by the Master of the Rolls; but I wish to express the hope that the President of the Family Division, who will no doubt be kept well informed about developments in this field, will soon feel able to relax the present requirement so as to limit applications for declarations to those cases in which there is a special need for the procedure to be invoked.

In the subsequent Court of Appeal decision of *Frenchay NHS Trust v S* [1994] 2 All ER 403, Sir Thomas Bingham MR made it clear that, while judges would attach great weight to medical opinion in deciding whether continued treatment was in a patient's best interests, the ultimate decision lay with the court:

Sir Thomas Bingham MR: Mr Munby ... submit[s] that the judge erred in attaching too much importance to the judgment of doctors as to what was in the patient's best interests. Mr Munby submits that the House of Lords' decision in *Airedale NHS Trust v Bland* ... left open whether the judgment was finally to be made by the doctors or by the court, his submission being that in the last resort it must be made by the court, albeit with great regard to the opinions of responsible medical men. It is true that the learned judge paid close attention to what members of the House of Lords had said about the subject in the course of their speeches in *Bland*'s case and did express the view that the conclusion at which S's consultant had arrived was reasonable and bona fide. He regarded the judgments which had been expressed by the doctors in this case as being fully in accord with criteria which their Lordships had laid down. It is, I think, important that there should not be a belief that what the doctor says is the patient's best interest is the patient's best interest. For my part I would certainly reserve to the court the ultimate power and duty to review the doctors' decision in the light of all the facts.

An important question is how far the courts must also be involved in similar decisions in relation to incompetent patients not in PVS. In *R (on the application of Burke) v GMC* [2004] EWHC 1879, Munby J suggested that, in the light of ECHR considerations, what had previously been a matter of good practice, was now at least in certain circumstances a legal requirement: the failure to involve the court would violate the patient's right to respect for his private and family life under Article 8 ECHR. He derived this principle in particular from the ECtHR's ruling in *Glass v UK* [2004] 1 FCR 553 (see Chapter 4 above).

This was however rejected in forthright terms by the Court of Appeal, which was dismissive as to the significance of the *Glass* ruling (implying that the ECtHR had misunderstood the applicable English law):

R (On the Application of Burke) v GMC [2005] EWCA 1003, CA (Lord Phillips MR, Waller and Wall LJJ)

Lord Phillips MR (delivering the judgment of the Court):

Is there a legal requirement to obtain court authorisation before withdrawing ANH?

[67] The judge's Declaration (6) suggests that "in certain circumstances" this question must be answered in the affirmative. What circumstances did the judge have in mind? The answer is given by paragraph 214(g) of his judgment:

> "(g) Where it is proposed to withhold or withdraw ANH the prior authorisation of the court is required as a matter of law (and thus ANH cannot be withheld or withdrawn without prior judicial authorisation): (i) where there is any dou bt or disagreement as to the capacity (competence) of the patient; or (ii) where there is a lack of unanimity amongst the attending medical professionals as to either (1) the patient's condition or prognosis or (2) the patient's best interests or (3) the likely outcome of ANH being either withheld or withdrawn or (4) otherwise as to whether or not ANH should be withheld or withdrawn; or (iii) where there is evidence that the patient when competent would have wanted ANH to continue in the relevant circumstances; or (iv) where there is evidence that the patient (even if a child or incompetent) resists or disputes the proposed withdrawal of ANH; or (v) where persons having a reasonable claim to have their views or evidence taken into account (such as parents or close relatives, partners, close friends, long-term carers) assert that withdrawal of ANH is contrary to the patient's wishes or not in the patient's best interests." ...

[69] Declaration (6) has caused considerable concern. The Intensive Care Society informed us that each year approximately 50,000 patients are admitted to intensive care units and of these 30% die in the unit or on the wards before hospital discharge. Most of these die because treatment is withdrawn or limited, albeit in circumstances where the clinicians conclude that such treatment would be likely merely to prolong the process of dying. There is not always agreement on the part of all concerned as to the withdrawal of treatment. This is hardly surprising. Grief stricken relatives may not be able to accept that the patient is beyond saving. The ICS calculates that, if Munby J's criteria were applied, approximately 10 applications a day would have to be made to the courts.

[70] In the event, we do not consider that the judge is right to postulate that there is a legal duty to obtain court approval to the withdrawal of ANH in the circumstances that he identifies ...

[75] [Munby J] concluded that [*Glass v UK*] converted what had previously been only "a matter of good practice" into "a matter of legal requirement" by reason of the Human Rights Act 1998 (judgment paragraph 210). He observed that this was 'a significant and potentially very important change'. If the judge was correct we would concur. Accordingly it is necessary to consider *Glass* with some care.

[76] The application in *Glass* was brought by a mother on behalf of her small child. The complaint related to the treatment of the child when in hospital. The doctors thought that the child was dying and administered diamorphine by way of palliative despite the objections of the mother, who thought that the intention of this treatment was to hasten the child's death. The disagreement culminated in a fight in the hospital and the removal of the child by the mother. The child recovered. The mother also complained that the doctors had imposed a 'do not resuscitate' direction in relation to the child without her consent, but the ECtHR did not give separate consideration to this complaint. They treated the case as one of the imposition of invasive treatment on a child contrary to the wishes of its parent.

[77] The ECtHR gave detailed consideration to the position under English law, as this was presented to the court. The ECtHR understood the position to be as follows. As a general proposition, medical treatment of a child requires the authorisation of the child's parents. Where the parents do not consent, the court can authorise such treatment. The doctors can, however, lawfully impose treatment without the consent of the parents or the authorisation of the court in a situation of emergency ...

[79] After considering the facts, the ECtHR concluded that the mother had not consented to the administration to her child of diamorphine and that, when this became apparent to the doctors, they had ample time to get the court to resolve the position ...

[80] This was not a decision which made "a significant and potentially very important change in English law". The ECtHR did no more than consider the implications of the doctors' conduct in the light of what the ECtHR understood to be English law. The true position is that the court does not "authorise" treatment that would otherwise be unlawful. The court makes a declaration as to whether or not proposed treatment, or the withdrawal of treatment, will be lawful. Good practice may require medical practitioners to seek such a declaration where the legality of proposed treatment is in doubt. This is not, however, something that they are required to do as a matter of law. For these reasons Declaration 6 made by Munby J misstated the law.

Guidance for doctors or relatives who are contemplating applying to the court for a declaration in such cases –including where the patient is in PVS- has been issued by the Official Solicitor: see *Practice Note (Official Solicitor: Declaratory Proceedings: Medical and Welfare Decisions for Adults Who Lack Capacity)* [2001] 2 FLR 158.

REFORMING THE LAW

In the wake of the *Bland* case, a Select Committee of the House of Lords was established to look into the current state of English law in relation to euthanasia. Whilst endorsing steps to facilitate the practice of passive euthanasia (although it avoided this term), such as by encouraging the greater use of advance directives, the

Committee was of the view that both assisted suicide and active euthanasia should remain offences, the latter continuing to be treated as murder:

House of Lords Select Committee, *Report of the Select Committee on Medical Ethics,* **HL Paper No 21, 1994, London: HMSO, Vol I:**

236 The right to refuse treatment is far removed from the right to request assistance in dying. We spent a long time considering the very strongly held and sincerely expressed views of those witnesses who advocated voluntary [active] euthanasia. Many of us have had the experience of relatives or friends whose dying days were less than peaceful or uplifting, or whose final stages of life were so disfigured that the loved one already seemed lost to us, or who were simply weary of life. Our thinking must inevitably be coloured by such experience. The accounts we received from individual members of the public about such experiences were particularly moving, as were the letters from those who themselves longed for the release of an early death. Our thinking must also be coloured by the wish of every individual for a peaceful and easy death, without prolonged suffering, and by a reluctance to contemplate the possibility of severe dementia or dependence. We gave much thought too to Professor [Ronald] Dworkin's opinion that, for those without religious belief, the individual is best able to decide what manner of death is fitting to the life that has been lived.

237 Ultimately, however, we do not believe that these arguments are sufficient reason to weaken society's prohibition of intentional killing. That prohibition is the cornerstone of law and social relationships. It protects each of us impartially, embodying the belief that all are equal. We do not wish that protection to be diminished and we therefore recommend that there be no change in the law to permit euthanasia. We acknowledge that there may be individual cases in which euthanasia may be seen by some to be appropriate. But individual cases cannot reasonably establish the foundation of a policy which would have such serious and widespread repercussions. Moreover dying is not only a personal or individual affair. The death of a person affects the lives of others, often in ways and to an extent that cannot be foreseen. We believe that the issue of euthanasia is one in which the interest of the individual cannot be separated from the interest of society as a whole.

238 One reason for this conclusion is that we do not think it possible to set secure limits on voluntary euthanasia. Some witnesses told us that to legalise voluntary euthanasia was a discrete step which need have no other consequences. But ... issues of life and death do not lend themselves to clear definition, and without that it would not be possible to frame adequate safeguards against non-voluntary euthanasia if voluntary euthanasia were to be legalised. It would be next to impossible to ensure that all acts of euthanasia were truly voluntary, and that any liberalisation of the law was not abused. Moreover to create an exception to the general prohibition of intentional killing would inevitably open the way to its further erosion whether by design, by inadvertence, or by the human tendency to test the limits of any regulation. These dangers are such that we believe that any decriminalisation of voluntary euthanasia would give rise to more, and more grave, problems than those it sought to address. Fear of what some witnesses referred to as a 'slippery slope' could in itself be damaging.

239 We are also concerned that vulnerable people – the elderly, lonely, sick or distressed – would feel pressure, whether real or imagined, to request early death. We accept that, for the most part, requests resulting from such pressure or from remediable depressive illness would be identified as such by doctors and managed appropriately. Nevertheless we believe that the message which society

sends to vulnerable and disadvantaged people should not, however obliquely, encourage them to seek death, but should assure them of our care and support in life.

240 Some of those who advocated voluntary euthanasia did so because they feared that lives were being prolonged by aggressive medical treatment beyond the point at which the individual felt that continued life was not a benefit but a burden. But, in the light of the consensus which is steadily emerging over the circumstances in which life-prolonging treatment may be withdrawn or not initiated, we consider that such fears may increasingly be allayed. We welcome moves by the medical professional bodies to ensure more senior oversight of practice in casualty departments, as a step towards discouraging inappropriately aggressive treatment by less experienced practitioners.

241 Furthermore there is good evidence that, through the outstanding achievements of those who work in the field of palliative care, the pain and distress of terminal illness can be adequately relieved in the vast majority of cases. Such care is available not only within hospices: thanks to the increasing dissemination of best practice by means of home-care teams and training for general practitioners, palliative care is becoming more widely available in the health service, in hospitals and in the community, though much remains to be done. With the necessary political will such care could be made available to all who could benefit from it. We strongly commend the development and growth of palliative care services.

However, the Committee also strongly endorsed the view of a previous Select Committee (*Murder and Life Imprisonment*, Session 1988–89, HL Paper 78, London: HMSO, Vol I), that the mandatory life sentence that follows a conviction for murder should be abolished; the discretion over sentencing thereby given to judges would clearly be highly significant in cases where the agent has killed on compassionate grounds ('mercy killing', as it is often termed).

The generally cautious approach in this country, and in particular the strong endorsement of the acts/omissions distinction central to the 'qualified sanctity of life' doctrine, contrasts with that adopted in certain other jurisdictions. Most well known is the policy in Holland of permitting active steps by doctors in some circumstances, which are directly intended to terminate the lives of their patients. The latter development, and the interest it has aroused within our own legal system, has been commented upon extrajudicially by Lord Goff:

Goff, R, 'A matter of life and death' (1995) 3 Med L Rev 1:

The distinction drawn by the House of Lords in the case of *Anthony Bland*, between on the one hand withholding or withdrawing life sustaining treatment or care and so allowing a patient to die, which may be lawful, and on the other hand actively causing a patient's death, which is not, is one which can readily be understood by lawyers. But it may not be so easily understood by members of the public; and an acute question which has arisen in the aftermath of the cases of *Dr Cox* and *Anthony Bland* is whether the distinction is one which is generally acceptable. Taking first the case of *Dr Cox*, there can be little doubt that, in the last days of her life, if the means had been available to her, Mrs Boyes would have taken her own life; and suicide is, as I have said, now lawful in England. Yet, when she was desperate to take that step because of the terrible nature of her illness, the same illness had the effect that she was unable to obtain the means to do so; furthermore, since in England aiding and abetting another to commit suicide is still a criminal offence, it would have been very difficult for others lawfully to provide her with the necessary assistance ... Then take the case of Anthony Bland. It was there decided that a person in Anthony's condition may lawfully be deprived of life support in the form of artificial feeding, with the inevitable consequence that he will die within a few days; yet, though his doctor has in these circumstances decided that he must inevitably die, the law does not permit him to take the humane step of accelerating that event by giving him a lethal injection. It is for reasons such as these that the two English cases have presented the British public with the question whether the law in its present form is acceptable to them.

To the members of the Voluntary Euthanasia Society, the answer to that question is an emphatic 'No'. The aim of the Society is to make it legal for a competent adult, who is suffering severe distress from an incurable illness, to receive medical help to die at his or her considered and persistent request. In advocating this change in the law, the Society invokes in particular the concept of personal autonomy, which is now reflected in the lawfulness of suicide, and the freedom of choice, inherent in that concept, for an individual to waive the right to his own life ... The Society asks that the law in England should be brought into line with what it believes to be good medical practice, to enable doctors to act in the best interests of their patients without fear of prosecution or the need to dissemble.

The rational force of this argument is very strong. Furthermore, the opinion polls provide at least some evidence of widespread popular support for the Society's proposal ... But certain comments should in any event be made. First, a concordat, such as that adopted in the Netherlands, is difficult to envisage in England; I doubt whether the Director of Public Prosecutions in England would feel free to enter into any such agreement ... The opinion expressed by the House of Lords [in *Bland*] was that only by legislation which expressed the democratic will could so fundamental a change be made in the common law; and attention was drawn to the fact that such legislation, if enacted, could make express provision designed to ensure that any such legalised killing could only be carried out subject to appropriate supervision and control.

Even so, we must be grateful when experiments of this kind are carried out in other jurisdictions, so that we ourselves can learn from them before deciding whether or not to proceed down the same road. I have hitherto regarded the United States as the legal laboratory of the world; but in the case of euthanasia we must all be watching developments in the Netherlands with great interest. However, judging by one account published in a very reputable journal in England ... in 1992, based upon research funded by the British Academy in London [Keown, J, 'The law and practice of euthanasia in the Netherlands' (1992) 108 LQR 51], the established criteria for euthanasia in the Netherlands have proved in practice to be neither so precise nor so strict as originally claimed. The criteria include requirements that the request for euthanasia must come from the patient and must be free and voluntary; that the request must be well considered, durable and persistent; that the patient must be experiencing intolerable (not necessarily physical) suffering; and that the physician must consult with an independent physician colleague who has experience in the field. The first requirement – that the request must be free and voluntary – is, perhaps inevitably, not the subject of further definition, it is not, for example, clear that a request for euthanasia on the ground that the patient is a nuisance to the patient's family is excluded. It is doubtful too whether doctors possess the means, or the expertise, to determine whether the requirement is fulfilled, or indeed the requirement that the request must be well considered, durable and persistent. A survey carried out among general practitioners in the Netherlands in 1990 raised doubts in particular about the efficacy of this latter requirement, revealing that in 22% of cases there had been only one request; in a further 30% of cases, the interval between the first and the last requests as between one hour and one week; and in almost 66% of cases the request was purely oral. The requirement of 'intolerable suffering' has also proved to be imprecise. The survey among general practitioners revealed that, although in 56% of cases the official notification certified intolerable suffering to be the most important reason for euthanasia, only 42% of the patients had mentioned it as a reason, and only 18% as the most important reason. Significantly, 24% of patients gave as their most important reason 'fear/anticipation of mental deterioration', which raises the inevitable but very difficult problem of euthanasia in cases of incipient Alzheimer's disease, a problem not directly addressed in the Dutch criteria. The requirement of consultation also appeared to be of doubtful value in practice, and frequently not complied with ...

In the Netherlands, the lawfulness of active voluntary euthanasia has now been formalised in the Termination of Life on Request and Assisted Suicide (Review Procedures) Act 2001. In September 2003 Belgium followed the Dutch example and introduced similar legislation.

Nevertheless, in the light of the concerns noted by Lord Goff, together with those identified by the Select Committee in its 1994 report, there currently seems little prospect of any similar reform in the UK. Although from time to time Private Members have proposed Bills to this end (a recent example is Lord Joffe's 'Patient (Assisted Dying) Bill of 2003), these have invariably failed for want of Government support. Indeed, in the report *Making Decisions*, issued by the Lord Chancellor's Department in October 1999, the Government stated that it wished 'to make absolutely clear its complete opposition to euthanasia, which is and will remain illegal' (para 18).

INDEX